Lecture Notes in Computer Science 3927

Commenced Publication in 1973
Founding and Former Series Editors:
Gerhard Goos, Juris Hartmanis, and Jan van Leeuwen

T0189735

João Hespanha   Ashish Tiwari (Eds.)

Hybrid Systems: Computation and Control

9th International Workshop, HSCC 2006
Santa Barbara, CA, USA, March 29-31, 2006
Proceedings

 Springer

Volume Editors

João Hespanha
University of California
Dept. of Electrical and Computer Engineering
Center for Control Dynamical Systems and Computation
Santa Barbara, CA 93106, USA
E-mail: hespanha@ece.ucsb.edu

Ashish Tiwari
SRI International
333 Ravenswood Ave, Menlo Park, CA 94025, USA
E-mail: tiwari@csl.sri.com

Library of Congress Control Number: 2006922526

CR Subject Classification (1998): C.3, C.1.m, F.3, D.2, F.1.2, J.2, I.6

LNCS Sublibrary: SL 1 – Theoretical Computer Science and General Issues

ISSN   0302-9743
ISBN-10   3-540-33170-0 Springer Berlin Heidelberg New York
ISBN-13   978-3-540-33170-4 Springer Berlin Heidelberg New York

Springer is a part of Springer Science+Business Media

springer.com

© Springer-Verlag Berlin Heidelberg 2006
Printed in Germany

Typesetting: Camera-ready by author, data conversion by Scientific Publishing Services, Chennai, India
Printed on acid-free paper   SPIN: 11730637   06/3142   5 4 3 2 1 0

Preface

This volume contains the proceedings of the 9th Workshop on Hybrid Systems: Computation and Control (HSCC 2006) held in Santa Barbara, California, during March 29-31, 2006. The annual workshop on hybrid systems attracts researchers from academia and industry interested in modeling, analysis, and implementation of dynamic and reactive systems involving both discrete and continuous behaviors. The previous workshops in the HSCC series were held in Berkeley, USA (1998), Nijmegen, The Netherlands (1999), Pittsburgh, USA (2000), Rome, Italy (2001), Palo Alto, USA (2002), Prague, Czech Republic (2003), Philadelphia, USA (2004), and Zurich, Switzerland (2005). This year's HSCC was organized in cooperation with the Special Interest Group on Embedded Systems (SIGBED) of ACM.

The program consisted of 3 invited talks and 39 regular papers selected from 79 regular submissions. The program covered topics such as tools for analysis and verification, control and optimization, modeling, engineering applications, and emerging directions in programming languages support and implementation.

We would like to thank the Program Committee members and reviewers for an excellent job of evaluating the submissions and participating in the online Program Committee discussions. Special thanks also go to Francesco Bullo (University of California at Santa Barbara), P. R. Kumar (University of Illinois at Urbana-Champaign), and John Rushby (SRI International) for their participation as invited speakers. We are also grateful to the Steering Committee for their helpful guidance and support. Many other people worked hard to make HSCC 2006 a success and we acknowledge their help. We would like to express our gratitude to the US National Science Foundation, SRI International, and University of California at Santa Barbara for their financial support.

March 2006

João Hespanha
Ashish Tiwari
Program Chair
HSCC 2006

Organization

Organizing Committee

Program Co-chairs: João Hespanha (UC, Santa Barbara)

                                Ashish Tiwari (SRI International)

Program Committee

Rajeev Alur (University of Pennsylvania)
Kartik Ariyur (Honeywell)
Eugene Asarin (University Paris 7)
Calin Belta (Drexel University)
Alberto Bemporad (University of Siena)
Antonio Bicchi (University of Pisa)
Gautam Biswas (Vanderbilt University)
Thao Dang (Verimag)
Jennifer Davoren (University of Melbourne)
Luca de Alfaro (UC Santa Cruz)
Magnus Egerstedt (Georgia Institute of Technology)
Karl Henrik Johansson (Royal Institute of Technology)
Eric Klavins (University of Washington)
John Koo (Vanderbilt University)
Kim Larsen (Aalborg University)
Nancy Lynch (MIT)
Bud Mishra (New York University)
Ian Mitchell (University of British Columbia)
George Pappas (University of Pennsylvania)
Maria Prandini (Politecnico di Milano)
Henny Sipma (Stanford University)
Paulo Tabuada (Notre Dame University)
P. S. Thiagarajan (National University of Singapore)
Claire Tomlin (Stanford University)
Arjan van der Schaft (University of Twente)
Sergio Yovine (CNRS)

Steering Committee

Rajeev Alur (University of Pennsylvania)
Bruce Krogh (Carnegie Mellon University)
Oded Maler (Verimag)
Manfred Morari (ETH Zurich)
George J. Pappas (University of Pennsylvania)
Anders Ravn (Aalborg University)

Sponsors

US National Science Foundation
SRI International, Menlo Park, California
University of California at Santa Barbara, California

Additional Referees

Sherif Abdelwahed	Nicolo Giorgetti	Lucia Pallottino
Manindra Agrawal	Antoine Girard	Luigi Palopoli
Alessandro Alessio	Luca Greco	Simone Paoletti
Mohamed Babaali	Adam Halasz	Bruno Picasso
Lei Bao	Gabe Hoffmann	Marc Pouzet
Ahmed Bouajjani	Agung Julius	Robin Raffard
Manuela Bujorianu	Jorge Julvez	Gerardo Schneider
Paul Caspi	Marina Kleptsyna	Enzo Scordio
Samarjit Chakraborty	Geoffrey Koh	Christos Sofronis
Stefano Di Cairano	Xenofon Koutsoukos	Alberto Speranzon
Alexandre Donz	Gerardo Lafferriere	Dusan Stipanovic
Adriano Fagiolini	Mircea Lazar	Herbert Tanner
Giancarlo Ferrari Trecate	Colas Le-Guernic	Sasa V. Rakovic
Oscar Flardh	Magnus Lindhe	Wang Yi
Daniele Fontanelli	Oded Maler	Jun Zhang
Goran Frehse	Sayan Mitra	

Table of Contents

Invited Talks

Regular Papers

Motion Coordination for Multi-agent Networks

Francesco Bullo

Mechanical Engineering,
University of California at Santa Barbara,
http://motion.mee.ucsb.edu

Abstract. Motion coordination is an extraordinary phenomenon in biological systems, such as schools of fishes, as well as a remarkable tool for man-made groups of robotic vehicles and active sensors. Even though each individual agent has no global knowledge of the system, complex coordinated behaviors emerge from local interactions. In this talk I will describe some recently-developed models, algorithms and tools for motion coordination. Building on concepts from distributed computation, robotics and control theory, I investigate notions of robotic network, joint control and communication laws, and time complexity of coordination tasks. From an algorithmic viewpoint, the focus is on various coordination problems such as network deployment over a given region, rendezvous at a point, and vehicle routing. The proposed control and communication laws achieve the various coordination objectives requiring only spatially-distributed information.

João Hespanha and A. Tiwari (Eds.): HSCC 2006, LNCS 3927, p. 1, 2006.
© Springer-Verlag Berlin Heidelberg 2006

Towards a Third Generation of Control Systems

P.R. Kumar

Department of Electrical and Computer Engineering,
University of Illinois, Urbana-Champaign

Abstract. The first generation of control systems can be regarded as analog control and the second generation as digital control. Over the past three decades since the advent of digital control, there have been great technological advances in computing hardware and software as well as in networking. We are therefore at the cusp of a third generation of control systems which consist of sensors and actuators connected by shared wired or wireless networks, and involving powerful computational nodes as well as software services.

How does one facilitate the proliferation of such next generation control systems? We argue that it is important to develop the appropriate abstractions and a matching architecture for the (re)convergence of control with communication and computation. We propose an abstraction of virtual collocation to be manufactured by the supporting middleware, and a principle of local temporal autonomy for enhancing reliability. We provide an overview of efforts in the Convergence Laboratory at the University of Illinois.

João Hespanha and A. Tiwari (Eds.): HSCC 2006, LNCS 3927, p. 2, 2006.
© Springer-Verlag Berlin Heidelberg 2006

Hybrid Systems—And Everything Else*

John Rushby

Computer Science Laboratory,
SRI International,
333 Ravenswood Avenue,
Menlo Park, CA 94025, USA

Abstract. Hybrid systems are at the core of most embedded and many other kinds of systems; formal methods for analysis of hybrid systems have made remarkable progress in the last decade and thus provide a strong foundation for assurance in the system core.

But there are many systems issues that interact with the hybrid systems core and complicate the overall system design and its assurance case. These include real time and fault tolerance, interaction with human operators, and the relationship between verification and certification.

For example, fault tolerance demands multiple redundant sensors, which are themselves prone to faults and inaccuracy, and whose precision degrades as real time progresses from the moment when the sample was taken to that when it is used. Fault tolerance generally also requires multiple independent channels of computation and this raises issues of their synchronization and coordination.

There are two broad classes of methods for dealing with these combined issues: one uses architectural means to separate them, so we can reason separately about hybrid control and fault tolerance, for example; the other integrates them, so that a single method is used to reason, for example, about real time and fault tolerance. I describe some of these methods and sketch some topics for further research.

In the larger systems context, the embedded core may be managed by a planning and execution system that uses AI techniques, and/or by a human operator. Both of these may have an imperfect model of the system and incomplete knowledge of its internal state. I outline these topics and some of the interesting research opportunities therein.

Finally, many of the systems we consider have the potential to do harm, and thus raise concern for informal or regulated certification. I outline recent developments in this area and their connection to verification.

The rich relationship between hybrid systems and everything else suggests a need to reason cooperatively across multiple domains. I sketch a proposal for "an evidential tool bus" to facilitate this.

---

* This work was supported by SRI International.

João Hespanha and A. Tiwari (Eds.): HSCC 2006, LNCS 3927, p. 3, 2006.

Behavioural Approximations for Restricted Linear Differential Hybrid Automata

Manindra Agrawal[1,*], Frank Stephan[2,**], P.S. Thiagarajan[3], and Shaofa Yang[3]

[1] Department of Computer Science and Engineering,
Indian Institute of Technology, Kanpur, India
`manindra@cse.iitk.ac.in`
[2] School of Computing and Department of Mathematics,
National University of Singapore (NUS), Singapore
`fstephan@comp.nus.edu.sg`
[3] School of Computing,
National University of Singapore, Singapore
`{thiagu, yangsf}@comp.nus.edu.sg`

Abstract. We show the regularity of the discrete time behaviour of hybrid automata in which the rates of continuous variables are governed by linear differential operators in a diagonal form and in which the values of the continuous variables can be observed only with finite precision. We do not demand resetting of the values of the continuous variables during mode changes. We can cope with polynomial guards and we can tolerate bounded delays both in sampling the values of the continuous variables and in effecting changes in their rates required by mode switchings. We also show that if the rates are governed by diagonalizable linear differential operators with rational eigenvalues *and* there is no delay in effecting rate changes, the discrete time behaviour of the hybrid automaton is recursive. However, the control state reachability problem in this setting is undecidable.

1 Introduction

We study the behaviour of hybrid automata in which the rate functions associated with the modes are restricted linear differential equations. We show that if the values of the continuous variables can be observed only with finite precision, then the discrete time behaviour of a large class of hybrid automata is regular. Further, these behaviours can be effectively computed. The key feature of our setting is that we do not demand that the value of a continuous variable be reset during a mode switch. Our results suggest that focusing on discrete time semantics and the realistic assumption of finite precision can lead to effective analysis methods for hybrid automata whose continuous dynamics is governed by (linear) differential equations.

---

* Part of this work was done when the author was a Distinguished Visiting Professor at NUS.

** Supported in part by NUS grant R252–000–212–112.

João Hespanha and A. Tiwari (Eds.): HSCC 2006, LNCS 3927, pp. 4–18, 2006.
© Springer-Verlag Berlin Heidelberg 2006

In the related literature, one often assumes that the rates are piecewise constant. This is so, at least in settings where one obtains positive verification results [7, 10, 13]. Even here, since the mode changes can take place over continuous time (a transition may be taken any time its guard is satisfied), basic verification problems often become undecidable [4, 9]. In contrast, it was shown in [8] that one can go much further in the positive direction for piecewise constant rate automata, if one defines their behaviour using a discrete time semantics. As argued in [8], if the hybrid automaton models the closed loop system consisting of a digital controller interacting with a continuous plant, then the discrete time semantics is the natural one; the controller will observe via sensors, the states of the plant and effect, via actuators, changes in the plant dynamics at discrete time points determined by its internal clock. In [2] it was shown that, in this setting, one can in fact tolerate bounded delays both in the observation of the plant states and in effecting changes in the plant dynamics.

Both in [8] and [2], the transition guards were required to be rectangular; conjunctions of simple linear inequalities involving just one variable. We showed in [3] that one can cope with much more expressive guards—essentially all effectively computable guards—if one assumes that the values of the continuous variables can be observed only with finite precision. In many settings including the one where the hybrid automaton models a digital controller interacting with a continuous plant, this is a natural assumption.

Here our goal is to show that the combination of discrete time semantics and finite precision can not only allow more expressive guards but can also take us beyond piecewise constant rates. One of our main results is that under finite precision, the discrete time behaviour of a hybrid automaton is regular and effectively computable even when the rate of a continuous variable in the control state q is governed by an equation of the form $dx/dt = c_q \cdot x(t)$. This holds even though we do not demand resetting of the values of the continuous variables during mode changes. Further, we can cope with arbitrary computable guards. We can also tolerate bounded delays in sampling the values of the continuous variables and in effecting changes in their rates required by mode switchings.

We also show that the discrete time behaviours of hybrid automata in a much richer setting are *recursive*. Specifically, the rates of continuous variables at the control state q are governed by a linear differential operator represented by a diagonalizable ([11]) matrix A_q with rational eigenvalues. Further, we allow polynomial guards but do not permit delays in effecting rates changes. A consequence of this positive result is that one can effectively solve a variety of bounded model checking problems [6] in this rich setting. However, we show that the control state reachability problem is undecidable for this class of automata; this is so, even if the guards are restricted to be rectangular.

The proofs of the above two results seem to suggest that one can hope to go much further if update delays are allowed. This will prevent the hybrid automaton from retaining an unbounded amount of information as its dynamics evolves. The key obstacle is that we do not know at present how to take advantage of this observation since we lack suitable techniques for tracking rational approximations of exponential terms with *real* exponents. In this connection, the fundamental theory presented in [5] may turn to be important. We also feel that the techniques presented in [14, 15] will turn out to be useful even though they are developed under a regime where continuous variables are reset during mode changes.

In the next two sections, we define our hybrid automata and develop their discrete time semantics. In section 4, we present our main result concerning hybrid automata whose discrete time behaviours are regular. In section 5, we study a subclass of hybrid automata whose discrete time behaviours are recursive but whose control state reachability problem is undecidable.

2   Hybrid Automata Preliminaries

Through the rest of the paper, we fix a positive integer n and one function symbol x_i for each i in $\{1, 2, \ldots, n\}$. We will often refer to the x_i's as "continuous" variables and will view each x_i as a function (of time) $x_i : \mathbb{R}_{\geq 0} \to \mathbb{R}$ with $\mathbb{R}$ being the set of reals and $\mathbb{R}_{\geq 0}$, the set of non-negative reals. We let $\mathbb{Q}$ denote the set of rationals.

The transitions of the hybrid automaton will have associated guards that need to be satisfied by the values of the continuous variables for the transitions to be enabled. A *polynomial constraint* is an inequality of the form $p(x_1, x_2, \ldots, x_n) \leq 0$ or $p(x_1, x_2, \ldots, x_n) < 0$ where $p(x_1, x_2, \ldots, x_n)$ is a polynomial over $x_1, x_2, \ldots, x_n$ with integer coefficients. A *polynomial guard* is a finite conjunction of polynomial constraints. We let *Grd* denote the set of polynomial guards. Unless otherwise stated, by a guard we will mean a polynomial guard.

A *valuation* V is just a member of $\mathbb{R}^n$. It will be viewed as prescribing the value $V(i)$ to each variable x_i. The notion of a valuation satisfying a guard is defined in the obvious way.

A *lazy finite-precision differential hybrid automaton* is a structure $\mathcal{A} = (Q, q_{in}, V_{in}, Delay, \epsilon, \{\rho_q\}_{q \in Q}, \{\gamma_{min}, \gamma_{max}\}, \longrightarrow)$ where:

- Q is a finite set of *control states* with q, q' ranging over Q.
- $q_{in} \in Q$ is the initial control state.
- $V_{in} \in \mathbb{Q}^n$ is the initial valuation.
- $Delay = \{\delta_{ob}^0, \delta_{ob}^1, \delta_{up}^0, \delta_{up}^1\} \subseteq \mathbb{Q}$ is the set of *delay parameters* such that $0 \leq \delta_{up}^0 \leq \delta_{up}^1 < \delta_{ob}^0 \leq \delta_{ob}^1 \leq 1$.
- ϵ, a positive rational, is the *precision of measurement*.
- $\{\rho_q\}_{q \in Q}$ is a family of rate functions associated with the control states. In the general case, ρ_q will be of the form $\dot{x} = A_q x + b_q$ where A_q is an $n \times n$ matrix with rational entries and $b_q \in \mathbb{Q}^n$. For each i in $\{1, 2, \ldots, n\}$ this specifies the rate function of x_i as the differential equation $dx_i/dt = \sum_{j=1}^n A_q(i, j) \cdot x_j(t) + b_q(i)$ where $A_q(i, j)$ is the (i, j)-th entry of A_q.
- $\gamma_{min}, \gamma_{max} \in \mathbb{Q}$ are *range parameters* such that $0 < \gamma_{min} < \gamma_{max}$.
- $\longrightarrow \subseteq Q \times Grd \times Q$ is a transition relation such that $q \neq q'$ for every (q, g, q') in $\longrightarrow$.

We shall study the discrete time behaviour of our automata. At each time instant T_k, the automaton receives a measurement regarding the current values of the x_i's. However, the value of x_i that is observed at time T_k is the value that held at some time $t \in [T_{k-1} + \delta_{ob}^0, T_{k-1} + \delta_{ob}^1]$. Further, the value is observed with a precision of ϵ. More specifically, any value of x_i in the half-open interval $[(m - 1/2)\epsilon, (m + 1/2)\epsilon)$ is reported as $m\epsilon$ where m is an integer. For a real number v, we will denote this rounded-off value relative to ϵ as $\langle v \rangle_\epsilon$ and often just write $\langle v \rangle$. More sophisticated rounding-off functions can be considered as in [3] but for ease of presentation, we shall not do so here.

If at T_k, the automaton is in control state q and the observed n-tuple of values $(\langle v_1 \rangle, \langle v_2 \rangle, \ldots, \langle v_n \rangle)$ satisfies the guard g with (q, g, q') being a transition, then the automaton may perform this transition instantaneously and move to the control state q'. As a result, the x_i's will cease to evolve according to the rate function ρ_q and instead start evolving according to the rate function $\rho_{q'}$. However, for each x_i, this change in the rate of evolution of each x_i will not kick in at T_k but at some time $t \in [T_k + \delta_{up}^0, T_k + \delta_{up}^1]$. In this sense, both the sensing of the x_i's and the rate changes associated with mode switching take place in a lazy fashion but with bounded delays. We expect $\delta_{ob}^0, \delta_{ob}^1$ to be close to 1 and $\delta_{up}^0, \delta_{up}^1$ to be close to 0 while both $\delta_{ob}^1 - \delta_{ob}^0$ and $\delta_{up}^1 - \delta_{up}^0$ to be small compared to 1.

In the idealized setting, the value observed at T_k is the value that holds at exactly T_k ($\delta_{ob}^0 = 1 = \delta_{ob}^1$) and the change in rates due to mode switching would kick in immediately ($\delta_{up}^0 = 0 = \delta_{up}^1$). In addition, assuming perfect precision would boil down to setting $\langle v \rangle = v$ for every real number v.

The parameters $\gamma_{min}, \gamma_{max}$ specify the relevant range of the absolute values of the continuous variables. The automaton gets stuck if $|x_i|$ gets outside the allowed range $[\gamma_{min}, \gamma_{max}]$ for any i. Loosely speaking, the γ_{max} bound is used to restrict the amount of information carried by a continuous variable evolving at a (positive or negative) constant rate ($\dot{x} = c$) and a continuous variable increasing at an exponential rate ($\dot{x} = c \cdot x(t)$, $c > 0$). On the other hand, γ_{min} is used to restrict the amount of information carried by a continuous variable decreasing at an exponential rate ($\dot{x} = c \cdot x(t)$, $c < 0$). We note that our setting is quite different from the classical continuous setting. Hence the standard control objective of driving a system variable to 0 is not relevant here and thus does not pose a serious limitation.

We will be mainly interested in the setting that each A_q is a diagonal matrix and in the more general case where each A_q is a diagonalizable matrix having n distinct rational eigenvalues. In the former setting we show that the control state sequence languages generated by our hybrid automata are regular and can be effectively computed provided every continuous variable either evolves at (possibly different) constant rates in all the control states or at (possibly different) exponential rates in all the control states. In the latter setting, with the additional restriction that there are no delays associated with rates update ($\delta_{up}^0 = 0 = \delta_{up}^1$), we show that the control state sequence languages generated by our hybrid automata are recursive, but the control state reachability problem is undecidable.

3   The Transition System Semantics

Through the rest of this paper we fix a lazy finite-precision differential hybrid automaton $\mathcal{A}$ and assume its associated notations and terminology as defined in the previous section. We shall often refer to "lazy finite-precision differential hybrid automata" simply as "hybrid automata". The behaviour of $\mathcal{A}$ will be defined in terms of an associated transition system. A *configuration* is a triple (q, V, q') where q, q' are control states and V is a valuation. q is the current control state, q' is the control state that held at the previous time instant and V captures the *actual* values of the variables at the current time instant. The valuation V is said to be *feasible* if $\gamma_{min} \leq |V(i)| \leq \gamma_{max}$ for every i in $\{1, 2, \ldots, n\}$. The configuration (q, V, q') is *feasible* iff V is a feasible valuation. The initial configuration is (q_{in}, V_{in}, q_{in}) and is assumed to be feasible. We let $Conf_{\mathcal{A}}$ denote the set of configurations. We assume that the unit of time has been fixed at some suitable level of granularity and that the rate functions $\{\rho_q\}_{q \in Q}$ have been scaled accordingly.

Suppose the automaton $\mathcal{A}$ is in the configuration (q_k, V_k, q'_k) at time T_k. Then one unit of time will be allowed to pass and at time instant T_{k+1}, the automaton $\mathcal{A}$ will make an instantaneous move by executing a transition or the silent action τ and move to a configuration $(q_{k+1}, V_{k+1}, q'_{k+1})$. The silent action τ will be used to record that no mode change has taken place during this move. The action μ will be used to record that a transition has been taken and as a result, a mode change has taken place. As is common, we will collapse the unit-time-passage followed by an instantaneous transition into one "time-abstract" transition labelled by τ or μ. We wish to formalize the transition relation $\Longrightarrow \subseteq Conf_{\mathcal{A}} \times \{\tau, \mu\} \times Conf_{\mathcal{A}}$. For doing so, we note that given a matrix $A \in \mathbb{Q}^{n \times n}$, a vector $b \in \mathbb{Q}^n$, a positive real T and a valuation V, we can find a unique family of curves (see [11]) $\{x_i\}_{1 \leq i \leq n}$ with $x_i : [0, T] \to \mathbb{R}$ such that for every i we have $x_i(0) = V(i)$ and for every $t \in [0, T]$ we have $dx_i/dt = \sum_{j=1}^{n} A_q(i, j) \cdot x_j(t) + b_q(i)$. In what follows, we shall denote the valuation $(x_1(T), x_2(T), \ldots, x_n(T))$ thus obtained as $Val(A, b, T, V)$ without explicitly displaying the curves x_i's.

Let (q, V, q'), $(q1, V1, q1')$ be in $Conf_{\mathcal{A}}$. Suppose there exist reals t_i^{up}, $i = 1, 2, \ldots, n$, in $[\delta_{up}^0, \delta_{up}^1]$ such that $V1$ is related to V as follows: Let $t_{\pi_1}^{up} \leq t_{\pi_2}^{up} \leq \cdots \leq t_{\pi_n}^{up}$ with $\pi_1, \pi_2, \ldots, \pi_n$ being a permutation of the indices $1, 2, \ldots, n$. Then there exist valuations U_i, $i = 1, 2, \ldots, n$, such that $U_1 = Val(A_{q'}, b_{q'}, t_{\pi_1}^{up}, V)$; $U_{i+1} = Val(A_i, b_i, t_{\pi_{i+1}}^{up} - t_{\pi_i}^{up}, U_i)$ for $i = 1, 2, \ldots, n - 1$; and $V1 = Val(A_n, b_n, 1 - t_{\pi_n}^{up}, U_n)$, where for $i = 1, 2, \ldots, n$, the matrix $A_i \in \mathbb{Q}^{n \times n}$ and the vector $b_i \in \mathbb{Q}^n$ are given by: if $j \in \{\pi_1, \pi_2, \ldots, \pi_i\}$, then the j-th row of A_i (b_i) equals the j-th row of A_q (b_q); otherwise the j-th row of A_i (b_i) equals the j-th row of $A_{q'}$ ($b_{q'}$).

The intuition is that at time T_{k+1} the continuous variables have valuation $V1$ while at time T_k, the continuous variables have valuation V and $\mathcal{A}$ resides at control state q. Further, at time T_{k-1}, the automaton was at control state q'. For each i, the real number $T_k + t_i^{up}$ is the time at which x_i ceases to evolve at the rate $dx_i/dt = \sum_{j=1}^{n} A_{q'}(i,j) \cdot x_j + b_{q'}(i)$ and starts to evolve at the rate $dx_i/dt = \sum_{j=1}^{n} A_q(i,j) \cdot x_j + b_q(i)$.

Now we state the condition that $\Longrightarrow$ must fulfil. Let (q, V, q'), $(q1, V1, q1')$ be in $Conf_{\mathcal{A}}$. Suppose there exist reals t_i^{up}, $i = 1, 2, \ldots, n$, in $[\delta_{up}^0, \delta_{up}^1]$ such that $V1$ is related to V as dictated above.

- Suppose $q1 = q1' = q$. Then $(q, V, q') \overset{\tau}{\Longrightarrow} (q1, V1, q1')$.
- Suppose $q1' = q$ and there exists a transition $(q, g, q1)$ in $\longrightarrow$ and reals t_i^{ob}, $i = 1, 2, \ldots, n$, in $[\delta_{ob}^0, \delta_{ob}^1]$ such that $(\langle w_1 \rangle, \langle w_2 \rangle, \ldots, \langle w_n \rangle)$ satisfies g, where w_i is the i-th component of the valuation $Val(A_n, b_n, t_i^{ob} - t_{\pi_n}^{up}, U_n)$ for $i = 1, 2, \ldots, n$. Then $(q, V, q') \overset{\mu}{\Longrightarrow}_{\mathcal{A}} (q1, V1, q1')$.

As might be expected, the real $T_k + t_i^{ob}$ is the time at which the value of x_i was observed for each $i = 1, 2, \ldots, n$.

Basically there are four possible transition types depending on whether $q = q'$ and whether τ or μ is the action label. For convenience, we have collapsed these four possibilities into two cases according to τ or μ being the action label, and in each case have handled the subcases $q = q'$ and $q \neq q'$ simultaneously.

Now define the transition system $TS_{\mathcal{A}} = (RC_{\mathcal{A}}, (q_{in}, V_{in}, q_{in}), \{\tau, \mu\}, \Longrightarrow_{\mathcal{A}})$ via:

- $RC_{\mathcal{A}}$, the set of *reachable configurations* of $\mathcal{A}$ is the least subset of $Conf_{\mathcal{A}}$ that contains the initial configuration (q_{in}, V_{in}, q_{in}) and satisfies: Suppose (q, V, q') is in $RC_{\mathcal{A}}$ and is a feasible configuration. Suppose further, $(q, V, q') \overset{\alpha}{\Longrightarrow} (q1, V1, q1')$ for some $\alpha \in \{\tau, \mu\}$. Then $(q1, V1, q1') \in RC_{\mathcal{A}}$.
- $\Longrightarrow_{\mathcal{A}}$ is $\Longrightarrow$ restricted to $RC_{\mathcal{A}} \times \{\tau, \mu\} \times RC_{\mathcal{A}}$.

We note that a reachable configuration can be the source of a transition in $TS_{\mathcal{A}}$ only if it is feasible. Thus infeasible reachable configurations will be deadlocked in $TS_{\mathcal{A}}$. A *run* of $TS_{\mathcal{A}}$ is a finite sequence of the form

$$\sigma = (q_0, V_0, q_0') \, \alpha_0 \, (q_1, V_1, q_1') \, \alpha_1 \, (q_2, V_2, q_2') \ldots (q_\ell, V_\ell, q_\ell')$$

where (q_0, V_0, q_0') is the initial configuration and $(q_k, V_k, q_k') \overset{\alpha_k}{\Longrightarrow}_{\mathcal{A}} (q_{k+1}, V_{k+1}, q_{k+1}')$ for $k = 0, 1, \ldots, \ell - 1$. The *state sequence* induced by the run σ above is the sequence $q_0 q_1 \ldots q_\ell$. We define the state sequence language of $\mathcal{A}$ denoted $\mathcal{L}(\mathcal{A})$ to be the set of state sequences induced by runs of $TS_{\mathcal{A}}$.

4 Diagonal Rate Matrices

We first study the setting where each A_q is a diagonal matrix and where every continuous variable either evolves at constant rates in all the modes or at exponential rates in all the modes. It turns out that the language of state sequences in this setting is always regular. More precisely:

Theorem 1. *Let $\mathcal{A}$ be a lazy finite-precision differential hybrid automaton such that A_q is a diagonal matrix for every control state q. Suppose there exists a fixed partition $\{DIF, CON\}$ of the indices $\{1, 2, \ldots, n\}$ such that for each control state q, $\dot{x}_i = A_q(i, i) \cdot x_i$ if $i \in DIF$ and $\dot{x}_i = b_q(i)$ if $i \in CON$. Then $\mathcal{L}(\mathcal{A})$ is a regular subset of $Q^\star$. Further, a finite state automaton accepting $\mathcal{L}(\mathcal{A})$ can be effectively computed from $\mathcal{A}$.*

Proof of Theorem 1: The basic strategy is to generalize the proof of the main result in [3]. As before, the proof consists of two major steps. The first one is to quotient the set of reachable configurations $RC_{\mathcal{A}}$ into a *finite number* of equivalence classes using a suitably chosen equivalence relation $\approx$. The crucial property required of $\approx$ is that it should be a congruence with respect to the transition relation of $TS_{\mathcal{A}}$. In other words, if $(q1, V1, q1') \approx (q2, V2, q2')$ and $(q1, V1, q1') \overset{\alpha}{\Longrightarrow}_{\mathcal{A}} (q3, V3, q3')$, then we require that there exists a configuration $(q4, V4, q4')$ such that $(q2, V2, q2') \overset{\alpha}{\Longrightarrow}_{\mathcal{A}} (q4, V4, q4')$ *and* $(q3, V3, q3') \approx (q4, V4, q4')$. The second step is to show that we can effectively compute these equivalence classes and a transition relation over them such that the resulting finite state automaton generates the language of state sequences.

For notational convenience, we assume $V_{in}(i) > 0$ for every $i \in DIF$. It will become clear that this involves no loss of generality. The key consequence of this assumption is that in any reachable configuration, the value of x_i for $i \in DIF$ will be positive.

We also assume without loss of generality that for each guard g in $\mathcal{A}$, the valuation V satisfies g only if V is feasible.

Let Δ be the largest positive rational number that *integrally* divides every number in the set of rational numbers $\{\delta_{ob}^0, \delta_{ob}^1, \delta_{up}^0, \delta_{up}^1, 1\}$. Define Γ to be the largest rational which *integrally* divides every number in the finite set of rational numbers $\{A_q(i, i) \cdot \Delta \mid q \in Q, i \in DIF\} \bigcup \{b_q(j) \cdot \Delta \mid q \in Q, j \in CON\} \bigcup \{\gamma_{min}, \gamma_{max}\} \bigcup \{\epsilon/2\}$.

Let $\mathbb{Z}$ denote the set of integers. Define Θ_{con} to be the *finite* set of rational numbers $\{h\Gamma \in [-\gamma_{max}, \gamma_{max}] \mid h \in \mathbb{Z}\}$. In other words, Θ_{con} contains integral multiples of Γ in the interval $[-\gamma_{max}, \gamma_{max}]$.

Let Θ_{IR} be the set of irrational numbers $\{\ln((m + 1/2)\epsilon) \mid m \in \mathbb{Z}, \langle \gamma_{min} \rangle \leq m\epsilon \leq \langle \gamma_{max} \rangle\} \bigcup \{\ln \gamma_{min}, \ln \gamma_{max}\}$. Define Θ_{dif} to be the *finite* set of real numbers $\{h\Gamma \in [\ln \gamma_{min}, \ln \gamma_{max}] \mid h \in \mathbb{Z}\} \bigcup \{\ell\Gamma + \theta \in [\ln \gamma_{min}, \ln \gamma_{max}] \mid \ell \in \mathbb{Z}, \theta \in \Theta_{IR}\}$. In other words, Θ_{dif} contains rational numbers of the form $h\Gamma$ in the interval $[\ln \gamma_{min}, \ln \gamma_{max}]$ where h is a (positive) integer, and irrational numbers of the form $\ell\Gamma + \theta$ in the interval $[\ln \gamma_{min}, \ln \gamma_{max}]$ where ℓ is an integer (that can be positive, zero or negative) and θ is a member of Θ_{IR}.

Loosely speaking, the set Θ_{con} (respectively Θ_{dif}) contains bounds relevant to the values of continuous variables x_i's for $i \in CON$ (respectively $i \in DIF$). The points in Θ_{con} (Θ_{dif}) cut the real line into a finite number of segments. We shall use this segmentation to in turn partition the set of reachable configurations into finitely many equivalence classes. The simple but key observation that enables this is, in the (natural) logarithmic scale, exponential rates get represented as *constant* rates.

In this light, let the members of Θ_{dif} be $\{\theta_1, \theta_2, \ldots, \theta_{|\Theta_{dif}|}\}$ where $\theta_1 < \theta_2 < \cdots < \theta_{|\Theta_{dif}|}$. We define the finite set of intervals $\mathcal{I}_{dif} = \{(-\infty, \theta_1), (\theta_1, \theta_2), \ldots, (\theta_{|\Theta_{dif}|-1}, \theta_{|\Theta_{dif}|}), (\theta_{|\Theta_{dif}|}, \infty)\} \cup \{[\theta_i, \theta_i] \mid i = 1, 2, \ldots, |\Theta_{dif}|\}$. In the same way, we define $\mathcal{I}_{con}$ from Θ_{con}.

Let $\mathbb{R}^+$ be the set of positive reals. Define the map $\|\cdot\|_{dif} : \mathbb{R}^+ \to \mathcal{I}_{dif}$ via: $\|v\| = I$ if $\ln v \in I$. Define $\|\cdot\|_{con} : \mathbb{R} \to \mathcal{I}_{con}$ via: $\|v\| = I$ if $v \in I$. Finally we define $\|\cdot\| : RC_{\mathcal{A}} \to (\mathcal{I}_{dif} \cup \mathcal{I}_{con})^n$ by: $\|V\| = (I_1, I_2, \ldots, I_n)$ where $I_i = \|V(i)\|_{dif}$ for $i \in DIF$ and $I_i = \|V(i)\|_{con}$ for $i \in CON$. We can now define the equivalence relation $\approx \subseteq RC_{\mathcal{A}} \times RC_{\mathcal{A}}$ by: $(q1, V1, q1') \approx (q2, V2, q2')$ iff $q1 = q2$, $\|V1\| = \|V2\|$ and $q1' = q2'$. The crucial property of $\approx$ is that it is a congruence relation with respect to the transition relation $\Longrightarrow_{\mathcal{A}}$.

Claim 2. *Suppose $(q1, V1, q1') \approx (q2, V2, q2')$ and $(q1, V1, q1') \overset{\alpha}{\Longrightarrow}_{\mathcal{A}} (q3, V3, q3')$, then there exists a reachable configuration $(q4, V4, q4')$ such that $(q2, V2, q2') \overset{\alpha}{\Longrightarrow}_{\mathcal{A}} (q4, V4, q4')$ and $(q3, V3, q3') \approx (q4, V4, q4')$.*

Proof of Claim 2: Clearly $q1 = q2$ and $q1' = q2'$. Set $q4 = q3$ and $q4' = q3'$. We show that $(q2, V2, q2')$ is a feasible configuration and there exists a valuation $V4$ such that $(q2, V2, q2') \overset{\alpha}{\Longrightarrow}_{\mathcal{A}} (q4, V4, q4')$ and $\|V4\| = \|V3\|$.

We first note that the configuration $(q2, V2, q2')$ is feasible. Fix an $i \in DIF$. Since the configuration $(q1, V1, q1')$ is feasible, we have $\ln \gamma_{min} \leq \ln V1(i) \leq \ln \gamma_{max}$. Since $\ln \gamma_{min}, \ln \gamma_{max}$ are members of Θ_{dif} and $\|V1(i)\|_{dif} = \|V2(i)\|_{dif}$, we conclude $\ln \gamma_{min} \leq \ln V2(i) \leq \ln \gamma_{max}$ and so $\gamma_{min} \leq |V2(i)| \leq \gamma_{max}$. Similarly it is easy to see that $\gamma_{min} \leq |V2(i)| \leq \gamma_{max}$ for $i \in CON$.

We show the existence of $V4$ by considering two cases according to $\alpha = \tau$ or $\alpha = \mu$.

—**Case 1:** $\alpha = \tau$

It follows from the definition of $TS_{\mathcal{A}}$ that there exist reals $t_i^{up} \in [\delta_{up}^0, \delta_{up}^1]$, $i = 1, 2, \ldots, n$, such that $\ln V3(i) = \ln V1(i) + A_{q'}(i, i) \cdot t_i^{up} + A_q(i, i) \cdot (1 - t_i^{up})$ for $i \in DIF$ and $V3(i) = V1(i) + b_{q'}(i) \cdot t_i^{up} + b_q(i) \cdot (1 - t_i^{up})$ for $i \in CON$. It suffices to show that there exist reals $s_i^{up} \in [\delta_{up}^0, \delta_{up}^1]$, $i = 1, 2, \ldots, n$, such that $\|V4\| = \|V3\|$, where $\ln V4(i) = \ln V2(i) + A_{q'}(i, i) \cdot s_i^{up} + A_q(i, i) \cdot (1 - s_i^{up})$ for $i \in DIF$ and $V4(i) = V2(i) + b_{q'}(i) \cdot s_i^{up} + b_q(i) \cdot (1 - s_i^{up})$ for $i \in CON$.

In what follows, we will often need to give similar arguments for $i \in DIF$ and $i \in CON$. To avoid repetition, we will omit the latter.

Fix an $i \in DIF$. We show the existence of s_i^{up}. Assume $\|V3(i)\|_{dif} = (\theta, \theta')$ where $\theta, \theta' \in \Theta_{dif}$ and $A_{q'}(i, i) > A_q(i, i)$. It will become clear that other cases can be similarly handled. For any real u, let $\Phi^\tau(u)$ be the condition

$$\exists t^{up} \in \mathbb{R}. \ \delta_{up}^0 \leq t^{up} \leq \delta_{up}^1$$
$$\wedge \ \theta < u + A_{q'}(i, i) \cdot t^{up} + A_q(i, i) \cdot (1 - t^{up}) < \theta' \ .$$

It is easy to see that $\Phi^\tau(u)$ holds iff $\eta < u < \eta'$ where $\eta = \theta - A_{q'}(i, i) \cdot \delta_{up}^1 - A_q(i, i) \cdot (1 - \delta_{up}^1)$ and $\eta' = \theta' - A_{q'}(i, i) \cdot \delta_{up}^0 - A_q(i, i) \cdot (1 - \delta_{up}^0)$.

Since $\Phi^\tau(\ln V1(i))$ holds, we have $\eta < \ln V1(i) < \eta'$. Note that η, η' are members of Θ_{dif} (if $\eta, \eta' \in [\ln \gamma_{min}, \ln \gamma_{max}]$). Applying $\|V2(i)\|_{dif} = \|V1(i)\|_{dif}$ then yields $\eta < \ln V2(i) < \eta'$ and consequently $\Phi^\tau(\ln V2(i))$ holds. This establishes the existence of s_i^{up} for $i \in DIF$.

—**Case 2:** $\alpha = \mu$

As in Case 1, it follows from the definition of $TS_\mathcal{A}$ that there exist reals t_i^{up} in $[\delta_{up}^0, \delta_{up}^1]$, $i = 1, 2, \ldots, n$, such that $\ln V3(i) = \ln V1(i) + A_{q'}(i,i) \cdot t_i^{up} + A_q(i,i) \cdot (1 - t_i^{up})$ for $i \in DIF$ and $V3(i) = V1(i) + b_{q'}(i) \cdot t_i^{up} + b_q(i) \cdot (1 - t_i^{up})$ for $i \in CON$. Further there exist reals $t_i^{ob} \in [\delta_{ob}^0, \delta_{ob}^1]$, $i = 1, 2, \ldots, n$, and a guard g such that the following conditions are satisfied: Firstly, $(q1, g, q3) \in \longrightarrow$. Secondly, $(\langle U(1) \rangle, \langle U(2) \rangle, \ldots, \langle U(n) \rangle)$ satisfies g, where U is the valuation with $\ln U(i) = \ln V1(i) + A_{q'}(i,i) \cdot t_i^{up} + A_q(i,i) \cdot (t_i^{ob} - t_i^{up})$ for $i \in DIF$; $U(i) = V1(i) + b_{q'}(i) \cdot t_i^{up} + b_q(i) \cdot (t_i^{ob} - t_i^{up})$ for $i \in CON$. We shall show the existence of reals $s_i^{up} \in [\delta_{up}^0, \delta_{up}^1]$, $s_i^{ob} \in [\delta_{ob}^0, \delta_{ob}^1]$, $i = 1, 2, \ldots, n$, such that $\|V4\| = \|V3\|$ and $\|U'\| = \|U\|$ where $V4$ is the valuation given by $\ln V4(i) = \ln V2(i) + A_{q'}(i,i) \cdot s_i^{up} + A_q(i,i) \cdot (1 - s_i^{up})$ for $i \in DIF$ and $V4(i) = V2(i) + b_{q'}(i) \cdot s_i^{up} + b_q(i) \cdot (1 - s_i^{up})$ for $i \in CON$. And U' is the valuation given by $\ln U'(i) = \ln V2(i) + A_{q'}(i,i) \cdot s_i^{up} + A_q(i,i) \cdot (s_i^{ob} - s_i^{up})$ for $i \in DIF$ and $U'(i) = V2(i) + b_{q'}(i) \cdot s_i^{up} + b_q(i) \cdot (s_i^{ob} - s_i^{up})$ for $i \in CON$. First we argue that the existence of U' satisfying $\|U'\| = \|U\|$ will guarantee $\langle U'(i) \rangle = \langle U(i) \rangle$ for $i = 1, 2, \ldots, n$. This follows from the fact $\ln((m + 1/2)\epsilon) \in \Theta_{dif}$ for integers m with $\langle \gamma_{min} \rangle \le m\epsilon \le \langle \gamma_{max} \rangle$ and $(m + 1/2)\epsilon \in \Theta_{con}$ for integers m with $\langle -\gamma_{max} \rangle \le m\epsilon \le \langle \gamma_{max} \rangle$. Thus U' also satisfies the guard g since U satisfies g. So the existence of s_i^{up}, s_i^{ob}, $i = 1, 2, \ldots, n$, suffices to establish the claim.

Fix an $i \in DIF$. Assume $\|V3(i)\|_{dif} = (\theta, \theta')$, $\|U(i)\|_{dif} = (\vartheta, \vartheta')$ where $\theta, \theta', \vartheta, \vartheta' \in \Theta_{dif}$ and $A_{q'}(i,i) > A_q(i,i) > 0$. Other cases can be similarly handled. For any real u, let $\Phi^\mu(u)$ be the condition

$$\exists t^{up} \in \mathbb{R}. \; \exists t^{ob} \in \mathbb{R}. \quad \delta_{up}^0 \le t^{up} \le \delta_{up}^1$$
$$\wedge \quad \theta < u + A_{q'}(i,i) \cdot t^{up} + A_q(i,i) \cdot (1 - t^{up}) < \theta'$$
$$\wedge \quad \delta_{ob}^0 \le t^{ob} \le \delta_{ob}^1$$
$$\wedge \quad \vartheta < u + A_{q'}(i,i) \cdot t^{up} + A_q(i,i) \cdot (t^{ob} - t^{up}) < \vartheta' \;.$$

As in Case 1, it is easy to see that $\Phi^\mu(u)$ holds iff $\eta < u < \eta'$, where η is the larger of $\theta - A_{q'}(i,i) \cdot \delta_{up}^1 - A_q(i,i) \cdot (1 - \delta_{up}^1)$ and $\vartheta - A_{q'}(i,i) \cdot \delta_{up}^1 - A_q(i,i) \cdot (\delta_{ob}^1 - \delta_{up}^1)$. On the other hand, η' is the smaller of $\theta' - A_{q'}(i,i) \cdot \delta_{up}^0 - A_q(i,i) \cdot (1 - \delta_{up}^0)$ and $\vartheta' - A_{q'}(i,i) \cdot \delta_{up}^0 - A_q(i,i) \cdot (\delta_{ob}^0 - \delta_{up}^0)$. It follows that η, η' are members of Θ_{dif} (if $\eta, \eta' \in [\ln \gamma_{min}, \ln \gamma_{max}]$). Thus, as in Case 1, one concludes that $\Phi^\mu(\ln V2(i))$ holds and the existence of s_i^{up}, s_i^{ob} for $i \in DIF$ is established.

By filling in similar but simpler arguments for $i \in CON$, we can complete the proof of Claim 2. □

Having established the claim that $\approx$ is a congruence with respect to $\Longrightarrow_\mathcal{A}$, we now argue that one can effectively construct a finite automaton which accepts $\mathcal{L}(\mathcal{A})$. Clearly, the members of Θ_{dif} and Θ_{con} can be effectively represented. Further, the members of Θ_{dif} (Θ_{con}) can be effectively ordered and thus the finitely many equivalence classes of $\approx$ can be effectively represented. Note that, to compare two members of Θ_{dif} one just needs to determine whether $e^{m_1} < m_2$ for integers m_1, m_2. This can be done by approximating e sufficiently precisely using for instance the power series expansion of e. Now construct a finite transition system $\mathcal{B}$ whose states are the finitely many equivalence classes of $\approx$. Further, there is a transition from $C1$ to $C2$ with label α iff there exists (q, V, q') in $C1$, $(q1, V1, q1')$ in $C2$ such that $(q, V, q') \overset{\alpha}{\Longrightarrow}_A (q1, V1, q1')$. From the proof of Claim 2, to determine whether there exists a transition from $C1$ to $C2$ with label α amounts to comparing members of Θ_{dif} (and Θ_{con}). Hence the transition system $\mathcal{B}$ can be effectively computed. It is now straightforward to construct from $\mathcal{B}$ a finite state automaton which accepts $\mathcal{L}(\mathcal{A})$. This completes the proof of Theorem 1. □

It is clear that the proof of Theorem 1 also holds for any effectively computable language of guards instead of just polynomial guards.

As usual, a variety of verification and controller synthesis problems become decidable for hybrid automata satisfying the conditions set out in Theorem 1 above. One basic verification problem in this context is the *control state reachability problem*; to decide, for a designated state q_f, whether there exists a state sequence whose last letter is q_f.

5 Diagonalizable Rate Matrices

The regularity result of the previous section requires the matrices A_q to be diagonal. A natural way to relax this requirement is just to demand that every A_q be *diagonalizable* [11]. We recall that the $n \times n$ matrix A is diagonalizable in case there is a basis of eigenvectors $\{f_1, f_2, \ldots, f_n\}$ so that under the associated coordinate transformation, A can be represented as the diagonal matrix $diag(\lambda_1, \lambda_2, \ldots, \lambda_n)$ with the λ_i's being the eigenvalues of A. Given our concern for effective computations, it then seems reasonable to demand that, in addition to being diagonalizable, every matrix A_q should also have (n distinct) rational eigenvalues.

We further restrict ourselves to the case that there is no delay associated with the update of rates of the continuous variables ($\delta_{up}^0 = 0 = \delta_{up}^1$). This is due to the fact at present we don't know how to deal with differential equations of the form $\dot{x} = Ax + b$. One will have to deal with such equations if update delays are present ($\delta_{up}^0 < \delta_{up}^1$). This is due to the fact that the rate changes of the continuous variables may kick in at *different* times in the interval $[T_k + \delta_{up}^0, T_k + \delta_{up}^1]$.

Assuming there are no update delays we first show that the state sequence language of every lazy finite-precision differential hybrid automaton is recursive. This result may be intuitively obvious it still requires an argument. This is so, since the decidability of the first order theory of the reals extended with the exponential operator is still open [17] and the results developed in [14] crucially exploit the resetting property. We then show that the control state reachability problem is undecidable in this setting.

Theorem 3. *Suppose $\mathcal{A}$ is a lazy finite-precision differential hybrid such that $\delta_{up}^0 = 0 = \delta_{up}^1$ and for every control state q, A_q is a diagonalizable matrix having n distinct rational eigenvalues. Then $\mathcal{L}(\mathcal{A})$ is a recursive subset of $Q^\star$.*

Proof. First we note that the first order theory of the reals augmented with the *constant e* is decidable. For convenience we shall denote this augmented structure as $(\mathbb{R}, +, \cdot, <, 0, 1, e)$ but emphasize that e, the base of the natural logarithm is being used as a constant and *not* as an operator. To see that the augmented theory is decidable, we observe that one can effectively determine whether $p(e) < 0$ for any given polynomial $p(e)$ with integer coefficients. Since $e = 1 + \sum_{h=1}^{\infty} 1/h!$, we have

$$1 + \sum_{h=1}^{k} \frac{1}{h!} < e < 1 + \sum_{h=1}^{k} \frac{1}{h!} + \sum_{h=k+1}^{\infty} \frac{1}{k^{h-k}} = 1 + \sum_{h=1}^{k} \frac{1}{h!} + \frac{1}{k-1}.$$

Note that the polynomial $p(u)$ with one variable has finitely many real roots. Hence for sufficiently large k, $p(u)$ has no root in the interval $[1 + \sum_{h=1}^{k} 1/h!,$ $1 + \sum_{h=1}^{k} 1/h! + 1/(k-1)]$ and so $p(e)$ has the same sign as $p(1 + \sum_{h=1}^{k} 1/h!)$. Clearly such a k can be effectively found. Now, given a sentence φ in $(\mathbb{R}, +, \cdot, <, 0, 1, e)$, one can apply Tarski's quantifier elimination algorithm [16] to obtain a quantifier-free sentence φ' such that φ is true iff φ' is true, and φ' is a boolean combination of formulas of the form $p(e) < 0$.

Next we show that given control states $q, q', q1, q1'$ and $\alpha \in \{\tau, \mu\}$, one can construct in $(\mathbb{R}, +, \cdot, <, 0, 1, e)$ a formula $\Phi_{q,q',q1,q1',\alpha}(V, V1)$ with free variables $V(i), V1(i), i = 1, 2, \ldots, n$, that asserts $(q, V, q') \xrightarrow{\alpha}_{\mathcal{A}} (q1, V1, q1')$. In what follows, we fix $q, q', q1, q1' \in Q$ and $\alpha \in \{\tau, \mu\}$.

Clearly we can effectively compute the rational eigenvalues $\lambda_i, i = 1, 2, \ldots, n$, of A_q, and for each $i = 1, 2, \ldots, n$ find a rational eigenvector $f_i \in \mathbb{Q}^n$ corresponding to λ_i (i.e. $A_q \cdot f_i = \lambda_i \cdot f_i$). Let $F = (f_1 \ f_2 \ \ldots \ f_n)$ be the matrix in $\mathbb{Q}^{n \times n}$ whose i-th column is f_i for $i = 1, 2, \ldots, n$. From [11] it is easy to see that for a real $T \in [0, 1]$, $Val(A_q, b_q, T, V) = H(e^T)$ where $H : \mathbb{R} \to \mathbb{R}^n$ is given by

$$H(u) = F \ diag(u^{\lambda_1}, u^{\lambda_2}, \ldots, u^{\lambda_n}) \ F^{-1}(V + A_q^{-1}b_q) - A_q^{-1}b_q.$$

It is easy to see that for $\alpha = \tau$, the formula $\Phi_{q,q',q1,q1',\alpha}(V, V1)$ can be constructed. The only point to note is that constants of the form e^r where $r \in \mathbb{Q}$ are definable in $(\mathbb{R}, +, \cdot, <, 0, 1, e)$. The case $\alpha = \mu$ will follow from two observations that we now outline.

Let $(q, V, q'), (q1, V1, q1')$ be reachable configurations of $\mathcal{A}$ such that $(q, V, q') \xrightarrow{\mu}_{\mathcal{A}} (q1, V1, q1')$. It follows from the definition of $TS_{\mathcal{A}}$ that $(q, V, q') \xrightarrow{\mu}_{\mathcal{A}} (q1, V1, q1')$ iff $V1 = Val(A_q, b_q, 1, V)$ and there exist reals t_i^{ob} in $[\delta_{ob}^0, \delta_{ob}^1], i = 1, 2, \ldots, n$, and a guard g such that $(q, g, q1)$ is a transition in $\longrightarrow$. Further, $(\langle w_1 \rangle, \langle w_2 \rangle, \ldots, \langle w_n \rangle)$ satisfies g, where w_i is the i-th component of $Val(A_q, b_q, t_i^{ob}, V)$ for $i = 1, 2, \ldots, n$. Firstly we note that the function $t \in [\delta_{ob}^0, \delta_{ob}^1] \to e^t \in [e^{\delta_{ob}^0}, e^{\delta_{ob}^1}]$ is continuous, increasing and onto. Thus there exist reals $t_i^{ob}, i = 1, 2, \ldots, n$, satisfying the desired condition iff there exist reals $u_i \in [e^{\delta_{ob}^0}, e^{\delta_{ob}^1}], i = 1, 2, \ldots, n$, such that w_i is the i-th component of $H(u_i)$ for each $i = 1, 2, \ldots, n$.

Secondly, we note that $-\gamma_{max} \le w_i \le \gamma_{max}$ for every $i = 1, 2, \ldots, n$. For a guard g in $\mathcal{A}$, let $Valuations(g)$ be the *finite* set of valuations given by:

$(v_1, v_2, \ldots, v_n)$ is in *Valuations(g)* iff for each i, $v_i = m_i\epsilon$ where m_i is an integer with $\langle -\gamma_{max} \rangle \leq m_i\epsilon \leq \langle \gamma_{max} \rangle$, and $(v_1, v_2, \ldots, v_n)$ satisfies g. It follows that $(w_1, w_2, \ldots, w_n)$ satisfies g iff $(\langle w_1 \rangle, \langle w_2 \rangle, \ldots, \langle w_n \rangle)$ is in *Valuations(g)*.

Putting together the above two observations, it is now clear how the formula $\Phi_{q,q',q1,q1',\mu}(V, V1)$ can be constructed. It is then also straightforward to see that given a state sequence $q_0 q_1 \ldots q_\ell$ one can construct a sentence $\Phi_{q_0 q_1 \ldots q_\ell}$ such that $\Phi_{q_0 q_1 \ldots q_\ell}$ is true iff $q_0 q_1 \ldots q_\ell$ is in $\mathcal{L}(\mathcal{A})$. □

Theorem 3 implies that one can in principle solve *bounded model checking* problems [6] for the class of hybrid automata satisfying the conditions set out in the statement of the theorem. The next result shows that one can not hope to do much better in this setting.

Theorem 4. *There is no effective procedure which can, given a lazy finite-precision differential hybrid automaton $\mathcal{A}$ satisfying the restrictions stated in Theorem 3 and a control state q_f of $\mathcal{A}$, determine whether q_f is reachable in $\mathcal{A}$. In other words, whether there exists a reachable configuration (q, V, q') of $\mathcal{A}$ such that $q = q_f$.*

Proof. We shall reduce the halting problem of two-counter automata ([12]) to the control state reachability problem of the class of hybrid automata stated in the theorem.

Let $\mathcal{C} = (S, s_{in}, s_{halt}, \leadsto)$ be a two-counter automaton where S is a finite set of states, $s_{in} \in S$ the initial state, $s_{halt} \in S$ the halting state and $\leadsto \subseteq S \times \{ZERO, POS\}^2 \times \{INC, DEC\}^2 \times S$ the instruction table. The instruction $(s, O_1, O_2, \alpha_1, \alpha_2, s')$ indicates that at state s, if the sign of the integer stored in counter i is O_i then $\mathcal{C}$ can perform action α_i (increment or decrement) on counter i and move to state s'. For example, the instruction $(s, ZERO, POS, INC, DEC, s')$ specifies that at state s, if counter 1 is zero and counter 2 is positive, then $\mathcal{C}$ can increment counter 1, decrement counter 2 and move to state s'. The semantics of $\mathcal{C}$ is defined in the obvious way.

In what follows, we construct a lazy finite-precision differential hybrid automaton $\mathcal{A} = (Q, q_{in}, V_{in}, \{\delta_{ob}^0, \delta_{ob}^1, \delta_{up}^0, \delta_{up}^1\}, \epsilon, \{\rho_q\}_{q \in Q}, \{\gamma_{min}, \gamma_{max}\}, \longrightarrow)$ over continuous variables $x_1, \ldots, x_n$ such that $\delta_{up}^0 = 0 = \delta_{up}^1$ and every ρ_q is of the form $\dot{x} = A_q x + b_q$, where A_q is a diagonalizable matrix having n distinct rational eigenvalues. Further, a designated control state $q_f \in Q$ is reachable in $\mathcal{A}$ iff the halting state $s_{halt} \in S$ is reachable in $\mathcal{C}$. In fact, we will construct $\{\rho_q\}_{q \in Q}$ in such a way that every A_q is a diagonal matrix.

We set $n = 3$ and hence $\mathcal{A}$ will be over x_1, x_2, x_3. We first outline the construction of $Q, q_{in}, V_{in}, \{\rho_q\}_{q \in Q}, \longrightarrow$ and later discuss the choice of the parameters $\delta_{ob}^0, \delta_{ob}^1, \epsilon, \gamma_{min}, \gamma_{max}$.

The set of control states Q is $S \bigcup \{s_\xi^\sharp, s_\xi^{\sharp\sharp} \mid \xi \in \leadsto\}$ where for $\xi = (s, O_1, O_2, \alpha_1, \alpha_2, s')$ in $\leadsto$, $s_\xi^\sharp = (s, O_1, O_2, \alpha_1, \alpha_2, s', \sharp)$ and $s_\xi^{\sharp\sharp} = (s, O_1, O_2, \alpha_1, \alpha_2, s', \sharp\sharp)$. Intuitively, the continuous variable x_1 (x_2) will represent values of counter 1 (2). A counter having value h will be represented by the corresponding continuous variable taking the value $1 + e^{-1} + e^{-2} + \cdots + e^{-h}$. In particular, a counter with value zero will be represented by the corresponding continuous variable taking the value 1.

Suppose at time T_k, the hybrid automaton $\mathcal{A}$ is at control state s and wants to "execute" the instruction $(s, O_1, O_2, \alpha_1, \alpha_2, s')$. This is to be done by moving first to $(s, O_1, O_2, \alpha_1, \alpha_2, s', \sharp)$ at time T_{k+1}, and then to $(s, O_1, O_2, \alpha_1, \alpha_2, s', \sharp\sharp)$ at *exactly* time T_{k+2}, and finally to land at s' at *exactly* time T_{k+3}. In this process, the variable x_3 will be used to control that $\mathcal{A}$ "stays" for exactly one time unit at each of $(s, O_1, O_2, \alpha_1, \alpha_2, s', \sharp)$, $(s, O_1, O_2, \alpha_1, \alpha_2, s', \sharp\sharp)$.

The initial control state is s_{in}. The initial valuation is $(1, 1, 1)$.

The rate functions are as follows. For $s \in S$, we set ρ_s to be $\dot{x}_1 = 0 = \dot{x}_2 = \dot{x}_3$. Suppose $(s, O_1, O_2, \alpha_1, \alpha_2, s') \in \leadsto$ is an instruction of $\mathcal{C}$ and $step \in \{\sharp, \sharp\sharp\}$, then the rate function of $(s, O_1, O_2, \alpha_1, \alpha_2, s', step)$ is: $\dot{x}_1 = F_{\alpha_1}^{step}(x_1)$, $\dot{x}_2 = F_{\alpha_2}^{step}(x_2)$, $\dot{x}_3 = H^{step}(x_3)$ where:

- $F_{INC}^{\sharp}(x_i) = -x_i$ and $F_{INC}^{\sharp\sharp}(x_i) = 1$ for $i = 1, 2$.
- $F_{DEC}^{\sharp}(x_i) = -1$ and $F_{DEC}^{\sharp\sharp}(x_i) = x_i$ for $i = 1, 2$.
- $H^{\sharp}(x_3) = 1$ and $H^{\sharp\sharp}(x_3) = -1$.

The transition relation $\longrightarrow$ of $\mathcal{A}$ is $\bigcup_{\xi \in \leadsto} TR_\xi$, where for each $\xi = (s, O_1, O_2, \alpha_1, \alpha_2, s')$ in $\leadsto$, the members of TR_ξ are

$$\left(s, \; g_\xi^s, \; (s, O_1, O_2, \alpha_1, \alpha_2, s', \sharp)\right),$$

$$\left((s, O_1, O_2, \alpha_1, \alpha_2, s', \sharp), \; g_\xi^\sharp, \; (s, O_1, O_2, \alpha_1, \alpha_2, s', \sharp\sharp)\right),$$

$$\left((s, O_1, O_2, \alpha_1, \alpha_2, s', \sharp\sharp), \; g_\xi^{\sharp\sharp}, \; s'\right),$$

with the guards $g_\xi^s, g_\xi^\sharp, g_\xi^{\sharp\sharp}$ being specified as follows. The guard g_ξ^s is $\Phi_{O_1}(x_1) \wedge \Phi_{O_2}(x_2)$ where $\Phi_{ZERO}(x_i)$ is $x_i \leq 1$ and $\Phi_{POS}(x_i)$ is $x_i > 1$ for $i = 1, 2$. The guard $g_\xi^\sharp$ is $x_3 \leq 2$ and $g_\xi^{\sharp\sharp}$ is $x_3 \geq 1$.

It remains to choose the parameters $\delta_{ob}^0, \delta_{ob}^1, \epsilon, \gamma_{min}, \gamma_{max}$ appropriately. Recall that a valuation $(v_1, v_2, \ldots, v_n)$ satisfies a polynomial constraint $p(x_1, x_2, \ldots, x_n) < 0$ iff $p(\langle v_1 \rangle_\epsilon, \langle v_2 \rangle_\epsilon, \ldots, \langle v_n \rangle_\epsilon) < 0$. Thus the main technicality is to ensure that the guards are "stable" even with finite precision measurement of values. The only restriction we need for the choice of $\delta_{ob}^0, \delta_{ob}^1, \epsilon, \gamma_{min}, \gamma_{max}$ is that ϵ integrally divides every member of $\{1, \delta_{ob}^0, \delta_{ob}^1\}$, $\langle 1 + e^{-1} \rangle_\epsilon > 1$, $\gamma_{min} \leq 1$, $\gamma_{max} \geq 2$. We emphasize that we need not demand $\delta_{ob}^0 = 1 = \delta_{ob}^1$.

It is now straightforward to establish that the halting state s_{halt} is reachable in the two-counter automaton $\mathcal{C}$ iff the control state s_{halt} is reachable in the hybrid automaton $\mathcal{A}$. $\qquad\square$

We note that the above proof shows that the undecidability result goes through even if we restrict ourselves to just rectangular guards. This is not surprising since we have the undecidability result of [10]. From the above proof, it is also easy to construct a lazy finite-precision hybrid automaton $\mathcal{A}_1$ satisfying the conditions in Theorem 4 such that $\mathcal{L}(\mathcal{A}_1)$ is *not* regular. For example, let $\mathcal{C}_1$ be the two-counter automaton $(\{s_{DEC}, s_{INC}, s_{halt}\}, s_{DEC}, s_{halt}, \leadsto)$ where the members of $\leadsto$ are: $(s_{DEC}, ZERO, ZERO, INC, INC, s_{INC})$, $(s_{INC}, POS, POS,$

INC, INC, s_{INC}), $(s_{INC}, POS, POS, DEC, DEC, s_{DEC})$, $(s_{DEC}, POS, POS, DEC, DEC, s_{DEC})$. Let $\mathcal{A}_1$ be the hybrid automaton constructed from $\mathcal{C}_1$ as in the proof of Theorem 4. It is easy to show that $\mathcal{L}(\mathcal{A}_1)$ is not regular.

6 Summary

We have shown here that the twin features of discrete time semantics and finite precision can be used to cope with hybrid automata whose dynamics are governed by restricted linear differential operators and whose transitions have polynomial guards. It is easy to show (see [1]) that each of our results, namely Theorem 1, 3, 4, also holds if the combination of finite precision and polynomial guards is replaced by that of perfect precision and rectangular guards.

Our results seem to suggest that once observational and update delays are included to further reduce the expressive power of these automata, one may be able to handle much richer continuous dynamics. The key obstacle here is the lack of means for constructing suitable rational approximations of the continuous dynamics. Here, the mathematical foundations provided in [5] and the logical underpinnings developed in [14, 15] promise to be good starting points.

References

[1] M. Agrawal, F. Stephan, P.S. Thiagarajan, and S. Yang. Behavioural approximations for restricted linear differential hybrid automata. Technical Report TR42/05, School of Computing, National University of Singapore, Singapore, 2005.

[2] M. Agrawal and P.S. Thiagarajan. Lazy rectangular hybrid automata. In *7th HSCC, LNCS 2993*, pages 1–15. Springer, 2003.

[3] M. Agrawal and P.S. Thiagarajan. The discrete time behaviour of lazy linear hybrid automata. In *8th HSCC, LNCS 3414*, pages 55–69. Springer, 2005.

[4] R. Alur, T.A. Henzinger, G. Lafferriere, and G.J. Pappas. Discrete abstractions of hybrid systems. *Proc. of the IEEE*, 88:971–984, 2000.

[5] A. Baker. *Transcendental Number Theory*. Cambridge University Press, 1979.

[6] A. Biere, A. Cimatti, E.M. Clarke, O. Strichman, and Y. Zhu. *Bounded Model Checking*. Advances in Computers 58. Academic Press, 2003.

[7] V. Gupta, T.A. Henzinger, and R. Jagadeesan. Robust timed automata. In *HART '97, LNCS 1201*, pages 331–345. Springer, 1997.

[8] T.A. Henzinger. The theory of hybrid automata. In *11th LICS*, pages 278–292. IEEE Press, 1996.

[9] T.A. Henzinger and P.W. Kopke. State equivalences for rectangular hybrid automata. In *7th CONCUR, LNCS 1119*, pages 530–545. Springer, 1996.

[10] T.A. Henzinger, P.W. Kopke, A. Puri, and P. Varaiya. What's decidable about hybrid automata? *J. of Comp. and Sys. Sci.*, 57:94–124, 1998.

[11] M. Hirsch and S. Smale. *Differential Equations, Dynamical Systems and Linear Algebra*. Academic Press, 1974.

[12] J.E. Hopcroft and J.D. Ullman. *Introduction to Automata Theory, Languages and Computation*. Addison-Wesley, 1979.

[13] Y. Kesten, A. Pnueli, J. Sifakis, and S. Yovine. Integration graphs: A class of decidable hybrid systems. In *Hybrid Systems, LNCS 736*, pages 179–208. Springer, 1993.

[14] G. Lafferriere, G.J. Pappas, and S. Sastry. O-minimal hybrid systems. *Math. Control Signals Systems*, 13:1–21, 2000.

[15] G. Lafferriere, G.J. Pappas, and S. Yovine. Symbolic reachability computation for families of linear vector fields. *J. Symbolic Computation*, 32:231–253, 2001.

[16] A. Tarski. *A Decision Method for Elementary Algebra and Geometry.* University of California Press, 1951.

[17] A. Wilkie. Schanuel's conjecture and the decidability of the real exponential field. In *Algebraic Model Theory*, pages 223–230. Kluwer, 1997.

Bounded Model Checking for GSMP Models of Stochastic Real-Time Systems*

Rajeev Alur and Mikhail Bernadsky

Department of Computer and Information Science,
University of Pennsylvania
{alur, mbernads}@cis.upenn.edu

Abstract. Model checking is a popular algorithmic verification technique for checking temporal requirements of mathematical models of systems. In this paper, we consider the problem of verifying bounded reachability properties of stochastic real-time systems modeled as generalized semi-Markov processes (GSMP). While GSMPs is a rich model for stochastic systems widely used in performance evaluation, existing model checking algorithms are applicable only to subclasses such as discrete-time or continuous-time Markov chains. The main contribution of the paper is an algorithm to compute the probability that a given GSMP satisfies a property of the form "can the system reach a target before time T within k discrete events, while staying within a set of safe states". For this, we show that the probability density function for the remaining firing times of different events in a GSMP after k discrete events can be effectively partitioned into finitely many regions and represented by exponentials and polynomials. We report on illustrative examples and their analysis using our techniques.

1   Introduction

Probabilistic modeling is commonly used in the design and performance evaluation of a wide range of real-time systems such as communication protocols and multi-media systems ([11, 8]). Traditional analysis of probabilistic models involves simulations, and is used to obtain estimates of quality-of-service metrics such as mean delivery time for a message. In contrast, formal verification techniques are aimed at checking whether or not a system model satisfies a functional correctness property such as "every message is eventually delivered." Model checking has emerged as a viable method for formal verification for debugging critical components in industrial settings ([6, 5, 12]). The goal of probabilistic model checking is to integrate the two approaches so that a probabilistic model of a real-time system can be algorithmically checked against a specification such as "every message is delivered within 1ms with probability 0.9."

Early work on probabilistic model checking considers discrete models such as finite-state Markov chains or Markov decision processes, and requirements given by temporal logics or automata, and shows how to algorithmically compute the probability that a model satisfies the requirement ([19, 7, 10]). More recent work allows modeling using continuous-time Markov chains (CTMCs), and specifications written in temporal logics

* This research was supported by the US National Science Foundation via grants CCR-0410662 and ITR/SY 0121431.

João Hespanha and A. Tiwari (Eds.): HSCC 2006, LNCS 3927, pp. 19–33, 2006.
© Springer-Verlag Berlin Heidelberg 2006

such as CSL and PCTL that allow requirements with time and probability ([3, 15, 16]). Issues concerning symbolic representation and efficient implementation have also been studied leading to a number of probabilistic model checkers ([13, 17]). In particular, the model checker PRISM has been applied to a number of case studies in distributed protocols and embedded systems (see http://www.cs.bham.ac.uk/~dxp/prism).

In this paper, we consider the probabilistic model checking problem for systems modeled as *Generalized Semi-Markov Processes* (GSMPs) ([9, 18, 8]). In our model of *finite-state* GSMPs, the system can be in one of the finitely many states, and can have a finite number of scheduled events. When the event(s) with the least remaining firing time happens, the state is updated probabilistically, and new events can be scheduled at times chosen randomly according to distributions described by exponential and polynomial density functions with finitely many discontinuities, which we call *expolynomial region distributions* (ERDs). Unlike CTMCs, such distributions need not be memoryless, and the class of ERDs includes uniform or polynomial distributions over finite intervals, point distributions over finitely many constant values, and exponentials.

The classical way to analyze GSMP models involves Monte Carlo simulations. In [1], the authors show how to check *qualitative* probabilistic properties, that is, whether a GSMP satisfies a property with probability 0 or 1, and this analysis is based on the so-called region graph introduced for analysis of non-probabilistic real-time systems modeled using timed automata [2]. Region graph, however, is not adequate for computing *quantitative* probabilistic properties as different configurations in the same region have different probabilities of satisfaction of properties. In [14], the authors show that by refining the region graph, one can approximate the satisfaction of quantitative probabilistic properties, while [20] shows that statistical sampling can be adopted to compute estimates for the model checking problem. The literature on stochastic Petri nets shows how GSMPs can be approximated by Markovian models [8]. In this paper, we show that if we are given a bound on the number of events, then exact symbolic analysis for verifying quantitative probabilistic properties of GSMPs is possible. More specifically, given a finite-state GSMP M, a target set F, a safety set S, a bound k on the number of discrete events, we show how to compute the probability that M will reach F, while staying within the set S, within k discrete events (and also, within a time bound T, if specified). The bound k is analogous to the bound on the lengths of paths used in recent work on *bounded model checking* of discrete Boolean systems using SAT solvers [4].

For quantitative analysis of a GSMP, we need to effectively represent and compute the distribution on the remaining firing times of scheduled events when the event(s) with the least firing time happens. For this purpose, we consider multidimensional expolynomial region distributions: the space of configurations is divided into finitely many regions using axis-parallel and diagonal constraints similar to the region graph, and with each region, the density function is continuous represented by a combination of exponential and polynomial functions. Our main technical construction shows that the class of ERDs is effectively closed under expiration of events and scheduling of new events. This leads to an iterative symbolic algorithm which computes the probability distribution after each discrete step.

We are implementing our modeling and analysis approach in a tool called *Event Horizon Verifier*, and we illustrate it using a classical example from queuing networks.

Consider a buffer for which the interarrival time between successive messages from the producer, and the processing time for a message by the consumer, are described by ERDs. Given a capacity N, suppose we want to calculate the probability that the number of unprocessed messages exceeds N. Then, our analysis allows us to compute this probability, given a bound on the total number of events.

2 Generalized Semi-Markov Processes

Let $\mathbb{N}$ be the set of all natural numbers, $\mathbb{N}_0$ be $\mathbb{N} \cup \{0\}$, $\mathbb{R}$ be the set of reals, and $\mathbb{R}_+$ be the set of all non-negative reals.

In a GSMP the time between scheduling an event and its occurrence (or firing time) is modeled as a positive random variable. For this reason we briefly review related terminology. A random variable X is characterized by its *cumulative distribution function* (cdf) $distr(x) = \Pr(X < x)$, and if $distr(x)$ is continuous then also by *probability density function* (pdf) $dens(x)$ defined by the equation $distr(x) = \int_0^x dens(y)\, dy$. For many modeling purposes, however, it is convenient to use random variables whose cdf's are not continuous. For instance, it may be necessary to model the firing time of an event by a random variable that takes only a finite number of possible values. We say that $x \in \mathbb{R}_+$ is a *mass point* of X if $\Pr(X = x) > 0$[1]. We will see that for random variables with a finite number of mass points it is still possible to define a function with properties similar to those of the pdf of a random variable with continuous cdf.

We say that an expression $e(x)$ is *expolynomial* if it can be written as $\sum_{k=1}^{r} c_k x^{m_k} e^{\lambda_k x}$, where $c_k, \lambda_k \in \mathbb{R}$, $m_k \in \mathbb{N}_0$, for all $k = 1, \ldots, r$. Let $Expr(x)$ be the set of all expolynomial expressions. Consider a partition R_a of $\mathbb{R}_+$, which consists of a bounded intervals followed by an unbounded interval and the points between them: $R_a = \cup_{i=0}^{a-1}\{i, (i, i+1)\} \cup \{a, (a, +\infty)\}$. The constant a is the *width* of R_a. We say that a function $f(x)$ is *expolynomial* with finite support on R_a if there exists a map $M_f \colon R_a \to Expr(x)$, such that for all $x \in \mathbb{R}_+$, $f(x) = M(r)(x)$, where $x \in r$ and $r \in R_a$ (i.e. r is either an interval or a point).

Definition 1. *A (unidimensional) random variable X has an expolynomial region distribution of width a, if there exists an expolynomial function $dens(x) \geq 0$ on R_a, such that for all $t \in \mathbb{R}_+$, $\Pr(X < t) = \sum_{I \in I_{R_a}} \int_{I \cap (y < t)} dens(y)\, dy + \sum_{i=1}^{\min(a, \lfloor t \rfloor)} dens(i)$ $= \int_0^t dens(y)\, dy + \sum_{i=1}^{\min(a, \lfloor t \rfloor)} dens(i)$, where I_{R_a} is the set of all intervals in R_a, and $\lfloor t \rfloor$ denotes the largest integer no greater than t.*

We call $dens(x)$ the pdf of X. Notice, that X has a mass point at i iff $dens(i) > 0$ and $i \in \{1, \ldots, a\}$.

Uniform distributions, exponential and truncated exponential distributions, finite discrete distributions are all examples of expolynomial region distributions. Many other distributions with continuous and discrete components can be approximated by expolynomial distributions. Our definition requires finite intervals to be of the unit length and

---

[1] Mass points can also be treated using Dirac delta function $\delta(x)$. We have chosen not to do so because this approach leads to cumbersome expressions in the multidimensional settings.

mass points to occur at a finite number of points in $\mathbb{N}$, however this is done only to simplify the presentation of the results. In general, it is sufficient if a distribution is defined by expolynomial expressions on a finite number of intervals with rational endpoints, and has only a finite number of mass points.

Now we are ready to give a formal definition of the class of stochastic processes that we study in this paper.

Definition 2. *A finite-state generalized semi-Markov process (GSMP) is a tuple $A = (Q, \Sigma, E, init, distr, next)$ where:*

- *Q is a finite set of locations;*
- *Σ is a finite set of events;*
- *$E \colon Q \to 2^\Sigma$ assigns to each location $q \in Q$ a set of events that are active in q. A location q is absorbing iff $E(q) = \emptyset$.*
- *$init \colon Q \to [0,1]$ is a probability measure on Q, which for each location $q \in Q$ gives the probability that q is the initial location of A;*
- *$distr \colon \Sigma \to (\mathbb{R}_+ \to [0,1])$ assigns to each event its firing time distribution, which is an expolynomial region distribution. For a cdf $distr(e)$, $dens(e)$ denotes the corresponding pdf.*
- *$next \colon Q \times (2^\Sigma \setminus \{\emptyset\}) \to (Q \to [0,1])$ defines transitions between the locations of A. This function takes as its arguments a source location q and a non-empty subset G of the active events of q, and returns a probability measure on Q. For each location q', this measure gives the probability that A will move from q to q' if all events in G occur simultaneously; we require that $\sum_{q' \in Q} next(q, G)(q') = 1$ for all $G \subseteq 2^{E(q)} \setminus \{\emptyset\}$.*

It is convenient to think that a clock is assigned to each event e. Upon (re-)scheduling of e we update its clock to a new valuation chosen independently at random according to $distr(e)$. The clock shows the time remaining until the next occurrence of e. Every clock runs down with the same rate equal to 1. Let us say that $\nu \colon \Sigma \to \mathbb{R}_+$ is a clock valuation (or simply valuation) if ν maps events to the values of their clocks. If an event is not active in the current location we assume that its value is undefined.

A *configuration* of the GSMP A is a pair $s = (q, \nu)$, where $q \in Q$ and ν is a clock valuation. Given a configuration $s = (q, \nu)$, let $t^*(s) = \min\{\nu(e), e \in E(q)\}$ be the time until the next transition and $E^*(s) = \{e^* \mid e^* = \arg\min\{\nu(e), e \in E(q)\}\}$ be the set of events that causes the transition (the clocks of these events expire simultaneously). For any $t \le t^*(s)$ we denote by $\nu - t$ the valuation ν' such that for all $e \in E(q)$, $\nu'(e) = \nu(e) - t$. We say that $s \xrightarrow{t} s'$ is a *timed transition* between the configurations $s = (q, \nu)$ and $s' = (q, \nu')$ if $\nu' = \nu - t$. If $t^*(s) = 0$, then $E^* = \{e^* \mid \nu(e^*) = 0\}$, and $s \xrightarrow{\mu} s'$ denotes a *discrete transition* between the configurations $s = (q, \nu)$ and $s' = (q', \nu')$, where q' is chosen according to the probability measure $\mu = next(q, E^*)$, and the valuation ν' is constructed as follows:

1. if an event $e \in E_{old}(q, E^*, q')$, where $E_{old}(q, E^*, q') = E(q') \cap [E(q) \setminus E^*]$ is the set of events, excluding the events in E^*, that were active in q and continue to be active in q', then $\nu'(e) = \nu(e)$;

2. if $e \in E_{\text{new}}(q, E^*, q')$, where $E_{\text{new}}(q, E^*, q') = E(q') \setminus E_{\text{old}}(q, E^*, q')$ is the set of events that were not active in q but become active in q' and events that are in $E^* \cap E(q')$ (i.e. events that fired in q and are active in q'), then valuations $\nu'(e)$ are chosen independently at random according to $distr(e)$ (i.e. the events in $E_{\text{new}}(q, E^*, q')$ are (re-)scheduled);

3. if $e \in E_{\text{cancelled}}(q, E^*, q')$, where $E_{\text{cancelled}}(q, E^*, q') = E(q) \setminus E(q')$ is the set of cancelled events that were active in q but no longer active in q', then $\nu'(e)$ is undefined.

A *run* σ of A is a sequence of alternating timed and discrete transitions:

$$\sigma = s_0 \xrightarrow{t^*(s_0)} s_0' \xrightarrow{\mu_0} s_1 \xrightarrow{t^*(s_1)} s_1' \xrightarrow{\mu_1} s_2 \xrightarrow{t^*(s_2)} s_2' \xrightarrow{\mu_2} \ldots$$

The run σ starts at the initial configuration $s_0 = (q_0, \nu_0)$, q_0 is the initial location, which is chosen according to *init*, and ν_0 is the initial valuations of the events in $E(q_0)$, scheduled according to the corresponding firing time distributions. A run can have a finite or infinite number of transitions; a run that has reached an absorbing location will stay in that location forever.

The time of the nth transition is the time $T_n(\sigma) = \sum_{i=0}^{n-1} t^*(s_i)$ that elapsed since the start of σ and until the nth discrete transition.

Example 1. Let us describe a GSMP A_s, which we will use as our running example. A_s has six locations, q_0 is the initial location (i.e. *init* picks this location with probability one), and locations q_2, q_3, q_4, and q_5 are absorbing. In q_0 two events e_1 and e_2 are active, the initial clock valuations for these events are chosen according to their firing time density functions: $dens(e_1)(t_1) = Dt_1 e^{-t_1}$ when $t_1 \in (0, 1)$ and 0 otherwise (the normalizing constant D is equal to $1/(1 - 2e^{-1})$), and $dens(e_2)(t_2) = 1/2$ when $t_2 \in (0, 1) \cup (1, 2)$ and 0 otherwise, i.e. it is uniformly distributed on $(0, 2)$. If e_1 fires first, then the process moves to q_1 with probability 1, otherwise it moves to q_2 and stays there forever. In q_1 three events are active — e_2 whose clock keeps its valuation from q_0 and events e_1 and e_3 whose clocks obtain new valuations upon entering q_1. The firing time density function for e_3 is $dens(e_3)(t_3) = 1$ when $t_3 \in (0, 1)$ and 0 otherwise, and it describes the uniform distribution on $(0, 1)$. Firings of e_1, e_2 and e_3 in q_1 lead to locations q_3, q_4 and q_5, respectively.

A *history* π of the length n of a run σ is a sequence of tuples and transitions between them marked with sets of events:

$$\pi = (q_0, \mathcal{O}_0, \mathcal{N}_0) \xrightarrow{E_1} (q_1, \mathcal{O}_1, \mathcal{N}_1) \xrightarrow{E_2} \ldots \xrightarrow{E_n} (q_n, \mathcal{O}_n, \mathcal{N}_n)$$

Each tuple $(q_i, \mathcal{O}_i, \mathcal{N}_i)$ consists of a visited location and two sets that partition the set of active events of that location. The set $\mathcal{O}_i$ consists of active events that were not scheduled upon arriving to q_i and the set $\mathcal{N}_i$ consists of active events that were scheduled. For the tuple $(q_0, \mathcal{O}_0, \mathcal{N}_0)$, we have that $\mathcal{O}_0 = \emptyset$ and $\mathcal{N}_0 = E(q_0)$, and for any $i > 0$, $\mathcal{O}_i = E_{\text{old}}(q_{i-1}, E_i, q_i)$ and $\mathcal{N}_i = E_{\text{new}}(q_{i-1}, E_i, q_i)$.

By $last(\pi) = q_n$ we will denote the last visited location in a history π, and by Π we will denote the set of all finite histories.

It easy to see that two runs share the same history π of length n if they visit the same sequence of n locations and transitions between those locations are caused by firing of the same sets of events.

We say that a history π' is a *successor* of π along an edge marked by a set of events E iff there exists a tuple $(q_{l'}, \mathcal{O}_{l'}, \mathcal{N}_{l'})$ such that $\pi' = \pi \xrightarrow{E} (q_{l'}, \mathcal{O}_{l'}, \mathcal{N}_{l'})$.

Definition 3. *Let π be a history of length n and let $l = |E(last(\pi))|$ be the number of the active events in the last location of π, then the event clock valuations of π (abbreviated as ecv of π) is an l-dimensional random variable of values of the active clocks in the location $last(\pi)$, immediately after it has been reached by the nth transition.*

Given a history π, we denote by $f^\pi(x_1, \ldots, x_l)$ the pdf of the event clock valuations of π. We will show how to use $f^\pi(x_1, \ldots, x_l)$ to compute probability p_π, which is called the *occurrence probability* of π and which is equal to the probability that a run of A has π as its history.

3   Computing Probabilities of Bounded Until Properties

Suppose that we are given a GSMP A. The locations of A are partitioned into two sets: Q_s and Q_u which are called the sets of *safe* and *unsafe* locations, respectively. Furthermore, a subset Q_d of Q_s is called the set of *destination locations*.

Let $\Pi^n_{\text{until}} \subseteq \Pi$ be a set of histories of length less than or equal to n, and such that for every $\pi \in \Pi^n_{\text{until}}$ all locations of π belong to Q_s and the only location that belongs to Q_d is $last(\pi)$; let $\Pi_{\text{until}} = \cup_{n>0}\Pi^n_{\text{until}}$.

Given two parameters — a real number $p \in [0, 1]$ and an integer $n > 0$, we consider the *bounded until problem*:

- Is the probability that a run σ of A has a history $\pi \in \Pi^n_{\text{until}}$ greater than p?

Algorithm 1. is a generic algorithm to solve this problem. The algorithm works on tuples (π, f^π, p_π), the first element of a tuple is a history π, the second element is the ecv density f^π of π, and the last element p_π is the occurrence probability of π. Given f^π and p_π, we assume (and we will prove later) that for any successor history π' of π, we are able to compute $f^{\pi'}$ and $p_{\pi'|\pi}$ (which is the occurrence probability of π' conditioned on the probabilistic event that π has happened).

HistorySet is the set of tuples that the algorithm has to process. The set is initialized with the tuples $(\pi_0^i, f^{\pi_0^i}, p_{\pi_0^i})$, where $\pi_0^i = (q_i, \mathcal{O}_0^i, \mathcal{N}_0^i)$ for locations q_i of A, such that $init(q_i) > 0$. The algorithm also sets to zero two real numbers P_d and P_u, which are the lower bounds of reaching a destination location and an unsafe location, respectively. In the main loop, the algorithm picks a history from *HistorySet* and checks if its last location is a destination or an unsafe location. If this is the case then it increases P_d or P_u. If the last location is a safe location but not a destination location and the length of the history is less than n, then the algorithm computes $f^{\pi'}$ and $p_{\pi'|\pi}$ for every successor history π' of π and updates *HistorySet* with the computed tuples. When the loop is completed, the algorithm outputs "*YES*" if $P_d > p$ and "*NO*" otherwise.

Algorithm 1. Genereric iterative algorithm

---

for all $q_i : q_i \in Q \wedge init(q_i) > 0$ **do**
  $HistorySet \leftarrow (\pi_0^i, f^{\pi_0^i}, p_{\pi_0^i})$
end for
$P_d \leftarrow 0, P_u \leftarrow 0$
while $HistorySet \neq \emptyset \wedge P_d \leq p \wedge P_u \leq (1 - p)$ **do**
  pick (π, f^π, p_π) in $HistorySet$
  if $last(\pi) \in Q_d$ **then**
    $P_d \leftarrow P_d + p_\pi$
  else if $last(\pi) \in Q_u$ **then**
    $P_u \leftarrow P_u + p_\pi$
  else if length of $\pi < n$ **then**
    for all $\pi_s : \pi_s$ is a successor of π **do**
      compute f^{π_s} and $p_{\pi_s | \pi}$
      add $(\pi_s, f^{\pi_s}, p_\pi \cdot p_{\pi_s | \pi})$ to $HistorySet$
    end for
  end if
end while
if $P_d > p$ **then**
  return YES
else
  return NO
end if

Suppose that in addition to the numbers p and n, we are given a positive real number T. Then, applying our algorithm, we can also solve the *bounded timed-until problem*:

– *Is the probability that a run σ of A has a history $\pi \in \Pi_{until}^n$ and $T_{|\pi|}(\sigma) < T$ greater than p?*

The bounded timed-until problem can be reduced to the bounded until problem by introducing a new event e_t and a new unsafe absorbing location q_t. The random variable that models firing time distribution for e_t is equal to T with probability one. For every location q and every set of events E, such that $e_t \in E$, $next(q, E)$ returns a probability measure concentrated on q_t. Thus, if a destination location is reached then it is reached before time T has elapsed.

3.1 A Sample Computation

Consider the GSMP A_s from Example 1 of Section 2. Given a history $\pi_1 = \pi_0 \xrightarrow{\{e_1\}}$ $(q_1, \{e_2\}, \{e_1, e_3\})$, $\pi_0 = (q_0, \emptyset, \{e_1, e_2\})$, we want to compute p_{π_1} and f^{π_1}.

Later, in Section 4, we will prove that to find p_{π_1} and f^{π_1} we need to compute three formulas:

$$\tilde{f}^{\pi_1}(t_2) = \int_0^{+\infty} dens(e_2)(t_1 + t_2) dens(e_1)(t_1) \, dt_1, \qquad p_{\pi_1} = \int_0^{+\infty} \tilde{f}^{\pi_1}(t_2) \, dt_2,$$

$$f^{\pi_1}(t_1, t_2, t_3) = dens(e_1)(t_1) \frac{\tilde{f}^{\pi_1}(t_2)}{p_{\pi_1}} dens(e_3)(t_3).$$

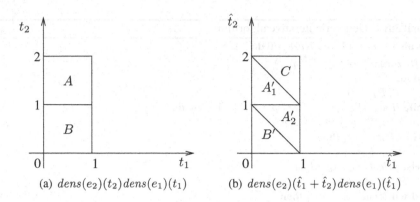

(a) $dens(e_2)(t_2)dens(e_1)(t_1)$ (b) $dens(e_2)(\hat{t}_1 + \hat{t}_2)dens(e_1)(\hat{t}_1)$

Fig. 1. Computing f^{π_1}

Intuitively, the first formula captures the necessary information on the distribution of values of the clock of e_2 in q_1, given that e_1 has fired before e_2. The second formula shows that we can find p_{π_1} by integrating $\tilde{f}^{\pi_1}(t_2)$ over all possible values. And the last formula gives an expression for $f^{\pi_1}(t_1, t_2, t_3)$ as a product of three density functions, each corresponds to an active clock of q_1. Even though the formulas above use integrals we will not use numerical computations, but instead we will obtain the formulas in an explicit form. This suitability for symbolic computations is a distinctive property of the expolynomial functions and we will use it throughout the paper.

We show two ways to compute the first formula. Let $1_{[a<t<b]}$ denote a function of t, which is 1 if $a < t < b$ and 0 otherwise. We know that $dens(e_1)(t_1) = Dt_1e^{-t_1}1_{[0<t_1<1]}$ and $dens(e_2)(t_2) = \frac{1}{2}1_{[0<t_2<2]}$, thus $\tilde{f}^{\pi_1}(t_2) = \frac{D}{2}\int_0^{+\infty} t_1e^{-t_1}1_{[0<t_1<1]}1_{[0<t_1+t_2<2]} \, dt_1 = \frac{D}{2}\int_0^1 t_1e^{-t_1}1_{[0<t_1+t_2<2]} \, dt_1$. We consider two cases:

- if $t_2 \in (0,1)$, then $\tilde{f}^{\pi_1}(t_2) = \frac{D}{2}\int_0^1 t_1e^{-t_1} \, dt_1 = \frac{1}{2}$;
- if $t_2 \in (1,2)$, then $\tilde{f}^{\pi_1}(t_2) = \frac{D}{2}\int_0^{2-t_2} t_1e^{-t_1} \, dt_1 = \frac{D}{2}(t_2e^{t_2-2} - 3e^{t_2-2} + 1)$.

Note that computing $\tilde{f}^{\pi_1}(t_2)$ requires analysis of different possible cases and the number of cases quickly becomes intractable with the increase in the number of active events in a location and complexity of firing time distributions. To deal with these difficulties we present now a more convenient "geometric" way to compute $\tilde{f}^{\pi_1}(t_2)$.

In Figure 1(a), the support for the function $dens(e_2)(t_2)dens(e_1)(t_1)$ is shown. It consists of two squares A and B (without the borders), and in each of these squares the function is equal to $\frac{D}{2}t_1e^{-t_1}$. Now consider a linear transformation $t_1 = \hat{t}_1$, $t_2 = \hat{t}_1 + \hat{t}_2$. Under this transformation the squares A and B are transformed into areas $A'_1 \cup A'_2$ and B', respectively (see Figure 1(b)). The original function did not depend on t_2, and after the transformation the function will not depend on $\hat{t}_2$ either — it is equal to $\frac{D}{2}\hat{t}_1e^{-\hat{t}_1}$ in the areas A'_1, A'_2 and B', and it is 0 in C. Now it is easy to see that if $\hat{t}_2 \in (0,1)$ then we have to compute two integrals, one over B' and the other over A'_2: $\tilde{f}^{\pi_1}(\hat{t}_2) = \frac{D}{2}\int_0^{1-\hat{t}_2} \hat{t}_1e^{-\hat{t}_1} \, d\hat{t}_1 + \frac{D}{2}\int_{1-\hat{t}_2}^1 \hat{t}_1e^{-\hat{t}_1} \, d\hat{t}_1 = \frac{1}{2}$; and if $\hat{t}_2 \in (1,2)$

then we need to compute only one integral over A_1': $\tilde{f}^{\pi_1}(\hat{t}_2) = \frac{D}{2} \int_0^{2-\hat{t}_2} \hat{t}_1 e^{-\hat{t}_1}\, dt_1 = \frac{D}{2}(\hat{t}_2 e^{\hat{t}_2 - 2} - 3e^{\hat{t}_2 - 2} + 1)$.

Now, using the second formula and renaming the variable $\hat{t}_2$ back to t_2, we obtain that

$$p_{\pi_1} = \int_0^2 \tilde{f}^{\pi_1}(t_2)\, dt = \int_0^1 \frac{1}{2}\, dt_2 + \frac{D}{2}\int_1^2 (t_2 e^{t_2 - 2} - 3e^{t_2 - 2} + 1)\, dt_2$$

$$= \frac{1}{2} + \frac{D}{2}(3e^{-1} - 1) \approx 0.7$$

Finally, $f^{\pi_1}(t_1, t_2, t_3) = Dt_1 e^{-t_1} 1_{[0 < t_1 < 1]} \cdot \left(\frac{1}{2p_\pi} 1_{[0 < t_2 < 1]} + \frac{D}{2p_\pi}(t_2 e^{t_2 - 2} - 3e^{t_2 - 2} + 1) 1_{[1 < t_2 < 2]}\right) \cdot 1_{[0 < t_3 < 1]}$. Again, for this function we can have a convenient geometric representation but this time in three dimensions.

4   Multidimensional Expolynomial Region Distributions

In this section we introduce multidimensional expolynomial region distributions. We are interested in this class because it is closed under symbolic computations that we will use. It follows that if the firing time distributions of the events are (one-dimensional) ERDs then all the distributions that we will encounter will also be ERDs. Before giving a formal definition, we describe a class of partitions of the clock valuation space that we will call *diagonal mesh partitions*. These partitions serve as domains for the ERDs — in each region of a diagonal mesh partition, an ERD is given by a multidimensional *expolynomial expression*.

4.1   Diagonal and Inverse Diagonal Mesh Partitions

For a set of variables $t_1, \ldots, t_n$ an n-dimensional diagonal mesh partition R_a of width $a \in \mathbb{N}$ is a partition of $\mathbb{R}_+^n$ into regions such that each region is described by:

- *mesh constraints:* for each variable t, by a constraint of the form $b - 1 < t < b$ (we say that such a constraint is *bounded*), or $t = b$, or $t > a$ (an *unbounded* constraint), where $b \in \mathbb{N}$ and $b \leq a$;
- *diagonal constraints:* for every pair of different variables t and t', such that both of them have bounded mesh constraints in the region, by an ordering on the fractional parts of the variables, i.e. by a constraint of the form $(t - \lfloor t \rfloor) \sim (t' - \lfloor t' \rfloor)$, where $\sim \in \{<, >, =\}$. Equivalently, if there are constraints $b - 1 < t < b$ and $c - 1 < t' < c$, then the diagonal constraint can be written as $t \sim t' + (b - c)$.

Given a region r of an n-dimensional diagonal mesh partition R_a, let m be the number of independent constraints of the form $t = b$ or $t = t' + b$, then we say that the dimension of r is $n - m$. The regions that have dimension n are called *full dimensional regions*, and regions that have less than n dimensions are called *mass regions*.

For technical reasons, we will be also interested in the *inverse diagonal mesh partitions*. Compared to the diagonal mesh partitions these partitions have one designated variable t^*, which cannot form diagonal constraints with any other variable but, instead, it forms inverse diagonal constraints. Formally, for a set of variables $t_1, \ldots, t_{n-1}, t^*$ an n-dimensional inverse diagonal mesh partition $\tilde{R}_a$ of width $a \in \mathbb{N}$ is a partition of $\mathbb{R}_+^n$ into regions such that each region is described by:

- *mesh constraints:* for each variable $t \in \{t_1, \ldots, t_{n-1}, t^*\}$ by a mesh constraint, as described in the definition of diagonal mesh partition;
- *diagonal constraints:* for every pair of different variables $t \neq t^*$ and $t' \neq t^*$ with bounded mesh constraints, by a diagonal constraint, as described in the definition of diagonal mesh partition;
- *inverse diagonal constraints:* for every pair of variables t and t^*, such that for each of them there is a bounded mesh constraint, by a constraint of the form $(t - \lfloor t \rfloor) + (t^* - \lfloor t^* \rfloor) \sim 1$, where $\sim \in \{<, >, =\}$. Equivalently, if there are constraints $b - 1 < t < b$ and $c - 1 < t^* < c$, then the inverse diagonal constraint can be written as $t + t^* + 1 \sim b + c$.

Note that the number of the regions in every diagonal or inverse diagonal mesh partition is finite, and exponential in the number of variables. Note also that the constraints can be seen as hyperplanes in $\mathbb{R}_+^n$.

Next we will consider an important linear transformation $\mathcal{L} \colon \mathbb{R}_+^n \to \mathbb{R}_+^n$. Let $p = (t_1, \ldots, t_{n-1}, t^*)$ be a point that $\mathcal{L}$ maps to a point $\hat{p} = (\hat{t}_1, \ldots, \hat{t}_{n-1}, \hat{t}^*)$, then coordinates of p and $\hat{p}$ are related by the following equations: $t_i = \hat{t}_i + \hat{t}^*$, for $i = 1, \ldots, n-1$ and $t^* = \hat{t}^*$. We have seen an application of $\mathcal{L}$ in Section 3.1. The properties of the partitions are given by the following lemmas. Due to the lack of space, we omit the proofs.

Lemma 1. *Let R_a be an n-dimensional diagonal mesh partition of width a. Then $\mathcal{L}$ transforms R_a into an n-dimensional inverse diagonal mesh partition $\hat{R}_a$ of the same width. The pre-image of any l-dimensional region in $\hat{R}_a$, for $l = 0, \ldots, n$, is a (part of) l-dimensional region in R_a.*

Lemma 2. *Let $\hat{R}_a$ be an n-dimensional inverse diagonal mesh partition with the variables $(t_1, \ldots, t_{n-1}, t^*)$, then the projection R'_a of $\hat{R}_a$ on the subspace $\mathbb{R}_+^{n-1}$ that corresponds to the variables $(t_1, \ldots, t_{n-1})$ is $(n-1)$-dimensional diagonal mesh partition of width a.*

Our interest in diagonal and inverse diagonal mesh partitions is justified by the following example. Let us revisit the GSMP A_s from Example 1. In Section 3.1 we have computed p_{π_1} and $f^{\pi_1}(t_1, t_2, t_3)$ and showed that f^{π_1} had its support on cubes in $\mathbb{R}_+^3$. Now we want to show that it is necessary to have diagonal constraints too. Consider the history π_2, which is a successor of π_1: $\pi_2 = \pi_1 \xrightarrow{\{e_3\}} (q_5, \emptyset, \emptyset)$. We want to compute p_{π_2}. Similarly to the formula for $\tilde{f}^{\pi_1}(t_2)$, we can write $\tilde{f}^{\pi_2}(t_1, t_2) = \int_0^{+\infty} f^{\pi_1}(t_1 + t_3, t_1 + t_3, t_3)\, dt_3$. Evaluating this formula using, for example, MAPLE we will see that in two regions $(0 < t_1 < 1, 0 < t_2 < 1, t_1 < t_2)$ and $(0 < t_1 < 1, 0 < t_2 < 1, t_1 > t_2)$, $\tilde{f}^{\pi_2}(t_1, t_2)$ is given by two *different* expolynomial expressions.

4.2 Expolynomial Expressions, Functions, and Distributions

We say that $e(x_1, \ldots, x_n)$ is an expolynomial expression if it is of the form $\sum_{k=1}^r c_k x_1^{m_{k1}} \cdots x_n^{m_{kn}} e^{\lambda_{k1} x_{k1} + \cdots + \lambda_{kn} x_{kn}}$, where $c_k, \lambda_{k1}, \ldots, \lambda_{kn} \in \mathbb{R}$,

$m_{k1}, \ldots, m_{kn} \in \mathbb{N}_0$ for all $k = 1, \ldots, r$. By $Expr(x_1, \ldots, x_n)$ we denote the class of all expolynomial expressions in the variables $x_1, \ldots, x_n$.

A function $f_a(x_1, \ldots, x_n)$ is a *multidimensional expolynomial function* of width a with finite support on a diagonal mesh partition R_a if there exists a map $M_f : R_a \rightarrow Expr(x_1, \ldots, x_n)$ such that if a point $(x_1, \ldots, x_n) \in r$, r is a region in R_a, then $f(x_1, \ldots, x_n) = M_f(r)(x_1, \ldots, x_n)$.

Given an expolynomial function $f(\bar{x}) = f(x_1, \ldots, x_n)$ and an m-dimensional region $r \in R_a$, $1 \leq m \leq n$, we want to define the integral of f on r (denoted as $\int_r f$). It is easy to see that due to the region's constraints, each point in r can be determined by only m independent parameters $\bar{y} = (y_1, \ldots, y_m)$, and we can express $\bar{x}$ as a function of $\bar{y}$, i.e. $x_i = x_i(\bar{y})$ for $i = 1, \ldots, n$. Thus we can define $\int_r f$ as a multiple integral $\int_{(x_1(\bar{y}), \ldots, x_n(\bar{y})) \in r} f(\bar{y}) \, d\bar{y}$ taken over m variables.

Definition 4. *Multidimensional random variable $\bar{X} = (X_1, \ldots, X_n)$ has an expolynomial region distribution (ERD) of width a if there exists an expolynomial function $f_a(\bar{x}) = f_a(x_1, \ldots, x_n) \geq 0$ on R_a such that for all $\bar{t} = (t_1, \ldots, t_n) \in \mathbb{R}_+^n$, $\Pr(\bar{X} < \bar{t}) = \Pr(X_1 < t_1, \ldots, X_n < t_n) = \sum_{r \in I_{R_a}} \int_{r \cap (x_1(\bar{y}) < t_1, \ldots, x_n(\bar{y}) < t_n)} f_a(\bar{y}) \, d\bar{y} + \sum_{\substack{(x_1, \ldots, x_n) \in P_{R_a} \\ x_1 < t_1, \ldots, x_n < t_n}} f(x_1, \ldots, x_n)$, where I_{R_a} is the set of all regions of dimension one or higher in R_a, and P_{R_a} is the set of all zero-dimensional regions (points).*

We call $f_a(\bar{x})$ the pdf of $\bar{X}$. Note, that for every region $r \in R_a$, $\Pr(\bar{X} \in r) = \int_r f$.

Let us give a simple example. Consider two one-dimensional independent random variables with ERDs given by their density functions:

$$f_1(x) = \begin{cases} 0, \text{ if } x = 0 \text{ or } x = 1 \\ 1, \text{ if } 0 < x < 1 \end{cases}, \qquad f_2(y) = \begin{cases} 0, & \text{if } y = 0 \\ 1/2, \text{ if } 0 < y < 1 \text{ or } y = 1 \end{cases}.$$

The first random variable X is uniformly distributed on $(0, 1)$. The second random variable Y is uniformly distributed on $(0, 1)$ and has a mass point at $y = 1$. Then the random variable $Z = XY$ is a two-dimensional random variable with the pdf

$$f_3(x, y) = \begin{cases} 0, & \text{if } (x = i, y = j) \text{ or } (x = i, 0 < y < 1), i, j = 0, 1 \\ 1/2, \text{ if } (0 < x < 1, 0 < y < 1, x \sim y), \sim \in \{<, >\} \\ 1/2, \text{ if } (y = 1, 0 < x < 1) \\ 0, & \text{if } (0 < x < 1, 0 < y < 1, x = y) \text{ or } (y = 0, 0 < x < 1) \end{cases}$$

We see that $f_3(x, y)$ is not zero in both full dimensional regions and in one mass region $(y = 1, 0 < x < 1)$.

5   Image Computation

In this section we will prove our main technical result.

Theorem 1. *Let A be a GSMP, such that the firing time distributions of all events are ERDs of width a. Let $\pi \in \Pi$ be a history of A, f^π be the pdf of the ecv of π, $\pi' = \pi \xrightarrow{E^*} (q_{l'}, \mathcal{O}_{l'}, \mathcal{N}_{l'})$ be a successor of π, $f^{\pi'}$ be the pdf of the ecv of π', and m' be the number of active events in $q_{l'}$, then:*

1. $f^{\pi'}$ is an m'-dimensional ERD of width a;
2. given f^π, $f^{\pi'}$ can be computed symbolically.

The theorem will follow from the steps described below.

To simplify complex expressions we will use a convenient shorthand notation. Suppose that $B = \{b_1, \ldots, b_q\}$ is a set of indices, then instead of writing $f(x_{b_1}, \ldots, x_{b_q}, y)$ we will write $f_{b \in B}(x_b, y)$. We will also slightly abuse notation by writing $f_{b \in B}(x_b + z, y)$ (where z is a variable) instead of writing $f_{b \in B}(\hat{x}_b, y)$, $\hat{x}_b = x_b + z$.

Suppose a non-negative n-dimensional random variable X with pdf $f(\bar{x})$ is divided into two random variables X_1 and X_2, such that $X_1 \in \mathbb{R}_+^s$ and $X_2 \in \mathbb{R}_+^{n-s}$. Then the pdf of X_1 is $f_{X_1}(\bar{x}_1) = \int_0^{+\infty} \cdots \int_0^{+\infty} f(y_1, \ldots, y_s, y_{s+1}, \ldots, y_n)\, dy_{s+1} \cdots dy_n$. The function $f_{X_1}(\bar{x}_1)$ is called a *marginal pdf* of X.

Analysis of $f^{\pi'}$: Notice that $f^{\pi'}$ can be written as

$$f^{\pi'}_{e \in \mathcal{O}_{l'} \cup \mathcal{N}_{l'}}(t_e) = \check{f}^{\pi'}_{e \in \mathcal{O}_{l'}}(t_e) \prod_{e \in \mathcal{N}_{l'}} dens(e)(t_e),$$

where $\check{f}^{\pi'}_{e \in \mathcal{O}_{l'}}(t_e)$ is the joint density function of the clock values of the events in $\mathcal{O}_{l'}$. Thus, obtaining $\check{f}^{\pi'}$ is sufficient for the construction of $f^{\pi'}$. It is also easy to see that if $\check{f}^{\pi'}$ is an expolynomial function of width a, then $f^{\pi'}$ is also an expolynomial function of width a (but of a higher dimension).

Computation of $\tilde{f}^{\pi,e^*}$: Let us pick any event $e^* \in E^*$ and let $(q_l, \mathcal{O}_l, \mathcal{N}_l)$ be the last tuple of π. Suppose that A has followed π and now is in q_l. Let $G = \{t_e \geq t_{e^*} \mid e \in (\mathcal{O}_l \cup \mathcal{N}_l) \setminus \{e^*\}\}$ be a probabilistic event that the clock of the event e^* expires before or simultaneously with the other clocks and $\Pr(G)$ be its probability. Then let $\tilde{f}^{\pi,e^*}_{e \in (\mathcal{O}_l \cup \mathcal{N}_l) \setminus \{e^*\}}(\hat{t}_e)$ be the pdf of clock values of all events in $(\mathcal{O}_l \cup \mathcal{N}_l) \setminus \{e^*\}$ at the moment when $t_{e^*} = 0$, conditioned on occurrence of G.

Let $\hat{t}_e = t_e - t_{e^*}$ and define

$$g_{e \in (\mathcal{O}_l \cup \mathcal{N}_l) \setminus \{e^*\}}(\hat{t}_e, t_{e^*}) = f^\pi_{e \in (\mathcal{O}_l \cup \mathcal{N}_l) \setminus \{e^*\}}(\hat{t}_e + t_{e^*}, t_{e^*}). \tag{1}$$

Then g can be seen as the joint density function of t_{e^*} and the *differences* between the values of the other event clocks and t_{e^*} (these differences may be positive or negative).

Now let $g'_{e \in (\mathcal{O}_l \cup \mathcal{N}_l) \setminus \{e^*\}}(\hat{t}_e) = \int_0^{+\infty} g_{e \in (\mathcal{O}_l \cup \mathcal{N}_l) \setminus \{e^*\}}(\hat{t}_e, t_{e^*})\, dt_{e^*}$ be a marginal pdf. Then, given the definition of G that states that all differences $\hat{t}_e$ should be non-negative we obtain that

$$\tilde{f}^{\pi,e^*}_{e \in (\mathcal{O}_l \cup \mathcal{N}_l) \setminus \{e^*\}}(\hat{t}_e) = \frac{g'_{e \in (\mathcal{O}_l \cup \mathcal{N}_l) \setminus \{e^*\}}(\hat{t}_e)}{\Pr(G)} = \frac{\displaystyle\int_0^{+\infty} g_{e \in (\mathcal{O}_l \cup \mathcal{N}_l) \setminus \{e^*\}}(\hat{t}_e, t_{e^*})\, dt_{e^*}}{\Pr(G)} \tag{2}$$

If we know how to compute g', it is easy to compute $\Pr(G)$. Since $\tilde{f}^{\pi,e^*}$ is a pdf then if we integrate over all its variables we should obtain 1. Hence, from (2):

$$\Pr(G) = \int_0^{+\infty} \cdots \int_0^{+\infty} g'_{e_i \in (\mathcal{O}_l \cup \mathcal{N}_l) \setminus \{e^*\}}(\hat{t}_{e_i})\, d\hat{t}_{e_1} \cdots d\hat{t}_{e_{m-1}},$$

where m is the number of active events in q_l.

It remains to show how, given $f^{\pi}_{e \in (\mathcal{O}_l \cup \mathcal{N}_l)}(t_e)$, we can compute g' and to examine properties of this computation. Let us introduce a new variable $\hat{t}_{e^*} = t_{e^*}$, then from (1) we see that to compute g from f^{π} we need to apply the linear transformation $\mathcal{L}$ from Section 4.1. The expolynomial expressions are closed under linear transformations, and we also saw that diagonal mesh partitions are transformed into inverse diagonal mesh partitions of the same width (Lemma 1). So we conclude that g is an expolynomial function on an inverse diagonal partition $\hat{R}^g_a$.

Now we have to obtain g' from g. First, notice that by Lemma 2, g' is defined on a diagonal partition $R^{g'}_a$ of the dimension one less than $\hat{R}^g_a$ and of the same width a. As in the example of Section 3.1, at each region r it is given as a sum of integrals of expolynomial expressions of regions of $\hat{R}^g_a$ that are projected on r. These integrals can be computed symbolically using the formula $\int Dx^m e^{cx}\, dx = D(\frac{1}{c}x^m e^{cx} - \frac{m}{c} \int x^{m-1} e^{cx}\, dx)$, which can be easily derived by applying the integration by parts method. Thus, g' (and therefore $\check{f}^{\pi,e^*}$) are computable expolynomial functions of width a.

Computation of $\check{f}^{\pi'}$: First, we "integrate out" of $\check{f}^{\pi,e^*}$ all clocks that were cancelled upon transition from q_l to $q_{l'}$:

$$\tilde{\tilde{f}}^{\pi,e^*}_{e \in \mathcal{O}_{l'}}(t_e) = \int_0^{+\infty} \cdots \int_0^{+\infty} \tilde{f}^{\pi,e^*}_{e \in (\mathcal{O}_l \cup \mathcal{N}_l) \setminus \{e^*\}}(t_e)\, dt_{e_1} \cdots dt_{e_s},$$

where $e_1, \ldots, e_s \in E_{\text{cancelled}}(q, E^*, q')$, thus $\tilde{\tilde{f}}^{\pi}$ is a marginal pdf, and it easy to check that it is also an expolynomial function of width a.

We are almost done. It is left to extract from $\tilde{\tilde{f}}^{\pi,e^*}$ information that is pertinent only to the transition that was caused by firing of the events E^* and not to the transitions that are triggered by the sets of events that properly contain E^*. Let $\check{E}^* = E^* \setminus \{e^*\}$, then we construct $\check{f}^{\pi'}$ from $\tilde{\tilde{f}}^{\pi,e^*}$ by extracting exactly those regions that have a constraint of the form $t_e = 0$ if and only if $e \in \check{E}^*$. For example, if e^* is the only event in E^*, then $\check{E}^* = \emptyset$ and we obtain $\check{f}^{\pi'}$ from $\tilde{\tilde{f}}^{\pi,e^*}$ by setting to zero all regions that have a constraint $t_e = 0$ for any event e. Similarly, if $\check{E}^* = \{e_1\}$ then we extract all those regions that are defined by the constraint $t_{e_1} = 0$ (and set to zero the expolynomial expressions for regions that in addition to $t_{e_1} = 0$ have a constraint $t_{e'} = 0$ for any other event e').

Note, that $\check{f}^{\pi'}$ constructed from $\tilde{\tilde{f}}^{\pi,e^*}$ may no longer be a pdf, so we have to divide it by a normalizing constant $0 < H < 1$, which is easily computable.

Computation of $p_{\pi'|\pi}$: As a consequence of our previous computations, we obtain the formula for $p_{\pi'|\pi}$:

$$p_{\pi'|\pi} = \Pr(G) \cdot H \cdot next(q_l, E^*, q_{l'}).$$

6 Illustrative Example

We are developing a tool called EHV (Event Horizon Verifier) that implements the algorithm of Section 5. The tool is written in JAVA and relies on JSCIENCE open source library for the symbolic computations.

As an application of our method we consider a queueing problem. The producer generates messages and the consumer processes them. The messages that await processing are stored in a buffer of capacity K (initially the buffer is empty). The interarrival time between successive messages is modeled by ERD with the pdf: $f_1(t)$ is p if $t \in (0,1)$, is $a(p) + b(p)x$ if $t \in (1,2)$, and 0 otherwise, where $p \in (0,1)$ is a parameter. With $f_1(t)$ we can model a situation when the interval between any two successive messages are at most two time units, the probability that a message arrives during the first time unit is uniform and the probability that a message would arrive during the second time unit is "skewed" towards the end of the interval.

The time that the consumer needs to process a message is uniformly distributed on $(0,1)$. It is also known that the producer can produce at most $N > K$ messages and we want to find the probability P_{overflow} that the buffer exceeds its capacity.

Notice, that if the difference between N and K is small, then P_{overflow} can also be very small. Simulation techniques to estimate small probabilities are involved, they require a large number of simulations and give only statistical guarantees. To the contrary, the running time of our method does not depend on the absolute value of P_{overflow}, and, in fact, performance improves if there are only a few paths that lead to the unsafe locations.

The problem can be reduced to the bounded until problem for the GSMP B defined as follows. The locations of B are encoded with pairs (k,n), where $k = 0, \ldots, K+1$ is the number of messages in the buffer and $n = 0, \ldots, N$ is the total number of messages received so far. The location $(0,0)$ is the initial location. For any n, the locations $(K+1,n)$ are "unsafe", and all locations (k',n'), such that $N - n' \leq K - k'$ are destinations (if B is in such a location then the buffer cannot overflow). B has two events e_p and e_c. For all $n = 0, \ldots, N-1$, the locations $(0,n)$ have e_p as their only active event and upon firing of that event B moves to the location $(1, n+1)$. Unsafe and destination locations are absorbing, and all the other locations have both e_p and e_c as their active events. When B is in such a location (i,j), firing of e_p or e_c causes a transition to $(i+1, j+1)$ or $(i-1, j)$, respectively.

We performed experiments for some sets of parameters. The computer that we used for our experiments was a Linux server equipped with dual Pentium III processors operating at $1400\,\text{MHz}$ and with $2\,\text{GB}$ of RAM. For each set of parameters we analyzed all histories in Π_{until} (the total number of them is in the "Dest. reached" column) and all histories that end in an unsafe location (the "Unsafe reached" column). Below is the summary of results.

Parameter values: $(\mathbf{K}, \mathbf{N})$, p	Results			
	P_{overflow}	Running time	Dest. reached	Unsafe reached
$(5, 11), 1/2$	9.0897×10^{-4}	1 min. 23 sec.	2380	1040
$(7, 11), 1/2$	7.5504×10^{-6}	36 sec.	560	185
$(7, 11), 1/5$	4.1124×10^{-9}	3 min. 7 sec.	560	185
$(7, 11), 1/10$	1.9335×10^{-11}	3 min. 17 sec.	560	185
$(30, 31), 1/10$	1.2161×10^{-64}	23 sec.	30	1

References

1. R. Alur, C. Courcoubetis, and D.L. Dill. Model-checking for probabilistic real-time systems. In *Automata, Languages and Programming: Proceedings of the 18th ICALP*, LNCS 510, pages 115–136. Springer-Verlag, 1991.
2. R. Alur and D.L. Dill. A theory of timed automata. *Theoretical Computer Science*, 126: 183–235, 1994.
3. A. Aziz, K. Sanwal, V. Singhal, and R.K. Brayton. Model-checking continuous-time markov chains. *ACM Transactions on Computational Logic*, 1(1):162–170, 2000.
4. A. Biere, A. Cimatti, E. Clarke, M. Fujita, and Y. Zhu. Symbolic model checking using SAT procedures instead of BDDs. In *Proceedings of the 36th ACM/IEEE Design Automation Conference*, pages 317–320, 1999.
5. E.M. Clarke, O. Grumberg, and D.A. Peled. *Model checking*. MIT Press, 2000.
6. E.M. Clarke and R.P. Kurshan. Computer-aided verification. *IEEE Spectrum*, 33(6):61–67, 1996.
7. C. Courcoubetis and M. Yannakakis. The complexity of probabilistic verification. *Journal of the ACM*, 42(4):857–907, 1995.
8. R. German. *Performance analysis of communication systems: Modeling with non-Markovian stochastic Petri nets*. J. Wiley & Sons, 2000.
9. P.W. Glynn. A GSMP formalism for discrete event systems. *Proceedings of the IEEE*, 77(1):14–23, 1988.
10. H. Hansson and B. Jonsson. A framework for reasoning about time and reliability. In *Proceedings of the Tenth IEEE Real-Time Systems Symposium*, pages 102–111, 1989.
11. B. Haverkort. *Performance of computer-communication systems: A model-based approach*. Wiley & Sons, 1998.
12. G.J. Holzmann. The model checker SPIN. *IEEE Transactions on Software Engineering*, 23(5):279–295, 1997.
13. M. Kwiatkowska, G. Norman, and D. Parker. PRISM: Probabilistic symbolic model checker. In *Proceedings of Computer Performance Evaluation/Tools 2002*, LNCS 2324, pages 200–204, 2002.
14. M. Kwiatkowska, G. Norman, R. Segala, and J. Sproston. Verifying quantitative properties of continuous probabilistic timed automata. In *Proceedings of the 11th International Conference on Concurrency Theory*, LNCS 1877, pages 123–137. Springer, 2000.
15. M.Z. Kwiatkowska. Model checking for probability and time: from theory to pratice. In *Proceedings of the 18th IEEE Symposium on Logic in Computer Science*, pages 351–360, 2003.
16. M.Z. Kwiatkowska, G. Norman, and D. Parker. Probabilistic symbolic model checking with PRISM: a hybrid approach. *Software Tools for Technology Transfer*, 6(2):128–142, 2004.
17. P.D'Argenio, H. Hermanns, J.-P. Katoen, and R. Klaren. Modest - a modeling and description language for stochastic timed systems. In *Proceedings of the PAPM-PROBMIV Joint International Workshop*, LNCS 2165, pages 87–104. Springer, 2001.
18. G.S. Shedler. *Regenerative stochastic simulation*. Academic Press, 1993.
19. M.Y. Vardi. Automatic verification of probabilistic concurrent finite-state programs. In *Proceedings of the 26th IEEE Symposium on Foundations of Computer Science*, pages 327–338, 1985.
20. H. Younes and R. Simmons. Probabilistic verification of discrete event systems using acceptance sampling. In *Computer Aided Verification, 14th International Conference*, LNCS 2404, pages 223–235, 2002.

On the Stability of Zeno Equilibria*

Aaron D. Ames[1], Paulo Tabuada[2], and Shankar Sastry[1]

[1] Department of Electrical Engineering and Computer Sciences,
University of California at Berkeley, Berkeley, CA 94720
{adames, sastry}@eecs.berkeley.edu
[2] Department of Electrical Engineering,
University of Notre Dame, Notre Dame, IN 46556
ptabuada@nd.edu

Abstract. Zeno behaviors are one of the (perhaps unintended) features of many hybrid models of physical systems. They have no counterpart in traditional dynamical systems or automata theory and yet they have remained relatively unexplored over the years. In this paper we address the stability properties of a class of Zeno equilibria, and we introduce a necessary paradigm shift in the study of hybrid stability. Motivated by the peculiarities of Zeno equilibria, we consider a form of asymptotic stability that is global in the continuous state, but local in the discrete state. We provide sufficient conditions for stability of these equilibria, resulting in sufficient conditions for the existence of Zeno behavior.

1   Introduction

Hybrid models have been used successfully during the past decade to describe systems exhibiting both discrete and continuous dynamics, while they have simultaneously allowed complex models of continuous systems to be simplified. We are interested in the rich dynamical behavior of hybrid models of physical systems. These hybrid models admit a kind of equilibria that is not found in continuous dynamical systems or in automata theory: *Zeno equilibria*. Zeno equilibria are collections of points which are invariant under the discrete component of the hybrid dynamics, and which can be stable is many cases of interest.

Mechanical systems undergoing impacts are naturally modeled as hybrid systems (cf. [1] and [2]). The convergent behavior of these systems is often of interest—even if this convergence is not to "classical" notions of equilibrium points. This motivates the study of Zeno equilibria because even if the convergence is not classical, it still is important. For example, simulating trajectories of these systems is an important component in their analysis, yet this may not be possible due to the relationship between Zeno equilibria and Zeno behavior.

An equally important reason to address the stability of Zeno equilibria is to be able to assess the existence of Zeno trajectories. This behavior is infamous in the hybrid system community for its ability to halt simulations. The only way to

---

* This research is supported by the National Science Foundation (award numbers CCR-0225610 and CSR-EHS-0509313).

João Hespanha and A. Tiwari (Eds.): HSCC 2006, LNCS 3927, pp. 34–48, 2006.

prevent this undesirable outcome is to give *a priori* conditions on the existence of Zeno behavior. This has motivated a profuse study of Zeno hybrid systems (see [1, 3, 4, 5, 6, 7, 8] to name a few) but a concrete notion of convergence (in the sense of stability) has not yet been introduced. As a result, there is a noticeable lack of sufficient conditions for the existence of Zeno behavior. We refer the reader to [3, 7, 8] for a more thorough introduction to Zeno behavior.

Our investigations into the stability of Zeno equilibria are made possible through a categorical framework for hybrid systems (as first introduced in [9] and later utilized in [10]). This theory allows "non-hybrid" objects to be generalized to a hybrid setting. Specifically, let T be a category, i.e., a collection of mathematical objects that share a certain property together with morphisms between these objects. A *hybrid object* over this category is a special type of small category H, termed an *H-category*, together with a functor (either covariant or contravariant) $S : H \to T$. Morphisms between objects of T are generalized to a hybrid setting through the use of natural transformations.

The main contribution of this paper is sufficient conditions for the stability of Zeno equilibria. As a byproduct, we are able to give sufficient conditions for the existence of Zeno behavior. The categorical approach to hybrid systems allows us to decompose the study of stability into two manageable steps. The first step consists of identifying a sufficiently rich, yet sufficiently simple, class of hybrid systems embodying the desired stability properties: *first quadrant hybrid systems*. The second step is to understand the stability of general hybrid systems by understanding the relationships between these systems and first quadrant hybrid systems described by morphisms (in the category of hybrid systems).

2   Classical Stability: A Categorical Approach

In this section we revisit classical stability theory under a categorical light. The new perspective afforded by category theory is more than a simple exercise in abstract nonsense because it motivates the development of an analogous stability theory for hybrid systems and hybrid equilibria to be presented in Sections 4 and 5. We shall work on Dyn, the category of dynamical systems, which has as objects pairs (M, X), where M is a smooth manifold[1] and $X : M \to TM$ is a smooth vector field. The morphisms are smooth maps $f : N \to M$ making the following diagram commutative:

$$
\begin{array}{ccc}
TN & \xrightarrow{Tf} & TM \\
\Big\uparrow Y & & \Big\uparrow X \\
N & \xrightarrow{f} & M
\end{array}
\qquad (1)
$$

The subcategory Interval(Dyn) of Dyn will play an especially important role in the theory developed in this paper. This subcategory is the full subcategory of Dyn

---

[1] We assume that M is a Riemannian manifold, and so has a metric $d(x, y) = \|x - y\|$. Alternatively, we could assume that M is a subset of $\mathbb{R}^n$.

defined by objects[2] $(I, \frac{d}{dt})$ with I a subset of $\mathbb{R}$ of the form $[t, t'], (t, t'], [t, t'), (t, t')$ and $\{t\}$, where $[t, t']$ is a manifold with boundary (and so is $(t, t']$ and $[t, t')$) and $\{t\}$ is a zero-dimensional manifold consisting of the single point t (which is trivially a smooth manifold). The following observation shows the relevance of Interval(Dyn). A morphism $c : (I, d/dt) \to (M, X)$ is a smooth map $c : I \to M$ making diagram (1) commutative and thus satisfying:

$$\dot{c}(t) = Tc \cdot \frac{d}{dt} = X \circ c(t).$$

We can therefore identify a morphism $c : (I, d/dt) \to (M, X)$ with a trajectory of (M, X). Furthermore, the existence of a morphism $f : (N, Y) \to (M, X)$ implies that for every trajectory $c : (I, d/dt) \to (N, Y)$, the composite $f \circ c : (I, d/dt) \to (M, X)$ is a trajectory of (M, X). In other words, a morphism $f : (N, Y) \to (M, X)$ carries trajectories of (N, Y) into trajectories of (M, X).

Remarkably, stability also can be described through the existence of certain morphisms. Let us first recall the definition of globally asymptotically stable equilibria.

Definition 1. *Let (M, X) be an object of* Dyn. *An equilibrium point $x^* \in M$ of X is said to be globally asymptotically stable when for any morphism $c : ([t, \infty), \frac{d}{dt}) \to (M, X)$, for any $t_1 > t$ and for any $\varepsilon > 0$ there exists a $\delta > 0$ satisfying:*

1. $\|c(t_1) - x^*\| < \delta \quad \Rightarrow \quad \|c(t_2) - x^*\| < \varepsilon \qquad \forall t_2 \geq t_1 \geq t$,
2. $\lim_{\tau \to \infty} c(\tau) = x^*$.

Consider now the full subcategory of Dyn denoted by GasDyn and defined by objects $(\mathbb{R}_0^+, -\alpha)$ where α is a class $\mathcal{K}_\infty$ function. Lyapunov's second method can then be described as follows:

Theorem 1. *Let (M, X) be an object of* Dyn. *An equilibrium point $x^* \in M$ of X is globally asymptotically stable if there exists a morphism:*

$$(M, X) \xrightarrow{\ v\ } (\mathbb{R}_0^+, -\alpha) \in \mathsf{GasDyn}$$

in Dyn *satisfying:*

1. $v(x) = 0$ implies $x = x^*$,
2. $v : M \to \mathbb{R}_0^+$ is a proper (radially unbounded) function.

The previous result suggests that the study of stability properties can be carried out in two steps. In the first step we identify a suitable subcategory having the desired stability properties. In the case of global asymptotic stability, this subcategory is GasDyn; for local stability we could consider the full subcategory defined by objects of the form $(\mathbb{R}_0^+, -\alpha)$ with α a non-negative definite function.

---

[2] We do not consider more general objects of the form $(J, g(t)d/dt)$ with $g > 0$ since each such object is isomorphic to $(I, d/dt)$.

The chosen category corresponds in some sense to the simplest possible objects having the desired stability properties. In the second step we show that existence of a morphism from a general object (M, X) to an object in the chosen subcategory implies that the desired stability properties also hold in (M, X). This is precisely the approach we will develop in Sections 4 and 5 for the study of Zeno equilibria.

3 Categorical Hybrid Systems

This section is devoted to the study of first quadrant hybrid systems, categorical hybrid systems, and their interplay. We begin by defining a very simple class of hybrid systems; these systems are easy to understand and analyze, but lack generality. We then proceed to define general hybrid systems through the framework of hybrid category theory; these systems are general but difficult to analyze. The advantage of introducing these two concepts is that not only can they be related through explicit constructions, but also through the more general framework of morphisms in the category of hybrid systems. This relationship will be important in understanding the stability of general hybrid systems.

First Quadrant Systems. In order to understand the stability of general hybrid systems, we must consider a class of hybrid systems analogous to the objects of GasDyn; these are termed *first quadrant hybrid systems*. It is not surprising that these would be chosen as the "canonical" hybrid systems with which to understand the stability of Zeno equilibria as they already have been used to derive sufficient conditions for the existence of Zeno behavior in [3].

A *first quadrant hybrid system* is a tuple:

$$\mathscr{H}_{\mathbf{FQ}} = (\Gamma, D, G, R, F),$$

where

- $\Gamma = (Q, E)$ is an oriented cycle, with

$$Q = \{1, \ldots, k\}, \qquad E = \{e_1 = (1,2), e_2 = (2,3), \ldots, e_k = (k,1)\}.$$

- $D = \{D_i\}_{i \in Q}$, where for all $i \in Q$,

$$D_i = (\mathbb{R}_0^+)^2 = \{(x_1, x_2) \in \mathbb{R}^2 : x_1 \geq 0 \text{ and } x_2 \geq 0\}.$$

- $G = \{G_e\}_{e \in E}$, where for all $e \in E$

$$G_e = \{(x_1, x_2) \in \mathbb{R}^2 : x_1 = 0 \text{ and } x_2 \geq 0\}.$$

- $R = \{R_e\}_{e \in E}$, where $R_e : G_e \rightarrow (\mathbb{R}_0^+)^2$ and for all $e \in E$ there exists a function $r_e : \mathbb{R}_0^+ \rightarrow \mathbb{R}_0^+$ with

$$R_e(0, x_2) = (r_e(x_2), 0).$$

- $F = \{f_i\}_{i \in Q}$, where f_i is a Lipshitz vector field on $(\mathbb{R}_0^+)^2$.

Before discussing the stability properties of first quadrant hybrid systems, we need to relate them to more general hybrid systems. This is accomplished by introducing a categorical framework for hybrid systems. As outlined in the introduction, a hybrid object over a category is a pair $S : H \to T$. Since we allow S to be any functor, the main component of the definition is the small category H which must be an H-category; the special form of this small category directly reflects its ability to describe "hybrid objects." Therefore, in order to define hybrid objects over a category, we must invest a rather sizable amount of effort in understanding the definition and structure of H-categories.

H-Cateogries. We start by defining a specific type of small category termed an *oriented H-category* and denoted by H. This is a small category (cf. [11]) in which every diagram has the form:[3]

That is, an H-category has as its basic atomic unit a diagram of the form: $\bullet \longleftarrow \bullet \longrightarrow \bullet$, and any other diagram in this category must be obtainable by gluing such atomic units along the target of a morphism (and not the source). In addition, we require the existence of an orientation on H. Before defining such an orientation, some additional definitions are needed. Denote by $Ob(H)$ the objects of H, denote by $Mor(H)$ the morphisms of H, and by $Mor_{id}(H)$ the set of non-identity morphisms of H. For a morphism $\alpha : a \to b$ in H, its domain (or source) is denoted by $dom(\alpha) = a$ and its codomain (or target) is denoted by $cod(\alpha) = b$. For H-categories, there are two sets of objects that are of particular interest; these are subsets of the set $Ob(H)$. The first of these is called the *edge set of* H, is denoted by $Ob_{(\leftarrow\cdot\rightarrow)}(H)$, and is defined to be

$$Ob_{(\leftarrow\cdot\rightarrow)}(H) = \{a \in Ob(H) : \ a = dom(\alpha) = dom(\beta),$$
$$\alpha, \beta \in Mor_{id}(H), \ \alpha \neq \beta\}.$$

The symbol $Ob_{(\leftarrow\cdot\rightarrow)}(\ \cdot\ )$ is used because every object $a \in Ob_{(\leftarrow\cdot\rightarrow)}(H)$ sits in a diagram of the form:

$$cod(\alpha_a) = b \xleftarrow{\ \alpha_a\ } dom(\alpha_a) = a = dom(\beta_a) \xrightarrow{\ \beta_a\ } c = cod(\beta_a)$$

called a *bac-diagram*. Note that giving all diagrams of this form (of which there is one for each $a \in Ob_{(\leftarrow\cdot\rightarrow)}(H)$) gives all the objects in H, i.e., every object of H is the target of α_a or β_a, or their source, for some $a \in Ob_{(\leftarrow\cdot\rightarrow)}(H)$. More specifically, we can define the *vertex set of* H by

$$Ob_{(\rightarrow\cdot\leftarrow)}(H) = \left(Ob_{(\leftarrow\cdot\rightarrow)}(H)\right)^c$$

where $\left(Ob_{(\leftarrow\cdot\rightarrow)}(H)\right)^c$ is the complement of $Ob_{(\leftarrow\cdot\rightarrow)}(H)$ in the set $Ob(H)$.

---

[3] Where $\bullet$ denotes an arbitrary object in H and $\longrightarrow$ denotes an arbitrary morphism.

Oriented H-Categories. We can orient an H-category by picking a specific labeling of its morphisms. Specifically, we define an *orientation* of an H-category H as a pair of maps (α, β) between sets:

$$Ob_{(\leftarrow\cdot\rightarrow)}(H) \underset{\beta}{\overset{\alpha}{\rightrightarrows}} Mor_{id}(H)$$

such that for every $a \in Ob_{(\leftarrow\cdot\rightarrow)}(H)$, there is a bac-diagram in H:

$$b \xleftarrow{\ \alpha_a\ } a \xrightarrow{\ \beta_a\ } c. \tag{2}$$

We can form the category of oriented H-categories: Hcat. A morphism between two oriented H-categories, H and H′ (with orientations (α, β) and (α', β'), respectively), is a functor $F : H \to H'$ such that the following diagrams

$$
\begin{array}{ccc}
Ob_{(\leftarrow\cdot\rightarrow)}(H) & \xrightarrow{F} & Ob_{(\leftarrow\cdot\rightarrow)}(H') \\
{\scriptstyle\alpha}\downarrow & & \downarrow{\scriptstyle\alpha'} \\
Mor_{id}(H) & \xrightarrow{F} & Mor_{id}(H')
\end{array}
\qquad
\begin{array}{ccc}
Ob_{(\leftarrow\cdot\rightarrow)}(H) & \xrightarrow{F} & Ob_{(\leftarrow\cdot\rightarrow)}(H') \\
{\scriptstyle\beta}\downarrow & & \downarrow{\scriptstyle\beta'} \\
Mor_{id}(H) & \xrightarrow{F} & Mor_{id}(H')
\end{array}
\tag{3}
$$

commute. This requirement implies that, if $a \in Ob_{(\leftarrow\cdot\rightarrow)}(H)$ with corresponding bac-diagram (2) in H, there is a corresponding bac-diagram:

$$F(b) \xleftarrow{\ F(\alpha_a) = \alpha'_{F(a)}\ } F(a) \xrightarrow{\ F(\beta_a) = \beta'_{F(a)}\ } F(c)$$

where $F(a) \in Ob_{(\leftarrow\cdot\rightarrow)}(H')$.

From Graphs to H-Categories. To every oriented H-category, we can associate (a possibly infinite) oriented graph, and vice versa. That is, we have functors (see [12] for the explicit construction of these functors):

$$
\begin{array}{cc}
\Gamma : Grph \longrightarrow Hcat & H : Hcat \longrightarrow Grph \\
\Gamma \mapsto \Gamma(\Gamma) := H_\Gamma & H \mapsto H(H) := \Gamma_H
\end{array}
$$

where Grph is the category of oriented graphs. The functor Γ is, roughly speaking, defined on every edge $e_i \in E$ by:

$$\Gamma\left(i \xrightarrow{\ e_i\ } j \right) = i \xleftarrow{\ \alpha_{e_i}\ } e_i \xrightarrow{\ \beta_{e_i}\ } j.$$

The relationship between oriented H-categories and oriented graphs is made more precise in the following theorem (again, see [12]).

Theorem 2. *There is an isomorphism of categories,*

$$Grph \cong Hcat, \tag{4}$$

where this isomorphism is given by the functor $H : Hcat \to Grph$ *with inverse* $\Gamma : Grph \to Hcat.$

Example 1. For the hybrid system $\mathscr{H}_{\mathbf{FQ}}$, and by utilizing (4), we can associate to the graph Γ a H-category H_Γ. Both Γ and the corresponding H-category are given in the following diagrams:

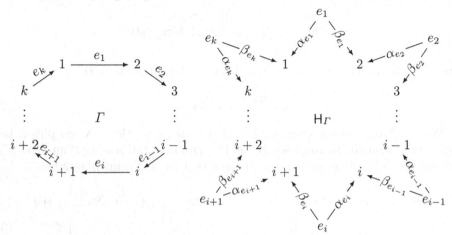

We now have the necessary framework in which to introduce hybrid objects over a category.

Definition 2. *Let* T *be a category. Then a hybrid object over* T *is a pair* $(\mathsf{H}, \boldsymbol{S})$, *where* H *is an H-category and*

$$\boldsymbol{S} : \mathsf{H} \to \mathsf{T}$$

is a functor (either covariant or contravariant). Given two hybrid objects, $(\mathsf{H}, \boldsymbol{S})$ *and* $(\mathsf{H}', \boldsymbol{S}')$, *a morphism between these objects is a functor and a natural transformation* $(\boldsymbol{F}, \boldsymbol{f}) : (\mathsf{H}, \boldsymbol{S}) \to (\mathsf{H}', \boldsymbol{S}')$ *where* $\boldsymbol{F} : \mathsf{H} \to \mathsf{H}'$ *is a morphism in* Hcat *and* $\boldsymbol{f} : \boldsymbol{S} \overset{\cdot}{\longrightarrow} \boldsymbol{S}' \circ \boldsymbol{F}$.

Hybrid Manifolds. An important example of a hybrid object is a hybrid manifold, defined to be a functor $\boldsymbol{M} : \mathsf{H}_M \to \mathsf{Man}$ where H_M is an H-category and Man is the category of smooth manifolds; in this paper, we assume that for every diagram (2), there is the following diagram:

$$\boldsymbol{M}_b \xleftarrow{\boldsymbol{M}_{\alpha_a} = i_{\alpha_a}} \boldsymbol{M}_a \xrightarrow{\boldsymbol{M}_{\beta_a}} \boldsymbol{M}_c$$

in Man, where $\boldsymbol{M}_a \subseteq \boldsymbol{M}_b$ and i_{α_a} is the natural inclusion. If $(\mathsf{H}_N, \boldsymbol{N})$ is another hybrid manifold, a morphism of hybrid manifolds is a pair $(\boldsymbol{F}, \boldsymbol{f}) : (\mathsf{H}_N, \boldsymbol{N}) \to (\mathsf{H}_M, \boldsymbol{M})$ where $\boldsymbol{F} : \mathsf{H}_N \to \mathsf{H}_M$ is a morphism in Hcat and $\boldsymbol{f}$ is a natural transformation: $\boldsymbol{f} : \boldsymbol{N} \overset{\cdot}{\longrightarrow} \boldsymbol{M} \circ \boldsymbol{F}$.

Example 2. For $\mathscr{H}_{\mathbf{FQ}}$, the "hybrid manifold" portion of this hybrid system corresponds to the tuple (Γ, D, G, R). To make this explicit, the hybrid manifold associated to $\mathscr{H}_{\mathbf{FQ}}$ is given by the pair $(\mathsf{H}_\Gamma, \boldsymbol{M}^{\mathscr{H}_{\mathbf{FQ}}})$ where $\boldsymbol{M}^{\mathscr{H}_{\mathbf{FQ}}}$ is the functor defined on each bac-diagram in H_Γ to be

$$\boldsymbol{M}^{\mathscr{H}_{\mathbf{FQ}}}\left(i \xleftarrow{\alpha_{e_i}} e_i \xrightarrow{\beta_{e_i}} i+1 \right) = D_i \xleftarrow{i} G_{e_i} \xrightarrow{R_{e_i}} D_{i+1}.$$

Hybrid Systems. A hybrid system is a tuple (H_M, M, X), where (H_M, M) is a hybrid manifold and $X = \{X_b\}_{b \in \mathrm{Ob}_{(\to \cdot \leftarrow)}(H)}$ with $X_b : M_b \to TM_b$ a Lipschitz vector field on M_b. With this formulation of hybrid systems (it can be verified that this definition is consistent with the standard one), we can form the category of hybrid systems, HySys. The objects are hybrid systems and the morphisms are pairs $(F, f) : (\mathsf{H}_N, N, Y) \to (\mathsf{H}_M, M, X)$, where (F, f) is a morphism from the hybrid manifold (H_N, N) to the hybrid manifold (H_M, M) such that there is a commuting diagram for all $b \in \mathrm{Ob}_{(\to \cdot \leftarrow)}(\mathsf{H}_N)$

$$
\begin{array}{ccc}
TN_b & \xrightarrow{\; Tf_b \;} & TM_{F(b)} \\
{\scriptstyle Y_b}\big\uparrow & & \big\uparrow{\scriptstyle X_{F(b)}} \\
N_b & \xrightarrow{\; f_b \;} & M_{F(b)}
\end{array}
$$

That is, for all $b \in \mathrm{Ob}_{(\to \cdot \leftarrow)}(\mathsf{H}_N)$, $f_b : (N_b, Y_b) \to (M_{F(b)}, X_{F(b)})$ is a morphism in Dyn.

Morphisms of hybrid systems are composed by composing the associated functor and natural transformation, respectively.

Example 3. The categorical hybrid system associated to $\mathscr{H}_{\mathbf{FQ}}$ is given by

$$
(\mathsf{H}_\Gamma, M^{\mathscr{H}_{\mathbf{FQ}}}, X^{\mathscr{H}_{\mathbf{FQ}}}),
$$

where $(\mathsf{H}_\Gamma, M^{\mathscr{H}_{\mathbf{FQ}}})$ is the hybrid manifold defined in the previous example and $X^{\mathscr{H}_{\mathbf{FQ}}} = \{f_i\}_{i \in \mathrm{Ob}_{(\to \cdot \leftarrow)}(\mathsf{H}_\Gamma) = Q}$.

Hybrid Intervals. As with the continuous case discussed in Section 2, we need to introduce a notion of intervals for hybrid systems. Let $\Lambda = \{0, 1, 2, \ldots\} \subseteq \mathbb{N}$ be a finite or infinite indexing set, from which we can associate a graph $\Gamma_\Lambda = (Q_\Lambda, E_\Lambda)$, where $Q_\Lambda = \Lambda$ and E_Λ is the set of pairs $\eta_{j+1} = (j, j+1)$ such that $j, j+1 \in \Lambda$. From this graph we obtain an H-category $\mathsf{H}_{\Gamma_\Lambda}$ via (4); this implies that every bac-diagram in this H-category must have the form:

$$
j - 1 \xleftarrow{\; \alpha_j \;} \eta_j = (j-1, j) \xrightarrow{\; \beta_j \;} j, \tag{5}
$$

and so we denote by 0 the object of $\mathsf{H}_{\Gamma_\Lambda}$ corresponding to the vertex $0 \in Q_\Lambda = \Lambda$. Define Interval(Hcat) to be the subcategory of Hcat consisting of all H-categories obtained from graphs of this form. A hybrid interval now can be defined as a pair:

$$
I : \mathsf{H}_I \to \mathrm{Interval(Dyn)},
$$

where H_I is an object of Interval(Hcat), and we assume that for every bac-diagram in H_I, there exist (switching times) $\tau_{j-1}, \tau_j, \tau_{j+1} \in \mathbb{R} \cup \{\infty\}$, with $\tau_{j-1} \leq \tau_j \leq \tau_{j+1}$ such that:

$$
I_{j-1} = [\tau_{j-1}, \tau_j] \xleftarrow{\; I_{\alpha_j} = \iota \;} I_{\eta_j} = \{\tau_j\} \xrightarrow{\; I_{\beta_j} = \iota \;} I_j = [\tau_j, \tau_{j+1}] \text{ or } [\tau_j, \tau_{j+1}).
$$

We also suppose that $I_0 = [0, \tau_1]$ or $[0, \tau_1)$.

Trajectories of Hybrid Systems. The importance of hybrid intervals is that, like classical intervals, they can be used to define trajectories of hybrid systems (which correspond to the classical notion of an execution for a hybrid system). The interval category of HySys, denoted by Interval(HySys), is the full subcategory of HySys with objects consisting of hybrid systems of the form $(\mathsf{H}_I, I, d/dt)$ where (H_I, I) is a hybrid interval and $d/dt_j = d/dt$ for all $j \in \Lambda = \mathsf{Ob}_{(\rightarrow \cdot \leftarrow)}(\mathsf{H}_I)$.

Definition 3. *A* trajectory *of a hybrid system* (H_M, M, X) *is a morphism* (C, c) *in* HySys:

$$(C, c) : (\mathsf{H}_I, I, d/dt) \to (\mathsf{H}_M, M, X),$$

where $(\mathsf{H}_I, I, d/dt)$ *is an object of* Interval(HySys). *In particular, this implies that* $\dot{c}_j(t) = X_{C(j)}(c_j(t))$ *for every object* $j \in \Lambda = \mathsf{Ob}_{(\rightarrow \cdot \leftarrow)}(\mathsf{H}_I)$.

Note that the functor C corresponds to the "discrete" portion of the trajectory, while the natural transformation c corresponds to the "continuous" portion. The discrete initial condition is given by $C(0)$ and the continuous initial condition is given by $c_0(0) \in M_{C(0)}$, i.e., the initial condition to the trajectory is $(c_0(0), C(0))$.

Example 4. To better understand the categorical formulation of trajectories, we enumerate the consequences of Definition 3 for first quadrant hybrid systems. Let

$$(C, c) : (\mathsf{H}_I, I, d/dt) \to (\mathsf{H}_\Gamma, M^{\mathscr{H}_{\mathrm{FQ}}}, X^{\mathscr{H}_{\mathrm{FQ}}})$$

be a trajectory of the hybrid system $(\mathsf{H}_\Gamma, M^{\mathscr{H}_{\mathrm{FQ}}}, X^{\mathscr{H}_{\mathrm{FQ}}})$. Since c is a natural transformation, we have a commuting diagram:

$$
\begin{array}{ccccc}
I_{j-1} = [\tau_{j-1}, \tau_j] & \xleftarrow{\ I_{\alpha_j} = \iota\ } & I_{\eta_j} = \{\tau_j\} & \xrightarrow{\ I_{\beta_j} = \iota\ } & I_j = [\tau_j, \tau_{j+1}] \text{ or } [\tau_j, \tau_{j+1}) \\
\Big\downarrow c_{j-1} & & \Big\downarrow c_{\eta_j} & & \Big\downarrow c_j \\
D_{C(j-1)} & \xleftarrow{\ \ \iota\ \ } & G_{C(\eta_j)} & \xrightarrow{\ R_{C(\beta_j)}\ } & D_{C(j)}
\end{array}
$$

This in turn implies that a trajectory must satisfy the following conditions:

$$c_{j-1}(\tau_j) \in G_{C(\eta_j)}, \qquad R_{C(\beta_j)}(c_{j-1}(\tau_j)) = c_j(\tau_j),$$

which are the standard requirements on a trajectory.

We end this section by noting that, as with the continuous case, if (F, f): $(\mathsf{H}_N, N, Y) \to (\mathsf{H}_M, M, X)$ is a morphism of hybrid systems, and (C, c): $(\mathsf{H}_I, I, d/dt) \to (\mathsf{H}_N, N, Y)$ is a trajectory of (H_N, N, Y), then

$$(F \circ C, f \bullet c) : (\mathsf{H}_I, I, d/dt) \to (\mathsf{H}_M, M, X)$$

is a trajectory of (H_M, M, X).

4 Stability of Zeno Equilibria

The purpose of this section is to study the stability of a type of equilibria that is unique to hybrid systems: Zeno equilibria. The uniqueness of these equilibria necessitates a paradigm shift in the current notions of stability, i.e., we must introduce a type of stability that is both local and global in nature and, therefore, has no direct analogue in continuous and discrete systems. The main result of this section is sufficient conditions for the stability of Zeno equilibria in first quadrant hybrid systems.

It is important to note that we do not claim that Zeno equilibria are the most general form of equilibria corresponding to Zeno behavior. We do claim that the type of Zeno equilibria considered are general enough to cover a wide range of interesting (and somewhat peculiar) behavior, while being specific enough to allow for analysis.

Definition 4. *Let* (H_M, M, X) *be a hybrid system. A Zeno equilibria* (H_M^Γ, z) *is a H-subcategory* H_M^Γ *of* H_M *obtained from a cycle* Γ *together with a set* $z = \{z_a\}_{a \in \mathrm{Ob}(\mathsf{H}_M^\Gamma)}$ *such that*

- $z_a \in M_a$ *for all* $a \in \mathrm{Ob}(\mathsf{H}_M^\Gamma)$,
- $z_b = M_\gamma(z_a)$ *for all* $\gamma : a \to b$ *in* H_M^Γ,
- $X_a(z_a) \neq 0$ *for all* $a \in \mathrm{Ob}(\mathsf{H}_M^\Gamma)$.

Another Interpretation of Zeno Equilibria. There is a more categorical definition of a Zeno equilibria. Starting with the one point set $*$, we obtain a hybrid manifold $(\mathsf{H}_M^\Gamma, \triangle(*))$ where $\triangle(*) : \mathsf{H}_M^\Gamma \to \mathsf{Man}$ with $\triangle$ the diagonal functor. Denoting by $\mathbf{Inc} : \mathsf{H}_M^\Gamma \to \mathsf{H}_M$ the inclusion functor, a Zeno equilibria is a morphism of hybrid manifolds:

$$(\mathbf{Inc}, z) : (\mathsf{H}_M^\Gamma, \triangle(*)) \to (\mathsf{H}_M, M)$$

such that $X_a(z_a) \neq 0$; in this case (and by slight abuse of notation) $z_a(*) := z_a$.

Example 5. For the hybrid system $\mathscr{H}_{\mathbf{FQ}}$, and since we are assuming the underlying graph to be a cycle, the conditions expressed in Definition 4 imply that a set $z = \{z_1, \ldots, z_k\}$ is a Zeno equilibria if for all $i = 1, \ldots, k$, $z_i \in G_{e_i}$ and

$$R_{e_{i-1}} \circ \cdots \circ R_{e_1} \circ R_{e_k} \circ \cdots \circ R_{e_i}(z_i) = z_i. \tag{6}$$

Because of the special structure of $\mathscr{H}_{\mathbf{FQ}}$, (6) holds iff $z_i = 0$ for all i. That is, the only Zeno equilibria of $\mathscr{H}_{\mathbf{FQ}}$ is the singleton set $z = \{0\}$.

Induced Hybrid Subsystems. Let (H_M, M, X) be a hybrid system, H_M^Γ be an H-subcategory of H_M, and $\mathbf{Inc} : \mathsf{H}_M^\Gamma \to \mathsf{H}_M$ be the inclusion functor. In this case, there is a hybrid subsystem $(\mathsf{H}_M^\Gamma, M^\Gamma, X^\Gamma)$ of (H_M, M, X) corresponding to this inclusion, i.e., there is an inclusion in HySys:

$$(\mathbf{Inc}, \mathbf{id}) : (\mathsf{H}_M^\Gamma, M^\Gamma, X^\Gamma) \hookrightarrow (\mathsf{H}_M, M, X)$$

where $\mathbf{id}$ is the identity natural transformation.

Definition 5. *A Zeno equilibria* (H_M^Γ, z) *of* (H_M, M, X) *is globally asymptotically stable relative to* $(\mathsf{H}_M^\Gamma, M^\Gamma, X^\Gamma)$ *if the inclusion* $\mathbf{Inc} : \mathsf{H}_M^\Gamma \to \mathsf{H}_M$ *satisfies: for all* $b \in \mathrm{Ob}_{(\to \cdot \leftarrow)}(\mathsf{H}_M^\Gamma)$,

$$\mathbf{cod}(\alpha_{a_1}) = \mathbf{Inc}(b) = \mathbf{cod}(\alpha_{a_2}) \quad \Rightarrow \quad a_1 = a_2,$$

and for every trajectory:

$$(C, c) : (\mathsf{H}_I, I, d/dt) \to (\mathsf{H}_M^\Gamma, M^\Gamma, X^\Gamma),$$

with $\Lambda = \mathbb{N}$, *and for any* $\varepsilon_{C(j)}$ *there exists* $\delta_{C(i)}$ *such that:*

1. *If* $\|c_i(\tau_i) - z_{C(i)}\| < \delta_{C(i)}$ *for* $i = 0, 1, \ldots, k \in Q$ *then*

$$\|c_j(t) - z_{C(j)}\| < \varepsilon_{C(j)}$$

   with $j \in \Lambda$ *and* $t \in I_j = [\tau_j, \tau_{j+1}]$.
2. *For all* $a \in \mathrm{Ob}_{(\to \cdot \leftarrow)}(\mathsf{H}_M^\Gamma)$

$$\lim_{\substack{j \to \infty \\ C(j) = a}} c_j(\tau_j) = z_a, \qquad \lim_{\substack{j \to \infty \\ C(j) = a}} c_j(\tau_{j+1}) = z_a.$$

We say that a Zeno equilibria (H_M^Γ, z) *of* (H_M, M, X) *is globally asymptotically stable if it is globally asymptotically stable relative to* $(\mathsf{H}_M^\Gamma, M^\Gamma, X^\Gamma)$ *and* $(\mathsf{H}_M, M, X) = (\mathsf{H}_M^\Gamma, M^\Gamma, X^\Gamma)$.

The definition of relative global asymptotic stability implicitly makes some very subtle points. The first is that this type of stability is both local and global in nature—hence the use of the words "global" and "relative" in the definition. While for traditional dynamical systems this would seem contradictory, the complexity of hybrid systems requires us to view stability in a much different light, i.e., we must expand the paradigm for stability.

To better explain the mixed global and local nature of relatively globally asymptotically stable Zeno equilibria, we note that the term "global" is used because the hybrid subsystem $(\mathsf{H}_M^\Gamma, M^\Gamma, X^\Gamma)$ is globally stable to the Zeno equilibria; this also motivates the use of the word "relative" as (H_M, M, X) is stable relative to a hybrid subsystem. Finally, the local nature of this form of stability is in the discrete portion of the hybrid system, rather than the continuous one. That is, the H-subcategory H_M^Γ can be thought of as a neighborhood inside the H-category (see Fig. 1, where the H-categories H_M^Γ and H_M are represented by graphs in order to make their orientations explicit). The condition on the inclusion functor given in the definition is a condition that all edges (or morphisms) are pointing into the neighborhood.

Definition 6. *A trajectory of a hybrid system* (H_M, M, X):

$$(C, c) : (\mathsf{H}_I, I, d/dt) \to (\mathsf{H}_M, M, X)$$

is Zeno if $\Lambda = \mathrm{Ob}_{(\to \cdot \leftarrow)}(\mathsf{H}_I) = \mathbb{N}$ *and*

$$\lim_{j \to \infty} \tau_j = \tau_\infty$$

for a finite τ_∞.

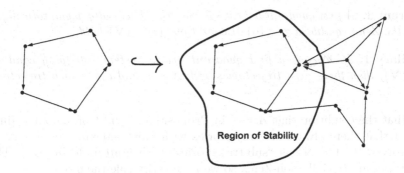

Fig. 1. A graphical representation of the "local" nature of relatively globally asymptotically stable Zeno equilibria

Zeno equilibria are intimately related to Zeno behavior for first quadrant hybrid systems.

Proposition 1. *If a first quadrant hybrid system $\mathscr{H}_{FQ}$ is globally asymptotically stable at the Zeno equilibria $z = \{0\}$, then every trajectory with $\Lambda = \mathbb{N}$ is Zeno.*

Conditions for the Stability of $\mathscr{H}_{FQ}$. In order to give conditions on the stability of Zeno equilibria, it is necessary to give conditions on both the continuous and discrete portions of the hybrid system. That is, the conditions on stability will relate to three aspects of the behavior of the hybrid system: the continuous portion, the existence of events and the discrete portion.

Continuous conditions: For all $i \in Q$,
- **(I)** $f_i(x) \neq 0$ for all $x \in (\mathbb{R}_0^+)^2$.
- **(II)** There exists a function $v_i : (\mathbb{R}_0^+)^2 \to \mathbb{R}_0^+$ of class $\mathcal{K}_\infty$ along each ray emanating from the origin in D_i and $dv_i(x)f_i(x) \leq 0$ for all $x \in (\mathbb{R}_0^+)^2$.

Event conditions: For all $i \in Q$,
- **(III)** $(f_i(x_1, 0))_2 \geq 0$.

Now consider the map ψ_i defined by requiring that:

$$\psi_i(x) = y \quad \text{if} \quad (0, y) = v_i^{-1}(v_i(x, 0)) \cap \{x_1 = 0 \text{ and } x_2 \geq 0\}$$

which is well-defined by condition **(II)**. Using ψ_i we introduce the function $P_i : \mathbb{R}_0^+ \to \mathbb{R}_0^+$ given by:

$$P_i(x) = r_{e_{i-1}} \circ \psi_{i-1} \circ \cdots \circ r_{e_1} \circ \psi_{e_1} \circ r_{e_k} \circ \psi_{e_k} \circ \cdots \circ r_{e_1} \circ \psi_1(x).$$

The map P_i can be thought of as both a Poincaré map or a discrete Lyapunov function depending on the perspective taken. The final conditions are given by:

Discrete conditions: For all $i \in Q$ and $e \in E$,
- **(IV)** r_e is order preserving.
- **(V)** There exists a class $\mathcal{K}_\infty$ function α such that $P_i(x) - x \leq -\alpha(x)$.

Theorem 3. *A first quadrant hybrid system $\mathscr{H}_{\mathbf{FQ}}$ is globally asymptotically stable at the Zeno equilibria $z = \{0\}$ if conditions (**I**) − (**V**) hold.*

Corollary 1. *If $\mathscr{H}_{\mathbf{FQ}}$ is a first quadrant hybrid system satisfying conditions (**I**) − (**V**), then there exist trajectories with $\Lambda = \mathbb{N}$ and every such trajectory is Zeno.*

Note that the condition that $\Lambda = \mathbb{N}$ in Proposition 1 and Corollary 1 is due to the fact that there always are trajectories with finite indexing set Λ, e.g., any trajectory with $\Lambda = \mathbb{N}$ has "sub-trajectories" with finite indexing sets. These trajectories are trivially non-Zeno, so we necessarily rule them out.

5   Hybrid Stability: A Categorical Approach

Building upon the results of the previous section, we are able to derive sufficient conditions for the stability of general hybrid systems. Mirroring the continuous case, we simply find a morphism to the "simplest stable object," i.e., a first quadrant hybrid system.

Theorem 4. *A Zeno equilibria (H_Γ, z) of (H_M, M, X) is globally asymptotically stable relative to $(\mathsf{H}_\Gamma, M^\Gamma, X^\Gamma)$ if there exists a morphism of hybrid systems:*

$$(\mathsf{H}_\Gamma, M^\Gamma, X^\Gamma) \xrightarrow{(V, v)} (\mathsf{H}^{\mathbf{SFQ}}, M^{\mathbf{SFQ}}, X^{\mathbf{SFQ}})$$

where $(\mathsf{H}^{\mathbf{SFQ}}, M^{\mathbf{SFQ}}, X^{\mathbf{SFQ}})$ is the object of HySys corresponding to a stable first quadrant hybrid system, and for all $a \in \mathrm{Ob}(\mathsf{H}_\Gamma)$ the following holds:

1. *$v_a(x) = 0$ implies $x = z_a$,*
2. *v_a is a proper (radially unbounded) function.*

Furthermore, there exist trajectories

$$(\mathsf{H}_I, I, d/dt) \xrightarrow{(C, c)} (\mathsf{H}_\Gamma, M^\Gamma, X^\Gamma)$$

with $\Lambda = \mathrm{Ob}_{(\rightarrow \cdot \leftarrow)}(\mathsf{H}_I) = \mathbb{N}$ and every such trajectory is Zeno.

Example 6. The bouncing ball is the classical example of a hybrid system that is Zeno (cf. [6]). Although it is possible to show that the bouncing ball is Zeno by explicitly solving for the vector fields, we will demonstrate that it is Zeno by applying our results on the stability of Zeno equilibria. In order to do so, we can view the classical model of a bouncing ball as a first quadrant hybrid system by adding an additional discrete mode; we then will apply Theorem 3.

The classical hybrid model for the bouncing ball has $(\{q\}, \{e = (q, q)\})$ as its graph. The domain is given by the set of positive positions:

$$D_q = \{(x_1, x_2) \in \mathbb{R}^2 : x_1 \geq 0\}$$

and the guard is given by the ground together with the condition that the velocity is not positive:

$$G_e = \{(x_1, x_2) \in \mathbb{R}^2 : x_1 = 0 \text{ and } x_2 \leq 0\}.$$

The equations of motion for the bouncing ball are given by the Hamiltonian

$$H(x_1, x_2) = \frac{1}{2}x_2^2 + mgx_1,$$

where x_1 is the position of the ball and x_2 is its velocity; here we have assumed that the mass of the ball is $m = 1$ for simplicity. This can be used (see [2]) to define both the vector field on D_q and the reset map $R_e : G_e \to D_q$:

$$f_q(x_1, x_2) = \begin{pmatrix} x_2 \\ -g \end{pmatrix}, \qquad R_e(x_1, x_2) = \begin{pmatrix} x_1 \\ -ex_2 \end{pmatrix},$$

where $0 \leq e \leq 1$ is the coefficient of restitution.

The bouncing ball can be viewed as a first quadrant hybrid system $\mathscr{H}_B = (\Gamma, D, G, R, F)$ by dividing the original domain into two components, and changing the vector fields accordingly. We first define

$$\Gamma = (\{1, 2\}, \{e_1 = (1, 2), e_2 = (2, 1)\}).$$

Since it is a first quadrant hybrid system, the domains and guards are given as in Section 3. The domain D_1 is obtained from the top half of the original domain for the bouncing ball by reflecting it around the line $x_1 = x_2$. The domain D_2 is obtained from the bottom half of the original domain by reflecting it around the line $x_2 = 0$. This implies that the reset maps are given by:

$$R_{e_1}(x_1, x_2) = (x_2, x_1), \qquad R_{e_2}(x_1, x_2) = (ex_2, x_1).$$

Finally, the transformed vector fields are given by

$$f_1(x_1, x_2) = \begin{pmatrix} -g \\ x_1 \end{pmatrix}, \qquad f_2(x_1, x_2) = \begin{pmatrix} -x_2 \\ g \end{pmatrix}$$

as pictured in Fig. 2.

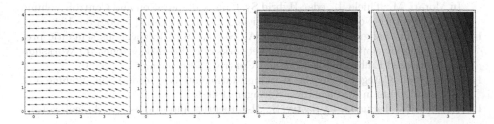

Fig. 2. (Left) Vector fields for the modified bouncing ball hybrid system. (Right) Level sets of the Lyapunov functions on each domain.

To verify that $\mathscr{H}_B$ is globally asymptotically stable at the Zeno point $z = \{0\}$, and hence Zeno by Proposition 1, we need only show that conditions $(\mathbf{I})-(\mathbf{V})$ are satisfied. It is easy to see that conditions $(\mathbf{I})$ and $(\mathbf{III})$ are satisfied. Since $r_{e_1}(x)$ $= x$ and $r_{e_2}(x) = ex$, condition $(\mathbf{IV})$ holds. We use the original Hamiltonian, suitably transformed, for the Lyapunov type functions given in $(\mathbf{II})$, i.e., we pick:

$$v_1(x_1, x_2) = \frac{1}{2}x_1^2 + gx_2, \qquad v_2(x_1, x_2) = \frac{1}{2}x_2^2 + gx_1.$$

It is easy to see that these functions meet the specifications given in $(\mathbf{II})$; some of the level sets of these functions can be seen in Fig. 2. Note that the level sets on one domain increase, but this is compensated for by the decreasing level sets on the other domain. Finally, condition $(\mathbf{V})$ is satisfied when $e < 1$ since $P_1(x) = P_2(x) = ex$.

References

1. Ames, A.D., Zheng, H., Gregg, R.D., Sastry, S.: Is there life after Zeno? Taking executions past the breaking (Zeno) point. (Submitted to the 2006 American Control Conference)
2. Brogliato, B.: Nonsmooth Mechanics. Springer-Verlag (1999)
3. Ames, A.D., Abate, A., Sastry, S.: Sufficient conditions for the existence of Zeno behavior. 44th IEEE Conference on Decision and Control and European Control Conference ECC (2005)
4. Branicky, M.S.: Stability of hybrid systems: State of the art. In: Proceedings of the 36th IEEE Conference on Decision and Control, San Diego, CA (1997)
5. Heymann, M., Lin, F., Meyer, G., Resmerita, S.: Analysis of Zeno behaviors in hybrid systems. In: Proceedings of the 41st IEEE Conference on Decision and Control, Las Vagas, NV (2002)
6. Johansson, K.H., Lygeros, J., Sastry, S., Egerstedt, M.: Simulation of Zeno hybrid automata. In: Proceedings of the 38th IEEE Conference on Decision and Control, Phoenix, AZ (1999)
7. Zhang, J., Johansson, K.H., Lygeros, J., Sastry, S.: Zeno hybrid systems. Int. J. Robust and Nonlinear Control **11**(2) (2001) 435–451
8. Zheng, H., Lee, E.A., Ames, A.D.: Beyond Zeno: Get on with it! (To appear in Hybrid Systems: Computation and Control, 2006)
9. Ames, A.D., Sastry, S.: A homology theory for hybrid systems: Hybrid homology. In Morari, M., Thiele, L., eds.: Hybrid Systems: Computation and Control. Volume 3414 of Lecture Notes in Computer Science., Springer-Verlag (2005) 86–102
10. Ames, A.D., Sangiovanni-Vincentelli, A., Sastry., S.: Homogenous semantic preserving deployments of heterogenous networks of embedded systems. In: Workshop on Networked Embedded Sensing and Control, Notre Dame, IN (2005)
11. Lane, S.M.: Categories for the Working Mathematician. second edn. Volume 5 of Graduate Texts in Mathematics. Springer (1998)
12. Ames, A.D., Tabuada, P., Sastry, S.: H-categories and graphs. (Technical Note)

Reachability Analysis for Controlled Discrete Time Stochastic Hybrid Systems

Saurabh Amin[1], Alessandro Abate[1], Maria Prandini[2],
John Lygeros[3], and Shankar Sastry[1]

[1] University of California at Berkeley - Berkeley, USA
{saurabh, aabate, sastry}@eecs.berkeley.edu
[2] Politecnico di Milano - Milano, Italy
prandini@elet.polimi.it
[3] University of Patras - Patras, Greece
lygeros@ee.upatras.gr

Abstract. A model for discrete time stochastic hybrid systems whose evolution can be influenced by some control input is proposed in this paper. With reference to the introduced class of systems, a methodology for probabilistic reachability analysis is developed that is relevant to safety verification. This methodology is based on the interpretation of the safety verification problem as an optimal control problem for a certain controlled Markov process. In particular, this allows to characterize through some optimal cost function the set of initial conditions for the system such that safety is guaranteed with sufficiently high probability. The proposed methodology is applied to the problem of regulating the average temperature in a room by a thermostat controlling a heater.

1 Introduction

Engineering systems like air traffic control systems or infrastructure networks, and natural systems like biological networks exhibit complex behaviors which can often be naturally described by hybrid dynamical models– systems with interacting discrete and continuous dynamics. In many situations the system dynamics are uncertain, and the evolution of the discrete and continuous dynamics as well as the interactions between them are of stochastic nature.

An important problem in hybrid systems theory is that of reachability analysis. In general terms, a reachability analysis problem consists in evaluating if a given system will reach a certain set during some time horizon, starting from some set of initial conditions. This problem arises, for instance, in connection with those safety verification problems where the unsafe conditions for the system can be characterized in terms of its state entering some unsafe set: if the state of the system cannot enter the unsafe set, then the system is declared to be "safe". In a stochastic setting, the safety verification problem can be formulated as that of estimating the probability that the state of the system remains outside the unsafe set for a given time horizon. If the evolution of the state can be influenced by some control input, the problem becomes verifying if it is possible to keep the state of the system outside the unsafe set with sufficiently high probability by selecting a suitable control input.

João Hespanha and A. Tiwari (Eds.): HSCC 2006, LNCS 3927, pp. 49–63, 2006.
© Springer-Verlag Berlin Heidelberg 2006

Reachability analysis for stochastic hybrid systems has been a recent focus of research, e.g., in [1, 2, 3, 4]. Most of the approaches consider the problem of reachability analysis for continuous time stochastic hybrid systems (CTSHS), wherein the effect of control actions is not directly taken into account. The theory of CTSHS, developed for instance in [5, 6, 7], is used in [1] to address the theoretical issues regarding measurability of the reachability events. On the computational side, a stochastic approximation method is used in [2, 4] to compute the probability of entering into the unsafe set (reach probability). More recently, in [3], certain functions of the state of the system known as barrier certificates are used to compute an upper bound on the reach probability. In the discrete time framework, [8] computes the reach probability using randomized algorithms.

This study adopts the discrete time setting in order to gain a deeper understanding of the theoretical and computational issues associated with the reachability analysis of stochastic hybrid systems. The present work extends the above mentioned approaches to controlled systems, by developing a methodology to compute the maximum probability of remaining in a safe set for a discrete time stochastic hybrid system (DTSHS) whose dynamics is affected by a control input. The approach is based on formulating the reachability analysis problem as an optimal control problem. The maximum probability of remaining in a safe set for a certain time horizon can then be computed by dynamic programming. In addition, the optimal value function obtained through the dynamic programming approach directly enables one to compute the maximal safe set for a specified threshold probability, which is the largest set of all initial conditions such that the probability of remaining in the safe set during a certain time horizon is greater than or equal to the threshold probability.

The paper is organized as follows: Section 2 introduces a model for a DTSHS. This model is inspired by the stochastic hybrid systems models previously introduced in [5, 6, 7] in continuous time. An equivalent representation of the DTSHS in the form of a controlled Markov process is derived. In Section 3, the notion of stochastic reachability for a DTSHS is introduced. The problem of determining probabilistic maximal safe sets for a DTSHS is formulated as a stochastic reachability analysis problem, which can be solved by dynamic programming. The representation of the DTSHS as a controlled Markov process is useful in this respect. In Section 4 we apply the proposed methodology to the problem of regulating the temperature of a room by a thermostat that controls a heater. Concluding remarks are drawn in Section 5.

2   Discrete Time Stochastic Hybrid System

In this section, we introduce a definition of discrete time stochastic hybrid system (DTSHS). This definition is inspired by the continuous time stochastic hybrid system (CTSHS) model described in [9].

The hybrid state of the DTSHS is characterized by a discrete and a continuous component. The discrete state component takes values in a finite set $\mathcal{Q}$. In each mode $q \in \mathcal{Q}$, the continuous state component takes values in the Euclidean space

$\mathbb{R}^{n(q)}$, whose dimension is determined by the map $n : \mathcal{Q} \to \mathbb{N}$. Thus the hybrid state space is $\mathcal{S} := \cup_{q \in \mathcal{Q}}\{q\} \times \mathbb{R}^{n(q)}$. Let $\mathcal{B}(\mathcal{S})$ be the σ-field generated by the subsets of $\mathcal{S}$ of the form $\cup_q\{q\} \times A_q$, where A_q is a Borel set in $\mathbb{R}^{n(q)}$. It can be shown (see [5, page 58]) that $(\mathcal{S}, \mathcal{B}(\mathcal{S}))$ is a Borel space.

The continuous state evolves according to a probabilistic law that depends on the discrete state. A transition from one discrete state to another may occur during the continuous state evolution, according to some probabilistic law. This will then cause a modification of the probabilistic law governing the continuous state evolution. A control input can affect both the continuous and discrete probabilistic evolutions. After a transition in the discrete state has occurred, the continuous state is subject to a probabilistic reset that is also influenced by some control input. Following the reference CTSHS model in [9], we distinguish this latter input from the former one. We call them transition input and reset input, respectively.

Definition 1 (DTSHS). *A discrete time stochastic hybrid system (DTSHS) is a tuple $\mathcal{H} = (\mathcal{Q}, n, \mathcal{U}, \Sigma, T_x, T_q, R)$, where*

- $\mathcal{Q} := \{q_1, q_2, \ldots, q_m\}$, *for some $m \in \mathbb{N}$, represents the discrete state space;*
- $n : \mathcal{Q} \to \mathbb{N}$ *assigns to each discrete state value $q \in \mathcal{Q}$ the dimension of the continuous state space $\mathbb{R}^{n(q)}$. The hybrid state space is then given by $\mathcal{S} := \cup_{q \in \mathcal{Q}}\{q\} \times \mathbb{R}^{n(q)}$;*
- $\mathcal{U}$ *is a compact Borel space representing the transition control space;*
- Σ *is a compact Borel space representing the reset control space;*
- $T_x : \mathcal{B}(\mathbb{R}^{n(\cdot)}) \times \mathcal{S} \times \mathcal{U} \to [0,1]$ *is a Borel-measurable stochastic kernel on $\mathbb{R}^{n(\cdot)}$ given $\mathcal{S} \times \mathcal{U}$, which assigns to each $s = (q, x) \in \mathcal{S}$ and $u \in \mathcal{U}$ a probability measure on the Borel space $(\mathbb{R}^{n(q)}, \mathcal{B}(\mathbb{R}^{n(q)}))$: $T_x(dx|(q,x),u)$;*
- $T_q : \mathcal{Q} \times \mathcal{S} \times \mathcal{U} \to [0,1]$ *is a discrete stochastic kernel on $\mathcal{Q}$ given $\mathcal{S} \times \mathcal{U}$, which assigns to each $s \in \mathcal{S}$ and $u \in \mathcal{U}$, a probability distribution over $\mathcal{Q}$: $T_q(q|s,u)$;*
- $R : \mathcal{B}(\mathbb{R}^{n(\cdot)}) \times \mathcal{S} \times \Sigma \times \mathcal{Q} \to [0,1]$ *is a Borel-measurable stochastic kernel on $\mathbb{R}^{n(\cdot)}$ given $\mathcal{S} \times \Sigma \times \mathcal{Q}$, that assigns to each $s = (q,x) \in \mathcal{S}$, $\sigma \in \Sigma$, and $q' \in \mathcal{Q}$, a probability measure on the Borel space $(\mathbb{R}^{n(q')}, \mathcal{B}(\mathbb{R}^{n(q')}))$: $R(dx|(q,x),\sigma,q')$.* □

In order to define the semantics of a DTSHS, we need first to specify how the system is initialized and how the reset and transition inputs are selected. The system initialization can be specified through some probability measure $\pi : \mathcal{B}(\mathcal{S}) \to [0,1]$ on the Borel space $(\mathcal{S}, \mathcal{B}(\mathcal{S}))$. When the initial state of the system is $s \in \mathcal{S}$, then, the probability measure π is concentrated at $\{s\}$. As for the choice of the reset and transition inputs, we need to specify which is the rule to determine their values at every time step during the DTSHS evolution (control policy). Here, we consider a DTSHS evolving over a finite horizon $[0, N]$ $(N < \infty)$. If the values for the control inputs at each time $k \in [0, N)$ are determined based on the values taken by the past inputs and the state up to the current time k, then the policy is said to be a feedback policy.

Definition 2 (Feedback policy). *Let* $\mathcal{H} = (\mathcal{Q}, n, \mathcal{U}, \Sigma, T_x, T_q, R)$ *be a DTSHS. A feedback policy* μ *for* $\mathcal{H}$ *is a sequence* $\mu = (\mu_0, \mu_1, \ldots, \mu_{N-1})$ *of universally measurable maps* $\mu_k : S \times (S \times \mathcal{U} \times \Sigma)^k \to \mathcal{U} \times \Sigma$, $k = 0, 1, \ldots, N-1$. *We denote the set of feedback policies as* $\mathcal{M}$. □

Definition 3 (Execution). *Consider a DTSHS* $\mathcal{H} = (\mathcal{Q}, n, \mathcal{U}, \Sigma, T_x, T_q, R)$. *A stochastic process* $\{\mathbf{s}(k) = (\mathbf{q}(k), \mathbf{x}(k)), \ k \in [0, N]\}$ *with values in* $S = \cup_{q \in \mathcal{Q}}\{q\} \times \mathbb{R}^{n(q)}$ *is an execution of* $\mathcal{H}$ *associated with a policy* $\mu \in \mathcal{M}$ *and an initial distribution* π *if its sample paths are obtained according to the following algorithm, where all the random extractions involved are independent:*

DTSHS algorithm:

Extract from S *a value* $s_0 = (q_0, x_0)$ *for the random variable* $\mathbf{s}(0) = (\mathbf{q}(0), \mathbf{x}(0))$ *according to* π;

set $k=0$

while $k < N$ *do*

> *set* $(u_k, \sigma_k) = \mu_k(s_k, s_{k-1}, u_{k-1}, \sigma_{k-1}, \ldots)$;
>
> *extract from* Q *a value* q_{k+1} *for the random variable* $\mathbf{q}(k+1)$ *according to* $T_q(\cdot | (q_k, x_k), u_k)$;
>
> *if* $q_{k+1} = q_k$, *then*
>
>> *extract from* $\mathbb{R}^{n(q_{k+1})}$ *a value* x_{k+1} *for* $\mathbf{x}(k+1)$ *according to* $T_x(\cdot | (q_k, x_k), u_k)$
>
> *else*
>
>> *extract from* $\mathbb{R}^{n(q_{k+1})}$ *a value* x_{k+1} *for* $\mathbf{x}(k+1)$ *according to* $R(\cdot | (q_k, x_k), \sigma_k, q_{k+1})$
>
> *set* $s_{k+1} = (q_{k+1}, x_{k+1})$
>
> $k \to k+1$

end □

If the values for the control inputs are determined only based on the value taken by the state at the current time step, i.e., $(u_k, \sigma_k) = \mu_k(s_k)$, then the policy is said to be a Markov policy.

Definition 4 (Markov Policy). *Consider a DTSHS* $\mathcal{H} = (\mathcal{Q}, n, \mathcal{U}, \Sigma, T_x, T_q, R)$. *A Markov policy* μ *for* $\mathcal{H}$ *is a sequence* $\mu = (\mu_0, \mu_1, \ldots, \mu_{N-1})$ *of universally measurable maps* $\mu_k : S \to \mathcal{U} \times \Sigma$, $k = 0, 1, \ldots, N-1$. *We denote the set of Markov policies as* $\mathcal{M}_m$.

Note that Markov policies are a subset of the feedback policies: $\mathcal{M}_m \subseteq \mathcal{M}$.

Remark 1. It is worth noticing that the map T_q can model both the spontaneous transitions that might occur during the continuous state evolution, and the forced transitions that must occur when the continuous state exits some prescribed set.

As for spontaneous transitions, if at some hybrid state $(q, x) \in S$ a transition to the discrete state q' is allowed by the control input $u \in \mathcal{U}$, then this is modeled by $T_q(q'|(q, x), u) > 0$. T_q also encodes a possible delay in the actual occurrence of a transition: if $T_q(q'|(q, x), u) = 1$, then the transition must occur, the smaller is $T_q(q'|(q, x), u)$, the more likely is that the transition will be postponed to a later time.

The invariant set $Dom(q)$ of a discrete state $q \in \mathcal{Q}$, namely the set of all the admissible values for the continuous state within mode q, can be expressed in terms of T_q by forcing $T_q(q|(q, x), u)$ to be zero irrespectively of the value of the control input u in $\mathcal{U}$, for all the continuous state values $x \in \mathbb{R}^{n(q)}$ outside $Dom(q)$. Thus $Dom(q) := \mathbb{R}^{n(q)} \setminus \{x \in \mathbb{R}^{n(q)} : T_q(q|(q, x), u) = 0, \forall u \in \mathcal{U}\}$.   □

Define the stochastic kernel $\tau_x : \mathcal{B}(\mathbb{R}^{n(\cdot)}) \times S \times \mathcal{U} \times \Sigma \times \mathcal{Q} \to [0, 1]$ on $\mathbb{R}^{n(\cdot)}$ given $S \times \mathcal{U} \times \Sigma \times \mathcal{Q}$, which assigns to each $s = (q, x) \in S$, $u \in \mathcal{U}$, $\sigma \in \Sigma$ and $q' \in \mathcal{Q}$ a probability measure on the Borel space $(\mathbb{R}^{n(q')}, \mathcal{B}(\mathbb{R}^{n(q')}))$ as follows:

$$\tau_x(dx' \,|(q, x), u, \sigma, q') = \begin{cases} T_x(dx'|(q, x), u), & \text{if } q' = q \\ R(dx'|(q, x), \sigma, q'), & \text{if } q' \neq q. \end{cases}$$

In the DTSHS algorithm, τ_x is used to extract a value for the continuous state at time $k + 1$ given the values taken by the hybrid state and the control inputs at time k, and the value extracted for the discrete state at time $k + 1$.

Based on τ_x we can define the Borel-measurable stochastic kernel $T_s : \mathcal{B}(S) \times S \times \mathcal{U} \times \Sigma \to [0, 1]$ on S given $S \times \mathcal{U} \times \Sigma$, which assigns to each $s = (q, x) \in S$, $(u, \sigma) \in \mathcal{U} \times \Sigma$ a probability measure on the Borel space $(S, \mathcal{B}(S))$ as follows:

$$T_s(ds' \,|s, (u, \sigma)) = \tau_x(dx' \,|s, u, \sigma, q') T_q(q'|s, u), \tag{1}$$

$s, s' = (q', x') \in S$, $(u, \sigma) \in \mathcal{U} \times \Sigma$. Then, the DTSHS algorithm can be rewritten in a more compact form as:

extract from S a value s_0 for the random variable $\mathbf{s}(0)$ according to π;

set k=0

while $k < N$ do

    set $(u_k, \sigma_k) = \mu_k(s_k, s_{k-1}, u_{k-1}, \sigma_{k-1}, \dots)$;

    extract from S a value s_{k+1} for $\mathbf{s}(k + 1)$ according to $T_s(\cdot \,|s_k, (u_k, \sigma_k))$;

    $k \to k + 1$

end   □

This shows that a DTSHS $\mathcal{H} = (\mathcal{Q}, n, \mathcal{U}, \Sigma, T_x, T_q, R)$ can be described as a controlled Markov process with state space $S = \cup_{q \in \mathcal{Q}} \{q\} \times \mathbb{R}^{n(q)}$, control space $\mathcal{A} := \mathcal{U} \times \Sigma$, and controlled transition probability function $T_s : \mathcal{B}(S) \times S \times \mathcal{A} \to [0, 1]$ defined in (1). This will be referred to in the following as "embedded controlled Markov process" (see, e.g., [10] for an extensive treatment on controlled Markov processes).

As a consequence of this representation of $\mathcal{H}$, the execution $\{\mathbf{s}(k) = (\mathbf{q}(k),$ $\mathbf{x}(k)), k \in [0, N]\}$ associated with $\mu \in \mathcal{M}$ and π is a stochastic process defined on the canonical sample space $\Omega = \mathcal{S}^N$, endowed with its product topology $\mathcal{B}(\Omega)$, with probability measure P_π^μ uniquely defined by the transition kernel T_s, the policy $\mu \in \mathcal{M}$, and the initial probability measure π (see [11, Proposition 7.45]). When π is concentrated at $\{s\}$, $s \in \mathcal{S}$, we shall write simply P_s^μ. From the embedded Markov process representation of a DTSHS it also follows that the execution of a DTSHS associated with a Markov policy μ and an initial condition π is a Markov process. In the sequel, only Markovian policies will be considered.

Example 1 (The thermostat). Consider the problem of regulating the temperature of a room by a thermostat that can switch a heater on and off.

The state of the controlled system is naturally described as a hybrid state. The discrete state component is represented by the heater being in either the "on" or the "off" condition. The continuous state component is represented by the average temperature of the room.

We next show how the controlled system can be described through a DTSHS model $\mathcal{H} = (\mathcal{Q}, n, \mathcal{U}, \Sigma, T_x, T_q, R)$. We then formulate the temperature regulation problem with reference to this model.

Concerning the state space of the DTSHS, the discrete component of the hybrid state space is $\mathcal{Q} = \{\texttt{ON}, \texttt{OFF}\}$, whereas $n : \mathcal{Q} \to \mathbb{N}$ defining the dimension of the continuous component of the hybrid state space is the constant map $n(q) = 1, \forall q \in \mathcal{Q}$. We assume that the heater can be turned on or off, and that this is the only available control on the system. We then define $\Sigma = \emptyset$ and $\mathcal{U} = \{0, 1\}$ with the understanding that "1" means that a switching command is issued, "0" that no switching command is issued. Regarding the continuous state evolution, in the stochastic model proposed in [12], the average temperature of the room evolves according to the following stochastic differential equations (SDEs)

$$dx(t) = \begin{cases} -\frac{a}{C}(\mathbf{x}(t) - x_a)dt + \frac{1}{C}d\mathbf{w}(t), & \text{if the heater is off} \\ -\frac{a}{C}(\mathbf{x}(t) - x_a)dt + \frac{r}{C}dt + \frac{1}{C}d\mathbf{w}(t), & \text{if the heater is on,} \end{cases} \quad (2)$$

where a is the average heat loss rate; C is the average thermal capacity of the room; x_a is the ambient temperature (assumed to be constant); r is the rate of heat gain supplied by the heater; $\mathbf{w}(t)$ is a standard Wiener process modeling the noise affecting the temperature evolution. By applying the constant-step Euler-Maruyama discretization scheme [13] to the SDEs in (2), with time step Δt, we obtain the stochastic difference equation

$$\mathbf{x}(k+1) = \begin{cases} \mathbf{x}(k) - \frac{a}{C}(\mathbf{x}(k) - x_a)\Delta t + \mathbf{n}(k), & \text{if the heater is off} \\ \mathbf{x}(k) - \frac{a}{C}(\mathbf{x}(k) - x_a)\Delta t + \frac{r}{C}\Delta t + \mathbf{n}(k) & \text{if the heater is on,} \end{cases} \quad (3)$$

where $\{\mathbf{n}(k), k \geq 0\}$ is a sequence of i.i.d. Gaussian random variables with zero mean and variance $\nu^2 := \frac{1}{C^2}\Delta t$.

Let $\mathcal{N}(\cdot; m, \sigma^2)$ denote the probability measure over $(\mathbb{R}, \mathcal{B}(\mathbb{R}))$ associated with a Gaussian density function with mean m and variance σ^2. Then, the continuous transition kernel T_x implicitly defined in (3) can be expressed as follows:

$$T_x(\cdot\,|(q,x),u) = \begin{cases} \mathcal{N}(\cdot\,;x - \frac{a}{C}(x - x_a)\Delta t, \nu^2), & q = \text{OFF} \\ \mathcal{N}(\cdot\,;x - \frac{a}{C}(x - x_a)\Delta t + \frac{r}{C}\Delta t, \nu^2), & q = \text{ON} \end{cases} \quad (4)$$

Note that the evolution of the temperature within each mode is uncontrolled and so the continuous transition kernel T_x does not depend on the value u of the transition control input.

We assume that it takes some (random) time for the heater to actually switch between its two operating conditions, after a switching command has been issued. This is modeled by defining the discrete transition kernel T_q as follows

$$T_q(q'|(q,x),0) = \begin{cases} 1, & q' = q \\ 0, & q' \neq q \end{cases}$$

$$T_q(q'|(q,x),1) = \begin{cases} \alpha, & q' = \text{OFF}, q = \text{ON} \\ 1 - \alpha, & q' = q = \text{ON} \\ \beta, & q' = \text{ON}, q = \text{OFF} \\ 1 - \beta, & q' = q = \text{OFF} \end{cases} \quad (5)$$

$\forall x \in \mathbb{R}$, where $\alpha \in [0,1]$ represents the probability of switching from the ON to the OFF mode in one time-step. Similarly for $\beta \in [0,1]$.

We assume that the actual switching between the two operating conditions of the heater takes a time step. During this time step the temperature keeps evolving according to the dynamics referring to the starting condition. This is modeled by defining the reset kernel as follows

$$R(\cdot\,|(q,x),q') = \begin{cases} \mathcal{N}(\cdot\,;x - \frac{a}{C}(x - x_a)\Delta t, \nu^2), & q = \text{OFF} \\ \mathcal{N}(\cdot\,;x - \frac{a}{C}(x - x_a)\Delta t + \frac{r}{C}\Delta t, \nu^2), & q = \text{ON}. \end{cases} \quad (6)$$

Let $\bar{x}^-$, $\bar{x}^+ \in \mathbb{R}$, with $\bar{x}^- < \bar{x}^+$. Consider the (stationary) Markov policy $\mu_k : \mathcal{S} \to \mathcal{U}$ defined by

$$\mu_k((q,x)) = \begin{cases} 1, & q = \text{ON}, x \geq \bar{x}^+ \text{ or } q = \text{OFF}, x \leq \bar{x}^- \\ 0, & q = \text{ON}, x < \bar{x}^+ \text{ or } q = \text{OFF}, x > \bar{x}^- \end{cases}$$

that switches the heater on when the temperature drops below $\bar{x}^-$ and off when the temperature goes beyond $\bar{x}^+$.

Suppose that initially the heater is off and the temperature is uniformly distributed in the interval between $\bar{x}^-$ and $\bar{x}^+$, independently of the noise process affecting its evolution. In Figure 1, we report some sample paths of the execution of the DTSHS associated with this policy and initial condition. We plot only the continuous state realizations. The temperature is measured in Fahrenheit degrees ($^\circ F$) and the time in minutes (min). The time horizon N is taken to be 600 min. The discretization time step Δt is chosen to be 1 min. The parameters in equations (4) and (6) are assigned the following values: $x_a = 10.5^\circ F$, $a/C = 0.1\ min^{-1}$, $r/C = 10^\circ F/min$, and $\nu = 1^\circ F$. The switching probabilities

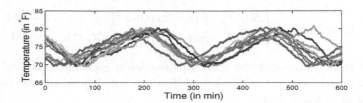

Fig. 1. Sample paths of the temperature for the execution corresponding to a Markov policy switching the heater on/off when the temperature drops below $70°F$/goes above $80°F$, starting with heater off and temperature uniformly distributed on $[70, 80]°F$

α and β in equation (5) are both chosen to be equal to 0.8. Finally, $\bar{x}^-$ and $\bar{x}^+$ are set equal to $70°F$ and $80°F$, respectively.

Note that some of the sample paths exit the set $[70, 80]°F$. This is due partly to the delay in turning the heater on/off and partly to the noise entering the system. If the objective is keeping the temperature within the set $[70, 80]°$F, more effective control policies can be found. In the following section we consider the problem of determining those initial conditions for the system such that it is possible to keep the temperature of the room within prescribed limits over a certain time horizon $[0, N]$, by appropriately acting on the only available control input. Due to the stochastic nature of the controlled system, we relax our requirement to that of keeping the temperature within prescribed limits over $[0, N]$ with sufficiently high probability. We shall see how this problem can be formulated as a stochastic reachability analysis problem.   □

3   Stochastic Reachability

We consider the issue of verifying if it is possible to maintain the state of a stochastic hybrid system outside some unsafe set with sufficiently high probability, by choosing an appropriate control policy. This problem can be reinterpreted as a stochastic reachability analysis problem.

With reference to the introduced stochastic hybrid model $\mathcal{H}$, for a given Markov policy $\mu \in \mathcal{M}_m$ and initial state distribution π, a reachability analysis problem consists in determining the probability that the execution associated with the policy μ and initialization π will enter a Borel set $A \in \mathcal{B}(S)$ during the time horizon $[0, N]$:

$$\mathcal{P}_\pi^\mu(A) := P_\pi^\mu(\mathbf{s}(k) \in A \text{ for some } k \in [0, N]). \tag{7}$$

If π is concentrated at $\{s\}$, $s \in \mathcal{S}$, then this is the probability of entering A starting from s, which we denote by $\mathcal{P}_s^\mu(A)$.

Suppose that A represents an unsafe set for $\mathcal{H}$. Different initial conditions are characterized by a different probability of entering A: if the system starts from an initial condition that corresponds to a probability $\epsilon \in (0, 1)$ of entering the unsafe set A, then the system is said to be "safe with probability $1 - \epsilon$". It is then possible to define sets of initial conditions corresponding to different safety levels, that is sets of states such that the value for the probability of entering the unsafe set starting from them is smaller than or equal to a given value ϵ.

The set of initial conditions that guarantees a safety level $1 - \epsilon$, when the control policy $\mu \in \mathcal{M}_m$ is assigned,

$$S^\mu(\epsilon) = \{s \in \mathcal{S} : \mathcal{P}_s^\mu(A) \leq \epsilon\} \tag{8}$$

is referred to as *probabilistic safe set* with safety level $1 - \epsilon$. If the control policy can be selected so as to minimize the probability of entering A, then

$$S^\star(\epsilon) = \{s \in \mathcal{S} : \inf_{\mu \in \mathcal{M}_m} \mathcal{P}_s^\mu(A) \leq \epsilon\}. \tag{9}$$

is the *maximal probabilistic safe set* with safety level $1 - \epsilon$. By comparing the expressions for $S^\mu(\epsilon)$ and $S^\star(\epsilon)$, it is in fact clear that $S^\mu(\epsilon) \subseteq S^\star(\epsilon)$, for each $\mu \in \mathcal{M}_m$, $\epsilon \in (0, 1)$.

In the rest of the section, we show that (i) the problem of computing $\mathcal{P}_s^\mu(A)$ and $S^\mu(\epsilon)$ for $\mu \in \mathcal{M}_m$ can be solved by using a backward iterative procedure; and (ii) the problem of computing $S^\star(\epsilon)$ can be reduced to an optimal control problem. This, in turn, can be solved by dynamic programming. These results are obtained based on the representation of $\mathcal{P}_\pi^\mu(A)$ as a multiplicative cost function.

The probability $\mathcal{P}_\pi^\mu(A)$ defined in (7) can be expressed as $\mathcal{P}_\pi^\mu(A) = 1 - p_\pi^\mu(\bar{A})$, where $\bar{A}$ denotes the complement of A in $\mathcal{S}$ and $p_\pi^\mu(\bar{A}) := P_\pi^\mu(\mathbf{s}(k) \in \bar{A}$ for all $k \in [0, N])$. Let $\mathbf{1}_C : \mathcal{S} \rightarrow \{0, 1\}$ denote the indicator function of a set $C \subseteq \mathcal{S}$: $\mathbf{1}_C(s) = 1$, if $s \in C$, and 0, if $s \notin C$. Observe that

$$\prod_{k=0}^{N} \mathbf{1}_{\bar{A}}(s_k) = \begin{cases} 1, & \text{if } s_k \in \bar{A} \text{ for all } k \in [0, N] \\ 0, & \text{otherwise}, \end{cases}$$

where $s_k \in \mathcal{S}$, $k \in [0, N]$. Then,

$$p_\pi^\mu(\bar{A}) = P_\pi^\mu(\prod_{k=0}^{N} \mathbf{1}_{\bar{A}}(\mathbf{s}(k)) = 1) = E_\pi^\mu[\prod_{k=0}^{N} \mathbf{1}_{\bar{A}}(\mathbf{s}(k))]. \tag{10}$$

From this expression it follows that

$$p_\pi^\mu(\bar{A}) = \int_{\mathcal{S}} E_\pi^\mu\Big[\prod_{k=0}^{N} \mathbf{1}_{\bar{A}}(\mathbf{s}(k))|\, s(0) = s\Big] \pi(ds), \tag{11}$$

where the conditional mean $E_\pi^\mu[\prod_{k=0}^{N} \mathbf{1}_{\bar{A}}(\mathbf{s}(k))|\, s(0) = s]$ is well defined over the support of the probability measure π representing the distribution of $\mathbf{s}(0)$.

3.1 Backward Reachability Computations

We next show how it is possible to compute $p_\pi^\mu(\bar{A})$ through a backward iterative procedure for a given Markov policy $\mu = (\mu_0, \mu_1, \ldots, \mu_{N-1}) \in \mathcal{M}_m$, with $\mu_k :$

$\mathcal{S} \to \mathcal{U} \times \Sigma$, $k = 0, 1, \ldots, N - 1$. For each $k \in [0, N]$, define the map $V_k^\mu : \mathcal{S} \to [0, 1]$ as follows

$$V_k^\mu(s) := \mathbf{1}_{\bar{A}}(s) \int_{\mathcal{S}^{N-k}} \prod_{l=k+1}^{N} \mathbf{1}_{\bar{A}}(s_l) \prod_{h=k+1}^{N-1} T_s(ds_{h+1}|s_h, \mu_h(s_h)) T_s(ds_{k+1}|s, \mu_k(s)),$$

(12)

$\forall s \in \mathcal{S}$, where T_s is the controlled transition function of the embedded controlled Markov process, and $\int_{\mathcal{S}^0}(\ldots) = 1$. If s belongs to the support of π, then, $E_\pi^\mu\left[\prod_{l=k}^{N} \mathbf{1}_{\bar{A}}(\mathbf{s}(l)) | \mathbf{s}(k) = s\right]$ is well-defined and equal to the right-hand-side of (12), so that

$$V_k^\mu(s) = E_\pi^\mu\left[\prod_{l=k}^{N} \mathbf{1}_{\bar{A}}(\mathbf{s}(l)) | \mathbf{s}(k) = s\right]$$

(13)

denotes the probability of remaining outside A during the (residual) time horizon $[k, N]$ starting from s at time k, under policy μ applied from π.

By (11) and (13), $p_\pi^\mu(\bar{A})$ can be expressed as $p_\pi^\mu(\bar{A}) = \int_\mathcal{S} V_0^\mu(s)\pi(ds)$. If π is concentrated at $\{s\}$, $p_s^\mu(\bar{A}) = V_0^\mu(s)$. Since $\mathcal{P}_s^\mu(A) = 1 - p_s^\mu(\bar{A})$, then the probabilistic safe set with safety level $1 - \epsilon$, $\epsilon \in (0, 1)$, defined in (8) can be computed as $S^\mu(\epsilon) = \{s \in \mathcal{S} : V_0^\mu(s) \geq 1 - \epsilon\}$.

By a reasoning similar to [14] for additive costs, we prove the following lemma.

Lemma 1. *Fix a Markov policy μ. The maps $V_k^\mu : \mathcal{S} \to [0, 1]$, $k = 0, 1 \ldots, N$, can be computed by the backward recursion:*

$$V_k^\mu(s) = \mathbf{1}_{\bar{A}}(s)\left[T_q(q|s, u_k^\mu(s)) \int_{\mathbb{R}^{n(q)}} V_{k+1}^\mu((q, x')) T_x(dx'|s, u_k^\mu(s))\right.$$

$$\left. + \sum_{q' \neq q} T_q(q'|s, u_k^\mu(s)) \int_{\mathbb{R}^{n(q')}} V_{k+1}^\mu((q', x')) R(dx'|s, \sigma_k^\mu(s), q')\right], s = (q, x) \in \mathcal{S},$$

where $\mu_k = (u_k^\mu, \sigma_k^\mu) : \mathcal{S} \to \mathcal{U} \times \Sigma$, initialized with $V_N^\mu(s) = \mathbf{1}_{\bar{A}}(s)$, $s \in \mathcal{S}$.

Proof. From definition (12) of V_k^μ, we get that $V_N^\mu(s) = \mathbf{1}_{\bar{A}}(s)$, $s \in \mathcal{S}$. For $k < N$,

$$V_k^\mu(s) = \mathbf{1}_{\bar{A}}(s) \int_{\mathcal{S}^{N-k}} \prod_{l=k+1}^{N} \mathbf{1}_{\bar{A}}(s_l) \prod_{h=k+1}^{N-1} T_s(ds_{h+1}|s_h, \mu_h(s_h)) T_s(ds_{k+1}|s, \mu_k(s))$$

$$= \mathbf{1}_{\bar{A}}(s) \int_\mathcal{S} \mathbf{1}_{\bar{A}}(s_{k+1})\left(\int_{\mathcal{S}^{N-k-1}} \prod_{l=k+2}^{N} \mathbf{1}_{\bar{A}}(s_l) \prod_{h=k+2}^{N-1} T_s(ds_{h+1}|s_h, \mu_h(s_h))\right.$$

$$\left. T_s(ds_{k+2}|s_{k+1}, \mu_{k+1}(s_{k+1}))\right) T_s(ds_{k+1}|s, \mu_k(s))$$

$$= \mathbf{1}_{\bar{A}}(s) \int_\mathcal{S} V_{k+1}^\mu(s_{k+1}) T_s(ds_{k+1}|s, \mu_k(s)).$$

Recalling the definition of T_s the thesis immediately follows. □

3.2   Maximal Probabilistic Safe Set Computation

The calculation of the maximal probabilistic safe set $S^\star(\epsilon)$ defined in (9) amounts to finding the infimum over the Markov policies of the probability $\mathcal{P}_s^\mu(A)$ of entering the unsafe set A starting from s, for all s outside A (the probability of entering A starting from $s \in A$ is 1 for any policy). A policy that achieves this infimum is said to be *maximally safe*.

Definition 5 (Maximally safe policy). *Let* $\mathcal{H} = (\mathcal{Q}, n, \mathcal{U}, \Sigma, T_x, T_q, R)$ *be a DTSHS, and* $A \in \mathcal{B}(\mathcal{S})$ *an unsafe set. A policy* $\mu^* \in \mathcal{M}_m$ *is maximally safe if* $\mathcal{P}_s^{\mu^*}(A) = \inf_{\mu \in \mathcal{M}_m} \mathcal{P}_s^\mu(A)$, $\forall s \in \bar{A}$.

Given that $\mathcal{P}_s^\mu(A) = 1 - p_s^\mu(\bar{A})$, finding the infimum of the probability $\mathcal{P}_s^\mu(A)$ is equivalent to computing the supremum of the probability $p_s^\mu(\bar{A})$ of remaining within the safe set $\bar{A}$. In the following theorem, we describe an algorithm to compute $\sup_{\mu \in \mathcal{M}_m} p_s^\mu(\bar{A})$ and give a condition for the existence of a maximally safe policy. The proof is based on [11, Proposition 11.7].

Theorem 1. *Define the maps* $V_k^* : \mathcal{S} \to [0,1]$, $k = 0, 1, \ldots, N$, *by the backward recursion:*

$$V_k^*(s) = \sup_{(u,\sigma) \in \mathcal{U} \times \Sigma} \mathbf{1}_{\bar{A}}(s) \int_{\mathcal{S}} V_{k+1}^*(s_{k+1}) T_s(ds_{k+1} | s, (u,\sigma)), \; s \in \mathcal{S},$$

initialized with $V_N^*(s) = \mathbf{1}_{\bar{A}}(s)$, $s \in \mathcal{S}$.
    Then, $V_0^*(s) = \sup_{\mu \in \mathcal{M}_m} p_s^\mu(\bar{A})$ *for all* $s \in \mathcal{S}$. *Moreover, if* $U_k(s, \lambda) = \{(u, \sigma) \in \mathcal{U} \times \Sigma | \mathbf{1}_{\bar{A}}(s) \int_{\mathcal{S}} V_{k+1}^*(s_{k+1}) T_s(ds_{k+1} | s, (u,\sigma)) \leq \lambda\}$ *is compact for all* $s \in \mathcal{S}$, $\lambda \in \mathbb{R}$, $k \in [0, N-1]$, *then there exists a maximally safe policy* $\mu^* = (\mu_0^*, \ldots, \mu_{N-1}^*)$, *with* $\mu_k^* : \mathcal{S} \to \mathcal{U} \times \Sigma$, $k \in [0, N-1]$, *given by*

$$\mu_k^*(s) = \arg \sup_{(u,\sigma) \in \mathcal{U} \times \Sigma} \mathbf{1}_{\bar{A}}(s) \int_{\mathcal{S}} V_{k+1}^*(s_{k+1}) T_s(ds_{k+1} | s, (u,\sigma)), \forall s \in \mathcal{S}. \quad (14)$$

Proof. Note that we deal with Borel spaces and with Borel measurable stochastic kernels. The one-stage cost function $\mathbf{1}_{\bar{A}}(s)$ is Borel measurable, non negative and bounded for all $s \in \mathcal{S}$. In particular, $V_N^*(s) = \mathbf{1}_{\bar{A}}(s)$ is Borel measurable, hence universally measurable. It can be directly checked that the mapping $H : \mathcal{S} \times \mathcal{U} \times \Sigma \times V \to \mathbb{R}$ defined as $H(s, (u,\sigma), V) = \mathbf{1}_{\bar{A}}(s) \int_{\mathcal{S}} V(s') T_s(ds' | s, (u,\sigma))$ satisfies the *monotonicity assumption* when applied to universally measurable functions V (cf. [11, Section 6.1]). Then $V_k^*(s) = \sup_{(u,\sigma) \in \mathcal{U} \times \Sigma} H(s, (u,\sigma), V_{k+1}^*)$ is universally measurable for every $k \in [0, N-1]$. The functions $V_k^*(s)$ are also lower semi-analytic. This holds because the product of a lower semi-analytic function by a positive Borel measurable function is lower semi-analytic; furthermore, the integration of a lower semi-analytic function with respect to a stochastic kernel and its supremization with respect to one of its arguments (in this specific instance, the control input) is lower semi-analytic (cf. [11, Propositions 7.30, 7.47 and 7.48]). The preceding measurability arguments provide a solid ground

for the *exact selection assumption* to hold ([11, Section 6.2]), which finally leads
to the statement of the theorem by the application of [11, Proposition 11.7].   □

Remark 2. When $\mathcal{U}$ and Σ are finite sets, then the compactness assumption
required in the theorem is trivially satisfied.

The maximal probabilistic safe set $S^\star(\epsilon)$ with safety level $1 - \epsilon$ defined in (9)
can be determined as $S^\star(\epsilon) = \{s \in \mathcal{S} : V_0^*(s) \geq 1 - \epsilon\}$.

4   The Thermostat Example

In this section we apply the proposed methodology to the problem of regulating
the temperature of a room by a thermostat controlling a heater. We refer to the
DTSHS description of the system given in Example 1 of Section 2. The system
parameters and time horizon are set equal to the values reported at the end of
Example 1. Three safe sets are considered: $\bar{A}_1 = (70, 80)°F$, $\bar{A}_2 = (72, 78)°F$,
and $\bar{A}_3 = (74, 76)°F$. The dynamic programming recursion described in Section
3.2 is used to compute maximally safe policies and maximal probabilistic safe
sets. The implementation is done in MATLAB. The temperature is discretized
into 100 equally spaced values within the safe set.

Figure 2 show the plots of 100 temperature sample paths resulting from sampling the initial temperature from the uniform distribution over the safe sets,

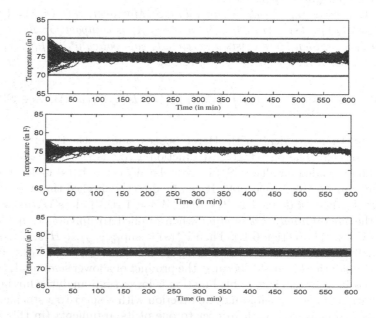

Fig. 2. Sample paths of the temperature for the execution corresponding to maximally
safe policies, when the safe set is: $\bar{A}_1$ (top), $\bar{A}_2$ (middle), and $\bar{A}_3$ (bottom)

and using the corresponding maximally safe policy. The initial operating mode is chosen at random between the equiprobable ON and OFF values.

It can be observed from each of the plots that the maximally safe policy computed by the dynamic programming recursion leads to an optimal behavior in the following sense: regardless of the initial state, most of the temperature sample paths tend toward the middle of the corresponding safe set. As for the $\bar{A}_1$ and $\bar{A}_2$ safe sets, the temperature actually remain confined within the safe set in almost all the sample paths, whereas this is not the case for $\bar{A}_3$. The set $\bar{A}_3$ is too small to enable the control input to counteract the drifts and the randomness in the execution in order to maintain the temperature within the safe set. The maximal probability of remaining in the safe set $p_\pi^{\mu^*}(\bar{A}_i)$ for π uniform over $\mathcal{Q} \times \bar{A}_i$, $i = 1, 2, 3$, is computed. The value is 0.991 for $\bar{A}_1$, 0.978 for $\bar{A}_2$ and 0.802 for $\bar{A}_3$.

The maximal probabilistic safe sets $S^*(\epsilon)$ corresponding to different safety levels $1 - \epsilon$ are also calculated. The results obtained are reported in Figure 3 with reference to the heater initially off (plot on the left) and on (plot on the right). In all cases, as expected, the maximal probabilistic safe sets get smaller as the required safety level $1 - \epsilon$ grows. When the safe set is $\bar{A}_3$, there is no policy that can guarantee a safety probability greater than about 0.86.

The maximally safe policies at some time instances $k \in [0, 600]$ $\mu_k^* : \mathcal{S} \to \mathcal{U}$ are shown in Figure 4, as a function of the continuous state and discrete state (the red crossed line refers to the OFF mode, whereas the blue circled line refers to the ON mode). The obtained result is quite intuitive. For example, at time $k = 599$, close to the end of the time horizon, and in the OFF mode, the maximally safe policy prescribes to stay in same mode for most of the continuos state values except near the lower boundary of the safe set, in which case it prescribes to change the mode to ON since there is a possibility of entering the unsafe set in the residual one-step time horizon. However, at earlier times (for instance, time $k = 1$), the maximally safe policy prescribes to change the mode even for states that are distant from the safe set boundary. Similar comments apply to

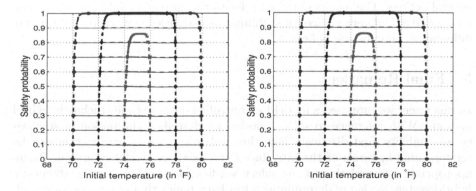

Fig. 3. Maximal probabilistic safe sets: heater initially off (left) and on (right). Blue, black, and red colors refer to cases when the safe sets are $\bar{A}_1$, $\bar{A}_2$, and $\bar{A}_3$, respectively.

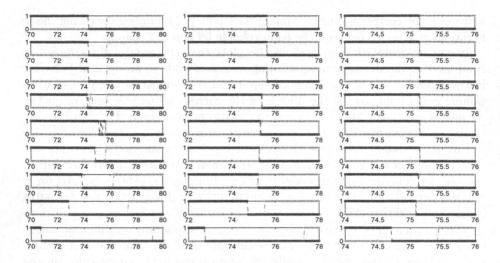

Fig. 4. Maximally safe policy as a function of the temperature at times $k = 1$, 250, 500, 575, 580, 585, 590, 595, and 599 (from top to bottom) for the safe sets $\bar{A}_1$, $\bar{A}_2$, and $\bar{A}_3$ (from left to right). The darker (blue) circled line corresponds to the OFF mode and the lighter (red) crossed line corresponds to the ON mode.

the ON mode. This shows that a maximally safe policy is not stationary. By observing from top to bottom each column of Figure 4, one can see that this non-stationary behavior appears limited to a time interval at the end of the time horizon. Also, by comparing the columns of Figure 4, this time interval gets progressively smaller moving from $\bar{A}_1$ to $\bar{A}_2$ and $\bar{A}_3$.

It is interesting to note the behavior of the maximally safe policy corresponding to the safe set $\bar{A}_1$ at $k = 575$ and $k = 580$. For example, for $k = 580$, the maximally safe policy for the OFF mode fluctuates between actions 0 and 1 when the temperature is around $75°F$. This is because the corresponding values taken by the function to be optimized in (14) are almost equal for the two control actions. The results obtained refer to the case of switching probabilities $\alpha = \beta = 0.8$. Different choices of switching probabilities may yield qualitatively different maximally safe policies.

5   Final Remarks

In this paper we proposed a model for controlled discrete time stochastic hybrid systems. With reference to such a model, we described the notion of stochastic reachability, and discussed how the problem of safety verification can be reinterpreted in terms of the introduced stochastic reachability notion. By an appropriate reformulation of the safety verification problem for the stochastic hybrid system as that of determining a feedback policy that optimizes some multiplicative cost function for a certain controlled Markov process, we were able to suggest a solution based on dynamic programming. Temperature regulation of a room by a heater that can be repeatedly switched on and off was presented as a simple example to illustrate the model capabilities and the reachability analysis methodology.

Further work is needed to extend the current approach to the infinite horizon and partial information cases. The more challenging problem of stochastic reachability analysis for continuous time stochastic hybrid systems is an interesting subject of future research.

References

1. Bujorianu, M.L., Lygeros, J.: Reachability questions in piecewise deterministic Markov processes. In Maler, O., Pnueli, A., eds.: Hybrid Systems: Computation and Control. Lecture Notes in Computer Science 2623. Springer Verlag (2003) 126–140
2. Hu, J., Prandini, M., Sastry, S.: Probabilistic safety analysis in three-dimensional aircraft flight. In: Proc. of the IEEE Conf. on Decision and Control (2003)
3. Prajna, S., Jadbabaie, A., J.Pappas, G.: Stochastic safety verification using barrier certificates. In: Proc. of the IEEE Conf. on Decision and Control (2004)
4. Hu, J., Prandini, M., Sastry, S.: Aircraft conflict prediction in the presence of a spatially correlated wind field. IEEE Trans. on Intelligent Transportation Systems 6(3) (2005) 326–340
5. Davis, M.H.A.: Markov Models and Optimization. Chapman & Hall, London (1993)
6. Ghosh, M.K., Araposthasis, A., Marcus, S.I.: Ergodic control of switching diffusions. SIAM Journal of Control and Optimization 35(6) (1997) 1952–1988
7. Hu, J., Lygeros, J., Sastry, S.: Towards a theory of stochastic hybrid systems. In Lynch, N., Krogh, B., eds.: Hybrid Systems: Computation and Control. Lecture Notes in Computer Science 1790. Springer Verlag (2000) 160–173
8. Lygeros, J., Watkins, O.: Stochastic reachability for discrete time systems: an application to aircraft collision avoidance. In: Proc. of the IEEE Conf. on Decision and Control (2003)
9. Bujorianu, M., Lygeros, J.: General stochastic hybrid systems: Modelling and optimal control. In: Proc. of the IEEE Conf. on Decision and Control. (2004)
10. Puterman, M.: Markov decision processes. John Wiley & Sons, Inc (1994)
11. Bertsekas, D.P., Shreve, S.E.: Stochastic optimal control: the discrete-time case. Athena Scientific (1996)
12. Malhame, R., Chong, C.Y.: Electric load model synthesis by diffusion approximation of a high-order hybrid-state stochastic system. IEEE Transactions on Automatic Control AC-30(9) (1985) 854–860
13. Milstein, G.: Numerical Integration of Stochastic Differential Equations. Kluver Academic Press (1995)
14. Kumar, P.R., Varaiya, P.P.: Stochastic Systems: Estimation, Identification, and Adaptive Control. Prentice Hall, Inc., New Jersey (1986)

Output-Based Optimal Timing Control
of Switched Systems*

Shun-ichi Azuma[1], Magnus Egerstedt[2], and Yorai Wardi[2]

[1] Graduate School of Informatics, Kyoto University, Uji, Kyoto 611-0011, Japan
sazuma@i.kyoto-u.ac.jp
[2] School of Electrical and Computer Engineering,
Georgia Institute of Technology, Atlanta, GA 30332, USA
{magnus, ywardi}@ece.gatech.edu

Abstract. Optimal switch-time control is an area that investigates how best to switch between different control modes. In this paper we present an algorithm for solving the optimal switch-time control problem for nonlinear systems where the state is only partially known through the outputs. A method is presented that both guarantees that the current switch-time estimates remain optimal as the state estimates evolve, and that ensures this in a computationally feasible manner, thus rendering the method applicable to real-time applications. The viability of the proposed method is illustrated through a number of examples.

1 Introduction

The basic question behind the work in this paper can be summarized as follows: *If only incomplete information about the state of the system is available, and one would like to solve an optimal switch-time control problem with respect to the true state of the system, how can this be achieved in real-time, i.e. in a computationally feasible manner?* The solution that we propose consists of three main building-blocks. The first building block is given by the solution to the optimization problem for a given, initial state estimate/guess. This is computationally expensive and is a price one can only afford to pay "off-line" in the sense that once the system starts evolving, the exact solution can no longer be obtained from scratch due to computational real-time constraints. The second building-block is the construction of a set of dynamical equations that dictate how the current solution to the optimization problem evolves as the state estimate evolves. This "solution dynamics" must satisfy two properties, namely: *(i)* It must be computationally cheap, i.e. no extensive computations are allowed as the solution evolves over time. *(ii)* It must be optimal with respect to the current state estimate. In other words, at all times the best possible solution to the optimization problem must be obtained. The final building block that is needed is a safe-guard against undesirable behaviors that may arise due to the transient response of the state estimate, e.g. observer over-shoots. We will achieve this by

---

* This work was supported by the National Science Foundation through grant #0509064.

João Hespanha and A. Tiwari (Eds.): HSCC 2006, LNCS 3927, pp. 64–78, 2006.
© Springer-Verlag Berlin Heidelberg 2006

imposing constraints on the possible switching times, thus producing a solution to a constrained rather than a free parameter optimization problem.

This idea has been investigated in [10] for *single*-switch, *linear* systems, and provides us with some initial guidance. However, this paper considerably extends the results in [10] in order to complete the framework of computationally feasible optimal switch-time control with partial information. In other words, in this paper we deal with the problem in its full generality, namely, the *multiple*-switch, *nonlinear* case.

The outline of this paper is as follows: In Section 2, the solution to the complete state-information problem is recalled and the strategy of using observer-based switch-time control for the partial information case is introduced. The next section (Section 3) presents the solution to the observer-based problem. Section 4 presents a method for dealing with constrained switch-times in order to avoid undesirable switch-time behaviors caused by nonlinear observer dynamics. The resulting, constrained optimization problem is solved, and a number of examples illustrate the viability of the proposed solution.

2 Background

2.1 State-Based Switch-Time Optimization

Consider the problem of finding the switch-times $\tau^{\star} = (\tau_1^{\star}, \tau_2^{\star}, \ldots, \tau_N^{\star})^T$ that solves the optimization problem $\Sigma_1(t_0, x_0)$:

$$\min_{\tau} J(t_0, x_0, \tau) = \frac{1}{2} \int_{t_0}^{T} L(x(t)) dt$$

$$\Sigma_1(t_0, x_0): \quad \text{subject to} \begin{cases} \dot{x}(t) = \begin{cases} f_1(x(t)), \ t \in [t_0, \tau_1) \\ f_2(x(t)), \ t \in [\tau_1, \tau_2) \\ \vdots \\ f_N(x(t)), \ t \in [\tau_{N-1}, \tau_N) \\ f_{N+1}(x(t)), \ t \in [\tau_N, T] \end{cases} \\ x(t_0) = x_0. \end{cases}$$

Here x is the n-dimensional state vector, L and f_i ($i = 1, 2, \ldots, N+1$) are continuously differentiable functions from $\mathbb{R}^n$ to $\mathbb{R}$ and from $\mathbb{R}^n$ to $\mathbb{R}^n$, respectively, N is the number of switch-times, and τ is the collection of switch-times, i.e. $\tau = (\tau_1, \tau_2, \ldots, \tau_N)^T$. The interpretation here is that the system evolves according to $\dot{x} = f_1(x(t))$ on the time interval $[t_0, \tau_1)$, to $\dot{x} = f_{i+1}(x(t))$ on $[\tau_i, \tau_{i+1})$ ($i \in \{1, 2, \ldots, N-1\}$), and to $\dot{x} = f_{N+1}(x(t))$ on $[\tau_{N+1}, T]$. Such systems arise in a variety of applications, including situations where a control module has to switch its attention among a number of subsystems [14, 17, 21], or collect data sequentially from a number of sensory sources [5, 7, 13].

Recently, there has been a growing interest in optimal switching time control of such hybrid systems, where the control variable consists of a proper switching law as well as the input function $u(t)$ (see [4, 6, 11, 12, 18, 19, 20, 22]). In particular, in [4] a framework is established for optimal control, while [18, 19, 20] present suitable variants of the maximum principle to the setting of hybrid systems. In [2, 3, 11, 16] piecewise-linear or affine systems are considered, while the special case of autonomous systems, where the term $u(t)$ is absent and the control variable consists solely of the switching times, is considered in [11, 13, 23, 24]. In particular, in [8, 23, 24] general nonlinear systems are considered together with nonlinear-programming algorithms that compute the gradient and second-order derivatives of the cost functional. Note that we, in this paper, follow this line of work by not having an explicit input u affect the system. This restriction will have the effect that the gradient of the cost with respect to the control parameters (the switch-times) can be quickly computed without having to solve any boundary value problems. However, the reason why we focus on this model is not entirely driven by this computational concern, but it also stems from the fact that in a number of applciations, a collection of control laws have already been designed (i.e. u has already been given in terms of x) and the remaining problem is simply the problem of determining the duration of each individual control mode.

In particular, in [8], the Calculus of Variations were used for finding the first order, necessary optimality conditions for $\tau^\star$, namely

$$\frac{\partial J}{\partial \tau_i}(t_0, x_0, \tau^\star) = \lambda_i(\tau_i^\star)\Big(f_i(x(\tau_i^\star)) - f_{i+1}(x(\tau_i^\star))\Big) = 0$$

for every $i \in \{1, 2, \ldots, N\}$, where the costate λ_i satisfies

$$\dot{\lambda}_i(t) = -\lambda_i(t)\frac{\partial f_{i+1}}{\partial x}(x(t)) - \frac{\partial L}{\partial x}(x(t)), \ t \in [\tau_i, \tau_{i+1}]$$
$$\lambda_i(\tau_{i+1}) = 0.$$

Here we have used the convention that the costate is an n-dimensional row vector. Note that we only obtain locally optimal and not globally optimal solutions, which is all we can hope for in general since J is nonconvex in τ.

In this case, i.e. in the case where the complete state information is available, we can thus easily produce a gradient descent-based algorithm for actually finding the optimal switching time, e.g.:

Algorithm 1:
$\tau = \tau_0$ (initial guess)
repeat
    solve for $x(t)$, $t \in [t_0, T]$ forwards
    solve for $\lambda_i(t)$, $t \in [\tau_i, \tau_{i+1}]$ backwards for every i
    compute $\partial J/\partial \tau = \left[\frac{\partial J}{\partial \tau_1} \ \frac{\partial J}{\partial \tau_2} \ \cdots \ \frac{\partial J}{\partial \tau_N}\right]$ with
$$\frac{\partial J}{\partial \tau_i} = \lambda_i(\tau_i)\Big(f_i(x(\tau_i)) - f_{i+1}(x(\tau_i))\Big)$$
    $\tau := \tau - \gamma(\partial J/\partial \tau)^T$
until $\|\partial J/\partial \tau(\tau)\| \le \epsilon$

Here $\epsilon > 0$ is the termination thresh-hold, and γ is the step length in the gradient descent. Note that γ could possibly be varying, e.g. using the Armijo stepsize [1], which was the case in [8, 9]. Note also that such an algorithm involves solving for $x(t)$ and $\lambda(t)$ a number of times until the optimal τ has been found. In other words, if δ is the stepsize used in the numerical integration algorithm, and if a total number of M gradient descent iterations are needed, the computational complexity is $\mathcal{O}(M/\delta)$, which is a non-trivial computational burden if the optimal τ has to be found in real-time, i.e. fast enough with respect to the particular application that is being considered.

2.2 Partial State Information

We now turn our attention to a slightly different problem, namely the problem of finding the optimal τ when only partial information is available. By this we understand that only $y(t) \in \mathbb{R}^p$ (and not $x(t)$) is known, where

$$
y(t) = \begin{cases} g_1(x(t)), & t \in [t_0, \tau_1) \\ g_2(x(t)), & t \in [\tau_1, \tau_2) \\ \vdots \\ g_N(x(t)), & t \in [\tau_{N-1}, \tau_N) \\ g_{N+1}(x(t)), & t \in [\tau_N, T] \end{cases}
$$

and g_i $(i = 1, 2, \ldots, N+1)$ are continuously differentiable output functions from $\mathbb{R}^n$ to $\mathbb{R}^p$.

The strategy that we will use is to guess an initial state value, $\hat{x}(t_0)$ and then solve the computational resource intense optimal control problem for this initial state using the gradient descent algorithm in Algorithm 1, resulting in an optimal switching time $\hat{\tau}(t_0)$. The idea is that this computation can be performed off-line, i.e. before the system actually starts evolving. Once this happens, we will use an observer for estimating the state. Moreover, the main idea of this paper is to also update $\hat{\tau}(t)$ in such a way that the following two conditions hold:

1. For all times $t \in [t_0, T]$, $\hat{\tau}(t)$ is optimal given the current state estimate $\hat{x}(t)$.
2. The time evolution of $\hat{\tau}(t)$ must be computationally reasonable.

What these two conditions thus say is that we should only pay the high computational price associated with solving the optimal switch-time control problem for the initial state estimate guess. After that, the switch-time estimates should evolve in such a way that they remain optimal as well as are easy to compute.

3 Observer-Based Switch-Time Optimization

This section is concerned with the problem of solving $\Sigma_1(t, \hat{x}(t))$, where $\hat{x}(t)$ is the state of the previously defined observer. First, for simplicity of discussion, we derive the switch-time dynamics for the case $N = 1$ (single switch time), i.e. $\tau = \tau_1$. This will clearly show the key idea behind switch-time optimization based on observers. Next, observers are introduced for executing our technique, and then the validity is demonstrated by a numerical example. We finally extend the result to the multiple switch-time problem (with $N \geq 2$).

3.1   Switch-Time Dynamics

Let us consider the dynamics of the optimal switch-time for the current state estimate $\hat{x}(t)$ under $N = 1$. For this, we assume that we have been able to compute $\hat{\tau}(t_0)$ as the solution to $\Sigma_1(t_0, \hat{x}(t_0))$ using Algorithm 1, where $\hat{x}(t_0)$ is the initial state estimate. Now, let

$$\dot{\hat{\tau}}(t) = -\frac{1}{\frac{\partial^2 J}{\partial \tau^2}(t, \hat{x}(t), \hat{\tau}(t))}\left(\frac{\partial^2 J}{\partial t \partial \tau}(t, \hat{x}(t), \hat{\tau}(t)) + \frac{\partial^2 J}{\partial x \partial \tau}(t, \hat{x}(t), \hat{\tau}(t))\dot{\hat{x}}(t)\right). \quad (1)$$

Throughout this paper we will make the explicit assumption that $\hat{\tau}(t)$ is a local minimum to $\Sigma_1(t, \hat{x}(t))$ for all $t \in [t_0, T]$, and hence that the Hessian, i.e. the second derivative matrix of J with respect to τ is positive definite, which in turn implies that the above expression is well-defined. This assumption may not always hold since extrema are known to not always be continuous across system parameters even though the cost and the constraints may be arbitrarily smooth. In fact, this is a potential weakness of the proposed approach but at present, we state it as an assumption and leave further investigations of this issue to the future.

That this is in fact the correct evolution of $\hat{\tau}(t)$ follows directly from the fact that

$$\frac{d}{dt}\left(\frac{\partial J}{\partial \tau}(t, \hat{x}(t), \hat{\tau}(t))\right)$$

$$= \frac{\partial^2 J}{\partial \tau^2}(t, \hat{x}(t), \hat{\tau}(t))\dot{\hat{\tau}}(t) + \frac{\partial^2 J}{\partial t \partial \tau}(t, \hat{x}(t), \hat{\tau}(t)) + \frac{\partial^2 J}{\partial x \partial \tau}(t, \hat{x}(t), \hat{\tau}(t))\dot{\hat{x}}(t)$$

$$= -\frac{\frac{\partial^2 J}{\partial \tau^2}(t, \hat{x}(t), \hat{\tau}(t))}{\frac{\partial^2 J}{\partial \tau^2}(t, \hat{x}(t), \hat{\tau}(t))}\left(\frac{\partial^2 J}{\partial t \partial \tau}(t, \hat{x}(t), \hat{\tau}(t)) + \frac{\partial^2 J}{\partial x \partial \tau}(t, \hat{x}(t), \hat{\tau}(t))\dot{\hat{x}}(t)\right)$$

$$+ \frac{\partial^2 J}{\partial t \partial \tau}(t, \hat{x}(t), \hat{\tau}(t)) + \frac{\partial^2 J}{\partial x \partial \tau}(t, \hat{x}(t), \hat{\tau}(t))\dot{\hat{x}}(t) = 0.$$

Hence, as long as $\partial J/\partial \tau = 0$ initially it will remain zero and $\hat{\tau}(t)$ will in fact remain optimal. In the following paragraphs we will compute an explicit expression for this update rule as well as show that it does in fact satisfy the second condition that we imposed, namely that the computational burden associated with evolving $\hat{\tau}(t)$ is low.

From Section 2.1 we know that

$$\frac{\partial J}{\partial \tau}(t, x, \tau) = \lambda(\tau)(f_1(x(\tau)) - f_2(x(\tau))),$$

where

$$\begin{cases} \dot{x}(s) = \begin{cases} f_1(x(s)), & s \in [t, \tau) \\ f_2(x(s)), & s \in [\tau, T] \end{cases} \\ x(t) = x \\ \dot{\lambda}(s) = -\lambda(s)\frac{\partial f_2}{\partial x}(x(s)) - \frac{\partial L}{\partial x}(x(s)), & s \in [\tau, T] \\ \lambda(T) = 0, \end{cases}$$

where the costate λ_1 is simply denoted by λ.

By letting $\Phi_2(s,\tau)$ be the state transition matrix on $s \in [\tau,T]$ of the autonomous linear system

$$\dot{z} = \frac{\partial f_2}{\partial x} z,$$

it is straightforward to solve the above costate equation with respect to λ, giving

$$\lambda(\tau) = \int_\tau^T \frac{\partial L}{\partial x}(x(s))\Phi_2(s,\tau)ds.$$

By plugging this into the expression for $\partial J/\partial \tau$ we obtain

$$\frac{\partial J}{\partial \tau}(t,x,\tau) = \int_\tau^T \frac{\partial L}{\partial x}(x(s))\Phi_2(s,\tau)ds(f_1(x(\tau)) - f_2(x(\tau))).$$

Now, in order to compute the update rule for $\hat{\tau}(t)$, we need the partial derivatives of $\partial J/\partial \tau$, for which it is convenient to define $p(t,x,\tau)$ and $q(t,x,\tau)$ as

$$p(t,x,\tau) = \int_\tau^T \frac{\partial L}{\partial x}(x(s))\Phi_2(s,\tau)ds,$$
$$q(t,x,\tau) = f_1(x(\tau)) - f_2(x(\tau)),$$

where, as before, $x(t) = x$. Using this notation, the partial derivative with respect to x becomes

$$\frac{\partial^2 J}{\partial x \partial \tau}(t,x,\tau) = q^T(t,x,\tau)\frac{\partial p}{\partial x}(t,x,\tau) + p(t,x,\tau)\frac{\partial q}{\partial x}(t,x,\tau),$$

and then

$$\frac{\partial p}{\partial x}(t,x,\tau) = \int_\tau^T \left(\frac{\partial x(s)}{\partial x}\right)^T \frac{\partial^2 L}{\partial x^2}(x(s))\Phi_2(s,\tau)ds$$
$$= \int_\tau^T (\Phi_2(s,\tau)\Phi_1(\tau,t))^T \frac{\partial^2 L}{\partial x^2}(x(s))\Phi_2(s,\tau)ds$$
$$\frac{\partial q}{\partial x}(t,x,\tau) = \left(\frac{\partial f_1}{\partial x}(x(\tau)) - \frac{\partial f_2}{\partial x}(x(\tau))\right)\frac{\partial x(\tau)}{\partial x}$$
$$= \left(\frac{\partial f_1}{\partial x}(x(\tau)) - \frac{\partial f_2}{\partial x}(x(\tau))\right)\Phi_1(\tau,t),$$

where the facts $\partial x(s)/\partial x = \Phi_2(s,\tau)\Phi_1(\tau,t)$ and $\partial x(\tau)/\partial x = \Phi_1(\tau,t)$ are used.

It should be noted that this form of the partial derivative $\partial J/\partial \tau$ can be easily computed. In fact, we mainly need to calculate the five integrations for obtaining Φ_1, Φ_2, x, p, and $\partial p/\partial x$, in which the three integrations are required for the differential equations on Φ_1, Φ_2, and x. Hence, we have a computationally feasible method for computing $\partial J/\partial \tau$ that does not involve any iterations in a gradient descent algorithm.

In a similar way, the partial derivatives with respect to t and τ are given by

$$\frac{\partial^2 J}{\partial t \partial \tau}(t,x,\tau) = \frac{\partial p}{\partial t}(t,x,\tau)q(t,x,\tau) + p(t,x,\tau)\frac{\partial q}{\partial t}(t,x,\tau)$$

$$\frac{\partial^2 J}{\partial \tau^2}(t,x,\tau) = \frac{\partial p}{\partial \tau}(t,x,\tau)q(t,x,\tau) + p(t,x,\tau)\frac{\partial q}{\partial \tau}(t,x,\tau)$$

where

$$\frac{\partial p}{\partial t}(t,x,\tau) = \int_\tau^T \frac{\partial x(s)}{\partial t}\frac{\partial^2 L}{\partial x^2}(x(s))\Phi_2(s,\tau)ds$$

$$= -\int_\tau^T \Phi_2(s,\tau)\Phi_1(\tau,t)f_1(x)\frac{\partial^2 L}{\partial x^2}(x(s))\Phi_2(s,\tau)ds$$

$$\frac{\partial q}{\partial t}(t,x,\tau) = \left(\frac{\partial f_1}{\partial t}(x(\tau)) - \frac{\partial f_2}{\partial t}(x(\tau))\right)\frac{\partial x(\tau)}{\partial t}$$

$$= -\left(\frac{\partial f_1}{\partial x}(x(\tau)) - \frac{\partial f_2}{\partial x}(x(\tau))\right)\Phi_1(\tau,t)f(x)$$

$$\frac{\partial p}{\partial \tau}(t,x,\tau)$$

$$= -\frac{\partial L}{\partial x}(x(\tau))\Phi_2(\tau,\tau) + \int_\tau^T \frac{\partial^2 L}{\partial \tau \partial x}(x(s))\Phi_2(s,\tau) + \frac{\partial L}{\partial x}(x(s))\frac{\partial}{\partial \tau}\Phi_2(s,\tau)ds$$

$$= -\frac{\partial L}{\partial x}(x(\tau)) + \int_\tau^T \Phi_2(s,t)q\frac{\partial^2 L}{\partial x^2}(x(s))\Phi_2(s,\tau) - \frac{\partial L}{\partial x}(x(s))\Phi_2(s,\tau)\frac{\partial f_2}{\partial x}(x(\tau))ds$$

$$\frac{\partial q}{\partial \tau}(t,x,\tau) = \left(\frac{\partial f_1}{\partial x}(x(\tau)) - \frac{\partial f_2}{\partial x}(x(\tau))\right)\frac{\partial x(\tau)}{\partial \tau}$$

$$= \left(\frac{\partial f_1}{\partial x}(x(\tau)) - \frac{\partial f_2}{\partial x}(x(\tau))\right)f_1(x(\tau)),$$

and the relations $\partial x(s)/\partial t = -\Phi_2(s,\tau)\Phi_1(\tau,t)f_1(x)$, $\partial x(\tau)/\partial t = -\Phi_1(\tau,t)f_1(x)$, $\partial x(s)/\partial \tau = \Phi_2(s,\tau)q$, and $\partial x(\tau)/\partial \tau = f_1(x(\tau))$ are used. It is moreover easy to see that these partial derivatives can be obtained in a computationally feasible manner.

Under the assumption that we have a strict local minimum (i.e. that the Hessian is positive definite), this expression is well-defined, and, as previously shown, $\hat{\tau}(t)$ is a solution to $\Sigma_1(t,\hat{x}(t))$, which establishes the first property that our solution needed to satisfy. The second property involves the computational burden associated with computing $\hat{\tau}(t)$. And, the pieces needed for the computation of the partial derivatives are given by a bounded number of integrations. Hence we have an algorithm for updating the optimal switching time that satisfies both properties required from the solution, namely (i) optimality, and (ii) computational feasibility.

3.2   Observers for Switch-Time Optimization

The observers underlying this switch-time optimization strategy should (if possible) provide good estimates of the state, i.e. the estimated state should quickly converge to the real system state. We here outline two possible such observers:

If the system is in fact composed of linear subsystems, i.e.,

$$\dot{x}(t) = \begin{cases} A_1 x(t), \ t \in [t_0, \tau) \\ A_2 x(t), \ t \in [\tau, T] \end{cases}$$

$$y(t) = \begin{cases} C_1 x(t), \ t \in [t_0, \tau) \\ C_2 x(t), \ t \in [\tau, T] \end{cases}$$

$$x(t_0) = x_0,$$

we can use a standard switched-type Luenberger observer, defined as

$$\dot{\hat{x}}(t) = \begin{cases} A_1 \hat{x}(t) - K_1(C_1 \hat{x}(t) - y(t)), \ t \in [t_0, \tau) \\ A_2 \hat{x}(t) - K_2(C_2 \hat{x}(t) - y(t)), \ t \in [\tau, T], \end{cases}$$

where K_1, K_2 are appropriately chosen observer gain matrices. This observer has the advantage that the convergence of the observer state to the real system state can be specified by choosing K_1, K_2.

On the other hand, for systems with nonlinear subsystems:

$$\dot{x}(t) = f(x(t)) = \begin{cases} f_1(x(t)), \ t \in [t_0, \tau) \\ f_2(x(t)), \ t \in [\tau, T] \end{cases}$$

$$y(t) = g(x(t)) = \begin{cases} g_1(x(t)), \ t \in [t_0, \tau) \\ g_2(x(t)), \ t \in [\tau, T] \end{cases}$$

$$x(t_0) = x_0,$$

the Grizzle-Moraal Newton observer, originally proposed in [15], provides a good candidate. This observer is based on Newton's method for solving nonlinear equations, and we recall this method below for the non-switched case:

Given the state $x(t)$ and a (sufficiently) small positive scalar Δ, then $x(t+\Delta)$ can be approximately expressed as $x(t + \Delta) \simeq x(t) + \Delta f(x(t))$. Then we have an approximation of $x(t + k\Delta)$ for a natural number k as $x(t + k\Delta) \simeq F^k(x(t))$, where $F(x(t)) = x(t) + \Delta f(x(t))$ and

$$F^k(x(t)) = \underbrace{F \circ F \circ \cdots \circ F}_{k \text{ times}}(x(t)).$$

Using this notation, $y(t + k\Delta)$ can be approximated by $y(t + k\Delta) \simeq g(F^k(x(t)))$. Next, define $G_m(\hat{x}_0(t)) = \tilde{Y}_m - Y_m(\hat{x}_0(t))$, where

$$\tilde{Y}_m = \begin{bmatrix} y(t) \\ y(t + \Delta) \\ y(t + 2\Delta) \\ \vdots \\ y(t + (m-1)\Delta) \end{bmatrix}, \quad Y_m(\hat{x}_0(t)) = \begin{bmatrix} g(\hat{x}_0(t)) \\ g(F(\hat{x}_0(t))) \\ g(F^2(\hat{x}_0(t))) \\ \vdots \\ g(F^{m-1}(\hat{x}_0(t))) \end{bmatrix}.$$

Then the Grizzle-Moraal Newton observer is given by the following predictor-corrector step:

$$\hat{x}_k^- = f(\hat{x}(t + (k-1)\Delta)) \tag{2}$$

$$\hat{x}(t + k\Delta) = \hat{x}_k^- - \left\{\frac{\partial G_m}{\partial \hat{x}_0}(\hat{x}_k^-)\right\}^{\dagger} G_m(\hat{x}_k^-), \tag{3}$$

where the symbol "$\dagger$" denotes the pseudo-inverse. Although this observer is not always guaranteed to globally converge to the real system state, this observer can be applied to a broad class of the nonlinear systems, and the estimated state often converges very quickly to the real system state.

3.3 Example

Consider the system defined by

$$\dot{x} = \begin{cases} \begin{pmatrix} 2\sqrt{x_1} - \sqrt{x_2} \\ -\sqrt{x_2} \end{pmatrix} & t \in [t_0, \tau) \\ \begin{pmatrix} -\sqrt{x_1} + \sqrt{x_2} \\ \sqrt{x_2} \end{pmatrix} & t \in [\tau, T] \end{cases}$$

$$y = (1 \ \ 1)x \quad t \in [t_0, T],$$

where $t_0 = 0$, $T = 1$ and the cost function given by

$$L(x) = \left(x - \begin{pmatrix} 2 \\ 2 \end{pmatrix}\right)^T \left(x - \begin{pmatrix} 2 \\ 2 \end{pmatrix}\right). \tag{4}$$

The initial state of the system is given as $(1.3, 1.8)^T$, and the observer used here is a switched version of the Grizzle-Moraal Newton observer whose initial state is $(1.2, 1.9)^T$.

Figure 1 shows that, as the observer state approaches to the real system state, the switch time converges from $\hat{\tau}(0) = 0.365$ to the true optimal switch-time $\tau^* = 0.337$. In this way, even if the complete state information cannot be used, the switch-time is optimized when using the switch-time dynamics together with a suitable observer.

3.4 Extension to the Multiple Switch-Time Case

The switch-time optimization technique derived in the previous paragraphs will here be extended to the multiple switch-time case as follows:

Recall the relation for the single-switch case

$$\frac{\partial^2 J}{\partial \tau^2}(t, \hat{x}(t), \hat{\tau}(t))\dot{\hat{\tau}}(t) + \frac{\partial^2 J}{\partial t \partial \tau}(t, \hat{x}(t), \hat{\tau}(t)) + \frac{\partial^2 J}{\partial x \partial \tau}(t, \hat{x}(t), \hat{\tau}(t))\dot{\hat{x}}(t) = 0,$$

where the left hand side corresponds to the time derivative of $\frac{\partial J}{\partial \tau}(t, \hat{x}(t), \hat{\tau}(t))$, i.e. $\frac{d}{dt}\left(\frac{\partial J}{\partial \tau}(t, \hat{x}(t), \hat{\tau}(t))\right)$. It can be directly shown in exactly the same way as for

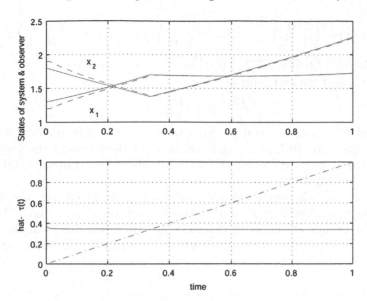

Fig. 1. The upper figure shows the state and observer trajectories (solid lines and dotted lines), while the lower figure shows $\hat{\tau}(t)$ in which it is illustrated how $\hat{\tau}(t)$ (solid line) evolves until $\hat{\tau}(t) = t$ (dotted line), at which point the system switches

the single-switch case that this relation still holds for the multiple switch-time case ($N \geq 2$) and then $\partial^2 J/\partial \tau^2 \in \mathbb{R}^{N \times N}$, $\partial^2 J/\partial t \partial \tau \in \mathbb{R}^{N \times 1}$, and $\partial^2 J/\partial x \partial \tau \in \mathbb{R}^{N \times n}$. Thus we obtain the following expression for the multiple switch-time dynamics.

$$\dot{\hat{\tau}}(t) = -\left(\frac{\partial^2 J}{\partial \tau^2}(t, \hat{x}(t), \hat{\tau}(t))\right)^{-1}\left(\frac{\partial^2 J}{\partial t \partial \tau}(t, \hat{x}(t), \hat{\tau}(t)) + \frac{\partial^2 J}{\partial x \partial \tau}(t, \hat{x}(t), \hat{\tau}(t))\dot{\hat{x}}(t)\right).$$
$$(5)$$

Here the partial derivatives of $\partial J/\partial \tau$, i.e. $\partial^2 J/\partial \tau^2$, $\partial^2 J/\partial t \partial \tau$, and $\partial^2 J/\partial x \partial \tau$, can be expressed as similar explicit forms to the case of $N = 1$. In fact, this is seen by computing the gradient

$$\frac{\partial J}{\partial \tau_i}(t, x, \tau) = \int_{\tau_i}^{\tau_{i+1}} \frac{\partial L}{\partial x}(x(s))\Phi_{i+1}(s, \tau)ds(f_i(x(\tau_i)) - f_{i+1}(x(\tau_i)))$$

$$\lambda(\tau) = \int_{\tau_i}^{\tau_{i+1}} \frac{\partial L}{\partial x}(x(s))\Phi_{i+1}(s, \tau)ds.$$

Furthermore, the observers supporting the switch-time optimization can also be obtained through a straightforward extension of the results in Section 3.2. Therefore, the switch-time optimization method works also for the multiple switch-time case.

The multiple switch-case can best be illustrated through an example. Consider the system defined as

$$f_1(x) = \begin{pmatrix} 1 & 0 \\ 0 & -1 \end{pmatrix} x, \quad f_2(x) = \begin{pmatrix} -1 & 0 \\ 0 & 1 \end{pmatrix} x, \quad f_3(x) = \begin{pmatrix} 1 & 0 \\ 0 & -1 \end{pmatrix} x,$$

$$g_1(x) = g_2(x) = g_3(x) = (1, \ 1),$$

with $N = 2$, and the cost function

$$L(x) = x^T \begin{pmatrix} 1 & 0 \\ 0 & 1 \end{pmatrix} x.$$

The initial time is $t_0 = 0$ and the final time is $T = 1$. The initial state of the system is given by $(0.7, 1.4)^T$, and the observer used here is the Luenberger observer whose poles are all set at -13, while the initial state is $(1, 1)^T$, which gives $\hat{\tau}(t_0) = (0.2, 0.6)^T$.

Figure 2 shows that even multiple switch-time case, we can still optimize the switch-times by estimating the state with a suitable observer. It should be noted that the dynamics are linear in this example. However, this example is to be thought of as illustrating the transition from $N = 1$ to $N \geq 2$ rather than linear vs. nonlinear.

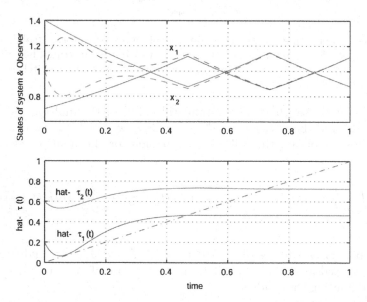

Fig. 2. The upper figure illustrates the state and observer trajectories (solid lines and dotted lines), while the lower figure shows $\hat{\tau}(t)$ (solid lines) evolving until $\hat{\tau}(t) = t$ (dotted line). The first switch occurs at $t \simeq 0.468$ and the second at $t \simeq 0.736$.

4   Constrained Switch-Time Optimization

As noted in our previous paper [10], it is possible that the transient behavior (e.g. over-shoot) of the observer dynamics will force the system to switch very quickly. This should not be taken as a fault with the proposed method since we are in fact guaranteeing that the resulting switch-times $\hat{\tau}(t)$ are optimal with respect to the current state estimate. Instead this implies that the optimality with respect to the current state estimate may not always be desirable unless additional constraints are imposed on the system. Thus as proposed in [10], it is quite natural to introduce the constraint on the switch-times for making sure that the observer is given enough time to settle.

On the other hand, this is just a special case of the more challenging problem that we will address in this paper. Namely, when multiple switches are present, we must enforce that $t_0 \leq \tau_1 \leq \tau_2 \leq \cdots \leq \tau_N \leq T$. This is the case since otherwise the transient observer behavior may change the switch-time sequence. Thus we deal with the following problem: How is the problem $\Sigma_1(t_0, x_0)$ solved under the switch-time sequence constraint $t_0 \leq \tau_1 \leq \tau_2 \leq \cdots \leq \tau_N \leq T$?

4.1   Optimality Conditions

We first assume $N = 2$ for simplicity of notation. Then the following problem arises.

$$\Sigma_2(t, x) : \quad \text{subject to} \begin{cases} \min_\tau J(t, x, \tau) = \frac{1}{2} \int_t^T L(x(s)) ds \\ \dot{x}(s) = \begin{cases} f_1(x(s)), & s \in [t, \tau_1) \\ f_2(x(s)), & s \in [\tau_1, \tau_2) \\ f_3(x(s)), & s \in [\tau_2, T] \end{cases} \\ x(t) = x \\ \tau_1 \leq \tau_2. \end{cases}$$

Now, in order to solve $\Sigma_2(t, x)$ it is no longer enough to find $\hat{\tau}(t)$ such that $\partial J / \partial \tau = 0$. Instead, the first order necessary Kuhn-Tucker condition will have to serve as the optimality function. In other words, we must have that $\partial L / \partial \tau = 0$, where the Lagrangian L is given by

$$L(t, x, \tau, \mu) = J(t, x, \tau) + \mu(\tau_1 - \tau_2),$$

where the multiplier satisfies

$$\mu = \begin{cases} 0, & \tau_1 < \tau_2 \\ \geq 0, & \tau_1 = \tau_2. \end{cases}$$

It is straightforward to see that the Kuhn-Tucker condition becomes

$$\begin{cases} \frac{\partial J}{\partial \tau_1} = 0, \quad \frac{\partial J}{\partial \tau_2} = 0 & \text{if } \tau_1 < \tau_2 \\ \frac{\partial J}{\partial \tau_1} \leq 0, \quad \frac{\partial J}{\partial \tau_2} \geq 0, \quad \frac{\partial J}{\partial \tau_1} + \frac{\partial J}{\partial \tau_2} = 0 & \text{if } \tau_1 = \tau_2, \end{cases}$$

which provides the following switch-time dynamics.

$$\begin{cases} \dot{\hat{\tau}}(t) = -\dfrac{1}{\frac{\partial^2 J}{\partial \tau_1^2} + \frac{\partial^2 J}{\partial \tau_2 \partial \tau_1} + \frac{\partial^2 J}{\partial \tau_1 \partial \tau_2} + \frac{\partial^2 J}{\partial \tau_2^2}} \left(\frac{\partial^2 J}{\partial t \partial \tau_1} + \frac{\partial^2 J}{\partial t \partial \tau_2} + \left(\frac{\partial^2 J}{\partial x \partial \tau_1} + \frac{\partial^2 J}{\partial x \partial \tau_2} \right) \dot{x}(t) \right) \begin{bmatrix} 1 \\ 1 \end{bmatrix} \\ \hspace{10cm} \text{if } \begin{cases} \tau_1 = \tau_2 \\ \dot{\hat{\tau}}_1(t) > \dot{\hat{\tau}}_2(t) \end{cases} \\ \dot{\hat{\tau}}(t) = -\left(\frac{\partial^2 J}{\partial \tau^2} \right)^{-1} \left(\frac{\partial^2 J}{\partial t \partial \tau} + \frac{\partial^2 J}{\partial x \partial \tau} \dot{x}(t) \right) \hspace{2cm} \text{otherwise} \end{cases}$$

The switching time $\hat{\tau}(t)$ obtained according to the above dynamics is a solution to $\Sigma_2(t, \hat{x}(t))$, i.e., it satisfies the first order necessary Kuhn-Tucker condition. This can be shown as follows.

First, as discussed in Sections 3.1 and 3.4, the second switch-time dynamics satisfies the Kuhn-Tucker condition when (a) $\tau_1(t) < \tau_2(t)$ or (b) $\tau_1(t) = \tau_2(t)$, $\dot{\tau}_1(t) \leq \dot{\tau}_2(t)$.

Next, it is proven by the reduction to absurdity that the Kuhn-Tucker condition at the boundary point is satisfied by the first switch-time dynamics, obtained from $\frac{d}{dt}\left(\frac{\partial J}{\partial \tau_1} + \frac{\partial J}{\partial \tau_2}\right) = 0$, namely, we will show that the first switch-time dynamics provides $\hat{\tau}(t+\delta)$ for some $\delta > 0$ satisfying the Kuhn-Tucker condition:

Let $\tau^*(t)$ be an optimal solution satisfying $\tau_1^*(t) = \tau_2^*(t)$, $\frac{\partial L}{\partial \tau_i}(t, x, \tau^*(t)) = 0$ for all $i \in \{1, 2\}$, and $\tau_1^*(t+\delta) = \tau_2^*(t+\delta)$ for some $\delta > 0$, where $\tau_i^*(t)$ is the i-th element of $\tau^*(t)$. Note that $\tau^*(t)$ is the switch time satisfying the Kuhn-Tucker condition at the boundary point and remains on the boundary for a while. If we assume $\dot{\hat{\tau}}(t) \neq \dot{\tau}^*(t)$, we have

$$\frac{d}{dt}\left(\frac{\partial J}{\partial \tau_1}(t, x(t), \tau^*(t))\right) > 0, \quad \frac{d}{dt}\left(\frac{\partial J}{\partial \tau_2}(t, x(t), \tau^*(t))\right) < 0, \tag{6}$$

since the Kuhn-Tucker condition at the boundary point is violated and $\frac{\partial J}{\partial \tau_1} + \frac{\partial J}{\partial \tau_2} = 0$ holds for $\dot{\hat{\tau}}(t)$. This gives

$$\frac{\partial J}{\partial \tau_1}(t+\delta, x(t+\delta), \tau^*(t) + \dot{\hat{\tau}}(t)\delta + o(\delta)) > 0 \tag{7}$$

$$\frac{\partial J}{\partial \tau_2}(t+\delta, x(t+\delta), \tau^*(t) + \dot{\hat{\tau}}(t)\delta + o(\delta)) < 0, \tag{8}$$

for a small positive scalar δ, which implies that

$$\tau_1^*(t+\delta) < \tau_1^*(t) + \dot{\hat{\tau}}_1(t)\delta + o(\delta) \tag{9}$$
$$\tau_2^*(t+\delta) > \tau_2^*(t) + \dot{\hat{\tau}}_2(t)\delta + o(\delta). \tag{10}$$

Note here that (7) and (8) mean $J(t+\delta, x(t+\delta), \tau^*(t) + \dot{\hat{\tau}}(t)\delta + o(\delta)) > J(t+\delta, x(t+\delta), \tau)$ for a τ satisfying $\tau_1 < \tau_1^*(t) + \hat{\dot{1}}(t)\delta + o(\delta)$, $\tau_2 > \tau_2^*(t) + \hat{\dot{2}}(t)\delta + o(\delta)$, and thus (9) and (10) are provided. Then, because $\tau_1^*(t) = \tau_2^*(t)$ and $\dot{\hat{\tau}}_1(t) = \dot{\hat{\tau}}_2(t)$, it follows that $\tau_1^*(t+\delta) < \tau_2^*(t+\delta)$, namely, it contradicts $\tau_1^*(t+\delta) = \tau_2^*(t+\delta)$ for some $\delta > 0$. Hence, $\dot{\hat{\tau}}(t) = \dot{\tau}^*(t)$. Therefore, this choice of $\dot{\hat{\tau}}(t)$ does in fact guarantee that the resulting solution is locally optimal to $\Sigma_2(t, \hat{x}(t))$, and thus we use the new $\dot{\hat{\tau}}(t)$ instead of the old one.

For the case $N > 2$, we can derive the corresponding update rule based on the first order necessary Kuhn-Tucker condition. More precisely, $\dot{\hat{\tau}}(t)$ can be provided as the time-derivative of $\hat{\tau}(t)$ satisfying the equality condition in the corresponding Kuhn-Tucker condition at the boundary point.

4.2   Example: The Constrained Case

Let us return to the example in Section 3.4. Here we consider the initial state $(1.2, 0.3)^T$.

Figure 3 shows a situation where $\hat{\tau}_1(t)$ approaches to $\hat{\tau}_2(t)$ as the time proceeds, and $\hat{\tau}_1(t) = \hat{\tau}_2(t)$ holds on $[0.022, 0.147]$. On this time interval, the

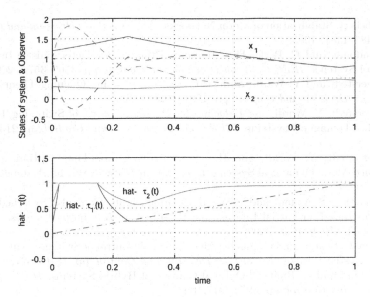

Fig. 3. A situation is shown where although $\hat{\tau}_1(t)$ approaches to $\hat{\tau}_2(t)$, $\hat{\tau}_1(t) = \hat{\tau}_2(t)$ holds on $[0.022, 0.147]$ and the switch-time optimization is achieved with the proper switching sequence

switch-time dynamics newly obtained in Section 4.1 is used. It is thus clear that the switch-times can be optimized while maintaining the switching sequence.

5   Conclusions

An algorithm was presented for solving the optimal switch-time control problem when the state of the system is only partially known through the output. This algorithm was constructed in such a way that it both guarantees that the current switch-time remains optimal as the state estimates evolve, and that it ensures this in a computationally feasible manner, thus rendering the method applicable for real-time applications. An extension was moreover considered where the switching-times ensure that they do not cross each other, thus maintaining the correct switching sequence.

References

1. L. Armijo. Minimization of Functions Having Lipschitz Continuous First-Partial Derivatives. *Pacific J. of Mathematics*, Vol. 16, pp. 1-3, 1966.
2. A. Bemporad, F. Borrelli, and M. Morari. Piecewise Linear Optimal Controllers for Hybrid Systems. *American Control Conf.*, pp. 1190-1194, 2000.
3. A. Bemporad, F. Borrelli, and M. Morari. On the Optimal Control Law for Linear Discrete Time Hybrid Systems. *Hybrid Systems: Computation and Control*, M. Greenstreet and C. Tomlin, Editors, Springer-Verlag, pp. 105-119, 2002.
4. M.S. Branicky, V.S. Borkar, and S.K. Mitter. A Unified Framework for Hybrid Control: Model and Optimal Control Theory. *IEEE Trans. on Automatic Control*, Vol. 43, pp. 31-45, 1998.

5. R. Brockett. Stabilization of Motor Networks. *IEEE Conf. on Decision and Control*, pp. 1484–1488, 1995.
6. J. Chudoung and C. Beck. The Minimum Principle for Deterministic Impulsive Control Systems. *IEEE Conf. on Decision and Control*, pp. 3569–3574, 2001.
7. M. Egerstedt and Y. Wardi. Multi-Process Control Using Queuing Theory. *IEEE Conf. on Decision and Control*, pp. 1991–1996, 2002.
8. M. Egerstedt, Y. Wardi, and F. Delmotte. Optimal Control of Switching Times in Switched Dynamical Systems. *IEEE Conf. on Decision and Control*, pp. 2138-2143, 2003.
9. M. Egerstedt, Y. Wardi, and H. Axelsson. Transition-Time Optimization for Switched-Mode Dynamical Systems. to appear in *IEEE Trans. on Automatic Control*, 2005.
10. M. Egerstedt, S. Azuma, and Y. Wardi. Optimal Timing Control of Switched Linear Systems Based on Partial Information. to appear in *Nonlinear Analysis: Theory, Methods & Applications*, 2006.
11. A. Guia, C. Seatzu, and C. Van der Mee. Optimal Control of Switched Autonomous Linear Systems. In *IEEE Conf. on Decision and Control*, pp. 1816-1821, 1999.
12. S. Hedlund and A. Rantzer. Optimal Control of Hybrid Systems. *IEEE Conf. on Decision and Control*, pp. 3972-3977, 1999.
13. D. Hristu-Varsakelis. Feedback Control Systems as Users of Shared Network: Communication Sequences that Guarantee Stability. *IEEE Conf. on Decision and Control*, pp. 3631–3631, 2001.
14. B. Lincoln and A. Rantzer. Optimizing Linear Systems Switching. *IEEE Conf. on Decision and Control*, pp. 2063–2068, 2001.
15. P. E. Moraal and J. W. Grizzle. Observer Design for Nonlinear Systems with Discrete-Time Measurements. *IEEE Trans. on Automatic Control*, vol. 40, pp. 395–404, 1995.
16. A. Rantzer and M. Johansson. Piecewise Linear Quadratic Optimal Control. *IEEE Trans. on Automatic Control*, Vol. 54, pp. 629-637, 2000.
17. H. Rehbinder and M. Sanfirdson. Scheduling of a Limited Communication Channel for Optimal Control. *IEEE Conf. on Decision and Control*, pp. 1011–1016, 2000.
18. M.S. Shaikh and P. Caines. On Trajectory Optimization for Hybrid Systems: Theory and Algorithms for Fixed Schedules. *IEEE Conf. on Decision and Control*, pp. 1997–1998, 2002.
19. M.S. Shaikh and P.E. Caines. On the Optimal Control of Hybrid Systems: Optimization of Trajectories, Switching Times and Location Schedules. In *6th International Workshop on Hybrid Systems: Computation and Control*, 2003.
20. H.J. Sussmann. Set-Valued Differentials and the Hybrid Maximum Principle. *IEEE Conf. on Decision and Control*, pp. 558–563, 2000.
21. G. Walsh, H. Ye, and L. Bushnell. Stability Analysis of Networked Control Systems. *American Control Conf.*, pp. 2876–2880, 1999.
22. L.Y. Wang, A. Beydoun, J. Cook, J. Sun, and I. Kolmanovsky. Optimal Hybrid Control with Applications to Automotive Powertrain Systems. *Control Using Logic-Based Switching*, Vol. 222 of LNCIS, pp. 190-200, Springer-Verlag, 1997.
23. X. Xu and P. Antsaklis. Optimal Control of Switched Autonomous Systems. *IEEE Conf. on Decision and Control*, pp. 4401–4406, 2002.
24. X. Xu and P.J. Antsaklis. Optimal Control of Switched Systems via Nonlinear Optimization Based on Direct Differentiations of Value Functions. *Int. J. of Control*, Vol. 75, pp. 1406-1426, 2002.

Hybrid Modelling and Control of the Common Rail Injection System

Andrea Balluchi[1,2], Antonio Bicchi[2], Emanuele Mazzi[1,2],
Alberto L. Sangiovanni Vincentelli[1,3], and Gabriele Serra[4]

[1] PARADES, Via S. Pantaleo, 66, 00186 Roma, Italy
{balluchi, emazzi, alberto}@parades.rm.cnr.it
[2] Centro Interdipartimentale di Ricerca "Enrico Piaggio",
Università di Pisa, 56100 Pisa, Italy
bicchi@ing.unipi.it
[3] Dept. of EECS., University of California at Berkeley, CA 94720, USA
alberto@eecs.berkeley.edu
[4] Magneti Marelli Powertrain, Via del Timavo 33, 40134 Bologna, Italy
Gabriele.Serra@bologna.marelli.it

Abstract. We present an industrial case study in automotive control of significant complexity: the new common rail fuel injection system for Diesel engines, currently under production by Magneti Marelli Powertrain. In this system, a flow–rate valve, introduced before the High Pressure (HP) pump, regulates the fuel flow that supplies the common rail according to the engine operating point. The standard approach followed in automotive control is to use a mean–value model for the plant and to develop a controller based on this model. In this particular case, this approach does not provide a satisfactory solution as the discrete–continuous interactions in the fuel injection system, due to the slow time–varying frequency of the HP pump cycles and the fast sampling frequency of sensing and actuation, play a fundamental role. We present a design approach based on a hybrid model of the Magneti Marelli Powertrain common–rail fuel–injection system for four-cylinder multi–jet engines and a hybrid approach to the design of a rail pressure controller. The hybrid controller is compared with a classical mean–value based approach to automotive control design whereby the quality of the hybrid solution is demonstrated.

1 Introduction

Common–rail fuel–injection is the dominant system in diesel engine control. In common–rail fuel–injection systems (see Figure 1), a low-pressure pump located in the tank supplies an HP pump with a fuel flow at the pressure of 4–6 bars. The HP pump delivers the fuel at high pressure (from 150 to 1600 bars) to the common rail, which supplies all the injectors. The fuel pressure in the common rail depends on the balance between the inlet fuel flow from the HP pump and the outlet fuel flow to the injectors. The common–rail pressure is controlled to achieve tracking of a reference signal that is generated on–line (it depends on the engine operating point) to optimize fuel injection and to obtain proper combustion with low emissions and noise.

João Hespanha and A. Tiwari (Eds.): HSCC 2006, LNCS 3927, pp. 79–92, 2006.

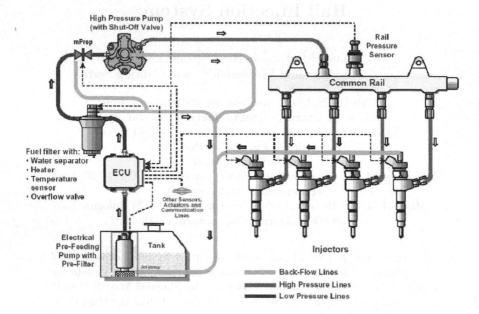

Fig. 1. Common rail fuel injection system developed by Magneti Marelli Powertrain

In the novel fuel–injection system developed by Magneti Marelli Powertrain, a flow–rate valve located before the HP pump allows for effective control of the amount of fuel that is compressed to high pressure and delivered to the rail. The HP pump and, hence, the rail are supplied with the precise amount of fuel flow that is necessary for fuel injection, achieving high efficiency of the injection system. The previous fuel injection system, which was not equipped with the flow–rate valve, was characterized by a high power consumption by the HP pump, which always supplied with the maximum fuel flow for the current operating condition (rail pressure control was achieved by a regulation valve located on the rail).

To control the rail pressure efficiently, we need to model accurately the interaction between discrete and continuous behaviours of the injection system components, exhibiting the pulsating evolution of the rail pressure due the discontinuous inlet fuel flow from the HP pump and outlet fuel flows to the injectors. To do so, we present in this paper a hybrid model of the Magneti Marelli Powertrain common–rail fuel–injection system for four-cylinder multi–jet engines. Motivated by the success in solving other automotive control problems using hybrid system methodologies, e.g. cut-off control [1], intake throttle valve control [2], actual engaged gear identification [3], and adaptive cruise control [4], we developed a hybrid rail pressure controller that exhibits excellent performance. To compare our solution with the standard design methodology adopted in the automotive industry based on mean–value models of the plant, we present a classical Smith Predictor discrete–time controller. Simulations of the closed–loop system show that the mean–value model design approach does not achieve the same quality of design as the hybrid approach.

We believe this paper underlines the important role played by hybrid systems in solving complex industrial control problems in a domain as economically relevant as the automotive sector.

2 Hybrid Model of the Common Rail Injection System

The proposed hybrid model of the injection system, shown in Figure 2, consists of: the flow–rate valve, the HP pump, the injectors and the common rail [5]. The proposed hybrid model describes accurately the interacting discrete and continuous behaviours of the injection system components, reproducing the pulsating evolution of the rail pressure due the discontinuous inlet fuel flow from the HP pump and outlet fuel flows to the injectors. The rail pressure p [bar] is the controlled output. The flow–rate valve duty cycle $u \in [0, 1]$ is the control input. The injectors fuel flow q^{INJ} [mm^3/sec] , which depends on the injectors opening times ET [sec], is considered as a disturbance to be compensated. The models of the components of the system are described in the next sections using the hybrid automaton formalism [6].

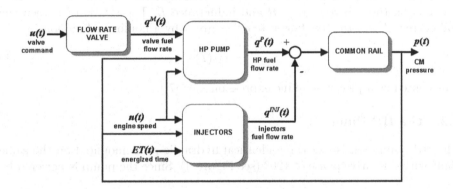

Fig. 2. Hybrid model of the fuel injection system

2.1 The Flow–Rate Valve

The hybrid model of the flow–rate valve is depicted in Figure 3 and includes: the valve PWM[1] electrical driver; the dynamics of the coil current I [A]; and the relation between the coil current and the fuel flow–rate q^M [mm^3/sec] across the valve.

The PWM electrical driver model is a hybrid model with as output a square wave voltage $v^{PWM}(t) \in \{0, V_{bat}\}$ given by pulse–width modulation of the battery voltage V_{bat} with duty cycle defined by the control input signal $u(t) \in [0, 1]$. Its implementation is based on a triangular wave generator with period T_0 and

---

[1] Pulse Width Modulation.

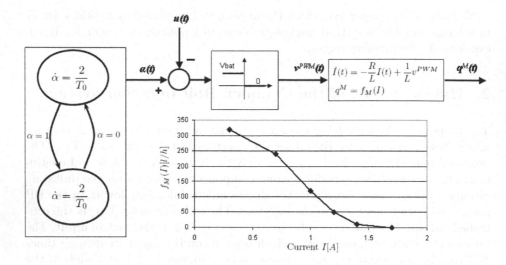

Fig. 3. Flow–rate valve hybrid model

output $\alpha(t)$, modelled as a hybrid system. The dynamics of the coil current I depends on the coil resistance R and inductance L. The relation between the coil current I and the fuel flow rate q^M is given by a nonlinear function

$$q^M = f_M(I) \tag{1}$$

represented as a piecewise affine expression (see [7]).

2.2   The HP Pump

The HP pump consists of three identical hydraulic rams mounted on the same shaft with a relative phase of 120° (see Figure 4). Since the pump is powered by

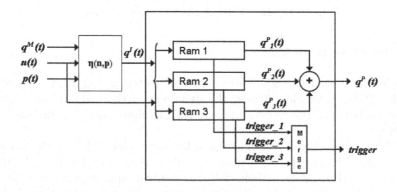

Fig. 4. HP pump hybrid model

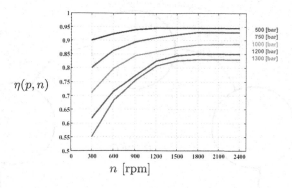

$\eta(p, n)$

n [rpm]

Fig. 5. HP pump efficiency

the camshaft, its revolution speed depends on the engine speed n [rpm]. Pump efficiency reduces the fuel flow q^I [mm^3/sec] to the rams, i.e.

$$q^I = \eta(p, n)q^M \qquad (2)$$

where the efficiency $\eta(p, n)$ depends on the rail pressure and the engine speed as depicted in Figure 5. The HP pump fuel flow to the rail q^P [mm^3/sec] is obtained by adding the contributions q_i^P of the three rams: $q^P = q_1^P + q_2^P + q_3^P$.

The partial closure of the flow–rate regulation valve produces the cavitation phenomenon in the pump, which affects both the intake and compression phases. For small effective area of the flow–rate valve, the pressure reduction in the ram during the intake phase causes fuel vaporization [8]. As a consequence, the amount of fuel charge in volume is lower than the geometric displacement of the cylinder. The partial fuel charge depends on the amount of fuel vapor in the cylinder. In a first part of the compression phase, the ram does not deliver any fuel to the rail. In fact, at the beginning of the compression phase, the increase of pressure inside the cylinder causes fuel condensation only. The outlet flow to the rail starts when the fuel is completely in the liquid state, i.e. when the geometric volume of the cylinder (which decreases during compression) equals the fuel charge in volume. From this time on, pressure increase in the ram produces the opening of outlet valve and the exit of the compressed fuel to the rail.

The hybrid model of the i-th ram of the HP pump is depicted in Figure 6. Its evolution is determined by the ram angle ϕ_i [^{o}]. Since the camshaft revolution speed is half the engine speed n, then the ram angle dynamics is $\dot{\phi}_i = \frac{360}{2}\frac{n}{60} = 3n$, where n is the engine speed in rpm.

The hybrid model contains two macro discrete states corresponding to the intake and compress phases, which have durations of half camshaft cycle. The pumping cycle starts with the beginning of the intake phase, which is triggered by the guard $\phi_i = 180^o$. The camshaft sensor detects the beginning of the pumping cycle by emitting the output event $trigger_i$ at transition time.

Since the intake duration is 180° and the three rams are mounted with a relative phase of 120°, then the intake phases of the rams partially overlap. Intake overlapping results in different supplying fuel flow to the rams. Rams

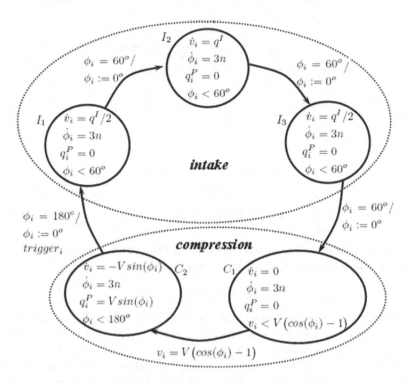

Fig. 6. Hybrid model of the i-th ram of the HP pump

overlapping is modelled in the i-th ram hybrid model by including three discrete states $\mathbf{I}_1$, $\mathbf{I}_2$ and $\mathbf{I}_3$ inside the **intake** state. In each state the model dwells for a duration of 60° of the ram angle ϕ_i. Concurrent intake with one of the other rams occurs in the first and the last part of the intake, i.e. in $\mathbf{I}_1$ and $\mathbf{I}_3$. Assuming that, in case of concurrent intake, both rams receive half of the flow q^I given by (2), then the amount of fuel v_i [mm^3] inside the i-th ram is subject to the dynamics: $\dot{v}_i = q^I/2$ in $\mathbf{I}_1$ and $\mathbf{I}_3$; and $\dot{v}_i = q^I$ in $\mathbf{I}_2$.

The **compression** state consists of two different states: $\mathbf{C}_1$, modeling fuel condensation, and $\mathbf{C}_2$, modeling fuel delivery to the rail. On entering the **compression** state, the ram angle ϕ_i is reset. During fuel condensation in state $\mathbf{C}_1$, the fuel charge in the ram remains constant ($\dot{v}_i = 0$) and the fuel flow–rate to the rail q_i^P is zero. The system remains in state $\mathbf{C}_1$ while the geometric volume of the ram $V(cos(\phi_i) - 1)$ is greater than the fuel charge v_i. When all fuel is at the liquid state (i.e. $v_i = V(cos(\phi_i) - 1)$), the model switches to state $\mathbf{C}_2$ where: the outlet valve is open, the compressed fuel flows towards the rail with flow–rate $q_i^P = V\sin(\phi_i)$, and the ram fuel charge decreases as $\dot{v}_i = -V\sin(\phi_i)$. The **compression** state is left when the ram angle ϕ_i reaches 180°.

2.3 Injectors

The common rail supplies four injectors, one for each cylinder of the engine. In multi–jet engines, each injection phase is composed by a sequence of 3 to 5 distinct injections. However, in most of the engine operating conditions only three injections are used. For the sake of simplicity, we consider this case. The three injections are: a pilot injection (applied to reduce combustion time by increasing cylinder temperature and pressure), a pre-injection (used to reduce production of emissions by optimizing combustion conditions) and a main injection (which produces the desired engine torque). Having the engine four cylinders, the frequency of injection sequences is twice the engine speed. The engine torque controller implemented in the engine control unit defines the amount of fuel to be injected and, consequently, the durations $ET = (\tau^{PIL}, \tau^{PRE}, \tau^{MAIN})$ [sec] and phases $(\theta^{PIL}, \theta^{PRE}, \theta^{MAIN})$ (expressed in crank angle) of each fuel injection, depending on the engine operating condition.

The amount of fuel that flows from the common rail to each injector is the sum of three different terms: the flow that enters the combustion chamber Q_{inj}, a flow necessary to keep the injector open Q_{serv}, and a leakage flow Q_{leak}. The latter two are collected into the tank. While the leakage flow–rate Q_{leak} is a continuous signal, the flow–rate Q_{inj} and Q_{serv} are not zero only when the injector is open. Since the common rail model is zero-dimensional and in each engine stroke only an injector is operated, then there is no loss of generality in referring the quantities Q_{inj}, Q_{serv}, Q_{leak} to the overall contribution of the four injectors to the common rail balance, with injection frequency twice the engine speed.

The fuel flow–rate q^{INJ} [mm^3/sec] out of the common rail is represented by the hybrid model reported in Figure 7, where q^L denotes the leakage flow Q_{leak} and q^J stands for the sum of the Q_{inj} and Q_{serv} flows.

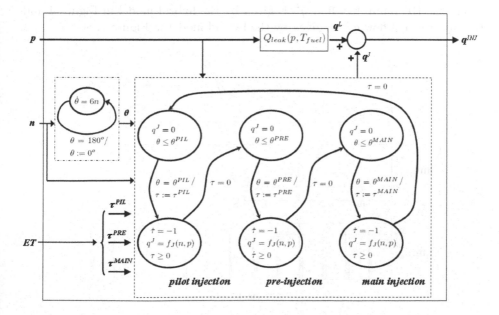

Fig. 7. Hybrid model of the injectors

The three states on the top of the model represent the synchronization phases for the opening of the injectors, which are defined in terms of guards on the crankshaft angle θ [^{o}] that evolves from 0 to 180° with dynamics $\dot{\theta} = 6n$. Parameters θ^{PIL}, θ^{PRE}, θ^{MAIN} denote the corresponding start of injection angles. In these states, the fuel flow to the injectors is due to leakage only, i.e. $q^J = 0$.

As soon as the guard conditions $\theta = \theta^{PIL}$, $\theta = \theta^{PRE}$, $\theta = \theta^{MAIN}$ become true, a transition to the corresponding state on the bottom takes place, and the timer τ is initialized to the current injection duration time τ^{PIL}, τ^{PRE}, τ^{MAIN}. The three states on the bottom model the system with one injector open. The flow to the open injector depends on the engine speed and the rail pressure: $q^J = f_J(n, p) = Q_{inj}(p, n) + Q_{serv}(p, n)$. The system remains in the injection states until the injection time elapses, i.e. $\tau = 0$.

2.4 Common Rail

The dynamics of the rail pressure is obtained by considering the balance between the HP pump inlet flow and injectors outlet flows. Under the assumption of not deformable rail, the fuel volume is constant, while the capacity depends on the pressure and temperature of the fuel in the rail according the Bulk module, which takes into account fuel compressibility. The evolution of the rail pressure is given by:

$$\dot{p}(t) = \frac{K_{Bulk}}{V_{rail}} \left(q^P(t) - q^{INJ}(t) \right), \tag{3}$$

where the HP pump fuel flow q^P is given by the hybrid model in Figure 4 and the injector fuel flow q^{INJ} is given by the hybrid model in Figure 7.

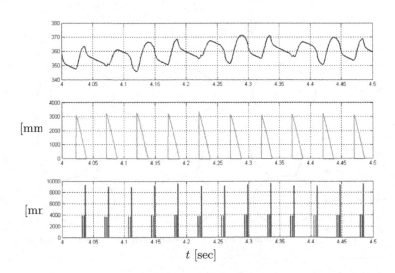

Fig. 8. Rail pressure pulsating profile and HP pump and injectors fuel flows

Simulation results obtained with the proposed common rail hybrid model show that it nicely represents the pulsating behaviour of the common rail pressure due to the HP pump and injectors discontinuous evolutions. Figure 8 reports a typical evolution of the common rail pressure, along with the pulsating fuel flows of the HP pump and the injectors. When the pump delivers the fuel, the pressure increases while when the injectors open, the pressure decreases.

3   Control Design

The objective is to design a feedback controller for the rail pressure that achieves tracking of a reference pressure signal. The latter is generated on-line by an outer loop control algorithm so to optimize fuel injection and obtain proper fuel combustion, with low emissions and noise, for the current engine operating point. The specifications for the rail pressure controller are:

- steady state rail pressure error lower than 30 bar;
- settling time lower than 150 mseconds;
- undershoot/overshot lower than 50 bar, for a ramp of rail pressure reference with rate 800 bar/sec, at 1000 rpm, with 15 mm^3/stroke fuel injection.

The most important aspect to be taken into account in the design of the control algorithm is the varying time delay between the flow–rate valve control command u and the pulsating fuel flow from the HP pump to the rail. This delay is due to HP pump cycles and is roughly in inverse proportion to engine speed. As a consequence, the control task is particularly critical during cranking and at low engine speed.

3.1   Controller Based on the Smith Predictor

In this section, we develop a "standard" controller based on a mean–value model of the plant. To cope with the large and time–varying loop delay, the controller is based on the Smith Predictor. The rail pressure Smith Predictor controller (see e.g. [9, 10]) is obtained following the standard approach to controller design adopted in the automotive industry that is based on mean–value modelling of the plant. The following continuous time model is considered:

$$\dot{I}(t) = -\frac{R}{L}I(t) + \frac{v^{PWM}(t)}{L} \tag{4}$$

$$\dot{p}(t) = \frac{K_{bulk}(p)}{V_{rail}} \left[(q^P(t - \hat{T}_d) - q^{INJ}(t) \right] \tag{5}$$

where $\hat{T}_d = 120/n$ is an estimate of the loop delay. The controller includes a model of the high pressure circuit and a PID with anti–windup and feedforward terms. The control algorithm is implemented in discrete time, with a sampling time of 5 mseconds. Satisfactory rail pressure tracking is achieved provided that the rate of variation of the reference pressure is not too large. Figure 9 reports a typical rail pressure evolution.

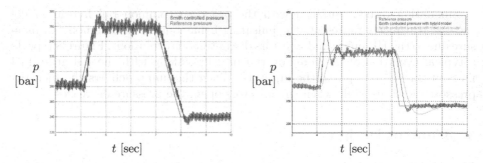

Fig. 9. Closed–loop hybrid system simulation results with the Smith Predictor: for slow (left) and fast (right) pressure references

However, the tracking performance significantly degrades and large overshoots are produced for fast rail pressure reference signals, as described in Figure 9. On the other hand, the simulation of the Smith Predictor controller against the mean–value model exhibits the expected behaviour showing that the controller is able to compensate properly the time delay. Hence, the poor tracking performances shown in the simulations with the common rail hybrid model demonstrate that mean–value modelling is not accurate enough to design high quality control. In fact, major difficulties in the calibration of mean–value model–based controllers for fast reference pressure signals were observed by Magneti Marelli Powertrain. From the closed-loop hybrid model simulation shown in Figure 9, to be able to efficiently track fast pressure references, the controller should be designed taking into account each single fuel delivery of the HP pump. In fact, in the reported simulation, only three compression phases of the HP pump drive the pressure close to the target value. From a physical point of view, the HP pump combines a sequence of control actions to determine the fuel charge for each single cycle. However, this behaviour is not taken into account by the pressure controller designed on the basis of the mean–value model of the system, which then exhibits large overshoot.

This analysis motivates the search for a better solution that can be offered by designing a hybrid controller that is based on the accurate hybrid model presented above.

3.2   Hybrid Multi–rate Controller

During the intake phases, the HP pump combines a sequence of control actions to determine the fuel charge for each single cycle. Hence, the HP pump introduces an under–sampling of the control actions. The slow frequency of intake and delivery of the HP pump is time varying since it depends on the engine speed. A hybrid system approach to controller design allows us to effectively handle the under–sampling produced by the HP pump cycles and properly handle the drift between the fast frequency of sensing and actuation (at 5 mseconds) and frequency of the HP pump [11].

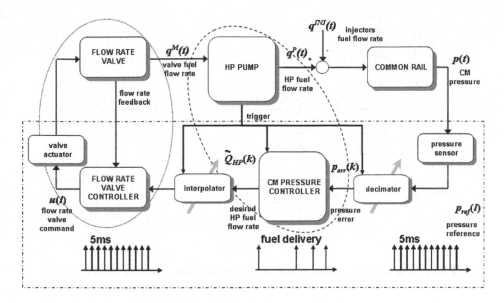

Fig. 10. Hybrid multi–rate controller

The proposed hybrid multi–rate controller, showed in Figure 10, consists on two regulators:

- The *CM pressure controller* is event–based and is synchronous with the HP pump fuel intake phases (it receives the HP pump *trigger* event from the camshaft sensor). This controller defines the desired fuel mass $\tilde{Q}_{HP}(k)$ [mm^3/stroke] needed to control the rail pressure error $p_{err}(k)$ to zero. A PI control with anti-windup and feedforward terms is used for this purpose.
- The *flow–rate valve controller* runs at 5 mseconds. Its task is to feed the high pressure circuit with the amount of fuel $\tilde{Q}_{HP}(l)$ requested by the outer loop controller. Due to the lack of a fuel flow–rate sensor downstream the valve, the flow–rate valve controller has to be open-loop. The duty cycle control u is obtained by abstracting away the coil current dynamics and inverting the flow–rate valve characteristic (1) and the PWM model, i.e.

$$u = \frac{2}{3} \frac{R}{V_{batt}} f_M^{-1}(\tilde{Q}_{HP}(l)). \qquad (6)$$

The factor $\frac{2}{3}$ is introduced to take into account the partial overlapping of the intakes phases of the rams in HP pump.

Smooth and effective coupling between the different time domains of pressure sensing, CM pressure control and flow–rate valve control is achieved by using a decimator and an interpolator [12].

- The decimator converts the high frequency pressure error $p_{err}(l) = p(l) - p_{ref}(l)$, having sampling time 5 mseconds, to the time–varying HP pump frequency. An IIR low–pass filter is employed (see Figure 11).

$p_{ref}(l)$
$p_{ref}(k)$
[bar]

$\tilde{Q}_{HP}(k)$
$\tilde{Q}_{HP}(l)$
[mm^3/sec]

t [sec]

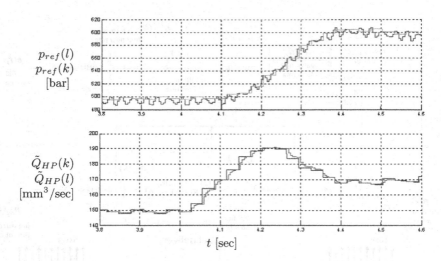

Fig. 11. Signal conversions provided by the decimator and the interpolator

p
[bar]

t [sec]

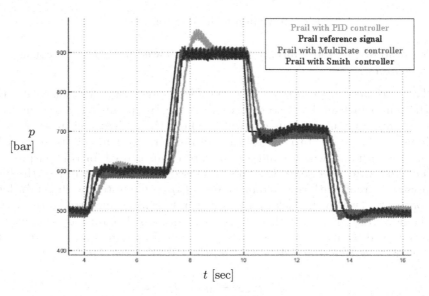

Fig. 12. Comparison between the proposed hybrid multi-rate controller and a controller based on the Smith Predictor developed using a mean–value model of the plant

– The interpolator converts the fuel mass signal $\tilde{Q}_{HP}(k)$ in [mm^3/stroke], synchronous with the time–varying HP pump frequency to the 5 msecond discrete–time domain, $\tilde{Q}_{HP}(l)$ in [mm^3/sec] used by the flow–rate valve controller. An IIR low–pass filter is employed in the interpolator. The interpolator produces a smooth and uniform input signal to the flow–rate valve controller as illustrated in Figure 11.

Both the decimator and the interpolator implement a gain scheduling of the cut–off frequency based on engine speed to compensate the variation of the HP pump frequency.

The simulation results presented in Figure 12 show the improvement obtained by the proposed hybrid multi–rate controller with respect to a controller based on the Smith Predictor presented in the previous section. Both controllers have been tuned to meet the specification on bounded overshoot. The settling time of the hybrid multi–rate controller is significantly shorter than the one of the Smith Predictor controller. Moreover, the hybrid multi–rate regulator, which implements a PI algorithm and two low–pass filters, is significantly simpler than the Smith Predictor that includes an internal model of the plant. Finally, while the Smith Predictor is affected by a time delay estimation error, in the multi-rate controller the loop delay is simply represented by a one step delay. Simulation results show that the hybrid multi–rate controller is robust to phase errors between the CM pressure controller execution and the beginning of intake phases of the rams.

4   Conclusions

We presented a relevant problem in diesel engine control that has been solved with a hybrid system approach. We first developed a hybrid model that takes into account the interactions between the discrete dynamics of the components of the common rail system.

Then we demonstrated the superiority of a hybrid multi–rate control algorithm versus the standard mean-value model approach to controller design adopted in the automotive industry. To do so, we designed a Smith Predictor controller to compensate the loop delay. Simulation results show that such controller achieves satisfactory tracking only for slow rail pressure reference signals. Figure 12 illustrates the improvement achieved by using the multi–rate controller.

In summary, we demonstrated how the use of hybrid models and control algorithms can produce superior results versus standard control approaches based on mean–value models for a relevant and complex industrial problem.

References

1. Balluchi, A., Benedetto, M.D.D., Pinello, C., Rossi, C., Sangiovanni-Vincentelli, A.L.: Hybrid control in automotive applications: the cut-off control. Automatica: a Journal of IFAC **35** (1999) 519–535
2. Baotic, M., Vasak, M., Morari, M., Peric, N.: Hybrid theory based optimal control of electronic throttle. In: In Proc. of the IEEE American Control Conference, Denver, Colorado, USA, ACC (2003) 5209–5214
3. Balluchi, A., Benvenuti, L., Lemma, C., Sangiovanni-Vincentelli, A.L., Serra, G.: Actual engaged gear identification: a hybrid observer approach. In: 16th IFAC World Congress, Prague, CZ, IFAC (2005)

4. Mobus, R., Baotic, M., Morari, M.: Multi-object adaptive cruise control. Hybrid Systems: Computation and Control **2623** (2003) 359–374
5. Millo, F.: Il sistema common rail. Technical report, Dipartimento di Energetica, Politecnico di Torino (2002)
6. Henzingerz, T.A.: The theory of hybrid automata. Technical report, Electrical Engineering and Computer Sciences University of California, (Berkeley)
7. Bosch: Injection Systems for Diesel Engines. Technical Customer Documents. (2003)
8. Knapp, R.: Cavitation. McGraw-Hill (1970)
9. Rath, G.: Smith's method for dead time control. Technical report (2000)
10. Mirkin, L.: Control of dead-time systems, K.U.Leuven - Belgium, Mathematical Theory of Networks and Systems (2004)
11. Glasson, D.: Development and applications of multirate digital control. IEEE Control Systems Magazine **3** (1983) 2–8
12. Vaidyanathan, P.: Multirate digital filters, filter banks, polyphase networks and applications: a tutorial. Proceedings of the IEEE **78** (1990) 56–92

Event-Based Model Predictive Control and Verification of Integral Continuous-Time Hybrid Automata

Alberto Bemporad[1], Stefano Di Cairano[1,*], and Jorge Júlvez[2]

[1] Dip. Ingegneria dell'Informazione, Universit di Siena, Italy
{bemporad, dicairano}@dii.unisi.it
[2] Dep. Informática e Ingeniería de Sistemas, Universidad de Zaragoza,
julvez@unizar.es

Abstract. This paper proposes an event-driven model predictive control scheme with guaranteed closed-loop convergence properties for the class of integral continuous-time hybrid automata (icHA). After converting icHA to a corresponding event-driven representation that allows one to compute the model predictive control action by mixed integer programming, sufficient conditions ensuring event-asymptotic and time-asymptotic convergence are proven. The paper also shows how the same modeling methodology can be employed to efficiently solve problems of verification of safety properties.

1 Introduction

Hybrid systems are complex dynamical systems in which continuous and discrete variables coexist and are mutually dependent. The trajectory of a continuous-time hybrid system can be represented as a sequence of continuous evolutions interleaved by discrete events [1,2], which cause changes in the equations defining the continuous flow, thus changing the operating mode of the system. The continuous flows and the instants at which the discrete events occur are further influenced by exogenous discrete and continuous input signals.

When optimal control is applied to continuous-time hybrid systems [3,4,5], the resulting computational problem is usually hard to solve, since it involves the solution of non-convex problems [5]. A numerically efficient approach is based on the application of mixed-integer programming (MIP) to a discrete-time representation of the system, in order to solve finite-horizon optimal control problems [6]. A drawback of this technique is that events (such as mode switches) can only occur at sampling instants, which can induce non-negligible modeling errors [7]. Modeling precision can be clearly improved by reducing the chosen sampling period; however, in a model predictive control (MPC) context [8,9], the obvious disadvantage is that, for a given time-horizon of prediction, a larger number of control variables is involved in the optimization problem. Better model accuracy is paid by increased computation complexity.

---

* Corresponding author. This work was partially supported by the European Community through the HYCON Network of Excellence, contract number FP6-IST-511368.

João Hespanha and A. Tiwari (Eds.): HSCC 2006, LNCS 3927, pp. 93–107, 2006.
© Springer-Verlag Berlin Heidelberg 2006

A different approach recently proposed in [7] exploits a continuous-time model of the hybrid system, called integral continuous-time hybrid automaton, and abstracts an event-driven representation of it, in which the time is an additional state variable and the events, which can occur at any time instant, cause a change of the speed of the continuous states. Moreover, constraints on state and input variables are enforced along the whole continuous-time trajectory, contrarily to discrete-time approaches that do not ensure constraint satisfaction during the inter-sampling period.

Under the modeling assumption that dynamics are piecewise integral ($\dot{x} = B_i u + f_i$) and input functions u are piecewise constant over time, continuous-time optimal control problems over a finite horizon on integral continuous-time hybrid automata can be solved by MIP, by exploiting an event-driven representation of the system [7].

In this paper, after defining the integral continuous-time hybrid automaton in Section 2, we explain in Section 3 how to represent it as an event-driven model that can be exploited for formulating optimal control problems as mixed-integer programs. In Section 4 we discuss an event-driven model predictive control scheme, providing sufficient convergence conditions and presenting a simple numerical example. Finally, in Section 5 we show how the event-driven model can be exploited for verification of hybrid systems, and test the approach on the well-known train-gate benchmark [10].

2   Integral Continuous Hybrid Automaton

In this paper we consider the class of *integral continuous (-time) Hybrid Automata* (icHA) [7]. Such systems are a continuous-time version of the Discrete Hybrid Automaton (DHA) [11], with integral continuous-state dynamics. The icHA has the same structure of the DHA, consisting of the four components reported in Figure 1: the integral Switched Affine System (iSAS), the Event Generator (EG), the Mode Selector (MS) and the asynchronous Finite State Machine (aFSM). The iSAS represents a collection of possible continuous-time integral dynamics (i.e., the system modes) for the continuous states,

$$\dot{x}_c(t) = B_{i(t)} u_c(t) + f_{i(t)}, \tag{1}$$

where $x_c \in \mathbb{R}^{n_c}$ and $u_c \in \mathbb{R}^{m_c}$ are the continuous components of the state and input vectors, respectively, and $i \in \mathcal{I} = \{1, 2, \ldots s\}$ is the system mode. While the main reason for focusing the attention to integral dynamics is computational (see [7] and Equation (6) below), the class of continuous-state dynamics (1) has been widely exploited for modeling and verification of hybrid systems [1, 10], showing to be powerful enough for modeling many practical problems[1].

---

[1] Given a nonlinear (possibly discontinuous) dynamical model $\dot{x} = f(x, u)$, model (1) can be interpreted as a zero-order approximation of the state-transition function with respect to the state vector x and a first-order approximation with respect to the input vector u. Piecewise affine (PWA) models $\dot{x} = A_i x + B_i u + f_i$ are first-order approximations with respect to both x and u.

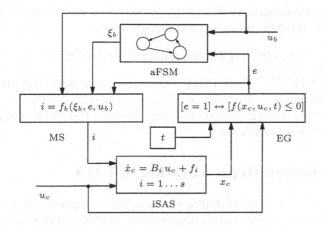

Fig. 1. Integral continuous-time Hybrid Automaton (icHA)

The EG defines the endogenous binary inputs e by linear threshold conditions

$$[e_i^x(t) = 1] \leftrightarrow \left[E_i^x \left[\begin{smallmatrix} x_c(t) \\ t \end{smallmatrix} \right] \leq F_i^x \right], \ i = 1, \ldots n_e^x \tag{2a}$$

$$[e_i^u(t) = 1] \leftrightarrow [E_i^u u_c(t) \leq F_i^u], \ i = 1, \ldots n_e^u \tag{2b}$$

where $n_e^x + n_e^u = n_e$ and $e = [e_1^x \ldots e_{n_e^x}^x \ e_1^u \ldots e_{n_e^u}^x]^T \in \{0,1\}^{n_e}$ is the vector of endogenous binary input variables. The icHA is also excited by exogenous binary input signals $u_b \in \{0,1\}^{m_b}$. We say that an *event* occurs whenever an endogenous input e or an exogenous input (u_c, u_b) changes its value. Accordingly, event instants $t_0 < t_1 < \ldots$ are defined as

$$t_k = \min_{t > t_{k-1}} \{t : (u_c(t), u_b(t), e(t)) \neq (u_c(t_{k-1}), u_b(t_{k-1}), e(t_{k-1}))\}, \tag{3}$$

where we assume that the minimum in (3) exists. As a consequence, the set of admissible input functions is the set $\mathcal{PC}_{(m_c, m_b)}$ of piecewise constant functions $u = [\begin{smallmatrix} u_c \\ u_b \end{smallmatrix}]$, $u : \mathbb{R} \to \mathbb{R}^{m_c} \times \{0,1\}^{m_b}$ such that $u(t) = u(t_k)$, $\forall t \in [t_k, t_{k+1})$, $\forall k = 0, 1, \ldots$.

The Boolean state $\xi_b \in \{0,1\}^{n_b}$ is defined as $\xi_b(t) \triangleq x_b(t_k)$ for $t_{k-1} \leq t < t_k$ and

$$x_b(t_{k+1}) = f_{\text{aFSM}}(x_b(t_k), u_b(t_k), e(t_k)), \tag{4}$$

where $f_{\text{aFSM}} : \{0,1\}^{n_b + m_b + n_e} \to \{0,1\}^{n_b}$ is a Boolean function. The Boolean state $\xi_b(t)$ remains constant, $\xi_b(t) \equiv x_b(t_k)$, during the whole interval $t_{k-1} \leq t < t_k$. At the event instant t_k, the Boolean state switches to the new value $f_{\text{aFSM}}(x_b(t_k), e(t_k), u_b(t_k))$, and remains at that value for $t_k \leq t < t_{k+1}$. While we are assuming that the transitions of the aFSM are instantaneous, delays can be easily modeled by introducing additional events and states. Note that transitions of icHA can occur at any time instant, not only at multiples of a given sampling period as in DHA [11].

The different operating modes of the system represented by the variable $i(t)$ are selected by the MS through the scalar product

$$i(t) = [1 \, 2 \dots s] \cdot f_{\mathrm{MS}}(\xi_b(t), u_b(t), e(t)), \tag{5}$$

where $f_{\mathrm{MS}} : \{0,1\}^{n_b+m_b+n_e} \to \{0,1\}^s$ is a Boolean function satisfying the mutual exclusivity relation $[1 \dots 1] \cdot f_{\mathrm{MS}} = 1$, $\forall (\xi_b(t), u_b(t), e(t)) \in \{0,1\}^{n_b+m_b+n_e}$. Note that if the inputs and the e variables are constant, the Boolean state and the system mode are also constant.

3   Event-Driven Representation of icHA

An icHA (1)-(5) can be converted to an event-driven representation that is suitable for computing solutions to optimal control problems. If the system mode $i(t)$ and the input $u_c(t)$ are constant for $t \in [t_k, \, t_{k+1})$, $k = 1, \dots, h$, the continuous state at t_h is [7]

$$x_c(t_h) \;=\; x_c(t_0) + \sum_{k=0}^{h-1} \Big(B_{i(t_k)}(t_{k+1} - t_k)u_c(t_k) + f_{i(t_k)}(t_{k+1} - t_k) \Big). \tag{6}$$

Thus, the system dynamics can be rewritten as the linear difference equations

$$x_c(k+1) = x_c(k) + B_{i(k)}v_c(k) + f_{i(k)}q(k) \tag{7a}$$
$$t(k+1) = t(k) + q(k) \tag{7b}$$

where k is the event counter, $x_c(k) = x_c(t_k)$, $t(k) = t_k$, $i(k) = i(t_k)$, $q(k)$ is the time interval between events k and $k+1$, $v_c(k) = q(k)u_c(k)$ is the integral over time period $q(k)$ of the input $u_c(k) = u_c(t_k)$, and time t is an additional state variable. The controlled variables are the input integral $v_c(k)$ and the input duration $q(k)$; the input $u_c(k) = \frac{v_c(k)}{q(k)}$ applied to the continuous-time system is computed from them.

The event generator becomes

$$[e_i^x(k) = 1] \leftrightarrow \left[E_i^x \begin{bmatrix} x_c(k) \\ t(k) \end{bmatrix} \leq F_i^x \right], \, i = 1, \dots n_e^x \tag{8a}$$
$$[e_i^u(k) = 1] \leftrightarrow [E_i^u v_c(k) \leq F_i^u q(k)] , \, i = 1, \dots n_e^u \tag{8b}$$

where $e(k) = e(t_k)$, and $e(t) = e(t_k)$, $\forall t \in [t_k, t_{k+1})$ by the definition of t_k in (3). Note that the dependence on time becomes a dependence on a state variable, because of (7b) and (8b) is obtained from (2b) by multiplying by $q(k)$ both sides. The mode selector equation becomes

$$i(k) = [1 \, 2 \dots s] \cdot \tilde{f}_{\mathrm{MS}}(x_b(k), u_b(k), e(k)), \tag{9}$$

where $i(t) = i(k)$, $\forall t \in [t_k, t_{k+1})$ as a consequence of the event definition, and $\tilde{f}_{\mathrm{MS}}(x_b(k), u_b(k), e(k)) = f_{\mathrm{MS}}(f_{\mathrm{aFSM}}(x_b(k), u_b(k), e(t_k)), u_b(k), e(k))$ because of

(5) and the definition of $\xi(t)$. Equation (4), is already defined with respect to the events.

Equations (4), (7), (8), (9) define the behavior of the components of the icHA in an event-driven representation. To take into account (3), however, the following condition must be ensured:

$$[(e(t_k), u_c(t_k), u_b(t_k)) = (\bar{e}, \bar{u}_c, \bar{u}_b)] \rightarrow [(e(t), u_c(t), u_b(t)) = (\bar{e}, \bar{u}_c, \bar{u}_b), \forall t \in [t_k, t_{k+1})]. \tag{10}$$

We consider two different cases: (i) the value u_c or u_b changes, so that an event is externally forced, (ii) an endogenous event occurs (e changes its value). The first case is caused by an arbitrary decision (e.g., by a controller), and no additional constraints are needed. Thus, we only need to ensure that

$$[e(t_k) = \bar{e}] \rightarrow [(e(t) = \bar{e}), \forall t \in [t_k, t_{k+1})]. \tag{11}$$

Note that the e variables in (2b) can change only when the input changes, thus they can be dealt with as for externally forced events. Hence, we only need to enforce (11) for (2a).

Let the mapping $\text{cod}() : \{0, 1\}^{n_e^x} \rightarrow \mathbb{N}$ associate an integer number j to each allowed value of vector $e^x = [e_1^x \ldots e_{n_e^x}^x]^T$ defined in (2a). For example j may be the integer whose binary encoding is e^x. Define the matrix $\bar{E}^x(j)$ and the vector $\bar{F}^x(j)$ by collecting the rows in the inequalities of the EG (8) which are satisfied for e^x such that $\text{cod}(e^x) = j$. In addition, define $\hat{E}^x(j)$, $\hat{F}^x(j)$ by collecting as rows the inequalities of the EG (8), which are not satisfied for e^x such that $\text{cod}(e^x) = j$. In this way, for all the values of state and input such that $\text{cod}(e^x(k)) = j$, $\bar{E}^x(j) [\begin{smallmatrix} x \\ t \end{smallmatrix}] \leq \bar{F}^x(j)$, $\hat{E}^x(j) [\begin{smallmatrix} x \\ t \end{smallmatrix}] > \hat{F}^x(j)$. As an example, consider two thresholds $[e_1^x = 1] \leftrightarrow [x \leq 0]$, $[e_2^x = 1] \leftrightarrow [x \leq 1]$. The matrices associated to $e^x = [0\ 1]'$, where $\text{cod}(e^x) = 1$, are $\bar{E}^x(1) = 1$, $\bar{F}^x(1) = 1$, collecting the second threshold condition (satisfied), and $\hat{E}^x(1) = 1$, $\hat{F}^x(1) = 0$.

As detailed in [7], in case of integral dynamics, (11) is guaranteed by the mixed-logical constraint

$$[\text{cod}(e^x(t_k)) = j] \rightarrow \left[\begin{bmatrix} \bar{E}^x(j) \\ -\hat{E}^x(j) \end{bmatrix} \begin{bmatrix} x(t_{k+1}) \\ t(k+1) \end{bmatrix} \leq \begin{bmatrix} \bar{F}^x(j) \\ -\hat{F}^x(j) \end{bmatrix} + \varepsilon \mathbf{1} \right], \tag{12}$$

in which ε is an arbitrary small positive constant that ensures that $e(t) = e(t_k)$, $\forall t \in [t_k, t_{k+1} - \sigma(\varepsilon)]$, and $\sigma(\varepsilon)$ tends to zero as ε tends to zero. Note that $x(t_{k+1})$ is a linear function of $x(k)$, $q(k)$, and $v(k) = \begin{bmatrix} v_c(k) \\ v_b(k) \end{bmatrix}$, where $v_b(k) = u_b(k)$, so that (12) is reformulated as mixed-integer inequalities on $x(k)$, $q(k)$, $v(k)$, $e(k)$.

Equations (4), (7), (8), (9), (12) represent a DHA that can be modeled in HYSDEL [11] through which we can obtain an event-driven MLD (eMLD) system

$$x(k + 1) = Ax(k) + B_1 w(k) + B_2 e(k) + B_3 z(k) + B_5, \tag{13a}$$

$$t(k + 1) = t(k) + q(k), \tag{13b}$$

$$E_2 e(k) + E_3 z(k) \leq E_1 w(k) + E_4 x(k) + E_5. \tag{13c}$$

where $w(k) = \begin{bmatrix} v(k) \\ q(k) \end{bmatrix}$. Differently from the standard discrete-time MLD system [6], in (13) k is an event counter while time t is an additional state variable.

Remark 1. Discontinuities of the continuous state trajectory can be introduced by resets. To model resets, additional *reset modes* $i \in \{s+1, \ldots, s_r\}$ are included, (7a) is modified into $x_c(k+1) = (E_i x_c(k) + h_i) + B_{i(k)} v(k) + f_{i(k)} q(k)$, and (7b) into $t(k+1) = t(k) + G_i q(k)$. In modes $i = \{1 \ldots s\}$, $E_i = I$ (where I is the identity matrix), $h_i = 0$ and $G_i = 1$, while in reset modes $i = \{s+1 \ldots s_r\}$ $B_i = 0$, $f_i = 0$ and $G_i = 0$. Note that resets are instantaneous.

The definition of the event-driven dynamics of the icHA by an eMLD system allows the definition of finite horizon optimal control problems that can be solved by mixed-integer programming (MIP) as shown in [6]. With respect to MLD models, the only difference is that the horizon represents the number of events occurred, and the time elapsed along the horizon is a continuous state variable.

4 Event-Driven Model Predictive Control

In [7] event-driven open-loop optimal control strategies are proposed with different cost functions: minimum-time, minimum-effort, and minimum displacement. They are computationally less expensive than their discrete-time counterparts and the system's constraints are satisfied along the whole trajectory instead of only at sampling instants. However, the approach of [7] is an open-loop control strategy. We introduce an event-driven MPC closed-loop strategy here.

Given an icHA, the eMLD model is obtained as explained in Section 3 so that a finite horizon optimal control problem can be formulated as in [6]

$$\min_{q,v} \quad J(x,t,v,q) \tag{14a}$$

$$\text{s.t.} \quad \text{system dynamics (13)} \tag{14b}$$

$$g(x,t,q,v) \leq 0, \tag{14c}$$

$$x(0) = x_0, \quad t(0) = t_0, \tag{14d}$$

where $t = \{t(k)\}_{k=0}^{N}$ are the event instants, $x = \{x(k)\}_{k=0}^{N}$ are the corresponding state values, $q = \{q(k)\}_{k=0}^{N-1}$ are the durations of the time intervals between two consecutive events and $v = \{v(k)\}_{k=0}^{N-1}$ are the input integrals during $[t_k, t_{k+1})$. We consider cost functions of the form

$$J(x,t,v,q) = F(x(N)) + \sum_{k=0}^{N-1} L(x(k), t(k), v_c(k), q(k)) \tag{15}$$

where $L(x(k), t(k), v_c(k), q(k)) = \|x(k) - \hat{x}\|_p^{Q_1} + \|t(k) - \hat{t}\|_p^{Q_2} + \|v(k) - \hat{v}\|_p^{R_1} + \|q(k) - \hat{q}\|_p^{R_2}$ is the stage cost, $F(x(N)) = \|x(N) - \hat{x}\|_p^{Q_N}$ is the terminal cost, $p = 1, 2, \infty$, $\|z\|_\infty^Q = \max_i |(Qz)_i|$, $\|z\|_1^Q = \sum_i |(Qz)_i|$ and $\|z\|_2^Q = z^T Q z$, and if not differently stated $\hat{q} = 0$, $\hat{v} = 0$. In (15), N is the number of allowed events, and as a consequence, the time period considered in the optimization problem will depend on the chosen input profile through the system dynamics: For a fixed N, when the continuous state evolves quickly and switches are frequent, the resulting time horizon will shrink because the system requires a tighter control action; on the contrary, when the dynamics is slow and few mode switches occur, the time-horizon will increase without increasing the complexity of the optimization problem, so that a smaller amount of computation per time unit is required.

Constraint (14c) represents additional constraints in the optimal control problem that have different purposes. Bounds on the continuous-time input value $\underline{u} \leq u_c(t) \leq \overline{u}$ can be cast as the linear constraints

$$\underline{u}q(k) \leq v(k) \leq \overline{u}q(k). \tag{16}$$

Different input bounds for different modes can be enforced as $[i(k) = \overline{i}] \rightarrow [\underline{u}_{\overline{i}}q(k) \leq v(k) \leq \overline{u}_{\overline{i}}q(k)]$, where $\underline{u}_{\overline{i}}$ and $\overline{u}_{\overline{i}}$ are the input upper and lower bounds while the system remains in mode $\overline{i}$. Additional operating constraints may be imposed on time intervals between two events

$$\underline{q} \leq q(k) \leq \overline{q}. \tag{17}$$

A finite value of $\overline{q}$ imposes a maximum time for each control action, in order to prevent the system from running in open-loop with a constant input for too long, because of the receding horizon mechanism. A minimum duration $\underline{q}$ ensures a minimum time interval between two events (thus, between two mode switches), therefore avoiding undesirable effects such as high frequency chattering and Zeno behaviors. Additional constraints in (14c) may concern terminal constraints on the final state and on the final time of the optimization problem. In this case, we consider

$$x(N) \in \mathcal{X}_T, \qquad t(N) \in \mathcal{T}_T, \tag{18}$$

as terminal constraints, where $\mathcal{X}_T$, $\mathcal{T}_T$ can be either polyhedra or isolated points.

The event-driven Model Predictive Control (eMPC) strategy is defined as follows:

1. Let N be the event horizon, and consider the initial instant $\tilde{t}$ and the corresponding state value $x(\tilde{t})$.
2. Solve the optimal control problem (14) with $t_0 = \tilde{t}$ and $x_0 = x(\tilde{t})$ and let $[v^*(0), \ldots, v^*(N-1)]$ be the sequence of optimal input integral values, $[q^*(0), \ldots, q^*(N-1)]$ be the sequence of input action durations, $[x^*(1), \ldots, x^*(N)]$ be the predicted state values at event instants and $[t^*(0), \ldots, t^*(N)]$ be the corresponding time instants at which the events occur.
3. Compute the input value $u_c(\tilde{t}) = \frac{v_c^*(0)}{q^*(0)}$, and apply $u(t) \equiv \begin{bmatrix} u_c(\tilde{t}) \\ v_b^*(0) \end{bmatrix}$ to the icHA during the time interval $[\tilde{t}, \tilde{t} + q^*(0)]$. [2]
4. Set $\tilde{t} \leftarrow \tilde{t} + q(0)$, $x(\tilde{t}) \leftarrow \check{x} = x(\tilde{t} + q(0))$ and go to 2.

---

[2] Different strategies may be proposed here, for example apply $u_c(t) \equiv \frac{v_c^*(0)}{q^*(0)}$ for $t \in [\tilde{t}, \tilde{t} + \max\{q(0), T_s\}]$, where T_s is a given minimum time interval (possibly covering more than one optimal event instants) to prevent out-of-time computation problems due to an excessively small duration $q^*(0)$.

Note that the actual state $\check{x}$ at the end of each control action can be different from the predicted one $x^*(1)$, because of external disturbances and modeling errors. Clearly, the main advantage of the eMPC strategy with respect to open-loop optimal control [7] is its closed-loop nature, since after each predicted event the real state is read or estimated again and a new optimal input sequence is computed from it. In the current event-driven approach also the prediction of the time instants at which events occur can be updated.

4.1   eMPC Example

In this section we present a simple numerical example showing the behavior of the eMPC strategy and its robustness with respect to disturbances. We consider a system having two continuous states x_1 and x_2, and two state thresholds $[e_1^x = 1] \leftrightarrow [x_1 \leq 0]$, $[e_2^x = 1] \leftrightarrow [x_2 \leq 0]$, so that the system has four modes. Each mode corresponds to an orthant of the Cartesian plane, where $i = 1$ corresponds to the positive orthant and the other orthants are numbered clockwise. The system has two inputs $-50 \leq u_1 \leq 50$ and $-50 \leq u_2 \leq 50$, and the vectors and matrices that define Equation (1) for $i = 1, \ldots, 4$ are $f_1 = f_4 = [\begin{smallmatrix} 1 \\ 0 \end{smallmatrix}]$, $f_2 = f_3 = [\begin{smallmatrix} -1 \\ 0 \end{smallmatrix}]$, $B_1 = [\begin{smallmatrix} 0 & 0 \\ 0 & 1.4 \end{smallmatrix}]$, $B_2 = [\begin{smallmatrix} 0 & 0 \\ 0 & 1.5 \end{smallmatrix}]$, $B_3 = [\begin{smallmatrix} 0 & 0 \\ 0 & 1.15 \end{smallmatrix}]$, $B_4 = [\begin{smallmatrix} 1 & 0 \\ 0 & 2.3 \end{smallmatrix}]$. Moreover, there are additional constraints on the inputs: when in mode $i = 1$ it must hold that $u_2 \geq -2$, for $i = 2$ $u_2 \leq -0.5$, for $i = 3$ $u_2 \leq 2$, and for $i = 4$ $u_1 \leq 2$ and $-0.5 \leq u_2 \leq 2$.

We want to bring the state of the system from $x_0 = [\begin{smallmatrix} 0.1 \\ 2 \end{smallmatrix}]$ to $x_f = [\begin{smallmatrix} -1 \\ 3 \end{smallmatrix}]$ while minimizing function (14a), where $p = \infty$, $Q_1 = [\begin{smallmatrix} 10 & 0 \\ 0 & 10 \end{smallmatrix}]$, $Q_2 = [\begin{smallmatrix} 0 & 0 \\ 0 & 0 \end{smallmatrix}]$, $R_1 = [\begin{smallmatrix} 10^{-3} & 10^{-3} \end{smallmatrix}]$, $R_2 = 1$, $\hat{x} = x_f$ and $0.1 \leq q \leq 50$. We have set $\hat{q} = 0.1$, $\hat{v} = u_\infty \hat{q}$, where $u_\infty = [\begin{smallmatrix} -1 \\ 0 \end{smallmatrix}]$. The system is perturbed by input-additive disturbances, so that the continuous state dynamics is $\dot{x}(t) = B_{i(t_k)}\big(u(t_k) + \xi_k\big) + f_{i(t_k)}$, $\forall t \in [t_k, t_{k+1})$, where ξ_k is a sequence of time-uncorrelated stochastic vectors in which each component is independent from the other and uniformly distributed in $[-0.1, 0.1]$.

Figure 2 reports the continuous-time trajectories generated by the eMPC controller with a prediction horizon of 4 events applied for 8 steps. In the undisturbed case (Figure 2(a)) the closed-loop eMPC strategy trajectory coincides with the open-loop optimal one; four control actions, corresponding to four mode switches, are required to bring the system to the target state. In the presence

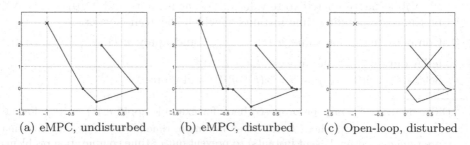

(a) eMPC, undisturbed   (b) eMPC, disturbed   (c) Open-loop, disturbed

Fig. 2. Example, controlled system trajectory

of disturbances (Figure 2(b)) the eMPC is able to counteract them, and to still bring the system close to x_f, even if a larger number of control actions with respect to the undisturbed case is required. The trajectory obtained by the open-loop optimal policy under the effect of the same disturbance realization is reported in Figure 2(c), showing that the effects of the interaction of the disturbance with the switching nature of the system are not negligible.

4.2 Conditions for Convergence of eMPC

We consider the case in which the terminal sets $\mathcal{X}_T$, $\mathcal{T}_T$ are isolated points or polytopes separately.

Definition 1. *A state value* $\bar{x} = \begin{bmatrix} \bar{x}_c \\ \bar{x}_b \end{bmatrix}$ *is an equilibrium point for the icHA in mode* $\bar{\imath}$ *if and only if there exists a steady state input value* $\bar{u}_\infty = \begin{bmatrix} \bar{u}_{c,\infty} \\ \bar{u}_{b,\infty} \end{bmatrix}$ *and* $\bar{e}_\infty$ *such that:*

1. $\bar{e}_\infty = f_{EG}(\bar{x}_c, \bar{u}_{c,\infty}, t)$, $\forall t \geq 0$, *where* f_{EG} *is the event generator (2);*
2. $\bar{x}_b = f_{aFSM}(\bar{x}_b, \bar{u}_{b,\infty}, \bar{e}_\infty)$;
3. $\bar{\imath} = [0, 1, \ldots s] \cdot f_{MS}(\bar{x}_b, \bar{u}_{b,\infty}, \bar{e}_\infty)$;
4. $B_{\bar{\imath}} \bar{u}_{c,\infty} + f_{\bar{\imath}} = 0$.

This definition of equilibrium requires that the input $\bar{u}_\infty$ maintains the continuous state, the discrete state, and the mode constant. Note that the target state x_f in the example of Section 4.1 is an equilibrium point of mode $i = 4$ with steady-state input $u_\infty = \begin{bmatrix} -1 \\ 0 \end{bmatrix}$.

Terminal equality constraint. If the terminal set reduces to a point, Constraint (18) can be written as

$$x(N) = \hat{x}, \qquad t(N) = \hat{t}, \qquad (19)$$

where $\hat{x}$ and $\hat{t}$ are referred to as target state and target time, respectively. As a consequence, the terminal cost can be removed from (15). In the following we denote by $\chi(k) = \begin{bmatrix} x(k) \\ t(k) \end{bmatrix}$ the state of the eMLD system.

Consider an initial state $\chi_0 = \chi(k)$ and solve Problem (14), obtaining the optimal cost $J^*(\chi_0)$, the optimal state trajectory $X^*(\chi_0) = [\chi_1^*(\chi_0) \cdots \chi_N^*(\chi_0)]$ and the optimal input $\mathbf{w}^*(\chi_0) = [w_0^*(\chi_0), \ldots w_{N-1}^*(\chi_0)]$, where $w_i = \begin{bmatrix} v_i \\ q_i \end{bmatrix}$. Let the eMPC control action at step k be $w_{MPC}(k) = w_0^*(\chi_0)$ and let the initial state for the next optimization problem be $\chi_1 = \chi(k+1) = G(\chi_0, w_{MPC}(k))$, where $G(\chi(k), w(k))$ is the state update function (13).

Theorem 1. *Let* $\underline{q} = 0$ *in (17),* $\hat{x}$ *be an equilibrium point with steady-state input* $\bar{u}_\infty$, $\hat{q} = 0$, $\hat{v} = \begin{bmatrix} 0 \\ \bar{u}_{b,\infty} \end{bmatrix}$, *and* Q_1, Q_2, R_1, R_2 *full rank. If Problem (14) is feasible for* $x_0 = x(k)$, $t_0 = t(k)$, *then it is feasible for* $x_0 = x_1^*(x(k))$, $t_0 = t_1^*(x(k))$ *and the state and time converge to the target state* $\hat{x}$ *and target time* $\hat{t}$, *respectively, as the number of events tends to infinity.*

Proof. Let $\chi_1 = \chi_1^*(\chi(k))$. The input sequence $\tilde{\mathbf{w}}(\chi_1) = [w_1^*(\chi_0), \ldots w_{N-1}^*(\chi_0),$ $\begin{bmatrix} 0 \\ \bar{u}_{b,\infty} \\ 0 \end{bmatrix}]$ obtained by shifting $\mathbf{w}^*(\chi_0)$ to the left is feasible for Problem (14), when χ_0 is replaced by χ_1. Then $\chi_i(\chi_1) = \chi_{i+1}(\chi_0)$ for $i = 0, \ldots, N-1$ and $\chi_N(\chi_1) = G\left(\chi_{N-1}^*(\chi_1), \begin{bmatrix} 0 \\ \bar{u}_{b,\infty} \\ 0 \end{bmatrix}\right)$ is equal to $\chi_{N-1}(\chi_1) = \chi_N(\chi_0)$. Thus, the dynamics and the operating constraints are satisfied at $\chi_N(\chi_1)$ and the sequence $\tilde{\mathbf{w}}(\chi_1)$ satisfies the constraints in (14).

Next, we show that the sequence of cost values is decreasing by applying the same approach of [6]. Because of optimality, $J^*(\chi_1) \leq J(\chi_1, \tilde{\mathbf{w}}(\chi_1))$, where

$$J(\chi_1, \tilde{\mathbf{w}}(\chi_1)) = J^*(\chi_0) - L(x(0), t(0), v(0), q(0)), \tag{20}$$

and hence $J^*(\chi_1) \leq J^*(\chi_0)$. Since $J(\chi(k))$ is lower bounded by 0 and the sequence is not increasing, $\lim_{k \to \infty} J(\chi(k)) = J_\infty$, so that $\lim_{k \to \infty} J(\chi(k+1)) - J(\chi(k)) = 0$, implying that $\lim_{k \to \infty} x(k) = \hat{x}$, $\lim_{k \to \infty} v(k) = \hat{v}$, $\lim_{k \to \infty} q(k) = 0$, $\lim_{k \to \infty} t(k) = \hat{t}$. □

Note that convergence is asymptotic with respect to the number of events, but nonetheless the state converges to the target state $\hat{x}$ in the finite time $\hat{t}$. In the more common case of $t(N)$ unconstrained and $Q_2 = 0$, $\lim_{k \to \infty} x(k) = \hat{x}$ but it is possible that $\lim_{k \to \infty} t(k) = \infty$, thus having time-asymptotic convergence; the proof follows directly from the previous one.

Remark 2. When q_0^* is very small the time required for solving the next optimization problem may be insufficient An approach to avoid $q(k) \to 0$ is to set $\hat{q} = q_\infty > 0$, $Q_2 = 0$, $\hat{v} = 0$ and $R_1 = 0$. In this way, if a steady state input $\bar{u}_\infty$ exists, eventually unknown, then $w_{MPC}(k) = \begin{bmatrix} \bar{u}_{c,\infty} q_\infty \\ \bar{u}_{b,\infty} \\ q_\infty \end{bmatrix}$ when $x(k) = \hat{x}$, which has zero cost. It must be noted that solutions in which $q(k) = 0$ are still feasible, but not optimal.

Next, we consider the case $\underline{q} > 0$ in (17), that ensures a minimum dwell time.

Theorem 2. *Let $\bar{u}_\infty$ be the steady-state input corresponding to the equilibrium point $\hat{x}$, let $\hat{v} = \begin{bmatrix} \bar{u}_{c,\infty} \hat{q} \\ \bar{u}_{b,\infty} \end{bmatrix}$ and $\underline{q} \leq \hat{q} \leq \bar{q}$. Let $Q_2 = 0$ and $t(N)$ be unconstrained. If Problem (14) is feasible for $\chi_0 = \chi(k)$, it is also feasible for $\chi(0) = \chi_1 = G(\chi_0, w_{MPC}(k))$ and the state converges to $\hat{x}$.*

Proof. Let $\mathbf{w}^*(\chi_0)$ be the optimal input sequence of the problem with initial state χ_0. Then $\tilde{\mathbf{w}}(\chi_1) = [w_1^*(\chi_0), \ldots w_{N-1}^*(\chi_0), [\begin{smallmatrix} \hat{v} \\ \hat{q} \end{smallmatrix}]]$ is feasible since $x(N+1) = x(N) = \hat{x}$, while fulfilling also all the other constraints. Furthermore, (20) holds and convergence is ensured. □

Note that the eMPC controller in the example of Section 4.1 was designed basing on the hypotheses of Theorem 2.

Remark 3. When the constraint $q \geq \underline{q} > 0$ is added, the optimal control problem might become unfeasible. A sufficient condition for feasibility is that $\forall i$, $\exists \bar{u}_i$ that satisfies the constraints of mode i and verifies $B_i \bar{u}_i + f_i = 0$. Such condition ensures the existence of an input that blocks the system state in each mode.

Terminal cost and terminal set. The terminal constraints are defined by

$$Sx(N) \leq M, \quad S_T t(N) \leq M_T, \tag{21}$$

where S is a suitable matrix and M, S_T, M_T are suitable vectors. For the sake of simplicity, we discuss the case in which the target time is not constrained nor weighted (thus S_T, M_T are empty and $Q_2 = 0$), $\hat{x} = 0$ and $\hat{v} = 0$, and the icHA system is time invariant (i.e. conditions in (2) do not depend on t), so that we can disregard the eMLD additional state t (the extensions are straightforward). We assume that there are no Boolean inputs, and that in a neighborhood of the origin the mode i is such that $f_i = 0$ in (1) and the discrete state is constantly $x_b = [0 \ldots 0]^T$. The last two conditions ensure that the translation of the eMLD yields an equivalent piecewise affine (PWA) model [12] that is linear in a neighborhood of the origin. We use here the results of [13] for convergence of MPC in discrete-time.

Let $\mathcal{X}_T$ be the polytope $\{x : Sx \leq M\}$, $W(x) = \{V(x) \times Q\}$ be the set of feasible solutions $w_0^*(x) = \begin{bmatrix} v_0^*(x) \\ q_0^*(x) \end{bmatrix}$ to Problem (14) when $x_0 = x$, and consider an auxiliary state-feedback controller

$$\tilde{w}(k) = h\big(x(k)\big). \tag{22}$$

The results on [13] ensure that if (i) $h\big(x(k)\big) \in W(x) \; \forall x \in \mathcal{X}_T$, (ii) $\mathcal{X}_T$ is a positively invariant set for system (13) in closed loop with (22), and (iii) the inequality

$$F(G(x(k), h(x(k)))) - F(x(k)) + L(x(k), h(x(k))) \leq 0, \tag{23}$$

is satisfied, then if Problem (14) is feasible at step k, it is feasible at step $k+1$ and the state converges asymptotically to the target state.

The problem reduces to computing the auxiliary controller, that for the event-driven approach of this paper has the structure

$$w(x) = \begin{bmatrix} v(x) \\ q(x) \end{bmatrix} = \begin{bmatrix} f_1(x(k)) \\ f_2(x(k)) \end{bmatrix}. \tag{24}$$

Consider the discrete-time system Σ_d with sampling time T_s described by equations (13a), (13c) in which $q(k) = T_s$ and the index k represents the sampling step counter. Let $J_d(x, v) = F_d(x(N)) + \sum_{k=0}^{N-1} L_d(x(k), v(k))$ be the cost function, where $L_d(x(k), v_c(k)) = \|x_c(k) - \hat{x}\|_p^{Q_1} + \|v_c(k) - \hat{v}\|_p^{R_1}$, $F_d(x(N)) = F(x(N))$, and $h_d(x(k))$ be an auxiliary piecewise linear (PWL) state-feedback controller. The decreasing cost condition of [13] for asymptotic stability is

$$F_d(G_d(x(k), h_d(x(k)))) - F_d(x(k)) + L_d(x(k), h_d(x(k))) \leq 0. \tag{25}$$

The following proposition shows that the auxiliary controller for Σ_d allows proving convergence of the event-driven system.

Proposition 1. *Let T_s be such that $\underline{q} \leq T_s \leq \overline{q}$, $\hat{q} = T_s$, $Q_2 = 0$ and $h_d(x(k))$ be a discrete-time PWL controller with sampling time T_s, such that $h_d(x) \in V(x) \; \forall x \in \mathcal{X}_T$. Let $\mathcal{X}_T$ be a positively invariant set for system Σ_d in closed-loop with $h_d(x)$, and (25) be satisfied. Then $x(k) \rightarrow 0$ for $k \rightarrow \infty$.*

Proof. System (13a), (13c), when $q(k) = T_s$ is a discrete-time MLD system of the form $x((k+1)T_s) = G_d(x(kT_s), v(kT_s))$ for which an equivalent PWA system can be computed [12]. Since we have supposed that in a neighborhood of the origin the continuous-time system has no affine terms and that the Boolean state is $[0, \ldots, 0]$, also the discrete-time PWA system is linear in such a region and the results of [13] hold. The discrete-time controller is equivalent to an event-driven controller that raises an event every T_s time units. Then the controller $w(k) = h(x(k)) = \begin{bmatrix} \frac{h_d(x(k))}{T_s} \end{bmatrix}$ is an auxiliary event-driven controller for system (13) that respects condition (23), since (23) is equal to (25) because of the chosen cost function ($\hat{q} = T_s$, $Q_2 = 0$).

Thus $h(x(k))$ is a state-feedback controller that respect hypotheses of [13] for system (13) interpreted as discrete-time systems, proving convergence of $x(k) \rightarrow 0$ as $k \rightarrow \infty$. $\qquad\square$

Proposition 1 ensures that if a discrete-time PWL controller respecting the hypotheses of [13] exists, for instance computed as in [14], then the eMPC controller is converging. The sampling time of the auxiliary controller is used to compute a valid $\mathcal{X}_T$ and can be changed in the design phase, without changing anything in the event-driven system but the parameter $\hat{q}$. In order to relax the assumption $x_b = [0, \ldots, 0]^T$, one may require convergence only for the continuous state as in [15], thus without weighting x_b in the cost function.

5   Event-Based Verification of icHA

In Section 4 we have exploited the icHA and its discrete-event reformulation for MPC design. However, this model can be conveniently exploited also for verification of safety and liveness properties. The main advantage of the event-based approach is that verification queries, whenever their negation can be formulated as a combination of linear and logical constraints, can be posed as feasibility problems of mixed-integer programs

$$\min_{q,v} \; 0$$

$$\begin{aligned}
\text{s.t.} \quad & \text{system dynamics (13)} & \text{(26a)} \\
& g(x, t, q, v) \leq 0, & \text{(26b)} \\
& x(0) \in \mathcal{X}_0, \quad t(0) \in \mathcal{T}_0. & \text{(26c)} \\
& H(x(N), t(N)) \leq 0 & \text{(26d)}
\end{aligned}$$

where (26a) and (26b) are the same as in (14), (26c) defines the set of possible initial states and (26d) is the region in which the query to be verified is false and it is enforced on the system's final state. Note that since we are considering mixed integer programming, $H()$ can be any combination of linear and logical constraints and $\mathcal{X}_0$, $\mathcal{T}_0$ can be any union of polyhedra. The event-horizon on which the property is verified is defined by the constant N. If Problem (26) admits a feasible solution, then there exists a trajectory departing from a valid initial state that violates the query to be verified, thus, the query is false. Note that if $q = 0$, (26d) ensures safety $\forall k = 1, \ldots, N$, even if it is formulated only with respect to the Nth step. In fact, if a feasible solution to Problem (26) for a horizon $k < N$ exists, then a feasible solution of (26) also exists, by extending the solution on k steps by "fictitious" events separated by $q = 0$ time units. Thus, the infeasibility implies that at any event instant constraint (26d) is unsatisfied. This implies also the safety of the whole trajectory, since trajectories are piecewise-linear because of the integral dynamics [7]. An intuitive explanation of this property is the following. In order to reach an interior point of the unsafe region, one of the thresholds delimiting such a region must be crossed. However, every time a threshold is crossed an event occurs and the state at such instant is inside the new region. If no state values at the event instants reside in the unsafe region, then the thresholds delimiting such a region cannot have been crossed. Note that if this approach is applied to standard discrete-time models, the infeasibility of the mixed-integer program would only ensure safety at sampling instants.

It is easy to recognize similarities between the icHA and the Linear Hybrid Automaton (LHA) [1,10], a model which has been widely exploited for verification of hybrid systems [10]. The LHA considers discrete and continuous states, the continuous dynamics are defined by discrete state dependent differential inclusions in the form $\sum_i a_i^j \dot{x}_i \in [b^j, c^j]$, where j is the discrete state index, i is the continuous state index, a_i^j, b^j, c^j are constants and x_i are the continuous state variables. The discrete states have associated invariant sets, defined by linear constraints over continuous state variables, the discrete state transitions are enabled by linear conditions over continuous state variables and after each of them the continuous state can be reset. The discrete state dynamics are defined by an aFSM with resets in both models, and the equations of the continuous dynamics switch according to the discrete state. For any given discrete state, all admissible continuous state trajectories of an LHA can be produced by an icHA by a proper selection of the input functions $u \in \mathcal{PC}$ and, viceversa, all icHA trajectories can be generated by an LHA by appropriately choosing the ranges of the differential inclusion. For instance, the dynamics $a \leq \dot{x}(t) + \dot{y}(t) \leq b$ can be modeled as $\dot{x} = u_1(t)$, $\dot{y} = u_2(t)$ along with $a \leq u_1(t) + u_2(t) \leq b$. The discrete state transitions of icHA are deterministic, those of LHA are not. However, in an icHA the non-determinism can be modeled by adding external signals $\eta(k)$[3] in (13). For instance, a transition of an LHA that can be fired whenever $a \leq x(t) \leq b$ can be modeled by adding the input $-\frac{b-a}{2} \leq \eta(k) \leq \frac{b-a}{2}$ and by setting the transition to occur when $x(k) + \eta(k) = \frac{b+a}{2}$.

---

[3] $\eta(k)$ is added in (13) as an additional component of $v(k)$.

The practical consequence of the similarities between LHA and icHA is that many systems that are modeled as LHA can be modeled also as icHA and verified by solving problem (26) by mixed integer programming, for which efficient algorithms and tools exist. A formal proof of equivalence between subclasses of LHA and of icHA is currently under study, and it is beyond the scope of this paper.

5.1   Verification Example

Consider the "train-gate" system [10], with small modifications. The system consists of a train that must safely cross a gate, meaning that when the train is crossing the gate, this must be closed. The gate can be *idle (I)*, *closing (Cl)*, *closed (C)* or *opening (O)*. A train can be *arriving (Ar)*, *crossing (Cr)*, *leaving (L)* or *far (F)*, depending on its position with respect to the gate. The corresponding automata with continuous-time differential inclusions are reported in Figure 3, where x is the train position and y is the gate position. Note that the signal *app* forces a transition in which x is reset. We performed the tests on a Pentium IV-M 2 GHz, equipped with 1 GB Ram, running MATLAB 6.5 and CPLEX 9.0.

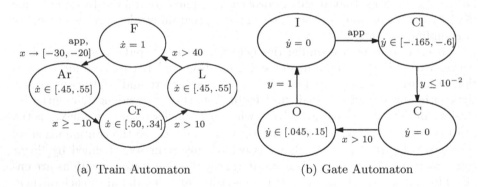

(a) Train Automaton   (b) Gate Automaton

Fig. 3. Train-Gate system

The system is modeled as an icHA and converted to eMLD form. Let the initial state be (x_0, y_0), where $x_0 \in [-25, -20]$ and $y_0 = 1$, and (Ar,Cl) as discrete state, and the query be: *"Does the system always stay out of the unsafe state (Cr, Cl)?"*. Problem (26) is solved for $N = 6$ proving its infeasibility, meaning that an unsafe trajectory does not exist. The computation required 0.984 seconds. If the differential inclusion in state Cl is changed to $\dot{y} = [-0.145, -0.4]$ a solution is found, meaning that the gate is closing too slowly.

Another query that can be verified is the following: *"Does the train always reach the state F in less than 100 time units, when departing from x_0?"*. The answer is no, since there exists a feasible solution to problem (26) in which (26d) is $x \leq 40$ and $-t \leq -100$. This query was tested in 0.312 seconds. Differently from the previous one, this query involves the capability of the system to reach its objective, thus it is related to the system liveness.

6   Conclusions

In this paper we have shown how to obtain an event-driven representation of an integral continuous-time hybrid automaton and we have analyzed model predictive control and verification schemes for such systems. The main advantage is that a continuous-time hybrid system can be analyzed as a discretely evolving one, so that MIP techniques can be exploited for computing the eMPC control action and for verification of safety properties. In addition, a lighter computational burden may result with respect to the discrete-time approach.

References

1. Henzinger, T.A.: The theory of hybrid automata. In: Proceedings of the 11th Annual IEEE Symposium on Logic in Computer Science, New Brunswick, New Jersey (1996) 278–292
2. Lygeros, J., Johansson, K.H., Simic, S.N., Zhang, J., Sastry, S.: Dynamical properties of hybrid automata. IEEE Tr. Automatic Control **48** (2003) 2–17
3. Gokbayrak, K., Cassandras, C.: Hybrid controllers for hierarchically decomposed systems. In Krogh, B., Lynch, N., eds.: Hybrid Systems: Computation and Control. Springer-Verlag (2000) 117–129
4. Shaikh, M.S., Caines, P.E.: On the optimal control of hybrid systems: Optimization of trajectories, switching times, and location schedules. In: Hybrid Systems: Computation and Control, Springer-Verlag (2003) 466–481
5. Xu, X., Antsaklis, P.J.: Results and perspectives on computational methods for optimal control of switched systems. In: Hybrid Systems: Computation and Control, Springer-Verlag (2003) 540–555
6. Bemporad, A., Morari, M.: Control of systems integrating logic, dynamics, and constraints. Automatica **35**(3) (1999) 407–427
7. Bemporad, A., Di Cairano, S., Júlvez, J.: Event-driven optimal control of integral continuous-time hybrid automata. In: Proc. 44th IEEE Conf. on Decision and Control, Seville, Spain (2005) 1409–1414
8. Maciejowski, J.: Predictive control with constraints. Englewood Cliffs, NJ: Prentice Hall. (2002)
9. Qin, S., Badgwell, T.: A survey of industrial model predictive control technology. Control Engineering Practice **11** (2003) 733–764
10. Henzinger, T.A., Ho, P.H., Wong-Toi, H.: HyTech: A model checker for hybrid systems. Int. J. on Software Tools for Technology Transfer **1**(1–2) (1997) 110–122
11. Torrisi, F.D., Bemporad, A.: HYSDEL — A tool for generating computational hybrid models. IEEE Tr. Contr. Systems Technology **12**(2) (2004) 235–249
12. Bemporad, A.: Efficient conversion of mixed logical dynamical systems into equivalent piecewise affine form. IEEE Tr. Automatic Control **49**(5) (2004) 832–838
13. Lazar, M., Heemels, W., Weiland, S., Bemporad, A.: Stability of hybrid model predictive control. In: Proc. of Int. Workshop on Assessment and Future Directions of NMPC, Germany (2005)
14. Lazar, M., Heemels, W., Weiland, S., Bemporad, A.: Stability of hybrid model predictive control. In: Proc. 43th IEEE Conf. on Decision and Control, Paradise Island, Bahamas (2004) 4595–4560
15. Ferrari-Trecate, G., Cuzzola, F.A., Morari, M.: Lagrange stability and performance analysis of discrete-time piecewise affine systems with logic states. Int. J. Control **76**(16) (2003) 1585–1598

Improving Efficiency of Finite Plans by Optimal Choice of Input Sets

Antonio Bicchi[1], Alessia Marigo[2], and Benedetto Piccoli[3]

[1] Interdepartmental Research Center "Enrico Piaggio", University of Pisa, Italy
[2] Department of Mathematics, Università di Roma - La Sapienza, Rome, Italy
[3] C.N.R. Istituto per le Applicazioni del Calcolo "E. Picone", Rome, Italy

Abstract. Finite plans proved to be an efficient method to steer complex control systems via feedback quantization. Such finite plans can be encoded by finite–length words constructed on suitable alphabets, thus permitting transmission on limited capacity channels. In particular flat systems can be steered computing arbitrarily close approximations of a desired equilibrium in polynomial time.

The paper investigates how the efficiency of planning is affected by the choice of inputs, and provides some results as to optimal performance in terms of accuracy and range. Efficiency is here measured in terms of computational complexity and description length (in number of bits) of finite plans.

1 Introduction

Consider the problem of planning inputs to efficiently steer a controllable dynamical system of the type

$$\dot{x} = f(x, u), \ x \in X \subseteq \mathbb{R}^n, u \in U \subset \mathbb{R}^r \tag{1}$$

between neighborhoods of given initial and final equilibria. By any approximation procedure, one may achieve finite plans (for specific choice of initial and finite states). However, we aim at designing finite plans, among equilibria of the system, with short description length (measured in bits) and low computational complexity.

Concerns about the complexity of describing plans show up whenever communication or storage limitations are in place. Particularly fitting to this perspective are examples from robotics, where input symbols may represent commands (aka *behaviors*, or *modes*.) For instance, for autonomous mobile rovers, high level plans may be comprised of sequences of motion primitives such as `wander`, `look_for`, `avoid_wall`, etc.; in the control of humanoids (see e.g. [17]), symbols are encountered such as `walk`, `run`, `stop`, `squat`, etc.. To deal with real implementations, such languages must be able to encode the richest variety of tasks by words of the shortest length. Consider for instance the case where the robotic agent receives its reference plans from a remote high-level control center through a finite capacity communication channel, or plans are exchanged in a

João Hespanha and A. Tiwari (Eds.): HSCC 2006, LNCS 3927, pp. 108–122, 2006.

networked system of a large number of simple semi-autonomous agents. In general, it can be assumed that robots are capable of accepting finitely-described reference signals, and can implement a finite number of possible different feedback strategies via the use of embedded controllers, according to the received messages.

Finite plans steering was considered by many authors in recent years, e.g. [15, 9, 12]. A general framework was proposed by introducing Motion Description Languages in [4]. The line of research addressing finite hyerarchic abstractions of continuous systems via bi-simulations ([21, 22, 20]) has several contact points with the one presented in this paper. Of direct relevance to work presented here is the quantitative analysis of the specification complexity of input sequences for a class of automata, presented in [10]. The key result there is that feedback can substantially reduce the specification complexity (i.e., the description length of the shortest admissible plan) to reach a certain goal state.

In this paper we treat the more complex case of controlled dynamical systems and, by introducing *control encoding* of a symbolic input language, we can compute in polynomial time plans for flat systems, whose specification complexity is logarithmic in the size of the region to be covered. In our context, we postulate that control decoders are available and embedded on the remotely controlled plant. Decoders receive symbols from the planner, and translate them in suitable control actions, possibly based on locally available state information.

The result is obtained following this reasoning. First we seek for a symbolic encoding so that there exists a sublanguage, whose action on the system has the desirable properties of additive groups, i.e. the actions of control words are invertible and commute. Furthermore, under the action of words in this language, the reachable set becomes a lattice. More precisely, a suitable (dynamic) feedback encoding permits us to transform any flat system to:

$$z^+ = z + \bar{H}\mu, \quad \bar{H} \in \mathbb{R}^{n \times n}, \ \mu \in \mathbb{Z}^n. \tag{2}$$

Once reduced to this special form, we address the problem of optimally choosing finite input sets in order to optimize the efficiency of plans. This objective is achieved by the study on the minimal specification complexity for interval-filling controls, derived from concurrent work of number-theoretic nature.

The effectiveness of the method is illustrate by Proposition 4.

1.1   Problem Description

Assume that system (1) is completely controllable, i.e. for any given two points x_0, x_f, a *plan* (i.e., a finite-support input function $u : [t, T + t] \to U$) exists that steers (1) from x_0 to x_f. An exact plan among initial and final point would generically require an infinite–length description, thus we consider approximate steering and address the following question:

Problem Π: Given a compact subset $\mathcal{M} \subseteq X$ and a tolerance ε, provide a specification P of plans such that, for every pair $(x_0, x_f) \in \mathcal{M}^2$, it exists a plan in P steering the system (1) from x_0 to within an ε-neighborhood of x_f.

We look for an *efficient* solution to this problem, where efficiency is intended in terms of low computational complexity, i.e. minimal number of elementary computations to be executed, and in terms of low specification complexity, i.e. minimal number of bits necessary to represent the plan (cf. [10]).

2   Encoding Control Quanta

Symbolic control is inherently related to the definition of elementary control events, or atoms, or *quanta*:

Definition 1. *A control quantum is a couple* (u, T) *where* $u : X \to L^\infty(\mathbb{R}^+ \times X, U)$ *and* $T : X \to \mathbb{R}^+$. *The set of control quanta is denoted by* $\widetilde{\mathcal{U}}$.

Hence, a control quantum is essentially a feedback that is applied to the system, starting at point x_0 at time t_0, until time $t_0 + T(x_0)$. To each control quantum it is natural to associate the map $\phi_{(u,T)} : X \to X$, where $\phi_{(u,T)}(x_0)$ is the solution at time $T(x_0)$ of the Cauchy problem corresponding to initial data x_0 and control $u(x_0)$.

Definition 2. *A control quantization consists in assigning a finite set* $\mathcal{U} \subset \widetilde{\mathcal{U}}$. *A (symbolic) control encoding on a control quantization is a map* $E : \Sigma \to \mathcal{U}$, *where* $\Sigma = \{\sigma_1, \sigma_2, \ldots\}$ *is a finite set of symbols.*

Given a control quantization and an encoder, we have the diagram $\Sigma \xrightarrow{E} \mathcal{U} \xrightarrow{\phi} \mathcal{D}(X)$, where $\mathcal{D}(X)$ denotes the group of automorphisms on X. This can be extended in an obvious way to $\Sigma^* \xrightarrow{E^*} \mathcal{U}^* \xrightarrow{\phi^*} \mathcal{D}(X)$, where Σ^* is the set of words formed with letters from the alphabet Σ, including the empty string ϵ. We assume $\phi \circ E(\epsilon) = Id(X)$, i.e. the identity map in $\mathcal{D}(X)$. An action of the monoid Σ^* on X is thus defined. In general, being the action of Σ^* just a monoid, the analysis of its action on the state space can be quite hard, and the structure of the reachable set under generic quantized controls can be very intricated (even for linear systems: see e.g. [1, 6, 2]). However, we will show that, appropriately choosing the quantization, for every flat system it is possible to find a sub-language Ω of Σ^* acting on $\mathbb{R}^n$ as $\mathbb{Z}^n$. Therefore, in suitable state and input coordinates, the system takes the form (2).

To reach the desired special form (2), we focus our attention on designing encodings that achieve simple composition rules for the action of words in a sublanguage $\Omega \subset \Sigma^*$:

$$\forall \omega \in \Omega, \exists h(\omega) \in \mathbb{R}^n : \forall x \in X, (\phi^* \circ E^*(\omega))(x) = x + h(\omega), \qquad (3)$$

and

$$\forall \omega_1 \in \Omega, \exists \bar{\omega}_1 \in \Omega : (\phi^* \circ E^*(\omega_1)) \circ (\phi^* \circ E^*(\bar{\omega}_1)) = Id(X). \qquad (4)$$

The additivity rule (3) implies that actions commute, therefore, the global action is independent from the order of application of control words in Ω. Moreover we have the following:

Proposition 1. *Under rules (3), (4), there exists a sublanguage $\Omega' \subset \Omega$ such that the corresponding reachable sets are lattices.*

Proof. First notice that, by rules (3) and (4), Ω acts on the states as an additive group. As a consequence, the reachable set from any point in X under the concatenation of words in Ω is a set Λ generated by vectors $h(\omega), \omega \in \Omega$,

$$\Lambda = \{h(\omega_1)\lambda_1 + \cdots + h(\omega_N)\lambda_N | \lambda_i \in \mathbf{Z}, N \in \mathbb{N}\}.$$

If $h(\omega) \in \mathbf{Q}^n$, $\forall \omega \in \Omega$, then we can choose $\Omega' = \Omega$. Otherwise, we choose Ω' to consist of concatenations of only n words in Σ^* which produce independent vectors $h(\omega)$.

A further important concern is that system (1) under symbolic control, maintains the possibility of approximating arbitrarily well all reachable equilibria in its state space, for suitable choices of symbols.

Definition 3. *A control system $\dot{x} = f(x, u)$ is additively (or lattice) approachable if, for every $\varepsilon > 0$, there exist a control quantization $\mathcal{U}_\varepsilon$ and an encoding $E^* : \Omega \mapsto \mathcal{U}_\varepsilon^*$ with $card(\mathcal{U}_\varepsilon) = q \in \mathbb{N}$, such that: i) the action of Ω obeys (3), (4), and ii) for every $x_0, x_f \in X$, there exists x in the Ω-orbit of x_0 with $\|x - x_f\| < \varepsilon$.*

Remark 1. The reachable set being a lattice under quantization does not imply additive approachability. For instance, consider the example used in [14] to illustrate the so-called kinodynamic planning method. This consists of a double integrator $\ddot{q} = u$ with piecewise constant encoding $\mathcal{U} = \{u_0 = 0, u_1 = 1, u_2 = -1\}$ on intervals of fixed length $T = 1$. The sampled system reads

$$q^+ = q + \dot{q} + \frac{u}{2}, \qquad \dot{q}^+ = \dot{q} + u,$$

hence $q(N) = q(0) + N\dot{q}(0) + \sum_{i=1}^{N} \frac{2(N-i)+1}{2} u(i)$, $\dot{q}(N) = \dot{q}(0) + \sum_{i=1}^{N} u(i)$. The reachable set from $q(0) = \dot{q}(0) = 0$ is

$$R(\mathcal{U}, 0) = \left\{ \begin{bmatrix} q \\ \dot{q} \end{bmatrix} = \begin{bmatrix} \frac{1}{2} & 0 \\ 0 & 1 \end{bmatrix} \lambda, \lambda \in \mathbf{Z}^2 \right\}.$$

The quantization thus induces a lattice structure on the reachable set. The lattice mesh can be reduced to any desired ε resolution by scaling U or T. However, the actions of control quanta do not compose according to rule (3): indeed, $\phi^*(u_1 u_2) \neq \phi^*(u_2 u_1)$ (for instance, $\phi^*(u_1 u_2)(0, 0) = (1, 0)$, while $\phi^*(u_2 u_1)(0, 0) = (-1, 0)$).

The following theorem motivates the interest in seeking control encodings for additive approachability, moreover Theorem 3 below shows the applicability of the method.

Theorem 1. *For an additively approachable system, a specification P for problem Π can be given in polynomial time.*

Proof. Consider a feedback encoding ensuring additive approachability. Arrange a sufficient number q of action vectors $h(\omega_i)$, $\omega_i \in \Omega$ in the columns of a matrix $H \in \mathbb{R}^{n \times q}$. The reachable set from x_0 is thus a lattice $x_0 + \Lambda$, where $\Lambda = \{H\lambda | \lambda \in \mathbb{Z}^q\}$. Additive approachability guarantees that the dispersion of Λ can be bounded by $\frac{1}{2}\varepsilon$, hence, $\forall x_f$, $\exists y \in \Lambda : \|x_f - x_0 - y\| \leq \varepsilon$. Finding a plan to x_f is thus reduced to solving the system of diophantine equations

$$y = H\lambda. \tag{5}$$

Each lattice coordinate λ_i represent directly the number of times the control word ω_i, hence the corresponding sequence of control quanta, is to be used to reach the goal. Due to additivity of the action, the order of application of the ω_i is ininfluent. The linear integer programming problem (5) can be solved in polynomial time with respect to the state space dimension n and p. Indeed, write H in Hermite normal form, $H = [L\ 0]\ U$, where $L \in \mathbb{R}^{n \times n}$ is a nonnegative, lower triangular, nonsingular matrix, and $U \in \mathbb{Q}^{m \times m}$ is unimodular (i.e., obtained from the identity matrix through elementary column operations). Once the Hermite normal form of H has been computed (which can be done off-line in polynomial time [18, 23]), all possible plans to reach any desired configuration y are easily obtained as $\lambda = U^{-1}[L^{-1}y, \mu]$, $\forall \mu \in \mathbb{Z}^{m-n}$.

2.1   Reducing the Specification Complexity

We now address the specification complexity for problem Π for a system in form (2). Without loss of generality to the purposes of this section, we can set the tolerance $\varepsilon = 1$ and assume $\bar{H} = Id$, thus reducing to system

$$z^+ = z + u. \tag{6}$$

This system can be treated componentwise, hence it will be sufficient to consider (6) with $z \in \mathbb{R}$. To deal with problem Π we introduce the following problems. Consider system (6) and fix integers $m > 0$, $N > 0$ and $M > 0$. Our aim is to study, for every integer control set $W = \{0, \pm v_1, \ldots, \pm v_m\}$, the reachable set $R(0, N)$ from the origin in N steps . More precisely we want to determine the maximal M such that the interval of integers $I(M) = [-M, -M+1, \ldots, M] \subset \mathbb{Z}$ is contained in $R(0, N)$.

We can thus state three significant problems:

Problem 1. Given a fixed number m and a symmetric interval of integers $I(M)$, find the minimal number N of steps and the set of $2m+1$ control values to completely fill $I(M)$ in at most N steps.

Problem 2. Given a fixed number N of steps and a symmetric interval of integers $I(M)$, find the minimal m such that there exists a control set with $2m+1$ elements which completely fills $I(M)$ in at most N steps.

Problem 3. Given a fixed number m and N of steps, find the optimal choice of $2m+1$ control values to completely fill a maximal symmetric interval of integers $I(M)$ in at most N step.

Notice that each problem is obtained fixing two of the three parameters m, N and M and optimizing over the other two. To treat Problem Π, Problems 1 and 2 are relevant: in both cases M is fixed and the optimization reduces the specification complexity. However, it is exactly Problem 3 which is mostly treatable. Thus we now focus on Problem 3 and, later, derive some information on Problems 1 and 2 from the solution of Problem 3.

Problem 3 is a number theoretical problem, related but not equivalent to the well-known "Frobenius postage stamp problem". More precisely, the postage problem seeks to maximize the minimum postage fee not realizable using stamps from a finite set of m possible denominations. For the classical postage problem, only results for small values of m are known, see [13]. The main difference with Problem 3 is the positivity of stamp denominations, while control values from $\mathcal{W}$ are also negative. Although this difference has substantial technical implications, the difficulty of the two problems is comparable.

Problem 3 was first studied in [5], then solved for $m = 2, 3, 4$ and any N in [7], where a general asymptotic formula was conjectured for every m. We report here the explicit formulae for the optimal choice of controls for $m = 2, 3$. For $m = 2$ we simply obtain $v_1 = N$ and $v_2 = N + 1$. For $m = 3$ we get:

$$
v_3 = \begin{cases} N^2/4 + 3/2\,N + 5/4 & \text{if } N \text{ is odd} \\ N^2/4 + 3/2\,N + 1 & \text{if } N \text{ is even,} \end{cases}
$$

$$
v_2 = v_3 - 1,
$$

$$
v_1 = \begin{cases} v_3 - \frac{N+1}{2} - 1 & \text{if } N \text{ is odd} \\ v_3 - \frac{N}{2} - 2 & \text{if } N \text{ is even.} \end{cases}
$$

Table 1 reports the maximum interval of the horizontal line which can be covered with unit resolution and different word lengths N, along with the actual values of the different control sets, for $m = 3$ and $m = 4$.

Table 1. Optimal interval-filling input values for system (6) for $m = 3$ (above) and $m = 4$ (below)

N	1	2	3	4	5	6	7
v_1	1	3	5	8	11	15	19
v_2	2	4	7	10	14	18	23
v_3	3	5	8	11	15	19	24
M	3	10	24	44	75	114	168

N	1	2	3	4	5	6	7
v_1	1	3	7	13	19	29	41
v_2	2	6	9	18	27	36	52
v_3	3	7	11	20	29	39	55
v_4	4	8	12	21	30	40	56
M	4	16	36	84	150	240	392

For $m = 2, 3, 4$ and $N >> m$, for the largest value in $\mathcal{W}$ it holds asymptotically $v_m \sim (\frac{N}{m-1})^{(m-1)}$. Given $2m+1$ controls one can thus reach in N steps a region of size

$$M \sim N^m / m^m. \tag{7}$$

In [7], it is conjectured that (7) holds for every m.

Consider now again Problem 1. In this case m and M are fixed. From (7), we know that we can cover $I(M)$, taking the $2m + 1$ optimal control values for Problem 3, in

$$N \sim m M^{\frac{1}{m}} \tag{8}$$

steps. This gives an approximate solution to Problem 1.

On the other hand, for Problem 2 (now N and M are fixed), taking the $2m+1$ optimal control values for Problem 3, we can cover $I(M)$ in N steps using $2m+1$ controls where

$$m \sim \frac{N}{M^{\frac{1}{m}}}. \tag{9}$$

Again this gives an approximate solution to Problem 2.

To efficiently solve Problem Π we need to reduce the specification complexity of finite plans. In order to achieve that we may either use the solution to Problem 1 or to Problem 2 In both cases, to describe plans covering the region of size M, a sequence of length N of symbols from an alphabet of size $2m + 1$ should be given. This results on a specification complexity of $N \lceil \log_2(2m + 1) \rceil$. Therefore we immediately get the following:

Proposition 2. *Using the (approximate) solutions to Problems 1 and 2, we can cover the region $I(M)$ by finite plans with specification complexities asymptotically given by (respectively):*

$$m M^{\frac{1}{m}} \lceil \log_2(2m + 1) \rceil, \tag{10}$$

$$N \left\lceil \log_2(\frac{2N}{M^{\frac{1}{m}}} + 1) \right\rceil \tag{11}$$

Clearly the two expressions (10) and (11) have the same asymptotic behavior (for $M \to \infty$), thus we focus on the first which depends only on two parameters m and M.

One can check, by formal computations, that (10) admits a minimum in m. We report in figure 1 the graph of (10) for $M = 10^3$: note the discontinuities produced by the function $\lceil \cdot \rceil$. An exact expression for the minimum is not possible, however we can compute the derivative of (10) (replacing the function $\lceil \cdot \rceil$ with the identity) and thus obtaining:

$$\frac{M^{\frac{1}{m}}}{\ln(2)} \left(\ln(2m + 1) \left(1 - \frac{\ln(M)}{m} \right) + \frac{2m}{2m + 1} \right).$$

From this expression, we see that the optimal value m^* satisfies $m^* < \ln(M)$. Finally, replacing this value in (10) we obtain:

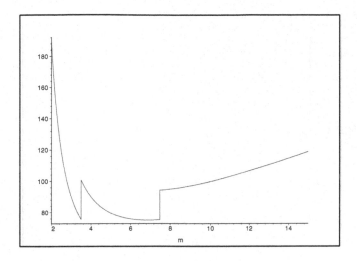

Fig. 1. Graph of (10) for $M = 1000$

Proposition 3. *Using the (approximate) solutions to Problems 1, the specification complexity asymptotically satisfies:*

$$\mathcal{C} \leq \ln(M)\, M^{\frac{1}{\ln(M)}} \lceil \log_2(2\ln(M) + 1) \rceil,$$

A compact representation of control sequences is obtained by using Run–Length Encoding (RLE). RLE consists in replacing repeated runs of a single symbol in an input stream by a single instance of the symbol and a run count. This compression method is particularly well suited for our method, because of the commutativity of symbols in control strings. In fact, we can assign, for each possible control value, an integer of size at most N, specifying how many times the corresponding control must be used. In this way, the control sequence requires $(2m + 1)\lceil \log_2(N) \rceil$ bits, or rather, by exploiting the symmetry of the symbol set and using sign-magnitude representation, $(m + 1)(1 + \lceil \log_2(N + 1) \rceil)$ bits. (We are assuming that control values are already computed off-line.) Using Proposition 3 and again (7), we thus get:

Proposition 4. *For Problem II, using feedback encoding, the approximate solution to Problem 1 and RLE, the specification complexity $\mathcal{C}$ satisfies:*

$$\mathcal{C} \sim (m + 1)\left(1 + \lceil \log_2(mM^{\frac{1}{m}} + 1) \rceil\right) \tag{12}$$

We can study this expression as above to determine an optimal value m^* of m: see in figure 2 the graph of (12) for $M = 10^3$. However, in this case we can only estimate $m^* = o(\ln(M))$, thus

$$\mathcal{C} = o(\ln(M))\log_2(o(\ln(M))M)$$

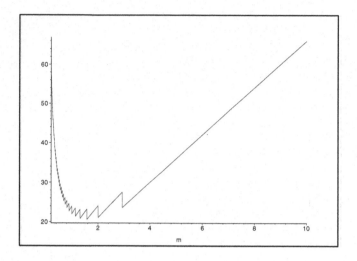

Fig. 2. Graph of (12) for $M = 1000$

3   Feedback Encoding for Flat Systems

Feedback encoding consists in associating to each symbol a control input u that depends on the symbol itself, on the current state of the system, and on its structure. If the encoding incorporates memory elements, e.g. additional states ξ are used to define the feedback, the feedback encoding is referred to as dynamic. The method of feedback encoding avails symbolic control with powerful results from the literature on feedback equivalence of dynamical systems. We show how this can be exploited to apply the planning method of theorem 1 to the rather general class of flat systems.

We start treating the case of linear systems:

$$\dot{x} = Fx + Gu \tag{13}$$

with $x \in \mathbb{R}^n$, $u \in U = \mathbb{R}^r$ and rank $G = r$. Application to (13) of piecewise constant encoding of symbolic inputs with durations $T_i = T$, $\forall i$, generates the discrete-time linear system

$$x^+ = Ax + Bu, \tag{14}$$

with $A = e^{FT}$, $B = (\int_0^T e^{(T-s)F} ds)G$. Let us recall the definition of Brunovsky form (see e.g. [19]). For a controllable system (14), there exist a change of coordinates S in the state space and V in the input space, and a linear feedback matrix K_0 such that the new system with drift $\tilde{A} = S^{-1}(A + BK_0)S$ and control matrix $\tilde{B} = S^{-1}BV$ has the following properties. The state $\xi = S^{-1}x$ can be split in r subvectors $\xi = (\xi_1, \ldots, \xi_r)$ for which the dynamics are written as

$$\dot{\xi}_i = A_{\kappa_i}\xi_i + b_{\kappa_i}v_i', \ i = 1, \ldots, r \tag{15}$$

where $\xi_i \in \mathbb{R}^{\kappa_i}$,

$$A_{\kappa_i} = \begin{bmatrix} 0 & 1 & \cdots & 0 & 0 \\ 0 & 0 & 1 & \cdots & 0 \\ \vdots & \vdots & \ddots & \ddots & \vdots \\ 0 & 0 & \cdots & 0 & 1 \\ 0 & 0 & \cdots & 0 & 0 \end{bmatrix} \in \mathbb{R}^{\kappa_i \times \kappa_i}, \qquad b_{\kappa_i} = \begin{bmatrix} 0 \\ \vdots \\ 0 \\ 1 \end{bmatrix} \in \mathbb{R}^{\kappa_i},$$

$v_i' \in \mathbb{R}$ and $\sum_{i=1}^{r} \kappa_i = n$.

Theorem 2. *For a controllable linear discrete-time system $x^+ = Ax + Bu$, there exists an integer $\ell > 1$ and a linear feedback encoding $E : \sigma_i \mapsto Kx + w_i$ with constant $K \in \mathbb{R}^{n \times n}$ and $w_i \in \mathcal{W}$, $\mathcal{W} \subset \mathbb{R}^r$ a quantized control set, such that, for all subsequences of period ℓT extracted from $x(\cdot)$, the reachable set is a lattice of arbitrarily fine mesh. In other words the all controllable linear discrete-time systems are additively approachable.*

We recall preliminarily a result which can be derived directly from [2].

Lemma 1. *The reachable set of the scalar discrete time linear system $\xi^+ = \xi + v$, $\xi \in \mathbb{R}$, $v \in \mathcal{W} := \gamma W$ with $\gamma > 0$ and $W = \{0, \pm w_1, \ldots, \pm w_m\}$, $w_i \in \mathbb{N}$ with at least two elements w_i w_j coprime, is a lattice of mesh size γ.*

Proof. Theorem 2.
For the controllable pair (A, B), let S, V, and K_0 be matrices such that $(S^{-1}(A + BK_0)S, S^{-1}BV)$ is in Brunovsky form. Let $v' = K_1 \xi + v$, where:

- $v \in \mathcal{W} = \gamma_1 \, {}^1W \times \cdots \times \gamma_r \, {}^rW$, with ${}^kW = \{0, \pm^k w_1, \ldots, \pm^k w_{m_k}\}$, ${}^k w_j \in \mathbb{N}$ $k = 1, \ldots, r$, $j = 1, \ldots, m_k$, each ${}^kW$ including at least two coprime elements ${}^k w_i \, {}^k w_j$;
- $K_1 \in \mathbb{R}^{r \times n}$ such that its i-th row (denoted K_{1i}) contains all zeroes except for the element in the $(\kappa_{i-1} + 1)$-th column which is equal to one (recall that by definition $\kappa_0 = 0$).

Using notation as in (15), it can be easily observed that $(A_{\kappa_i} + B_{\kappa_i} K_{1i})^{\kappa_i} = I_{\kappa_i}$, the $\kappa_i \times \kappa_i$ identity matrix. Hence, if we let $\ell = $ l.c.m. $\{\kappa_i : i = 1, \ldots, r\}$, we get $[S^{-1}((A + BK_0)S + BVK_1)]^{\ell} = I_n$.

Let $\xi_i \in \mathbb{R}^{\kappa_i}$ denote the i-th component of the state vector relative to the pair $(A_{\kappa_i}, B_{\kappa_i})$. For any $\tau \in \mathbb{N}$ we have $\xi_i(\tau + \kappa_i) = \xi_i(\tau) + [v_i(\tau), \ldots, v_i(\tau + \kappa_i - 1)]$. On the longer period of ℓT, we have

$$\xi_i(\tau + \ell) = \xi_i(\tau) + \begin{bmatrix} \sum_{k=0}^{\frac{\ell}{\kappa_i} - 1} v_i(\tau + k\kappa_i) \\ \vdots \\ \sum_{k=0}^{\frac{\ell}{\kappa_i} - 1} v_i(\tau + \kappa_i - 1 + k\kappa_i) \end{bmatrix}$$
$$:= \xi_i(\tau) + \bar{v}_i(\tau),$$

hence, in the initial coordinates,

$$x(\tau + \ell) = x(\tau) + S\bar{v}.$$

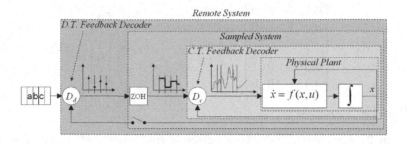

Fig. 3. Nested discrete-time continuous-time feedback encoding

It is also clear that, for any ε, it is possible to choose Γ such that z can be driven in a finite number of steps (multiple of ℓ) to within an ε-neighborhood of any point in $\mathbb{R}^n$.

Let us now pass to treat a general system (1) and let the equilibrium set be $\mathcal{E} = \{x \in X | \exists u \in U, f(x, u) = 0\}$. The focus on equilibria is consistent with usual practice in control, where equilibrium configurations typically correspond to nominal working conditions for a system (possibly up to group symmetries, see e.g. [12]).

Among systems with drift, linear systems are the simplest, yet their analysis encompasses the key features and difficulties of planning. Indeed, our strategy to attack the general case consists of reducing to planning for linear systems via feedback encoding. To achieve this, we introduce a further generalized encoder (still encompassed by the above definition of control quanta), i.e. the *nested feedback encoding* described in fig. 3. In this case, an inner continuous (possibly dynamic) feedback loop and an outer discrete-time loop – both embedded on the remote system – are used to achieve richer encoding of transmitted symbols. Since additive approachability for linear systems is proved in theorem 2, using nested feedback encoding, all feedback linearizable systems are hence additively approachable. Recalling results from [11], we can state the following

Theorem 3. *Every differentially flat system is locally additively approachable.*

4   Example

We illustrate the power of the proposed method by solving the steering problem for an example in the class of underactuated mechanical systems, which have attracted wide attention in the recent literature (see e.g. [8]).

In particular, we consider the class of underactuated mechanisms identified as "$(n-1)X_a - R_u$ planar robots", i.e. mechanisms having $n-1$ active joints of any type, and a passive rotational joint. In order to simplify the model analysis and control design, it is convenient to use a specific set of generalized coordinates. In particular, let $q = (q_1, ..., q_{n-3}, x, y, \theta) = (q_a, \theta)$ where (x, y) are the cartesian coordinates of the base of the last link. Assuming motion in a horizontal plane (or zero gravity), the dynamic model takes on the partitioned form

$$
\begin{bmatrix}
B_a(q_a) & \begin{matrix} 0_{(n-3)\times 1} \\ -m_n d_n s_\theta \\ m_n d_n c_\theta \end{matrix} \\
0_{1\times(n-3)} \;\; -m_n d_n s_\theta \;\; m_n d_n c_\theta & I_n + m_n d_n^2
\end{bmatrix}
\begin{bmatrix} \ddot{q}_a \\ \ddot{\theta} \end{bmatrix} +
$$

$$
+ \begin{bmatrix} c_a(q,\dot{q}) \\ 0 \end{bmatrix} = \begin{bmatrix} F_a \\ 0 \end{bmatrix} \tag{16}
$$

where $F_a = (F_1, ..., F_{n-3}, F_x, F_y)$ are the generalized forces performing work on the q_a coordinates, $s_\theta = \sin\theta$ and $c_\theta = \cos\theta$. For the n–th link, I_n, m_n and d_n are the baricentral inertia, the mass and the distance of the center of mass from its base.

In order to make the analysis independent from the nature of the $n-1$ active joints, the relative dynamics in (16) can be linearized via a globally defined partial static feedback, thus reducing them to a chain of two integrators per actuated joint. The dynamics of the coordinates q_i, $i = 1, ..., n-3$ are completely decoupled from the dynamics of the remaining coordinates (x, y, θ). Therefore, we will henceforth only consider the case $n = 3$. Following [8], we choose the cartesian coordinates of the center of percussion as the system's (flat) outputs:

$$
\begin{bmatrix} y_1 \\ y_2 \end{bmatrix} = \begin{bmatrix} x \\ y \end{bmatrix} + K_{CP} \begin{bmatrix} c_\theta \\ s_\theta \end{bmatrix}. \tag{17}
$$

The dynamics of the system after the dynamic feedback linearization are written as $y_1^{(4)} = v_1$, $y_2^{(4)} = v_2$. Choosing a sample time $t = 1s$ we obtain the following discrete time linear system:

$$
x_i^+ = Ax_i + Bv_i =
$$

$$
= \begin{bmatrix} 1 & 1 & \frac{1}{2} & \frac{1}{6} \\ 0 & 1 & 1 & \frac{1}{2} \\ 0 & 0 & 1 & 1 \\ 0 & 0 & 0 & 1 \end{bmatrix} x_i + \begin{bmatrix} \frac{1}{24} \\ \frac{1}{6} \\ \frac{1}{2} \\ 1 \end{bmatrix} v_i
$$

where $x_i = \left(y_i, y_i^{(1)}, y_i^{(2)}, y_i^{(3)} \right)$, $i = 1, 2$. Being each subsystem controllable, there exist S such that $(S^{-1}AS, S^{-1}B)$ is in control canonical form. For each subsystem in control canonical form, the set of equilibria is given by $\{\alpha 1_4 \in \mathbb{R}^4 : \alpha \in \mathbb{R}\}$. Then, in the initial coordinates, the set of equilibria is given by $\{\alpha S 1_4 \in \mathbb{R}^4 : \alpha \in \mathbb{R}\}$. For a given $\alpha \in \mathbb{R}$ we obtain the equilibrium $\alpha 1_4$ for the control canonical form and the equilibrium $(\alpha, 0, 0, 0)$ for the original subsystem, hence a constant position of the considered coordinate of the center of percussion. The scale factor is 1 in this case.

To obtain a reachable lattice of size $\gamma_1, \gamma_2 > 0$, ^1W, ^2W can be chosen to be any finite sets of integers, such that at least two of its elements are coprime, and and inputs scaled as $^i v \in \gamma_i\, ^i W$, $i = 1, 2$.

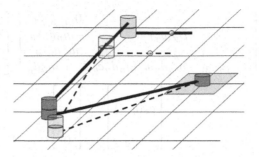

Fig. 4. An underactuated robot arm of type $2R_a - R_u$ used in example 2: the given initial and final configurations are shown by dashed and solid lines, respectively

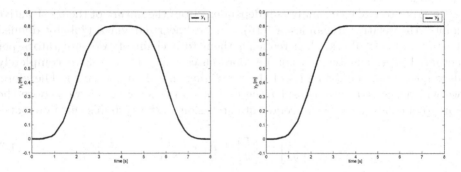

Fig. 5. Coordinates y_1 (left) and y_2 (right) of the center of percussion

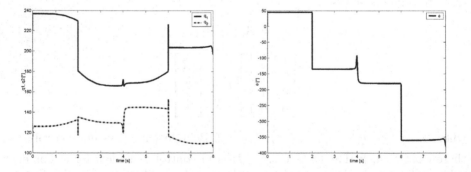

Fig. 6. Active joints angles (left) and orientation of the last passive link (right)

Given an initial robot pose $(y_1, y_2, \theta) = (0, 0, 0)$, consider three maneuvers: translation along the x axis, translation along the straight line $y = x$ and translation along the y axis. The first one can be achieved with a single symbol w applied on the input ^1v for $n = 4$ periods. The second maneuver is similar to the first one: we apply the previous command on the two inputs ^1v and ^2v for $n = 4$ periods. We can split the third maneuver in two maneuvers of the previous types.

Initial and final positions of a 3R robot are shown in fig. 4. Simulations were performed setting $l1 = l2 = 3m$, $K_{CP} = 1m$, $T = 1s$, and $w = 0.8\text{m/s}^2$. Fig. 5 shows the coordinates of the Center of Percussion of the last link while fig. 6 shows the angles of the active joints and the orientation of the last passive link, respectively.

5   Conclusions

In this paper, we addressed the issue of designing efficient finite plans to steer controlled dynamical systems. Efficiency is measured by specification and computational complexities.

Via suitable feedback encoding, based on control quanta, we showed how to reduce flat systems to a special form. Once this is obtained, we can use number-theoretic results to improve efficiency. It seems fair to affirm that few practically interesting classes of controllable systems remain outside the scope of application of the presented methods.

Connections to state observers in planning are unexplored at this stage.

Acknowledgments

This work was partially supported by EC through the Network of Excellence contract IST-2004-511368 "HYCON - HYbrid CONtrol: Taming Heterogeneity and Complexity of Networked Embedded Systems", and Integrated Project contract IST-2004-004536 "RUNES - Reconfigurable Ubiquitous Networked Embedded Systems". Authors would like to thank Adriano Fagiolini and Luca Greco for useful discussions.

References

1. Y. Anzai. A note on reachability of discrete–time quantized control systems. *IEEE Trans. on Automatic Control*, 19(5):575–577, 1974.
2. A. Bicchi, A. Marigo, and B. Piccoli. On the reachability of quantized control systems. *IEEE Trans. on Automatic Control*, 47(4):546–563, April 2002.
3. A. Marigo A. Bicchi and B. Piccoli. Encoding steering control with symbols. In *Proc. IEEE Int. Conf. on Decision and Control*, 2003.
4. R. Brockett. On the computer control of movement. In *Proc. IEEE Conf. on Robotics and Automation*, pages 534–540, April 1988.
5. Y. Chitour, A. Marigo, and B. Piccoli. Time optimal control for quantized input systems. In *Proc. IFAC Workshop on Nonlinear Control Systems (NOLCOS'04)*, 2004.
6. Y. Chitour and B. Piccoli. Controllability for discrete systems with a finite control set. *Math. Control Signals Systems*, 14(2):173–193, 2001.
7. A. Marigo. Optimal choice of input sets for quantized systems. *Mathematics of Control Signal and Systems*, to appear 2005.

8. A. De Luca and G. Oriolo. Trajectory Planning and Control for Planar Robots with Passive Last Joint. *The Internation Journal of Robotics Research*, Vol. 21, No. 5-6, 2002.
9. M. Egerstedt. Motion description languages for multimodal control in robotics. In A. Bicchi, H. Christensen, and D. Prattichizzo, editors, *Control Problems in Robotics*, number 4 in STAR, pages 75–89. Springer-Verlag, 2003.
10. M. Egerstedt and R. W. Brockett, Feedback Can Reduce the Specification Complexity of Motor Programs, IEEE Transaction on Automatic Control 48, 2003, 213-223.
11. M. Fliess, J. Lévine, P. Martin and P. Rouchon, Flatness and Defect of Nonlinear Systems: Introductory Theory and Examples, Int. J. of Control 61, 1995, 1327-1361.
12. E. Frazzoli, M. A. Dahleh, and E. Feron. Maneuver-Based Motion Planning for Nonlinear Systems with Symmetries. In *IEEE Trans. on Robotics*, to appear 2005.
13. R. K. Guy. Unsolved problems in number theory. Springer Verlag, 1994.
14. S. M. LaValle, Planning Algorithms, Cambridge University Press (also available at http://msl.cs.uiuc.edu/planning/), in print 2005.
15. V. Manikonda, P. S. Krishnaprasad, and J. Hendler. A motion description language and hybrid architecture for motion planning with nonholonomic robots. In *Proc. Int. Conf. on Robotics and Automation*, 1995.
16. A. Marigo, B. Piccoli, and A. Bicchi. A group-theoretic characterization of quantized control systems. In *Proc. IEEE Int. Conf. on Decision and Control*, pages 811–816, 2002.
17. M. Okada and Y. Nakamura. Polynomial design of dynamics-based infomration processing system. In A. Bicchi, H. Christensen, and D. Prattichizzo, editors, *Control Problems in Robotics*, number 4 in STAR, pages 91–104. Springer-Verlag, 2003.
18. A. Schrijver, *Theory of Linear and Integer Programming*. Wiley Interscience Publ., 1986.
19. E. D. Sontag, *Mathematical Control Theory*. Springer, 1998.
20. P. Tabuada, Sensor/actuator abstractions for symbolic embedded control design, in Hybrid Systems: Computation and Control, Lecture Notes in Computer Science 3414, Springer, 2005, 640-654.
21. P. Tabuada and G. J. Pappas, Bisimilar Control Affine Systems, Systems & Control Letters 52, 2004, 49-58.
22. P. Tabuada and G. J. Pappas, Hierarchical trajectory generation for a class of nonlinear systems, Automatica 41, 2005, 701-708.
23. L. A. Wolsey, *Integer Programming*. Wiley Interscience Publ., 1998.

Optimality Zone Algorithms for Hybrid Systems: Efficient Algorithms for Optimal Location and Control Computation

Peter E. Caines and M. Shahid Shaikh*

Department of Electrical & Computer Engineering,
Centre for Intelligent Machines, McGill University, Montréal,
Québec, H3A 2A7, Canada
{peterc, msshaikh}@cim.mcgill.ca

Abstract. A general Hybrid Minimum Principle (HMP) for hybrid optimal control problems (HOCPs) is presented in [1, 2, 3, 4] and in [4, 5], a class of efficient, provably convergent Hybrid Minimum Principle (HMP) algorithms were obtained based upon the HMP. The notion of optimality zones (OZs) ([3, 4]) provides a theoretical framework for the computation of optimal location (i.e. discrete state) schedules for HOCPs (i.e. discrete state sequences with the associated switching times and states). This paper presents the algorithm HMPOZ which fully integrates the prior computation of the OZs into the HMP algorithms class. Summing (a) the computational investment in the construction of the OZs for a given HOCP, and (b) the complexity of (i) the computation of the optimal schedule, (ii) the optimal switching time and optimal switching state sequence, and (iii) the optimal continuous control input, yields a complexity estimate for the algorithm HMPOZ which is linear (i.e. $O(L)$) in the number of switching times L.

1 Introduction

Over the last few years the notion of a hybrid control system with continuous and discrete states and dynamics has crystallized and various classes of optimal control problems for such systems have been formalized (see for example [3, 6, 2, 1, 7, 8, 9]). In particular, generalizing the standard Minimum Principle (MP), Sussmann [10] and Riedinger et al. [11], among other authors, have given versions of the Hybrid Minimum Principle (HMP) with indications of proof methods. An explicit theory for the two stage controlled switching optimal control problem was given by Tomiyama in [12] and a complete, rigorous treatment of the HMP is given in [13, 14] for the case of *a priori* fixed location sequences. In [1, 2, 3, 4] a set of necessary conditions for hybrid optimal control problems (HOCPs) was derived which constitutes a general Hybrid Minimum Principle (HMP); based upon this, a class of efficient Hybrid Minimum Principle (HMP)

---

* Work supported by NSERC Grant 1329-00.

João Hespanha and A. Tiwari (Eds.): HSCC 2006, LNCS 3927, pp. 123–137, 2006.

algorithms has been constructed [5] and their convergence established. Next, in [3, 4] the notion of optimality zones (OZs) was introduced as a theoretical framework enabling the computation of optimal schedules (i.e. location sequences with the associated switching times and states) for HOCPs. A distinct approach to the computational solution of HOCPs with fixed schedules is to be found in [7], while [15, 16, 17] present progress on parallel work on the solution of HOCPs including schedule optimization using a location (i.e. discrete state) insertion method.

The contributions of this paper include: (i) the algorithm HMPOZ which fully integrates the prior computation (termed the PREP computation) of the OZs into the HMP algorithms of [4, 5]; and (ii) computed examples of the application of HMPOZ to a bilinear quadratic regulator HOCP, demonstrating the efficacy of HMPOZ.

The computational complexity of HMPOZ has two components: (a) the complexity of the construction of the optimality zones for a given HOCP, which depends upon the cardinality of the discrete state set Q and the number of grid points $|G|$ but is independent of the number of switchings, and (b) the complexity of a single run of the HMP algorithm which is linear (i.e. $O(L)$) in the number of switchings L. This gives the overall complexity of HMPOZ as $O(|G|^2 \cdot |Q|) + O(L)$; this is to be compared with the geometric (i.e. $O(|Q|^L)$) growth of a direct combinatoric search over the set of location sequences.

Efficient Dynamic Programming (DP) based computational methods exist for certain classes of standard optimal control problems (see [18, 19]); furthermore, in case the upper bound $\bar{L}$ on the number of switchings is infinite (see [8, 4]) or the switchings occur at fixed instants, numerical methods for HOCP may, in principle, be formulated within a DP framework. However, severe complexity issues arise for DP based methods when the constraint $\bar{L} < \infty$ must be taken into account at each iterative step of a DP procedure; these do not arise for local optima seeking methods such as HMPOZ.

While the computational complexity of PREP for HMPOZ and DP methods increases geometrically with the dimension of the continuous state space $\mathbb{R}^n$, the complexity of HMPOZ implementations increase proportionally to that of the TPBVP methods used by HMP. For reasons of space, and to concentrate on the dependence on $\bar{L}$, the examples in this paper concern scalar systems.

The notion of optimality zones must be distinguished from the so-called "switching regions" presented in [20, 21, 22]; switching regions partition the continuous state space of autonomous (steady state) hybrid systems whereas optimality zones partition the Cartesian product of the system's time and state space $(\mathbb{R}^1 \times \mathbb{R}^n)$ with itself, that is to say, they partition $(\mathbb{R}^1 \times \mathbb{R}^n)^2$. As explained in Section 4, these partitions are defined for any given finite horizon hybrid optimal control problem (HOCP) and their specification is completely independent of the number of switchings L in the associated HOCP.

2   Hybrid Optimal Control Theory

In this paper we consider hybrid systems which in each location are governed by globally controllable non-linear dynamics of the form

$$\mathbb{H} : \dot{x}_q = f_q(x_q, u), \quad q \in Q \triangleq \{1, 2, \dots, |Q|\}.$$

At a controlled location transition at an instant t, $t \in [t_0, t_f]$, the piecewise constant, right continuous, Q valued, discrete state (component) trajectory satisfies

$$\mathbb{H} : q(t-) = q_i \in Q, \quad q(t) = q_j \in Q, \quad q_i \neq q_j.$$

In this paper no constraints are imposed on the dynamics of the location transition while in [4, 5] the controlled transitions satisfy the Q-dependent dynamics of the form $q_j = \Gamma(q_i, \sigma_{ij})$, where σ_{ij} is a partially defined discrete input; however, the algorithms presented here are easily extended to the more general case.

Consider the initial time t_0, final time $t_f < \infty$, initial hybrid state $h_0 = (q_0, x_0)$, and an upper bound on the number of switchings $\bar{L} \leq \infty$. Let $S_L = ((t_0, q_0), (t_1, q_1), \dots, (t_L, q_L))$ be a hybrid switching sequence and let $I_L \triangleq (S_L, u)$, $u \in \mathcal{U}^{\text{cpt}}$, $\bar{L} \leq \infty$, be a hybrid input trajectory which (subject to the assumptions of [4, 5]) results in a (necessarily unique) hybrid execution and is such that $L \leq \bar{L}$ switchings occur on the time interval $[t_0, t_f]$. Here the set of *admissible input control functions* is $\mathcal{U}^{\text{cpt}} \triangleq \mathcal{U}(U^{\text{cpt}}, L_\infty([0, t_f]))$, the set of all bounded measurable functions on some interval $[0, t_f]$, taking values in the compact set U^{cpt}. Further let the collection of such inputs be denoted $\{I_L\}$. We define the hybrid cost function as:

$$J : J(t_0, t_f, h_0; I_L, \bar{L}, \mathcal{U}^{\text{cpt}}) \triangleq \sum_{i=0}^{L} \int_{t_i}^{t_{i+1}} l_{q_i}(x_{q_i}(s), u(s)) \, ds + g(x_{q_L}(t_f)), \quad (1)$$

where for $i = 0, 1, \dots, L$,

$$\dot{x}_{q_i}(t) = f_{q_i}(x_{q_i}(t), u(t)), \quad a.e.\, t \in [t_i, t_{i+1}),$$
$$u(t) \in U^{\text{cpt}} \subset \mathbb{R}^n,$$
$$u(\cdot) \in L_\infty(U^{\text{cpt}}),$$
$$h_0 = (q_0, x_{q_0}(t_0)) = (q_0, x_0),$$
$$x_{q_{i+1}}(t_{i+1}) = \lim_{t \uparrow t_{i+1}} x_{q_i}(t), \text{ and}$$
$$t_{L+1} = t_f < \infty, \qquad L \leq \bar{L} \leq \infty.$$

Definition 1. *([4, 5], Hybrid Optimal Control Problem (HOCP)) Given a hybrid system $\mathbb{H}$, loss functions $\{l_q, q \in Q\}$, initial and final times, t_0, t_f, the initial hybrid state $h_0 = (q_0, x_0)$, and an upper bound on the number of switchings $\bar{L} \leq \infty$, the hybrid optimal control problem (HOCP$(t_0, t_f, x_0, \bar{L}, \mathcal{U}^{\text{cpt}})$), is to find the infimum $J^0(t_0, t_f, h_0, \bar{L}, \mathcal{U}^{\text{cpt}})$ of the hybrid cost function $J(t_0, t_f, h_0; I_L, \bar{L}, \mathcal{U}^{\text{cpt}})$ over the family of input trajectories $\{I_L\}$.*

If a hybrid input trajectory I_{L^0} exists which realizes $J^0(t_0, t_f, h_0, \bar{L}, \mathcal{U}^{\text{cpt}})$ it is called a hybrid optimal control for the HOCP$(t_0, t_f, x_0, \bar{L}, \mathcal{U}^{\text{cpt}})$. □

In Theorem 1 we state the necessary conditions, for the controlled switchings case, upon which the algorithms of this paper are based; the theorem is stated for the cases where the control takes values in the compact set U^{cpt}. The reader is referred to [4] and the associated paper [5] for a complete exposition of the HMP necessary conditions covering compact and open bounded control value sets and both the autonomous and controlled switchings cases.

Theorem 1. *([4, 5]) Consider a hybrid system $\mathbb{H}$ and the HOCP($t_0, t_f, x_0, \bar{L},$ U^{cpt}), and define*

$$H_q(x, \lambda, u) = \lambda^T f_q(x, u) + l(x, u), \quad x, \lambda \in \mathbb{R}^n, \quad u \in U^{\text{cpt}}, \quad q \in Q.$$

1) Let $J^0(t_0, t_f, h_0, U^{\text{cpt}}) = \inf_{\{I_L\}} J^0(t_0, t_f, h_0, I_L, \bar{L}, U^{\text{cpt}})$ be realized at $I_{L^0}^0$, (x^0, q^0).
2) Let $t_1, t_2, \ldots, t_{L^0}$, denote the switching times along the optimal trajectory (x^0, q^0).
3) Assume that either (a) $\bar{L} < \infty$ and $L^0 + 2 \leq \bar{L}$, or (b) $\bar{L} = \infty$ and $L^0 < \infty$.

Then

(i) There exists a (continuous to the right), piecewise absolutely continuous adjoint process λ^0 satisfying

$$\dot{\lambda}^0 = -\frac{\partial H_{q^0(t)}}{\partial x}(x^0, \lambda^0, u^0), \quad t \in (t_j, t_{j+1}), \quad j \in \{0, 1, 2, \ldots, L^0\}, \quad (2)$$

where $t_{L^0+1} = t_f$ and where the following boundary value conditions hold with $\lambda^0(t_0)$ free:
(a) $\lambda^0(t_f) = \nabla_x g(x^0(t_f))$.
(b) If t_j is a switching time, then

$$\lambda^0(t_j-) \equiv \lambda^0(t_j) = \lambda^0(t_j+), \quad j \in \{0, 1, 2, \ldots, L^0\}. \quad (3)$$

(ii) The Hamiltonian minimization conditions are satisfied, i.e.
(a)

$$H_{q^0(t)}(x^0(t), \lambda^0(t), u^0(t)) \leq H_{q^0(t)}(x^0(t), \lambda^0(t), v),$$
$$\text{a.e. } t \in [t_j, t_{j+1}), \forall v \in U^{\text{cpt}}, j \in \{0, 1, 2, \ldots, L^0\}. \quad (4)$$

(b)

$$H_{q^0(t)}(x^0(t), \lambda^0(t), u^0(t)) \leq H_q(x^0(t), \lambda^0(t), u^0(t)),$$
$$\text{a.e. } t \in [t_j, t_{j+1}), j \in \{0, 1, 2, \ldots, L^0\}, \forall q \in Q. \quad (5)$$

(iii) The following Hamiltonian continuity condition holds at a controlled switching time $t = t_j$

$$H(t_j-) \equiv H_{q^0(t_j-)}(t_j-) = H_{q^0(t_j-)}(t_j) = H_{q^0(t_j)}(t_j)$$
$$= H_{q^0(t_j+)}(t_j+) \equiv H(t_j+), \quad j \in \{1, 2, \ldots, L^0\}.$$

$\square$

3 HMP Conceptual Algorithm

Based on the necessary conditions for hybrid optimality in Theorem 1 we proposed the HMP algorithm in [4, 5] and established its convergence properties. This algorithm is presented below for the single switching time case but can be generalized to multiple switching times case in an obvious manner. This algorithm forms the basis of the algorithm HMPOZ which is given in Section 5.

We reproduce the HMP algorithm below; in Steps 3 and 4 $\{r_k\}$ is either a constant sequence of strictly positive numbers or is an unbounded monotonically increasing sequence.

0. Algorithm Initialization: Fix $0 < \epsilon_f \ll 1$. Let (t_s, x_s) be a nominal switching time-state pair such that $t_0 < t_s < t_f$. Set the iteration counter $k = 0$. Set $t_s^k = t_s$ and $x_s^k = x_s$. Compute the optimal control functions $u_1^k(t)$, $t_0 \le t < t_s$ and $u_2^k(t)$, $t_s \le t \le t_f$. Compute the associated state and costate trajectories and Hamiltonians over the two intervals $[t_0, t_s^k]$ and $[t_s^k, t_f]$, with the terminal state pairs (x_0, x_s^k) and (x_s^k, x_f) respectively. Also compute the new total cost $J^k(t_s^k, x_s^k)$.

1. Increment k by 1.

2. Let $z_s^k \triangleq (t_s^k, x_s^k)$ and set

$$z_s^k = z_s^{k-1} - r_k \left(\begin{array}{c} H_1^k(t_s^{k-1}) - H_2^k(t_s^{k-1}) \\ \lambda_2^k(t_s^{k-1}) - \lambda_1^k(t_s^{k-1}) \end{array} \right).$$

3. Compute the optimal control functions $u_1^k(t)$, $t_0 \le t < t_s$ and $u_2^k(t)$, $t_s \le t \le t_f$. Compute the associated state and costate trajectories and Hamiltonians over the two intervals $[t_0, t_s^k]$ and $[t_s^k, t_f]$ with the terminal state pairs (x_0, x_s^k) and (x_s^k, x_f) respectively. Next, compute the $J^k \triangleq J^k(t_s^k, x_s^k)$.

4. If $|J^k - J^{k-1}| < \epsilon_f$, then Stop; else go to Step 1.

The convergence of the HMP algorithm is established in [4, 5, 23] for the case of unbounded increasing $\{r_k\}$ by use of penalty function methods and Ekeland's variational principle. The efficiency of the HMP algorithm in comparison with other fixed discrete state sequence hybrid optimal control algorithms is discussed with illustrative examples in [4, 5].

4 Optimality Zones, Location Sequences and the HMPOZ Algorithm

Henceforth in this paper the HMP algorithm shall be treated as a modular unit in more general algorithmic procedures. In this section, the properties of optimal hybrid controlled trajectories are shown to permit the exploitation of the HMP algorithm in computational methods which converge to discrete and continuous control functions with certain local and global optimality properties.

4.1   Fundamental Implications of the DP Principle for Optimal Location Sequences

DP Principle. Along an optimal hybrid execution $(I_{L^0}^0, x^0)$ the Dynamic Programming Principle implies that the part of the hybrid input $I_{L^0}^0$ (and correspondingly the hybrid trajectory (q^0, x^0)) from the j-th switching time and state pair to the $j + 1$-st switching time and state pair, $(t_j^0, x_j^0) \to (t_{j+1}^0, x_{j+1}^0)$, $0 \le j \le L^0$, is optimal. Hence, in particular, $q^0(t)$, $t \in [t_j^0, t_{j+1}^0)$, must be an optimal location for the trajectory from (t_j^0, x_j^0) to (t_{j+1}^0, x_{j+1}^0).

Non-hybrid Optimal Control Problem. It is to be noted that for each $q((t_j^0, x_j^0), (t_{j+1}^0, x_{j+1}^0)) \in Q$ the optimization above is a standard (non-hybrid) optimal control problem which is not linked to an analogous optimization over any other interval.

$|Q|$ Complexity Search. We further note that for each time and state pair $\{(t_j, x_j), (t_{j+1}, x_{j+1})\}$ the set-up cost of a search over a set Q to find the optimal $q^0((t_j, x_j), (t_{j+1}, x_{j+1}))$ is proportional to $|Q|$ and is not linked to an analogous search over any other interval.

4.2   Variations in Switching Time and State and Local Optimality with respect to Discrete Location

Local Optimality for fixed $q \in Q$. In [4, 23] we show that under weak assumptions the value function $v(t, x, q)$ of HOCP is bounded and continuous in (t, x) for each $q \in Q$. For simplicity, consider the case where we have two locations, $Q = \{q_1, q_2\}$, and two controlled switchings at (t_1, x_1) and (t_2, x_2) with $t_0 \le t_1 < t_2 \le t_f$. Further assume that over the interval $[t_1, t_2]$ the optimal cost $J_{q_1}^0((t_1, x_1), (t_2, x_2))$ of a trajectory from x_1 to x_2 in location q_1 is strictly smaller than the corresponding cost $J_{q_2}^0((t_1, x_1), (t_2, x_2))$ in location q_2. Hence by the continuity of each $J_{q_i}^0$, $i = 1, 2$, in $((t_1, x_1), (t_2, x_2))$, there is a neighbourhood $N_{((t_1, x_1), (t_2, x_2))}$ of $((t_1, x_1), (t_2, x_2))$ such that for any $((t_1', x_1'), (t_2', x_2')) \in N_{((t_1, x_1), (t_2, x_2))}$ the optimality of location q_1 is preserved.

Specification of OZs. The preservation of the optimality of location q_1 with respect to the perturbations of $((t_1, x_1), (t_2, x_2))$ gives rise to the notion of (the set of) optimality zones (OZs).

   Under the assumptions generating the class of hybrid systems $\mathbb{H}$ (and the associated HOCP) the value function $J^0((t_1, x_1), (t_2, x_2), q)$ of HOCP is bounded and continuous in $((t_1, x_1), (t_2, x_2))$ for each $q \in Q$ (see [4]). So it is possible to define a region OZ_q of points $((t_1, x_1), (t_2, x_2))$ in the space $(\mathbb{R} \times \mathbb{R}^n)^2$ for which a specific location $q \in Q$ corresponds to the optimal hybrid system trajectory starting at (t_1, x_1) and terminating at (t_2, x_2).

   We adopt the convention that if (t_2, x_2) is not accessible from (t_1, x_1) and similarly if (t_1, x_1) is not co-accessible to (t_2, x_2)) when the system $\mathbb{H}$ is in the location $q \in Q$ then $J_q((t_1, x_1), (t_2, x_2)) = \infty$.

Definition 2. *For $t_0 \leq t_1 < t_2 \leq t_f$, the optimality zone OZ_q, corresponding to the location $q \in Q$, is given by*

$$OZ_q \underset{=}{\triangle} \{((t_1, x_1), (t_2, x_2)) \in ((t_0, t_f) \times \mathbb{R}^n)^2 :$$
$$J_q^0((t_1, x_1), (t_2, x_2)) \leq J_{q'}^0((t_1, x_1), (t_2, x_2)), \ t_1 < t_2, \ \forall q' \in Q\}. \quad \square$$

Under reasonable conditions [5, 24] optimality zones are closed sets with disjoint interiors.

4.3   Formulation of the HMPOZ Algorithm

Discretization of Space-Time. For simplicity and for the purpose of estimation of computational complexity assume that Γ is a rectangular region in $\mathbb{R}^{n+1}$:

$$\Gamma \underset{=}{\triangle} [t_0, t_f] \times [x_i^1, x_f^1] \times \cdots \times [x_i^n, x_f^n]$$

Let a grid G on Γ be defined as follows. The time interval $[t_0, t_f] \in \mathbb{R}$ is divided into N_0 uniform subintervals and let $\delta_0 \underset{=}{\triangle} (t_f - t_0)/N_0$. For each point $t_0 + \delta_0 k$, $k = 0, 1, \ldots, N_0$, let each edge of Γ be divided into N_i uniform subintervals and let $\delta_i \underset{=}{\triangle} (x_f^i - x_0^i)/N_i$, $i = 1, 2, \ldots, n$. Then

$$G \underset{=}{\triangle} \{t_0, \ldots, t_f\} \times \left(\times_{k=1}^n \{x_i^k, \ldots, x_f^k\} \right).$$

Set-Up Computation. We shall adopt the name $PREP(G)$ for an algorithm performing the following calculation: find the optimal location $q^0 = q^0((t_1, x_1), (t_2, x_2)) \in Q$, $((t_1, x_1), (t_2, x_2)) \in G$, $t_0 \leq t_1 < t_2 \leq t_f$, for all such strictly ordered t_r, t_s on the lattice points of the grid G with $|G|$ elements, where the envelope of G is assumed to contain the optimal trajectory $(x^0(t); t_0 \leq t \leq t_f)$.

HMP with OZ Data; Conceptual Algorithm. Let the execution of the basic HOCP algorithm HMP (see [4, 5]) be modified so that, after an iterative shift of the vector of switching time and state pairs $(t_j, x_j)^{[k]}$ to $(t_j, x_j)^{[k+1]}$ in $\mathbb{R}^{L(n+1)}$, the location $q_j^{[k+1]}$ on the interval $[t_j^{[k+1]}, t_{j+1}^{[k+1]})$ is chosen so as to be optimal among all trajectories from $x_j^{[k+1]}$ to $x_{j+1}^{[k+1]}$ (such a location is generated by $PREP(G)$). Upon incrementing k to $k+1$ the HMPOZ algorithm repeats its basic HMP operation if the halting rule of HMP has not been satisfied.

4.4   Optimality and Complexity of HMPOZ

Based upon the conceptual specification of Algorithm HMPOZ above, and invoking the DP Principle 4.1 together with the global convergence analysis (subject to the associated conditions) of the Algorithm HMP in [4, 5], it is shown in Theorem 2 below that if HMPOZ halts at some $(x^H, u^H, q^H) \equiv (u^H, q^H)$ then neither (i) a change in q^H with the given $\{t_s^H, x_s^H\}$, nor (ii) a change in u^H for the given q^H can strictly decrease the cost J.

The algorithm $PREP(G)$ solves one standard (i.e. non-hybrid) optimal control problem for each pair of points in the grid G, for each location $q \in Q$. Hence the computational cost of the determination of the optimality zones for HOCP by use of $PREP(G)$ in $\mathbb{R}^{2(n+1)}$ is $O(|G|^2 \cdot |Q|)$ which is independent of the number of switchings L. The HMPOZ algorithm resulting from the enhancement of HMP with $PREP$ computes (i) the optimal continuous variables and controls, and (ii) the optimal discrete location sequence with an overall complexity cost of $O(|G|^2 \cdot |Q|) + O(L)$, where $O(L)$ corresponds to the complexity of a single run of the HMP algorithm. Hence, over k HOCP problems with possibly differing initial and terminal data, the complexity comparison between the repeated application of HMPOZ and of a full combinatorial search method employing HMP is given by:

$$\alpha |Q||G|^{2|x|+1} + \beta k |\text{Pont}(|x|)|(L+1) < \gamma k |\text{Pont}(|x|)|(L+1)|Q|^L,$$

where α, β, γ are constants, k = number of problems, $|G|$ = space-time sample point density, L = number of switchings, $|Q|$ = cardinality of Q, $|x|$ = dimension of x, and $|\text{Pont}(|x|)|$ denotes the complexity of solving one classical optimal control problem by application of a TPBVP algorithm (which constitutes the basic module of HMP).

Figure 1 shows the projections $\mathbf{P_1}(OZ_q)$ and $\mathbf{P_2}(OZ_q)$ of the optimality zone OZ_q on (t_1, x_1) and (t_2, x_2) spaces respectively.

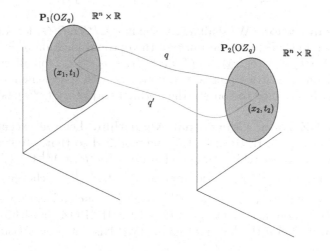

Fig. 1. Optimality zones

5   Halting and Convergence of HMPOZ Algorithms

Let $z_i \underline{\Delta} (t_i, x_i)$ and let $OZ : \mathbb{R}^{(n+1)L} \to Q^{L+1}$ be such that $OZ(\{z_i\}_{i=1}^L) = \{q_i\}_{i=0}^L$, i.e. for a given HOCP, the function OZ takes a sequence of time and state pairs and returns a sequence of locations from the precomputed Optimality Zones database computed by $PREP(G)$. Notice that the initial and final time-state are not passed to the OZ as they are part of the specification of HOCP.

Let $HMP : \mathbb{R}^{(n+1)L} \times Q^{L+1} \to \mathbb{R}^{(n+1)L}$ be such that for a given HOCP it performs the switching time and switching state update step of the Algorithm HMP of [4, 5].

Also, let $SC : \mathbb{R}^{2(n+1)L} \times Q^{2(L+1)} \times \mathbb{Z}_+ \to \mathbb{R}_+$ be a function which, for a given HOCP, computes a quantity to be compared to the stopping condition tolerance $\epsilon > 0$ of the Algorithm HMP of [4, 5].

Then the Algorithm HMPOZ may be specified as follows:

1. Initialization: Fix $0 < \epsilon \ll 1$. Set the iteration counter $k = 0$. Let $\{z_i\}_{i=1}^L \triangleq \{(t_i, x_i)\}_{i=1}^L$ be initial switching time and state pairs satisfying $t_0 < t_1 < t_2 < \cdots < t_L < t_f$. Also let $\{q_i\}_{i=0}^L = OZ(\{z_i\}_{i=1}^L)$ be the initial location sequence.
2. $\{z_i\}_{i=1}^L \leftarrow HMP\left(\{z_i\}_{i=1}^L, \{q_i\}_{i=0}^L\right)$.
3. $\{q_i\}_{i=0}^L \leftarrow OZ(\{z_i\}_{i=1}^L)$.
4. If $SC\left(\{z_i\}_{i=1}^L, \{q_i\}_{i=0}^L; k, k-1\right) \le \epsilon$ then STOP;
   else $k \leftarrow k+1$, go to Step 2. □

Figures 2 and 3 show a typical iteration of the Algorithm HMPOZ where an OZ boundary crossing takes place.

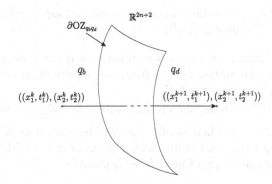

Fig. 2. An iteration of the Algorithm HMPOZ: ∂OZ crossing

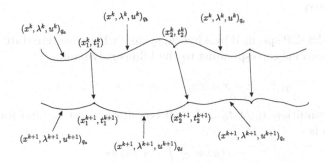

Fig. 3. An iteration of the Algorithm HMPOZ: switching time and switching state update

5.1   Convergence of HMPOZ

For brevity let us denote the sequence of switching times, switching states and locations $(\{(t_i, x_i)\}_{i=1}^L, \{q_i\}_{i=0}^L)$ as (z, q). Also let $u^0(z, q)$ denote the optimal continuous control for the sequence (z, q), i.e. for $i = 0, 1, \cdots, L$, the restriction of $u^0(z, q)$ to the interval $[t_i, t_{i+1}]$ is optimal for transferring the system from the continuous state x_i to continuous state x_{i+1} when the discrete state of the system is q_i. We define a product optimality zone OZ_q corresponding to the location sequence $\{q_i\}_{i=0}^L$ as

$$OZ_q \triangleq OZ_{q_0} \times OZ_{q_1} \times \cdots \times OZ_{q_L} \subset \mathbb{R}^{2(n+1)(L+1)},$$

and denote its interior as $\overset{\circ}{OZ}_q$. Then the following theorem gives the properties of the halting point of the Algorithm HMPOZ.

Theorem 2. *Assume A1 and A2 hold and assume HMPOZ halts at (z^H, q^H), then (z^H, q^H) has the following properties:*

(i) *For all $q \in Q^{N+1}$: $J(u^0(z^H, q^H)) \leq J(u^0(z^H, q))$.*

(ii) *Let $z^H \in \overset{\circ}{OZ}_{q^H}$, then there exists a neighbourhood $N(z^H)$ of z^H such that for all $z \in N(z^H)$: $J(u^0(z^H, q^H)) \leq J(u^0(z, q^H))$.*

Proof. (i) The optimality with respect to location sequence, for a given sequence of switching times and states, follows from the specification of $PREP(G)$ and the construction of the function OZ.

(ii) In this case $N(z^H)$ can be taken to be a subset of $\overset{\circ}{OZ}_{q^H}$ for which necessarily $N(z^H) \cap \overset{\circ}{OZ}_{q^H} = N(z^H)$. Then locally (i.e. for the iterations of HMPOZ which result in switching times and states which lie in $N(z^H)$) HMPOZ behaves as HMP and its convergence proof in [4, 5] is applicable.   □

6   The Hybrid Bilinear Quadratic Regulator (BLQR) Problem

Consider the HOCP specified by a hybrid system whose discrete state set consists of the two locations corresponding to the bilinear dynamics:

$$q_1: \quad \dot{x} = x + xu, \qquad q_2: \quad \dot{x} = -x + xu,$$

with initial condition x_0 at t_0 and final condition x_f at t_f, and for which the cost function is

$$J(u) = \frac{1}{2} \int_{t_0}^{t_f} u^2(s)\, ds.$$

In the set of computational experiments applying HMPOZ to this problem, the program $PREP$ was first applied to the product time-space $(R^{1+1})^2$ and this generated the OZ region data which was stored in the main program look-up

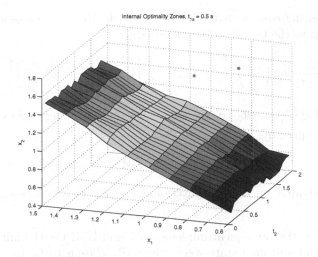

Fig. 4. OZ boundary for x_1, x_2, t_2 varying with $t_1 = 0.5$

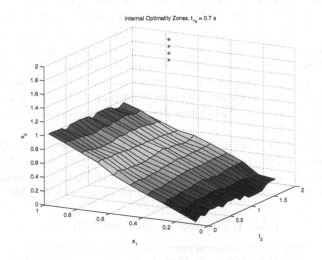

Fig. 5. OZ boundary for x_1, x_2, t_2 varying with $t_1 = 0.7$

table. The zonal boundary for the OZs corresponding to $Q = \{q_1, q_2\}$ is shown in Figures 4 and 5.

For this particular HOCP it is possible to obtain closed form expressions for the optimal cost of transferring the system from a general (t_1, x_1) to a general (t_2, x_2) under the two dynamics ($i = 1, 2$) respectively:

$$
J_i((t_1, x_1), (t_2, x_2)) = \begin{cases} \frac{1}{2}\left[1 + \frac{(-1)^i}{t_2 - t_1} \log\left(\frac{x_2}{x_1}\right)\right]^2 (t_2 - t_1), & \text{if } t_1 \neq t_2 \wedge x_1 x_2 > 0 \\ 0, & \text{if } t_1 = t_2 \wedge x_1 = x_2 \wedge x_1 x_2 > 0 \\ \infty, & \text{if } (t_1 = t_2 \wedge x_1 \neq x_2) \vee (x_1 x_2 \leq 0). \end{cases}
$$

The interesting case is that of $t_1 \neq t_2$ and in this case equating the costs corresponding to the two distinct dynamics gives:

$$\frac{1}{2}\left[1 - \frac{1}{t_2 - t_1}\log\left(\frac{x_2}{x_1}\right)\right]^2(t_2 - t_1) = \frac{1}{2}\left[1 + \frac{1}{t_2 - t_1}\log\left(\frac{x_2}{x_1}\right)\right]^2(t_2 - t_1),$$

Hence $\frac{1}{t_2 - t_1}\log\left(\frac{x_2}{x_1}\right) = 0$, so $x_1 = x_2$, and the switching surface is given in (t_1, t_2, x_1, x_2)-space by:

$$\partial OZ = \{(t_1, t_2, x_1, x_2) \in \mathbb{R}^4 : x_1 = x_2\},$$

which is illustrated by the computational experiments in Examples 1 and 2 below.

Example 1. For the subsequent implementation of HMPOZ the initial and final time and initial and final state were arbitrarily chosen to be $t_0 = 0$, $t_f = 2$, $x_0 = -1.2$, and $x_0 = -1.4$ respectively.

The control objective was to transfer the continuous state from its initial value at the initial time to the final value at the final time while minimizing the cost function $J(u) = \frac{1}{2}\int_0^2 u^2(s)\,ds$. After two iterations of HMP the second and third switching time and state pairs passed through the OZ boundary; in each case this corresponded to the ratio of the subsequent switching state values passing through the value 1 as specified in the exact analysis above. These transitions resulted in the location sequence evolving from $(2, 1, 1, 2)$ to $(2, 2, 2, 2)$ as shown in the third line of Table 1. After three iterations the algorithm converged giving the optimal cost 1.21587.

The computational time for *PREP* in this experiment was 7231 seconds (about two hours). For the HMPOZ implementation the computation time was 2.5637 seconds. All computations were performed in Matlab 6.5 under Windows 2000 SP4 operating system on a P4 3.2 GHz machine with 512 MB of RAM. $\square$

Table 1. Execution of Algorithm HMPOZ

Iter.	Loc. sequence	Cost	x_{s_1}	x_{s_2}	x_{s_3}
1	$(2, 1, 1, 2)$	1.33775	-1.3329	-1.3000	-1.2684
2	$(2, 1, 1, 2)$	1.27524	-1.3159	-1.3000	-1.2862
3	$(2, 2, 2, 2)$	1.21587	-1.2979	-1.3000	-1.3042

Example 2. To demonstrate the power of the HMPOZ algorithm we applied it to solve an HOCP involving the BLQR of Example 1 with ten switchings. *It is to be noted that the specification of the Optimality Zones for the three switchings case (Example 1) is reused for this ten switchings example without any modification. This would have been the case even if the zones had been obtained numerically.* The problem data was: $t_0 = 0$, $t_f = 2$, $x_0 = 2.4$, $x_f = 2.6$ and number of

Table 2. Execution of Algorithm HMPOZ: Ten switchings case

Iteration	Location sequence	Cost
1	$(1,1,1,1,2,1,1,2,2,1,1)$	0.75653
2	$(1,1,1,1,2,1,1,2,2,1,1)$	0.70324
3	$(1,1,1,1,2,1,1,2,2,1,1)$	0.68563
4	$(1,1,1,1,2,1,1,2,2,1,1)$	0.63887
5	$(1,1,1,1,2,1,1,2,2,1,1)$	0.61678
6	$(1,1,1,1,2,1,1,2,2,1,1)$	0.60291
7	$(1,1,1,1,2,1,1,2,2,1,1)$	0.58548
8	$(1,1,1,1,2,1,1,2,2,1,1)$	0.54783
9	$(1,1,1,1,2,1,1,2,2,1,1)$	0.49985
10	$(1,1,1,1,2,1,1,2,2,1,1)$	0.47789
11	$(1,1,1,1,2,1,1,2,2,1,1)$	0.43679
12	$(1,1,1,1,2,1,1,2,2,1,1)$	0.39453
13	$(1,1,1,1,2,1,1,2,2,1,1)$	0.35672
14	$(1,1,1,1,2,1,1,2,2,1,1)$	0.33756
15	$(1,1,1,1,2,1,1,2,2,1,1)$	0.31957
16	$(1,1,2,2,1,1,2,1,2,1,1)$	0.21986
17	$(1,1,2,2,1,1,2,1,2,1,1)$	0.21897
18	$(1,1,2,2,1,1,2,1,2,1,1)$	0.21897

switchings was set to 10. The algorithm initially computed (i) ten uniformly distributed switching times between $t_0 = 0$ and $t_f = 2$, (ii) ten randomly distributed switching states between $x_0 = 2.4$ and $x_f = 2.6$, and (iii) the initial switching sequence: $(1,1,1,1,2,1,1,2,2,1,1)$ which corresponds to the initial choice of switching times and states. The initial cost as computed by the algorithm is $J = 0.75653$ which drops down to $J = 0.31957$ by the 15th iteration. In the next (i.e. 16th) iteration the algorithm switches to the zone corresponding to the optimal switching sequence: $(1,1,2,2,1,1,2,1,2,1,1)$ giving the optimal cost $J = 0.21897$ at the 18th iteration. The running time was 45.596 seconds. The iterations of the program execution are shown in Table 2. □

Acknowledgment

The authors would like to thank Sean Meyn of University of Illinois at Urbana-Champaign, and Sebastian Engell of Universität Dortmund for valuable discussions.

References

1. Shaikh, M.S., Caines, P.E.: On trajectory optimization for hybrid systems: Theory and algorithms for fixed schedules. In: Proc. 41st IEEE Int. Conf. Decision and Control, Las Vegas, NV (2002) 1997–1998
2. Shaikh, M.S., Caines, P.E.: On the optimal control of hybrid systems: Optimization of trajectories, switching times, and location schedules. In Maler, O., Pnueli, A., eds.: Proc. sixth international workshop, Hybrid Systems: Computation and Control, LNCS 2623, Berlin, Germany, Springer-Verlag (2003) 466–481
3. Shaikh, M.S., Caines, P.E.: On the optimal control of hybrid systems: Analysis and algorithms for trajectory and schedule optimization. In: Proc. 42nd IEEE Int. Conf. Decision and Control, Maui, Hawaii (2003) 2144–2149
4. Shaikh, M.S.: Optimal Control of Hybrid Systems: Theory and Algorithms. PhD thesis, Department of Electrical and Computer Engineering, McGill University, Montréal, Canada (2004) Available: http://www.cim.mcgill.ca/~msshaikh/publications/thesis.pdf.
5. Shaikh, M.S., Caines, P.E.: On the hybrid optimal control problem: Theory and algorithms. revised for IEEE Trans. Automat. Contr. (2005)
6. Shaikh, M.S., Caines, P.E.: On the optimal control of hybrid systems: Optimization of switching times and combinatoric location schedules. In: Proc. American Control Conference, Denver, CO (2003) 2773–2778
7. Xu, X., Antsaklis, P.J.: Optimal control of switched systems based on parameterization of the switching instants. IEEE Trans. Automat. Contr. **49**(1) (2004) 2–16
8. Branicky, M.S., Borkar, V.S., Mitter, S.K.: A unified framework for hybrid control: model and optimal control theory. IEEE Trans. Automat. Contr. **43**(1) (1998) 31–45
9. Branicky, M.S., Mitter, S.K.: Algorithms for optimal hybrid control. In: Proc. 34th IEEE Int. Conf. Decision and Control, New Orleans, LA (1995) 2661–2666
10. Sussmann, H.: A maximum principle for hybrid optimal control problems. In: Proc. 38th IEEE Int. Conf. Decision and Control, Phoenix, AZ (1999) 425–430
11. Riedinger, P., Kratz, F., Iung, C., Zanne, C.: Linear quadratic optimization of hybrid systems. In: Proc. 38th IEEE Int. Conf. Decision and Control, Phoenix, AZ (1999) 3059–3064
12. Tomiyama, K.: Two-stage optimal control problems and optimality conditions. J. Economic Dynamics and Control **9**(3) (1985) 317–337
13. Clarke, F.H., Vinter, R.B.: Optimal multiprocesses. SIAM J. Control and Optimization **27**(5) (1989) 1072–1079
14. Clarke, F.H., Vinter, R.B.: Applications of optimal multiprocesses. SIAM J. Control and Optimization **27**(5) (1989) 1048–1071
15. Egerstedt, M., Wardi, Y., Delmotte, F.: Optimal control of switching times in switched dynamical systems. In: Proc. 42nd IEEE Int. Conf. Decision and Control, Maui, HI (2003) 2138–2143
16. Wardi, Y., Egerstedt, M., Boccadoro, M., Verriest, E.: Optimal control of switching surfaces. In: Proc. 43rd IEEE Int. Conf. Decision and Control, Atlantis, Paradise Island, Bahamas (2004) 1854–1859
17. Axelsson, H., Egerstedt, M., Wardi, Y., Vachtsevanos, G.: Algorithm for switching-time optimization in hybrid dynamical systems. In: Proc. 2005 International Symposium on Intelligent Control/13th Mediterranean Conference on Control and Automation, Cypres (2005) 256–261

18. Tsitsiklis, J.N.: Efficient algorithms for globally optimal trajectories. IEEE Trans. Automat. Contr. **40**(9) (1995) 1528–1538
19. Sethian, J.A., Vladimirsky, A.: Ordered upwind methods for hybrid control. In Tomlin, C., Greenstreet, M.R., eds.: Proc. fifth international workshop, Hybrid Systems: Computation and Control, LNCS 2289, Berlin, Germany, Springer-Verlag (2002) 393–406
20. Giua, A., Seatzu, C., Mee, C.V.D.: Optimal control of autonomous linear systems switched with a pre-assigned finite sequence. In: Proc. 2001 IEEE International Symposium on Intelligent Control. (2001) 144–149
21. Giua, A., Seatzu, C., Mee, C.V.D.: Optimal control of switched autonomous linear systems. In: Proc. 40th IEEE Int. Conf. Decision and Control, Orlando, FL (2001) 2472–2477
22. Bemporad, A., Giua, A., Seatzu, C.: A master-slave algorithm for the optimal control of continuous-time switched affine systems. In: Proc. 41st IEEE Int. Conf. Decision and Control, Las Vegas, NV (2002) 1976–1981
23. Shaikh, M.S., Caines, P.E.: Optimality zone algorithms for hybrid systems computation and control. Technical report, ECE Department, McGill University (2005)
24. Caines, P.E., Shaikh, M.S.: Optimality zone algorithms for hybrid control systems. submitted to IEEE Trans. Automat. Contr. (2005)

Approximate Reachability Computation for Polynomial Systems

Thao Dang

VERIMAG, Centre Equation, 2 avenue de Vignate,
38610 Gières, France
Thao.Dang@imag.fr

Abstract. In this paper we propose an algorithm for approximating the reachable sets of systems defined by polynomial differential equations. Such systems can be used to model a variety of physical phenomena. We first derive an integration scheme that approximates the state reachable in one time step by applying some polynomial map to the current state. In order to use this scheme to compute all the states reachable by the system starting from some initial set, we then consider the problem of computing the image of a set by a multivariate polynomial. We propose a method to do so using the Bézier control net of the polynomial map and the blossoming technique to compute this control net. We also prove that our overall method is of order 2. In addition, we have successfully applied our reachability algorithm to two models of a biological system.

1   Introduction

Reachability analysis is an important problem in formal verification of hybrid systems. A major ingredient in designing a reachability analysis algorithm for hybrid systems is an efficient method to handle their continuous dynamics described by differential equations (since their discrete dynamics can be handled using existing discrete verification methods). Reachability computation methods for a special class of systems with constant derivatives are well-developed. On the other hand, while many well-known properties of linear differential equations can be exploited to design relatively efficient methods, non-linear systems are much more difficult to analyze. Numerical integration is a common method to solve non-linear differential equations. Its goal is to derive a scheme to approximate the solution at each time step based on the solution at one or several previous steps. In general, a typical numerical integration scheme can be written as: $\mathbf{x}_{k+1} = \mathcal{Y}_k(f, h, \mathbf{x}_0, \mathbf{x}_1, \ldots, \mathbf{x}_k)$ where f is the derivative and h is the step size. Nevertheless, while this approach is concerned with computing a single solution at a time and each $\mathbf{x}_k$ in this scheme is a point, in reachability analysis one has to deal with sets of all possible solutions (due to non-determinism in initial conditions and in the dynamics of the system). Therefore, wishing to exploit the numerical integration idea for reachable set computation purposes, a question that arises is how to perform such schemes with sets, that is, when each $\mathbf{x}_k$ is a set of points. The essence behind the approach we propose in this paper can be

João Hespanha and A. Tiwari (Eds.): HSCC 2006, LNCS 3927, pp. 138–152, 2006.

described as extending traditional numerical integration to set integration. In particular, we are interested in systems defined by polynomial differential equations. Such systems can be used to model a variety of physical phenomena, in particular the dynamics of bio-chemical networks. We first derive an integration scheme that approximates the reachable state $\mathbf{x}_{k+1}$ by applying some polynomial map to $\mathbf{x}_k$. In order to use this scheme to approximate the reachable set, we then consider the problem of computing the image of a set by a multivariate polynomial. To do so, we employ the techniques from computer aided geometric design, in particular the Bézier techniques and the blossoming principle. We also prove that our overall method is of order 2. Although this paper focuses on continuous systems, the proposed method can be extended to hybrid systems, since reachable sets are represented by convex polyhedra, and Boolean operations (required to deal with discrete transitions) over such polyhedra can be computed using a variety of existing algorithms. This is illustrated through an example in Section 3.

Before continuing, we present a brief review of related work. The reachability problem for continuous systems described by differential equations has motivated much research both for theoretical problems, such as computability (see for example [1]), and for the development of computation methods and tools. If the goal is to exactly compute the reachable set or approximate it as accurately as possible, one can use a variety of methods for tracking the evolution of the reachable set under the continuous flows using some set representation (such as polyhedra, ellipsoids, level sets) [2,3,4,5,6,7,8,9]. Since high quality approximations are hard to compute, other methods seek approximations that are sufficiently good to prove the property of interest[1] (such as barrier certificates [10], polynomial invariants [11]). Abstraction methods for hybrid systems are also close in spirit to these methods. Indeed, their main idea is to approximate the original system with a simpler system (that one can handle more efficiently) and refine it if the analysis result obtained for the approximate system is too conservative (see for example [12,13,14,15,16]).

The paper is organized as follows. In Section 2, after stating our problem, we describe an integration scheme for polynomial differential equations. This scheme requires computing the image of a set by a polynomial map, the problem we discuss in Section 3. We then present our reachability algorithm and some experimental results obtained using the algorithm on the models of gene transcription control of the bacteria Vibrio Fisheri.

2   Reachability Analysis of Polynomial Systems

Throughout the paper, vectors are often written using bold letters. Given a vector $\mathbf{x}$, $\mathbf{x}[i]$ denotes its ith component.

We consider a polynomial system:

$$\dot{\mathbf{x}}(t) = g(\mathbf{x}(t)). \tag{1}$$

---

[1] It should be noted that reachable set computations can also be used for controller synthesis where the accuracy criterion is important.

We first rewrite the dynamics of the system as the sum of its linear part $A\mathbf{x}(t)$ and its non-linear part $f(\mathbf{x}(t))$, that is,

$$\dot{\mathbf{x}}(t) = g(\mathbf{x}(t)) = A\mathbf{x}(t) + f(\mathbf{x}(t)). \tag{2}$$

We then consider the non-linear term as independent input. In other words, the system is treated as a linear system with input $f(\mathbf{x}(t))$. This trick is to separate the linear part for which we can derive the exact closed-form solution. The interest in doing so will become clearer when we discuss the approximation error. We now develop a numerical solution for (2). Let $h > 0$ be a time step and $t_k = kh$ where $k = 0, 1, 2, \ldots$. Then, we have

$$\mathbf{x}(t_{k+1}) = e^{Ah}\mathbf{x}(t_k) + \int_0^h e^{A(h-\tau)} f(\mathbf{x}(t_k + \tau)) \, d\tau. \tag{3}$$

The idea is to approximate $\mathbf{x}(t_k + \tau)$ inside the above integral by its Taylor expansion around t_k to the first order, that is $\boldsymbol{\alpha}(t_k + \tau) = \mathbf{x}(t_k) + g(\mathbf{x}(t_k))\tau$. Denoting $\mathbf{x}(t_k) = \mathbf{x}_k$, $f(\mathbf{x}(t_k)) = f_k$ and $g(\mathbf{x}(t_k)) = g_k$, we have $\boldsymbol{\alpha}(t_k + \tau) = \mathbf{x}_k + g_k\tau = \mathbf{x}_k + (A\mathbf{x}_k + f_k)\tau$. Replacing $\mathbf{x}(t_k + \tau)$ with $\boldsymbol{\alpha}(t_k + \tau)$, we obtain an approximation $\bar{\mathbf{x}}_{k+1}$ of the exact solution $\mathbf{x}_{k+1}$:

$$\bar{\mathbf{x}}_{k+1} = e^{Ah}\mathbf{x}_k + \int_0^h e^{A(h-\tau)} f(\boldsymbol{\alpha}(t_k + \tau)) \, d\tau. \tag{4}$$

The integral in the above equation is a function of $\mathbf{x}_k$, and we denote it by $Q(\mathbf{x}_k) = \int_0^h e^{A(h-\tau)} f(\boldsymbol{\alpha}(t_k + \tau)) \, d\tau$.

Proposition 1. *The map $Q(\mathbf{x}_k)$ can be written as a polynomial in $\mathbf{x}_k$.*

Proof. The proof of the proposition is straightforward, however we present it here for the clarity of the development that follows. It is easy to see that if the total degree of $f(\mathbf{x})$ is d in $\mathbf{x}$, then $\boldsymbol{\alpha}(t_k + \tau)$ is a multivariate polynomial of total degree d in $\mathbf{x}_k$, and therefore $f(\boldsymbol{\alpha}(t_k + \tau))$ is a polynomial of degree d in τ. We can write $f(\boldsymbol{\alpha}(t_k + \tau)) = \sum_{l=0}^d \psi_l(\mathbf{x}_k)\tau^l$ where for every $l \in \{0, 1, \ldots, d\}$, $\psi_l(\mathbf{x}_k)$ is a polynomial in $\mathbf{x}_k$. We then denote $\Gamma_l = \int_0^h e^{A(h-\tau)}\tau^l \, d\tau$, which can be written in a closed form. It then follows that $\int_0^h e^{A(h-\tau)} f(\boldsymbol{\alpha}(t_k + \tau)) \, d\tau = \sum_{l=0}^d \Gamma_l \psi_l(\mathbf{x}_k)$. $\square$

The resulting integration scheme to approximate the solution of (1) is:

$$\begin{cases} \bar{\mathbf{x}}_{k+1} = e^{Ah}\bar{\mathbf{x}}_k + Q(\bar{\mathbf{x}}_k) = P(\bar{\mathbf{x}}_k), \\ \bar{\mathbf{x}}_0 \quad = \mathbf{x}(0). \end{cases}$$

We call $P(\mathbf{x}_k)$ the *integration map*.

Example of multi-affine systems. Let us illustrate the proof with a simple case where $g(\mathbf{x})$ is a multi-affine function of degree 2. This is the case of a biological model we study in Section 5. The function $f(\mathbf{x})$ can be written as:

$f(\mathbf{x}) = \sum_{i,j \in \{1,\ldots,n\}, i \neq j} \mathbf{x}[i]\mathbf{x}[j]\mathbf{c}_{ij}$ with $\mathbf{c}_{ij} \in \mathbb{R}^n$. Then, replacing $\mathbf{x}(t_k + \tau)$ with $\boldsymbol{\alpha}(t_k + \tau) = \mathbf{x}_k + g_k\tau$, we have:

$$f(\boldsymbol{\alpha}(t_k + \tau)) = \sum_{i \neq j \in \{1,\ldots,n\}} (g_k[i]g_k[j]\tau^2 + (\mathbf{x}_k[i]g_k[j] + g_k[i]\mathbf{x}_k[j])\tau + \mathbf{x}_k[i]\mathbf{x}_k[j])\mathbf{c}_{ij}$$

Therefore, the equation (4) becomes:

$$\bar{\mathbf{x}}_{k+1} = P(\mathbf{x}_k) = \Phi\mathbf{x}_k + \sum_{i \neq j \in \{1,\ldots,n\}} (\gamma_2\Gamma_2 + \gamma_1\Gamma_1 + \gamma_0\Gamma_0)\mathbf{c}_{ij}. \tag{5}$$

where $\Phi = e^{Ah}$ and $\gamma_2 = g_k[i]g_k[j]$, $\gamma_1 = g_k[i]\mathbf{x}_k[j] + \mathbf{x}_k[i]g_k[j]$, $\gamma_0 = \mathbf{x}_k[i]\mathbf{x}_k[j]$. After straightforward calculations, we obtain:

$$\Gamma_l = l! \sum_{i=0}^{\infty} \frac{A^i h^{i+l+1}}{(i+l+1)!} \tag{6}$$

It is thus easy to see that, due to the term γ_2, $P(\mathbf{x}_k)$ in (5) is a polynomial of degree 4 in $\mathbf{x}_k$. The equation (5) can be readily used as a scheme specialized for multi-affine systems of degree 2.

Convergence. A bound on the error in our approximation is given in the following theorem.

Theorem 1. *Let $\bar{\mathbf{x}}(t_{k+1})$ be the approximate solution at time t_{k+1} (computed by (4)) and $\mathbf{x}(\cdot)$ be the corresponding exact solution such that $\bar{\mathbf{x}}(t_k) = \mathbf{x}(t_k)$. Then, a bound on the local error is given by: $\|\bar{\mathbf{x}}(t_{k+1}) - \mathbf{x}(t_{k+1})\| = \mathcal{O}(h^3)$.*

The proof of this result is presented in Appendix. This theorem shows that the equation (4) is a *second order scheme*. In addition. we can show that the global error is also convergent. As one can see from the proof, the error bound depends on the Lipschitz constant of the non-linear function f. So now we can see the interest in separating the linear part since the Lipschitz constant of f is smaller than that of g.

Higher order integration schemes. Note that we have used an approximation of the exact solution $\mathbf{x}(t_k + \tau)$ by the its first order Taylor expansion around t_k. To obtain better convergence orders, we can use higher order expansions which results in integration schemes involving high order derivatives of $f(\mathbf{x})$. The derivation of such schemes is similar to the above development, but the degree of the resulting integration map $P(\mathbf{x}_k)$ can be higher. In the other direction, if we use a simpler approximation $\boldsymbol{\alpha}(t_k + \tau) = \mathbf{x}_k$ for all $\tau \in [t_k, t_{k+1})$, then $Q(\mathbf{x}_k) = \Gamma_0 f(\mathbf{x}_k)$ and we obtain the classic Euler scheme for the non-linear part. The advantage of this scheme is that the resulting polynomial $Q(\mathbf{x}_k)$ has the same degree as $f(\mathbf{x})$. As we shall see later, the degree of the integration map is one of the factors determining the complexity of the reachability algorithm. It remains to compute the polynomial map $Q(\mathbf{x}_k)$, the problem we tackle in the next section.

3   Computing Polynomial Maps

The problem we are interested in can be formally stated as follows. Given a polynomial map $\pi : \mathbb{R}^n \to \mathbb{R}^n$ of total degree d and a bounded set $X \subset \mathbb{R}^n$, we want to compute the image $\pi(X)$ defined as: $\pi(X) = \{\pi(\mathbf{x}) \mid \mathbf{x} \in X\}$. We shall focus on the case where X is a simplex in $\mathbb{R}^n$.

3.1   Bézier Simplices

To determine the image of a simplex by a polynomial map, we use the results on *Bézier simplices* [17]. We need to introduce first some notation.

A multi-index $\mathbf{i} = (\mathbf{i}[1], \ldots, \mathbf{i}[n+1])$ is a vector of $(n+1)$ non-negative integers. We define the norm of $\mathbf{i}$ by $||\mathbf{i}|| = \sum_{j=1}^{n+1} \mathbf{i}[j]$ and let $\mathcal{I}_n^d$ denote the set of all multi-indices $\mathbf{i} = (\mathbf{i}[1], \ldots, \mathbf{i}[n+1])$ with $||\mathbf{i}|| = d$. We define two special multi-indices: $\mathbf{e}_j$ is a multi-index that has all the components equal to 0 except for the jth component which is equal to 1, and $\mathbf{o}$ is a multi-index that has all the components equal to 0. We call $\mathbf{o}$ the zero multi-index.

Let Δ be a full-dimensional simplex in $\mathbb{R}^n$ with vertices $\{\mathbf{v}_1, \ldots, \mathbf{v}_{n+1}\}$. Given a point $\mathbf{x} \in \Delta$, let $\lambda(\mathbf{x}) = (\lambda_1(\mathbf{x}), \ldots, \lambda_{n+1}(\mathbf{x}))$ be the function that gives the barycentric coordinates of $\mathbf{x}$ with respect to the vertices of Δ, that is, $\mathbf{x} = \sum_{j=1}^{n+1} \lambda_j(\mathbf{x})\mathbf{v}_j$ and $\sum_{j=1}^{n+1} \lambda_j(\mathbf{x}) = 1$. A *Bézier simplex* of degree d of the form $\pi : \mathbb{R}^n \to \mathbb{R}^n$ is defined as[2]:

$$\pi(\mathbf{x}) = \sum_{||\mathbf{i}||=d} \mathbf{b_i} B_{\mathbf{i}}^d(\lambda_1(\mathbf{x}), \ldots, \lambda_{n+1}(\mathbf{x})) \tag{7}$$

where for a given multi-index $\mathbf{i}$, $\mathbf{b_i}$ is a vector in $\mathbb{R}^n$ and $B_{\mathbf{i}}^d : \mathbb{R}^n \to \mathbb{R}$ is a *Bernstein polynomial* of degree d defined as:

$$B_{\mathbf{i}}^d(y_1, \ldots, y_{n+1}) = \binom{d}{\mathbf{i}} y_1^{\mathbf{i}[1]} y_2^{\mathbf{i}[2]} \ldots y_{n+1}^{\mathbf{i}[n+1]} \tag{8}$$

with the multimonial coefficient $\binom{d}{\mathbf{i}} = \frac{d!}{\mathbf{i}[1]! \, \mathbf{i}[2]! \, \ldots \, \mathbf{i}[n+1]!}$. In the above formula (7), each vector $\mathbf{b_i}$ is called a *Bézier control point* and the set of all such $\mathbf{b_i}$ form the *Bézier control net* of π with respect to Δ.

Any polynomial can be written in form of a Bézier simplex, as in formula (7). This form is a popular way to write polynomials in computer aided geometric design (see [17] and references therein). The following properties of Bernstein polynomials are well-known. The Bernstein polynomials form a partition of unity, that is, $\sum_{||\mathbf{i}||=d} B_{\mathbf{i}}^d(y_1, \ldots, y_{n+1}) = 1$, and they are non-negative, that is, $B_{\mathbf{i}}^d(y_1, \ldots, y_{n+1}) \geq 0$ for all $0 \leq y_1, \ldots, y_{n+1} \leq 1$. These properties of Bernstein polynomials imply the following *shape properties* of Bézier simplices, which we shall use for reachability computation purposes.

---

[2] The definition holds for more general polynomials of the form $\pi : \mathbb{R}^n \to \mathbb{R}^m$.

Lemma 1. *Given an arbitrary point* $\mathbf{x} \in \Delta$,

1. **[Convex hull property]** *the point* $\pi(\mathbf{x})$ *lies inside the convex hull of the control net, that is* $\pi(\mathbf{x}) \in conv\{\mathbf{b_i} \mid \mathbf{i} \in \mathcal{I}_n^d\}$.
2. **[End-point interpolation property]** π *interpolates the control net at the corner control points specified by* $\mathbf{b}_{\mathbf{de}_k}$ *for all* $k \in \{1, \ldots, n+1\}$.

Note that the number of multi-indices in $\mathcal{I}_k^d$ is $\binom{d+n}{n}$; therefore, the number of points $\mathbf{b_i}$ is exactly $\binom{d+n}{n} = \frac{(d+n)!}{d!\,n!}$. We denote this number by $\beta(n, d)$.

These shape properties can be used to approximate polynomial maps. Indeed, the *convex hull property* in Lemma 1 shows that one can over-approximate $\pi(\Delta)$ by taking the convex hull of the Bézier control net of π with respect to Δ. In addition, this *over-approximation is tight* due to the above *end-point interpolation property*. In the rest of this section we focus on the problem of computing the Bézier control net of the polynomial π. To avoid confusion, it is worthy to emphasize that for reachability computation purposes, we are dealing with the systems whose vector fields are given in monomial form (i.e. sums of monomials), hence the integration map is also defined in this form. To compute the control points of a polynomial given in monomial forms, we shall exploit the techniques for approximating and designing polynomial curves and surfaces. However, it is important to mention that most of such existing tools deal with univariate or bivariate polynomials (often expressed in terms of control points), their application to solve our problem requires an adaptation to multivariate polynomials as well as geometric manipulation in general dimension.

3.2   Computing the Bézier Control Net

Our goal is to obtain the Bézier control net of a polynomial π given in monomial form. By the definition (7), the most natural approach is to solve the following interpolation problem. Let S be a set of $\beta(n, d)$ points in Δ. For each $\mathbf{x} \in S$, we evaluate $\pi(\mathbf{x})$ and use (7) to obtain a system of linear equations with the coordinates of the Bézier control points $\mathbf{b_i}$ as unknown variables. One can choose the set S such that the unique solution to these linear equations exists [18]. Although this method is conceptually simple, it may require solving a large linear system[3] (which is of size $n * \beta(n, d)$). We shall use a more efficient approach based on the blossoming principle, which is summarized in the following theorem. A thorough description of this principle and its various applications can be found in [19, 20].

Theorem 2 (Blossoming principle). *For any polynomial* $\pi : \mathbb{R}^n \to \mathbb{R}^n$ *of degree* d, *there is a unique symmetric* d-*affine map* $p : (\mathbb{R}^n)^d \to \mathbb{R}^n$ *such that for all* $\mathbf{x} \in \mathbb{R}^n$ $p(\mathbf{x}, \ldots, \mathbf{x}) = \pi(\mathbf{x})$. *The map* p *is called the* blossom *or the* polar form *of* π.

---

[3] The Gaussian elimination algorithm to solve a linear system of size $m \times m$ has the time complexity $O(m^3)$.

We recall that a map $q(\mathbf{x}_1, \ldots, \mathbf{x}_d)$ is called *d-affine* if it is affine when all but one of its arguments are kept fixed; it is said to be symmetric if its value does not depend on the ordering of the arguments, that is, for any permutation $(\mathbf{y}_1, \ldots, \mathbf{y}_d)$ of $(\mathbf{x}_1, \ldots, \mathbf{x}_d)$ we have $q(\mathbf{y}_1, \ldots, \mathbf{y}_d) = q(\mathbf{x}_1, \ldots, \mathbf{x}_d)$. Given a polynomial π, the connection between its Bézier control net relative to a simplex Δ and its blossom p is described by the following lemma.

Lemma 2. *For all* $\mathbf{i} \in \mathcal{I}_n^d$, $\mathbf{b_i} = p(\underbrace{\mathbf{v}_1, \ldots, \mathbf{v}_1}_{\mathbf{i}[1]}, \underbrace{\mathbf{v}_2, \ldots, \mathbf{v}_2}_{\mathbf{i}[2]}, \ldots, \underbrace{\mathbf{v}_{n+1}, \ldots, \mathbf{v}_{n+1}}_{\mathbf{i}[n+1]})$
where $\{\mathbf{v}_1, \ldots, \mathbf{v}_{n+1}\}$ *are the vertices of* Δ.

This fact is also well-known [19], and we present its proof in Appendix, which can facilitate understanding the subsequent development.

Computing the blossom. We have seen that the Bézier control points can be computed by evaluating the blossom values at some particular points shown in Lemma 2. To compute them, we first derive an analytic expression of the polar form and then show how to compute this expression efficiently. We do so by extending the results for bivariate polynomial surfaces [21] to multivariate polynomials.

Before proceeding, we mention that the problem of computing the Bézier control net can be formulated as a problem of changing from the monomial basis to the Bézier basis, which can be solved using the algorithms proposed in [22, 23]. These algorithms also make use of the blossoming principle. The idea is to express the coordinates of the new basis vectors in the old basis, and then apply the transformation matrix to the old coefficients. However, when the polynomial representation is "sparse", that is it contains many zero coefficients, this sparsity is not exploited. The method discussed in the following deals better with such sparsity since it considers only the monomials with non-null coefficients. More precisely, by "sparse polynomial representations" we mean those where the number of monomials (with non-null coefficients) is much smaller than the number of all combinations of coordinate variables up to degree d. The sparse case indeed happens in many practical applications we have encountered.

Let us now show how to compute the blossom of monomials which are products of only two variables, such as $\mathbf{x}[i]^h \mathbf{x}[j]^k$. Similar treatment can be used for monomials involving more variables, but due to the length of the involved formulas we do not detail it here. On the other hand, using linearity, we can obtain the blossom of any polynomial expressed as a sum of monomials.

The blossom of degree d of the monomial $(\mathbf{x}[i])^h (\mathbf{x}[j])^k$ is given by:

$$p_{h,k}^d(\mathbf{u}_1, \mathbf{u}_2, \ldots, \mathbf{u}_d) = \frac{1}{\binom{d}{h}\binom{d-h}{k}} \sum_{\substack{I \cup J \subset \{1, \ldots, d\}, \\ |I| = h, |J| = k, I \cap J = \emptyset}} \prod_{r \in I} \mathbf{u}_r[i] \prod_{s \in J} \mathbf{u}_s[j].$$

To prove this, it suffices to check that the right hand side is a symmetric multi-affine function, and moreover $p_{h,k}^d(\mathbf{u}, \mathbf{u}, \ldots, \mathbf{u}) = (\mathbf{u}[i])^h (\mathbf{u}[j])^k$. $\square$

To compute the blossom values using the above expression, we make use of a recurrence equation on p, as proposed in [21]. We first denote

$$\sigma_{h,k}^d = \frac{1}{\binom{d}{h}\binom{d-h}{k}} p_{h,k}^d(\mathbf{u}_1, \mathbf{u}_2, \ldots, \mathbf{u}_d).$$

The function σ is symmetric and has the following interpretation: this function is computed by choosing h i^{th} coordinates of the argument points and k i^{th} coordinates and forming their product, then summing these products over all possible choices. We can thus derive the following recurrence formula:

$$\begin{cases} \sigma_{h,k}^d = \sigma_{h,k}^{d-1} + \mathbf{u}_d[i]\sigma_{h-1,k}^{d-1} + \mathbf{u}_d[j]\sigma_{h,k-1}^{d-1} & \text{if } h, k \geq 0 \text{ and } h + k \geq 1, \\ \sigma_{0,0}^d = 0 \end{cases} \tag{9}$$

This means that to compute the required blossom value $p_{h,k}^d(\mathbf{u}_1, \mathbf{u}_2, \ldots, \mathbf{u}_d)$ we compute all the intermediate values $p_{h',k'}^{d'}(\mathbf{u}_1, \ldots, \mathbf{u}_{d'})$ with $d' \leq d$, $h' + k' \leq d'$. This computation can be done in time $O(d^3)$.

3.3   Approximation Error and Subdivision

We proceed to estimate an error bound for the approximation of the polynomial map π by its the Bézier control points.

Theorem 3. *For each Bézier control point $\mathbf{b_i}$ there exists a point $\mathbf{y} \in \pi(\Delta)$ such that $||\mathbf{b_i} - \mathbf{y}|| \leq K\rho^2$ where ρ be the maximal side length of Δ and K is some constant not depending on Δ.*

The proof of this theorem can be found in Appendix.

Consequently, when the simplicial domain Δ is large, to achieve the desired accuracy we may need to subdivide it into smaller simplices. This subdivision creates new Bézier bases and therefore new control points. However, due to the properties of multi-affine maps, one can compute the new control nets in a clever way which reuses the computations performed for the original simplex. Suppose that we want to partition the simplex Δ by adding a point $\mathbf{x} \in \Delta$ and forming $(n+1)$ new smaller simplices. Then, we can use de Catesljau algorithm [24, 17] to compute the value of the polynomial π at $\mathbf{x}$. It turns out that this computation also produces the control net for the new simplices. Note that this algorithm can only be applied when the Bézier control points of the polynomial are known. We denote $\mathbf{b_i}^l = p(\underbrace{\mathbf{v}_1, \ldots, \mathbf{v}_1}_{\mathbf{i}[1]}, \ldots, \underbrace{\mathbf{v}_{n+1}, \ldots, \mathbf{v}_{n+1}}_{\mathbf{i}[n+1]}, \underbrace{\mathbf{x}_1, \ldots, \mathbf{x}_l}_{l})$ with $\mathbf{i}[1] + \ldots + \mathbf{i}[n+1] + l = d$. Since p is symmetric and multi-affine, we have:

$$\mathbf{b_i}^l = \lambda_1(\mathbf{x}_l)\mathbf{b}_{\mathbf{i}+\mathbf{e}_1}^{l-1} + \ldots + \lambda_n(\mathbf{x}_l)\mathbf{b}_{\mathbf{i}+\mathbf{e}_n}^{l-1} \tag{10}$$

Note that $\mathbf{b_o}^n = p(\mathbf{x}_1, \ldots, \mathbf{x}_n)$ where $\mathbf{o}$ is the zero multi-index. In addition, with $l = 0$, $\mathbf{b_i}^0$ are exactly the Bézier control points of the polynomial. Therefore, by running the above recursion starting from $l = 0$ until $l = n$ we obtain the blossom value at $(\mathbf{x}_1, \ldots, \mathbf{x}_n)$. If all the argument points of the blossom are equal

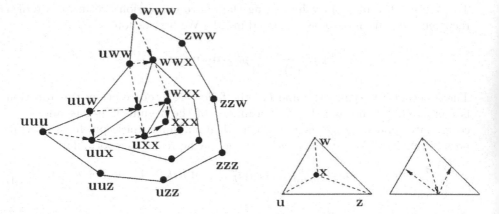

Fig. 1. Subdividing a Bézier control net

to $\mathbf{x}$, the result of the algorithm is $\pi(\mathbf{x})$. The de Catesljau algorithm is illustrated with a 2-dimensional example in Figure 1 where each node is annotated with the arguments of the blossom to evaluate. The nodes on the outermost layer correspond to the control points for the original triangle $\mathbf{uzw}$. The incoming arrows of $\mathbf{uux}$ show that the blossom value at this point is computed from the blossom values at $\mathbf{uuu}$ and $\mathbf{uuw}$. As mentioned earlier, we can see that the computation of $\pi(\mathbf{x})$ indeed produces the Bézier control points for the sub-simplices. Figure 1 shows the values $p(\underbrace{\mathbf{u},\ldots,\mathbf{u}}_{i[1]},\underbrace{\mathbf{x},\ldots,\mathbf{x}}_{i[2]},\underbrace{\mathbf{w},\ldots,\mathbf{w}}_{i[3]})$ which are the Bézier control points for the triangle $\mathbf{uxw}$.

One important remark is that the subdivision at the center of the simplex does not reduce the maximal side length of the simplices. By Theorem 3 this means that the convergence of the Bézier control net towards the polynomial is not guaranteed. However, one can repeat the bisection at the mid-point of the logest edge, as shown in Figure 1 to achieve the desired accuracy. More generally, the subdivision of a simplex can be defined as follows. For each barycentric coordinate $\lambda_i(\mathbf{x}) > 0$ of a point $\mathbf{x} \in \Delta$ we define a simplex Δ_i obtained from Δ by replacing the vertex $\mathbf{v}_i$ with $\mathbf{x}$. Hence, when the point $\mathbf{x}$ is the mid-point of an edge we obtain a bisection. It was proved in [25] that using the bisection at the mid-point of the longest edge, after n steps (where n is the dimension of the simplex) the simplex diameter is reduced at least by $\sqrt{3}/2$ times. In two dimensions, another method of subdivision via all the mid-points of the edges was discussed in [21]. This method is however more complex to implement for dimensions higher than 2.

4   Reachability Algorithm

Let us summarize our development so far. In Section 2, we presented a scheme to approximate the successor in one time step by applying a polynomial, called the integration map, to the current state. We then showed in Section 3 how to over-approximate the image of a simplex by a polynomial map using the Bézier control net. The result of this approximation is in general a polyhedron.

We are now ready to describe our reachability algorithm for polynomial systems. In Algorithm 1, X_0 is the initial set which is assumed to be a convex polyhedron in $\mathbb{R}^n$, each R_k is a set of convex polyhedra. The function Bez over-approximates the image of a simplex Δ by the integration map P, using the method presented in Section 3. The goal of the function $triangulation$ is to triangulate a set of convex polyhedra and return the set of all simplices of the triangulation. To do so, we collect all the vertices of the polyhedra and compute a triangulation of this set. We then exclude all the simplices in the triangulation whose interior does not intersect with R_k. Let us briefly discuss the precision of

---

Algorithm 1. Reachable set computation

$R_0 = \{X_0\}$, $k = 0$
repeat
   $S_\Delta = triangulation(R_k)$
   $C = \emptyset$
   for all $\Delta \in S_\Delta$ **do**
      $C = C \cup Bez(\Delta)$
   end for
   $R_{k+1} = C$
   $k = k + 1$
until $R_{k+1} = R_k$

---

the algorithm. We suppose that ρ is the maximal size of the simplices that are produced by the function $triangulation$ and h is the integration time step. If the integration map P can be exactly computed, using Theorem 1, the integration error is $\mathcal{O}(h^3)$. In addition, Theorem 3 shows that our approximation of the integration map P induces an error $\mathcal{O}(\rho^2)$. By the triangle inequality, the total error in each iteration of Algorithm 1 is bounded by $(\mathcal{O}(h^3) + \mathcal{O}(\rho^2))$. Therefore, by choosing appropriate values ρ in function of h, we can guarantee a bound $\mathcal{O}(h^3)$ on the local error and thus the order 2 of Algorithm 1.

We now discuss some computation issues. The first remark is that the total number of the Bézier control points is $\beta(n, d)$, but the actual number of vertices of their convex hull (that is, $Bez(\Delta)$) is often much smaller, depending on the geometric structure of the polynomial map P. On the other hand, in order to speed up the computation (at the price of less precise results), one can approximate C by its convex hull or even by a simplex. Algorithms for doing so have been developed and some algorithms can compute a minimal volume enclosing simplex (such as, [26, 27]).

Let us now briefly discuss the relation between our new algorithm and the reachability algorithm based on hybridization, proposed in [15]. The latter first approximates the (general) non-linear dynamics by a piecewise linear dynamics, using a simplicial decomposition of the state space. Hence, for the approximate system, one can indeed compute the reachable set of each linear dynamics more accurately. However, the treatement of discrete transitions (i.e. the dynamics changes) makes the overall computation very expensive due to the geometric complexity of the intersection between the reachable set and the switching hyperplanes. In the algorithm of this paper, the one-step computation for polynomial systems is in general more costly than that for linear systems, but discrete transitions are avoided. Nevertheless, more experimentation is needed to draw conclusions about the advantages and inconvenients of these two approaches.

5   Application to a Biological System

We have implemented Algorithm 1 and applied it to a well-known biological system. The initial motivation of our study of polynomial systems come from the interest in applying hybrid systems techniques to biological systems. Indeed, the continuous dynamics of many such systems can be described using multi-affine or more generally polynomial differential equations. We have experimented the implementation of our algorithm on two simplified models of gene transcription control in the bacteria Vibrio Fisheri. The reader is refered to the papers [28, 29] for a detailed description of the models and the related gene control problems. The first model corresponds to one mode of a simplified hybrid system where the continuous dynamics is described by the following multi-affine system:

$$\begin{cases} \dot{x}_1 = k_2 x_2 - k_1 x_1 x_3 + u_1 \\ \dot{x}_2 = k_1 x_1 x_3 - k_2 x_2 \\ \dot{x}_3 = k_2 x_2 - k_1 x_1 x_3 - n x_3 + n u_2 \end{cases} \tag{11}$$

The state variables $\mathbf{x} = (x_1, x_2, x_3)$ represent the cellular concentrations of different species, and the parameters k_1, k_2, n are the binding, dissociation and diffusion constants. The variables u_1 and u_2 are control variables, which respectively represent the plasmid and external source of autoinducer. In [29] the following control law for steering all the states in the rectangle $[1, 2] \times [1, 2] \times [1, 2]$

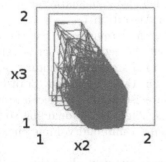 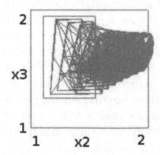

Fig. 2. Reachable sets: with $u_1 = u_2 = 0$ (left) and with the specified control law (right). The control law indeed drives the system to the face $x_2 = 2$.

to the face $x_2 = 2$ was proposed: $u_1(\mathbf{x}) = -10(x_2 + x_1(-1 + 3) - 4x_3)$ and $u_2(\mathbf{x}) = x_1(3 + x_2(-1 + x_3)) - (-2 + x_2)x_3$. This control objective corresponds to the activation of some genes in the system. We consider two cases: with no control (i.e. $u_1 = u_2 = 0$) and with the above control law. Figure 2 shows the projection on x_2 and x_3 of the reachable sets obtained using our algorithm for polynomial systems. In [16] we have already treated this model using an abstraction method based on projection. This method approximates the multi-affine system by a lower dimensional bilinear system. Comparing with the result presented in [16], one can see that our new algorithm for polynomial systems is more accurate, and in addition we have observed that it is also more time-efficient.

The second model is taken from [28]. It is a hybrid model[4] with two modes and one additional continuous variable x_4. The continuous dynamics is $\dot{\mathbf{x}} = A\mathbf{x} + g(\mathbf{x}) + b_{ij}$ where b_{01} and b_{10} correspond respectively to the non-luminescent and luminescent modes, and

$$A = \begin{pmatrix} \frac{-1}{H_{sp}} & 0 & 0 & r_{Co} \\ 0 & 0 & 0 & \frac{-1}{H_{sp}} - r_{Co} \\ 0 & x_0 r_{AII} & \frac{-1}{H_{AI}} & x_0 r_{Co} \\ 0 & \frac{-1}{H_{sp}} & 0 & 0 \end{pmatrix} ; \; g(\mathbf{x}) = \begin{pmatrix} -1 \\ 1 \\ -x_0 \\ 0 \end{pmatrix} r_{AIR} x_1 x_3$$

We are interested in the question of how to determine the sets of states from which the system can reach the luminescent equilibrium. The condition for switching between the two modes is $x_2 = x_{2sw}$. This problem was also previously studied in [28] using the tool $\mathbf{d/dt}$. However, in [28] the multi-affine dynamics was approximated by a 3-dimensional linear system, assuming that x_1 remains constant. Using our new algorithm for polynomial systems, we can now handle the non-linearity in the dynamics. To deal with the discrete dynamics of the model, it suffices to implement some Boolean operations over the reachable set by the continuous dynamics, which are represented in form of convex polyhedra. Concerning qualitative behavior, the result obtained for the 4-dimensional multi-affine model is compatible with the result for the linear approximate model in [28], that is, from the non-luminescent mode the system can reach the guard to switch to the luminescent mode and then converge to the equilibrium. However, the new result obtained for the 4-dimensional model shows a larger set of states that can reach the equilibrium. This can be explained by the fact that in this model the variable x_1 is not kept constant and can evolve in time.

6   Concluding Remarks

In this paper, we presented a new approach to approximate reachability analysis of polynomial systems by combining the ideas from numerical integration and techniques from computer aided geometric design. The reachability algorithm we proposed is of order 2, and these results can be straightforwardly applied to safety verification of hybrid systems. This work opens interesting directions to

---

[4] The numbering of variables is different from that in [28].

explore. Indeed, different tools from geometric modeling (such as, splines) could be exploited to approximate polynomial maps more efficiently. In addition, we plan to do more experimentation on other case studies, such as a model of metabolic mechanism of a plant.

References

1. Alur, R., Henzinger, T., Lafferriere, G., Pappas, G.: Discrete abstractions of hybrid systems. Proc. of the IEEE (2000)
2. Greenstreet, M., Mitchell, I.: Integrating projections. In Henzinger, T., Sastry, S., eds.: Hybrid Systems: Computation and Control. LNCS 1386, Springer (1998) 159–1740
3. Dang, T., Maler, O.: Reachability analysis via face lifting. In Henzinger, T., Sastry, S., eds.: Hybrid Systems: Computation and Control. LNCS 1386, Springer (1998) 96–109
4. Chutinan, A., Krogh, B.: Verification of polyhedral invariant hybrid automata using polygonal flow pipe approximations. In Vaandrager, F., van Schuppen, J., eds.: Hybrid Systems: Computation and Control. LNCS 1569, Springer (1999) 76–90
5. Kurzhanski, A., Varaiya, P.: Ellipsoidal techniques for reachability analysis. In Krogh, B., Lynch, N., eds.: Hybrid Systems: Computation and Control. LNCS 1790, Springer (2000) 202–214
6. Asarin, E., Bournez, O., Dang, T., Maler, O.: Approximate reachability analysis of piecewise-linear dynamical systems. In Krogh, B., Lynch, N., eds.: Hybrid Systems: Computation and Control. LNCS 1790, Springer (2000) 20–31
7. Tomlin, C., Mitchell, I., Bayen, A., Oishi, M.: Computational techniques for the verification of hybrid systems. Proceedings of the IEEE 91(7) (2003) 986–1001
8. Mitchell, I.M., Templeton, J.A.: A toolbox of Hamilton-Jacobi solvers for analysis of nondeterministic continuous and hybrid systems. In: Hybrid Systems: Computation and Control. LNCS, Springer (2005, to appear)
9. Girard, A.: Reachability of uncertain linear systems using zonotopes. In: Hybrid Systems : Computation and Control. LNCS 3414, Springer (2005) 291–305
10. Prajna, S., Jadbabaie, A.: Safety verification of hybrid systems using barrier certificates. In Alur, R., Pappas, G.J., eds.: Hybrid Systems: Computation and Control. LNCS 2993, Springer (2004) 477–492
11. Tiwari, A., Khanna, G.: Nonlinear systems: Approximating reach sets. In: Hybrid Systems: Computation and Control. LNCS 2993, Springer (2004) 600–614
12. Tiwari, A., Khanna, G.: Series of abstractions for hybrid automata. In Tomlin, C., Greenstreet, M., eds.: Hybrid Systems: Computation and Control. LNCS 2289, Springer (2002) 465–478
13. Alur, R., Dang, T., Ivancic, F.: Reachability analysis via predicate abstraction. In Greenstreet, M., Tomlin, C., eds.: Hybrid Systems: Computation and Control. LNCS 2289, Springer (2002)
14. Clarke, E.M., Fehnker, A., Han, Z., Krogh, B.H., Ouaknine, J., Stursberg, O., Theobald, M.: Abstraction and counterexample-guided refinement in model checking of hybrid systems. Int. J. Found. Comput. Sci. 14(4) (2003) 583–604
15. Asarin, E., Dang, T., Girard, A.: Reachability analysis of nonlinear systems using conservative approximation. In Maler, O., Pnueli, A., eds.: Hybrid Systems: Computation and Control. LNCS 2623, Springer (2003) 20–35

16. Asarin, E., Dang, T.: Abstraction by projection. In Alur, R., Pappas, G., eds.: Hybrid Systems: Computation and Control. LNCS 2993, Springer (2004) 32–47
17. Farin, G.: Curves and Surfaces for Computer Aided Geometric Design. Academic Press (1990)
18. Davyrov, O., M.Sommer, H.Strauss: On almost interpolation by multivariate splines. In G.Nürnberger, J., G.Walz, eds.: Multivariate Approximation and Splines, ISNM, Birkhäuser (1997) 45–58
19. Ramshaw, L.: Blossoms are polar forms. Computer Aided Geometric Design **6** (1989) 323–358
20. Seidel, H.P.: Polar forms and triangular B-spline surfaces. In: Blossoming: The New Polar-Form Approach to Spline Curves and Surfaces, SIGGRAPH '91 Course Notes 26, ACM SIGGRAPH. (1991) 8.1–8.52
21. Gallier, J.: Curves and surfaces in geometric modeling: theory and algorithms. Series In Computer Graphics and Geometric Modeling. Morgan Kaufmann (1999)
22. DeRose, T., Goldman, R., Hagen, H., Mann, S.: Functional composition via blossoming. ACM Transactions on Graphics **12**(2) (April 1993)
23. Lodha, S., Goldman, R.: Change of basis algorithms for surfaces in cagd. Computer Aided Geometric Design **12** (1995) 801–824
24. de Casteljau, P.: Formes à pôles. Hermes, Paris (1985)
25. Rivara, M.C.: Mesh refinement process based on the generalized bisection of simplices. SIAM Journal on Numerical Analysis **21** (1984) 604–613
26. Vegter, G., Yap, C.: Minimal circumscribing simplices. In: Proc. of the 3rd Canadian Conference on Computational Geometry, Vancouver, Canada. (1991) 58–61
27. Fuhrmann, D.R.: A simplex shrink-wrap algorithm. In: Proceedings of SPIE, AeroSense (1999)
28. Belta, C., Schug, J., Dang, T., Kumar, V., Pappas, G., Rubin, H., Dunlap, P.: Stability and reachability analysis of a hybrid model of luminescence in the marine bacterium *vibrio fisheri*. In: Proc. of CDC. (2001)
29. Belta, C., Habets, L.C.G.J.M., Kumar, V.: Control of multi-affine systems on rectangles with an application to gene transcription control. In: Proc. of CDC. (2003)

Proof of Theorem 1. From (3) and (4), the local error can be written as:

$$\mathbf{x}(t_k + \tau) - \bar{\mathbf{x}}(t_k + \tau) = \int_0^h e^{A(h-\tau)}[f(\mathbf{x}(t_k + \tau)) - f(\alpha(t_k + \tau))]\, d\tau.$$

On the other hand, due to the Taylor expansion, we have $\|\mathbf{x}(t_k + \tau) - \alpha(t_k + \tau)\|$ $\leq M\tau^2$ where M is some constant. We then have $\| f(\mathbf{x}(t_k+\tau)) - f(\alpha(t_k+\tau)) \| \leq$ $LM\tau^2$ where L is the Lipschitz constant of f. Using the expression (6), we have $\Gamma_2 = \int_0^h e^{A(h-\tau)}\tau^2\, d\tau = \frac{A^3}{3!}h^3 + \mathcal{O}(h^4)$, it then follows that

$$\|\mathbf{x}(t_k + \tau) - \bar{\mathbf{x}}(t_k + \tau)\| = \mathcal{O}(h^3).$$

This completes the proof of the theorem.   □

Proof of Lemma 2. We consider $p(\mathbf{x}_1, \mathbf{x}_2, \ldots, \mathbf{x}_d)$ where each argument $\mathbf{x}_j$ can be expressed using the barycentric coordinates as: $\mathbf{x}_j = \lambda_1(\mathbf{x}_j)\mathbf{v}_1 + \ldots +$

$\lambda_{n+1}(\mathbf{x}_j)\mathbf{v}_{n+1}$. Due to the property of multi-affine maps, replacing the first argument $\mathbf{x}_1$ with its barycentric coordinates, we have:

$$p(\mathbf{x}_1, \mathbf{x}_2, \ldots, \mathbf{x}_d) = \lambda_1(\mathbf{x}_1)p(\mathbf{v}_1, \mathbf{x}_2, \ldots, \mathbf{x}_{n+1}) + \ldots + \lambda_{n+1}(\mathbf{x}_1)p(\mathbf{v}_{n+1}, \mathbf{x}_2, \ldots, \mathbf{x}_{n+1}).$$

We then do the same with other arguments to obtain:

$$p(\mathbf{x}_1, \ldots, \mathbf{x}_d) = \sum_{I \in \Xi} \prod_{k \in I_1} \lambda_1(\mathbf{x}_k) \ldots \prod_{k \in I_{n+1}} \lambda_{n+1}(\mathbf{x}_k) p(\underbrace{\mathbf{v}_1, \ldots, \mathbf{v}_1}_{i[1]}, \ldots, \underbrace{\mathbf{v}_{n+1}, \ldots, \mathbf{v}_{n+1}}_{i[n+1]})$$
(12)

where Ξ is the set of all partitions of $\{1, 2, \ldots, d\}$ defined as follows. We say that $I = \{I_k\}_{k=1,2\ldots,n+1}$ is a partition of $\{1, 2, \ldots, d\}$ iff all I_k are pairwise disjoint and $\cup_{k \in \{1,\ldots,n+1\}} I_k = \{1, 2, \ldots, d\}$. We write $|I_k|$ to denote the cardinality of I_k. Then, by letting the arguments $\mathbf{x}_i$ to be equal, it is not hard to see that the equation (12) becomes:

$$p(\mathbf{x}, \ldots, \mathbf{x}) = \sum_{||\mathbf{i}||=d} \binom{d}{\mathbf{i}} \lambda_1^{i[0]}(\mathbf{x}) \lambda_2^{i[1]}(\mathbf{x}) \ldots \lambda_n^{i[n]}(\mathbf{x}) p(\underbrace{\mathbf{v}_1, \ldots, \mathbf{v}_1}_{i[1]}, \ldots, \underbrace{\mathbf{v}_{n+1}, \ldots, \mathbf{v}_{n+1}}_{i[n+1]})$$

Comparing the above with the definition of Bézier simplices (7), it is easy to see that all the points $p(\underbrace{\mathbf{v}_1, \ldots, \mathbf{v}_1}_{i[1]}, \ldots, \underbrace{\mathbf{v}_{n+1}, \ldots, \mathbf{v}_{n+1}}_{i[n+1]})$ form the control net of a π whose polar form is p.   □

Proof of Theorem 3. Given a multi-index $\mathbf{i}$ with $||\mathbf{i}|| = d$, we consider a point $\mathbf{y} \in \Delta$ which is written as $\mathbf{y} = \sum_{i \in \{1,\ldots,n\}} \frac{i[i]}{d} \mathbf{v}_i$. We first observe that due to symmetry, $p(\mathbf{x}, \mathbf{y}, \ldots, \mathbf{y}) = p(\mathbf{y}, \mathbf{x}, \ldots, \mathbf{y}) = \ldots = p(\mathbf{y}, \mathbf{y}, \ldots, \mathbf{x})$. Let D denote the partial derivative of these functions at $\mathbf{x} = \mathbf{y}$. Using the Taylor expansion of $p(\mathbf{x}_1, \mathbf{x}_2, \ldots, \mathbf{x}_d)$ around $(\mathbf{y}, \mathbf{y}, \ldots, \mathbf{y})$, we have:

$$\mathbf{b_i} = p(\underbrace{\mathbf{v}_1, \ldots, \mathbf{v}_1}_{i[1]}, \ldots, \underbrace{\mathbf{v}_{n+1}, \ldots, \mathbf{v}_{n+1}}_{i[n+1]})$$

$$= p(\mathbf{y}, \mathbf{y}, \ldots, \mathbf{y}) + i[1]D(\mathbf{v}_1 - \mathbf{y}) + \ldots + i[n+1]D(\mathbf{v}_{n+1} - \mathbf{y}) + O(\rho^2)$$

Note that $i[0](\mathbf{v}_0 - \mathbf{y}) + \ldots + i[n+1](\mathbf{v}_{n+1} - \mathbf{y}) = 0$. It then follows that $\mathbf{b_i} = \pi(\mathbf{y}) + O(\rho^2)$. This means that $||\mathbf{b_i} - \pi(\mathbf{y})||$ is indeed of order $O(\rho^2)$.   □

A Lattice Theory for Solving Games of Imperfect Information*

Martin De Wulf, Laurent Doyen**, and Jean-François Raskin

Département d'Informatique,
Université Libre de Bruxelles

Abstract. In this paper, we propose a fixed point theory to solve games of imperfect information. The fixed point theory is defined on the lattice of antichains of sets of states. Contrary to the classical solution proposed by Reif [Rei84], our new solution does not involve determinization. As a consequence, it is readily applicable to classes of systems that do not admit determinization. Notable examples of such systems are timed and hybrid automata. As an application, we show that the discrete control problem for games of imperfect information defined by rectangular automata is decidable. This result extends a result by Henzinger and Kopke in [HK99].

1 Introduction

Timed and hybrid systems are dynamical systems with both discrete and continuous components. A paradigmatic example of a hybrid system is a digital control program for an analog plant environment, like a furnace or an airplane: the controller state moves discretely between control modes, and in each control mode, the plant state evolves continuously according to physical laws. A natural model for hybrid systems is the *hybrid automaton*, which represents discrete components using finite-state machines and continuous components using real-numbered variables whose evolution is governed by differential equations or differential inclusions [ACH+95].

The distinction between continuous evolutions of the plant state (which is given by the real-numbered variables of a hybrid automaton) and discrete switches of the controller state (which is given by the location, or control mode, of the hybrid automaton) permits a natural formulation of the *safety control problem*: given an unsafe set U of plant states, is there a strategy to switch the controller state in real time so that the plant can be prevented from entering U? In other words, the hybrid automaton specifies a set of possible control modes, together with the plant behavior resulting from each mode, and the control problem asks for deriving a *switching strategy* between control modes that keeps the plant out of trouble.

In the literature, there are algorithms or semi-algorithms (termination is not always guaranteed) to derive such switching strategy. Those semi-algorithms usually comes in the form of symbolic fixed point computations that manipulate sets of

---

* Supported by the FRFC project "Centre Fédéré en Vérification" funded by the Belgian National Science Foundation (FNRS) under grant nr 2.4530.02.
** Research fellow supported by the Belgian National Science Foundation (FNRS).

João Hespanha and A. Tiwari (Eds.): HSCC 2006, LNCS 3927, pp. 153–168, 2006.

states using a well-suited monotonic function like the controllable predecessor operator [AHK02, MPS95]. Those algorithms make a strong hypothesis: they consider that the controller that executes the switching strategy has a *perfect information* about the state of the controlled system. Unfortunately, this is usually an unreasonable hypothesis. Indeed, when the switching strategy has to be implemented by a real hardware, the controller typically acquires information about the state of the system by reading values on sensors. Those sensors have finite precision, and so the information about the state in which the system lies is *imperfect*. Let us illustrate this. Consider a controller that monitors the temperature of a tank, and has to maintain the temperature between given bounds by switching on and off a gas burner. The temperature of the tank is the state of the continuous system to control. Assume that the temperature is sensed through a thermometer that returns an integer number and ensures a deviation bounded by one degree Celsius. So, when the sensor returns the temperature c, the controller only knows that the temperature lies in the interval $(c-1, c+1)$ degrees. We say that the sensor reading is an *observation* of the system. This observation gives an imperfect information about the state of the system.

Now, if we fix a set of possible observations of the system to control, the control problem that we want to solve is the *safety control problem with imperfect information*: "given an unsafe set U of plant states, a set of observations, is there an observation based strategy to switch the controller state in real time so that the plant can be prevented from entering U?". While it is well-known that safety games of perfect information can be won using *memoryless strategies*, it is not the case for games of imperfect information [Rei84]. In that paper, Reif studies *games of incomplete information* which are a subclass of safety games of imperfect information where the set of observations is a partition of the state space. Notice that this is not the case of our tank example since when the temperature of the water is d, the thermometer may return either $\lceil d \rceil$ or $\lfloor d \rfloor$. To win such games, memory is sometimes necessary: the controller has to remember (part of) the history of observations that it has made so far. In the finite state case, games of incomplete information can be solved algorithmically. Reif proposes an algorithm that first transforms the game of incomplete information into a game of perfect information using a kind of determinization procedure.

In this paper, we propose an alternative method to solve games of imperfect (and incomplete) information. Our method comes in the form of a fixed point (semi-)algorithm that iterates a monotone operator on the lattice of antichains of sets of states. The greatest fixed point of this operator contains exactly the information needed to determine the states from which an observation based control strategy exists and to synthesize such a strategy. We prove that our algorithm has an optimal complexity for finite state games and we identify a class of infinite state games for which the greatest fixed point of the operator is computable. Using this class of games and results from [HK99], we show that the discrete-time control problem with imperfect information is decidable for the class of rectangular automata. Strategies that win those games are robust as they can be implemented using hardware that senses its environment with finite precision.

Our fixed point method has several advantages over the algorithmic method proposed by Reif. First, as it does not require determinization, our (semi-)algorithm is readily applicable to classes of systems for which determinization is not effective: timed and hybrid automata are notable examples [AD94]. Second, we show that there are families of games on which the Reif's algorithm needs exponential time when our algorithm only needs polynomial time. Third, as our method is based on a lattice theory, abstract interpretation methods can be used to derive in a systematic way approximation algorithms [CC77].

Our paper is structured as follows. In Section 2, we recall the definition of the lattice of antichains. In Section 3, we show how to use this lattice to solve games of imperfect information. In Section 4, we give a fixed point algorithm that is EXPTIME for finite state games and we compare with the technique of Reif. Finally, in Section 5, we solve games of imperfect information for rectangular automata. Due to lack of space, the proofs of most of the theorems have been omitted and can be found in [DDR06].

2   The Lattice of Antichains of Sets of States

First we recall the notion of antichain. An *antichain* on a partially ordered set $\langle X, \leq \rangle$ is a set $X' \subseteq X$ such that for any $x_1, x_2 \in X'$ with $x_1 \neq x_2$ we have neither $x_1 \leq x_2$ nor $x_2 \leq x_1$, that is X' is a set of incomparable elements of X. We define similarly a *chain* to be a set of comparable elements of X.

Let $q, q' \in 2^{2^S}$ and define $q \sqsubseteq q'$ if and only if $\forall s \in q : \exists s' \in q' : s \subseteq s'$. This relation is a preorder but is not antisymmetric. Since we need a partial order, we construct the set $L \subseteq 2^{2^S}$ for which $\sqsubseteq$ is antisymmetric on L. The set L is the set of antichains on $\langle 2^S, \subseteq \rangle$.

We say that a set $s \subseteq S$ is *dominated* in q if and only if $\exists s' \in q : s \subset s'$. The set of dominated elements of q is denoted $\mathsf{Dom}(q)$. The *reduced form* of q is $\lceil q \rceil = q \backslash \mathsf{Dom}(q)$ and dually the *expanded* form of q is $\rceil q \lceil = q \cup \mathsf{Dom}(q)$. The set $\lceil q \rceil$ is an antichain of $\langle 2^S, \subseteq \rangle$. Observe that $\mathsf{Dom}(\lceil q \rceil) = \emptyset$, that is $\forall s, s' \in \lceil q \rceil$: if $s_1 \subseteq s_2$ then $s_1 = s_2$. The relation $\sqsubseteq$ has the useful following properties:

Lemma 1. *Let* $q, q' \in 2^{2^S}$. *If* $q \subseteq q'$ *then* $q \sqsubseteq q'$.

Lemma 2. $\forall q, q' \in 2^{2^S}, \forall q_1, q_2 \in \{q, \lceil q \rceil, \rceil q \lceil \}, \forall q_1', q_2' \in \{q', \lceil q' \rceil, \rceil q' \lceil \} : q_1 \sqsubseteq q_2$ *is equivalent to* $q_1' \sqsubseteq q_2'$.

We can now define formally L as the set $\{\lceil q \rceil \mid q \in 2^{2^S}\}$.

Lemma 3. *The relation* $\sqsubseteq \subseteq L \times L$ *is a partial ordering and* $\langle L, \sqsubseteq \rangle$ *is a partially ordered set.*

Lemma 4. *For* $q, q' \in L$, *the greatest lower bound of* q *and* q' *is* $q \sqcap q' = \lceil \{s \cap s' \mid s \in q \wedge s' \in q'\} \rceil$ *and the least upper bound of* q *and* q' *is* $q \sqcup q' = \lceil \{s \mid s \in q \vee s \in q'\} \rceil$.

For $Q \subseteq L$, we have $\sqcap Q = \lceil \{\bigcap_{q \in Q} s_q \mid s_q \in q\} \rceil$ and $\sqcup Q = \lceil \{s \mid \exists q \in Q : s \in q\} \rceil$. The least element of L is $\bot = \sqcap L = \emptyset$ and the greatest element of L is $\top = \sqcup L = \{S\}$.

Lemma 5. $\langle L, \sqsubseteq, \sqcup, \sqcap, \bot, \top \rangle$ *is a complete lattice.*

This lattice is the *lattice of antichains of sets of states*.

3 Games of Imperfect Information

3.1 Definitions

Notations. Given a finite sequence $\bar{a} = a_0, a_1, \ldots, a_n$, we denote by $|\bar{a}| = n + 1$ the length of $\bar{a}$, by $\bar{a}_k = a_0, \ldots, a_k$ the sequence of the first $k + 1$ elements of $\bar{a}$ (and $\bar{a}_{-1}$ is the empty sequence) and by $\mathsf{last}(\bar{a}) = a_n$ the last element of $\bar{a}$.

Definition 6 [Two-player games]. *A two-player game* is a tuple $\langle S, S_0, \Sigma^c, \Sigma^u, \rightarrow \rangle$ where S is a (non-empty) set of *states*, $S_0 \subseteq S$ is the set of *initial states*, Σ^c (resp. Σ^u) is a finite alphabet of *controllable* (resp. *uncontrollable*) *actions*, and $\rightarrow \subseteq S \times (\Sigma^c \cup \Sigma^u) \times S$ is a transition relation.

The game is turn-based and played by a controller against an environment. To initialize the game, the environment chooses a state $x \in S_0$ and the controller takes the first turn. A turn of the controller consists of choosing a controllable action σ that is enabled in the current state x. If no such action exists, the controllers loses. A turn of the environment then consists of determining a state y such that $x \xrightarrow{\sigma} y$ and of choosing an uncontrollable action u and a state z such that $y \xrightarrow{u} z$. If no enabled action u exists the environment loses. If the game continues forever, the controller wins.

For $\sigma \in \Sigma^c \cup \Sigma^u$, let $\mathsf{Enabled}(\sigma) = \{x \in S \mid \exists x' \in S : (x, \sigma, x') \in \rightarrow\}$ be the set of states in which the action σ is *enabled*, and for $s \subseteq S$ let $\mathsf{Post}_\sigma(s) = \{x' \in S \mid \exists x \in s : (x, \sigma, x') \in \rightarrow\}$ be the set of *successor states* of s by the action σ. Furthermore, given a set $\Sigma \subseteq \Sigma^c \cup \Sigma^u$, we define the notation $\mathsf{Post}_\Sigma(s)$ to mean $\bigcup_{\sigma \in \Sigma} \mathsf{Post}_\sigma(s)$.

The controller has an imperfect view of the game state space in that his/her choices are based on imprecise observations of the states.

Definition 7 [Observation set]. *An observation set* of the state space S is a couple (Obs, γ) where $\gamma : \mathsf{Obs} \rightarrow 2^S$ is such that for all $x \in S$, there exists $\mathsf{obs} \in \mathsf{Obs}$ such that $x \in \gamma(\mathsf{obs})$.

An observation obs is *compatible* with a state x if $x \in \gamma(\mathsf{obs})$. When the controller observes the current state x of the game, he/she receives *one* observation compatible with x. The observation is non-deterministically chosen by the environment.

Definition 8 [Imperfect information]. A two-player game $\langle S, S_0, \Sigma^c, \Sigma^u, \rightarrow \rangle$ equipped with an observation set (Obs, γ) of its state space defines a *game of imperfect information* $\langle S, S_0, \Sigma^c, \Sigma^u, \rightarrow, \mathsf{Obs}, \gamma \rangle$. The *size* of the game is the sum of the sizes of the transition relation $\rightarrow$ and the set Obs.

Let $G = \langle S, S_0, \Sigma^c, \Sigma^u, \rightarrow, \mathsf{Obs}, \gamma \rangle$ be a game of imperfect information. We say that G is a *game of incomplete information* if for any $\mathsf{obs}_1, \mathsf{obs}_2 \in \mathsf{Obs}$, if $\mathsf{obs}_1 \neq \mathsf{obs}_2$ then $\gamma(\mathsf{obs}_1) \cap \gamma(\mathsf{obs}_2) = \emptyset$, that is the observations are disjoint, thus partitioning the state space. We say that G is a *game of perfect information* if $\mathsf{Obs} = S$ and γ is the identity function.

The drawback of games of incomplete information is that they are not suited for a robust modelization of sensors. Indeed, real sensors are imprecise and may return different observations for a given state.

An *observation based strategy* for a game of imperfect information $G = \langle S, S_0, \Sigma^c, \Sigma^u, \rightarrow, \text{Obs}, \gamma \rangle$ is a function $\lambda : \text{Obs}^+ \rightarrow \Sigma^c$. The *outcome* of λ on G is the set $\text{Outcome}_\lambda(G)$ of couples $(\overline{x}, \overline{\text{obs}}) \in S^+ \times \text{Obs}^+$ such that (i) $|x| = |\text{obs}|$, (ii) $x_0 \in S_0$, (iii) for all $0 \leq i \leq |x|$, $x_i \in \gamma(\text{obs}_i)$, and (iv) for all $1 \leq i \leq |x|$, there exists $u \in \Sigma^u$ such that $x_i \in \text{Post}_u(\text{Post}_{\lambda(\overline{\text{obs}}_{i-1})}(\{x_{i-1}\}))$.

Definition 9 [Winning strategy]. We say that an observation based strategy λ for a game G of imperfect information is *winning* if for every $(\overline{x}, \overline{\text{obs}}) \in \text{Outcome}_\lambda(G)$, we have $\text{last}(\overline{x}) \in \text{Enabled}(\lambda(\overline{\text{obs}}))$.

Let us call an *history* a couple $(\overline{\text{obs}}_k, \overline{\sigma}_{k-1}) \in \text{Obs}^+ \times \Sigma^{c+}$ such that $\exists \overline{x} \in S^+ : x_0 \in S_0$ and for all $0 \leq i \leq k$ we have $x_i \in \gamma(\text{obs}_i)$) and for all $0 \leq i < k$ we have $x_{i+1} \in \text{Post}_{\Sigma^u}(\text{Post}_{\sigma_i}(x_i))$. Let us call *knowledge* after an history $(\overline{\text{obs}}_k, \overline{\sigma}_{k-1})$ the function $K : \text{Obs}^+ \times \Sigma^{c+} \rightarrow 2^S$ defined inductively as follows.

$$\begin{cases} K(\overline{\text{obs}}_0, \overline{\sigma}_{-1}) = \gamma(\text{obs}_0) \cap S_0 \\ K(\overline{\text{obs}}_k, \overline{\sigma}_{k-1}) = \gamma(\text{obs}_k) \cap \text{Post}_{\Sigma^u}(\text{Post}_{\sigma_{k-1}}(K(\overline{\text{obs}}_{k-1}, \overline{\sigma}_{k-2}))) \quad \text{for } k > 0 \end{cases}$$

Thus, the *knowledge* after an history $(\overline{\text{obs}}_k, \overline{\sigma}_{k-1})$ is the set of states the player can be sure the game is in after this history.

The *imperfect information control problem* for a class $\mathcal{C}$ of games of imperfect information is defined as follows: given a game $G \in \mathcal{C}$, determine whether there exists a winning observation based strategy for G. We define similarly the *incomplete information control problem* and the *perfect information control problem*.

Safety games. We can encode the classical safety games using our winning condition. To show that, we first need some definitions. Given a game of imperfect information G we say that a set of state S_b is *final* if $\forall \sigma \in \Sigma^c \cup \Sigma^u : \text{Post}_\sigma(S_b) \subseteq S_b$.

We say that a strategy λ is *safe* on a game of imperfect information G w.r.t. a final set of bad states $S_b \subseteq S$ if for every $(\overline{x}, \overline{\text{obs}}) \in \text{Outcome}_\lambda(G)$ we have $\text{last}(\overline{x}) \notin S_b$.

The *imperfect information safety control problem* for a class $\mathcal{C}$ of games of imperfect information is defined as follows: given a two-player game $G \in \mathcal{C}$ and a final set of states S_b of G, determine whether there exists an observation based strategy λ which is safe w.r.t S_b.

Theorem 10. *The imperfect information safety control problem can be reduced to the imperfect information control problem.*

3.2 Using the Lattice of Antichains

We show how the lattice of antichains that we have introduced in Section 2 can be used to solve games of imperfect information by iterating a predecessor operator.

Controllable predecessors. For $q \in L$, define the set of *controllable predecessors* of q as follows:

$$\text{CPre}(q) = \lceil \{ s \subseteq S \mid \exists \sigma \in \Sigma^c \cdot \forall \text{obs} \in \text{Obs} \cdot \exists s' \in q : \\ s \subseteq \text{Enabled}(\sigma) \wedge \text{Post}_{\Sigma^u}(\text{Post}_\sigma(s)) \cap \gamma(\text{obs}) \subseteq s' \} \rceil$$

Let us consider an antichain $q = \{s'_0, s'_1, \dots\}$. A set s belongs to $\mathsf{CPre}(q)$ iff (i) there is a controllable action σ that is enabled in each state of s, (ii) when the controller plays σ, any observation compatible with the next state reached by the game (after the environment has played) suffices to determine in which set s'_i of q that next state lies [1], and (iii) s is maximal.

Lemma 11. *The operator* $\mathsf{CPre} : L \to L$ *is monotone for the partial ordering* $\sqsubseteq$.

Remark. The controllable predecessor operator is also *monotone w.r.t. the set of observations* in the following sense: given a two-player game G, let CPre_1 (resp. CPre_2) be the operator defined on the set of observations $(\mathsf{Obs}_1, \gamma_1)$ (resp. $(\mathsf{Obs}_2, \gamma_2)$). If $\{\gamma_2(\mathsf{obs}) \mid \mathsf{obs} \in \mathsf{Obs}_2\} \sqsubseteq \{\gamma_1(\mathsf{obs}) \mid \mathsf{obs} \in \mathsf{Obs}_1\}$, then for any $q \in L$ we have $\mathsf{CPre}_1(q) \sqsubseteq \mathsf{CPre}_2(q)$. That corresponds to the informal statement that it is easier to control a system with more precise observations.

Theorem 12. *Let* $G = \langle S, S_0, \Sigma^c, \Sigma^u, \to, \mathsf{Obs}, \gamma \rangle$ *be a game of imperfect information. There exists an observation based strategy winning on G if and only if*

$$\{S_0 \cap \gamma(\mathsf{obs}) \mid \mathsf{obs} \in \mathsf{Obs}\} \sqsubseteq \bigsqcup\{q \mid q = \mathsf{CPre}(q)\}. \tag{1}$$

Before proving this theorem, we give some intuition. We denote by Win the set $\bigsqcup\{q \mid q = \mathsf{CPre}(q)\}$ which is the greatest fixed point of CPre. Condition (1) states that any observation of the initial state x_0 suffices to determine in which set s of Win the game has been started. Since Win is a fixed point of the controllable predecessor operator, we know that in each set s of Win we have a controllable action that can be played by the controller in every state $x \in s$ such that (i) the state z reached after the move of the environment lies in one of the sets s' of Win whatever the environment does and, such that (ii) the set s' can be determined using any observation compatible with z. Following this, there exists a winning strategy if Condition (1) holds. The other direction of the theorem is a direct consequence of Tarski's Theorem.

Proof of Theorem 12. First, we give an effective construction of a winning strategy for G, in the form of a finite automaton. For $q \in L$ and $\sigma \in \Sigma^c$, let $\phi(q, \sigma) = \lceil \{s \in S \mid s \subseteq \mathsf{Enabled}(\sigma) \text{ and } \forall \mathsf{obs} \in \mathsf{Obs}, \exists s' \in q : \mathsf{Post}_{\Sigma^u}(\mathsf{Post}_\sigma(s)) \cap \gamma(\mathsf{obs}) \subseteq s'\} \rceil$ be the set of controllable predecessors of q for the action σ. From the greatest fixed point Win of CPre, we define the finite state automaton $A = \langle Q, q_0, \mathcal{L}, \delta \rangle$ where

- $Q = \mathsf{Win} \cup \{q_0\}$ where $q_0 \notin \mathsf{Win}$,
- q_0 is the initial state,
- $\mathcal{L} : Q \backslash \{q_0\} \to \Sigma^c$ is a labeling of the states. For each $s \in \mathsf{Win}$, we choose $\sigma \in \Sigma^c$ such that $s \in \phi(\mathsf{Win}, \sigma)$ and we fix $\mathcal{L}(s) = \sigma$ (such a σ exists since Win is a fixed point of CPre).
- $\delta : Q \times \mathsf{Obs} \to Q$ is a transition function.

---

[1] The quantification over obs is universal since for observations that are incompatible with the new state, the condition holds trivially.

- For each obs $\in$ Obs, choose $s \in$ Win such that $S_0 \cap \gamma(\text{obs}) \subseteq s$ and fix $\delta(q_0, \text{obs}) = s$;
- For each $s \in$ Win and obs $\in$ Obs, choose $s' \in$ Win such that $\text{Post}_{\Sigma^u}(\text{Post}_\sigma(s)) \cap \gamma(\text{obs}) \subseteq s'$ where $\sigma = \mathcal{L}(s)$ and fix $\delta(s, \text{obs}) = s'$.

Such sets s, s' exist by condition (1).

In this automaton, states are labelled with actions and transitions are labelled with observations. Intuitively, a state s of A corresponds to the minimal knowledge that is sufficient to control the system and the label $\mathcal{L}(s)$ is a winning move the controller can play having this knowledge. The next state s' is determined by the observation obs according to the transition relation.

Let $\hat{\delta} : Q \times \text{Obs}^+ \to Q$ be an extension of the transition function δ on words defined recursively by $\hat{\delta}(s, \text{obs}) = \delta(s, \text{obs})$ and $\hat{\delta}(s, \overline{\text{obs}}.\text{obs}) = \delta(\hat{\delta}(s, \overline{\text{obs}}), \text{obs})$.

The strategy defined by A is $\lambda : \text{Obs}^+ \to \Sigma^c$ such that $\lambda(\overline{\text{obs}}) = \mathcal{L}(s)$ if $\hat{\delta}(q_0, \overline{\text{obs}}) = s$. If for some $\overline{\text{obs}}$ there is no s such that $\hat{\delta}(q_0, \overline{\text{obs}}) = s$, then the sequence of observations $\overline{\text{obs}}$ is impossible. In this case, we can set $\lambda(\overline{\text{obs}})$ to any value.

Now we proceed with the proof of the theorem.

- If (1) holds. We show that the strategy λ defined by A is such that for any $(\overline{x}, \overline{\text{obs}}) \in \text{Outcome}_\lambda(G)$, we have (i) $\text{last}(\overline{x}) \in \hat{\delta}(q_0, \overline{\text{obs}})$ and (ii) $\text{last}(\overline{x}) \in \text{Enabled}(\lambda(\overline{\text{obs}}))$ (thus λ is winning). We show this by induction on the length of $\overline{x}$ and $\overline{\text{obs}}$.

  1. $|\overline{x}| = 1$. We have $\overline{x} = x_0$ and $\overline{\text{obs}} = \text{obs}_0$ with $x_0 \in S_0$ and $x_0 \in \gamma(\text{obs}_0)$. Let $s = \hat{\delta}(q_0, \text{obs}_0)$ and $\sigma = \mathcal{L}(s) = \lambda(\text{obs}_0)$. By construction of A, we have $S_0 \cap \gamma(\text{obs}_0) \subseteq s$ and $s \in$ Win.

     As $x_0 \in s$ and Win is a fixed point of CPre, we have (i) $\text{last}(\overline{x}) \in \hat{\delta}(q_0, \text{obs}_0)$ and (ii) $x_0 \in \text{Enabled}(\lambda(\text{obs}_0))$.

  2. $|\overline{x}| > 0$. We have $\overline{x} = x_0, x_1, \ldots, x_k$ and $\overline{\text{obs}} = \text{obs}_0, \text{obs}_1, \ldots, \text{obs}_k$ with $x_k \in \gamma(\text{obs}_k)$. Let $s_{k-1} = \hat{\delta}(q_0, \overline{\text{obs}}_{k-1})$ and $\sigma = \mathcal{L}(s_{k-1}) = \lambda(\overline{\text{obs}}_{k-1})$.

     By the induction hypothesis, we have $x_{k-1} \in s_{k-1}$. For obs $= \text{obs}_k$, let $s_k = \delta(s_{k-1}, \text{obs})$. By construction of A, we have $s_k \in$ Win and $\text{Post}_{\Sigma^u}(\text{Post}_\sigma(s_{k-1})) \cap \gamma(\text{obs}) \subseteq s_k$. Therefore, we have $x_k \in s_k$ and by definition of $\mathcal{L}$, we have $s_k \subseteq \text{Enabled}(\sigma')$ where $\sigma' = \mathcal{L}(s_k) = \lambda(\overline{\text{obs}}_k)$. This yields (i) $\text{last}(\overline{x}) \in \hat{\delta}(q_0, \overline{\text{obs}})$ and (ii) $x_k \in \text{Enabled}(\lambda(\overline{\text{obs}}_k))$.

- If λ is an observation based strategy that is winning on G. We must show that (1) holds. Let $V_\lambda \subseteq 2^S \times \text{Obs}^+$ be the smallest set (w.r.t. to $\subseteq$) such that:
  - $(S_0 \cap \gamma(\text{obs}), \text{obs}) \in V_\lambda$ for every obs $\in$ Obs, and
  - if $(s, \overline{\text{obs}}) \in V_\lambda$ then $(\text{Post}_{\Sigma^u}(\text{Post}_{\lambda(\overline{\text{obs}})}(s)) \cap \gamma(\text{obs}), \overline{\text{obs}}.\text{obs}) \in V_\lambda$ for every obs $\in$ Obs.

  Let $W_\lambda = \{s \mid (s, \overline{\text{obs}}) \in V_\lambda\}$. Let us show that $W_\lambda \sqsubseteq \text{CPre}(W_\lambda)$. By Lemma 1, it suffices to show that $W_\lambda \subseteq \lceil \text{CPre}(W_\lambda) \rceil$. Let $(s, \overline{\text{obs}}) \in V_\lambda$ with $\overline{\text{obs}} = \text{obs}_0, \text{obs}_1, \ldots, \text{obs}_k$ and let us show that $s \in \text{CPre}(W_\lambda)$.

  By definition of V_λ, there exist $s_0, s_1, \ldots, s_k$ such that $s_0 = S_0 \cap \gamma(\text{obs}_0)$, $s_k = s$, and for each $1 \le i \le k$: $s_i = \text{Post}_{\Sigma^u}(\text{Post}_{\sigma_i}(s_{i-1})) \cap \gamma(\text{obs}_i)$ with $\sigma_i = \lambda(\text{obs}_0 \text{obs}_1 \ldots \text{obs}_{i-1})$. For any sequence of states $\overline{x} = x_0, x_1, \ldots, x_k$

with $x_i \in s_i$ and $(\overline{x}_k, \overline{obs}_k) \in \mathsf{Outcome}_\lambda(G)$, since λ is winning on G, we have $x_k \in \mathsf{Enabled}(\lambda(\overline{obs}))$ and thus $s \subseteq \mathsf{Enabled}(\lambda(\overline{obs}))$. Also we have $\mathsf{Post}_{\Sigma^u}(\mathsf{Post}_{\lambda(\overline{obs})}(s)) \cap \gamma(obs) \in W_\lambda$ for every obs $\in$ Obs by construction of V_λ. This entails that $s \in \lceil \mathsf{CPre}(W_\lambda) \rceil$, showing that $W_\lambda \sqsubseteq \mathsf{CPre}(W_\lambda)$, that is CPre is extensive at W_λ and by the Tarski's fixed point Theorem $W_\lambda \sqsubseteq \mathsf{Win}$. The conclusion follows since $\{S_0 \cap \gamma(obs) \mid obs \in \mathsf{Obs}\} \subseteq W_\lambda$. $\blacksquare$

4   Games with Finite State Space

In this section we show that computing the greatest fixed point of CPre for finite state games can be done in EXPTIME. We also compare our algorithm based on the lattice of antichains with the classical technique of [Rei84].

4.1   Fixed Point Algorithm

To compute the greatest fixed point of CPre, we iterate CPre from S using Algorithm 1. This algorithm constructs systematically subsets of S and checks at line 1 whether they belong to $\mathsf{CPre}(q)$. This is done by treating all subsets of size i before the subsets of size $i - 1$, so we avoid to treat the subsets of the already included subsets and the result is in reduced form. Therefore, Algorithm 1 uses the following operator $\mathsf{Children}(s) = \{s \backslash \{x\} \mid x \in s\}$ which returns the subsets of s of cardinality $|s| - 1$.

Lemma 13. *Algorithm 1 computes* CPre *in EXPTIME in the size of the game.*

Lemma 14. *An ascending (or descending) chain in $\langle L, \sqsubseteq, \bigsqcup, \bigsqcap, \bot, \top \rangle$ has at most $2^n + 1$ elements where $n = |S|$.*

Algorithm 1. Algorithm for CPre .

| | **Data** | : A game of imperfect information $G = \langle S, S_0, \Sigma^c, \Sigma^u, \rightarrow, \mathsf{Obs}, \gamma \rangle$ and a set $q \in L$. |

Result   : The set $Z = \mathsf{CPre}(q)$.

begin

1     $Z \leftarrow \emptyset$;

2   Wait $\leftarrow \{S\}$;

3   **while** Wait $\neq \emptyset$ **do**

4   Pick $s \in$ Wait of maximal cardinality ;

5   Wait $\leftarrow$ Wait$\backslash \{s\}$;

6   **if** *for some $\sigma \in \Sigma^c$ we have :*
       (1) $s \subseteq \mathsf{Enabled}(\sigma)$ and
       (2) for all obs $\in$ Obs, *there exists $s' \in q$ such that $\mathsf{Post}_{\Sigma^u}(\mathsf{Post}_\sigma(s)) \cap \gamma(obs) \subseteq s'$*
       then

7           $Z \leftarrow Z \cup \{s\}$;

       else

8   Wait $\leftarrow$ Wait $\cup \{s' \mid s' \in \mathsf{Children}(s) \wedge \forall s'' \in Z \cup \mathsf{Wait} : s' \not\subseteq s''\}$;

9   **return** Z;

end

Theorem 15. *The imperfect information control problem is EXPTIME-complete.*

Proof. We first prove the upper bound. From Lemma 14 and since CPre is monotone, we reach the greatest fixed point Win after at most $O(2^n)$ iterations of CPre. From Lemma 13 computing CPre can be done in EXPTIME. The conclusion follows. For the lower bound, since we solve a more general problem than Reif [Rei84], we have the EXPTIME-hardness. ∎

4.2 Example

Consider the two-player game G_1 on Fig. 1 with state space $S = \{1, 1', 2, 2', 3, 3', \text{Bad}\}$, initial state $S_0 = \{2, 3\}$, actions $\Sigma^c = \{a, b\}$ and $\Sigma^u = \{u\}$. The observation set is Obs $= \{\text{obs}_1, \text{obs}_2\}$ with $\gamma(\text{obs}_1) = \{1, 1', 2, 2', \text{Bad}\}$ and $\gamma(\text{obs}_2) = \{1, 1', 3, 3'\}$.

For the controller, the goal is to avoid state Bad in which there is no controllable action. So the controller must play an a in state 1 and 3 and a b in state 2. However the controller cannot distinguish 1 from 2 using only the current observation. Thus, to discriminate those states, the controller has to rely on its memory of the past observations.

We show below the iterations of the fixed point algorithm and the construction of the strategy. The fixed point computation starts from $\top = \{S\}$. Each set is paired with an action that can be played in all the states of that set:

$$S_1 = \text{CPre}(\{S\}) = \{\{1, 2, 3\}_a\}$$
$$S_2 = \text{CPre}(S_1) \quad = \{\{2\}_b, \{1, 3\}_a\}$$
$$S_3 = \text{CPre}(S_2) \quad = \{\{1\}_a, \{2\}_b, \{3\}_a\}$$
$$S_4 = \text{CPre}(S_3) \quad = S_3$$

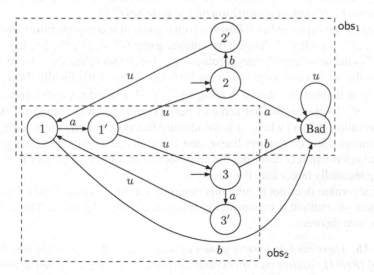

Fig. 1. A two-player game G_1 with observation set $\{\text{obs}_1, \text{obs}_2\}$

Since $S_4 = S_3$, we have Win $= S_3 = \{\{1\}, \{2\}, \{3\}\}$. The existence of a winning strategy is established by condition (1) of Theorem 12 since the sets $S_0 \cap \gamma(\mathrm{obs}_1) = \{2\}$ and $S_0 \cap \gamma(\mathrm{obs}_2) = \{3\}$ are dominated in Win.

From the fixed point, using the construction given in the proof of Theorem 12, we construct the automaton of Fig. 2 which encodes a winning strategy. Indeed, when the game starts the control is either in state 2 if the given observation is obs_1 or in state 3 if the given observation is obs_2. In the first case, the controller plays b and in the second case, it plays a. Then the game lies in state 1. According to the strategy automaton, the controller plays an a and receives a new observation that allows it to determine if the game lies now in state 2 (obs_1) or in state 3 (obs_2). From there, the controller can clearly iterate this strategy.

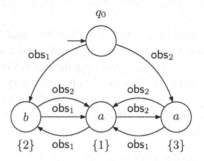

Fig. 2. A finite state automaton A defining a winning strategy for G_1

4.3   Comparison with the Classical Technique of [Rei84]

In [Rei84] the author gives an algorithm to transform a game of incomplete information G into a game G' of perfect information on the histories of G.

The idea can be expressed as follows : given a game of incomplete information $G = \langle S, S_0, \Sigma^c, \Sigma^u, \rightarrow_1, \mathrm{Obs}, \gamma \rangle$ define a two-player game $G'' = \langle S', S'_0, \Sigma^c, \{\varepsilon\}, \rightarrow_2 \rangle$ as follows: S' is the set of knowledges $K(\overline{\mathrm{obs}}_k, \overline{\sigma}_{k-1})$ such that $(\overline{\mathrm{obs}}_k, \overline{\sigma}_{k-1})$ is an history of G. S'_0 is the set of knowledges $\{K(\mathrm{obs}_0)|\gamma(\mathrm{obs}_0) \cap S_0 \neq \emptyset\}$. Finally the transition relation $\rightarrow_2$ is defined as follows: $K(\overline{\mathrm{obs}}_k, \overline{\sigma}_{k-1}) \xrightarrow{\sigma_k}_2 K(\overline{\mathrm{obs}}_{k+1}, \overline{\sigma}_k)$ and $s \xrightarrow{\varepsilon}_2 s$ for all $s \in S'$. To obtain the final game of perfect information G', equip G'' with the set of observation (S', γ_I) where γ_I is the identity function. Solving the resulting game of perfect information G' requires linear time in the size of S' but there exist games of incomplete information G requiring the construction of a game of perfect information of size exponentially larger than the size of G.

As our algorithm does not require this determinization, it is easy to find families of games where our method is exponentially faster than Reif's algorithm. This is formalized in the next theorem.

Theorem 16. *There exist finite state games of incomplete information for which the algorithm of [Rei84] requires an exponential time where our algorithm needs only polynomial time.*

5   Control with Imperfect Information of Rectangular Automata

In this section, we introduce the notion of infinite games with finite stable quotient. We use this notion to show that the *discrete control problem for games of imperfect information defined by rectangular automata* is decidable. This result extends the results in [HK99].

5.1   Games with Finite R-Stable Quotient

Here we drop the assumption that S is finite and we consider the case where there exists a finite quotient of S over which the game is *stable*. We obtain a general decidability result for games of imperfect information with finite stable quotients.

Let $R = \{r_1, r_2, \ldots, r_l\}$ be a finite partition of S. A set $s \subseteq S$ is R-*definable* if $s = \bigcup_{r \in Z} r$ for some $Z \subseteq R$. An antichain $q \in L$ is R-definable if for every $s \in q$, s is R-definable.

Definition 17 [R-stable]. A game of imperfect information $\langle S, S_0, \Sigma^c, \Sigma^u, \rightarrow, \mathsf{Obs}, \gamma \rangle$ is R-*stable* if for every $\sigma \in \Sigma^c$ the following conditions hold:

  (i) Enabled(σ) is R-definable;
  (ii) for every $r \in R$, $\mathsf{Post}_{\Sigma^u}(\mathsf{Post}_\sigma(r))$ is R-definable;
  (iii) for any $r, r' \in R$, if for some $x \in r$ and $u \in \Sigma^u$, $\mathsf{Post}_u(\mathsf{Post}_\sigma)(\{x\}) \cap r' \neq \emptyset$
          then for any $x \in r$, there exists $u \in \Sigma^u$ such that $\mathsf{Post}_{\Sigma^u}(\mathsf{Post}_\sigma)(\{x\}) \cap r' \neq \emptyset$;
  (iv) furthermore, for every obs $\in$ Obs, $\gamma(\mathsf{obs})$ is R-definable.

The next lemma states properties of R-stable games of imperfect information. They are useful for the proof of the next theorem.

Lemma 18. *Let* $G = \langle S, S_0, \Sigma^c, \Sigma^u, \rightarrow, \mathsf{Obs}, \gamma \rangle$ *be a* R-*stable game of imperfect information. Let* $s, s', s'' \subseteq S$ *and* $r \in R$ *such that* (i) s' *and* s'' *are* R-*definable and* (ii) $s \cap r \neq \emptyset$. *If there exists* $\sigma \in \Sigma^c$ *such that* (iii) $s \subseteq$ Enabled(σ) *and* (iv) $\mathsf{Post}_{\Sigma^u}(\mathsf{Post}_\sigma(s)) \cap s' \subseteq s''$ *then* (v) $r \subseteq$ Enabled(σ) *and* (vi) $\mathsf{Post}_{\Sigma^u}(\mathsf{Post}_\sigma(s \cup r)) \cap s' \subseteq s''$.

Theorem 19. *Let* $G = \langle S, S_0, \Sigma^c, \Sigma^u, \rightarrow, \mathsf{Obs}, \gamma \rangle$ *be a* R-*stable game of imperfect information. The greatest fixed point of* CPre *is a* R-*definable antichain and is computable.*

Proof. We show that for any R-definable antichain $q \in L$, the antichain CPre(q) is also R-definable. Let $s \in$ CPre(q). For any $r \in R$ such that $s \cap r \neq \emptyset$, we have by Lemma 18 that $s \cup r \in$ CPre(q). Since $s \subseteq s \cup r$, we must have $s = s \cup r$. This shows that s is R-definable. The number of R-definable antichains is finite, and so, using Tarski's theorem, we can compute the greatest fixed point of CPre in a finite number of iterations.   ∎

5.2   Rectangular Automata

We first recall the definition of rectangular automata and we define their associated game semantics. We recall a result of [HK99] that establishes the existence of a finite bisimulation quotient for this game semantics.

Let $X = \{x_1, \ldots, x_n\}$ be a set of real-valued variables. A *rectangular inequality* over X is a formula of the form $x_i \sim c$, where c is an integer constant, and $\sim$ is one of the following: $<, \leq, >, \geq$. A *rectangular predicate* over X is a conjunction of rectangular inequalities. The set of all rectangular predicates over X is denoted $\mathsf{Rect}(X)$. The rectangular predicate ϕ defines the set of vectors $[\![\phi]\!] = \{y \in \mathbb{R}^n | \phi[X := y]$ is true$\}$. For $1 \leq i \leq n$, let $[\![\phi]\!]_i$ be the projection on variable x_i of the set $[\![\phi]\!]$. A set of the form $[\![\phi]\!]$, where ϕ is a rectangular predicate, is called a *rectangle*. Given a nonnegative integer $m \in \mathbb{N}$, the rectangular predicate ϕ and the rectangle $[\![\phi]\!]$ are *m-bounded* if $|c| \leq m$ for every conjunct $x_i \sim c$ of ϕ. Let us denote $\mathsf{Rect}_m(X)$ the set of m-bounded rectangular predicate on X.

Definition 20 [Rectangular automaton]. A *rectangular automaton* H is a tuple $\langle \mathsf{Loc}, \mathsf{Lab}, \mathsf{Edg}, X, \mathsf{Init}, \mathsf{Inv}, \mathsf{Flow}, \mathsf{Jump} \rangle$ where:

- $\mathsf{Loc} = \{\ell_1, \ldots, \ell_m\}$ is a finite set of *locations*;
- Lab is a finite set of *labels*;
- $\mathsf{Edg} \subseteq \mathsf{Loc} \times \mathsf{Lab} \times \mathsf{Loc}$ is a finite set of *edges*;
- $X = \{x_1, \ldots, x_n\}$ is a finite set of *variables*;
- $\mathsf{Init} : \mathsf{Loc} \to \mathsf{Rect}(X)$ gives the *initial condition* $\mathsf{Init}(\ell)$ of location ℓ. The automaton can start in ℓ with an initial valuation v lying in $[\![\mathsf{Init}(\ell)]\!]$;
- $\mathsf{Inv} : \mathsf{Loc} \to \mathsf{Rect}(X)$ gives the *invariant condition* $\mathsf{Inv}(\ell)$ of location ℓ. The automaton can stay in ℓ as long as the values of its variables lie in $[\![\mathsf{Inv}(\ell)]\!]$;
- $\mathsf{Flow} : \mathsf{Loc} \to \mathsf{Rect}(\dot{X})$ governs the evolution of the variables in each location.
- Jump maps each edge $e \in \mathsf{Edg}$ to a predicate $\mathsf{Jump}(e)$ of the form $\phi \wedge \phi' \wedge \bigwedge_{i \notin \mathsf{Update}(e)} (x_i' = x_i)$, where $\phi \in \mathsf{Rect}(X)$ and $\phi' \in \mathsf{Rect}(X')$ and $\mathsf{Update}(e) \subseteq \{1, \ldots, n\}$. The variables in X' refer to the updated values of the variables after the edge has been traversed. Each variable x_i with $i \in \mathsf{Update}(e)$ is updated nondeterministically to an arbitrary new value in the interval $[\![\phi']\!]_i$.

A rectangular automaton is *m-bounded* if all its rectangular constraints are m-bounded.

Definition 21 [Nondecreasing and bounded variables]. Let H be a rectangular automaton, and let $i \in \{1, \ldots, n\}$. The variable x_i of H is *nondecreasing* if for every control mode $\ell \in \mathsf{Loc}$, the invariant interval $[\![\mathsf{Inv}(\ell)]\!]_i$ and the flow interval $[\![\mathsf{Flow}(\ell)]\!]_i$ are subsets of the nonnegative reals. The variable x_i is *bounded* if for every control mode $\ell \in \mathsf{Loc}$, the invariant interval $[\![\mathsf{Inv}(\ell)]\!]_i$ is a bounded set. The automaton H has *nondecreasing* (resp. *bounded; nondecreasing or bounded*) *variables* if all n variables of H are nondecreasing (resp. bounded; either nondecreasing or bounded).

In the sequel, all the rectangular automata that we consider are assumed to be with nondecreasing or bounded variables.

We now associate a game semantics to each rectangular automaton.

Definition 22 [Discrete game semantics of rectangular automata]. The game *semantics* of a rectangular automaton $H = \langle \text{Loc}, \text{Lab}, \text{Edg}, X, \text{Init}, \text{Inv}, \text{Flow}, \text{Jump} \rangle$ is the game $[\![H]\!] = \langle S, S_0, \Sigma^c, \Sigma^u, \rightarrow \rangle$ where $S = \text{Loc} \times \mathbb{R}^n$ is the *state space* (with $n = |X|$), $S_0 = \{(\ell, v) \in S \mid v \in [\![\text{Init}(\ell)]\!]\}$ is the *initial space*, $\Sigma^c = \text{Lab}$, $\Sigma^u = \{1\}$ and $\rightarrow$ contains all the tuples $((\ell, v), \sigma, (\ell', v'))$ such that:

- either there exists $e = (\ell, \sigma, \ell') \in \text{Edg}$ such that $(v, v') \in [\![\text{Jump}(e)]\!]$,
- *or* $\ell = \ell'$ and $\sigma = 1$ and there exists a continuously differentiable function f : $[0, 1] \rightarrow [\![\text{Inv}(\ell)]\!]$ such that $f(0) = v$, $f(1) = v'$ and for all $t \in (0, 1)$: $\dot{f}(t) \in [\![\text{Flow}(\ell)]\!]$.

Games constructed from rectangular automata are played as follows. The game is started in a location ℓ with a valuation v for the continuous variables such that $v \in [\![\text{Init}(\ell)]\!]$. At each round, the controller decides to take one of the enabled edges if one exists. Then the environment updates the continuous variables by letting time elapse for 1 time unit as specified by the (nondeterministic) flow predicates. A new round is started from there. As for the games that we have considered previously, the goal of the controller is to avoid to reach states where he does not have an enabled transition to propose.

The next definition recalls the notion of bisimulation.

Definition 23 [Bisimulation]. A *simulation* on the game $G = \langle S, S_0, \Sigma^c, \Sigma^u, \rightarrow \rangle$ is a binary relation $\sim$ on the state set S such that $s_1 \sim s_2$ implies that $\forall \sigma \in \Sigma^c \cup \Sigma^u$, if $s_1 \xrightarrow{\sigma} s_1'$ then there exists s_2' such that $s_2 \xrightarrow{\sigma} s_2'$ and $s_1' \sim s_2'$. Such a relation is called a *bisimulation* if it is symmetric.

We consider the following equivalence relation between states of rectangular automata.

Definition 24 . Given the game semantics $[\![H]\!] = \langle S, S_0, \text{Lab}, \{1\}, \rightarrow \rangle$ of a m-bounded rectangular automaton H, define the equivalence relation $\approx_m$ on S by $(\ell, v) \approx_m (\ell', v')$ iff $\ell = \ell'$ and for all $1 \leq i \leq n$ either $\lfloor v_i \rfloor = \lfloor v_i' \rfloor$ and $\lceil v_i \rceil = \lceil v_i' \rceil$ or both v_i and v_i' are greater than m. Let us call $R_{\approx_m}$ the set of equivalence classes of $\approx_m$ on S.

The next lemma states that the number of equivalence classes for this relation is finite for any rectangular automata.

Lemma 25. *[HK99] Let H be a m-bounded rectangular automaton. The equivalence relation $\approx_m$ is the largest bisimulation of the game semantics $[\![H]\!]$.*

5.3 Control of Rectangular Automata with Imperfect Information

We are now in position to extend the result of [HK99] to the case of imperfect information.

Given $H = \langle \text{Loc}, \text{Lab}, \text{Edg}, X, \text{Init}, \text{Inv}, \text{Flow}, \text{Jump} \rangle$, a m-bounded rectangular automaton, we say that the observation set (Obs, γ) is m-bounded if for each obs $\in \text{Obs}$, $\gamma(\text{obs})$ is definable as a finite union of sets of the form $\{(l, v) \mid v \in g\}$ where g is m-bounded rectangle.

Theorem 26. *For any m-bounded rectangular automaton H with game semantics* $[\![H]\!]= \langle S, S_0, \Sigma^c, \Sigma^u, \rightarrow \rangle$, *for any m-bounded observation set* (Obs, γ), *the game of imperfect information* $\langle S, S_0, \Sigma^c, \Sigma^u, \rightarrow, \mathsf{Obs}, \gamma \rangle$ *is* $R_{\approx_m}$-*stable.*

As corollary of Theorem 19 and Theorem 26, we have that:

Corollary 1. *The discrete control problem for games of imperfect information defined by m bounded rectangular automata and m-bounded observation sets is decidable (in 2EXPTIME).*

So far, we do not have a hardness result but we conjecture that the problem is 2EXPTIME-complete. Now, let us illustrate the discrete control problem for games of imperfect information defined by rectangular automata on an example.

Example. We have implemented our fixed point algorithm using HYTECH and its script language [HHWT95]. We illustrate the use of the algorithm on a simple example. Fig. 3 shows a rectangular automaton with four locations and one continuous variable x.

In this example, the game models a cooling system that controls the temperature x. When requested to start, the system begins to cool down. There are two modes of cooling, either fast or slow, among which the environment chooses. The controller can only observe the system through two observations: H with $\gamma(\mathsf{H}) = \{(\ell, x) \mid x \geq 280\}$ and L with $\gamma(\mathsf{L}) = \{(\ell, x) \mid x \leq 285\}$. Thus, only the continuous variable x can be observed imperfectly, not the modes. Depending on the mode however, the timing and action to stop the system are different. In the slow mode, the controller has to issue an action a when the temperature is below 280. In the fast mode, the controller has to issue an action b when the temperature is below 270.

The controller must use its memory of the past observations to make the correct action in time. If the first two observations are H, H then the controller knows that the

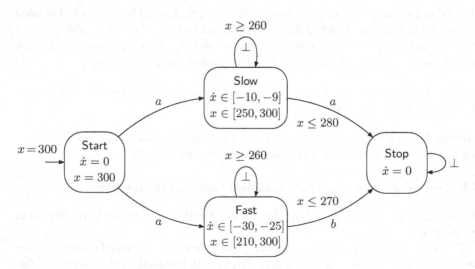

Fig. 3. A rectangular automaton modeling a cooling system

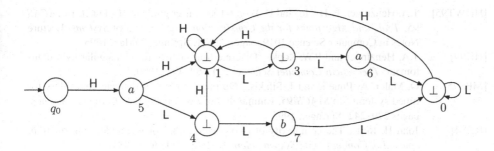

Fig. 4. A finite state automaton defining a winning strategy for the cooling system

mode is Slow. If the first two observations are H, L then the controller knows that the mode is Fast.

The greatest fixed point, given below, allows the computation of the deterministic strategy depicted in Fig. 4. The whole process has been automated in HYTECH. The correspondence between state numbers in the figure and states of the fixed point is the following:

- State $0 \equiv (\mathsf{Stop}, x = 0), (\mathsf{Slow}, 295 < x \leq 300)$
- State $1 \equiv (\mathsf{Slow}, 270 \leq x \leq 300)$
- (Not depicted) State $2 \equiv (\mathsf{Slow}, 295 < x \leq 300), (\mathsf{Fast}, 290 \leq x \leq 300)$
- State $3 \equiv (\mathsf{Slow}, 260 \leq x \leq 289), (\mathsf{Slow}, 295 < x \leq 300)$
- State $4 \equiv (\mathsf{Slow}, 295 < x \leq 300), (\mathsf{Fast}, 260 \leq x \leq 295)$
- State $5 \equiv (\mathsf{Start}, x = 300)$
- State $6 \equiv (\mathsf{Slow}, 250 \leq x \leq 280)$
- State $7 \equiv (\mathsf{Fast}, 210 \leq x \leq 270)$

As before, the strategy associates an action to each set of the fixed point and the observations give the next state of the strategy.

References

[ACH+95] R. Alur, C. Courcoubetis, N. Halbwachs, T.A. Henzinger, P.-H. Ho, X. Nicollin, A. Olivero, J. Sifakis, and S. Yovine. The algorithmic analysis of hybrid systems. *Theoretical Computer Science*, 138:3–34, 1995.

[AD94]   Rajeev Alur and David L. Dill. A theory of timed automata. *Theoretical Computer Science*, 126(2):183–235, 1994.

[AHK02]   R. Alur, T.A. Henzinger, and O. Kupferman. Alternating-time temporal logic. *Journal of the ACM*, 49:672–713, 2002.

[CC77]   Patrick Cousot and Radhia Cousot. Abstract interpretation: A unified lattice model for static analysis of programs by construction or approximation of fixpoints. In *POPL*, pages 238–252, 1977.

[DDR06]   M. De Wulf, L. Doyen, and J.-F. Raskin. A lattice theory for solving games of imperfect information (extended version). Technical Report 58, U.L.B. – Federated Center in Verification, 2006. http://www.ulb.ac.be/di/ssd/cfv/publications.html.

[HHWT95]   T.A. Henzinger, P.-H. Ho, and H. Wong-Toi. A user guide to HYTECH. In *TACAS 95: Tools and Algorithms for the Construction and Analysis of Systems*, Lecture Notes in Computer Science 1019, pages 41–71. Springer-Verlag, 1995.

[HK99]   T.A. Henzinger and P.W. Kopke. Discrete-time control for rectangular hybrid automata. *Theoretical Computer Science*, 221:369–392, 1999.

[MPS95]   O. Maler, A. Pnueli, and J. Sifakis. On the synthesis of discrete controllers for timed systems. In *STACS'95*, volume 900 of *Lecture Notes in Computer Science*, pages 229–242. Springer, 1995.

[Rei84]   John H. Reif. The complexity of two-player games of incomplete information. *Journal of Computer and System Sciences*, 29(2):274–301, 1984.

Observability of Hybrid Automata
by Abstraction*

A. D'Innocenzo, M.D. Di Benedetto, and S. Di Gennaro

Department of Electrical Engineering and Computer Science, University of L'Aquila
{adinnoce, dibenede, digennar}@ing.univaq.it

Abstract. In this paper, we deal with the observability problem of a class of Hybrid Systems whose output is a timed string on a finite alphabet. We determine under which conditions it is always possible to immediately detect, using the observed output, when the system enters a given discrete state. We illustrate how to construct a Timed Automaton that is an abstraction of the given Hybrid System, and that preserves its observability properties. Moreover, we propose a verification algorithm with polynomial complexity for checking the observability of the Timed Automaton, and a constructive procedure for an observer of the discrete state.

1 Introduction

The issue of observability is an interesting open problem in the context of Hybrid Systems, whose significance is widely recognized in safety critical applications (e.g. Air Traffic Management) or failure detection applications (e.g. software monitoring and telecommunications). Observability of Hybrid Systems was extensively studied in the literature (see e.g. in [3],[8],[14] and [17]), while observer design was considered e.g. in [4]. In this work, we provide a definition of observability of a hybrid system with respect to a discrete state (or set of discrete states): given a hybrid model, we mark as "critical" some discrete states that correspond to an unsafe behavior or to a failure. For each of such critical locations, the system is required to be observable.

In [9] and [10], Hybrid Systems with no Guards and Resets were considered and the discrete outputs of the system were used to characterize observability of a discrete location. The continuous inputs and outputs were used to enrich the measurable information with new discrete outputs (signatures) characteristic of a specific continuous dynamics. However, the generation of a signature requires a finite and non-zero time to be generated, so that the detection of an unsafe operation or a failure is given with delay. In this paper, we analyze observability of Hybrid Systems where the observable output is a timed string on a finite alphabet, the discrete transitions are triggered by guards and resets, and no continuous and discrete disturbances are present. The discrete transitions are

---

* This work has been partially supported by European Commission under NoE HYCON (contract n.511368).

João Hespanha and A. Tiwari (Eds.): HSCC 2006, LNCS 3927, pp. 169–183, 2006.
© Springer-Verlag Berlin Heidelberg 2006

possibly non deterministic if the guard sets intersect, and we suppose that a transition may not occur even if the continuous state enters a guard set. Also, no delay is accepted for the detection of a critical location. Building upon the results achieved in [5], [11] and [18] on reachability in a given time interval of Continuous and Hybrid Systems, the basic idea is to abstract a Hybrid Automaton $\mathcal{H}$ by a Timed Automaton $\mathcal{T}$, so that the timed output language generated by the former is contained in or equal to the timed output language generated by the latter. In other words, we propose a procedure to construct a Timed Automaton that is an abstraction of the given Hybrid Automaton and preserves observability of a given discrete state. Necessary and sufficient observability conditions for a class of Timed Automata are given, and we prove that observability of the given Hybrid Automaton is implied by observability of the constructed Timed Automaton.

In Section 2, we define the class of Hybrid Systems of interest, the languages given by all timed executions and the associated timed observations. Then, we define observability of a given discrete state. In Section 3, we define a class of Timed Automata, provide necessary and sufficient observability conditions, and propose an algorithm with polynomial complexity to verify observability of a given discrete state. We also relate this work to the results obtained in [16] on Diagnosability of Timed Automata. Moreover, we construct an observer of a given discrete state. In Section 4, we provide a procedure to construct a Timed Automaton from a given Hybrid Automaton, and prove that observability of the former implies observability of the latter.Some concluding remarks are offered in the last section.

2   Basic Definitions

2.1   Hybrid Automata

We consider a class of Hybrid Systems, where the continuous state evolves following linear autonomous dynamics, and the discrete state evolution depends only on the continuous state according to guard maps, possibly with non deterministic transitions. We suppose that the only measurable output is the discrete one (the continuous output is not measurable), so that the observed output is a timed string on a finite alphabet. Formally,

Definition 1. *A Hybrid Automaton is a tuple*
$\mathcal{H} = (\Xi, \Xi_0, S, E, \Sigma, \eta, G, Inv, R)$ *(see [13]) where:*

- $\Xi = Q \times X$ *is the hybrid state space, where Q is a finite set of discrete states* $q_1, q_2, \cdots q_N$, *and $X \subseteq \mathbb{R}^n$ is the continuous state space.*
- $\Xi_0 = Q_0 \times X_0 \subseteq Q \times X$ *is the set of initial discrete and continuous conditions.*
- *S associates to each discrete state $q \in Q$ autonomous continuous-time linear dynamics as $\dot{x} = A(q)x$, where $A(q) \in \mathbb{R}^{n \times n}$.*
- *Σ is the finite alphabet of discrete output symbols $\{\varepsilon, \sigma_1, \sigma_2, \cdots \sigma_r\}$, where ε is the null symbol that corresponds to an unobservable output.*

– $E \subseteq Q \times Q$ is a collection of edges.
– $\eta : E \to \Sigma$ is the output function.
– $G : E \to 2^X$ associates a guard set to each edge.
– $Inv : Q \to 2^X$ is the invariant mapping.
– $R : X \times E \to 2^X$ is the reset mapping.

Note that the discrete output symbols are associated with discrete transitions, and not with discrete states. We assume that $Inv(q) = X$, $\forall q \in Q$, and that guard conditions are enabling conditions: even if the continuous state enters a guard set, the corresponding transition may not take place. This assumption guarantees that the system is non-blocking. Moreover, we assume that there is no cycle of edges associated with unobservable output. Let $E_{q \to} = \{(q, \bar{q}) \in E : \bar{q} \in Q\}$ be the set of all edges starting from q, and $E_{\to q} = \{(\bar{q}, q) \in E : \bar{q} \in Q\}$ the set of all edges ending in q. Furthermore, let $E_{q \to}^{\varepsilon} = \{e \in E_{q \to} : \eta(e) = \varepsilon\}$ be the set of all edges starting from q and whose output is the empty string, and $E_{\to q}^{\varepsilon} = \{e \in E_{\to q} : \eta(e) = \varepsilon\}$ the set of all edges ending in q and whose output is the empty string.

We introduce a hybrid time basis $\tau = \{I_i\}_{i \geq 0}$ of $\mathcal{H}$ as a finite or infinite sequence of intervals $I_i = [t_i, t_i']$ such that [13]

1. I_i is closed if τ is infinite; I_i might be right-open if it is the last interval of a finite sequence τ;
2. $t_i \leq t_i'$ for all i and $t_{i-1}' \leq t_i$ for $i > 0$.

An execution of $\mathcal{H}$ is a collection $\chi = (\tau, x, q)$, with x, q satisfying the continuous and discrete dynamics of $\mathcal{H}$ and their interactions (Invariant, Guard and Reset functions). To each execution χ we associate a unique timed string ρ as a finite or infinite sequence $q(I_0), \Delta_0, q(I_1), \Delta_1, \cdots$ where $q(I_i) \in Q$ and $\Delta_i = (t_{i+1} - t_i) \in \mathbb{R}^+ \cup \{0, \infty\}$. Namely, ρ is a timed execution of the discrete state of $\mathcal{H}$, where $q(I_i)$ is the discrete state in the time interval $I_i = [t_i, t_{i+1})$ and Δ_i the dwell time in that state.

We define $\mathcal{L}(\mathcal{H})$ the language of all finite prefixes of all timed executions ρ associated to all executions χ of $\mathcal{H}$. Given a discrete state $q_c \in Q$, we define $\mathcal{L}_{q_c}(\mathcal{H})$ the language of timed strings ρ in $\mathcal{L}(\mathcal{H})$ such that the last discrete state visited is q_c. More formally

$$\mathcal{L}_{q_c}(\mathcal{H}) = \{\rho = q(I_0), \Delta_0, \cdots, q(I_s), \Delta_s \in \mathcal{L}(\mathcal{H}) : q(I_s) = q_c, \Delta_s \in \mathbb{R}^+\}$$

Clearly,

$$\mathcal{L}_{q_i}(\mathcal{H}) \cap \mathcal{L}_{q_j}(\mathcal{H}) = \varnothing$$

for each $q_i \neq q_j$ with $i, j = 1, \cdots, N$ and $i \neq j$. Furthermore,

$$\bigcup_{q \in Q} \mathcal{L}_q(\mathcal{H}) = \mathcal{L}(\mathcal{H})$$

Thus, $\mathcal{L}_{q_i}(\mathcal{H})$ for $i = 1, \cdots, N$ partitions $\mathcal{L}(\mathcal{H})$. Let $\tilde{Q} \subseteq Q$. Then,

$$\mathcal{L}_{\tilde{Q}}(\mathcal{H}) = \bigcup_{\tilde{q} \in \tilde{Q}} \mathcal{L}_{\tilde{q}}(\mathcal{H})$$

Given a finite discrete execution $\rho = q(I_0), \Delta_0, \cdots, q(I_s), \Delta_s$ we define the *associated observed timed string* as follows. Consider the projection $P(\rho)$, obtained from ρ first by replacing $q(I_0)$ with ε and $q(I_i)$ with $\sigma_i = \eta(q(I_{i-1}), q(I_i))$ for $i = 1, \cdots, s$, then by erasing all ε (unobservable) symbols and adding the delays between successive symbols. The resulting string is a finite sequence $P(\rho) = \Delta_0, \sigma_1, \Delta_1, \cdots, \sigma_{s'}, \Delta_{s'}$ with $s' \leq s$ and $\Delta_{s'} \geq \Delta_s$. We call $P(\rho)$ the observed output timed string of ρ, and $\mathcal{P}(\mathcal{H}) = \{P(\rho) : \rho \in \mathcal{L}(\mathcal{H})\}$ the language given by the projections of all strings in $\mathcal{L}(\mathcal{H})$. $\mathcal{P}(\mathcal{H})$ is the language that contains all finite length observed output timed strings of $\mathcal{H}$.

2.2   Observability of Hybrid Automata

Given a Hybrid Automaton $\mathcal{H}$ and a discrete state $q_c \in Q$, our objective is to detect immediately whether the current state is q_c. This property of q_c is called *observability* and is formally defined as follows:

Definition 2. *Given a Hybrid Automaton $\mathcal{H}$, a discrete state $q_c \in Q$ is observable if*

$$\rho \in \mathcal{L}_{q_c}(\mathcal{H}), \rho' \in \mathcal{L}(\mathcal{H}) \smallsetminus \mathcal{L}_{q_c}(\mathcal{H}) \Rightarrow P(\rho) \neq P(\rho') \tag{1}$$

Definition 2 states that a state q_c is observable if, for each execution that drives the system to q_c, there exists no other execution with the same observed output such that the system may be in a different discrete state at the same time. In other words, a state q_c is observable if, for each execution of $\mathcal{H}$, the timed output of the system allows to detect at each time instant whether the current state is q_c. Conversely, if the condition of Definition 2 does not hold, there exist two executions ρ' and ρ'' of the same time length $\bar{t}$ and the same observed output such that, at time $\bar{t}$, the current state is respectively $q' = q_c$ for the execution ρ', and $q'' \neq q_c$ for the execution ρ''. It is then clearly impossible to decide whether the system is currently in q_c at time $\bar{t}$.

If we are interested in detecting immediately whether the current state belongs to a set Q_c, then a similar definition can be given:

Definition 3. *Given a Hybrid Automaton $\mathcal{H}$, the set $Q_c \subset Q$ is observable if*

$$\rho \in \mathcal{L}_{Q_c}(\mathcal{H}), \rho' \in \mathcal{L}(\mathcal{H}) \smallsetminus \mathcal{L}_{Q_c}(\mathcal{H}) \Rightarrow P(\rho) \neq P(\rho')$$

Our results are given with respect to Definition 2 but can be trivially extended to Definition 3 (see Section 4).

Given a Hybrid Automaton $\mathcal{H}$, an observer of the discrete state q_c is a decision block whose input is the timed observed output of $\mathcal{H}$ and whose output is 1 (or *true*) if the current state of $\mathcal{H}$ is q_c and 0 (or *false*) if the current state of $\mathcal{H}$ is not q_c.

Definition 4. *Given a Hybrid Automaton $\mathcal{H}$, an observer of the discrete state $q_c \in Q$ is a function*

$$\mathcal{O} : \mathcal{P}(\mathcal{H}) \rightarrow \{0,1\}$$

such that

$$\mathcal{O}(P(\rho)) = \begin{cases} 1 \ if \ \rho \in \mathcal{L}_{q_c}(\mathcal{H}) \\ 0 \ if \ \rho \notin \mathcal{L}_{q_c}(\mathcal{H}) \end{cases}$$

The following proposition formalizes the equivalence between observability and the existence of an observer.

Proposition 1. *Given a Hybrid Automaton $\mathcal{H}$, a state q_c is observable if and only if an observer of q_c exists.*

3   Observability of Timed Automata

The flow chart diagram in Figure 1 shows the whole verification procedure of observability of a discrete state q_c of a given Hybrid Automaton $\mathcal{H}$. The first step is the construction of an abstraction $\mathcal{T}$ of $\mathcal{H}$: Algorithm 4 will be defined in Section 4, and we will see that $\mathcal{T}$ belongs to a special class of Timed Automata. In this section, we first define this class. Then, starting from $\mathcal{T}$, we show in Algorithm 1 how to construct a system $\tilde{\mathcal{T}}$ that does not contain unobservable outputs and preserves the observability property of $\mathcal{T}$. Algorithm 3 applied to the system $\mathcal{T}$ or $\tilde{\mathcal{T}}$ verifies whether a given discrete state q_c is observable for $\mathcal{T}$. Once we have solved the observability problem on the special class of timed automata of interest, we will state in Section 4 the main result of this work: observability of $\mathcal{T}$ implies observability of $\mathcal{H}$.

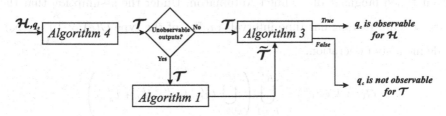

Fig. 1. Verification procedure of observability for the Hybrid Automaton $\mathcal{H}$

A Timed Automaton is a class of Hybrid Automata where the dynamics of the continuous variables have constant slope 1 for each discrete location (e.g. clocks), the initial continuous state is a singleton set for each discrete location, the guards are rectangular sets, and the reset map is a function (deterministic reset):

Definition 5. *A Timed Automaton $\mathcal{T}$ is a Hybrid Automaton $\mathcal{H}$ such that [1]:*

- *the continuous state space $X = (\mathbb{R}^+)^n$.*
- *for all $q_0 \in Q_0$, if $(X_0, q_0) \subset \Xi_0$ then X_0 is a singleton set.*
- *$S = S_{\mathbb{I}}$ is such that $A(q) = I_{n \times n} \ \forall q \in Q$.*
- *for any edge e the set $G(e)$ is a rectangular set.*

    – *for any discrete state q the set Inv(q) is a rectangular set.*
    – *for any edge e and any $x \in G(e)$ the set $R(x, e)$ is a singleton set.*

As such, definitions of executions and languages $\mathcal{L}(\mathcal{T})$ and $\mathcal{P}(\mathcal{T})$, and of observability and observer can be given as in the previous section.

Remark 1. In [16] a procedure is proposed to verify if a Timed Automaton is diagnosable, and it is proved that the diagnosability verification problem is in PSPACE. By Definitions 2 and 4, and by definition of 0-Diagnosability ([16]), it is possible to prove that, given a Timed Automaton $\mathcal{T}$, a discrete state $q_c \in Q$ is observable if and only if all edges $e \in E_{\rightarrow q} \cup E_{q \rightarrow}$ are 0-Diagnosable.

As a consequence Remark 1, the observability verification problem of Timed Automata is in PSPACE. However, the Timed Automaton $\mathcal{T}$ that will be constructed in Section 4 as an abstraction of a given Hybrid Automaton $\mathcal{H}$ has the following properties: $X = \mathbb{R}^+$, $Inv(q) = X \ \forall q \in Q$, and $R(x, e) = 0 \ \forall e \in E, x \in G(e)$. We will prove in Proposition 5 that the observability verification problem for this subclass of Timed Automata is in PTIME. To this purpose, we first introduce a procedure (Algorithm 1) that constructs, given $\mathcal{T}$, a Timed Automaton $\tilde{\mathcal{T}}$ without unobservable outputs, such that q_c is observable for $\tilde{\mathcal{T}}$ if and only if q_c is observable for $\mathcal{T}$. This procedure is necessary since Algorithm 3 that is proposed later for checking observability of a state of $\mathcal{T}$ can only be applied if the system does not contain edges associated to unobservable outputs. Removing unobservable edges from a Discrete Event System in order to preserve the output language is a classical problem [15]. We define here a procedure to preserve the output timed language of a Timed Automaton. Under the assumption that the guard sets are rectangular time intervals on $\mathbb{R}^+$ of the type $G(e) = \bigcup\limits_{k=1}^{K} \langle a_k, b_k \rangle$, we define a sum operation:

$$G(e') + G(e'') = \bigcup_{k'=1}^{K'} \left(\bigcup_{k''=1}^{K''} \langle a'_{k'} + a''_{k''}, b'_{k'} + b''_{k''} \rangle \right)$$

where $\langle \cdot, \cdot \rangle$ can be open or closed intervals.

    It is easy to prove that $G(e') + G(e'')$ is still a rectangular interval, and that the commutative, associative and transitive properties hold. Given a sequence of edges $e_1, \cdots, e_n$, we define

$$\delta(e_1, \cdots, e_n) = \sum_{i=1}^{n} G(e_i)$$

Remark 2. $\delta(e_1, \cdots, e_n)$ is a rectangular interval, and

$$t \in \delta(e_1, \cdots, e_n) \Leftrightarrow \exists t_1 \in G(e_1), \cdots, \exists t_n \in G(e_n) : t = \sum_{i=1}^{n} t_i$$

Algorithm 1. Given a Timed Automaton T, define
$\tilde{T} := (\tilde{\Xi}, \tilde{\Xi}_0, \tilde{S}, \tilde{E}, \tilde{\Sigma}, \tilde{\eta}, \tilde{G}, \tilde{Inv}, \tilde{R}) = T$, then proceed as follows:

1. For all $q \in Q$ such that $E^{\varepsilon}_{q \to} \neq \varnothing$ and $E_{\to q} \setminus E^{\varepsilon}_{\to q} \neq \varnothing$, do:

   1.1. For all $e_1 = (q, q_1), \cdots, e_n = (q_{n-1}, q_n), e_{n+1} = (q_n, \bar{q})$ such that $\eta(e_1) = \cdots = \eta(e_n) = \varepsilon$ and $\eta(e_{n+1}) = \bar{\sigma} \neq \varepsilon$, do:

      1.1.1. If there exists $\bar{e} = (q, \bar{q})$ such that $\eta(\bar{e}) = \bar{\sigma}$ is not in $\tilde{E}$, then add $\bar{e}$ to $\tilde{E}$, and let $\tilde{\eta}(\bar{e}) = \bar{\sigma}$ and $\tilde{G}(\bar{e}) = \delta(e_1, \cdots, e_{n+1})$.

      1.1.2. Else If $\bar{e} = (q, \bar{q})$ such that $\eta(\bar{e}) = \bar{\sigma}$ is in $\tilde{E}$, then $\tilde{G}(\bar{e}) = \tilde{G}(\bar{e}) \cup \delta(e_1, \cdots, e_{n+1})$.

2. Erase all states $q \in \tilde{Q}$ such that $\tilde{E}_{\to q} \setminus \tilde{E}^{\varepsilon}_{\to q} \neq \emptyset$;
3. Erase all hanging and unobservable edges.

By construction, $\tilde{T}$ does not contain any edge associated with an unobservable output.

Remark 3. By construction of $\tilde{T}$, it is possible that some edge $e = (q', q'')$ is associated to many output symbols $\sigma_1, \cdots, \sigma_m$ and guards $G(e, \sigma_1), \cdots, G(e, \sigma_m)$. In order to associate only a single output symbol and a guard to each edge, we can split q' (or q'') in the set of states $q'_1, \cdots, q'_m$ such that $\eta(q'_i, q'') = \sigma_i$ and $G(q'_i, q'') = G(e, \sigma_i)$. Since we can equivalently split q' or q'', we assume without loss of generality that a critical state q_c is never split in $\tilde{T}$.

Remark 4. Let T_ε be the restriction of the graph (Q, E) of T induced by the edges associated with an unobservable output. We define N_ε the maximum cardinality of the connected components of T_ε: with the assumption that there are no cycles of edges associated to unobservable output, the complexity of Algorithm 1 is polynomial with N_ε.

Remark 5. $E^{\varepsilon}_{\to q_c} = E^{\varepsilon}_{q_c \to} = \varnothing$ is clearly a necessary condition for q_c to be observable. Thus, it is reasonable to apply Algorithm 1 only if $E^{\varepsilon}_{\to q_c} = E^{\varepsilon}_{q_c \to} = \varnothing$, so that q_c is never erased from $\tilde{T}$.

Proposition 2. *Given a Timed Automaton T, let $\tilde{T}$ be obtained by Algorithm 1 and $q_c \in Q$ such that $E^{\varepsilon}_{\to q_c} = E^{\varepsilon}_{q_c \to} = \varnothing$. Then, for each execution $\rho \in \mathcal{L}(T)$, there exists an execution $\tilde{\rho} \in \mathcal{L}(\tilde{T})$ such that:*

1. $P(\rho) = P(\tilde{\rho})$;
2. $\rho \in \mathcal{L}_{q_c}(T) \Rightarrow \tilde{\rho} \in \mathcal{L}_{q_c}(\tilde{T})$ *and* $\rho \notin \mathcal{L}_{q_c}(T) \Rightarrow \tilde{\rho} \notin \mathcal{L}_{q_c}(\tilde{T})$

Viceversa, for each execution $\tilde{\rho} \in \mathcal{L}(\tilde{T})$ there exists an execution $\rho \in \mathcal{L}(T)$ such that:

1. $P(\rho) = P(\tilde{\rho})$;
2. $\tilde{\rho} \in \mathcal{L}_{q_c}(\tilde{T}) \Rightarrow \rho \in \mathcal{L}_{q_c}(T)$ *and* $\tilde{\rho} \notin \mathcal{L}_{q_c}(\tilde{T}) \Rightarrow \rho \notin \mathcal{L}_{q_c}(T)$

Proof. Let $\rho \in \mathcal{L}(\mathcal{T})$: if there is no edge $e : \eta(e) = \varepsilon$ in ρ, then $\tilde{\rho} = \rho \in \mathcal{L}(\tilde{\mathcal{T}})$, because Algorithm 1 does not modify edges with observable outputs. Otherwise, let $\rho = \cdots q_{i-1}, \Delta_{i-1}, q_i, \Delta_i, \cdots q_{i+n}, \Delta_{i+n}, q_{i+n+1} \cdots$ where $e_k = (q_{k-1}, q_k)$. If $\eta(e_i) = \sigma_i \neq \varepsilon$, $\eta(e_{i+1}) = \cdots = \eta(e_{i+n}) = \varepsilon$ and $\eta(e_{i+n+1}) = \sigma_{i+n+1} \neq \varepsilon$, then $P(\rho) = \cdots \sigma_i, \sum_{k=i}^{i+n} \Delta_k, \sigma_{i+n+1} \cdots$. By construction of $\tilde{\mathcal{T}}$, and for each $\Delta \in \delta(e_{i+1}, \cdots, e_{i+n+1})$, there exists a path $\tilde{\rho} = \cdots \tilde{q}_i, \Delta, \tilde{q}_{i+n+1} \cdots$ such that $P(\tilde{\rho}) = \cdots, \sigma_i, \Delta, \sigma_{i+n+1}, \cdots$. The first part of this proof shows that $\exists \tilde{\rho} : P(\rho)$ and $P(\tilde{\rho})$ are equal for all symbols except Δ. However, Remark 2 shows that $\sum_{k=i}^{i+n} \Delta_k \in \delta(e_{i+1}, \cdots, e_{i+n+1})$, thus $\exists \tilde{\rho} : \Delta = \sum_{k=i}^{i+n} \Delta_k$. Consider now ρ and the constructed string $\tilde{\rho}$: if $\rho \in \mathcal{L}_{q_c}(\mathcal{T})$ then $\tilde{\rho} \in \mathcal{L}_{q_c}(\tilde{\mathcal{T}})$ because q_c is not erased by Algorithm 1; otherwise, if $\rho \in \mathcal{L}_q(\mathcal{T})$ where $q \neq q_c$, then $\tilde{\rho} \in \mathcal{L}_{\tilde{q}}(\tilde{\mathcal{T}})$ where $\tilde{q} = q$ or q is erased by Algorithm 1, and thus $\tilde{q} \neq q_c$. The inverse can be proved similarly.

Some consequences of Proposition 2 are stated below. In particular, it is possible to study the observability of a given Timed Automaton on a new Timed Automaton without unobservable outputs.

Corollary 1. *Given $\mathcal{T}$, and $\tilde{\mathcal{T}}$ constructed by Algorithm 1, the following hold:*

1. *$\mathcal{P}(\mathcal{T}) = \mathcal{P}(\tilde{\mathcal{T}})$.*
2. *Given a discrete state $q_c \in \tilde{Q}$, then q_c is observable for $\mathcal{T}$ if and only if q_c is observable for $\tilde{\mathcal{T}}$.*

Proof. (1) By Proposition 2. (2) Let q_c be observable for $\tilde{\mathcal{T}}$ but not for $\mathcal{T}$. Then there exist $\rho', \rho'' \in \mathcal{L}(\mathcal{T})$ such that $\rho' \in \mathcal{L}_{q_c}(\mathcal{T})$, $\rho'' \in \mathcal{L}(\mathcal{T}) \setminus \mathcal{L}_{q_c}(\mathcal{T})$ and $P(\rho') = P(\rho'')$. By Proposition 2, there exist $\tilde{\rho}'$ and $\tilde{\rho}'' \in \mathcal{L}(\tilde{\mathcal{T}})$ such that $\tilde{\rho}' \in \mathcal{L}_{q_c}(\tilde{\mathcal{T}})$, $\tilde{\rho}'' \in \mathcal{L}(\tilde{\mathcal{T}}) \setminus \mathcal{L}_{q_c}(\tilde{\mathcal{T}})$ and $P(\tilde{\rho}') = P(\tilde{\rho}'')$, that is a contradiction. The same holds assuming q_c observable for $\mathcal{T}$ but not for $\tilde{\mathcal{T}}$.

In what follows, we assume without loss of generality that the Timed Automaton $\mathcal{T}$ does not contain any unobservable output symbol. We give now a method for verifying observability of a discrete state q_c of $\mathcal{T}$: the idea of the proposed procedure is intuitively described as follows: given $q_c \in Q$ and a pair of initial states $q'_0, q''_0 \in Q_0$, we construct the Timed Automata $\mathcal{T}_{q'_0}$ and $\mathcal{T}_{q''_0}$, that are equal to $\mathcal{T}$ except for the set of initial states: more precisely, $Q'_0 = \{q'_0\}$ and $Q''_0 = \{q''_0\}$. From $\mathcal{T}_{q'_0}$ and $\mathcal{T}_{q''_0}$, we construct a system $\mathcal{T}_{q'_0, q''_0}$, whose discrete state space is $Q \times Q$, and such that $\mathcal{L}_{(q_c, q)}(\mathcal{T}_{q'_0, q''_0})$ is the language of all executions $\rho' \in \mathcal{L}_{q_c}(\mathcal{T}_{q'_0})$ and $\rho'' \in \mathcal{L}_q(\mathcal{T}_{q''_0})$ with $P(\rho') = P(\rho'')$. We will prove that checking emptiness of $\mathcal{L}_{(q_c, q)}(\mathcal{T}_{q'_0, q''_0})$ for each $q \in Q \setminus \{q_c\}$ and for each $(q'_0, q''_0) \in Q_0 \times Q_0$ verifies observability of q_c.

Given two Timed Automata $\mathcal{T}_{q'_0}$ and $\mathcal{T}_{q''_0}$ as defined above, we propose a procedure to construct a Timed Automaton $\mathcal{T}_{q'_0, q''_0}$:

Algorithm 2. Given $\mathcal{T}_{q'_0} = (Q \times \mathbb{R}^+, (q'_0, 0), S_{\mathbb{I}}, E, \Sigma, \eta, G, Inv, R)$ and $\mathcal{T}_{q''_0} = (Q \times \mathbb{R}^+, (q''_0, 0), S_{\mathbb{I}}, E, \Sigma, \eta, G, Inv, R)$, proceed as follows:

1. Initialize $\mathcal{T}_{q'_0, q''_0} := (\tilde{Q} \times \mathbb{R}^+, (\tilde{Q}_0 \times 0), S_{\mathbb{I}}, \tilde{E}, \Sigma, \tilde{\eta}, \tilde{G}, \tilde{Inv}, \tilde{R})$, where $\tilde{Q} \subseteq Q \times Q$;
2. Initialize $\tilde{Q} = \tilde{Q}_0 := (q'_0, q''_0)$, $\tilde{E} := \varnothing$;
3. For each unvisited state $q = (q', q'') \in \tilde{Q}$ do:
    1.1. For each $e', e'' \in E : e' = (q', \bar{q}'), e'' = (q'', \bar{q}'') \wedge \eta(e') = \eta(e'') = \sigma$ do:
        1.1.1. $\tilde{Q} := \tilde{Q} \cup (\bar{q}', \bar{q}'')$ and $\tilde{Inv}((\bar{q}', \bar{q}'')) = Inv(\bar{q}') \cap Inv(\bar{q}'')$;
        1.1.2. $\tilde{E} := \tilde{E} \cup \tilde{e} := ((q', q''), (\bar{q}', \bar{q}''))$;
        1.1.3. $\tilde{\eta}(\tilde{e}) := \sigma$, $\tilde{G}(\tilde{e}) := G(e') \cap G(e'')$ and $\tilde{R}(\tilde{x}, \tilde{e}) = 0$;
    1.2 Mark q as visited;

Lemma 1. *Given a Timed Automaton $\mathcal{T}$ without unobservable outputs and two strings $\rho' = q'_0, \Delta'_0, \cdots, q'_s, \Delta'_s, \rho'' = q''_0, \Delta''_0, \cdots, q''_s, \Delta''_s$ of the language $\mathcal{L}(\mathcal{T})$ such that $P(\rho') = P(\rho'')$, then $\Delta'_i = \Delta''_i \ \forall i = 1, \cdots, s$.*

Proof. Trivial, because no symbols are erased from $P(\rho')$ and $P(\rho'')$.

Proposition 3. *Let $\mathcal{T}_{q'_0}, \mathcal{T}_{q''_0}$ be given and $\mathcal{T}_{q'_0, q''_0}$ computed with Algorithm 2, then $\tilde{\rho} \in \mathcal{L}_{(q', q'')}(\mathcal{T}_{q'_0, q''_0})$ if and only if there exist two executions $\rho' \in \mathcal{L}_{q'}(\mathcal{T}_{q'_0})$, $\rho'' \in \mathcal{L}_{q''}(\mathcal{T}_{q''_0})$ such that $P(\rho') = P(\rho'') = P(\tilde{\rho})$.*

Proof. ($\Leftarrow$) Consider the strings $\rho' = q'_0, \Delta_0, q'_1, \Delta_1, \cdots, q', \Delta \in \mathcal{L}_{q'}(\mathcal{T}_{q'_0})$ and $\rho'' = q''_0, \Delta_0, q''_1, \Delta_1, \cdots, q'', \Delta \in \mathcal{L}_{q''}(\mathcal{T}_{q''_0})$ such that $P(\rho') = P(\rho'')$. By construction of $\mathcal{T}_{q'_0, q''_0}$, $\tilde{q}_0 = (q'_0, q''_0) \in \tilde{Q}_0$, $\tilde{q}_1 = (q'_1, q''_1) \in \tilde{Q}$ and $\tilde{e} = ((q'_0, q''_0), (q'_1, q''_1)) \in \tilde{E}$. Clearly, $\Delta_0 \in G((q'_0, q'_1)) \cap G((q''_0, q''_1)) = \tilde{G}(\tilde{e})$, thus the string $\tilde{\rho} = \tilde{q}_0, \Delta, \tilde{q}_1, 0 \in \mathcal{L}_{(q'_1, q''_1)}(\mathcal{T}_{q'_0, q''_0})$. Furthermore, by construction, $\tilde{\eta}(\tilde{e}) = \eta((q'_0, q'_1)) = \eta((q''_0, q''_1))$. Iterating, we construct a string $\tilde{\rho} = \tilde{q}_0, \Delta_0, \cdots, \tilde{q}, \Delta \in \mathcal{L}_{(q', q'')}(\mathcal{T}_{q'_0, q''_0})$ such that $P(\tilde{\rho}) = P(\rho') = P(\rho'')$ and $\tilde{q} = (q', q'')$.

($\Rightarrow$) As above, given $\tilde{\rho} \in \mathcal{L}_{(q', q'')}(\mathcal{T}_{q'_0, q''_0})$ we can construct $\rho' \in \mathcal{L}_{q'}(\mathcal{T}_{q'_0})$ and $\rho'' \in \mathcal{L}_{q''}(\mathcal{T}_{q''_0})$ such that $P(\rho') = P(\rho'') = P(\tilde{\rho})$.

The following proposition provides necessary and sufficient conditions of observability of $q_c \in Q$:

Proposition 4. *Given a Timed Automaton $\mathcal{T}$, a discrete state q_c is observable if and only if*

$$\forall q \in Q \setminus \{q_c\}, \ \forall (q'_0, q''_0) \in Q_0 \times Q_0, \mathcal{L}_{(q_c, q)}(\mathcal{T}_{q'_0, q''_0}) = \varnothing \ .$$

Proof. (Necessity) Suppose q_c is observable, and suppose there exist (q'_0, q''_0) and $q \neq q_c$ such that $\mathcal{L}_{(q_c, q)}(\mathcal{T}_{q'_0, q''_0}) \neq \varnothing$: it implies that there exist two executions ρ' starting from q'_0 and ending in q_c and ρ'' starting from q''_0 and ending in q such that $P(\rho') = P(\rho'')$, that is a contradiction.

(Sufficiency) Suppose q_c is not observable. Then there exist two executions ρ' starting from q'_0 and ending in q_c and ρ'' starting from q''_0 and ending in q such that $P(\rho') = P(\rho'')$, thus $\mathcal{L}_{(q_c, q)}(\mathcal{T}_{q'_0, q''_0}) \neq \varnothing$, that is a contradiction.

Intuitively, we compute, for each pair of initial states q'_0, q''_0 and for each $q \neq q_c$ the language $\mathcal{L}_{(q_c, q)}(\mathcal{T}_{q'_0, q''_0})$, that is the intersection between the language of executions starting from q'_0 and ending in q_c, and the language of executions starting from q_0'' and ending in $q \neq q_c$, such that the observation string is equal. If such language is not empty, there exist two executions with the same observation, such that the first drives the system in q_c, but not the second. Checking emptiness of $\mathcal{L}_{(q_c,q)}(\mathcal{T}_{q_0',q_0''})$ for each pair $(q_0', q_0'') \in Q_0 \times Q_0$ and for each $q \in Q \backslash \{q_c\}$ verifies observability of q_c. We define now an algorithm that checks if a discrete state q_c is observable for a given Timed Automaton $\mathcal{T}$:

Algorithm 3. Let a Timed Automaton $\mathcal{T} = (\Xi, \Xi_0, S_\mathbb{I}, E, \Sigma, \eta, G, Inv, R)$ be given:

1. For each pair $(q_0', q_0'') \in Q_0 \times Q_0$ do:
   1.1. Compute $\mathcal{T}_{q_0',q_0''}$ by Algorithm 2: for each $q \neq q_c$ do:
       1.2.1. If $\mathcal{L}_{(q_c,q)}(\mathcal{T}_{q_0',q_0''}) \neq \varnothing$, then return **False**;
2. return **True**;

Remark 6. Consider a graph G obtained removing from the graph $(\tilde{Q}, \tilde{E})$ of $\mathcal{T}_{q_0',q_0''}$ all edges whose guard set is the empty set: it is clear, because of the assumption that the clocks are always reset to zero, that checking emptiness of $\mathcal{L}_{(q_c,q)}(\mathcal{T}_{q_0',q_0''})$ can be reduced to a reachability problem on G.

We now show that the complexity of Algorithm 3 is polynomial with the number of discrete states of $\mathcal{T}$:

Proposition 5. *The observability verification problem for the studied class of Timed Automata is in PTIME.*

Proof. The first loop on $Q_0 \times Q_0$ requires N_0^2 iterations, where $N_0 = |Q_0| \leq |Q| = N$. Algorithm 2 has complexity $o(N^4)$. Remark 6 implies that checking emptiness of $\mathcal{L}_{(q_c,q)}(\mathcal{T}_{q_0',q_0''})$ has quadratic complexity with the number of discrete states of $\mathcal{T}_{q_0',q_0''}$, that is $(N^2)^2$. Iterating for each $q \neq q_c$ requires $N - 1$ steps. Therefore, the overall complexity of Algorithm 3 is $o(N_0^2 \cdot N^4 \cdot N^4 \cdot N) \leq o(N^{11})$.

We conclude this section proposing an observer of a discrete state of $\mathcal{T}$. Given an output string $p = \Delta_0, \sigma_1, \Delta_1, \cdots, \sigma_s, \Delta_s$, we define a function $\hat{q} : \mathcal{P}(\mathcal{T}) \to 2^Q$. For, let $\hat{q}_0(p) = Q_0$ and

$$\hat{q}_{k+1}(p) = \{q \in Q | \exists e \in E, \bar{q} \in \hat{q}_k(p) : e = (\bar{q}, q) \wedge \Delta_k \in G(e) \wedge \eta(e) = \sigma_{k+1}\}$$

for $k = 0, 1, \cdots, s$. We define $\hat{q}(p) := \hat{q}_s(p)$. Clearly, $\hat{q}(p) = \{q \in Q | \exists \rho \in \mathcal{L}_q(\mathcal{T}) : P(\rho) = p\}$. That is, $\hat{q}(p)$ is the set of discrete states where $\mathcal{T}$ can be driven by an execution starting from some $q_0 \in Q_0$ and whose output is p. Let us define a function $\mathcal{O}_{q_c} : \mathcal{P}(\mathcal{T}) \to \{0, 1\}$ as follows:

$$\mathcal{O}_{q_c}(P(\rho)) = \begin{cases} 1 \text{ if } \hat{q}(P(\rho)) = \{q_c\} \\ 0 \text{ if } \hat{q}(P(\rho)) \neq \{q_c\} \end{cases} \tag{2}$$

for each execution $\rho \in \mathcal{L}(\mathcal{T})$. The following holds:

Proposition 6. *Let q_c be observable for $\mathcal{T}$, then $\mathcal{O}_{q_c}$ defined by (2) is an observer of the discrete state q_c for $\mathcal{T}$.*

Proof. It is clear that for each $P(\rho) \in \mathcal{P}(\mathcal{T})$, then $\rho \in \mathcal{L}_{\hat{q}(P(\rho))}(\mathcal{T})$. Furthermore, let q_c is observable for $\mathcal{T}$: Definition 2 clearly implies that if $q_c \in \hat{q}(P(\rho))$, then $\hat{q}(P(\rho)) = \{q_c\}$. By these considerations follows that if $\hat{q}(P(\rho)) = \{q_c\}$ then $\rho \in \mathcal{L}_{q_c}(\mathcal{T})$, and if $\hat{q}(P(\rho)) \neq \{q_c\}$ then $\rho \notin \mathcal{L}_{q_c}(\mathcal{T})$, thus Definition 4 is fulfilled.

4   Abstraction of Hybrid Automata

In this section, for a given Hybrid Automaton $\mathcal{H}$, we propose a procedure to construct a Timed Automaton $\mathcal{T}$ that is an abstraction of $\mathcal{H}$, and prove that observability of $\mathcal{T}$ implies observability of $\mathcal{H}$.

Let a discrete state $q \in Q$ and the associated continuous dynamics $\dot{x} = A(q)x$ be given. We define $\mathcal{R}_{e_i}(q) = \Re(R(\cdot, e_i))$ as the range of the reset associated to an edge $e_i \in E_{\rightarrow q}$ and $\mathcal{G}_{e_j}(q) = G(e_j)$ as the domain of the reset associated to an edge $e_j \in E_{q \rightarrow}$. Furthermore, we define $\mathcal{R}_{e_0}(q_0) = X_0$ for $(X_0, q_0) \in \Xi_0$ as the set of initial continuous states for each initial discrete state.

From [18], given a set of initial states X_0, we can define the reach set of the linear system $\dot{x} = Ax$ on the interval $[t_1, t_2]$ as

$$Reach_{[t_1, t_2]}(A, X_0) = \{x_f \in X | \exists t \in [t_1, t_2], \exists x_0 \in X_0 : x_f = e^{At}x_0\}.$$

Given a set of final states $X_f \subseteq X$, we define $[t_{min}, t_{max}]$ as the time interval such that

$$Reach_{[0, t_{min}]}(A, X_0) \cap X_f = \varnothing$$

$$Reach_{[t_{min}, t_{max}]}(A, X_0) \cap X_f \neq \varnothing$$

$$Reach_{[t_{max}, \infty)}(A, X_0) \cap X_f = \varnothing$$

With the assumption that X_0, X_f are polytopes, and following [18], it is possible to compute an interval $[t^*_{min}, t^*_{max}] \supseteq [t_{min}, t_{max}]$, such that if $e^{At}x_0 \in X_f$ and $x_0 \in X_0$, then $t \in [t^*_{min}, t^*_{max}]$. On the basis of this result, and assuming that $\mathcal{G}_{e_j}(q)$ and $\mathcal{R}_{e_i}(q)$ are polytopes, it is possible to compute a rectangular time interval $\Delta_{e_i, e_j}(q)$ such that

$$\forall x_0 \in \mathcal{R}_{e_i}(q), \forall t \in \mathbb{R}^+ : e^{A(q)t}x_0 \in \mathcal{G}_{e_j}(q) \Rightarrow t \in \Delta_{e_i, e_j}(q) \qquad (3)$$

The algorithm proposed in [18] is very fast, even for high dimensional continuous state spaces, but there is no analysis on the size of the over-approximation error. Then, in order to calculate $\Delta_{e_i, e_j}(q)$, we can use the result in [5], which provides a procedure to compute a sequence of polytopes (a flow pipe) that are over-approximations of the reach sets

$$Reach_{[0, \Delta t]}(A, X_0), Reach_{[\Delta t, 2\Delta t]}(A, X_0), \cdots$$

for arbitrary small Δt. By computing, for each of these sets, the intersection with X_f, it is possible to determine each $\Delta_{e_i, e_j}(q)$ with an arbitrary small error, but with an explosion of the computation time. An interesting point of this method is that it can be applied to non-linear continuous dynamics. Another similar procedure is presented in [11]: with the assumption that $\mathcal{G}_{e_j}(q)$ and $\mathcal{R}_{e_i}(q)$ are zonotopes (that is a subclass of polytopes), the computation time considerably decreases. In what follows, we assume the knowledge of $\Delta_{e_i,e_j}(q)$ $\forall q \in Q, e_i \in E_{\to q}, e_j \in E_{q \to}$, and of $\Delta_{e_0,e_j}(q_0)$ $\forall q_0 \in Q_0, e_j \in E_{q_0 \to}$.

Given a Hybrid Automaton $\mathcal{H}$, we now propose an algorithm to construct a Timed Automaton $\mathcal{T}$. Then, we will prove that observability of $\mathcal{T}$ implies observability of $\mathcal{H}$. In this algorithm, we will define a function $T : \tilde{Q} \to Q$, that is a surjection from the discrete state space of $\tilde{T}$ to the discrete state space of $\mathcal{H}$.

Algorithm 4. Let $\mathcal{H} = (Q \times X, Q_0 \times X_0, S, E, \Sigma, \eta, G, Inv, R)$ be a given Hybrid Automaton:

1. Initialize $\tilde{T} := (\tilde{Q} \times \mathbb{R}^+, \tilde{Q}_0 \times \{0\}, S_\mathbb{I}, \tilde{E}, \Sigma, \tilde{\eta}, \tilde{G}, \tilde{Inv}, \tilde{R})$, where $\tilde{Q} = \tilde{Q}_0 = E = \emptyset$;
2. For each $q_k \in Q$ do:
   - 2.1. Let $E_{\to q_k} = \{e_1, \cdots e_r\}$: assign $\tilde{Q} := \tilde{Q} \cup \{\tilde{q}_{k,e_1}, \cdots, \tilde{q}_{k,e_r}\}$;
   - 2.2. $T(\tilde{q}_{k,e_i}) := q_k$ $\forall e_i \in E_{\to q_k}$;
   - 2.3. If $q_k \in Q_0$ then $\tilde{Q} := \tilde{Q} \cup \{\tilde{q}_{k,e_0}\}$, $\tilde{Q}_0 := \tilde{Q}_0 \cup \{\tilde{q}_{k,e_0}\}$ and $T(\tilde{q}_{k,e_0}) := q_k$;
2. If $e_j = (q_k, q_{k'}) \in E$ then $(\tilde{q}_{k,e_i}, \tilde{q}_{k',e_j}) \in \tilde{E}$;
3. $\tilde{\eta}(\tilde{q}_{k,e_i}, \tilde{q}_{k',e_j}) = \eta((q_k, q_{k'}))$;
4. $\tilde{G}(\tilde{q}_{k,e_i}, \tilde{q}_{k',e_j}) = \Delta_{e_i,e_j}(q_k)$;
5. $\tilde{Inv} = \mathbb{R}^+$ $\forall \tilde{q} \in \tilde{Q}$;
6. $\tilde{R}(\tilde{x}, \tilde{e}) = 0$ $\forall \tilde{e} \in \tilde{E}$;

Proposition 7. *Given a Hybrid Automaton $\mathcal{H}$, let $\tilde{T}$ be obtained by Algorithm 4 and $q_c \in Q$. Then, for each execution $\rho \in \mathcal{L}(\mathcal{H})$, there exists an execution $\tilde{\rho} \in \mathcal{L}(\tilde{T})$ such that*

1. $P(\rho) = P(\tilde{\rho})$
2. $\rho \in \mathcal{L}_{q_c}(\mathcal{H}) \Rightarrow \tilde{\rho} \in \mathcal{L}_{T^{-1}(q_c)}(\tilde{T})$ *and* $\rho \notin \mathcal{L}_{q_c}(\mathcal{H}) \Rightarrow \tilde{\rho} \notin \mathcal{L}_{T^{-1}(q_c)}(\tilde{T})$

Proof. Consider the string $\rho = q_{k_0}, \Delta_0, q_{k_1}, \Delta_1, \cdots, q_{k_s}, \Delta_s \in \mathcal{L}_{q_{k_s}}(\mathcal{H})$ and let $e_1 = (q_{k_0}, q_{k_1}) \in E$. By construction of $\tilde{T}$, $\tilde{q}_{k_0,e_0} \in \tilde{Q}_0$, $\exists \tilde{e}_1 \in \tilde{E}$ and $\tilde{q}_{k_1,e_1} \in T^{-1}(q_{k_1})$ such that $\tilde{e}_1 = ((\tilde{q}_{k_0,e_0}, \tilde{q}_{k_1,e_1}))$. (3) implies that $\Delta_0 \in \Delta_{e_0,e_1}(q_{k_0}) = \tilde{G}(\tilde{e}_1)$. Thus, for each $q_{k_1} \in Q$ the string $\tilde{\rho} = \tilde{q}_{k_0,e_0}, \Delta_0, \tilde{q}_{k_1,e_1}, 0 \in \mathcal{L}_{T^{-1}(q_{k_1})}(\tilde{T})$. Furthermore, by construction, $\tilde{\eta}(\tilde{e}_1) = \eta((q_{k_0}, q_{k_1}))$. Iterating, we construct from ρ a string

$$\tilde{\rho} = \tilde{q}_{k_0,e_0}, \Delta_0, \cdots, \tilde{q}_{k_s,e_s}, \Delta_s \in \mathcal{L}_{T^{-1}(q_{k_s})}(\tilde{T}) \text{ such that } P(\rho) = P(\tilde{\rho}).$$

Given a Hybrid Automaton $\mathcal{H}$, we assume the Timed Automaton $\tilde{T}$ be given by Algorithm 4.

Corollary 2. $\mathcal{P}(\mathcal{H}) \subseteq \mathcal{P}(\tilde{T})$.

Proof. The statement of Proposition 7 is clearly an inclusion of the languages of observations.

The following proposition is a generalization of Proposition 4 according to Definition 3:

Proposition 8. *Given a Timed Automaton $\mathcal{T}$, a set of discrete states $Q_c \subset Q$ is observable if and only if*

$$\forall q_c \in Q_c, q \in Q \setminus Q_c, \ \forall (q_0', q_0'') \in Q_0 \times Q_0, \mathcal{L}_{(q_c,q)}(\mathcal{T}_{q_0',q_0''}) = \varnothing \qquad (4)$$

Proof. Similar to Proposition 4.

It is easy to see that checking condition (4) can be done with a slight modification to Algorithm 3, namely by replacing line 1.2 with the following:

1.1. Compute $\mathcal{T}_{q_0',q_0''}$ by Algorithm 2: for each $q_c \in Q_c$ and for each $q \in Q \setminus Q_c$ do:

We can now state the main result:

Theorem 1. *Given $\mathcal{H}$ and $\tilde{\mathcal{T}}$, then q_c is observable for $\mathcal{H}$ if $T^{-1}(q_c)$ is observable for $\tilde{\mathcal{T}}$.*

Proof. Let $T^{-1}(q_c)$ be observable for $\tilde{\mathcal{T}}$ but q_c is not for $\mathcal{H}$. Then $\exists \rho', \rho'' \in \mathcal{L}(\mathcal{H})$ such that $\rho' \in \mathcal{L}_{q_c}(\mathcal{H})$, $\rho'' \in \mathcal{L}(\mathcal{H}) \setminus \mathcal{L}_{q_c}(\mathcal{H})$ and $P(\rho') = P(\rho'')$. By Proposition 7, $\exists \tilde{\rho}', \tilde{\rho}'' \in \mathcal{L}(\tilde{\mathcal{T}})$ such that $\tilde{\rho}' \in \mathcal{L}_{T^{-1}(q_c)}(\tilde{\mathcal{T}})$, $\tilde{\rho}'' \in \mathcal{L}(\tilde{\mathcal{T}}) \setminus \mathcal{L}_{T^{-1}(q_c)}(\tilde{\mathcal{T}})$ and $P(\tilde{\rho}') = P(\tilde{\rho}'')$, that is a contradiction.

If we assume that

(i) The time intervals $\Delta_{e_i,e_j}(q)$ can be computed exactly, that is when the linear system has a certain structure [2],[12].
(ii) For the system $\mathcal{H}$ the following holds:

$$R(x, e) = \Re(R(\cdot, e)) \ \forall e \in E, \ \forall x \in G(e)$$

that is, given an edge e and guard set $G(e)$, then each continuous state $x \in G(e)$ is non-deterministically reset by $R(x, e)$ to the set $\Re(R(\cdot, e))$.

then, we can state the following:

Proposition 9. *Given $\mathcal{H}$, $\tilde{\mathcal{T}}$ and $q_c \in Q$, and assume that (i) and (ii) hold. Then, for each execution $\tilde{\rho} \in \mathcal{L}(\tilde{\mathcal{T}})$, there exists an execution $\rho \in \mathcal{L}(\mathcal{H})$ such that*

1. $P(\rho) = P(\tilde{\rho})$
2. $\tilde{\rho} \in \mathcal{L}_{T^{-1}(q_c)}(\tilde{\mathcal{T}}) \Rightarrow \rho \in \mathcal{L}_{q_c}(\mathcal{H})$ and $\tilde{\rho} \notin \mathcal{L}_{T^{-1}(q_c)}(\tilde{\mathcal{T}}) \Rightarrow \rho \notin \mathcal{L}_{q_c}(\mathcal{H})$

Proof. Consider the string $\tilde{\rho} = \tilde{q}_{k_0,e_0}, \Delta_0, \tilde{q}_{k_1,e_1}, \Delta_1, \cdots, \tilde{q}_{k_s,e_s}, \Delta_s \in \mathcal{L}_{T^{-1}(q_{k_s})}(\tilde{\mathcal{T}})$ and let $\tilde{e}_1 = (\tilde{q}_{k_0,e_0}, \tilde{q}_{k_1,e_1}) \in \tilde{E}$. By construction of $\tilde{\mathcal{T}}$, $q_{k_0} = T(q_{k_0,e_0}) \in Q_0$, $q_{k_1} = T(q_{k_1,e_1}) \in Q$ and $e_1 = (q_{k_0}, q_{k_1}) \in E$. By assumption (i), follows that if $\Delta_0 \in \tilde{G}(\tilde{e}_1) = \Delta_{e_0,e_1}(q_{k_0})$, then $\exists x_0 \in \mathcal{R}_{e_0}(q_{k_0}) : e^{A(q_{k_0})\Delta_0} x_0 \in \mathcal{G}_{e_1}(q_{k_0})$.

Since $\mathcal{R}_{e_0}(q_{k_0})$ is the set of initial continuous states of $\mathcal{H}$ for the initial discrete state q_{k_0}, then for each $q_{k_1,e_1} \in \tilde{Q}$ the string $\rho = q_{k_0}, \Delta_0, q_{k_1}, 0 \in \mathcal{L}_{q_{k_1}}(\mathcal{H})$. Furthermore, by construction, $\eta(q_{k_0}, q_{k_1}) = \tilde{\eta}(\tilde{q}_{k_0,e_0}, \tilde{q}_{k_1,e_1})$. These considerations can be iterated to the rest of the string $\tilde{\rho}$ since, under assumption (ii), each $x \in G(e_i)$ is non-deterministically reset by the function $R(x, e_i)$ to the same set $\Re(R(\cdot, e_i))$ when the transition $e_i = (q_{k_{i-1}}, q_{k_i})$ has occurred. Therefore, we can construct from $\tilde{\rho}$, by iteration, a string $\rho = q_{k_0}, \Delta_0, \cdots, q_{k_s}, \Delta_s \in \mathcal{L}_{q_{k_s}}(\mathcal{H})$ such that $P(\rho) = P(\tilde{\rho})$.

Proposition 9 has the following consequences:

Corollary 3. $\mathcal{P}(\mathcal{H}) = \mathcal{P}(\tilde{T})$.

Theorem 2. Given $\mathcal{H}$ and $\tilde{T}$, let assumptions (i) and (ii) hold. Then, q_c is observable for $\mathcal{H}$ if and only if $T^{-1}(q_c)$ is observable for $\tilde{T}$.

Proof. By Theorem 1 and Propositions 7 and 9.

5   Conclusions

In this work, we tackled the problem of immediate detection of a critical state - corresponding to a dangerous situation - by providing a definition of observability of the discrete state for a class of Hybrid Systems whose output is a timed string on a finite alphabet. We proposed a procedure to construct a Timed Automaton that is an abstraction of the given system, and for which observability is easier to determine. We provided algorithms to check observability of the abstraction and to construct an observer of a given discrete state. Finally, we proved that observability of the abstraction implies observability of the given hybrid system, and provided conditions under which this implication can be reversed. In some future work, the authors wish to extend these results to Hybrid Systems with continuous output, and to simple classes of Stochastic Hybrid Systems.

Acknowledgement

The first author wishes to thank George Pappas and Antoine Girard for the interesting discussions on bisimulation and observability of Hybrid Systems that originated this work, during a visiting period at the Department of Electrical and Systems Engineering at the University of Pennsylvania.

References

1. R. Alur, T. Henzinger, G. Lafferriere, and G. Pappas. *Discrete abstractions of hybrid systems*, Proccedings of the IEEE, 88(2), July 2000, pp. 971-984.
2. H. Anai and V.Weispfenning. *Reach set computations using real quantifier elimination*, Hybrid Systems: Computation and Control 2001, Lecture Notes in Computer Science, M. D. Di Benedetto and A. L. Sangiovanni-Vincentelli, Eds., vol. 2034, Springer Verlag, 2001, pp. 63-76.

3. M. Babaali and G. J. Pappas. *Observability of switched linear systems in continuous time*. Hybrid Systems: Computation and Control 2005, In Lecture Notes in Computer Science, M. Morari and L. Thiele, Eds., vol. 3414, Springer-Verlag, 2005, pp. 103–117.
4. A. Balluchi, L. Benvenuti, M.D. Di Benedetto, A.L. Sangiovanni-Vincentelli. *Design of Observers for Hybrid Systems*, Hybrid Systems: Computation and Control 2002, In Lecture Notes in Computer Science, C.J. Tomlin and M.R. Greensreet, Eds., vol. 2289, Springer-Verlag, 2002, pp.76-89.
5. A. Chutinan and B. Krogh. Computing polyhedral approximations to flow pipes for dynamic systems, In Proceedings of the 37th IEEE Conference on Decision and Control, Tampa, FL, Dec. 1998, pp. 2089-2094.
6. A. Chutinan, and B.H. Krogh. *Computing approximating automata for a class of linear hybrid systems*. In Hybrid Systems V, Lecture Notes in Computer Science, Springer-Verlag, 1998, pp.16-37.
7. E.M. Clarke, O. Grumberg, and D.A. Peled. *Model Checking*, The MIT Press, Cambridge, Massachusetts, 2002.
8. E. De Santis, M.D. Di Benedetto, and G. Pola. *On Observability and Detectability of continuous-time Switching Linear Systems*. In Proceedings of the 42nd IEEE Conference on Decision and Control, CDC 03, Maui, Hawaii, USA, Dec. 2003, pp. 5777 - 5782.
9. M.D. Di Benedetto, S. Di Gennaro, and A.D'Innocenzo. *Critical Observability and Hybrid Observers for Error Detection in Air Traffic Management*, 13th Mediterranean Conference on Control and Automation, Limassol, Cyprus, June 27-29, 2005.
10. M.D. Di Benedetto, S. Di Gennaro, and A.D'Innocenzo. *Error Detection within a Specific Time Horizon and Application to Air Traffic Management*. In Proceedings of the Joint 44th IEEE Conference on Decision and Control and European Control Conference (CDC-ECC'05), Seville, Spain, Dec. 2005, pp. 7472-7477.
11. A. Girard. *Reachability of Uncertain Linear Systems using Zonotopes*, Hybrid Systems: Computation and Control 2005, In Lecture Notes in Computer Science, M. Morari and L. Thiele, Eds., vol. 3414, Springer-Verlag, 2005, pp. 291-305.
12. G. Lafferriere, G. J. Pappas, and S. Yovine, *Symbolic reachability computations for families of linear vector fields*, Journal of Symbolic Computation, vol. 32, no. 3, September 2001, pp. 231-253.
13. J. Lygeros, C. Tomlin, S. Sastry, *Controllers for reachability specications for hybrid systems*, Automatica, Special Issue on Hybrid Systems, vol. 35, 1999.
14. M. Oishi, I. Hwang and C. Tomlin, *Immediate Observability of Discrete Event Systems with Application to User-Interface Design*. In Proceedings of the 42nd IEEE Conference on Decision and Control, Maui, Hawaii USA, Dec. 2003, pp. 2665-2672.
15. C.M. Ozveren, and A.S. Willsky. *Observability of Discrete Event Dynamic Systems*, IEEE Transactions on Automatic Control, Vol. 35, 1990, pp. 797-806.
16. S. Tripakis. *Fault Diagnosis for Timed Automata*, In Lecture Notes in Computer Science, 2469, W. Damm and E.-R. Olderog, Eds., Springer-Verlag, 2002, pp. 205-221.
17. R. Vidal, A. Chiuso, S. Soatto and S. Sastry. *Observability of Linear Hybrid Systems*. Hybrid Systems: Computation and Control, Lecture Notes in Computer Science, A. Pnueli and O. Maler, Eds., vol. 2623, Springer Verlag, 2003, pp. 526-539.
18. H. Yazarel and G. J. Pappas. *Geometric programming relaxations for linear system reachability*. In Proceedings of the 2004 American Control Conference, Boston, MA, June 2004.
19. T. Yoo and S. Lafortune, *On The Computational Complexity Of Some Problems Arising In Partially-observed Discrete-Event Systems*, In Proceedings of the 2001 American Control Conference, Arlington , Virginia , June, 25-27, 2001.

Reconstruction of Switching Thresholds in Piecewise-Affine Models of Genetic Regulatory Networks

S. Drulhe[1], G. Ferrari-Trecate[2,3], H. de Jong[1], and A. Viari[1]

[1] INRIA Rhône-Alpes, 655 avenue de l'Europe, Montbonnot,
38334 Saint Ismier Cedex, France
{Samuel.Drulhe, Hidde.de-Jong, Alain.Viari}@inrialpes.fr
[2] INRIA, Domaine de Voluceau, Rocquencourt - B.P.105,
78153, Le Chesnay Cedex, France
Giancarlo.Ferrari-Trecate@inria.fr
[3] Dipartimento di Informatica e Sistemistica, Università degli Studi di Pavia,
Via Ferrata 1, 27100 Pavia, Italy

Abstract. Recent advances of experimental techniques in biology have led to the production of enormous amounts of data on the dynamics of genetic regulatory networks. In this paper, we present an approach for the identification of PieceWise-Affine (PWA) models of genetic regulatory networks from experimental data, focusing on the reconstruction of switching thresholds associated with regulatory interactions. In particular, our method takes into account geometric constraints specific to models of genetic regulatory networks. We show the feasibility of our approach by the reconstruction of switching thresholds in a PWA model of the carbon starvation response in the bacterium *Escherichia coli*.

1 Introduction

Recent advances of experimental techniques in biology have led to the production of enormous amounts of data on the dynamics of cellular processes. Prominent examples of such techniques are DNA microarrays and gene reporter systems, which allow gene expression to be measured with varying degrees of precision and throughput. One of the major challenges in biology today consists in the analysis and interpretation of these data, with a view to identifying the networks of interactions between genes, proteins, and small molecules that regulate the observed processes. The mapping of these *genetic regulatory networks* is a key issue for understanding the functioning of a cell and for designing interventions of biotechnological or biomedical relevance.

The problem of identifying genetic regulatory networks from gene expression data has attracted much attention over the last ten years. Most approaches are based on the use of *linear* models (*e.g.*, [1, 2, 3]), for which powerful identification algorithms exist. However, given that the underlying biological processes are usually strongly nonlinear, the models are valid only near an equilibrium

João Hespanha and A. Tiwari (Eds.): HSCC 2006, LNCS 3927, pp. 184–199, 2006.

point (see [4] for an exception). While there have been some approaches based on *nonlinear* models of genetic regulatory networks, the practical applicability of these models is often compromised by the intrinsic mathematical and computational difficulty of nonlinear system identification. Not surprisingly, most authors have therefore focused on specific classes of nonlinear models, with restrictions that reduce the number of parameters and simplify the mathematical form (*e.g.*, [5, 6]).

Another class of models that seems to strike a good compromise between the advantages and disadvantages of linear and nonlinear models are the *Piece Wise-Affine (PWA)* models of genetic regulatory networks introduced by Glass and Kauffman in the 1970s [7]. The study of these models and their generalizations has been an active research area in both mathematical biology and hybrid systems theory (*e.g.*, [8, 9, 10, 11, 12, 13]). Notwithstanding their simple mathematical form, PWA systems capture essential aspects of gene regulation, as demonstrated by several modeling studies of regulatory networks of biological interest [12, 14]. Moreover, powerful techniques for the identification of PWA systems have been developed in the field of hybrid systems (see [15] and the references therein), which might be profitably applied to the reconstruction of genetic regulatory networks from experimental data.

Although the available hybrid identification algorithms provide a good starting point, they are generic in nature and therefore not well-adapted to a number of constraints specific to PWA models of genetic regulatory networks. First of all, the state space regions associated with modes of the system are hyperrectangular, as they are defined by switching thresholds of the concentration variables. Second, there exist strong dependencies between the modes of the system, as a consequence of the coordinated control of gene expression. Third, the aim of the system identification process is not to generate a single model, but *all* models with a minimal number of regulatory interactions that are consistent with the experimental data.

The aim of our paper is to make a first step towards the adaptation of existing algorithms for the identification of PWA models so as to take into account the above constraints. In particular, we focus on a crucial stage of the identification process: the estimation of the switching thresholds that partition the state space into hyperrectangular regions. We introduce an algorithm that, given gene expression time-series data classified according to the regulatory modes, produces all minimal sets of switching thresholds. We thus assume here that the preliminary problem of detecting mode switches in time-series data has been solved [15], although we are of course well aware that the underlying classification algorithms will probably have to be tailored to gene expression data as well. In order to illustrate the feasibility of our approach, we apply the threshold reconstruction algorithm to a PWA model of the carbon starvation response in *Escherichia coli* [8, 14]. The gene expression data has been obtained by simulation, while adjusting the noise level and the sampling frequency to the real data that will ultimately be available to us. The work presented in this paper is complementary to the approach of Perkins and colleagues [16], who focus on the reconstruction of the regulatory modes once the switching thresholds of the system are known.

In the next two sections, we will review PWA models of genetic regulatory networks and discuss the use of hybrid identification techniques for their reconstruction. In Sections 4 to 6 we introduce the notions of cut and multicut, formulate the switching threshold reconstructing problem in terms of these concepts, and introduce a so-called multicut algorithm that, under suitable assumptions, reconstructs minimal sets of switching thresholds from gene expression data. Section 7 presents the results of the multicut algorithm in the context of the *E. coli* carbon starvation model. In the final section we summarize our contributions and indicate directions for further research.

2   Piecewise-Affine Models of Genetic Regulatory Networks

A variety of model formalisms have been proposed to describe the dynamics of genetic regulatory networks (see [17] for a review). One particularly well-adapted to the currently available experimental data is the following class of *PWA differential equations* [7]:

$$\dot{x} = h(x) = f(x) - g(x)x, \tag{1}$$

where $x = [x_1, \ldots, x_n]' \in \Omega \subset \mathbb{R}^n_{\geq 0}$ is a vector of cellular protein concentrations, $f = [f_1, \ldots, f_n]'$, $g = \text{diag}(g_1, \ldots, g_n)$, and Ω is a bounded, n-dimensional hyperrectangle. In (1), the rate of change of each protein concentration x_i is the difference of the rate of synthesis $f_i(x)$ and the rate of degradation $g_i(x)x_i$. The map f_i is defined as a sum of terms having the general form $\kappa_i^l b_i^l(x)$, where $\kappa_i^l > 0$ is a rate parameter and $b_i^l(x) : \Omega \to \{0, 1\}$ a piecewise-constant function defined in terms of the scalar step functions s^+ and s^- defined as

$$s^+(x_i, \theta_i) = \begin{cases} 1 \text{ if } x_i > \theta_i \\ 0 \text{ if } x_i < \theta_i \end{cases} \quad and \quad s^-(x_i, \theta_i) = 1 - s^+(x_i, \theta_i), \tag{2}$$

with $\theta_i > 0$ a constant denoting a threshold concentration for x_i. The step functions are reasonable approximations of sigmoid functions, which represent the switch-like character of the interactions found in gene regulation. The map g_i, which expresses regulation of protein degradation, is defined analogously, except that it is required to be strictly positive. Examples of PWA models of genetic networks are given in [8, 10].

We now show how model (1) can be recast into a standard PWA system. Consider the union of threshold hyperplanes $\Theta = \cup_{i \in \{1, \ldots, n\}, l_i \in \{1, \ldots, p_i\}} \{x \in \Omega : x_i = \theta_i^{l_i}\}$, where p_i denotes the number of thresholds for x_i. Θ splits Ω in open hyperrectangular regions Δ^j, $j = 1, \ldots, s$, $s = \prod_{i=1}^n (p_i + 1)$, called *regulatory domains*. One can show that if $x \in \Delta^j$, then model (1) reduces to $\dot{x} = \mu^j - \nu^j x$, where $\mu^j = f(x)$ is a constant vector and $\nu^j = g(x)$ is a constant diagonal matrix. In summary, when $x \in \Omega \backslash \Theta$, model (1) is equivalent to the PWA system

$$\dot{x} = h(x) = \mu^j - \nu^j x, \quad \text{if} \quad \lambda(x) = j, \quad j = 1, \dots, s, \qquad (3)$$

where the switching function λ is defined as: $\lambda(x) = j$, if and only if $x \in \Delta^j$. Note that in every domain Δ^j, the map $h(x)$ is affine and in each mode of operation the state variables evolve independently of each other.

3   Hybrid System Identification of Genetic Regulatory Networks

Experimental techniques in biology, like DNA microarrays and gene reporter systems, allow gene expression to be measured at discrete time instants. In what follows, we assume that data are obtained with a uniform sampling period $T > 0$, where T is small with respect to the time constants of gene expression. We denote by $\hat{x}(k)$, $k = 1, \dots, N + 1$, the measured vectors of concentrations $\hat{x}(kT)$. By approximating derivatives through first-order differences, from (3) one obtains the following data model:

$$\hat{x}(k + 1) = (I - T\nu^j)\,\hat{x}(k) + T\mu^j + \epsilon(k), \quad \text{if} \quad \lambda(\hat{x}(k)) = j, \qquad (4)$$

where $\epsilon(k)$ is an additive noise corrupting the measurements. By focusing on the dynamics of a single protein concentration, say $\hat{x}_i$, model (4) becomes

$$\hat{x}_i(k + 1) = \begin{bmatrix} \hat{x}_i(k) & 1 \end{bmatrix} \phi^j + \epsilon(k), \quad \text{if} \quad \lambda(\hat{x}(k)) = j, \qquad (5)$$

where $\phi^j = \begin{bmatrix} 1 - T(\nu^j)_{ii} & T(\mu^j)_i \end{bmatrix}'$. [1]

Over the last few years, several hybrid system identification algorithms have been proposed for the reconstruction of so-called PieceWise AutoRegressive eXogenous (PWARX) models (see [15] for a review). Without going into details (which can be found in [18]), we just highlight that (5) is a PWARX system with input $u(k) = [\hat{x}_1(k), \dots, \hat{x}_{l \neq i}(k), \dots, \hat{x}_n(k)]'$ and output $y(k) = \hat{x}_i(k)$.

The identification of model (5) involves various tasks [15, 18]. In the sequel, we focus on the estimation of the hyperrectangular domains Δ^j, which usually requires an intermediate result produced by all of the above algorithms: the reconstruction of the *switching sequence* $\lambda(\hat{x}(k))$, $k = 1, \dots, N$. More specifically, as illustrated in [18], a domain Δ^j is found by looking for the $s-1$ hyperplanes separating the set $\mathcal{F}_j = \{\hat{x}(k) : \lambda(\hat{x}(k)) = j\}$ from all sets $\mathcal{F}_l = \{\hat{x}(k) : \lambda(\hat{x}(k)) = l\}$, $l \neq j$. These hyperplanes can be obtained through pattern-recognition techniques such as Multicategory Robust Linear Programming (MRLP) [19] or Support Vector Classifiers (SVC) [20].

A problem with this approach is that both MRLP and SVC do not impose any constraints on the hyperplanes to be estimated. As a consequence, even if the

---

[1] $(\nu^j)_{ii}$ is the element at position (i, i) of ν^j, $(\mu^j)_i$ is the ith element of μ^j.

switching sequence is perfectly known, there is no guarantee that the estimated domains Δ^j will be hyperrectangular. This may result in hybrid models that are meaningless from a biological point of view, since they do not preserve the concept of a switching threshold associated with a concentration variable. Another problem with existing techniques is that they produce a single model. This is not realistic in our case, because only a fraction of the modes are encountered in the experiments. As a consequence, several hybrid models of the network, each characterized by a different combination of thresholds for the variables, may be consistent with the data and need to be considered.

For all of these reasons, we propose a pattern recognition algorithm tailored to the features of PWARX models of genetic regulatory networks in the next three sections.

4   Switching Thresholds and Multicuts

Let $\mathcal{F}_1, \ldots, \mathcal{F}_s$ be disjoint sets collecting finitely-many points in $\mathbb{R}^n$ and $\mathcal{F}^* = \{\mathcal{F}_1, \ldots, \mathcal{F}_s\}$. Hereafter, we focus on the problem of separating the sets in $\mathcal{F}^*$ with hyperplanes parallel to the linear combination of $n-1$ axes. In order to illustrate the main concepts, we will use the collection $\mathcal{F}^*$ depicted in Figure 1(a). Pairs of distinct sets in $\mathcal{F}^*$ will often be indexed by means of pairs in $U = \{(p,q) \in \{1,\ldots,s\}^2 : p < q\}$.

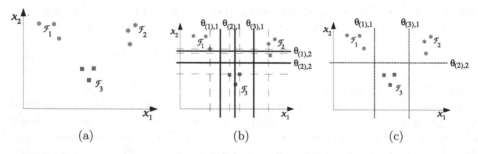

$$(a) \qquad\qquad\qquad (b) \qquad\qquad\qquad (c)$$

Fig. 1. Simple example of multicuts. (a) Data sets $\mathcal{F}^*$. (b) Multicut $\mathcal{C}^*$: bold lines correspond to cuts and dotted lines are the limits of their equivalence class. (c) Multicut $Max_{\preceq}\mathcal{C}^*$.

Definition 1 (Ap-hyperplane). *An* axis-parallel (ap-) hyperplane *in* $\mathbb{R}^n$ *with direction* $i \in \{1,\ldots,n\}$ *is a hyperplane of equation* $x_i = \alpha$, $\alpha \in \mathbb{R}$, *or equivalently, the zero level set of the function* $\theta(x) = x_i - \alpha$.

By abuse of notation, θ will denote both an ap-hyperplane and its associated function. The function $dir(\theta)$ gives the direction i of the ap-hyperplane θ, while the function $Z(\theta)$ gives the zero-level α. We introduce the following set-valued functions that will turn out to be useful below:

$$\mathcal{I}_-(\theta) = \{j : \forall x \in \mathcal{F}_j, \theta(x) < 0\}, \quad \mathcal{B}_-(\theta) = \cup_{j \in \mathcal{I}_-(\theta)} \mathcal{F}_j,$$
$$\mathcal{I}_+(\theta) = \{j : \forall x \in \mathcal{F}_j, \theta(x) > 0\}, \quad \mathcal{B}_+(\theta) = \cup_{j \in \mathcal{I}_+(\theta)} \mathcal{F}_j.$$

Definition 2 (Separability). *Let $\mathcal{F}_p$ and $\mathcal{F}_q$ be disjoint sets collecting finitely many points in $\mathbb{R}^n$. An ap-hyperplane θ in $\mathbb{R}^n$ separates $\mathcal{F}_p$ and $\mathcal{F}_q$ if there exists $\delta \in \{+1, -1\}$ such that for all $x \in \mathcal{F}_p \cup \mathcal{F}_q$ one has $\delta\,\theta(x) > 0$, if $x \in \mathcal{F}_p$, and $\delta\,\theta(x) < 0$, if $x \in \mathcal{F}_q$. In this case, we write $\mathcal{F}_p \overset{\theta}{\curlyvee} \mathcal{F}_q$. $\mathcal{F}_p$ and $\mathcal{F}_q$ are separable if there exists an ap-hyperplane separating the sets.*

We introduce two additional functions on sets $\mathcal{F}_p$ and $\mathcal{F}_q$, for $i \in \{1, \ldots, n\}$,

$$Inf_i(\mathcal{F}_p, \mathcal{F}_q) = \min(\max_{x \in \mathcal{F}_p} x_i, \max_{x \in \mathcal{F}_q} x_i),$$
$$Sup_i(\mathcal{F}_p, \mathcal{F}_q) = \max(\min_{x \in \mathcal{F}_p} x_i, \min_{x \in \mathcal{F}_q} x_i).$$

In Figure 1, $\mathcal{F}_1$ and $\mathcal{F}_2$ are separable since there exist ap-hyperplanes in the x_1-direction (*e.g.*, $\theta_{(1),1}$ and $\theta_{(2),1}$), such that all points in $\mathcal{F}_1$ lie on one side of the hyperplane $\theta_{(1),1}$ and all points of $\mathcal{F}_2$ on the other side. Notice that the sets $\mathcal{F}_1$ and $\mathcal{F}_2$ are not separable in the x_2-direction. As can be verified in Figure 1, the ap-hyperplane $\theta_{(1),1}$ separates more sets than the ap-hyperplane $\theta_{(2),1}$. The difference in separation power of ap-hyperplanes can be formally defined as follows.

Definition 3 (Separation power). *The* separation power *of an ap-hyperplane θ is the set-valued function $S(\theta) = \{(p,q) \in U : \mathcal{F}_p \overset{\theta}{\curlyvee} \mathcal{F}_q\}$.*

In the remainder of this section, we focus on ap-hyperplanes in the set $\Theta = \{\theta : S(\theta) \neq \emptyset\}$. The comparison of the separation power of ap-hyperplanes in Θ in a given direction motivates the introduction of equivalence classes of ap-hyperplanes.

Definition 4 (Equivalence). *Two ap-hyperplanes $\theta, \theta' \in \Theta$ are equivalent if $dir(\theta) = dir(\theta')$ and $S(\theta) = S(\theta')$. Equivalent ap-hyperplanes will be denoted by $\theta \sim \theta'$ and the equivalence class of θ by $[\theta] = \{\theta' : \theta' \sim \theta\}$.*

Following the above definition, the ap-hyperplanes $\theta_{(1),1}$ and $\theta_{(2),1}$ in Figure 1 are not equivalent.

We recall that, given an equivalence relation $\sim$ on a set X and a function $f : X \to Y$, f is *invariant* under $\sim$ if $x \sim y$ implies $f(x) = f(y)$. It is not difficult to show that the functions dir, S, $\mathcal{I}_+$, $\mathcal{I}_-$, $\mathcal{B}_+$ and $\mathcal{B}_-$ are invariant under the equivalence relation $\sim$ defined in Definition 4. This implies that we can generalize these functions to the *quotient set* $\mathcal{E}^* = \Theta/\sim$. Note also that the cardinality of $\mathcal{E}^*$ is finite [21].

Although all ap-hyperplanes in an equivalence class $\mathcal{E} \in \mathcal{E}^*$ have the same separation power, only one is optimal in a statistical sense [20]. This ap-hyperplane will be called a *cut*.

Definition 5 (Cut). *Let $\mathcal{E} \in \mathcal{E}^*$ and $i = dir(\mathcal{E})$. The cut associated to $\mathcal{E}$ is the ap-hyperplane $\theta \in \Theta$ such that*

$$Z(\theta) = Inf_i(\mathcal{B}_+(\mathcal{E}), \mathcal{B}_-(\mathcal{E})) + \frac{Sup_i(\mathcal{B}_+(\mathcal{E}), \mathcal{B}_-(\mathcal{E})) - Inf_i(\mathcal{B}_+(\mathcal{E}), \mathcal{B}_-(\mathcal{E}))}{2}. \quad (6)$$

In what follows the set of all cuts is denoted by C^*. Since $\mathcal{E}^*$ and C^* are isomorphic, the cardinality of C^* is also finite. In the example with three data sets in Figure 1(a), C^* is composed of five cuts ($\theta_{(1),1}$, $\theta_{(2),1}$, $\theta_{(3),1}$, $\theta_{(1),2}$, and $\theta_{(2),2}$), which are represented in Figure 1(b) by means of bold lines.

Intuitively, we would be inclined to say that the cut $\theta_{(1),1}$ is more powerful than $\theta_{(2),1}$, in the sense that the former separates $\mathcal{F}_1$ and $\mathcal{F}_2$ as well as $\mathcal{F}_1$ and $\mathcal{F}_3$, whereas the latter separates only $\mathcal{F}_1$ and $\mathcal{F}_2$ (that is, $S(\theta_{(1),1}) = \{(1,2),(1,3)\}$ and $S(\theta_{(2),1}) = \{(1,2)\}$). This motivates the introduction of the following relation on C^*, denoted by $\preceq$:

$$\theta \preceq \theta' \text{ if } S(\theta) \subseteq S(\theta') \text{ and } dir(\theta) = dir(\theta'). \tag{7}$$

It is straightforward to show that $\preceq$ is reflexive, antisymmetric, and transitive, and hence that $\preceq$ is a partial order on C^*. That is, C^* is a poset (partially ordered set).

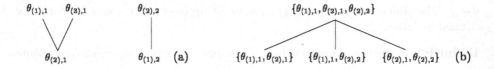

Fig. 2. (a) Poset diagram for the set of cuts C^* in Figure 1. The diagram shows, *e.g.*, $\theta_{(2),1} \preceq \theta_{(1),1}$. (b) Poset diagram for the down-set of $\mathcal{M} = \{\theta_{(1),1}, \theta_{(3),1}, \theta_{(2),2}\}$, which is a multicut for Figure 1. In fact, $\mathcal{M}$ equals $\mathrm{Max}_{\preceq} C^*$.

The poset diagram corresponding to the example in Figure 1 is shown in Figure 2(a). As for any poset, C^* admits maximal and minimal elements. The sets of maximal and minimal elements of C^* are denoted by $\mathrm{Max}_{\preceq} C^*$ and $\mathrm{Min}_{\preceq} C^*$, respectively. For instance, in Figure 2(a) $\mathrm{Max}_{\preceq} C^* = \{\theta_{(1),1}, \theta_{(3),1}, \theta_{(2),2}\}$.

In general, several cuts will be required to separate all sets in $\mathcal{F}^*$. This motivates the introduction of multicuts.

Definition 6 (Multicut). *A multicut $\mathcal{M}$ of $\mathcal{F}^*$ is a finite set of cuts such that for all $(p,q) \in U$ there exists a $\theta \in \mathcal{M}$, such that $\mathcal{F}_p \overset{\theta}{\curlyvee} \mathcal{F}_q$. A collection $\mathcal{F}^*$ is said to be* m-separable *if there exists a multicut of $\mathcal{F}^*$ or, equivalently, if $U = \cup_{\theta \in \mathcal{M}} S(\theta)$.*

We call $\mathcal{M}^*$ the set of multicuts. Due to the fact that C^* is finite, $\mathcal{M}^*$ is finite as well. Notice that $\mathcal{M}^*$ may be empty, that is, $\mathcal{F}^*$ may not be m-separable. In the example of Figure 1, $\mathcal{M} = \{\theta_{(3),1}, \theta_{(2),2}\}$ is a multicut since we have $S(\theta_{(3),1}) = \{(1,2),(2,3)\}$ and $S(\theta_{(2),2}) = \{(1,3)\}$.

The following proposition, proven in [21], states a relevant property of C^*.

Proposition 1. *$\mathcal{F}^*$ is m-separable if and only if C^* is a multicut.*

We define an obvious partial order relation on the set of multicuts $\mathcal{M}^*$, the set inclusion $\subseteq$. The poset $\mathcal{M}^*$ for the example in Figure 1 consists of 20 multicuts (figure not shown).

To every subset $\mathcal{B}$ of $\mathcal{M}^*$ we can associate a down-set, which consists of the multicuts in $\mathcal{M}^*$ upper bounded (according to $\subseteq$) by some multicut in $\mathcal{B}$. For reasons that will become clear below, we focus here on the down-set of singletons $\mathcal{B} = \{\mathcal{M}\}$, for some $\mathcal{M} \in \mathcal{M}^*$.

Definition 7 (Down-set of multicut set). *The* down-set *of* $\{\mathcal{M}\}$, $\mathcal{M} \in \mathcal{M}^*$, *denoted by* $\downarrow \{\mathcal{M}\}$, *is defined by* $\downarrow \{\mathcal{M}\} = \{\mathcal{M}' \in \mathcal{M}^* : \mathcal{M}' \subseteq \mathcal{M}\}$.

Consider the multicut $\mathrm{Max}_{\preceq} \mathcal{C}^*$ in the example (Figure 2(a)). The down-set of $\{\mathrm{Max}_{\preceq} \mathcal{C}^*\}$ is the union of all sets appearing in Figure 2(b). We note that $\downarrow \{\mathcal{M}\}$ is also a poset with respect to set inclusion.

5 Formulation of Switching Threshold Reconstruction Problem

The introduction of the concepts of cut and multicut, and the partial orders defined on them, allows us to formulate the problem of reconstructing switching thresholds in a more precise way. In general, the available data are consistent with a large number of multicuts, and thus with a large number of PWA models of the genetic regulatory network. *A priori* there is no reason to prefer one of these models above the others. However, in practice we are most interested in the minimal models that account for the available data, that is, those models that contain a minimal number of thresholds and separate all pairs of sets in $\mathcal{F}^*$. Assuming that the set of data points is m-separable, so that $\mathcal{C}^*$ is a multicut, it seems reasonable to accept as solutions all multicuts in $\mathrm{Min}_{\subseteq} \downarrow \{\mathcal{C}^*\}$.

Notice though that $\mathcal{C}^*$ may contain many cuts with a weak separation power that could be eliminated beforehand if we are only interested in finding minimal multicuts. That is, we can remove cuts $\theta \in \mathcal{C}^*$ if there exists another $\theta' \in \mathcal{C}^*$, $\theta' \neq \theta$, such that $\theta \preceq \theta'$. Eliminating these cuts does not affect the m-separability of the sets of data points, as indicated by the following proposition (proven in [21]), which should be compared with Proposition 1.

Proposition 2. *$Max_{\preceq} \mathcal{C}^*$ is a multicut if and only if $\mathcal{F}^*$ is m-separable.*

Once $\mathcal{C}^*$ has been reduced to $\mathrm{Max}_{\preceq} \mathcal{C}^*$, our switching threshold reconstruction problem can be recast into the problem of computing the set

$$\mathrm{Min}_{\subseteq} \downarrow \{\mathrm{Max}_{\preceq} \mathcal{C}^*\}. \tag{8}$$

Notice that $\mathrm{Max}_{\subseteq} \downarrow \{\mathrm{Max}_{\preceq} \mathcal{C}^*\}$ is $\{\mathrm{Max}_{\preceq} \mathcal{C}^*\}$ itself, so that we will call $\mathrm{Max}_{\preceq} \mathcal{C}^*$ the *maximal multicut*. In the example of Figure 1, $\mathrm{Max}_{\preceq} \mathcal{C}^*$ consists of three cuts, as shown in Figure 2(a). That is, two cuts with obvious weaker separation power have been eliminated ($\theta_{(2),1}$ and $\theta_{(1),2}$). The down-set of $\{\mathrm{Max}_{\preceq} \mathcal{C}^*\}$ is shown in Figure 2(b). It has three minimal multicuts: $\{\theta_{(1),1}, \theta_{(3),1}\}$, $\{\theta_{(1),1}, \theta_{(2),2}\}$, and $\{\theta_{(3),1}, \theta_{(2),2}\}$. As illustrated by the example, there will generally be several minimal multicuts. We can distinguish between *locally* and *globally* minimal multicuts.

Definition 8. *Let* $\mathcal{M}$ *be a multicut of* $\mathcal{F}^*$. $\mathcal{M}$ *is* locally minimal *if for all* $\theta \in \mathcal{M}$, *the set* $\mathcal{M} \backslash \{\theta\}$ *is not a multicut of* $\mathcal{F}^*$. $\mathcal{M}$ *is* globally minimal *if*

$$|\mathcal{M}| = \min_{\tilde{\mathcal{M}} \in \mathcal{M}_{min}} |\tilde{\mathcal{M}}|, \tag{9}$$

where $\mathcal{M}_{min}$ *is the set of all locally minimal multicuts of* $\mathcal{F}^*$.

It can be shown (see [21]) that the elements of $\text{Min}_{\subseteq} \downarrow \{\text{Max}_{\preceq} \mathcal{C}^*\}$ are locally minimal multicuts, but they are not necessarily globally minimal.

The above remarks lead us to a final refinement of the problem statement:

find *all* globally minimal multicuts in $\text{Min}_{\subseteq} \downarrow \{\text{Max}_{\preceq} \mathcal{C}^*\}$. (10)

6 Algorithms for Computing Switching Thresholds

In this section we present an approach to compute the multicuts satisfying criterion (10), and thus infer the minimal set of switching thresholds for a PWA model of a genetic regulatory network from a classified data set $\mathcal{F}^*$.

The computation of the set of all cuts ($\mathcal{C}^*$) is rather straightforward, based on the definition of a cut (Definition 5). For sake of brevity, we omit the algorithm which can be found in [21]. Similarly, the set of maximal cuts ($\text{Max}_{\preceq} \mathcal{C}^*$) can be computed by applying directly the definition of maximal element of $\mathcal{C}^*$ with respect to the partial order (7) (see [21] for further details).

A more challenging task is the computation of all globally minimal multicuts. In order to find them, we could in principle enumerate all subsets of $Max_{\preceq} \mathcal{C}^*$ and verify minimality by means of Definitions 6 and 8. However, this procedure is computationally prohibitive even for simple examples. Therefore, in the sequel, we present an additional result on multicuts that will allow us to reduce the dimension of the search space.

Definition 9 (Redundancy). *Let* $\mathcal{M}$ *be a multicut of* $\mathcal{F}^*$. *A cut* $\theta \in \mathcal{M}$ *is* redundant *in* $\mathcal{M}$, *if* $S(\theta) \subseteq \cup_{\theta' \in \mathcal{M} \backslash \{\theta\}} S(\theta')$.

In the example of Figure 1, each of the three cuts in the multicut $\{\theta_{(1),1}, \theta_{(3),1}, \theta_{(2),2}\}$ is redundant. The following proposition (proven in [21]), shows that redundant cuts can be safely ignored.

Proposition 3. *A multicut* $\mathcal{M}$ *of* $\mathcal{F}^*$ *is locally minimal if and only if no* $\theta \in \mathcal{M}$ *is redundant in* $\mathcal{M}$.

Definition 10 (Kernel). *Let* $\mathcal{M}$ *be a multicut of* $\mathcal{F}^*$. *The* kernel *of* $\mathcal{M}$ *is defined as* $\ker(\mathcal{M}) = \{\theta \in \mathcal{M} : \exists u \in S(\theta), \nexists \theta' \in \mathcal{M} \backslash \{\theta\}, u \in S(\theta')\}$.

From Definition 10, it is apparent that $\ker(Max_{\preceq} \mathcal{C}^*)$ collects the cuts in $\mathcal{M}$ that must belong to every minimal multicut, otherwise at least one pair of sets in $\mathcal{F}^*$ will not be separated. In the case of $\mathcal{M} = \{\theta_{(1),1}, \theta_{(3),1}, \theta_{(2),2}\}$ in the example of Figure 1, the kernel is empty: none of the cuts is indispensable.

Algorithm 1. Create the set $\mathcal{M}^*_{min}$ of all globally minimal multicuts

---

1: Initialize the global variables $\mathcal{M}^*_{min} = \emptyset$ and $best = |Max_{\preceq}\mathcal{C}^*|$. Initialize $\mathcal{M}_{in} = \ker(Max_{\preceq}\mathcal{C}^*)$

2: **if** $U = \cup_{\theta \in \mathcal{M}_{in}} S(\theta)$ **then**

3:     Append $\ker(Max_{\preceq}\mathcal{C}^*)$ to $\mathcal{M}^*_{min}$ and exit

4: **else**

5:     $Branch(\mathcal{M}_{in})$

6: **end if**

function $Branch(\mathcal{M}_{in})$

1: **for all** $\theta \in Max_{\preceq}\mathcal{C}^* \backslash \mathcal{M}_{in}$ **do**

2:     **if** $S(\theta) \not\subseteq \cup_{\theta' \in \mathcal{M}_{in}} S(\theta')$ **then** $//\theta$ is not redundant in $\mathcal{M}_{in} \cup \{\theta\}$.

3:         Set $\mathcal{M}_{out} = \mathcal{M}_{in} \cup \{\theta\}$

4:         **if** $U = \cup_{\theta' \in \mathcal{M}_{out}} S(\theta')$ **then** $//\mathcal{M}_{out}$ is a multicut.

5:             **if** $|\mathcal{M}_{out}| = best$ and $\mathcal{M}_{out} \notin \mathcal{M}^*_{min}$ **then**

6:                 Append $\mathcal{M}_{out}$ to $\mathcal{M}^*_{min}$

7:             **else if** $|\mathcal{M}_{out}| < best$ **then**

8:                 Set $\mathcal{M}^*_{min} = \{\mathcal{M}_{out}\}$ and $best = |\mathcal{M}_{out}|$ $//$Reset $\mathcal{M}^*_{min}$ and update $best$.

9:             **end if**

10:         **else if** $|\mathcal{M}_{out}| < best$ **then**

11:             $Branch(\mathcal{M}_{out})$

12:         **end if**

13:     **end if**

14: **end for**

The notions of redundancy and kernel are used to speed up the branch-and-bound strategy of Algorithm 1 below, computing the set $\mathcal{M}^*_{min} \subseteq \mathcal{M}^*$ of globally minimal multicuts. The basic idea is to start with a small subset of $Max_{\preceq}\mathcal{C}^*$, given by $\ker(Max_{\preceq}\mathcal{C}^*)$, and add new cuts iteratively.

During the execution of Algorithm 1, the global variable $best$ stores the size of the smaller multicut found so far. If $\ker(Max_{\preceq}\mathcal{C}^*)$ is a multicut, it is also the only globally minimal multicut in $Max_{\preceq}\mathcal{C}^*$ and the algorithm terminates (lines 1 and 1 of the main procedure). Otherwise, the function $Branch$ is called in order to add suitable cuts to $\ker(Max_{\preceq}\mathcal{C}^*)$. At line 1 of the function $Branch$, the addition of a new cut θ to $\mathcal{M}_{in}$ is considered only if θ is not redundant in $\mathcal{M}_{out} = \mathcal{M}_{in} \cup \{\theta\}$ (following Proposition 3). Lines 1-1 process sets $\mathcal{M}_{out}$ that are multicuts and modify the set $\mathcal{M}^*_{min}$ accordingly. More specifically, a multicut of size $best$ is added to $\mathcal{M}^*_{min}$ (line 1), while a multicut of size less than $best$ causes the reset of the set $\mathcal{M}^*_{min}$ (line 1) and the update of $best$. These operations guarantee that only globally minimal multicuts will be stored in $\mathcal{M}^*_{min}$.

7   Reconstruction of Switching Thresholds in PWA Model of Carbon Starvation Response of *E. coli*

In order to test the applicability of the multicut approach, we have used it for the reconstruction of switching thresholds in a PWA model of the carbon starvation response in the bacterium *Escherichia coli.* In the absence of essential carbon sources, an *E. coli* population abandons exponential growth and enters a non-growth state called *stationary phase.* On the molecular level, the transition from exponential phase to stationary phase in response to a carbon stress is controlled by a complex genetic regulatory network.

A PWA model of the carbon starvation response has been developed in *E. coli* [14]. The model describes how a carbon stress signal is propagated through a network of interactions between global transcriptional regulators of the bacterium, so as to influence the synthesis of stable RNAs and thereby adapt the growth of the cell. For this study, we have used a simplified version of this model (Figure 3), which preserves essential properties of the qualitative dynamics

$$\dot{x}_{CRP} = \kappa^0_{CRP} + \kappa^1_{CRP}\, s^-(x_{Fis}, \theta^1_{Fis})\, s^+(x_{CRP}, \theta^1_{CRP})\, s^+(x_S, \theta_S) - \gamma_{CRP}\, x_{CRP}$$

$$\dot{x}_{Fis} = \kappa^1_{Fis}\, (1 - s^+(x_{CRP}, \theta^2_{CRP})\, s^+(x_S, \theta_S))$$
$$\quad + \kappa^2_{Fis}\, s^+(x_{GyrAB}, \theta_{GyrAB})\, (1 - s^+(x_{CRP}, \theta^2_{CRP})\, s^+(x_S, \theta_S)) - \gamma_{Fis}\, x_{Fis}$$

$$\dot{x}_{GyrAB} = \kappa_{GyrAB}\, s^-(x_{Fis}, \theta^3_{Fis}) - \gamma_{GyrAB}\, x_{GyrAB}$$

$$\dot{x}_{rrn} = \kappa_{rrn}\, s^+(x_{Fis}, \theta^2_{Fis}) - \gamma_{rrn}\, x_{rrn}$$

$$\dot{x}_S = 0 \tag{a}$$

(b)

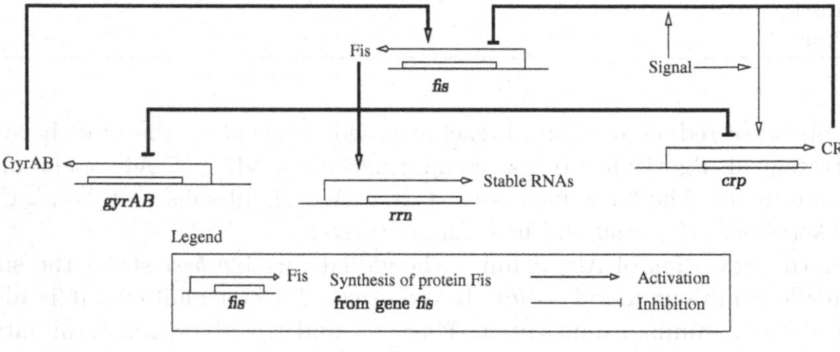

Fig. 3. (a) Simplified PWA model of the carbon starvation network in *E. coli* [14]. The variables x_{CRP}, x_{Fis}, x_{GyrAB}, and x_{rrn} denote the concentrations of CRP, Fis, GyrAB, and stable RNAs, while x_S represents the carbon starvation signal ($s^+(x_S, \theta_S) = 1$ means that the carbon starvation signal is present). The variables have been rescaled to the interval $[0, 1]$, and the following parameter values have been used for the simulations: $\theta^1_{CRP} = 0.33$, $\theta^2_{CRP} = 0.67$, $\theta^1_{Fis} = 0.1$, $\theta^2_{Fis} = 0.5$, $\theta^3_{Fis} = 0.75$, $\theta_{GyrAB} = 0.5$, $\theta_{rrn} = 0.5$, $\theta_S = 0.5$, $\gamma_{CRP} = 0.5;$, $\gamma_{Fis} = 2$, $\gamma_{GyrAB} = 1$, $\gamma_{rrn} = 1.5$, $\gamma_S = 0.5$, $\kappa^0_{CRP} = 0.25$, $\kappa^1_{CRP} = 0.4$, $\kappa^1_{Fis} = 0.6$, $\kappa^2_{Fis} = 1.15$, $\kappa_{GyrAB} = 0.75$, $\kappa_{rrn} = 1.12$, (b) Graphical representation of the PWA model, indicating genes and their regulatory interactions. The interactions in bold have been correctly identified by the best globally minimal multicuts obtained from the data for the reentry into exponential phase after a carbon upshift (MC_2 in Figure 5(c)) and for the entry into stationary phase (results not shown).

predicted by the original model, as verified by means of the approach described in [8]. In response to a carbon starvation signal, the system switches from an equilibrium point characteristic for exponential growth to another equilibrium point, corresponding to stationary phase. Reentry into exponential phase after a carbon upshift gives rise to a damped oscillation towards the exponential-phase equilibrium point.

The use of reporter genes encoding fluorescent and luminescent proteins makes it possible to obtain precise and densely-spaced measurements of the expression of the genes in the carbon starvation response network. This kind of data is well-suited for system identification purposes, as shown previously in [2, 6]. In this paper, we use simulated data to test the multicut approach, staying close to the expected noise and sample density of the real measurements.

Figure 4 gives an indication of the data obtained from simulating the reentry into exponential phase after a carbon upshift. In order to separate the threshold reconstruction problem from the classification problem for the purpose of this paper, we have generated the correct classification by detecting mode switches during simulation.

The resulting datasets have been analyzed by means of a Matlab implementation of the algorithms presented in Section 6. The results for the transition from stationary to exponential phase after a carbon upshift are summarized in Figure 5. The algorithm finds the maximal multicut $\mathcal{C}^*$, consisting of six cuts $(\theta_1, \ldots, \theta_6)$. In order to get an idea of the separation power of the cuts, Figure 5(b) pictures the projection of the data points on the (x_{Fis}, x_{GyrAB})-subspace. As can be seen, the cuts θ_2, θ_5, and θ_6 nicely separate the classes generated from the damped oscillation (Figure 4).

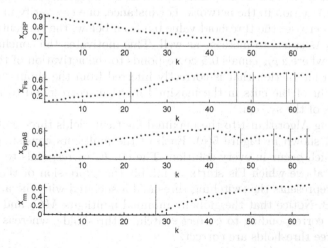

Fig. 4. Simulation of the reentry into exponential phase following a carbon upshift, using the PWA model in Figure 3(a). In order to mimic the absence of a carbon stress, $x_S(0)$ has been set to 0. For each protein concentration variable, the mode switches are indicated by means of vertical bars.

Cut	Variable	Threshold value	Interaction	Correct? (Y/N)
θ_1	x_{Fis}	0.26	Fis activates fis	N
θ_2	x_{GyrAB}	0.49	GyrAB activates fis	Y
θ_3	x_{rrn}	0.03	Stable RNAs activate rrn	N
θ_4	x_{CRP}	0.65	CRP inhibits fis	Y
θ_5	x_{Fis}	0.5	Fis activates rrn	Y
θ_6	x_{Fis}	0.74	Fis inhibits $gyrAB$	Y

(a)

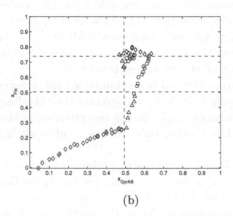

Multicut	Composing cuts	Correct?
MC_1	$\{\theta_2, \theta_3, \theta_6\}$	$\{Y, N, Y\}$
MC_2	$\{\theta_2, \theta_4, \theta_6\}$	$\{Y, Y, Y\}$
MC_3	$\{\theta_2, \theta_5, \theta_6\}$	$\{Y, Y, Y\}$

(b)   (c)

Fig. 5. (a) Maximal multicut for the data in Figure 4. (b) Illustration of the separation power of the cuts θ_2, θ_5, and θ_6, included in the globally minimal multicut MC_3 in (c). The data have been projected on the (x_{Fis}, x_{GyrAB})-subspace. (c) Globally minimal multicuts generated by Algorithm 1 from the maximal multicut in (a).

To each of the cuts corresponds a switching threshold, associated with a regulatory interaction in the network. For instance, one can verify in Figure 4 that when x_{Fis} crosses the threshold value 0.5 from below, the concentration x_{rrn} of stable RNAs starts to increase as well. This motivates the conclusion that the threshold where x_{Fis} equals 0.5 corresponds to the activation of the rrn operon by Fis, an interaction that is correctly inferred from the simulation data (Figure 4). Four of the cuts in the maximal multicut correspond to real switching thresholds of the system.

Applying Algorithm 1 to the maximal multicut yields three globally minimal multicuts, shown in Figure 5(c). Each of the multicuts consists of three cuts, two of which occur in every solution. The cut θ_6 corresponds to the switching threshold above which Fis starts to inhibit the expression of the gene $gyrAB$, while θ_2 represents the switching threshold associated with the activation of fis by GyrAB. Notice that the globally minimal multicuts MC_2 and MC_3 contain only cuts corresponding to correct switching thresholds, whereas for MC_1 two out of three thresholds are correct.

Repeating the above procedure for the second set of simulation data, corresponding to the entry into stationary phase, yields a maximal multicut consisting of four cuts, three of which correspond to a real switching threshold of the system (results not shown). From this information, Algorithm 1 generates four globally minimal multicuts, each composed of two cuts. Two of the globally minimal multicuts entirely consist of cuts corresponding to correct switching thresholds, whereas in the other two cases one of the cuts corresponds to a non-existing threshold.

Summarizing the results of the switching threshold reconstruction process, the best globally minimal multicuts for the first and second data series have been projected on the graphical representation of the carbon starvation network in Figure 3. As can be seen, the multicut approach has inferred five out of six interactions from the data (only the autoactivation of CRP is missing). As for the worst globally minimal multicuts found by the algorithm, they nevertheless achieve the correct identification of three of the switching thresholds in the model. These results confirm the in-principle applicability of our approach.

8 Conclusions

In this paper we have proposed a pattern recognition technique for reconstructing all combinations of switching thresholds that are consistent with measured data in PWA models of genetic regulatory networks. We have shown how to recast this problem into finding all globally minimal multicuts of maximal cuts that separate different sets of points within a given collection. This algorithm is intended to be used in combination with hybrid identification procedures for classifying the data (i.e., partitioning temporal gene expression data into subsets associated with different regulatory modes) and for reconstructing the values of synthesis/degradation parameters characterizing the dynamics of the network in different regulatory domains.

A potential pitfall of the multicut approach is that the algorithms presented in Section 6 have been derived under the assumption that the sets of points considered are m-separable. Although this assumption is satisfied in the example of Section 7, it may be violated in other situations for two main reasons. The first one is that noisy data may affect the quality of the results obtained through hybrid systems identification, and lead to a misclassification of some data points [15]. The second reason is that genetic regulatory networks may exhibit the same dynamics on different regulatory domains, a fact that may result in a structural loss of m-separability. However, we stress that even if some pairs of sets are not separable, this does not prevent the multicut algorithm from finding *some* of the thresholds. Most importantly, the m-separability assumption can be verified once C^* has been found. We also believe that even if the mathematical framework for multicuts developed in Sections 4 to 6 is tailored to an idealized case, it provides a sound background for developing new methods capable of dealing with m-inseparable collections of sets.

Acknowledgments. This research has been supported by the European Commission under project HYGEIA (NEST-4995).

References

1. D'haeseleer, P., Liang, S., Somogyi, R.: Genetic network inference: From co-expression clustering to reverse engineering. Bioinformatics **16** (2000) 707–726
2. Gardner, T., di Bernardo, D., Lorenz, D., Collins, J.: Inferring genetic networks and identifying compound mode of action via expression profiling. Science **301** (2003) 102–105
3. van Someren, E., Wessels, L., Reinders, M.: Linear modeling of genetic networks from experimental data. In Altman, R., et al., eds.: Proc. Eight Int. Conf. Intell. Syst. Mol. Biol., ISMB 2000, Menlo Park, CA, AAAI Press (2000) 355–366
4. Lemeille, S., Latifi, A., Geiselmann, J.: Inferring the connectivity of a regulatory network from mRNA quantification in *Synechocystis* PCC6803. Nucleic Acids Res. **33** (2005) 3381–3389
5. Jaeger, J., Surkova, S., Blagov, M., Janssens, H., Kosman, D., Kozlov, K., Manu, Myasnikova, E., Vanario-Alonso, C., Samsonova, M., Sharp, D., Reinitz, J.: Dynamic control of positional information in the early *Drosophila* embryo. Nature **430** (2004) 368–371
6. Ronen, M., Rosenberg, R., Shraiman, B., Alon, U.: Assigning numbers to the arrows: Parameterizing a gene regulation network by using accurate expression kinetics. Proc. Natl. Acad. Sci. USA **99** (2002) 10555–10560
7. Glass, L., Kauffman, S.: The logical analysis of continuous non-linear biochemical control networks. J. Theor. Biol. **39** (1973) 103–129
8. Batt, G., Ropers, D., de Jong, H., Geiselmann, J., Page, M., Schneider, D.: Qualitative analysis and verification of hybrid models of genetic regulatory networks: Nutritional stress response in *Escherichia coli*. In Morari, M., Thiele, L., eds.: Proc. Hybrid Systems: Computation and Control (HSCC 2005). Volume 3414 of LNCS. Springer-Verlag, Berlin (2005) 134–150
9. Belta, C., Finin, P., Habets, L., Halász, A., Imiliński, M., Kumar, R., Rubin, H.: Understanding the bacterial stringent response using reachability analysis of hybrid systems. In Alur, R., Pappas, G., eds.: Proc. Hybrid Systems: Computation and Control (HSCC 2004). Volume 2993 of LNCS. Springer-Verlag, Berlin (2004) 111–125
10. de Jong, H., Gouzé, J.L., Hernandez, C., Page, M., Sari, T., Geiselmann, J.: Qualitative simulation of genetic regulatory networks using piecewise-linear models. Bull. Math. Biol. **66** (2004) 301–340
11. Edwards, R., Siegelmann, H., Aziza, K., Glass, L.: Symbolic dynamics and computation in model gene networks. Chaos **11** (2001) 160–169
12. Ghosh, R., Tomlin, C.: Symbolic reachable set computation of piecewise affine hybrid automata and its application to biological modelling: Delta-Notch protein signalling. Syst. Biol. **1** (2004) 170–183
13. Mestl, T., Plahte, E., Omholt, S.: A mathematical framework for describing and analysing gene regulatory networks. J. Theor. Biol. **176** (1995) 291–300
14. Ropers, D., de Jong, H., Page, M., Schneider, D., Geiselmann, J.: Qualitative simulation of the carbon starvation response in *Escherichia coli*. BioSystems (2006) In press.
15. Juloski, A., W.P.M.H. Heemels, W., Ferrari-Trecate, G., Vidal, R., Paoletti, S., Niessen, J.: Comparison of four procedures for the identification of hybrid systems. In Morari, M., Thiele, L., eds.: Proc. Hybrid Systems: Computation and Control (HSCC-05). Volume 3414 of LNCS., Springer-Verlag, Berlin (2005) 354–369

16. Perkins, T., Hallett, M., Glass, L.: Inferring models of gene expression dynamics. J. Theor. Biol. **230** (2004) 289–299
17. de Jong, H.: Modeling and simulation of genetic regulatory systems: A literature review. J. Comput. Biol. **9** (2002) 67–103
18. Ferrari-Trecate, G., Muselli, M., Liberati, D., Morari, M.: A clustering technique for the identification of piecewise affine and hybrid systems. Automatica **39** (2003) 205–217
19. Bennett, K., Mangasarian, O.: Multicategory discrimination via linear programming. Optimization Methods and Software **3** (1993) 27–39
20. Vapnik, V.: Statistical Learning Theory. John Wiley, NY (1998)
21. Drulhe, S., Ferrari-Trecate, G., de Jong, H., Viari, A.: Reconstruction of switching thresholds in piecewise-affine models of genetic regulatory networks. Technical report, INRIA (2005) http://www.inria.fr/rrrt/index.en.html.

Decision Problems for the Verification of Real-Time Software⋆

Michael Emmi and Rupak Majumdar

University of California, Los Angeles
{mje, rupak}@cs.ucla.edu

Abstract. We study two questions in the theory of timed automata concerning timed language inclusion of real-time programs modeled as timed pushdown automata in real-time specifications with just one clock. We show that if the specification B is modeled as a timed automaton with one clock, then the language inclusion problem $L(A) \subseteq L(B)$ for a timed pushdown automaton A is decidable. On the other hand, we show that the universality problem of timed visibly pushdown automata with only one clock is undecidable. Thus there is no algorithm to check language inclusion of real-time programs for specifications given by visibly pushdown specifications with just one clock.

1 Introduction

Timed automata [4] are a standard modeling formalism for real-time systems. Alur and Dill [4] showed the untimed reachability problem for timed automata is decidable. However, the universality problem (whether all timed traces are accepted) is undecidable, and therefore the timed language inclusion problem (whether all finite timed traces accepted by A are also accepted by B) is also undecidable. These bounds were recently tightened. The timed language inclusion problem $L(A) \subseteq L(B)$ for timed automata A and B *is* decidable if B has at most one clock [13], while the proof of [4] shows two clocks are sufficient for the universality problem to become undecidable. On the other hand, over infinite timed words, one clock is enough to make the language inclusion problem undecidable [2].

When verifying real-time software, the basic model of timed automata must be augmented by a program stack to model procedure calls. In this case, the model is a timed pushdown automaton: a timed automaton augmented with a stack. Untimed reachability is decidable for timed pushdown automata [8], in fact, the binary reachability relation for timed pushdown automata is also decidable [9]. Since the timed language inclusion problem $L(A) \subseteq L(B)$ is undecidable for timed automata if B has more than one clock, one remaining open question is when A is a timed pushdown automaton and B is a timed automaton that has exactly one clock (if B has no clocks, then the question

---

⋆ This research was supported in part by the grants NSF CCR-0427202 and NSF CNS-0541606.

João Hespanha and A. Tiwari (Eds.): HSCC 2006, LNCS 3927, pp. 200–211, 2006.

is decidable by a reduction to reachability, using closure properties of finite automata). We show that this problem is decidable, by extending the proof of [13]. The question is not just of theoretical interest. Many network protocol specifications can be modeled as timed automata with just one clock, and their software implementations are usually modeled as timed pushdown automata [12].

The main technical content of our proof is a generic decidability result for well-structured infinite software systems that is of independent interest in software verification. A large class of infinite state systems have been shown decidable using *well quasi-ordering* relations on the state space [1, 3, 10]. However, these formalisms are not immediately applicable to software verification, where a program is organized into procedures with possibly recursive calls. For software with a *finite* data state space, the standard technique to compute the set of reachable states is context free reachability [14, 7]. Our result unifies the two worlds by providing a context free reachability algorithm for infinite data state spaces, whose termination is proved using well quasi-ordering relations of [1, 10].

What if we extend the expressive power of the specification formalism beyond timed automata? The universality (and so language inclusion) problem for timed pushdown automata is undecidable, since the corresponding problems are already undecidable for (untimed) pushdown automata. We must therefore contend ourselves with formalisms of lesser expressive power. One such candidate is *visibly* pushdown automata [6] —where the stack pushes and pops are determined explicitly by the input alphabet. (Untimed) visibly pushdown automata are already sufficient to specify many interesting properties of software systems [6, 5]. Moreover, they have the nice decidability properties akin to regular languages: for example, universality and language inclusion problems are decidable for (untimed) visibly pushdown automata, and one can hope for similar decidability results in the timed case. We therefore study the universality problem for *timed* visibly pushdown automata with one clock. Unfortunately, we exhibit that this problem (and hence the language inclusion problem even when there is exactly one clock) is undecidable, thus precluding algorithmic solutions to the problem.

Our undecidability result encodes the operation of two counter machines using a timed visibly pushdown automaton with exactly one clock. We cannot directly apply the undecidability proof for the universality of pushdown automata, since the standard proof [11] is not *visibly* pushdown (indeed, universality is decidable for visibly pushdown automata). Instead, we represent a configuration of a two counter machine using two "identical" copies, one with the pop alphabet of the visibly pushdown automaton, and the other with the push alphabet, and use the single clock to make sure that the two copies are identical.

Thus, our results show that model checking real-time software modeled as timed pushdown automata against real time specifications with one clock and no stack remains decidable, however, the problem becomes undecidable as soon as the specification formalism is allowed a visibly pushdown stack.

2   Timed Pushdown Automata

Given an alphabet Σ, a *timed word* $(\sigma, \tau) \in \Sigma^* \times \mathbb{R}^*$ of length n is a word $\sigma = \sigma_1\sigma_2\ldots\sigma_n$ paired with a time sequence $\tau = \tau_1\tau_2\ldots\tau_n$ such that τ is monotonically increasing. A *timed language* is a set of timed words.

Let C be a set of *clock variables*. A *clock constraint* ϕ is defined inductively by

$$\phi := x \leq c \mid c \leq x \mid \neg\phi \mid \phi_1 \wedge \phi_2$$

where $x \in C$ and $c \in \mathbb{Q}$. $\Phi(C)$ is the set of all clock constraints over C. For a set of clocks C, a *clock valuation* is a function $\nu : C \to \mathbb{R}$ which describes the values of each clock $c \in C$ at an instant. A clock constraint $\phi \in \Phi(C)$ is *satisfied* by the clock valuation ν (written $\nu \vdash \phi$) if $[\nu(c)/c]_{c \in C}\phi$ is true. Given a set of clocks λ and a clock valuation ν, let $\nu \downarrow \lambda$ be defined as

$$(\nu \downarrow \lambda)(c) = \begin{cases} 0 & \text{when } c \in \lambda \\ \nu(c) & \text{otherwise} \end{cases}$$

Given a clock valuation ν and a time $t \in \mathbb{R}$ define $(\nu + t)(c) = \nu(c) + t$.

A *timed pushdown automaton* (TPDA) is a tuple $M = (\tilde{\Sigma}, \Gamma, Q, S, F, C, \delta)$, where $\tilde{\Sigma}$ is a finite alphabet of input symbols, Γ is finite stack alphabet (we write $\Gamma_\epsilon = \Gamma \cup \{\epsilon\}$ where ϵ is a fresh symbol not in Γ), Q is a finite set of states, $S \subseteq Q$ is a set of start states, $F \subseteq Q$ is a set of final states, C is a finite set of real-valued clocks, and $\delta \subseteq (Q \times \Sigma \times \Gamma_\epsilon \times \Phi(C) \times Q \times \Gamma_\epsilon \times 2^C)$ is a discrete transition relation.

A transition $(q, a, \gamma, \phi, q', \gamma', \lambda) \in \delta$ is taken if the current location is q, the input symbol is a, the stack is popped and the popped symbol is γ (if $\gamma = \epsilon$, then the stack is not popped), and the current valuation ν satisfies ϕ, and then the new location is q', the symbol γ' is pushed on the stack (if $\gamma' = \epsilon$, then no symbol is pushed) and the new clock valuation is $\nu' = \nu \downarrow \lambda$. Given a timed word (σ, τ) of length n, a *run* of a TPDA M on (σ, τ) is a sequence $(q_1, \nu_1, \gamma_1), (q_2, \nu_2, \gamma_2), \ldots, (q_{n+1}, \nu_{n+1}, \gamma_{n+1}) \in (Q \times (C \to \mathbb{R}) \times \Gamma^*)^*$ if for each $i \in \{1, \ldots, n\}$ there exists $t \in \mathbb{R}$ such that $(q_i, \sigma_i, \gamma, \phi, q_{i+1}, \hat{\gamma}, \lambda) \in \delta$, $\nu_i \vdash \phi$, $\nu_{i+1} = \nu_i \downarrow \lambda + t$, and there is some $\gamma' \in \Gamma^*$ such that $\gamma_i = \gamma' \cdot \gamma$ and $\gamma_{i+1} = \gamma' \cdot \hat{\gamma}$. A run $\rho = (q_1, \nu_1, \gamma_1) \ldots (q_{n+1}, \nu_{n+1}, \gamma_{n+1})$ of a TPDA M is *initialized* if $q_1 \in S$, $\nu_1(c) = 0$ for all $c \in C$, and $\gamma_1 = \epsilon$. The run ρ is *accepting* if $q_{n+1} \in F$. A timed word (σ, τ) of length n is accepted by a TVPA M if there exists a run of M on (σ, τ) that is initialized and accepting. The timed language of a TPDA M, denoted $L(M)$, is the set of all timed words that are accepted by M. A TPDA M is called *universal* if $L(M) = (\tilde{\Sigma} \times \mathbb{R})^*$, i.e., if it accepts all timed words.

A TPDA M is *visibly pushdown* (TVPA) if the input alphabet $\tilde{\Sigma}$ can be partitioned into three disjoint sets $\tilde{\Sigma} = \Sigma_{int} \cup \Sigma_c \cup \Sigma_r$ of internal, call, and return input symbols respectively, and $\delta \subseteq (Q \times \Sigma_{int} \times \Phi(C) \times Q \times 2^C) \cup (Q \times \Sigma_c \times \Phi(C) \times Q \times \Gamma \times 2^C) \cup (Q \times \Sigma_r \times \Gamma \times \Phi(C) \times Q \times 2^C)$ is the visible pushdown transition relation. The transitions of a TVPA come in three varieties. Let ν be a clock valuation. An *internal transition* $(q, a, \phi, q', \lambda) \in \delta$ at clock valuation ν is a move on the (internal) input symbol a from the state q to q' such that ν satisfies

ϕ and the resulting clock valuation $\nu' = \nu \downarrow \lambda$. A *call transition* $(q, a, \phi, q', \gamma, \lambda)$ is a move on the (call) input symbol a from q to q' where ν satisfies ϕ, the clock valuation is updated from ν to $\nu \downarrow \lambda$, and γ is pushed on the stack. A *return transition* $(q, a, \gamma, \phi, q', \lambda)$ is a move on the (return) input symbol a and stack symbol γ, from q to q' where ϕ is satisfied and ν is updated to $\nu \downarrow \lambda$. Given a timed word (σ, τ) of length n, a *run* of the TVPA M on (σ, τ) is a sequence $(q_1, \nu_1, \gamma_1), (q_2, \nu_2, \gamma_2), \ldots, (q_{n+1}, \nu_{n+1}, \gamma_{n+1}) \in (Q \times (C \to \mathbb{R}) \times \Gamma^*)^*$ if for each $i \in \{1, \ldots, n\}$ there exists $t \in \mathbb{R}$ such that one of the following holds:

1. $(q_i, \sigma_i, \phi, q_{i+1}, \lambda) \in \delta$, $\nu_i \vdash \phi$, $\nu_{i+1} = \nu_i \downarrow \lambda + t$, and $\gamma_{i+1} = \gamma_i$
2. $(q_i, \sigma_i, \phi, q_{i+1}, \gamma, \lambda) \in \delta$, $\nu_i \vdash \phi$, $\nu_{i+1} = \nu_i \downarrow \lambda + t$, and $\gamma_{i+1} = \gamma_i \gamma$
3. $(q_i, \sigma_i, \gamma, \phi, q_{i+1}, \lambda) \in \delta$, $\nu_i \vdash \phi$, $\nu_{i+1} = \nu_i \downarrow \lambda + t$, and $\gamma_{i+1} \gamma = \gamma_i$

Initialized and accepted runs, languages, and universality for TVPAs are defined by restriction from TPDAs. A TVPA is a timed automaton if $\Sigma_c = \Sigma_r = \emptyset$.

The *universality problem* for TPDAs (resp. TVPAs) takes as input a TPDA (resp. TVPA) M, and returns "yes" if M is universal, and returns "no" otherwise. Notice that the universality problem for TPDAs is undecidable, even if there is no clock, i.e., if $C = \emptyset$, since the universality of PDAs is undecidable [11].

3 One-Clock Language Inclusion Problem

We now show that the language inclusion problem $L(B) \subseteq L(A)$ where B is a TPDA and A is a timed automaton with one clock is decidable. This extends the result of [13]. Our main technical tool is a decidability result for context free reachability for well-structured transition systems.

3.1 Well-Structured Infinite Pushdown Automata

A *quasi-order* (or *preorder*) $\leq$ over a set A is a reflexive and transitive relation $\leq \subseteq A \times A$. A *well-quasi-order* (wqo) is a quasi-order where for every infinite sequence $a_1, a_2, a_3, \ldots$ from A, there exist $i, j \in \mathbb{N}$ where $i < j$ and $a_i \leq a_j$. We say that a *dominates* a' if $a' \leq a$.

An *infinite pushdown automaton* (∞PDA) M is a quintuple $M = (Q, \Sigma, \Gamma, S, \delta)$ where Q is an infinite set of states, Σ and Γ are input and tape alphabets, $S \subseteq Q$ is a finite set of initial states, and $\delta \subseteq (Q \times \Sigma \times Q) \cup (Q \times \Sigma \times Q \times \Gamma) \cup (Q \times \Sigma \times \Gamma \times Q)$ is a transition relation. We say M is *finitely branching* if for all $q \in Q$, $\{(q, \sigma, q') \in \delta \mid \sigma \in \Sigma, q' \in Q\} \cup \{(q, \sigma, q', \gamma) \in \delta \mid \sigma \in \Sigma, q' \in Q, \gamma \in \Gamma\} \cup \{(q, \sigma, \gamma, q') \in \delta \mid \sigma \in \Sigma, \gamma \in \Gamma, q' \in Q\}$ is a finite set. Given a quasi-order $\leq \subseteq Q \times Q$ we say that $\leq$ is *strictly (downward) compatible* with δ if for all $p \leq q$:

(i) if $(q, \sigma, q') \in \delta$ for some $q' \in Q$ then there exists $p' \in Q$ such that $(p, \sigma, p') \in \delta$ and $p' \leq q'$;
(ii) if $(q, \sigma, q', \gamma) \in \delta$ for some $q' \in Q$ and $\gamma \in \Gamma$ then there exists $p' \in Q$ such that $(p, \sigma, p', \gamma) \in \delta$ and $p' \leq q'$; and
(iii) if $(q, \sigma, \gamma, q') \in \delta$ for some $q' \in Q$ and $\gamma \in \Gamma$ then there exists $p' \in Q$ such that $(p, \sigma, \gamma, p') \in \delta$ and $p' \leq q'$.

A *well-structured infinite pushdown automaton* ($\infty_{\sqsubseteq}$PDA) $M = (Q, \Sigma, \Gamma, S, \delta, \sqsubseteq)$ is a finitely branching infinite pushdown automaton where $\sqsubseteq \subseteq Q \times Q$ is a wqo over the set of states Q that is strictly compatible with δ.

Let M be a well-structured infinite pushdown automaton over states Q, and let $\sqsubseteq$ be a well-quasi-order over Q. Define $\sqsubseteq$-*reachability* to be the decision problem of whether or not for a given state $q \in Q$ there exists a state $q' \in Q$ such that $q' \sqsubseteq q$ and q' is reachable from an initial state of M.

Theorem 1. *The $\sqsubseteq$-reachability problem is decidable for well-structured infinite pushdown automata with decidable $\sqsubseteq$.*

Proof. The algorithm $\sqsubseteq$-*Reachability* shown in Figure 1 computes the set *Paths* $\subseteq S \times Q$. The set *Paths* contains pairs of states (s, q) where s is a start state, and there is some series of transitions from M in which to arrive at q, taking into account constraints on stack symbols. Thus the pair $(s, q) \in$ *Paths* corresponds to the existence of a path from s to q. To see that there is a corresponding pair in *Paths* for every reachable state, if a state q remains unexplored either *Update*

```
subroutine Update(q, p, s)
    if ∄b ∈ Basis.b ⊑ q then
        Basis := Basis ∪ {q}
    if q ∈ Basis and ( p ⊄ Paths or s ⊄ Summaries ) then
        Paths := Paths ∪ p
        Summaries := Summaries ∪ s
        ToExplore := ToExplore ∪ {q}

algorithm ⊑-Reachability(M = (Q, Σ, Γ, S, δ, ⊑))
    let Basis := {q | q ∈ S}
        ToExplore := {q | q ∈ S}
        Paths := {(q, q) | q ∈ S}
        Summaries := ∅
    in until ToExplore = ∅ repeat
        remove some q from ToExplore
        for each q' ∈ Q and σ ∈ Σ where (q, σ, q') ∈ δ do
            let p = {(q'', q') | (q'', q) ∈ Paths}
                s = {(q'', q')_γ | (q'', q)_γ ∈ Summaries}
            in Update(q', p, s)
        for each q' ∈ Q and σ ∈ Σ and γ ∈ Γ where (q, σ, q', γ) ∈ δ do
            let p = {(q'', q') | (q'', q) ∈ Paths}
                s = {(q, q')_γ}
            in Update(q', p, s)
        for each q' ∈ Q and σ ∈ Σ and γ ∈ Γ where (q, σ, γ, q') ∈ δ do
            let p = {(q'', q') | ∃q''' ∈ Q where
                                (q'', q''') ∈ Paths and (q''', q)_γ ∈ Summaries}
                s = {⌈q'', q'⌉_γ | (q'', q)_γ ∈ Summaries}
            in Update(q', p, s)
```

Fig. 1. Algorithm to decide $\sqsubseteq$-reachability

was never invoked with q, or there is some state q' which is dominated by q, and q' is explored. In the latter case, since $\sqsubseteq$ is compatible with δ, we can be sure that for any state p which q could have transitioned to, there will be some state $p' \sqsubseteq p$ which q' could transition to. If $Update$ is never invoked with q then either there is no explored state which made a transition to q, or at some point along a path to q there is a state which dominates a state that is explored. Thus to decide whether a given state $p \in Q$ is $\sqsubseteq$-reachable in M, it suffices to find a pair (s, p') from the finite set $Paths$ such that $p' \sqsubseteq p$.

To show that the algorithm $\sqsubseteq$-$Reachability$ indeed terminates in a finite number of steps, consider the following argument. Since $\sqsubseteq$ is a wqo, there is no infinite strictly decreasing sequence $q_1 \sqsupset q_2 \sqsupset q_3 \sqsupset \ldots$ from Q, and so any number of repeated invocations of the subroutine $Update$ can only add a finite number of states to the set $Basis$. Because $Basis$ is always a finite set, and only states from $Basis$ are considered in the sets $Paths$, $Summaries$ and $ToExplore$, these sets are also finite; thus the second phase of the subroutine $Update$ is only invoked a finite number of times, and only a finite sequence of states is added to $ToExplore$. For each state that is explored there are only a finite number of successors (by the definition of ∞PDA.) Combined with a finite bound on the number of states inserted into $ToExplore$, it is clear that the algorithm $\sqsubseteq$-$Reachability$ terminates in a finite number of steps. ∎

3.2   Decidability of Language Inclusion

We now show the decidability of language inclusion when the specification is a timed automaton with one clock and the implementation a TPDA. Our proof follows that of [13]. The idea is to construct an infinite pushdown automaton by a product construction between A and B, in which we identify "bad" states as product states which are accepting in B, and non-accepting in A. Then we apply Theorem 1 to decide if any bad states are reachable. If some bad state is reachable, then B accepts some string which A does not, and $L(B) \not\subseteq L(A)$. If there are no reachable bad states, then we know $L(B) \subseteq L(A)$.

Theorem 2. *For a single-clock timed automaton A and timed pushdown automaton B, $L(B) \subseteq L(A)$ is decidable.*

Proof. Given a single-clock timed automaton $A = (Q_A, \Sigma, S_A, F_A, C_A = \{x\}, \delta_A)$, and a TPDA $B = (Q_B, \Sigma, \Gamma, S_B, F_B, C_B, \delta_B)$, we now define a $\infty_\sqsubseteq$PDA P which is the product automaton of a determinized A and non-deterministic B. We define the product as $P = (Q, \Sigma, \Gamma, S, \delta, \sqsubseteq)$ where

$$Q = \mathcal{P}(Q_A \times (C_A \to \mathbb{R})) \times Q_B \times (C_B \to \mathbb{R})$$
$$S = \mathcal{P}(S_A \times (C_A \to \{0\})) \times S_B \times (C_B \to \{0\})$$
$$\delta = \{((q_A, q_B), \sigma, (q'_A, q'_B)) \mid q'_B \in \delta'_B(q_B, \sigma), q'_A = \delta'_A(q_A, \sigma)\}$$
$$\cup \{((q_A, q_B), \sigma, (q'_A, q'_B), \gamma) \mid (q'_B, \gamma) \in \delta'_B(q_B, \sigma), q'_A = \delta'_A(q_A, \sigma)\}$$
$$\cup \{((q_A, q_B), \sigma, \gamma, (q'_A, q'_B)) \mid q'_B \in \delta'_B(q_B, \sigma, \gamma), q'_A = \delta'_A(q_A, \sigma)\}$$

and

$$\delta'_A(q_A, \sigma) \quad = \{(q', \nu') \mid (q, \nu) \in q_A, (q, \sigma, \phi, q', \lambda) \in \delta_A, \nu \vdash \phi, \nu' = \nu \downarrow \lambda\}$$
$$\delta'_B((q, \nu), \sigma) \quad = \{(q', \nu') \mid (q, \sigma, \phi, q', \lambda) \in \delta_B, \nu \vdash \phi, \nu' = \nu \downarrow \lambda\}$$
$$\qquad\qquad\quad \cup \{(q', \nu', \gamma) \mid (q, \sigma, \phi, q', \lambda, \gamma) \in \delta_B, \nu \vdash \phi, \nu' = \nu \downarrow \lambda\}$$
$$\delta'_B((q, \nu), \sigma, \gamma) = \{(q', \nu') \mid (q, \sigma, \gamma, \phi, q', \lambda) \in \delta_B, \nu \vdash \phi, \nu' = \nu \downarrow \lambda\}$$

are defined for convenience. Note that P is finitely branching since clock valuations are not arbitrarily increased by a transition of A or B; rather they must either remain constant or be (partially) reset.

As in [13], the wqo $\sqsubseteq$ over Q is defined as follows. Without loss of generality we assume that all numeric values in the clock constraints of A and B are integral. Define the set of regions $Reg = \{r_0, r_0^1, r_1, r_1^2, \ldots, r_K\}$, where K is the largest constant appearing in a clock constraint of A and B. For all $t \in \mathbb{R}$, let $\bar{t} \in [0, 1)$ be the fractional part of t (i.e., $\bar{t} = t - \lfloor t \rfloor$). Let $reg : \mathbb{R} \to Reg$ be the function mapping clock values to regions defined by

$$reg(t) = \begin{cases} r_K & \text{when } t \geq K \\ r_i & \text{when } t < K, \bar{t} = 0 \text{ and } t = i \\ r_i^{i+1} & \text{when } t < K, \bar{t} \neq 0 \text{ and } i < t < i+1 \end{cases}.$$

Let $F : Q \to \mathcal{P}((Q_A \times Reg \times [0, 1)) \cup (Q_B \times C_B \times Reg \times [0, 1)))$ be a function which disassembles the state structure of Q into sets of its constituents:

$$F((q_A, q_B, \nu_B)) = \{(\eta, \overline{\nu(x)}) \mid (q, \nu) \in q_A, \{x\} = C_A \text{ and } \eta = (q, reg(\nu(x)))\}$$
$$\cup \{(\eta, \overline{\nu_B(y)}) \mid y \in C_B \text{ and } \eta = (q_B, y, reg(\nu_B(y)))\}$$

Now define G to group together tuples with the same clock fraction:

$$G(q) = \left\{ \left(\bigcup \{\rho' \mid (\rho', t) \in F(q)\}, t \right) \middle| (\rho, t) \in F(q) \right\}$$

and finally let H be defined as

$$H(q) = \rho_1 \rho_2 \cdots \rho_{|G(q)|},$$

where $(\rho_i, t_i) \in G(q)$ for $1 \leq i \leq |G(q)|$ and $t_i < t_{i+1}$ for $1 \leq i < |G(q)|$. The codomain of H is the set of finite words on a finite alphabet. By Higman's Lemma, this set is well quasi-ordered with respect to the subword ordering $\preceq$. We define the quasi-order $\sqsubseteq$ as $q_1 \sqsubseteq q_2$ if and only if $H(q_1) \preceq H(q_2)$. As shown in [13], this is a well quasi-ordering on states.

To see that $\sqsubseteq$ is strictly compatible with δ consider two states $p \sqsubseteq q$. By the definition of $\sqsubseteq$, p and q are in the same Q_A and Q_B states, and the valuations of their corresponding clocks are in the same regions (i.e., they satisfy the same clock constraints.) Thus any transition that is enabled out of q has a corresponding transition enabled out of p.

Define $Bad = \mathcal{P}((Q_A \setminus F_A) \times (C_A \to \mathbb{R})) \times F_B \times (C_B \to \mathbb{R})$ to be the set of "bad" states of P. Since P is a $\infty_{\sqsubseteq}$PDA with decidable $\sqsubseteq$, Theorem 1 states that $\sqsubseteq$-reachability is decidable on P. Let $Paths$ be computed from $\sqsubseteq$-$Reachability(P)$. Now the language containment question $L(B) \subseteq L(A)$ is reduced to finding a state from the finite set $\{q \mid (s, q) \in Paths\}$ which also belongs to Bad, and is thus decidable.   ∎

4 Universality of Timed Visibly Pushdown Automata

We now prove a negative result that shows that the specification formalism cannot be extended from finite state one-clock timed automata to one-clock TVPA. The universality problem for (untimed) visibly pushdown automata is decidable [6]. On the other hand, the universality problem for timed automata with two clocks is undecidable, and (from [13]) the universality problem for timed automata with one clock is decidable. We now show that the universality problem for TVPAs with one clock is undecidable, thus completing the decidability picture.

The proof is by a reduction from the halting problem for two counter machines. A *two counter machine* is a tuple $M = (I, C, D)$ where $I : \mathbb{N} \rightarrow (\{C, D\} \times \mathbb{N} \times \mathbb{N}) \cup (\{Inc, Dec\} \times \{C, D\})$ and the domain of I is finite. That is, M has a finite set of instructions I and counters C and D and at each instruction M can either increment or decrement one counter and proceed to the next instruction, or conditionally jump to another instruction upon a given counter having the value 0. For example the instruction $(3, (C, 5, 7)) \in I$ means that the instruction at location 3 is a jump to location 5 if the value of C is 0, and is otherwise a jump to location 7. The instruction $(5, (Dec, D)) \in I$ means that at location 5 the value of counter D is decremented before advancing to location 6.

A configuration of M is represented by the triple $(l, c, d) \in \mathbb{N} \times \mathbb{N} \times \mathbb{N}$ where l is a location and $c, d \geq 0$ are the values of counters C and D. The unique *initial configuration* is the triple $(1, 0, 0)$. The set of *final configurations* is $\{(2, c, d) \mid c, d \in \mathbb{N}\}$. A *run* of the two-counter machine $M = (I, C, D)$ is a sequence of configurations $(l_1, c_1, d_1)(l_2, c_2, d_2) \ldots (l_n, c_n, d_n) \in (\mathbb{N} \times \mathbb{N} \times \mathbb{N})^*$ where for each $i \in \{1, 2, \ldots, n-1\}$, we have

$$(l_{i+1}, c_{i+1}, d_{i+1}) = \begin{cases} (l_i + 1, c_i + 1, d_i) & \text{when } I(l_i) = (Inc, C) \\ (l_i + 1, c_i - 1, d_i) & \text{when } I(l_i) = (Dec, C) \\ (l_i + 1, c_i, d_i + 1) & \text{when } I(l_i) = (Inc, D) \\ (l_i + 1, c_i, d_i - 1) & \text{when } I(l_i) = (Dec, D) \\ (b_1, c_i, d_i) & \text{when } I(l_i) = (C, b_1, b_2) \text{ and } c_i = 0 \\ (b_2, c_i, d_i) & \text{when } I(l_i) = (C, b_1, b_2) \text{ and } c_i \neq 0 \\ (b_1, c_i, d_i) & \text{when } I(l_i) = (D, b_1, b_2) \text{ and } d_i = 0 \\ (b_2, c_i, d_i) & \text{when } I(l_i) = (D, b_1, b_2) \text{ and } d_i \neq 0 \end{cases}$$

A run $\alpha_1 \ldots \alpha_n$ of M is accepting if α_1 an initial configuration and α_n is a final configuration.

Theorem 3. *Universality of single clock TVPA's is undecidable.*

Proof. We reduce from the accepting problem for two counter machines. For a two-counter machine $M = (I, C, D)$, fix $\Sigma_{int} = \{h_i \mid i \in dom(I)\}$, $\Sigma_c = \{f_c, g_c\}$, $\Sigma_r = \{f_r, g_r\}$ and $\tilde{\Sigma} = \Sigma_{int} \cup \Sigma_c \cup \Sigma_r$. Given a two-counter machine M, we build a TVPA N that accepts any string in $w \in (\tilde{\Sigma} \times \mathbb{R})^*$ such that w does not represent an accepting run of M. The problem of finding the existence of an accepting run of M is then reduced to verifying that N is not universal (i.e., if the language of N is the universe, then M has no accepting run).

We represent each configuration (i, j, k) of the two-counter machine M by a timed word $\Pi(i, j, k) = (h_i f_r^j g_r^k g_c^k f_c^j, \tau)$ where $\tau_1 \in \mathbb{N}$, and $\tau_1 \leq \tau_{j+1} < (\tau_1 + \frac{1}{4})$ $< \tau_{j+2} \leq \tau_{j+k+1} < (\tau_1 + \frac{1}{2}) < \tau_{j+k+2} \leq \tau_{j+2k+1} < (\tau_1 + \frac{3}{4}) < \tau_{j+2k+2} \leq \tau_{2j+2k+1} < (\tau_1 + 1)$. In addition we require that for every g_r there is a g_c that follows at exactly $\frac{1}{4}$ time units, and for every f_r there is a f_c that follows at exactly $\frac{3}{4}$ time units. A sequence of configurations $\beta_1 \beta_2 \ldots \beta_n$ is represented as the concatenation of timed words $\Pi(\beta_1)\Pi(\beta_2) \ldots \Pi(\beta_n)$ where for each $1 \leq i < n$ we have $\beta_i = (\alpha^i, \tau^i)$, $\tau_1^{i+1} = \tau_1^i + 1$, and $\tau_1^1 = 1$.

We will build N to be a disjunction of several smaller TVPA's which each try to find a particular reason why the input string is not an accepting run of M. The input alphabet of N is $\tilde{\Sigma}$, the stack alphabet is $\Gamma = \{C, D, X, Y\}$, and there is one clock x. The state and transition structure is taken as the disjunction of the smaller automata that we now describe.

One possibility is that the input string does not represent some sequence of configurations. The regular automaton $N_{\neg format}$ accepts strings that are not matched by the regular expression $R_{format} = ((h_1 \cup h_2 \cup \ldots h_m) f_r^* g_r^* g_c^* f_c^*)^*$, where $m = |dom(I)|$.

Another possibility is that at least one timing constraint is broken in the input string. The single-clock automaton $N_{\neg schedule}$ accepts any string in which either the first symbol does not occur at time 1, or there exist $h_i, h_j \in \Sigma_{int}$ from successive configurations where h_i does not occur exactly one time unit before h_j, or any of the symbols f_r, g_r, f_c, g_c don't fit into the intervals $(\tau + 0, \tau + \frac{1}{4})$, $(\tau + \frac{1}{4}, \tau + \frac{1}{2})$, $(\tau + \frac{3}{4}, \tau + 1)$, and $(\tau + \frac{1}{2}, \tau + \frac{3}{4})$ respectively, where τ is the time of the nearest preceding h_i. The single-clock automaton $N_{\neg schedule}$ is shown in Figure 2.

The regular automaton $N_{\neg init}$ accepts strings that start with a configuration which is not initial. Since an initial configuration has location 1 and both counter values of 0, the regular expression $R_{init} = h_1 (h_1 \cup h_2 \cup \ldots \cup h_m) (h_1 \cup h_2 \cup \ldots \cup h_m \cup f_c \cup f_r \cup g_c \cup g_r)^*$ matches all strings that represent correct initial configurations, where $m = |dom(I)|$.

The regular automaton $N_{\neg final}$ accepts strings that end with a configuration that is not final. Since a final configuration has location 2, the regular expression

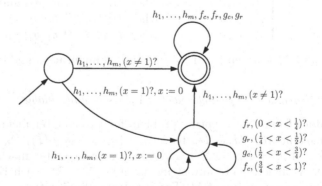

Fig. 2. The one-counter automaton $N_{\neg schedule}$ recognizes strings that are not properly timed configuration sequences

$R_{final} = (h_1 \cup h_2 \cup \ldots \cup h_m \cup f_c \cup f_r \cup g_c \cup g_r)^* h_2 (f_c \cup f_r \cup g_c \cup g_r)^*$ matches all strings that represent correct final configurations, where $m = |dom(I)|$.

In our textual representation of a configuration there should be a f_c following each f_r by $\frac{3}{4}$ time units, a f_r $\frac{3}{4}$ time units before each f_c, and g_r if and only if there is a g_c following at $\frac{1}{4}$ time units. The single-clock automata $N_{\neg f_r \to f_c}$, $N_{\neg f_r \leftarrow f_c}$, $N_{\neg g_r \to g_c}$ and $N_{\neg g_r \leftarrow g_c}$ accept strings with unpaired f_r's and f_c's (or g_r's and g_c's) within a configuration. As an example $N_{\neg f_r \to f_c}$ is shown in Figure 3.

The automata that have been described so far accept when there is some problem with the format of a particular configuration representation, and accept timed (or untimed) regular languages. The remaining automata will accept when there is a particular problem with a sequence of two configurations and will use the pushdown stack of a visibly pushdown automaton.

For each instruction/location we will use several automata to recognize an invalid sequence. For each instruction i that is not a branch instruction, the regular automaton $N_{\neg step}^i$ accepts when the following instruction in the configuration sequence is not $i + 1$ (e.g., represented by h_{i+1}). For each instruction i which increments counter C, the automata $N_{\neg c\uparrow}^i$ and $N_{c\uparrow \wedge \neg d=}^i$ accept when counter C is not incremented, or C is incremented and D does not remain the same. These automata function by using the pushdown stack to remember how many g_c's and f_c's appear before the f_r's and g_r's of the following configuration. Note that the pushdown stack can only compare the counters of successive configurations, since

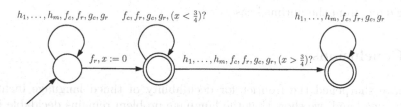

Fig. 3. The single-clock automaton $N_{\neg f_r \to f_c}$ recognizes strings in which some configuration has a symbol f_r without a matching symbol f_c following at $\frac{3}{4}$ time units

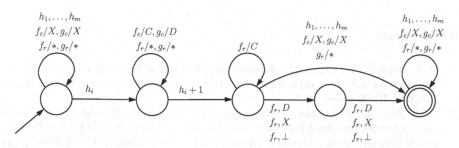

Fig. 4. The visibly pushdown automaton $N_{\neg c\uparrow}^i$ recognizes strings in which a configuration invoking instruction (Inc, C) is followed by a configuration where the C counter is not properly incremented

symbols can only be pushed on the stack when f_c or g_c are read, and can only be popped from the stack when f_r or g_r are read. Figure 4 depicts this functionality.

The remaining $N^i_{c\uparrow \wedge \neg d=}$, $N^i_{\neg c\downarrow}$, $N^i_{c\downarrow \wedge \neg d=}$, $N^i_{\neg c=}$, $N^i_{c=\wedge \neg d\uparrow}$, $N^i_{c=\wedge \neg d\downarrow}$, and $N^i_{c=\wedge \neg d=}$ automata all function in a similar manner, by counting between configurations using the pushdown stack.

The automata $N^i_{c=0\wedge \neg goto-l_1}$ and $N^i_{c\neq 0\wedge \neg goto-l_2}$ require no clock or stack, and simply recognize when the configuration following a branch has a location that does not match with the branch location.

As mentioned earlier, N is simply the disjunction of each of the machines mentioned above. Since each automaton uses at most one clock, and are either regular or visibly pushdown, the resulting disjunction N is a single-clock visibly pushdown automaton. By construction N accepts any string that either doesn't encode a sequence of configurations of M, or encodes a sequence of configurations that is not an initialized and accepting run of M. Thus by reduction, the universality problem for N decides membership for M.   ∎

As a corollary, the language inclusion problem $L(A) \subseteq L(B)$ where B is a timed visibly-pushdown automaton with at least one clock is undecidable. What can we say if the specification automaton B has no clocks (i.e., is an untimed visibly pushdown automaton)? If A is a TVPA, then the language inclusion problem is decidable using the closure properties of visibly pushdown automata (i.e., we can reduce the problem to the emptiness question $L(A \cap \neg B) = \emptyset$, and $A \cap \neg B$ is again a TVPA). On the other hand, if A is a PDA, then the problem is already undecidable from the untimed case.

5 Conclusions

We have sharpened the frontier for decidability of timed language inclusion. On the one hand, we show that the language problem remains decidable if the implementation is strengthened to be a TPDA and the specification is a timed automaton with at most one clock. On the other hand, if we strengthen the specification to TVPA with one clock, the problem becomes undecidable.

References

1. P. A. Abdulla, K. Čerāns, B. Jonsson, and Yih-Kuan Tsay. General decidability theorems for infinite-state systems. In *LICS 96: Logic in Computer Science*, pages 313–321. IEEE Press, 1996.
2. P. A. Abdulla, J. Deneux, J. Ouaknine, and J. Worrell. Decidability and complexity results for timed automata via channel machines. In *ICALP 05: International Conference on Automata, Languages, and Programming*, LNCS 3580, pages 1089–1101. Springer-Verlag, 2005.
3. P. A. Abdulla, K. Čerāns, B. Jonsson, and Yih-Kuan Tsay. Algorithmic analysis of programs with well quasi-ordered domains. *Information and Computation*, 160:109–127, 2000.

4. R. Alur and D.L. Dill. A theory of timed automata. *Theoretical Computer Science*, 126:183–235, 1994.
5. R. Alur, K. Etessami, and P. Madhusudan. A temporal logic of nested calls and returns. In *TACAS 04: Tools and Algorithms for the Construction and Analysis of Systems*, LNCS 2988, pages 467–481. Springer-Verlag, 2004.
6. R. Alur and P. Madhusudan. Visibly pushdown automata. In *STOC 04: Symposium on Theory of Computing*, pages 202–211. ACM Press, 2004.
7. T. Ball and S. K. Rajamani. Bebop: A symbolic model checker for Boolean programs. In *SPIN 00: SPIN Workshop*, LNCS 1885, pages 113–130. Springer-Verlag, 2000.
8. A. Bouajjani, R. Echahed, and R. Robbana. On the automatic verification of systems with continuous variables and unbounded discrete data structures. In *Hybrid Systems II*, LNCS 999, pages 64–85. Springer-Verlag, 1994.
9. Z. Dang. Pushdown timed automata: a binary reachability characterization and safety verification. *Theoretical Computer Science*, 302:93–121, 2003.
10. A. Finkel and Ph. Schnoebelen. Well-structured transition systems everywhere. *Theoretical Computer Science*, 256:63–92, 2001.
11. J.E. Hopcroft and J.D. Ullman. *Introduction to Automata Theory, Languages, and Computation*. Addison-Wesley Publishing Company, 1979.
12. V.K. Nandivada and J. Palsberg. Timing analysis of TCP servers for surviving denial-of-service attacks. In *RTAS 05: IEEE Real-Time and Embedded Technology and Applications Symposium*, pages 541–549. IEEE Press, 2005.
13. J. Ouaknine and J. Worrell. On the language inclusion problem for timed automata: Closing a decidability gap. In *LICS 2004: Logic in Computer Science*, pages 54–63. IEEE Press, 2004.
14. T. Reps, S. Horwitz, and M. Sagiv. Precise interprocedural dataflow analysis via graph reachability. In *POPL 95: Principles of Programming Languages*, pages 49–61. ACM, 1995.

Laplacian Sheep: A Hybrid, Stop-Go Policy for Leader-Based Containment Control

G. Ferrari-Trecate[1,2], M. Egerstedt[3], A. Buffa[4], and M. Ji[3]

[1] INRIA, Domaine de Voluceau, Rocquencourt - B.P.105,
78153, Le Chesnay Cedex, France
[2] Dipartimento di Informatica e Sistemistica,
Universitá degli Studi di Pavia, Via Ferrata 1, 27100 Pavia, Italy
giancarlo.ferrari@unipv.it
[3] Georgia Institute of Technology,
School of Electrical and Computer Engineering,
Atlanta, GA 30332, USA
{magnus, mengji}@ece.gatech.edu
[4] Istituto di Matematica Applicata e Tecnologie Informatiche, C.N.R.,
Via Ferrata, 1, 27100 Pavia, Italy
annalisa@imati.cnr.it

Abstract. The problem of driving a collection of mobile robots to a given target location is studied in the context of partial difference equations. In particular, we are interested in achieving this transfer while ensuring that the agents stay in the convex polytope spanned by dedicated leader-agents, whose dynamics will be given by a hybrid Stop-Go policy. The resulting system ensures containment through the enabling result that under a Laplacian, decentralized control strategy for the followers, these followers will converge to a location in the convex leader polytope, as long as the leaders are stationary and the interaction graph is connected. Simulation results testify to the viability of the proposed, hybrid control strategy.

1 Introduction

This paper investigates a particular subarea of multi-agent control, namely the so-called *containment* problem. (See for example [1, 2].) The problem is to drive a collection of autonomous, mobile agents to a given target location while guaranteeing that their motion satisfies certain geometric constraints. These constraints are there to ensure that the agents are contained in a particular area during their transportation. These types of issues arise for example when a collection of autonomous robots are to secure and then remove hazardous materials. This removal must be secure in the sense that the robots should not venture into populated areas or in other ways contaminate their surroundings.

We approach this problem from a leader-follower point-of-view [3, 4, 5]. In particular, we will let the agents move autonomously based on local, consensus-like interaction rules, commonly found in the literature under the banner of

João Hespanha and A. Tiwari (Eds.): HSCC 2006, LNCS 3927, pp. 212–226, 2006.
© Springer-Verlag Berlin Heidelberg 2006

algebraic graph theory [6, 7, 8]. The reason for this is that the robot motion can be described using the graph Laplacian. However, we will augment this control structure with the addition of leader-agents. These leaders are to define vertexes in a convex polytope (the leader-polytope) and they are to move in such a way that the target area is reached while ensuring that the follower-agents stay in the convex polytope spanned by the leaders, as shown in Fig. 1. As such, the followers movements are calculated in a decentralized manner according to a fixed interaction topology, while the leaders are assumed to be able to detect if any of the followers violate the containment property. This strategy also explains the title "Laplacian Sheep" since the followers are moving using a "Laplacian-based" control strategy. However, they are to be "herded" like sheep by the leaders, and hence the title.

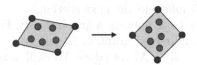

Fig. 1. The containment problem: The leaders are to move in such a way that the followers remain in the convex leader-polytope for all times

It should be noted already at this point that although the subject matter is multi-agent control, our proposed solution to the problem of selecting the leader dynamics will be hybrid. In particular, we will use a Stop-Go policy [9, 10], in which the leaders move according to a decentralized formation control strategy until the containment property is about to be violated. At this point, they stop and let the followers settle back into the leader-polytope before they start moving again. For such a strategy to be successful, a number of results are needed, including a guarantee that the Laplacian-based follower-control will in fact drive the followers back into the leader-polytope. Moreover, we must also ensure that such a control strategy is feasible in the sense of non-Zeno, live in the sense of not staying in the Stop mode indefinitely, and convergent in the sense that the target area is in fact reached. These are the main issues under investigation in this paper.

In order to properly understand the behavior of such a control system, some initial results in multi-agent control are needed. We will use the recently developed framework of Partial difference Equations (PdEs) [11] for this, and, in particular, we will show that as long as the interaction graph is connected and the leaders are stationary, the followers will always converge to locations in the convex hull spanned by the leaders. This result enables the use of a Stop-Go policy since by halting the evolution of the leaders, the containment property can be ensured.

The outline of this paper is as follows: In Section 2 we present the mathematical preliminaries needed to prove the main convergence result for the case with stationary leaders, in Section 3. The hybrid Stop-Go control policy is given in Section 4, followed by an illustrative example, in Section 5. Additional extensions to the proposed control strategy, including a hierarchical layering of the formation, are given in Section 6.

2   Background and Mathematical Preliminaries

Even though the main focus of this paper is the development of hybrid control strategies for the leader-agents in charge of "herding" the followers, this task will rely on a collection of enabling results in (non-hybrid) multi-agent control. These enabling results will allow us to structure the hybrid Stop-Go controller in such a way that containment is achieved. Hence, before we can start defining any hybrid control laws, some room must be given to multi-agent control. In this section we will present the basic mathematical framework, and the main containment results will follow in the next section.

We start summarizing basic notions of graph theory. For more details we defer the reader to [12]. An undirected graph G is defined by a set $\mathcal{N}_G = \{1, \ldots N\}$ of *nodes* and a set $\mathcal{E}_G \subset \mathcal{N}_G \times \mathcal{N}_G$ of *edges*. We will also use $|\mathcal{N}_G|$ for denoting the cardinality of $\mathcal{N}_G$. Two nodes x and y are *neighbors* if $(x, y) \in \mathcal{E}_G$. The neighboring relation is indicated with $x \sim y$ and $\mathcal{P}(x) = \{y \in \mathcal{N}_G : y \sim x\}$ collects all neighbors to the node x. A *path* $x_0 x_1 \ldots x_L$ is a finite sequence of nodes such that $x_{i-1} \sim x_i$, $i = 1, \ldots, L$. A graph G is *connected* if there is a path connecting every pair of distinct nodes. G is *complete* if $\mathcal{E}_G = \mathcal{N}_G \times \mathcal{N}_G$.

Definition 1. *Let* $S = (\mathcal{N}_S, \mathcal{E}_S)$ *be an undirected host graph and* $\mathcal{N}_{S'} \subset \mathcal{N}_S$. *The subgraph* S' *associated with* $\mathcal{N}_{S'}$ *is the pair* $(\mathcal{N}_{S'}, \mathcal{E}_{S'})$ *where* $\mathcal{E}_{S'} = \{(x, y) \in \mathcal{E}_S : x \in \mathcal{N}_{S'}, y \in \mathcal{N}_{S'}\}$.

Definition 1 allows basic operations in set theory to be extended to graphs.

Definition 2. *Let* S_1 *and* S_2 *be to subgraphs of the graph* S. *Then,* $S_1 \cup S_2$, $S_1 \cap S_2$, $S_1 \backslash S_2$ *are the graph associated with* $\mathcal{N}_{S_1} \cup \mathcal{N}_{S_2}$, $\mathcal{N}_{S_1} \cap \mathcal{N}_{S_2}$, *and* $\mathcal{N}_{S_1} \backslash \mathcal{N}_{S_2}$, *respectively.*

For our purposes, we will often use graphs with a boundary.

Definition 3. *Let* S *be a subgraph of* G. *The boundary of* S *is the subgraph* $\partial S \subset G$ *associated with* $\mathcal{N}_{\partial S} \doteq \{y \in \mathcal{N}_G \backslash \mathcal{N}_S : \exists x \in \mathcal{N}_S : x \sim y\}$. *The closure of* S *is* $\bar{S} = \partial S \cup S$.

Note that the definition of the boundary of a graph depends upon the host graph G. This implies that if one considers three graphs $S' \subset S \subset G$, the boundaries of S' in S and in G may differ.

In our case, the nodes of the host graph G represent agents and the edges are communication links. In particular, an agent x has access to the states of all its neighbors and can use this piece of information to compute its control law. In this setting, partial communication amounts to considering incomplete graphs. However, we always assume that the host graph is connected, otherwise the agents are split in one or more sub-groups that do not exchange information.

In order to model the collective behavior of the agents we will use functions $f : \mathcal{N}_G \mapsto \mathbb{R}^d$ defined over a graph G [13]. The *partial derivative* of f is defined as $\partial_y f(x) \doteq f(y) - f(x)$ and enjoys the following properties: (i) $\partial_y f(x) = -\partial_x f(y)$, (ii) $\partial_x f(x) = 0$ and (iii) $\partial_y^2 f(x) = -\partial_y f(x)$. The Laplacian of f is given by

$$\Delta f(x) \doteq - \sum_{y \in \mathcal{N}_G, y \sim x} \partial_y^2 f(x) = + \sum_{y \in \mathcal{N}_G, y \sim x} \partial_y f(x), \tag{1}$$

where the last identity follows from property (iii). The integral and the average of f are defined, respectively, as

$$\int_G f \, dx \doteq \sum_{x \in \mathcal{N}_G} f(x), \quad \langle f \rangle \doteq \frac{1}{|\mathcal{N}_G|} \int_G f \, dx. \tag{2}$$

Let $L^2(G|\mathbb{R}^d)$ be the Hilbert space composed by all functions $f : \mathcal{N}_G \mapsto \mathbb{R}^d$ endowed with the norm $\|f\|_{L^2}^2 = \int_G \|f\|^2$. We will use the shorthand notation L^2 when there is no ambiguity on the underlying domain and range of the functions.

Let S be a subgraph of G and ∂S its boundary in G, such that $S \cup \partial S = G$ As in [13], we also consider the Hilbert space $H_0^1(S) = \{f \in L^2(G) : f_{|\partial S} = 0\}$ (see [13] for the definition of a suitable norm on $H_0^1(S)$). Note that a function $f \in H_0^1(S)$ is defined on $\bar{S}$ and possibly non null only on S.

The next theorem, proved in [13], characterize the eigenstructure of the Laplacian operator defined on $H_0^1(S)$.

Theorem 1. *Let G be a connected graph and S a proper subgraph of G. Then, the operator $\Delta : H_0^1(S|\mathbb{R}^d) \mapsto L^2(\bar{S}|\mathbb{R}^d)$ has $|\mathcal{N}_S|d$ strictly negative eigenvalues. Moreover, the corresponding eigenfunctions form a basis for $H_0^1(S|\mathbb{R}^d)$.*

3   Multiple Stationary Leaders

In this section we use PdEs for modeling and analyzing a group of agents with multiple leaders. A leader is just a vehicle that moves along a prescribed trajectory, independently of the motion of all other vehicles. However, followers that are neighbors to the leader can use the leader state in order to compute their control inputs.

Let $r(x, t)$ be the position of the agent x at time $t \geq 0$, where[1] $r \in L^2$. The communication network is represented by the undirected and connected graph G. For distinguishing between leaders and followers, we consider two subgraphs S_F and S_L of G such that $S_F \cup S_L = G$ and $\partial S_F = S_L$, where the subscripts denote "Leaders" and "Followers" respectively. Note that we assume that all agents are either designated as leaders or followers.

As already mentioned in the introduction, we will assume that the followers obey the simple dynamics $\dot{r}(x, t) = u(x, t)$, where

$$u(x, t) \doteq \Delta r(x, t) \tag{3}$$

---

[1] For sake of conciseness, for a function $f(x, t) : \mathcal{N}_G \times \mathbb{R}^+ \to \mathbb{R}^d$ we will often write $f \in L^2$ instead of $f(\cdot, t) \in L^2$.

is the *Laplacian* control law. Let $\hat{r}(x,t)$, $x \in \mathcal{N}_{\partial S_F}$ (i.e. in the set of leaders, $\mathcal{N}_{S_L}$) be the trajectory of the leaders. Then, the collective dynamics is represented by the model

$$\dot{r}(x,t) = \Delta r(x,t) \qquad x \in \mathcal{N}_{S_F} \qquad (4a)$$

$$r(x,t) = \hat{r}(x,t) \qquad x \in \mathcal{N}_{\partial S_F} \qquad (4b)$$

endowed with the initial conditions $r(\cdot,0) = \tilde{r} \in L^2(S_F)$.

Model (4) is an example of a continuous-time Partial difference Equation (PdE) with non-homogeneous Dirichlet boundary conditions. We defer the reader to [13, 11, 14] for an introduction to PdEs.

Laplacian control has been one of the most studied control paradigms for multi-agent systems. The main reason is that Laplacian control allows the agents to achieve globally coordinated behaviors, despite its decentralized nature. The main results on Laplacian control available in the literature and specialized to model (4) are:

- in the leaderless case (i.e. $\partial S_F = \emptyset$), the Laplacian control solves the rendez-vous problem, i.e. $r(x,t) \rightarrow r^* \in \mathbb{R}^d$, $\forall x \in \mathcal{N}_G$ as $t \rightarrow +\infty$. Moreover, the agents achieve *average* consensus, i.e. $r^* = \langle \tilde{r} \rangle$. These results have been established in [15, 16] through the joint use of tools in control theory and algebraic graph theory. A formal analysis of the PdE (4a) has been conducted in [11, 14] showing a complete accordance with results available within the theory of the heat equation [17];

- in the case of a single leader (i.e. $\mathcal{N}_{\partial S_F} = \{x_L\}$) with fixed position (i.e. $\hat{r}(x_L,t) = \bar{r} \in \mathbb{R}^d$), Laplacian control solves the rendez-vous problem with $r^* = \bar{r}$ [15]. This property has also been shown in [11, 14] within the PdE framework, thus highlighting the profound links between model (4) and the heat equation with Dirichlet boundary conditions [17].

A first aim of this paper is to characterize the asymptotic behavior of the followers in the presence of multiple leaders with fixed positions. To this end, for the remainder of this section, we will assume that $\hat{r}(x,t) = \bar{r}(x) \in L^2(\partial S_F)$. The equilibria of (4) are then given by the solutions to the PdE

$$\Delta h(x) = 0 \qquad x \in \mathcal{N}_{S_F} \qquad (5a)$$

$$h(x) = \bar{r}(x) \qquad x \in \mathcal{N}_{\partial S_F} \qquad (5b)$$

and they have been studied in [13]. In particular, [13, Theorem 3.5] shows that if the hosting graph G is connected and $\mathcal{N}_{\partial S_F} \neq \emptyset$ then, the PdE (5) has a unique solution[2] $h(x)$. By analogy with the jargon of Partial Differential Equations, h is termed the *harmonic extension of the boundary conditions* $\bar{r}$.

Our next aim is to verify that $r \rightarrow h$ as $t \rightarrow +\infty$. Let us consider the decomposition

$$r(x,t) = r_0(x,t) + h(x), \qquad r_0 \in H_0^1(S_F) \qquad (6)$$

---

[2] [13, Theorem 3.5] assumes that the subgraph S is *induced* (see [13] for the definition of induced subgraphs). However, a careful examination of the proof, reveals that this assumption is unnecessary.

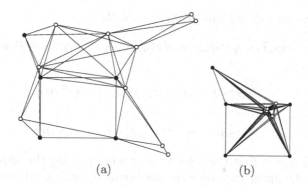

(a)   (b)

Fig. 2. An example of the application of Theorem 2 is given. Initially, some of the followers (white) are located outside Ω_L but after a while they have all reached Ω_L, spanned by the stationary leaders (black). The edges between agents capture the information flow in this static interaction graph.

Since h does not depend upon time and $\Delta h = 0$, $\forall x \in \mathcal{N}_{S_F}$, the PdE (4) is equivalent to the following one

$$\dot{r}_0(x,t) = \Delta r_0(x,t) \qquad x \in \mathcal{N}_{S_F} \tag{7a}$$

$$r_0(x,t) = 0 \qquad x \in \mathcal{N}_{\partial S_F} \tag{7b}$$

From (6), it is apparent that the problem of checking if $r \to h$ as $t \to +\infty$ can be recast into the problem of studying the convergence to zero of the solutions to the PdE (7). The fact that $r_0 \to 0$ as $t \to +\infty$ follows from Theorem 1 and it can be shown by proceeding exactly as in the proof of [11, Theorem 7][3].

The next Theorem, proved in Appendix A, highlights a key geometrical feature of $h(x)$. For a set X of points in $\mathbb{R}^d$, $\mathrm{Co}(X)$ will denote its convex hull. Moreover, the set Ω_L is the convex hull of leaders positions, i.e. $\Omega_L \doteq \mathrm{Co}(\{\bar{r}(y),\ y \in \mathcal{N}_{\partial S_F}\})$.

Theorem 2. *Let S_1 be a nonempty connected subgraph of S_F and ∂S_1 be its boundary in G. Then, $\forall x \in \mathcal{N}_{S_1}$ it holds*

$$h(x) \in \mathrm{Co}(\{h(y),\ y \in \mathcal{N}_{\partial S_1}\}). \tag{8}$$

Moreover, one has that $h(x) \in \Omega_L$, i.e. that the position of each follower lies in the convex hull of the leaders positions. Finally, if Ω_L is full dimensional, then $h(x) \in \Omega_L \backslash \partial \Omega_L$, $\forall x \in \mathcal{N}_{S_F}$.

This result is illustrated in Fig. 2.

Another geometrical feature which we need is the following:

Theorem 3. *Suppose that Ω_L is fully dimensional and that $r(x,t)$ is evolving according to (4). Suppose that, at a given time $t = \bar{t}$, there is an agent $x \in \mathcal{N}_{S_F}$ such that $r(x,\bar{t}) \in \partial \Omega_L$. Then, two situations may occur:*

---

[3] Actually, [11, Theorem 7] proves a stronger property, namely that the origin of (7) is "exponentially stable on the space $H_0^1(S)$". The definition of stability of equilibria on subspaces is provided in [11].

1. *there exists an (affine) hyperplane χ such that*

$$r(x, \bar{t}) \in \chi \cap \partial\Omega_L, \text{ and } r(y, \bar{t}) \in \chi \cap \partial\Omega_L \; \forall y \in \mathcal{P}(x).$$

   Then:
$$\exists \alpha > 0 \; : \; r(x, \bar{t}) + \alpha \dot{r}(x, \bar{t}) \in \chi \cap \partial\Omega_L, \tag{9}$$

2. *otherwise,*
$$\exists \alpha > 0 \; : \; r(x, \bar{t}) + \alpha \dot{r}(x, \bar{t}) \in \Omega_L \setminus \partial\Omega_L. \tag{10}$$

Note that (9) means that the velocity of x will be along the hyperplane χ (in other words, the agent may slide on the boundary $\partial\Omega_L$), whereas (10) means that the velocity of x is pointing inside the polytope Ω_L.

Proof: (Theorem 3)
   Since $r(x, t)$ obeys to (4), by rearranging terms we obtain:

$$\dot{r}(x, \bar{t}) = -|\mathcal{P}(x)|r(x, \bar{t}) + \sum_{y \in \mathcal{P}(x)} r(y, \bar{t}).$$

Then, setting $\alpha = |\mathcal{P}(x)|^{-1}$, it holds:

$$r(x, \bar{t}) + \alpha \dot{r}(x, \bar{t}) = |\mathcal{P}(x)|^{-1} \sum_{y \in \mathcal{P}(x)} r(y, \bar{t}),$$

i.e., $r(x, \bar{t}) + \alpha \dot{r}(x, \bar{t})$ is the barycenter $b(\mathcal{Y}_x)$ of the polytope $\mathcal{Y}_x \doteq \text{Co}(\{r(y, \bar{t}), y \in \mathcal{P}(x)\})$. Note that: first $\mathcal{Y}_x \in \Omega_L$, second, thanks to convexity, the barycenter of $\mathcal{Y}_x$ lies in the relative interior of $\mathcal{Y}_x$. Thus, if all $y \in \mathcal{P}(x)$ verify that $r(y, \bar{t}) \in \chi \cap \partial\Omega_L$ then $\mathcal{Y}_x \subset \chi \cap \partial\Omega_L$ and so does $b(\mathcal{Y}_x)$, i.e. $b(\mathcal{Y}_x) \in \chi \cap \partial\Omega_L$; otherwise $b(\mathcal{Y}_x) \in \Omega_L \setminus \partial\Omega_L$. ∎

4   Hybrid Containment Control

Since the motion of the followers is governed directly by the Laplacian control in (4a), what the system designers have control over is the motion of the leaders. In particular, we would like to endow the leaders with a motion that requires as little information sharing as possible while still ensuring containment. For this, we define two distinctly different control modes for the evolution of the leaders. The first of the two control modes is the Stop mode. As the name indicates, this mode corresponds to the leaders halting their movements altogether in order to prohibit a break in the containment:

$$STOP :$$
$$\dot{r}(x, t) = \Delta r(x, t) \qquad x \in \mathcal{N}_{S_F} \tag{11a}$$
$$r(x, t) = \hat{r}(x, t) \qquad x \in \mathcal{N}_{\partial S_F} \tag{11b}$$
$$\dot{r}(x, t) = 0 \qquad x \in \mathcal{N}_{\partial S_F} \tag{11c}$$

It is clear that in order to execute this mode, no information is needed for the leaders whatsoever.

The second control mode under consider is the Go mode, in which the leaders move toward a given target location/formation/shape. A number of different control laws can be defined for this, but we, for the sake of conceptual unification, let the Go mode be given by a Laplacian-based control strategy as well.

$$GO:$$
$$\dot{r}(x,t) = \Delta r(x,t) \qquad\qquad x \in \mathcal{N}_{S_F} \qquad\qquad (12a)$$
$$r(x,t) = \hat{r}(x,t) \qquad\qquad x \in \mathcal{N}_{\partial S_F} \qquad\qquad (12b)$$
$$\dot{\hat{r}}(x,t) = \Delta_{S_L}(\hat{r}(x,t) - r_T(x)) \quad x \in \mathcal{N}_{\partial S_F} \qquad (12c)$$

where $r_T(x)$, $x \in \mathcal{N}_{\partial S_F}$ denotes the desired target position of leader x, and where we use Δ_{S_L} to denote the Laplacian operator defined solely over the subgraph S_L, i.e.

$$\Delta_{S_L} f(x) \doteq - \sum_{y \sim x,\ y \in \mathcal{N}_{S_L}} \partial_y^2 f(x).$$

Now, under the assumption that S_L is connected, and, by exactly the same reasoning as for the standard rendez-vous problem, the leaders will converge to positions $r_L(x)$ such that $\partial_y r_L(x) = \partial_y r_T(x)$, $\forall x, y \in \mathcal{N}_{S_L}$. In other words, no convergence to a predefined point is achieved. Rather, this control law ensures that the leaders arrive at a translationally invariant target formation.

Note that the details of the leaders' motion is not crucial and this particular choice is but one of many possibilities. However, this choice is appealing in that it makes the information flow explicit, and the leaders only need access to the positions (and target locations) of their neighboring leaders in order to compute their motion. As such the decentralized character of the algorithm is maintained.

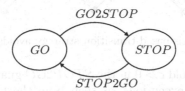

Fig. 3. The hybrid automaton implementing the Stop-Go policy

In order for fully specify the hybrid Stop-Go leader policy depicted in Fig. 3, transition rules are needed as well. As before, let Ω_L denote the leader-polytope and let $d(\mu, \Omega_L)$ denote the signed distance

$$d(\mu, \Omega_L) \doteq \zeta_{\Omega_L}(\mu) \min_{x \in \partial \Omega_L} \|\mu - x\|_2,$$

where $\|\cdot\|_2$ denotes the Euclidean 2-norm, and where $\zeta_{\Omega_L}(\mu) = -1$ if $\mu \in \Omega_L$ and $+1$ otherwise. Using this distance measure we let the two guards be given by

$$GUARD_{GO2STOP} : \exists y \in \mathcal{N}_{S_F} \mid d(r(y,t),\Omega_L) \geq 0? \tag{13}$$

$$GUARD_{STOP2GO} : d(r(y,t),\Omega_L) < -\epsilon \; \forall y \in \mathcal{N}_{S_F}? \tag{14}$$

Note that the guard $STOP2GO$ is crossed only if the following assumptions are verified:

Assumption 1. *Let $\hat{h}(\cdot,t)$ be the solution to (5) for $\bar{r}(\cdot) = \hat{r}(\cdot,t)$, $\forall t \geq 0$ and consider the set $\Omega_L^{\epsilon}(t) = \{y \in \Omega_L(t) : \mathrm{dist}(y,\partial\Omega_L(t)) > \epsilon\}$. Then*

1. $\Omega_L^{\epsilon}(t)$ *is nonempty, $\forall t \geq 0$;*
2. $\mathrm{Co}(\{\hat{h}(x,t), x \in \mathcal{N}_{S_F}\}) \subset \Omega_L^{\epsilon}(t)$.

In particular, Assumption 1 implies that Ω_L must be full-dimensional at all times and "sufficiently fat" along every direction. Conditions relating property 2 of Assumption 1 to the graph topology are currently under investigation. A few comments must be made about the computation and communication requirements that these guards give rise to. If two leaders are located at the end-points of the same face of Ω_L, then they must be able to determine if any of the followers are in fact on this face. This can be achieved through a number of range sensing devices, such as ultrasonic, infra-red, or laser-based range-sensors. Moreover, in order for all leaders to transition between modes in unison, they must communicate between them, which means that either ∂S_F is a complete graph, or that multi-hop strategies are needed. In either way, a minimal requirement for these mode transitions to be able to occur synchronously, without having to rely on information flow across follower-agents, is that ∂S_F must be connected.

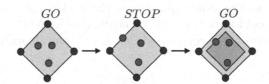

Fig. 4. A hysteresis-based transition strategy avoids Zeno executions

The hysteresis threshold $\epsilon > 0$ in the $STOP2GO$ guard (see Fig. 4) is needed in order to avoid Zeno executions, as seen from the following argument: The distance between any points in Ω_L is less than the diameter of Ω_L. We let ρ_{Ω_L} denote the supremum of these diameters during an execution, and note that since the leaders are under our control, ρ_{Ω_L} can be prevented from being unbounded, and we state this as an assumption:

Assumption 2. $\exists M < \infty$ *such that* $\rho_{\Omega_L} \leq M$.

Note that the Laplacian control law used for controlling the leaders is but one of many possible control strategies. As such, we can always use for example a plan-based leader control law if the Laplacian control law was to violate the assumption.

Under the above-mentioned assumption we have

$$\|\dot{r}(x,t)\| = \|\Delta r(x,t)\| \le \sum_{y \sim x} \|\partial_y r(x)\| \le \sum_{y \sim x} \rho_{\Omega_L} \le N\rho_{\Omega_L}, \quad \forall x \in \mathcal{N}_{S_F}.$$

Now, in order for the system to leave the Stop mode, at least one follower agent must have traveled at least a distance ϵ, which in turn implies that the system will always stay for a time greater than or equal to $\epsilon/N\rho_{\Omega_L}$ in the Stop mode. And, in order for the system to exhibit Zeno executions, a necessary condition is that the difference between the transition times must approach zero [18]. And, since this is not the case here, the non-Zeno property is established.

In the following section, an example is given that describes the operation and the feasibility of the proposed Stop-Go control policy.

5   Examples

The previous sections show that the polytope spanned by the leaders is invariant to the followers and the hybrid control strategy is non-Zeno. In this section, an example is given to show the validity of the proposed control method.

A scenario where three leaders (black) maneuver four followers (white) is investigated here. The initial position and final position of the leaders are $r(x,0) = \{(1,-3),(0,-1),(0,1)\}$ and $r_T(x) = \{(0,-2),(1,2),(2,-2)\}$ respectively. The followers are indexed from 1 to 4 and the leaders from 5 to 7.

During the maneuvering, the Stop-Go policy is adopted, i.e. the followers are governed by the Laplacian control, while the leaders dynamics are only affected by other leaders, as in (12c).

In Fig. 5, the snap-shots of the herding process are shown. The magnitude of the velocities of the agents are shown in Fig. 6, where we can see the instances when the leaders stop to make sure that the followers remain inside the leader-polytope. The snap-shots of the transition instances are shown in Fig. 7.

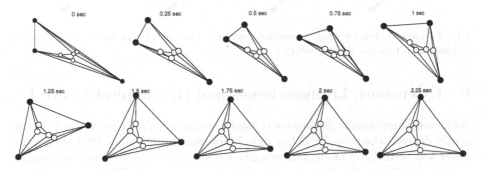

Fig. 5. A herding process where 4 followers (white) are herded by 3 leaders (black), who use the hybrid Stop-Go control policy

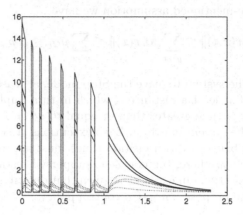

Fig. 6. The magnitude of the velocities of the agents in the Stop-Go herding process. Solid lines correspond the velocity of the leaders while dashed lines correspond to those of the followers.

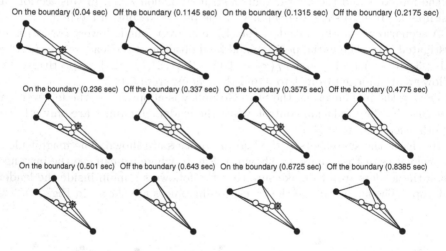

Fig. 7. Time instances when transitions occur. (The asterisk denotes the particular follower who touches the boundary.)

6   Extensions: Liveness Issues and Hierarchical Control

As already mentioned, the proposed solution is non-Zeno. However, as it is currently defined, the Stop-Go policy may be blocking in the sense that the system never leaves the Stop mode. One remedy to this problem is to allow the containment to be slightly less tight. In other words, we can select different guards, e.g.

$$GUARD_{GO2STOP} : \exists y \in \mathcal{N}_{S_F} \mid d(r(t, y), \Omega_L) > \delta? \tag{15}$$

$$GUARD_{STOP2GO} : d(r(t, y), \Omega_L) \leq 0 \; \forall y \in \mathcal{N}_{S_F}? \tag{16}$$

What this means is that we do not enter the Stop mode until a follower is $\delta > 0$ outside Ω_L.

Assumption 3. *The set Ω_L is full dimensional at all times and $\mathrm{Co}(\{\hat{r}_T(x), x \in \mathcal{N}_{\partial S_F}\})$ is full dimensional.*

Under Assumption 3, the size of Ω_L is lower bounded at all times by a positive constant and hence, by virtue of Theorem 2, every follower will eventually get back in Ω_L in finite time (since the leaders are stationary in the Stop mode). This argument proves that the system is live in the sense of always leaving the Stop mode eventually.

However, liveness is not enough. We moreover must ensure that we do in fact reach the target location.

Under Assumption 2, it holds $\|\dot{r}(x,t)\| \leq N(\rho_{\Omega_L} + \delta)$ and we can repeat the non-Zeno argument from Section 4 in order to see that the system always stays in the Go mode for a time greater than or equal to $\delta/(N(\rho_{\Omega_L} + \delta))$. In fact, this bound can be made tighter by virtue of Theorem 3, since we do not need to take the followers on $\partial\Omega_L$ into account because the motion of the followers is such that their velocities will never point away from Ω_L. In other words, a transition from Go to Stop occurs when the leaders "catch up" with the followers rather than when the followers move away from Ω_L. As a result, in a non-blocking system the leaders will be given infinitely many opportunities to move during a finite (bounded away from zero) time horizon, which implies convergence to the target location as long as the the leaders would in fact end up at the target location under the influence of the Go mode alone without the leader polytope degenerating to a convex polytope of a reduced dimension.

Another direction in which additional improvements can be expected is to reduce the necessary information flow by imposing a hierarchical structure on the formation. This can for instance be achieved by organizing the agents into M layers such that each agent in layer i, $i = 1, 2, \ldots, M-1$, is a follower of the agents in its upper layer, $i+1$, i.e. $\mathcal{N}_{\partial S_{i+1}} \subseteq \mathcal{N}_{S_i} \cup \mathcal{N}_{S_{i+2}} \; \forall \, i = 1, \cdots, M-2$, where S_i denotes the subgraph corresponding to layer i and ∂S_{i-1} is the (non-empty) boundary of S_{i-1} in the host graph G. In such a setting, the Stop-Go control policy would still be applicable. Only the agents of the outermost layer would be given target locations, $r_T(x)$. All other layers simply obey the Laplacian control strategy unless that layer's boundary is intersected by an agent belonging to layer $i - 1$, at which point they would halt their motion. This, however, is a research direction that is left to the future, and we simply mention it here as a possible and promising extension.

7   Conclusions

In this paper we present a hybrid Stop-Go control policy for the leaders in a multi-agent containment scenario. In particular, the control strategy allows us to transport a collection of follower-agents to a target area while ensuring that they stay in the convex polytope spanned by the leaders. The enabling results needed in order to achieve this is that, for stationary leaders, the followers in a connected interaction graph will always converge to locations in the leader-polytope. Additional extensions to the proposed control strategy are given in order to ensure certain liveness properties and we outline how the proposed methods lend themselves easily to generalizations to hierarchical information exchange strategies. Examples are moreover presented in order to stress the viability of the proposed approach.

Acknowledgment

The work by Giancarlo Ferrari-Trecate was partially supported by the European Commission under the Network of Excellence HYCON, contract number FP6-IST-511368. The work by Magnus Egerstedt and Meng Ji was supported by the U.S. Army Research Office through Grant #99838.

References

1. Parker, L.E., Kannan, B., Fu, X., Tang, Y.: Heterogeneous mobile sensor net deployment using robot herding and line-of-sight formations. In: Proceedings of IEEE International Conference on Intelligent Robots and Systems. (2003) 681–689
2. Vaughan, R., Sumpter, N., Henderson, J., Frost, A., Cameron, S.: Experiments in automatic flock control. Journal of Robotics and Autonomous Systems **31** (2000) 109–117
3. Desai, J., Ostrowski, J.P., Kumar, V.: Controlling formations of multiple mobile robots. In: Proc. IEEE Int. Conf. Robot. Automat. (1998) 2864–2869
4. Ji, M., Muhammad, A., Egerstedt, M.: Leader-based multi-agent coordination: Controllability and optimal control. (Submitted to the American Control Conference, Minneapolis, MN, June 2006)
5. Tanner, H., Pappas, G., Kumar, V.: Leader to formation stability. IEEE Transactions on Robotics and Automation **20**(3) (2004) 443–455
6. Tanner, H., Jadbabaie, A., Pappas, G.: Flocking in fixed and switching networks. (2005) http://www.seas.upenn.edu/~pappasg/publications.html#journals. Submitted.
7. Saber, R.O.: A unified analytical look at Reynolds flocking rules. Technical Report CIT-CDS 03-014, California Institute of Technology (2003)
8. Muhammad, A., Egerstedt, M.: Connectivity graphs as models of local interactions. (To appear in Journal of Applied Mathematics and Computation, 2005)
9. Egerstedt, M., Martin, C.: Conflict resolution for autonomous vehicles: A case study in hierarchical control design. International Journal of Hybrid Systems **2**(3) (2002) 221–234
10. Sussmann, H.: A maximum principle for hybrid optimal control problems. 38th IEEE Conference on Decision and Control (1999)
11. Ferrari-Trecate, G., Buffa, A., Gati, M.: Analysis of coordination in multiple agents formations through Partial difference Equations. Technical Report 5-PV, IMATI-CNR (2004) http://www-rocq.inria.fr/who/Giancarlo.Ferrari-Trecate/publications.html.
12. Bollobás, B.: Modern graph theory. Graduate texts in Mathematics. Springer-Verlag (1998)

13. Bensoussan, A., Menaldi, J.L.: Difference equations on weighted graphs. Journal of Convex Analysis (Special issue in honor of Claude Lemaréchal) **12**(1) (2005) 13–44
14. Ferrari-Trecate, G., Buffa, A., Gati, M.: Analysis of coordination in multi-agent systems through partial difference equations. Part I: The Laplacian control. 16th IFAC World Congress on Automatic Control (2005)
15. Jadbabaie, A., Lin, J., Morse, A.S.: Coordination of groups of mobile autonomous agents using nearest neighbor rules. IEEE Trans. on Automatic Control **48**(6) (2003) 988 – 1001
16. Olfati-Saber, R., Murray, R.: Consensus problems in networks of agents with switching topology and time-delays. IEEE Trans on Autom. Control **49**(9) (2004) 101–115
17. Dautray, R., Lions, J.L.: Mathematical analysis and numerical methods for science and technology. Vol. 5-6: Evolution problems I-II. Springer-Verlag, Berlin (1992)
18. Johansson, K., Egerstedt, M., Lygeros, J., Sastry., S.: Regularization of zeno hybrid automata. Systems and Control Letters **38** (1999) 141–150

Appendix A

This Appendix is devoted to the proof of Theorem 2. We start by introducing a basic result on polytopes.

Lemma 1. *Consider the polytope $P = \text{Co}(X)$ where $X = \{x_i \in \mathbb{R}^d : i = 1, \ldots, L\}$ and let X_1 be a proper subset of X. If $x \in \text{Co}(X_1)$, $\forall x \in X \backslash X_1$, then $P = \text{Co}(X_1)$.*

Proof: The conditions $x \in X \backslash X_1$ and $x \in \text{Co}(X_1)$ imply that x is not a vertex of P. Then, X_1 includes all vertexes of P, thus proving that $P = \text{Co}(X_1)$. ∎

Lemma 2. *Let G be a host graph, S a subgraph of G and T_1 a proper subgraph of S and ∂T_1 the boundary of T_1 in G. Consider $\bar{x} \in \mathcal{N}_{\partial T_1} \cap \mathcal{N}_S$, and let $r \in L^2(G)$ be a function verifying*

$$r(\bar{x}) \in \text{Co}(\{r(y) : y \in \mathcal{P}(\bar{x})\}) \tag{17}$$

$$r(x) \in \text{Co}(\{r(y) : y \in \mathcal{N}_{\partial T_1}\}), \quad \forall x \in \mathcal{N}_{T_1} \tag{18}$$

Let T_2 be the subgraph associated with $\mathcal{N}_{T_1} \cup \{\bar{x}\}$ and ∂T_2 be the boundary of T_2 in G. Then, for all $x' \in \mathcal{N}_{T_2}$ it holds

$$r(x') \in \text{Co}(\{r(y) : y \in \mathcal{N}_{\partial T_2}\}). \tag{19}$$

Proof: From (17), one has that all $\bar{r} \in \{r(y) : y \in \mathcal{N}_{T_2}\}$ verify $\bar{r} \in P$ where $P = \text{Co}(\{r(y) : y \in \mathcal{N}_{\partial T_1} \cup \mathcal{P}(\bar{x})\})$. In particular, if $x \in \mathcal{P}(\bar{x}) \cap T_1$ one has that $r(x) \in \text{Co}(\{r(y) : y \in \mathcal{N}_{\partial T_1}\})$. Recalling (18) and that $\bar{x} \in \mathcal{N}_{\partial T_1}$ one can apply Lemma 1 and obtain

$$P = \text{Co}(\{r(y) : y \in (\mathcal{N}_{\partial T_1} \backslash \{\bar{x}\}) \cup (\mathcal{P}(\bar{x}) \backslash \mathcal{N}_{T_1})\}).$$

The proof is concluded by realizing that

$$\mathcal{N}_{\partial T_2} = (\mathcal{N}_{\partial T_1} \backslash \{\bar{x}\}) \cup (\mathcal{P}(\bar{x}) \backslash \mathcal{N}_{T_1}). \qquad\blacksquare$$

We are now in a position to prove Theorem 2.

Proof: (Theorem 2.)

Let $p = x_0 x_1 \ldots x_L$ be a path going through all nodes of S_1. Since $\Delta h(x) = 0$, $\forall x \in \mathcal{N}_{S_F}$ from (1) one has

$$h(x) = \frac{1}{|\mathcal{P}(x)|} \sum_{y \in \mathcal{P}(x)} h(y), \ \forall x \in \mathcal{N}_{S_F}$$

which implies that

$$h(x) \in \mathrm{Co}\{h(y) : y \in \mathcal{P}(x)\} \tag{20}$$

We will prove the theorem using a recursive argument on the nodes composing $\mathcal{P}$. First, note that $x_1 \in \mathcal{P}(x_0)$. Let T_1 and T_2 be the subgraphs associated with $\{x_0\}$ and $\mathcal{N}_{S_1} \cup \{x_1\}$, respectively. Lemma (2) can be applied with $\bar{x} = x_1$. Indeed, (17) amounts to (20) for $x = x_0$ and (18) amounts to (20) for $x = x_1$. Then, from (19) we have

$$h(x) \in \mathrm{Co}(\{h(y) : y \in \mathcal{N}_{\partial T_2}\}), \ \forall x \in \mathcal{N}_{T_2}$$

Now, we denote by $S^{(i)}$, $i < L$ the subgraph of S_1 associated with the $i+1$ nodes $\{x_0, x_1, \ldots, x_i\}$ and by $\partial S^{(i)}$ its boundary in G. Assume now that at the i-th step, $i < L$ we have

$$h(x) \in \mathrm{Co}(\{h(y) : y \in \mathcal{N}_{\partial S^{(i)}}\}), \ \forall x \in \mathcal{N}_{S^{(i)}} \tag{21}$$

We need to prove that:

$$h(x) \in \mathrm{Co}(\{h(y) : y \in \mathcal{N}_{\partial S^{(i+1)}}\}), \ \forall x \in \mathcal{N}_{S^{(i+1)}}. \tag{22}$$

Note that $x_{i+1} \in \mathcal{P}(x_i)$. Set $T_1 = S^{(i)}$ and let T_2 be the graph associated with $\mathcal{N}_{S^{(i)}} \cup \{x_{i+1}\}$. Lemma (2) can be applied with $\bar{x} = x_{i+1}$. Indeed, (17) amounts to (20) for $\bar{x} = x_{i+1}$ and (18) amounts to (21). Then, from (19) we have

$$h(x) \in \mathrm{Co}(\{h(y) : y \in \mathcal{N}_{\partial T_2}\}), \ \forall x \in \mathcal{N}_{T_2}.$$

Since, $T_2 = S^{(i+1)}$, formula (8) is proved. If S is connected, the result holds also for $S = S_1$. If S is not connected, we apply (8) on each connected component S_i, $1 \leq i \leq n$, and, by simple algebra, obtain

$$h(x) \in \mathrm{Co}(\{h(y), \ y \in \mathcal{N}_{\partial S_1} \cup \mathcal{N}_{\partial S_2} \cup \ldots \cup \mathcal{N}_{\partial S_n}\}).$$

The proof that each follower lies in the convex hull of the leaders positions is ended by realizing that $\mathcal{N}_{\partial S} = \mathcal{N}_{\partial S_1} \cup \mathcal{N}_{\partial S_2} \cup \ldots \cup \mathcal{N}_{\partial S_n}$.

The fact that the full dimensionality of Ω_L implies that $h(x) \in \Omega_L \backslash \partial \Omega_L$, $\forall x \in \mathcal{N}_{S_F}$ is proved by contradiction. Let $x \in \mathcal{N}_{S_F}$ be such that $h(x) \in \partial \Omega_L$ and denote with χ the supporting hyperplane of Ω_L such that $h(x) \in \Omega_L \cap \chi$. Then, since $h(x) \in \mathrm{Co}(\{h(y), \ y \in \mathcal{P}(x)\})$, all $y \in \mathcal{P}(x)$ verify $h(y) \in \partial \Omega_L \cap \chi$. Iterating the argument over the followers lying on χ, one would find that also all leaders $x \in \mathcal{N}_{\partial S_F}$ lie on χ and this contradicts the fact that Ω_L is full dimensional. ∎

Optimal Control of Piece-Wise Polynomial Hybrid Systems Using Cylindrical Algebraic Decomposition

Ioannis A. Fotiou, A. Giovanni Beccuti,
Georgios Papafotiou, and Manfred Morari

Automatic Control Laboratory, Swiss Federal Institute of Technology (ETH),
CH–8092 Zürich, Switzerland
{fotiou, beccuti, papafotiou, morari}@control.ee.ethz.ch
http://control.ethz.ch

Abstract. We present a new method to solve the constrained finite-time optimal control (CFTOC) problem for piece-wise polynomial (PWP) hybrid systems, based on Cylindrical Algebraic Decomposition (CAD). The computational approach consists of two parts. The off-line, where the method re-formulates the original CFTOC optimization problem in algebraic form, decomposes it into smaller subproblems and then independently pre-processes each subproblem to obtain certain structural information, and the on-line, where this available precomputed information is used to efficiently compute the optimal solution of the original problem in real time. The method is illustrated through its application to the control of a boost dc-dc converter.

1 Introduction

In this paper we present a new solution approach to the constrained finite-time optimal control (CFTOC) problem for discrete-time piece-wise polynomial systems. The latter term refers to systems defined over a semi-algebraic partition of the state-input space, where a polynomial state-update and output equation is associated with each semi-algebraic set. In particular, we are going to show how algebraic tools can be used to solve the optimization problem that results from the CFTOC formulation and obtain the optimal control law by combining an off-line precomputation stage using algebraic techniques and the on-line solution of univariate polynomial equations.

The problem considered has been motivated by the successful application of Model Predictive Control (MPC) [1] for the optimal control of linear, non-linear and hybrid systems. In MPC, a CFTOC problem is set up and solved, based on a model of the controlled plant that is used to predict the plant's behavior over a prediction horizon. The control objectives are expressed in an objective function and the control law is obtained by minimizing this objective function subject to the plant's model and the physical constraints that are present. By employing a receding horizon strategy, feedback is achieved.

João Hespanha and A. Tiwari (Eds.): HSCC 2006, LNCS 3927, pp. 227–241, 2006.
© Springer-Verlag Berlin Heidelberg 2006

In many applications, however, the use of MPC is restricted due to its increased computational cost. The restrictions arise either from the need to use hardware of limited cost in the control loop, or from the very small sampling times that are present, making the time-consuming on-line solution of the optimization problem an inviable option. Such cases have motivated the development of new solution methods to the optimization problem, that allow one to pre-compute off-line the optimal control law for all feasible states using the state vector as a parameter. Such methods have been reported in [2] for linear systems with quadratic cost and have been extended in [3] to linear systems with linear cost expressions, and in [4, 5, 6] to linear hybrid systems in a piece-wise affine (PWA) representation.

On the other hand, deriving an exact closed-form expression giving the solution of the CFTOC problem for non-linear systems is in the general case not possible. The authors in [7] have proposed a method to obtain an approximate explicit solution, by partitioning the state-space into polyhedral regions and locally approximating the multi-parametric non-linear program with a multi-parametric quadratic program (mp-QP) over each polyhedron. An algorithm is presented that creates and iteratively refines the above mentioned partition such that the approximation error introduced is kept below a certain specified threshold.

More recently, the authors of [8] have shown how to parameterize the optimal solution of the CFTOC problem for nonlinear polynomial systems, i.e. systems that comprise polynomial state-update and output equations, by combining a precomputation stage using algebraic techniques and the on-line solution of univariate polynomial equations. The CFTOC problem is reformulated in algebraic form and then solved using cylindrical algebraic decomposition (CAD) [9]. The CAD falls within the frame of symbolic-algebraic computation techniques. In the recent past, numerous publications have reported on the use of such algebraic methods to tackle computational issues in hybrid systems. As representative examples, one can refer to the application of quantifier elimination (a process that can be performed using CAD) for the reachability analysis of hybrid automata [10], the use of symbolic computations for the construction of abstractions of hybrid systems [11] and the application of algebraic methods to the identification of hybrid systems [12]. Due to space limitations, a more extensive literature review of this area cannot be provided in this paper; the reader is referred to [11] and references therein for a more extended coverage.

CAD is a method that given a set of multivariate polynomials in n variables, creates a special partition of $\mathbb{R}^n$ into components, called *cells*, over which all the polynomials have constant signs. When using CAD for solving the optimization problem, the set of polynomials comprises the objective function, together with a real variable expressing the optimal cost, and the constraints. Therefore, the cells provide information for the feasible region of the CFTOC problem and the boundaries of the feasible cells give a number of candidate solutions to the optimization problem. This method is extended in this paper to the case of piece-wise polynomial (PWP) systems. Here, the CFTOC problem is also first reformulated in algebraic form and subsequently decomposed into subproblems that are solved independently using an approach similar to the above method. The proposed approach consists of two stages, an off-line and an on-line. The off-line stage comprises the algebraic reformulation, the decomposition of the CFTOC problem, and the independent solution of each subproblem. What is obtained is a set of polynomials whose roots yield candidate optimal solutions and optimizers to the original problem. In the on-line stage, the candidate solutions are extracted from each subproblem and a comparison procedure selects the one with the minimum cost.

The method is illustrated through its application to CFTOC problem of the boost dc-dc converter, which, as shown in [13], can be modelled for controller design purposes as a PWP system. On the one hand, it becomes evident that the method suffers from the excessive computational burden associated with the off-line stage. On the other hand, despite the inherent difficulties associated with the method, the authors express the belief that there is still a lot of potential in it, since.

The rest of the paper is structured as follows. In Section 2 the PWP systems are formally defined. Section 3 derives the formulation of the CFTOC problem and demonstrates the connection with parametric optimization. In Section 4, the computational approach is presented and Section 5 illustrates it with an application example. Finally, the paper is concluded in Section 6, where future research directions are pointed out.

2   Piece-Wise Polynomial (PWP) Hybrid Systems

In this section, we formally define the class of piece-wise polynomial (PWP) hybrid systems. This class is fairly general and the physical systems it can describe can be abundantly found in various disciplines (nonlinear oscillators, friction models and battery charge characteristics to name a few).

Before defining the PWP class of systems, some definitions are in order. Let $\mathbb{R}[y_1, \ldots, y_n]$ denote the ring of scalar-valued polynomials in n variables with coefficients in the field of real numbers $\mathbb{R}$. The ring of vector-valued real polynomial functions in n variables is accordingly denoted with $\mathbb{R}[y_1, \ldots, y_n]^q$, where q is the dimension of the range of the functions.

Definition 1 (Semi-algebraic set). *A subset S of $\mathbb{R}^n$ is semi-algebraic if it can be constructed by finitely many applications of the union, intersection and complementation operations, starting from sets of the form*

$$\{y \in \mathbb{R}^n \mid F(y) \leq 0\}$$

where F is an element of $\mathbb{R}[y_1, \ldots, y_n]$, the ring of real polynomials in n variables.

Consider now the class of discrete time hybrid systems that can be described as constrained piece-wise polynomial systems of the following form:

$$x(k+1) = f_{PWP}(x(k), u(k)) := f_i(x(k), u(k)), \text{ if } \begin{bmatrix} x(k) \\ u(k) \end{bmatrix} \in \mathcal{D}_i, \quad (1)$$

where $x \in \mathbb{R}^n$ is the continuous state vector, $u \in \mathbb{R}^m$ is the continuous input vector, $\{f_i\}_{i=1}^s \in \mathbb{R}[x, u]$ are real, vector-valued polynomial functions in vectors x and u and $\{\mathcal{D}_i\}_{i=1}^s$ is a partition of the joint state-input space $\mathbb{R}^{n+m}$ into s disjoint semi-algebraic sets. We furthermore assume that the origin is contained in some $\mathcal{D}_i$. We call the class of systems defined by equation (1) Piece-wise Polynomial Systems (PWP).

3   The CFTOC Problem for PWP Systems

We consider the problem of regulating system (1) to the origin. Based on the model of system (1), and given a control input sequence $\{u(0), u(1), \ldots, u(N-1)\}$, with $u(k) \in \mathbb{R}^m$, we predict the system evolution over a prediction horizon of N future moves. With a slight abuse of notation, from now on we consider u to be an r-vector, with $u := [u(0)^T, \ldots, u(N-1)^T]^T \in \mathbb{R}^r$, where $r = mN$. Therefore, u denotes the vector of all control inputs over the prediction horizon. Let also $x_0 := x(0) = [x_1(0), \ldots, x_n(0)]^T \in \mathbb{R}^n$ denote the initial state vector of the system. We introduce then a cost function that penalizes the control action and the deviation of state from the origin over the prediction horizon as follows:

$$J(u, x_0) = L_N(x(N)) + \sum_{k=0}^{N-1} L_k(x(k), u(k)) , \qquad (2)$$

where L_k are polynomial functions of the state x and control u called *stage costs*, whereas L_N – a polynomial function of the terminal state $x(N)$ – is called *terminal cost*. Note that the cost function $J(u, x_0)$ depends only on the input control sequence and the initial condition $x_0 \in \mathbb{R}^n$. This is because state update equation (1) implicitly expresses all states $x(k)$ for $k > 1$ with respect to x_0 and the input control sequence. Solving the CFTOC problem amounts to the following optimization problem:

$$\min_u \; J(u, x_0)$$
$$\text{s.t.} \begin{cases} x(k+1) = f_{PWP}(x(k), u(k)) \\ g(u(k), x(k)) \le 0, \quad k = 0, \ldots, N , \end{cases} \qquad (3)$$

where $g(u(k), x(k)) \in \mathbb{R}[x_1(k), \ldots, x_n(k), u_1(k), \ldots, u_m(k)]^q$ is a vector-valued polynomial function representing the system constraints in the joint input-state space $\mathbb{R}^{m+n}$.

In the case where the objective function $J(u, x_0)$ is linear with respect to the decision variable $u \in \mathbb{R}^r$ and the submodels f_i of system (1) are affine, the resulting optimization problem (3) is an instance of a parametric mixed-integer linear programming problem that has been extensively studied in the literature [4]. Closed-form formulas for problem (3) that give the optimal solution and corresponding optimizer as a function of the parameter x_0 can then be computed. It turns out that these expressions are piece-wise affine (PWA) functions of the parameter x_0.

3.1   Parametric Optimization and PWP Systems

For the more general class of polynomial systems we study in this paper, however, such closed-form formulas do not always exist. In contrast to the PWA case with linear cost [14], no "simple" expression of the optimal solution is possible, as it necessarily involves implicit algebraic functions. Nevertheless, a parametrization of the optimal solution is still possible by combining a precomputation stage using cylindrical algebraic decomposition and the on-line solution of univariate polynomial equations [8].

Namely, our goal is to minimize the function $J(u, x_0)$ with respect to u for any given value of the parameter x_0 in the region of interest. Therefore, the polynomial parametric optimization problem consists of finding a computational procedure for evaluating the maps

$$
\begin{aligned}
u^*(x_0) : \mathbb{R}^n &\longrightarrow \mathbb{R}^r \\
x_0 &\longmapsto u^*
\end{aligned}
\quad \text{and} \quad
\begin{aligned}
J^*(x_0) : \mathbb{R}^n &\longrightarrow \mathbb{R} \\
x_0 &\longmapsto J^*,
\end{aligned}
\tag{4}
$$

where $u^* = \arg\min_u J(u, x_0)$ and $J^* = \min_u J(u, x_0)$. Generally speaking, a nonlinear optimization problem is not guaranteed to have a unique optimizer. Consequently, in order for (4) not to be point-to-set maps, we focus our attention to one (any) optimizer. In addition, we assume that the minimum is attained[1]. Moreover, it has to be noted that the proposed approach is applicable without the need for any convexity assumptions on the optimization problem.

4   Computation of the Optimal Control Law

In order to parametrically solve the optimal control problem (3), we first translate the problem into an algebraic form. Then, the translated problem is decomposed into smaller subproblems, each of which is a nonlinear optimization problem (NLP).

4.1   Posing the Problem in Algebraic Form

Consider again system (1). For simplicity and without loss of generality, we assume that the semi-algebraic sets $\mathcal{D}_i$ are described by vector polynomial functions $h_i(u, x)$ as

$$
\mathcal{D}_i = \{(x, u) \in \mathbb{R}^{m+n} \mid h_i(x, u) \leq 0\} \quad \forall\, i = 1, \ldots, s .
\tag{5}
$$

Because in every region $\mathcal{D}_i$ a different vector field f_i is active, we can describe the system evolution over the finite prediction horizon N by the following relation:

$$
\bigwedge_{k=0}^{N-1} \bigvee_{i=1}^{s} \left[\begin{array}{l} h_i(x(k), u(k)) \leq 0 \,\wedge \\ f_i(x(k), u(k)) = x(k+1) \end{array} \right] = \text{true} .
\tag{6}
$$

---

[1] That is, there exists a feasible $u^* \in \mathbb{R}^r$ such that $J(u^*, x_0) = \inf_u J(u, x_0)$.

Using (6), CFTOC problem (3) can be written in the following form:

$$\min_{u} J(u, x_0)$$

$$\text{s.t.} \quad \left\{ \bigwedge_{k=0}^{N-1} \bigvee_{i=1}^{s} \left[\begin{matrix} h_i(x(k), u(k)) \leq 0 \wedge \\ f_i(x(k), u(k)) = x(k+1) \end{matrix} \right] \right\} \wedge \left\{ \bigwedge_{k=0}^{N} [g(u(k), x(k)) \leq 0] \right\}. \quad (7)$$

4.2 Decomposing the Problem

To break the problem into smaller subproblems, we convert the logic expression appearing in (7) into *disjunctive normal form* (DNF), by repeatedly applying the distributive law. Thus, we obtain the following optimization problem:

$$\min_{u} J(u, x_0) \quad \text{s.t.}$$

$$\bigvee_{j=1}^{s^N} \left\{ \bigwedge_{\substack{k \in [1\ N] \\ t_j \in \mathcal{Q}_{[1\ s]}^{N}}} \left[\begin{matrix} h_{t_j(k)}(x(k), u(k)) \leq 0 \wedge \\ f_{t_j(k)}(x(k), u(k)) = x(k+1) \end{matrix} \right] \right\} \wedge \left\{ \bigwedge_{k=0}^{N} [g(u(k), x(k)) \leq 0] \right\},$$

$$(8)$$

where $t_j := [t_j(1), \ldots, t_j(N)]$ is an index vector, $[1\ s]$ denotes all the integers from 1 to s, s being the number of polynomial system submodels, and $\mathcal{Q}_{[1\ s]}^{N}$ is the set of all permutations of the elements of the set

$$\left\{ \underbrace{1, \ldots, 1}_{N \text{ elements}}, \underbrace{2, \ldots, 2}_{N \text{ elements}}, \ldots \underbrace{s, \ldots, s}_{N \text{ elements}} \right\},$$

taken N at a time. The permutation set $\mathcal{Q}$ expresses all possible - feasible or infeasible - transitions of the system from one sub-model region $\mathcal{D}_i$ to another.

For ease of notation, we define $G_k \subset \mathbb{R}^{n+r}$ to be the subset of the feasible joint (u, x_0)-space, provided that the system will follow a predefined sub-model transition sequence. As a consequence, equation (8) gives rise to s^N subproblems SP_k of the form:

$$\mathbf{SP_k} : \quad \min_{u} J(u, x_0) \quad \text{s.t.} \quad (u, x_0) \in G_k, \quad (9)$$

where

$$G_k = \{ (u, x_0) \in \mathbb{R}^{n+r} \mid$$

$$\left\{ \bigwedge_{\substack{k \in [1\ N] \\ t_j \in \mathcal{Q}_{[1\ s]}^{N}}} \left[\begin{matrix} h_{t_j(k)}(x(k), u(k)) \leq 0 \wedge \\ f_{t_j(k)}(x(k), u(k)) = x(k+1) \end{matrix} \right] \right\} \wedge \left\{ \bigwedge_{k=0}^{N} [g(u(k), x(k)) \leq 0] \right\} \}.$$

$$(10)$$

The subproblems SP_k are solved using cylindrical algebraic decomposition, as shown in the next Section.

4.3   Solving the Subproblems

Before showing how CAD can be used to parametrically solve sub-problems (9) and present the full MPC algorithm for PWP systems, we have to introduce some basic algebraic notions associated to CAD.

Cylindrical Algebraic Decomposition. The notion of CAD was initially conceived in the breakthrough paper by Collins [9]. Given a set $P \subset \mathbb{R}[y_1, \ldots, y_n]$ of multivariate polynomials in n variables, a CAD is a special partition of $\mathbb{R}^n$ into components, called *cells*, over which all the polynomials have constant sign. The algorithm for computing a CAD also provides a point in each cell, called *sample point*, which can be used to determine the sign of the polynomials in the cell.

To perform optimization, a CAD is associated with a Boolean formula. This Boolean formula can either be quantified or quantifier-free. By a quantifier-free Boolean formula we mean a formula consisting of polynomial equations $\{f_i(y) = 0\}$ and inequalities $\{f_j(y) \leq 0\}$ combined using the Boolean operators $\wedge$ (and), $\vee$ (or), and $\rightarrow$ (implies). In general, a *formula* is an expression in the variables $y = (y_1, ..., y_n)$ of the following type:

$$Q_1 y_1 ... Q_n y_n \quad \mathcal{F}(f_1(y), ..., f_\phi(y)) \tag{11}$$

where $\mathcal{F}(f_1(y), ..., f_\phi(y))$ is assumed to be a quantifier-free Boolean formula and Q_i is one of the quantifiers $\forall$ (for all) and $\exists$ (there exists).

Construction of the CAD. The construction of the CAD involves three phases. The first, the *projection phase* computes successive sets of polynomials in $n - 1, n - 2, \ldots, 1$ variables. The second phase is the *base phase* and it constructs a decomposition of $\mathbb{R}$, at the lowest level of projection, after all variables but one have been eliminated. The last phase is the *extension phase* where the $\mathbb{R}$-decomposition is successively extended to a decomposition of $\mathbb{R}^2$, $\mathbb{R}^2$ to $\mathbb{R}^3$,...,$\mathbb{R}^{n-1}$ to $\mathbb{R}^n$. In this way, a decomposition of the full $\mathbb{R}^n$-space is obtained.

Additionally, along with every set of polynomials $\mathcal{P}_k(f_i(y))$, the CAD construction algorithm returns a special set of polynomials attached to each projection level d, called the *projection level factors* denoted by $\{L_i^d\}_{i=1..t_d}$. The set of the real roots of these polynomials contains critical information about the CAD, defining the boundaries of its cells. These roots can be isolated points in $\mathbb{R}^n$, curves, surfaces or hypersurfaces, depending on the dimension of the projection space. In Figure 1, for example, the zero sets of the level factors of a CAD are depicted as three n-dimensional hypersurfaces. The level factor polynomials are also called *level factors*. Moreover, every cell c in every projection level of a CAD has an associated *truth value* $v(c)$. The truth value of a cell is "true" if $\mathcal{F}(f_1(y), ..., f_\phi(y))$ in (11) is true in that cell and "false" otherwise.

CAD and Parametric Optimization. Suppose we have to solve problem (9). We associate with problem (9) the following boolean expression:

$$[(u, x_0) \in G_k] \wedge [\gamma - J(u, x_0) \geq 0] , \tag{12}$$

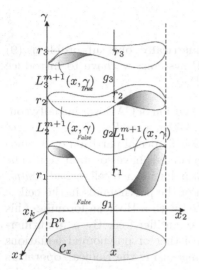
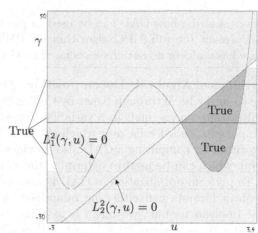

Fig. 1. The zero sets of the level factors are represented with three surfaces and mark the boundaries of the cells. The Figure is based on Christopher Brown's ISSAC 2004 CAD tutorial slides.

Fig. 2. A simple cylindrical algebraic decomposition in $\mathbb{R}^2$. The true cells are specially marked. The Figure is taken from the example in [8].

where γ is a new variable associated with the cost function. We then compute the CAD defined by the polynomial expressions in (12). For this, we use the software tool QEPCAD B [15]. The signs of the polynomials appearing in (12) as well as of $\mathcal{P}_k(f_i(x))$ resulting from the projection steps are determined in each cell. These signs, in turn, determine the truth value of (12) in each cell – see also Figure 2. All we need to solve problem (9) is the level factor polynomials associated with the CAD of system (12), and the truth value of the cells. The input formula to the CAD construction algorithm is (12). The projection phase of the CAD is carried out up to the point where all decision variables u plus the cost-associated variable γ have been eliminated. The resulting level factors at this last projection level are parameterized in the variable x_0, which is the optimization problem parameter.

4.4   The MPC Algorithm

The MPC algorithm for PWP systems consists of two parts. The off-line, where the CAD's for systems (12) associated to optimization problems (9) are constructed and the associated level factor information is extracted, and the on-line, where this precomputed information is used to obtain the solution of the original CFTOC problem (3) in real time. It has to be emphasized that the on-line algorithm needs only solve univariate polynomial equations and perform a search over a discrete set of candidate solutions to select the optimal.

We have to note, however, a difference of our approach as compared to the algorithm presented in [8]. Here, we *partially* construct the CAD by projecting (eliminating) only the decision variables and the variable γ. The drawback of this "partial" approach is that in the on-line implementation one has to compare more candidate solutions. This is because one lacks the sample point information that comes with a full projection [8], that would enable us to immediately determine the solution of each subproblem SP_k. The benefit, however, is that the off-line computations become much easier.

The on-line process repeatedly calls Algorithm 1 to solve each of the SP_k problems. Algorithm 1 uses then the precomputed CAD information to obtain the optimizer and optimal solution for each one of the subproblems [8] and returns these to the calling on-line process. Subsequently, the on-line process compares all the candidate solutions returned and selects the one with the minimum optimal cost J_k^* as *the* optimal solution for CFTOC problem (3).

Algorithm 1. *(Subroutine called by the on-line algorithm)*

Input: Value of the parameter x_0 (state measurement taken in real time).
Output: Optimal cost J_k^* and optimizer u_k^* for sub-problem SP_k.
1: Specialize parameter x_0 in level factor polynomials $\{L_i^{n+1}\}$ and solve resulting univariate equations to obtain roots $\{r_k\}$ (candidate optimal costs J_k^*).
2: **for all** $j = 1, \ldots, r$ **do**
3:     specialize x_0 and solve $L_i^{n+1+j} = 0$ to obtain candidate optimizers u_j.
4: **end for**
5: Check feasibility of candidate solutions and discard infeasible ones
6: Among the feasible ones, select minimum candidate optimal cost J_k^* and related optimizer u_k^*.
7: **return:** optimal cost J_k^* and optimizer u_k^*.

Remark 1. The feasibility check in step 5 of Algorithm 1 can lead to a search of exponential complexity with respect to the dimension m of the control input vector. This would be avoided if one were to have the associated sample point information that comes with the full projection of all variables (decision variables and cost associated variable *plus* parameters) [8]. Therefore, the practical relevance of the proposed partial projection scheme is restricted to problems with a relatively small dimension m. The reader is referred to [8] for a more detailed description of Algorithm 1.

5   Application Example

Dc-dc converters are a class of electronic power circuits that is used extensively in regulated dc power supplies and dc motor drive applications due to its advantageous features in terms of size, weight and reliable performance. In this paper the controller synthesis problem of the fixed-frequency boost dc-dc converter is considered, where the semiconductor switch is operated by a pulse sequence with constant switching frequency f_s (resp. period T_s). It is then possible to regulate the

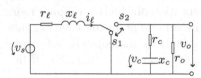

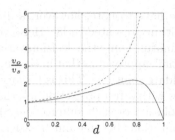

Fig. 3. Topology of the boost converter. r_o denotes the output load resistance, r_c and r_ℓ are the parasitic resistances of the capacitor and the inductor and x_c and x_ℓ represent the capacitance and inductance of the converter.

Fig. 4. Steady state characteristic of the boost converter with (continuous) and without (dashed) parasitics

dc component of the output voltage via the duty cycle $d = \frac{t_{on}}{T_s}$, where t_{on} denotes the interval within the switching period during which the switch is in conduction.

5.1   Modelling

Operation Principle. The circuit topology of the boost converter is shown in Fig. 3; only the continuous conduction mode will be considered, that is operating points for which the inductor current remains positive. The boost converter features two operation modes with two different affine dynamics. The controller selects the control input, the duty cycle $d(k)$, for each period k, determining when the switch from the first mode to the second takes place. During the time interval $kT_s \le t < (k+d(k))T_s$ the switch S is in the s_1 position and the inductor is charged. At the end of this interval S is switched to s_2 and power is transferred to the load. Subsequently, at the end of the period, the switch is set back to the s_1 position.

Hybrid PWP Model. As shown in [13], one can formulate a discrete-time PWP hybrid model of the boost converter, to be used for the design of the controller. The model monitors the behaviour of the states within a single switching period, thus providing an expression approximating the average inductor current, required for reasons further detailed in Section 5.2. By taking $x(t) = [i_\ell(t) \; v_c(t)]^T$ as the state vector, where $i_\ell(t)$ is the inductor current and $v_c(t)$ the capacitor voltage, and $d(k)$ being the manipulated variable of the control problem, this PWP model can be written in the form introduced in Section 2

$$x(k+1) = f_j(x(k), d(k)) \tag{13}$$

$$y(k) = g_j(x(k), d(k)), \text{ if } d(k) \in [\frac{j-1}{\nu}, \frac{j}{\nu}], j = 1, \ldots, \nu, \tag{14}$$

where f_j and g_j are polynomial functions and ν is a design parameter that determines the accuracy of the PWP model with respect to the exact discrete-time map describing the converter [13].

5.2   Control

Objectives. The main control objective is to regulate the dc component of the output voltage v_o to its reference. This regulation has to be achieved in the presence of the hard constraints on the manipulated variable (the duty cycle) which is bounded between 0 and 1, and needs to be maintained despite changes in the voltage source v_s. The controller must also render a steady state operation under a constant duty cycle, thus avoiding the occurrence of fast-scale instabilities (subharmonic oscillations). Due to some peculiarities of the specific converter, detailed in [13], the control problem is formulated as a current (rather than a voltage) regulation problem, aiming at steering the average value of the inductor current i_ℓ to a reference $i_{\ell,ref}$. This approach is the common industrial practice [16], and yields satisfactory results in terms of the closed-loop performance.

CFTOC. For the formulation of the CFTOC, the control objectives are to regulate the average inductor current to its reference, despite changes in the voltage source v_s, which we assume to be measurable, consistently with industrial practice. At every time-instant k the measurements of the states and the current reference are then normalized with respect to v_s, so that a variation in the voltage source is directly mirrored in an updated value for the current reference. Let $\Delta d(k) = |d(k) - d(k-1)|$ indicate the absolute value of the difference between two consecutive duty cycles. This term is introduced in order to reduce the presence of unwanted chattering in the input when the system has almost reached stationary conditions.

We define the penalty matrix $Q = \text{diag}(q_1, q_2)$ with $q_1, q_2 \in \mathbb{R}^+$ and the vector $\varepsilon(k) = [i_{\ell,err}(k), \Delta d(k)]^T$, with $i_{\ell,err}(k)$ being the deviation of the average inductor current from its reference (see [13] for details). Consider the objective function

$$J(D(k), x(k), d(k-1)) = \sum_{\ell=0}^{N-1} \|Q\ \varepsilon(k+\ell|k)\|_2^2 \tag{15}$$

which penalizes the predicted evolution of $\varepsilon(k+\ell|k)$ from time-instant k on over the finite horizon N using the quadratic cost. The control law at time-instant k is then obtained by minimizing the objective function (15) over the sequence of control moves $D(k) = [d(k), \ldots, d(k+N-1)]^T$ subject to the related system equations and constraints for the PWP model.

Computation. For the numerical simulation of the proposed scheme, we employ a PWP model with $\nu = 3$. The circuit parameters are as in [13], the penalty matrix is chosen to be $Q = \text{diag}(5, 2)$ and the prediction horizon is set to $N = 2$.

Initially, to keep the computational cost relatively low, we employ a move blocking [17] scheme of length two, i.e. we consider the control input to be constant over the horizon. The x_0 parameter of the problem is then $x_0 = [i_\ell\ v_c\ i_{\ell,ref}\ d_0]^T$, where d_0 is the duty cycle input of the previous time step. The move blocking renders the decision variable space $\mathbb{R}^r$ one-dimensional, that is $r = 1$. After decomposing the algebraic formulation (8) of the CFTOC problem into subproblems, we obtain three nonlinear programs SP_k. Normally one would expect $s^N = 9$ subproblems, since $s = 3$ and $N = 2$. Due to the move block-ing, however, and because the dynamics of the system are partitioned along the d-space only, the subproblems that we get are only three, since the same mode of the piece-wise dynamics will be active throughout the horizon.

The projection phase of the CAD construction algorithm constructs three level factor polynomials for each SP_k. The degree of these polynomials is three, one and one. Their coefficients are polynomial functions of the parameters i_ℓ, v_c, $i_{\ell,ref}$ and d_0. In real time, these parameters are specified and the roots com-puted provide the candidate optimal cost and optimizer to the original CFTOC problem. The optimal solution is then determined by searching over this finite set of candidate solutions.

Subsequently, we increase the complexity of the considered example by abandoning the move blocking strategy. The decision variable becomes then a two-dimensional vector. In this case, the CAD construction involves two projec-tion steps instead of one. In the second step, the CAD off-line procedure tries to symbolically expand the determinant of Sylvester matrices as large as 23×23, whose elements are polynomials of up to approximately 2000 monomials. This is a highly demanding task, impossible with today's commonly available com-putational power. This complex step is central to the CAD procedure, since the latter eliminates variables step by step [9] and therefore needs the level factor polynomials of the previous step, which are determinants of Sylvester matrices. To alleviate this bottleneck, we modify the last projection step of the CAD pro-cedure as follows. We choose *not to expand* the determinants of the Sylvester matrices, since it is only the roots of the determinant polynomials that are needed for the on-line algorithm, not the polynomials themselves. Their com-putation can be achieved through the use of *generalized eigenvalues*, which is a highly efficient numerical linear algebra procedure. In the last projection step, the Sylvester matrices are matrix polynomials in the cost-associated variable γ. If we write them in the form

$$M(\gamma) = M_0 + M_1\gamma + \cdots + M_\xi\gamma^\xi , \qquad (16)$$

where ξ is the maximum degree of the polynomials in $M(\gamma)$, it turns out that

$$\{\gamma \in \mathbb{C} \mid \det M(\gamma) = 0\} = \{\lambda \in \mathbb{C} \mid \exists x : Ax = \lambda Bx\} , \qquad (17)$$

where A and B are certain square block matrices whose blocks are the coeffi-cient matrices M_j, $j = 1, \ldots, \xi$, arranged with a certain structure [18]. In other words, the roots of the determinant of a univariate matrix polynomial (w.r.t. γ in this case) are equal to the generalized eigenvalues of its linearization [18]. By taking this step the problem is rendered computationally feasible. However, there are two issues that arise. First, the sheer size of the matrices in terms of storage needed is prohibitive. Therefore, one has to use floating point arithmetic to reduce it within the limits that modern computer algebra systems can handle. There is an inevitable loss of accuracy involved in this operation. Secondly, this loss of accuracy creates numerical instabilities to such an extent, that the on-line computations, although feasible from a complexity point of view, yield results that can no longer be meaningfully used. For this second approach, a simple version of the CAD algorithm was implemented in Maple. The level factors obtained were transferred to Matlab, where the on-line algorithm was implemented using YALMIP [19].

5.3 Simulation Results

In this section, simulation results demonstrating the performance of the proposed scheme (with move blocking) are presented. All results presented in the following figures are normalized, including the time scale where one time unit is equal to one switching period.

The first case to be examined is that of the transient behavior during startup. Fig.5(a) and Fig.5(b) depict the step responses of the different schemes during start-up. The initial state is given by $x(0) = [0,0]^T$, the voltage source is

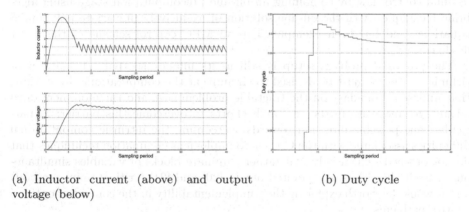

(a) Inductor current (above) and output voltage (below)
      (b) Duty cycle

Fig. 5. Simulation results for the startup scenario

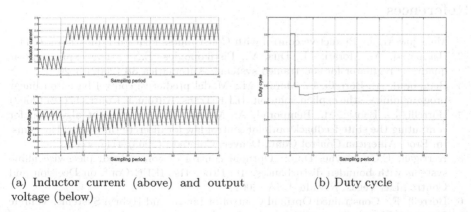

(a) Inductor current (above) and output voltage (below)
      (b) Duty cycle

Fig. 6. Simulation results for the scenario featuring the step-down of v_s from 0.8 p.u. to 0.55 p.u.

$v_s = 0.8$ p.u. and the reference for the output is 1 p.u. This translates to a current reference $i_{\ell,ref} = 1.3889$. The output voltage reaches its steady state within approximately 30 switching periods with an overshoot of just over 10%.

In the second case, the behavior of the converter under a step change in the voltage source is analyzed. In the example presented, the converter is initially at steady state when a step change in the voltage source from $v_s = 0.8$ p.u. to $v_s = 0.55$ p.u. is applied at time-instant $k = 5$. This is shown in Fig.6(a) and Fig.6(b), where one can see that the output voltage remains practically unaffected and the controller finds the new steady-state duty cycle within 15 switching periods.

6   Conclusions and Future Outlook

A new solution approach to the CFTOC problem for discrete-time PWP systems has been proposed. The described technique is based on CAD to compute the optimal control law by combining an off-line precomputation stage using algebraic techniques with the on-line solution of exclusively univariate polynomial equations, and has been exemplified in an MPC control scheme of the boost dc-dc converter.

The proposed problem setup is still in its infancy so that adequate algorithmic strategies must be devised to circumvent the computational limitations that impose a boundary on the tractable problem size, and the aforementioned advantages motivate further research efforts to overcome this barrier; in particular, one possible direction towards overcoming the intrinsic computational difficulties associated with the CAD is to implement elimination techniques that do not proceed sequentially, but rather eliminate blocks of variables simultaneously. Such algorithms are pointed out in [20] and [21] (critical point method) and it would be worth exploring their implementability in the context of optimal control problems.

References

1. Maciejowski, J.: Predictive control with Constraints. Pearson Education (2001)
2. Bemporad, A., Morari, M., Dua, V., Pistikopoulos, E.N.: The explicit linear quadratic regulator for constrained systems. Automatica **38** (2002) 3–20
3. Bemporad, A., Borrelli, F., Morari, M.: Model predictive control based on linear programming — the explicit solution. IEEE Trans. Automat. Contr. **47**(12) (2002)
4. Borrelli, F., Baotić, M., Bemporad, A., Morari, M.: An efficient algorithm for computing the state feedback optimal control law for discrete time hybrid systems. In: Proc. American Control Conf., Denver, Colorado (2003) 4717–4722
5. Kerrigan, E.C., Mayne, D.Q.: Optimal control of constrained, piecewise affine systems with bounded disturbances. In: Proc. 41st IEEE Conf. on Decision and Control, Las Vegas, Nevada, USA (2002)
6. Borrelli, F.: Constrained Optimal Control of Linear and Hybrid Systems. Volume 290 of LNCIS. Springer (2003)
7. Johansen, T.A.: Approximate explicit receding horizon control of constrained nonlinear systems. Automatica **40**(2) (2004) 293–300

8. Fotiou, I.A., Parrilo, P.A., Morari, M.: Nonlinear parametric optimization using cylindrical algebraic decomposition. In: Proc. of the Conf. on Decision & Control, Seville, Spain (2005) 3735–3740
9. Collins, G.: Quantifier elimination for real closed fields by cylindrical algebraic decomposition. Number 33 in Lecture Notes in Computer Science, London, UK, Springer-Verlag (1975) 134–183
10. Lafferriere, G., Pappas, G., Yovine, S.: Reach set computation for linear vector fields using quantifier elimination. In: Electronic Proceedings of the IMAC Conference on Applications of Computer Algebra, El Escorial, Spain (1999)
11. Alur, R., Henzinger, T., Lafferriere, G., Pappas, G.: Discrete abstractions of hybrid systems. Proceedings of the IEEE **88**(7) (2000) 971–984
12. Vidal, R., Soatto, S., Ma, Y., Sastry, S.: An Algebraic Geometric Approach to the Identification of a Class of Linear Hybrid Systems. In: Proc. of the Conf. on Decision & Control, Maui, HI (2003)
13. Beccuti, A.G., Papafotiou, G., Morari, M.: Optimal Control of the Boost dc-dc Converter. In: Proc. of the Conf. on Decision & Control, Seville, Spain (2005)
14. Baotić, M., Christophersen, F.J., Morari, M.: A new Algorithm for Constrained Finite Time Optimal Control of Hybrid Systems with a Linear Performance Index. In: Proc. of the European Control Conference, Cambridge, UK (2003)
15. Brown, C.W.: QEPCAD B: a program for computing with semialgebraic sets using CADs. ACM SIGSAM Bulletin **37** (2003) 97–108
16. Mohan, N., Undeland, T.M., Robbins, W.P.: Power Electronics: Converters, Applications and Design. Wiley, London (1989)
17. Qin, S.J., Badgwell, T.A.: A survey of industrial model predictive control technology. Control Engineering Practice **11** (2003) 733–764
18. Gohberg, I., Lancaster, P., Rodman, L.: Matrix Polynomials. Academic Press, New York (1982)
19. Löfberg, J.: YALMIP : A toolbox for modeling and optimization in MATLAB. In: Proceedings of the CACSD Conference, Taipei, Taiwan (2004) Available from `http://control.ee.ethz.ch/~joloef/yalmip.php`.
20. Mishra, B.: Computational Real Algebraic Geometry. Handbook of discrete and computational geometry (1997) 537–556
21. Basu, S., Pollack, R., Roy, M.F.: Algorithms in real algebraic geometry. Springer Verlag, New York (2003)

The Reachability Problem for Uncertain Hybrid Systems Revisited: A Viability Theory Perspective

Yan Gao[1], John Lygeros[2], and Marc Quincapoix[3]

[1] School of Management, University of Shanghai for Science and Technology,
200093 Shanghai, China
gaoyan1962@263.net
[2] Department of Electrical Engineering, University of Patras,
Rio, 26500 Patras, Greece
lygeros@ee.upatras.gr
[3] Laboratoire de Mathematiques, Université de Bretagne Occidentale,
6 Avenue Le Gorgeu, 29200 Brest Cedex, France
Marc.Quincampoix@univ-brest.fr

Abstract. We revisit the problem of designing controllers to meet safety specifications for hybrid systems, whose evolution is affected by both control and disturbance inputs. The problem is formulated as a dynamic game and an appropriate notion of hybrid strategy for the control inputs is developed. The design of hybrid strategies to meet safety specifications is based on an iteration of alternating discrete and continuous safety calculations. We show that, under certain assumptions, the iteration converges to a fixed point, which turns out to be the maximal set of states for which the safety specifications can be met. The continuous part of the calculation relies on the computation of the set of winning states for one player in a two player, two target, pursuit evasion differential game. We develop a characterization of these winning states using methods from non-smooth analysis and viability theory.

1 Introduction

Problems of controller synthesis for discrete and hybrid systems have been an important topic of research in the automatic control and computer theory communities for a number of years. Initial work concentrated on purely discrete systems, first from a computer theoretic perspective (see [1] and the references therein) and, more recently, from an automatic control perspective [2]. The discrete results were subsequently extended to timed automata [3,4] and classes of hybrid automata where the continuous dynamics are described by constant differential inclusions (the so-called linear hybrid automata) [5]. Of particular interest have been problems of controller synthesis under safety specifications, where the objective of the controller is to keep the system state in a "safe" part of the state space.

João Hespanha and A. Tiwari (Eds.): HSCC 2006, LNCS 3927, pp. 242–256, 2006.

If the system evolution is influenced by both control and disturbance inputs, the problem of controller synthesis is naturally formulated in the context of dynamic games. Specifically for controller synthesis problems under safety specifications, this gives rise to pursuit-evasion games, where it is assumed that the disturbance is trying to lead the state to the unsafe part of the state space and the controller is trying to prevent it from doing so. Such a pursuit evasion approach to safe controller synthesis for general classes hybrid systems was adopted in [6, 7, 8, 9, 10]. The procedure proposed in these references revolves around an iteration of two coupled reachability computations, one involving the discrete dynamics and one involving the continuous dynamics. The discrete reachability computation requires only the inversion of the maps encoding the discrete dynamics. The continuous reachability computation, however, requires the solution of a pursuit-evasion differential game with two players and two targets (what is referred to in [8] as a "reach-avoid" computation). In [8, 9, 10] the solution to these pursuit evasion games is characterized using dynamic programming, through the level sets of an appropriate value function.

Though conceptually appealing, the approach of [8, 9, 10] suffers from two drawbacks. The first is that each step of the iterative procedure establishes a set of states where the controller can ensure that the system solutions remain in the safe set for an interval of continuous evolution, followed by a discrete transition. Iterating, establishes sets of states for which the controller can ensure that the state remains in the safe set for 2, 3, ... such continuous-discrete operations. There is, however, no guarantee that this procedure will converge to a kernel of states for which there exists a controller such that all solutions stay in the kernel for ever. This kernel is what is referred to as the "maximal control invariant" subset of the safe states [7].

The second draw back of the approach of [8, 9, 10] is that the dynamic programming argument in these references only applies to differentiable value functions. In [8, 9], the value function for the reach-avoid computation is characterized as a solution to a pair of coupled variational inequalities. In [10], a simpler characterization is developed, that involves one Hamilton-Jacobi type partial differential equation, together with an inequality constraint. Even though classical (differentiable) solutions may exist for some of these variational problems, it is well known that this is not the case in general; even for purely continuous pursuit evasion games one typically has to allow viscosity solutions [11, 12, 13]. Moreover, the Hamiltonians used in the characterizations of [8, 9, 10] are only lower semi-continuous functions. Therefore, even if one allows viscosity solutions, a very complicated mathematical argument will be necessary to ensure the existence and uniqueness of the solutions, and hence the well-posedness of the characterization.

In this paper we rethink the safe controller synthesis problem for uncertain hybrid systems formulated in [6, 7, 8, 9, 10]. Instead of relying on dynamic programming and viscosity solutions, we follow the approach of [14, 15, 16, 17] and formulate the gaming problem in the context of viability theory. We then use non-smooth analysis tools to characterize the solution. This approach not only does not suffer from the technical complications that arise with viscosity solutions of the partial differential equation with lower semi-continuous Hamiltonian, but also allows us to establish convergence results for the iterative procedure. Finally, it opens the door for the use of powerful numerical algorithms that have been developed based on non-smooth analysis to numerically approximate discontinuous value functions [18, 19]. A related approach to safety problems for hybrid systems under either only control or only disturbance inputs was developed in [20]. Approximate stabilization of the class of systems considered in this paper was studied in [21].

In summary, the main contributions of this paper are:

1. The definition of an appropriate notion of strategy for a class of hybrid pursuit evasion games (Definition 6). This allows one to characterize control invariant sets as fixed points of an appropriate operator (Theorem 1) and hence the maximal control invariant set as the limit point of an intuitive iteration (Theorem 2).
2. The characterization of the continuous part of the operator using non-smooth analysis tools. To the best of our knowledge this is the only complete characterization of this operator at this level of generality.

In Section 2 we provide some background definitions on hybrid systems necessary to formulate our results. We then define pursuit-evasion games for a class of hybrid systems and provide an appropriate notion of strategy. In Section 3 we develop an iterative procedure closely related to that of [8, 9, 10] for approximating the solution to the hybrid pursuit evasion games and provide convergence results. Then, in Section 4, we provide a characterization of the continuous part of the iteration as a two player, two target differential game, based on non-smooth analysis tools. The proofs of the continuous results are rather lengthy and technical and are omitted in the interest of space; proof sketches are provided for the hybrid argument.

2   Hybrid Dynamics and Reachability Problem Formulation

2.1   Notation and Terminology

We briefly review a few concepts from non-smooth analysis and viability theory needed to develop our results; for a more thorough treatment the reader is referred to [22]. Let $\langle \cdot, \cdot \rangle$ denote the standard inner product in $\mathbb{R}^n$ and let $|\cdot|$ denote the corresponding metric. We assume that $\mathbb{R}^n$ is endowed with the standard Euclidean topology generated by open balls in the metric. We assume that finite sets are endowed with the discrete topology (i.e. all subsets are open). We assume that product spaces of the form $Q \times X$, where Q is a finite set and X is a subset of Euclidean space, are endowed with the product topology generated by the products of the corresponding open sets. For a set K we use 2^K to denote the set of all subsets (power set) of K.

For $x \in \mathbb{R}^n$ and $K \subseteq \mathbb{R}^n$, let $d_K(x)$ denote the *distance* of the point x to the set K defined by

$$d_K(x) = \inf_{y \in K} |x - y|.$$

Clearly $d_K(x) = 0$ if x is in the closure of K. The set of *proximal normals* to the set $K \subseteq \mathbb{R}^n$ at the point $x \in K$ is defined by

$$\mathrm{NP}_K(x) = \{y \in \mathbb{R}^n \mid d_K(y + x) = |y|\}.$$

Clearly $\mathrm{NP}_K(x) = \{0\}$ if x is in the interior of K. For $y \in \mathbb{R}^n$, we denote by $\varPi_K(y)$ the *projection* of y onto K, i.e. the set

$$\varPi_K(y) = \{x \in K \mid d_K(y) = |x - y|\}.$$

Clearly $\varPi_K(y) = \{y\}$ if $y \in K$.

For variables u and d taking values in sets $U \subseteq \mathbb{R}^m$ and $D \subseteq \mathbb{R}^p$ respectively we use $\mathcal{U}$ and $\mathcal{D}$ to denote the sets of Lebesgue measurable functions $u(\cdot) : \mathbb{R}_+ \rightarrow U$ and $d(\cdot) : \mathbb{R}_+ \rightarrow D$ respectively. For $u(\cdot) \in \mathcal{U}$ and $T \geq 0$ we use $u \downarrow_T (\cdot) \in \mathcal{U}$ to denote the function $u \downarrow_T (t) = u(t + T)$.

In logic formulas we use $\wedge$ as a shorthand for "and", $\vee$ as a shorthand for "or" and $\Rightarrow$ as a shorthand for "implies".

2.2   Dynamics and Solutions

We consider dynamical systems that involve both a continuous state (denoted by x) and a discrete state (denoted by q). The evolution of the state is influenced by two different kinds of inputs: controls and disturbances. We partition the inputs of each kind into two classes, those used to control the discrete evolution (v and δ respectively) and those used to control continuous evolution (u and d). The inputs v and δ can be further partitioned into discrete valued and continuous valued, we will not, however, make this distinction explicit in the notation.

The dynamics of the state are determined through four functions: a vector field f that determines the continuous evolution, a reset map r that determines the outcome of the discrete transitions, a "guard" set that determines when discrete transitions can take place and a "domain" set Dom that determines when continuous evolution is possible. The following definition formalizes the details.

Definition 1 (Hybrid game automaton). *A hybrid game automaton characterizes the evolution of*

- *discrete state variables $q \in Q$ and continuous state variables $x \in X$,*
- *control inputs $v \in \varUpsilon$ and $u \in U$, and*
- *disturbance inputs $\delta \in \varDelta$ and $d \in D$*

by means of four functions

- *a vector field $f : Q \times X \times U \times D \rightarrow X$,*
- *a domain set $Dom : Q \rightarrow 2^X$,*
- *guard sets $G : Q \times Q \rightarrow 2^X$ and*
- *a reset function $r : Q \times Q \times X \times \varUpsilon \times \varDelta \rightarrow X$.*

To formally define the solutions of this class of hybrid systems, we recall the following notion from [23, 20]; an effectively equivalent notion of hybrid time can be found in [24].

Definition 2 (Hybrid time set). *A hybrid time set $\tau = \{I_i\}_{i=0}^{N}$ is a finite or infinite sequence of intervals of the real line, such that*

- *for all $i < N$, $I_i = [\tau_i, \tau_i']$;*
- *if $N < \infty$, then $I_N = [\tau_N, \tau_N']$, or $I_N = [\tau_N, \tau_N')$, possibly with $\tau_N' = \infty$;*
- *for all i, $\tau_i \leq \tau_i' = \tau_{i+1}$.*

Since all the primitives in Definition 1 are time invariant, we can assume that $\tau_0 = 0$ without loss of generality.

Roughly speaking, the solution of a hybrid game automaton (called a "run") is defined over a hybrid time set τ and involves a sequence of intervals of continuous evolution followed by discrete transitions. Starting at some initial state (q_0, x_0) the continuous state moves along the solution of the differential equation

$$\dot{x} = f(q_0, x, u, d)$$

as long as it does not leave the set $\text{Dom}(q_0)$. The discrete state remains constant throughout this time. If at some point x reaches a set $G(q_0, q')$ for some $q' \in Q$, a discrete transition can take place. The first interval of τ ends and the second one begins with a new state (q', x') where x' is determined by the reset map r. The process is then repeated. Notice that considerable freedom is allowed when defining the solution in this "declarative" way: in addition to the effect of the input variables, there may also be a choice between evolving continuously or taking a discrete transition (if the continuous state is in both the domain set and a guard set) or between multiple discrete transitions (if the continuous state is in many guard sets at the same time).

The following concept helps to formalize the above discussion.

Definition 3 (Hybrid trajectory). *A hybrid trajectory over a set of variables that take values in a set A is a pair (τ, a) where $\tau = \{I_i\}_{i=0}^{N}$ is a hybrid time set and $a = \{a_i(\cdot)\}_{i=0}^{N}$ is a sequence of functions $a_i(\cdot) : I_i \to A$.*

Notice that given a function $\hat{u}(\cdot) \in \mathcal{U}$ and a hybrid time set $\tau = \{I_i\}_{i=0}^{N}$ one can naturally define a hybrid trajectory (τ, u) by $u_i(t) = \hat{u}(t)$ for all $i \in \{0, 1, \ldots, N\}$ and all $t \in I_i$. Likewise, given a sequence $\{\hat{v}_i\}_{i=0}^{\infty}$ with $\hat{v}_i \in \Upsilon$ and a hybrid time set $\tau = \{I_i\}_{i=0}^{N}$ one can define a hybrid trajectory (τ, v) by $v_i(t) = \hat{v}_i$ for all $i \in \{0, 1, \ldots, N\}$ and all $t \in I_i$. Constructions like these will be used repeatedly in the definition of runs, hybrid strategies, etc.

Definition 4 (Run). *A run of a hybrid game automaton is a hybrid trajectory $(\tau, q, x, v, u, \delta, d)$ over its state and input variables that satisfies the following conditions:*

- *Discrete Evolution: for $i < N$,*
    1. *$x_i(\tau_i') \in G(q_i(\tau_i'), q_{i+1}(\tau_{i+1}))$.*
    2. *$x_{i+1}(\tau_{i+1}) = r(q_i(\tau_i'), q_{i+1}(\tau_{i+1}), x_i(\tau_i'), v_{i+1}(\tau_{i+1}), \delta_{i+1}(\tau_{i+1}))$.*

- *Continuous Evolution: for all i with $\tau_i < \tau_i'$*
  1. *$u_i(\cdot)$ and $d_i(\cdot)$ are measurable functions on I_i.*
  2. *$q_i(t) = q_i(\tau_i)$, $v_i(t) = v_i(\tau_i)$ and $\delta_i(t) = \delta_i(\tau_i)$ for all $t \in I_i$.*
  3. *$x_i(\cdot)$ is the solution of the differential equation*

$$\dot{x}_i(t) = f(q_i(t), x_i(t), u_i(t), d_i(t)) \tag{1}$$

  over the interval I_i with initial condition $x_i(\tau_i)$.
  4. *$x_i(t) \in Dom(q_i(t))$ for all $t \in [\tau_i, \tau_i')$.*

Notice that since the discrete state and inputs remain constant throughout the continuous evolution, we can identify the discrete elements of a run with sequences of discrete states and inputs in the obvious way. Definition 4 suggests that hybrid game automata can encode a very rich class of hybrid dynamics. There are two main limitations, however.

1. The inputs cannot force discrete transitions to take place. Since Dom is independent of both control and disturbance inputs (and will be assumed to be open below), if $x \in Dom(q)$ continuous evolution is possible from (q, x), irrespective of the values of the input variables.
2. The inputs cannot determine the discrete state after a discrete transition. Since $G(q, q')$ is independent of both control and disturbance inputs, if x is in multiple guards, say $x \in G(q, q') \cap G(q, q'')$, any of the q', q'' is a possible destination of a discrete transition from (q, x). The inputs have no way of influencing the choice.

In the context of the safety problems considered below, these are not a very severe limitation from the point of view of the disturbance inputs. The design procedure we develop is naturally conservative and assumes that all non-deterministic choices are resolved in favor of the disturbance. In other words, if there is a possibility of unfavorable continuous evolution, or an unfavorable discrete transition, the algorithm assumes that the system will follow that evolution without the disturbance having to force it to do so. The same argument, however, suggests that these limitation can be quite severe for the control inputs; if both favorable and unfavorable alternatives are possible the control inputs have no way of forcing the system to take the favorable path.

   The results given below rely on a number of assumptions needed to ensure well posedness of the models and convergence of the algorithms. These assumptions are summarized below; not all assumptions are needed for all results though.

Assumption 1. *1. The continuous state space is $X = \mathbb{R}^n$. The set Q is finite. The sets U, Υ, D and Δ are compact subsets of Euclidean spaces.*
2. For all $q \in Q$ the function $f(q, x, u, d)$ is globally Lipschitz continuous in x, continuous in u and d and bounded. For all $(q, x) \in Q \times X$, the set $\bigcup_{d \in D} f(q, x, u, d)$ is convex and compact for all $u \in U$. U is convex and f is affine in u, i.e., $f(q, x, u, d) = g(x, d) + h(x, d)u$.
3. For all $q, q' \in Q$, the function $r(q, q', x, v, \delta)$ is continuous in x, v and δ.
4. For all $q, q' \in Q$, the set $G(q, q')$ is open (possibly the empty set).
5. For all $q \in Q$, the set $Dom(q)$ is open and $Dom(q) \cup \bigcup_{q' \in Q} G(q, q') = X$.

Under Assumption 1 one can show that infinite (possibly Zeno) runs exist for all choices of inputs and disturbance.

2.3   Pursuit-Evasion Games and Strategies

In this paper we concentrate on reachability problems for hybrid game automata. Following [7, 8] we assume that we are given a hybrid game automaton and a set of desirable states, $F \subseteq Q \times X$, and are asked to select the control inputs to keep the state in F whenever possible; borrowing notation from temporal logic we will say that runs that have this property meet the safety specification $\Box[(q, x) \in F]$.

Since there are both control and disturbance inputs involved, the reachability problems can be cast in the framework of pursuit evasion games. Formulating these games precisely requires one to introduce an appropriate notion of strategy. To this end, we first recall the standard notion of non-anticipative strategy for continuous, differential games [25, 11, 15].

Definition 5 (Non-anticipative). *A function $\alpha(\cdot, \cdot, \cdot) : \mathcal{D} \times Q \times X \to \mathcal{U}$ is called non-anticipative (with respect to the first variable) if for all $(q, x) \in Q \times X$, $d(\cdot), d'(\cdot) \in \mathcal{D}$ and $T \geq 0$, if $d(t) = d'(t)$ for almost every $t \in [0, T]$ then $\alpha(d, q, x)(t) = \alpha(d', q, x)(t)$ for almost every $t \in [0, T]$.*

A non-anticipative function $\beta(\cdot, \cdot, \cdot) : \mathcal{U} \times Q \times X \to \mathcal{D}$ can be defined analogously. As will soon become apparent, (q, x) in Definition 5 plays the role of the initial condition. Definition 5 coincides effectively with the classical definition of non-anticipative strategy for differential two player games [25, 11, 15]. The only difference is that we have made explicit the dependence of the control input generated by the strategy at time t not only on the disturbance input up to time t, but also on the initial condition (q, x). Given an initial condition $(\hat{q}, \hat{x}) \in Q \times X$, an $\alpha(\cdot, \cdot, \cdot) : \mathcal{D} \times Q \times X \to \mathcal{U}$ non-anticipative and a $d(\cdot) \in \mathcal{D}$ we use $\phi(t, \hat{q}, \hat{x}, \alpha, d)$ to denote the unique solution of

$$\dot{x}(t) = f(\hat{q}, x(t), \alpha(d, \hat{q}, \hat{x})(t), d(t))$$

starting at $x(0) = \hat{x}$. Notice that since any "open-loop" $u(\cdot) \in \mathcal{U}$, $d(\cdot) \in \mathcal{D}$ can also be thought of as trivial non-anticipative strategies we will also use $\phi(t, \hat{q}, \hat{x}, u, d)$ to denote the solution to the differential equation $\dot{x}(t) = f(\hat{q}, x(t), u(t), d(t))$ starting at $x(0) = \hat{x}$. We also use $\phi(t, \hat{q}, \hat{x}, u, d)$ with $u \in U$ and/or $d \in D$ to denote the solution under constant inputs. The interpretation should be clear from the context.

Building on the non-anticipative notion, we can now define a notion of strategy for hybrid game automata.

Definition 6 (Hybrid strategy). *A hybrid strategy (α, γ) for the control inputs v and u consists of a non-anticipative function, $\alpha(\cdot, \cdot, \cdot) : \mathcal{D} \times Q \times X \to \mathcal{U}$ and a feedback function $\gamma(\cdot, \cdot) : Q \times X \to \Upsilon$.*

Given a hybrid strategy (α, γ) for the control inputs one can define the "closed-loop" runs of the hybrid game automaton. These will be runs $(\tau, q, x, v, u, \delta, d)$ of the hybrid game automaton that for some disturbance inputs $\hat{d}(\cdot) \in \mathcal{D}$ and $\{\hat{\delta}_i\}_{i=0}^{\infty}$ satisfy:

- For all $I_i \in \tau$ and all $t \in I_i$, $d_i(t) = \hat{d}(t)$, $\delta_i(t) = \hat{\delta}_i$, $u_i(t) = \alpha(d \downarrow_{\tau_i}$
  $(\cdot), q_i(\tau_i), x_i(\tau_i))(t - \tau_i)$.
- For $i < N$, $v_{i+1}(\tau_{i+1}) = \gamma(q_i(\tau_i'), x_i(\tau_i'))$.

(In addition to the constraints imposed by Definition 4).

Coming back to the reachability problem, we would like to find a strategy for the control inputs to keep the state in F for all actions of the disturbance.

Definition 7 (Hybrid discriminating domain). *A closed set $K \subseteq Q \times X$ is called a hybrid discriminating domain if there exists a hybrid strategy (α, γ) for the control inputs such that all the closed loop runs, $(\tau, q, x, v, u, \delta, d)$, with $(q_0(\tau_0), x_0(\tau_0)) \in K$ are such that $(q_i(t), x_i(t)) \in K$ for all $I_i \in \tau$ and all $t \in I_i$.*

In general, the set F in the safety specification $\Box[(q, x) \in F]$ will not be a discriminating domain, and therefore it will be impossible to meet the safety specification for all initial conditions in F. We call the largest subset of F for which it is possible to meet the specification the discriminating kernel of F.

Definition 8 (Hybrid discriminating kernel). *The hybrid discriminating kernel, $\mathrm{Disc}(F)$, of a closed set $F \subseteq Q \times X$ is the set*

$$\{(q, x) \in F \mid \exists \text{ hybrid strategy } (\alpha, \gamma) \text{ such that } \forall d(\cdot) \in \mathcal{D}, \forall \{\delta_i\}_{i=0}^{\infty},$$
$$\text{all closed loop runs starting at } (q, x) \text{ remain in } F\}.$$

We shall see (Theorem 2) that the hybrid discriminating kernel is closed and it is the largest closed hybrid discriminating domain contained in F. Note that here we have defined hybrid discriminating kernels and domains by properties of the trajectories, while usually ([14, 15, 16, 17] and Definition 10 of the present paper) they are defined through Hamiltonians. This ambiguity will disappear when we show that both definitions coincide under our assumptions, as can be deduced from Theorems 2, 3 and 4.

3   Main Procedure and Results

Following [8, 9] we define two operators, $\mathrm{Pre}^{\exists} : 2^{Q \times X} \to 2^{Q \times X}$ and $\mathrm{Pre}^{\forall} : 2^{Q \times X} \to 2^{Q \times X}$ by

$$\mathrm{Pre}^{\exists}(K) = \{(q, x) \in K \mid [x \notin \mathrm{Dom}(q)] \wedge [\exists v \in \Upsilon, \forall \delta \in \Delta, \forall q' \in Q,$$
$$x \in G(q, q') \Rightarrow (q', r(q, q', x, v, \delta)) \in K]\}$$
$$\mathrm{Pre}^{\forall}(K) = K^c \cup \{(q, x) \in K \mid \forall v \in \Upsilon, \exists \delta \in \Delta, \exists q' \in Q,$$
$$[x \in G(q, q')] \wedge [(q', r(q, q', x, v, \delta)) \notin K]\}$$

In words, $\mathrm{Pre}^{\exists}(K)$ contains all states in K for which a discrete transition is forced to take place and there exists a choice for the discrete controls such that for all choices of the discrete disturbance the state after the discrete transition is bound to also be in the set K. $\mathrm{Pre}^{\forall}(K)$, on the other hand, contains all states outside of K, plus all states for which for all choices of the discrete controls there exists a choice for the discrete disturbance such that a transition to a state outside of K is possible.

The operators $\mathrm{Pre}^{\exists}$ and $\mathrm{Pre}^{\forall}$ encode the reachability implications of the discrete dynamics. To capture the reachability implications of the continuous dynamics we introduce a third operator, Reach : $2^{Q \times X} \times 2^{Q \times X} \to 2^{Q \times X}$ given by[1]:

$$\mathrm{Reach}(K, L) = \{(q, x) \in Q \times X \mid \exists \alpha(\cdot, q, x) : \mathcal{D} \to \mathcal{U} \text{ non-anticipative, } \forall d(\cdot) \in \mathcal{D},$$
$$[\forall t \geq 0, \ (q, x(t)) \notin L]$$
$$\vee [\exists T \geq 0, \ ((q, x(T)) \in K) \wedge (\forall t \in [0, T], \ (q, x(t)) \notin L)]\},$$

where we abbreviate $x(\cdot) = \phi(\cdot, q, x, \alpha, d)$. In words, the operator Reach returns the set of states for which there exists a non-anticipative strategy for the controls such that whatever the disturbance does the state will evolve continuously and either avoid the set L altogether, or reach the set K before reaching L.

The hybrid discriminating kernel of a set can now be characterized in terms of the three operators, $\mathrm{Pre}^{\exists}$, $\mathrm{Pre}^{\forall}$ and Reach. The first step is to show all hybrid discriminating domains are fixed points of an appropriate operator.

Theorem 1. *A closed set K is a hybrid discriminating domain if and only if $Reach(Pre^{\exists}(K), Pre^{\forall}(K)) = K$.*

Proof (sketch): *Sufficiency:* Assume that K is a hybrid discriminating domain. Let (α, γ) denote the strategy of Definition 7 and $R = \mathrm{Reach}(\mathrm{Pre}^{\exists}(K), \mathrm{Pre}^{\forall}(K))$. It is easy to show that $R \subseteq K$. To prove that $K \subseteq R$, consider an arbitrary $(\hat{q}, \hat{x}) \in K$. Notice that if $(\hat{q}, \hat{x}) \in \mathrm{Pre}^{\exists}(K)$, then $(\hat{q}, \hat{x}) \in R$ and the sufficiency proof is complete. Assume now that $(\hat{q}, \hat{x}) \in K \setminus \mathrm{Pre}^{\exists}(K)$. By the definition of $\mathrm{Pre}^{\exists}$ either $\hat{x} \in \mathrm{Dom}(\hat{q})$, or there exists $\hat{\delta}$ and $\hat{q}'$ such that $\hat{x} \in G(\hat{q}, \hat{q}')$ and $(\hat{q}', r(\hat{q}, \hat{q}', \hat{x}, \gamma(\hat{q}, \hat{x}), \hat{\delta})) \notin K$. In the latter case, there exists a run with $\tau_0 = \tau_0' = 0$, $q_0(\tau_0) = \hat{q}$, $x_0(\tau_0) = \hat{x}$, $q_1(\tau_1) = \hat{q}'$, $v_1(\tau_1) = \gamma(\hat{q}, \hat{x})$, $\delta(\tau_1) = \hat{\delta}$ and $x_1(\tau_1) = r(\hat{q}, \hat{q}', \hat{x}, \gamma(\hat{q}, \hat{x}), \hat{\delta})$ that leaves K immediately by a discrete transition. This violates the assumption that K is a hybrid discriminating domain.

Finally, assume that $(\hat{q}, \hat{x}) \in K \setminus \mathrm{Pre}^{\exists}(K)$ and $\hat{x} \in \mathrm{Dom}(\hat{q})$. For arbitrary $d(\cdot) \in \mathcal{D}$ let $x(\cdot) = \phi(\cdot, \hat{q}, \hat{x}, \alpha, d)$. Since $\mathrm{Dom}(\hat{q})$ is open, under Assumption 1 there exists $\theta > 0$ such that $x(t) \in \mathrm{Dom}(\hat{q})$ for all $t \in [0, \theta]$. Let $\hat{\theta}$ denote the sup of such θ. Notice that for all $t \in [0, \hat{\theta})$ we must have $(\hat{q}, x(t)) \notin \mathrm{Pre}^{\forall}(K)$. If $\hat{\theta} = \infty$ then we are done. Otherwise, $x(\hat{\theta}) \notin \mathrm{Dom}(\hat{q})$ and $(\hat{q}, x(\hat{\theta})) \in \mathrm{Pre}^{\exists}(K) \cup \mathrm{Pre}^{\forall}(K)$. If $(\hat{q}, x(\hat{\theta})) \in \mathrm{Pre}^{\exists}(K)$ the sufficiency proof is complete. The case $(\hat{q}, x(\hat{\theta})) \in \mathrm{Pre}^{\forall}(K)$ is impossible.

Necessity: We assume that $\mathrm{Reach}(\mathrm{Pre}^{\exists}(K), \mathrm{Pre}^{\forall}(K)) = K$ and construct a hybrid strategy, (α, γ) satisfying Definition 7. For $(\hat{q}, \hat{x}) \notin K$ take $\alpha(d, \hat{q}, \hat{x})$ and $\gamma(\hat{q}, \hat{x})$ arbitrary. For $(\hat{q}, \hat{x}) \in K$, we first define $\gamma : Q \times X \to \Upsilon$. If

---

[1] This operator is different (in a sense dual) from the Reach-Avoid operator defined in [8, 9].

$(\hat{q}, \hat{x}) \notin \mathrm{Pre}^{\exists}(K)$ take $\gamma(\hat{q}, \hat{x})$ to be any $\hat{\upsilon} \in \Upsilon$. If $(\hat{q}, \hat{x}) \in \mathrm{Pre}^{\exists}(K)$ then there exists a $\hat{\upsilon}$ such that for all δ and for all $\hat{q}'$ with $\hat{x} \in G(\hat{q}, \hat{q}')$ we have that $(\hat{q}', r(\hat{q}, \hat{q}', \hat{x}, \hat{\upsilon}, \delta)) \in K$. We take $\gamma(\hat{q}, \hat{x}) = \hat{\upsilon}$. To define α for $(\hat{q}, \hat{x}) \in K = \mathrm{Reach}(\mathrm{Pre}^{\exists}(K), \mathrm{Pre}^{\forall}(K))$, notice that, by definition of Reach, there exists a non-anticipative strategy such that for all $d(\cdot) \in \mathcal{D}$ the solution either never reaches $\mathrm{Pre}^{\forall}(K)$ or reaches $\mathrm{Pre}^{\exists}(K)$ before it reaches $\mathrm{Pre}^{\forall}(K)$. We let α be the strategy that achieves this. One can easily show that under the strategy (α, γ) all runs starting in K stay in K for ever.   ∎

Theorem 1 suggests that one should be able to compute the hybrid discriminating kernel of a set F as the maximal fixed point of the operator $\mathrm{Reach}(\mathrm{Pre}^{\exists}(\cdot), \mathrm{Pre}^{\forall}(\cdot))$. A standard procedure for doing this is by recursive application of the operator, as shown in the following algorithm.

Algorithm 1 (Discriminating kernel approximation)

> **initialization:** $W_0 = F$, $i = 0$
> **repeat**
> $$W_{i+1} = \mathrm{Reach}(\mathrm{Pre}^{\exists}(W_i), \mathrm{Pre}^{\forall}(W_i))$$
> $$i = i + 1$$
> **until** $W_i = W_{i-1}$
> **set** $W_\infty = \bigcap_{i=0}^{\infty} W_i$

Theorem 2. W_∞ is the hybrid discriminating kernel of F. Moreover, it is the largest closed hybrid discriminating domain contained in F.

Proof (sketch): We show first that $\mathrm{Disc}(F) \subseteq W_\infty$. Since $\mathrm{Disc}(F) \subseteq F$ and $W_\infty \subseteq F$, it suffices to show that $F \setminus W_\infty \subseteq F \setminus \mathrm{Disc}(F)$. Take $(\hat{q}, \hat{x}) \in F \setminus W_\infty$. Fix any hybrid strategy (α, γ). We show that we can find a closed loop run starting at $(q_0(\tau_0), x_0(\tau_0)) = (\hat{q}, \hat{x})$ leaving F in finite time and after a finite number of discrete transitions, thus proving that $(\hat{q}, \hat{x}) \notin \mathrm{Disc}(F)$.

Since $(\hat{q}, \hat{x}) \notin W_\infty$, there exists i such that $(\hat{q}, \hat{x}) \notin W_i$. Note that $(\hat{q}, \hat{x}) \notin \mathrm{Pre}^{\exists}(W_{i-1})$. Therefore, either $\hat{x} \in \mathrm{Dom}(\hat{q})$, or there exists $\hat{\delta}$ and $\hat{q}'$ such that $\hat{x} \in G(\hat{q}, \hat{q}')$ and $(\hat{q}', r(\hat{q}, \hat{q}', \hat{x}, \gamma(\hat{q}, \hat{x}), \hat{\delta})) \notin W_{i-1}$. In the latter case, set $\tau_0' = 0$, $q_1(\tau_1) = \hat{q}'$, $x_1(\tau_1) = r(\hat{q}, \hat{q}', \hat{x}, \gamma(\hat{q}, \hat{x}), \hat{\delta}))$ and notice that $(q_1(\tau_1), x_1(\tau_1)) \notin W_{i-1}$. If now $\hat{x} \in \mathrm{Dom}(\hat{q})$, there exists $d(\cdot)$ such that the solution to $\phi(\cdot, \hat{q}, \hat{x}, \alpha, d)$ reaches $\mathrm{Pre}^{\forall}(W_{i-1})$ without first reaching $\mathrm{Pre}^{\exists}(W_{i-1})$. It is easy to see that there exists $T \geq 0$ such that $x(T) \in \mathrm{Pre}^{\forall}(W_{i-1})$ and for all $t \in [0, T)$, $x(t) \in \mathrm{Dom}(\hat{q}) \setminus \mathrm{Pre}^{\exists}(W_{i-1})$. Let $x_0(t) = x(t)$ for all $t \in [0, T]$. By the definition of $\mathrm{Pre}^{\forall}$, either $(q(T), x_0(T)) \notin W_{i-1}$ or there exist $\hat{\delta}$ and $\hat{q}'$ such that $x_0(T) \in G(\hat{q}, \hat{q}')$ and $(\hat{q}', r(\hat{q}, \hat{q}', x_0(T), \gamma(\hat{q}, x_0(T)), \hat{\delta})) \notin W_{i-1}$. In the latter case, set $\tau_0' = T$, $q_1(\tau_1) = \hat{q}'$ and $x_1(\tau_1) = r(\hat{q}, \hat{q}', x_0(T), \gamma(\hat{q}, x_0(T)), \hat{\delta})$ and notice that $\tau_1 = T < \infty$ and $(q_1(\tau_1), x_1(\tau_1)) \notin W_{i-1}$.

Iterating i times we construct a run that leaves $W_0 = F$ in finite time and after at most i discrete transitions. Hence for any α we have found d and $\{\delta_i\}_i$ such that the associated run starting from $(\hat{q}, \hat{x})$, leaves F in finite time. Hence $(\hat{q}, \hat{x}) \notin \mathrm{Disc}(F)$.

To complete the proof we need to show that $W_\infty \subseteq \text{Disc}(F)$. This can be done as in the proof of Theorem 4 (argument omitted).   ∎

4 Characterization of the Reach Operator

In this section we provide a characterization of the set Reach based on non-smooth analysis tools. Note that $\text{Reach}(K, L)$ can be computed separately for each discrete state, by taking the disjoint union of the sets

$$\text{Reach}_q(K_q, L_q) = \{x \in X \mid \exists \alpha(\cdot, q, x) : \mathcal{D} \to \mathcal{U} \text{ non-anticipative}, \forall d(\cdot) \in \mathcal{D},$$
$$[\forall t \geq 0, \; x(t) \notin L_q]$$
$$\vee [\exists T \geq 0, \; (x(T) \in K_q) \wedge (\forall t \in [0, T], \; x(t) \notin L_q)]\},$$

where $K_q = \{x \in X \mid (q, x) \in K\}$ and $L_q = \{x \in X \mid (q, x) \in L\}$. Throughout this section we will therefore assume that the discrete state has a constant value.

The characterization of Reach is closely related to the characterization of the victory domains for two player, two target games developed in [16]. The key difference is that in [16] one of the two targets is treated as a state constraint that all trajectories are forced to respect. By contrast, the situation is more symmetric in our case: the dynamics do not constrain the system to stay out of either target set, it is the players that try to reach or avoid the target sets in order to win the game. In [16] the main goal was to deal with state constrained differential games. This required the introduction of a number of additional assumptions. For example, the continuous state was assumed to be separated into two parts, one controlled by u and the other by d. Moreover, transversality conditions on the constraint sets were imposed. In this section, because we do not deal with state constrained games, we show how these assumptions can be relaxed and hence obtain a more general characterization of the Reach operator.

Consider a continuous two target game with dynamics $\dot{x} = f(q, x, u, d)$, state $x \in X$ and players $u \in U$ (Ursula) and $d \in D$ (David). Let $K_q \subseteq X$ be a closed target for Ursula and $L_q \subseteq X$ an open evasion set for David. Ursula aims either to avoid L_q altogether, or to reach K_q before reaching L_q. David aims to reach L_q in finite time, without first reaching K_q. To achieve their aims for a given initial state $x_0 \in X$ the two players are allowed to play non-anticipative strategies, $\alpha(\cdot, q, x_0) : \mathcal{D} \to \mathcal{U}$ for Ursula and $\beta(\cdot, q, x_0) : \mathcal{U} \to \mathcal{D}$ for David.

Definition 9 (Ursula's victory domains). *Ursula's victory domain is the set of initial states $x_0 \in X$ for which she can find a non-anticipative strategy $\alpha(\cdot, q, x_0) : \mathcal{D} \to \mathcal{U}$ such that for all $d(\cdot) \in \mathcal{D}$ played by David, the trajectory $\phi(t, q, x_0, \alpha, d)$ either avoids L_q for ever, or avoids L_q as long as it does not reach K_q.*

David's victory domain can be defined in a similar way [26]. We will not provide the definition and characterization of this set here, because of the following fact.

Proposition 1. *The victory domain of Ursula is the desired set $Reach_q(K_q, L_q)$.*

Therefore to complete the characterization of the hybrid discriminating kernel of Section 3 if suffices to characterize Ursula's victory domain.

For a given closed set $K_q \subseteq \mathbb{R}^n$, let us introduce the following Hamiltonian.

$$H(x, p) = \begin{cases} \sup_{d \in D} \inf_{u \in U} \langle f(q, x, u, d), p \rangle, & \text{if } x \notin K_q, \\ \min\{0, \sup_{d \in D} \inf_{u \in U} \langle f(q, x, u, d), p \rangle\}, & \text{otherwise.} \end{cases} \tag{2}$$

It is easy to show that if K_q is closed, H is lower semi-continuous.

Definition 10. *A closed set $W \subseteq X$ is a discriminating domain for f if for all $x \in W$ and all $p \in NP_W(x)$, $H(x, p) \leq 0$.*

Because H is lower semi-continuous, it can be shown that [26] any closed $W \subseteq \mathbb{R}^n$ contains a maximal discriminating kernel for f, denoted by $\mathrm{Disc}_f(W)$. In the rest of this section we show that the desired set $Reach_q(K_q, L_q)$ is in fact the discriminating kernel of the set L_q^c. This completes the theoretical characterization of of the hybrid discriminating kernel and enables the use of numerical algorithms developed for viability computations in differential games [18, 19].

We first provide an interpretation of discriminating domains in terms of non-anticipative strategies for Ursula.

Theorem 3. *A closed set $W \subseteq \mathbb{R}^n$ is a discriminating domain for f if and only if for any initial position $x_0 \in W$, there exists a non-anticipative strategy $\alpha(\cdot, q, x_0) : \mathcal{D} \to \mathcal{U}$ such that for any d, the solution $\phi(t, q, x_0, \alpha, d)$ remains in W until it reaches K_q (or remains in W on $[0, +\infty)$ if it never reaches K_q).*

The following theorem provides a connection between the discriminating kernel of a set and the game winning positions for Ursula, and hence the computation of the operator $Reach_q$ needed for the hybrid discriminating kernel characterization.

Theorem 4. *The discriminating kernel of closed set $W \subseteq \mathbb{R}^n$, for f is the set of $x_0 \in W$, for which there exists a non-anticipative strategy $\alpha(\cdot, q, x_0) : \mathcal{D} \to \mathcal{U}$ such that for any $d(\cdot) \in \mathcal{D}$, the solution $\phi(t, q, x_0, \alpha, d)$ remains in W until it reaches K_q (or remains in W on $[0, +\infty)$ if it never reaches K_q).*

5 Example

To illustrate the construction of the hybrid discriminating kernel, we apply the algorithm to a toy example. For more realistic problems in highway automation and in air traffic management where our algorithm is applicable the reader is referred to [6, 8, 27, 10].

Consider a hybrid game automaton with $Q = \{q\}$, $X = \mathbb{R}$, $U = D = \Upsilon = \Delta = [-1, 1]$, $f(q, x, u, d) = u + |x|d$, $\mathrm{Dom}(q) = (-\infty, 2)$, $G(q, q) = (0, \infty)$ and $r(q, q, x, \upsilon, \delta) = 4(1 - |x - 1|)\delta$. Since there is only one discrete state, we drop the dependence on q everywhere to simplify the notation. We would like to compute the hybrid discriminating kernel of the set $[-2, 2]$. Notice that even though the system is very simple, it still possesses some challenging features: nonlinear continuous and discrete dynamics and a choice between continuous evolution and discrete transition in the interval $(0, 2)$.

Applying the algorithm, we set $W_0 = [-2, 2]$. It is easy to see that $\mathrm{Pre}^{\exists}(W_0) = \{2\}$. Moreover,

$$
\begin{aligned}
\mathrm{Pre}^{\forall}(W_0) =&(-\infty, 2) \cup (2, \infty) \\
&\cup \{x \in [0, 2] \mid \exists \delta \in [-1, 1], (r(x, \delta) < -2) \vee (r(x, \delta) > 2)\} \\
=&(-\infty, 2) \cup (2, \infty) \cup (1/2, 3/2).
\end{aligned}
$$

Because d can dominate u whenever $|x| > 1$, we then have $W_1 = [-1, 1/2] \cup \{2\}$.

At the second step of the algorithm we get $\mathrm{Pre}^{\exists}(W_1) = \{2\}$ and

$$
\mathrm{Pre}^{\forall}(W_1) = (-\infty, -1) \cup (1/8, 2) \cup (2, \infty).
$$

Therefore, $W_2 = [-1, 1/8] \cup \{2\}$.

More generally, it is easy to see that at step i of the algorithm we get the set

$$
W_i = \left[-1, \frac{2}{4^i}\right] \cup \{2\}.
$$

This sequence converges to the hybrid discriminating kernel

$$
\mathrm{Disc}([-2, 2]) = [-1, 0] \cup \{2\}.
$$

The strategy for u that keeps the state in $\mathrm{Disc}([-2, 2])$ can in this case be expressed in feedback terms: any $u(x)$ with $u(-1) = 1$, and $u(0) \leq 0$ is adequate for this task. Notice that v does not enter any of the equations.

6   Concluding Remarks

Motivated by problems of safe controller synthesis for hybrid systems, we developed an approach to pursuit-evasion games for a fairly general class of hybrid systems. We introduced a notion of a hybrid strategy and developed a characterization of the game winning positions for the control inputs. These are readily identified with what are known in the literature as maximal controlled invariant sets, i.e. the maximal set of states for which a controller that meets a given safety specification exists. The continuous part of the argument required an extension of classical results for two player, single target differential pursuit evasion games to a class of differential games with two players and two targets.

Even though the class of hybrid systems treated here are rather general, they are still not as general as one would like. The main limitation is that the models do not allow control inputs to force discrete transitions. Current work concentrates on alleviating this restriction.

With the approach adopted in this paper, control inputs view the disturbances as an adversary. As a consequence, the controller design methodology is worst case: the aim is to ensure that specifications are met for any realization of the disturbance inputs. Even though this is a standard approach for many problems in the literature (including pursuit-evasion games and robust control) it is too conservative for some applications, where substantial levels of uncertainty are present. In such cases it may be more realistic to assume a probabilistic characterization of the disturbances and design controllers that take this into account (e.g. work "on the average", or guarantee specifications with certain probability). An approach to safety problems for such stochastic hybrid systems is another topic of our current research.

Acknowledgment. The authors are grateful to Eva Crück for helpful discussions on appropriate notions of strategy for hybrid games. The work was supported by the EPSRC under grant GR/R51575/01 and by the European Commission under the project COLUMBUS, IST-2001-38314 and the Network of Excellence HYCON, IST-511368.

References

1. W. Thomas, "On the synthesis of strategies in infinite games," in *Proceedings of STACS 95*, ser. LNCS, E. Mayr and C. Puech, Eds. Berlin: Springer-Verlag, 1995, vol. 900, pp. 1–13.
2. P. J. G. Ramadge and W. M. Wonham, "The control of discrete event systems," *Proceedings of the IEEE*, vol. Vol.77, no. 1, pp. 81–98, 1989.
3. O. Maler, A. Pnueli, and J. Sifakis, "On the synthesis of discrete controllers for timed systems," in *Theoretical Aspects of Computer Science*, ser. LNCS, no. 900. Berlin: Springer-Verlag, 1995, pp. 229–242.
4. M. Heymann, F. Lin, and G. Meyer, "Synthesis and viability of minimally interventive legal controllers for hybrid systems," *Discrete Event Dynamic Systems: Theory and Applications*, vol. 8, no. 2, pp. 105–135, June 1998.
5. H. Wong-Toi, "The synthesis of controllers for linear hybrid automata," in *IEEE Conference on Decision and Control*, San Diego, California, December 10–12 1997, pp. 4607–4613.
6. J. Lygeros, D. Godbole, and S. Sastry, "Verified hybrid controllers for automated vehicles," *IEEE Transactions on Automatic Control*, vol. 43, no. 4, pp. 522–539, April 1998.
7. J. Lygeros, C. Tomlin, and S. Sastry, "Controllers for reachability specifications for hybrid systems," *Automatica*, vol. 35, no. 3, pp. 349–370, March 1999.
8. C. Tomlin, J. Lygeros, and S. Sastry, "A game theoretic approach to controller design for hybrid systems," *Proceedings of the IEEE*, vol. 88, no. 7, pp. 949–969, July 2000.
9. C. Tomlin, "Hybrid control of air traffic management systems," Ph.D. dissertation, Department of Electrical Engineering and Computer Sciences, University of California, Berkeley, 1998.
10. I. M. Mitchell, "Application of level set methods to control and reachability problems in continuous and hybrid systems," Ph.D. dissertation, Stanford University, 2002.
11. L. Evans and P. Souganidis, "Differential games and representation formulas for solutions of Hamilton–Jacobi–Isaacs equations," *Indiana University Mathematics Journal*, vol. 33, no. 5, pp. 773–797, 1984.

12. J. Lygeros, "On reachability and minimum cost optimal control," *Automatica*, vol. 40, no. 6, pp. 917–927, 2004.

13. I. Mitchell, A. Bayen, and C. Tomlin, "A time-dependent Hamilton–Jacobi formulation of reachable sets for continuous dynamic games," *IEEE Transactions on Automatic Control*, vol. 70, no. 7, pp. 947–957, 2005.

14. P. Cardaliaguet, "Domaines discriminants et jeux différentiels," Ph.D. dissertation, Université Paris IX Dauphine, 1993.

15. ——, "A differential game with two players and one target," *SIAM Journal on Control and Optimization*, vol. 34, no. 4, pp. 1441–1460, 1996.

16. P. Cardaliaguet, M. Quincampoix, and P. Saint-Pierre, "Pursuit differential games with state constraints," *SIAM Journal on Control and Optimization*, vol. 39, no. 5, pp. 1615–1632, 2001.

17. E. Crück, "Contrôle et jeux différentiels des systèmes hybrides et impulsionnels: Problèmes de cible at de viabilité," Ph.D. dissertation, Université de Bretagne Occidentale, 2003.

18. P. Cardaliaguet, M. Quincampoix, and P. Saint-Pierre, "Set-valued numerical analysis for optimal control and differential games," in *Stochastic and Differential Games: Theory and Numerical Methods*, ser. Annals of the International Society of Dynamic Games, M. Bardi, T. Raghavan, and T. Parthasarathy, Eds. Boston, MA: Birkhäuser, 1999, no. 4, pp. 177–247.

19. ——, "Numerical schemes for discontinuous value functions of optimal control," *Set-Valued Analysis*, vol. 8, pp. 111–126, 2000.

20. J.-P. Aubin, J. Lygeros, M. Quincampoix, S. Sastry, and N. Seube, "Impulse differential inclusions: A viability approach to hybrid systems," *IEEE Transactions on Automatic Control*, vol. 47, no. 1, pp. 2–20, January 2002.

21. Y. Gao, J. Lygeros, M. Quincampoix, and N. Seube, "On the control of uncertain impulsive systems: Approximate stabilization and controlled invariance," *International Journal of Control*, vol. 77, no. 16, pp. 1393–1407, 2004.

22. J.-P. Aubin and H. Frankowska, *Set-Valued Analysis*. Boston, MA: Birkhäuser, 1990.

23. J. Lygeros, K. Johansson, S. Simić, J. Zhang, and S. Sastry, "Dynamical properties of hybrid automata," *IEEE Transactions on Automatic Control*, vol. 48, no. 1, pp. 2–17, January 2003.

24. R. Goebel, J. Hespanha, A. Teel, C. Cai, and R. Sanfelice, "Hybrid systems: Generalized solutions and robust stability," in *IFAC Symposium on Nonlinear Control Systems*, September 2004.

25. P. Varaiya, "On the existance of solutions to a differential game," *SIAM Journal on Control*, vol. 5, no. 1, pp. 153–162, 1967.

26. P. Cardaliaguet, "Nonsmooth semi-permeable barriers, isaacs equation and application to a differential game with one target and two players," *Applied Mathematics and Optimization*, vol. 36, pp. 125–146, 1997.

27. C. Tomlin, I. Mitchell, and R. Ghosh, "Safety verification of conflict resolution manoeuvres," *IEEE Transactions on Intelligent Transportation Systems*, vol. 2, no. 2, pp. 110–120, June 2001.

Efficient Computation of Reachable Sets of Linear Time-Invariant Systems with Inputs[*]

Antoine Girard[1], Colas Le Guernic[2], and Oded Maler[3]

[1] Department of Electrical and Systems Engineering,
University of Pennsylvania, PA 19104, Philadelphia
agirard@seas.upenn.edu
[2] École Normale Supérieure,
45 rue d'Ulm, 75005 Paris, France
Colas.Le.Guernic@ens.fr
[3] VERIMAG, 2 avenue de Vignate, 38610 Gières, France
Oded.Maler@imag.fr

Abstract. This work is concerned with the problem of computing the set of reachable states for linear time-invariant systems with bounded inputs. Our main contribution is a novel algorithm which improves significantly the computational complexity of reachability analysis. Algorithms to compute over and under-approximations of the reachable sets are proposed as well. These algorithms are not subject to the *wrapping effect* and therefore our approximations are *tight*. We show that these approximations are useful in the context of hybrid systems verification and control synthesis. The performance of a prototype implementation of the algorithm confirms its qualities and gives hope for scaling up verification technology for continuous and hybrid systems.

1 Introduction

Computing reachable states for continuous or hybrid systems subject to bounded disturbances has become a major research issue in hybrid systems [ACH+95], [G96], [CK98], [DM98], [CK03], [GM99], [ABDM00], [BT00], [MT00], [KV00], [D00] [ADG03], [G05], [F05]. One may argue that focusing on this question, which is concerned with *transient* behaviors of dynamical systems, can be seen as a major contribution of computer science to enriching the ensemble of standard questions (stability, controllability) traditionally posed in control [ABD+00], [M02]. For hybrid systems in which the continuous dynamics has constant derivatives in every discrete state, such as timed automata or "linear" hybrid automata, the computation of the reachable states in a continuous phase is simply a matter of linear algebra [ACH+95], [AMP95], [HHW97], [F05]. For systems with a non-trivial continuous dynamics, an approximation of the reachable states is generally computed by a combination of numerical integration and geometrical algorithms [GM99], [CK03], [ABDM00], [D00], [BT00], [KV00] [G05].

[*] This work was partially supported by the European Community projects IST-2001-33520 CC (Control and Computation) and IST-2003-507219 PROSYD (Property-based System Design) as well as by the project CalCel of région Rhône-Alpes.

João Hespanha and A. Tiwari (Eds.): HSCC 2006, LNCS 3927, pp. 257–271, 2006.

As an illustration consider a continuous linear time-invariant system of the form $\dot{x}(t) = Ax(t)$. The computation of the set of states reachable from an initial set I within a time interval $[0, T]$ can be handled as follows. We choose an integration step $r = T/(N+1)$ and compute a sequence of sets $\Omega_0, \ldots, \Omega_N$ such that Ω_i contains all the states reachable from I within $[ir, (i+1)r]$ time. The first set of the sequence, Ω_0, can be obtained by bloating the convex hull of the sets I and ΦI where $\Phi = e^{rA}$ (see [CK03], [ABDM00], [D00], [G05]). Then, the other elements of the sequence can be computed from the recurrence relation $\Omega_{i+1} = \Phi\Omega_i$. For obvious reasons, the choice of the representation of the sets Ω_i usually consists of classes of sets closed under linear transformations such as polytopes [CK03], [ABDM00], ellipsoids [KV97], [KV00], [BT00] or zonotopes [G05].

When dealing with continuous linear time-invariant systems with bounded inputs of the form $\dot{x}(t) = Ax(t) + Bu(t)$, where the value of $u(t)$ is constrained in some bounded convex set, a similar algorithm is possible. The computation of the influence of the inputs on the reachable sets can be handled according to two main approaches. The first one uses techniques borrowed from optimal control [V98], [ABDM00], [KV00] to compute for each point on the boundary of Ω_i the input u that transforms it in the most "outward" manner. The second approach consists in computing the reachable set using the autonomous dynamics $\dot{x}(t) = Ax(t)$ and then adding (in the sense of the Minkowski sum) a set which accounts for the influence of the inputs [ADG03], [G05]. The recurrence relation between Ω_i and Ω_{i+1} is then of the form $\Omega_{i+1} = \Phi\Omega_i \oplus U$ where U is a bounded convex set. This is the approach considered in this paper.

The major contribution of this paper is a new implementation scheme for the recurrence relation $\Omega_{i+1} = \Phi\Omega_i \oplus U$ which improves significantly (both theoretically and empirically) the computation of the reachable sets of linear time-invariant (LTI) systems with bounded inputs. A version of this algorithm based on *zonotopes* decisively outperforms related algorithms. In addition, algorithms for the computation of over- and under-approximations of the reachable sets are proposed. These algorithms are not subject to the *wrapping effect* (propagation of approximation errors through the computations [K98], [K99]) and therefore our approximations are *tight* in the sense of [KV00]. In the context of hybrid systems, we show that over- and under-approximations can be computed such that they both intersect the guards if and only if the exact reachable set does. We also show that our under-approximations can be used for control synthesis.

2   Reachability Computations for LTI Systems

We consider the problem of computing an over-approximation of the reachable set of a linear time-invariant system over $\mathbb{R}^d$ with bounded inputs within a bounded time interval. As explained in the introduction, this can be done with arbitrary precision by computing the first N elements of a sequence of sets defined by a recurrence relation of the form:

$$\Omega_{i+1} = \Phi\Omega_i \oplus U, \ i \in \mathbb{N} \tag{1}$$

where Φ is a $d \times d$ matrix, U is a convex bounded subset of $\mathbb{R}^d$ (not necessarily full dimensional) and $\oplus$ denotes the Minkowski sum. The derivation of this recurrence relation from the continuous-time system is not detailed in the present paper but can be found, for instance, in [ADG03], [G05]. Note that since the system is time-invariant, the matrix Φ and the set of inputs U resulting from time discretization are independent of i.

For representations closed under linear transformation and Minkowski sum such as polytopes or zonotopes, the complexity of Ω_i grows due to the Minkowski sum. As a consequence, the computation of the next element of the sequence becomes more expensive as the cost of the linear transformation is proportional to the complexity of the set to which it is applied. For representations with bounded complexity such as oriented rectangular hulls, ellipsoids or zonotopes with bounded order, the Minkowski sum enforces us to make over-approximations at each step. The propagation of these errors through the computations, known as the *wrapping effect* [K98], [K99], can lead to dramatic over-approximations when considering reachability problems for large time horizons.

For linear time-invariant systems we present an algorithm free of any of these problems. Let us remark that from the recurrence relation (1), we have:

$$\Omega_{i+1} = \Phi^{i+1}\Omega_0 \oplus \Phi^i U \oplus \ldots \oplus U, \ i \in \mathbb{N}.$$

Then, let us define the auxiliary sequences of sets:

$$\begin{aligned}
X_0 &= \Omega_0, & X_{i+1} &= \Phi X_i, \\
V_0 &= U, & V_{i+1} &= \Phi V_i, \\
S_0 &= \{0\}, & S_{i+1} &= S_i \oplus V_i.
\end{aligned} \tag{2}$$

Equivalently, we have

$$X_{i+1} = \Phi^{i+1}\Omega_0, \ V_{i+1} = \Phi^{i+1}U \text{ and } S_{i+1} = \Phi^i U \oplus \ldots \oplus U.$$

Therefore, $\Omega_{i+1} = X_{i+1} \oplus S_{i+1}$ where X_{i+1} is the reachable set of the autonomous system from the set of initial states Ω_0, and S_{i+1} is the reachable set of the system with inputs from the initial set $\{0\}$. Note that the decomposition of the linear transformation and the Minkowski sum in the computation of S_{i+1} is possible only because the system is time-invariant. Algorithm 1 implements the reachable set computation based on the recurrence relations (2).

Let us remark that this algorithm does not depend on the class of sets chosen for the representing of the reachable sets. However, this class has to be closed under linear transformation and Minkowski sum (*e.g.* polytopes, zonotopes). The main advantage of this algorithm is that the linear transformations are applied to sets whose complexity *does not increase* at each iteration and this constitutes a significant improvement over existing algorithmic realizations of the recurrence relation (1). Thus, the time complexity of Algorithm 1 is bounded by $\mathcal{O}(N\mathcal{L}(n_{in}) + N\mathcal{K}(n_{out}))$, where $\mathcal{L}$ is the complexity of performing a linear

---

Algorithm 1. Reachability of linear time-invariant systems.

Input: The matrix Φ, the sets Ω_0 and U, an integer N.
Output: The first N terms of the sequence defined in equation (1).
1: $X_0 \leftarrow \Omega_0$
2: $V_0 \leftarrow U$
3: $S_0 \leftarrow \{0\}$
4: **for** i from 0 to $N - 1$ **do**
5:     $X_{i+1} \leftarrow \Phi X_i$ ▷ $X_{i+1} = \Phi^{i+1} \Omega_0$
6:     $S_{i+1} \leftarrow S_i \oplus V_i$ ▷ $S_{i+1} = \Phi^i U \oplus \cdots \oplus U$
7:     $V_{i+1} \leftarrow \Phi V_i$ ▷ $V_{i+1} = \Phi^{i+1} U$
8:     $\Omega_{i+1} \leftarrow X_{i+1} \oplus S_{i+1}$ ▷ $\Omega_{i+1} = \Phi^{i+1} \Omega_0 \oplus \Phi^i U \oplus \cdots \oplus U$
9: **end for**
10: **return** $\{\Omega_1, \ldots, \Omega_N\}$

---

transformation, $\mathcal{K}$ is the complexity of performing a Minkowski sum, n_{in} bounds the size of Ω_0 and U, and n_{out} bounds the size of Ω_N. These parameters depend obviously on the class of sets chosen for the representation.

Due to the Minkowski sum, the size of the output may actually be very large. Hence, for an efficient implementation of Algorithm 1, the class of sets used for the representation of the reachable sets has to satisfy one of the following properties. Either the representation size of the Minkowski sum of two sets equals the representation size of the operands, or the computational complexity of the Minkowski sum is independent of the size of the operands.

General polytopes, for example, do not satisfy any of these requirements. As far as we know, there is no reasonable representation satisfying the first property which is closed under Minkowski sum and linear transformations. The second property is satisfied by the class of zonotopes for which the complexity of Minkowski sum does not depend on the description complexity of the sets. In the following section, the implementation of Algorithm 1 using zonotopes is discussed.

3   Reachability Using Zonotopes

The class of zonotopes has already been suggested for efficient reachability computations in [K98], [K99], [G05]. Indeed, zonotopes have a compact representation and are closed under linear transformation and Minkowski sum[1]. A zonotope is defined as the Minkowski sum of a finite set of segments. Equivalently it can be seen as the image of a cube by an affine transformation.

Definition 1 (Zonotope). *A zonotope is a subset of $\mathbb{R}^d$ represented by its center $u \in \mathbb{R}^d$ and its generators $v_1, \ldots, v_m \in \mathbb{R}^d$:*

---

[1] Actually, the class of zonotopes is the smallest class of sets closed under linear transformation and Minkowski sum and which contains a connected set with a non-empty interior.

$$(u, \langle v_1, \ldots, v_m \rangle) = \left\{ u + \sum_{j=1}^{m} \alpha_j v_j \mid \alpha_j \in [-1, 1], \; j = 1, \ldots, m \right\}.$$

A *zonotope with m generators is said to have order $\frac{m}{d}$.*

Each zonotope is a centrally-symmetric convex polytope. Parallelepipeds are zonotopes of order one. A planar zonotope with three generators is depicted in Figure 1. Zonotopes admit a very compact representations relative to their number of vertices or faces. A generic zonotope of order p, though it is encoded by only $pd^2 + d$ numbers, has more than $(2p)^{d-1}/\sqrt{d}$ vertices [Z75]. Hence, zonotopes are perfectly suited for the representation of high dimensional sets.

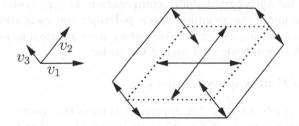

Fig. 1. A planar zonotope with three generators

The image of a zonotope $Z = (u, \langle v_1, \ldots, v_m \rangle)$ under a linear transformation Φ is given by:

$$\Phi Z = (\Phi u, \langle \Phi v_1, \ldots, \Phi v_m \rangle).$$

Then, the computational complexity of a linear transformation applied to a zonotope is $\mathcal{O}(p\mathcal{M}(d))$, where $\mathcal{M}(d)$ is the complexity of the multiplication of two $d \times d$ matrices. Using standard matrix multiplication the computational complexity of the linear transformation is[2] $\mathcal{O}(pd^3)$. In comparison, if the zonotope Z was to be represented by its vertices, the linear transformation would require at least $(2p)^{d-1}d^{3/2}$ operations.

The property which really makes zonotopes interesting for the implementation of Algorithm 1 is that their Minkowski sum can be computed in $\mathcal{O}(d)$, independently of the order of the operands. Indeed, the sum of two zonotopes $Z_1 = (u_1, \langle v_1, \ldots, v_m \rangle)$ and $Z_2 = (u_2, \langle w_1, \ldots, w_n \rangle)$ is

$$Z_1 \oplus Z_2 = (u_1 + u_2, \langle v_1, \ldots, v_m, w_1, \ldots, w_n \rangle).$$

Hence, the computation of the Minkowski sum consists of summing two vectors and concatenating two lists. Therefore, zonotopes satisfy the requirements for an efficient implementation of Algorithm 1. Assuming Ω_0 and U are zonotopes of orders p and q, respectively, the time complexity of Algorithm 1 becomes $\mathcal{O}(N(p + q)d^3)$. Moreover, since the Minkowski sum essentially consists of a

---

[2] Note that, theoretically, the complexity can be further reduced down to $\mathcal{O}(pd^{2.376})$ by using a more sophisticate matrix multiplication algorithm [CW90].

concatenation of lists, it is not necessary to store the sequence S_i since it can be computed very easily from the sequence V_i. Therefore, the space complexity of a zonotope implementation of Algorithm 1 is $\mathcal{O}(N(p+q)d^2)$.

4   Tight Over-Approximations of the Reachable Sets

The implementation of Algorithm 1 using zonotopes provides for an efficient (in time and in space) computation of the sets $\Omega_1, \ldots, \Omega_N$ defined by (1). Nevertheless, the result of this algorithm, which is typically a set of high-order zonotopes, does not lend itself easily to operations other than linear transformations and Minkowski sum. For example, intersecting a zonotpe with another set, a crucial operation for *hybrid* reachability computation, is very costly as it involves the transformation of the zonotope into a polytopic representation. In this section, we propose an algorithm for computing over-approximations of the sets $\Omega_1, \ldots, \Omega_N$ which are both tight and of low order.

4.1   Interval Hull Approximations

We first consider interval hull over-approximations of the reachable sets. Let Box be a function that maps a set $E \subseteq \mathbb{R}^d$ to its interval hull, that is, to the smallest Cartesian product of intervals containing E. Note that for every $E_1, E_2 \subseteq \mathbb{R}^d$ we have

$$\text{Box}(E_1 \oplus E_2) = \text{Box}(E_1) \oplus \text{Box}(E_2). \tag{3}$$

Algorithm 2 computes the interval hulls of the reachable sets $\Omega_1, \ldots, \Omega_N$.

Algorithm 2. Interval hull approximation of the reachable sets

---

Input: The matrix Φ, the sets Ω_0 and U, and an integer N.
Output: The interval hulls of the N first terms of the sequence defined in (1).
1: $X_0 \leftarrow \Omega_0$
2: $V_0 \leftarrow U$
3: $S_0 \leftarrow \{0\}$
4: **for** i from 0 to $N-1$ **do**
5:      $X_{i+1} \leftarrow \Phi X_i$ $\triangleright X_{i+1} = \Phi^{i+1}\Omega_0$
6:      $S_{i+1} \leftarrow S_i \oplus \text{Box}(V_i)$ $\triangleright S_{i+1} = \text{Box}(\Phi^i U \oplus \cdots \oplus U)$
7:      $V_{i+1} \leftarrow \Phi V_i$ $\triangleright V_{i+1} = \Phi^{i+1} U$
8:      $\overline{\Omega}_{i+1} \leftarrow \text{Box}(X_{i+1}) \oplus S_{i+1}$ $\triangleright \overline{\Omega}_{i+1} = \text{Box}(\Omega_{i+1})$
9: **end for**
10: **return** $\{\overline{\Omega}_1, \ldots, \overline{\Omega}_N\}$

The sequences $X_0, \ldots, X_N$ and $V_0, \ldots, V_N$ are represented as zonotopes which allow to benefit from the low computational complexity of the linear transformations. The sequences $S_0, \ldots, S_N$ and $\overline{\Omega}_1, \ldots, \overline{\Omega}_N$ are represented as interval products ($2d$ numbers). The computation of the interval hull of a zonotope is particularly easy since the projection of a zonotope on a coordinate axis can be computed by projecting each of its generators on that axis. Then, the time complexity of Algorithm 2 is equivalent to that of Algorithm 1, but its space complexity drops to $\mathcal{O}(Nd + (p+q)d^2)$.

Let us remark that in Algorithm 2, approximations occur only when the function Box is invoked. Note that Box is always applied to *exact* sets and that other operations are computed exactly. Thus, approximation errors do not propagate further through the computations and Algorithm 2 does not suffer from the wrapping effect. Particularly, we have the following result:

Proposition 1. *For all $i \in \{1, \ldots, N\}$, $\overline{\Omega}_i$ is the interval hull of the set Ω_i.*

Proof. From equation (3), we have that

$$\overline{\Omega}_i = \text{Box}(\Phi^i \Omega_0) \oplus \text{Box}(\Phi^{i-1}U) \oplus \ldots \oplus \text{Box}(U)$$
$$= \text{Box}\left(\Phi^i \Omega_0 \oplus \Phi^{i-1}U \oplus \ldots \oplus U\right) = \text{Box}(\Omega_i). \qquad \blacksquare$$

Thus, each face of $\overline{\Omega}_i$ has at least one common point with the set Ω_i and the over-approximations $\overline{\Omega}_1, \ldots, \overline{\Omega}_N$ computed by Algorithm 2 are *tight* in the sense of [KV00].

Remark 1. Algorithm 2 is not specific to zonotopes and interval products. It can be implemented using any pair of classes of sets, the first of which closed under linear transformation and the second closed under the Minkowski sum and admitting a constant size representation. Then, the function Box has to be replaced by a function that approximates an object from the first class by an object from the second. For accurate over-approximations, this function has to satisfy a property similar to that of equation (3). For instance, we can replace zonotopes by ellipsoids or general polytopes. The choice of the second class is more restricted. In the following, we show that a class of polytopes defined as *intersections of bands* can be used advantageously in the hybrid systems context.

4.2   Guards-Oriented Over-Approximations for Hybrid Systems

Let us consider the class of hybrid systems where the continuous dynamics is linear and time-invariant, and where transition guards are specified by hyperplanes:

$$G_e = \left\{x \in \mathbb{R}^d \mid n_e \cdot x = f_e\right\} \text{ where } n_e \in \mathbb{R}^d, \ f_e \in \mathbb{R}.$$

In this section we present a variant of Algorithm 2 whose output can be intersected efficiently with such transition guards. The algorithm computes tight over-approximations of the sets $\Omega_1, \ldots, \Omega_N$ in a class of polytopes defined as intersections of bands.

Definition 2. *Let $\mathcal{S} = \{s_1, \ldots, s_\ell\}$ be a set of vectors. An $\mathcal{S}$-band intersection, represented by two vectors $m, M \in \mathbb{R}^\ell$, is the set defined by:*

$$[m, M]_\mathcal{S} = \left\{x \in \mathbb{R}^d \mid m_i \leq s_i \cdot x \leq M_i, \ i = 1, \ldots, \ell\right\}.$$

Let us remark that interval products constitute a subclass of $\mathcal{S}$-band intersections where $\mathcal{S}$ is the set of coordinate vectors, and that parallelepipeds are obtained when $\mathcal{S}$ is a set of d linearly independent vectors. For a given set of vectors $\mathcal{S}$, it is easy to show that the class of $\mathcal{S}$-band intersections is closed under the Minkowski sum:

$$[m_1, M_1]_{\mathcal{S}} \oplus [m_2, M_2]_{\mathcal{S}} = [m_1 + m_2, M_1 + M_2]_{\mathcal{S}}.$$

To use $\mathcal{S}$-band intersections in Algorithm 2, we need an over-approximation function which maps a zonotope to its smallest enclosing $\mathcal{S}$-band intersection.

Proposition 2. *Let* $Z = (u, \langle v_1, \ldots, v_m \rangle)$ *be a zonotope, then the* $\mathcal{S}$-*band intersection* $\mathrm{Box}_{\mathcal{S}}(Z) = [m, M]_{\mathcal{S}}$ *given by*

$$m_i = s_i \cdot u - \sum_{j=1}^{m} |s_i \cdot v_j|, \ M_i = s_i \cdot u + \sum_{j=1}^{m} |s_i \cdot v_j|, \ i = 1, \ldots, \ell$$

is an over-approximation of Z. *Moreover, each face of* $\mathrm{Box}_{\mathcal{S}}(Z)$ *has at least one common point with* Z.

Proof. Let $x \in Z$, then for all $i \in \{1, \ldots, \ell\}$,

$$s_i \cdot x = s_i \cdot \left(u + \sum_{j=1}^{m} \alpha_j v_j \right) = s_i \cdot u + \sum_{j=1}^{m} \alpha_j s_i \cdot v_j.$$

Since, for all $j \in \{1, \ldots, m\}$, $\alpha_j \in [-1, 1]$, $x \in \mathrm{Box}_{\mathcal{S}}(Z)$. Moreover, let $x_{i,1}$ and $x_{i,2}$ be the elements of Z given by

$$x_{i,1} = u - \sum_{j=1}^{m} \mathrm{sign}(s_i \cdot v_j)v_j, \ x_{i,2} = u + \sum_{j=1}^{m} \mathrm{sign}(s_i \cdot v_j)v_j.$$

Then, $s_i \cdot x_{i,1} = m_i$ and $s_i \cdot x_{i,2} = M_i$. ∎

Thus, the function $\mathrm{Box}_{\mathcal{S}}$ maps a zonotope Z to a tight over-approximation in the class of $\mathcal{S}$-band intersections (see Figure 2). Moreover, it is straightforward to show that $\mathrm{Box}_{\mathcal{S}}$ satisfies the following property:

$$\mathrm{Box}_{\mathcal{S}}(Z_1 \oplus Z_2) = \mathrm{Box}_{\mathcal{S}}(Z_1) \oplus \mathrm{Box}_{\mathcal{S}}(Z_2).$$

Hence, $\mathcal{S}$-band intersections can replace interval hulls in Algorithm 2. The time complexity of the algorithm becomes $\mathcal{O}(k(p + q)(d^3 + \ell d^2))$ and the space complexity $\mathcal{O}(k\ell + (p + q)d^2 + \ell d)$. Similar to Proposition 1, we can show that the sets computed by Algorithm 2 indeed satisfy $\overline{\Omega}_i = \mathrm{Box}_{\mathcal{S}}(\Omega_i)$, $i = 1, \ldots, N$.

The following result demonstrates some advantage in using band intersections in Algorithm 2 in the context of hybrid systems verification:

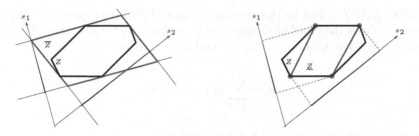

Fig. 2. A zonotope Z, a set of directions $\mathcal{S} = \{s_1, s_2\}$, an over-approximation $\overline{Z} \supset Z$ by an $\mathcal{S}$-band intersection and an under-approximation $\underline{Z} \subset Z$ by the convex-hull of points in Z which are extremal with respect to projections on $\mathcal{S}$

Proposition 3. *Let $\overline{\Omega}_i$ denote the over-approximation of Ω_i computed by Algorithm 2 using $\mathcal{S}$-band intersections, i.e. $\overline{\Omega}_i = Box_{\mathcal{S}}(\Omega_i)$. If the normal vector n_e to the guard G_e is an element of $\mathcal{S}$ then:*

$$\overline{\Omega}_i \text{ intersects } G_e \Longleftrightarrow \Omega_i \text{ intersects } G_e.$$

Proof. Let $s_j \in \mathcal{S}$, such that $s_j = n_e$. Let us assume that $\overline{\Omega}_i$ intersects G_e. This is equivalent to saying that $m_j \leq f_e \leq M_j$. From Proposition 2, we have that there exist points $x_{j,1}, x_{j,2} \in \Omega_i$ such that $m_j = s_j \cdot x_{j,1}$ and $M_j = s_j \cdot x_{j,2}$. Hence, there exists $x \in \Omega_i$ such that $s_j \cdot x = f_e$ and Ω_i intersects G_e. The other direction of the equivalence is trivial since $\Omega_i \subseteq \overline{\Omega}_i$.   ∎

Remark 2. Although Proposition 3 implies that a set computed by a step of Algorithm 2 will intersect a guard exactly when a set computed by Algorithm 1 would (when started from the same set), the corresponding intersections will differ and after the transition, Algorithm 2 will start from a larger set and will generate more behaviors. In other words, the wrapping effect manifests itself during discrete transitions.

5   Tight Under-Approximations and Control Synthesis

When the input U is interpreted as control rather than disturbance, reachability computation can be used to solve controller synthesis problems: find a sequence of input values that drives the system to a desired state while avoiding undesired ones. In this section we show how such control sequences can be extracted from tight *under-approximations* of the reachable sets. Previous work on applying reachability computation to controller synthesis was restricted to synthesizing mode switching conditions for hybrid systems [ABD+00].

5.1   Under-Approximation of the Reachable Sets

Let $\mathcal{S} = \{s_1, \ldots, s_\ell\}$ be a set of vectors. A zonotope $Z = (u, \langle v_1, \ldots, v_m \rangle)$ can be under-approximated by a polytope defined as the convex hull of the finite set of points corresponding to the extremal points of Z in the directions of S (see Figure 2). From the proof of Proposition 2, we know that the extremal points of Z in the direction s_i are $x_{i,1} = u - g_i$ and $x_{i,2} = u + g_i$ where:

$$g_i = \sum_{j=1}^{m} \text{sign}(s_i \cdot v_j) v_j.$$

The under-approximation of Z will be denoted by:

$$\underline{Z} = (u, [g_1, \dots, g_\ell]_S) = \text{ConvexHull}\left(\{u \pm g_i, \ i \in \{1, \dots, \ell\}\}\right)$$

$$= \left\{u + \sum_{i=1}^{\ell} \alpha_i g_i : \sum_{i=1}^{\ell} |\alpha_i| \leq 1\right\}.$$

Let us remark that the indices have their importance since $u \pm g_i$ are the extremal points in the direction given by s_i. In order to use this under-approximation in a reachability algorithm, we need to express the under-approximation of the Minkowski sum of two zonotopes as a function of the under-approximations of each zonotope.

Lemma 1. *Let us define the following operation*

$$(u, [g_1, \dots, g_\ell]_S) \boxplus (u', [g'_1, \dots, g'_\ell]_S) = (u + u', [g_1 + g'_1, \dots, g_\ell + g'_\ell]_S).$$

Then, for two zonotopes Z and Z', we have $\underline{Z \oplus Z'} = \underline{Z} \boxplus \underline{Z'}$.

Proof. The extremal points of $Z \oplus Z'$ in the direction s_i are $u + u' - h_i$ and $u + u' + h_i$ where

$$h_i = \sum_{j=1}^{m} sign(s_i \cdot v_j) v_j + \sum_{j=1}^{m'} sign(s_i \cdot v'_j) v'_j = g_i + g'_i. \qquad \blacksquare$$

Thus, we can adapt Algorithm 2 to compute under-approximations of the sets $\Omega_1, \dots, \Omega_N$. This is done by replacing Box by the under-approximation function defined above. Then, from Lemma 1, the output of the algorithm is exactly the sequence $\underline{\Omega_1}, \dots, \underline{\Omega_N}$. These under-approximations are *tight* since the extremal points of Ω_i in each direction $s_i \in S$ are vertices of $\underline{\Omega_i}$. Furthermore, it is easy to see that they have the same S-band over-approximation. Then, the following result is straightforward.

Theorem 1. *Let $\overline{\Omega_i}$ denote the S-band over-approximation of Ω_i and let $\underline{\Omega_i}$ denote its under-approximation. If the normal vector n_e to the guard G_e is an element of S then:*

$$\underline{\Omega_i} \text{ intersects } G_e \Longleftrightarrow \overline{\Omega_i} \text{ intersects } G_e \Longleftrightarrow \Omega_i \text{ intersects } G_e.$$

5.2   Application to Control Synthesis

The under-approximation of Ω_i can be used for control synthesis when U is interpreted as control rather than disturbance. Let y be a point of $\underline{\Omega}_N$ and therefore of Ω_N, we want to determine an initial state $x_0 \in \Omega_0$ and a sequence of inputs $v_0, \ldots, v_{N-1}$ in U, such that the discrete-time system defined by equation (1) reaches y in N steps. Since $y \in \underline{\Omega}_N = (u, [g_1, \ldots, g_\ell]_S)$, it can be written under the form:

$$y = u + \sum_{j=1}^{\ell} \alpha_j g_j, \text{ with } \sum_{j=1}^{\ell} |\alpha_j| \leq 1.$$

If $\ell = d$ and $\underline{\Omega}_k$ is full dimensional, this is equivalent to a change of variable. The under-approximations $\underline{\Phi^N \Omega_0} = (u^N, [g_1^N, \ldots, g_\ell^N]_S)$ and $\underline{\Phi^i U} = (u^i, [g_1^i, \ldots, g_\ell^i]_S)$ ($i \in \{0, \ldots, N-1\}$) are computed by Algorithm 2 while computing $\underline{\Omega}_N$. Let us remark that from Lemma 1, we have $u = u^N + u^{N-1} + \ldots + u^0$ and $g_j = g_j^N + g_j^{N-1} + \ldots + g_j^0$. Then, if Φ is invertible (which is the case if the discrete-time system is achieved by discretization of a continuous-time system), we can choose

$$x_0 = \Phi^{-N}(u^N + \sum_{j=1}^{\ell} \alpha_j g_j^N),$$

$$v_i = \Phi^{i+1-N}(u^{N-1-i} + \sum_{j=1}^{\ell} \alpha_j g_j^{N-1-i}), \ i = 0, \ldots, N-1.$$

It is clear that $x_0 \in \Omega_0$, $v_0, \ldots, v_{N-1} \in U$ and, moreover, the sequence $x_{i+1} = \Phi x_i + v_i$ satisfies $x_N = y$.

6   Experimental Results

Algorithms 1 and 2 have been implemented in OCaml [C05]. For the sake of comparison, we have also implemented the zonotope-based reachability algorithm presented in [G05]. This algorithm, which obtained the best accuracy/performance tradeoffs reported so far, computes an over-approximation of the reachable sets using the recurrence relation (1). At each step, in order to avoid computational explosion, it reduces the complexity of the reachable set by over-approximating it by a zonotope of fixed order p. In the following, we refer to this algorithm by Zono-p. Zonotopes and linear algebra operations were implemented in separate modules so that all algorithms use the same subroutines. All computations were performed on a Pentium III 800MHz with 256MB RAM.

6.1   A Five-Dimensional Linear System

As a first benchmark consider the five-dimensional example borrowed from [G05]. Over-approximations of the reachable sets of this system have been computed using Algorithms 1, 2 and Zono-20.

The approximation obtained by Algorithm 1 is always the most accurate because it consists of the exact sequence $\Omega_1, \ldots, \Omega_N$ defined by the recurrence relation (1). For short time horizons, the over-approximations computed by Zono-20 are more accurate than the ones computed by Algorithm 2. However, as we consider longer time horizons, the errors introduced at each step of Zono-20 start propagating through the computations and the wrapping effect becomes too significant to actually say anything interesting about the reachable states of the system. In comparison, the over-approximations obtained by Algorithm 2 are tight and remain accurate even for long time horizons. Moreover, since Algorithm 2 uses interval hull over-approximations, the output of this algorithm is much easier to manipulate than the output of Zono-20 which consists of a sequence of zonotopes of order 20.

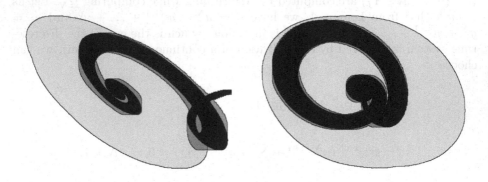

Fig. 3. Reachable states of a five-dimensional linear system after 1000 iterations: projections on coordinates x_1 and x_2 (left), x_4 and x_5 (right). In light gray: set computed by Zono-20 (maximum order allowed for the zonotopes is 20). In dark gray: set computed by Algorithm 2. In black: set computed by Algorithm 1.

Figure 3 shows the over-approximations of the reachable sets obtained by the three algorithms for a long time horizon ($N = 1000$). It is clear that Algorithms 1 and 2 have a much better precision than Algorithm Zono-20, an obvious victim of the wrapping effect. Computation time and memory consumption of the three algorithms for different time horizons N are reported in Table 1. We can see that Algorithms 1 and 2 are fast and require much less memory. Algorithm 2, which computes interval-hulls approximation, is about 100 times faster, and needs 25 times less memory than Algorithm Zono-20, while producing approximations of higher quality.

6.2   High-Dimensional Linear Systems

The three algorithms were also tested on continuous linear time-invariant systems which were randomly generated according to the following procedure: the matrix A was chosen at random and then normalized for the infinity norm and the inputs were chosen bounded for the infinity norm. In [G05], it is explained

Table 1. Time and memory consumptions of reachability computations for a five-dimensional linear system, for different time horizons

$N =$	200	400	600	800	1000
Algorithm 1	0.01s	0.02s	0.04s	0.05s	0.07s
Algorithm 1	0.s	0.s	0.01s	0.01s	0.02s
Zono-20	0.34s	0.74s	1.14s	1.46s	2.16s

$N =$	200	400	600	800	1000
Algorithm 1	492KB	737KB	983KB	1.23MB	1.47MB
Algorithm 1	246KB	246KB	246KB	246KB	246KB
Zono-20	1.47MB	2.95MB	4.18MB	5.65MB	6.88MB

Table 2. Time and memory consumption for $N = 100$ for several linear time-invariant systems of different dimensions

$d =$	5	10	20	50	100	150	200
Algorithm 1	0.0s	0.02s	0.11s	1.11s	8.43s	35.9s	136s
Algorithm 2	0.0s	0.01s	0.07s	0.91s	8.08s	28.8s	131s
Zono-20	0.16s	0.61s	3.32s	22.6s	152s		

$d =$	5	10	20	50	100	150	200
Algorithm 1	246KB	492KB	1.72MB	8.85MB	33.7MB	75.2MB	133MB
Algorithm 2	246KB	246KB	246KB	492KB	983KB	2.21MB	3.69MB
Zono-20	737KB	2.46MB	8.36MB	44.5MB	177MB		

how the recurrence relation given by equation (1) can be obtained. The discretization time step was $r = 0.01$ and the number of iterations is $N = 100$. Computation times and memory consumptions of the three algorithms for linear systems of several dimensions d are reported in Table 2.

Algorithms 1 and 2 appear to be extremely scalable in terms of both time and space, which confirms the theoretical complexity estimations. Let us remark that using Algorithm 2, we can compute a tight over-approximation of the reachable set of a 100-dimensional system after 100 time steps in less than 10 seconds using less than 1MB memory. To the best of our knowledge, there is no report in the literature of algorithms with similar performances for such high-dimensional systems.

6.3   Varying the Time Step

When the recurrence relation (1) is obtained by discretization of a continuous-time system, we expect that the smaller is the time step, the more accurate will be the over-approximation we compute. However, is not always the case for algorithms suffering from the wrapping effects because reducing the time steps increases the number of iterations of the reachability algorithm in order to cover the same time interval. As we can see in Figure 4, reducing the time step improves the quality of the over-approximations obtained by Algorithm 2 whereas the over-approximations obtained by Algorithm Zono-5 blows up beyond usefulness.

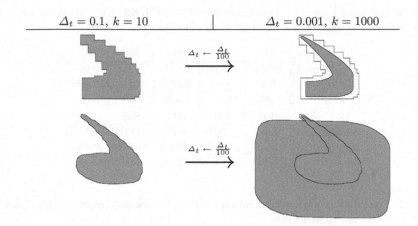

Fig. 4. Reducing the timestep in a 20-dimensional example improves the quality of the over-approximation obtained by Algorithm 2 (top) but increase the *wrapping effect* on the algorithm Zono-5 (bottom)

7   Conclusions

We have presented an extremely-efficient and exact algorithm for computing reachable states of a discrete-time LTI systems, as well as several variants of this algorithm for computing tight over- and under-approximation of these sets, which do not suffer from the wrapping effect. We showed that we can compute over-approximations that facilitate guard intersections, and that our under-approximations can be used to solve control synthesis problems. The prototype implementation of our algorithms has outperfromed previously reported algorithms in terms of execution time, memory consumption and approximation tightness. The implementation will be improved by using efficient linear algebra libraries. Future work will focus on the application to hybrid systems and, in particular, on computing intersections with guards.

References

[ACH+95]   R. Alur, C. Courcoubetis, N. Halbwachs, T.A. Henzinger, P.-H. Ho, X. Nicollin, A. Olivero, J. Sifakis, and S. Yovine, The Algorithmic Analysis of Hybrid Systems, *Theoretical Computer Science* **138**, 3–34, 1995.

[ABDM00]   A. Asarin, O. Bournez, T. Dang, and O. Maler, Approximate Reachability Analysis of Piecewise-linear Dynamical Systems, *HSCC'00*, LNCS 1790, 20–31, Springer, 2000.

[ABD+00]   E. Asarin, O. Bournez, T. Dang, O. Maler and A. Pnueli, Effective Synthesis of Switching Controllers for Linear Systems, *Proceedings of the IEEE* **88**, 1011-1025, 2000.

[ADG03]   E. Asarin, T. Dang, and A. Girard, Reachability Analysis of Nonlinear Systems using Conservative Approximation, *HSCC'03*, LNCS 2623, 20–35, Springer, 2003.

[AMP95]   E. Asarin, O. Maler and A. Pnueli, Reachability Analysis of Dynamical Systems having Piecewise-Constant Derivatives, *Theoretical Computer Science* **138**, 35–65, 1995.

[BT00]   O. Botchkarev and S. Tripakis, Verification of Hybrid Systems with Linear Differential Inclusions using Ellipsoidal Approximations, *HSCC'00*, LNCS 1790, 73–88, Springer, 2000.

[C05]   *The Caml Language webpage*, 2005. http://caml.inria.fr/ .

[CK98]   A. Chutinan and B.H. Krogh, Computing Polyhedral Approximations to Dynamic Flow Pipes, *CDC'98*, IEEE, 1998.

[CK03]   A. Chutinan and B.H. Krogh, Computational Techniques for Hybrid System Verification, *IEEE Trans. on Automatic Control* **48**, 64–75, 2003

[CW90]   D. Coppersmith and S. Winograd, Matrix Multiplication via Arithmetic Progressions, *J. Symbolic Computation* **9**, 251–280, 1990.

[D00]   T. Dang, *Verification and Synthesis of Hybrid Systems*, PhD thesis, Institut National Polytechnique de Grenoble, Laboratoire Verimag, 2000.

[DM98]   T. Dang and O. Maler, Reachability Analysis via Face Lifting, *HSCC'98*, LNCS 1386, 96–109, Springer, 1998

[F05]   PHAVer: Algorithmic Verification of Hybrid Systems Past HyTech, *HSCC'05*, LNCS 3414, 258–273, Springer, 2005.

[G05]   A. Girard, Reachability of Uncertain Linear Systems using Zonotopes, *HSCC'05*, LNCS 3414, 291–305, Springer, 2005.

[G96]   M.R. Greenstreet, Verifying Safety Properties of Differential Equations, *CAV'96*, LNCS 1102, 277–287, Springer, 1996.

[GM99]   M.R. Greenstreet, and I. Mitchell, Reachability Analysis using Polygonal Projections, *HSCC'99*, LNCS 1569, 103–116, Springer, 1999.

[HHW97]   T.A Henzinger, P.-H. Ho, and H. Wong-Toi, Hytech: A Model Checker for Hybrid Systems, *Software Tools for Technology Transfer* **1**, 110–122, 1997.

[K98]   W. Kühn, Rigorously Computed Orbits of Dynamical Systems without the Wrapping Rffect. *Computing* **61**, 47–68, 1998.

[K99]   W. Kühn, Towards an Optimal Control of the Wrapping Effect, *SCAN 98, Developments in Reliable Computing*, 43–51, Kluwer, 1999.

[KV97]   A. Kurzhanski and I. Valyi, *Ellipsoidal Calculus for Estimation and Control*. Birkhauser, 1997.

[KV00]   A.B Kurzhanski and P. Varaiya, Ellipsoidal Techniques for Reachability Analysis, *HSCC'00*, LNCS 1790, 202–214, Springer, 2000.

[M02]   O. Maler, Control from Computer Science, *Annual Reviews in Control* **26**, 175-187, 2002.

[MT00]   I. Mitchell and C. Tomlin, Level Set Methods for Computation in Hybrid Systems, *HSCC'00*, LNCS 1790, 310–323, Springer, 2000.

[V98]   P. Varaiya, Reach Set computation using Optimal Control, *KIT Workshop, Verimag, Grenoble*, 377–383, 1998.

[Z75]   T. Zaslavsky, Facing Up to Arrangements: Face-Count Formulas for Partitions of Space by Hyperplanes, *Memoirs of the AMS* **154**, American Mathematical Society, 1975.

Verification Using Simulation*

Antoine Girard and George J. Pappas

Department of Electrical and Systems Engineering,
University of Pennsylvania,
Philadelphia, PA 19104
{agirard, pappasg}@seas.upenn.edu

Abstract. Verification and simulation have always been complementary, if not competing, approaches to system design. In this paper, we present a novel method for so-called metric transition systems that bridges the gap between verification and simulation, enabling system verification using a finite number of simulations. The existence of metrics on the system state and observation spaces, which is natural for continuous systems, allows us to capitalize on the recently developed framework of approximate bisimulations, and infer the behavior of neighborhood of system trajectories around a simulated trajectory. For nondeterministic linear systems that are robustly safe or robustly unsafe, we provide not only a completeness result but also an upper bound on the number of simulations required as a function of the distance between the reachable set and the unsafe set. Our framework is the first simulation-based verification method that enjoys completeness for infinite-state systems. The complexity is low for robustly safe or robustly unsafe systems, and increases for nonrobust problems. This provides strong evidence that robustness dramatically impacts the complexity of system verification and design.

1 Introduction

Given a system model and a desired specification, system designers rely on both analysis and simulation methods. Simulation-based approaches ensure that a finite number of user-defined system trajectories meet the desired specification. Even though computationally inexpensive simulation is ubiquitous in system design, it suffers from completeness as it is impossible or impractical to test all system trajectories. Furthermore, simulation-based testing is semi-automatic since the user must provide a large number of test cases. On the other hand, automated verification methods enjoy completeness by showing that all system trajectories satisfy the desired property. Despite great progress on verification tools for discrete software and hardware systems, the algorithmic complexity of verification tools makes them applicable to smaller scale problems.

The gap between simulation and verification is more extreme when considering systems with infinite states, such as continuous or hybrid systems.

---

* This research is partially supported by the Région Rhône-Alpes (Projet CalCel) and the NSF Presidential Early CAREER (PECASE) Grant 0132716.

João Hespanha and A. Tiwari (Eds.): HSCC 2006, LNCS 3927, pp. 272–286, 2006.

Whereas traditional simulation techniques for discrete and continuous systems can be naturally extended for hybrid systems [1, 2, 3], verification techniques have been much more challenging to extend due to the complexity of computing reachable sets for continuous systems. This has resulted in a variety of computationally intensive approaches for hybrid system verification using predicate abstraction [4, 5], barrier certificates [6], level sets [7], and exact arithmetic [8]. Even though these approaches can handle low-dimensional hybrid systems, for the class of uncertain linear systems, promising scalable results have been obtained using zonotope computations [9].

In this paper, we present a novel method that bridges the gap between verification and simulation methods, enabling system verification using a finite number of simulations. This is achieved for so-called metric transition systems, that are transition systems that are equipped with metrics on the system state and observation spaces. Whereas choosing metrics may not be natural for purely combinatorial discrete problems, they are very natural for continuous and hybrid systems. Having a notion of distance between states and observations, enables us to build on the recently developed framework of approximate bisimulation metrics [10, 11, 12, 13]. Bisimulation metrics measure how far two states are from being bisimilar, thus enabling the quantification of error between trajectories originating from approximately bisimilar states.

Equipping transition systems with bisimulation metrics enables the development of a simulation-based verification algorithm by inferring the behavior of neighborhood of system trajectories around a simulated trajectory, resulting in more robust simulations. By appropriately sampling the set of initial states, we can verify or falsify the desired property for all system trajectories. The more robust the simulations, the less simulations we have to perform. The pre-computed bisimulation metric is used for automatically guiding the choice of trajectories that will be simulated.

For the class of metric transition systems generated by nondeterministic linear systems that are robustly safe or robustly unsafe, a completeness result is provided. Our framework is the first simulation-based verification method that enjoys completeness for continuous systems. Furthermore, we obtain an upper bound on the number of simulations required as a function of the distance between the reachable set of the system and the unsafe set. Naturally, the complexity of our approach is low for robustly safe or robustly unsafe systems, and increases for nonrobust problems. This provides strong evidence that robustness dramatically impacts the complexity of system verification and design.

2   Bisimulation Metrics for Transition Systems

We consider the class of metric transition systems defined as follows:

Definition 1 (Metric transition system). *A transition system with observations is a tuple $T = (Q, \rightarrow, Q_0, \Pi, \langle\langle . \rangle\rangle)$ that consists of:*

- a (possibly infinite) set Q of states,
- a transition relation $\to \subseteq Q \times Q$,
- a (possibly infinite) set $Q_0 \subseteq Q$ of initial states,
- a (possibly infinite) set Π of observations,
- an observation map $\langle\langle . \rangle\rangle : Q \to \Pi$.

If (Q, d_Q) and (Π, d_Π) are metric spaces, then T is called a metric transition system.

A metric transition system is therefore a possibly nondeterministic transition system equipped with metrics for states and observations. A transition $(q, q') \in \to$ will be denoted $q \to q'$. The successor map is defined as the set valued map given by

$$\forall q \in Q, \ \mathrm{Post}(q) = \{q' \in Q \mid q \to q'\}.$$

We assume the set of initial values Q_0 is a compact subset of Q and for all $q \in Q$, $\mathrm{Post}(q)$ is a compact subset of Q. A state trajectory of T is a finite sequence of transitions, $q_0 \to \cdots \to q_k$, where $q_0 \in Q_0$. For $N \in \mathbb{N}$, $S_N(T)$ denotes the set of state trajectories of length less or equal to N. The reachable set of T within N transitions is the subset of Π defined by:

$$\mathrm{Reach}_N(T) = \{\pi \in \Pi \mid \exists\, q_0 \to \cdots \to q_k \in S_N(T),\ \langle\langle q_k \rangle\rangle = \pi\}.$$

An important problem for transition systems is the safety verification problem which asks whether the intersection of $\mathrm{Reach}_N(T)$ with an unsafe set $\mathcal{U} \subseteq \Pi$ is empty or not. When considering metric transition systems, more robust (i.e. quantitative) versions of this property can be formulated:

Definition 2. A metric transition system T is robustly safe if there exists $\delta > 0$ such that

$$\forall \pi \in \mathrm{Reach}_N(T),\ \mathcal{N}_\Pi(\pi, \delta) \cap \mathcal{U} = \emptyset,$$

and is robustly unsafe if there exists $\delta > 0$ such that

$$\exists \pi \in \mathrm{Reach}_N(T),\ \mathcal{N}_\Pi(\pi, \delta) \subseteq \mathcal{U},$$

where $\mathcal{N}_\Pi(\pi, \delta)$ denotes the δ-neighborhood of observation π for the metric d_Π. The supremum of the set of δ such that one of these equations holds is called the coefficient of robustness of T. If T is neither robustly safe nor robustly unsafe, we say that T is not robust with respect to the safety property.

Remark 1. Robustness with respect to the safety property is generic for metric transition systems. Indeed, T is not robust with respect to the safety property if and only if the intersection of the interior of $\mathrm{Reach}_N(T)$ and $\mathcal{U}$ is empty while the intersection of their closure is not.

For systems with a finite number of states, the safety verification problem can be solved by exhaustive simulation of the transition system. Though effective for systems with a reasonable number of states, this approach becomes much more computationally demanding when the number of states increases. For systems with a finite but large number of states, notions of systems refinement and equivalence, based on language inclusion, simulation and bisimulation relations [14], have been useful for simplifying the safety verification problem.

Definition 3 (Bisimulation relation). *A relation $\sim \subseteq Q \times Q$ is a bisimulation relation if for all $q_1 \sim q_2$:*

1. *$\langle\langle q_1 \rangle\rangle = \langle\langle q_2 \rangle\rangle$,*
2. *for all $q_1 \to q_1'$, there exists $q_2 \to q_2'$, such that $q_1' \sim q_2'$,*
3. *for all $q_2 \to q_2'$, there exists $q_1 \to q_1'$, such that $q_1' \sim q_2'$.*

From a bisimulation relation, we can construct an equivalent (but smaller) transition system T' defined on the quotient set of states $Q/\sim$. Particularly, the reachable sets of T and T' are equal and therefore the safety verification problem of both systems are equivalent though much simpler to solve for T'.

For transition systems with an infinite number of states such as those generated by dynamical and hybrid systems, exhaustive simulation is generally not possible. Extensions of the notion of simulation and bisimulation relations have recently been developed [15, 16, 17]. Though simpler, the quotient system generally still has an infinite number of states for which exhaustive simulation would require to compute an infinite number of trajectories. In the following, we show that an approach based on the computation of a finite number of trajectories is possible using more robust relations defined by metrics.

Definition 4 (Bisimulation metric). *A continuous function $d_{\mathcal{B}} : Q \times Q \to \mathbb{R}+$ is a bisimulation metric if it is a pseudo-metric:*

1. *for all $q \in Q$, $d_{\mathcal{B}}(q, q) = 0$,*
2. *for all $q_1, q_2 \in Q$, $d_{\mathcal{B}}(q_1, q_2) = d_{\mathcal{B}}(q_2, q_1)$,*
3. *for all $q_1, q_2, q_3 \in Q$, $d_{\mathcal{B}}(q_1, q_3) \leq d_{\mathcal{B}}(q_1, q_2) + d_{\mathcal{B}}(q_2, q_3)$,*

and if in addition, there exists $\lambda > 1$, such that for all $q_1, q_2 \in Q$,

$$d_{\mathcal{B}}(q_1, q_2) \geq \max(\, d_{\Pi}(\langle\langle q_1 \rangle\rangle, \langle\langle q_2 \rangle\rangle),\ \lambda \sup_{q_1 \to q_1'} \inf_{q_2 \to q_2'} d_{\mathcal{B}}(q_1', q_2')\,). \tag{1}$$

The notion of bisimulation metrics extends the notion of bisimulation relations. A bisimulation metric measures how far two states are from being bisimilar:

Proposition 1. *The zero set of a bisimulation metric is a bisimulation relation.*

Proof. Let $q_1, q_2 \in Q$ such that $d_{\mathcal{B}}(q_1, q_2) = 0$. Then, from equation (1), we have that $d_{\Pi}(\langle\langle q_1 \rangle\rangle, \langle\langle q_2 \rangle\rangle) = 0$. Since d_{Π} is a metric, this implies that $\langle\langle q_1 \rangle\rangle = \langle\langle q_2 \rangle\rangle$. Now, let $q_1 \to q_1'$, then since $d_{\mathcal{B}}$ is continuous and $\mathrm{Post}(q_2)$ is compact, equation (1) implies that there exists $q_2 \to q_2'$ such that $d_{\mathcal{B}}(q_1', q_2') = 0$. Similarly, since $d_{\mathcal{B}}(q_1, q_2) = d_{\mathcal{B}}(q_2, q_1)$, we have that for all $q_2 \to q_2'$, there exists $q_1 \to q_1'$ such that $d_{\mathcal{B}}(q_2', q_1') = d_{\mathcal{B}}(q_1', q_2') = 0$. ∎

Remark 2. The branching distance defined in [10] and [11] as the smallest function (but not necessarily metric) d satisfying the functional equation:

$$d(q_1, q_2) = \max(\ d_\Pi(\langle\langle q_1\rangle\rangle, \langle\langle q_2\rangle\rangle),$$
$$\lambda \sup_{q_1 \to q_1'} \inf_{q_2 \to q_2'} d(q_1', q_2'),\ \lambda \sup_{q_2 \to q_2'} \inf_{q_1 \to q_1'} d(q_1', q_2')\ )$$

is a bisimulation metric. Moreover, we have shown [11] that it is the smallest (or minimal) bisimulation metric which is the analog for metrics of the largest (or maximal) bisimulation relation for relations. Though it is possible to compute the minimal bisimulation metric for systems with a finite number of states [10], it becomes more problematic for systems with an infinite number of states. In that case, the relaxed conditions of Definition 4 allows to make computations easier [12, 13].

Given a bisimulation metric $d_\mathcal{B}$, we define state neighborhoods associated to this metric. For all $q \in Q$ and $\delta > 0$, $\mathcal{N}_\mathcal{B}(q, \delta) = \{q' \in Q \mid d_\mathcal{B}(q, q') \le \delta\}$.

3   Simulation-Based Reachability Computation

In this section, we show that for metric transition systems equipped with a bisimulation metric, we can compute an approximation (with any desired precision) of the reachable set of a metric transition system by simulating a finite number of its state trajectories. Let us assume that we have a discretization function *Disc* which associates to a compact set $\mathcal{C} \subseteq Q$ and a real number $\varepsilon > 0$, a finite set of points $Disc(\mathcal{C}, \varepsilon) = \{q_1, \dots, q_r\} \subseteq \mathcal{C}$ such that

$$\text{for all } q \in \mathcal{C}, \text{ there exists } q_i, \text{ such that } d_\mathcal{B}(q, q_i) \le \varepsilon.$$

Since $d_\mathcal{B}$ is assumed to be continuous, such a function always exists[1].

The reachable set of T can then be approximated with arbitrarily precision using a finite set of simulations, *i.e.* by computing a finite number of state trajectories of T. Let $\delta > 0$ be the desired precision of approximation for the reachable set. Let ε be a discretization parameter such that $\delta \ge \delta/\lambda + \varepsilon$. First, start with the discretization of the set of initial states of T, $P_0 = Disc(Q_0, \delta)$. Then, we compute some state trajectories of T from the following iteration:

$$P_{i+1} = P_i \cup \left(\bigcup_{q \in P_i} Disc(\text{Post}(q), \varepsilon) \right),\ i = 0, \dots, N-1.$$

Theorem 1. *Let us consider the finite set*

$$\text{Reach}_N^{\delta,\varepsilon}(T) = \{\pi \in \Pi \mid \exists q \in P_N,\ \langle\langle q \rangle\rangle = \pi\}.$$

Then, the following inclusions hold

$$\text{Reach}_N^{\delta,\varepsilon}(T) \subseteq \text{Reach}_N(T) \subseteq \mathcal{N}_\Pi \left(\text{Reach}_N^{\delta,\varepsilon}(T), \delta \right).$$

---

[1] The proof is not stated here because of the lack of space.

Proof. The first inclusion is obvious since P_N is obtained from simulations of T. Let $\pi \in \text{Reach}_N(T)$ and $q_0 \to \cdots \to q_k$ be a state trajectory of T, such that $\langle\langle q_k \rangle\rangle = \pi$ ($k \leq N$). Since $q_0 \in Q_0$, there exists $p_0 \in Disc(Q_0, \delta) = P_0$ such that $d_{\mathcal{B}}(p_0, q_0) \leq \delta$. Then, from equation (1), there exists $p'_1 \in \text{Post}(p_0)$ such that $d_{\mathcal{B}}(p'_1, q_1) \leq \delta/\lambda$. There also exists $p_1 \in Disc(\text{Post}(p_0), \varepsilon) \subseteq P_1$ such that $d_{\mathcal{B}}(p_1, p'_1) \leq \varepsilon$. From the triangular inequality, $d_{\mathcal{B}}(p_1, q_1) \leq \delta/\lambda + \varepsilon \leq \delta$. Recursively, we can show that there exists $p_k \in P_k \subseteq P_N$ such that $d_{\mathcal{B}}(p_k, q_k) \leq \delta$. Then, from equation (1), we also have $d_{\Pi}(\langle\langle p_k \rangle\rangle, \langle\langle q_k \rangle\rangle) \leq \delta$ which finally leads to the second inclusion.   ∎

If we assume that the number of elements $Disc(\text{Post}(q), \varepsilon)$ is always greater than an integer $r > 1$, then the set P_N contains $\mathcal{O}(r^N)$ elements. Then, the number of trajectories that we need to compute grows exponentially with the time horizon N. To overcome this problem and design a more efficient reachability algorithm, one can think of using an approach similar to the systematic simulation algorithm proposed in [2]. The main idea consists in merging, at each iteration, *neighbor* states in P_i. The algorithm in [2] used general ellipsoidal neighborhoods and requires several ellipsoidal operations at each step to determine which states need to be merged. An implementation of this method with neighborhoods associated to the bisimulation metric seems promising and will be explored in the future.

4   Simulation-Based Safety Verification

The method presented in the previous section can be dramatically improved in the context of safety verification. First, it is seldom the case that we need a uniform approximation (in space) of the reachable set. Whereas the previous approach uniformly covers the reachable set with δ neighborhoods, an approach allowing rough approximations where it is possible (*i.e.* far from the unsafe set) and an accurate estimation where it is necessary (*i.e.* near the unsafe set) would definitely give more accurate results for equivalent computations. Second, if the approximation with δ neighborhoods does not allow concluding the safety of the transition system T, the previous approach does not give any guidance for refining our approximation other than choose a smaller δ and start over. Motivated by these two remarks, we propose an algorithm for safety verification for the class of metric transition systems generated by discrete-time linear systems of the form:

$$\Sigma : \begin{cases} x(k+1) = Ax(k) + Bu(k), & x(k) \in \mathbb{R}^n, \ u(k) \in U, \ x(0) \in I, \\ y(k) \quad = Cx(k), & y(k) \in \mathbb{R}^p, \end{cases} \tag{2}$$

where U is a compact subset of $\mathbb{R}^m$ and I is a compact subset of $\mathbb{R}^n$. The input $u(.)$ is to be thought as a disturbance rather than a control.

Remark 3. The distance between the reachable set of a continuous-time system and the reachable set of its sampled version can be quantified. The presented approach can therefore be adapted for safety verification of a continuous-time system at the expense of a quantifiable error.

4.1 Bisimulation Metrics for Linear Systems

In the spirit of [16], the linear system can be written as a nondeterministic transition system $T = (Q, \rightarrow, Q^0, \Pi, \langle\langle . \rangle\rangle)$ where

- the set of states is $Q = \mathbb{R}^n$,
- the transition relation is given by

$$x \rightarrow x' \iff \exists u \in U \text{ such that } x' = Ax + Bu,$$

- the set of initial states is $Q_0 = I$,
- the set of observations is $\Pi = \mathbb{R}^p$,
- the observation map is given by $\langle\langle x \rangle\rangle = Cx$.

The set of states and observations are equipped with the traditional Euclidean metric. Our approach requires a bisimulation metric for our transition system. Following [12], we search for bisimulation metrics of the form:

$$d_\mathcal{B}(x_1, x_2) = \sqrt{(x_1 - x_2)^T M (x_1 - x_2)} \tag{3}$$

where M is a positive semi-definite symmetric matrix.

Theorem 2. *Let M be a positive semi-definite symmetric matrix, $\lambda > 1$ such that the following linear matrix inequalities hold:*

$$M \geq C^T C, \tag{4}$$
$$M - \lambda^2 A^T M A \geq 0. \tag{5}$$

Then, the function $d_\mathcal{B}(x_1, x_2)$ given by equation (3) is a bisimulation metric.

Proof. It is clear that $d_\mathcal{B}$ is pseudo-metric. The linear matrix inequality (4) implies that

$$d_\mathcal{B}(x_1, x_2) \geq \sqrt{(x_1 - x_2)^T C^T C (x_1 - x_2)} = \|Cx_1 - Cx_2\|.$$

The linear matrix inequality (5) implies that for all $u \in U$,

$$\lambda d_\mathcal{B}(Ax_1 + Bu, Ax_2 + Bu) = \lambda \sqrt{(x_1 - x_2)^T A^T M A (x_1 - x_2)}$$
$$\leq \sqrt{(x_1 - x_2)^T M (x_1 - x_2)} = d_\mathcal{B}(x_1, x_2).$$

It follows that $d_\mathcal{B}(x_1, x_2) \geq \lambda \sup_{x_1 \rightarrow x_1'} \inf_{x_2 \rightarrow x_2'} d_\mathcal{B}(x_1', x_2')$. ∎

Thus, a bisimulation metric can be computed by solving a set of linear matrix inequalities which can be done efficiently using semi-definite programming [18]. Moreover, for the class of asymptotically stable linear systems, bisimulation metrics of the form (3) are universal.

Theorem 3. *If Σ is asymptotically stable (i.e. all the eigenvalues of A lie inside the open unit disk), then there exists a bisimulation metric of the form (3).*

The proof is omitted here but a similar result has been proved in [12].

4.2   Safety Verification Algorithm

Let T be a metric transition system generated by a stable discrete-time linear system and $d_{\mathcal{B}}$ a bisimulation metric of form (3). We propose a safety verification algorithm consisting of two main phases. First, by simulating a single trajectory of T, we compute a rough finite-state abstraction $T_{\mathcal{A}}$ of our transition system. Then, the algorithm automatically decides which new trajectories need to be simulated (choice of the initial value and of the sequence of inputs) in order to refine the abstraction $T_{\mathcal{A}}$ and conclude the safety of T.

The states of our abstraction are of the form $q = (x, \mu)$ with $x \in \mathbb{R}^n$ and $\mu \geq 0$ and should be thought of as representing the points of the neighborhood $\mathcal{N}_{\mathcal{B}}(x, \mu)$. The abstraction of T is a transition system $T_{\mathcal{A}} = (Q_{\mathcal{A}}, \rightarrow_{\mathcal{A}}, Q_{\mathcal{A},0}, \Pi_{\mathcal{A}}, \langle\langle . \rangle\rangle_{\mathcal{A}})$ where the set of states $Q_{\mathcal{A}}$ is a finite subset of $\mathbb{R}^n \times \mathbb{R}^+$, the set of observations is $\Pi_{\mathcal{A}} = \Pi$ and the observation map is given by $\langle\langle (x, \mu) \rangle\rangle_{\mathcal{A}} = \langle\langle x \rangle\rangle$. We also need a set $Q_{\text{safe}} \subseteq Q_{\mathcal{A}}$ consisting of *safe* states of $T_{\mathcal{A}}$.

Algorithm 1 shows the structure of our safety verification algorithm. In the following, each step of the method is detailed.

Compute the initial abstraction $T_{\mathcal{A}}$
while $\text{Reach}_N(T_{\mathcal{A}}) \cap \mathcal{U} = \emptyset$ *and* $Q_{\mathcal{A}} \neq Q_{safe}$ **do**
  - *Main refinement loop:*
  Determine the states to split $\mathcal{S} \subseteq Q_{\mathcal{A}} \setminus Q_{\text{safe}}$
  foreach $q \in \mathcal{S}$ **do**
  | Split the state q - *refinement operation*
  end
end
if $\text{Reach}_N(T_{\mathcal{A}}) \cap \mathcal{U} \neq \emptyset$ **then**
| **return** *"The system is unsafe"*
else
| **return** *"The system is safe"*
end

Algorithm 1. Safety verification algorithm

Computation of the initial abstraction. The initial abstraction is computed according to the following procedure. Initially, the set of states $Q_{\mathcal{A}}$, the set of initial states $Q_{\mathcal{A},0}$ the set of *safe* states Q_{safe} as well as the transition relation $\rightarrow_{\mathcal{A}}$ are empty.

First, we choose an initial state $z_0 \in I$ and compute μ_0 such that for all $x_0 \in I$, $d_{\mathcal{B}}(x_0, z_0) \leq \mu_0$. We insert (z_0, μ_0) in $Q_{\mathcal{A}}$ and $Q_{\mathcal{A},0}$. Then, we choose an input $v \in U$ and compute ε such that for all $u \in U$, $d_{\mathcal{B}}(Bv, Bu) \leq \varepsilon$. For $i = 1 \ldots N$, we compute $z_i = Az_{i-1} + Bv$ and $\mu_i = \mu_{i-1}/\lambda + \varepsilon$. Note that this essentially consists in simulating system T for the initial state z_0 and the constant input v. We insert (z_i, μ_i) in $Q_{\mathcal{A}}$ and $((z_{i-1}, \mu_{i-1}), (z_i, \mu_i))$ in the transition relation $\rightarrow_{\mathcal{A}}$.

The second step consists in inserting *safe* states in Q_{safe}. A state (z_i, μ_i) of the abstraction is *safe* if $\mathcal{N}_{\Pi}(\langle\langle z_i \rangle\rangle, \mu_i) \cap \mathcal{U} = \emptyset$ (*i.e.* it is safe now) and its succesors are *safe* (*i.e.* it is safe in the future). We start from the state

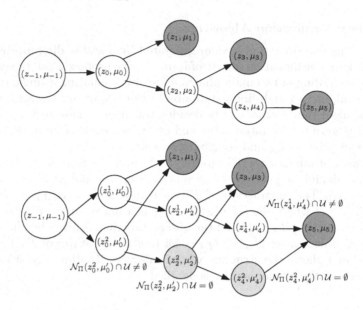

Fig. 1. Illustration of state splitting, the new states are obtained by simulation of the system. The grey states are *safe* states (elements of Q_{safe}): dark grey for states that were in Q_{safe} before state splitting and light grey for those that were added during state splitting.

(z_N, μ_N), if $\mathcal{N}_\Pi(\langle\langle z_N \rangle\rangle, \mu_N) \cap \mathcal{U} = \emptyset$, then we insert (z_N, μ_N) in Q_{safe}. We repeat this procedure for (z_{N-1}, μ_{N-1}) and so on until we find $(z_{N'}, \mu_{N'})$ such that $\mathcal{N}_\Pi(\langle\langle z_{N'} \rangle\rangle, \mu_N) \cap \mathcal{U} \neq \emptyset$.

Refinement operation: state splitting. If the initial abstraction is not sufficient to conclude safety ($Q_\mathcal{A} = Q_{\text{safe}}$) or unsafety ($\text{Reach}_N(T_\mathcal{A}) \cap \mathcal{U} \neq \emptyset$) then the abstraction needs to be refined by splitting states. Let $\rho \in (0,1)$ be a refinement parameter that determines how many states result from state splitting; the smaller ρ, the more new states are inserted in the abstraction. For simplicity, we assume that all the states in $Q_\mathcal{A} \setminus Q_{\text{safe}}$ have at most one predecessor for the transition relation $\to_\mathcal{A}$[2]. We split any state $q_0 = (z_0, \mu_0) \in Q_\mathcal{A} \setminus Q_{\text{safe}}$ according to the following procedure. State splitting is illustrated on Figure 1.

The first step consists in splitting the state q_0 into several states. If q_0 is an initial state (*i.e.* $q_0 \in Q_{\mathcal{A},0}$), then let $\mu_0' = \rho\mu_0$ and $\{z_0^1, \ldots, z_0^r\} = Disc(\mathcal{N}_\mathcal{B}(z_0, \mu_0) \cap I, \rho\mu_0)$. We replace (z_0, μ_0) by $(z_0^1, \mu_0'), \ldots, (z_0^r, \mu_0')$ in $Q_\mathcal{A}$ and $Q_{\mathcal{A},0}$. If q_0 is not an initial state (*i.e.* $q_0 \notin Q_{\mathcal{A},0}$), then let $(z_{-1}, \mu_{-1}) \in Q_\mathcal{A}$ be the predecessor of q_0 (*i.e.* $(z_{-1}, \mu_{-1}) \to_\mathcal{A} (z_0, \mu_0)$) and let $\{w_{-1}^1, \ldots, w_{-1}^r\} = Disc(\mathcal{N}_\mathcal{B}(Bv_{-1}, \varepsilon_{-1}) \cap BU, \rho\varepsilon_{-1})$ where $\varepsilon_{-1} = \mu_0 - \mu_{-1}/\lambda$ and $v_{-1} \in U$ is the input which leads T from z_{-1} to z_0. Let $v_{-1}^1, \ldots, v_{-1}^r \in U$ be inputs such that $Bv_{-1}^j = w_{-1}^j$ ($j = 1, \ldots, r$). Let $z_0^j = Az_{-1} + Bv_{-1}^j$ and $\mu_0' = \mu_{-1}/\lambda + \rho\varepsilon_{-1}$, we replace

---

[2] This assumption is not restrictive since we are performing finite-horizon verification and thus such cases can be handled by duplicating states.

(z_0, μ_0) by $(z_0^1, \mu_0'), \ldots, (z_0^r, \mu_0')$ in $Q_{\mathcal{A}}$ and $((z_{-1}, \mu_{-1}), (z_0, \mu_0))$ is replaced by $((z_{-1}, \mu_{-1}), (z_0^1, \mu_0')), \ldots, ((z_{-1}, \mu_{-1}), (z_0^r, \mu_0'))$ in the transition relation $\rightarrow_{\mathcal{A}}$.

We update $Q_{\mathcal{A}}$ and $\rightarrow_{\mathcal{A}}$, so that each sequence of transitions of the form $(z_0, \mu_0) \rightarrow_{\mathcal{A}} (z_1, \mu_1) \rightarrow_{\mathcal{A}} \cdots \rightarrow_{\mathcal{A}} (z_k, \mu_k)$ such that $(z_k, \mu_k) \notin Q_{\text{safe}}$ is replaced by r sequences:

$$(z_0^j, \mu_0') \rightarrow_{\mathcal{A}} (z_1^j, \mu_1') \rightarrow_{\mathcal{A}} \cdots \rightarrow_{\mathcal{A}} (z_k^j, \mu_k'), \ j = 1, \ldots, r$$

such that $z_{i+1}^j = A z_i^j + B v_i$ where $v_i \in BU$ is the input which leads the system T from z_i to z_{i+1} and $\mu_{i+1}' = \mu_i'/\lambda + \varepsilon_i$ where $\varepsilon_i = \mu_{i+1} - \mu_i/\lambda$. Hence, for each trajectory initiating from z_0 (associated to a sequence of inputs $v_0, \ldots, v_{k-1}$), we need to simulate the trajectories starting in $z_0^1, \ldots, z_0^r$ for the same sequence of inputs. For each *safe* successors of (z_k, μ_k), $(z_{k+1}, \mu_{k+1}) \in Q_{\text{safe}}$, the transition $((z_k, \mu_k), (z_{k+1}, \mu_{k+1}))$ is replaced by the transitions $((z_k^1, \mu_k'), (z_{k+1}, \mu_{k+1})), \ldots,$ $((z_k^r, \mu_k'), (z_{k+1}, \mu_{k+1}))$ in $T_{\mathcal{A}}$. The main idea is that since we already know that (z_{k+1}, μ_{k+1}) is safe, there is no need to split this state.

Finally, we update the set of *safe* states Q_{safe}. For each new state (z, μ) of $T_{\mathcal{A}}$, if all its successors are safe and $\mathcal{N}_{\Pi}(\langle\langle z \rangle\rangle, \mu) \cap \mathcal{U} \neq \emptyset$, then we insert (z, μ) in Q_{safe}. The same process is repeated for the predecessor of (z, μ).

Remark 4. The number of new states introduced by the splitting of q_0 depends critically on how many transitions separate q_0 from a state in Q_{safe}. For instance if all the successors of q_0 are in Q_{safe} then the refinement operation adds r new states. On the other hand, if q_0 is an initial state the total number of states of the abstraction can multiplied by r.

At each iteration of the main loop of Algorithm 1, we choose a set $\mathcal{S} \subseteq Q_{\mathcal{A}} \setminus Q_{\text{safe}}$ of states to be split according to a refinement policy. Then, we apply state splitting to each state in $\mathcal{S}$. The order in which we split the elements of $\mathcal{S}$ is in backward manner, that we split an element q of $\mathcal{S}$ if all the states $q' \in \mathcal{S}$ such that $q \rightarrow_{\mathcal{A}} \cdots \rightarrow_{\mathcal{A}} q'$ have already been split.

The refinement procedure defined by state splitting is such that after each refinement, the states q which remain in $Q_{\mathcal{A}} \setminus Q_{\text{safe}}$ are those for which there exists a sequence of transitions $q \rightarrow_{\mathcal{A}} \cdots \rightarrow_{\mathcal{A}} q'$ such that $q' = (z', \mu')$ and $\mathcal{N}_{\Pi}(\langle\langle z' \rangle\rangle, \mu) \cap \mathcal{U}$ is not empty. This means that all states of $Q_{\mathcal{A}} \setminus Q_{\text{safe}}$ are states which potentially lead to an unsafe state. Since only these states are refined, this approach is similar to counterexample guided abstraction refinement [19, 4, 5].

Soundness and completeness. Before stating results on soundness and completeness of Algorithm 1, we need two approximation results.

Lemma 1. *Let $T_{\mathcal{A}}$ be an abstraction of T obtained from the initial abstraction by a finite sequence of state splittings, let $x_0 \rightarrow \cdots \rightarrow x_k \in S_N(T)$. Then, there exists $(z_0, \mu_0) \rightarrow_{\mathcal{A}} \cdots \rightarrow_{\mathcal{A}} (z_k, \mu_k) \in S_N(T_A)$ such that one of the following holds*

1. $(z_k, \mu_k) \in Q_{safe}$ and $d_\mathcal{B}(x_k, z_k) \leq \mu_k$,
2. $(z_k, \mu_k) \notin Q_{safe}$, $d_\mathcal{B}(x_0, z_0) \leq \mu_0$ and $d_\mathcal{B}(Bu_i, Bv_i) \leq \varepsilon_i$ $(i = 0, \ldots, k-1)$, where $\varepsilon_i = \mu_{i+1} - \mu_i/\lambda$ and $u_0, \ldots, u_{k-1}$ (respectively $v_0, \ldots, v_{k-1}$) is the sequence of inputs associated to the trajectory $x_0 \to \cdots \to x_k$ (respectively $z_0 \to \cdots \to z_k$).

Proof. Let $x_0 \to \cdots \to x_k \in S_N(T)$, let $(z_0, \mu_0) \to_\mathcal{A} \cdots \to_\mathcal{A} (z_k, \mu_k)$ be the unique trajectory of length k of the initial abstraction $T_\mathcal{A}$. By construction, we have $d_\mathcal{B}(x_0, z_0) \leq \mu_0$ and $d_\mathcal{B}(Bu_i, Bv_i) \leq \varepsilon_i$ $(i = 0, \ldots, k-1)$. Then,

$$d_\mathcal{B}(x_{i+1}, z_{i+1}) \leq d_\mathcal{B}(Ax_i + Bu_i, Ax_i + Bv_i) + d_\mathcal{B}(Ax_i + Bv_i, Az_i + Bv_i)$$
$$\leq \varepsilon_i + d_\mathcal{B}(x_i, z_i)/\lambda.$$

By induction, we have that $d_\mathcal{B}(x_k, z_k) \leq \mu_k$. Hence, it is clear that the property holds for the initial abstraction. Let us assume that it holds after a finite sequence of refinements, and let $(z_0, \mu_0) \to_\mathcal{A} \cdots \to_\mathcal{A} (z_k, \mu_k)$ be the associated element of $S_N(T_\mathcal{A})$. We apply state splitting to an element $q \in Q_\mathcal{A} \setminus Q_{safe}$. If (z_k, μ_k) was in Q_{safe} before state splitting, then it is clear that the first assertion of the lemma still holds after state splitting. Let us assume that (z_k, μ_k) is not in Q_{safe} and that the second assertion of the lemma holds before state splitting. Particularly, it can be shown by induction that $d_\mathcal{B}(x_k, z_k) \leq \mu_k$. If for all $i \in \{0, \ldots, k\}$, $q \neq (z_i, \mu_i)$ then $(z_0, \mu_0) \to_\mathcal{A} \cdots \to_\mathcal{A} (z_k, \mu_k)$ is still a trajectory of $T_\mathcal{A}$ after state splitting and one of the two assertions of the lemma holds. If $q = (z_i, \mu_i)$ (for some $i \in \{1, \ldots, k\}$, the case $i = 0$ being similar), then after state splitting, we know by construction that there exists a trajectory of $T_\mathcal{A}$ of the form $(z_0, \mu_0) \to_\mathcal{A} \cdots \to_\mathcal{A} (z_{i-1}, \mu_{i-1}) \to_\mathcal{A} (z_i^j, \mu_i') \cdots \to_\mathcal{A} (z_k^j, \mu_k')$ such that $d_\mathcal{B}(x_0, z_0) \leq \mu_0$ and $d_\mathcal{B}(Bu_0, Bv_0) \leq \varepsilon_0, \ldots, d_\mathcal{B}(Bu_{i-2}, Bv_{i-2}) \leq \varepsilon_{i-2}$, $d_\mathcal{B}(Bu_{i-1}, Bv_{i-1}^j) \leq \varepsilon_{i-1}' = \rho\varepsilon_{i-1}$, $d_\mathcal{B}(Bu_i, Bv_i) \leq \varepsilon_i, \ldots, d_\mathcal{B}(Bu_{k-1}, Bv_{k-1}) \leq \varepsilon_{k-1}$. Note that this also implies that $d_\mathcal{B}(x_k, z_k^j) \leq \mu_k'$. Therefore, one of the assertions of the lemma holds after state splitting. Hence, Lemma 1 is proved by induction. ∎

Theorem 4. *Let $T_\mathcal{A}$ be an abstraction of T obtained from the initial abstraction by a finite sequence of state splittings. Let us define the following set*

$$\widetilde{\mathrm{Reach}_N}(T_\mathcal{A}) = \{\pi \in \Pi | \exists (z, \mu) \in Q_\mathcal{A}, \, d_\pi(\langle\langle z \rangle\rangle, \pi) \leq \mu\}.$$

Then, the following inclusions hold

$$\mathrm{Reach}_N(T_\mathcal{A}) \subseteq \mathrm{Reach}_N(T) \subseteq \widetilde{\mathrm{Reach}_N}(T_\mathcal{A}).$$

Proof. The first inclusion is obvious because the states of the abstraction are computed by simulation of T. Let $\pi \in \mathrm{Reach}_N(T)$ and $x_0 \to \cdots \to x_k$ be a state trajectory of T, such that $\langle\langle x_k \rangle\rangle = \pi$ $(k \leq N)$. From Lemma 1, there exists $(z_0, \mu_0) \to_\mathcal{A} \cdots \to_\mathcal{A} (z_k, \mu_k) \in S_N(T_\mathcal{A})$ such that one assertion of the lemma holds. Let us remark that in both cases, we have $d_\mathcal{B}(z_k, x_k) \leq \mu_k$ and therefore $d_\pi(\langle\langle z_k \rangle\rangle, \pi) \leq \mu_k$. ∎

The following soundness result is straightforward:

Theorem 5. *If Algorithm 1 terminates, then it provides the correct answer to the safety verification problem.*

Proof. If at the termination of Algorithm 1, we have $\text{Reach}_N(T_A) \cap \mathcal{U} \neq \emptyset$, then from the first inclusion of Theorem 4, we have that T is unsafe. If at the termination of Algorithm 1, we have $Q_A = Q_{\text{safe}}$, this particularly means that for all $(z, \mu) \in Q_A$, $\mathcal{N}_\pi(\langle\langle z \rangle\rangle, \mu) \cap \mathcal{U} = \emptyset$. From the second inclusion of Theorem 4, we have that T is safe. ∎

Guaranteed termination of Algorithm 1 requires defining more precisely the refinement policy. If at each iteration of the main loop of Algorithm 1, we split all the states of T_A ($\mathcal{S} = Q_A \setminus Q_{\text{safe}}$), then we have the following completeness result:

Theorem 6. *If we apply the refinement policy $\mathcal{S} = Q_A \setminus Q_{\text{safe}}$, and if the metric transition system T is either robustly safe or robustly unsafe with coefficient of robustness δ, then Algorithm 1 terminates after at most $\lceil (\log(\delta) - \log(\bar{\mu}_0)) / \log(\rho) \rceil$ iterations where $\bar{\mu}_0 = \max\{\mu \mid (z, \mu) \in Q_A \setminus Q_{\text{safe}}$ in the initial abstraction$\}$.*

Proof. Let $\bar{\mu}_i = \max\{\mu \mid (z, \mu) \in Q_A \setminus Q_{\text{safe}}$ after the i-th refinement loop$\}$. Since at each refinement loop, state splitting is applied to all the states in $Q_A \setminus Q_{\text{safe}}$, it is not hard to see that $\bar{\mu}_{i+1} \leq \rho\bar{\mu}_i$. Then, $\bar{\mu}_i \leq \rho^i\bar{\mu}_0$. It follows that for $i \geq (\log(\delta) - \log(\bar{\mu}_0)) / \log(\rho)$, $\bar{\mu}_i \leq \delta$. Let us assume that Algorithm 1 did not terminate after i iterations. Then, there exists $(z, \mu) \in Q_A \setminus Q_{\text{safe}}$ with $\mu \leq \delta$ and such that $\langle\langle z \rangle\rangle \notin \mathcal{U}$ and $\mathcal{N}_\Pi(\langle\langle z \rangle\rangle, \mu) \cap \mathcal{U}$ is not empty. From Theorem 4, we have that $\langle\langle z \rangle\rangle \in \text{Reach}_N(T)$, it follows that T cannot be robustly safe. If T was robustly unsafe, there would be a $\pi \in \text{Reach}_N(T)$ such that $\mathcal{N}_\Pi(\pi, \delta) \subseteq \mathcal{U}$, from Theorem 4, there exists $\pi' \in \text{Reach}_N(T_A)$ such that $d_\Pi(\pi, \pi') \leq \bar{\mu}_i$. Hence, $\pi' \in \mathcal{N}_\Pi(\pi, \bar{\mu}_i) \subseteq \mathcal{N}_\Pi(\pi, \delta) \subseteq \mathcal{U}$ which contradicts the fact that Algorithm 1 did not terminate. ∎

We can see that the more robust with respect to the safety property a system is, the less refinements are needed resulting in fewer computations and easier safety verification. Note that particularly, if $\bar{\mu}_0 \leq \delta$, no refinement is needed to decide wether T is safe or unsafe. This is an important advantage of the method.

In practice, it is seldom necessary to apply state splitting to all the states of the abstraction. Moreover, we have seen that applying state splitting to states that are separated by a large number of transitions of a state in Q_{safe} may result in a large increase of the number of states in Q_A. Hence, from this point of view it is better to apply state splitting to states that are within a small number of transitions from elements in Q_{safe}. A different refinement policy can be defined by $\mathcal{S} = \mathcal{P}(Q_A, p)$ which consists of the states $q = (z, \mu) \in Q_A$ such that there exists a sequence of transition of the form $q \rightarrow_A q_1 \rightarrow_A \cdots \rightarrow_A q_k$ with $q_k \in Q_{\text{safe}}$ and $k \leq p$. Note that for this refinement policy, Theorem 6 does not hold even if Algorithm 1 shows better performances in practice. For theoretical completeness, we can use a refinement policy which alternates $\mathcal{S} = \mathcal{P}(Q_A, p)$ and $\mathcal{S} = Q_A \setminus Q_{\text{safe}}$. In that case, a result similar to Theorem 6 holds.

Remark 5. It is clear from Lemma 1 that the abstraction $T_{\mathcal{A}}$ not only allows to approximate the reachable set of T but also its language. This is strong evidence that our approach can be generalized for the simulation-based verification of more complex properties such as those expressible in linear temporal logic [14].

4.3   Experimental Results

Let us consider the following continuous-time linear system:

$$\begin{cases} \dot{x}_1(t) = \quad 3x_1(t) + 20x_2(t) \\ \dot{x}_2(t) = -2x_1(t) - 9x_2(t) + x_3(t) + u(t) \\ \dot{x}_3(t) = -4x_3(t) + 2u(t) \end{cases}$$

For piecewise constant inputs with sampling period $\tau = 0.1$, the sampled system dynamics are given by

$$x(k+1) = Ax(k) + Bv(k), \text{ where}$$

$$A = \begin{bmatrix} 1.17 & 1.47 & 0.07 \\ -0.15 & 0.28 & 0.05 \\ 0 & 0 & 0.67 \end{bmatrix}, B = \begin{bmatrix} 0.09 \\ 0.07 \\ 0.16 \end{bmatrix}, x(k) = \begin{bmatrix} x_1(k\tau) \\ x_2(k\tau) \\ x_3(k\tau) \end{bmatrix},$$

and $v(k) = u(k\tau)$. Only the variable x_2 is observed (*i.e.* $C = [0\ 1\ 0]$). The set of initial states I and of inputs U are given by $I = [-0.05, 0.05] \times [9.95, 10.05] \times \{0\}$ and $U = [0, 2.5]$. T denotes the associated metric transition system. The safety

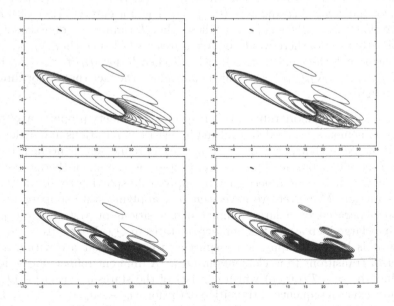

Fig. 2. Over approximation of the set reachable by x_1 and x_2, the red line represent the border of the unsafe set. The quality of the approximation is adapted automatically to the safety property we want to verify.

property we want to check is wether the reachable set $\text{Reach}_{20}(T)$ intersects the set $\{y \leq \theta\}$ or not. In order to apply our safety verification algorithm, we need to compute a bisimulation metric. This is done by solving linear matrix inequalities (4) and (5). Our safety verification algorithm has been implemented in MATLAB and used for several values of the parameter θ with the refinement parameter and the refinement policy $\mathcal{S} = \mathcal{P}(Q_{\mathcal{A}}, 5)$.

Figure 2 represents the over approximation of the set reachable by x_1 and x_2 computed by our algorithm for different values of θ. We can see that as the value of θ becomes larger, the system becomes less robustly safe and our over-approximation of the reachable set needs to be more precise. Let us remark that the state-splitting is effectively applied where it is needed, that is where the reachable set is close to the unsafe set. The results of our computations are presented in Figure 3. Experimentation confirms what we expected from Theorem 6. Indeed, we can check that if the system is very robust with respect to the safety property, the safety verification is performed using only one simulation and takes less than a second. As the system safety becomes less robust, the algorithm needs more time to decide if the system is safe or unsafe. On Figure 3, this is visible and we can expect that the curves of the CPU time and of the number of refinement loops have a vertical asymptote for some critical value of θ.

θ	Result	CPU time (s)	Refinements
-7.4	Safe	0.16	0
-7.0	Safe	0.25	1
-6.5	Safe	0.44	2
-5.8	Safe	74.77	3
-4.6	Unsafe	5.82	3
-4.5	Unsafe	0.16	0

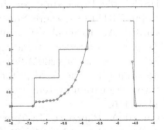

Fig. 3. Results of Algorithm 1 (table). Number of refinement loops needed by Algorithm 1 and CPU time in logarithmic scale against the parameter θ (figure).

5   Conclusion

In this paper we presented a simulation-based framework for verifying the safety of metric transition systems. Our algorithm critically relies on recently developed bisimulation metrics which can be used to approximate arbitrarily close the reachable set of metric transition systems by simulating a finite number of trajectories. For metric transition systems generated by nondeterministic linear systems, we proposed a safety verification algorithm which is complete for systems that are robustly safe or robustly unsafe. Future research will focus on lifting the completeness of the safety verification algorithm to general metric transition systems, including classes of hybrid systems.

References

1. Alur, R., Grosu, R., Hur, Y., Kumar, V., Lee, I.: Modular specification of hybrid systems in charon. In: HSCC '00: Proceedings of the 3rd International Workshop on Hybrid Systems. Volume 1790 of Lecture Notes In Computer Science., Springer-Verlag (2000) 6 – 19
2. Kapinski, J., Krogh, B.H., Maler, O., Stursberg, O.: On systematic simulation of open continuous systems. In: Hybrid Systems: Computation and Control. Volume 2623 of LNCS., Springer (2003) 283–297
3. Lee, E.A., Zheng, H.: Operational semantics of hybrid systems. In: HSCC '05: Proceedings of the 8th International Workshop on Hybrid Systems. Volume 3414 of Lecture Notes In Computer Science., Springer-Verlag (2005) 25 – 53
4. Alur, R., Dang, T., Ivancic, F.: Counter-example guided predicate abstraction of hybrid systems. In: Tools and Algorithms for the Construction and Analysis of Systems. Volume 2619 of LNCS., Springer (2003) 208–223
5. Clarke, E., Fehnker, A., Han, Z., Krogh, B., Ouaknine, J., Stursberg, O., Theobald, M.: Abstraction and counterexample-guided refinement in model checking of hybrid systems. International Journal of Foundations of Computer Science 14(4) (2003)
6. Prajna, S., Jadbabaie, A.: Safety verification of hybrid systems using barrier certificates. In: Hybrid Systems: Computation and Control. Volume 2993 of Lecture Notes in Computer Science., Springer (2004) 477 – 492
7. Mitchell, I., Tomlin, C.: Level set methods for computation in hybrid systems. In: Hybrid Systems: Computation and Control. Volume 1790 of LNCS., Springer (2000)
8. Frehse, G.: Phaver: Algorithmic verification of hybrid systems past hytech. In: HSCC '05: Proceedings of the 8th International Workshop on Hybrid Systems. Volume 3414 of Lecture Notes In Computer Science. (2005) 258–273
9. Girard, A.: Reachability of uncertain linear systems using zonotopes. In: Hybrid Systems: Computation and Control. Volume 3414 of Lecture Notes in Computer Science., Springer (2005) 291–305
10. de Alfaro, L., Faella, M., Stoelinga, M.: Linear and branching metrics for quantitative transition systems. In: ICALP'04. Volume 3142 of LNCS., Springer (2004) 1150–1162
11. Girard, A., Pappas, G.J.: Approximation metrics for discrete and continuous systems. Technical Report MS-CIS-05-10, Dept. of CIS, University of Pennsylvania (2005)
12. Girard, A., Pappas, G.J.: Approximate bisimulations for constrained linear systems. In: Proc. IEEE Conference on Decision and Control and European Control Conference, Seville, Spain (2005) 4700–4705
13. Girard, A., Pappas, G.J.: Approximate bisimulations for nonlinear dynamical systems. In: Proc. IEEE Conference on Decision and Control and European Control Conference, Seville, Spain (2005) 684–689
14. Clarke, E.M., Grumberg, O., Peled, D.A.: Model Checking. MIT Press (2000)
15. Haghverdi, E., Tabuada, P., Pappas, G.J.: Bisimulation relations for dynamical, control, and hybrid systems. Theoretical Computer Science 342(2-3) (2005) 229–262
16. Pappas, G.J.: Bisimilar linear systems. Automatica 39(12) (2003) 2035–2047
17. van der Schaft, A.: Equivalence of dynamical systems by bisimulation. IEEE Transactions on Automatic Control 49(12) (2004) 2160–2172
18. Sturm, J.F.: Using SEDUMI 1.02, a MATLAB toolbox for optimization over symmetric cones. Optimization Methods and Softwares 11-12 (1999) 625–653
19. Clarke, E., Grumberg, O., Jha, S., Lu, Y., Veith, H.: Counterexample-guided abstraction refinement. In: Computer Aided Verification. Volume 1855 of LNCS., Springer (2000) 154–169

Reachability Analysis of Large-Scale Affine Systems Using Low-Dimensional Polytopes*

Zhi Han and Bruce H. Krogh

Carnegie Mellon University, 5000 Forbes Ave, Pittsburgh PA 15213, USA
{zhih, krogh}@ece.cmu.edu

Abstract. This paper presents a method for computing the reach set of affine systems for sets of initial states given as low-dimensional polytopes. An affine representation for polytopes is introduced to improve the efficiency of set representations. Using the affine representation, we present a procedure to compute conservative over-approximations of the reach set, which uses the Krylov subspace approximation method to handle large-scale affine systems (systems of order over 100).

1 Introduction

Reachability analysis is an important problem in formal verification of continuous and hybrid dynamic systems. Reachability analysis concerns the computation of the system's *reach set*, the set of reachable states in the state space from a given set of initial states. Due to the complexity of representing and computing high-dimensional sets, most existing tools for reachability analysis have been limited to low-order systems (orders less than 10).

Recent progress on reachability analysis for linear systems has made it possible to compute over-approximations of reach sets for relatively high-order systems [1, 2, 3]. These methods can be categorized into two classes, which we refer to as *dimensional* methods and *representational* methods. Dimensional methods rely on the construction of reduced-order approximations for the given full-order linear system models [3, 4]. Reach sets are computed for the reduced-order models using existing computational tools, and analysis results for the full-order model are then inferred from the results obtained for the reduced-order models. Representational methods, on the other hand, reduce the computational complexity by using special representations of sets in the high-dimensional state space of the full-order model. For polytopes, this can be done by restricting the sets to special classes of polytopes, e.g., hyper-boxes [5], oriented rectangles [2], and zonotopes [1]. Besides polytopes, ellipsoids have been used successfully for reachability analysis of continuous and hybrid systems [6]. The reduction in computational complexity is due to the use of reduced-size representations in the reachability algorithms.

Both classes of methods still have difficulties when they are applied to large-scale systems. For dimensional methods, a good reduced-order model in practice may be of order 10 to 30, which is still beyond the capability of the current computational tools for reachability analysis. Representational methods suffer from

---

* Research supported in part by US Army Research Office (ARO).

João Hespanha and A. Tiwari (Eds.): HSCC 2006, LNCS 3927, pp. 287–301, 2006.

two problems. First, arbitrary polytopes can be only over-approximated using the reduced-size representations. Second, these special classes of polytopes are not closed under intersection, e.g., the intersection of a hyper-box with a halfspace is generally not a hyper-box. Since intersection is a necessary computation in reachability analysis for hybrid dynamic systems, additional post-processing is needed for these methods to be useful for applications.

This paper concerns reachability analysis for affine systems with sets of initial states given as *low-dimensional* polytopes. A polytope is low dimensional when the continuous variables are linearly correlated. Linearly correlated variables are common in linear systems [7, 8]. In applications, this class of problems arises in the following situations. If variations in a certain subset of continuous variables are of interest, the initial set is low-dimensional. Preliminary analysis of the system, e.g., using simulations and principal component analysis, can identify the variables of interest. Another possible situation is that there is strong correlation between the initial values of the state variables because of the dynamics, e.g., if the initial state of the system is an unknown but steady state, the initial state satisfies $Ax(0) = b$. This equality constraint enforces the initial polytope to be low-dimensional.

Our method of reachability analysis attacks the complexity issue from both the representational and the dimensional perspectives. From the representational perspective, we introduce an affine representation for polytopes to enable efficient set representations. The affine representation can describe arbitrary polytopes and is closed under intersection. From the dimensional perspective, we reduce the computational complexity of analyzing high-order models by approximating the reach set using the Krylov subspace approximations [9].

This paper is organized as follows. Section 2 presents mathematical background and notation used in this paper. Section 3 introduces the affine representation for polytopes. Section 4 describes the procedure to compute the reach set using affine representations. Section 5 considers the reach set computation using the Krylov subspace approximations. Section 6 presents a numeric example to illustrate the method. The paper concludes with a summary of the contribution and a discussion of the relationship of this work to zonotope computations [1].

2   Preliminaries

2.1   Polytopes

Let $\mathbb{R}^n$ denote the nth-order normed real space. The norm $\|\cdot\|$ denotes the infinity norm. The Hausdorff distance between two subsets $\mathcal{X}_1$ and $\mathcal{X}_2$ of $\mathbb{R}^n$ is defined as $d(\mathcal{X}_1, \mathcal{X}_2) = \max\{\sup_{x_1 \in \mathcal{X}_1} \inf_{x_2 \in \mathcal{X}_2} \|x_1 - x_2\|, \sup_{x_2 \in \mathcal{X}_2} \inf_{x_1 \in \mathcal{X}_1} \|x_1 - x_2\|\}$. A finite set of points $v_i \in \mathbb{R}^n$, $i = 1, \ldots, k$ is also represented by the matrix $V \subset \mathbb{R}^{n \times k} = [v_1\ v_2\ \ldots\ v_k]$. The subspace $span(V)$ is the linear subspace spanned by the set of points $v_1, \ldots, v_k$, that is, $span(V) = \{x | x = \sum_{i=1}^{k} \lambda_i v_i, \lambda_i \in \mathbb{R}\}$.

A *halfspace* is a set of the form $H(\pi^T, d) = \{x | \pi^T x \leq d, x \in \mathbb{R}^n\}$, where $\pi \in \mathbb{R}^n$ and $d \in \mathbb{R}$. A *polytope* in $\mathbb{R}^n$ is a bounded intersection of a finite set of halfspaces $\mathcal{P} = \{x | \pi_i^T x \le d_i, x \in \mathbb{R}^n\}$ where $\pi_i \in \mathbb{R}^n$, $d_i \in \mathbb{R}$ and $i = 1, \ldots, m$. Given $\Pi = \begin{bmatrix} \pi_1 \ldots \pi_m \end{bmatrix}^T \in \mathbb{R}^{m \times n}$, $d = \begin{bmatrix} d_1 \, d_2 \ldots d_m \end{bmatrix}^T \in \mathbb{R}^m$, we use $P(\Pi, d)$ as a short-hand notation for a polytope $\mathcal{P} = \{x | \Pi x \le d\} \subseteq \mathbb{R}^n$. The halfspace representation is also called the $\mathcal{H}$-representation of the polytope [10].

For a set $\mathcal{X} \subset \mathbb{R}^n$, the convex hull $CH(\mathcal{X})$ is the intersection of all the convex sets that contains $\mathcal{X}$ [10]. A polytope can be represented as the convex hull of a finite set of points $\mathcal{P} = CH(\{v_1, v_2 \ldots, v_k\}) := \{x | x = \sum_{i=1}^k \lambda_i v_i, \lambda_i \ge 0, \sum_{i=1}^k \lambda_i = 1\}$. Using the matrix notation we write $\mathcal{P} = CH(V)$, which is called the $\mathcal{V}$-representation for polytopes [10].

The *dimension* of a set of points, denoted $dim(\mathcal{X})$, is the dimension of the affine subspace $aff(\mathcal{X}) = \{z | z = \sum_{i=1}^k \lambda_i x_i, x_i \in \mathcal{X}, \lambda_i \in \mathbb{R}, \sum_{i=1}^k \lambda_i = 1\}$ [10]. A polytope $\mathcal{P}$ is *full-dimensional* if $dim(\mathcal{P}) = n$. A d-dimensional polytope is also called d-polytope.

For polytopes, the following operations are commonly used in reachability analysis. Polytopes are closed under these operations [10], i.e., the results of the operations are also polytopes.

– Affine transformation: For $A \in \mathbb{R}^{m \times n}$, $b \in \mathbb{R}^m$: $A\mathcal{P} + b = \{y | y = Ax + b, x \in \mathcal{P} \subset \mathbb{R}^n\} \subseteq \mathbb{R}^m$.
– Intersection: $\mathcal{P}_1 \cap \mathcal{P}_2 = \{x | x \in \mathcal{P}_1 \land x \in \mathcal{P}_2, \mathcal{P}_1 \subseteq \mathbb{R}^n, \mathcal{P}_2 \subseteq \mathbb{R}^n\} \subseteq \mathbb{R}^n$.
– Minkowski sum: $\mathcal{P}_1 \oplus \mathcal{P}_2 = \{y | y = x_1 + x_2, x_1 \in \mathcal{P}_1 \subseteq \mathbb{R}^n, x_2 \in \mathcal{P}_2 \subseteq \mathbb{R}^n\}$.
– Cartesian product: $\mathcal{P}_1 \otimes \mathcal{P}_2 = \{[x_1^T, x_2^T]^T | x_1 \in \mathcal{P}_1 \subseteq \mathbb{R}^n, x_2 \in \mathcal{P}_2 \subseteq \mathbb{R}^m\}$

If $\mathcal{P}_2$ is an affine transformation of $\mathcal{P}_1$ and the affine mapping $\mathcal{P}_1 \to \mathcal{P}_2 : x \mapsto Ax + b$ is bijective, then $\mathcal{P}_1$ and $\mathcal{P}_2$ are said to be *affinely equivalent* [10]. Every d-polytope in $\mathbb{R}^n$ is affinely equivalent to a d-polytope in $\mathbb{R}^d$.

2.2 Reach Sets for Affine Dynamic Systems

Affine systems are dynamic systems governed by affine differential equations of the form $\mathcal{S} : \dot{x}(t) = Ax(t) + b$, where $A \in \mathbb{R}^{n \times n}$, $b \in \mathbb{R}^n$, and $x(t) \in \mathbb{R}^n$ is a vector of state variables. For a given *initial set* $\mathcal{X}_0$, where $\mathcal{X}_0 \subseteq \mathbb{R}^n$ is a set of initial states, the *reach set* of an affine system $\mathcal{S}$ at time t is the set $Reach(\mathcal{S}, \mathcal{X}_0, t) = \{x(t) | x(t) = e^{At} x_0 + \int_0^t e^{A(t-\tau)} b \, d\tau, x_0 \in \mathcal{X}_0\}$, where $t > 0$. With a slight abuse of notation, the reach set of system $\mathcal{S}$ with initial set $\mathcal{X}_0$ over a time interval $[t_s, t_f]$ is defined as $Reach(\mathcal{S}, \mathcal{X}_0, [t_s, t_f]) = \bigcup_{t \in [t_s, t_f]} Reach(\mathcal{S}, \mathcal{X}_0, t)$, where $0 \le t_s < t_f < \infty$. We denote the reach set at t and $[t_s, t_f]$ as $Reach(t)$ and $Reach([t_s, t_f])$, if the other parameters are clear from the context. For a given time sequence t_0, $t_1, \ldots, t_N$, where $0 = t_0 < t_1 < \ldots < t_N$, the reach set $Reach(t_k)$ is also written as $\mathcal{X}_k$ as a short-hand notation.

In the sequel we let $\mathcal{X}_{k-1,k}$ be the set defined as $\mathcal{X}_{k-1,k} = \{x | x = \lambda x_{k-1} + (1-\lambda)x_k$ where $x_{k-1} = e^{At_{k-1}} x_0 + \int_0^{t_{k-1}} e^{A(t-\tau)} b \, d\tau, x_k = e^{At_k} x_0 + \int_0^{t_k} e^{A(t-\tau)} b \, d\tau, x_0 \in \mathcal{X}_0, \lambda \in [0, 1]\}$ and call it the *linear interpolation* of $\mathcal{X}_{k-1}$ and $\mathcal{X}_k$. The set $\mathcal{X}_{k-1,k}$ is in general non-convex. Over-approximations of the reach set segment can be computed by 'bloating' a convex over-approximation of the linear interpolation [11].

2.3 Krylov Subspace Approximations

To facilitate the discussion we introduce a series of matrix functions φ_i [9]. For matrix $A \in \mathbb{R}^{n \times n}$:

$$\varphi_i(A, t) = \begin{cases} e^{At} & = \sum_{j=0}^{\infty} \frac{1}{j!} A^j t^j, & i = 0 \\ \frac{1}{(i-1)! t^i} \int_0^t e^{A(t-\tau)} \tau^{i-1} d\tau & = \sum_{j=0}^{\infty} \frac{1}{(i+j)!} A^j t^j, & i \geq 1 \end{cases} \quad (1)$$

For matrix $A \in \mathbb{R}^{n \times n}$ and $B \in \mathbb{R}^{n \times m}$, we define the scalar-valued matrix function $\psi_i(A, B, t)$ as $\psi_i(A, B, t) = \sup_{s \in [0,t]} \|\varphi_i(A, s)B\|$, $i = 0, 1, \ldots$.

There are a collection of methods for computing the matrix functions φ_i [12]. The Krylov subspace approximation method is in particular a very efficient way to compute $\varphi_i(A, t)v$ for an arbitrary $v \in \mathbb{R}^n$ and a large-scale sparse matrix A [9, 13].

Consider the case $i = 0$, the matrix exponential $e^{At}v$ is the solution to the linear system $\dot{x}(t) = Ax(t)$, $x(0) = v$ at time t. For matrix $A \in \mathbb{R}^{n \times n}$ and vector $v \in \mathbb{R}^n$, the rth-order Krylov subspace is defined as $Kr(A, v, r) := span\{v, Av, \ldots, A^{r-1}v\}$. The solution of the full-order model can be approximated by its orthogonal *projection* to $K_r(A, v, r)$. Let $V_r \in \mathbb{R}^{n \times r}$ be a matrix whose column vectors $\{v_1, v_2, \ldots, v_r\}$ is an orthogonal basis of K_r. Then a reduced-order model is constructed as $\dot{z}(t) = H_r z(t)$, $z(0) = V_r^T v$, where $H_r = V_r^T A V_r \in \mathbb{R}^{r \times r}$ is a reduced-order system matrix. The trajectory of the full-order model is approximated by $x(t) \approx V_r z(t)$. In terms of matrix computations, the Krylov subspace method approximates the full-order matrix exponential using $e^{At}v \approx V_r e^{H_r t} V_r^T v =: (e^{At}v)^{\mathcal{K}}$. In this paper we use superscript $\mathcal{K}$ to denote the terms computed using Krylov subspace approximation. The projection matrix V_r can be computed using iterative methods, e.g., the Arnoldi procedure [14].

To compute approximations to $\varphi_i(A, t)v$, $i \geq 1$, it is shown in [13] that $\varphi_i(A, t)$ can be computed using $\varphi_0(A, t)v$ by augmenting the system matrix. Consider the $(n + i)^{th}$-order linear dynamic model

$$\dot{\overline{x}} = \overline{A}\overline{x} = \begin{bmatrix} A & v & 0 & \cdots & 0 \\ 0 & 0 & 1 & \ddots & 0 \\ \vdots & \vdots & \ddots & \ddots & \vdots \\ 0 & 0 & \cdots & 0 & 1 \\ 0 & 0 & \cdots & 0 & 0 \end{bmatrix} \overline{x}, \quad \overline{x}(0) = \overline{x}_0 = \begin{bmatrix} 0 \\ \vdots \\ 0 \\ 1 \end{bmatrix} \in \mathbb{R}^{n+i} \quad (2)$$

The first n-rows of the solution to the augmented system are $t^i \varphi_i(A, t)v$.

Krylov subspace approximation is usually good for small values of t. For large values of t, approximations to the solution of the linear system are computed through a time-stepping strategy [13]. At each step k, a small step size $h_k = t_k - t_{k-1}$ is chosen and the Krylov subspace approximation to $x(t_k)$ is computed using the Krylov subspace from previous results $Kr(A, x(t_{k-1}), r)$. The computation repeats until the time t is reached, giving an approximation of $e^{At}v$. Throughout the paper we neglect the numeric error caused by round-off and focus on the error introduced by Krylov subspace approximation. The following theorem provides a bound on the error of Krylov subspace approximation for matrix exponentials.

Theorem 1. *[9]. Let A be any square matrix and let $\rho = \|A\|$. Then the error of the rth-order Krylov subspace approximation for matrix exponential satisfies* $\|e^A v - V_r e^{H_r} V_r^T v\| \leq 2\|v\| \frac{\rho^r e^\rho}{r!}$.

3   Affine Representation for Polytopes

Affine representations are introduced for efficiently representing low-dimensional polytopes in the reachability analysis algorithms. Before introducing the affine representation, we note that operations on low-dimensional polytopes result in low-dimensional polytopes. Indeed,

- Affine transformation: $dim(A\mathcal{P} + b) \leq dim(\mathcal{P})$.
- Intersection: $dim(\mathcal{P}_1 \cap \mathcal{P}_2) \leq \min\{dim(\mathcal{P}_1), dim(\mathcal{P}_2)\}$.
- Minkowski sum: $dim(\mathcal{P}_1 \oplus \mathcal{P}_2) \leq dim(\mathcal{P}_1) + dim(\mathcal{P}_2)$.
- Cartesian product: $dim(\mathcal{P}_1 \otimes \mathcal{P}_2) = dim(\mathcal{P}_1) + dim(\mathcal{P}_2)$.

Since every d-polytope in $\mathbb{R}^n$ is affinely equivalent to a d-polytope in $\mathbb{R}^d$, it is convenient to represent the d-polytope in high-order space as an affine transformation of the d-polytope in low-order space. For polytope $\mathcal{P} \subseteq \mathbb{R}^n$ satisfying $\mathcal{P} = \Phi \mathcal{P}_w + \gamma$ where $\Phi \in \mathbb{R}^{n \times d}$ is full-column-rank, $\gamma \in \mathbb{R}^n$ and $\mathcal{P}_w$ is a d-polytope in $\mathbb{R}^d$. we write $\mathcal{P} = \langle \Phi, \gamma, \mathcal{P}_w \rangle$ and call it the *affine representation* for $\mathcal{P}$. We further enforce the following restrictions on affine representations

$$\mathcal{P}_w \text{ is full-dimensional,} \tag{3}$$
$$\mathbf{0} \in \mathcal{P}_w \text{ and } \sup_{w \in \mathcal{P}_w} \|w\| \leq 1.$$

Computation for operations on polytopes can be performed on their affine representations. The following proposition gives operations on polytopes in their affine representation.

Proposition 1. *For polytopes $\mathcal{P} = \langle \Phi, \gamma, \mathcal{P}_w \rangle$, $\mathcal{P}_1 = \langle \Phi_1, \gamma_1, \mathcal{P}_{w1} \rangle$ and $\mathcal{P}_2 = \langle \Phi_2, \gamma_2, \mathcal{P}_{w2} \rangle$ in their affine representations, the following relations hold.*

- *Affine transformation: $A\mathcal{P} + b = \langle A\Phi, A\gamma + b, \mathcal{P}_w \rangle$.*
- *Minkowski sum: $\mathcal{P}_1 \oplus \mathcal{P}_2 = \langle [\Phi_1 \ \Phi_2], \gamma_1 + \gamma_2, \mathcal{P}_{w1} \otimes \mathcal{P}_{w2} \rangle$.*
- *Cartesian product: $\mathcal{P}_1 \otimes \mathcal{P}_2 = \langle \begin{bmatrix} \Phi_1 & 0 \\ 0 & \Phi_2 \end{bmatrix}, \begin{bmatrix} \gamma_1 \\ \gamma_2 \end{bmatrix}, \mathcal{P}_{w1} \otimes \mathcal{P}_{w2} \rangle$.*
- *Intersection with halfspace: $\mathcal{P} \cap H(\pi^T, d) = \langle \Phi, \gamma, P(\begin{bmatrix} \Pi_w \\ \pi^T \Phi \end{bmatrix}, \begin{bmatrix} d \\ d - \pi^T \gamma \end{bmatrix}) \rangle$.*

Proof. The first three computations can be derived directly from their definition. For intersections, we first prove $\mathcal{P} \cap H(\pi^T, d) \subseteq \langle \Phi, \gamma, P(\begin{bmatrix} \Pi_w \\ \pi^T \Phi \end{bmatrix}, \begin{bmatrix} d \\ d - \pi^T \gamma \end{bmatrix}) \rangle$.
Assume $x \in \langle \Phi, \gamma, P(\Pi_w, d_w) \rangle \cap H(\pi^T, d)$, then there exists a $w \in P(\Pi_w, d_w)$

such that $x = \Phi w + \gamma \in H(\pi^T, d)$. From definition of halfspace we know $w \in H(\pi^T \Phi, d - \pi^T \gamma)$.

To prove $\langle \Phi, \gamma, P(\Pi_w, d_w) \rangle \cap H(\pi^T, d) \supseteq \langle \Phi, \gamma, P(\begin{bmatrix} \Pi_w \\ \pi^T \Phi \end{bmatrix}, \begin{bmatrix} d \\ d - \pi^T \gamma \end{bmatrix}) \rangle$, let $x \in \langle \Phi, \gamma, P(\begin{bmatrix} \Pi_w \\ \pi^T \Phi \end{bmatrix}, \begin{bmatrix} d \\ d - \pi^T \gamma \end{bmatrix}) \rangle$, then there exists a w such that $x = \Phi x + \gamma$. Then $x \in \langle \Phi, \gamma, P(\Pi_w, d_w) \rangle$ since $w \in P(\Pi_w, d_w)$. Also $x \in H(\pi^T, d)$ since $w \in H(\pi^T \Phi, d - \pi^T \gamma)$. □

The computations in Proposition 1 are efficient for low-dimensional polytopes. For affine transformations, the computation is reduced to matrix and vector computations. For the other computations, the polytope operations are performed in $\mathbb{R}^d$ instead of $\mathbb{R}^n$.

For affine systems, the reach set segments $Reach([t_{k-1}, t_k])$ are generally full-dimensional, even though $\mathcal{X}_{k-1}$ and $\mathcal{X}_k$ may be low-dimensional. Therefore, low-dimensional polytopes are *approximations* of the actual reach sets. Over-approximations can be computed from the low-dimensional polytopes by "bloating". Consider a set $\mathcal{X} \subseteq \mathbb{R}^n$ in the state space, let $\mathcal{P} = \langle \Phi, \gamma, \mathcal{P}_w \rangle$ be the low-dimensional polytope approximation and let δ denote a bound of the Hausdorff distance between the approximation and the set $\mathcal{X}$, i.e., $d(\mathcal{P}, \mathcal{X}) \leq \delta$. A conservative over-approximation can be constructed as $\mathcal{X} \subseteq \mathcal{P} \oplus \mathcal{B}_\delta$, where $\mathcal{B}_\delta = [-\delta, \delta]^n$ is a closed hyper-box with radius δ, which is called the *bloating factor* in this paper. Note that the bloated polytope $\mathcal{P} \oplus \mathcal{B}_\delta$ is an n-polytope in $\mathbb{R}^n$ since the hyper-box $\langle I, \gamma, \mathcal{B}_\delta \rangle \subseteq \mathcal{P} \oplus \mathcal{B}_\delta$. To reduce the complexity of the representation, we write $\overline{\mathcal{P}} = \mathcal{P} \oplus \mathcal{B}_\delta = \langle \Phi, \gamma, \mathcal{P}_w, \delta \rangle$ and call it an *approximate affine representation* for the n-polytope $\overline{\mathcal{P}}$. The following proposition provides over-approximations for operations of polytopes in their approximate affine representations.

Proposition 2. *For polytopes* $\mathcal{P} = \langle \Phi, \gamma, \mathcal{P}_w, \delta \rangle$, $\mathcal{P}_1 = \langle \Phi_1, \gamma_1, \mathcal{P}_{w1}, \delta_1 \rangle$ *and* $\mathcal{P}_2 = \langle \Phi_2, \gamma_2, \mathcal{P}_{w2}, \delta_2 \rangle$ *in their approximate affine representations, the following relations hold.*

- *Affine transformation:* $A\mathcal{P} + b \subseteq \langle A\Phi, A\gamma + b, \mathcal{P}_w, \|A\|\delta \rangle$.
- *Minkowski sum:* $\mathcal{P}_1 \oplus \mathcal{P}_2 = \langle [\Phi_1 \ \Phi_2], \gamma_1 + \gamma_2, \mathcal{P}_{w1} \otimes \mathcal{P}_{w2}, \delta_1 + \delta_2 \rangle$.
- *Cartesian product:* $\mathcal{P}_1 \otimes \mathcal{P}_2 \subseteq \langle \begin{bmatrix} \Phi_1 & 0 \\ 0 & \Phi_2 \end{bmatrix}, \begin{bmatrix} \gamma_1 \\ \gamma_2 \end{bmatrix}, \mathcal{P}_{w1} \otimes \mathcal{P}_{w2}, \max\{\delta_1, \delta_2\} \rangle$.
- *Intersection with halfspace:* $\mathcal{P} \cap H(\pi^T, d) \subseteq \langle \Phi, \gamma, P(\begin{bmatrix} \Pi_w \\ \pi^T \Phi \end{bmatrix}, \begin{bmatrix} d_w \\ d - \pi^T \gamma + \|\pi^T\|\delta \end{bmatrix}), \delta \rangle$.

Proof. See [15]. □

4   Reach Set Computation Using Affine Representations

For affine system $\mathcal{S}$, we consider the problem of computing $Reach([0, t_f])$ for the set of initial states $\mathcal{X}_0 = \langle \Phi_0, \gamma_0, \mathcal{P}_w \rangle$, which is a d-polytope. Note that the reach set $\mathcal{X}_k$ at a time t_k is an affine transformation of $\mathcal{X}_0$ given by:

$$\mathcal{X}_k = \varphi_0(A, t_k)\mathcal{X}_0 + t_k\varphi_1(A, t_k)b. \tag{4}$$

Thus,

$$\mathcal{X}_k = \langle \varphi_0(A, t_k)\Phi_0, \varphi_0(A, t_k)\gamma_0 + t_k\varphi_1(A, t_k)b, \mathcal{P}_w \rangle. \tag{5}$$

Figure 1 shows REACH_AFFINE$^{\mathcal{K}}$, a procedure to compute the reach set $Reach([0, t_f])$ using affine representations and Krylov subspace approximations. The procedure first computes $\mathcal{X}_k$ for $k = 1, \ldots, N$. Over-approximations of the reach set segment $Reach([t_{k-1}, t_k])$ are then computed by bloating over-approximations of the linear interpolations $\mathcal{X}_{k-1,k}$, $k = 1, \ldots, N$.

Input: $\mathcal{S}$, $\mathcal{X}_0$, 0, dt, t_f
Output: $Reach([0, t_f])$
ProcedureREACH_AFFINE$^{\mathcal{K}}$:
$t \leftarrow 0$, $k \leftarrow 1$, $\mathcal{R} \leftarrow \emptyset$
WHILE $t \leq t_f$
    IF $size(A)$ >MAX_ORDER
        Choose step size h based on the error tolerance ϵ_{OSE}
        Compute $\mathcal{X}_k \leftarrow \mathcal{X}_k^{\mathcal{K}}$
    ELSE
        Choose step size $h \leftarrow dt$
        Compute $\mathcal{X}_k$ using (5)
    END IF
    Compute low-dimensional polytope $\mathcal{P}_{k-1,k}$ s.t. $\mathcal{X}_{k-1,k} \subseteq \mathcal{P}_{k-1,k}$
    Compute bloating factor $\delta_{k-1,k}$
    IF $\mathcal{X}_k^{\mathcal{K}}$ is used
        Compute bloating factor δ_{AE} for the Krylov subspace approximation
    END IF
    $\mathcal{R} \leftarrow \mathcal{R} \cup (\mathcal{P} \oplus \mathcal{B}_{\delta_{k-1,k}+\delta_{AE}})$, $t \leftarrow t + h$, $k \leftarrow k + 1$
END FOR
RETURN $\mathcal{R}$

Fig. 1. Reach set computation using the Krylov subspace approximation

The parameter MAX_ORDER is the threshold for the Krylov subspace approximation method. If the size of the matrix A is smaller than MAX_ORDER, the set $\mathcal{X}_k$ is computed by first computing $\varphi_i(A, t_k)$ and then forming the affine representations for $\mathcal{X}_k$. If $size(A)$ > MAX_ORDER, the Krylov subspace approximation method is used to compute $\mathcal{X}_k$. The terms $\varphi_0(A, t_k)\Phi_0$, $\varphi_0(A, t_k)\gamma_0$ and $\varphi_1(A, t_k)b$ are computed approximately using the Krylov subspace method. The approximation of the reach set is $\mathcal{X}_k^{\mathcal{K}} = \langle [\varphi_0(A, t_k)\Phi_0]^{\mathcal{K}}, [\varphi_0(A, t_k)\gamma_0]^{\mathcal{K}} + t_k[\varphi_1(A, t_k)b]^{\mathcal{K}}, \mathcal{P}_w \rangle$. The step size is chosen based on computation of the error bound of the Krylov subspace approximations. The step size is chosen such that the *one-step error* $\delta_{OSE} \leq \epsilon_{OSE}$ where ϵ_{OSE} is the manually chosen tolerance. To incorporate the error caused by the Krylov subspace approximation, we compute a bound on the accumulated error δ_{AE} and incorporated it into the bloating factor to guarantee conservative results.

The remainder of this section explains the details of computing low-dimensional over-approximations of $\mathcal{X}_{k-1,k}$ and $\delta_{k-1,k}$. Section 5 presents the computation of a bound on the error of Krylov subspace approximation.

4.1   Low-Dimensional Polytope Over-Approximations of $\mathcal{X}_{k-1,k}$

The linear interpolation, $\mathcal{X}_{k-1,k}$, is contained in $CH(\mathcal{X}_{k-1} \cup \mathcal{X}_k)$. The following proposition establishes an upper bound on the dimension of $CH(\mathcal{X}_{k-1} \cup \mathcal{X}_k)$.

Proposition 3.
$$dim\,(CH(\mathcal{X}_{k-1} \cup \mathcal{X}_k)) \le 2d + 1.$$

Proof. For $\mathcal{X}_{k-1} = \langle \Phi_{k-1}, \gamma_{k-1}, \mathcal{P}_w \rangle$ and $\mathcal{X}_k = \langle \Phi_k, \gamma_k, \mathcal{P}_w \rangle$, each satisfying (3). $CH(\mathcal{X}_{k-1} \cup \mathcal{X}_k) = CH((\Phi_{k-1}\mathcal{P}_w + \gamma_{k-1}) \cup (\Phi_k \mathcal{P}_w + \gamma_k))$. Noticing the dimension of a set is invariant for any arbitrary displacement, we have $dim(CH((\Phi_{k-1}\mathcal{P}_w + \gamma_{k-1}) \cup (\Phi_k \mathcal{P}_w + \gamma_k))) = dim(CH((\Phi_k \mathcal{P}_w) \cup (\Phi_{k+1}\mathcal{P}_w + \gamma_k - \gamma_{k-1})))$. Hence the dimension of the set is bounded by $dim(CH(\mathcal{X}_{k-1} \cup \mathcal{X}_k)) = rank([\Phi_{k-1}\Phi_k\gamma_k - \gamma_{k-1}]) \le 2d + 1$. $\qquad\square$

Proposition 3 implies that the convex hull $CH(\mathcal{X}_{k-1} \cup \mathcal{X}_k)$ can be low-dimensional if the initial set is low-dimensional. As a corollary we know that the dimension of the linear interpolation $\mathcal{X}_{k-1,k}$ is also bounded by $2d+1$. Note that the bound is valid for any k, hence the dimension of $\mathcal{X}_{k-1,k}$ does not grow with time.

$CH(\mathcal{X}_{k-1} \cup \mathcal{X}_k)$ can be computed in the affine subspace, $aff(\mathcal{X}_{k-1} \cup \mathcal{X}_k)$. The computation is as follows. We compute a matrix $V \in \mathbb{R}^{n \times m}$, $m = rank([\Phi_{k-1}\ \Phi_k\ \gamma_k - \gamma_{k-1}]) \le 2d + 1$ whose columns form an orthogonal basis of $span$ $([\Phi_{k-1}\ \Phi_k\ \gamma_k - \gamma_{k-1}])$. This leads to the following affine representation for $CH(\mathcal{X}_{k-1} \cup \mathcal{X}_k)$:

$$CH(\mathcal{X}_{k-1} \cup \mathcal{X}_k) = \langle V, \gamma_{k-1}, CH(V^T \Phi_{k-1}\mathcal{P}_w \cup V^T(\Phi_k \mathcal{P}_w + \gamma_k - \gamma_{k-1})) \rangle.$$

The convex hull computation is performed in $\mathbb{R}^m$ instead of $\mathbb{R}^n$.

For the case where $m > 10$, the computation of convex hull of the points can be difficult [10]. The linear interpolation can be over-approximated by Minkowski sums of polytopes when the convex hull computation is too complex. We use the following over-approximations in our computations that avoid the computation of convex hull:

1. (Forward Approximation) $\mathcal{MS}_0 = \langle \Phi_{k-1}, \gamma_{k-1}, \mathcal{P}_w \rangle \oplus \langle \Phi_k - \Phi_{k-1}, 0, \mathcal{P}_w \rangle \oplus \langle \gamma_k - \gamma_{k-1}, 0, [0,1] \rangle$.
2. (Backward Approximation) $\mathcal{MS}_1 = \langle \Phi_k, \gamma_k, \mathcal{P}_w \rangle \oplus \langle \Phi_{k-1} - \Phi_k, 0, \mathcal{P}_w \rangle \oplus \langle \gamma_{k-1} - \gamma_k, 0, [0,1] \rangle$.
3. (Mid-point Approximation) $\mathcal{MS}_{1/2} = \langle \frac{1}{2}(\Phi_{k-1} + \Phi_k), \frac{1}{2}(\gamma_{k-1} + \gamma_k), \mathcal{P}_w \rangle \oplus \langle \frac{1}{2}(\Phi_k - \Phi_{k-1}), 0, \mathcal{P}_w \rangle \oplus \langle \frac{1}{2}(\gamma_k - \gamma_{k-1}), 0, [-\frac{1}{2}, \frac{1}{2}] \rangle$.

Note that $\mathcal{MS}_i$ is an m-polytope, $i = 0, 1, 1/2$. The following proposition claims the three polytopes are indeed over-approximations of $\mathcal{X}_{k-1,k}$.

Proposition 4. *All three approximations $\mathcal{MS}_0$, $\mathcal{MS}_1$ and $\mathcal{MS}_{1/2}$ are over-approximations of $\mathcal{X}_{k-1,k}$.*

Proof. See [15]. □

Since each approximation $\mathcal{MS}_i$ is convex and contains $\mathcal{X}_{k-1}$ and $\mathcal{X}_k$, these polytopes all contain the convex hull $CH(\mathcal{X}_{k-1} \cup \mathcal{X}_k)$. The over-approximations of $\mathcal{X}_{k-1,k}$ are illustrated in the following example.

Example 1. Consider approximating $\mathcal{X}_{k-1,k}$ where $\mathcal{X}_{k-1} = \langle [0.1\,0\,0]^T, [0\,0\,0]^T, [-1,1] \rangle$ and $\mathcal{X}_k = \langle [0\,0.1\,0]^T, [0\,0\,1]^T, [-1,1] \rangle$. Figure 2 shows the polytope over-approximations to the set $\mathcal{X}_{k-1,k}$. All of the polytope over-approximations are 3-polytopes. Among the polytopes, $CH(\mathcal{X}_{k-1} \cup \mathcal{X}_k)$ is the tightest since it is contained properly in any of the other three over-approximations. For this example, $\mathcal{MS}_{1/2}$ is tighter than $\mathcal{MS}_0$ and $\mathcal{MS}_1$.

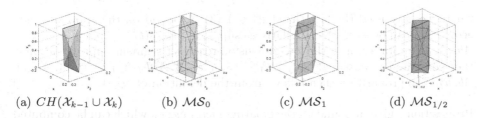

(a) $CH(\mathcal{X}_{k-1} \cup \mathcal{X}_k)$ (b) $\mathcal{MS}_0$ (c) $\mathcal{MS}_1$ (d) $\mathcal{MS}_{1/2}$

Fig. 2. Polytope over-approximations of $\mathcal{X}_{k-1,k}$

4.2   Bloating Factor $\delta_{k-1,k}$

Consider the problem of computing an over-approximation of the reach set segment $Reach([t_{k-1}, t_k])$. If the polytope approximation of $\mathcal{X}_{k-1,k}$ is $\mathcal{P}_{k-1,k} = \langle \Phi_{k-1,k}, \gamma_{k-1,k}, \mathcal{P}_w \rangle$, we want to compute $\delta_{k-1,k}$ such that $Reach([t_{k-1}, t_k]) \subseteq \langle \Phi_{k-1,k}, \gamma_{k-1,k}, \mathcal{P}_w, \delta_{k-1,k} \rangle$. Motivated by the analysis of the hump phenomenon [12, 13], we compute a bound on the bloating factor using the matrix functions ψ_i, which in turns are computed by computing matrix exponentials ϕ_i over time $[0, h]$. The following proposition gives a bloating factor for reach set segments.

Proposition 5 (Bloating factor for linear interpolation). *Given affine system $\mathcal{S}$ with the initial state set $\mathcal{X}_0 = \langle \Phi_0, \gamma_0, \mathcal{P}_w \rangle$ and t_0, $t_1 \in \mathbb{R}$ satisfying $0 = t_0 < t_1 = h$, let $\mathcal{P}_{0,1}$ be a polytope such that $\mathcal{X}_{0,1} \subseteq \mathcal{P}_{0,1}$, then $Reach([t_0, t_1]) \subseteq \mathcal{P}_{0,1} \oplus \mathcal{B}_\delta$ where*

$$\delta = 2h^2 \psi_2(A, A^2\Phi_0, h) + 2h^2 \psi_2(A, A^2\gamma_0 + Ab, h).$$

Proof. Let $x(\cdot)$ denote a trajectory of the actual system where $s \in [0, h]$, and let $x'(\cdot)$ denote the trajectory of the linear interpolation between $x'(t) = \frac{h-t}{h}x(0) + \frac{t}{h}x(h)$. Let $x(0) = x_0$, then $x(h) = e^{Ah}x_0 + h\varphi_1(A, h)b$, respectively. Consider the difference of $x(t)$ and $x'(t)$:

$$x(t) - x'(t)$$
$$= e^{At}x_0 - (\tfrac{h-t}{h}x_0 + \tfrac{t}{h}e^{Ah}x_0) + t\varphi_1(A,t)b - \tfrac{t}{h}h\varphi_1(A,h)b$$
$$= (t\varphi_2(A,t) - h\varphi_2(A,h))tA^2x_0 + (t\varphi_2(A,t) - h\varphi_2(A,h))tAb$$

For a set of initial states in the affine representation, $x_0 = \Phi_0 w + \gamma_0$ where $w \in \mathcal{P}_w$. The error is rewritten as

$$x(t) - x'(t)$$
$$= [(t\varphi_2(A,t) - h\varphi_2(A,h))tA^2\Phi_0 w] + [(t\varphi_2(A,t) - h\varphi_2(A,h))tA(A\gamma_0 + b)]$$
$$=: Err_1(t) + Err_2(t)$$

To compute the error bound Err_1, we have

$$\sup_{0 \le t \le h} \|Err_1(t)\| \le \sup_{0 \le t \le h} t\|(t\varphi_2(A,t) - h\varphi_2(A,h))A^2\Phi_0\|\|w\|$$
$$\le \sup_{0 \le t \le h} t(\|t\varphi_2(A,t)A^2\Phi_0\| + \|h\varphi_2(A,h)A^2\Phi_0\|)\|w\|$$
$$\le 2h^2\psi_2(A, A^2\Phi_0, h).$$

where we have used the fact that $\|w\| \le 1$ (3). A bound on the approximation error Err_2 can be estimated similarly as $\sup_{0 \le t \le h} \|Err_2(t)\| \le 2h^2\psi_2(A, A^2\gamma_0 + Ab, h)$. The total error in the low-dimension reach set segment approximation is then computed as $d(Reach([t_0, t_1]), \mathcal{P}_{0,1}) \le 2h^2\psi_2(A, A^2\Phi_0, h) + 2h^2\psi_2(A, A^2\gamma_0 + Ab, h)$. The proposition then follows from the definition of $d(\cdot, \cdot)$.   □

Proposition 5 gives a bound on the bloating factor $\delta_{k-1,k}$ which can be computed using matrix function ψ_2:

$$\delta_{k-1,k} = 2h_k^2\psi_2(A, A^2\Phi_{k-1}, h_k) + 2h_k^2\psi_2(A, A^2\gamma_{k-1} + Ab, h_k). \tag{6}$$

An alternative bloating factor is derived and used in [1]. The bloating factor given in [1] always grows exponentially with the step size h, even when the system is stable. In contrast our bloating factor depends on the hump, ψ_i, of the system matrix. When the system is stable, the hump is bounded [9]. In this case our bloating factor grows quadratically with the step size h.

5   Bloating Factor for the Krylov Subspace Approximation

We first consider the problem of estimating the error of the Krylov subspace approximation for matrix functions. The following lemma gives bound on the error of the Krylov subspace approximation of $\varphi_i(A, h)b$.

Lemma 1. *For $A \in \mathbb{R}^{n \times n}$, $v \in \mathbb{R}^n$, $\overline{A}$ given in (2), let $\rho = \|\overline{A}\|$. Then the error of the rth-order Krylov subspace approximation for $\varphi_j(A, h)$ is such that*

$$\|\varphi_j(A,h)v - V_r\varphi_j(H_r,h)V_r^T v\| \le 2\frac{h^r\rho^{r+j}e^{(h\rho)}}{(r+j)!}$$

Proof. To compute the approximation error for φ_j, consider first the augmented system (2). Observe that if the rth-order projection matrix for $Kr(A, v, r)$ is V_r, then the $(r + j)^{th}$-order projection matrix for $\overline{A}$ can be formed as $\overline{V}_{r+j} = \begin{bmatrix} V_r & 0 \\ 0 & I_j \end{bmatrix} \in \mathbb{R}^{(n+j) \times (r+j)}$. Note that $\overline{V}_{r+j}$ is orthonormal and spans $Kr(\overline{A}, \overline{x}_0, r + j)$, the Krylov subspace approximation is obtained for system with state matrix

$$\overline{H}_{r+j} = \overline{V}_{r+j}^T \overline{A} \, \overline{V}_{r+j} = \begin{bmatrix} H_r & V_r^T v & 0 & \dots & 0 \\ 0 & 0 & 1 & \ddots & 0 \\ \vdots & \vdots & \ddots & \ddots & \vdots \\ 0 & 0 & 0 & \ddots & 1 \\ 0 & 0 & 0 & 0 & 0 \end{bmatrix} \in \mathbb{R}^{(r+j) \times (r+j)}.$$

Using theorem 1 on the augmented matrix $\overline{A}$, $\overline{V}$ and $\overline{H}$. We have

$$\| e^{\overline{A}h} \overline{x}_0 - \overline{V}_{j+r}^T e^{\overline{H}h} \overline{V}_{j+r} \overline{x}_0 \| \le 2 \frac{(h\rho)^{r+j} e^{h\rho}}{(r+j)!}.$$

Since the Krylov subspace approximation of $\varphi(A, h)v$ is computed as $\frac{1}{h^j} e^{\overline{A}h} \overline{x}_0$, the error bound is obtained by dividing the above inequality by h^j. $\square$

To compute a bound on the error in the computed reach set, we first compute a bound on the error incurred in each step of the computation, which we call the one-step error (OSE), and then derive a bound on the *accumulated error* (AE) which includes the error propagated from the previous steps.

Proposition 6 (One-step Krylov approximation error). *For affine system S and initial set $\mathcal{X}_0 = \langle \Phi_0, \gamma_0, \mathcal{P}_w \rangle$ satisfying (3), let $\phi_i^{\mathcal{K}}$ and $\gamma^{\mathcal{K}}$ be the Krylov subspace approximation for the vector $e^{Ah} \phi_{0_i}$ and vector $\varphi_1(A, h)(A\gamma_0 + b)$, where ϕ_{0_i} is the ith-column of Φ_0. For $t \in [0, h]$, let $\Delta \phi_i$ and $\Delta \gamma$ denote the bounds on approximation errors of the vectors estimated using Theorem 1 and Lemma 1. Then*

$$\forall t \in [0, h] : Reach(t) \subseteq \langle \Phi_t^{\mathcal{K}}, \gamma_t^{\mathcal{K}}, \mathcal{P}_w, \delta_{OSE} \rangle$$

where $\delta_{OSE} := \sum_{i=1}^d \Delta \phi_i + \Delta \gamma$.

Proof. For any $x \in Reach(t)$, x can be written as $x = e^{At} \Phi_0 w + \gamma_0 + (e^{At} \gamma_0 - \gamma_0) + t\varphi_1(A, t)b = e^{At} \Phi_0 w + \gamma_0 + t\varphi_1(A, t)(A\gamma_0 + b)$, where $t \in [0, h]$ and $w \in \mathcal{P}_w$. Let $x^{\mathcal{K}} = \sum_{i=1}^d \phi_i^{\mathcal{K}} w + \gamma^{\mathcal{K}}$ be the Krylov subspace approximation, then $\| x - x^{\mathcal{K}} \| = \| \sum_{i=1}^d (\phi_i - \phi_{i_t}^{\mathcal{K}}) w + \gamma_i - \gamma_{i_t}^{\mathcal{K}} \| \le \sum_{i=1}^d \| \phi_i - \phi_{i_t}^{\mathcal{K}} \| \| w \| + \| \gamma_i - \gamma_{i_t}^{\mathcal{K}} \| \le \delta_{OSE}$. $\square$

The following proposition gives a bound on the AE of the reach set computed using the Krylov subspace approximations.

Proposition 7 (Accumulated Krylov approximation error). *For affine system S and initial set $\mathcal{X}_0 = \langle \Phi_0, \gamma_0, \mathcal{P}_w \rangle$, suppose the time steps for reach set*

computation are $0 = t_0 < t_1 < \ldots < t_N = t_f$. *Let* $\delta_{avg} = max_{1 \leq k \leq N} \frac{\delta_{OSE_k}}{t_k - t_{k-1}}$.
Then $\forall t \in [0, t_f] : Reach(t) \subseteq \langle \Phi_t^{\mathcal{K}}, \gamma_t^{\mathcal{K}}, \mathcal{P}_w, \delta_{AE} \rangle$, *where* $\delta_{AE} := t_f \max_{\tau \in [0, t_f]}$
$\|e^{\tau A}\| \delta_{avg}$.

Proof. Suppose $x(t) \in Reach(t)$ and $x'(t) \in Reach^{\mathcal{K}}(t)$ is an element of the approximation computed using the Krylov subspace approximation. For $t \in [t_{k-1}, t_k], \|x(t) - x'(t)\| \leq \sum_{i=0}^{k} \|e^{A(t-t_i)}\| \delta_{OSE_i}$.

Since every term in the summation is nonnegative, we have the AE bound as
$\|x(t) - x'(t)\| \leq \max_{\tau \in [0, t_f]} \|e^{\tau A}\| \cdot \sum_{i=1}^{N} \frac{\delta_{OSE_i}}{t_i - t_{i-1}} (t_i - t_{i-1}) \leq \delta_{AE}$.   □

For the reach set segments, the bloating factor is the sum of the bounds from Proposition 5 and Proposition 7.

Proposition 8 (Bloating factor for reach set segments). *For affine system* $\mathcal{S}$ *and initial set* $\mathcal{X}_0 = \langle \Phi_0, \gamma_0, \mathcal{P}_w \rangle$ *satisfying (3), suppose the time steps for reach set computation are* $0 = t_0 < t_1 < \ldots < t_N = t_f$ *and let* δ_{AE} *be the accumulated error estimated using Proposition 7. Then* $Reach([t_{k-1}, t_k]) \subseteq \langle \Phi_{k-1,k}^{\mathcal{K}}, \gamma_{k-1,k}^{\mathcal{K}}, \mathcal{P}_{w_{k-1,k}}, \delta_{k-1,k} + \delta_{AE} \rangle$ *for* $1 \leq k \leq N$, *where* $\delta_{k-1,k} = 2h_k^2 \psi_2^{\mathcal{K}}(A, A^2 \Phi_{k-1}^{\mathcal{K}}, h_k) + 2h_k^2 \psi_2^{\mathcal{K}}(A, A^2 \gamma_{k-1}^{\mathcal{K}} + Ab, h_k)$.

Proof. Let $t \in [t_{k-1}, t_k]$, and let $x(\cdot)$ be a trajectory of the system. Let $x^{\mathcal{K}}(\cdot)$ denote the trajectory of the corresponding Krylov subspace approximation model and $x^{\mathcal{K}'} = \frac{h_k - t}{h_k} x^{\mathcal{K}}(t_{k-1}) + \frac{t - h_{k-1}}{h_k} x^{\mathcal{K}}(t_k)$ be the linear interpolation. Then

$$\|x(t) - x^{\mathcal{K}'}(t)\| \leq \|x(t) - x^{\mathcal{K}}(t)\| + \|x^{\mathcal{K}}(t) - x^{\mathcal{K}'}(t)\| \leq \delta_{AE} + \delta_{k-1,k}.$$

Since $x(t) \in Reach([t_{k-1}, t_k])$ and $x^{\mathcal{K}}(t) \in \mathcal{P}_{k-1,k}^{\mathcal{K}}$. The proposition follows from the definition of $d(\cdot, \cdot)$.   □

6   Example: Heat Conduction

This section applies the reachability analysis procedure REACH_AFFINE$^{\mathcal{K}}$ to a numeric example. The reach set computation procedures are implemented in MATLAB. All the computations are performed on a Pentium4 PC with 1G RAM running Windows XP and MATLAB 7.0.1.

Figure 3(a) shows a metal plate insulated along three edges. The right edge is open, allowing heat exchange with the ambient environment. The left half of the bottom edge of the plate is connected to a constant heat source. Suppose the temperature of the environment is 0 °C, and the temperature of the heat source is 1 °C. Figure 3(b) shows a contour plot of the steady-state temperature for the plate.

The dynamics of the temperature in the metal plate is modeled as the partial differential equation (PDE) $\frac{\partial T}{\partial t}(x, t) = \alpha^2 \frac{\partial^2 T}{\partial x^2}(x, t)$, where $T(\cdot, \cdot)$ is the temperature. Linear system models are used to approximately model the dynamics by discretizing the PDE among the grid points of a rectangular mesh over the plate [16].

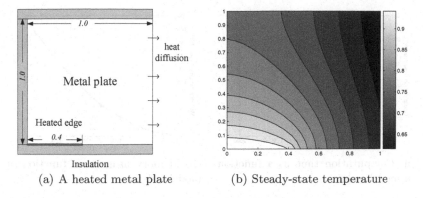

(a) A heated metal plate   (b) Steady-state temperature

Fig. 3. Heat conduction example

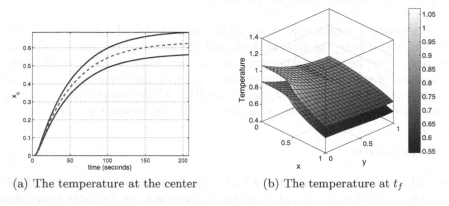

(a) The temperature at the center   (b) The temperature at t_f

Fig. 4. The reach set for the 400th-order model

The linear system has the form $\dot{x} = Ax + bu$ where $x \in \mathbb{R}^{p^2}$ is the temperature at the grid points, $u \in \mathbb{R}$ is the temperature of the heat source and p is the number of grid point along an edge.

Suppose the temperature of the plate is initially $0\,°C$, and the material has diffusion constant $1cm^2/sec$ and heat exchange coefficient $0.5cal/(cm\cdot sec\cdot°C)$. Consider the problem of computing the reach set for the system for $u(t) = T \in [0.9, 1.1]\,°C$. We apply REACH_AFFINE$^{\mathcal{K}}$ to compute the reach set $\mathcal{X}_1, \ldots, \mathcal{X}_k$ for $0 = t_0 < \ldots < t_N = 200$. 30th-order Krylov subspace approximation models are used for the computation. The tolerance ϵ_{OSE} is set to $1 \times 10^{-8}\,°C$ by hand. The accumulated error δ_{AE} is computed to be bounded by $4 \times 10^{-6}\,°C$ for the reach set.

Figure 4 shows the reach set computed for the 400th-order heat conduction model. Figure 4(a) shows the projection of the reach set to x_c, the temperature of the grid point at the center of the plate. The nominal trajectory for $u = 1°C$ is shown as the dashed line in the same figure. Figure 4(b) shows the temperature at t_f computed for all the states. For each grid point, the reach set is an interval. Figure 4(b) shows the upper bound curve and the lower bound curve of the temperature across the mesh grid.

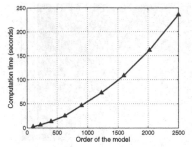
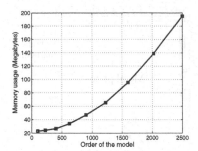
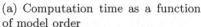

(a) Computation time as a function of model order

(b) Memory usage as a function of model order

Fig. 5. Computation time and memory usage of reachability analysis using the Krylov subspace approximations for fixed error bounds

We generated systems of various orders using meshes of different sizes. Note that although we vary the order of the model, the initial set remains a 1-polytope. Figure 5 shows the computation time and memory usage of REACH_AFFINE$^{\mathcal{K}}$ for systems of various orders. The computation time and memory increase with the order of the model. The increase is mainly due to the computations involving larger state vectors and smaller time steps in the reachability analysis.

7   Discussion

Reachability analysis for arbitrary high-order continuous systems is difficult. This paper presents a method to compute the reach set for large-scale affine systems for initial sets given as low-dimensional polytopes. With the aid of the Krylov subspace approximations we demonstrate that our method can be applied to a class of reachability analysis problems of large-scale affine systems. Methods to extend the approach to analyze hybrid system is currently under investigation.

There is an interesting relation between the affine representation in this paper and the representation for zonotopes in [1]. A zonotope is a polytope that is equivalent to the affine transformation of a unit cube [10] $\mathcal{Z} = \{y|y = \Phi x + \gamma$ where $x \in [-1,1]^p \subset \mathbb{R}^p\}$ for some $\Phi \in \mathbb{R}^{n \times p}$ and $\gamma \in \mathbb{R}^n$. The affine representation for zonotopes is $\mathcal{Z} = \langle \Phi, \gamma, [-1,1]^p \rangle$. Since the radius of the cube is always 1 and its dimension is equal to the number of columns of Φ, the cube can be dropped from the representation. This simplification gives rise to the generator representation in [1]. Using the generator representation, the procedure REACH_AFFINE$^{\mathcal{K}}$ can be applied to zonotope computations, which is similar to the procedure in [1] when applied to affine systems, except for the use of the Krylov subspace approximations.

This paper concerns affine systems. A more general reachability analysis problem is to compute the reach set for linear systems with uncertain inputs $\mathcal{S}_u : \dot{x} = Ax + Bu, u \in \mathcal{U}$. The reach set $Reach(\mathcal{S}_u, \mathcal{X}_0, t)$ for the system is the Minkowski sum $Reach(\mathcal{S}_1, \mathcal{X}_0, t) \oplus Reach(\mathcal{S}_u, 0, t)$, where $\mathcal{S}_1 : \dot{x} = Ax$. The reach set $Reach(S_1, X_0, t)$ can be computed using the method in this paper. Our method does not apply to the computation of $Reach(S_u, 0, t)$, since the reach set is not guaranteed to be low-dimensional. Over-approximations of the reach set can be computed using zonotopes computation for moderate-order models [1]. For large-scale systems, a promising way to compute the reach set is to first compute reduced-order models and then apply zonotope computations to compute the reach sets. Thus, over-approximations of $Reach(S_u, X_0, t)$ can be efficiently computed by combining our method with zonotope computation and model order reduction techniques.

References

1. Girard, A.: Reachability of uncertain linear systems using zonotopes. In: Hybrid Systems: Computation and Control (HSCC'05). (2005) 291–305
2. Stursberg, O., Krogh, B.H.: On efficient representation and computation of reachable sets for hybrid systems. In: Hybrid Systems: Computation and Control (HSCC'03). (2003) 482–497
3. Asarin, E., Dang, T.: Abstraction by projection and application to multi-affine systems. In: Proceedings of Hybrid Systems: Computation and Control (HSCC'04). (2004) 32–47
4. Girard, A., Pappas, G.J.: Approximation metrics for discrete and continuous systems. Technical Report MS-CIS-05-10, Dept. of CIS, University of Pennsylvania (2005)
5. Bemporad, A., Pilippi, C., Torrisi, F.D.: Inner and outer approximation of polytopes using boxes. Computational Geometry: Theory and Applications 27(2) (2003) 151–178
6. Kurzhanski, A.B., Varaiya, P.: Ellipsoidal techniques for reachability analysis. In: Hybrid Systems: Computation and Control (HSCC'00). (2000) 202–214
7. Ma, J.D., Rutenbar, R.A.: Interval-valued reduced order statistical interconnect modeling. In: Computer Aided Design, 2004. IEEE/ACM International Conference on. (2004) 1092–3152
8. de Figueiredo, L.H., Stolfi, J.: Self-Validated Numerical Methods and Applications. Brazilian Mathematics Colloquium monograph, IMPA, Rio de Janeiro, Brazil (1997)
9. Saad, Y.: Analysis of some Krylov subspace approximations to the matrix exponential operator. SIAM Journal of Numerical Analysis 20(1) (1992) 209–228
10. Grünbaum, B.: Convex Polytopes (Second Edition). Springer-Verlag New York, Inc. (2003)
11. Chutinan, A., Krogh, B.H.: Compuational techniques for hybrid system verification. IEEE Transaction on Automatic Control 48(1) (2003) 64–75
12. Moler, C., Van Loan, C.: Nineteen dubious ways to compute the exponential of a matrix, twenty-five years later. SIAM Review 45(1) (2003) 3–49
13. Sidje, R.B.: EXPOKIT: Software package for computing matrix exponentials. ACM Transactions on Mathematical Software 24(1) (1998) 130–156
14. Golub, G.H., Van Loan, C.F.: Matrix Computations (Third Edition). The John Hopkins University Press (1996)
15. Han, Z.: Reachability analysis of continuous dynamic systems using dimension reduction and decomposition. PhD thesis, Carnegie Mellon University (2005)
16. Farlow, S.J.: Partial Differential Equations for Scientists and Engineers. Dover Publications, Inc. (1993)

Simultaneous Optimization of Continuous Control Inputs and Discrete State Waypoints

Jun-ichi Imura and Hiromichi Matsushima

Tokyo Institute of Technology, Tokyo 152-8552, Japan
Tel.:+81.3.5734.3635; Fax:+81.3.5734.3635
imura@mei.titech.ac.jp

Abstract. This paper addresses the receding horizon control problem of continuous-time linear systems with respect to continuous control inputs and discrete state waypoints under discrete-dynamical constraints. First, a generalized version of our previous method is described, where a discretization technique is applied only for the constrained state variables. Next, it is proven that the problem is reduced to the finite-time optimal control problem of a certain discrete-time linear system with discrete-valued inputs. Finally, a new efficient algorithm for solving this optimization problem is proposed. Several numerical simulations show that this solver is much faster than the CPLEX solver.

1   Introduction

As in the case of bisimulation techniques (see e.g., [1, 2]), it is one of the natural approaches to approximately solve a complex problem by simplifying it via discretization/abstraction techniques. In such an approach, even if the original control problem involves only a dynamical system of continuous variables as a controlled plant, it may be often reduced to the control problem of some hybrid system; one of typical examples is an approximation of nonlinear systems via piecewise affine systems (see e.g., [3]).

From a similar (but rigorously different) point of view, we have addressed in [4] the obstacle avoidance problem (see e.g., [5, 6]) of continuous-time linear systems. In this problem, the admissible region of the state is in general given by a time-varying, non-convex set, which will make it quite difficult to determine an optimal control input in a short time interval. Thus, in order to solve this kind of problem approximately and efficiently, we have used there a directed graph (i.e., discrete dynamics) with respect to the waypoint of the state and the time at which the state coincides with the waypoint, and have derived a solution to the control problem of simultaneously optimizing the so-called continuous control input and the waypoints of the state constrained by the directed graph. However, a discretization technique has been used there for the waypoints of all the state variables (e.g., both position and velocity). In general, some of state variables, e.g., the velocity variable, may not be constrained via complex conditions. Furthermore, the computational amount exponentially increases with respect to the number of the discretized state variables, if the same resolution

João Hespanha and A. Tiwari (Eds.): HSCC 2006, LNCS 3927, pp. 302–317, 2006.
© Springer-Verlag Berlin Heidelberg 2006

is used for all state variables. This implies that it is not so easy to apply the proposed method to the class of large-dimensional systems. Hence it is more relevant to use a discretization technique only for the state variables constrained in a complex way such as the position variables in the obstacle avoidance case.

This paper addresses the model predictive control problem of continuous-time linear systems under the state constraints given by the directed graph, and gives a generalized version of the control method proposed in [4] in the sense that a discretization approach is applied for the constrained state variables, not for all state variables. First, after describing the control problem in a generalized setting, we prove that the problem is reduced to the finite-time optimal control problem of a certain discrete-time linear system with discrete-valued inputs constrained by a directed graph. Next, an efficient algorithm for solving the integer quadratic programming (IQP) problem subject to a kind of dynamical constraints on discrete variables, which is given from the above finite-time optimal control problem, is proposed. It is shown by numerical simulations that the proposed solver is much faster compared with the CPLEX solver, which is well known as one of the efficient commercial solvers. Numerical simulations also show that the proposed control method including the solver is effective.

The following notation is used: let $\mathbb{R}$ and $\mathcal{PC}$ denote the real number field and the set of all piecewise continuous functions, respectively. For the sets $\mathcal{S}$ and $\mathcal{T}$, let us denote by $\mathcal{S}/\mathcal{T}$ the difference set of $\mathcal{S}$ and $\mathcal{T}$, and by $|\mathcal{S}|$ the cardinality of the finite set $\mathcal{S}$.

2 Problem Statement

Consider the linear system

$$\dot{x} = Ax + Bu \tag{1}$$

where $x \in \mathbb{R}^n$ is the state, $u \in \mathbb{R}^m$ is the input, and the pair (A, B) is controllable. For this system, we study the model predictive control problem under a kind of state constraints that $x(t_i) = x_i$, $i = k, k+1, \ldots, k+N$, where t_i is the decision time (t_k is the current time), and x_i denotes the waypoint at time t_i selected from a finite set of the candidates for waypoints.

More specifically, the problem to be studied here is given as follows. We assume without loss of generality

$$x(t) = \begin{bmatrix} x^c(t) \\ x^u(t) \end{bmatrix}, \quad x^c(t) \in \mathbb{R}^{n_c}, \quad x^u(t) \in \mathbb{R}^{n-n_c}$$

where the subscripts "c" and "u" of x^c and x^u express the "constrained" and the "unconstrained" state, respectively. In a similar way, the waypoint of the state at time t_i is denoted by

$$x_i = \begin{bmatrix} x_i^c \\ x_i^u \end{bmatrix}, \quad x_i^c \in \mathbb{R}^{n_c}, \quad x_k^u \in \mathbb{R}^{n-n_c}.$$

We also consider a kind of directed graph on time axis and state space to express constraints on the state (see Fig. 1). So let $\mathcal{V}_i$, $i = k, k+1, \ldots, k+N$

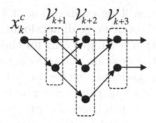

Fig. 1. Directed graph on time axis and state space

denote the finite set whose element takes a value in $\mathcal{R}^{n_c}$ and expresses a candidate for waypoints at time t_i. Furthermore, the finite set of all elements in $\mathcal{V}_{i+1}$ to which the system can be driven from $\xi \in \mathcal{V}_i$ is denoted by $\mathcal{E}_i(\xi)$. Note that $\mathcal{E}_i(x_i^c)$ expresses the set of all candidates for waypoints in $\mathcal{V}_{i+1}$ subject to $x^c(t_i) = x_i^c$. Thus a directed graph with its depth N, where the starting node is x_k^c, is generated by $x_{i+1}^c \in \mathcal{E}_i(x_i^c)$, $i = k, k+1, \ldots, k+N-1$, which we denote by $\mathcal{G}_k(x_k^c)$. Then the problem to be studied here is given as follows.

Problem 1. Suppose that the decision times t_i $(t_i < t_{i+1})$, $i = k, k+1, \ldots, k+N$, and a directed graph $\mathcal{G}_k(x_k^c)$ are given. Then for the system (1), find a state-feedback control $u(t) \in \mathcal{PC}^m$, $t \in [t_k, t_{k+N})$, and waypoints $x_i \in \mathbb{R}^n$, $i = k+1, k+2, \ldots, k+N$, of the state minimizing the cost

$$J(x(t_k), u(\cdot), \{x_i\}_{i=k+1,k+2\ldots,k+N}) = \sum_{i=k}^{k+N-1} J_i(x_i, u(\cdot), x_{i+1}) + g_i(x_i^c, x_{i+1}^c) \quad (2)$$

$$J_i(x_i, u(\cdot), x_{i+1}) := \int_{t_i}^{t_{i+1}} \left\{ (x(t) - x_{i+1})^T Q(x(t) - x_{i+1}) + u^T(t)Ru(t) \right\} dt$$

$$g_i(x_i^c, x_{i+1}^c) := \begin{bmatrix} x_i^c \\ x_{i+1}^c \end{bmatrix}^T G_i^a \begin{bmatrix} x_i^c \\ x_{i+1}^c \end{bmatrix} + \begin{bmatrix} x_i^c \\ x_{i+1}^c \end{bmatrix}^T G_i^b,$$

subject to

$$x^c(t_i) = x_i^c \in \mathcal{E}_{i-1}(x_{i-1}^c), \quad x^u(t_i) = x_i^u \in \mathbb{R}^{n-n_c},$$
$$i = k+1, k+2, \ldots, k+N$$

where $Q \geq 0$, $R > 0$, and $G_i^a \geq 0$. □

The cost function $g_i(x_i^c, x_{i+1}^c)$ is used for the geometrical distance between two waypoints x_i^c, x_{i+1}^c, e.g., $g_i = \| x_i^c - x_{i+1}^c \|^2$, where $\| \cdot \|$ is the Euclid norm.

The receding horizon policy is executed by solving Problem 1 at each time t_k as follows. Suppose that the optimal control input $u^*(t)$, $t \in [t_k, t_{k+N})$, and the optimal waypoint x_i^*, $i = k, k+1, \ldots, k+N$ are obtained by solving Problem 1 at $t = t_k$. Then after $u^*(t)$ with x_{k+1}^* is applied to the system for $t \in [t_k, t_{k+1})$, Problem 1 with t_k replaced by t_{k+1} is solved and the same strategy is repeated.

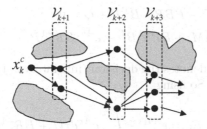

Fig. 2. Directed graph in the obstacle avoidance problem

Note that t_{k+N+1}, $\mathcal{V}_{k+N+1}$, and $\mathcal{E}_{k+N}(\xi)$ for every $\xi \in \mathcal{V}_{k+N}$ need to be generated at time t_{k+1} to realize the above receding horizon policy. However, in this paper, we will not address the generation problem of t_k and $\mathcal{G}_k(x_k^c)$ due to the limited space. This issue will be reported in the near future.

Problem 1 can be applied to various motion control problems of mechanical systems such as robots. In particular, it will be useful to solve the obstacle avoidance problem in an approximated way. For example, suppose that the vehicle, as a controlled plant, is given by $\dot{x}_p = x_v$, $\dot{x}_v = u$. In this case, the position x_p of the vehicle may be often restricted by some time-varying, non-convex set, while its velocity x_v is not. It will be difficult to rigorously solve such an optimal control problem in a real time. Thus we consider $x^c = x_p$, $x^u = x_v$, and $n_c = 1$ in Problem 1, and approximate the allowable region of the position in terms of the directed graph $\mathcal{G}_k(x_k^c)$ as in Fig. 2. Based on this graph and the state signal $x(t)$, both a sequence of waypoints x_i, $i = k, k+1, \ldots, k+N$ and a control input $u(t)$, $t \in [t_k, t_{k+N})$, are optimized. This corresponds to simultaneously optimize a kind of discrete decision such as the right- or left-side path by selecting a sequence of waypoints on x_p, and a continuous-time continuous-valued motion trajectory of the vehicle between two waypoints.

The first author has considered in [4] the case in which every element of the waypoints $x_i \in \mathcal{R}^n$ takes a value in a finite set. However, as in the obstacle avoidance problem, it will be natural to define a finite set only for elements of the waypoint corresponding to the state variables constrained in a complex way. In the following sections, a solution to such an extended version is given.

Note also that Problem 1 belongs to a special class of the optimal control problems of piecewise affine systems, since it can be considered the problem of finding switching actions of the affine terms as well as the so-called control inputs (see the first part of the proof of Theorem 1).

3   Derivation of an Optimal Controller

Problem 1 is reduced to a kind of discrete-time optimal control problem with discrete-valued inputs. Before showing this result, we prepare the following symbols.

Assume that the pair (A, B) is controllable. Then there exists positive-definite solutions P and M_i satisfying

$$PA + A^T P - PBR^{-1}B^T P + Q = 0 \tag{3}$$

$$M_i \tilde{A}^T + \tilde{A}M_i + BR^{-1}B^T - e^{\tilde{A}h_i}BR^{-1}B^T e^{\tilde{A}^T h_i} = 0 \tag{4}$$

respectively, where h_i denotes the decision time interval, i.e., $h_i := t_{i+1} - t_i$, and $\tilde{A} := A - BR^{-1}B^T P$. So using

$$D_i := e^{\tilde{A}h_i}, \quad E_i := e^{\tilde{A}h_i} - \int_0^{h_i} e^{\tilde{A}\tau} d\tau (I + BR^{-1}B^T \tilde{A}^{-T} P) A$$

we define the matrix given by

$$S^i = \begin{bmatrix} S_1^i & S_2^i \\ (S_2^i)^T & S_3^i \end{bmatrix}, \quad \begin{aligned} S_1^i &:= D_i^T M_i^{-1} D_i + P \in \mathbb{R}^{n \times n}, \\ S_2^i &:= -D_i^T M_i^{-1} E_i - P - \tilde{A}^{-T} PA \in \mathbb{R}^{n \times n}, \\ S_3^i &:= E_i^T M_i^{-1} E_i + P + \tilde{A}^{-T} PA + A^T P \tilde{A}^{-1} \\ &\quad + h_i A^T P \tilde{A}^{-1} P^{-1} Q P^{-1} \tilde{A}^{-T} PA \in \mathbb{R}^{n \times n}. \end{aligned} \tag{5}$$

Furthermore, we express S_2^i and S_3^i as

$$S_2^i = \begin{bmatrix} S_{21}^i & S_{22}^i \end{bmatrix}, \quad S_{22}^i \in \mathbb{R}^{n \times (n - n_c)},$$

$$S_3^i = \begin{bmatrix} S_{31}^i & S_{32}^i \\ (S_{32}^i)^T & S_{33}^i \end{bmatrix}, \quad S_{33}^i \in \mathbb{R}^{(n - n_c) \times (n - n_c)},$$

respectively. Then one of the main results in this paper is obtained.

Theorem 1. *For Problem 1, assume that the pair (A, B) is controllable. Then the optimal waypoints x_i^*, $i = k+1, k+2, \ldots, k+N$, are solutions of the optimal trajectory to the following optimal control problem of the discrete-time linear system with discrete-valued inputs:*

$$\text{Problem A:} \quad \min_{\substack{v_i^c, \, i = k, k+1, \\ \ldots, k+N-1}} \sum_{i=k}^{k+N-1} w_i(x_i, v_i^c) + g_i(x_i^c, v_i^c)$$

$$\text{subject to} \quad x_{i+1} = A_i^d x_i + B_i^d v_i^c, \quad x_k : \text{given}$$

$$v_i^c \in \mathcal{E}_i(v_{i-1}^c), \quad v_{k-1}^c = x_k^c$$

where

$$w_i(x_i, v_i^c) := \begin{bmatrix} x_i \\ v_i^c \end{bmatrix}^T W^i \begin{bmatrix} x_i \\ v_i^c \end{bmatrix}, \quad W^i = \begin{bmatrix} W_1^i & W_2^i \\ (W_2^i)^T & W_3^i \end{bmatrix},$$

$$W_1^i := S_1^i - S_{22}^i (S_{33}^i)^{-1} (S_{22}^i)^T \in \mathbb{R}^{n \times n},$$

$$W_2^i := S_{21}^i - S_{22}^i (S_{33}^i)^{-1} (S_{32}^i)^T \in \mathbb{R}^{n \times n_c},$$

$$W_3^i := S_{31}^i - S_{32}^i (S_{33}^i)^{-1} (S_{32}^i)^T \in \mathbb{R}^{n_c \times n_c}$$

$$A_i^d := \begin{bmatrix} 0_{n_c \times n} \\ -(S_{33}^i)^{-1} (S_{22}^i)^T \end{bmatrix}, \quad B_i^d := \begin{bmatrix} I_{n_c} \\ -(S_{33}^i)^{-1} (S_{32}^i)^T \end{bmatrix}.$$

Then the optimal control $u^*(t) \in \mathcal{PC}$, $t \in [t_k, t_{k+N})$, is given by

$$u^*(t) = -R^{-1}B^T P(x(t) - x^*_{i+1}) + R^{-1}B^T \tilde{A}^{-T} P A x^*_{i+1}$$
$$-R^{-1}B^T e^{\tilde{A}^T(t_{i+1}-t)} M_i^{-1}(D_i x(t_i) - E_i x^*_{i+1}),$$
$$t \in [t_i, t_{i+1}), i = k, k+1, \ldots, k+N-1. \qquad (6)$$

Proof. For $\bar{x}_i(t) := x(t) - x_{i+1}$, we obtain $\dot{\bar{x}}_i(t) = A\bar{x}_i(t) + Bu(t) + Ax_{i+1}$, and further for $\hat{x}_i(t) := [\bar{x}_i^T(t)\ 1]^T$, we obtain

$$\dot{\hat{x}}_i(t) = \hat{A}_i \hat{x}_i(t) + \hat{B}u(t), \quad \hat{A}_i := \begin{bmatrix} A & Ax_{i+1} \\ 0 & 0 \end{bmatrix}, \quad \hat{B} := \begin{bmatrix} B \\ 0 \end{bmatrix}.$$

Since, by (3), we have the relation $\hat{P}_i \hat{A}_i + \hat{A}_i^T \hat{P}_i - \hat{P}_i \hat{B} R^{-1} \hat{B}^T \hat{P}_i + \hat{Q}_i = 0$, where

$$\hat{Q}_i := \begin{bmatrix} Q & 0 \\ 0 & r_i \end{bmatrix}, \quad \hat{P}_i := \begin{bmatrix} P & q_i \\ q_i^T & 0 \end{bmatrix}$$

$$q_i := -\tilde{A}^{-T} P A x_{i+1}, \quad r_i := -x_{i+1}^T A^T P \tilde{A}^{-1} P^{-1} Q P^{-1} \tilde{A}^{-T} P A x_{i+1}$$

it follows that

$$J_i(x_i, u(\cdot), x_{i+1}) = \int_{t_i}^{t_{i+1}} \left[\hat{x}_i^T(t) \hat{Q}_i \hat{x}_i(t) + u^T(t) R u(t) \right] dt - h_i r_i,$$

$$= \hat{x}_i^T(t_i) \hat{P}_i \hat{x}_i(t_i) - \hat{x}_i^T(t_{i+1}) \hat{P}_i \hat{x}_i(t_{i+1}) + \int_{t_i}^{t_{i+1}} \bar{u}_i^T(t) R \bar{u}_i(t) dt - h_i r_i$$

where $\bar{u}_i(t) := u(t) + R^{-1}\hat{B}^T \hat{P}_i \hat{x}_i$. Then from $x(t_i) = x_i$, $\bar{x}_i(t_i) = x(t_i) - x_{i+1} = x_i - x_{i+1}$ and $\bar{x}_i(t_{i+1}) = x(t_{i+1}) - x_{i+1} = 0$, it follows that

$$J_i(x_i, u(\cdot), x_{i+1}) = (x_i - x_{i+1})^T P(x_i - x_{i+1})$$

$$-2(x_i - x_{i+1})^T \tilde{A}^{-T} P A x_{i+1} + \int_{t_i}^{t_{i+1}} \bar{u}_i^T(t) R \bar{u}_i(t) dt - h_i r_i. \qquad (7)$$

Thus the problem for fixed x_i and x_{i+1} is reduced into a minimum energy control problem with respect to $\bar{u}_i(t)$; for given x_i and x_{i+1}, find an input $\bar{u}_i^*(t)$ satisfying $(x(t_i), x(t_{i+1})) = (x_i, x_{i+1})$ and minimizing the cost $\hat{J} = \int_{t_i}^{t_{i+1}} \bar{u}_i^T(t) R \bar{u}_i(t) dt$. As is well known, the optimal controller and the minimum cost of this problem are given by $\bar{u}_i^*(t) = -R^{-1}B^T e^{\tilde{A}^T(t_{i+1}-t)} M_i^{-1}(D_i x_i - E_i x_{i+1})$ and min $\hat{J} = (D_i x_i - E_i x_{i+1})^T M_i^{-1}(D_i x_i - E_i x_{i+1})$, respectively (see e.g., [7, 8]). It is remarked here that M_i of (4) is a positive-definite matrix given by $M_i = \int_0^{h_i} e^{\tilde{A}\tau} B R^{-1} B^T e^{\tilde{A}^T \tau} d\tau$.

Thus by applying min $\hat{J} = (D_i x_i - E_i x_{i+1})^T M_i^{-1}(D_i x_i - E_i x_{i+1})$ to (7), we have

$$\min_u J_i = s_i(x_i, x_{i+1}), \quad s_i(x_i, x_{i+1}) := \begin{bmatrix} x_i \\ x_{i+1} \end{bmatrix}^T S^i \begin{bmatrix} x_i \\ x_{i+1} \end{bmatrix} \qquad (8)$$

where S^i is given in (5). Therefore, the original problem $\min_{u, \{x_i\}} J$ is rewritten as the following optimization problem with respect to the waypoints x_i, $i = k+1, k+2, \ldots, k+N$:

Problem A':
$$\min_{\substack{x_i,\ i=k+1,\\ k+2,\dots,k+N}} \sum_{i=k}^{k+N-1} s_i(x_i, x_{i+1}) + g_i(x_i^c, x_{i+1}^c)$$

subject to x_k : given, $x_i^c \in \mathcal{E}_{i-1}(x_{i-1}^c)$, $x_i^u \in \mathbb{R}^{n-n_c}$

Furthermore, if we set $x_{i+1} = v_i$, where v_i is a new input, Problem A' is expressed as the optimal control problem of the discrete-time linear system with input constraints:

Problem A'':
$$\min_{\substack{v_i,\ i=k,k+1,\\ \dots,k+N-1}} \sum_{i=k}^{k+N-1} s_i(x_i, v_i) + g_i(x_i^c, v_i^c)$$

subject to $x_{i+1} = v_i$, x_k : given

$$v_i = \begin{bmatrix} v_i^c \\ v_i^u \end{bmatrix},\ v_i^c \in \mathcal{E}_i(v_{i-1}^c),\ v_{k-1}^c = x_k^c,\ v_i^u \in \mathbb{R}^{n-n_c}.$$

Now suppose $x_i \equiv 0$ and $x_{i+1} \neq 0$ in (8). Then $\min_u J_i > 0$ holds because the input energy term $\int_{t_i}^{t_{i+1}} u^T(t)Ru(t)dt$ in J_i necessarily becomes positive. This proves that $S_3^i > 0$. Thus since $S_{33}^i > 0$ holds from $S_3^i > 0$, simple calculation shows that a minimizer $(v_i^u)^*$ of v_i^u for this problem with v_i^c fixed is given as $(v_i^u)^* = -(S_{33}^i)^{-1}\{(S_{22}^i)^T x_i + (S_{32}^i)^T v_i^c\}$. By substituting $v_i^u = (v_i^u)^*$ into $x_{i+1} = v_i$, we obtain $x_{i+1} = A_i^d x_i + B_i^d v_i^c$. This implies that Problem A'' is reduced to Problem A.   □

Theorem 1 gives the optimal input $u^*(t)$ in an explicit form parameterized with the waypoints, which are the solutions of Problem A. It is also remarked that $S^i \geq 0$, $S_1^i > 0$, $W^i \geq 0$, $W_1^i > 0$, $W_3^i > 0$ are also proven in addition to $S_3^i > 0$; $S^i \geq 0$ follows from $J_i \geq 0$, and $S_1^i > 0$ follows from the control problem of J_i with $x_{i+1} \equiv 0$. These facts also yield $W_1^i > 0$, $W_3^i > 0$, $W^i \geq 0$ by the property of positive definiteness of the block matrix.

Remark 1. Suppose $n = n_c$, that is, $x_i = x_i^c$, which has been studied in [4]. Then Problem A is reduced into the following problem:

Problem B:
$$\min_{\substack{v_i^c,\ i=k,k+1,\\ \dots,k+N-1}} \sum_{i=k}^{k+N-1} w_i^g(x_i, v_i^c)$$

subject to $x_{i+1} = v_i^c$, x_k : given

$$v_i^c \in \mathcal{E}_i(v_{i-1}^c),\ v_{k-1}^c = x_k$$

where $w_i^g = w_i + g_i$. Thus we can use the *forward dynamic programming* (F-DP) to solve Problem B as follows.

$$V_{j+1}(v_{k+j+1}^c) = \min_{v_{k+j}^c \in \mathcal{E}_{k+j}(v_{k+j-1}^c)} \{w_{k+j}^g(v_{k+j}^c, v_{k+j+1}^c) + V_j(v_{k+j}^c)\}$$

where

$$V_j(v_{k+j}^c) := \min_{\substack{v_i^c \in \mathcal{E}_i(v_{i-1}^c),\, i = k, \\ k+1\dots,\, k+j-1}} \sum_{i=k}^{k+j} w_i^g(x_i, v_i^c).$$

It is well-known that the computational cost in the above F-DP is $O(n_e)$, where n_e is the number of the edges of the directed graph $\mathcal{G}_k(x_k^c)$. However, under the assumption that the resolution of the discretized variables is all the same, n_e will grow exponentially with the dimension of the state, i.e., the computational effort will exponentially grow.

4 Optimization Algorithm of Discrete Inputs with Dynamical Constraints

In Theorem 1, the original problem has been reduced to Problem A. Thus, next, we discuss an efficient algorithm for solving Problem A.

Problem A may be solved by the "backward" dynamic programming. However, the computational effort in this case is much larger than the case in Remark 1. Thus such a kind of approach will not be practical, and a new efficient approach will be required.

By substituting

$$x_{k+i} = \left(\prod_{s=0}^{i-1} A_{k+i-1-s}^d\right) x_k + \sum_{j=0}^{i-1}\left(\prod_{s=0}^{i-2-j} A_{k+i-1-s}^d\right) B_{k+i} v_{k+i},$$

obtained from $x_{i+1} = A_i^d x_i + B_i^d v_i^c$, into the cost of Problem A, it is reduced to the following discrete quadratic programming problem:

$$\text{Problem C:} \quad \min_U U^T H U + U^T f$$

$$\text{subject to} \quad U \in \mathcal{U}$$

where H is a positive definite matrix (proven from $W_3^i > 0$, $W^i \geq 0$, and $G_a^i \geq 0$), f is a vector-valued function of x_k, and

$$\mathcal{U} := \{U \mid v_i^c \in \mathcal{E}_i(v_{i-1}^c),\ i = k, k+1, \dots, k+N-1,\ v_{k-1}^c = x_k \}, \qquad (9)$$

$$U := \begin{bmatrix} v_k^c \\ v_{k+1}^c \\ \vdots \\ v_{k+N-1}^c \end{bmatrix} \in \mathbb{R}^{N_c}, \quad N_c := N n_c.$$

Although the above symbols H, f, U, and $\mathcal{U}$ depend on the time t_k and/or the state x_k, we have omitted this information for simplicity of notation. Moreover, the ith element of U is denoted by u_i ($i = 1, 2, \dots, N_c$) and the condition $U \in \mathcal{U}$ is called the input sequence constraints hereafter.

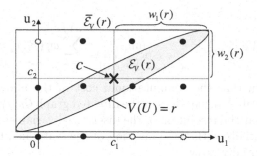

Fig. 3. A super-ellipsoid $\mathcal{E}_V(r)$ and a super-rectangular $\bar{\mathcal{E}}_V(r)$ for $N_c = 2$ (black points express inputs that belong to $\mathcal{U}$)

If the input sequence constraints are ignored, Problem C is rewritten as the 0-1 integer quadratic programming (IQP) problem by $v_i^c = \sum_{j=1}^{|\mathcal{E}_i(v_{i-1}^c)|} \alpha_j^i \delta_j^i$, $\delta_j^i \in \{0, 1\}$, $\sum_{j=1}^{|\mathcal{E}_i(v_{i-1}^c)|} \delta_j^i = 1$, and α_j^i is the element of $\mathcal{E}_i(v_{i-1}^c)$. So the efficient IQP solvers such as ILOG CPLEX solvers can be applied to this problem. However, in this case, the number of the binary variables increases in proportion to the cardinality of the finite set $\mathcal{E}_i(v_{i-1}^c)$, which makes the computation load exponentially increased. Furthermore, many additional inequalities are required to express the input sequence constraints in terms of δ_j^i; for example, the condition that "if $\delta_1 = 1$, then we can take $\delta_2 = 1$ or $\delta_3 = 1$" can be expressed as the four inequalities $\delta_1 - \theta \leq 0$, $\delta_2 - \theta \leq 0$, $\delta_3 - \theta \leq 0$, and $\delta_2 + \delta_3 - \theta \geq 0$ by using additional binary variable $\theta \in \{0, 1\}$.

Thus we will propose the other approach, that is, an enumeration approach based on the branch and bound method as follows. For a given positive constant r, consider the super-ellipsoid on $\mathbb{R}^{N_c}$ as follows:

$$\mathcal{E}_V(r) := \{U \in \mathbb{R}^{N_c} \mid V(U) \leq r\}$$

where $V(U) = U^T H U + U^T f$. Then for each enumerated $U \in \mathcal{U} \cap \mathcal{E}_V(r)$, we will compare the value $V(U)$ to find $U^* = \arg\min V(U)$. However, it will in general spend much time to find a $U \in \mathcal{U} \cap \mathcal{E}_V(r)$, otherwise to determine that there exists no $U \in \mathcal{U} \cap \mathcal{E}_V(r)$. So we will consider a super-rectangular, denoted by $\bar{\mathcal{E}}_V(r)$, that is circumscribed in the super-ellipsoid $\mathcal{E}_V(r)$, and whose side is parallel to some u_i-axis of U (see Fig. 3). Then the set $\bar{\mathcal{E}}_V(r)$ can be easily characterized as follows.

Lemma 1. *The center c of $\bar{\mathcal{E}}_V(r)$ (or equivalently the center of $\mathcal{E}_V(r)$) and the distance $w(r)$ between the center c and each face of $\bar{\mathcal{E}}_V(r)$ are given as follows:*

$$c = -\frac{1}{2}H^{-1}f, \quad w_i(r) = \sqrt{\left(r + \frac{1}{4}f^T H f\right)h_i^{inv}}, \quad i = 1, 2, \dots, N_c \quad (10)$$

where $w_i(r)$ denotes the ith element of $w(r)$, and h_i^{inv} the (i, i)th element of H^{-1}.

Proof. The first relation is trivial. We prove the second one. So for $\bar{V}(\bar{U}) :=$ $\bar{U}^T H \bar{U}$ with $\bar{U} := U + \frac{1}{2} H^{-1} f (= U - c)$, the super-ellipsoid $\mathcal{E}_V(r)$ is expressed as

$$\mathcal{E}_V(r) = \{U \in \mathbb{R}^{N_c} \mid \bar{V}(\bar{U}) \leq \bar{r}\}, \quad \bar{r} := r + \frac{1}{4} f^T H f.$$

Then defining for $\bar{U}$ and H the symbols given by

$$\bar{U} = \begin{bmatrix} \bar{U}_a \\ \bar{U}_b \\ \bar{U}_c \end{bmatrix}, \quad \bar{U}_a \in \mathbb{R}^{i-1}, \quad \bar{U}_b \in \mathbb{R}, \quad \bar{U}_c \in \mathbb{R}^{N_c - i},$$

$$H = \begin{bmatrix} h_{11} & h_{12} & h_{13} \\ h_{12}^T & h_{22} & h_{23} \\ h_{13}^T & h_{23}^T & h_{33} \end{bmatrix}, \quad \begin{array}{l} h_{11} \in \mathbb{R}^{(i-1)\times(i-1)}, \quad h_{12} \in \mathbb{R}^{i-1}, \quad h_{13} \in \mathbb{R}^{(i-1)\times(N_c-i)}, \\ h_{22} \in \mathbb{R}, \quad h_{23} \in \mathbb{R}^{1\times(N_c-i)}, \quad h_{33} \in \mathbb{R}^{(N_c-i)\times(N_c-i)}, \end{array}$$

$\bar{V}(\bar{U})$ is expressed as

$$\bar{V}(\bar{U}) = \hat{U}^T \hat{H} \hat{U} + 2\bar{U}_b \hat{U}^T \hat{f} + h_{22} \bar{U}_b^2$$

where

$$\hat{U} := \begin{bmatrix} \bar{U}_a \\ \bar{U}_c \end{bmatrix}, \quad \hat{H} := \begin{bmatrix} h_{11} & h_{13} \\ h_{13}^T & h_{33} \end{bmatrix}, \quad \hat{f} := \begin{bmatrix} h_{12} \\ h_{23}^T \end{bmatrix}.$$

Thus since $\hat{H} > 0$ follows from $H > 0$, we have

$$\bar{r} - \bar{V}(\bar{U}) = \bar{r} - (h_{22} - \hat{f}^T \hat{H}^{-1} \hat{f}) \bar{U}_b^2 - (\hat{U} + \hat{H}^{-1} \hat{f} \bar{U}_b)^T \hat{H} (\hat{U} + \hat{H}^{-1} \hat{f} \bar{U}_b) \geq 0 \quad (11)$$

which thus implies $\bar{r} \geq (h_{22} - \hat{f}^T \hat{H}^{-1} \hat{f}) \bar{U}_b^2$. Since $H > 0$, we can prove that the term $h_{22} - \hat{f}^T \hat{H}^{-1} \hat{f}$ is positive, and its reciprocal number $1/(h_{22} - \hat{f}^T \hat{H}^{-1} \hat{f})$ is equal to the (i,i)th element h_i^{inv} of H^{-1} (via the definition of the inverse matrix). Thus noting $\bar{U}_b = u_i - c_i$, we have for the ith element of U, $c_i - \sqrt{\bar{r} h_i^{inv}} \leq u_i \leq c_i + \sqrt{\bar{r} h_i^{inv}}$. Finally, we show that $w_i(r)$ of (10) expresses the distance between the center c and each face of $\bar{\mathcal{E}}_V(r)$. For $\hat{U} = -\hat{H}^{-1} \hat{f} \bar{U}_b$ in (11), we can take $\bar{U}_b$ as $\bar{U}_b = \sqrt{\bar{r}/(h_{22} - \hat{f}^T \hat{H}^{-1} \hat{f})}$ to satisfy $\bar{V}(\bar{U}) = \bar{r}$. This proves the second relation. $\qquad \square$

From this lemma, we can see that $\bar{\mathcal{E}}_V(r)$ is easily calculated by using H and f of $V(U)$; thus we can easily pick up an element $U \in \mathcal{U} \cap \bar{\mathcal{E}}_V(r)$ thanks to the fact that each side of $\bar{\mathcal{E}}_V(r)$ is parallel to its corresponding axis u_i. However, in general, the cardinality of $\mathcal{U} \cap \bar{\mathcal{E}}_V(r)$ is still much larger than that of $\mathcal{U} \cap \mathcal{E}_V(r)$.

So we will consider a section of the ellipsoid $\mathcal{E}_V(r)$ by fixing the values of u_i that belongs to $\bar{\mathcal{E}}_V(r)$. The main idea is as follows. Consider the case of $N_c = 2$. First, the value of u_1 is fixed as $u_1 = p_1$ for a certain constant p_1 in $\mathcal{U} \cap \bar{\mathcal{E}}_V(r)$. Then for a function $V(U)|_{u_1=p_1}$ on u_2, it will be quite easy to characterize all values of u_2 in $\mathcal{U} \cap \mathcal{E}_V(r)$, which enables us to check the minimum value of $V(U)$ for $u_1 = p_1$ in an easy way. A similar way for the other p_1 is repeated, and finally the minimum value of $V(U)$ is obtained. Even if $N_c \geq 3$, we can use the same technique by fixing the values of all variables except for one variable, although some proper strategy on how the variables are fixed is required. Thus if we can find a candidate U_{temp} in $\mathcal{U} \cap \mathcal{E}_V(r)$, we can reset the value of r as $r = V(U_{temp})$, which is denoted by r_{new}, to make the search region smaller. Then for a new super-rectangular $\mathcal{E}_V(r_{new})$, the same procedure is executed. In this way, the solution U^* will be determined by making r smaller until $\mathcal{U} \cap \mathcal{E}_V(r) = \emptyset$.

Of course, for the worst case, all elements in the finite set $\mathcal{U} \cap \bar{\mathcal{E}}_V(r)$ may have to be picked up; this is the same as that of all the other branch and bound algorithms. Thus by numerical comparisons with the other algorithms, the efficiency of the proposed algorithm will be shown in the next section, where we will see that this branch and bound method based on $\bar{\mathcal{E}}_V(r)$ dramatically decrease the number of the elements to be picked up.

First, we prepare the following notation. Using the new variable $U^i := [u_i\ u_{i+1}$ $\cdots\ u_{N_c}]^T$, let us consider the function

$$V_i(U^i;\ p^{i-1}) := V(U)\big|_{[u_1\ u_2\ \cdots\ u_{i-1}]^T = p^{i-1}}$$

where $p^{i-1} = [p_1\ p_2\ \cdots\ p_{i-1}]^T$ is any given $(i-1)$-dimensional constant vector. This function is expressed as

$$V_i(U^i;\ p^{i-1}) = (U^i)^T H^i U^i + (U^i)^T f^i(p^{i-1})$$
$$H^i = \begin{bmatrix} h_{11}^i & h_{12}^i \\ (h_{12}^i)^T & h_{22}^i \end{bmatrix}, \quad f^i(p^{i-1}) = \begin{bmatrix} f_1^i(p^{i-1}) \\ f_2^i(p^{i-1}) \end{bmatrix}.$$

where H^i and f^i are defined in an inductive way:

$$H^1 = H, \quad f^1(p^0) = f,$$
$$H^i = h_{22}^{i-1}, \quad f^i(p^{i-1}) = 2p_{i-1}(h_{12}^{i-1})^T + f_2^{i-1}(p^{i-2}), \quad i \geq 2. \tag{12}$$

Note that p^0 is used in a formal way, $p^1 = p_1$, and $p^i = [(p^{i-1})^T\ p_i]^T$, and also $V_1(U^1;\ p^0) = V(U)$. Furthermore, we define the following notation for $i \geq 2$:

$$r_i(p^{i-1}) = r_{i-1}(p^{i-2}) + h_{11}^{i-1}(p_{i-1})^2 + f_1^{i-1}(p^{i-2})p_{i-1}, \tag{13}$$

$$c^i(p^{i-1}) = -\frac{1}{2}(H^i)^{-1} f^i(p^{i-1}), \tag{14}$$

$$w^i(r, p^{i-1}) = [w_j^i(r, p^{i-1})], \quad w_j^i(r, p^{i-1}) = \sqrt{(r - r_i(p^{i-1}) + \tilde{f}^i)h_j^{i,inv}}, \tag{15}$$

$$\tilde{f}^i(p^{i-1}) = \frac{1}{4}\{f^i(p^{i-1})\}^T (H^i)^{-1} f^i(p^{i-1}), \tag{16}$$

$$\mathcal{D}^i(r, p^{i-1}) = \{\ u_i \in \mathcal{U}_i \mid c_i^i(p^{i-1}) - w_i^i(r, p^{i-1}) \leq u_i \leq c_i^i(p^{i-1}) + w_i^i(r, p^{i-1})\ \} \tag{17}$$

where $h_j^{i,inv}$ is the (j,j)th element of $(H^i)^{-1}$, c_i^i is the ith element of c^i, w_j^i (r, p^{i-1}) is the ith element of $w^i(r, p^{i-1})$, and $\mathcal{U}_i$ is the set of the ith element of $U \in \mathcal{U}$.

Note that $r_i(p^{i-1})$ characterizes the super-ellipsoid subject to $[u_1\ u_2\ \cdots\ u_{i-1}]^T = p^{i-1}$, i.e., $V_i(U^i; p^{i-1}) \leq r - r_i(p^{i-1})$. For this ellipsoid, its center is given by $c^i(p^{i-1})$, and $w^i(r, p^{i-1})$ expresses the distance between the center $c^i(p^{i-1})$ and each face of the super-rectangular $\bar{\mathcal{E}}_{V_i}(r_i(p^{i-1}))$ (see Lemma 1). Finally, $\mathcal{D}^i(r, p^{i-1})$ expresses, among all the points U^i within the ellipsoid $V_i(U^i; p^{i-1}) \leq r - r_i(p^{i-1})$, all the 1-st elements u_i of U^i such that $u_i \in \mathcal{U}_i$.

Now we are in a position to propose the following algorithm.

[Proposed algorithm]
Main routine:

Step 0: $H, f, \mathcal{U}$, and $U_{ini} \in \mathcal{U}$ are given.
Step 1: Calculate

$$r = V(U_{ini}),\quad H^1 = H,\quad f^1(p^0) = f,\quad r_1(p^0) = 0,$$
$$c^1(p^0) = -\frac{1}{2}H^{-1}f,\quad w^1(r, p^0) = w(r),$$
$$\mathcal{D}^1(r, p^0) = \{u_1 \in \mathcal{U}_1 \mid c_1^1(p^0) - w_1^1(r, p^0) \leq u_1 \leq c_1^1(p^0) + w_1^1(r, p^0)\},$$
$$\mathcal{B}^1 = \emptyset,\quad \mathcal{P}^1(r, p^0, \mathcal{B}^1) = \mathcal{D}^1(r, p^0),\quad i = 1$$

Step 2: One of (i)~(iii) is executed.
  (i) If $i < N_c$ and $\mathcal{P}^i(r, p^{i-1}, \mathcal{B}^i) \neq \emptyset$, then $p_i = \mathrm{mid}(\mathcal{P}^i(r, p^{i-1}, \mathcal{B}^i))$, $\mathcal{B}^i = \mathcal{B}^i \bigcup\{p_i\}$, $\mathcal{B}^{i+1} = \emptyset$, and then $i = i + 1$. Go to Substep 1.
  (ii) If $i = N_c$ and $\mathcal{P}^{N_c}(r, p^{N_c-1}, \mathcal{B}^{N_c}) \neq \emptyset$, then $p_{N_c} = \arg\min_{u_{N_c} \in \mathcal{P}^{N_c}} V_{N_c}$ $(u_{N_c}; p^{N_c-1})$, $p = [p_1\ p_2\ \cdots\ p_{N_c}]^T$, $r = V(p)$, and then $i = N_c - 1$. Go to Substep 2.
  (iii) If $i > 1$ and $\mathcal{P}^i(r, p^{i-1}, \mathcal{B}^i) = \emptyset$, then $i = i - 1$ and go to Substep 3.
  (iv) If $i = 1$ and $\mathcal{P}^1(r, p^0, \mathcal{B}^1) = \emptyset$, then output $U^* = p$.

Subroutine:

Substep 1: Calculate H^i and f^i of $V_i(U^i; p^{i-1})$ in (12), $r_i(p^{i-1})$ in (13), and $c_i(p^{i-1})$ in (14). Then go to Substep 2.
Substep 2: Calculate $w^i(r, p^{i-1})$ in (15) and $\mathcal{D}^i(r, p^{i-1})$ in (17), and then go to Substep 3.
Substep 3: Renew $\mathcal{P}^i(r, p^{i-1}, \mathcal{B}^i)$ as $\mathcal{P}^i(r, p^{i-1}, \mathcal{B}^i) = \mathcal{D}^i(r, p^{i-1})/\mathcal{B}^i$ and then go to Step 2.

Here the function $\mathrm{mid}(\mathcal{P})$ is defined for a finite set $\mathcal{P}$ on $\mathbb{R}$ as follows:

$$\mathrm{mid}(\mathcal{P}) = \arg\min_{p \in \mathcal{P}} \sum_{j=1}^{|\mathcal{P}|} |p - p_j|$$

which implies that $p^* = \mathrm{mid}(\mathcal{P})$ expresses the middle of $\mathcal{P}$ in the above sense.

Let us explain the procedures in the algorithm roughly. Suppose that $i = 1$ and that (i) holds in step 2. Then p_1 is determined as a middle of the set $\mathcal{P}^1(r, p^0, \mathcal{B}^1)$, i.e., $\mathcal{D}^1(r, p^0)$. Further, $\mathcal{B}^1 = \{p_1\}$, $\mathcal{B}^2 = \emptyset$, and $i = 2$ are set

($\mathcal{B}^i$ is used for memorizing the values of p_i that have been checked). In substeps 1 and 2, the ellipsoid $V_2(\mathsf{u}_2; p^1) \leq r - r_2(p^1)$ with $\mathsf{u}_1 = p_1$ and its parameters are calculated. In substep 3, we have $\mathcal{P}^2(r, p^1, \mathcal{B}^2) = \mathcal{D}^2(r, p^1)$ because of $\mathcal{B}^2 = \emptyset$.

Next, suppose that (ii) holds in step 2 (suppose $N_c = 2$). Then $p_2 \in \mathcal{P}^2(r, p^1, \mathcal{B}^2)$ is determined to minimize the value of $V_2(\mathsf{u}_2; p^1)$, and the value of r is renewed as $r = V(p)$, where $p = [p_1, p_2]^T$. Furthermore, we reset $i = 1$ and go to substeps 2 and 3. Thus $\mathcal{P}^1(r, p^0, \mathcal{B}^1)$ is given by deleting the element p_1, because $\mathcal{B}^1 = \{p_1\}$. So if (i) is satisfied, the same story is repeated for this new $\mathcal{P}^1(r, p^0, \mathcal{B}^1)$.

On the other hand, suppose that (iii) holds (assume $i = 2$), i.e., $\mathcal{P}^2(r, p^1, \mathcal{B}^2) = \emptyset$. which implies that no candidate for p_2 exists. Then we reset $i = 1$. Thus after the new $\mathcal{P}^1(r, p^0, \mathcal{B}^1)$ is obtained in substep 3, if (i) in step 2 holds, we can change the value of p_1.

Finally, if (iv) holds after repeating the above procedure, that is, r is decreasing and at last no possible new candidate for p_1 exists, we can obtain the optimal solution.

It is also stressed that the proposed approach has another advantage; it needs to take no special consideration for the constraints given by the directed graph, because the value p_i of u_i only has to be selected based on the directed graph. On the other hand, in the usual IQP solvers that cannot directly treat the constraints given by the directed graph, many binary variables and some inequalities will be required in general to express such constraints.

5   Simulation

5.1   Computation Time with No Constraints

First, it is shown that the discrete optimization algorithm is quite efficient by comparing the commercial solver "ILOG CPLEX solver", which is well known as one of efficient solvers, even if no constraints exist.

For fixed k, consider Problem C with

$$\mathcal{U} := \{U | \mathsf{u}_i \in \{-d, -(d-1), \ldots, d-1, d\}, \ i = 1, \ldots, N_c\}.$$

This corresponds to the so-called integer quadratic programming problem with no constraints. Fig. 4 shows the computation time with respect to the number of variables N_c for $d = 5$, where Linux (Kernel 2.4) is used on the computer with the Intel Pentium 4 2.53GHz processor and the 2048MB memory, and 20 different cases of H, f, which are generated in a random way, are used for each N_c. This figure shows that the proposed solver is about 30 times faster than the CPLEX solver at $N_c = 25 \sim 30$. For $d = 20$ and $N_c = 25$, the maximum computation time is about 0.6 (sec) for the proposed solver, while 12.76 (sec) for the CPLEX solver. In this way, the proposed solver is quite efficient compared with the CPLEX solver.

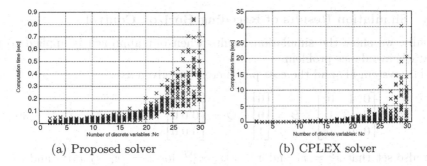

(a) Proposed solver   (b) CPLEX solver

Fig. 4. Computation time with no constraints for $d = 5$

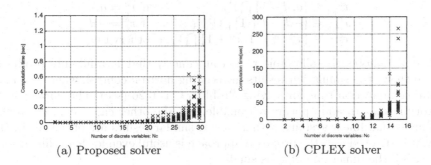

(a) Proposed solver   (b) CPLEX solver

Fig. 5. Computation time with the sequence constraints for $d = 5$

5.2   Computation Time Under the Sequence Constraints

Next, we consider Problem C with

$$\mathcal{U} := \{ \, U | \; \mathsf{u}_i \in \mathcal{E}(\mathsf{u}_{i-1}), \; i = 1, 2, \ldots, N_c, \; u_0 = 0 \, \}$$

where $\mathcal{E}$ is given by the rule that for $\mathsf{u}_i \in \{-d, -(d-1), \ldots, d-1, d\}$

$$
\begin{aligned}
\mathsf{u}_{i+1} &\in \{d, d-1, d-2\} & \text{if } \mathsf{u}_i = d, \\
\mathsf{u}_{i+1} &\in \{-d, -d+1, -d+2\} & \text{if } \mathsf{u}_i = -d, \\
\mathsf{u}_{i+1} &\in \{\mathsf{u}_i - 2, \mathsf{u}_i - 1, \mathsf{u}_i, \mathsf{u}_i + 1, \mathsf{u}_i + 2\} & \text{otherwise.}
\end{aligned}
$$

Note that $\mathcal{E}(\cdot)$ is a time-invariant function. Fig. 5 shows the computation time with respect to the number of variables N_c (2~30), where Linux (Kernel 2.4) is used on the computer with the Xenon 2.0GHz processor and the 2048MB memory, and 20 different cases of H, f, which are generated in a random way, are used for each N_c. From this result, we can see that the proposed algorithm can solve the problem with $N_c \le 29$ within 1 (sec). On the other hand, if the CPLEX solver (IQP solver) is applied to this problem by expressing the directed graph in terms of 0-1 inequalities and additional binary variables, the computational time is much larger than the case of the proposed method as in Fig. 5(b). For example, the proposed solver is more than 4000 times faster than the CPLEX solver at $N_c = 15$.

5.3   Simulation Results of Receding Horizon Control

Finally, we show the simulation results when our approach is applied to the obstacle avoidance problem.

The system (1) and the cost parameters are given as

$$A = \begin{bmatrix} 0 & 1 & 0 \\ 0 & -3 & 1 \\ 0 & 0 & -5 \end{bmatrix}, \; B = \begin{bmatrix} 0 \\ 0 \\ 1 \end{bmatrix}, \; Q = \begin{bmatrix} 1 & 0 & 0 \\ 0 & 0 & 0 \\ 0 & 0 & 0 \end{bmatrix}, \; R = 1, \; t_i = i, \; N = 30.$$

We also set that $x^c = x_1$ and $x^u = [x_2 \; x_3]^T$ for $x = [x_1 \; x_2 \; x_3]^T$, and assume that the graph $\mathcal{E}_i(x_i^c)$ is given by

$$\begin{aligned} x_{i+1}^c &\in \{d, d-1\} \cap \mathcal{V}_{i+1} & \text{if } x_i^c = d, \\ x_{i+1}^c &\in \{-d, -d+1\} \cap \mathcal{V}_{i+1} & \text{if } x_i^c = -d, \\ x_{i+1}^c &\in \{x_i^c, x_i^c - 1, x_i^c + 1\} \cap \mathcal{V}_{i+1} & \text{otherwise.} \end{aligned}$$

where $\mathcal{V}_i$ denotes the allowable region at time t_i that is randomly produced. Fig. 6 shows the simulation results in receding horizon control, where the maximum computation time for solving Problem C is 0.26 (sec). The obrained trajectory is smooth and appears reasonable. For the other cases, e.g., for several 4-dimensional linear systems with $x^c = x_1$, similar results are obtained. In this way, it is stressed that the proposed approach is useful even for high-dimensional systems if the dimension of x^c is small.

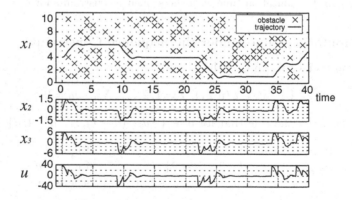

Fig. 6. Simulation results for the obstacle avoidance problem

6   Conclusion

This paper has proposed a generalized framework of simultaneous optimization of motion trajectories (continuous variables) and waypoints (discrete variables) subject to the linear system with discrete dynamical constraints. Although the problem of how to generate a directed graph from the admissible region, which is also an important issue, has not been addressed here, it will be reported in the near future.

References

1. G.J. Pappas, G. Lafferriere, and S. Sastry. Hierarchically consistent control systems. *IEEE Trans. Automatic Control, Vol.45*, pp. 1144–1160, 2000.
2. A.J. van der Schaft. Equivalence of dynamical systems by bisimulation. *IEEE Trans. Automatic Control, Vol.49*, pp. 2160–2172, 2004.
3. A. Rantzer and M. Johansson. Piecewise linear quadratic optimal control. *IEEE Trans. on Automatic Control, Vol.45*, pp. 629–637, 2000.
4. H.L. Hagenaars, J. Imura, and H. Nijmeijer. Approximate continuous-time optimal control in obstacle avoidance by time/space discretization of non-convex state constraints, *Proc. of IEEE Conf. on Control Applications*, 878/883 (2004)
5. Y.K. Hwang and N. Ahuja. Gross Motion Planning-A Survey *ACM Computing Surveys, Vol.24, No.3, pp.219–291*, 1992.
6. J.N. Tsitsklis. Efficient Algorithms for Globally Optimal Trajectories. *IEEE Trans. on Automatic Control, pp.1528–1538*, 1995.
7. R.W. Brockett. Finite dimensional linear systems. *New York, Wiley*, 1970.
8. M. Egerstedt and C. F. Martin. Optimal trajectory planning and smoothing splines. *Automatica, Vol. 37, pp.1057–1064*, 2001.

Approximate Abstraction of Stochastic Hybrid Automata[*]

A. Agung Julius

Dept. Electrical and Systems Engineering,
University of Pennsylvania,
200 South 33rd Street, Philadelphia PA-19104, USA
agung@seas.upenn.edu

Abstract. This paper discusses a notion of approximate abstraction for linear stochastic hybrid automata (LSHA). The idea is based on the construction of the so called stochastic bisimulation function. Such function can be used to quantify the distance between a system and its approximate abstraction. The work in this paper generalizes our earlier work for jump linear stochastic systems (JLSS). In this paper we demonstrate that linear stochastic hybrid automata can be cast as a modified JLSS and modify the procedure for constructing the stochastic bisimulation function accordingly. The construction of quadratic stochastic bisimulation functions is essentially a linear matrix inequality problem. In this paper, we also discuss possible extensions of the framework to handle nonlinear dynamics and variable rate Poisson processes. As an example, we apply the framework to a chain-like stochastic hybrid automaton.

1 Introduction

Stochastic hybrid systems are widely used to model physical and engineering systems, in which the continuous dynamics has many modes or discontinuities, as well as stochastic behavior [1]. Applications of stochastic hybrid systems can be found in telecommunication networks [2], systems biology [3], air traffic management [4], etc.

There are several available modelling formalisms for stochastic hybrid systems. One of the earliest frameworks is the one in [5], where a general type of stochastic hybrid systems, whose continuous dynamics is described by diffusion stochastic differential equation [6], is presented. Mode switching occurs when some invariant condition in the corresponding mode is violated. Another framework that involves multimodal diffusion equation is the switched diffusion processes [7]. There are also modelling frameworks, where the continuous dynamics is described by ordinary differential equation, such as the piecewise deterministic Markov processes [8], stochastic hybrid systems [2], etc. In these frameworks, the switching is modelled as a Poisson process. For a more thorough

---

[*] This research is supported by the National Science Foundation Presidential Early CAREER (PECASE) Grant 0132716.

survey on the modelling formalisms for stochastic hybrid systems, the interested reader is referred to [1].

Researchers have been working on how to tame the increasing complexity of system analysis. There are two approaches. The first approach is to develop a framework that allows the computation to be performed in a modular fashion. The other approach is to develop a framework that allows abstraction of the complex system. By abstraction we mean building a simpler system that is, in some sense, equivalent to the complex system. The computation is then performed on the simpler system and the equivalence guarantees that the results can be carried over into the complex system. The discussion in this paper pertains to the second approach.

Bisimulation is a concept of system equivalence that is widely used for abstraction of complex systems. Notions of exact bisimulation for some classes of stochastic hybrid systems have been recently developed in [9, 10]. In [9], a category theoretical notion exact bisimulation for general stochastic hybrid systems is discussed, while [10] treats the issue of exact bisimulation for the so called communicating piecewise deterministic hybrid systems. In this paper, we relax the requirement that the abstraction is exactly equivalent to the original system. Instead, we require that they are only *approximately* equivalent [11, 12]. We then need to define a metric, with which we can measure the distance between systems and hence the quality of the abstraction. In [13, 14], the authors develop some metrics for labelled Markov processes and probabilistic transition systems, inspired by the Hutchinson metric, which gives the distance between two distributions of the transition probability. The approach that we take in this paper differs from that, since we use a different kind of metric. The metric that we use is based on the L_∞ distance between the output trajectories of the systems. We develop a theory of approximate bisimulation for a class of stochastic hybrid automata, in which the continuous dynamics is modelled by stochastic differential equations and the switches are modelled as Poisson processes. This class of systems is called the *linear stochastic hybrid automata* (LSHA).

The approach that we take in this paper is by computing the so called *stochastic bisimulation function*. The stochastic bisimulation function is used to quantify the quality of the abstraction. This approach has been used in [15] for jump linear stochastic systems (JLSS). The jump linear stochastic systems are stochastic systems whose dynamics is described by a stochastic differential equation with Poisson jumps in the continuous state. Thus, an LSHA can be thought of as a generalization of JLSS, as in LSHA it is possible to have multiple modes for the continuous dynamics. However, in this paper we also show that it is possible to cast an LSHA as a modified JLSS, and hence we can compute the stochastic bisimulation function for LSHA by modifying the procedure for JLSS. We also demonstrate that the construction of quadratic stochastic bisimulation functions for LSHA can be cast as a tractable linear matrix inequality problem. Further, we also discuss possible extensions of the framework to deal with nonlinear dynamics and variable rate Poisson processes.

2   Linear Stochastic Hybrid Automata

In this paper, we formally define a linear stochastic hybrid automaton (LSHA) as a 5-tuple $\mathcal{A} = (L, n, m, T, F)$, where

- L is a finite set, which is the set of locations or discrete states. The number of locations is denoted by $|L|$.
- $n : L \to \mathbb{N}$, where for every $l \in L$, $n(l)$ is the dimension of the continuous state space in location l,
- $m \in \mathbb{N}$, is the dimension of the output of the automaton $\mathcal{A}$,
- T is the set of random transitions. A transition $\tau \in T$ can be written as a 4-tuple $(l, \lambda_\tau, l', R_\tau)$. This is a transition from location $l \in L$ to $l' \in L$ that is triggered by a Poisson process with intensity $\lambda_\tau \in \mathbb{R}_+$. The matrix $R_\tau \in \mathbb{R}^{n(l') \times n(l)}$ is the linear reset map associated with the transition τ. The number of transitions is denoted by $|T|$.
- F defines the continuous dynamics in each location. For every $l \in L$, $F(l)$ is a triple (A_l, G_l, C_l), where $A_l \in \mathbb{R}^{n(l) \times n(l)}$, $G_l \in \mathbb{R}^{n(l) \times n(l)}$ and $C_l \in \mathbb{R}^{m \times n(l)}$.

The state space of the automaton can be written as

$$\mathcal{X} = \bigcup_{i=1}^{|L|} \left(\{l_i\} \times \mathbb{R}^{n(l_i)} \right). \tag{1}$$

We also define the functions $\mathtt{source} : T \to L$ and $\mathtt{dest} : T \to L$, such that if $\tau \in T$ is $(l, \lambda_\tau, l', R_\tau)$ then

$$\mathtt{source}(\tau) = l, \ \mathtt{dest}(\tau) = l'. \tag{2}$$

The semantics of the linear stochastic hybrid automaton $\mathcal{A}$ can be explained as follows. The state trajectory $\xi_t = (l_t, x_t)$ of the LSHA $\mathcal{A}$ is inherently a stochastic process. Every state trajectory that the automaton executes is a realization of the process. In each location $l \in L$, the continuous state of the system satisfies the following stochastic differential equation (SDE).

$$dx_{l,t} = A_l x_{l,t} \ dt + G_l x_{l,t} \ dw_t, \tag{3a}$$

$$y_t = C_l x_{l,t}, \tag{3b}$$

$$x_{l,t} \in \mathbb{R}^{n(l)}, y_t \in \mathbb{R}^m. \tag{3c}$$

The process w_t is an $\mathbb{R}$ valued standard Brownian motion, where $E[w_t^2] = t$. The $\mathbb{R}^m$ valued stochastic process y_t is the output/observation of automaton A.

Remark 1. In general, it is possible to incorporate multi dimensional Brownian motions in the framework. In this case, the term $G_l x_{lt} \ dw_t$ in (3a) would be replaced by $\sum_{i=1}^N G_{l,i} x_{lt} \ dw_{i,t}$ to incorporate an N-dimensional Brownian motion. Hereafter, we stick to the one dimensional Brownian motion for simplicity.

Denote the set of outgoing transitions of a location as

$$\texttt{out} : L \to 2^T, \ \texttt{out}(l) := \{\tau \in T \mid \texttt{source}(\tau) = l\}, \tag{4}$$

and $|\texttt{out}(l)|$ as the number of outgoing transitions from location l. While the system is evolving in a location $l \in L$, each transition in $\texttt{out}(l)$ is represented by an active Poisson process. Each of these Poisson processes has a constant rate indicated by the transition. The first Poisson process to generate a point triggers a transition. Suppose that $\tau = (l, \lambda_\tau, l', R_\tau)$ is the transition that corresponds to the first process that generates a point (at time t), then the evolution of the system will switch to location l'. The matrix R_τ defines a linear reset map,

$$x_t = R_\tau x_{t^-}, \tag{5}$$

where $x_{t^-} := \lim_{s \uparrow t} x_s$.

Figure 1 illustrates a realization of the execution of an LSHA. In Figure 1, the execution starts in location l_0 by following the SDE that defines the dynamics in the location. The set of outgoing transitions from l_0, $\texttt{out}(l_0) = \{\tau, \theta\}$. In this particular realization, the Poisson process associated with τ generates a point before that of θ. Hence, a transition occurs that brings the trajectory to location $\texttt{dest}(\tau) = l_1$. The continuous state of the trajectory is reset by the linear map

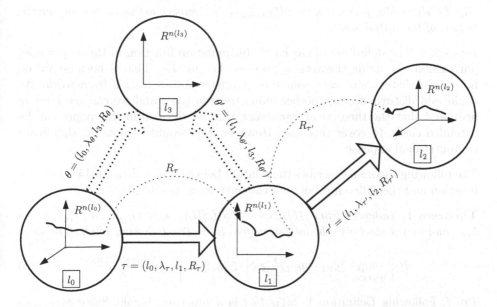

Fig. 1. An illustration of the execution of an LSHA. The solid bold arrows represent transitions between locations that occur. The dotted bold arrows indicate transitions that do not occur, since the associated Poisson process do not generate a point fast enough. The dotted arrows denote the linear reset maps associated with the transitions that occur.

R_τ. In the new location, the continuous dynamics proceeds with the SDE that defines the dynamics in location l_1. The set $\mathsf{out}(l_1) = \{\tau', \theta'\}$. In this particular realization, the Poisson process associated with τ' generates a point before that of θ'. Hence, a transition occurs that brings the trajectory to location l_2. The continuous state of the system is then subsequently reset by the linear map $R_{\tau'}$.

3   Approximate Abstraction of LSHA

In this paper we will develop the notion of approximate abstraction of linear stochastic hybrid automata. The notion of approximate abstraction is constructed using the concept of stochastic bisimulation functions [15][1].

A stochastic bisimulation function is defined between two LSHA, $\mathcal{A}_i = (L_i, n_i, m, T_i, F_i)$, $i = 1, 2$. Notice that we assume that the outputs of the automata have the same dimension. We denote the state space of $\mathcal{A}_i$ as $\mathcal{X}_i$, $i = 1, 2$. See (1).

Definition 1. *[15] A function* $\phi : \mathcal{X}_1 \times \mathcal{X}_2 \to \mathbb{R}_+ \cup \{+\infty\}$ *is a **stochastic bisimulation function** between* $\mathcal{A}_1$ *and* $\mathcal{A}_2$ *if the following statements hold.*
(i) Suppose that $\xi_i = (l_i, x_i) \in \mathcal{X}_i, i = 1, 2$, *then*

$$\phi(\xi_1, \xi_2) \geq \|C_{1,l_1} x_1 - C_{2,l_2} x_2\|^2 = \|y_1 - y_2\|^2,$$

where $\|\cdot\|$ *denotes the Euclidean distance in* $\mathbb{R}^m$,
(ii) the stochastic process $\phi_t := \phi(\xi_{1,t}, \xi_{2,t})$ *is a supermartingale for any distribution of the initial state.*

Remark 2. The definition of stochastic bisimulation function in this paper does not exhibit the game theoretic aspect as that in [15]. This is because we do not model disturbance as a source of nondeterminism in this framework. We could add disturbance as another affine term in (3a), and we can see later in Section 4 that the theoretical framework that we develop in this paper can be extended easily to cover this case. However, this would be done at significant computational expense.

The following theorem describes the relation between the stochastic bisimulation function and the difference between the output of $\mathcal{A}_1$ and $\mathcal{A}_2$.

Theorem 1. *(adapted from [15])Given two LSHA,* $\mathcal{A}_i = (L_i, n_i, m, T_i, F_i)$, $i = 1, 2$, *and* $\phi(\cdot)$ *a stochastic bisimulation function. The following relation holds.*

$$P\left\{ \sup_{0 \leq t < \infty} \|y_{1,t} - y_{2,t}\|^2 \geq \delta \,\middle|\, (\xi_{1,0}, \xi_{2,0}) \right\} \leq \frac{\phi(\xi_{1,0}, \xi_{2,0})}{\delta}. \tag{6}$$

Proof. Following Definition 1, $\phi(\xi_{1t}, \xi_{2t})$ is a supermartingale. Since $\phi(\xi_{1t}, \xi_{2t})$ is a nonnegative supermartingale, we have the following result [16].

$$P\left\{ \sup_{0 \leq t < \infty} \phi(\xi_{1,t}, \xi_{2,t}) \geq \delta \,\middle|\, (\xi_{1,0}, \xi_{2,0}) \right\} \leq \frac{\phi(\xi_{1,0}, \xi_{2,0})}{\delta}. \tag{7}$$

---

[1] The work is inspired by the nonstochastic version in [12].

Moreover, since $\phi(\xi_1, \xi_2) \geq \|y_1 - y_2\|^2$ by construction, we also have that

$$P\left\{ \sup_{0 \leq t < \infty} \|y_{1,t} - y_{2,t}\|^2 \geq \delta \,\Big|\, (\xi_{1,0}, \xi_{2,0}) \right\} \leq P\left\{ \sup_{0 \leq t < \infty} \phi(\xi_{1,t}, \xi_{2,t}) \geq \delta \,\Big|\, (\xi_{1,0}, \xi_{2,0}) \right\}. \tag{8}$$

Hence we have (6).

The stochastic bisimulation function can be used to guarantee that the difference between the output of the original system and its abstraction will not exceed a given bound, with a certain probability. The difference between the outputs is measured in the sense of L_∞. This makes this approach particularly suitable for analyzing safety/reachability property of the system, as it is illustrated in the following.

Given a complex system represented by an LSHA $\mathcal{A}_1$ and its simpler abstraction $\mathcal{A}_2$. Suppose that $\phi(\cdot)$ is a stochastic bisimulation function between the two automata, and that the initial condition of the composite system is $(\xi_{1,0}, \xi_{2,0})$. Given the unsafe set for the automaton $\mathcal{A}_1$, $\mathbf{unsafe}_1 \subset \mathbb{R}^m$, we can construct another set $\mathbf{unsafe}_2 \subset \mathbb{R}^m$, which is the δ neighborhood of $\mathbf{unsafe}_1$ for some $\delta > 0$. That is,

$$\mathbf{unsafe}_2 = \{y \mid \exists y' \in \mathbf{unsafe}_1, \|y - y'\| \leq \delta\}. \tag{9}$$

We define the events $\mathbf{unsafe}_i := \{\exists t \geq 0 \text{ s.t. } y_{i,t} \in \mathbf{unsafe}_i\}, i = 1, 2$. The following theorem holds [15].

Theorem 2. *The following relation between the safety properties of the automata holds.*

$$P\{\mathbf{unsafe}_1\} \leq P\{\mathbf{unsafe}_2\} + \frac{\phi(\xi_{1,0}, \xi_{2,0})}{\delta^2}. \tag{10}$$

Theorem 2 tells us that we can get an upper bound of the risk of the complex system by performing the risk calculation on the simple abstraction and adding a factor that depends on the stochastic bisimulation function.

4   Casting LSHA as Jump Linear Stochastic Systems

We have seen that we need to construct a stochastic bisimulation function between an LSHA and its abstraction, to measure the quality of abstraction. In this section, we demonstrate how an LSHA can be cast as a modified jump linear stochastic system (JLSS) [15]. We shall then use the tools that have been developed for JLSS to construct stochastic bisimulation functions for LSHA.

First, we introduce the structure of a jump linear stochastic system. A *jump linear stochastic system* (JLSS) can be modeled as a stochastic system that satisfies the following stochastic differential equation.

$$dx_t = Ax_t \, dt + Gx_t \, dw_t + \sum_{i=1}^{N} Q_i x_t \, dp_t^i, \tag{11a}$$

$$y_t = Cx_t. \tag{11b}$$

Here, y_t is the output of the system, the process w_t is a standard Brownian motion, while p_t^i is a Poisson process with a constant rate λ_i. We assume that the Poisson processes and the Brownian motion are independent of each other.

Remark 3. The model of jump linear stochastic system that we use here is slightly different from that in [15]. The difference is in the fact that the we use a linear diffusion term (i.e. Gx_t), while in [15] a constant term is used. With this modification, we make sure that the origin is an equilibrium with probability 1. That is, $P\{x_t \neq 0, t \geq 0|x_0 = 0\} = 0$. As we shall see later, this property is exploited to cast LSHA as JLSS.

Given an LSHA $\mathcal{A} = (L, n, m, T, F)$ as in Section 2, the following is an algorithm to define a JLSS, structured as in (11), that represents $\mathcal{A}$.

- The state space of the JLSS has the dimension of $\sum_{i=1}^{|L|} n(l_i)$, $l_i \in L$.
- The A and G matrices of the JLSS has a block diagonal structure, with $|L|$ blocks. That is,

$$A := \begin{bmatrix} A_1 & 0 & \cdots & 0 \\ 0 & A_2 & \cdots & 0 \\ \vdots & \vdots & \ddots & \vdots \\ 0 & 0 & \cdots & A_{|L|} \end{bmatrix}, G := \begin{bmatrix} G_1 & 0 & \cdots & 0 \\ 0 & G_2 & \cdots & 0 \\ \vdots & \vdots & \ddots & \vdots \\ 0 & 0 & \cdots & G_{|L|} \end{bmatrix}. \tag{12}$$

where $A_i := A_{l_i}$ and $G_i := G_{l_i}$ are the A and G matrices of the LSHA in location l_i.
- The C matrix of the JLSS is structured as $C := \begin{bmatrix} C_1 & C_2 & \cdots & C_{|L|} \end{bmatrix}$, where $C_i := C_{l_i}$ is the C matrix of the LSHA in location l_i.
- There are $|T|$ independent Poisson processes. Thus, $N = |T|$. Each Poisson process represents a transition in T. Denote the transitions as $T = \{\tau_i\}_{1 \leq i \leq |T|}$ and $\tau_i := (loc_i, \lambda_i, loc_i', R_i)$. Then the Poisson process p_t^i has the rate of λ_i, and the matrix Q_i has a block diagonal structure as A and G, where

$$Q_i := \begin{bmatrix} 0 & \cdots & 0 & 0 & \cdots & 0 \\ \vdots & \ddots & & & & \vdots \\ 0 & & -I & 0 & & 0 \\ 0 & & R_i & 0 & & 0 \\ \vdots & & & & \ddots & \vdots \\ 0 & \cdots & 0 & 0 & \cdots & 0 \end{bmatrix} \begin{matrix} \\ \\ \longleftarrow loc_i \\ \longleftarrow loc_i' \\ \\ \end{matrix}, \tag{13}$$

that is, almost all the blocks are zero, except for two blocks:
(i) the diagonal block associated with loc_i, which is $-I$, and
(ii) the block whose row is associated with loc_i' and its column with loc_i, which is R_i.

The idea behind this procedure is as follows. We formulate a JLSS with $|L|$ invariant dynamics. That is, the state space can be written as the direct sum of $|L|$ subspaces, each of which is invariant with respect to the following dynamics:

$$dx_t = Ax_t \, dt + Gx_t \, dw_t. \tag{14}$$

Each invariant subspace represents a location in the LSHA. Further, we can observe that the origin is also invariant with respect to (14) (see Remark 3). As the result, if we start the evolution of the system in one of the invariant subspaces (hence, in one of the locations of the LSHA), the trajectory will remain in the subspace. Let us call the location l. When a Poisson process generates a point, if the process does not correspond to a transition whose source location is l, then the reset map does not change the continuous state of the system. This is due to the construction of (13). If the source location is l and the target is, say, l', then the continuous state is reset to another invariant space that corresponds to the location l'.

One apparent difference between the JLSS realization of the system and the original LSHA is that in the LSHA, only the Poisson processes in the active location are active. However, this difference does not affect the probabilistic properties of the trajectories, since Poisson processes are memoryless [8]. When we enter a location, it does not matter if we assume that the Poisson processes in the location are just started or that they have been running before.

5   Computation of the Stochastic Bisimulation Function

In the previous section we demonstrate how we can cast a linear stochastic hybrid automaton (LSHA) as a jump linear stochastic system (JLSS). In general, we can then exploit the available construction of quadratic stochastic bisimulation function for JLSS [15], and apply it for LSHA. However, since we also modified the definition (see Remark 3), we also need to modify the procedure for constructing a stochastic bisimulation function.

Given two JLSS, for $i = 1, 2$,

$$S_i : \begin{cases} dx_{i,t} = A_i x_{i,t} \, dt + G_i x_{i,t} \, dw_t + \sum_{j=1}^{N} Q_{ij} x_t \, dp_t^j, \\ y_{it} = C_i x_{i,t}. \end{cases} \tag{15}$$

We define the following composite system

$$x_t := \begin{bmatrix} x_{1,t} \\ x_{2,t} \end{bmatrix}, y_t := y_{1,t} - y_{2,t}, A := \begin{bmatrix} A_1 & 0 \\ 0 & A_2 \end{bmatrix}, G := \begin{bmatrix} G_1 & 0 \\ 0 & G_2 \end{bmatrix}, \tag{16a}$$

$$Q_j := \begin{bmatrix} Q_{1j} & 0 \\ 0 & Q_{2j} \end{bmatrix}, C := \begin{bmatrix} C_1 & -C_2 \end{bmatrix}. \tag{16b}$$

Hence we have the following system:

$$S : \begin{cases} dx_t = A x_t \, dt + G x_t \, dw_t + \sum_{j=1}^{N} Q_j x_t \, dp_t^j, \\ y_t = C x_t. \end{cases} \tag{17}$$

As mentioned above, we want to construct a quadratic stochastic bisimulation function. Thus, we want to find the conditions for a function of the form

$$\phi(x) = x^T M x, \tag{18}$$

to satisfy Definition 1. We can observe that the process $\phi_t := \phi(x_t)$ satisfies the following SDE.

$$d\phi_t = \frac{\partial \phi}{\partial x} dx_t + \frac{1}{2} dx_t^T \frac{\partial^2 \phi}{\partial x^2} dx_t = 2x_t^T M \left(A x_t \, dt + G x_t \, dw_t + \sum_{j=1}^{N} Q_j x_t \, dp_t^j \right)$$
$$+ x_t^T G^T M G x_t \, dt + \sum_{i,j \in \{1,2,\cdots,N\}} x_t^T Q_i^T M Q_j x_t \, dp_t^i dp_t^j. \tag{19}$$

Using the fact that the Poisson processes are independent from each other, we can establish that the expectation of the last term of the right hand side satisfies the following relation,

$$E\left[x_t^T Q_i^T M Q_j x_t \, dp_t^i dp_t^j\right] = \begin{cases} E\left[x_t^T Q_i^T M Q_j x_t\right] \lambda_i \lambda_j dt^2, & i \neq j, \\ E\left[x_t^T Q_j^T M Q_j x_t\right] (\lambda_j dt + \lambda_j^2 dt^2), & i = j. \end{cases}$$

The expectation of ϕ_t then satisfies the following equation.

$$\frac{dE[\phi_t]}{dt} = E\left[x_t^T \Theta x_t\right], \tag{20}$$

where

$$\Theta := 2MA + 2M\sum_{i=1}^{N}\lambda_i Q_i + G^T M G + \sum_{i=1}^{N}\lambda_i Q_i^T M Q_i. \tag{21}$$

Theorem 3. *The function $\phi(x) = x^T M x$ is a stochastic bisimulation function for the systems in (15) if and only if $M \geq C^T C$, and $\Theta \leq 0$.*

This theorem in an immediate consequence of Definition 1. The problem of finding M such that the conditions in Theorem 3 hold is a linear matrix equality (LMI) problem.

Remark 4. If we see the quadratic stochastic bisimulation function as a stochastic Lyapunov function, then the conditions in Theorem 3 guarantee that y_t converges to 0 in probability. However, in this paper we are not interested in the asymptotic behavior of y_t (the convergence), rather we are interested in the bound on the magnitude of y_t.

6   Extensions of the LSHA

In this section we discuss two possible extensions of the linear stochastic hybrid automata, and the implications of the extensions to the computation of the stochastic bisimulation function.

6.1 Nonlinear Stochastic Hybrid Automata

Consider a linear stochastic hybrid automata $A = (L, n, m, T, F)$. Suppose that instead of the linear dynamics in (3), we assume that the dynamics in location $l \in L$ satisfies a nonlinear SDE of the following form.

$$dx_{l,t} = a_l(x_{l,t})\, dt + g_l(x_{l,t})\, dw_t, \qquad (22\text{a})$$

$$y_t = c_l(x_{l,t}), \qquad (22\text{b})$$

$$x_{l,t} \in \mathbb{R}^{n(l)}, y_t \in \mathbb{R}^m. \qquad (22\text{c})$$

We assume that for all $l \in L$,

$$a_l(0) = 0, g_l(0) = 0. \qquad (23)$$

This assumption renders the origin invariant under the dynamics described by (22). In general, we only need to have a point that is invariant under (22).

Furthermore, assume that instead of the linear reset map (5), the reset function of a given transition $\tau \in T$ follows the relation $x_t = r_\tau(x_{t-})$, where $x_{t-} := \lim_{s \uparrow t} x_t$.

Analogous to the discussion in Section 4, we can show that the nonlinear version of the stochastic hybrid automata can be cast as a nonlinear version of the jump linear stochastic systems, that is, systems of the form.

$$dx_t = a(x_t)\, dt + g(x_t)\, dw_t + \sum_{i=1}^{N} q_i(x_t)\, dp_t^i, \qquad (24\text{a})$$

$$y_t = c(x_t). \qquad (24\text{b})$$

Furthermore, given two systems, for $i = 1, 2$,

$$S_i : \begin{cases} dx_{i,t} = a_i(x_{i,t})\, dt + g_i(x_{i,t})\, dw_t + \sum_{j=1}^{N} q_{ij}(x_t)\, dp_t^j, \\ y_{i,t} = c_i(x_{i,t}), \end{cases} \qquad (25)$$

we can form a composite system in the form of (24), by following a construction analogous to (16).

Definition 1 is still valid for the nonlinear version of the stochastic hybrid automata. Hence, the results that relate the stochastic bisimulation function with approximate abstraction and safety verification still hold.

Suppose that we are given a smooth function $\phi(\cdot)$ of the state of the composite system (24). It can be verified that the evolution of the expectation of $\phi_t := \phi(x_t)$ can be written as:

$$\frac{dE\,[\phi_t]}{dt} = E\left[\frac{\partial \phi}{\partial x} a(x_t)\right] + \frac{1}{2} E\left[g^T(x_t) \frac{\partial^2 \phi}{\partial x^2} g(x_t)\right] + \sum_{j=1}^{N} \lambda_j E[\phi(x_t + q_j(x_t)) - \phi(x_t)].$$

$$(26)$$

Define

$$\Theta(x) := \frac{\partial \phi}{\partial x} a(x) + \frac{1}{2} g^T(x) \frac{\partial^2 \phi}{\partial x^2} g(x) + \sum_{j=1}^{N} \lambda_j (\phi(x + q_j(x)) - \phi(x)), \qquad (27)$$

then $\frac{dE[\phi_t]}{dt} = E[\Theta(x_t)]$.

Thus, to compute a general stochastic bisimulation function, we need to find a smooth function ϕ such that

$$\phi(x) \geq (c(x))^2, \; \Theta(x) \leq 0. \tag{28}$$

An automatic procedure for constructing such a function ϕ does not exist. However, if we assume that all the functions involved are polynomials, this problem can be cast as a *sum-of-squares* problem. There is a software tool that can be used to solve such problems, that is SOSTOOLS [17].

6.2   LSHA with Variable Rate Poisson Processes

In this subsection, we discuss the LSHA where the rate of the Poisson processes are assumed to be functions of the continuous state. This type of LSHA can still be cast as a JLSS of the form (11). The only difference is that now the Poisson processes $\{p_t^j\}_{1 \leq j \leq N}$ have rates that depend on the continuous state, $\lambda_j(x)$ instead of a constant rate. We also assume that for every $j \in \{1, 2, \cdots, N\}$, there exist $L_j \geq 0$ and $U_j \geq L_j$ such that for every continuous state x,

$$L_j \leq \lambda_j(x) \leq U_j. \tag{29}$$

Thus, for all x, the vector $\begin{bmatrix} \lambda_1(x) & \lambda_2(x) & \cdots & \lambda_N(x) \end{bmatrix}$ is contained in a hyper rectangle defined by the lower and upper bounds in (29). Let $\Gamma \in \mathbb{R}^{2^N \times N}$ be the matrix with all the 2^N vertices of the hyper rectangle. That is,

$$\Gamma := \begin{bmatrix} L_1 & L_2 & \cdots & L_{N-1} & L_N \\ L_1 & L_2 & \cdots & L_{N-1} & U_N \\ L_1 & L_2 & \cdots & U_{N-1} & L_N \\ \vdots & \vdots & & \vdots & \vdots \\ U_1 & U_2 & \cdots & U_{N-1} & U_N \end{bmatrix}.$$

Assuming quadratic stochastic bisimulation function $\phi(x) = x^T M x$, we can show that in the case of variable rate Poisson processes, equations (20) and (21) become

$$\frac{dE[\phi_t]}{dt} = E\left[x_t^T \Theta(x_t) x_t\right], \tag{30}$$

where

$$\Theta(x) := 2MA + 2M \sum_{i=1}^{N} \lambda_i(x) Q_i + G^T M G + \sum_{i=1}^{N} \lambda_i(x) Q_i^T M Q_i. \tag{31}$$

Theorem 4. *Let M be a symmetric matrix that satisfies*

$$M \geq C^T C, \tag{32a}$$

$$\Theta_i := 2MA + 2M \sum_{j=1}^{N} \Gamma_{ij} Q_i + G^T M G + \sum_{j=1}^{N} \Gamma_{ij} Q_i^T M Q_i \leq 0, \tag{32b}$$

for $1 \leq i \leq 2^N$, then $\phi(x) = x^T M x$ is a stochastic bisimulation function.

Proof. We need to show that (32b) implies that $\phi_t = \phi(x_t)$ is a supermartingale for any distribution of the initial state. Suppose that (32b) holds, then for any x, the matrix $\Theta(x)$ can be written as a convex combination of $\{\Theta_i\}_{1 \leq i \leq 2^N}$. Therefore, $\Theta(x) \leq 0$. From (30) we can infer that ϕ_t is a supermartingale for any distribution of the initial state.

The problem of finding M such that (32) holds can also be cast as a linear matrix inequality problem.

7   Example: Chain-Like Linear Stochastic Hybrid Automata

In this section we present an example, where we apply the framework of approximate abstraction of linear stochastic hybrid automata. The original automaton $\mathcal{A}$ has a chain like structure, with 21 locations. See Figure 2.

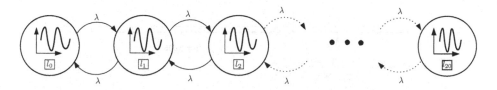

Fig. 2. The chain-like automaton $\mathcal{A}$ with 21 locations

Chain-like automata is a structure that can be found in modelling of systems that involve birth and death process. That is, each location represents the number of a certain object in the system, for example, persons in a queue or molecules in a chemical reaction. Researchers have been working towards approximating such systems in a way that allows for both fast and accurate simulations [18], as well as faster computation [19].

Adjacent locations in the automaton $\mathcal{A}$ are connected by a pair of transitions with constant rate $\lambda = 0.02$. The continuous dynamics of $\mathcal{A}$ is such that the dynamics changes gradually from location l_0 to location l_{20}. The stochastic differential equation that describes the dynamics in location l_i, $0 \leq i \leq 20$, is as follows.

$$dx_{i,t} = A_i x_{i,t}\, dt + G_i x_t\, dw_t,$$

$$y_t = C_i x_{i,t}, \text{ where}$$

$$A_i = \begin{bmatrix} -0.01 & -0.1(1 + \alpha \cdot i) \\ 0.1(1 + \alpha \cdot i) & -0.01 \end{bmatrix}, G_i = \begin{bmatrix} 0.1 & 0 \\ 0 & 0.1 \end{bmatrix},$$

$$C_i = \begin{bmatrix} 0 & 1 \end{bmatrix}, i = 0 \ldots 20.$$

We are going to apply the procedure for several values of α.

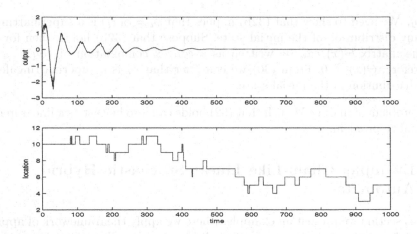

Fig. 3. A realization of the output trajectory (top) and the location (bottom) of the linear stochastic hybrid automaton $\mathcal{A}$

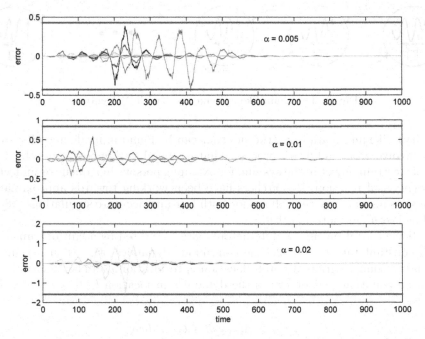

Fig. 4. Ten realizations of the error trajectory for each of the α value. The parallel lines indicate the 90% confidence interval stipulated by the stochastic bisimulation functions.

We can easily observe that the continuous dynamics in each location is a damped 2-dimensional oscillator driven by Brownian motion. A realization of the output of $\mathcal{A}$ is plotted in Figure 3. As we go from location l_0 to l_{20}, the frequency of the oscillation increases. We want to see if we can approximate $\mathcal{A}$ with another automaton $\mathcal{A}'$ that has only one location. The continuous dynamics of $\mathcal{A}'$ is the same as that in location l_{10} of $\mathcal{A}$. Hence we compute a stochastic bisimulation function between $\mathcal{A}$ and $\mathcal{A}'$. The computation is done by solving the linear matrix inequality problem explained in Section 5. We perform the computation using the tool YALMIP [20].

Three different values for α are used, namely 5×10^{-3}, 10^{-2}, and 2×10^{-2}. For these values of α, the ratio between the oscillation frequency in location l_{20} and l_0 are 1.1, 1.2, and 1.4 respectively. We simulate the execution of the original automaton $\mathcal{A}$ and its abstraction $\mathcal{A}'$. In the simulation we use $[1\ 1]^T$ as the initial condition for the continuous dynamics, and assume that automaton $\mathcal{A}$ starts in location l_{10}. With the computed stochastic bisimulation function, we can also compute the 90% confidence interval for the error between the outputs of $\mathcal{A}$ and $\mathcal{A}'$ (see Theorem 1).

In Figure 4 we can see ten realizations of the error trajectory for each of the value of α. The 90% confidence intervals are also shown. We can observe that the quadratic stochastic bisimulation function seems to give a good estimate for the error, as the confidence intervals seem quite tight. We can also observe that as the dynamics in the locations vary more, the error in the approximation becomes larger.

8   Conclusions

In this paper we develop the notion of approximate bisimulation for linear stochastic hybrid automata. The approach is based on the construction of a stochastic bisimulation function that can be used as a tool to quantify the distance between an automaton and its abstraction. We show that this notion of distance relates nicely with the safety properties of the automata (see Theorem 2). An example of the application of the results is provided at the end of the paper, where we evaluate approximate abstraction of a chain-like stochastic hybrid automaton.

We also discuss two possible extensions to the framework, namely when the continuous dynamics is nonlinear, and when the rates of the Poisson processes are not constant. In each case, we show how the computation of the stochastic bisimulation function will be. Future extensions of the work presented in this paper can be highlighted as follows. Issues such as incorporating nondeterminism (see Remark 2) and establishing necessary and sufficient conditions for the existence of the stochastic bisimulation function are possible research direction in the future. Another interesting direction is exploring different construction procedure for the stochastic bisimulation function, for example, using polynomial functions (which are generalization of quadratic functions).

Acknowledgements. The author would like to thank Antoine Girard and George Pappas for the discussions during the preparation of this paper, and Bruce Krogh for a valuable suggestion on relating JLSS and LSHA.

References

1. Pola, G., Bujorianu, M., Lygeros, J., Benedetto, M.D.: Stochastic hybrid models: an overview. In: Proc. IFAC Conf. Analysis and Design of Hybrid Systems, St. Malo, IFAC (2003)
2. Hespanha, J.P.: Stochastic hybrid systems: applications to communication networks. [21] 387 – 401
3. Hu, J., Wu, W.C., Sastry, S.: Modeling subtilin production in bacillus subtilis using stochastic hybrid systems. [21] 417 – 431
4. Glover, W., Lygeros, J.: A stochastic hybrid model for air traffic control simulation. [21] 372 – 386
5. Hu, J., Lygeros, J., Sastry, S.: Towards a theory of stochastic hybrid systems. In Lynch, N., Krogh, B.H., eds.: Hybrid Systems: Computation and Control. Volume 1790 of Lecture Notes in Computer Science., Springer Verlag (2000) 160–173
6. Oksendal, B.: Stochastic differential equations: an introduction with applications. Springer-Verlag, Berlin (2000)
7. Ghosh, M.K., Arapostathis, A., Marcus, S.: Ergodic control of switching diffusions. SIAM Journal on Control and Optimization 35(6) (1997) 1952–1988
8. Davis, M.H.A.: Markov models and optimization. Chapman and Hall, London (1993)
9. Bujorianu, M.L., Lygeros, J., Bujorianu, M.C.: Bisimulation for general stochastic hybrid systems. [22] 198–214
10. Strubbe, S., van der Schaft, A.J.: Bisimulation for communicating piecewise deterministic Markov processes. [22] 623–639
11. Ying, M., Wirsing, M.: Approximate bisimilarity. In Rus, T., ed.: AMAST 2000. Volume 1816 of Lecture Notes in Computer Science., Springer Verlag (2000) 309–322
12. Girard, A., Pappas, G.J.: Approximate bisimulation for constrained linear systems. to appear in the Proceedings of the IEEE Conf. Decision and Control (2005)
13. Desharnais, J., Gupta, V., Jagadeesan, R., Panangaden, P.: Metrics for labelled Markov processes. Theoretical Computer Science 318(3) (2004) 323–354
14. van Breugel, F., Worrell, J.: An algorithm for quantitative verification of probabilistic transition systems. In: Proc. of CONCUR, Aalborg, Springer-Verlag (2001) 336–350
15. Julius, A.A., Girard, A., Pappas, G.J.: Approximate bisimulation for a class of stochastic hybrid systems. submitted to the American Control Conference 2006 (2005)
16. Prajna, S., Jadbabaie, A., Pappas, G.J.: Stochastic safety verification using barrier certificates. In: Proc. 43rd IEEE Conference on Decision and Control, Bahamas, IEEE (2004)
17. Prajna, S., Papachristodoulou, A., Seiler, P., Parillo, P.A.: SOSTOOLS and its control application. In: Positive polynomials in control, Springer - Verlag (2005)
18. Neogi, N.A.: Dynamic partitioning of large discrete event biological systems for hybrid simulation and analysis. [21] 463 – 476
19. Hespanha, J.P.: Polynomial stochastic hybrid systems. [22] 322–338
20. Löfberg, J.: (http://control.ee.ethz.ch/~joloef/yalmip.php)
21. Alur, R., Pappas, G.J., eds.: Hybrid systems: computation and control. Volume 2993 of Lecture Notes in Computer Science., Springer Verlag (2004)
22. Morari, M., Thiele, L., eds.: Hybrid systems: computation and control. Volume 3414 of Lecture Notes in Computer Science., Springer Verlag (2005)

A Fully Automated Framework for Control of Linear Systems from LTL Specifications*

Marius Kloetzer and Calin Belta

Center for Information and Systems Engineering,
Boston University, 15 Saint Mary's Street,
Boston, MA 02446
{kmarius, cbelta}@bu.edu

Abstract. We consider the following problem: given a linear system and an LTL_{-X} formula over a set of linear predicates in its state variables, find a feedback control law with polyhedral bounds and a set of initial states so that all trajectories of the closed loop system satisfy the formula. Our solution to this problem consists of three main steps. First, we partition the state space in accordance with the predicates in the formula and construct a transition system over the partition quotient, which captures our capability of designing controllers. Second, using model checking, we determine runs of the transition system satisfying the formula. Third, we generate the control strategy. Illustrative examples are included.

1 Introduction

Temporal logic [1] is the natural framework for specifying and verifying the correctness of computer programs. However, due to their resemblance to natural language, their expressivity, and the existence of off-the-shelf algorithms for model checking, temporal logic has the potential to impact several other areas of engineering. Analysis of systems with continuous dynamics based on qualitative simulations and temporal logic was proposed in [2, 3, 4]. In the control-theoretic community, a framework for specifying and controlling the behavior of a discrete linear system has been developed in [5]. The use of temporal logic for task specification and controller synthesis in mobile robotics has been advocated as far back as [6], and recent results include [7, 8, 9]. In the area of systems biology, the qualitative behavior of genetic circuits can be expressed in temporal logic, and model checking can be used for analysis, as suggested in [10, 11].

We consider the following problem: *given a linear system $\dot{x} = Ax + b + Bu$ with polyhedral control constraints U, and given an arbitrary LTL_{-X} formula ϕ over an arbitrary set of linear predicates, find initial states and a feedback control strategy u so that the corresponding trajectories of the closed loop system verify the formula ϕ, while staying inside a given full-dimensional polytope P_N.*

Our approach to solving the above problem can be summarized as the following three steps. In the first step, we construct a finite state "generator" transition system T_g.

---

* This work is partially supported by NSF CAREER 0447721 and NSF 0410514.

João Hespanha and A. Tiwari (Eds.): HSCC 2006, LNCS 3927, pp. 333–347, 2006.

Its states are the equivalence classes produced by the feasible full-dimensional subpolytopes of P_N determined by the linear predicates appearing in the formula ϕ. The transitions of T_g are determined by adjacency of subpolytopes and existence of feedback controllers making such subpolytopes invariant or driving all states in a subpolytope to an adjacent subpolytope through a common facet [12]. In the second step, we produce runs of T_g that satisfy formula ϕ. This is in essence a model checking problem, and we use standard tools based on Büchi automata [13]. In the third step, we construct a feedback "control strategy", which leads to a closed loop hybrid system, whose continuous trajectories satisfy formula ϕ. We implemented our approach as a user friendly software package LTLCON [14] under Matlab.

Related work and contribution of the paper. In order to extend temporal logic techniques from purely discrete systems to continuous systems, two approaches are possible. First, a careful treatment of the semantics of temporal logic formulas in models with continuous or hybrid dynamics [4] can be performed. Second, finite quotients with respect to meaningful equivalence relations can be constructed. Such equivalence relations include language equivalences (preserving properties specified in linear temporal logic) and bisimulation relations (preserving specifications in both linear and branching time logic). The first success in this direction was the work on timed automata reported in [15], followed by multi-rate automata [16], and rectangular hybrid automata [17]. Other classes of systems for which finite bisimulation quotients exist are identified in [18]. The interested reader is referred to [19] for an excellent review of all these works. Linear dynamics are studied in [20], while nonlinear systems are considered in [21, 22]. Quotients that only simulate a continuous or hybrid system and can be used for conservative analysis are developed in [23].

This paper is inspired from [5, 9]. The problem of controller synthesis from LTL specifications for discrete-time continuous-space linear systems with semi-linear partitions are considered in [5], where it is shown that finite bisimulations exist for controllable systems with properly chosen observables. The focus in [5] is on existence and computability. Specifically, it is shown that the iterative (partitioning) bisimulation algorithm [18] terminates and each step is computable. However, no computational formulas for the controllers are provided. Another contribution of [5] is setting up the framework for producing runs of the finite quotient satisfying an LTL formula. This framework is further refined in [9], where the authors study the problem of controlling a planar robot in a polygon so that its trajectory satisfies an LTL_{-X} formula. In [9], it is assumed that a triangulation of the polygon is given, and vector fields are assigned in each triangle so that the produced trajectories satisfy a formula over the triangles. For construction of vector fields, the authors use the algorithms developed in [24].

This paper extends the results of [5, 9] in several ways. First, we consider continuous-time systems as opposed to discrete-time systems in [5]. Second, based on results on controlling a linear system to a facet of a polytope from [12], and an invariance theorem stated in this paper, we provide a fully computational and algorithmic approach to controller design consisting of polyhedral operations and searches on graphs only. Third, as opposed to [5], we can guarantee arbitrary polyhedral control bounds. Fourth, we extend the results [9] by approaching arbitrary dimensional problems and considering systems with (linear) drift. The feasibility of the partition induced by the predicates in the formula and the construction of the partition quotient is fully automated in our framework, rather than assuming a given triangulation. Finally, we provide a tighter connection between the continuous and the discrete part of the problem in two ways. First, the transitions of the discrete quotient capture the controllability properties of the continuous system. Second, the runs of the discrete system are shown to be of a particular form which is implementable by the continuous system.

2   Preliminaries

2.1   Polytopes

Let $N \in \mathbb{N}$ and consider the N - dimensional Euclidean space $\mathbb{R}^N$. A full dimensional *polytope* P_N is defined as the convex hull of at least $N + 1$ affinely independent points in $\mathbb{R}^N$. A set of $M \geq N + 1$ points $v_1, \ldots, v_M \in \mathbb{R}^N$ whose convex hull gives P_N and with the property that v_i, $i = 1, \ldots, M$ is not contained in the convex hull of $v_1, \ldots, v_{i-1}, v_{i+1}, \ldots, v_M$ is called the set of *vertices* of P_N. A polytope is completely described by its set of vertices:

$$P_N = conv(v_1, \ldots, v_M), \tag{1}$$

where $conv$ denotes the convex hull. Alternatively, P_N can be described as the intersection of at least $N + 1$ closed half spaces. In other words, there exist a $K \geq N + 1$ and $a_i \in \mathbb{R}^N$, $b_i \in \mathbb{R}$, $i = 1, \ldots, K$ such that

$$P_N = \{x \in \mathbb{R}^N \mid a_i^T x + b_i \leq 0, \ i = 1, \ldots, K\} \tag{2}$$

Forms (1) and (2) are referred to as V- and H- representations of the polytope, respectively. Given a full dimensional polytope P_N, there exist algorithms for translation from representation (1) to representation (2) [25, 26]. A *face* of P_N is the intersection of P_N with one or several of its supporting hyperplanes. If the dimension of the intersection is p (with $0 \leq p < N$), then the face is called a p-face. A $(N - 1)$-face obtained by intersecting P_N with one of its supporting hyperplanes is called a *facet*. The vertices of P_N are 0-faces. We denote by $int(P_N)$ the set of points of P_N which are not on its facets, *i.e.*, the region in $\mathbb{R}^N$ obtained if the inequalities in (2) were strict. If F is a facet of P_N, $int(F)$ is defined analogously, with the observation that F is full dimensional polytope in $\mathbb{R}^{N-1}$.

A full dimensional polytope with $N + 1$ vertices (and $N + 1$ facets) is called a full dimensional *simplex*. Arbitrary full dimensional polytopes can be *triangulized* [27]. In other words, for any full dimensional polytope P_N, there exist full dimensional simplices $S_1, \ldots, S_L$ such that: (i) $P_N = \bigcup_{i=1}^{L} S_i$, (ii) $S_i \cap S_j$ is either empty or a common face of S_i and S_j, for all $i, j = 1, \ldots, L$, $i \neq j$, and (iii) The set of vertices of simplex S_i is a subset of $\{v_1, \ldots, v_M\}$, for all $i = 1, \ldots, L$.

2.2   Transition Systems and Temporal Logic

Definition 1. *A transition system is a tuple* $T = (Q, Q_0, \rightarrow, \Pi, \models)$, *where* Q *is a set of states,* $Q_0 \subseteq Q$ *is a set of initial states,* $\rightarrow \subseteq Q \times Q$ *is a transition relation,* Π *is a finite set of atomic propositions, and* $\models \subseteq Q \times \Pi$ *is a satisfaction relation.*

In this work, we assume that the transition system is *finite* (Q is finite). For an arbitrary proposition $\pi \in \Pi$, we define $[[\pi]] = \{q \in Q | q \vDash \pi\}$ as the set of all states satisfying it. Conversely, for an arbitrary state $q \in Q$, let $\Pi_q = \{\pi \in \Pi \mid q \vDash \pi\}$, $\Pi_q \in 2^{\Pi}$, denote the set of all atomic propositions satisfied at q. A *trajectory* or *run* of T starting from q is an infinite sequence $r = r(1)r(2)r(3)\ldots$ with the property that $r(1) = q$, $r(i) \in Q$, and $(r(i), r(i+1)) \in \rightarrow$, for all $i \geq 1$. A trajectory $r = r(1)r(2)r(3)\ldots$ defines a *word* $w = w(1)w(2)w(3)\ldots$, where $w(i) = \Pi_{r(i)}$.

In the rest of this section, we give a brief review of a propositional linear temporal logic known as LTL_{-X} [1].

Definition 2 *[Syntax of LTL_{-X} formulas]. A linear temporal logic LTL_{-X} formula over Π is recursively defined as follows:*

- *Every atomic proposition π_i, $i = 1, \ldots, K$ is a formula, and*
- *If ϕ_1 and ϕ_2 are formulas, then $\phi_1 \vee \phi_2$, $\neg\phi_1$, $\phi_1\mathcal{U}\phi_2$ are also formulas.*

The semantics of LTL_{-X} formulas are given over words of transition system T.

Definition 3 *[Semantics of LTL_{-X} formulas]. The satisfaction of formula ϕ at position $i \in \mathbb{N}$ of word w, denoted by $w(i) \vDash \phi$, is defined recursively as follows:*

- *$w(i) \vDash \pi$ if $\pi \in w(i)$,*
- *$w(i) \vDash \neg\phi$ if $w(i) \nvDash \phi$,*
- *$w(i) \vDash \phi_1 \vee \phi_2$ if $w(i) \vDash \phi_1$ or $w(i) \vDash \phi_2$,*
- *$w(i) \vDash \phi_1\mathcal{U}\phi_2$ if there exist a $j \geq i$ such that $w(j) \vDash \phi_2$ and for all $i \leq k < j$ we have $w(k) \vDash \phi_1$*

A word w satisfies an LTL_{-X} formula ϕ, written as $w \vDash \phi$, if $w(1) \vDash \phi$.

The symbols $\neg$ and $\vee$ stand for negation and disjunction. The Boolean constants $\top$ and $\bot$ are defined as $\top = \pi \vee \neg\pi$ and $\bot = \neg\top$. The other Boolean connectors $\wedge$ (conjunction), $\Rightarrow$ (implication), and $\Leftrightarrow$ (equivalence) are defined from $\neg$ and $\vee$ in the usual way. The *temporal operator* $\mathcal{U}$ is called the *until* operator. Formula $\phi_1\mathcal{U}\phi_2$ intuitively means that (over a word) ϕ_2 will eventually become true and ϕ_1 is true until this happens. Two useful additional temporal operators, "eventually" and "always" can be defined as $\Diamond\phi = \top\mathcal{U}\phi$ and $\Box\phi = \phi\mathcal{U}\bot$, respectively. Formula $\Diamond\phi$ means that ϕ becomes eventually true, whereas $\Box\phi$ indicates that ϕ is true at all positions of w. More expressiveness can be achieved by combining the temporal operators. Examples include $\Box\Diamond\phi$ (ϕ is true infinitely often) and $\Diamond\Box\phi$ (ϕ becomes eventually true and stays true forever).

LTL [1], the most used propositional linear temporal logic, is richer than LTL_{-X} in the sense that it allows for an additional temporal operator $\bigcirc$, which is called the 'next' operator. Formally, the syntax of LTL is obtained by adding "$\bigcirc\phi_1$" to Definition 2 and its semantics is defined by adding "$w(i) \vDash \bigcirc\phi$ if $w(i+1) \vDash \phi$" to Definition 3. A careful examination of the LTL and LTL_{-X} semantics shows that the increased expressivity of LTL is manifested only over words with a finite number of repetitions of a symbol. Our choice of LTL_{-X} over LTL is motivated by our definition of the satisfaction of a formula by a continuous trajectory and by our approach to finding runs. Specifically, as it will become clear in Section 3, a word corresponding to a continuous trajectory will never have a finite number of successive repetitions of a symbol. In Section 4.3, we produce runs which will either have one or infinitely many successive appearances of a symbol (or finite sequences of symbols).

3 Problem Formulation and Approach

Consider the following affine control system in a full dimensional polytope P_N in $\mathbb{R}^N$:

$$\dot{x} = Ax + b + Bu, \; x \in P_N, \; u \in U \subset \mathbb{R}^m \tag{3}$$

where $A \in \mathbb{R}^{N \times N}$, $B \in \mathbb{R}^{N \times m}$, $b \in \mathbb{R}^N$, and U is a given polyhedral subset of $\mathbb{R}^m$ capturing control constraints. Let Π be a set of atomic propositions given as arbitrary strict linear inequalities in $\mathbb{R}^N$. Formally:

$$\Pi = \{\pi_i \mid i = 1, \ldots, n\}, \tag{4}$$

where each proposition π_i, $i = 1, \ldots, n$, denotes an open half-space of $mathbbR^N$:

$$[[\pi_i]] = \{x \in \mathbb{R}^N \mid c_i^T x + d_i < 0\} \tag{5}$$

The polytope P_N can be seen as a region of $\mathbb{R}^N$ capturing known physical bounds on the state of system (3), or as a region that is required to be an invariant for its trajectories. For example, P_2 can be a convex polygon giving the environment boundaries for a planar robot with kinematics given by (3). The predicates (5) describe other regions (properties) of interest. Note that, for technical reasons to become clear later, we only allow strict inequalities in (5). However, this assumption does not seem restrictive from an application point of view. If the predicates in Π model sensor information, it is unrealistic to check for the attainment of a specific value due to sensor noise. Moreover, if a specific value is of interest, it can be included in the interior of a polyhedron given by other predicates.

In this paper we consider the following problem:

Problem 1. For an arbitrary LTL_{-X} formula ϕ over Π, find a set of initial states and a feedback control strategy for system (3) so that all trajectories of the corresponding closed loop system satisfy ϕ, while always staying inside P_N.

To fully specify Problem 1, we need to define the satisfaction of an LTL_{-X} formula ϕ on Π by a trajectory of (3), which can be seen as a continuous curve $\alpha : [0, \infty) \to \mathbb{R}^N$. This curve can, in general, be non-smooth and can have self-intersections. For each symbol $\Theta \in 2^\Pi$, we define $[[\Theta]]$ as being the set of states in $\mathbb{R}^N$ satisfying all and only propositions $\pi \in \Theta$:

$$[[\Theta]] = \bigcap_{\pi \in \Theta} [[\pi]] \setminus \bigcup_{\pi \in \Pi \setminus \Theta} [[\pi]] \tag{6}$$

Definition 4. *The* word *corresponding to trajectory α is the sequence $w_\alpha = w_\alpha(1)$ $w_\alpha(2) w_\alpha(3) \ldots$, $w_\alpha(k) \in 2^\Pi$, $k \geq 1$, generated such that the following rules are satisfied for any $\tau \geq 0$ and any $k \in \mathbb{N}^*$:*

– $\alpha(0) \in [[w_\alpha(1)]]$,
– If $\alpha(\tau) \in [[w_\alpha(k)]]$ and $w_\alpha(k) \neq w_\alpha(k+1)$, then there exist $\tau' > \tau$ such that: (1) $\alpha(\tau') \in [[w_\alpha(k+1)]]$, (2) $\alpha(t) \notin [[\pi]]$, $\forall t \in [\tau, \tau']$, $\forall \pi \in \Pi \setminus (w_\alpha(k) \cup w_\alpha(k+1))$, and (3) $c_i^T \alpha(t') + d_i \neq 0$, for all $i \in \{1, \ldots, n\}$ and $t' \in \{\tau, \tau'\}$,
– If $\alpha(\tau) \in [[w_\alpha(k)]]$ and $w_\alpha(k) = w_\alpha(k+1)$, then $\alpha(t) \in [[w_\alpha(k)]]$, $\forall t \geq \tau$ (i.e. the region $[[w_\alpha(k)]]$ is a "sink" for trajectory α).

A careful examination of Definition 4 shows that the word produced by a continuous trajectory is exactly the sequence of sets of propositions satisfied by it as time evolves. Note that Definition 4 captures the situations when a trajectory hits a sink region, leave it and eventually come back and remains there, as well as Zeno-type behaviors, when a trajectory visits two adjacent regions infinitely often.

Remark 1. On the well posedness of Definition 4, first note that our assumption that trajectories of system (3) always stay inside P_N implies that the generated words have infinite length, so the problem of satisfaction of an LTL_{-X} by such a word is well-posed. Second, the predicates in (4) are given by strict linear inequalities, Definition 4 makes sense only if $c_i^T \alpha(0) + d_i \neq 0$ and $c_i^T \bar{\alpha} + d_i \neq 0$, where $\bar{\alpha} = \lim_{t \to \infty} \alpha(t)$ (if it exists), for all $i = 1, \ldots, n$. Third, Definition 4 is a proper characterization of satisfaction of sets of predicates from Π by $\alpha(t)$ as time evolves only if there does not exist $t_1 < t_2$ and $i = 1, \ldots, n$ such that $c_i^T \alpha(t) + d_i = 0$, for all $t \in (t_1, t_2)$. All these three requirements are guaranteed by the way we design controllers, as it will become clear in Sections 4.1 and 5.

Remark 2. According to Definition 4, the word w_α produced by a trajectory $\alpha(t)$ does not contain a finite number of successive repetitions of a symbol, which suggests using LTL without the 'next' operator, as stated in Section 2.2.

Definition 5. *A trajectory $\alpha : [0, \infty) \to \mathbb{R}^N$ of (3) satisfies LTL_{-X} formula ϕ, written as $\alpha \vDash \phi$, if and only if $w_\alpha \vDash \phi$, where w_α is the word generated by α in accordance with Definition 4.*

4   The Generator Transition System

4.1   Control of Affine Systems in Polytopes

Consider a full dimensional polytope P in $\mathbb{R}^N$ with vertices $v_1, \ldots, v_M$, $M \geq N+1$. Let $F_1, \ldots, F_K$ denote the facets of P with normal vectors $n_1, \ldots, n_K$ pointing out of the polytope P. For $i = 1, \ldots, K$, let $V_i \subset \{1, \ldots, M\}$ be the set of indexes of vertices belonging to facet F_i. For $j = 1, \ldots, M$, let $W_j \subset \{1, \ldots, K\}$ be the set of indexes of all facets containing vertex v_j.

Lemma 1 *[Lemma 4.6 from [12]]. There exists a continuous function $\lambda : P \to [0, 1]^M$ with $\sum_{j=1}^M \lambda_j(x) = 1$ such that, for all $x \in P$, $x = \sum_{j=1}^M \lambda_j(x) v_j$.*

Theorem 1 *[Theorem 4.7 plus Remark 4.8 from [12]]. Consider control system (3) defined on the full dimensional polytope P. Assume that there exist $u_1, \ldots, u_M \in U$ such that:*

(1) $\forall j \in V_1$:
    (a) $n_1^T(Av_j + Bu_j + b) > 0$,
    (b) $\forall i \in W_j \setminus \{1\}$: $n_i^T(Av_j + Bu_j + b) \leq 0$.
(2) $\forall j \in \{1, \ldots, M\} \setminus V_1$:
    (a) $\forall i \in W_j$: $n_i^T(Av_j + Bu_j + b) \leq 0$,
    (b) $n_1^T(Av_j + Bu_j + a) > 0$.

Then there exists a continuous feedback controller $u : P \to U$ *with the property that for any initial state* $x(0) \in P$, *there exist a* $T_0 > 0$ *such that (i)* $\forall t \in [0, T_0]$: $x(t) \in P$, *(ii)* $x(T_0) \in F_1$, *and (iii)* $n_1^T \dot{x}(T_0) > 0$.

In other words, Theorem 1 states that if linear inequalities (1)(a),(b) and (2)(a),(b) are satisfied by some $u_1, \ldots, u_M \in U$, then a continuous feedback controller driving all initial states from P out of P through facet F_1 in finite time exists (condition (iii) means that the velocity on the exit facet F_1 is oriented outside the facet).

Theorem 2. *Consider control system (3) defined on the full dimensional polytope* P. *There exists a continuous feedback controller* $u : P \to U$ *that makes* P *an invariant for (3) if and only if there exist* $u_1, \ldots, u_M \in U$ *such that:*

$$\forall j \in \{1, \ldots, M\}, \forall i \in W_j : n_i^T(Av_j + Bu_j + b) \leq 0$$

Proof. See [28].

For both Theorems 1 and 2, given the values $u_1, \ldots, u_M$ at the vertices, the construction of a continuous controller everywhere in P starts with a triangulation $S_1, \ldots, S_L$ of P. Let $v_1^i, \ldots, v_{N+1}^i \in \{v_1, \ldots, v_M\}$ be the vertices of the full dimensional simplex S_i, $i = 1, \ldots, L$ and $u_1^i, \ldots, u_{N+1}^i \in \{u_1, \ldots, u_M\}$ be the corresponding control values. Then everywhere in P, the feedback control is given by:

$$u(x) = u^i(x) \text{ if } x \in S_i, \ i = 1, \ldots, L \tag{7}$$

where the control in each simplex is given by [29]:

$$u^i(x) = \begin{bmatrix} u_1^i & \cdots & u_{N+1}^i \end{bmatrix} \begin{bmatrix} v_1^i & \cdots & v_{N+1}^i \\ 1 & \cdots & 1 \end{bmatrix}^{-1} \begin{bmatrix} x \\ 1 \end{bmatrix}, \ i = 1, \ldots, L. \tag{8}$$

Note that the controller given by (7) is well defined. It is obvious that the controller is well defined when (7) is restricted to the interior of the simplices, since the intersection of all such interiors is empty. The only problem that might appear is on the common facets. However, recall that an affine function defined on $\mathbb{R}^N$ is uniquely determined by its values at the vertices of a full dimensional simplex and the restriction of the function to the simplex is a unique convex combination of these values [12, 29]. Moreover, a facet of a full dimensional simplex in $\mathbb{R}^N$ is a full dimensional simplex in $\mathbb{R}^{N-1}$. It follows that, given a pair of adjacent simplices S_i and S_j, $u^i(x) = u^j(x)$ everywhere on the common facet of S_i and S_j. Therefore, formula (7) is well defined and the affine feedback controller is continuous everywhere in P. Moreover, $u(x)$ constructed using (7) is always a convex combination of the values $u_1, \ldots, u_M$. This guarantees that $u(x) \in U$ everywhere in P if and if $u_j \in U$, for all $j = 1, \ldots, M$.

If inequalities (1)(b) and (2)(a) from Theorem 1 are satisfied strictly, then it is easy to see that, for all $i = 2, \ldots, K$ and all $j \in V_i$, $n_i^T(Av_j + Bu_j + b) < 0$. Since with u constructed using (7) and (8), the restriction of $n_i^T(Ax + Bu + b)$ to F_i is a convex combination of $n_i^T(Av_j + Bu_j + b)$, $j \in V_i$, it follows that $n_i^T(Ax + Bu + b) < 0$ everywhere in F_i. We conclude that, if the system starts in $int(P)$, it will never reach F_i. Moreover, if it starts in F_i, it will instantaneously penetrate in $int(P)$. Similar reasoning applies the case when the inequalities of Theorem 2 are strict, leading to the following two Corollaries:

Corollary 1. *If inequalities (1)(b) and (2)(a) from Theorem 1 are satisfied strictly, the continuous controller constructed in accordance with (7), (8) produces trajectories that satisfy $x(t) \in int(P)$, for all $t \in (0, T_0)$, and $x(T_0) \in int(F_1)$.*

Corollary 2. *If the inequalities in Theorem 2 are satisfied strictly, then $int(P)$ is an invariant for system (3) with controls given by (7), (8).*

4.2   Construction of the Generator Transition System

Assume the polytope P_N is given in the inequality form (2). Assume there are $\mathcal{M}$, $1 \leq \mathcal{M} \leq 2^n$ feasible sets of the form $\bigwedge_{i=1}^{n}((-1)^{j_i}(c_i^T x + d_i) < 0) \bigwedge_{l=1}^{K}(a_l^T x + b_l < 0)$, where $j_1, \ldots, j_n \in \{0, 1\}$ (each of these sets is the interior of a full dimensional polytope included in P_N and corresponds to a feasible combination of all predicates from Π inside P_N). To each of them we attach a symbol q_i, $i = 1, \ldots, \mathcal{M}$. Let $\mathcal{P}$ denote the set of all such symbols $\mathcal{P} = \{q_i \mid i = 1, \ldots, \mathcal{M}\}$. Let $h : P_{N_-} \rightarrow \mathcal{P}$ be the quotient map corresponding to these nonempty sets, where $P_{N_-} = int(P_N) \backslash \bigcup_{i=1}^{n} \{x \in \mathbb{R}^n \mid c_i^T x + d_i = 0\}$. We also use the notations $h^{-1}(q)$ and $h^{-1}(h(x))$ to denote the set of all points in P_{N_-} with quotient q and the set of all points in P_{N_-} in the same equivalence class with x, respectively. Let $\overline{h^{-1}(q)}$ denote the closure of $h^{-1}(q)$. Note that $\overline{h^{-1}(q)}$, $q \in \mathcal{P}$ are full-dimensional subpolytopes of P_N. It is easy to see that $h^{-1}(q_i) \bigcap h^{-1}(q_j) = \emptyset$ for all $i, j = 1, \ldots, \mathcal{M}, i \neq j$ and $\bigcup_{i=1}^{\mathcal{M}} \overline{h^{-1}(q_i)} = P_N$.

Definition 6. *The transition system $T_g = (Q_g, Q_{g0}, \rightarrow_g, \Pi_g, \models_g)$ is defined by*

- $Q_g = Q_{g0} = \mathcal{P}$,
- *For all $i = 1, \ldots, \mathcal{M}$, $(q_i, q_i) \in \rightarrow_g$ if there exists a feedback controller $u_{q_i q_i} : \overline{h^{-1}(q_i)} \rightarrow U$ for the polytope $\overline{h^{-1}(q_i)}$, making $\overline{h^{-1}(q_i)}$ an invariant for the trajectories of (3) as in Corollary 2 of Theorem 2,*
- *For all $i, j = 1, \ldots, \mathcal{M}$, $i \neq j$, $(q_i, q_j) \in \rightarrow_g$ if $\overline{h^{-1}(q_i)}$ and $\overline{h^{-1}(q_j)}$ share a facet and there exists a feedback controller $u_{q_i q_j} : \overline{h^{-1}(q_i)} \rightarrow U$ for the polytope $\overline{h^{-1}(q_i)}$ with exit facet $\overline{h^{-1}(q_i)} \cap \overline{h^{-1}(q_j)}$ as in Corollary 1 of Theorem 1,*
- *$\Pi_g = \Pi$, with Π as defined in (4),*
- *$q \models_g \pi_i \in \Pi$ if $\exists x \in h^{-1}(q)$ so that $c_i^T x + d_i < 0$.*

On the computation of the transition system T_g, (i.e., checking the existence of affine controllers $u_{q_i q_i}$ and $u_{q_i q_j}$), it is important to note that it only consists of checking the non-emptiness of polyhedral sets (since U is polyhedral), for which there exists several powerful algorithms.

4.3 Determining Trajectories of the Generator Transition System

In this section, we will outline a procedure for finding runs of T_g satisfying an arbitrary LTL_{-X} formula ϕ over Π. Due to space constraints, we omit the details, and refer the reader to the technical report available at [28]. We start by translating ϕ into a Büchi automaton $\mathcal{B}_\phi$. To this goal, we use the conversion algorithm described in [13] and its freely downloadable implementation LTL2BA. Then we take the (synchronous) product of T_g with $\mathcal{B}_\phi$ to obtain a product automaton $\mathcal{A}_{g,\phi}$ [30]. We use standard algorithms for graph traversing on $\mathcal{A}_{g,\phi}$ and eventually project back to find the desired runs of T_g. Our approach is inspired by model checking algorithms, which are used to verify if a transition system satisfies a property expressed in terms of LTL. The difference is that a model checker constructs a Büchi automaton for the negation of the LTL formula and the product automaton is checked for emptiness (*i.e.* non-existence of accepted runs).

While we refer the reader to [28] for details, two important observations are in order. First, as opposed to related approaches reported in [30, 9], we consider possible self-transitions in states of T_g (Definition 6), and cannot use the "stutter extension" rule. In our case, the usage of this rule (adding self-loops to blocking final states of $\mathcal{A}_{g,\phi}$) could lead to incorrect results, because we could obtain runs which cannot be produced by T_g. Second, we consider only runs of T_g that have a special structure composed of one *prefix* and an infinite number of repetitions of a *suffix*. Note that this is not restrictive, since it can be proved [30] that, if there is an accepted run, then there is at least one accepted run with the above structure. If there are more such runs starting from the same state, we choose the "shortest" one, as defined in [28].

Let $r_i = r_i(1)r_i(2)r_i(3)\ldots, r_i(j) \in Q_g = \mathcal{P}$ denote the nonempty run of T_g starting from state q_i, *i.e.*, $r_i(1) = q_i$, $i \in I$, where $I \subseteq \{1,\ldots,\mathcal{M}\}$ is the set of indices of all nonempty runs. The fact that r_i has the prefix-suffix structure can be formally written as: for any $i \in I$, there exists n_p^i and n_s^i such that for any $j > n_p^i + n_s^i$, $r_i(j) = r_i((j - n_p^i - 1) \bmod n_s^i + n_p^i + 1)$. n_p^i and n_s^i are the number of states in prefix and suffix of r_i, respectively and thus the run r_i contains at most $n_p^i + n_s^i$ different states.

Proposition 1, proved in [28], states that, in a run r_i, $i \in I$ of T_g, none of the states can be succeeded by itself, except for the state of a suffix of length one (case in which this state will be infinitely repeated).

Proposition 1. *Each run $r_i = r_i(1)r_i(2)r_i(3)\ldots$, $i \in I$, satisfies the following property: $r_i(j) \neq r_i(j + 1)$, $\forall j \in \mathbb{N}^*$, $j \neq n_p^i + k\,n_s^i + 1$, $k \in \mathbb{N}$. Moreover, if $n_s^i \geq 2$, $r_i(j) \neq r_i(j + 1)$, $\forall j \in \mathbb{N}^*$.*

Remark 3. Proposition (1) and Remark 2 justifies our choice of LTL without the 'next' operator. Indeed, we do not need the increased expressiveness obtained by adding it.

5 Control Strategy

To provide a solution to Problem 1, we restrict the set of initial states of system (3) to

$$x(0) \in \cup_{i \in I} h^{-1}(q_i), \tag{9}$$

where $I \subseteq \{1,\ldots,\mathcal{M}\}$ is the set of indices of non-empty runs as defined in the previous section.

Definition 7 (Control strategy). *A control strategy for system (3) corresponding to an* LTL_{-X} *formula* ϕ *is a tuple* $C^\phi = (L, L_0, u, Inv, Rel)$, *where:*

- $L = \{l^i_{r_i(j)r_i(j+1)} \mid i \in I, j \geq 1\}$ *is its set of locations,*
- $L_0 = \{l^i_{q_i r_i(2)}, i \in I\}$ *is the set of initial locations,*
- $Inv : L \rightarrow 2^{P_N}$, $Inv(l^i_{r_i(j)r_i(j+1)}) = \overline{h^{-1}(r_i(j))}$ *gives the invariant for each location,*
- $u : L \times P_N \rightarrow U$ *is a map which assigns to each location* $l^i_{r_i(j)r_i(j+1)}$ *and state* $x \in Inv(l^i_{r_i(j)r_i(j+1)})$ *a feedback controller* $u(l^i_{r_i(j)r_i(j+1)}, x) = u_{r_i(j)r_i(j+1)}(x)$ ($u_{r_i(j)r_i(j+1)}$ *are defined in Section 4.2),*
- $Rel \subseteq L \times L$, $Rel = \{(l^i_{r_i(j)r_i(j+1)}, l^i_{r_i(j+1)r_i(j+2)}), i \in I, j \geq 1, r_i(j) \neq r_i(j+1)\}$

A location $l^i_{r_i(j)r_i(j+1)}$ corresponds to position j in run r_i. According to structure of runs described in Section 4.3, the set of locations L is finite, even though the runs are infinite. A location $l^i_{r_i(j)r_i(j+1)}$ corresponds to driving all states from $\overline{h^{-1}(r_i(j))}$ to $h^{-1}(r_i(j+1))$ in finite time (through the common facet of $\overline{h^{-1}(r_i(j))}$ and $h^{-1}(r_i(j+1))$) if $r_i(j) \neq r_i(j+1)$, or to keeping the state of the system in $h^{-1}(r_i(j))$ for all times if $r_i(j) = r_i(j+1)$, by using the control $u_{r_i(j)r_i(j+1)}(x)$. Note that there can be several locations mapped to the same physical region $\overline{h^{-1}(q)}$, $q \in Q$. These can correspond to different runs of T_g passing through q or to locations of the same run passing through q at different times and with different successors.

The semantics of control strategy from Definition 7 applied to system (3) with initial states (9) are as follows: starting from $x(0) \in h^{-1}(q_i)$ and location $l = l^i_{q_i r_i(2)} \in L_0$, feedback controller $u(l, x)$ is applied to system (3) as long as the state $x \in Inv(l)$. When (and if) $x \notin Inv(l)$, then the location of C^ϕ is updated to l' according to $(l, l') \in Rel$ and the process continues.

Remark 4. From the given semantics of the control strategy, it follows that the control is well defined on common facets: the one from the polytope that is left is always used. Also, with controllers $u_{q_i q_i}$ and $u_{q_i q_j}$ designed according to Corollaries 2 and 1, the produced trajectories are consistent with Definition 4 in the sense of Remark 1.

We are now ready to provide a solution to Problem 1:

Theorem 3. *All trajectories of system (3), with feedback control strategy given by Definition 7 and set of initial states as in (9), satisfy the LTL_{-X} formula ϕ and stay inside P_N for all times.*

Proof. The proof follows from the construction of C^ϕ from Definition 7, the satisfaction of an LTL_{-X} formula by a continuous trajectory given in Definition 5, and Corollaries 1 and 2 of Theorems 1 and 2. The details can be found in [28]. ∎

Remark 5. It is possible that the solution trajectories visit some states more than once, and have different velocities at the same state at different times. Therefore, the obtained feedback controllers are in general time-variant. The feedback controllers will be piece-wise affine and with a thin set of discontinuities - the common facets of full dimensional subpolytopes of P_N. The generated trajectories will be piecewise smooth and everywhere continuous.

To implement the control strategy described in Definition 7, we have in general infinitely many choices of controllers of the type $u_{q_i q_i}$ and $u_{q_i q_j}$. Indeed, for any polytope, Corollaries 2 and 1 return whole polyhedral sets of allowed controls at vertices. In order to construct a controller according to (7), (8), we need to choose a control at each vertex. To this goal, we solve a set of (maximization) linear programs obtained by attaching a cost to each vertex. If a controller of type $u_{q_i q_j}$ is desired in $h^{-1}(q_i)$, then the costs corresponding to the vertices of $h^{-1}(q_i)$ are the projections of the controls at the vertices along the unit vector connecting the center of $h^{-1}(q_i)$ to the center of $h^{-1}(q_j)$. If a controller of type $u_{q_i q_i}$ is desired in $h^{-1}(q_i)$, then the cost at a vertex is the projection of the control at the vertex along the unit vector from the vertex to the center of $h^{-1}(q_i)$.

Discussion. Our approach to solving Problem 1 is obviously conservative. If the model checking algorithm does not find any solution, this does not mean that there does not exist initial states and feedback controllers producing trajectories satisfying the formula. There are three sources of conservativeness in our approach. First, we look for whole sets (full dimensional polytopes) of initial states instead of investigating isolated ones. Second, we restrict our attention to affine feedback controllers, as opposed to allowing for any type of controllers. Third, Theorem 1 and Corollary 1 provide sufficient conditions for existence of controllers, as opposed to equivalent conditions.

On the positive side, working with sets of states instead of isolated states provides robustness with respect to uncertainty in initial conditions and measurement of the current state. As proved in [12], Theorem 1 can be replaced with a very similar result providing equivalent conditions for the existence of affine controllers if full dimensional simplices are considered instead of full dimensional polytopes. Therefore, if P_N was triangulized instead of partitioned into arbitrary polytopes, the third source of conservativeness would be eliminated. Another advantage of using simplices instead of polytopes would be the fact that we could produce smooth trajectories everywhere by matching the choice of controls at vertices on adjacent simplices [24]. We chose polytopes as opposed to simplices for two reasons. First, as far as we know, there does not exist algorithms for triangulation in dimension larger than 2 that preserve linear constraints (we need to produce proposition preserving partitions when we construct T_g). Second, triangulations can produce an explosion in the number of states of T_g. Due to space constraints, we do not give here an analysis of complexity. However, an example is included at the end of Section 6 for illustration.

6   Implementation and Simulation Results

We implemented our approach as a user friendly software package for LTL_{-X} control of linear systems LTLCon under Matlab. The tool, which is freely downloadable from [14], takes as input the polytope P_N, the matrices A, B, and b of system (3)), and the LTL_{-X} formula ϕ. If it finds a solution, it plots the produced trajectories corresponding to user defined initial states. Even though transparent to the user, LTLCon also uses two free packages. The first one is a mex-file calling CDD in Matlab [31] and it is used to convert a polytope expressed in form (1) to form (2) and vice-versa. The second one is LTL2BA [13], which is used to convert an LTL formula to a Büchi automaton.

To illustrate the use of LTLCon, we first consider a 2D case ($N = 2$), chosen for simplicity of graphical representation. We considered the following numerical values for system (3):

$$\dot{x} = \begin{bmatrix} 0.2 & -0.3 \\ 0.5 & -0.5 \end{bmatrix} x + \begin{bmatrix} 1 & 0 \\ 0 & 1 \end{bmatrix} u + \begin{bmatrix} 0.5 \\ 0.5 \end{bmatrix}, \quad x \in P_2, \ u \in U \qquad (10)$$

Polytope P_2 is specified in form (2), as the intersection of 8 closed half spaces, defined by: $a_1 = [-1 \ \ 0]^T$, $b_1 = -5$, $a_2 = [1 \ \ 0]^T$, $b_2 = -7$, $a_3 = [0 \ \ -1]^T$, $b_3 = -3$, $a_4 = [0 \ \ 1]^T$, $b_4 = -6$, $a_5 = [-3 \ \ -5]^T$, $b_5 = -15$, $a_6 = [1 \ \ -1]^T$, $b_6 = -7$, $a_7 = [-1 \ \ 2.5]^T$, $b_7 = -15$, $a_8 = [-2 \ \ 2.5]^T$, $b_8 = -17.5$. Control constraints are captured by the set $U = [-2, 2] \times [-2, 2]$.

We define a set Π containing 10 predicates, as in equations (4,5), where: $c_1 = [0 \ \ 1]^T$, $d_1 = 0$, $c_2 = [1 \ \ -1]^T$, $d_2 = 0$, $c_3 = [4 \ \ 1]^T$, $d_3 = 12$, $c_4 = [4 \ \ -7]^T$, $d_4 = 34$, $c_5 = [-2 \ \ -1]^T$, $d_5 = 4$, $c_6 = [-1 \ \ -12]^T$, $d_6 = 31$, $c_7 = [-1 \ \ -1]^T$, $d_7 = 11$, $c_8 = [1 \ \ 0]^T$, $d_8 = -3$, $c_9 = [0 \ \ -1]^T$, $d_9 = -1.5$, $c_{10} = [-6 \ \ -4.5]^T$, $d_{10} = -12$.

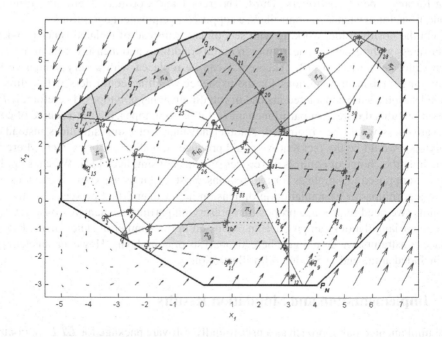

Fig. 1. The arrows represent the drift vector field of system (10). The yellow boxes mark the half-spaces corresponding to atomic propositions π_i, $i = 1, \ldots, 10$. The regions to be visited are green, while the obstacles are gray.

There are 33 feasible full-dimensional subpolytopes in P_2, and therefore 33 states in T_g. Figure 1 depicts the bounding polytope P_2, the vector field given by the drift of system (10), the predicates π_i, $i = 1, \ldots, 10$, and the feasible subpolytopes corresponding to states q_i, $i = 1, \ldots, 33$ of T_g. The red lines connecting the centroids of the polytopes in Figure 1 represent the transitions of T_g, with the following convention: for all $i \neq j$: a full line means that $(q_i, q_j), (q_j, q_i) \in \rightarrow_g$; a dashed line means that $(q_i, q_j) \in \rightarrow_g$ for $i < j$; a dotted line means that $(q_i, q_j) \in \rightarrow_g$ for $i > j$. A self-transition $(q_i, q_i) \in \rightarrow$ is represented by a red star in the center of $h^{-1}(q_i)$.

We have chosen an LTL_{-X} formula inspired from robot motion planning, which involves visiting a sequence of three regions infinitely often, while always avoiding three obstacles. The regions to be visited are, in order: $r_1 = h^{-1}(q_1)$, $r_2 = \bigcup_{i \in \{20,21,29\}} h^{-1}(q_i)$, and $r_3 = h^{-1}(q_{32})$. The obstacles are represented by the polyhedral regions $o_1 = \bigcup_{i \in \{13,14,16,17,18\}} h^{-1}(q_i)$, $o_2 = \bigcup_{i \in \{19,28\}} h^{-1}(q_i)$ and $o_3 = h^{-1}(q_{10})$. All regions to be visited and obstacles are represented in Figure 1. The LTL_{-X} formula can be written as $\phi = \Box(\Diamond(r_1 \wedge \Diamond(r_2 \wedge \Diamond r_3)) \wedge \neg(o_1 \vee o_2 \vee o_3))$. By expressing interesting regions r_i and o_i, $i = 1, 2, 3$ in terms of predicates π_j, $j = 1, \ldots, 10$ we obtain $\phi = \Box(\Diamond((\pi_3 \wedge \pi_{10}) \wedge \Diamond((\neg\pi_4 \wedge \pi_5 \wedge \pi_6 \wedge \pi_8) \wedge \Diamond(\neg\pi_1 \wedge \neg\pi_6 \wedge \neg\pi_8))) \wedge \neg(\pi_4 \vee \pi_7 \vee (\pi_1 \wedge \neg\pi_2 \wedge \neg\pi_5 \wedge \pi_9)))$.

The set of initial states from which there exist continuous trajectories satisfying the formula is the union of the yellow polytopes in Figure 2 (a). The set of initial states of T_g from which there exist runs satisfying the formula are the corresponding labels. The run r_{15} of T_g starting from q_{15} and satisfying ϕ is presented in Figure 2 (b). The prefix of run r_{15} of T_g is $q_{15}q_2$ (shown as green polytopes), while the suffix is $q_1q_3q_{26}q_{23}q_{20}q_{23}q_{31}q_{32}q_{30}q_{22}q_{20}q_{23}q_{26}q_3$ (red polytopes). A continuous trajectory starting from $x_0 = [-2.66 \quad -1.33]^T$ (blue diamond) is also shown in Figure 2 (b). It is colored in blue for prefix part and in red for suffix part.

The above case study was run on a Pentium 4 (2.66 GHz) machine with 1 GB RAM, Windows XP, and Matlab 7. The transition system T_g with 33 states was created in

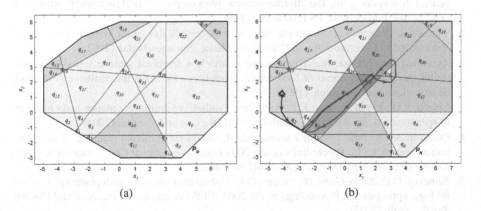

(a)   (b)

Fig. 2. (a) The union of the yellow polytopes represents the set of initial states from which there exist continuous trajectories satisfying formula ϕ. (b) An example of such a trajectory.

about 0.9 seconds. The Büchi automaton had 9 states and was created in 2.2 seconds. The desired runs of T_g were obtained in about 11 seconds. We also ran a four dimensional example ($N = 4$), with P_4 defined by 9 hyperplanes and Π containing $n = 15$ predicates. There were $\mathcal{M} = 295$ states in T_g - its construction took 68 seconds. A tesselation using the intersection points between hyperplanes defining the predicates would yield 17509 tetrahedra. As explained before, these simplices are not suitable for our problem, but even if they were, a transition system with so many states would be inefficient from a computational point of view.

7   Conclusion

In this paper, we described a fully automated framework for control of linear systems from specifications given in terms of LTL_{-X} formulas over linear predicates in its state variables. We expect that the method will find applications in several areas of engineering, where linear systems are used for modelling and temporal logic for specifying performance. Future directions of research include the extension of these techniques to piece-wise affine systems and hybrid systems with more complicated dynamics.

References

1. Emerson, E.A.: Temporal and modal logic. In van Leeuwen, J., ed.: Handbook of Theoretical Computer Science: Formal Models and Semantics. Volume B. North-Holland Pub. Co./MIT Press (1990) 995–1072
2. Shults, B., Kuipers, B.: Proving properties of continuous systems: Qualitative simulation and temporal logic. Artificial Intelligence **92** (1997) 91–130
3. Brajnik, G., Clancy, D.: Focusing qualitative simulation using temporal logic: theoretical foundations. Annals of Mathematics and Artificial Intelligence **22** (1998) 59–86
4. Davoren, J., Coulthard, V., Markey, N., Moor, T.: Non-deterministic temporal logics for general flow systems. In: The 7th International Workshop on Hybrid Systems: Computation and Control, Philadelphia, PA (2004) 280–295
5. Tabuada, P., Pappas, G.: Model checking ltl over controllable linear systems is decidable. Volume 2623 of Lecture Notes in Computer Science. Springer-Verlag (2003)
6. Antoniotti, M., Mishra, B.: Discrete event models + temporal logic = supervisory controller: Automatic synthesis of locomotion controllers. In: IEEE International Conference on Robotics and Automation. (1995)
7. Loizou, S.G., Kyriakopoulos, K.J.: Automatic synthesis of multiagent motion tasks based on ltl specifications. In: 43rd IEEE Conference on Decision and Control. (2004)
8. Quottrup, M.M., Bak, T., Izadi-Zamanabadi, R.: Multi-robot motion planning: A timed automata approach. In: Proceedings of the 2004 IEEE International Conference on Robotics and Automation, New Orleans, LA (2004) 44174422
9. Fainekos, G.E., Kress-Gazit, H., Pappas, G.J.: Hybrid controllers for path planning: a temporal logic approach. In: Proceedings of the 2005 IEEE Conference on Decision and Control, Seville, Spain (2005)
10. Antoniotti, M., Park, F., Policriti, A., Ugel, N., Mishra, B.: Foundations of a query and simulation system for the modeling of biochemical and biological processes. Proceedings of the Pacific Symposium on Biocomputing, Lihue, Hawaii (2003) 116–127

11. Batt, G., Ropers, D., de Jong, H., Geiselmann, J., Mateescu, R., Page, M., Schneider, D.: Validation of qualitative models of genetic regulatory networks by model checking: analysis of the nutritional stress response in e.coli. In: Thirteen International Conference on Intelligent Systems for Molecular Biology. (2005)

12. Habets, L., van Schuppen, J.: A control problem for affine dynamical systems on a full-dimensional polytope. Automatica **40** (2004) 21–35

13. Gastin, P., Oddoux, D.: Fast ltl to büchi automata translation. In G. Berry, H.C., Finkel, A., eds.: Proceedings of the 13th Conference on Computer Aided Verification (CAV'01). Number 2102 in LNCS, SPRINGER (2001) 53–65

14. Kloetzer, M., Belta, C.: Ltlcon, a matlab package for control of linear systems from linear temporal logic specifications. (2005) URL http//iasi.bu.edu/~software/LTL-control.htm.

15. Alur, R., Dill, D.L.: A theory of timed automata. Theoretical Computer Science **126** (1994) 183–235

16. Alur, R., C.Courcoubetis, Halbwachs, N., Henzinger, T., Ho, P., Nicollin, X., A.Olivero, Sifakis, J., Yovine, S.: Hybrid automata: An algorithmic approach to specification and verification of hybrid systems. Theoretical Computer Science **138** (1995) 3–34

17. Puri, A., Varaiya, P.: Decidability of hybrid systems with rectangular inclusions. Computer Aided Verification (1994) 95–104

18. Lafferriere, G., Pappas, G.J., Sastry, S.: O-minimal hybrid systems. Mathematics of Control, Signals and Systems **13** (2000) 1–21

19. Alur, R., Henzinger, T.A., Lafferriere, G., Pappas, G.J.: Discrete abstractions of hybrid systems. Proceedings of the IEEE **88** (2000) 971–984

20. Pappas, G.J.: Bisimilar linear systems. Automatica **39** (2003) 2035–2047

21. Broucke, M.: A geometric approach to bisimulation and verification of hybrid systems. In Vaandrager, F.W., van Schuppen, J.H., eds.: Hybrid Systems: Computation and Control. Volume 1569 of Lecture Notes in Computer Science. Springer-Verlag (1999) 61–75

22. Haghverdi, E., Tabuada, P., Pappas, G.: Bisimulation relations for dynamical and control systems. Volume 69 of Electronic Notes in Theoretical Computer Science. Elsevier (2003)

23. Tiwari, A., Khanna, G.: Series of abstractions for hybrid automata. In: Fifth International Workshop on Hybrid Systems: Computation and Control, Stanford, CA (2002)

24. Belta, C., Isler, V., Pappas, G.J.: Discrete abstractions for robot planning and control in polygonal environments. IEEE Transactions on Robotics **21** (2005) 864–874

25. Motzkin, T., H.Raiffa, Thompson, G., R.M.Thrall: The double description method. In Kuhn, H., Tucker, A., eds.: Contributions to theory of games. Volume 2. Princeton University Press, Princeton, NJ (1953)

26. Fukuda, K.: cdd/cdd+ package. (URL http://www.cs.mcgill.ca/~fukuda/soft/cdd_home/cdd.html)

27. Lee, C.W.: Subdivisions and triangulations of polytopes. In Goodman, J.E., ORourke, J., eds.: Handbook of discrete and computational geometry. CRC Press, Boca Raton, NY (1997) 271–290

28. Kloetzer, M., Belta, C.: A fully automated framework for controller synthesis from linear temporal logic specifications. Technical Report CISE 2005-IR-0050, Boston University (2005) http://www.bu.edu/systems/research/publications/2005/2005-IR-0050.pdf.

29. Belta, C., Habets, L.: Constructing decidable hybrid systems with velocity bounds. In: 43rd IEEE Conference on Decision and Control, Paradise Island, Bahamas (2004)

30. Holzmann, G.: The Spin Model Checker, Primer and Reference Manual. Addison-Wesley, Reading, Massachusetts (2004)

31. Torrisi, F., Baotic, M.: Matlab interface for the cdd solver. (URL http:// control.ee.ethz.ch/~hybrid/cdd.php)

Reachability Analysis of Multi-affine Systems

Marius Kloetzer and Calin Belta

Center for Information and Systems Engineering,
Boston University, 15 Saint Mary's Street,
Brookline, MA 02446
{kmarius, cbelta}@bu.edu

Abstract. We present a technique for reachability analysis of continuous multi-affine systems based on rectangular partitions. The method is iterative. At each step, finer partitions and larger discrete quotients are produced. We exploit some interesting convexity properties of multi-affine functions on rectangles to show that the construction of the discrete quotient at each step requires only the evaluation of the vector field at the set of all vertices of all rectangles in the partition and finding the roots of a finite set of scalar affine functions. The methodology promises to be easily extendable to rectangular hybrid automata with multi-affine vector fields and is expected to find important applications in analysis of biological networks and robot control.

1 Introduction

Reachability analysis is the problem of constructing the set of states reached by trajectories of a system originating in a given (possibly infinite dimensional) initial set. *Safety verification* is the problem of proving that a system does not have any trajectory from a given initial set to a given final (unsafe) set. For discrete systems with a finite number of states, these problems are *decidable*, *i.e.*, can be solved by a computer in a finite number of steps. For continuous and hybrid (*i.e.*, described by both continuous and discrete dynamics) systems, these problems are very difficult (in general undecidable) because of the uncountability of the state space.

One way to solve such problems for continuous and hybrid systems is to construct the set of states reached by the system, or an over-approximation of this set, by working directly in the continuous state space. Such methods are called *direct* and are not the subject of this paper. Our work can be included into the group of *indirect* methods, where a reachability problem for a continuous or hybrid system is mapped to a reachability problem for a finite state discrete system through *discrete abstractions*. The main idea in discrete abstractions is to iteratively partition the infinite dimensional continuous state space and produce partition quotients whose trajectories include the trajectories of the continuous or hybrid system. Such a discrete system is said to *simulate* the original system. If the converse is true, *i.e.*, the continuous or hybrid system simulate the discrete quotient, the two systems are called *bisimilar*, and the two

João Hespanha and A. Tiwari (Eds.): HSCC 2006, LNCS 3927, pp. 348–362, 2006.

reachability problems become equivalent. Therefore, in this case, the reachability problem for a continuous or hybrid system becomes decidable.

The bisimulation relation was introduced in [1], formally defined for linear systems in [2], and for nonlinear systems in a categorical context in [3]. In [4], it has been shown that reachability is undecidable for a very simple class of hybrid systems. Several decidable classes have been identified though by restricting the continuous behavior of the hybrid system, as in the case of timed automata [5], multirate automata [6], [7], and rectangular automata [4], [8], or by restricting the discrete behavior, as in order-minimal hybrid systems [9, 10, 11]. All these decidable classes are too weak to represent continuous and hybrid system models encountered in practice. Then one might be satisfied with sufficient abstractions, when a discrete quotient that simulates the original system is enough to prove a safety property. But even finding the discrete quotient is not at all trivial. Related work focuses on partitioning using linear functions of the continuous variables, as in the method of predicate abstractions [12, 13], or using polynomial functions as in [13, 14]. However, to derive the transitions of the discrete quotient, one has to be able to either integrate the vector fields of the initial system [12], or use computationally expensive decision procedures such as quantifier elimination for real closed fields and theorem proving [13], which severely limit the dimensions of the problems that can be approached.

In this paper, we focus on formal analysis of continuous systems with multi-affine vector fields, *i.e,* affine in each variable, defined on rectangular regions of the Euclidean space. The main idea behind this work is, as in [15, 16, 17], to exploit the specific form of the vector field and the particular shape of the invariant to infer reachability properties of infinite uncountable sets of states from properties verified by a finite set of states. Specifically, in [18], we proved that a multi-affine function is uniquely determined by its values at the vertices of a rectangle and its restriction to the rectangle is a convex combination of these values. In this paper, we use this result to develop a reachability analysis algorithm for multi-affine systems by iteratively constructing finer and finer discrete quotients.

Even though the abstraction procedure in this paper falls into the more general framework of [13], we show that if more structure is allowed, then reachabiltity and safety verification questions can be answered with much less computation. The calculation of the discrete quotient at a given iteration involves only finding the roots of scalar affine functions and evaluation of multi-affine functions at a finite number of points. This will allow us to approach much larger problems, as usually found in analysis of bio-molecular networks, where the multi-affine structure appears naturally when chemical reactions with unitary stoichiometric coefficients are modelled using mass action kinetics. Multi-affine dynamics are also found in other systems, including the celebrated Euler's equations for angular velocity of rotation of rigid bodies, the equations of motion of translating and rotating rigid bodies with rotation parameterized by quaternions [19], Volterra [20], and Lotka-Volterra equations [21].

2   Continuous Systems and Discrete Quotients

Definition 1 (Continuous system). *We represent a continuous dynamical system as a pair*

$$CS = (X, f), \tag{1}$$

where $X \subseteq \mathbb{R}^n$, $n \in \mathbb{N}$ is its continuous state space and f is a smooth vector field on X, i.e., the state $x \in X$ of system (1) evolves according to $\dot{x} = f(x)$.

We assume that X is a connected subset of $\mathbb{R}^n$ and introduce a *set partition* of X by defining the *abstraction map*: $abs : X \to L$, where L is a finite set of labels for all the elements in the partition. Let con be the *concretization map* of the partition induced by abs: $con : L \to X$, $con(l) = \{x \in X | abs(x) = l\}$.

In other words, for $l \in L$, we use $con(l) \subseteq X$ to denote the set of all $x \in X$ in the partition element with label l. Since abs induces a partition and con is its concretization map, we have $\bigcup_{l \in L} con(l) = X$ and $con(l) \cap con(l') = \emptyset$, for all $l, l' \in L$, $l \neq l'$. We use $con(l) \sim con(l')$, or simply $l \sim l'$ to denote adjacency of regions $con(l)$ and $con(l')$. For simplicity of notation, we use $con(I)$ to denote $\bigcup_{l \in I} con(l)$, $I \subset L$. For an arbitrary $I \subset L$, we denote by $\text{Post}(con(I))$ the set of all states in X reached by the trajectories of (1) originating in $con(I)$, for all times $t \geq 0$. The reachability problem for CS can be formulated as follows:

Problem 1 (Reachability). For an arbitrary $I \subset L$, determine $\text{Post}(con(I))$.

The safety verification problem for CS is the problem of deciding if (1) has trajectories between arbitrary regions in the partition induced by the map abs:

Problem 2 (Safety). Given $I, F \subset L$ with $I \cap F = \emptyset$, determine the truth value of the following assertion:

$$\text{Post}(con(I)) \cap con(F) = \emptyset \tag{2}$$

In a particular application, $con(I)$ corresponds to a set of states around initial or operating points of a system CS, while $con(F)$ might represent unsafe regions.

Note that our definition of 'Post' operator implies that the reachability and safety problems we are dealing with are time-abstract. It is obvious to see that the solution to Problem 1 immediately gives a solution to Problem 2, provided that we can calculate the intersection in Eqn. (2). However, in order to solve Problem 2, it is not necessary to solve Problem 1 - it is enough to construct an over-approximation of $\text{Post}(con(I))$ that has empty intersection with $con(F)$. To construct over-approximations of $\text{Post}(con(I))$, we use *discrete quotients*:

Definition 2 (Discrete quotient). *A discrete quotient of CS induced by the partition map 'abs' is a finite state transition system DS described by the pair*

$$DS = (L, T), \tag{3}$$

*where L is the set of labels produced by the abstraction map 'abs', and $T \subseteq L \times L$
is a set of transitions satisfying the following property:*

$$(l, l') \in T \text{ if } l \sim l' \text{ and there exist } t_1, t_2 \geq 0, t_1 < t_2 \text{ and}$$
$$\text{a trajectory } x(t) \text{ of } CS \text{ such that} \tag{4}$$
$$x(t_1) \in con(l), \; x(t_2) \in con(l') \text{ and } x(t) \in (con(l)) \cap con(l'), \; \forall t \in [t_1, t_2].$$

As before, for $I \subset L$, we denote by $\text{Post}(I) \subseteq L$ the set of all discrete states that
can be reached from I by DS. More formally, $\text{Post}(I) = \bigcup_{l \in I} \text{Post}(l)$.

Note that we use the same operator 'Post' for both CS and DS, with the
observation that they are easily distinguished by their arguments.

From (4) it follows that

$$\text{Post}(con(I)) \subseteq con(\text{Post}(I)) \tag{5}$$

Eqn. (5) implies that, if the transitions (4) of a discrete quotient (3) can be
computed, then an over-approximation $con(\text{Post}(I))$ of $\text{Post}(con(I))$ can be easily determined by a search on the transition system (3), which is a decidable
problem. If $\text{Post}(I) \cap F = \emptyset$ (equivalent with $con(\text{Post}(I)) \cap con(F) = \emptyset$, since
$con(L)$ is a partition of X), then the truth value of (2) is TRUE. Otherwise, we
cannot answer Problem 2, and a less conservative discrete quotient is necessary.

There are two sources of conservativeness in the definition of DS. The first
comes from the fact that, according to (4), there might exist a transition $(l, l') \in$
T even if CS does not have a trajectory from $con(l)$ to $con(l')$. A more correct
definition of the discrete quotient should have 'if and only if' instead of 'if' in
Eqn. (4). This would make CS and DS equivalent from the point of view of
reachability of adjacent regions in one step. However, even in this case, there
is a second source of conservativeness, which comes from lack of transitivity in
the following sense: if $(l, l') \in T$ and $(l', l'') \in T$, which implies that l, l', l'' is a
trajectory of DS, this does not imply that CS has a trajectory from $con(l)$ to
$con(l')$ and to $con(l'')$, simply because it is possible that all trajectories that go
from $con(l)$ to $con(l')$ escape to a region $con(l''')$, with $l''' \neq l''$. The conservativeness is completely eliminated, i.e., CS and DS are equivalent with respect
to reachability properties, if and only if, in (4), the 'if' statement is replaced by
'if and only if', and all initial states in $con(l)$ flow in finite time to $con(l')$ under
the dynamics of CS.

As outlined in Section 1, finding such non-conservative discrete quotients of
continuous systems is an extremely hard problem. Moreover, even finding discrete quotients with 'if and only if' in Eqn. (4) is very difficult. In this paper,
we use the relaxed Definition 2 of a discrete quotient to construct less and less
conservative over-approximations $con(\text{Post}(I))$ for the solutions to Problems 1
and 2. Formally, we define a refinement of a discrete quotient as follows:

Definition 3 (Refinement). *For a given continuous system CS, a discrete
quotient $\overline{DS} = (\bar{L}, \bar{T})$ induced by $\overline{abs} : X \to \bar{L}$ refines a discrete quotient $DS =$
(L, T) induced by $abs : X \to L$ if $|\bar{L}| > |L|$ and the following conditions hold:*

*(i) For any $l \in L$, there exists $\bar{I} \subset \bar{L}$ with $|\bar{I}| \geq 1$ so that $\overline{con}(\bar{I})$ is a partition
of $con(l)$. Any $\bar{l} \in \bar{I}$ is said to refine $l \in L$, and we denote this by $\bar{l} \leq l$.*

(ii) For any $\bar{l}, \bar{l}' \in \bar{L}$ with $(\bar{l}, \bar{l}') \in \bar{T}$, if there exist $l, l' \in L$, $l \neq l'$, so that $\bar{l} \leq l$
and $\bar{l}' \leq l'$, then $(l, l') \in T$.
(iii) There exist $l, l' \in L$ with $(l, l') \in T$ and $\bar{l}, \bar{l}' \in \bar{L}$ with $\bar{l} \sim \bar{l}'$, $\bar{l} \leq l$, $\bar{l}' \leq l'$,
and $(\bar{l}, \bar{l}') \notin \bar{T}$.

In other words, (i) states that each region in the partition produced by *abs*
is further partitioned by $\overline{abs}$. Note that, since $|\bar{L}| > |L|$, at least one region
$con(l)$ is strictly partitioned. Condition (ii) requires that the finer quotient $\overline{DS}$
can only have transitions between states refining states connected by transitions
in the coarser quotient DS and between states refining the same state of DS.
Conditions (i) and (ii) will guarantee that the over-approximation $con(\text{Post}(I))$
as in Eqn. (5) does not grow through refinement. Finally, (iii) means that there
exist at least one pair of states connected in the coarser DS for which refinement
determines two disconnected states in the finer description $\overline{DS}$.

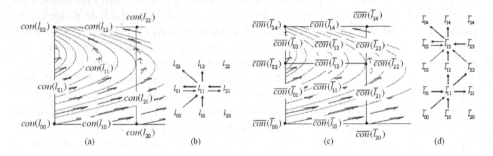

Fig. 1. Discrete quotients for a vector field $f = (f_1, f_2)$, $f_1 = 2 - x_1 x_2$, $f_2 = 1 + x_2 - x_1 x_2$
in a rectangular region $[1.5, 1.56] \times [1.1, 1.42]$ in plane. An initial partition and the
corresponding discrete quotient are shown in (a) and (b), respectively. A finer partition
is shown in (c), and the corresponding discrete quotient (d) refines the initial one
(b). The regions of partitions are "open" rectangles of dimension 0 (points), 1 (open
line segments), and 2 (rectangles without boundaries). The transitions of the discrete
quotients correspond to 'if and only if' in Eqn. (4).

An example is given in Fig. 1, where an initial partition $\bigcup_{i,j=0,1,2} con(l_{ij})$ of a
2-dimensional rectangle (containing its boundaries) is refined to $\bigcup_{i=0,1,2; j=0,\ldots,4} \overline{con}(\bar{l}_{ij})$. It is easy to see that condition (ii) of Definition 3 is satisfied, *i.e.*, no
"new" transitions are added. As it can be seen in Fig. 1(c), the refinement is
achieved by "cutting" with a horizontal line where the f_1 component of the
vector field becomes zero on the vertical open segment $con(l_{21})$. This leads to a
partition $\overline{con}(\bar{l}_{13})$, $\overline{con}(\bar{l}_{12})$, $\overline{con}(\bar{l}_{11})$ of $con(l_{11})$ and a partition $\overline{con}(\bar{l}_{23})$, $\overline{con}(\bar{l}_{22})$,
$\overline{con}(\bar{l}_{21})$ of $con(l_{21})$. In the finer quotient, it can be seen for example that there is
no transition from $\bar{l}_{21}$ to $\bar{l}_{11}$ and from $\bar{l}_{13}$ to $\bar{l}_{23}$, even though the coarser quotient
had transitions between l_{11} and l_{21} in both directions (condition (iii)).

Condition (iii) in Definition 3 is a necessary condition for strict shrinking of
the over-approximation $con(\text{Post}(I))$. However, it is not sufficient. Indeed, for
adjacent regions $\bar{l} \sim \bar{l}'$, if CS does not have trajectories penetrating directly from

$\overline{con}(\bar{l})$ to $\overline{con}(\bar{l}')$, this does not mean that $Post(\overline{con}(\bar{l})) \bigcap \overline{con}(\bar{l}') = \emptyset$. Trajectories originating in $\overline{con}(\bar{l})$ can loop around and eventually hit $\overline{con}(\bar{l}')$.

These ideas are formalized in Proposition 1. Due to the space constraints, the proof of Proposition 1 is not included here, and it can be found in [22].

Proposition 1 (Conservativeness reduction by refinement). *If* $\overline{DS} = (\bar{L}, \bar{T})$ *refines* $DS = (L, T)$, *and* $I \subset L$, $\bar{I} \subset \bar{L}$ *with the property that* $\overline{con}(\bar{I})$ *is a partition of* $con(I)$, *then we have*

$$Post(con(I)) = Post(\overline{con}(\bar{I})) \subseteq \overline{con}(Post(\bar{I})) \subseteq con(Post(I)) \qquad (6)$$

Moreover, if (iii) from Definition 3 is replaced by:

(iii)' There exist $l, l' \in L$ *with* $(l, l') \in T$ *and* $\bar{l}' \in \bar{L}$ *with* $\bar{l}' \leq l'$, *and* $\bar{l}' \notin Post(\bar{l})$, $\forall \bar{l} \in \bar{L}, \bar{l} \leq l$

and $l \in (I \cup Post(I))$, *then the last inclusion relation in (6) is strict, i.e., the over-approximation* $con(Post(I))$ *as in Eqn. (5) strictly shrinks through refinement.*

Remark 1 (Simulation and bisimulation). Both CS and DS defined above can be embedded into transition systems [2, 23] with set of observables L. In this framework, DS given by Definition 2 is said to simulate CS. When both sources of conservativeness mentioned above are eliminated, then CS simulates DS as well, and they are called bisimilar. The interested reader can refer to [1, 2, 23] for formal definitions of simulation and bisimulation relations.

In this paper, we assume that X is a full dimensional "closed" rectangle in $\mathbb{R}^n$ and the vector field f is multi-affine, *i.e.*, affine in each state component. We use iterative partitions of X into "open" rectangles and some interesting convexity properties of multi-affine functions on rectangles to calculate discrete quotients according to Definitions 2 and 3 and provide a solution to Problem 2 and a conservative solution to Problem 1. As it will be seen, we cannot guarantee the sufficient condition (iii)' for strict shrinking at each step of the refinement. Instead, we satisfy the necessary condition (iii), with the "hope" that the conservativeness is strictly reduced.

3   Rectangles and Multi-affine Functions

Two vectors $a = (a_1, \ldots, a_n) \in \mathbb{R}^n$ and $b = (b_1, \ldots, b_n) \in \mathbb{R}^n$ with the property that $a_i < b_i$ for all $i = 1, \ldots, n$ determine a set of 3^n rectangles in $\mathbb{R}^n$:

$$\mathcal{R}(a, b) = \{R_{(l_1, \ldots, l_n)}, \; l_i \in \{0, 1, 2\}, \; i = 1, \ldots, n\} \qquad (7)$$

where each rectangle $R_{(l_1, \ldots, l_n)}$, $l_i \in \{0, 1, 2\}$, $i = 1, \ldots, n$ is defined by

$$R_{(l_1, \ldots, l_n)} = \{x = (x_1, \ldots, x_n) \in \mathbb{R}^n \,|\, x_i = a_i \text{ if } l_i = 0,$$
$$a_i < x_i < b_i \text{ if } l_i = 1, \; x_i = b_i \text{ if } l_i = 2, \; i = 1, \ldots, n\} \qquad (8)$$

We define the order m of a rectangle $R_{(l_1,\ldots,l_n)}$ as being the number of '1' entries in its label $(l_1,\ldots,l_n)$. The number of m - order rectangles in $\mathcal{R}(a,b)$ is $2^{n-m}n!/((n-m)!m!)$. As particular cases, there is only one n - order (full dimensional) rectangle $R_{(1,\ldots,1)}$, and 2^n 0 - order rectangles, or *vertices* $R_{(l_1,\ldots,l_n)}$, $l_i \in \{0,2\}$, $i = 1,\ldots,n$. For a given rectangle $R_{(l_1,\ldots,l_n)}$, we can define

$$
\begin{aligned}
\mathcal{L}R_{(l_1,\ldots,l_n)} = \{R_{(l'_1,\ldots,l'_n)} \in \mathcal{R}(a,b) \,|\, \\
(l'_1,\ldots,l'_n) \neq (l_1,\ldots,l_n) \wedge l''_i = l_i \text{ if } l_i \in \{0,2\}\}
\end{aligned}
\tag{9}
$$

The set of vertices corresponding to $R_{(l_1,\ldots,l_n)}$ is a subset of $\mathcal{L}R_{(l_1,\ldots,l_n)}$ defined by

$$
\begin{aligned}
\mathcal{V}R_{(l_1,\ldots,l_n)} = \{R_{(l'_1,\ldots,l'_n)} \in \mathcal{R}(a,b) \,|\, (l'_1,\ldots,l'_n) \neq (l_1,\ldots,l_n) \wedge \\
l'_i = l_i \text{ if } l_i \in \{0,2\} \wedge l'_i \in \{0,2\} \text{ if } l_i = 1\}
\end{aligned}
\tag{10}
$$

If the order of $R_{(l_1,\ldots,l_n)}$ is m, there are $3^m - 1$ rectangles in $\mathcal{L}R_{(l_1,\ldots,l_n)}$, all of order less than or equal to $m-1$, and 2^m vertices (0-order rectangles) in $\mathcal{V}R_{(l_1,\ldots,l_n)}$. We call the rectangles defined by (8) *open* rectangles, with the observation that, except for $R_{(1,\ldots,1)}$, they are not open sets in $\mathbb{R}^n$. If all '<' in (8), if any, are replaced by '≤', then $R_{(l_1,\ldots,l_n)}$ becomes *closed*, and is denoted by $\bar{R}_{(l_1,\ldots,l_n)}$. It is easy to see that $\bar{R}_{(l_1,\ldots,l_n)} = R_{(l_1,\ldots,l_n)} \cup \mathcal{L}R_{(l_1,\ldots,l_n)}$. For a closed rectangle $\bar{R}$, sets $\mathcal{L}\bar{R}$ and $\mathcal{V}\bar{R}$ are defined as in (9,10) by replacing R with $\bar{R}$. It follows that the sets of vertices of open and closed rectangles are identical, *i.e.*, $\mathcal{V}R = \mathcal{V}\bar{R}$. Therefore we will use $\mathcal{V}R$ for the set of vertices of $\mathcal{V}\bar{R}$.

Definition 4 (Multi-affine function). *A multi-affine function $f : \mathbb{R}^n \longrightarrow \mathbb{R}^p$ (with $p \in \mathbb{N}$) is a polynomial in the indeterminates $x_1,\ldots,x_n$ with the property that the degree of f in any of the variables is less than or equal to 1. Stated differently, f has the form:*

$$
f(x_1,\ldots,x_n) = \sum_{i_1,\ldots,i_n \in \{0,1\}} c_{i_1,\ldots,i_n} x_1^{i_1} \cdots x_n^{i_n},
\tag{11}
$$

with $c_{i_1,\ldots,i_n} \in \mathbb{R}^p$ for all $i_1,\ldots,i_n \in \{0,1\}$ and using the convention that if $i_k = 0$, then $x_k^{i_k} = 1$.

The following proposition is proved in [18]:

Proposition 2. *A multi-affine function is uniquely determined by its values at the vertices $\mathcal{V}R_{(1,\ldots,1)}$ of a full dimensional closed rectangle $\bar{R}_{(1,\ldots,1)}$. Its restriction to the rectangle is a convex combination of the values at the vertices and has the following form:*

$$
\begin{aligned}
f|_{\bar{R}_{(1,\ldots,1)}}(x_1,\ldots,x_n) = \sum_{(v_1,\ldots,v_n) \in \mathcal{V}R_{(1,\ldots,1)}} \\
\prod_{k=1}^{n} \left(\frac{x_k - a_k}{b_k - a_k}\right)^{\xi(v_k)} \left(\frac{b_k - x_k}{b_k - a_k}\right)^{1-\xi(v_k)} f(v_1,\ldots,v_n),
\end{aligned}
\tag{12}
$$

where $\xi_k : \{a_1,\ldots,a_n,b_1,\ldots,b_n\} \to \{0,1\}$ is an indicator function defined by: $\xi_k(a_k) = 0$, $\xi_k(b_k) = 1$, $k = 1,\ldots,n$.

Since a multi-affine function remains multi-affine if some of its arguments are kept constant, Proposition 2 is true when a multi-affine function is restricted to a lower order closed rectangle, when Eqn. (12) becomes:

$$f|_{\bar{R}_{(l_1,\dots,l_n)}}(x_1,\dots,x_n) = \sum_{(v_1,\dots,v_n)\in VR_{(l_1,\dots,l_n)}}$$
$$\prod_{k,l_k=1}\left(\frac{x_k-a_k}{b_k-a_k}\right)^{\xi(v_k)}\left(\frac{b_k-x_k}{b_k-a_k}\right)^{1-\xi(v_k)} f(v_1,\dots,v_n), \tag{13}$$

Note that $f|_{\bar{R}_{(l_1,\dots,l_n)}}(x_1,\dots,x_n)$ is obtained from $f|_{\bar{R}_{(1,\dots,1)}}(x_1,\dots,x_n)$ by setting $x_i = a_i$ for $l_i = 0$ and $x_i = b_i$ for $l_i = 2$, $i = 1,\dots,n$.

A straightforward corollary of Proposition 2 can be stated as (the proof can be found in [22]):

Corollary 1. *If f is a scalar multi-affine function ($p = 1$ in Definition 4) and $R_{(l_1,\dots,l_n)}$ is an open rectangle of arbitrary order, then we have:*

(a) $f(x) > 0$ *everywhere in* $R_{(l_1,\dots,l_n)}$ *if and only if $f(v) \geq 0$ for all $v \in VR_{(l_1,\dots,l_n)}$, and there exists at least one $v \in VR_{(l_1,\dots,l_n)}$ for which $f(v) > 0$.*
(b) $f(x) < 0$ *everywhere in* $R_{(l_1,\dots,l_n)}$ *if and only if $f(v) \leq 0$ for all $v \in VR_{(l_1,\dots,l_n)}$, and there exists at least one $v \in VR_{(l_1,\dots,l_n)}$ for which $f(v) < 0$.*
(c) $f(x) = 0$ *everywhere in* $R_{(l_1,\dots,l_n)}$ *if and only if $f(v) = 0$ for all $v \in VR_{(l_1,\dots,l_n)}$.*
(d) *There exist $x, x' \in R_{(l_1,\dots,l_n)}$ with $f(x) > 0$ and $f(x') < 0$ if and only if there exist $v, v' \in VR_{(l_1,\dots,l_n)}$ with $f(v) > 0$ and $f(v') < 0$.*

4   Reachability Analysis of Multi-affine Systems

We now have all the necessary background to consider Problems 2 and 1 for a continuous system CS (Definition 1) , whose continuous state space is a closed rectangle in $\mathbb{R}^n$ defined by $a = (a_1,\dots,a_n) \in \mathbb{R}^n$ and $b = (b_1,\dots,b_n) \in \mathbb{R}^n$, $a_i < b_i$ for all $i = 1,\dots,n$:

$$X = \{x = (x_1,\dots,x_n) \in \mathbb{R}^n \,|\, a_i \leq x_i \leq b_i, \ i = 1,\dots,n\}, \tag{14}$$

and whose vector field f is multi-affine as in Definition 4 (with $p = n$).

We first define a partition of X into open rectangles, which gives the states of the discrete quotient DS (Definition 2). We then define the transitions of DS and a refinement procedure according to Definition 3. Finally, we collect all the results in an iterative algorithm for safety verification of multi-affine systems. Due to the space constraints, we give just some informal explanations of the involved algorithms, and we refer to [22] for pseudocodes.

4.1   The States of the Discrete Quotient

We assume that each axis Ox_i, $i = 1,\dots,n$ is divided into $n_i \geq 1$ intervals by the points $\theta_0^i < \theta_1^i < \dots < \theta_{n_i}^i$. This induces a partition of X into $\prod_{i=1}^n(2n_i+1)$

open rectangles. Using the same idea as in Section 3, we label the rectangles with n - uples $(l_1, \ldots, l_n)$ by defining an abstraction map as follows:

$$abs(x_1, \ldots, x_n) = (l_1, \ldots, l_n) \tag{15}$$

where, for each $i = 1, \ldots, n$ and $j_i = 0, 1, \ldots, n_i$,

$$l_i = 2j_i, \text{ if } x_i = \theta^i_{j_i} \quad , \quad l_i = 2j_i - 1, \text{ if } \theta^i_{j_i - 1} < x_i < \theta^i_{j_i} \tag{16}$$

Remark 2. The connection with the work in [13] can be seen as follows: the polynomials $x_i - \theta^i_{j_i}$, $j_i = 0, \ldots, n_i$, $i = 1, \ldots, n$ define a set of discrete variables, which generate the set L when interpreted over the set of symbols $\{pos, neg, zero\}$ (with the obvious significance). In this representation, each discrete state $l \in L$ is a word of length $\sum_{i=1}^{n} n_i + n$ over the set $\{pos, neg, zero\}$, and the cardinality of L becomes $|L| = 3^{\sum_{i=1}^{n} n_i + n}$. However, in our definition (15), $|L| = \prod_{i=1}^{n}(2n_i + 1)$. The dramatic reduction in the number of discrete states comes form the fact that, in the rectangular partition, infeasible combinations of polynomial interpretations are automatically eliminated.

As defined in Section 3, the number m of odd entries in $l = (l_1, \ldots, l_n)$ is the order of the rectangle. Moreover, $con(l)$ is an open m - rectangle in X. From now on, when we refer to rectangles we mean open rectangles. If all l_i's are odd, then $con(l)$ is a (full dimensional) n - order rectangle and if all l_i's are even, then $con(l)$ is a point (vertex), or 0 - order rectangle. Inspired by this observation, we define the *order* of a discrete state l as the number of its odd entries.

4.2   The Transitions of the Discrete Quotient

Before we start constructing the set T of transitions from all discrete states $l \in L$, note that, because of the rectangular partition, it is easy to identify a subset of L where transitions are possible, so we don't have to explore the whole L in search for successors. Let

$$\mathcal{H}(l) = \{l' = (l'_1, \ldots, l'_n) \in L \,|\, l' \neq l \,\wedge$$
$$l'_i = l_i \text{ if } l_i \text{ odd } \wedge l'_i \in \{l_i - 1, l_i, l_i + 1\} \text{ if } l_i \text{ even}\} \tag{17}$$

$$\mathcal{L}(l) = \{l' = (l'_1, \ldots, l'_n) \in L \,|\, l' \neq l \,\wedge$$
$$l'_i = l_i \text{ if } l_i \text{ even } \wedge l'_i \in \{l_i - 1, l_i, l_i + 1\} \text{ if } l_i \text{ odd}\} \tag{18}$$

Note that, if l is an m - order discrete state, then all the discrete states in $\mathcal{H}(l)$ are of order strictly greater than m and all the discrete states in $\mathcal{L}(l)$ are of order strictly less than m. For a m - order discrete state $l = (l_1, \ldots, l_n)$, $1 \leq l_i \leq 2n_i - 1$, the cardinality of $\mathcal{H}(l)$ and $\mathcal{L}(l)$ are $3^{n-m} - 1$ and $3^m - 1$, respectively. Given $l \in L$, it is only possible to have discrete transitions towards discrete states in $\mathcal{H}(l) \cup \mathcal{L}(l)$. For a state l with order $m \geq 1$, let $\mathcal{V}(l)$ denote the set of labels of vertices of $con(l)$. Formally,

$$\mathcal{V}(l) = \{l' = (l'_1, \ldots, l'_n) \in L \,|\, l' \neq l \,\wedge$$
$$l'_i = l_i \text{ if } l_i \text{ even } \wedge l'_i \in \{l_i - 1, l_i + 1\} \text{ if } l_i \text{ odd}\} \tag{19}$$

Before adding discrete transitions to complete the discrete system DS, we assign a *signature* to each discrete state $l \in L$.

Definition 5 (Signature of a discrete state). *For a discrete location $l = (l_1, \ldots, l_n) \in L$, the signature $s(l) = (s_1(l), \ldots, s_n(l))$ is a n-uple over the four-valued domain $\{po, ne, ze, in\}$ (i.e., positive, negative, zero, indefinite) with the following significance, for all $i = 1, \ldots, n$:*

- *$s_i(l) = po$, if $f_i(x) > 0$, $\forall x \in con(l)$*
- *$s_i(l) = ne$, if $f_i(x) < 0$, $\forall x \in con(l)$*
- *$s_i(l) = ze$, if $f_i(x) = 0$, $\forall x \in con(l)$*
- *$s_i(l) = in$, if $\exists x \in con(l)$ so that $f_i(x) > 0$ and $\exists x \in con(l)$ so that $f_i(x) < 0$*

where $f = (f_1, \ldots, f_n)$ is the vector field of CS.

The first and second cases correspond to the situation when $con(l)$ has an empty intersection with $f_i(x) = 0$. In the third case, $con(l)$ coincides with $f_i(x) = 0$ or $f_i(x) = 0$ contains $con(l)$. In the fourth, there is an intersection between $con(l)$ and $f_i(x) = 0$. The four cases from Definition 5 cover all possible choices for vector field f of CS.

Determining the signatures for 0 - order discrete states, *i.e.*, $l = (l_1, \ldots, l_n) \in L$ with all l_i even, is easy, because $con(l)$ is a point in X and determining the signatures reduces to evaluating the vector field f at $con(l)$ and determining its sign. Note that the symbol in in the signature of such a discrete state cannot appear. Based on Corollary 1, the signature $s_i(l)$ of an m - order discrete state $l = (l_1, \ldots, l_n)$, $m \geq 1$, is determined by checking what different symbols appear in each of the sets $\{s_i(l') \mid l' \in \mathcal{V}(l)\}$, $i = 1, \ldots, n$ [22].

We give here an informal and intuitive description of the algorithm from [22] for finding transitions of DS. For every state $l = (l_1, \ldots, l_n) \in L$, a set L' is created, such that $l \times L'$ contains transitions of DS starting from l, in accordance with Definition 2.

In order to easily describe the transitions from a state with signature entries in the set $\{po, ne, ze\}$, we introduce a map from these symbols to numbers: $eval : \{po, ne, ze\} \rightarrow \{+1, -1, 0\}$, $eval(po) = +1$, $eval(ne) = -1$, $eval(ze) = 0$. Each direction i, $i = 1, \ldots, n$ is considered separately and a set L_i containing all sub-labels l_i' of states l' in which l transits is constructed. The main idea in finding elements of set L_i is to decide the value of l_i' based only on the value of $s_i(l)$. Roughly speaking, if $s_i(l) \in \{po, ne, ze\}$, (*i.e.*, $f_i(x)$ has a well defined sign everywhere in $con(l)$ according to Definition 5), then $l_i' = l_i + eval(s_i(l))$. In this case, the added transitions correspond to Definition 2 in which the 'if' statement from Eqn. (4) is replaced by 'if and only if'. It is interesting to note here that our algorithm properly deals with situations in which, judged by the signature $s(l)$ of l, transitions to higher order neighbors l' are suggested, while in reality it is possible that $f(x)$ points towards $con(l')$ everywhere on $con(l)$, while the trajectories of CS only become tangent to $con(l')$ everywhere on $con(l)$ and flow to a even higher order neighbor. Each situation of this kind is signaled by a flag, some preliminary sets L_i, $i = 1, \ldots, n$ are constructed and later they are modified in a fixpoint manner.

If $s_i(l) = in$, then by Definition 5, in general there might exist points in $con(l)$ flowing to all neighbors in direction i, and therefore we let l_i' be any of $\{l_i - 1, l_i, l_i + 1\}$. In this case, it is possible that we add transitions in DS that do not correspond to trajectories of CS, *i.e.,* Eqn. (4) is satisfied in general with 'if'. However, this source of conservativeness is eliminated through refinement as described below.

After finding all sets L_i, since l can have transitions to its neighbors only, set L' is found by intersecting the cartesian product of sets L_i, $i = 1, \ldots, n$ with the set of neighbors of l.

4.3   Refinement

For a given partition $con(L)$ in which all entries $s_i(l)$, $i = 1, \ldots, n$, in the signatures $s(l)$ of all states $l \in L$ are in the set $\{po, ne, ze\}$, $con(Post(I))$ cannot be shrunk by finer partitioning, for any $I \subset L$. Therefore it does not make sense to partition such quotients.

On the contrary, if for a given partition $con(L)$ there exists a state $l \in L$ and a signature entry $s_i(l) = in$, we can show that proper partitioning produces a discrete quotient $\overline{DS} = (\bar{L}, \bar{T})$ that refines $DS = (L, T)$ in the sense of Definition 3. Therefore, "smaller" over-approximations of the reach set can be constructed (guaranteed strictly smaller if (iii)' in Proposition 1 holds). We give here the main ideas that lead to conclusion that Definition 3 is satisfied.

Rectangles of order 0 (vertices) always have well-defined signature entries $s_i(l)$ in all directions $i = 1, \ldots, n$. A rectangle l of order 1 from DS has indefinite signature entry $s_i(l)$ if $con(l)$ intersects the surface defined by $f_i(x) = 0$ in X. Let l_j be the only odd entry in l. Since f is multi-affine and $con(l)$ is parallel with axis Ox_j, the intersection is a point whose coordinates can be easily computed by solving a linear equation with respect to x_j. Let the solution be denoted by $\tilde{x}_j$. By splitting the current partition DS with respect to the hyperplane $x_j = \tilde{x}_j$, we obtain a new partition $\overline{DS}$. In this partition there are three states refining state l from the previous partition. All these states have well defined signature entry of index i, and by applying the transition algorithm described in Section 4.2 to these states, their discrete transitions will exactly correspond to continuous trajectories in direction i.

A finer quotient $\overline{DS}$ of DS can be found by using a refinement algorithm inspired by the above idea and available in [22]. The algorithm computes all possible intersections in X between all surfaces $f_i = 0$, $i = 1, \ldots, n$ and all $con(l)$, where l is a state of order 1 in DS. Rectangles with order greater than 1 are not split if they have an indefinite signature on a certain direction and all their neighbors of order 1 have well defined signatures on the same direction. From the tests we performed, we observed that if X contains no common points of any two surfaces $f_i = 0$ and $f_j = 0$, $i, j = 1, \ldots, n$, $i \neq j$, then, after a finite number of iterations, the refinement algorithm will not produce new points. In this case, all surfaces $f_i = 0$, $i = 1, \ldots, n$ will eventually have non-empty intersections only with some rectangles of order 0 and of order greater than 1.

4.4   Safety Verification Algorithm

We collect all the results in this paper in the form of an iterative algorithm, detailed in [22], for providing a solution to Problem 2. This safety verification algorithm starts with an initial rectangular partition determined by the sets I and F. A discrete quotient DS is constructed as described in Sections 4.1 and 4.2 and Post(I) is calculated using standard techniques from graph theory. If Post(I)$\bigcap F = \emptyset$, then assertion (2) is true, i.e., $con(F)$ cannot be reached by the continuous system initialized in $con(I)$. If Post(I)$\bigcap F \neq \emptyset$, then refinement is undertaken as described in Section 4.3. The algorithm is stopped if any of the following occurs: the safety property is satisfied, the refinement is finished, a partitioning precision is reached, or a user defined maximum number of iterations is exceeded. Otherwise, the algorithm iterates by using the finer quotient of DS. When the algorithm is stopped and the safety property is not verified, it returns a sub-region $con(S_F)$ of $con(F)$ which is safe for CS if initialized in $con(I)$. If only an over-approximation of the solution to Problem 1 is desired, then the safety verification algorithm can be run with $F = L$ ($con(F) = X$), where the initial partition L is induced by I only.

On the connection between the solutions to Problems 1 and 2, note that, even if the over-approximation of $con($Post(I)$)$ is guaranteed to strictly shrink, this does not necessarily imply that the safe sub-region $con(S_F)$ of $con(F)$ strictly grows. It is guaranteed not to shrink, but it might not grow if the refinement is made in a region of X which has empty intersection with $con(F)$ and/or the rectangles which are refined are not contained in a path from I to F in DS.

5   Case Studies

We have developed a user-friendly software package for Reachability Analysis of Multi-Affine Systems (RAMAS) in Matlab [24]. The program takes as inputs the dimension n, the closed rectangle X, the coefficients $c_{i_1,...,i_n}$ of a multi-affine vector field f as in Eqn. (11), and the sets $con(I)$ and $con(F)$ given in terms of unions of open sub-rectangles of arbitrary order in X. According to algorithm described in Section 4.4, it returns either a positive answer if there are no trajectories of the continuous system from $con(I)$ and $con(F)$, or a subset of $con(F)$ which is guaranteed to be safe with respect to $con(I)$. Even though our tries show that the algorithm works even for $n = 10$, in this paper we focus on a planar case ($n = 2$) so we can show illustrative pictures.

We first consider a nonlinear multi-affine vector field (Case Study 1). We then focus on a linear systems (i.e., $\dot{x} = Ax$) (Case Study 2), which is of course a particular case of multi-affine systems. The qualitative phase portraits for such planar linear systems are known, and reachability properties are almost intuitive. Applying our method to such systems gives us some idea on the conservativeness of our approach, as detailed in [22].

Case Study 1 (nonlinear multi-affine system). Consider $X = [1.5, 3] \times [0.4, 2]$, $f = (f_1, f_2)$ with $f_1 = 2 - x_1x_2$, and $f_2 = 1 + x_2 - x_1x_2$. The initial set is $con(I) = [1.5, 2.5] \times \{0.4\}$, which can be written as the union of two zero-order open rectangles $\{1.5, 0.4\}$, $\{2.5, 0.4\}$ and one first-order open rectangle $(1.5, 2.5) \times 0.4$. The final set is $con(F) = [1.5, 3] \times [0.8, 1.4]$, which in the initial partition can be seen as the union of 6 zero-order open rectangles, 7 first-order

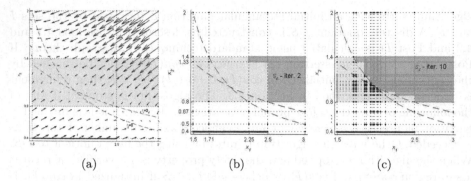

(a)   (b)   (c)

Fig. 2. Case Study 1: (a) Multi-affine vector field f, initial set $con(I)$ (blue - almost black on black and white printers), final set $con(F)$ (yellow - light grey), and initial partition induced by initial and final sets. (b,c) Iterations 2 and 10 from safety verification algorithm. The growing green (dark grey) area represents the safe sub-region $con(S_F)$ of $con(F)$.

open rectangles, and 2 second-order open rectangles. In Fig. 2(a), we plot the vector field f everywhere in X and the two curves $f_1 = 0$ and $f_2 = 0$. Note that the two curves intersect inside $con(F)$, and the refinement procedure will not terminate. At each iteration, the algorithm will produce strictly shrinking over-approximations of $\text{Post}(con(I))$ in X, which lead to strictly growing safe sub-regions in $con(F)$, as depicted by Fig. 2(b,c).

Case Study 2 (linear system). Consider the rectangular region $X = [-3, 4] \times [-3, 2]$ and the planar linear vector field $f_1 = 0.5x_1 + 1.5x_2$, $f_2 = 1.5x_1 + 0.5x_2$, for which the origin is an unstable node (saddle). The vector field is plotted in Fig. 3(a), together with the initial set $con(I) = [-1, 3] \times \{-2\}$ and the two

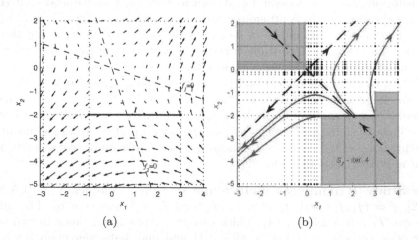

(a)   (b)

Fig. 3. Case Study 2: (a) Vector field f, lines $f_1 = 0$ and $f_2 = 0$, and initial set (b) Safe region (green - dark grey) obtained in 4 iterations by the reachability algorithm

lines $f_1 = 0$ and $f_2 = 0$, which intersect at the origin. The over-approximation of $Post(con(I))$ calculated in 4 iterations by our method is shown as the white region in Fig. 3(b), together with the eigenvectors and some illustrative trajectories. Note that the refinement does not terminate, but the result does not change significantly with the number of iterations.

6   Conclusion and Future Work

In this paper, we developed a computationally inexpensive method for reachability analysis of multi-affine continuous systems. The method is based on rectangular partitions and iterative constructions of discrete quotients which provide an over-approximation of the reach set of the continuous system, with guaranteed decrease of conservativeness. While falling into the more general framework of [13], where general polynomials are used for partition and polynomial vector fields are allowed, this paper shows that if more structure is allowed, then reachabiltity and safety verification questions can be answered with much less computation. Future work includes development of algorithms to check specifications given in terms of linear temporal logic and and applications to mathematical models found in areas such as biochemistry and control of aircraft and under-water vehicles.

Acknowledgements. This work is partially supported by NSF CAREER 0447721 and NSF 0410514. The second author wishes to thank Luc C.G.J.M. Habets for useful discussions on this topic.

References

1. R. Milner, *Communication and Concurrency*. Prentice Hall, 1989.
2. G. J. Pappas, "Bisimilar linear systems," *Automatica*, vol. 39, no. 12, pp. 2035–2047, 2003.
3. E. Haghverdi, P. Tabuada, and G. Pappas, *Bisimulation relations for dynamical and control systems*, ser. Electronic Notes in Theoretical Computer Science, Blute and e. Peter Selinger, Eds. Elsevier, 2003, vol. 69.
4. T. A. Henzinger, P. W. Kopke, A. Puri, and P. Varaiya, "What is decidable about hybrid automata?" *J. Comput. Syst. Sci.*, vol. 57, pp. 94–124, 1998.
5. R. Alur and D. L. Dill, "A theory of timed automata," *Theoret. Comput. Sci.*, vol. 126, pp. 183–235, 1994.
6. R. Alur, C. Courcoubetis, T. A. Henzinger, and P. H. Ho, "Hybrid automata: An algorithmic approach to the specification and verification of hybrid systems," in *Lecture Notes in Computer Science*. New York: Springer-Verlag, 1993, vol. 736, pp. 209–229.
7. X. Nicolin, A. Olivero, J. Sifakis, and S. Yovine, "An approach to the description and analysis of hybrid automata," in *Lecture Notes in Computer Science*. New York: Springer-Verlag, 1993, vol. 736, pp. 149–178.
8. A. Puri and P. Varaiya, "Decidability of hybrid systems with rectangular differential inclusions," *Computer Aided Verification*, pp. 95–104, 1994.

9. G. Lafferriere, G. J. Pappas, and S. Sastry, "O-minimal hybrid systems," *Math. Control, Signals, Syst*, vol. 13, no. 1, pp. 1–21, 2000.
10. G. Lafferriere, G. J. Pappas, and S. Yovine, "A new class of decidable hybrid systems," in *Lecture Notes in Computer Science*. New York: Springer-Verlag, 1999, vol. 1569, pp. 137–151.
11. ——, "Reachability computation for linear hybrid systems," in *Proc. 14th IFAC World Congress*, Beijing, P.R.C, July 1999.
12. R. Alur, T. Dang, and F. Ivancic, "Reachability analysis of hybrid systems via predicate abstraction," in *Fifth International Workshop on Hybrid Systems: Computation and Control*, Stanford, CA, 2002.
13. A. Tiwari and G. Khanna, "Series of abstractions for hybrid automata," in *Fifth International Workshop on Hybrid Systems: Computation and Control*, Stanford, CA, 2002.
14. R. Ghosh, A. Tiwari, and C. Tomlin, "Automated symbolic reachability analysis; with application to delta-notch signaling automata," in *Lecture Notes in Computer Science*. New York: Springer-Verlag, 2003, vol. 2623, pp. 233–248.
15. L. Habets and J. van Schuppen, "A control problem for affine dynamical systems on a full-dimensional polytope," *Automatica*, vol. 40, pp. 21–35, 2004.
16. C. Belta and L. Habets, "Constructing decidable hybrid systems with velocity bounds," in *43rd IEEE Conference on Decision and Control*, Paradise Island, Bahamas, 2004.
17. C. Belta, V. Isler, and G. J. Pappas, "Discrete abstractions for robot planning and control in polygonal environments," *IEEE Trans. on Robotics*, vol. 21, no. 5, pp. 864–874, 2005.
18. C. Belta and L. Habets, "Control of a class of nonlinear systems on rectangles," *IEEE Transactions on Automatic Control*, 2005, to appear.
19. C. Belta, "On controlling aircraft and underwater vehicles," in *IEEE International Conference on Robotics and Automation*, New Orleans, LA, 2004.
20. V. Volterra, "Fluctuations in the abundance of a species considered mathematically," *Nature*, vol. 118, pp. 558–560, 1926.
21. A. Lotka, *Elements of physical biology*. New York: Dover Publications, Inc., 1925.
22. M. Kloetzer and C. Belta, "Reachability analysis of multi-affine systems," Boston University, Brookline, MA, Technical report CISE-2005-IR-0070, October 2005. [Online]. Available: http://www.bu.edu/systems/research/publications/2005/2005-IR-0070.pdf
23. P. Tabuada and G. Pappas, "Model checking LTL over controlable linear systems is decidable," in *Hybrid Systems : Computation and Control*, ser. Lecture Notes in Computer Science. Springer Verlag, 2003, vol. 2623.
24. M. Kloetzer and C. Belta, "Reachability analysis of multi-affine systems (ramas)," URL http://iasi.bu.edu/~software/reach-ma.htm.

Approximation, Sampling and Voting in Hybrid Computing Systems[*]

Chiheb Kossentini[1] and Paul Caspi[2]

[1] Airbus
chiheb.kossentini@airbus.com
[2] Verimag (CNRS)
caspi@imag.fr

Abstract. This paper addresses the question of extending the usual approximation and sampling theory of continuous signals and systems to those encompassing discontinuities, such as found in modern distributed control systems. We provide a topological framework dealing with continuous, discrete and mixed systems in a uniform manner. We show how this theoretical framework can be used for voting on hybrid signals in critical real-time systems.

1 Introduction

Though the theory of distributed fault-tolerant systems advocates the use of clock synchronization [16, 11], still many critical real-time systems are based on the GALS (globally asynchronous, locally synchronous), and more precisely the "Quasi-Synchronous" [6] paradigm: in this framework, each computer is time-triggered but the clocks associated with each computer are not synchronized and communication is based on periodic sampling: each computer has its own clock and periodically samples its environment, *i.e.*, the physical environment but, also, the activities of the other computers with which it communicates. When such an architecture is used in critical systems, there is a need for a thorough formalization of fault tolerance in this framework. In a previous paper [7] we already formalized the concepts of threshold and delay voters. However there was in this paper some lack of symmetry between the two concepts: sampling continuous signals and threshold voting were very simply based on topological notions like uniform continuity and L_∞ norm. On the contrary, sampling discrete event signals and associated delay voting were based on more *ad-hoc* notions.

Later [5], we found that the use of the Skorokhod distance [3] was a way to overcome this lack of symmetry. More precisely, we showed that the discrete signals that could be sampled were those that were uniformly continuous with respect to this distance. This opened the way toward a generalization to hybrid (mixed continuous-discrete) signals. Moreover, we remarked that our previous study on voters was incomplete: in practice, it appears that people do not only use threshold voters and delay voters but also, and mainly, mixed threshold and delay voters. In these voters, a failure is detected if two signals differ for more than a given threshold during more than a given delay. But, when

---

[*] This work has been supported by the European Network of Excellence Artist and by the Airbus-Verimag CIFRE grant 2003-2006.

we tried to relate those two issues [12] we found unexpected difficulties linked to the fact that the Skorokhod topology is too fine and distinguishes too many systems. It should be noted that this would be also the case for another topology which has also been proposed for robust hybrid systems [9].

In this paper, we propose a simpler topology which seems to better meet our needs in that it:

- generalizes the L_∞ norm to non continuous signals and systems;
- allows us to uniformly handle errors and bounded delays;
- provides a setting where samplable signals are those uniformly continuous with respect to this topology, and where asymptotically stable systems and combinational boolean systems are uniformly continuous systems;
- provides a foundation to mixed error and delay voters.

More precisely, we show that if two signals are within a given neighborhood and if both of them are uniformly continuous with respect to that topology, then we can design a 2x2 hybrid voter which will not raise an alarm as long as these conditions are fulfilled. In practice, this result allows us to finely tune the voter parameters as a function of the nominal (non-faulty) errors and delays resulting from:

- the numerical and delay analysis of sensors,
- the algorithms used for computing outputs[1]
- and the architecture of communication between computing locations.

The paper is organized as follows: in a second section, we provide basic definitions. Section 3 addresses the classical theory of sampling continuous signals and systems. Section 4 recalls basic voting schemes and presents the mixed (hybrid) voter. In Section 5, we define our topology and prove the paper main result on the property of signals and systems which are uniformly continuous with respect to that topology. Finally, section 6 applies this result to hybrid voters and to mixed error and delay analysis of combinational systems.

1.1   Related Works

Several approaches seem to have been followed for addressing the question:

- The topological approach initiated by Nerode [17, 4] explicitly introduces the approximation and then tries to characterise it as a continuous mapping. This leads to equip the approximation space with an *ad-hoc* (small) topology.
- The equivalence or property preserving approaches followed for instance in [15, 1, 8, 10] tries to construct an approximation of a given system and to check whether it is equivalent to or preserves some properties of the original system expressed in some logic.
- Finally, M. Broucke [14] mixes the two approaches and uses the Skorokhod distance in order to define an approximate bisimulation between several classes of hybrid systems. In this sense, her work is quite close from ours. However, the motivations are slightly different: it doesn't seem that uniformity is addressed and that a result similar to proposition 6.1 is obtained.

---

[1] We can remark that this kind of method allows the use of diverse programming [2] which is one of the ways for tolerating design and software faults.

2 Basic Definitions

2.1 Signals and Systems

We consider systems that have to operate continuously for a long time, for instance a nuclear plant control that is in operation for weeks or an aircraft control that flies for several hours. Thus, the horizon of our signals is not bounded. Hence, a *signal x* is for us simply a piece-wise continuous function from $\mathbb{R}$ to $\mathbb{R}$, that is to say, a function which is continuous but on a finite or diverging sequence of times $\{t_0, \ldots t_n, \ldots\}$. This means, in particular, that left and right limits exist at each point in time. Furthermore, we assume that discontinuities are only of the first kind, such that the value at a given time is always within the interval made of left and right limits:

For all t,

$$x(t) \in [\inf(x(t^-), x(t^+)), \sup(x(t^-), x(t^+))]$$

where, as usual, $x(t^-), (x(t^+))$ is the left (right) limit of x at t.

Finally, we assume that the signal remains constant before the first discontinuity time t_0.

Concerning boolean signals, the fact that the sequence of discontinuity points diverges does not prevent there being two consecutive discontinuity points arbitrarily close together. This is why, in many cases we may need a stronger restriction:

Definition 1. *A boolean signal x has uniform bounded variability (UBV) if the interval between two consecutive discontinuities is lower bounded, i.e., there exists a positive (stable time) T_x between any two successive discontinuities of x.*

A *system* is simply a function S causally transforming signals, that is to say, such that $S(x)(t)$ is only function of $x(t'), t' < t$.

The *delay operator* Δ^τ is such that $(\Delta^\tau x)(t) = x(t-\tau)$, and a system is *stationary* (or time invariant) if $\forall \tau, S(\Delta^\tau x) = \Delta^\tau(S x)$.

An even more restricted class of systems is the class of *static or combinational* systems, that is to say, systems that are the "unfolding" of a scalar function:

$$S_f(x)(t) = f(x(t))$$

3 A Sampling Theory for Continuous Signals and Systems [12]

3.1 Uniformly Continuous Signals

A signal x is *uniformly continuous (UC)* (figure 1) if there exists a positive function[2] η_x from errors to delays, such that:

$$\forall \epsilon > 0, \forall t, t', |t - t'| \leq \eta_x(\epsilon) \Rightarrow |x(t) - x(t')| \leq \epsilon$$

---

[2] A Skolemisation of the usual textbook definition $\forall \epsilon \exists \eta$: there exists therefore a function providing η, given ϵ.

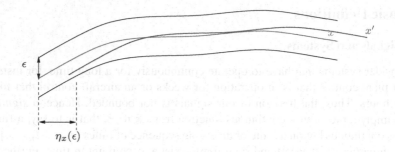

Fig. 1. A uniformly continuous signal

Such a definition can be rephrased in a functional way by introducing the $|| \ ||_\infty$ norm on signals, *i.e.,* for our piece-wise continuous signals with only first kind discontinuities: $||x||_\infty = \sup_t |x(t)|$.

Then, a signal x is uniformly continuous if there exists a positive function η_x from errors to delays, such that:

$$\forall \epsilon > 0, \forall \tau, |\tau| \leq \eta_x(\epsilon) \Rightarrow ||x - \Delta^\tau x||_\infty \leq \epsilon$$

3.2 Retiming and Sampling

A *retiming* function r is a non decreasing function from $\mathbb{R}$ to $\mathbb{R}$. Let Ret be the set of such functions. This is a very general definition which provides many possibilities. For instance, a piece-wise constant retiming function can be seen as a sampler: if $x' = x \circ r$, and if r is piece-wise constant, then, at each jump of r, a new value of x is taken and maintained up to the next jump. This allows us to define a periodic sampler r, of period T_r as the piece-wise constant function (see figure 2):

$$r(t) = \lfloor t/T_r \rfloor T_r$$

where $\lfloor \ \rfloor$ is the floor function.

Finally, retimings allow us to characterize static (or combinational) systems as those systems which commute with retiming:

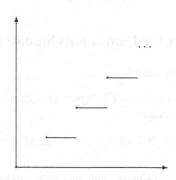

Fig. 2. A periodic sampling retiming

Proposition 3.1 (Static systems). *A static system S is such that, for any $r \in Ret$,*

$$S \circ r = r \circ S$$

3.3 Sampling

Retiming allows us to restate the uniformly continuous signal definition, by saying that a signal x is uniformly continuous if there exists a positive function η_x from errors to delays, such that:

$$\forall \epsilon > 0, \forall\, retiming\ r, ||r - id||_\infty \leq \eta_x(\epsilon) \Rightarrow ||x - x \circ r||_\infty \leq \epsilon$$

where id is the identity function (neutral retiming).

We can then define a *samplable* signal as a signal such that the sampling error can be controlled by tuning the sampling period:

Definition 2 (Samplable Signal). *A signal x is samplable if there exists a positive function η_x from errors to sampling periods, such that:*

$$\forall \epsilon > 0, \forall\, periodic\ sampling\ r, T_r \leq \eta_x(\epsilon) \Rightarrow ||x - x \circ r||_\infty \leq \epsilon$$

Then the following property obviously holds:

Proposition 3.2. *A signal is samplable if and only if it is uniformly continuous.*

3.4 From Signals to Systems

This framework extends quite straightforwardly to systems by saying that a system S is uniformly continuous (figure 3) if there exists a positive function η_S from errors to errors such that:

$$\forall \epsilon > 0, \forall x, x', ||x - x'||_\infty \leq \eta_S(\epsilon) \Rightarrow ||(S\ x) - (S\ x')||_\infty \leq \epsilon$$

and state the following proposition:

Proposition 3.3. *A uniformly continuous stationary system, fed with a uniformly continuous signal outputs a uniformly continuous signal.*

The proof is straightforward and can be found in [5, 13]. This property says that given an acyclic network of UC systems, one can compute maximum delays on system interconnection, sampling periods and maximum errors on input signals such that errors on output signals be lower than given bounds. This provides us thus with a nice approximation theory.

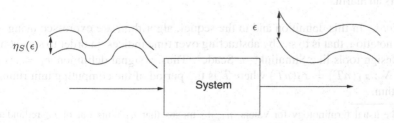

Fig. 3. A uniformly continuous system

4 Hybrid Voting

In this section we recall the classical threshold and delay voting schemes. Then we propose a 2/2 hybrid voter[3] which is a mixture of these two aspects.

4.1 Threshold Voting

Threshold voting is a classical voting scheme. Assume that signals x, x' are redundantly computed signals. In theory, the two signals should be equal but, because they are not computed at the same time, in the same computer, from the same sensor values, and possibly by dissimilar algorithms, their values can be slightly different. The figure 4 shows a tolerance tube around the reference signal x. Whenever the signal x' remains within the tolerance tube, the voted value is the reference one. If the signal x' gets out the tube, an alarm is raised.

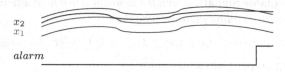

Fig. 4. Threshold voting

Knowing bounds on the normal deviation between values that should be equal, easily allows the design of threshold voters. For instance, if x is uniformly continuous and if

$$x' = x \circ r + e$$

with

- $||r - id||_\infty \leq \eta_x(\epsilon)$
- $||e||_\infty \leq \epsilon$

we can find a threshold $\epsilon' = 2\epsilon$ and design a 2/2-voter:

$$voter2/2(x, x', \epsilon') = \text{if } |x - x'| \leq \epsilon'$$
$$\text{then } x$$
$$\text{else } alarm$$

such that the voter delivers a correct output in the absence of failure and, otherwise, delivers an alarm.

Notations: In this definition and in the sequel, algorithms are expressed using a functional notation, that is to say by abstracting over time indices, in order to stay consistent with design tools like Simulink[4] or Scade[5]. Thus, a signal definition $x_1 = x_2$ means $\forall n \in N : x_1(nT) = x_2(nT)$ where T is the period of the computing unit running the algorithm.

---

[3] In the usual terminology for voters, n_1/n_2 means that n_1 units out of n_2 redundant ones should operate correctly in order that the redundant system operates correctly.

[4] http://www.mathworks.com

[5] http://www.esterel-technologies.com

4.2   Delay Voting

Delay voting is the discontinuous equivalent to the threshold one. The figure 5 shows this scheme principle. Whenever the two signals are equal, the voted value is the common one. Else, the voter holds its output and waits for a new agreement during a predefined temporal window. If there is no agreement, an alarm is latched.

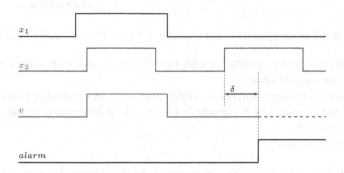

Fig. 5. Bounded delay voting

Let us consider boolean UBV signals x_1 and x_2 which is, in normal operation, a delayed image of x_1:

$$x_2 = x_1 \circ r$$

with a bound τ on the delay in correct operation:

$$||r - id||_\infty \leq \tau$$

There signals are received by some unit of period T. However, the assumption that correct computers have perfect clocks, is clearly not realistic. To be more realistic, one should consider clock drifts. A frequent assumption is that clock drifts are bounded, either because the mission time is bounded or extra mechanisms allow for detecting exceedingly large drifts. Then there exist lower (T_m) and upper (T_M) bounds for T and, in each condition involving T, it should be replaced by the bound which makes it more pessimistic. We thus assume $T_m \leq T \leq T_M$.

We also assume $\tau + T_M < T_x$ where T_x is the stable time of signal x (cf. definition 1). This assumption guarantees that the joint effect of the delay and the sampling at rate T (which can induce an additional delay) cannot lead to miss any change of input value (which, by assumption lasts at least T_x). Then,

- the maximum time interval during which the two signals may continuously disagree is obviously τ,
- the maximum number of samples where two correct copies continuously disagree is

$$nmax = \left\lfloor \frac{\tau}{T_m} \right\rfloor + 1$$

This allows us to design **delay voters** for delay booleans signals. For instance, a 2/2 voter could be:

Definition 3 (2/2 delay voter)

$$voter2/2(x_1, x_2, nmax) = x \text{ where } x, \quad n = \text{if } x_1 = x_2$$
$$\text{then } x_1, \quad 0$$
$$\text{else if } \Delta_0^T n < nmax - 1$$
$$\text{then } \Delta_{x_0}^T x, \quad \Delta_0^T n + 1$$
$$\text{else } alarm$$

where $\Delta_{x_0}^T$ is the *delay operator* such that $\Delta_{x_0}^T x(t) = x(t - \tau)$ with initial value x_0.

- this voter maintains a counter n with initial value 0, and its previous output, with some known initial value x_0,
- whenever the two inputs agree, it outputs one input and resets the counter,
- else, if the counter has not reached $nmax - 1$, it increments it and outputs the previous output,
- else it raises an alarm.

Proposition 4.1. *voter2/2 raises an alarm if the two inputs disagree for more than $nmaxT_M$ and otherwise delivers the correct value with maximum delay $(nmax + 1)T_M$.*

4.3   Hybrid Delay-Threshold Voting

Can we mix now the two previous voters, the threshold and the delay one? This would amount to define an hybrid voter that is illustrated at figure 6:

Definition 4 (2/2hybrid voter)

$$hyb\_voter2/2(x, x', nmax, \epsilon') = y \text{ where } y, \quad n = \text{if } |x - x'| \le \epsilon'$$
$$\text{then } x, \quad 0$$
$$\text{else if } \Delta_0^T n < nmax - 1$$
$$\text{then } \Delta_{x_0}^T y, \quad \Delta_0^T n + 1$$
$$\text{else } alarm$$

- this voter maintains a counter n with initial value 0, and its previous output, with some known initial value x_0,
- whenever the two inputs threshold-agree, it outputs one input and resets the counter,
- else, if the counter has not reached $nmax - 1$, it increments it and outputs the previous output,
- else it raises an alarm.

On which condition could we state the following desirable proposition?

Proposition 4.2 (Hybrid voter property). *hyb_voter2/2 raises an alarm if the two inputs differ for more than ϵ' during more than $nmaxT_M$ and otherwise delivers the correct value with maximum delay $(nmax + 1)T_M$.*

Answering this question is the object of the next section.

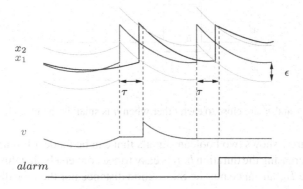

Fig. 6. Hybrid threshold-delay voting

5   A Hybrid Topology

The difficulties met with the Skorxokhod topology have led us to propose the following definition:

5.1   Topology Definition

Let us consider the following family of open balls centered at arbitrary signals x, with positive parameters T, ϵ:

$$B(x; T, \epsilon) = \{y \mid \sup_t \int_t^{t+T} \frac{|x-y|}{T} < \epsilon\}$$

Proposition 5.1. *This family defines a topology.*

Proof. It suffices to show that any point of a ball is the center of another ball which is a subset of the former.

Let $x' \in B(x; T, \epsilon)$. It yields:

$$\sup_t \int_t^{t+T} \frac{|x'-x|}{T} = d < \epsilon$$

Let us take

- $T' = T$
- $\epsilon' = (\epsilon - d)$

Let $x'' \in B(x'; T', \epsilon')$ and let us show that x'' belongs to $B(x; T, \epsilon)$: for any t,

$$\int_t^{t+T} |x'' - x| \leq \int_t^{t+T} |x'' - x'| + \int_t^{t+T} |x' - x|$$

$$\int_t^{t+T} |x'' - x| < \epsilon'T + dT = (\epsilon - d)T + dT = \epsilon T$$

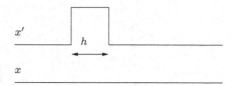

Fig. 7. x and x' are close to each other when h is small in the given topology

Example: Figure 7 shows two boolean signals that can be made arbitrarily close in this topology by decreasing the duration h. It is easy to see conversely that this is not the case, neither with the L_∞ distance nor the Skorokhod distance nor the tube distance of [9].

Closed Balls: Let us denote as $\bar{B}(x; T, \epsilon)$ the corresponding closed balls.

$$\bar{B}(x; T, \epsilon) = \{y \mid \sup_t \int_t^{t+T} \frac{|x - y|}{T} \leq \epsilon\}$$

5.2 Product Topology

When dealing with signal tuples, we consider product topologies. For instance, the topology associated with couples (x, x') will be defined by the balls:

$$B((x, x'); T, \epsilon, T', \epsilon') = B(x; T, \epsilon) \times B(x'; T', \epsilon')$$

In order to deal with these cases in a uniform way, we adopt the following convention: in a ball $B(x; T, \epsilon)$, x can be a n-tuple and T, ϵ two n-vector parameters $(T_1, T_2, \ldots T_n), (\epsilon_1, \epsilon_2, \ldots \epsilon_n)$.

5.3 Uniformly Continuous Signals

Definition 5. *A signal x is uniformly continuous with respect to the hybrid topology (UC_{ht}) if there exists a positive function $\eta_x(T, \epsilon)$ such that*

- *For all $\epsilon, T > 0$,*
- *For all r with $\sup_t |r(t) - t| \leq \eta_x(T, \epsilon)$*

$x \circ r$ belongs to $\bar{B}(x; T, \epsilon)$

Examples:

- Uniform bounded variability signals are UC_{ht}.
- Uniformly continuous signals in the usual sense are UC_{ht}.

5.4 Fundamental Property of UC_{ht} signals

Proposition 5.2. *Let x be a UC_{ht} signal, fix $T > 0$ and $\epsilon > 0$ and let*

$$n = \left\lceil \frac{T}{\inf\{T, \eta_x(T, \epsilon)\}} \right\rceil$$

Then, there exists in any interval of duration T, a sub-interval of duration $h = \frac{T}{n}$ such that, for any t, t' in this interval

$$|x(t) - x(t')| \leq 2\epsilon$$

Proof. Let us divide an arbitrary interval I of duration T into n equal sub-intervals $I_i, i = 1, n$ of duration h. Let:

- $x_i^M = \sup_{t \in I_i} x(t)$
- $x_i^m = \inf_{t \in I_i} x(t)$
- $e_i = x_i^M - x_i^m$

It is easy to design two retimings r^M et r^m such that :

- for all $t \in I_i$, $x \circ r^M(t) = x_i^M$ and $x \circ r^m(t) = x_i^m$

We have moreover for all r in $\{r^M, r^m\}$:

$$\sup_t |r(t) - t| \leq \eta_x(T, \epsilon)$$

Thus, for r in $\{r^M, r^m\}$:

$$\int_I \frac{|x - x \circ r|}{T} \leq \epsilon$$

By triangular inequality, we get:

$$\int_I \frac{|x \circ r^M - x \circ r^m|}{T} \leq 2\epsilon$$

Finally,

$$\sum_1^n \frac{h}{T} e_i \leq 2\epsilon$$

If all e_i were larger than 2ϵ, this would be also true for their mean value. Thus, at least one e_i is smaller than or equal to 2ϵ.

We clearly see now how our new topology generalizes the usual one concerning uniform continuity: In the usual definition, for any ϵ, we can find η such that, in any interval of duration η, the signal variation is smaller than or equal to ϵ. In our new framework, for any T, ϵ, we can find η such that, in any interval of duration T, there exists a sub-interval of duration η where the signal variation is smaller than or equal to ϵ. This is clearly a generalization and it is the price to be paid for tolerating the discontinuities inherent to discontinuous signals like booleans and for encompassing in the same framework continuous signals and boolean signals. Furthermore, having been able to encompass both classes of signals allows us to also deal with hybrid piece-wise continuous ones.

Moreover, we can show that this property is quite tight by considering the example of a boolean signal x with uniform bounded variability, *i.e.*, such that the interval between two discontinuities is larger than T.

It is easy to show, by taking a delay $r(t) = t - T\epsilon$, with $\epsilon < 1/2$, that

$$\eta_x(T, \epsilon) = T\epsilon$$

Now, in any interval of duration T, there truly exists an interval of duration $T\epsilon < T/2$ where the boolean signal remains constant and, thus,

$$x^M - x^m \leq 2\epsilon < 1$$

6   Applications

6.1 UC_{ht} Signals and Votes

We can now state this proposition which provides a positive answer to the question raised in 4.2:

Proposition 6.1. *If x and x' are UC_{ht} and*

$$x' \in \bar{B}(x; T, \epsilon)$$

then there exists some T' such that, in any interval of duration T, there exists a sub-interval of duration T' over which any t yields

$$|x(t) - x'(t)| \leq 3\epsilon$$

We omit here the proof which is very similar to the one of proposition 5.2 and can be found in [13]. Clearly this proposition provides a foundation to the use of mixed threshold and delay voters.

6.2 UC_{ht} Systems

This framework also allows us to provide elements of a sampling and approximation theory for hybrid systems.

Definition 6. *A system S is UC_{ht} if there exists a positive function $\eta_S(T, \epsilon)$ such that:*

- *for all $T, \epsilon > 0$,*
- *for all x, x' where x' belongs to $\bar{B}(x; \eta_S(T, \epsilon))$*

$S(x')$ belongs to $\bar{B}(S(x); T, \epsilon)$

Clearly,

Proposition 6.2. *Asymptotically stable linear time-invariant systems are UC_{ht}.*

The proof is simple and can be found in [13]. But we also have this very nice property:

Proposition 6.3. *Boolean combinational systems are UC_{ht}.*

Proof. Let us show the proof for a boolean function f with two inputs. It suffices to take:

$$\eta_f(T, \epsilon) = (T, T), (\epsilon/2, \epsilon/2)$$

Let us first remark that if $\epsilon \geq 1$ the property is obvious.

Let us assume $\epsilon < 1$ and $x_1' \in \bar{B}(x_1; T, \epsilon/2), x_2' \in \bar{B}(x_2; T, \epsilon/2)$. This amounts to saying that in any interval of duration T, x_1' differs from x_1 for some fraction of time $\epsilon/2 < 0.5$ and similarly for x_2, x_2'. It is then clear that the couple x_1', x_2' differs from couple x_1, x_2 for a fraction of time at most equal to ϵ. This is also the case for $f(x_1', x_2')$ and $f(x_1, x_2)$.

Noting that combinational functions commute with retiming, we can reuse the proof of 3.3 to state a similar property for networks of boolean functions:

Proposition 6.4. *A uniformly continuous combinational system, fed with a uniformly continuous signal outputs a uniformly continuous signal.*

This property says that given an acyclic network of UC_{ht} combinational systems, one can compute maximum delays on system interconnection, sampling periods and maximum errors on input signals such that errors on output signals, in the sense of our topology, be lower than given bounds. This provides us thus with a nice approximation theory which also nicely combines with voting, in that this "error calculus" allows voter parameters to be correctly set.

7 Conclusion

This paper has intended to provide a satisfactory theory for merging together threshold voters adapted to continuous signals and delay voters adapted to boolean signals in order to cope with hybrid piece-wise continuous signals. One problem in performing this merge was that, while threshold voters are based on uniform continuity, delay voters are based on a more *ad-hoc* notion of uniform bounded variability. After having previously tried the Skorokhod topology, we propose here a new topology for hybrid systems which seems to better match our purpose. In particular, it allows us to merge in a very uniform way the theory of threshold voters and the theory of delay voters and to build a theory of hybrid mixed threshold and delay voters.

Moreover, this voting problem is clearly related to the more general sampling problem for hybrid systems and the results provided here may also help in defining which classes of hybrid systems can be accurately sampled. This can be a subject for future work.

Identifying uniformly continuous signals and systems enables us to handle in a safe way reconfiguration issues by using finely tuned voting schemes. These schemes guarantee recovering the overall stability of switched hybrid systems. The "error calculus" introduced in this paper is a starting point for a further work closely linking uniform continuity to the more general field of robustness.

References

1. A.Chutinan and B.H.Krogh. Computing approximating automata for a class of hybrid systems. *Mathematical and Computer Modeling of Dynamical Systems*, 6:30–50, March 2000. Special Issue on Discrete Event Models of Continuous Systems.
2. A. Avizienis. The methodology of *n*-version programming. In M.R. Lyu, editor, *Software Fault Tolerance*, pages 23–46. John Wiley, 1995.
3. P. Billingsley. *Convergence of probability measures*. John Wiley & Sons, 1999.
4. M.S. Branicky. Topology of hybrid systems. In *32nd Conference on Decision and Control*, pages 2309–2311. IEEE, 1993.
5. P. Caspi and A. Benveniste. Toward an approximation theory for computerised control. In A. Sangiovanni-Vincentelli and J. Sifakis, editors, *2nd International Workshop on Embedded Software, EMSOFT02*, volume 2491 of *Lecture Notes in Computer Science*, 2002.
6. P. Caspi, C. Mazuet, R. Salem, and D. Weber. Formal design of distributed control systems with Lustre. In *Proc. Safecomp'99*, volume 1698 of *Lecture Notes in Computer Science*. Springer Verlag, September 1999.
7. P. Caspi and R. Salem. Threshold and bounded-delay voting in critical control systems. In Mathai Joseph, editor, *Formal Techniques in Real-Time and Fault-Tolerant Systems*, volume 1926 of *Lecture Notes in Computer Science*, pages 68–81, September 2000.
8. E.Asarin, O.Maler, and A.Pnueli. On discretization of delays in timed automata and digital circuits. In R.de Simone and D.Sangiorgi, editors, *Concur'98*, volume 1466 of *Lecture Notes in Computer Science*, pages 470–484. Springer, 1998.
9. V. Gupta, T.A. Henzinger, and R. Jagadeesan. Robust timed automata. In O. Maler, editor, *Hybrid and Real-Time Systems, HART'97*, volume 1201 of *Lecture Notes in Computer Science*, pages 331–345. Springer Verlag, 1997.
10. J.Ouaknine. Digitisation and full abstraction for dense-time model checking. In *TACAS 02*, volume 2280 of *Lecture Notes In Computer Science*, pages 37–51. Springer, 2002.
11. H. Kopetz. *Real-Time Systems Design Principles for Distributed Embedded Applications*. Kluwer, 1997.
12. Ch. Kossentini and P. Caspi. Mixed delay and threshold voters in critical real-time systems. In S. Yovine Y. Lakhnech, editor, *Formal Techniques in Real-Time and Fault-Tolerant Systems, FTRTFT04*, volume 3253 of *Lecture Notes in Computer Science*. Springer Verlag, 2004.
13. Ch. Kossentini and P. Caspi. Approximation, sampling and voting in hybrid computing systems. Research Report TR-2005-19, Verimag, December 2005. Available at http://www-verimag.imag.fr/TR/TR-2005-17.pdf.
14. M.Broucke. Regularity of solutions and homotopic equivalence for hybrid systems. In *Proceedings of the 37th IEEE Conference on Decision and Control*, volume 4, pages 4283–4288, 1998.
15. R.Alur, T.A.Henzinger, G.Lafferriere, and G.J.Pappas. Discrete abstractions of hybrid systems. *Proceedings of the IEEE*, 88:971–984, 2000.
16. J.H. Wensley, L. Lamport, J. Goldberg, M.W. Green, K.N. Lewitt, P.M. Melliar-Smith, R.E Shostak, and Ch.B. Weinstock. SIFT: Design and analysis of a fault-tolerant computer for aircraft control. *Proceedings of the IEEE*, 66(10):1240–1255, 1978.
17. W.Kohn and A.Nerode. Models for hybrid systems: automata, topologies, controllability and observability. In *Hybrid Systems*, volume 732 of *Lecture Notes in Computer Science*. Springer, 1993.

Computational Methods for Reachability Analysis of Stochastic Hybrid Systems

Xenofon Koutsoukos and Derek Riley

Institute for Software Integrated Systems,
Department of Electrical Engineering and Computer Science,
Vanderbilt University, Nashville, TN 37235, USA
{Xenofon.Koutsoukos, Derek.Riley}@vanderbilt.edu

Abstract. Stochastic hybrid system models can be used to analyze and design complex embedded systems that operate in the presence of uncertainty and variability. Verification of reachability properties for such systems is a critical problem. Developing algorithms for reachability analysis is challenging because of the interaction between the discrete and continuous stochastic dynamics. In this paper, we propose a probabilistic method for reachability analysis based on discrete approximations. The contribution of the paper is twofold. First, we show that reachability can be characterized as a viscosity solution of a system of coupled Hamilton-Jacobi-Bellman equations. Second, we present a numerical method for computing the solution based on discrete approximations and we show that this solution converges to the one for the original system as the discretization becomes finer. Finally, we illustrate the approach with a navigation benchmark that has been proposed for hybrid system verification.

1 Introduction

Stochastic hybrid system models can be used to analyze and design complex embedded systems that operate in the presence of uncertainty and variability because they incorporate complex dynamics, uncertainty, multiple modes of operations, and they can support high-level control specifications that are required for design of autonomous or semi-autonomous applications. Reachability analysis for such systems is a critical problem because of the interaction between the discrete and continuous stochastic dynamics. Reachability properties are usually expressed as formulas in appropriate logics. Given a specification formula encoding a property, the task is to determine whether the formal model of the system satisfies the property or generate a counterexample that violates the formula. In this paper, we proposed a probabilistic method for reachability analysis. Instead of encoding the reachability property with a logical formula that can be evaluated to be true or false, we consider a representation using measurable functions taking values in $[0, 1]$ that characterize the probability that the system will satisfy the property.

In this paper, we show that reachability for stochastic hybrid systems can be represented by a measurable function that is the viscosity solution of a system of coupled Hamilton-Jacobi-Bellman (HJB) equations. This function is similar to

João Hespanha and A. Tiwari (Eds.): HSCC 2006, LNCS 3927, pp. 377–391, 2006.
© Springer-Verlag Berlin Heidelberg 2006

the value function for the exit problem of a standard stochastic diffusion but the running and terminal costs depend on the function itself. Using a non-degeneracy assumption for the diffusion term of the stochastic dynamics, we show that the viscosity solution is continuous and bounded which allows us to extend standard results for Markov diffusions to stochastic hybrid systems.

One of the advantages of characterizing reachability properties using viscosity solutions is that for computational purposes we can employ numerical methods based on discrete approximations. We use an approximation method based on finite differences and we present an iterative algorithm based on dynamic programming for computing the solution. We show that the algorithm converges for appropriate initial conditions. Further, we show that the solution based on the discrete approximations converges to the one for the original stochastic hybrid system as the discretization becomes finer. Finally, we illustrate the approach with a navigation benchmark which has been proposed for hybrid system verification.

In this paper, we adopt the model presented in [3] which can be viewed as an extension of the stochastic hybrid systems described in [12]. An important characteristic of this model used in our analysis is that it satisfies the strong Markov property [3]. Related models have been presented in [11] with the emphasis on modeling and analysis of communication networks and in [1] for simulation of concurrent systems. Stochastic hybrid systems can be viewed as an extension of piecewise-deterministic processes [6] that incorporate stochastic continuous dynamics. Reachability of such systems has been studied in [4]. Communicating piecewise Markov processes have been presented in [20] with an emphasis on concurrency. Viscosity solution techniques in optimal control of piecewise deterministic processes have been studied in [7]. Our approach extends the results of [7] for reachability analysis of stochastic hybrid systems.

Reachability properties for continuous and hybrid systems have been characterized as viscosity solutions of variants of HJB equations in [16, 17]. Extensions of this approach to stochastic hybrid systems and a toolbox based on level set methods have been presented in [18]. Level set methods are also based on a discretization of the state space but they may offer computational advantages since the computation is limited to a boundary of the reachable set. The dynamic programming approach described in this paper is simpler to implement and capture the dependency of the value function between discrete modes. The approach allows us to show the convergence of solution obtained using the numerical solutions to the solution of the stochastic hybrid system.

Discrete approximation methods based on finite differences have been studied extensively in [15] and the references therein. Based on discrete approximations, the reachability problem can be solved using algorithms for discrete processes [19, 5, 8]. The approach has been applied for optimal control of stochastic hybrid systems given a discounted cost criterion in [14]. For reachability analysis, the discount term cannot be used and convergence of the value function can be ensured only for appropriate initial conditions. A grid-based method for safety analysis of stochastic systems with applications to air traffic management has been presented in [13]. Our approach is similar but using viscosity solutions we show the convergence of the discrete approximation methods.

The paper is organized as follows. Section 2 describes the stochastic hybrid system model. Section 3 formulates the reachability problem and characterizes its solution. Section 4 presents and analyzes the numerical methods based on discrete approximations. Section 5 illustrates the approach using a navigation benchmark and Section 6 concludes the paper.

2 Stochastic Hybrid Systems

We adopt the General Stochastic Hybrid System (GSHS) model presented in [3]. We briefly describe the model to establish the notation.

Let Q be a set of discrete states. For each $q \in Q$, we consider the Euclidean space $\mathbb{R}^{d(q)}$ with dimension $d(q)$ and we define an invariant as an open set $X^q \subseteq \mathbb{R}^{d(q)}$. The hybrid state space is denoted as $S = \bigcup_{q \in Q} \{q\} \times X^q$. Let $\bar{S} = S \cup \partial S$ and $\partial S = \bigcup_{q \in Q} \{q\} \times \partial X^q$ denote the completion and the boundary of S respectively. The Borel σ-field in S is denoted as $\mathcal{B}(S)$.

Definition 1. *A GSHS is defined as $H = ((Q, d, \mathcal{X}), b, \sigma, Init, \lambda, R)$ where*

- *Q is a set of discrete states,*
- *$d : Q \to \mathbb{N}$ is a map that defines the continuous state space dimension for each $q \in Q$,*
- *$\mathcal{X} : Q \to \mathbb{R}^{d(\cdot)}$ is a map that describes the invariant for each $q \in Q$ as an open set $X^q \subseteq \mathbb{R}^{d(q)}$,*
- *$b : Q \times X^q \to \mathbb{R}^{d(q)}$ and $\sigma : Q \times X^q \to \mathbb{R}^{d(q) \times p}$ are drift vectors and dispersion matrices respectively,*
- *$Init : \mathcal{B}(S) \to [0, 1]$ is an initial probability measure on S,*
- *$\lambda : \bar{S} \to \mathbb{R}_+$ is a nonnegative transition rate function, and*
- *$R : \bar{S} \times \mathcal{B}(\bar{S}) \to [0, 1]$ is a transition measure.*

To define the execution of the system, denote $(\Omega, \mathcal{F}, P)$ the underlying probability space and consider an $\mathbb{R}^p$-valued Wiener process $w(t)$ and a sequence of *stopping times* $\{t_0 = 0, t_1, t_2, \ldots\}$ that represent the times when the continuous and discrete dynamics interact. Let the state at time t_i be $s(t_i) = (q(t_i), x(t_i))$[1] with $x(t_i) \in X^{q(t_i)}$. While the continuous state stays in $X^{q(t_i)}$, $x(t)$ evolves according to the stochastic differential equation (SDE)

$$dx = b(q, x)dt + \sigma(q, x)dw \tag{1}$$

where the discrete state $q(t) = q(t_i)$ remains constant and the solution of (1) is understood using the Itô stochastic integral.

---

[1] When there is no confusion, we will use interchangeably the notation (q, x) and s for the hybrid state to simplify complex formulas and often we will use the notation $s_{t_i} = (q_{t_i}, x_{t_i})$ for brevity.

Let $t_{i+1}^* = \inf\{t \geq t_i, x(t) \in \partial X^{q(t_i)}\}$. The next stopping time t_{i+1} is defined as the minimum between t_{i+1}^* and a stopping time τ_{i+1} with survivor function $\exp\left(-\int_{t_i}^{t} \lambda(q(t_i), x_z(\omega)dz,\right)$, $\omega \in \Omega$. Thus, the survivor function of t_{i+1} can be written as

$$F(t, \omega) = I_{(t < t_{i+1}^*)} \exp\left(-\int_{t_i}^{t} \lambda(q(t_i), x_z(\omega))dz\right)$$

where I denotes the indicator function. If $t_{i+1} = \infty$, the system continues to evolve according to (1) with $q(t) = q(t_i)$. If $t_{i+1} < \infty$, the system jumps at t_{i+1} to a new state $s(t_{i+1}) = (q(t_{i+1}), x(t_{i+1}))$ according to the transition measure $R(s(t_{i+1}^-), A)$ with $A \in \mathcal{B}(S)$. The evolution of the system is then governed by (1) with $q(t) = q(t_{i+1})$ until the next stopping time.

The following assumptions are imposed on the model. The functions $b(q, x)$ and $\sigma(q, x)$ are bounded and Lipschitz continuous in x for every q, and thus the SDE (1) has a unique solution. The transition rate function λ is a bounded and measurable function which is assumed to be integrable for every $x_t(\omega)$. For the transition measure, it is assumed that $R(\cdot, A)$ is measurable for all $A \in \mathcal{B}(S)$, $R(s, \cdot)$ is a probability measure for all $s \in \bar{S}$, and $R((q, x), dz)$ is a stochastic continuous kernel.

Let $N_t = \sum_i I_{t \geq t_i}$ denote the number of jumps in the interval $[0, t]$. It is assumed that $E_s[N_t] < \infty$ for every initial state $s \in S$. Sufficient conditions for ensuring finitely many jumps can be formulated by imposing restrictions on the transition measure $R(s, A)$ [1].

Additionally, in this paper we consider the two following assumptions:

Assumption 1: Non-degeneracy. The boundaries ∂X^q are assumed to be sufficiently smooth and the trajectories of the system satisfy a non-tangency condition with respect to the boundaries. A sufficient condition for the non-tangency assumption is that the diffusion term is non-degenerate, i.e. $a(q, x) = \sigma(q, x)\sigma^T(q, x)$ is positive definite. This assumption is used to show the continuity of the viscosity solution close to the boundaries [10]. It should be noted that it is possible to show the continuity of the viscosity solution close to the boundaries even with degenerate variance by imposing appropriate conditions [10, 15].

Assumption 2: Boundness. It is assumed that the set Q is finite and that X^q is bounded for every q. This is a reasonable assumption for many systems that have finitely many modes and saturation constraints on the continuous state. Even if the state space is unbounded, often it is desirable to approximate it for applying numerical methods. By defining appropriately the boundary conditions, it can be shown that the effect of the numerical cutoff is small [10]. This assumption is used for approximating the hybrid system by a finite Markov chain and employing numerical methods based on dynamic programming.

We refer to the class of GSHS that satisfies the assumptions above simply as stochastic hybrid systems (SHS).

3   Probabilistic Reachability

In this section, we show that the probability that a state will reach a set of target states while avoiding an unsafe set can be characterized as the viscosity solution of a system of coupled HJB equations.

Let $T = \cup_{q \in Q_T} \{q\} \times T^q$ and $U = \cup_{q \in Q_U} \{q\} \times U^q$ be subsets of S representing the set of target and unsafe states respectively. We assume that T^q and U^q are proper subsets of X^q for each q, i.e. $\partial T^q \cap \partial X^q = \partial U^q \cap \partial X^q = \emptyset$ and the boundaries ∂T^q and ∂U^q are sufficiently smooth. We define $\Gamma^q = X^q \setminus (T^q \cup U^q)$ and $\Gamma = \cup_{q \in Q} \{q\} \times \Gamma^q$. The initial state (which, in general, is a probability distribution) must lie outside the sets T and U. The transition measure $R(s, A)$ is assumed to be defined so that the system cannot jump directly to U or T.

Consider the stopping time $\tau = \inf\{t \geq 0 : s(\tau^-) \in \partial T \cup \partial U\}$. Let s be an initial state in Γ, then we define the function $V : \bar{\Gamma} \to \mathbb{R}_+$ by

$$V(s) = \begin{cases} E_s[I_{(s(\tau^-)\in\partial T)}], & s \in \Gamma \\ 1, & s \in \partial T \\ 0, & s \in \partial U \end{cases}.$$

The function $V(s)$ can be interpreted as the probability that a trajectory starting at s will reach the set T while avoiding the set U.

Inspired by [6], we add a new state Δ and we denote $\Gamma' = \Gamma \cup \Delta$. The system transitions to Δ according to the measure

$$R(s, \Delta) = \begin{cases} 1, & \text{if } s \in \partial T \cup \partial U \\ 0, & \text{otherwise} \end{cases}.$$

The new process is indistinguishable from the original process $s(t)$ for $t < \tau$ and at time τ it jumps to Δ and stays there forever. The system dies immediately after transitioning to Δ, i.e. $b(\Delta) = \sigma(\Delta) = \lambda(\Delta) = 0$. Finally, we extend V to Γ' by defining $V(\Delta) = 0$ which agrees with the probabilistic interpretation of V. By abuse of notation, we will denote the new process also by $s(t)$.

Given the assumptions on the sets T and U and their boundaries, we can construct a bounded function $c : \bar{S} \to \mathbb{R}_+$ continuous in x such that

$$c(q, x) = \begin{cases} 1, & \text{if } s = (q, x) \in \partial T^q \\ 0, & \text{if } s = (q, x) \in \partial U^q \cup \partial X^q \end{cases}.$$

Then, the value function V can be written as

$$V(s) = E_s \left[\int_0^\infty c(q_{t-}, x_{t-}) dp^*(t) \right] \tag{2}$$

where $p^*(t) = \sum_{i=1}^\infty I_{(t \geq t_i)} I_{((q_{t_{i_-}}, x_{t_{i_-}}) \in \partial S)}$ is a counting process counting the number of times the trajectory hits the boundary and jumps.

Consider the set of nonnegative Borel measurable functions $\mathcal{B}(S)_+$ and define the operator $\mathcal{G} : \mathcal{B}(S)_+ \to \mathcal{B}(S)_+$ by

$$Gg(q, x) = E_s[c(q_{t_1^-}, x_{t_1^-}) I_{(t_1 = t_1^*)} + g(q_{t_1}, x_{t_1})]. \tag{3}$$

where t_1 is the stopping time of the first jump. We will show that V is a fixed point of $\mathcal{G}$.

Lemma 1. $G^n g(q, x) = E_s \left[\int_0^{t_n} c(q_{t-}, x_{t-}) dp^*(t) + g(q_{t_n}, x_{t_n}) \right].$

Proof. By the strong Markov property [3] and the construction of the SHS process we have[2]

$$E_s[c(q_{t_2^-}, x_{t_2^-}) I_{(t_2=t_2^*)} + g(q_{t_2}, x_{t_2}) | \mathcal{F}_{t_1}] = E_s[c(q_{t_1}, x_{t_1^-}) I_{(t_2=t_2^*)} + g(q_{t_2}, x_{t_2}) | \mathcal{F}_{t_1}]$$
$$= E_s[g(q_{t_1}, x_{t_1})].$$

Therefore,

$$\mathcal{G}^2 g(q, x) = \mathcal{G}(\mathcal{G}g(q, x)) = E_s[c(q_{t_1^-}, x_{t_1^-}) I_{(t_1=t_1^*)} + \mathcal{G}g(q_{t_1}, x_{t_1})]$$
$$= E_s[c(q_{t_1^-}, x_{t_1^-}) I_{(t_1=t_1^*)} + E_s[c(q_{t_2^-}, x_{t_2^-}) I_{(t_2=t_3^*)} + g(q_{t_2}, x_{t_2}) | \mathcal{F}_{t_1}]]$$
$$= E_s[c(q_{t_1^-}, x_{t_1^-}) I_{(t_1=t_1^*)} + c(q_{t_2^-}, x_{t_2^-}) I_{(t_2=t_2^*)} + g(q_{t_2}, x_{t_2})].$$

By induction, we get

$$G^n g(q, x) = E_s[\sum_{i=1}^{n} c(q_{t_i^-}, x_{t_i^-}) I_{(t_i=t_{i*})} + g(q_{t_n}, x_{t_n})]$$
$$= E_s[\int_0^{t_n} c(q_{t-}, x_{t-}) dp^*(t) + g(q_{t_n}, x_{t_n})].$$

Theorem 1. *The value function V is a fixed point of the operator $\mathcal{G}$.*

Proof. By definition of $\mathcal{G}$, for any $\psi_1 \leq \psi_2$ we have $\mathcal{G}\psi_1 \leq \mathcal{G}\psi_2$. Let $v^0(q, x) = 0$ for every q and every x and set $v^{n+1}(q, x) = \mathcal{G}v^n(q, x)$. Then $\{v^n\}$ increases monotonically and v^n takes values in $[0, 1]$ for every n. Therefore, $\lim_{n \to \infty} v^n(q, x) = v(q, x)$ exists. Note that convergence is not guaranteed for other choices of v^0.

Since $v \geq v^n$, we have $\mathcal{G}v \geq \mathcal{G}v^n$ and thus $\mathcal{G}v \geq v^{n+1}$ for all n, therefore $\mathcal{G}v \geq v$. In addition, $\mathcal{G}v^n = v^{n+1} \leq v \leq \mathcal{G}v$ and $\lim_{n \to \infty} v^n = v$, therefore $\mathcal{G}v \leq v \leq \mathcal{G}v$ and $v = \lim_{n \to \infty} v^n$ is a fixed point of $\mathcal{G}$.

Finally by Lemma 1, $v = \lim_{n \to \infty} G^n v^0 = E_s[\int_0^\infty c(q_{t-}, x_{t-}) dp^*(t)]$ therefore V is a fixed point of $\mathcal{G}$, i.e. $V(s) = \mathcal{G}V(s)$.

Next, we show that the value function V can be represented as a discounted cost criterion with a target set where the running and the terminal cost depend on V itself.

Theorem 2. *Consider the value function $V(s)$ defined by (2) and define $L^V(q, x) = \lambda(q, x) \int_\Gamma V(y) R((q, x), dy)$ and $\psi^V(q, x) = c(q, x) + \int_\Gamma V(y) R((q, x), dy)$. Then, for $s \in \Gamma$*

$$V(s) = E_s \left[\int_0^{t_1^*} \Lambda(t) L^V(q_{t-}, x_{t-}) dt + \Lambda(t_1^*) \psi^V(q_{t_1^*}, x_{t_1^*}) \right]. \tag{4}$$

---

[2] $\mathcal{F}_t$ denotes the filtration of the SHS process.

Proof. The SHS satisfies the strong Markov property [3], and therefore, the Markov property can be applied not only for constant times but also for random stopping times. Let t_1 be the time of the first jump and $t_1^* = \inf\{t \geq 0 : x(t) \in \partial X^{q(t_0)}\}$, then, using a standard dynamic programming argument, we can write

$$V(s) = E_s \left[I_{(t_1 < t_1^*)} \int_\Gamma V(y) R((q_{t_1^-}, x_{t_1^-}), dy) dt \right.$$
$$\left. + I_{(t_1 = t_1^*)} \left(c(q_{t_1^*}, x_{t_1^*}) + \int_\Gamma V(y) R((q_{t_1^*}, x_{t_1^*}), dy) \right) \right]. \qquad (5)$$

By construction of the transition rate λ, t_1 and x_t are not independent (unless λ is constant). Denote $\mathcal{F}_\infty$ the σ-field $\sigma(x_t, t \geq 0)$ generated by x_t. The conditional distribution of t_1 given $\mathcal{F}_\infty$ is $P[t_1 > t | \mathcal{F}_\infty] = I_{t < t_1^*} \Lambda(t)$, where $\Lambda(t) = \exp\left\{ -\int_0^t \lambda(q_0, x_z) dz \right\}$, and the conditional density is

$$\frac{dP[t_1 \leq t | \mathcal{F}_\infty]}{dt} = \lambda(q_0, x_t) \Lambda(t) I_{(t < t_1^*)} + \Lambda(t_1^*) \delta(t - t_1^*).$$

Thus, equation (5) can be written as

$$V(s) = E_s \left[E_s \left[I_{(t_1 < t_1^*)} \int_\Gamma V(y) R((q_{t_1^-}, x_{t_1^-}), dy) dt \right. \right.$$
$$\left. \left. + I_{(t_1 = t_1^*)} \left(c(q_{t_1^*}, x_{t_1^*}) + \int_\Gamma V(y) R((q_{t_1^*}, x_{t_1^*}), dy) \right) | \mathcal{F}_\infty \right] \right]$$
$$= E_s \left[\int_0^{t_1^*} \lambda(q_t, x_t) \Lambda(t) \int_\Gamma V(y) R((q_{t-}, x_{t-}), dy) dt \right.$$
$$\left. + \Lambda(t_1^*) c(q_{t_1^*}, x_{t_1^*}) + \Lambda(t_1^*) \int_\Gamma V(y) R((q_{t_1*}, x_{t_1*}), dy) \right].$$

Using the definitions of $L^V(q, x)$ and $\psi^V(q, x)$ we have

$$V(s) = E_s \left[\int_0^{t_1^*} \Lambda(t) L^V(q_{t-}, x_{t-}) dt + \Lambda(t_1^*) \psi^V(q_{t_1^*}, x_{t_1^*}) \right].$$

Assuming that the transition measure $R(s, A)$ is a continuous stochastic kernel, the map $(q, x) \to \int_\Gamma f(y) R((q, x), dy)$ is bounded uniformly continuous for every bounded and continuous function f [2]. Then, if V is continuous in $\bar{X}^{q(t_0)}$, equation (4) is very similar to the discounted cost criterion with a target set [15]. The main difference is that the running cost $L^V(q, x)$ and the terminal cost $\psi^V(q, x)$ depend on the value function. Since the SHS satisfies the strong Markov property, the same procedure can be repeated every time a jump occurs. Next, we show that under the non-degeneracy assumption V is continuous.

Theorem 3. V *is bounded and continuous in* x *on* $\bar{\Gamma}$.

Proof. The $\mathcal{G}$ operator defined by (3) can be written as

$$\mathcal{G}g(q,x) = E_s \left[\int_0^{t_1} c(q_{t-}, x_{t-}) dp^*(t) + g(q_{t_1}, x_{t_1}) \right].$$

Since the SHS satisfies the strong Markov property, we can apply the same transformation as in Theorem 2 to get

$$\mathcal{G}q(q,x) = E_s \left[\int_0^{t_1^*} \Lambda(t) L^g(q_{t-}, x_{t-}) dt + \Lambda(t_1^*) \psi^g(q_{t_1^*}, x_{t_1^*}) \right]. \tag{6}$$

Therefore

$$v^{n+1}(q,x) = \mathcal{G}v^n(q,x)$$
$$= E_s \left[\int_0^{t_n^*} \Lambda(t) L^{v^n}(q_{t-}, x_{t-}) dt + \Lambda(t_1^*) \psi^{v^n}(q_{t_n^*}, x_{t_n^*}) \right].$$

Because of the non-degeneracy assumption, the exit times t_i^* are continuous at the sample paths of the process [15]. Therefore, all the functions in the sequence v^n are continuous and further, we have $v^n \geq v^0$ for every n. By applying the results of [2] (Chapter 7) we can conclude that $V = \lim_{n \to \infty} v^n$ is lower semi-continuous and bounded below.

Next, define a new function $\tilde{V} : \bar{\Gamma} \to \mathbb{R}_+$ by

$$V(s) = \begin{cases} E_s[I_{(s(\tau-) \in \partial U)}], & s \in \Gamma \\ 1, & s \in \partial U \\ 0, & s \in \partial T \end{cases}.$$

The function $\tilde{V}$ can be interpreted as the probability that a trajectory starting at s will reach U before T and it can be written as

$$\tilde{V}(s) = E_s \left[\int_0^\infty \tilde{c}(q_{t-}, x_{t-}) dp^*(t) \right]$$

where

$$\tilde{c}(q,x) = \begin{cases} 0, & \text{if } s = (q,x) \in \partial T^q \cup \partial X^q \\ 1, & \text{if } s = (q,x) \in \partial U^q \end{cases}.$$

From the non-degeneracy assumption, we have that $\tilde{V} = 1 - V(s)$. By applying the argument given in the first part of the proof to $\tilde{V}$, it follows that $\tilde{V}$ is lower semi-continuous and bounded below and therefore, $V = 1 + (-\tilde{V})$ is upper semi-continuous and bounded above. Thus, V is continuous and bounded in $\bar{\Gamma}$.

Next, we prove the main result of this section that characterizes V as the viscosity solution of a system of HJB equations. We use the results of [15] to derive the HJB equations (similar results can be found also in [10]).

Theorem 4. *Assume that f and σ are continuously differentiable w.r.t. x in Γ^q for each q and for suitable C_1 and C_2 satisfy $|f_x| \leq C_1$, $|\sigma_x| \leq C_1$, and $|f(q,0)| + |\sigma(q,x)| \leq C_2$. Then V is the unique viscosity solution of the system of equations*

$$\mathcal{H}_V\left((q,x), V, D_x V, D_x^2 V\right) = 0 \; in \; \Gamma^q, \; q \in Q \tag{7}$$

with boundary conditions

$$V(q,x) = \psi^V(q,x) \; on \; \partial\Gamma^q, \; q \in Q \tag{8}$$

where

$$\mathcal{H}_V\left((q,x), V, D_x V, D_x^2 V\right) = f(q,x)D_x V + \frac{1}{2}tr(a(q,x)D_x^2 V) + \lambda(q,x)V + L^V(q,x).$$

Proof. Consider the function

$$v(q,x) = \begin{cases} \mathcal{G}g(q,x) & \text{in } \Gamma^q \\ \psi^g(q,x) & \text{on } \partial\Gamma^q \end{cases}$$

where $g \in \mathcal{B}(S)_+$ is a continuous and bounded function. From (6), it follows that $v(q,x)$ is the value function of an exit-time problem in Γ^q for the diffusion (1) where $L^g : \Gamma \rightarrow \mathbb{R}_+$ and $\psi^g : \partial\Gamma \rightarrow \mathbb{R}_+$ are bounded continuous functions. Under the assumptions of f and σ, we can apply the results for standard Markov diffusions [10] (Thm V.2.1 and Cor. V.3.1) and therefore, $v(q,x)$ a viscosity solution of

$$\mathcal{H}_g\left((q,x), V, D_x V, D_x^2 V\right) = 0 \; in \; \Gamma^q \tag{9}$$
$$V(q,x) = \psi^g(q,x) \; on \; \partial\Gamma^q. \tag{10}$$

By Theorem 3, V is bounded and continuous. Therefore,

$$\bar{V}(q,x) = \begin{cases} \mathcal{G}V(q,x) & \text{in } \Gamma^q \\ \psi^V(q,x) & \text{on } \partial\Gamma^q \end{cases}$$

is a viscosity solution of

$$\mathcal{H}_V\left((q,x), \bar{V}, D_x \bar{V}, D_x^2 \bar{V}\right) = 0 \; in \; \Gamma^q$$
$$\bar{V}(q,x) = \psi^V(q,x) \; on \; \partial\Gamma^q.$$

where V is considered known and $\bar{V}$ unknown. But V is a fixed point of $\mathcal{G}$, and thus $V = \mathcal{G}V = \bar{V}$ in Γ^q and $\psi^V = \psi^{\bar{V}}$ on $\partial\Gamma^q$, which means $V = \bar{V}$ is a viscosity solution of (7 - 8). Further, V is continuous, and therefore, is the unique viscosity solution which is continuous in $\bar{\Gamma}$.

4   Numerical Methods for Reachability Analysis

4.1   Locally Consistent Markov Chains

In this section, we employ the finite difference method presented in [15] to compute locally consistent Markov chains (MCs) that approximate the SHS while preserving local mean and variance. We consider a discretization of the state space denoted by $\bar{S}^h = \cup_{q \in Q}\{q\} \times \bar{S}_q^h$ where $\bar{S}_q^h$ is a set of discrete points approximating X^q and $h > 0$ is an approximation parameter characterizing the distance between neighboring points. By abuse of notation, we denote the sets of boundary and interior points of $\bar{S}_q^h$ by ∂S_q^h and S_q^h respectively. The state of the approximating MC is denoted by $s_n^h = (q_n^h, \xi_n^h)$, $n = 0, 1, 2, \ldots$.

Consider the continuous evolution of the SHS between jumps and assume that the state is (q, x). The local mean and variance given the SDE (1) on the interval $[0, \delta]$ are

$$E[x(\delta) - x] = b(q(t), x(t))\delta + o(\delta)$$
$$E[(x(\delta) - x)(x(\delta) - x)^T] = a(q(t), x(t))\delta + o(\delta).$$

Let $\{q_n^h = q, \xi_n^h\}$ describe the MC on $S_q^h \subset X^q$ with transition probabilities denoted by $p_D^h((q, x), (q, y))$. A locally consistent MC must satisfy

$$E[\Delta \xi_n^h] = b(q, x)\Delta t^h(q, x) + o(\Delta t^h(q, x))$$

$$E[(\Delta \xi_n^h - E[\Delta \xi_n^h])(\Delta \xi_n^h - E[\Delta \xi_n^h])^T] = \\ a(q(t), x(t))\Delta t^h(q, x) + o(\Delta t^h(q, x))$$

where $\Delta \xi_n^h = \xi_{n+1}^h - \xi_n^h, \xi_n^h = x$ and $\Delta t^h(q, x)$ are appropriate interpolation intervals (or the "holding times") for the MC.

The diffusion transition probabilities $p_D^h((q, x), (q', x'))$ and the interpolation intervals can be computed systematically from the parameters of the SDE (details can be found in [15]). If the diffusion matrix $a(q, x)$ is diagonal and we consider a uniform grid with e_i denoting the unit vector in the ith direction, the transition probabilities are

$$p_D^h((q, x), (q, x \pm he_i)) = \frac{a_{ii}(q, x)/2 + hb_i^\pm(q, x)}{Q(q, x)}$$

and the interpolation intervals are $\Delta t(q, x) = h^2/Q(q, x)$ where $Q(q, x) = \sum_i [a_{ii}$ $(q, x) + h|b_i(q, x)|]$ and $a^+ = \max\{a, 0\}$ and $a^- = \max\{-a, 0\}$ denote the positive and negative parts of a real number.

Next, consider the jumps with transition rate $\lambda(q, x)$ and transition measure $R((q, x), A)$. Suppose that at time t the state has just changed to $\{q_n^h = q, \xi_n^h = x\}$. The probability that a jump will occur on $[t, t + \delta)$ conditioned on the past data can be approximated by

$$P[(q, x) \text{ jumps on } [t, t + \delta)|q(s), x(s), w(s), s \leq t] = \lambda(q, x)\delta + o(\delta).$$

The ith jump of the approximating process is denoted by $\zeta((q, x), \rho_i)$ where ρ_i are independent random variables with distribution $\bar{R} = \{\rho : \zeta((q, x), \rho_i) \in A\} = R((q, x), A)$ with compact support Θ. Let ζ_h be a bounded measurable function such that $|\zeta_h((q, x), \rho) - \zeta(q, x), \rho)| \to 0$ uniformly in x for each ρ and which satisfies $\zeta_h((q,x),\rho) \in \bar{S}^h$. If $x \in S_q^h$, then with probability $1 - \lambda(q,x)\Delta t^h(q,x) - o(\Delta t^h(q,x))$ the next state is determined by the diffusion probabilities p_D^h and with probability $\lambda(q,x)\Delta t^h(q,x) + o(\Delta t^h(q,x))$ there is a jump and the next state is $(q_{n+1}^h, \xi_{n+1}^h) = \zeta((q,x),\rho_i)$. For the points in ∂S_q^h, the next state is determined by $\zeta((q,x),\rho_i)$ with probability 1. Therefore, the transition probabilities are defined by

$$p^h((q,x),(q',x')) =$$
$$\begin{cases} (1 - \lambda(q,x)\Delta t^h(q,x) - o(\Delta t^h(q,x)))p_D^h((q,x),(q',x')) \\ \quad + (\lambda(q,x)\Delta t^h(q,x) + o(\Delta t^h(q,x)))\bar{R}\{\rho : \zeta_h((q,x),\rho) = (q',x'-x)\} & \text{if } x \in S_q^h \\ \bar{R}\{\rho : \zeta_h((q,x),\rho) = (q',x'-x)\} & \text{if } x \in \partial S_q^h \end{cases}$$
$$(11)$$

4.2 Iterative Methods for Reachability Analysis

This section describes the approximation of the value function, formulates the problem for the discrete approximations, and presents the convergence results for the numerical methods.

Consider the approximating MC $\{s_n^h\} = \{\xi_n^h, q_n^h\}$ with transition probabilities $p^h((q,x),(q',x'))$ defined in (11). Let $\bar{T}^h = \bar{S}^h \cap \bar{T}$ and $\bar{U}^h = \bar{S}^h \cap \bar{U}$ and denote by n_i the jump times and ν_h the stopping time representing that $(q_n^h, \xi_n^h) \in \bar{T}^h \cup \bar{U}^h$, then the value function V can be approximated by

$$V^h(s) = E_s\left[\sum_{n=0}^{\nu_h} c(q_n^h, \xi_n^h)I_{(n=n_i)}\right].$$

The function V^h can be computed using a value iteration algorithm. To show the convergence of the algorithm, we consider a terminal state Δ similar to Section 3. The state space of the MC becomes $\tilde{S}^h = \bar{S}^h \cup \{\Delta\}$ and the transition probabilities are defined so that $\tilde{p}^h((q,x),\Delta) = 1$ if $x \in \bar{T}^h \cup \bar{U}^h$, $\tilde{p}^h(\Delta,\Delta) = 1$, and $\tilde{p}^h((q,x),(q',x')) = p^h((q,x),(q',x'))$ otherwise. This means that when the state reaches T or U, it transitions to Δ and stays there for ever. Consider the function $\tilde{c} : \tilde{S}^h \to \mathbb{R}_+$ with $\tilde{c}(\Delta) = 1$ and $\tilde{c}(q,x) = 0$ for every (q,x) and the value function

$$\tilde{V}^h(s) = E_s[\sum_{n=0}^{\infty} \tilde{c}(s_n)]. \tag{12}$$

Clearly, this sum is well-defined, bounded, and we have $\tilde{V}^h = V^h$.

Proposition 1. *Let $\tilde{V}_0^h(q,x) = 0$ for every (q,x), then the iteration*

$$\tilde{V}_{n+1}^h(q,x) = \left[\sum_{q',x'} \tilde{p}^h((q,x),(q',x'))\tilde{V}_n^h(q',x')\right] \tag{13}$$

converges pointwise and monotonically to $\tilde{V}^h = V^h$.

Proof. Consider the value function defined by (12) for $\{s_n\}$. We have that $\tilde{V}^h(q, x) \in [0, 1] < \infty$ and $\tilde{c}(s) \geq 0$ for all $s \in \tilde{S}^h$. Therefore, computing $\tilde{V}$ is a special case of the total expected reward criterion for positive models [19]. If v is a fixed point of the iteration (13), then $v + k[1, \ldots, 1]^T$, $k > 0$ is also a fixed point. Thus, the iteration may have multiple fixed points but if we pick $\tilde{V}_0^h = 0$ it converges to the least fixed point $\tilde{V}$ [19] (Thm 7.2.12).

4.3   Convergence Results

Finally, we show that the value function V^h obtained using the approximating MC converges to the value function V of the SHS as $h \to 0$. Let $g \in \mathcal{B}(S)_+$ be a continuous and bounded function and suppose that V is the unique viscosity solution of (9-10) that is bounded and continuous in $\bar{\Gamma}^q$. Consider $\bar{\Sigma}_q^h$ to be a discretization of $\bar{\Gamma}^q$ and denote Σ_q^h and $\partial \Sigma_q^h$ the set of interior and boundary points respectively. Using the approximation described in Subsection 4.1, the dynamic programming equation for $\bar{\Sigma}_q^h$ can be written as

$$V^h(q, x) = \begin{cases} F_g^h[V^h(\cdot)](q, x) & \text{if } x \in \Sigma_q^h \\ \psi_g^h(q, x) & \text{if } x \in \partial \Sigma_q^h \end{cases}$$

where

$$F_g^h[V^h(\cdot)](q, x) =$$
$$(1 - \lambda(q, x)\Delta t^h(q, x) - o(\Delta t^h(q, x)) \sum_{q', x'} p_D^h((q, x), (q', x'))V^h(q', x')$$
$$+ (\lambda(q, x)\Delta t^h(q, x) + o(\Delta t^h(q, x)) \int_{\Theta} g(\zeta_h((q, x), \rho))\bar{R}(d\rho)$$

and

$$\psi_g^h(q, x) = c(q, x) + \int_{\Theta} g(\zeta_h((q, x), \rho))\bar{R}(d\rho).$$

Lemma 2. $\lim_{y \to x, h \to 0} V^h(q, y) = V(q, x)$ *uniformly in* $\bar{\Gamma}^q$.

Proof. V is continuous and bounded viscosity solution of (9-10) and $\psi^g(q, x)$ is continuous. Therefore, for each q we have a standard exit problem from Γ^q for the SDE (1) and by applying the results of [10] (Sec. IX.5) we have that V^h converges uniformly to V.

To show convergence of V^h for the SHS, we replace g by V and we follow an argument similar to the proof of Theorem 1.

Theorem 5. *Let*

$$V^h(q, x) = \begin{cases} F_V^h[V^h(\cdot)](q, x) & \text{if } x \in \Sigma_q^h \\ \psi_V^h(q, x) & \text{if } x \in \partial \Sigma_q^h \end{cases}$$

then $\lim_{y \to x, h \to 0} V^h(q, y) = V(q, x)$.

Proof. Assume that V is given and define

$$\bar{V}^h(q, x) = \begin{cases} F_V^h[\bar{V}^h(\cdot)](q, x) & \text{if } x \in \Sigma_q^h \\ \psi_V^h(q, x) & \text{if } x \in \partial \Sigma_q^h \end{cases}.$$

By Lemma 2, since V is bounded and continuous we have $\lim_{y \to x, h \to 0} \bar{V}^h(q, y) = \bar{V}(q, x)$. Assume that for each h, $\bar{V}^h$ is computed by a value iteration algorithm with $v^0 = 0$. Then, V^h is a fixed point of F_V^h and therefore, $\bar{V}^h = V^h$ for every h and $\bar{V} = V$.

5 Navigation Benchmark

This section illustrates the approach using a stochastic version of the navigation benchmark presented in [9]. The benchmark describes an object moving within a bounded 2-dimensional region partitioned into cells X^q, $q \in \{0, 1, \ldots, N\}$ as shown in Figure 1. Let $[x_1, x_2]^T$ and $v = [v_1, v_2]^T$ denote the position and the velocity of the object respectively. The behavior is defined by the ODE $\dot{v} = A(v - v_d^q)$ where $A \in \mathbb{R}^{2 \times 2}$ and $v_d^q = [sin(q\pi/4), cos(q\pi/4)]^T$. Selecting the matrix A and adding a diffusion term, the dynamics of the object are described by the SDE

$$dx = (\tilde{A}x + \tilde{B}u_d^q)dt + \Sigma dw$$

where $x = [x_1, x_2, v_1, v_2]^T$, $u_d^q = [0, 0, v_d^q]^T$, $w(t)$ is an $\mathbb{R}^4$-valued Wiener process,

$$\tilde{A} = \begin{bmatrix} 0 & I_2 \\ 0 & A \end{bmatrix}, \quad A = \begin{bmatrix} -1.2 & 0.1 \\ 0.1 & -1.2 \end{bmatrix}, \quad \text{and } \Sigma = 0.1I_4.$$

Consider the target set T and the unsafe set U shown in Figure 1. Given initial state $s_0 = (q_0, x_0)$, we want to compute the probability that the state will reach T while avoiding U. Sample trajectories are shown in Figure 1. In order to apply the approach described in this paper, we under-approximate each cell X^q by $\tilde{X}^q$ by considering a smooth boundary $\partial \tilde{X}^q$. We also define a transition

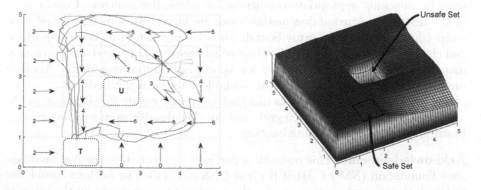

Fig. 1. The navigation benchmark, sample trajectories, and the value function

Table 1. Performance Data

h	Time (minutes)	Number of States
.5	.5	2500
.25	7	32400
.1	200	1147041
.05	5110	17147881

measure $R((q,x),A)$ so that the state jumps into an adjacent cell if it hits an "inner" boundary and jumps into the same cell if it hits on "outer" boundary. The transition rate is assumed to be zero. We discretize the state space using a uniform grid with approximation parameter $h > 0$ and apply the method described in Section 4 to compute $V^h(q,x)$. As $h \to 0$, $V^h(q,x)$ converges to the solution $V(q,x)$ of the stochastic approximation of the benchmark problem.

Since the continuous state space of the example is 4-dimensional, we select to plot a projection of V^h for initial velocity $v_0 = [0,0]^T$. Figure 1 shows this projection for $h = 0.1$ that describes the probability that a trajectory starting from $(q,[x_1,x_2,0,0]^T)$ will reach T while avoiding U. The computational performance of the algorithm is illustrated in Table 1. All data was collected using a 3.0 GHz desktop computer with 1 Gb RAM. A more exact characterization is more involved since the operator F_V^h of the value iteration algorithm is not a contraction mapping and convergence is guaranteed only for $V_0^h = 0$.

6 Conclusions and Future Work

The paper characterizes reachability of stochastic hybrid systems as a viscosity solution of a system of coupled Hamilton-Jacobi-Bellman equations and employs a numerical method based on discrete approximations for reachability analysis. The main advantage of the approach is that it guarantees the convergence of the solution based on the discrete approximation to the solution of the original problem. The approach can be extended to controlled stochastic hybrid systems by imposing appropriate conditions for admissible controls. Convergence of the discrete approximation methods can be investigated using relaxed controls. Characterization of error bounds and convergence rates is an important and challenging problem especially since convergence is not based on contraction mappings but it is guaranteed only for appropriate initial conditions. Another fundamental challenge is to develop scalable numerical methods that can be applied to large systems. Towards this goal, currently we are investigating methods based on variable resolution grids and parallel algorithms as well as methods based on value function approximation.

Acknowledgements. This research is partially supported by the National Science Foundation (NSF) CAREER grant CNS-0347440. The authors would like to thank the anonymous reviewer for the constructive comments on the proof of Theorem 2.

References

1. M. Bernadskiy, R. Sharykin, and R. Alur Structured Modeling of Concurrent Stochastic Hybrid Systems. *FORMATS'04*, LNCS 3253, pp. 309-324, Springer, 2004.
2. D.P. Bertsekas and S.E. Shreve *Stochastic Optimal Control: The Discrete Time Case.* Academic Press, 1978.
3. M. Bujorianu, J. Lygeros, General Stochastic Hybrid Systems: Modeling and Optimal Control, *In Proc. of 43rd IEEE Conf. on Decision and Control*, 2004.
4. M.L. Bujorianu and J. Lygeros. Reachability Questions in Piecewise Deterministic Markov Processes. In *Hybrid Systems: Computation and Control - HSCC 2003*, LNCS 2623, pp. 126-140, Springer, 2003.
5. C. Courcoubetis and M. Yannakakis, The complexity of probabilistic verification, *Journal of ACM*, 42(4), pp, 857-907, 1995.
6. M. Davis, *Markov Models and Optimization*, Chapman and Hall, 1993.
7. M. Davis and M. Farid, Piecewise-deterministic processes and viscosity solutions, In *Stochastic Analysis, Control, Optimization and Applications: A Volume in Honor of W.H. Fleming*, pp. 249-268, Birkhauser, 1999.
8. L. de Alfaro, Computing Minimum and Maximum Reachability Times in Probabilistic Systems, In *CONCUR'99*, LNCS 1664, pp. 66-81, 1999.
9. A. Fehnker and F. Ivancic, Benchmarks for Hybrid Systems Verification, *HSCC 2004*, LNCS 2993, pp. 326-341, Springer, 2004.
10. W. Fleming, H. Soner, *Controlled Markov Processes and Viscosity Solutions*, Springer-Verlag, 1993.
11. J.P. Hespanha. Stochastic Hybrid Systems: Application to Communication Networks. In *HSCC 2004*, LNCS 2993, pp. 387-401, Springer, 2004.
12. J. Hu, J. Lygeros, and S. Sastry. Towards a Theory of Stochastic Hybrid Systems. In *HSCC 2000*, LNCS 1790, pp. 160-173, Springer, 2000.
13. J. Hu, M. Prandini, and S. Sastry, Probabilistic Safety Analysis in Three Dimensional Aircraft Flight, *In Proc. of 42nd IEEE Conf. on Decision and Control*, pp. 5335-5340, 2003.
14. X. Koutsoukos, Optimal Control of Stochastic Hybrid Systems Based on Locally Consistent Markov Decision Processes, *Int. J. of Hybrid Systems*, 4, 301-318, 2004.
15. H.J. Kushner and P. Dupuis. *Numerical Methods for Stochastic Control Problems in Continuous Time*. Springer, 2001.
16. J. Lygeros, On reachability and minimum cost optimal control, *Automatica*, 40(6), 917-927, 2004.
17. I.M. Mitchell, A.M. Bayen, and C.J. Tomlin, A Time-Dependent Hamilton-Jacobi Formulation of Reachable Sets for Continuous Dynamic Games, *IEEE Trans. on Automatic Control*, 50(7), 947-957, 2005.
18. I.M. Mitchell and J.A. Templeton, A Toolbox of Hamilton-Jacobi Solvers for Analysis of Nondeterministic Continuous and Hybrid Systems, In *HSCC 2005*, LNCS 3414, pp. 480-494, 2005.
19. M. Puterman, *Markov Decision Processes-Discrete Stochastic Dynamic Programming*, Wiley: Hoboken, New Jersey, 2005.
20. S.N. Strubbe, A.A. Julius, and A.J. van der Schaft. Communicating piecewise deterministic Markov processes. In *ADHS03*, June 2003.

R-Charon, a Modeling Language for Reconfigurable Hybrid Systems*

Fabian Kratz[1], Oleg Sokolsky[2], George J. Pappas[2], and Insup Lee[2]

[1] Eindhoven University of Technology (TU/e), Eindhoven, The Netherlands
[2] University of Pennsylvania, Philadelphia, USA

Abstract. This paper describes the modeling language R-Charon as an extension for architectural reconfiguration to the existing distributed hybrid system modeling language Charon. The target application domain of R-Charon includes but is not limited to modular reconfigurable robots and large-scale transportation systems. While largely leaving the Charon syntax and semantics intact, R-Charon allows dynamic creation and destruction of components (agents) as well as of links (references) between the agents. As such, R-Charon is the first formal, hybrid automata based modeling language which also addresses dynamic reconfiguration. We develop and present the syntax and operational semantics for R-Charon on three levels: behavior (modes), structure (agents) and configuration (system).

1   Introduction

A hybrid system typically consists of a collection of components interacting with each other and with an analog environment. In many real world systems, the collection of components as well as the components they interact with may change dynamically, i.e., reconfigure [1].

In the world of software design the concept of reconfiguration is well recognized. Object orientation is (becoming) the main design and implementation paradigm. Creation and destruction of objects as well as changing the communication structure of the objects are at the core of the object oriented design paradigm.

Traditional object oriented design methodologies and languages, however, only support the modeling of discrete systems. Despite the growth of hybrid modeling languages [2, 3, 4, 5, 6], most hybrid modeling languages do not support reconfiguration. To properly describe and analyze reconfigurable hybrid systems, a formal approach is necessary which integrates reconfigurable discrete behaviors with continuous behaviors. In this paper we present a reconfiguration extension for the hierarchical hybrid modeling language Charon [2, 3].

Charon is a hybrid modeling language with support for architectural as well as behavioral hierarchy. The building block for describing a system architecture is an *agent*, which can communicate with other agents. Concurrency of agents and hiding of information is provided by a composition and a hiding operator.

---

* This research was supported in part by NSF CNS-0509327 and ARO DAAD19-01-1-0473.

João Hespanha and A. Tiwari (Eds.): HSCC 2006, LNCS 3927, pp. 392–406, 2006.

The building block for describing behavior in an agent is a *mode*. A mode is a hierarchical hybrid state machine, i.e., it can have submodes and transitions connecting them. An agent alternates between taking a discrete and a continuous step. A discrete step consists of a series of transitions leading from the currently active atomic mode, to another atomic mode. This flow of control is determined by mode invariants, transition guards, and transition actions possibly changing mode variables. A continuous step amounts to passage of time, during which the continuous variables evolve according to the algebraic and differential constraints of the active modes.

There could be many notions of (re)configuration for hybrid systems. We focus on reconfiguration in two, in a sense similar, application domains: large-scale transportation systems and modular reconfigurable robots. A transportation system typically consists of a large number of possibly mobile entities, competing for bounded resources. These entities can enter and leave an environment dynamically. Furthermore, (groups of) entities nearing each other may dynamically set up a communication connection to prevent a collision or to continue as a group to allow for a more efficient use of the resources. Examples of large-scale transportation systems include highway control systems [7], unmanned aerial vehicles [8], and air traffic control systems [9]. A modular robot is built up from homogeneous modules which can be connected to each other [10, 11]. Typically there are only a few different types of modules, where each type is designed to be very orthogonal with respect to the connection to other modules. In this way a number of many relative simple modules can be connected to form a sophisticated robot. A comprehensive overview of the different existing modular robot systems can be found in Chapter 4 of [12].

The main contribution of this paper is the formal definition of R-Charon and its features. In addition to the Charon features, our extension supports agent creation and destruction as well as dynamic communication connections between the agents. This makes R-Charon the first formal, hybrid automata based modeling language with explicit support for reconfiguration. We used two guidelines in the design of R-Charon: minimize the amount of changes to Charon and minimize the number of restrictions on the use of the syntax. Note that the latter comes at the expense of more sophisticated semantics.

Related work. An early approach to hierarchical hybrid modeling with support for reconfiguration is SHIFT [13]. R-Charon is inspired by its features while enjoying the formal Charon semantics. The Φ-calculus [6] is a process algebraic based hybrid reconfigurable modeling language. As an extension of Milner's π-calculus [14] it inherits the powerful reconfiguration primitives on process algebra terms. However, as pointed out in [4] the Φ-calculus considers continuous behavior to be a property of an explicit environment instead of being part of an agent as we do. Furthermore a process algebraic approach has the disadvantage that it is difficult to learn and use due to some of its technicalities [15]. Besides a hybrid extension to I/O Automata [5], also a reconfiguration extension [16] exists, though not both are combined into a single framework. Some work has been done on reconfiguration in discrete state machines [17] for programmable hardware. The state machines are reconfigured by adding and removing states and transitions, i.e., take place at the behaviorial level in contrast to the architectural level we aim at.

2   Reconfiguration

Before we present R-Charon, we first formalize the notion of reconfiguration we use. The definition is based on the reconfiguration possibilities of modular robots and large-scale transportation systems, and is inspired by SHIFT [13].

A model of a system consists of a set of components C. Each component $c \in C$ consists of a single set of links L, containing links to other components to which the component is either logically or physically connected. The set of links L of a specific component c is denoted by $c.L$. A component c having at least one link to a component d, means that c can communicate with d, where we consider linking not to be reciprocal.

Given a system with a set of components C, the reconfiguration primitives given below can take place. More complex operations can be performed by a series of primitives. Since a reconfiguration-only view is presented, the time instant or the event at which the reconfiguration happens is not relevant.

1. **Adding a component:** A component $c \in C$ can create a new component c_{new} and add it to the set C, i.e., $C := C \cup \{c_{new}\}$. As a consequence components can now link to c_{new}. We assume that c_{new} is of a certain type, which is known beforehand and defines the structure of the new component.
2. **Removing a component:** A component $c \in C$ can remove an arbitrary $c_r \in C$ from the set C, i.e., $C := C - \{c_r\}$.
3. **Adding a link:** A component $c \in C$ can add an arbitrary $c_a \in C$ to its set $c.L$, i.e., $c.L := c.L \cup \{c_a\}$. As a consequence component c can now communicate with c_a.
4. **Removing a link:** A component $c \in C$ can remove an arbitrary $c_r \in c.L$ from $c.L$, i.e., $c.L := c.L - \{c_r\}$.

The configuration of the world is determined by the set of components C and the specific values of the sets of links L of all components. To keep a system consistent after removal of a component, all links to the removed component are removed as well.

3   Application Example

In this section we present an application example that exhibits the new features of R-Charon. In the course of the example, we introduce some graphical R-Charon syntax, and point out the difficulties in defining the semantics for R-Charon. Our example is inspired by next generation air-traffic control supporting free flight for commercial airplanes [9], which allows airplanes to navigate themselves to their target with minimal air-traffic control interaction. We focus on a section of airspace (*center*) in which airplanes enter and leave, see Figure 1.

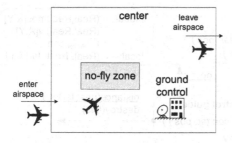

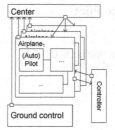

Fig. 1. Air-traffic control example   **Fig. 2.** Configuration snapshot

The center has a designated no-fly zone, e.g. a military training operation area off limit to commercial airplanes. In case an airplane approaches the designated no-fly zone, ground control takes over the navigation of the airplane by giving way-points, directing the airplane around the no-fly zone. Collision avoidance is not considered in this example.

Figure 2 presents a snapshot of the hierarchical agents and the configuration of the system. The arrows originating from a white box depict the links from one agent to another. The *Center* agent represents the section of the airspace and stores links to all airplanes in the airspace. Airplanes entering and leaving the center are modeled by creation and destruction of *Airplane* agents. The *Ground control* agent monitors the airspace in the center. In case an *Airplane* agent approaches the no-fly zone, the *Ground control* agents creates a new controller agent. The *Controller* agent contacts the corresponding airplane and guides it around the no-fly zone. As in Charon, each agent consists of one or more top-level modes, which can contain submodes. Figures 3 and 4 depict simplified views of the top-level modes of a *Ground control* agent, a *Controller* agent, and a number of *Airplane* agents, respectively. Modes not specified in detail are marked with a fat line. Assume that in the mode *Monitor center*, an airplane approaching the no-fly zone will be assigned to the *nfzPlane* reference variable. This triggers the creation of a new controller referred to by the *newController* variable. In the discrete initialization step of a *Controller* agent, the no-fly zone violating airplane is notified by setting a reference of the *Airplane* agent to itself.

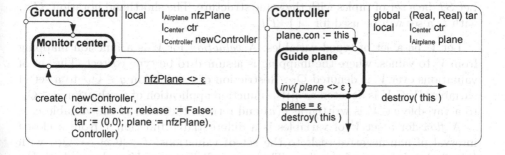

Fig. 3. Top-level modes of a *Ground control* and *Controller* agent

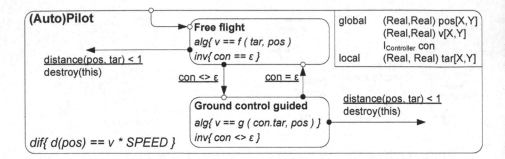

Fig. 4. Top-level mode of an airplane agent

Note that this reference represents a link from *Airplane* to *Controller*. The airplane switches to *Ground control guided* mode and follows a target coordinate given by the controller, which is computed in the *Guide plane* mode. As soon as either the airplane leaves the center or the controller decides that the airplane has maneuvered successfully around the no-fly zone, the controller is destroyed. In the latter case, the airplane switches back to the *Free flight* mode.

The most prominent semantic difficulties are related to agent creation and destruction. With agent creation the question arises when new agents take their discrete initialization step. Moreover, agent creation during initialization of a created agent leads to questions about creation and initialization order. With agent deletion the question arises how and when to update affected reference variables to reflect the deletion. The common difficulty lies in the compositional and hierarchial structure of Charon and the fact that creation or destruction is an action of a mode that has an effect on the much higher system level.

4   R-Charon

4.1   Notation

Let T be a tuple $(t_1, t_2, \ldots, t_n)$. The ith element of T is identified by $T.t_i$. In other words, the tuple element-names are used as record names and the period is used as a selector operator. This notation is extended to sets of tuples as follows. Let ST be a set of tuples with the same structure. The shorthand notation $ST.t_i$ with t_i a set will be used for $\bigcup_{T \in ST} T.t_i$.

Let V be a set of typed variables. A *valuation* for V is a function mapping from V to values, where the mapping is assumed to be type correct. The set of valuations over V is denoted $\mathcal{Q}_V$. Restriction of a valuation $q \in \mathcal{Q}_V$ to a set of variables $W \subseteq V$ is denoted as $q[W]$. Function application of a valuation $q \in \mathcal{Q}_V$ to a variable $v \in V$ is written as $q(v)$ and returns the value of the variable v.

A *flow* for a set V of variables is a differentiable function f from a closed interval of non-negative reals to the set of valuations: $f : [0, \delta] \rightarrow \mathcal{Q}_V$, with $\delta \geq 0$ the *duration* of the flow. The set of all flows for V is denoted as $\mathcal{F}_V$. Restriction of a flow $f \in \mathcal{F}_V$ to a set of variables $W \subseteq V$ is denoted as $f[W]$.

A list l with elements $a_1, \ldots, a_n$ is written as $\langle a_1, \ldots, a_n \rangle$. A list with zero elements is written as $\langle \rangle$. Concatenation of two lists $l_a = \langle a_1, \ldots, a_n \rangle, l_b = \langle b_1, \ldots, b_m \rangle$ is denoted by $l_a \frown l_b$ and results in the list $\langle a_1, \ldots, a_n, b_1, \ldots, b_m \rangle$.

4.2   Syntax

The syntax of Charon is extended to accommodate the proposed (re)configuration concept. The syntax is presented in a top-down fashion. Although counterintuitive for a modular modeling language, this approach is more suitable since the reconfiguration infrastructure is defined on the higher system and agent levels and used in the lower mode level.

System. The components of Section 2 are mapped onto Charon agents. Consequently, agents can be created and destroyed. Moreover, when creating new agents dynamically, the structure of the agent has to be known beforehand. To capture the dynamic set of agents and the possible structures of new agents, we define an R-Charon system as:

Definition 1 (System). *An R-Charon system is a tuple* $(\mathcal{S}, \mathcal{A})$*, where* $\mathcal{S}$ *is a set of structures and* $\mathcal{A}$ *is a set of parallelly composed agents. Each agent is an instantiation of a structure from the set* $\mathcal{S}$*.*

Structures and Agents. Assume that a system $Sys = (\mathcal{S}, \mathcal{A})$ is given. A structure is then defined as:

Definition 2 (Structure). *A structure* $S \in \mathcal{S}$ *is a tuple* (TM, V)*, where* TM *is a set of top-level modes and* V *is a set of typed variables.*

A structure is a blueprint for agents. The set of top-level modes consists of R-Charon modes, which are Charon modes extended as described in the mode syntax section further below. The top-level modes of the structure collectively define the behavior of each R-Charon agent which is an instance of the structure. The set of variables V is partitioned into two sets: a set of local variables V_l and a set of global variables V_g. All global variables of the structure have to originate in some top-level mode, i.e., $V_g \subseteq TM.V_g$. As in Charon, a variable can be of any type, as long as it has a type correct valuation.

To facilitate the concept of adding and removing links between agents, we introduce reference variables. Each instantiated reference variable represents a link to an agent. This introduces another partitioning of the set of variables V of a structure into two sets: the set of reference variables variables V_r and the set of non-reference variables V_{nr}. A reference variable which is instantiated to point to an agent A can be used to access the global variables of A. Note that a reference variable can be a global or a local variable.

A straightforward choice for the type of reference variables would be any $S \in \mathcal{S}$. However, to allow for a greater flexibility we introduce and use the notion of *interface*. The interface of an Agent A of structure S is defined to be the set of global variables of S, $S.V_g$. The set of interfaces $\mathcal{I}$ is then $\mathcal{I} = \{S.V_g | S \in \mathcal{S}\}$. The type of a reference variable can be any $I \in \mathcal{I}$, possibly representing a link to an agent with a *compatible* interface J. An agent with interface I_1 is compatible to a reference variable of type interface I_2, if all variables available in I_2 are also present in I_1, i.e., $I_2 \subseteq I_1$. These definitions enable interface specialization, allowing a single reference variable to link to agents with compatible interfaces but different behaviors.

Each agent $A \in \mathcal{A}$ is an instantiation of a certain structure $S \in \mathcal{S}$, i.e., there exists a function $s : \mathcal{A} \to \mathcal{S}$ mapping each agent to a structure. The structure of each agent remains fixed throughout its entire lifespan. An agent is defined as :

Definition 3 (Agent). *An agent $A \in \mathcal{A}$ of structure $s(A)$ is a tuple (TM, V, I), where TM is a set of top-level modes, V a set of variables, and I is a set of possible initialization assignments to the variables of A.*

The set of top-level modes is a copy of the set of top-level modes of the structure of the agent. The set of variables is a copy of the set of variables of the structure of the agent. The set V is extended with a special fixed variable *this*, always referring to the agent itself. The use of this variable will become apparent in the mode syntax presented below.

Modes. The high-level definition of the mode is identical to a Charon mode:

Definition 4 (Mode). *A mode M is a tuple $(E, X, V, SM, Cons, T)$, where E is a set of entry control points, X is a set of exit control points, V is a set of variables, SM is a set of submodes, $Cons$ is a set of constraints, and T is a set of transitions.*

The entry and exit control points and the submodes are the same as in Charon modes. A mode M is called *atomic* if $M.SM = \emptyset$ and *composite* otherwise. The syntax of the sets of variables, constraints, and transitions is extended to facilitate reconfiguration.

In R-Charon the configuration of the agents and the system can change as the system evolves. Hence, the Charon concept of using fixed agent input and output variables in the description of a mode is changed. Now modes can use the global variables of all agents to which they have a reference. To prevent undesirable behavior, all global variables of agents except for the (discrete) global reference variables are defined to be single writer variables, i.e., read-only for the modes in other agents. Allowing to write to global reference variables provides more flexibility in modeling reconfiguration.

To use the global variables of referenced agents in a mode, some additional syntax is introduced. Consider an agent A with the global variables $A.V_g$. Any mode in an agent with a reference variable v_r pointing to A, can use any global variable $v \in A.V_g$ of A by putting $v_r.v$ in its constraint or transition definitions.

The set of variables V of a mode is partitioned into subsets V_a and V_d, the sets of analog and discrete variables, respectively. In addition, V is partitioned into subsets V_g and V_l of global and local variables, respectively. Let $V_{ref} \subseteq V_d$ be the subset of V containing all reference variables of the mode. Define V_+ to be the set of the readable variables, i.e., the union of V and the sets of global variables V_g of the interfaces of the reference variables in V_{ref}. Moreover define the set V_{act} to be the set of writable variables, i.e., the union of V and the subsets of global reference variables of the interfaces of the reference variables in V_{ref}. The set of derivatives of the variables in V is denoted as $d(V)$.

To enable creation and destruction of agents, the syntax of the action part of the transitions is extended with two special operations: *create* and *destroy*. The create operation has a three tuple argument of the form $(v_r, Init, S)$. With v_r a reference variable afterwards pointing to the new agent, $Init \in \mathcal{Q}_{S.V}$ an initialization of the variables of the agent, and S the structure of the agent to be created. Similar to assignments to reference variables, the interface of S is required to be compatible to the interface type of v_r. The destroy action has one argument, a reference variable pointing to the agent that has to be destructed. Note that self-destruction of an agent is possible using the *this*-variable.

As already formalized in the Charon semantics, T is a set of transitions of the form (e, α, x), where $e \in E \cup SM.X$ and $x \in X \cup SM.E$. The action α has a guard γ attached to it, which in turn is a predicate over the set of valuations of V_+, $\mathcal{Q}_{V_+}$. The action α is a sequence of assignments to the variables V_{act} or create or destroy statements.

Each assignment is of the form $x = g(x_1, \ldots, x_n)$ with $x \in V_{act}$ and $x_1, \ldots, x_n \in V_+$. The function g might be any function on the given arguments, which returns a value with the same type as x. Note that by the definition of V_{act} new links to agents can be created either through assignments to reference variables of the mode or through assignments to global reference variables of referenced agents. A reference to an agent can be removed by assigning a special value ϵ to the reference variable representing the link. Adding as well as removing a link are demonstrated in the *Controller* mode of Figure 3.

As in Charon, the set of constraints consists of a set of invariants, a set of algebraic constraints, and a set of differential constraints, which together define the flow permitted in the mode. Similar to transition actions, the right-hand side of constraints can include variables from the set of global variables of referenced agents, V_+.

4.3   Informal Semantics

The extensions to Charon consist of two parts. The first part consists of the reference variables and the use of global variables of referenced agents in the mode constraints and transitions. This combination enables creation and destruction of links. The second part consists of the creation and destruction of agents. The semantics are defined on three levels: mode, agent, and system. An extensive discussion on the informal semantics and the motivated choices made, can be found in Section 4.4 of [18].

Upon agent creation, a new agent of the specified structure will be created and initialized according to the given initialization assignment on the mode level. The reference variable passed along as a parameter of the create command will point to the newly created agent. On the system level, the newly created agent will be added to the set of agents of the system.

Upon agent destruction, the agent referred to by the argument of the destroy operation, is removed from the set of agents of the system. The passed reference variable is set to ϵ. Upon deleting an agent, all reference variables in the system referring to the deleted agent are set to ϵ.

4.4 Semantics

Mode Operational Semantics. The set of all variables of a mode M as well as all variables of the submodes of M is defined recursively as $M.V_* = M.V \cup M.SM.V_*$. A subset of $M.V_*$ containing all reference variables of a mode M and its submodes, is defined recursively as $M.V_{ref*} = M.V_{ref} \cup M.SM.V_{ref*}$. Assuming that q is the current valuation of the variables in V_*, the set $V_\sharp$ is defined as $M.V_\sharp = M.V_* \cup \bigcup_{v \in M.V_{ref*}} q(v).V_g$. For every composite mode, the set $V_\sharp$ is extended with a local variable h which stores the currently active submode. In case no submode is active, h is valued ϵ. The state of the mode consists of a valuation of $V_\sharp$, denoted by various forms of q. The configuration state is captured by the valuation of the reference variables of the mode.

For any transition $(e, \alpha, x) \in M.T$ of a mode M, the action α is defined as a relation between the states of the variables. As described in the syntax, agents can be created or destroyed in α and as such also affect the system level. Respecting the hierarchy, however, the mode semantics cannot capture this directly. Therefore the relation defining the action is augmented with a list of agents created and destroyed in the action. Such a list will be denoted by various forms of L. The relation part of the action is a relation between $\mathcal{Q}_{V_{act} \setminus V_l}$ and $\mathcal{Q}_{V_{act}}$ if $e \in M.E$ and between $\mathcal{Q}_{V_{act}}$ and $\mathcal{Q}_{V_{act}}$ otherwise. All operations and assignments in α are executed sequentially, atomically, and instantaneously. An augmented pair $((q, q'), L) \in \alpha$ if and only if:

- q satisfies the guard γ attached to α.
- Assuming that α contains k operations, there is a sequence of pairs of a state and a list of created and destroyed agents $(q_1, L_1), (q_2, L_2), \ldots, (q_{k+1}, L_{k+1})$ such that $q_1 = q$, $L_1 = \langle \rangle$, and for every operation i, $1 \leq i \leq k$:
  - Unless specified otherwise, for every $v \in V_\sharp$, $q_{i+1}(v) = q_i(v)$.
  - If operation i is a create operation $(v_r, Init, S)$, then $L_{i+1} = L_i \frown \langle A_{new} \rangle$ with agent $A_{new} = (S.TM, S.V, Init)$ of structure S. Moreover $q_{i+1}(v_r) = A_{new}$ and $q_{i+1}[A_{new}.V] = Init$. Note that A_{new} is created instantly and can be used in operations of the remainder of the transition.
  - If operation i is a destroy operation with argument v_d, then $L_{i+1} = L_i \frown \langle q_i(v_d) \rangle$. Moreover $q_{i+1}(v_d) = \epsilon$ and $q_{i+1}(v) = \epsilon$ for every reference variable $v \in V_\sharp$ with $q_i(v) = q_i(v_d)$.
  - If operation i is neither a create nor a destroy operation, then $L_{i+1} = L_i$ and q_{i+1} is the result of the assignment operation performed in q_i.
- $q' = q_{k+1}$ and $L = L_{k+1}$.

The relations which capture the discrete steps of a mode M (R_D, R_e for $e \in M.E$, and R_x, for $x \in M.X$) are constructed from one or more transitions. As in Charon, the relations are constructed by sequentially aggregating the actions of the transitions, including the added lists of created and destroyed agents.

An atomic mode has a single internal step, which is the idling step. It is enabled if and only if the invariant of the mode is satisfied. Obviously, no agents are created or destroyed. So, for each state q such that $I(q)$, $((q,q),\langle\rangle) \in R_D$. Further an atomic mode can be entered and exited at any time. Since it does not have any entry or exit transitions, neither the state is changed nor agents are created or destroyed. That is, for all q, $((q,q),\langle\rangle) \in R_{de}$ and $((q,q),\langle\rangle) \in R_{dx}$.

For a composite mode M, the entry relations R_e and the exit relations R_x are constructed from the actions of entry, respectively exit transitions of the submodes of M. For each entry transition (e,α,e'), it holds that $((q,q'),L) \in R_e$ if for some q'', $((q,q''),L'') \in \alpha$, e' is an entry point of a submode M', $(q'',q',L') \in M'.R_{e'}$ and $L = L'' \frown L'$. For the default entry point, $((q,q),\langle\rangle) \in R_{de}$ whenever $q(h) \neq \epsilon$, which means that the execution of M has been previously interrupted by a group transition. None of the group transitions added in Charon contains a create or destroy operation and hence the create and destroy list is empty. When $q(h) = \epsilon$, a non-deterministic initialization occurs and thus $((q,q'),L) \in R_{de}$ whenever $((q,q'),L) \in R_e$ for some non-default entry point e. Similarly, for each exit transition (x',α,x) of a composite mode, $((q,q'),L) \in R_x$ if for some q'', $((q,q''),L'') \in M'.R_{x'}$, $((q'',q'),L') \in \alpha$ and $L = L'' \frown L'$. Also, M can be interrupted by a group transition at any moment during its execution and thus always has to be ready to exit through the default exit. Therefore, for every q such that $q(h) \neq \epsilon$, $((q,q),\langle\rangle) \in R_{dx}$.

Internal steps of a composite mode M are either internal steps of M changing the currently active submode or internal steps of the currently active submode of M. If a transition of the mode is involved in the step, then the source submode of the transition should be the active submode and allow an exit step that matches the transition, and also the target submode of the transition should allow a matching entry step. Similar to entry and exit steps, the create and destroy lists are constructed straightforwardly from the create and destroy lists of the transitions within the step. Consequently, $((q,q'),L) \in R_D$ if there exists a state q_0 such that $q_0[V] = q[V]$ and

- For an active submode $N \in M.SM$, it holds that $((q_0[N.V_\sharp], q'[N.V_\sharp]), L) \in N.R_D$ and $q_0[V_\sharp \backslash N.V_\sharp] = q'[V_\sharp \backslash N.V_\sharp]$, or
- The following four conditions hold:
  - There exists an exit point x of the active submode N such that for some q_1 and L_1, $((q_0[N.V_\sharp], q_1[N.V_\sharp]), L_1) \in N.R_x$.
  - There exists an entry point e of a submode N' such that for some q_2 and L_2, $((q_2[N'.V_*], q'[N'.V_*]), L_2) \in N'.R_e$.
  - There exists a transition $(x,\alpha,e) \in M.T$ such that for some L_3, $((q_1,q_2),L_3) \in \alpha$.
  - $L = (L_1 \frown L_3) \frown L_2$.

Similar to the Charon mode semantics, the continuous steps are captured by the relation R_C. The relation $R_C \subseteq \mathcal{Q}_{V_+} \times \mathcal{F}_{V_+}$ gives for every state q of M, the set of flows from q. R_C is obtained from the constraints of a mode and relation

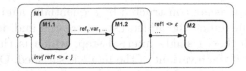

Fig. 5. Example of an additionally required invariant for a used reference variable

$N.R_C$ of its active sub-mode. Given a state Q of a mode M, $(q, f) \in R_C$ if and only if the following three conditions hold:

- The flow f is permitted by M, i.e., f satisfies all constraints in $M.Cons$.
- $(q[N.V_\sharp], f[N.V_\sharp]) \in N.R_C$.
- For each variable x, $q(x) = f(0)(x)$ unless M has an algebraic constraint A_x.

To be able to define the semantics for a mode, all reference variables used in a mode must be initialized, i.e., be unequal to ϵ, at all times at which the mode is active. A reference variable is used if it either appears in a destroy operation or a global variable of the referenced agent appears in the constraints or transitions. Consequently, every mode should have an invariant for each used reference variable, which states that the reference variable is unequal to ϵ. Figure 5 shows an example of a mode $M1$ with one reference variable ref_1 complying to this requirement.

Definition 5 (Mode Operational semantics). *The operational semantics of the mode M, $OS(M)$ is defined to be a six tuple consisting of its control points, its variables and the discrete and continuous relations: $OS(M) = (M.E \cup M.X, M.V_\sharp, M.R_C, M.R_D, \{M.R_e | e \in M.E\}, \{M.R_x | x \in M.X\})$.*

Agent Operational Semantics. Assume that q is the current valuation of the variables in V. Denote the set of all variables as well as all global variables of referenced agents as $V_\sharp$, formally $V_\sharp = V \bigcup_{v \in V_r} q(v).V_g$. The state of the agent consists of a valuation of $V_\sharp$, denoted by various forms of q.

To improve the clarity of the semantics of the system level, we lift the discrete and continuous step relations defined in the mode semantics to the level of the agent semantics. The discrete and continuous relations RA_{init}, RA_D, and RA_C are constructed from the relations R_{init}, R_D, and R_C respectively of the top-level modes of the agent[1]. For $o \in \{init, D\}$, $((q_1, q_2), L) \in RA_o$ if and only if there is an $M \in TM$ such that $((q_1[M.V_\sharp], q_2[M.V_\sharp]), L) \in M.R_o$. For the continuous steps, $(q_1, f) \in RA_C$ if and if only for every mode $M \in TM$, $(q_1[M.V], f[M.V]) \in M.R_C$.

Definition 6 (Agent Operational semantics). *The operational semantics of the agent A, $OS(A)$ is defined to be a five tuple consisting of the control points of its top-level modes, its variables, the continuous step relation, and the discrete step relations: $OS(A) = (A.TM.E \cup A.TM.X, A.V_\sharp, A.RA_C, A.RA_D, A.RA_{init})$.*

---

[1] A Charon top-level mode only has a single entry point *init* and no exit points.

System Operational Semantics. The state of a system consists of a two tuple $(q, \mathcal{A})$. The first element of this tuple is a valuation of all variables of all agents in $\mathcal{A}$. The set of variables $V_\sharp$ of the system is defined as $V_\sharp = \mathcal{A}.V$. The second element of the tuple is the set of all agents that currently exist in the system.

Definition 7 (System operational semantics). *The operational semantics of a system Sys, SO(Sys) consist of the set of structures and the set of agents of the system: $SO(Sys) = (\mathcal{S}, \mathcal{A})$.*

The operational semantics define a transition system $\mathcal{RS}$ over the states of the system Sys. A transition of the system $\mathcal{RS}$ representing a continuous step is denoted by $(q_1, \mathcal{A}) \overset{(f,t)}{\rightarrow} (q_2, \mathcal{A})$ if for all $A \in \mathcal{A}$, $(q_1[A.V], f[A.V]) \in A.RA_C$ with f defined on the interval $[0, t]$ and $f(t) = q_2$. Agents created and destroyed in a discrete step will be added, respectively deleted from the system subsequent to the discrete step. Each destroyed agent will be deleted from the system in a system update delete step. Each created agent will be added in a system update add step which is immediately followed by the discrete initialization steps of the top-level modes of the created agent. System update steps and discrete initialization steps of agents created or destroyed during a discrete initialization step are handled in a depth-first approach. A discrete step and its aftermath are thus best described recursively. For this purpose we introduce the recursive function Γ with as arguments a state $(q, \mathcal{A})$ and a list L of created and destroyed agents. The function $\Gamma((q, \mathcal{A}), L)$ returns all possible parts of the transition system dealing with recursively adding and initializing the agents created and deleting the agents destroyed during the discrete step.

Assuming the function Γ, a transition of the system representing a discrete step and its aftermath is denoted by $(q_1, \mathcal{A}) \overset{o}{\rightarrow} \Gamma((q_2, \mathcal{A}), L)$ if there is an $A \in \mathcal{A}$ such that $((q_1[A.V], q_2[A.V]), L) \in A.RA_o$ for $o \in \{init, D\}$. In a discrete step only one top-level mode of one agent takes a discrete step.

Both the system update add and delete step only occur in the parts of the transition system defined by Γ and are defined in the context of Γ. The function Γ is defined based on the pattern of the list of created and destroyed agents argument. In case the list is empty, no agents have been created or destroyed during the discrete step: $\Gamma((q, \mathcal{A}), \langle \rangle) = (q, \mathcal{A})$. In case the first element of the list is a destroyed agent A_d, first a system update delete step is taken: $\Gamma((q_1, \mathcal{A}), \langle A_d \rangle \frown L) = (q_1, \mathcal{A}) \overset{u_d}{\rightarrow} \Gamma((q_2, \mathcal{A} \backslash \{A_d\}), L)$ if

- $q_2[V_\sharp \backslash \mathcal{A}.V_r] = q_1[V_\sharp \backslash \mathcal{A}.V_r]$.
- For all $v \in \mathcal{A}.V_r$, if $q_1(v) = A_d$ then $q_2(v) = \epsilon$ otherwise $q_2(v) = q_1(v)$. That is, all references to the destroyed agent are removed.

In case the first element of the list is a created agent A_c:

$$\Gamma((q, \mathcal{A}), \langle A_c \rangle \frown L) = (q, \mathcal{A}) \overset{u_a}{\rightarrow} (q_0, \mathcal{A}_0) \overset{init}{\rightarrow}$$

$$\Gamma((q_1, \mathcal{A}_1), L_1) \overset{init}{\rightarrow} \ldots \overset{init}{\rightarrow} \Gamma((q_{k-1}, \mathcal{A}_{k-1}), L_{k-1}) \overset{init}{\rightarrow} \Gamma((q_k, \mathcal{A}_k), L_k \frown L)$$

if

- Agent A_c has k top-level modes, i.e., $|A_c.TM| = k$.
- $q_0[A.c\backslash(A_c.V_r \cap A_c.V_g)] \in A_c.I[A.c\backslash(A_c.V_r \cap A_c.V_g)]$. Note that the valuation of global reference variables of A_c already might have been changed by the remainder of the discrete step in which the agent has been created.
- The created agent is added to the set of agents in the system update step, i.e., $\mathcal{A}_0 = \mathcal{A}_1 = \mathcal{A} \cup \{A_c\}$.
- There is an $M \in A_c.TM$ such that $((q_0[A_c.V], q_1[A_c.V]), L_1) \in M.R_{init}$. That is, the first discrete step initializes one of the top-level modes of the added agent.
- For every $2 \le i \le k$:
  - Denote the last state of the transition system part defined by $\Gamma((q_i, \mathcal{A}_i), L_i)$ as $(q'_i, \mathcal{A}'_i)$.
  - There is an $M' \in A_c.TM\backslash M$ such that $((q'_{i-1}, q_i), L_i) \in M'.R_{init}$. That is, the remaining top-level modes of the added agent are initialized.
  - $\mathcal{A}_i = \mathcal{A}'_{i-1}$.

An execution of a system $Sys = (\mathcal{S}, \mathcal{A})$ is a path through the transition graph of $\mathcal{RS}$ and starts with:

$$(q_0, \mathcal{A}_0) \overset{init}{\to} \Gamma((q_1, \mathcal{A}_1), L_1) \overset{init}{\to} \Gamma((q_2, \mathcal{A}_2), L_2) \overset{init}{\to} \ldots \overset{init}{\to} \Gamma((q_k, \mathcal{A}_k), L_k)$$

such that if we define $(q'_i, \mathcal{A}'_i)$ to denote the last state of a transition system part defined by $\Gamma((q_i, \mathcal{A}_i), L_i)$:

- $\mathcal{A}_0 = \mathcal{A}$ and for all $A \in \mathcal{A}$ it holds that $q_0[A] \in A.I$.
- The number k equals the total number of top-level modes initially in the system, i.e., $k = \sum_{A \in \mathcal{A}} |A.TM|$.
- Each of the k top-level modes initially in the system takes one of the k explicitly described discrete initialization steps.
- For any i, $2 \le i \le k$ it holds that $q_i = q'_{i-1}$ and $\mathcal{A}_i = \mathcal{A}'_{i-1}$.

From that point on the execution continues as follows:

$$\overset{(f_1, t_1)}{\to} (q_{k+1}, \mathcal{A}_{k+1}) \overset{o}{\to} \Gamma((q_{k+2}, \mathcal{A}_{k+2}), L_{k+2}) \overset{f_2, t_2}{\to} \ldots$$

such that for any $i > 0$, i odd, it holds that $\mathcal{A}_{k+i} = \mathcal{A}'_{k+i-1}$.

5   Example Revisited

We discuss a part of a trace of the air-traffic control example system of Section 3:

$$\ldots (q_0, \mathcal{A}) \overset{D}{\to} (q_1, \mathcal{A}) \overset{u_a}{\to} (q_1, \mathcal{A}') \overset{init}{\to} (q_2, \mathcal{A}') \overset{(f_1, 0)}{\to} (q_2, \mathcal{A}') \overset{D}{\to}$$

$$(q_3, \mathcal{A}') \overset{(f_2, t_2)}{\to} (q_4, \mathcal{A}') \overset{D}{\to} (q_5, \mathcal{A}') \overset{u_d}{\to} (q_6, \mathcal{A}) \overset{(f_3, 0)}{\to} (q_6, \mathcal{A}) \overset{D}{\to} (q_7, \mathcal{A}) \overset{(f_3, 0)}{\to} \ldots$$

We consider the system at a stage with three agents: a ground control agent, a center agent, and an airplane agent, i.e., $\mathcal{A} = \{gc, ctr, a\}$. Assuming the airplane is approaching the no-fly zone, a discrete step in the gc agent occurs. In this step, gc creates a new controller c to guide a which results in a system update add step and $\mathcal{A}' = \{gc, ctr, a, c\}$. Note that the valuation q_1 does not change in this step. As described in the semantics, the add step is followed by the discrete initialization step of c. In this initialization step a link from a to c is created, i.e., $q_2(a.con) = c$. The continuous step with flow f_1 has a duration of 0 because the invariant of the *Free flight* mode of a evaluates to false now. The next discrete step is then a mode switch in a to the *Ground control guided* mode. After some time t_2 the airplane has been navigated successfully around the no-fly zone and the controller c destroys itself in a discrete step. This leads to the system update delete step in which the link from a to c is removed ($q_6(a.con) = \epsilon$) and c is removed from the system. Because the invariant in the active mode of a has become false again, the next continuous step has a duration of 0. In the following discrete step, a is forced back into the *Free flight* mode.

6   Conclusion and Future Work

We have presented an extension for reconfigurability to Charon, the hierarchical modular language for hybrid systems. The presented extension is a semi-conservative extension of Charon. i.e., an embedding of a Charon model to an R-Charon model exists [18]. The language extension is designed to support physical as well as communication-wise reconfiguration as encountered in large-scale transportation systems and in modular reconfigurable robots. Applicability of the reconfiguration notion inspired by SHIFT has already been shown [19].

The compositionality results of R-Charon modes can be taken over and extended straightforwardly from the mode compositionality results in [3]. A logical next step is to come up with a sound notion of agent compositionality and to prove that it holds for R-Charon agents. Other relevant work includes extending the Charon toolkit to support the presented reconfiguration concept, applying R-Charon to real modular robot models and use the models for analysis, exploring explicit agent hierarchy and reconfiguration between sub-agents within an agent, and adding a location model as a first class language element.

References

1. Fromherz, M.P.J., Crawford, L.S., Hindi, H.A.: Coordinated control for highly reconfigurable systems. In: HSCC '05: Proceedings of the 8th International Workshop on Hybrid Systems. Volume 3414 of LNCS. Springer-Verlag (2005) 1 – 24
2. Alur, R., Grosu, R., Hur, Y., Kumar, V., Lee, I.: Modular specification of hybrid systems in Charon. In: HSCC '00: Proceedings of the 3rd International Workshop on Hybrid Systems. Volume 1790 of LNCS., Springer-Verlag (2000) 6 – 19
3. Alur, R., Grosu, R., Lee, I., Sokolsky, O.: Compositional modeling and refinement for hierarchical hybrid systems. Journal of Logic and Algebraic Programming (**To appear**)

4. Cuijpers, P.J.L., Reniers, M.A.: Hybrid process algebra. Journal of Logic and Algebraic Programming **62**(2) (2005) 191 – 245
5. Lynch, N.A., Segala, R., Vaandrager, F.W.: Hybrid I/O automata. Information and Computation **185**(1) (2003) 105 – 157
6. Rounds, W.C., Song, H.: The ϕ-calculus: A language for distributed control of reconfigurable embedded systems. In: HSCC '03: Proceedings of the 6th International Workshop on Hybrid Systems. Volume 2623 of LNCS., Springer-Verlag (2003) 435 – 449
7. Varaiya, P.: Smart cars on smart roads: problems of control. IEEE Transactions on Automatic Control **38**(2) (1993) 195 – 207
8. Zelinski, S., Koo, T.J., Sastry, S.: Hybrid system design for formations of autonomous vehicles. In: 42nd IEEE Conference on Decision and Control. Volume 1. (2003) 1 – 6
9. Perry, T.S.: In search of the future of air traffic control. IEEE Spectrum **34**(8) (1997) 18 – 35
10. Bishop, J., Burden, S., Klavins, E., Kreisberg, R., Malone, W., Napp, N., Nguyen, T.: Self-organizing programmable parts. In: International Conference on Intelligent Robots and Systems. (2005)
11. Yim, M., Zhang, Z., Duff, D.: Modular robots. IEEE Spectrum **39**(2) (2002) 30 – 34
12. Østergaard, E.H.: Distributed Control of the ATRON Self-Reconfigurable Robot. PhD thesis, Maersk McKinney Moller Institute for Production Technology, University of Southern Denmark (2004)
13. Deshpande, A., Göllü, A., Semenzato, L.: The SHIFT programming language and run-time system for dynamic networks of hybrid systems. IEEE Transactions on Automatic Control **43**(4) (1998) 584 – 587
14. Milner, R.: Communicating and Mobile Systems: the π-calculus. Cambridge University Press (1999)
15. Aldini, A., Bernardo, M.: On the usability of process algebra: An architectural view. Theoretical Computer Science **335**(2-3) (2005) 281 – 329
16. Attie, P.C., Lynch, N.A.: Dynamic input/output automata: a formal model for dynamic systems. In: CONCUR 2001: 12th International Conference on Concurrency Theory, Aaalborg, Denmark. Volume 2154 of LNCS., Springer-Verlag (2001) 137–151
17. Teich, J., Koster, M.: (Self-)reconfigurable finite state machines: Theory and implementation. In: Proceedings of the conference on Design, automation and test in Europe. (2002) 559 – 568
18. Kratz, F.: A modeling language for reconfigurable distributed hybrid systems. Master's thesis, Technische Universiteit Eindhoven (2005)
19. Antoniotti, M., Göllü, A.: SHIFT and SmartAHS: A language for hybrid systems engineering, modeling, and simulation. In: Proceedings of the USENIX Conference of Domain Specific Languages. (1997)

Estimation and Conflict Detection in Human Controlled Systems

Charles Lesire[1,2] and Catherine Tessier[2]

[1] ENSAE-Supaero, Toulouse, France
charles.lesire@onera.fr
[2] Onera-DCSD, Toulouse, France
catherine.tessier@onera.fr

Abstract. Monitoring a hybrid system subjected to human actions needs both an estimation of the system state and an analysis of the possible conflicts in order to guarantee a safe behavior of the system. Such a monitoring principle is presented in this paper. The estimation of the hybrid system state is performed using the *particle Petri net* model. Then the estimated state is analysed by checking its consistency with respect to the reachable markings of the Petri net. The principle is applied to aircraft pilot's activity tracking and conflict detection.

1 Conflict Detection in Hybrid Systems

Monitoring hybrid systems is a major topic of research in complex applications. Indeed most of the real systems have a hybrid behavior – i.e. a continuous/discrete evolution of the state – induced both by the dynamics of the system (discontinuities, linear approximations) and by external actions that may be performed by a human operator. Moreover a real system is sensitive to environment modifications such as noises, defects... Therefore such a system needs its state to be estimated and its behavior to be analysed so as to ensure that it remains safe.

The work presented in this paper rests both on an estimation of the hybrid state of a system and on a detection of inconsistent behaviors. The monitoring principle is applied to the detection of *conflicts* [1] in the pilot's activities: during a flight, a misunderstanding between two agents (e.g. the pilot and the copilot, the crew and the controller, the crew and the autopilot...) may induce a dangerous situation. The case we are focusing on is the autopilot-pilot conflict: the aircraft state and the pilot's actions on the autopilot are monitored jointly to detect and anticipate possible inconsistencies.

In the next section, hybrid estimators are presented and discussed, and some prerequisites are given in Sect. 3. Then Sect. 4 presents the estimation process which is based on an iterative prediction–correction loop. The conflict detection principle is presented in Sect. 5. The estimation process is illustrated both with a thermostat example and an aircraft approach simulation (Sect. 6).

João Hespanha and A. Tiwari (Eds.): HSCC 2006, LNCS 3927, pp. 407–420, 2006.

2   Hybrid State Estimation

Estimating the state of a hybrid system is widely studied in the literature and involves a large amount of techniques, from numerical filters to network models.

In [2] the estimation rests on a set of Kalman filters, each one tracking a linear mode of the system. The most probable states allow to determine the most probable filter and then the most probable mode of the system (i.e. the most probable behavior of a car like turning, accelerating, etc.) In the same way, [3] propose an estimator based both on hybrid automata to represent the mode evolution and on a particle filter to estimate the continuous state of the system. The estimated mode is then the most probable mode of the system with respect to the estimated continuous states. A similar principle is applied in [4] that uses a concurrent probabilistic hybrid automaton (cPHA) to estimate the mode of the system using Kalman filters.

Bayesian networks are also used to represent hybrid systems by modeling the links between discrete and continuous variables in terms of conditional probabilities over time. Inference rules [5] or particle filtering [6] can be used to estimate the state of a hybrid system. However Bayesian networks suffer from:

1. the necessity to define a measure (probability, possibility...) on the (continuous and discrete) state. This is sometimes impossible to do for instance in case of complete uncertainty (see [7]);
2. the fact that consistency analysis is difficult to perform as the estimations on discrete and continuous states are aggregated within the probability distribution.

In the same way, the analysis of conflicts, or conversely consistency, is mainly based on the study of continuous variables. In [8] the hybrid system must satisfy constraints that are checked on the continuous estimated states of the system. Del Vecchio and Murray [9] use lattices to identify the discrete mode of a hybrid system when only continuous variables are observed. In [10], the reachability analysis, based on hybrid automata, allows to identify safe and dangerous behaviors of the system and is applied to an aircraft collision problem. Nielsen and Jensen [11] define a conflict measure on the estimated state of a Bayesian network; nevertheless this method still suffers from the need to define a measure on totally uncertain states, and from the fact that the conflict measure is continuous, which leads to a threshold effect. In [12] an aircraft procedure and pilot's actions are jointly modeled using a *particle Petri net* that allows the procedure to be simulated using a Monte-Carlo method and the results to be analysed using the Petri net properties. Hence only the nominal procedure is modeled and the analysis is based on qualitative properties and does not involve any continuous measure.

The monitoring system presented in this paper is based on the later work: it allows both the estimation to be computed and the consistency of the estimated states to be analysed without defining *a priori* measures on unknown states. Indeed it is the structure of the Petri net-based model itself which allows the consistency to be checked. The next section mentions the main definitions of particle Petri nets.

3   Prerequisites

3.1   Particle Filtering

The particle filter [13] allows the state x_k at time k of a dynamic system subject to deterministic and random inputs to be estimated from observations z_k spoilt with stochastic errors. It is based on a discretization of the uncertainty on the state value: the probability distribution function of the estimate $\hat{x}_{k|k}$ – meaning the state estimated at time k knowing the observation at time k – is represented by a set of N particles $x_{k|k}^{(1)}, \ldots, x_{k|k}^{(N)}$ (see Fig. 1). The estimation is achieved through a two-step process : the *prediction*, that consists of estimating the next particles $x_{k+1|k}^{(i)}$ according to the evolution model, and the *correction*, that is based on a comparison of the expected particle values with the observation: the closer the expected particles are to the most probable value of the observation, the bigger weight they are assigned. Then N new particles $x_{k+1|k+1}^{(i)}$ are generated from a resampling of the weighted corrected particles.

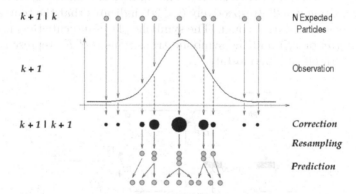

Fig. 1. Particle filtering (from [14])

3.2   Particle Petri Nets

A Petri net $< P, T, F, B >$ is a bipartite graph with two types of nodes: P is a finite set of places; T is a finite set of transitions [15]. Arcs are directed and represent the forward incidence function $F : P \times T \rightarrow \mathbb{N}$ and the backward incidence function $B : P \times T \rightarrow \mathbb{N}$ respectively. An *interpreted Petri net* is such that conditions and events are associated with places and transitions. When the conditions corresponding to some places are satisfied, tokens are assigned to those places and the net is said to be marked. The evolution of tokens within the net follows transition firing rules. Petri nets allow sequencing, parallelism and synchronization to be easily represented.

A *particle Petri net* [12] is a hybrid Petri net model where places and transitions are either numerical or symbolic:

1. *numerical places* P_N are associated with differential equations representing the continuous evolution of the system;
2. *numerical transitions* T_N are associated with conditions and represent mode changes in the system dynamics;
3. *symbolic places* P_S and *transitions* T_S are associated with symbolic states and actions respectively.

The state of the system is represented by a set of tokens, that are *particles* $\pi_{k+1|k}^{(i)}$ – meaning particle number i at time $k+1$ knowing the observation at time k –, evolving within the numerical places, and a set of *configurations* $\delta_{k+1|k}^{(j)}$ evolving within symbolic places. A marking $m_{i,j} = (\pi^{(i)}, \delta^{(j)})$ represents a possible state of the system. The firing rules [12] associated with numerical and symbolic transitions allow all the expected states of the system to be computed whatever the actions.

Figure 2 is the particle Petri net of a thermostat. The thermostat manages temperature[1] θ between $20°C$ and $25°C$. The numerical places p_0, p_1 and p_2 are associated with differential equations modeling heating ($\dot{\theta} = -0.2\theta + 5.4$) and cooling ($\dot{\theta} = -0.1\theta + 1.2$) respectively. The numerical transitions correspond to guards: transition $\theta > 25$ (respectively $\theta < 20$) indicates that the temperature is (respectively is not) warm enough. The symbolic places indicate the modes of the thermostat (*on* or *off*) and the symbolic transitions (*OFF*) represent external actions to turn off the thermostat.

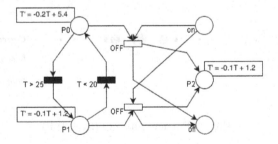

Fig. 2. The thermostat Petri net

4   Estimation of Particle Petri Net Marking

The estimator presented here is based on the particle filtering principle and computes the expected markings of a particle Petri net. The estimation is achieved through a two-step process:

---

[1] The temperature is noted θ in the text and T on figures as the θ character is not available in the estimation software and T is already the set of transitions of the particle Petri net.

1. a prediction of the expected markings, according to the particle Petri net firing rules, that computes all the possible combinations of numerical and symbolic states;
2. a correction of the markings according to an observation made on the system.

4.1   Prediction

The prediction is achieved through the computation of the *reachable markings* of the particle Petri net, i.e. the set of the expected states. It is based both on an *isoparticle evolution*, i.e. an evolution of the tokens within the net to model mode changes according to actions, and an *isomarking evolution*, i.e. an evolution of the particles according to differential equations.

Let us consider the example of the thermostat (Fig. 2), and let the initial marking be $\pi_{0|0}^{(0)} = 20°C$ marking place p_0 and $\delta^{(0)}$ marking place *on*. Then the expected marking at time 1 is the marking shown on Fig. 3, where

1. in place p_0, particle $\pi^{(0)} = 21.4°C$ has evolved according to the heating differential equation;
2. in place p_2, particle $\pi^{(1)} = 19.2°C$ has evolved according to the cooling differential equation, predicting the situation corresponding to the thermostat being turned off;
3. configurations $\delta^{(0)}$ and $\delta^{(1)}$ in symbolic places *on* and *off* respectively indicate that the thermostat may be either on or off at time 1.

Thereby the marking at time k represents the estimated states as a set of tokens – the set of particles being a discretization of the probability distribution on the continuous state –, and the prediction step computes the expected marking at time $k + 1$.

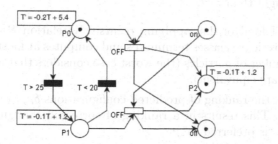

Fig. 3. Predicted marking at time 1

4.2   Correction

The correction consists in comparing matchings between the predicted tokens and the incoming observation and selecting the "best" ones. The correction process:

1. weights the predicted particles according to the noisy observation:

$$w(\pi_{k+1|k}^{(i)}) = \frac{p(z_{k+1}|\pi_{k+1|k}^{(i)})}{\displaystyle\sum_{j=0}^{N} p(z_{k+1}|\pi_{k+1|k}^{(j)})} \tag{1}$$

where z_{k+1} is the observation at time $k+1$, $w(\pi)$ is the weight of particle π and $p(z|\pi)$ is the conditional probability to observe z knowing the expected state π;

2. groups the weighted particles according to the equivalence relation $\mathcal{R}$:

$$\pi^{(i)}\mathcal{R}\pi^{(j)} \Leftrightarrow \begin{cases} \forall p \in P_N, (\pi^{(i)} \in \mathcal{M}(p) \Leftrightarrow \pi^{(j)} \in \mathcal{M}(p)) \\ \forall \pi^{(k)} \in \Pi \ / \ \forall p \in P_N(\pi^{(i)} \in \mathcal{M}(p) \Rightarrow \pi^{(k)} \notin \mathcal{M}(p)), \\ \quad (w(\pi^{(i)}) \geq w(\pi^{(k)}) \Leftrightarrow w(\pi^{(j)}) \geq w(\pi^{(k)})) \end{cases} \tag{2}$$

where $\Pi = \{\pi^{(i)}, i \in [\![1; N]\!]\}$ and $\mathcal{M}(p)$ is the marking of place p. The equivalence classes are noted $\Gamma = \{\gamma_{k+1|k}^{(i)}\}$, and their weights are defined by

$$w(\gamma_{k+1|k}^{(i)}) = \sum_{\pi \in \gamma_{k+1|k}^{(i)}} w(\pi) \tag{3}$$

The process is then recursively applied on Γ to group the equivalence classes until they are restricted to singletons;

Remark 1. The equivalence relation $\mathcal{R}$ is designed to help diagnose the state of the system by reducing the size of the data to be analysed. (2) means that particles $\pi^{(i)}$ and $\pi^{(j)}$ are equivalent if they mark the same place p and for each particle $\pi^{(k)}$ which is not in p, both $\pi^{(i)}$ and $\pi^{(j)}$ have either a higher or lower weight than $\pi^{(k)}$.

Remark 2. The algorithm applying recursively relation $\mathcal{R}$ on particles and then on equivalence classes terminates and computes at most N steps, where N is the number of particles (the worst case considers that at each step only two classes are equivalent).

3. updates [16] the ranking of predicted configurations $\delta_{k+1|k}$ according to the observation. This results in a ranking of corrected configurations $\delta_{k+1|k+1}$ ($\prec_\Delta$ means "is preferred to"):

$$(z_{k+1} \to \delta_{k+1|k}^{(i)}) \wedge (z_{k+1} \not\to \delta_{k+1|k}^{(j)}) \Rightarrow \delta_{k+1|k+1}^{(i)} \prec_\Delta \delta_{k+1|k+1}^{(j)} \tag{4}$$

where $z \to \delta$ means that configuration δ matches observation z (see Example 1 below). (4) means that the configurations matching the observation are preferred to the configurations not matching the observation.

If both $\delta_{k+1|k}^{(i)}$ and $\delta_{k+1|k}^{(j)}$ match (or do not match) the configuration, the ranking is not changed, the relation between $\delta_{k+1|k+1}^{(i)}$ and $\delta_{k+1|k+1}^{(j)}$ is the same as between $\delta_{k+1|k}^{(i)}$ and $\delta_{k+1|k}^{(j)}$:

$$
(z_{k+1} \to \delta_{k+1|k}^{(i)} \wedge z_{k+1} \to \delta_{k+1|k}^{(j)})
$$
$$
\Rightarrow (\delta_{k+1|k+1}^{(i)} \precsim_\Delta \delta_{k+1|k+1}^{(j)} \Leftrightarrow \delta_{k+1|k}^{(i)} \precsim_\Delta \delta_{k+1|k}^{(j)}) \tag{5}
$$

$$
(z_{k+1} \not\to \delta_{k+1|k}^{(i)} \wedge z_{k+1} \not\to \delta_{k+1|k}^{(j)})
$$
$$
\Rightarrow (\delta_{k+1|k+1}^{(i)} \precsim_\Delta \delta_{k+1|k+1}^{(j)} \Leftrightarrow \delta_{k+1|k}^{(i)} \precsim_\Delta \delta_{k+1|k}^{(j)}) \tag{6}
$$

The relation $\precsim_\Delta$ (meaning "is preferred or equivalent to") is a partial pre-order on the set of configurations;

Example 1. In the thermostat example, relation $\to$, representing the matching between predicted configurations and the observation, is defined by :

(a) *on* $\to$ *on* and *on* $\not\to$ *off*,
(b) *off* $\to$ *off* and *off* $\not\to$ *on*,
(c) *on* $\wedge$ *off* $\to$ *on* and *on* $\wedge$ *off* $\to$ *off*
(d) *false* $\to$ *on* and *false* $\to$ *off*

where case (c) corresponds to an observation of both modes *on* and *off*, that may come from a sensor error, and case (d) corresponds to an empty observation (*false*) that may come from a sensor failure.

4. constructs the *correction graph* by ranking (relation $\precsim$) the markings $m_{i,j} = (\gamma^{(i)}, \delta^{(j)})$, according to the weights on $\gamma^{(i)}$ and to relation $\precsim_\Delta$ on configurations $\delta^{(j)}$:

$$
m_{i,j} \prec m_{k,l} \Leftrightarrow \begin{cases} w(\gamma^{(i)}) \geq w(\gamma^{(k)}) \wedge \delta^{(j)} \precsim_\Delta \delta^{(l)} \\ w(\gamma^{(i)}) > w(\gamma^{(k)}) \vee \delta^{(j)} \prec_\Delta \delta^{(l)} \end{cases} \tag{7}
$$
$$
m_{i,j} \sim m_{k,l} \Leftrightarrow (w(\gamma^{(i)}) = w(\gamma^{(k)}) \wedge \delta^{(j)} \sim_\Delta \delta^{(l)}) \tag{8}
$$

5. resamples the particles : N new particles $\pi_{k+1|k+1}^{(i)}$ are drawn from the discrete probability law $\{\pi_{k+1|k}^{(i)}, w(\pi_{k+1|k}^{(i)})\}$. The particles are then spoilt with the model noise to represent the model approximation.

The resampled particles represent the estimated numerical states of the system at time $k+1$ and are introduced in the next prediction step. The correction graph built from predicted tokens is analysed to detect inconsistencies. This analysis is presented in the next section. The whole estimation process is illustrated in Sect. 6 on the thermostat example.

5   Consistency Analysis and Conflict Detection

A state of the system is said to be consistent if it is a possible state with respect to the initial state and to the model of the nominal behavior of the system. The set of possible states can be computed before the on-line estimation and consists in computing the reachable states of the particle Petri net.

Hence an ordinary safe Petri net[4] is associated with the particle Petri net of the system such as one ordinary token is associated to each place corresponding to a marked (by particles or by configurations) place in the particle Petri net.

Let the initial marking of the ordinary safe Petri net of the thermostat (Fig. 2) be $\mathcal{M}_0 = (1\,0\,0\,1\,0)$: places p_0 and *on* are marked, places p_1, p_2 and *off* are empty. Then marking $\mathcal{M}_0$ represents the initial state of the Petri net: the thermostat is on and heating.

The reachable states of the particle Petri net correspond to the *reachable markings* of the safe Petri net represented in Fig. 4. This graph is the classical automaton of a thermostat, with three modes: *on* (marking $\mathcal{M}_0$), *idle* (marking $\mathcal{M}_1$) and *off* (marking $\mathcal{M}_2$). Consequently the markings that are inconsistent in the estimation process are:

1. $\mathcal{M}_4 = (0\,0\,1\,1\,0)$, meaning that the thermostat is *on* but the temperature decreases;
2. $\mathcal{M}_5 = (1\,0\,0\,0\,1)$, meaning that the thermostat is *off* but is still heating;
3. $\mathcal{M}_6 = (0\,1\,0\,0\,1)$, meaning that the thermostat is *off* but will heat as soon as the temperature is under 20.

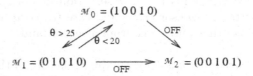

Fig. 4. Reachable markings of the thermostat Petri net

Remark 3. The computation of the reachable markings may be complex in general as the set of reachable markings may be infinite. Nevertheless the set of reachable markings of a safe Petri net is finite.

The consistency analysis is achieved through the study of the correction graph computed during the correction process:

1. Each marking $m_{i,j} = (\gamma^{(i)}, \delta^{(j)})$ is associated with a marking $\widetilde{m}_{i,j}$ in the associated safe Petri net:

$$\forall p \in P = P_N \cup P_S, \quad \widetilde{m}_{i,j}(p) = \begin{cases} 1 \text{ if } \gamma^{(i)} \in \mathcal{M}(p)^5 \text{ or } \delta^{(j)} \in \mathcal{M}(p) \\ 0 \text{ otherwise} \end{cases} \quad (9)$$

---

[4] An ordinary Petri net is a Petri net with no interpretation containing undifferentiated classical tokens. A Petri net is said to be *safe* for an initial marking $\mathcal{M}_0$ if for all reachable markings, each place contains zero or one token.

2. Then the consistency of $m_{i,j}$ is checked:

$$m_{i,j} \text{ is consistent } \Leftrightarrow \tilde{m}_{i,j} \in \mathcal{G} \tag{10}$$

where $\mathcal{G}$ is the graph of the reachable markings of the safe Petri net.

Knowing the (in)consistent markings of the correction graph is a first step towards the detection of conflictual situations. Some issues in analysing such a graph are currently under study, for instance about using the graph in the resampling strategy or identifying patterns in the correction graph to detect well-known conflictual situations.

The next section presents some examples and results about the estimation principle and the consistency analysis.

6   Simulations

6.1   Thermostat Monitoring

This subsection illustrates the estimation process and the consistency analysis presented in the previous section. The initial marking of the thermostat is represented in Fig. 5 where 50 particles have been drawn from the normal distribution $\mathcal{N}(22°C, 1)$ – $22°C$ is the initially observed temperature.

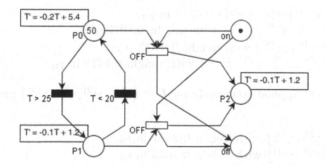

Fig. 5. Initial estimated state of the thermostat: the thermostat is on, heating, and the temperature is approximatively $22°C$

Temperature Estimation. Figure 6 is the result of the estimation process launched on the Petri net of Fig. 5 with a new observation of the temperature and the thermostat mode every second. The dashed line represents the (noisy) observations and the crosses are the particles.

We can notice that the shape of the estimated temperature smoothly fits the observed temperature, meaning that the estimation well corresponds to the

---

[5] By abuse of notation, $\gamma^{(i)} \in \mathcal{M}(p)$ means that all the particles in $\gamma^{(i)}$ are marking place p (which is true by construction of $\gamma^{(i)}$).

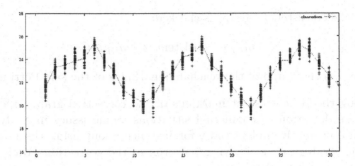

Fig. 6. Estimation of the temperature

thermostat behavior. To illustrate the estimation process, let us consider the correction step at time 1.

The observation at time 1 is $z_1 = (21.567°C, \ on)$. Table 1 contains the ten best predicted particles according to z_1 and their associated weights. As far as the consistency analysis is concerned, it is easily guessed that analysing the whole table, containing fifty columns (one per particle), is not obvious. Then the particles are grouped in equivalence classes according to relation $\mathcal{R}$ applied recursively: when the particles are ranked by weight, (2) consists in making classes by grouping the particles by place following the ranking. The first step of the construction results in the following equivalence classes:

1. $\gamma^{(1)} = \{\pi^{(11)}\}$ with weight 0.0361 in p_2,
2. $\gamma^{(2)} = \{\pi^{(12)}, \pi^{(25)}, \pi^{(17)}\}$ with weight 0.1077 in p_0,
3. $\gamma^{(3)} = \{\pi^{(41)}, \pi^{(18)}\}$ with weight 0.0702 in p_2,
4. $\gamma^{(4)} = \{\pi^{(8)}, \pi^{(29)}, \pi^{(1)}, \pi^{(42)}\}$ with weight 0.1410 in p_0.

Relation (2) applied recursively on $\Gamma = \{\gamma^{(1)}, \gamma^{(2)}, \gamma^{(3)}, \gamma^{(4)}\}$ gives as a final result:

1. $\gamma^{(5)} = \{\gamma^{(4)}, \gamma^{(2)}\}$ with weight 0.2487 in p_0,
2. $\gamma^{(6)} = \{\gamma^{(3)}, \gamma^{(1)}\}$ with weight 0.1063 in p_2.

The associated correction graph is drawn in Fig. 7 where $\delta^{(0)} = on$ and $\delta^{(1)} = off$: as the observation is on, $\delta^{(0)} \prec \delta^{(1)}$, and as $w(\gamma^{(5)}) > w(\gamma^{(6)})$, the marking relation is $m_{5,0} \prec m_{5,1}$, $m_{5,0} \prec m_{6,0}$, $m_{5,0} \prec m_{6,1}$, $m_{5,1} \prec m_{6,1}$ and $m_{6,0} \prec m_{6,1}$.

The framed markings are consistent. As a result, the best marking (the root of the graph) is consistent and matches the on state (thermostat on and heating).

Table 1. Best weighted particles at time 1

particle number	11	12	25	41	17	18	8	29	1	42
θ	21.581	21.594	21.535	21.615	21.618	21.624	21.630	21.502	21.638	21.642
weight	0.0361	0.0360	0.0360	0.0357	0.0357	0.0355	0.0354	0.0353	0.0352	0.0351
place	p_2	p_0	p_0	p_2	p_0	p_2	p_0	p_0	p_0	p_0

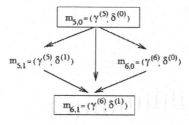

Fig. 7. Correction graph at time 1

Inconsistent Behaviors. In order to study the consistency of the thermostat behavior, two faulty cases are considered. Both consist in a wrong behavior of the thermostat that stops heating at temperatures $26°C$ and $24°C$ respectively.

Figure 8 is the result of the estimation of the thermostat that stops heating at $26°C$. At time 7, the best marking (given the observation at time 7) has a weight of 0.9985 and matches the state *idle* (places p_1 and *on*). At time 8, the best marking has a weight of 0.9970 and matches the state *on* (places p_0 and *on*). The difficulty to estimate the right state can be explained by the fact that the behavior is misunderstood by the estimator as no particle has a temperature around $26°C$.

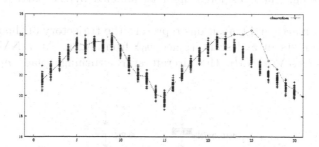

Fig. 8. Conflict detection: the behavior of the thermostat is unknown

At time 22, the best marking matches the *idle* state (place p_1 and *on*) with a weight of 1. Then from time 23, the best markings match state *off* (places p_2 and *off*) and consequently are inconsistent as the observation is *on*. The difficulty to track the behavior results in the fact that the estimation is completely wrong: all the particles are out of the main part of the Gaussian observation – 99% of the probability of a Gaussian distribution is within $[\mu - 3\sigma; \mu + 3\sigma]$ where μ is the mean value and σ the standard deviation.

This case shows that the prediction does not match the observations very well as nearly no particle has a temperature around $26°C$. Nevertheless the estimation is able to track the temperature over $25°C$. Switching from consistent to inconsistent matchings (times 7 and 8) reveals an inconsistent behavior.

Figure 9(a) is the result of the estimation of the thermostat that stops heating at $24°C$. In that case the estimation is completely different: all the correction graphs

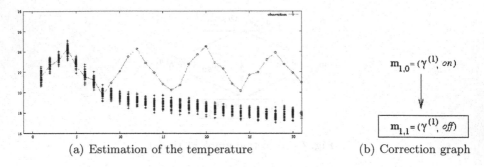

(a) Estimation of the temperature   (b) Correction graph

Fig. 9. Conflict detection: the behavior of the thermostat corresponds to the *off* mode

from time 4 are the same (Fig. 9(b), where $\gamma^{(1)} \in p_2$). Indeed the numerical observations can be explained as they match the particles within place p_2. However the symbolic observation is *on*. Then the best corrected marking is inconsistent and reveals a fault: the temperature evolves as if the thermostat was off.

6.2   Estimation of the Pilot's Activity

This section presents an application of the estimation principle to aircraft pilot's activity tracking. The considered flight is modeled by the particle Petri net of Fig. 10.

Numerical places and transitions represent the trajectory of the aircraft. The procedure consists of a descent (place p_0) from Agen. At 7 NM from Agen (transition $d(AGN){>}7NM$), the aircraft starts turning (place p_1) and when

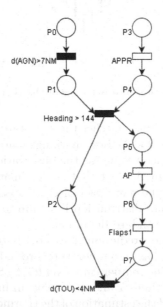

Fig. 10. The particle Petri net of the Approach from Agen to Toulouse

intercepting heading 144° (transition *Heading>144*), the aircraft has to perform a deceleration (place p_2). At 4 NM from Toulouse (transition *d(TOU)<4NM*), the Approach procedure is finished: the next phase is the Landing procedure. The symbolic transitions correspond to pressing the Approach button (transition APPR while descending or turning), engaging the autopilot and setting flaps 1 (transitions AP and Flaps1 while decelerating). Then the configurations have attributes *APPR*, *AP* and *Flaps*. The particles have attributes x, y, z (the 3-D coordinates of the aircraft), s (the speed) and h (the heading).

The estimation of the aircraft position (x and y coordinates) is represented in Fig. 11. The dashed lines represent the nominal trajectory of the aircraft and the dots represent the estimated particles. At time 0, the aircraft position is quite uncertain: the initial distribution is diffuse. The estimation becomes more precise from time 10.

At time 220, some particles mark place p_2 (the aircraft may be decelerating) but the main corrected state matches place p_1: the aircraft is still turning. At this time the observation states that the Approach button is not pressed. The correction graph at time 220 is shown in Fig. 12, with $\gamma^{(i)} \in p_i$ for $i \in \{1, 2\}$ and $\delta^{(j)} \in p_j$ for $j \in \{3, 4, 5, 6, 7\}$. Marking $m_{2,3}$ is close to the best marking $m_{1,3}$ and is inconsistent: it has to be studied and tracked while estimating the system state. Indeed it allows to anticipate a possible conflict that may occur if the Approach button is not pressed in a near future.

At time 230 most of the corrected particles are in p_2 and the Approach button is pressed (according to the observation): a safe state is recovered.

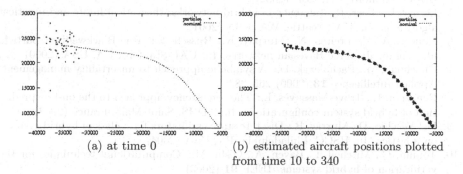

(a) at time 0

(b) estimated aircraft positions plotted from time 10 to 340

Fig. 11. Estimation of the aircraft position

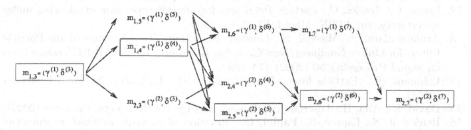

Fig. 12. Correction graph of the Approach at time 220

7   Conclusion

The particle Petri net-based estimation principle that is presented in this paper paves the way to the detection of inconsistent behaviors in systems subjected to discrete actions – e.g. human actions on the system interface. Therefore the paper has focused on the ability of the estimation principle to track and diagnose hybrid systems. Computational issues will be studied and discussed on future works.

Ongoing work is focusing on the analysis of the correction graph, and more specifically on inconsistent states. What is considered is to study the dynamics of inconsistent states within the correction graph while monitoring the system in order to design an automatic monitoring agent for hybrid systems that would allow an early detection of conflicts.

Experiments are being prepared with the flight simulator at Supaero in order to assess conflict detection in procedures involving complex autopilot modes.

References

1. Dehais, F., Tessier, C., Chaudron, L.: GHOST: experimenting conflicts counter-measures in the pilot's activity. In: IJCAI, Acapulco, Mexico (2003)
2. Veeraraghavan, H., Papanikolopoulos, N.: Combining multiple tracking modalities for vehicle tracking in traffic intersections. In: ICRA, New Orleans, LA, USA (2004)
3. Koutsoukos, X., Kurien, J., Zhao, F.: Estimation of distributed hybrid systems using particle filtering methods. In: HSCC, Prague, Czech Republic (2003)
4. Hofbaur, M., Williams, B.: Mode estimation of probabilistic hybrid systems. In: HSCC, Stanford, CA, USA (2002)
5. Lerner, U., Parr, R.: Inference in hybrid networks: theoretical limits and practical algorithms. In: UAI, Seattle, WA, USA (2001)
6. Doucet, A., de Freitas, N., Murphy, K., Russell, S.: Rao-Blackwellised particle filtering for dynamic Bayesian networks. In: UAI, Stanford, CA, USA (2000)
7. Chachoua, M., Pacholczyk, D.: A symbolic approach to uncertainty management. Applied Intelligence 13 (2000) 265–283
8. Benazera, E., Travé-Massuyès, L.: The consistency approach to the on-line prediction of hybrid system configurations. In: ADHS, Saint-Malo, France (2003)
9. Del Vecchio, D., Murray, R.: Discrete state estimators for a class of hybrid systems on a lattice. In: HSCC, Philadelphia, PA, USA (2004)
10. Tomlin, C., Mitchell, I., Bayen, A., Oishi, M.: Computational techniques for the verification of hybrid systems. IEEE 91 (2003)
11. Nielsen, T., Jensen, F.: Alert systems for production plants: a methodology based on conflict analysis. In: ECSQARU, Barcelona, Spain (2005)
12. Lesire, C., Tessier, C.: Particle Petri nets for aircraft procedure monitoring under uncertainty. In: ATPN, Miami, FL, USA (2005)
13. Arulampalam, S., Maskell, S., Gordon, N., Clapp, T.: A Tutorial on Particle Filters for Online Nonlinear/Non-Gaussian Bayesian Tracking. IEEE Transactions on Signal Processing 50 (2002) 174–188
14. Lehmann, E.: Particle filter. Ph.D. Coursework, Australian National Unversity (2003)
15. David, R., Alla, H.: Discrete, continuous, and hybrid Petri nets. Springer (2005)
16. Benferhat, S., Lagrue, S., Papini, O.: Revision of partially ordered information: axiomatisation, semantics and iteration. In: IJCAI, Edinburgh, UK (2005)

Stability Analysis of Hybrid Systems Via Small-Gain Theorems

Daniel Liberzon[1,*] and Dragan Nešić[2,**]

[1] Coordinated Science Laboratory,
University of Illinois at Urbana-Champaign,
Urbana, IL 61801, USA
liberzon@uiuc.edu
[2] Department of Electrical and Electronic Engineering,
University of Melbourne, Parkville, 3052, Victoria, Australia
d.nesic@ee.unimelb.edu.au

Abstract. We present a general approach to analyzing stability of hybrid systems, based on input-to-state stability (ISS) and small-gain theorems. We demonstrate that the ISS small-gain analysis framework is very naturally applicable in the context of hybrid systems. Novel Lyapunov-based and LaSalle-based small-gain theorems for hybrid systems are presented. The reader does not need to be familiar with ISS or small-gain theorems to be able to follow the paper.

1 Introduction

The small-gain theorem is a classical tool for analyzing input-output stability of feedback systems; see, e.g., [1]. More recently, small-gain tools have been used extensively to study feedback interconnections of nonlinear state-space systems in the presence of disturbances; see, e.g., [2]. Hybrid systems can be naturally viewed as feedback interconnections of simpler subsystems. For example, every hybrid system can be regarded as a feedback interconnection of its continuous and discrete dynamics. This makes small-gain theorems a very natural tool to use for studying internal and external stability of hybrid systems. However, we are not aware of any systematic application of this idea in the literature.

The purpose of this paper is to bring the small-gain analysis method to the attention of the hybrid systems community. We review, in a tutorial fashion, the concept of input-to-state stability (ISS) introduced by Sontag [3] and a nonlinear small-gain theorem from [2] based on this concept. The ISS small-gain theorem states that a feedback interconnection of two ISS systems is ISS if an appropriate composition of their respective ISS gain functions is smaller than the identity function. Since a proof of this theorem can be based entirely on time-domain analysis of system signals, the result is valid for general dynamical systems, thus

---

* Supported by NSF ECS-0134115 CAR and DARPA/AFOSR MURI F49620-02-1-0325 Awards.
** Supported by the Australian Research Council under the Discovery Grants and Australian Professorial Fellow schemes.

João Hespanha and A. Tiwari (Eds.): HSCC 2006, LNCS 3927, pp. 421–435, 2006.

providing an "off-the-shelf" method for verifying stability of hybrid systems. We also discuss Lyapunov-based tools for checking the hypotheses of this theorem.

As an alternative to time-domain proofs, Lyapunov function constructions for interconnected systems under small-gain conditions were studied for continuous-time systems in [4] and for discrete-time systems in [5]. It is well known that having a Lyapunov function provides additional insight into the behavior of a stable system and is important for tasks such as perturbation analysis and estimating the region of attraction. In this paper, we present a novel construction of a Lyapunov function for a class of hybrid systems satisfying the conditions of the ISS small-gain theorem. We also describe another approach, based on constructing a "weak" (non-strictly decreasing) Lyapunov function and applying the LaSalle invariance principle for hybrid systems from [6]. While the basic idea of the small-gain stability analysis for hybrid systems was announced and initially examined by the authors in [7], the Lyapunov function constructions reported here are new and represent the main technical contribution of this work.

In the companion paper [7], we illustrate the power of the proposed method through a detailed treatment of several specific problems in the context of hybrid control with communication constraints. As demonstrated there, the small-gain analysis provides insightful interpretations of existing results, immediately leads to generalizations, and allows a unified treatment of problems that so far have been studied separately. Due to the pervasive nature of hybrid systems in applications, we expect that the main ideas described in this paper will be useful in many other areas as well.

2   Preliminaries

In what follows, *id* denotes the identity function and ∘ denotes function composition. We write $a \vee b$ for $\max\{a, b\}$ and $a \wedge b$ for $\min\{a, b\}$. The class of continuously differentiable functions is denoted by C^1 (the domain will be specified separately). The gradient operator is denoted by ∇. Given some vectors $x_1 \in \mathbb{R}^{n_1}$ and $x_2 \in \mathbb{R}^{n_2}$, we often use the simplified notation (x_1, x_2) for the "stack" vector $(x_1^T, x_2^T)^T \in \mathbb{R}^{n_1 + n_2}$.

2.1   Hybrid System Model

We begin by describing the model of a hybrid system to which our subsequent results will apply. This model easily fits into standard modeling frameworks for hybrid systems (see, e.g., [8, 6, 9]), and the reader can consult these references for background and further technical details. The description to be provided here is somewhat informal, but it is sufficient for presenting the results.

We label the hybrid system to be defined below as $\mathcal{H}$. The *state variables* of $\mathcal{H}$ are divided into continuous variables $x \in \mathbb{R}^n$ and discrete variables $\mu \in \mathbb{R}^k$. We note that μ actually takes values in a discrete subset of $\mathbb{R}^k$ along every trajectory of the hybrid system, but this set need not be fixed a priori and may vary with initial conditions. The *time* is continuous: $t \in [t_0, \infty)$. We also consider *external variables* $w \in \mathbb{R}^s$, viewed as disturbances.

The *state dynamics* describing the evolution of these variables with respect to time are composed of *continuous evolution* and *discrete events*. During continuous evolution (i.e., while no discrete events occur), μ is held constant and x satisfies the ordinary differential equation $\dot{x} = f(x, \mu, w)$ with $f : \mathbb{R}^n \times \mathbb{R}^k \times \mathbb{R}^s \to \mathbb{R}^n$ locally Lipschitz. We now describe the discrete events. Given an arbitrary time t, we will denote by $x^-(t)$, or simply by x^- when the time arguments are omitted, the quantity $x(t^-) = \lim_{s \nearrow t} x(s)$, and similarly for the other state variables. Consider a *guard map* $G : \mathbb{R}^{n+k} \to \mathbb{R}^p$ (where p is a positive integer) and a *reset map* $R : \mathbb{R}^{n+k} \to \mathbb{R}^{n+k}$. The discrete events are defined as follows: whenever $G(x^-, \mu^-) \geq 0$ (component-wise), we let $(x, \mu) = R(x^-, \mu^-) = \big(R_x(x^-, \mu^-), R_\mu(x^-, \mu^-)\big)$. By construction, all signals are right-continuous.

Some remarks on the above relations are in order. In many situations, the continuous state does not jump at the event times: $R_x(x, \mu) \equiv x$. The guard map often depends on time and/or auxiliary clock variables, which we do not explicitly model here (they can be incorporated into x). We want inequality rather than equality in the reset triggering condition because for a discrete event to occur, we might need several conditions which do not become valid simultaneously (e.g., some relation between x and μ holds *and* a clock has reached a certain value). Of course, equality conditions are easily described by pairs of inequalities. Note that we allow the disturbances w to affect the discrete events only indirectly, through the continuous state x. This assumption will simplify the Lyapunov-based conditions in Sections 4 and 5; it is typically reasonable in the context of hybrid control design (see [7, 10]).

Well-posedness (existence and uniqueness of solutions) of the hybrid system $\mathcal{H}$ is an issue; see, e.g., [8]. At the general level of the present discussion, we are going to assume it. For example, by using clocks, we can ensure that a bounded number of discrete events occurs in any bounded time interval. Then, to obtain a solution (in the sense of Carathéodory), we simply flow the continuous dynamics until either the end of their domain is reached (finite escape) or a discrete event occurs; in the latter case, we repeat from the new state, and so on. See also [11] for an interesting alternative definition of solutions of hybrid systems.

2.2   Feedback Interconnection Structure

The starting point for our results is the observation that we can view the hybrid system $\mathcal{H}$ as a feedback interconnection of its continuous and discrete parts, as shown in Figure 1(a). For simplicity, we ignore the roles of the guard map G and the continuous state reset map R_x in the diagram.

It is clear that the above decomposition is just one possible way to split the hybrid system $\mathcal{H}$ into a feedback interconnection of two subsystems. There may be many ways to do it; the best choice will depend on the structure of the problem and will be one for which the small-gain approach described below will work. Each subsystem in the decomposition can be continuous, discrete, or hybrid, and may be affected by the disturbances. This more general situation is illustrated in Figure 1(b). Here, the state variables and the external signals of $\mathcal{H}$ are split as $x = (x_1, x_2)$, $\mu = (\mu_1, \mu_2)$, $w = (w_1, w_2)$, the first subsystem $\mathcal{H}_1$

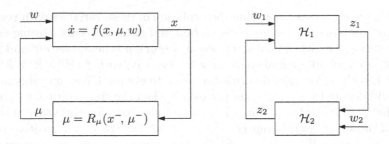

Fig. 1. Hybrid system viewed as feedback interconnection: (a) special decomposition, (b) general decomposition

has states $z_1 := (x_1, \mu_1)$ and inputs $v_1 = (z_2, w_1)$, and the second subsystem $\mathcal{H}_2$ has states $z_2 := (x_2, \mu_2)$ and inputs $v_2 = (z_1, w_2)$.

In the approach discussed here, coming up with a decomposition of the above kind is the first step in the analysis of a given hybrid system. As we pointed out, at least one such decomposition always exists. It can also happen that the hybrid system model is given from the beginning as an interconnection of several hybrid systems. Thus the structure we consider is very general and not restrictive.

2.3 Stability Definitions

A function $\alpha : [0, \infty) \to [0, \infty)$ is said to be of *class* $\mathcal{K}$ (which we write as $\alpha \in \mathcal{K}$) if it is continuous, strictly increasing, and $\alpha(0) = 0$. If α is also unbounded, then it is said to be of *class* $\mathcal{K}_\infty$ ($\alpha \in \mathcal{K}_\infty$). A function $\beta : [0, \infty) \times [0, \infty) \to [0, \infty)$ is said to be of *class* $\mathcal{KL}$ ($\beta \in \mathcal{KL}$) if $\beta(\cdot, t)$ is of class $\mathcal{K}$ for each fixed $t \geq 0$ and $\beta(r, t)$ is decreasing to zero as $t \to \infty$ for each fixed $r \geq 0$.

We now define the stability notions of interest in this paper. Consider a hybrid system with state $z = (x, \mu)$ and input v (as a special case, it can have only continuous dynamics or only discrete events). Following [3], we say that this system is *input-to-state stable* (ISS) with respect to v if there exist functions $\beta \in \mathcal{KL}$ and $\gamma \in \mathcal{K}_\infty$ such that for every initial state $z(t_0)$ and every input $v(\cdot)$ the corresponding solution satisfies the inequality

$$|z(t)| \leq \beta(|z(t_0)|, t - t_0) + \gamma(\|v\|_{[t_0, t]}) \tag{1}$$

for all $t \geq t_0$, where $\|v\|_{[t_0, t]} := \sup\{|v(s)| : s \in [t_0, t]\}$ (except possibly on a set of measure 0). We will refer to γ as an *ISS gain function*, or just a *gain* if clear from the context. For time-invariant systems, we can take $t_0 = 0$ without loss of generality. If the inputs are split as $v = (v_1, v_2)$, then (1) is equivalent to $|z(t)| \leq \beta(|z(t_0)|, t - t_0) + \gamma_1(\|v_1\|_{[t_0, t]}) + \gamma_2(\|v_2\|_{[t_0, t]})$ for some functions $\gamma_1, \gamma_2 \in \mathcal{K}_\infty$. In this case, we will call γ_1 the ISS gain from v_1 to z, and so on.

In the case of no inputs ($v \equiv 0$), the inequality (1) reduces to $|z(t)| \leq \beta(|z(t_0)|, t)$ for all $t \geq t_0$, which corresponds to the standard notion[1] of *global asymptotic stability* (GAS). In the presence of inputs, ISS captures the property

---

[1] This can also be equivalently restated in the more classical ε–δ style (cf. [12]).

that bounded inputs and inputs converging to 0 produce states that are also bounded and converging to 0, respectively. We note that asymptotic stability of a *linear* system (continuous or sampled-data) can always be characterized by a class $\mathcal{KL}$ function of the form $\beta(r,t) = cre^{-\lambda t}$, $c, \lambda > 0$. Moreover, an asymptotically stable linear system is automatically ISS with respect to external inputs, with a linear ISS gain function $\gamma(r) = cr$, $c > 0$.

3   ISS Small-Gain Theorem

Consider the hybrid system $\mathcal{H}$ defined in Section 2.1, and suppose that it has been represented as a feedback interconnection of two subsystems $\mathcal{H}_1$ and $\mathcal{H}_2$ in the way described in Section 2.2 and shown in Figure 1(b). The small-gain theorem stated next reduces the problem of verifying ISS of $\mathcal{H}$ to that of verifying ISS of $\mathcal{H}_1$ and $\mathcal{H}_2$ and checking a condition that relates their respective ISS gains. The result we give is a special case of the small-gain theorem from [2]. That paper treats continuous systems, but since the statement and the proof given there involve only properties of system signals, the fact that the dynamics are hybrid in our case does not change the validity of the result. We note that the small-gain theorem presented in [2] is much more general in that it treats partial measurements (input-to-output-stability, in conjunction with detectability) and deals with practical stability notions. Many other versions are also possible, e.g., we can replace the sup norm used in (1) by an L_p norm [13].

Theorem 1. *Suppose that:*
1. $\mathcal{H}_1$ is ISS with respect to $v_1 = (z_2, w_1)$, with gain γ_1 from z_2 to z_1, i.e.,

$$|z_1(t)| \le \beta_1(|z_1(t_0)|, t - t_0) + \gamma_1(\|z_2\|_{[t_0,t]}) + \bar{\gamma}_1(\|w_1\|_{[t_0,t]})$$

for some $\beta_1 \in \mathcal{KL}$, $\gamma_1, \bar{\gamma}_1 \in \mathcal{K}_\infty$.
2. $\mathcal{H}_2$ is ISS with respect to $v_2 = (z_1, w_2)$, with gain γ_2 from z_1 to z_2, i.e.,

$$|z_2(t)| \le \beta_2(|z_2(t_0)|, t - t_0) + \gamma_2(\|z_1\|_{[t_0,t]}) + \bar{\gamma}_2(\|w_2\|_{[t_0,t]})$$

for some $\beta_2 \in \mathcal{KL}$, $\gamma_2, \bar{\gamma}_2 \in \mathcal{K}_\infty$.
3. There exists a function $\rho \in \mathcal{K}_\infty$ such that[2]

$$(id + \rho) \circ \gamma_1 \circ (id + \rho) \circ \gamma_2(r) \le r \qquad \forall r \ge 0. \tag{2}$$

Then $\mathcal{H}$ is ISS with respect to the input $w = (w_1, w_2)$.

Three special cases are worth mentioning explicitly. First, in the case of no external signals ($w_1 = w_2 \equiv 0$), we conclude that $\mathcal{H}$ is GAS. Second, when the two ISS gain functions are linear: $\gamma_i(r) = c_i r$, $i = 1, 2$, the small-gain condition (2) reduces to the simple one $c_1 c_2 < 1$. Third, the theorem covers the case

---

[2] If one replaces $\beta + \gamma$ with $\beta \vee \gamma$ in the definition (1) of ISS, then the small-gain condition (2) can be simplified to $\gamma_1 \circ \gamma_2(r) < r$ for all $r > 0$.

of a cascade connection, where one of the gains is 0 and hence the small-gain condition (2) is automatically satisfied.

Sometimes one wants to concentrate only on some states of the overall system, excluding the other states from the feedback interconnection. For example, one might ignore some auxiliary variables (such as clocks) which have very simple dynamics and remain bounded for all time. Theorem 1 is still valid if z_1 and z_2 include only the states of interest for each subsystem.[3]

Small-gain theorems have been widely used for analysis of continuous-time as well as discrete-time systems with feedback interconnection structure. The discussion of Section 2.2 suggests that it is also very natural to use this idea to analyze (internal or external) stability of hybrid systems. Of course, one needs to show that the subsystems in a feedback decomposition satisfy suitable ISS properties, and calculate the ISS gains in order to check the small-gain condition (2). There exist efficient tools for doing this, as exemplified in the next section.

4   Sufficient Conditions for ISS

Consider the hybrid system $\mathcal{H}$ defined in Section 2.1, and suppose that it has been represented as a special feedback interconnection shown in Figure 1(a). The two lemmas stated below provide Lyapunov-based conditions which guarantee ISS of the continuous and discrete dynamics, respectively, and give expressions for the ISS gains. Thus they can be used for verifying the hypotheses of Theorem 1 in this particular case. The first result is well established [3]; the second one is a slightly sharpened version of Theorem 4 from the recent paper [15].

Lemma 1. *Suppose that there exists a C^1 function $V_1 : \mathbb{R}^n \to \mathbb{R}$, class $\mathcal{K}_\infty$ functions $\alpha_{1,x}, \alpha_{2,x}, \rho_x, \sigma$, and a continuous positive definite function $\alpha_{3,x} : [0, \infty) \to [0, \infty)$ satisfying*

$$\alpha_{1,x}(|x|) \leq V_1(x) \leq \alpha_{2,x}(|x|) \tag{3}$$

and

$$V_1(x) \geq \rho_x(|\mu|) \vee \sigma(|w|) \quad \Rightarrow \quad \nabla V_1(x) f(x, \mu, w) \leq -\alpha_{3,x}(V_1(x)). \tag{4}$$

Then the x-subsystem is ISS with respect to (μ, w), with gain $\gamma_x := \alpha_{1,x}^{-1} \circ \rho_x$ from μ to x.

The condition (3) simply says that V_1 is positive definite and radially unbounded. We can take $\alpha_{3,x}$ to be of class $\mathcal{K}_\infty$ with no loss of generality [3]. The condition (4) can be equivalently rewritten as $\nabla V_1(x) f(x, \mu, w) \leq -\alpha_{4,x}(V_1(x)) + \chi_x(|\mu|)$ for some $\alpha_{4,x}, \chi_x \in \mathcal{K}_\infty$. However, using the latter condition instead of (4) in the lemma would in general lead to a more conservative ISS gain. We also note that Lemma 1 can be easily generalized by allowing V_1 to depend on t as well as on x, leaving the bounds in (3) unchanged, and adding the time derivative of V_1 in (4); we will work with a Lyapunov function of this kind in Theorem 2 below.

---

[3] This amounts to modifying the hypotheses by replacing ISS with a suitable input-to-output stability notion (cf. [2, 14]) and requiring that the ISS gain from the "hidden" states in each subsystem to the states of interest in the other subsystem be 0.

Lemma 2. *Suppose that there exists a C^1 function $V_2 : \mathbb{R}^k \to \mathbb{R}$, class $\mathcal{K}_\infty$ functions $\alpha_{1,\mu}, \alpha_{2,\mu}, \rho_\mu$, and a continuous positive definite function $\alpha_{3,\mu} : [0, \infty) \to [0, \infty)$ satisfying*

$$\alpha_{1,\mu}(|\mu|) \leq V_2(\mu) \leq \alpha_{2,\mu}(|\mu|) \tag{5}$$

such that we have

$$V_2(\mu) \geq \rho_\mu(|x|) \quad \Rightarrow \quad V_2(R_\mu(x,\mu)) - V_2(\mu) \leq -\alpha_{3,\mu}(V_2(\mu)) \tag{6}$$

and

$$V_2(\mu) \leq \rho_\mu(r) \text{ and } |x| \leq r \quad \Rightarrow \quad V_2(R_\mu(x,\mu)) \leq \rho_\mu(r). \tag{7}$$

Suppose also that for each $t > t_0$ such that $V_2(\mu(s)) \geq \rho_\mu(\|x\|_{[t_0,s]})$ for all $s \in [t_0, t)$, the number $N(t, t_0)$ of discrete events in the interval $[t_0, t]$ satisfies

$$N(t, t_0) \geq \eta(t - t_0) \tag{8}$$

where $\eta : [0, \infty) \to [0, \infty)$ is an increasing function. Then the μ-subsystem is ISS with respect to x, with gain $\gamma_\mu := \alpha_{1,\mu}^{-1} \circ \rho_\mu$.

We can assume that $\alpha_{3,\mu} \in \mathcal{K}_\infty$ with no loss of generality [16]. The conditions (6) and (7) are both satisfied if we have

$$V_2(R_\mu(x,\mu)) - V_2(\mu) \leq -\alpha_{4,\mu}(V_2(\mu)) + \chi_\mu(|x|) \tag{9}$$

for some $\alpha_{4,\mu}, \chi_\mu \in \mathcal{K}_\infty$. Indeed, letting $\rho_\mu(r) := \alpha_{4,\mu}^{-1}(2\chi_\mu(r))$, we see that (6) holds with $\alpha_{3,\mu} := \alpha_{4,\mu}/2$. Decreasing $\alpha_{4,\mu}$ if necessary, assume with no loss of generality that $id - \alpha_{4,\mu} \in \mathcal{K}$ (cf. [17]). We then have

$$V_2(\mu) \leq \alpha_{4,\mu}^{-1}(2\chi_\mu(r)) \text{ and } |x| \leq r \quad \Rightarrow$$

$$V_2(R_\mu(x,\mu)) \leq \chi_\mu(|x|) + (id - \alpha_{4,\mu})\big(\alpha_{4,\mu}^{-1}(2\chi_\mu(r))\big) < \alpha_{4,\mu}^{-1}(2\chi_\mu(|x|))$$

and so (7) holds with the same ρ_μ. Moreover, (6) implies (9) and consequently (7) if the map R_μ is continuous at $(x, \mu) = (0, 0)$. Still, it is useful to write two separate conditions (6) and (7) if we want the least conservative expression for the ISS gain. The former condition coupled with (8) is the main ingredient for obtaining ISS, while the latter is automatically enforced if, for example, discrete events can only decrease $V_2(\mu)$. An example of a function η that can be used in (8) is $\eta(r) = \frac{r}{\delta_a} - N_0$, where δ_a and N_0 are positive numbers (see [15]). In this case, (8) says that discrete events must happen at least every δ_a units of time on the average, modulo a finite number of events that can be "missed".

Proof of Lemma 2. Let $\bar{t} := \min\{t \geq t_0 : V_2(\mu(t)) \leq \rho_\mu(\|x\|_{[t_0,t]})\} \leq \infty$ (this is well defined in view of right-continuity). By virtue of (6), we have $V_2(\mu) - V_2(\mu^-) \leq -\alpha_{3,\mu}(V_2(\mu^-))$ at each event time in the interval $[t_0, \bar{t})$. Therefore, there exists a function $\bar{\beta} \in \mathcal{KL}$ such that $V_2(\mu(t)) \leq \bar{\beta}(V_2(\mu(t_0)), N(t, t_0))$ for all $t \in [t_0, \bar{t})$; cf. [17]. Invoking (8), we have $V_2(\mu(t)) \leq \bar{\beta}(V_2(\mu(t_0)), \eta(t - t_0))$ hence $|\mu(t)| \leq \alpha_{1,\mu}^{-1}(\bar{\beta}(\alpha_{2,\mu}(|\mu(t_0)|), \eta(t - t_0))) =: \beta_\mu(|\mu(t_0)|, t - t_0)$ for all $t \in [t_0, \bar{t})$. Next, (7) applied with $r := \|x\|_{[t_0,t]}$ at each event time guarantees that $V_2(\mu(t)) \leq \rho_\mu(\|x\|_{[t_0,t]})$ hence $|\mu(t)| \leq \alpha_{1,\mu}^{-1} \circ \rho_\mu(\|x\|_{[t_0,t]})$ for all $t \geq \bar{t}$. Combining the two bounds for $|\mu(t)|$ gives the desired estimate. $\square$

5 Lyapunov-Based Small-Gain Theorems

Consider again the hybrid system $\mathcal{H}$ defined in Section 2.1 and decomposed as in Figure 1(a). Here we assume for simplicity that $R_x(x, \mu) \equiv x$ (continuous state does not jump at the event times). Theorem 1, applied to this special feedback decomposition, provides sufficient conditions for ISS. The proof of this theorem is based on trajectory analysis. Lemmas 1 and 2 can be used to check the hypotheses of Theorem 1, and involve ISS-Lyapunov functions for the two subsystems. The question naturally arises whether Theorem 1 can be formulated and proved entirely in terms of such Lyapunov functions. Such alternative formulations are available for continuous-time as well as discrete-time small-gain theorems [4,5], but this issue has not been pursued for hybrid systems.

Here we present a preliminary result in this direction. We denote by t_k, $k = 1, 2, \ldots$ the discrete event times, which we assume to be distinct (with no significant changes, we could allow finitely many discrete events to occur simultaneously). It is also convenient to introduce a special clock variable τ, which counts the time since the most recent discrete event and is reset to 0 at the event times: $\tau(t) := t - t_k$ for $t \in [t_k, t_{k+1})$. It must be noted that the Lyapunov function V constructed in Theorem 2 below depends, besides x and μ, on this variable τ. Therefore, it can really be viewed as a Lyapunov function only if the sequence $\{t_k\}$ is independent of the initial state. Otherwise, the proof of ISS using this function is actually a trajectory-based argument (but it still represents an interesting alternative to a purely time-domain one).

Theorem 2. *Suppose that there exist positive definite, radially unbounded C^1 functions $V_1 : \mathbb{R}^n \to \mathbb{R}$ and $V_2 : \mathbb{R}^k \to \mathbb{R}$, class $\mathcal{K}_\infty$ functions χ_1, χ_2, σ, and positive constants b_1, b_2, c, d, T such that we have*

$$V_1(x) \geq \chi_1(V_2(\mu)) \vee \sigma(|w|) \quad \Rightarrow \quad \nabla V_1(x)f(x, \mu, w) \leq -cV_1(x), \tag{10}$$

$$V_2(\mu) \geq \chi_2(V_1(x)) \quad \Rightarrow \quad V_2(R_\mu(x, \mu)) \leq e^{-d}V_2(\mu), \tag{11}$$

$$V_2(\mu) \leq e^{b_2}\chi_2(e^{b_1}V_1(x)) \quad \Rightarrow \quad V_2(R_\mu(x, \mu)) \leq \chi_2(V_1(x)), \tag{12}$$

the small-gain condition

$$e^{b_1}\chi_1(e^{b_2}\chi_2(r)) < r \qquad \forall r > 0 \tag{13}$$

holds, and the discrete events satisfy

$$t_{k+1} - t_k \leq T \qquad \forall k \geq 0. \tag{14}$$

Then there exist a locally Lipschitz function $V : [0, T] \times \mathbb{R}^n \times \mathbb{R}^k \to \mathbb{R}$, class $\mathcal{K}_\infty$ functions $\alpha_1, \alpha_2, \bar{\sigma}$, a continuous positive definite function $\alpha_3 : [0, \infty) \to [0, \infty)$, and a continuous function $\alpha_4 : [0, T] \times [0, \infty) \to [0, \infty)$ satisfying $\alpha_4(\tau, r) > 0$ when $\tau r \neq 0$, such that for all $\tau \in [0, T]$ and all $(x, \mu) \in \mathbb{R}^n \times \mathbb{R}^k$ the bound

$$\alpha_1(|(x, \mu)|) \leq V(\tau, x, \mu) \leq \alpha_2(|(x, \mu)|) \tag{15}$$

holds and we have

$$V(\tau, x, \mu) \geq \bar{\sigma}(|w|) \quad \Rightarrow$$

$$\dot{V}(\tau, x, \mu) := \frac{\partial V}{\partial \tau}(\tau, x, \mu) + \frac{\partial V}{\partial x}(\tau, x, \mu) f(x, \mu, w) \leq -\alpha_3(|(x, \mu)|) \quad (16)$$

for the continuous dynamics[4] and

$$V(0, x, R_\mu(x, \mu)) - V(\tau, x, \mu) \leq -\alpha_4(\tau, |(x, \mu)|) \quad (17)$$

for the discrete events. Consequently, $\mathcal{H}$ is ISS with respect to w.

In spirit, the hypotheses of Theorem 2 match the hypotheses of Theorem 1 and Lemmas 1 and 2, although there are some differences. We note that the condition (14) can be written as $N(t, s) \geq \frac{t-s}{T}$ for all $t > s \geq t_0$, i.e., it is a strengthened version of (8). For simplicity, we assumed in (10) and (11) that V_1 and V_2 decay at exponential rates. In the special case when the gain functions χ_1 and χ_2 are also linear, b_1 and b_2 in (12) and (13) can be set to 0. Note also that (10) only needs to hold for those states where we have continuous evolution, i.e., where $G(x, \mu) < 0$, while (11) and (12) only need to hold for those states where discrete events occur, i.e., where $G(x, \mu) \geq 0$.

Proof of Theorem 2. We have that V_1 stays constant during the discrete events while V_2 stays constant along the continuous dynamics. First, we want to construct modified functions $\overline{V}_1$ and $\overline{V}_2$ which strictly decrease during the discrete events and the continuous dynamics, respectively, while also enjoying decreasing properties similar to (10)–(12). Pick a number $L_1 \in (0, c \wedge (b_1/T))$ and define

$$\overline{V}_1(\tau, x) := e^{L_1 \tau} V_1(x). \quad (18)$$

Using (14), we have

$$V_1(x) \leq \overline{V}_1(\tau(t), x) \leq e^{L_1 T} V_1(x) \quad \forall t, x. \quad (19)$$

Similarly, pick a number $L_2 \in (0, (d \wedge b_2)/T)$ and define

$$\overline{V}_2(\tau, \mu) := e^{-L_2 \tau} V_2(\mu) \quad (20)$$

to obtain

$$e^{-L_2 T} V_2(\mu) \leq \overline{V}_2(\tau(t), \mu) \leq V_2(\mu) \quad \forall t, \mu. \quad (21)$$

Define $\bar{\chi}_1(r) := e^{L_1 T} \chi_1(e^{L_2 T} r)$ and $\bar{\sigma}(r) := e^{L_1 T} \sigma(r)$. Combining (10), (18), (19), and (21), we have for the continuous dynamics

$$\overline{V}_1(\tau, x) \geq \bar{\chi}_1(\overline{V}_2(\tau, \mu)) \vee \bar{\sigma}(|w|) \quad \Rightarrow$$

$$\frac{\partial \overline{V}_1}{\partial \tau}(\tau, x) + \frac{\partial \overline{V}_1}{\partial x}(\tau, x) f(x, \mu, w) \leq -(c - L_1)\overline{V}_1(\tau, x) \quad (22)$$

and for the discrete events

---

[4] We will define V as a maximum of two C^1 functions, hence the gradient $\partial V/\partial x$ is in general not defined at the points where these two functions are equal. However, the derivative of $V(x(\cdot))$ with respect to time exists everywhere and is continuous almost everywhere along each trajectory. This is sufficient for establishing ISS; cf. [4].

$$\overline{V}_1(0, x) = e^{-L_1 \tau} \overline{V}_1(\tau, x). \tag{23}$$

Similarly, the evolution of $\overline{V}_2$ satisfies

$$\frac{\partial \overline{V}_2}{\partial \tau}(\tau, \mu) = -L_2 \overline{V}_2(\tau, \mu), \tag{24}$$

$$\overline{V}_2(\tau, \mu) \geq \chi_2(\overline{V}_1(\tau, x)) \quad \Rightarrow \quad \overline{V}_2(0, R_\mu(x, \mu)) \leq e^{-(d - L_2 T)} \overline{V}_2(\tau, \mu), \tag{25}$$

$$\overline{V}_2(\tau, \mu) \leq \chi_2(\overline{V}_1(\tau, x)) \quad \Rightarrow \quad \overline{V}_2(0, R_\mu(x, \mu)) \leq \chi_2(\overline{V}_1(\tau, x)). \tag{26}$$

The condition (13) implies $\bar\chi_1 \circ \chi_2(r) < r$ for all $r > 0$, which is equivalent to $\chi_2(r) < \bar\chi_1^{-1}(r)$ for all $r > 0$. As in [4], pick a C^1, class $\mathcal{K}_\infty$ function ρ with

$$\rho'(r) > 0 \qquad \forall\, r > 0 \tag{27}$$

such that

$$\chi_2(r) < \rho(r) < \bar\chi_1^{-1}(r) \qquad \forall\, r > 0. \tag{28}$$

We are now ready to define a (time-varying) candidate ISS-Lyapunov function for the closed-loop system $\mathcal{H}$ as

$$V(\tau, x, \mu) := \begin{cases} \rho(\overline{V}_1(\tau, x)) & \text{if } \rho(\overline{V}_1(\tau, x)) \geq \overline{V}_2(\tau, \mu) \\ \overline{V}_2(\tau, \mu) & \text{if } \rho(\overline{V}_1(\tau, x)) < \overline{V}_2(\tau, \mu) \end{cases} \tag{29}$$

We claim that it satisfies (15)–(17). To prove this, pick arbitrary $\tau \in [0, T]$ and $(x, \mu) \neq (0, 0)$. Let us first consider the case when $V(\tau, x, \mu) \geq \bar\sigma(|w|)$. We further distinguish between the following two cases.

Case 1: $\rho(\overline{V}_1(\tau, x)) \geq \overline{V}_2(\tau, \mu)$, so that $V(\tau, x, \mu) = \rho(\overline{V}_1(\tau, x))$. If $\rho(\overline{V}_1(\tau, x)) > \overline{V}_2(\tau, \mu)$, then we have, using (22), (27), (28), and positive definiteness of V_1 and V_2, that $x \neq 0$ and

$$\dot{V}(\tau, x, \mu) = \rho'(\overline{V}_1(\tau, x)) \left(\frac{\partial \overline{V}_1}{\partial \tau}(\tau, x) + \frac{\partial \overline{V}_1}{\partial x}(\tau, x) f(x, \mu, w) \right)$$

$$\leq -\rho'(\overline{V}_1(\tau, x))(c - L_1) \overline{V}_1(\tau, x) < 0$$

If $\rho(\overline{V}_1(\tau, x)) = \overline{V}_2(\tau, \mu)$, then by positive definiteness of V_1 and V_2 both x and μ are nonzero and, invoking also (24), we have

$$\dot{V}(\tau, x, \mu) = \rho'(\overline{V}_1(\tau, x)) \left(\frac{\partial \overline{V}_1}{\partial \tau}(\tau, x) + \frac{\partial \overline{V}_1}{\partial x}(\tau, x) f(x, \mu, w) \right) \vee \frac{\partial \overline{V}_2}{\partial \tau}(\tau, \mu)$$

$$\leq -\rho'(\overline{V}_1(\tau, x))(c - L_1) \overline{V}_1(\tau, x) \vee -L_2 \overline{V}_2(\tau, \mu) < 0$$

Turning to the discrete events, we have three possible cases. If $\rho(\overline{V}_1(0, x)) \geq \overline{V}_2(0, R_\mu(x, \mu))$, then from (23) we have $V(0, x, R_\mu(x, \mu)) = \rho(\overline{V}_1(0, x)) = \rho(e^{-L_1 \tau} \overline{V}_1(\tau, x)) \leq \rho(\overline{V}_1(\tau, x)) = V(\tau, x, \mu)$, and the inequality is strict if

$\tau > 0$. If $\rho(\overline{V}_1(0, x)) < \overline{V}_2(0, R_\mu(x, \mu))$ and $\overline{V}_2(\tau, \mu) \geq \chi_2(\overline{V}_1(\tau, x))$, then (25) gives $V(0, x, R_\mu(x, \mu)) = \overline{V}_2(0, x, R_\mu(x, \mu)) < \overline{V}_2(\tau, \mu) \leq \rho(\overline{V}_1(\tau, x)) = V(\tau, x, \mu)$. Finally, if $\rho(\overline{V}_1(0, x)) < \overline{V}_2(0, R_\mu(x, \mu))$ and $\overline{V}_2(\tau, \mu) \leq \chi_2(\overline{V}_1(\tau, x))$, then using (26) we obtain $V(0, x, R_\mu(x, \mu)) = \overline{V}_2(0, x, R_\mu(x, \mu)) \leq \chi_2(\overline{V}_1(\tau, x)) < \rho(\overline{V}_1(\tau, x)) = V(\tau, x, \mu)$.

Case 2: $\rho(\overline{V}_1(\tau, x)) < \overline{V}_2(\tau, \mu)$, so that $V(\tau, x, \mu) = \overline{V}_2(\tau, \mu)$. Using (24) and positive definiteness of V_2, we have $\mu \neq 0$ and $\dot{V}(\tau, x, \mu) = \frac{\partial \overline{V}_2}{\partial \tau}(\tau, \mu) = -L_2 \overline{V}_2(\tau, \mu) < 0$. As for the discrete events, (25) and (28) imply that $\overline{V}_2(0, R_\mu(x, \mu)) < \overline{V}_2(\tau, \mu)$. If $\overline{V}_2(0, R_\mu(x, \mu)) > \rho(\overline{V}_1(0, x))$, then we have $V(0, x, R_\mu(x, \mu)) = \overline{V}_2(0, R_\mu(x, \mu)) < \overline{V}_2(\tau, \mu) = V(\tau, x, \mu)$. On the other hand, if $\overline{V}_2(0, R_\mu(x, \mu)) \leq \rho(\overline{V}_1(0, x))$, then by virtue of (23) we have $V(0, x, R_\mu(x, \mu)) = \rho(\overline{V}_1(0, x)) \leq \rho(\overline{V}_1(\tau, x)) < \overline{V}_2(\tau, \mu) = V(\tau, x, \mu)$.

Since V_1 and V_2 are positive definite and radially unbounded, there exist functions $\alpha_{1,x}, \alpha_{2,x}, \alpha_{1,\mu}, \alpha_{2,\mu} \in \mathcal{K}_\infty$ such that (3) and (5) hold. Using (19), (21), and (29), we obtain

$$\rho(\alpha_{1,x}(|x|)) \vee e^{-L_2 T} \alpha_{1,\mu}(|\mu|) \leq V(\tau, x, \mu) \leq \rho(e^{L_1 T} \alpha_{2,x}(|x|)) \vee \alpha_{2,\mu}(|\mu|).$$

It is now a routine exercise to construct functions $\alpha_1, \alpha_2 \in \mathcal{K}_\infty$ for which (15) holds. Next, observe that the condition $V(\tau, x, \mu) \geq \bar{\sigma}(|w|)$ was used, via (22), only to prove the decrease of V along the continuous dynamics but not during the discrete events. Thus (16) and (17) are established (constructing α_3 and α_4 is again a simple exercise). Finally, ISS of $\mathcal{H}$ with respect to w follows from (15)–(17) via standard arguments (cf. [3, 15]).   □

Remark 1. ISS of $\mathcal{H}$ would still hold if instead of (17) we had the weaker condition $V(0, x, R_\mu(x, \mu)) \leq V(\tau, x, \mu)$, with (16) unchanged. To construct a function V with these properties, we could set $L_1 = 0$ in the above proof, i.e., work with the original function V_1 in place of $\overline{V}_1$; accordingly, we could set $b_1 = 0$, and also the linearity of the right-hand side of (10) in V_1 would not be important. On the other hand, the stronger condition (17) makes the Lyapunov function V more useful for quantifying the effect of the discrete events. In particular, if we impose a dwell-time constraint $t_{k+1} - t_k \geq \varepsilon > 0$ for all $k \geq 0$, then a uniform decrease condition of the form $V - V^- \leq -\bar{\alpha}_4(V^-)$, with $\bar{\alpha}_4$ continuous positive definite, holds for all discrete events, yielding the stronger property of ISS with respect to a "hybrid time domain" in which the continuous time t and the discrete event index k play essentially equivalent roles (see [11]).   □

As an alternative to constructing a Lyapunov function strictly decreasing along solutions, we can work with a *weak* Lyapunov function non-strictly decreasing along solutions and apply a LaSalle invariance principle for hybrid systems, such as the one proved in [6] (see also [18] for recent generalizations and improvements). As can be seen from the proof of the result given next, such an approach is perhaps simpler and more natural in the situation at hand, and the relevant hypotheses more closely match those of Theorem 1 and Lemmas 1 and 2.

However, the result has inherent limitations characteristic of LaSalle theorems; in particular, it is restricted to disturbance-free, time-invariant dynamics.

Consider the same hybrid system $\mathcal{H}$ as in Theorem 2, but assume that there are no disturbances, i.e., the continuous dynamics are described by $\dot{x} = f(x, \mu)$. We assume as before that the resulting discrete event times are distinct (the extension to the case when a finite number of discrete events can occur simultaneously is straightforward). We also assume that the behavior of $\mathcal{H}$ is continuous with respect to initial conditions, in the sense defined and characterized in [6].

Theorem 3. *Suppose that there exist positive definite, radially unbounded C^1 functions $V_1 : \mathbb{R}^n \to \mathbb{R}$ and $V_2 : \mathbb{R}^k \to \mathbb{R}$, class $\mathcal{K}_\infty$ functions χ_1, χ_2, and continuous positive definite functions $\alpha_1, \alpha_2 : [0, \infty) \to [0, \infty)$ such that we have*

$$V_1(x) \geq \chi_1(V_2(\mu)) \quad \Rightarrow \quad \nabla V_1(x) f(x, \mu) \leq -\alpha_1(V_1(x)), \tag{30}$$

$$V_2(\mu) \geq \chi_2(V_1(x)) \quad \Rightarrow \quad V_2(R_\mu(x, \mu)) - V_2(\mu) \leq -\alpha_2(V_2(\mu)), \tag{31}$$

$$V_2(\mu) \leq \chi_2(V_1(x)) \quad \Rightarrow \quad V_2(R_\mu(x, \mu)) \leq \chi_2(V_1(x)), \tag{32}$$

the small-gain condition

$$\chi_1 \circ \chi_2(r) < r \qquad \forall r > 0 \tag{33}$$

holds, and for each $t > t_0$ such that $V_2(\mu(s)) \geq \chi_2(V_1(x(s)))$ for all $s \in [t_0, t)$, the number $N(t, t_0)$ of discrete events in the interval $[t_0, t]$ satisfies (8) for some increasing function $\eta : [0, \infty) \to [0, \infty)$. Then there exists a positive definite, radially unbounded, locally Lipschitz function $V : \mathbb{R}^n \times \mathbb{R}^k \to \mathbb{R}$ such that for all $(x, \mu) \in \mathbb{R}^n \times \mathbb{R}^k$ we have

$$\dot{V}(x, \mu) := \frac{\partial V}{\partial x}(x, \mu) f(x, \mu) \leq 0 \tag{34}$$

for the continuous dynamics,[5]

$$V(x, R_\mu(x, \mu)) \leq V(x, \mu) \tag{35}$$

for the discrete events, and there is no forward invariant set except for the origin inside the set $S_1 \cup S_2$, where $S_1 := \{(x, \mu) : \dot{V}(x, \mu) = 0, G(x, \mu) < 0\}$ and $S_2 := \{(x, \mu) : V(x, R_\mu(x, \mu)) = V(x, \mu), G(x, \mu) \geq 0\}$. Consequently, $\mathcal{H}$ is GAS.

As in Theorem 2, the condition (30) only needs to hold for those states where we have continuous evolution, i.e., where $G(x, \mu) < 0$, while (31) and (32) only need to hold for those states where discrete events occur, i.e., where $G(x, \mu) \geq 0$.

Proof of Theorem 3. The condition (33) is equivalent to $\chi_2(r) < \chi_1^{-1}(r)$ for all $r > 0$. As in [6], pick a C^1, class $\mathcal{K}_\infty$ function ρ satisfying (27) and

$$\chi_2(r) < \rho(r) < \chi_1^{-1}(r) \qquad \forall r > 0. \tag{36}$$

---

[5] See footnote 4.

Define a candidate weak Lyapunov function for $\mathcal{H}$ as

$$V(x, \mu) := \begin{cases} \rho(V_1(x)) & \text{if } \rho(V_1(x)) \geq V_2(\mu) \\ V_2(\mu) & \text{if } \rho(V_1(x)) < V_2(\mu) \end{cases}$$

This function is positive definite and radially unbounded by construction. We now prove that it satisfies (34) and (35). We consider two cases, similarly to the proof of Theorem 2.

Case 1: $\rho(V_1(x)) \geq V_2(\mu)$, so that $V(x, \mu) = \rho(V_1(x))$. If $\rho(V_1(x)) > V_2(\mu)$, then we have, using (27), (30), (36), and positive definiteness of V_1 and V_2, that $x \neq 0$ and

$$\dot{V}(x, \mu) = \rho'(V_1(x)) \frac{\partial V_1}{\partial x}(x) f(x, \mu) \leq -\rho'(V_1(x)) \alpha_1(V_1(x)) < 0.$$

If $\rho(V_1(x)) = V_2(\mu)$ then, since V_2 stays constant along the continuous dynamics, we have $\dot{V}(x, \mu) \leq -\rho'(V_1(x)) \alpha_1(V_1(x)) \vee 0 \leq 0$. We know that the discrete events do not change the value of $\rho(V_1(x))$. If $V_2(\mu) \geq \chi_2(V_1(x))$, then using (31) we have $V_2(x, R_\mu(x, \mu)) \leq V_2(\mu) \leq \rho(V_1(x))$. If $V_2(\mu) \leq \chi_2(V_1(x))$, then with the help of (32) we obtain $V_2(x, R_\mu(x, \mu)) \leq \chi_2(V_1(x)) \leq \rho(V_1(x))$. In either case we have $V_2(R_\mu(x, \mu)) \leq \rho(V_1(x))$, hence $V(x, R_\mu(x, \mu)) = \rho(V_1(x)) = V(x, \mu)$.

Case 2: $\rho(V_1(x)) < V_2(\mu)$, so that $V(x, \mu) = V_2(\mu)$. For the continuous dynamics, we have $\dot{V}(x, \mu) = 0$. As for the discrete events, (31) and (36) imply that $V_2(R_\mu(x, \mu)) < V_2(\mu)$. If $V_2(R_\mu(x, \mu)) > \rho(V_1(x))$, then $V(x, R_\mu(x, \mu)) = V_2(R_\mu(x, \mu)) < V_2(\mu) = V(x, \mu)$. If $V_2(R_\mu(x, \mu)) \leq \rho(V_1(x))$, then we have $V(x, R_\mu(x, \mu)) = \rho(V_1(x)) < V_2(\mu) = V(x, \mu)$.

The properties (34) and (35) are therefore established. Next, we turn to the claim about the absence of a nonzero invariant set inside $S_1 \cup S_2$. The previous analysis implies that we have $S_1 \subseteq \tilde{S}_1$ and $S_2 \subseteq \tilde{S}_2$, where $\tilde{S}_1 := \{(x, \mu) : \rho(V_1(x)) \leq V_2(\mu), G(x, \mu) < 0\}$ and $\tilde{S}_2 := \{(x, \mu) : \rho(V_1(x)) \geq V_2(\mu), G(x, \mu) \geq 0\}$. Hence it is enough to prove the claim for $\tilde{S}_1 \cup \tilde{S}_2$. By (36) and the hypotheses placed on the discrete events, no subset of either $\tilde{S}_1$ or $\tilde{S}_2$ can be invariant. Indeed, while the state is in $\tilde{S}_1$, (8) holds and so a discrete event must eventually occur, which means that the state must leave $\tilde{S}_1$. On the other hand, since consecutive discrete events are assumed to be separated by positive intervals of continuous evolution, $\tilde{S}_2$ is not invariant. It remains to show that discrete events cannot take the state from $\tilde{S}_2 \setminus \{(0, 0)\}$ to $\tilde{S}_1$. Consider an arbitrary $(x, \mu) \in \tilde{S}_2 \setminus \{(0, 0)\}$. If $V_2(\mu) \geq \chi_2(V_1(x))$, then from (31) we have $V_2(x, R_\mu(x, \mu)) < V_2(\mu) \leq \rho(V_1(x))$. If $V_2(\mu) \leq \chi_2(V_1(x))$, then from (32) we have $V_2(x, R_\mu(x, \mu)) \leq \chi_2(V_1(x)) < \rho(V_1(x))$. We conclude that $(x, R_\mu(x, \mu))$ cannot be in $\tilde{S}_1$, which establishes the claim.

Stability in the sense of Lyapunov and boundedness of all solutions follow from (34), (35), and the fact that V is positive definite and radially unbounded. Since $\mathcal{H}$ is non-blocking and deterministic by construction, the invariance principle for hybrid systems from [6] applies. To conclude GAS, we need to rule out the existence of an invariant set other than the origin inside the set on which V does not strictly decrease. But this latter set is $S_1 \cup S_2$, and we are done.   □

We see that although the function V in Theorem 3 is a weak Lyapunov function, it has the right properties for applying the LaSalle invariance principle and concluding GAS. However, for other purposes (such as, for example, analyzing stability under perturbations of the right-hand side) it is still desirable to have a strictly decreasing Lyapunov function. One may try to construct such a Lyapunov function by modifying V (e.g., see results of this kind for continuous systems under appropriate "detectability" conditions in [19] and "observability" conditions in [20]).

6   Conclusions and Future Work

The main purpose of this paper was to bring the small-gain analysis method to the attention of the hybrid systems community. We argued that general hybrid systems can be viewed as feedback interconnections of simpler subsystems, and thus the small-gain analysis framework is very naturally applicable to them. While the small gain theorem based on time-domain analysis provides an "off-the-shelf" tool for studying stability of hybrid systems, Lyapunov function constructions are also of interest and were addressed in this paper. For a class of hybrid systems satisfying the conditions of the small-gain theorem, we described a construction of a Lyapunov function and another construction of a weak Lyapunov function, each of which can be used to establish stability.

Further research is needed for improving Lyapunov function constructions of Section 5, which are currently not quite satisfactory. First, Theorem 2 falls short of recovering the result of Theorem 1. Second, both Theorem 2 and Theorem 3 are restricted to the special feedback interconnection shown in Figure 1(a). Another direction for future work is to systematically exploit the proposed method in application-motivated contexts. As demonstrated in the companion paper [7] (see also [13] and the subsequent work [21]), quantized control and networked control systems represent very promising application areas, but we expect the small-gain analysis to be useful for hybrid systems arising in many other areas as well.

References

1. Zames, G.: On the input-output stability of time-varying nonlinear feedback systems, part 1: conditions derived using concepts of loop gain, conicity, and positivity. IEEE Trans. Automat. Control **11** (1966) 228–238
2. Jiang, Z.P., Teel, A.R., Praly, L.: Small-gain theorem for ISS systems and applications. Math. Control Signals Systems **7** (1994) 95–120
3. Sontag, E.D.: Smooth stabilization implies coprime factorization. IEEE Trans. Automat. Control **34** (1989) 435–443
4. Jiang, Z.P., Mareels, I.M.Y., Wang, Y.: A Lyapunov formulation of the nonlinear small-gain theorem for interconnected ISS systems. Automatica **32** (1996) 1211–1215

5. Laila, D.S., Nešić, D.:   Lyapunov based small-gain theorem for parameterized discrete-time interconnected ISS systems. IEEE Trans. Automat. Control 48 (2003) 1783–1788
6. Lygeros, J., Johansson, K.H., Simić, S.N., Zhang, J., Sastry, S.S.: Dynamical properties of hybrid automata. IEEE Trans. Automat. Control 48 (2003) 2–17
7. Nešić, D., Liberzon, D.:   A small-gain approach to stability analysis of hybrid systems. In: Proc. 44th IEEE Conf. on Decision and Control. (2005) To appear. Available at http://decision.csl.uiuc.edu/~liberzon/publications.html.
8. van der Schaft, A., Schumacher, H.: An Introduction to Hybrid Dynamical Systems. Springer, London (2000)
9. Lynch, N., Segala, R., Vaandrager, F.: Hybrid I/O automata. Information and Computation 185 (2003) 105–157
10. Liberzon, D., Nešić, D.: Input-to-state stabilization of linear systems with quantized state measurements. (IEEE Trans. Automat. Control) To appear. Preliminary version in Proc. 44th IEEE Conf. on Decision and Control, 2005, to appear. Available at http://decision.csl.uiuc.edu/~liberzon/publications.html.
11. Goebel, R., Hespanha, J.P., Teel, A.R., Cai, C., Sanfelice, R.: Hybrid systems: generalized solutions and robust stability. In: Proc. 6th IFAC Symp. on Nonlinear Control Systems (NOLCOS). (2004) 1–12
12. Khalil, H.K.: Nonlinear Systems. 3rd edn. Prentice Hall, New Jersey (2002)
13. Nešić, D., Teel, A.R.: Input-output stability properties of networked control systems. IEEE Trans. Automat. Control 49 (2004) 1650–1667
14. Sontag, E.D., Wang, Y.: Notions of input to output stability. Systems Control Lett. 38 (1999) 235–248
15. Hespanha, J.P., Liberzon, D., Teel, A.R.: On input-to-state stability of impulsive systems. In: Proc. 44th IEEE Conf. on Decision and Control. (2005) To appear.
16. Jiang, Z.P., Wang, Y.: A converse Lyapunov theorem for discrete-time systems with disturbances. Systems Control Lett. 45 (2002) 49–58
17. Jiang, Z.P., Wang, Y.: Input-to-state stability for discrete-time nonlinear systems. Automatica 37 (2001) 857–869
18. Sanfelice, R.G., Goebel, R., Teel, A.R.: Invariance principles for hybrid systems with connections to detectability and asymptotic stability. (2005) Submitted. Preliminary version appeared as "Results on convergence in hybrid systems via detectability and an invariance principle" in Proc. 2005 American Control Conf.
19. Angeli, D.: Input-to-state stability of PD-controlled robotic systems. Automatica 35 (1999) 1285–1290
20. Mazenc, F., Nešić, D.: Strong Lyapunov functions for systems satisfying the conditions of La Salle. IEEE Trans. Automat. Control 49 (2004) 1026–1030
21. Carnevale, D., Teel, A.R., Nešić, D.: A Lyapunov proof of an improved maximum allowable transfer interval for networked control systems. (IEEE Trans. Automat. Control) Submitted.

Stochastic Hybrid Delay Population Dynamics

John Lygeros[1], Xuerong Mao[2], and Chenggui Yuan[3],*

[1] Department of Electrical and Computer Engineering,
University of Patras, Patras, GR 26500, Greece
[2] Department of Statistics and Modelling Science,
University of Strathclyde, Glasgow G1 1XH, UK
[3] Department of Mathematics,
University of Wales Swansea, Swansea SA2 8PP, UK
C.Yuan@swansea.ac.uk

Abstract. In this paper we will investigate a stochastic hybrid delay population dynamics (SHDPD) and show under certain conditions, the SHDPD will have global positive solution. Ultimate boundedness and extinction, two important properties in a population systems, are discussed.

Keywords: Brownian motion, Itô's formula, ultimate boundedness, extinction.

1   Introduction

Population dynamics have been of interest in a number of years. Starting with the early work of Lotka-Volterra, the delay differential equation

$$\frac{dx(t)}{dt} = x(t)[\mu + \alpha x(t) + \delta x(t - \tau)] \tag{1.1}$$

has been used to model the population growth of certain species and is known as the delay Lotka-Volterra model or the delay logistic equation. To allow the introduction of uncertainty in the influence of the environment, the delay Lotka-Volterra model for n interacting species is decribed by the n-dimensional delay differential equation

$$\frac{dx(t)}{dt} = \operatorname{diag}(x_1(t), \cdots, x_n(t))[b + Ax(t) + Bx(t - \tau)], \tag{1.2}$$

where

$$x = (x_1, \cdots, x_n)^T, \quad b = (b_1, \cdots, b_n)^T, \quad A = (a_{ij})_{n \times n}, \quad B = (b_{ij})_{n \times n}.$$

There is an extensive literature concerned with the dynamics of this delay model and we here only mention Ahmad and Rao [1], Bereketoglu and Gyori [4], Freedman and Ruan [6], He and Gopalsamy [8], Kuang and Smith [13], Teng

---

* Corresponding author.

João Hespanha and A. Tiwari (Eds.): HSCC 2006, LNCS 3927, pp. 436–450, 2006.
© Springer-Verlag Berlin Heidelberg 2006

and Yu [18] among many others. In particular, the books by Gopalsamy [7], Kolmanovskii and Myshkis [11] as well as Kuang [12] are good references in this area.

Taking the environmental disturbances into account, Bahar and Mao [5] discussed stochastic differential delay population dynamics

$$dx(t) = \text{diag}(x_1(t), \cdots, x_n(t))\Big([b + Ax(t) + Bx(t - \tau)]dt + \sigma dw(t)\Big), \quad (1.3)$$

where $\sigma = (\sigma_1, \ldots, \sigma_n)^T$ and $w(t)$ is a scalar Bownian motion.

On the other hand, many practical systems may experience abrupt changes in their structure and parameters caused by phenomena such as component failures or repairs, changing subsystem interconnections, and abrupt environmental disturbances. The hybrid systems driven by continuous-time Markov chains have recently been developed to cope with such situation. The hybrid systems combine a part of the state that takes values continuously and another part of the state that takes discrete values. Kazangey and Sworder [10] presented a jump system, where a macroeconomic model of the national economy was used to study the effect of federal housing removal policies on the stabilization of the housing sector. The term describing the influence of interest rates was modeled by a finite-state Markov chain to provide a quantitative measure of the effect of interest rate uncertainty on optimal policy. Athans [2] suggested that the hybrid systems would become a basic framework in posing and solving control-related issues in Battle Management Command, Control and Communications (BM/C^3) systems. The hybrid systems were also considered for the modeling of electric power systems by Willsky & Levy [19] as well as for the control of a solar thermal central receiver by Sworder & Rogers [17]. Hu, Wu and Sastry [9] studied modeled subtilin production in bacillus subtilis by using stochastic hybrid systems. In his book [15], Mariton explained that the hybrid systems had been emerging as a convenient mathematical framework for the formulation of various design problems in different fields such as target tracking (evasive target tracking problem), fault tolerant control and manufacturing processes. An important class of hybrid systems is the jump linear systems

$$\dot{x}(t) = A(r(t))x(t) \quad (1.4)$$

where a part of the state $x(t)$ takes values in $\mathbb{R}^n$ while another part of the state $r(t)$ is a Markov chain taking values in $S = \{1, 2, \ldots, N\}$.

Motivated by hybrid systems, let us return to the Eq. (1.3). If this system experiences abrupt changes in its structure and parameters and we use the continuous-time Markov chains to model these abrupt changes, we then need to deal with stochastic hybrid delay population dynamics (SHDPD)

$$dx(t) = \text{diag}(x_1(t), \cdots, x_n(t))\Big([(b(r(t)) + A(r(t))x(t) + B(r(t))x(t - \tau)]dt$$
$$+ \sigma(r(t))dw(t)\Big). \quad (1.5)$$

To ensure models are realistic one needs to check certain properties, e.g. they never predict that populations become negative or that they will grow unbounded. The first contribution of this paper is to establish a number of such well posedness conditions for a class of delay population models. For analysis, the most important question is extinction, i.e. whether a species is doomed. The second contribution of the paper is to determine extinction conditions. These are formulated in terms of stability results for the delayed SDEs that arise in the population dynamics.

2   Stochastic Hybrid Delay Population Dynamics

2.1   Generalised Itô Formula

Throughout this paper, unless otherwise specified, we let $(\Omega, \mathcal{F}, \mathcal{F}_t, P)$ be a complete probability space with a filtration $\mathcal{F}_t$ satisfying the usual conditions (i.e. it is increasing and right continuous while $\mathcal{F}_0$ contains all P-null sets). Let $w(t)$ be a scalar Brownian motion defined on the probability space. Let $\mathbb{R}_+^n = \{x = (x_1, \ldots, x_n) \in \mathbb{R}^n : x_m > 0, 1 \leq m \leq n\}$. Let $|\cdot|$ denote the Euclidean norm for vectors or the trace norm for matrices. If A is a symmetric matrix, denote by $\lambda_{\max}(A)$ and $\lambda_{\min}(A)$ its biggest and smallest eigenvalue respectively. Let $\tau > 0$ and $C([-\tau, 0]; \mathbb{R}^n)$ denote the family of all continuous $\mathbb{R}^n$-valued functions on $[-\tau, 0]$. Let $C_{\mathcal{F}_0}^b([-\tau, 0]; \mathbb{R}^n)$ be the family of all $\mathcal{F}_0$-measurable bounded $C([-\tau, 0]; \mathbb{R}^n)$-valued random variables $\xi = \{\xi(\theta) : -\tau \leq \theta \leq 0\}$.

Let $r(t), t \geq 0$, be a right-continuous Markov chain on the probability space taking values in a finite state space $S = \{1, 2, \ldots, N\}$ with generator $\Gamma = (\gamma_{ij})_{N \times N}$ given by

$$P\{r(t + \Delta) = j | r(t) = i\} = \begin{cases} \gamma_{ij} \Delta + o(\Delta) & : \quad \text{if } i \neq j \\ 1 + \gamma_{ij} \Delta + o(\Delta) & : \quad \text{if } i = j \end{cases}$$

where $\Delta > 0$. Here $\gamma_{ij} \geq 0$ is transition rate from i to j if $i \neq j$ while

$$\gamma_{ii} = -\sum_{j \neq i} \gamma_{ij}.$$

We assume that the Markov chain $r(\cdot)$ is independent of the Brownian motion $w(\cdot)$. It is well known that almost every sample path of $r(t)$ is a right continuous step function.

In this paper we consider the following stochastic hybrid delay population dynamics

$$dx(t) = \text{diag}(x_1(t), \cdots, x_n(t)) \Big([b(r(t)) + A(r(t))x(t) + B(r(t))x(t - \tau)]dt$$

$$+ \sigma(r(t))dw(t) \Big), \tag{2.1}$$

where $\forall i \in S$, $b(i) = (b_1(i), \ldots, b_n(i))^T$, $A(i) = (a_{kl}(i))_{n \times n}$, $B(i) = (b_{kl}(i))_{n \times n}$, $\sigma(i) = (\sigma_1(i), \ldots, \sigma_n(i))^T$. Let $C^{2,1}(\mathbb{R}^n \times \mathbb{R}_+ \times S; \mathbb{R}_+)$ denote the all the family of non-negative functions $V(x, t, i)$ on $\mathbb{R}^n \times \mathbb{R}_+ \times S$ which are continuously twice differentiable in x and once in t. If $V \in C^{2,1}(\mathbb{R}^n \times \mathbb{R}_+ \times S; \mathbb{R}_+)$, define an operator LV associated with Eq. (2.1) from $\mathbb{R}^n \times \mathbb{R}^n \times \mathbb{R}_+ \times S$ to $\mathbb{R}$ by

$$LV(x, y, t, i) = V_t(x, t, i) + V_x(x, t, i)\text{diag}(x_1, \cdots, x_n)[b(i) + A(i)x + B(i)y]$$
$$+ \frac{1}{2}\text{trace}[\sigma^T(i)\text{diag}(x_1, \cdots, x_n)V_{xx}(x, t, i)\text{diag}(x_1, \cdots, x_n)\sigma(i)]$$
$$+ \sum_{j=1}^{N} \gamma_{ij} V(x, t, j), \tag{2.2}$$

where

$$V_t(x, t, i) = \frac{\partial V(x, t, i)}{\partial t}, \quad V_x(x, t, i) = \left(\frac{\partial V(x, t, i)}{\partial x_1}, \ldots, \frac{\partial V(x, t, i)}{\partial x_n}\right)$$

and

$$V_{xx}(x, t, i) = \left(\frac{\partial^2 V(x, t, i)}{\partial x_i \partial x_j}\right)_{n \times n}.$$

By recalling that a continuous time Markov chain $r(t)$ with generator $\Gamma = \{\gamma_{ij}\}_{N \times N}$ can be represented as a stochastic integral with respect to a Poisson random measure (cf. [3]). Indeed, let Δ_{ij} be consecutive, left closed, right open intervals of the real line each having length γ_{ij} and define a function

$$h : S \times \mathbb{R} \to \mathbb{R} \tag{2.3}$$

by

$$h(i, y) = \begin{cases} j - i & : \quad \text{if } y \in \Delta_{ij}, \\ 0 & : \quad \text{otherwise.} \end{cases} \tag{2.4}$$

Then

$$dr(t) = \int_{\mathbb{R}} h(r(t-), y)\nu(dt, dy), r(0) = i_0, \tag{2.5}$$

where $\nu(dt, dy)$ is a Poisson random measure with intensity $dt \times m(dy)$, m being the Lebesgue measure on $\mathbb{R}$. Let $x(t)$ be the solution of Eq. (2.1). For the convenience of the reader we cite the the generalised Ito's formula (cf. [16]): If $V \in C^{2,1}(R^n \times R_+ \times S)$, then for any $t \geq 0$

$$V(x(t), t, r(t)) = V(x(0), 0, r(0))$$
$$+ \int_0^t LV(x(s), x(s - \tau), s, r(s))ds + \int_0^t V_x(x(s), s, r(s))\sigma(r(s))dB(s)$$
$$+ \int_0^t \int_{\mathbb{R}} (V(x(s), s, i_0 + h(r(s), l)) - V(x(s), s, r(s)))\mu(ds, dl), \tag{2.6}$$

where the function h is defined as in (2.4) and $\mu(ds, dl) = \nu(ds, dl) - m(dl)ds$ is a martingale measure.

2.2   Global Positive Solutions

Generally speaking, to the existence and the uniqueness of a stochastic differential equation for any given initial data, the coefficients of the equation are required to satisfy the linear growth condition and local Lipschitz condition. However, the coefficients of Eq. (2.1) do not satisfy the linear growth condition, though they are locally Lipschitz continuous, so the solution of Eq. (2.1) may explode at a finite time. It is therefore useful to establish some conditions under which the solution of Eq. (2.1) is not only positive but will also not explode to infinite at any finite time.

Theorem 1. *Assume that there are positive numbers $c_1(i), \ldots, c_n(i), i \in S$ and θ such that*

$$\lambda_{\max}\left(\frac{1}{2}[C(i)A(i) + A^T(i)C(i)] + \frac{1}{4\theta}C(i)B(i)B^T(i)C(i) + \theta I\right) \leq 0, \quad (2.7)$$

where $C(i) = \mathrm{diag}(c_1(i), \ldots, c_n(i))$ and I is the $n \times n$ identity matrix. Then for any given initial data $\{x(t) : -\tau \leq t \leq 0\} \in C^b_{\mathcal{F}_0}([-\tau, 0]; R^n_+)$, there is a unique solution $x(t)$ to equation (2.1) on $t \geq -\tau$ and the solution will remain in $\mathbb{R}^n_+$ with probability 1, namely $x(t) \in \mathbb{R}^n_+$ for all $t \geq -\tau$ almost surely.

Proof of Theorem 1.   Since the coefficients of the SHDPD (2.1) are locally Lipschitz continuous, for any given initial data $\xi(t) = \{x(t) : -\tau \leq t \leq 0\} \in C\mathcal{F}_0{}^b([-\tau, 0]; \mathbb{R}^n)$ and $r(0) = i_0 \in S$ there is a unique maximal local solution $x(t)$ on $t \in [-\tau, \tau_e)$, where τ_e is the explosion time. To show this solution is global, we need to show that $\tau_e = \infty$ a.s. Let k_0 be sufficiently large for

$$\frac{1}{k_0} < \min_{-\tau \leq t \leq 0} |\xi(t)| \leq \max_{-\tau \leq t \leq 0} |\xi(t)| < k_0$$

For $k \geq k_0$, define the stopping time

$$\rho_k = \inf\{t \in [0, \tau_e) : x_m(t) \notin (1/k, k) \text{ for some } m = 1, \ldots, n\}.$$

Also define V on $\mathbb{R}^n_+ \times S$ such that

$$V(x, i) = \sum_{m=1}^{n} c_m(i)h(x_m), \quad (x, i) \in \mathbb{R}^n_+ \times S, \quad (2.8)$$

where $h(u) = u - 1 - \ln(u)$. The operator associated with Eq. (2.1)

$$LV(x, y, i) = x^T C(i)b + \frac{1}{2}x^T[C(i)A(i) + A^T(i)C(i)]x + x^T C(i)B(i)y$$

$$- \bar{C}(i)(b(i) + A(i)x + B(i)y) + \frac{1}{2}\sigma^T(i)C(i)\sigma(i) + \sum_{j=1}^{N} \gamma_{ij}V(x, j), \quad (2.9)$$

where $\bar{C}(i) = (c_1(i), \ldots, c_n(i))$. Noting that

$$x^T C(i)B(i)y \le \frac{1}{4\theta}x^T C(i)B(i)B^T(i)C(i)x + \theta|y|^2$$

and the condition (2.7), we have

$$\frac{1}{2}x^T[C(i)A(i) + A^T(i)C(i)]x + x^T C(i)B(i)y$$

$$\le \frac{1}{2}x^T[C(i)A(i) + A^T(i)C(i)]x + \frac{1}{4\theta}x^T C(i)B(i)B^T(i)C(i)x + \theta|y|^2$$

$$= x^T\left[\frac{1}{2}(C(i)A(i) + A^T(i)C(i)) + \frac{1}{4\theta}C(i)B(i)B^T(i)C(i) + \theta I\right]x - \theta|x|^2 + \theta|y|^2$$

$$\le -\theta|x|^2 + \theta|y|^2. \tag{2.10}$$

Moreover, there is a constant $K_1 > 0$ such that

$$x^T C(i)b - \bar{C}(i)(b(i) + A(i)x + B(i)y) + \frac{1}{2}\sigma^T(i)C(i)\sigma(i) \le K_1(1 + |x| + |y|).$$

Substituting these into (2.9) yields we have

$$LV(x,y,i) \le K_1(1 + |x| + |y|) - \theta|x|^2 + \theta|y|^2 + \sum_{j=1}^{N}\gamma_{ij}V(x,j). \tag{2.11}$$

Let

$$\hat{q} = \max\left\{\frac{c_m(i)}{c_m(j)} : m = 1, \ldots, n, i, j \in S\right\}.$$

By the definition of V, for any $i, j \in S$, we have

$$\hat{q}V(x,i) = \sum_{m=1}^{n}\hat{q}c_m(i)[x_m - 1 - \ln x_m]$$

$$\ge \sum_{m=1}^{n}c_m(j)[x_m - 1 - \ln x_m] = V(x,j)$$

and

$$|x| \le \sum_{m=1}^{n}x_i \le \sum_{m=1}^{n}[2(x_m - 1 - \log x - m) + 2]$$

$$\le 2n + \frac{2}{\min\{c_m(i) : 1 \le m \le n, i \in S\}}\sum_{m=1}^{n}c_m(i)(x_m - 1 - \log x - m)$$

$$= 2n + \frac{2}{\min\{c_m(i) : 1 \le m \le n, i \in S\}}V(x,i).$$

Hence there is a constant $K_2 > 0$ such that

$$LV(x,y,i) \le K_2(1 + V(x,i) + V(y,i)) - \theta|x|^2 + \theta|y|^2. \tag{2.12}$$

$$E \int_0^{\rho_k \wedge t} LV(x(s), x(s-\tau), r(s)) ds \le E \int_0^{\rho_k \wedge t} \Big[- \theta |x(s)|^2 + \theta |x(s-\tau)|^2$$

$$+ K_2(1 + V(x(s), r(s)) + V(x(s-\tau), r(s))) \Big] ds. \qquad (2.13)$$

Compute

$$E \int_0^{\rho_k \wedge t} |x(s-\tau)|^2 ds = E \int_{-\tau}^{\rho_k \wedge t - \tau} |x(s)|^2 ds$$

$$\le \int_{-\tau}^0 |x(s)|^2 ds + E \int_0^{\rho_k \wedge t} |x(s)|^2 ds$$

and

$$E \int_0^{\rho_k \wedge t} V(x(s-\tau), r(s))) ds$$

$$\le E \int_{-\tau}^0 V(x(s), r(0)) ds + E \int_0^{\rho_k \wedge t} V(x(s), r(s-\tau)) ds$$

$$\le E \int_{-\tau}^0 V(x(s), r(0)) ds + \hat{q} E \int_0^{\rho_k \wedge t} V(x(s), r(s)) ds.$$

Substituting these into (2.13) gives

$$E \int_0^{\rho_k \wedge t} LV(x(s), x(s-\tau), r(s)) ds$$

$$\le K_3 + K_2(1 + \hat{q}) E \int_0^{\rho_k \wedge t} V(x(\rho_k \wedge s), r(\rho_k \wedge s)) ds, \qquad (2.14)$$

where

$$K_3 = K_2 T + \int_{-\tau}^0 |x(s) - \bar{x}|^2 ds + K_2 E \int_{-\tau}^0 V(x(s), r(0)) ds.$$

Using the generalised Itô formula and taking the expectation

$$EV(x(\rho_k \wedge t), r(\rho_k \wedge t))$$

$$= EV(\xi(0), r(0)) + E \int_0^{\rho_k \wedge t} LV(x(s), x(s-\tau), r(s)) ds$$

$$\le EV(\xi(0), r(0)) + K_3 + K_2(1 + \hat{q}) E \int_0^{\rho_k \wedge t} V(x(\rho_k \wedge s), r(\rho_k \wedge s)) ds. \qquad (2.15)$$

By the Gronwall inequality,

$$EV(x(\rho_k \wedge T), r(\rho_k \wedge T)) \le K := e^{K_2(1+\hat{q})} \left[EV(\xi(0), r(0)) + K_3 \right].$$

Note that for every $\omega \in \{\rho_k \le T\}$, there is some m such that $x_m(\rho_k, \omega)$ equals either k or $1/k$, hence

$$K \ge E[I_{\{\rho_k \le T\}} V(x(\rho_k, \omega), r(\rho_k, \omega))]$$

$$\ge P(\rho_k \le T) \min_{i \in S, 1 \le m \le n} \left\{ c_m(i)[k - 1 - \ln k] \wedge c_m(i) \left[\frac{1}{k} - 1 - \ln k \right] \right\}.$$

Letting $k \to \infty$ gives

$$\lim_{k \to \infty} P(\rho_k \leq T) = 0,$$

this implies that $y(t) \in \mathbb{R}_+^n$ and $\tau_e = \infty$ a.s. The proof is therefore complete. $\square$

We observe from the proof above that condition (2.7) is used to derive (2.11) from (2.9). But there are several different ways to estimate (2.9) which will lead to different alternative conditions for the global positive solution. For example, we know that

$$x^T \bar{C}(i)B(i)y \leq \frac{1}{2\theta}x^T C(i)x + \frac{\theta}{2}y^T B^T(i)C(i)B(i)y$$

holds for any $\theta > 0$. So

$$
\begin{aligned}
LV(x,y,i) \leq \frac{1}{2}x^T \Big[& C(i)A(i) + A^T(i)C(i) \\
& + \theta^{-1}C(i) + \theta B^T(i)C(i)B(i) \Big]x \\
& - \frac{\theta}{2}x^T B^T(i)C(i)B(i)x + \frac{\theta}{2}y^T B^T(i)C(i)B(i)y \\
& + K_1(1 + |x| + |y|) + \sum_{j=1}^N \gamma_{ij}V(x,j)
\end{aligned}
\tag{2.16}
$$

If we assume that

$$\lambda_{\max}\Big(C(i)A(i) + A^T(i)C(i) + \theta^{-1}C(i) + \theta B^T(i)C(i)B(i) \Big) \leq 0,$$

we will then have

$$
\begin{aligned}
LV(x,y,i) \leq & -\frac{\theta}{2}x^T B^T(i)C(i)B(i)x + \frac{\theta}{2}y^T B^T(i)C(i)B(i)y \\
& + K_1(1 + |x| + |y|) + \sum_{j=1}^N \gamma_{ij}V(x,j)
\end{aligned}
\tag{2.17}
$$

From this can we show in the same way as in the proof of Theorem 1 that the solution of equation (2.1) is positive and global. In other words, the arguments above give us an alternative result which we describe as a theorem below.

Theorem 2. *Assume that there are positive numbers $c_1(i), \cdots, c_n(i)$ and θ such that*

$$\lambda_{\max}\Big(C(i)A(i) + A^T(i)C(i) + \theta^{-1}C(i) + \theta B^T(i)C(i)B(i) \Big) \leq 0, \tag{2.18}$$

where $C(i)$ are the same as defined in Theorem 1. Then for any given initial data $\{x(t) : -\tau \leq t \leq 0\} \in C([-\tau, 0]; R_+^n)$, $i_0 \in S$, there is a unique solution $x(t)$ to equation (2.1) on $t \geq -\tau$ and the solution will remain in $\mathbb{R}_+^n$ with probability 1, namely $x(t) \in \mathbb{R}_+^n$ for all $t \geq -\tau$ almost surely.

3   Ultimate Boundedness

From now on we shall denote by $x(t; \xi, i_0)$ the unique global positive solution of the SHDPD (2.1) given initial data $\xi = \{\xi(t) : -\tau \leq t \leq 0\} \in C^b_{\mathcal{F}_0}([-\tau, 0]; \mathbb{R}^n_+), i_0 \in S$. One of the important properties for a population dynamics is the ultimate boundedness in mean. To be precise, let us give the definition.

Definition 3.1. *The SHDPD* (2.1) *is said to be ultimately bounded in mean if there is a positive constant K such that*

$$\limsup_{t \to \infty} E|x(t)| \leq K.$$

Theorem 3. *Assume that there are positive numbers $c_1(i), \cdots, c_n(i)$ and θ such that*

$$-\lambda := \lambda_{\max}\left(\frac{1}{2}[C(i)A(i) + A^T(i)C(i)] + \frac{1}{4\theta}C(i)B(i)B^T(i)C(i) + \theta I\right) < 0 \tag{3.1}$$

Then for any initial data $\xi = \{\xi(t) : -\tau \leq t \leq 0\} \in C^b_{\mathcal{F}_0}([-\tau, 0]; R^n_+), i_0 \in S$, the solution $x(t; \xi, i_0)$ is ultimately bounded in mean.

Proof. By Theorem 1, the solution $x(t)$ will remain in $\mathbb{R}^n_+$ for all $t \geq -\tau$ with probability 1. Let $\bar{C}(i) = (c_1(i), \ldots, c_n(i))$ and define

$$V(x, i) = \bar{C}(i)x = \sum_{m=1}^n c_m(i)x_m \quad \forall x \in \mathbb{R}^n_+.$$

The operator with Eq. (2.1)

$$LV(x, y, i) = x^T C(i)b + \frac{1}{2}x^T[C(i)A(i) + A^T(i)C(i)]x + x^T C(i)B(i)y$$

$$+ \sum_{j=1}^N \gamma_{ij}V(x, j), \tag{3.2}$$

By (2.10) we have

$$x^T C(i)[A(i)x + B(i)y] \leq -(\lambda + \theta)|x|^2 + \theta|y|^2.$$

Therefore

$$LV(x, y, i) \leq (|C(i)b| + \gamma|\bar{C}(i)|)|x| - (\lambda + \theta)|x|^2 + \theta|y|^2 \tag{3.3}$$

where $\gamma = \max_{j \in S} \sum_{i=1}^N |\gamma_{ij}|$.

By the generalised Itô formula and taking the expactation, we have

$$e^{\alpha t} EV(x(t), r(t)) = EV(x(0), r(0))$$

$$+ E \int_0^t x^T(s) e^{\alpha s} [\alpha V(x(s), r(s)) + LV(x(s)), x(s-\tau) r(s))] ds$$

$$\leq E \int_0^t e^{\alpha s} \left[\beta |x(s)| - (\lambda + \theta)|x(s)|^2 + \theta |x(s-\tau)|^2 \right] ds$$

$$\leq E \int_0^t e^{\alpha s} \beta |x(s)| ds - E \int_0^t e^{\alpha s} (\lambda + \theta)|x(s)|^2 ds$$

$$+ \theta e^{\alpha \tau} E \int_0^t e^{\alpha s} |x(s)|^2 ds + \theta e^{\alpha \tau} E \int_{-\tau}^0 |x(s)|^2 ds. \qquad (3.4)$$

where $\beta = \max_{i \in S}(|C(i)b(i)| + (\gamma + \alpha)|\bar{C}(i)|)$.

Let

$$\alpha = \frac{1}{\tau} \log \frac{\lambda + 2\theta}{2\theta},$$

we obtain that

$$e^{\alpha t} EV(x(t), r(t)) \leq EV(x(0), r(0)) + \theta e^{\alpha \tau} E \int_{-\tau}^0 |x(s)|^2 ds$$

$$+ E \int_0^t e^{\alpha s} \left(\beta |x(s)| - \frac{\lambda}{2}|x(s)|^2 \right) ds$$

$$\leq EV(x(0), r(0)) + \theta e^{\alpha \tau} E \int_{-\tau}^0 |x(s)|^2 ds + \frac{\beta^2}{2\lambda} \int_0^t e^{\alpha s} ds.$$

Hence

$$\limsup_{t \to \infty} EV(x(t), r(t)) \leq \frac{\beta^2}{2\alpha\lambda}.$$

But

$$|x(t)| \leq \sum_{m=1}^n x_m(t) \leq \frac{V(x(t), r(t))}{\min\{c_m(i) : 1 \leq m \leq n, i \in S\}}.$$

This yields

$$\limsup_{t \to \infty} E|x(t)| \leq \frac{\beta^2}{2\alpha\lambda \min\{c_m(i) : 1 \leq m \leq n, i \in S\}},$$

as required. The proof is therefore finished. $\qquad \square$

In the proof above, we not only prove that the solution is ultimately bounded in mean, but also we give a upper-bound. As the same way we obtain Theorem 2, we have the following theorem.

Theorem 4. *Assume that there are positive numbers $c_1(i), \cdots, c_n(i)$ and θ such that*

$$-\lambda := \lambda_{\max}\left(C(i)A(i) + A^T(i)C(i) + \theta^{-1}C(i) + \theta B^T(i)C(i)B(i)\right) < 0 \quad (3.5)$$

Then for any initial data $\xi = \{\xi(t) : -\tau \leq t \leq 0\} \in C([-\tau, 0]; R_+^n), i_0 \in S$, the solution $x(t; \xi, i_0)$ is ultimately bounded in mean.

4   Extinction

One of the important properties for a population dynamics is the extinction which means every species will become extinct. The most natural analogue for the stochastic population dynamics (2.1) is that every species will become extinct with probability 1. To be precise, let us give the definition.

Definition 4.1. *The SHDPD (2.1) is said to be extinct with probability 1 if, for every initial data $\xi = \{\xi(t) : -\tau \leq t \leq 0\} \in C([-\tau, 0]; R_+^n), i_0 \in S$, the solution $x(t; \xi, i_0)$ has the property that*

$$\lim_{t \to \infty} x_m(t) = 0 \quad a.s. \text{ for all } 1 \leq m \leq n. \tag{4.1}$$

In the previous section we have shown that either condition (2.7) or (2.18) guarantees the unique global positive solution. We shall now show that either of them together with the other condition below also guarantees the extinction with probability 1.

Theorem 5. *Assume that there are positive numbers $c_1(i), \cdots, c_n(i)$ and θ such that either (2.7) or (2.18) holds and*

$$b^T(i)C^T(i) + \sum_{j=1}^{N} \gamma_{ij} \bar{C}(j) \leq 0 \tag{4.2}$$

Then the SHDPD (2.1) is extinct.

To prove this theorem we will need the nonnegative semimartingale convergence theorem (see e.g. [14, Theorem 7 on p.139]) which we cite as a lemma below.

Lemma 1. *Let $A(t)$ and $U(t)$ be two continuous $\mathcal{F}_t$-adapted increasing processes on $t \geq 0$ with $A(0) = U(0) = 0$ a.s. Let $M(t)$ be a real-valued continuous local martingale with $M(0) = 0$ a.s. Let ζ be a nonnegative $\mathcal{F}_0$-measurable random variable such that $E\zeta < \infty$. Define*

$$X(t) = \zeta + A(t) - U(t) + M(t) \quad for \ t \geq 0.$$

Then, if $X(t)$ is nonnegative,

$$\left\{ \lim_{t \to \infty} A(t) < \infty \right\} \subset \left\{ \lim_{t \to \infty} X(t) < \infty \right\} \cap \left\{ \lim_{t \to \infty} U(t) < \infty \right\} \quad a.s.,$$

where $B \subset D$ a.s. means $P(B \cap D^c) = 0$. In particular, if $\lim_{t \to \infty} A(t) < \infty$ a.s., then for almost all $\omega \in \Omega$

$$\lim_{t \to \infty} X(t, \omega) < \infty, \quad \lim_{t \to \infty} U(t, \omega) < \infty$$

and

$$-\infty < \lim_{t \to \infty} M(t, \omega) < \infty.$$

Proof of Theorem 5. By Theorem 5, the solution $x(t)$ will remain in $\mathbb{R}_+^n$ for all $t \geq -\tau$ with probability 1. define

$$V(x, i) = \bar{C}(i)x = \sum_{m=1}^{n} c_m(i)x_i \quad \forall x \in \mathbb{R}_+^n.$$

By the generalised Itô formula, we have

$$V(x(t), r(t)) = V(x(0), r(0))$$
$$+ \int_0^t \left(x^T(s)C(r(s))[b(r(s)) + A(r(s))x(s) + B(r(s))x(s - \tau)] \right.$$
$$+ \sum_{j=1}^{N} \gamma_{r(s)j} \bar{C}(j)x(s) \right) ds + M_1(t) + M_2(t), \tag{4.3}$$

where

$$M_1(t) = \int_0^t \int_R (V(x(s), s, i_0 + h(r(s), l)) - V(x(s), s, r(s))) \mu(ds, dl)$$
$$M_2(t) = \int_0^t x^T(s)C(r(s))\sigma(r(s))dw(s).$$

By (2.10) we have

$$x^T(s)C(r(s))[A(r(s))x(s) + B(r(s))x(s - \tau)] \leq -\theta|x(s)|^2 + \theta|x(s - \tau)|^2.$$

This, together with the condition (4.2), yields

$$V(x(t), r(t)) \leq V(x(0), r(0))$$
$$+ \int_0^t \left(x^T(s)C(r(s))b(r(s)) + \sum_{j=1}^{N} \gamma_{r(s)j} \bar{C}(j)x(s) - \theta|x(s)|^2 + \theta|x(s - \tau)|^2 \right) ds$$
$$+ M_1(t) + M_2(t) \leq \theta \int_{-\tau}^{0} |x(s)|^2 ds + M_1(t) + M_2(t) \tag{4.4}$$

By Lemma 1,

$$-\infty < \lim_{t \to \infty} (M_1(t) + M_2(t)) < \infty \text{ a.s.} \tag{4.5}$$

For any positive constant K, define the stopping time

$$\rho_K = \inf\{t \geq 0 : |M_1(t) + M_2(t)| \geq K\}.$$

where here and throughout this paper we set $\inf \emptyset = \infty$. Obviously τ_K is increasing. In particular, by (4.5), there is a subset Ω_1 of Ω with $P(\Omega_1) = 1$ such that for every $\omega \in \Omega_1$ there is a finite number $K(\omega)$ such that $\rho_K(\omega) = \infty$ for all $K \geq K(\omega)$. On the other hand, since $M_1(t)$ is continuous martingale and $M_2(t)$ is discontinuous martingale, we have, for any $t > 0$, $E[M_1(t \wedge \rho_K)M_2(t \wedge \rho_K)] = 0$. Therefore

$$K^2 \geq E|M_1(t \wedge \rho_K) + M_2(t \wedge \rho_K)|^2 = E\int_0^{t \wedge \rho_K} |x^T(s)C(r(s))\sigma(r(s))|^2 ds.$$

Letting $t \to \infty$ yields

$$E\int_0^{\rho_K} |x^T(s)C(r(s))\sigma(r(s))|^2 ds \leq K^2,$$

which implies that

$$\int_0^{\rho_K} |x^T(s)C(r(s))\sigma(r(s))|^2 ds < \infty \tag{4.6}$$

holds with probability 1. Hence there is another subset Ω_2 of Ω with $P(\Omega_2) = 1$ such that if $\omega \in \Omega_2$, (4.6) holds for every $K \geq 1$. Therefore, for any $\omega \in \Omega_1 \cap \Omega_2$, we have

$$\int_0^\infty |x^T(s)C(r(s))\sigma(r(s))|^2 ds = \int_0^{\rho_{K(\omega)}(\omega)} |x^T(s)C(r(s))\sigma(r(s))|^2 ds < \infty.$$

It is straightforward to see that

$$\liminf_{t \to \infty} |x(t)| = 0 \quad \text{a.s.} \tag{4.7}$$

and

$$\lim_{t \to \infty} \int_{t-\tau}^t |x(s)|^2 ds = 0 \quad \text{a.s.} \tag{4.8}$$

Define $\mu : \mathbb{R}_+ \to \mathbb{R}_+$ by

$$\mu(u) = \inf_{|x| \geq u, i \in S} V(x, i).$$

By the definition of $V(x,i)$, it is clear that $\mu(u) \downarrow 0$ as $u \downarrow 0$. Let $\varepsilon > 0$ be arbitrary and set $\delta = \varepsilon\mu(\varepsilon)/2$. Define the stopping time:

$$\rho_1 = \inf\left\{t \geq 0 : V(x(t), r(t)) + \theta \int_{t-\tau}^t |x(s)|^2 ds \leq \delta\right\}.$$

It follows from (4.7) and (4.8) that $P\{\rho_1 < \infty\} = 1$. We can therefore find a positive constant T sufficiently large for

$$P\{\rho_1 \leq T\} \geq 1 - \frac{\varepsilon}{2}. \tag{4.9}$$

Now, define two stopping times

$$\rho_2 = \begin{cases} \rho_1 & \text{if } \rho_1 \leq T, \\ \infty & \text{otherwise} \end{cases}$$

and
$$\rho_3 = \inf\{t \geq \rho_2 : |x(t)| \geq \varepsilon\}.$$

We then derive from (4.4) that for any $t \geq T$,

$EV(x(t \wedge \rho_3), r(t \wedge \rho_3))$
$$\leq E\left(V(x((t \wedge \rho_2), r((t \wedge \rho_2)) + \int_{t \wedge \rho_2}^{t \wedge \rho_3} (-\theta|x(s)|^2 + \theta|x(s - \tau)|^2)ds\right). \quad (4.10)$$

Noting that $\rho_2 > T$ means $\rho_2 = \infty$ and $\rho_3 = \infty$, therefore

$$E\left\{I_{\{\rho_2 > T\}}\left(V(x((t \wedge \rho_2), r((t \wedge \rho_2)) + \int_{t \wedge \rho_2}^{t \wedge \rho_3} (-\theta|x(s)|^2 + \theta|x(s - \tau)|^2)ds\right)\right\}$$
$$= E\{I_{\{\rho_2 > T\}}V(x((t), r((t))\} = E\{I_{\{\rho_2 > T\}}V(x((t \wedge \rho_3), r((t \wedge \rho_3))\}.$$

By (4.10) we have
$$E\{I_{\{\rho_2 \leq T\}}V(x((t \wedge \rho_3), r((t \wedge \rho_3))\} \leq \delta.$$

Noting $\{\rho_3 \leq t\} \subset \{\rho_2 \leq T\}$ and recalling the definition of $\mu(\cdot)$, we further obtain
$$\mu(\varepsilon)P\{\rho_3 \leq t\} \leq \delta.$$

Using the definition of δ, we obtain
$$P\{\rho_3 < \infty\} \leq \frac{\varepsilon}{2}.$$

Hence, by (4.9) and the definition of ρ_2,
$$P\{\rho_2 < \infty \text{ and } \rho_3 = \infty\} \geq P\{\rho_2 < T\} - P\{\rho_3 < \infty\} \geq 1 - \varepsilon.$$

This yields
$$P\{\limsup_{t \to \infty} |x(t)| \leq \varepsilon\} \geq 1 - \varepsilon.$$

Since ε is arbitrary, we must have
$$P\{\limsup_{t \to \infty} |x(t)| = 0\} = 1.$$

The Proof is therefore complete.   □

We only prove the Theorem 5 under condition (2.7) since it can be done in the same way under condition (2.18). We omit it here and leave to the reader.

5   Conclusion

It is interesting to observe that the conditions imposed in all Theorems are independent of the noise intensity vector $\sigma(i), i \in S$. This means all properties which we studied for the SHDPD (2.1) will not change no matter the environmental noise is large or small. In other words, these properties of Eq. (2.1) are very robust under the noise. The logic next step is to investigate environmental noise effect on the SHDPD.

References

1. Ahmad, A. and Rao, M.R.M., Asymptotically periodic solutions of n-competing species problem with time delay, *J. Math. Anal. Appl.* 186 (1994), 557–571.
2. Athans, M., *Command and control (c2) theory: A challenge to control science,* IEEE Trans. Automat. Control 32(1987), 286-293.
3. Basak, G. K., Bisi, A. and Ghosh, M.K., *Stability of a random diffusion with linear drift,* J. Math. Anal. Appl. 202 (1996), 604–622.
4. Bereketoglu, H. and Gyori, I., Global asymptotic stability in a nonautonomous Lotka-Volterra type system with infinite delay, *J. Math. Anal. Appl.* 210 (1997), 279–291.
5. Bahar, A. and Mao, X., *Stochastic delay Lotka-Volterra model,* J. Math. Anal. Appl. 292 (2004), 364–380.
6. Freedman, H.I. and Ruan, S., Uniform persistence in functional differential equations, *J. Differential Equations* 115 (1995), 173–192.
7. Gopalsamy, K., *Stability and Oscillations in Delay Differential Equations of Population Dynamics,* Kluwer Academic, Dordrecht, 1992.
8. He, X. and Gopalsamy, K., Persistence, attractivity, and delay in facultative mutualism, *J. Math. Anal. Appl.* 215 (1997), 154–173.
9. Hu, J., Wu W. and Sastry S., *Modeling subtilin production in bacillus subtilis using stochastic hybrid systems.* In R. Alur, G. Pappas Eds., Hybrid Systems: Computation and Control, 7th International Workshop, HSCC 2004, 417-431. Springer LNCS vol. 2993, 2004.
10. T. Kazangey and D.D. Sworder, Effective federal policies for regulating residential housing, in: Proc. Summer Computer Simulation Conference, San diego, 1971, 1120–1128.
11. Kolmanovskii, V. and Myshkis, A., *Applied Theory of Functional Differential Equations,* Kluwer Academic Publishers, 1992.
12. Kuang, Y., *Delay Differential Equations with Applications in Population Dynamics,* Academic Press, Boston, 1993.
13. Kuang, Y. and Smith, H.L., Global stability for infinite delay Lotka-Volterra type systems, *J. Differential Equations* 103 (1993), 221–246.
14. Liptser, R.Sh. and Shiryayev, A.N., *Theory of Martingales,* Kluwer Academic Publishers, 1989. (Translation of the Russian edition, Nauka, Moscow, 1986).
15. Mariton, M., *Jump Linear Systems in Automatic Control,* Marcel Dekker, New York, 1990.
16. Skorohod, A.V., *Asymptotic Methods in the Theory of Stochastic Differential Equations,* American Mathematical Society, Providence, 1989.
17. Sworder, D. D. and Rogers, R. O., *An LQ-solution to a control problem associated with a solar thermal central receiver,* IEEE Trans. Automat. Control 28(1983), 971-978.
18. Teng, Z and Yu, Y., Some new results of nonautomomous Lotka-Volterra competitive systems with delays, *J. Math. Anal. Appl.* 241 (2000), 254–275.
19. A.S. Willsky and B.C. Levy, *Stochastic stability research for complex power systems,* DOE Contract, LIDS, MIT, Rep. ET-76-C-01-2295, 1979.

Finite Gain l_p Stabilization Is Impossible by Bit-Rate Constrained Feedback

Nuno C. Martins

ISR and ECE Dept., University of Maryland, College Park

Abstract. In this paper, we show that the finite gain (FG) l_p stabilization, with $1 \leq p \leq \infty$, of a discrete-time, linear and time-invariant unstable plant is impossible by bit rate constrained feedback. In addition, we show that, under bit rate constrained feedback, weaker (local) versions of FG l_p stability are also impossible. These facts are not obvious, since recent results have shown that input to state stabilization (ISS) is viable by bit-rate constrained control. We establish a comparison with existing work, leading to two conclusions: (1) in spite of ISS stability being attainable under bit rate constrained feedback, small changes in the *amplitude* of the external excitation may cause, in relative terms, a large increase in the *amplitude* of the state (2) FG l_p stabilization requires logarithmic precision around zero, implying that even without bit-rate constraints FG l_p stabilization is impossible in practice. Since our conclusions hold with no assumptions on the feedback structure, they cannot be derived from existing results. We adopt an information theoretic viewpoint, which also brings new insights into the problem of stabilization.

1 Introduction

Consider the following feedback system:

$$X(k+1) = AX(k) + \mathcal{F}(X^k, k) + W(k), \ X(0) = 0, \ k \in \mathbb{N}_+ \tag{1}$$

where $W(k) \in \mathbb{R}^n$ represents the input, $X(k) \in \mathbb{R}^n$, $X^k = (X(0), \ldots, X(k))$, $A \in \mathbb{R}^{n \times n}$ and $\mathcal{F}(\cdot, k) : \mathbb{R}^{n \times (k+1)} \to \mathbb{R}$ represents a feedback strategy.

Definition 1 (*Bit-Rate constrained feedback*). *Let $\mathcal{F}^k$ be defined as:*

$$\mathcal{F}^k(X^k) = \big(\mathcal{F}(X(0), 0), \ldots, \mathcal{F}(X^k, k)\big), X(k) \in \mathbb{R}^n, k \in \mathbb{N}_+$$

*We say that (1) has **bit-rate constrained feedback** if, for a given $R \in \mathbb{R}_+$, the range of $\mathcal{F}^k$ has at most $2^{(k+1)R}$ elements.*

Stabilization under bit-rate constrained feedback involves, implicitly, quantization. The work in [3] has motivated the careful study of the effects of quantization in feedback, where it is shown that the naive quantization noise model is not appropriate. The formulation in [3] adopts a discrete-time, time-invariant, memory-less and finite valued quantization of the state, under which it is shown that asymptotic internal stabilization is impossible. The analysis in [2], gives a complete solution to the problem of finding

João Hespanha and A. Tiwari (Eds.): HSCC 2006, LNCS 3927, pp. 451–459, 2006.

a quadratic control Lyapunov function (QCLF) in the presence of memoryless quantization of either the state, or of the observation estimation error (output feedback). In [2], it is shown that, under the aforementioned framework, the existence of a QCLF requires a quantizer with an infinite number of levels, whose resolution increases logarithmically around zero. On the other hand, it is reported in [1] that, by allowing analog processing before and after quantization, global asymptotic stability can be achieved in the presence of bit-rate constraints. A meticulous analysis of internal stabilization for discrete-time linear systems, in the presence of memoryless piecewise non-linearities, is given in [4]. The stabilization of nonlinear systems is studied in [9].

Most external stability bounds, for bit-rate constrained feedback, assume that the amplitude of the external excitation is known [5], [17], [8], [14],[6]. Therefore, in all of the aforementioned publications, the notions of stability are not compatible with finite gain (FG) l_p, nor with the more general notion of input to state stability (ISS) [13]. Recently, the authors of [10] have addressed this issue, by devising a bit-rate constrained feedback scheme that guarantees stabilization in the ISS sense. In order to attain ISS, the controller must not depend on prior knowledge of the amplitude of the external excitation. In addition, ISS guarantees that the amplitude of the state decreases, as the amplitude of the external signals decreases. However, the sensitivity, in terms of how the state is amplified with respect to the external excitation, has to be characterized using *gain* notions such as FG l_p stability, where $1 \leq p \leq \infty$. These facts have motivated the investigation reported in this paper, i.e., the derivation of necessary conditions for FG l_p stabilization.

Regarding the framework, the approaches in [2], [3] and [4] are significantly different from [1], [5], [17], [8] and [14]. The former addresses stabilization, under a given class of quantization schemes, while the latter is about control with bit-rate constraints. Each approach has its own motivation: specific quantization schemes are well suited for modeling measurement resolution, while bit-rate constraints describe an information-rate bottleneck in the feedback loop. It is important to make this distinction because necessary conditions for stabilization, derived for a given class of quantization schemes, cannot be used in deriving necessary conditions in terms of bit-rate constraints. For instance, [1] achieves global asymptotic stabilization by bit-rate constrained feedback, while in the scheme of [3] the state trajectory always converges to a chaotic orbit.

Our contribution is to show that FG l_p stabilization in not possible by bit-rate constrained feedback, and that includes bit-rate constrained control as a particular case. In addition, it follows from our analysis that bit-rate constrained feedback also rules out weaker (local) versions of FG l_p stabilization, and that, even though ISS is achievable [10], the amplitude of the state may increase arbitrarily with only a small change in the amplitude of the external excitation. The concept of logarithmic resolution was introduced in [2] for a class of quantization schemes. Our work comes in support of such fundamental notion, by proving that, regardless of the quantization scheme, the aforementioned weaker (local) versions of FG l_p stability also requires logarithmic resolution. Any quantization scheme requiring logarithmic resolution is not implementable in practice[1] and, for that reason, it introduces further limits to stability, even in the

---

[1] For instance, logarithmic resolution can be achieved by non-linear gains before and after uniform quantization, without amplitude constraints. On the other hand, such non-linear gains will *explode* around zero.

absence of bit-rate constraints. Our conclusions cannot be derived from existing results because they hold with no assumptions on the feedback structure. In particular, we allow arbitrary analog or digital pre-quantization processing (encoding) as well as post-quantization processing (decoding). In addition, we allow quantizers which may be time-varying and have infinite memory, or no quantizer at all. We use standard properties of information theory, which makes our proofs short and very general.

This paper has four sections. Section 2 discusses, without proofs, the necessary conditions for FG l_p stability and its implications on ISS, while detailed proofs may be found in [18]. Section 4 finalizes the paper with conclusions.

We adopt the following notation: Complex (or real) variables are represented by small caps letters, while vectors use large caps letters, such as $Z \in \mathbb{C}^n$, where the element at the i-th coordinate is presented as Z_i. Exception to this rule is A, which is used to denote the dynamic matrix of the state space representation in (1). Sequences of complex (or real) variables are indicated as $z^k = (z(0), \ldots, z(k))$, $k \in \mathbb{N}_+ \bigcup \{\infty\}$. Similarly, a sequence of vectors is represented as $Z^k = (Z(0), \ldots, Z(k))$, $k \in \mathbb{N}_+ \bigcup \{\infty\}$. The absolute value is given by $|z| = \sqrt{Re\{z\}^2 + Im\{z\}^2}$. The p-norm of a vector $Z \in \mathbb{C}^n$ is defined as $\|Z\|_p = (\sum_{i=1}^n |Z_i|^p)^{\frac{1}{p}}$. Likewise, the ∞-norm of Z is computed as $\|Z\|_\infty = \max_{i \in \{1,\ldots,n\}} |Z_i|$. Infinite complex (real) sequences are indicated as $\bar{z} = (z(0), z(1), \ldots)$, while infinite vector sequences are represented as $\bar{Z} = (Z(0), Z(1), \ldots)$. The l_p norm of an infinite sequence is defined as $\|\bar{Z}\|_p = (\sum_{i=0}^\infty \|Z(i)\|_p^p)^{\frac{1}{p}}$ and the l_∞ norm is given by $\|\bar{Z}\|_\infty = \sup_{k \geq 0} \|Z(k)\|_\infty$. Complex (or real) random variables and vectors are represented by bold face letters, such as $\mathbf{z}$ and $\mathbf{Z}$. With the exception of $\mathcal{K}$ (reserved), functions and maps are represented in calligraphic font, e.g., $\mathcal{Q}$. We denote $\mathbb{R}_+ \bigcup \{\infty\}$ as $\bar{\mathbb{R}}_+$. We also adopt the convention $0 \log_2 0 = 0$.

2 Necessary Conditions for FG l_p Stability

In this section, we explain why FG l_p stabilization cannot be achieved with bit-rate constrained feedback. In addition, we define a weaker (local) version of FG stabilization, which we prove is also not possible by bit-rate constrained feedback. At a later point, we argue that logarithmic resolution is needed for such weak notion of stability. The implications of our results, in input to state stability (ISS), are discussed at the end of this section.

The following are reasons why feedback may be bit-rate constrained. (1) If the feedback loop comprises a uniform quantizer with amplitude constraints then the feedback is finite set. Notice that, without amplitude constraints, a uniform quantizer has infinite range. (2) Another case of finite set feedback is when the controller is implemented by a dynamical system operating on a finite alphabet, such as a digital computer. (3) Furthermore, control over networks is necessarily bit-rate constrained. This scenario is specially relevant to remote control applications, where information can be reliably transmitted only at a finite rate. Besides being finite, the rate of transmission might also be low due to security reasons, because of the communication medium (under-water missions) or in the presence of fading.

Our results hold for the following parameterized notion of stability:

Definition 2 ((ϵ, δ) **FGI stability**). *Let $\bar{X}$ be the solution of (1) and the constants $\epsilon, \delta \in \bar{\mathbb{R}}_+$ be given. The system represented by (1) is (ϵ, δ) FGI (finite gain internally) stable, if the following holds:*

$$\exists k_{min} > 0, \ \mathcal{G}(k_{min}, \epsilon, \delta) \stackrel{def}{=} \sup_{k > k_{min}} \left(\sup_{\bar{W} \in \mathbb{D}_{\epsilon, \delta}} \frac{\|X(k)\|_\infty}{\|W(0)\|_\infty} \right) < \infty \qquad (2)$$

where $\mathbb{D}_{\epsilon, \delta} \stackrel{def}{=} \{\bar{W} \in \mathbb{R}^{n \times \infty} : 2^{-\epsilon} < \|W(0)\|_\infty < 2^\delta \text{ and } \forall k \geq 1, W(k) = 0\}$.

The following Theorem represents one of the main results of this paper.

Theorem 1 *[18]. Assume that the dynamical system represented by (1) has a non-Hurwitz (unstable) matrix A. In addition, consider the following conditions: **(C1)** there exists a real and positive δ such that (1) is (∞, δ) FGI stable; **(C2)** there exists a real and positive ϵ such that (1) is (ϵ, ∞) FGI stable; **(C3)** (1) is (∞, ∞) FGI stable. If at least one of these conditions holds, then there exists k_{min} such that the range of $\mathcal{F}^{k_{min}}$ is an infinite set.*

Definition 3. *The feedback system specified by (1) is FG l_p stable, if the following holds:*

$$\sup_{\bar{W} \in \mathbb{R}^{n \times \infty} - \{0\}} \frac{\|\bar{X}\|_p}{\|\bar{W}\|_p} = \beta_p < \infty \qquad (3)$$

Notice that if there is at least one p, with $1 \leq p \leq \infty$, such that (1) is FG l_p stable then (1) is also (ϵ, δ) FGI stable for all $\epsilon, \delta \in \bar{\mathbb{R}}_+$. Therefore, Theorem 1 is sufficiently general to prove the following corollary.

Corollary 1. *Consider that A, the dynamic matrix of the dynamical system represented by (1), is non-Hurwitz (unstable). If there exists p, satisfying $1 \leq p \leq \infty$, such that (1) is FG l_p stable then there exists k_{min} such that the range of $\mathcal{F}^{k_{min}}$ is an infinite set.*

2.1   Comparative Analysis Between ISS and (ϵ, δ) FGI Stability

We start by defining input to state stability (ISS) in discrete time [12], which is analogous to the continuous time version found in [13].

Definition 4 *(ISS). Let $\bar{x}$ be the solution of (1). We denote by $\mathcal{K}$ the set of positive, continuous, strictly increasing and unbounded functions $\mathcal{B}$ satisfying $\mathcal{B}(0) = 0$. We qualify the feedback loop (1) as input to state stable (ISS) (with zero initial conditions), if there exists $\mathcal{B} \in \mathcal{K}$ such that the following holds:*

$$\forall \bar{W} \in \mathbb{R}^{n \times \infty}, \|\bar{X}\|_\infty \leq \mathcal{B}\left(\|\bar{W}\|_\infty\right) \qquad (4)$$

The following Remark follows readily from definitions 2 and 4, and it establishes a connection between ISS and (ϵ, δ) FGI stability.

Remark 1. Consider that the system (1) is ISS and that $\mathcal{B} \in \mathcal{K}$ satisfies (4). For any arbitrary $\epsilon, \delta \in \bar{\mathbb{R}}_+$, the following holds:

$$\sup_{\varrho \in (2^{-\epsilon}, 2^{\delta})} \frac{\mathcal{B}(\varrho)}{\varrho} \geq \sup_{\bar{W} \in \mathbb{D}_{\epsilon, \delta}} \frac{\|\bar{X}\|_\infty}{\|\bar{W}\|_\infty} \geq \sup_{k \geq 0} \mathcal{G}(k, \epsilon, \delta) \tag{5}$$

The following Corollary, shows that finite set feedback may impose fundamental constraints on the non-linear gain $\mathcal{B}$. Its proof follows from definition 2, Remark 1 and Theorem 1.

Corollary 2. *Consider that the matrix A, of the dynamical system represented by (1), is non-Hurwitz (unstable) and that the feedback loop is ISS, with $\mathcal{B} \in \mathcal{K}$ satisfying (4). If $\mathcal{F}$ implements a finite set feedback strategy, then the function $\mathcal{B}$ satisfies the following:*

$$\forall \delta > 0, \quad \sup_{\varrho \in (0, 2^\delta)} \frac{\mathcal{B}(\varrho)}{\varrho} = \infty$$

$$\forall \epsilon > 0, \quad \sup_{\varrho > 2^{-\epsilon}} \frac{\mathcal{B}(\varrho)}{\varrho} = \infty$$

Since $\mathcal{B}$ is continuous and increasing, the unbounded growth-rate at zero creates a *cusp-like* shape (see Fig. 1) which has been confirmed empirically by the authors[2] of [10].

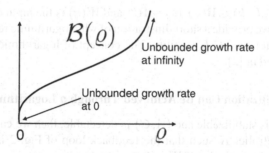

Fig. 1. Illustration of a function $\mathcal{B} \in \mathcal{K}$ which is not differentiable at zero and has unbounded sub-differential at infinity

The work in [17] addresses the problem of robustness in the presence of operator uncertainty, using induced norms, under the assumption that an upper bound on the amplitude of the external excitation is known. An alternative framework, in the absence of external excitation, can also be found in [7]. In the absence of a-priori bounds, Corollary 2 has further implications to robustness analysis. Since FG l_p stabilization is impossible under bit-rate constrained feedback, it follows that small gain arguments using l_p based induced norms are not viable. Thus, our results further support the use of ISS approaches to robustness, such as the work in [11].

---

[2] The author would like to thank Daniel Liberzon (UIUC) for sharing this information.

2.2 (∞, δ) FGI Stabilization Requires a Logarithmically Increasing Resolution

In this subsection, we argue that any (∞, δ) FGI stabilizing feedback requires a logarithmically increasing *resolution* as the infinity norm of $\bar{W}$ decreases.

Definition 5. *Let $\mathcal{F}$ be the causal feedback map in (1). Clearly $\mathcal{F}$ is ultimately a function of $\bar{W}$ and we can define $\mathcal{F}|_{\mathbb{D}_{\epsilon,\delta}}$ by restricting the domain of $\mathcal{F}$ to $\bar{W} \in \mathbb{D}_{\epsilon,\delta}$.*

Corollary 3 *[18]. Let δ be a given and $\bar{x}$ be the solution of (1). Consider that $\mathcal{F}$ stabilizes (1) in the (∞, δ) ISS sense, for some k_{min} and gain $\alpha > 0$. The following holds:*

$$\exists k_\infty > 0, \limsup_{\epsilon \to \infty} \frac{\log \left(\sharp Range \left(\mathcal{F}|_{\mathbb{D}_{\epsilon,\delta}}^{k_\infty} \right) \right)}{\log \epsilon} \geq 1 \qquad (6)$$

where $\mathcal{F}|_{\mathbb{D}_{\epsilon,\delta}}$ is the restricted $\mathcal{F}$ of definition 5 and $\sharp Range(\mathcal{F}|_{\mathbb{D}_{\epsilon,\delta}}^{k_\infty})$ is the cardinality of the range of $\mathcal{F}|_{\mathbb{D}_{\epsilon,\delta}}^{k_\infty}$.

3   Sufficient Conditions for FG l_p Stabilizability, with $1 \leq p \leq \infty$

In this section, we study the stability of the following system:

$$X(k+1) = AX(k) + BU(k) + W(k), X(0) = 0 \qquad (7)$$

$$Y(k) = CX(k) + DU(k) \qquad (8)$$

where $X(k) \in \mathbb{R}^n$, $U(k) \in \mathbf{R}^q$, $Y(k) \in \mathbf{R}^m$ and $W(k)$ is the input of the system.

In this section, we provide a short illustration of why logarithmic resolution feedback is sufficient to guarantee FG l_p stability. The concept of logarithmic quantization was originally presented in [2].

3.1   FG l_p Stabilization Can Be Achieved Through a Logarithmic Quantizer

If the pair (A, B) is stabilizable and (A, C) is detectable, then we can find a linear and time-invariant controller K such that the feedback loop of Fig. 2 is FG l_p stable for every $1 \leq p \leq \infty$. In particular, if $\bar{W} = 0$ then we have:

$$\sup_{\bar{E} \neq 0} \frac{\|\bar{Y}\|_p}{\|\bar{E}\|_p} = \alpha_p < \infty \qquad (9)$$

The diagram in Fig. 3 represents the feedback loop of Fig. 2 when a memory-less quantizer $\mathcal{Q}$ is placed between the output of the plant and the controller. By representing the quantization effect as $E(k) = \mathcal{Q}(Y(k)) - Y(k)$, we can use the small gain theorem to infer that FG l_p stability, with $1 \leq p \leq \infty$, is preserved in the presence of $\mathcal{Q}$, provided that the following holds:

$$\left(\sup_{V \in \mathbb{R}^m - \{0\}} \frac{\|\mathcal{Q}(V) - V\|_p}{\|V\|_p} \right) \alpha_p < 1 \qquad (10)$$

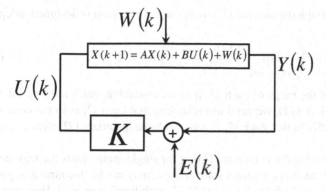

Fig. 2. Feedback system without quantization

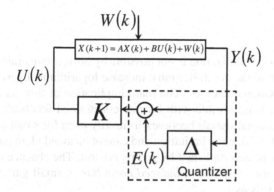

Fig. 3. Feedback system with quantization

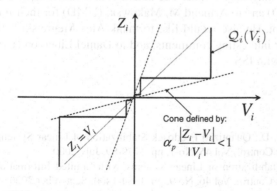

Fig. 4. Cone defined by (11), superimposed with a logarithmic quantizer $\mathcal{Q}_i$

We can adopt a decoupled quantizer $\mathcal{Q}$, where each component is designed independently according to:

$$\left(\sup_{V_i \in \mathbb{R} - \{0\}} \frac{|\mathcal{Q}_i(V_i) - V_i|}{|V_i|} \right) \alpha_p < 1 \tag{11}$$

It is easy to see that the range of each $\mathcal{Q}_i$ may be countable, but it must be infinite. Indeed, in order to satisfy (11), we need to make sure that each $\mathcal{Q}_i$ is in the cone represented in Fig 4. It suffices that each $\mathcal{Q}_i$ is a logarithmic quantizer [2], with a density strictly smaller than α_p^{-1}.

For the framework in Fig 3 it is known [2] that for single input plants the least dense quantizer, required for quadratic internal stabilization, may not be decoupled, suggesting that (11) might not be the *best* choice for FG l_p stabilization as well. However, we are not concerned about the density of $\mathcal{Q}$ because we only intended to illustrate that logarithmic quantization is sufficient to guarantee FG l_p stabilization.

4 Conclusions

We have established that FG l_p stabilization is not possible by bit-rate constrained feedback, and that the resolution of the controller must increase logarithmically as the amplitude of the external excitation decreases. The main implication of this result is the following: ISS stabilization is achievable with bit-rate constrained feedback, but the sensitivity with respect to external signals becomes arbitrarily large for small and large disturbances. This fact is a fundamental limitation and cannot be avoided, in particular, FG l_p stabilization can only be accomplished by analog control. The absence of FG l_p stability also precludes the use of standard, *induced norm based*, small gain theorem approaches for robustness analysis.

Acknowledgements. The author is grateful to Sridevi Sarma (MIT) and to Munther A. Dahleh (MIT) for interesting suggestions. The author is also indebted to Ola Ayaso (MIT), to Andre Tits (UMD) and to Armand M. Makowski (UMD) for their important feedback on this manuscript. He also would like to thank Alex Megretski (MIT) and Sanjoy K. Mitter (MIT) for interesting comments, and to Daniel Liberzon (UIUC) for suggesting the connection with ISS.

References

1. Brocket, R. W., Liberzon, D.: Quantized Feedback Stabilization of Linear Systems; IEEE Transaction on Automatic Control, Vol 45, No 7, pp. 1279-89, July 2000
2. Elia, N., Mitter, S. K.: Stabilization of Linear Systems With Limited Information; IEEE Transaction on Automatic Control, Vol 46, No 9, pp. 1384-1400, September 2000
3. Delchamps, D.: Stabilizing a Linear System with Quantized State Feedback; IEEE Transaction on Automatic Control, Vol 35, No 8, pp. 916-24, August 1990
4. Fagnani, F., Zampieri, S.: Stability Analysis and Synthesis for Linear Systems with Quantized State Feedback; IEEE Transaction on Automatic Control, Vol 48, No 9, pp. 1569-84, September 2003

5. Nair, G. N., Evans, R.J.: Stabilizability of Stochastic Linear Systems with Finite Feedback Data Rates; SIAM Journal Control and Optim., vol 43, No 2, pp. 413-36, 2004
6. Sarma, S., Dahleh, M., Salapaka, S.: On time-varying Bit-Allocation Maintaining Stability:A convex parameterization; Proceedings of the IEEE CDC 2004,
7. Phat, Vu N.;Jiang J.;Savkin, A. V.; Petersen, I.: Robust Stabilization of Linear Uncertain Discrete-Time Systems Via a Limited Capacity Communication Channel.; Systems and Control Letters 53(2004), pp. 347-360
8. Tatikonda, S., Mitter, S.: Control under communication constraints; IEEE Transaction on Automatic Control, Vol 49, No 7, pp. 1056-68, July 2004
9. Liberzon, D., Hespanha, J. P. : Stabilization of Nonlinear Systems with Limited Information Feedback; IEEE Transaction on Automatic Control (To Appear)
10. Liberzon, D., Nesic, D.: Input-to-state stabilization of linear systems with quantized feedback; Submitted to the IEEE Transactions on Automatic Control
11. Liberzon, D.: On Quantization and Delay Effects in Nonlinear Control Systems; Proceedings of the Workshop on Netorked Embeded Sensing and Control, University of Notre Dame, 2005 (to appear at the Springer LNCS series)
12. Jiang, Z. P.; Wang Y., " Input-to-state stability for discrete-time nonlinear systems", Automatica, vol. 37, pp. 857-869, 2001.
13. E. D. Sontag: Input to state stability: Basic concepts and results ; Springer Lecture Notes in Mathematics (CIME Course, Cetraro, June 2004), 2005, to appear.
14. Baillieul, J.: Feedback designs in information-based control; Proceedings of the Workshop on Stochastic Theory and Control, NY, pp. 35-57, 2001
15. Vidyasagar, M.: Nonlinear Systems Analysis (Classics in Applied Mathematics, 42) ; Society for Industrial and Applied Mathematic; 2nd edition (October, 2002)
16. Martins, N. C.,Dahleh, M. A.: Fundamental Limitations in The Presence of Finite Capacity Feedback; Proceedings of the ACC, 2005
17. Martins, N. C.,Dahleh, M. A., Elia, N.: Feedback Stabilization of Uncertain Systems inthe Presence of a Direct Link; Accepted for publication in the IEEE TAC.
18. Martins, N. C.; "Finite Gain lp Stabilization Requires Analog Control", Institute for Systems Research Technical Report TR 2005-111
19. Pinsker, M. S.: Information and Information Stability of Random Variables and Processes, Holden Day, 1964
20. Cover, T.M; Thomas, J. A.: Elements of Information Theory Wiley-Iterscience Publication, 1991

Specification and Analysis of Distributed Object-Based Stochastic Hybrid Systems

José Meseguer and Raman Sharykin

University of Illinois at Urbana-Champaign, USA

Abstract. In practice, many stochastic hybrid systems are not autonomous: they are objects that communicate with other objects by exchanging messages through an asynchronous medium such as a network. Issues such as: how to compositionally specify distributed object-based stochastic hybrid systems (OBSHS), how to formally model them, and how to verify their properties seem therefore quite important. This paper addresses these issues by: (i) defining a mathematical model for such systems that can be naturally regarded as a generalized stochastic hybrid system (GSHS) in the sense of [6]; (ii) proposing a formal OBSHS specification language in which system transitions are specified in a modular way by probabilistic rewrite rules; and (iii) showing how these systems can be subjected to statistical model checking analysis to verify their probabilistic temporal logic properties.

1 Introduction

Stochastic hybrid systems (see the survey [28] and references there) generalize ordinary hybrid systems (see, for example, [23, 3, 22, 4]) by allowing continuous evolution to be governed by stochastic differential equations (SDE's) and/or by allowing instantaneous changes in system modes to be probabilistic. This fits well the intrinsic uncertainty of the environments in which many hybrid systems must operate, and is also very useful when some of the system's algorithms are probabilistic. Indeed, there is a wide range of application areas, including communication networks [16], air traffic [18, 19], economics [9], fault tolerant control [13], and so on. Bioinformatics, where symbolic, hybrid, and probabilistic cell models are used, e.g., [11, 21, 15], seems also a field ripe for stochastic hybrid system applications.

While a solid foundation already exists about the mathematical properties of stochastic hybrid system models, such as being a strong Markov process, the question of how to *specify* such systems in a compositional way, so that larger systems can be described and understood in terms of smaller subsystems, remains to a good extent open, although some proposals discussed below and in Section 6 have already been made. Likewise, the question of how to *formally analyze* such systems in ways that substantially extend the analytic power of current simulation methods seems very much open. Since some application areas (for example, air traffic control) require very high assurance, specification and verification are important issues to address.

João Hespanha and A. Tiwari (Eds.): HSCC 2006, LNCS 3927, pp. 460–475, 2006.

The main goal of this paper is to address these specification and verification issues, presenting a concrete proposal for how to formally specify and verify stochastic hybrid systems that are *distributed*, and consist of different kinds of stochastic hybrid *objects* that interact with each other by asynchronous message passing. A distributed object-oriented style with asynchronous communication seems very natural for specifying many such systems: for example, networked embedded systems, or systems made out of aircraft and other, possibly unmanned, vehicles. However, we are not aware of any formal model currently supporting this specification style for stochastic hybrid systems. Our contributions in this regard include: (i) a mathematical model of distributed and asynchronous object-based stochastic hybrid systems (OBSHS) that has the strong Markov property and can be mapped to the GSHS model of [6] (Section 3); and (ii) a formal specification language in which such systems can be specified in a modular and natural way using probabilistic rewrite rules (Section 4).

We also address formal verification issues in Section 5. Our specifications can be simulated by translating them into Maude rewriting logic specifications [7]. They can also be subjected to statistical model checking analysis using the VeStA tool [29]. In this way, probabilistic temporal logic properties of a stochastic hybrid system can be model checked with a desired degree of statistical confidence, based on Monte Carlo simulations. We explain and illustrate this kind of model checking analysis with two case studies.

In Section 6 we discuss related work and make some concluding remarks. In particular, we discuss three other models that also address composition and concurrency issues for stochastic hybrid systems, namely, those proposed in [2, 31, 12]. As we further explain in Section 6 , although the model in [2] supports objects, and that in [12] supports delayed interaction, none of these models supports distributed object communication by asynchronous message passing. To make the paper reasonably self-contained and ease the presentation in Sections 3–4, we provide basic background on term rewriting, probabilistic rewriting, and object-based specification in Section 2.

2   Probabilistic Rewriting and Distributed Objects

We review basic concepts on term rewriting, probabilistic rewriting, and distributed objects. This will help motivate our mathematical model of OBSHS in Section 3 and our proposed OBSHS specification language in Section 4. The exposition below is informal; we refer to [10] for more details on term rewriting, and to [1] for more details on probabilistic rewriting.

We assume a *signature* Σ of function symbols, say, $f, g, h, a, b, \ldots \in \Sigma$, having an arity function $ar : \Sigma \longrightarrow \mathbb{N}$ specifying the number of arguments of each function symbol. We then denote by $T_\Sigma(X)$ the algebra of Σ-terms on a set X of variables. For example, $f(x, g(b, y)) \in T_\Sigma(X)$ is a Σ-term with $ar(f) = ar(g) = 2$, $ar(b) = 0$, and $x \in X$. We illustrate with an example the notions of *subterm, subterm position*, and *subterm replacement* For example, x, $g(b, y)$, and b are subterms of $f(x, g(b, y))$. If we think of a term as a labeled tree, then its subterms are its subtrees. We can indicate subterm positions by finite strings of natural numbers denoting paths from the root of the tree. For example, the above three subterms are at positions 1, 2, and 2.1, respectively. Given a position p in a term t, t/p denotes the subterm at position p. Given terms t and u, and a position p in t, we denote by $t[u]_p$ the new term obtained by replacing the subterm t/p by u at position p. For example, for t our example term and $u = h(a)$ we have $t[u]_2 = f(x, h(a))$. Note that each term t has a set $vars(t)$ of variables appearing in it. A *substitution* θ is a function $\theta : Y \longrightarrow T_\Sigma(X)$ with Y a set of variables. It extends in a unique way to a Σ-homomorphism $\theta : T_\Sigma(Y) \longrightarrow T_\Sigma(X)$. For our example term t, if $\theta(x) = h(z)$ and $\theta(y) = c$, then $\theta(t) = f(h(z), g(b, c))$. A *rewrite rule* is a sequent $l \longrightarrow r$ with $l, r \in T_\Sigma(X)$. We call l the rule's *lefthand side*, and r its *righthand side*, Let R be a set of rewrite rules. We say that a term t is *rewritten in one step* by R to t', denoted $t \longrightarrow_R t'$, if there is a position p in t and a substitution θ such that $t/p = \theta(l)$ and $t' = t[\theta(r)]_p$. We denote by $\longrightarrow_R^*$ the reflexive and transitive closure of R. Intuitively, we will think of terms as the *states* of a system. Then a set R of rewrite rules can be understood as a set of parametric state *transitions*, and $\longrightarrow_R^*$ as the system's *reachability relation*. We call a rewrite rule $l \longrightarrow r$ *nondeterministic* if $vars(r) \not\subseteq vars(l)$.

We can generalize this picture by rewriting not just terms, but equivalence classes of terms *modulo* an equational theory E. This is accomplished by the notion of a *rewrite theory* (Σ, E, R) [24], with Σ a signature, E a set of Σ-equations, and R a set of rewrite rules. Intuitively, the idea is to view the states of our system as elements of the *algebraic data type* $T_{\Sigma/E}$ specified by the equations E, its so-called initial algebra. The elements of $T_{\Sigma/E}$ are E-equivalence classes $[t]$ of Σ-terms t without variables modulo the equations E. Now R rewrites such equivalence classes instead of rewriting just terms. This is particularly useful for modeling distributed object systems that communicate with each other by message passing. We can view an object, say of a given object class C, as a record-like term of the form $\langle o : C \mid a_1 : v_1, \ldots, a_n : v_n \rangle$, where o is the object's name or identifier, C is its class name, and the a_i are its state variables (each of an appropriate type) with the v_i the corresponding values. We can similarly view a message addressed to o as another term of the form $\langle o \leftarrow c \rangle$ with c its contents and o its addressee. We can then model the distributed state of an object system as a multiset or "soup" of objects and messages. We denote multiset union with the parallel composition operator $\_\|\_$, where the two underbars indicate argument positions. For example the distributed state

$$\langle o : C \mid a_1 : v_1, \ldots, a_n : v_n \rangle \parallel \langle o \leftarrow c \rangle \parallel \langle o' : C' \mid b_1 : v_1', \ldots, b_k : v_k' \rangle \parallel \langle o' \leftarrow c' \rangle$$

has two objects o and o' of classes C and C', each with a message addressed to it and not yet received. Since multiset union is *associative and commutative*, the order of objects and messages is immaterial. In the case of objects in an OBSHS, the only additional fact is that some of the variables a_i of an object $\langle o : C \mid a_1 : v_1, \ldots, a_n : v_n \rangle$ are *continuous*, that is, they take real numbers as values, while other variables can be *discrete*. Since for OBSHS real time is of the essence, in addition to ordinary messages ready for instantaneous reception, there will also be *scheduled messages* of the form $[d, \langle o \leftarrow c \rangle]$, where d is a time called the *deadline*, which is decreased by time elapse. This allows us to model the fact that *asynchronous communication in a distributed system takes time*, so that a message sent is not immediately available for reception. In an OBSHS at any given time there will be *at most one* message available for reception, called the *active message*: all other messages will be scheduled messages.

The discrete transitions of a distributed object systems typically take place in response to messages: an object, upon receiving a message, may change its state, send other messages, and may disappear and/or spawn new objects. Such discrete concurrent transitions, as we will illustrate in a moment, can be naturally specified by rewrite rules. The point, however, is that for such systems the rewriting should be *multiset rewriting*, in which the order of objects and messages in the "soup" is immaterial. This can be neatly captured by a rewrite theory $(\Sigma, AC \cup E, R)$, where Σ specifies all the operators building up objects and messages, and the parallel composition operator $\_\|\_$, AC are equations of associativity and commutativity for $\_\|\_$, and E are other equations specifying auxiliary functions.

However, in an OBSHS the rewrite rules R specifying the instantaneous object transitions are typically *probabilistic*. A *probabilistic rewrite rule* [20, 1] is a rewrite rule of the form

$$l(\boldsymbol{x}) \rightarrow r(\boldsymbol{x}, \boldsymbol{y}) \;\; with \;\; probability \;\; \boldsymbol{y} := p(\boldsymbol{x})$$

The first thing to observe is that such a rule is *nondeterministic*, because the term r has new variables $\boldsymbol{y}$ disjoint from the variables $\boldsymbol{x}$ appearing in l. Therefore, a substitution θ for the variables $\boldsymbol{x}$ appearing in l that matches a subterm of a term t at position p does not uniquely determine the next state after the rewrite: there can be many different choices for the next state, depending on how we instantiate the extra variables $\boldsymbol{y}$ in r. In fact, we can denote the different next states by expressions of the form $t[r(\theta(\boldsymbol{x}), \rho(\boldsymbol{y}))]_p$, where θ is fixed as the given matching substitution, but ρ ranges over all the possible substitutions for the new variables $\boldsymbol{y}$. The probabilistic nature of the rule is expressed by the notation: *with probability* $\boldsymbol{y} := p(\boldsymbol{x})$, where $p(\boldsymbol{x})$ is a probability measure on the set of substitutions ρ (modulo the equations E in the given rewrite theory). However, the probability measure $p(\boldsymbol{x})$ *may depend on the matching substitution* θ. We sample $\boldsymbol{y}$, that is, the substitution ρ, probabilistically according to the probability measure $p(\theta(\boldsymbol{x}))$.

A simple example can illustrate many of the ideas presented so far. A possible object in an OBSHS can be a *bidder* object in an auction (Section 5.1). This is an object of the form $\langle o : Bidder \mid motivation : m \rangle$, with *motivation* a continuous variable measuring the bidder's degree of interest in the auction. The bidder sends bids to the auction at random times, but a bidder with greater motivation will bid more often. This can be modeled by the probabilistic rewrite rule

$$\langle X : Bidder \mid motivation : M \rangle \parallel \langle X \leftarrow schedule.bid \rangle \longrightarrow$$
$$\langle X : Bidder \mid motivation : M \rangle \parallel [T, \langle X \leftarrow place.bid \rangle]$$
$$with \;\; probability \;\; T := Exp(0.1 * duration / 0.1 + M)$$

were upon receiving a message $\langle X \leftarrow schedule.bid \rangle$ the bidder X schedules its next bid according to an exponential distribution whose rate involves both the auction duration and its own motivation. The probability measure crucially depends on the bidder's motivation, which is determined in each rule instance by the substitution θ instantiating the lefthand side variable M.

3   Object-Based Stochastic Hybrid Systems

This section presents our OBSHS model and shows its relation to the GSHS model. To simplify the mathematical details, we adopt a more Spartan notation for object states as tuples (o, q, v), with o the objects name, q a single discrete element that tuples together the class name and the discrete variables, and v the vector of values of the continuous variables. For $(X, \mathcal{O})$ a topological space, $(X, \mathfrak{B}(X))$ denotes its associated measurable space.

Definition 1. *Given measurable spaces* $(X, \mathfrak{F}_X)$, $(Y, \mathfrak{F}_Y)$, *we call a function* $K : X \times \mathfrak{F}_Y \to [0, 1]$ *a Markov kernel (from* $(X, \mathfrak{F}_X)$ *to* $(Y, \mathfrak{F}_Y)$*) iff* K *satisfies:* *(i)* $\forall x \in X$, $K(x, \cdot)$ *is a probability measure, and (ii)* $\forall B \in \mathfrak{F}_Y$, $K(\cdot, B)$ *is measurable. Intuitively, we think of* K *as a "probabilistic transition relation" from* X *to* Y. $\blacksquare$

Definition 2. *A* stochastic hybrid object class *(OBSHS class)* C *is a tuple* $C = (Q_C, Oid, Inv_C, \mu, \sigma, Jump_C)$, *where:*

Discrete States: Q_C *is a countable set of discrete states.*
Object Identifiers: *A countable set* Oid *of object names.*
Invariants: *For a fixed dimension* l, *a function* $Inv_C : Q_C \to \mathcal{O}(\mathbb{R}^l)$, *where* $\mathcal{O}(\mathbb{R}^l)$ *is the set of open sets of the Euclidean space* $\mathbb{R}^l$.
Object States: *The state of an object* o, *with* $o \in Oid$, *is a triple* $s = (o, q, v)$ *with* $q \in Q_C$ *and* $v \in Inv_C(q)$. *The set of all such states for all objects in the class* C *is denoted*

$$S_C = \bigcup_{o \in Oid, \; q \in Q_C} \{o\} \times \{q\} \times Inv_C(q)$$

we also define its closure $\overline{S}_C$ *as the set*

$$\overline{S}_C = \bigcup_{o \in Oid, \; q \in Q_C} \{o\} \times \{q\} \times \overline{Inv_C(q)}$$

with $\overline{Inv_C(q)}$ *the topological closure of the open set* $Inv_C(q)$, *and its boundary* $\partial S_C = \overline{S}_C \setminus S_C$. *Note that* S_C *is a disjoint union of metric spaces and therefore has an associated measurable space* $(S_C, \mathfrak{B}(S_C))$.
SDE Dynamics: *is specified by a pair of functions* $\mu : D_C \to \mathbb{R}^l$ *and* $\sigma : D_C \to \mathbb{R}^{l \times m}$, *with* $D_C = \bigcup_{q \in Q_C} \{q\} \times Inv_C(q)$, *and with* $\mu(q, x)$, $\sigma(q, x)$ *bounded and Lipschitz continuous in* x.
Jump Kernel: *a Markov kernel* $Jump_C : \partial S_C \times \mathfrak{B}(S_C) \to [0, 1]$. $\blacksquare$

A message has an object o from some class C as its addressee, and can also contain discrete and continuous parameters.

Definition 3. *Given an OBSHS class C, a message type M for objects of class C is a tuple $M = (Oid_C, Q', d)$ with Oid_C the object names of class C, Q' a countable set of discrete parameters, and $d \in \mathbb{N}$ the dimension of the set of continuous parameters $\mathbb{R}^d$. The set S_M of messages of type M is then $S_M = Oid_C \times Q' \times \mathbb{R}^d$. Similarly, the set S_{SM} of scheduled messages of type M is $S_{SM} = S_M \times \mathbb{R}_{\geq 0}$.* ∎

Definition 4. *An* Object-Based Stochastic Hybrid System (OBSHS) *A is given by:*

- *a set $C_1, \ldots, C_n$ of OBSHS classes.*
- *a set $M_1, \ldots, M_m$ of message types, each involving some C_i among the $C_1, \ldots, C_n$.*

The states of an OBSHS are multisets which contain objects in $C_1, \ldots, C_n$, scheduled messages in $M_1, \ldots, M_m$, and at most one message in one of the M_j:

$$s = \{((o_1, q_1, v_1), \ldots, (o_k, q_k, v_k), [(o', q', v')], ((o'_1, q'_1, v'_1), t_1), \ldots, ((o'_s, q'_s, v'_s), t_s))\}$$

where the object identities $o_1, \ldots, o_k$ are all different, we have a set inclusion $\{o', o'_1, \ldots, o'_s\} \subseteq \{o_1, \ldots, o_k\}$, and $[(o', q', v')]$ means that the single message (o', q', v') may not be present. The discrete component of the above state is the multiset

$$q = disc(s) = \{(o_1, q_1), \ldots, (o_k, q_k), < (o', q') >, (o'_1, q'_1), \ldots, (o'_s, q'_s)\}$$

where the angle bracket operator $< (o', q') >$ acts as a marker to distinguish the discrete part of the unique active message (o', q', v') if such a message is present. The set Q_A of all discrete components $disc(s)$ of the states s of an OBSHS A is by construction a countable set. The continuous component of the state s is of course scattered through the different objects and messages, but we can easily consolidate it into a single component as follows. Without loss of generality we may assume that the sets $Oid_{C_1}, \ldots, Oid_{C_n}$ and $Q'_{M_1}, \ldots, Q'_{M_m}$ are all disjoint and that the discrete message parts $q', q'_1, \ldots, q'_s$ are all different[1]. Then, by linearly ordering the $C_1, \ldots, C_n$, $M_1, \ldots, M_m$, and assuming linear orders in the Oid_{C_i} and Q'_{M_j}, we can lexicographically sort the elements of any discrete state $disc(s)$ in a unique way. Suppose that the sorted form of the state s above is exactly the order in which its elements are listed. Then, the continuous component of s is the vector

$$v = cont(s) = (v_1, \ldots, v_k, v', v'_1, t_1, \ldots, v'_s, t_s)$$

This means that we can represent the set of all states of the OBSHS A as a disjoint union

$$S_A = \bigcup_{q \in Q_A} \{q\} \times Inv(q)$$

---

[1] They can always be made different, for example, by including a message identifier in each message.

where if $(o_1, q_1), \ldots, (o_k, q_k)$ *(of classes* $C_{i_1}, \ldots C_{i_k}$) *are the discrete objects parts of the state* q, *then*

$$Inv(q) = Inv_{C_{i_1}}(q_1) \times \ldots \times Inv_{C_{i_k}}(q_k) \times \mathbb{R}^{md(q)}$$

where $md(q)$, *the* message dimension *of* q, *is obtained by adding all the dimensions of the continuous components in the optional active message and in the scheduled messages.*

• *a Markov kernel* $Msg : \widehat{S}_A \times \mathfrak{B}(S_A) \to [0, 1]$ *called the* instantaneous message reception kernel, *with* $\widehat{S}_A \subset S_A$ *the measurable subset of states containing exactly one active message.*

• *an* initial probability measure $Init : \mathfrak{B}(S_A) \to [0, 1]$. ∎

Assumption 1. *(i)* Msg, *when thought of as a "probabilistic transition relation" leaves all scheduled messages untouched, and all new scheduled messages introduced by the transition have a deadline in* $\mathbb{R}_{>0}{}^2$. *(ii) From a state in* $\widehat{S}_A$, *a state in* $S_A \setminus \widehat{S}_A$ *(no active messages) is reached in a finite number of* Msg *"transitions" with probability 1; therefore, all* Msg *transition sequences almost surely terminate.*

Since S_A is a disjoint union of metric spaces, it has a measurable space structure $(S_A, \mathfrak{B}(S_A))$. The $Jump_{C_i}$ kernels specified for each class $C_1, \ldots, C_n$ in an OBSHS A can be "glued together" to define a jump kernel $Jump_A : \partial S_A \times \mathfrak{B}(S_A) \to [0, 1]$, where, by definition, $\overline{S}_A = \bigcup_{q \in Q_A} \{q\} \times \overline{Inv(q)}$, and $\partial S_A = \overline{S}_A \setminus S_A$. The proof of the following proposition can be found in Appendix B of [25].

Proposition 1. *Given an OBSHS* A *with classes* $C_1, \ldots, C_n$, *the jump kernels* $Jump_{C_1}, \ldots, Jump_{C_n}$ *can be extended to a jump kernel* $Jump_A : \partial S_A \times \mathfrak{B}(S_A) \to [0, 1]$ *in such a way that for states in* ∂S_A *consisting of a single object* (o, q, v) *of class* C_i, *then* $Jump_{C_i}((o, q, v), \cdot)$ *and* $Jump_A(\{o, q, v\}, \cdot)$ *agree, when* ∂S_{C_i} *is homeomorphically embedded as a subspace of* ∂S_A. ∎

An *execution* of an OBSHS is a trajectory of a stochastic process P. The state space of P is S_A. The initial state is chosen according to the initial distribution $Init$. The system has evolutions of two types: *continuous evolution* and *discrete evolution*.

The system follows the *continuous evolution* (CE) when in its state all objects have their continuous states inside their boundaries, there is no active message, and there are no scheduled messages with their deadline times equal to zero. We denote the set of all such states by S_A^{CE}. During its continuous evolution the system evolves with each object evolution governed by the SDE of its class. The deadline time of each scheduled message decreases by the time elapsed.

When some objects reach their boundary or the deadline times of some scheduled messages reach zero, the system starts its *discrete evolution*. We denote by

---

[2] Note that, by definition of S_A, Msg will introduce at most one active message.

S_A! the set of states in S_A such that at least one scheduled message has reached its deadline. Therefore, discrete evolution begins when the process hits $\partial S_A \cup S_A$!. During the discrete evolution the system proceeds as follows:

(i) if there are some objects whose continuous state is in the boundary of their invariants, the $Jump_A$ kernel is used to perform a transition to the new state.
(ii) if there are no objects in the boundary, and there is an active message in the state, then the Msg kernel is used to perform a transition to the new state[3].
(iii) if there are no objects in the boundary and no active message, but some scheduled messages have their deadline time equal to 0, a scheduled message is chosen uniformly among the scheduled messages with 0 deadline and becomes the active message.

By the fact that $Jump_A$ moves states outside ∂S_A, plus Assumption 1, plus the fact that each transition of type (iii) decreases the number of zero-deadline messages, we know that after a finite number of iterations of transitions (i)-(iii) a state in S_A^{CE} (which is an absorbing state for transitions (i)-(iii)) is reached with probability 1. Therefore, all such transition sequences almost surely terminate.

After reaching a state in S_A^{CE} through a finite number of instantaneous transitions (i)-(iii), the system continues in time according to its continuous dynamics until a new time T_{i+1} is reached in which P hits $\partial S_A \cup S_A$!. Therefore, instantaneous transitions happen at discrete times $T_1 < T_2 < T_3 < \ldots..$

Assumption 2 *(Non-Zeno Dynamics). The expectation of N_t, the number of instantaneous transition times on $[0, t]$ is finite for all t.*

We are now ready to relate the OBSHS model to a very general model proposed by Bujorianu and Lygeros, namely, *General Stochastic Hybrid Systems* (GSHS) [6]. Intuitively, the key observation is that the sequence of instantaneous transitions (i)-(iii) after a process hits a state in $\partial S_A \cup S_A$! can be packed together into a single Markov kernel. The proof of the following proposition is given in Appendix B of [25].

Proposition 2. *Under Assumptions 1-2 an OBSHS A can be naturally understood as a GSHS.*[4]   ∎

As corollary of the above proposition, by using the same results proven for GSHS's in [6], we immediately obtain

Theorem 1. *Under Assumptions 1-2 an OBSHS A is a Borel right process.*   ∎

4 Specifying OBSHS's with Rewrite Rules

The different components of an OBSHS should be specified in a simple and highly reusable way by means of class specifications that are then composed into

---

[3] Note that, by the definition of Msg, the resulting state will have no objects in the boundary.
[4] In fact, by GSHS we mean a slight generalization of the model introduced in [6]. See Appendix B of [25] for details.

overall OBSHS specifications involving different class objects and messages and specifying their message-passing communication. We discuss below an object-based stochastic hybrid system example specified in SHYMaude, an extension of the PMaude language [1] supporting OBSHS features. PMaude itself supports specification of probabilistic rewrite theories in the Maude style; and simulation of such theories in the underlying Maude rewriting logic language [7].

A SHYMaude (Stochastic HYbrid Maude) *module* specifies an OBSHS and may contain several class declarations. It is introduced with the keyword **shymod** followed by its name and ends with the keyword **endshy**. In this example, the module is called **ROOM&SENSOR** and contains two classes: a class **Room** of rooms endowed with a thermostat control which can handle stochastic changes in room temperature, and a class **Sensor** of sensor objects that collect temperature information from rooms for statistical purposes. A module may import other modules, such as the **NAT** natural number module importation declared with the **protecting** keyword. Different types, called *sorts*, can also be declared; here we declare a sort **RMode** of room modes with two constants (**heat** and **cool**) introduced with the **ops** keyword. Similarly, several constants of sort **Real** are declared. Inside such a module, several stochastic hybrid object *classes* may be declared, each beginning with the **class** keyword followed by its name, and ending with **endclass**. After the class name, the discrete (**disc**) and continuous (**cont**) variables of objects in the class are declared, with the separation between both sets of variables marked by a vertical bar. For each discrete variable its corresponding sort is specified. **Room** objects have just one discrete variable (**mode**) holding the current mode, and one continuous variable (**temp**) holding the current temperature.

The invariant, SDE dynamics, and jump kernel of the class are declared with the **inv**, **dyn**, and **jump** keywords, with each declaration finished by a respective end keyword. The invariants are specified by equations identifying each invariant with a boolean predicate. The SDE dynamics is specified by a finite set of (in general parametric on the discrete state) SDE's with self-explanatory notation. Here we have just two discrete states for each object; therefore and SDE is specified for the temperature changes in each case. The Jump kernel specification is specified by probabilistic rewrite rules whose lefthand sides specify object states that have reached the boundary of their invariant, and with the corresponding righthand side specifying the state to which the object jumps according to a certain probability measure. Since for this class the jump outcomes are deterministic, the rules in this case are ordinary rewrite rules and the righthand side states are reached with probability 1.

Before specifying the **Sensor** class, its two **sleep** and **wait** modes are declared as constants of sort **SMode**. This class is very simple. It has three discrete variables: its mode, the oid of the room object it is sensing, and a counter, its only continuous variable (a temperature average) has no SDE dynamics, no invariants, and no jumps. The syntax for messages and for their contents are specified with operators of sorts **Msg** and **Contents**. Here a sensor **S** can send to its room **R** a message asking to report its temperature, and the room answers back with a temperature report. These message exchanges are specified by the first two rules. We assume that the sensor and the room are contiguous, so the reply message sent back by the room in the first rule has no delay. In the second rule, the sensor, upon receiving a temperature report, schedules a **check** message with delay chosen according to an exponential probability measure. The third rule shows how the sensor wakes up upon receiving a **check** message and queries the room again. Note that, by convention, variables not modified by a rule need not be mentioned. Note also that such message reception rules are *implicitly conditional* to the corresponding object being inside its current invariant. For example, the first rule must satisfy the implicit condition Inv(mode : M, temp : T) = true for M the current mode. Note finally, that the parallel composition operator (_‖_) is denoted here with empty (juxtaposition) syntax (_ _).

```
shymod ROOM&SENSOR is protecting NAT . sort RMode . ops heat cool
: -> RMode . ops T_max T_min intensity epsilon : -> Real .

class Room is disc mode : RMode | cont temp .

inv
  Inv(mode : heat, temp : T) = T < T_max .
  Inv(mode : cool, temp : T) = T > T_min .
endinv

dyn
  sde(mode : heat) d(temp) = intensity * dt + epsilon * dW(t) .
  sde(mode : cool) d(temp) = - intensity * dt + epsilon * dW(t) .
enddyn

jump
  rl < O : Room | mode : heat, temp : T_max > => < O : Room | mode: cool, temp : T_max > .
  rl < O : Room | mode : cool, temp : T_min > => < O : Room | mode :heat, temp : T_min > .
endjump endclass

sort SMode .  ops sleep wait : -> SMode .

class Sensor is disc mode : SMode, room : Oid, count : Nat | cont
average . endclass

op < _ <- _ > : Oid Contents -> Msg . op report : Oid -> Contents
. op temp :_ : Real -> Contents . op check : -> Contents .

rl  < R : Room | temp : T > < R <- report(S) > => < R : Room |
temp : T > < S <- temp : T > .

rl  < S : Sensor | mode : wait, average : A, count : N > < S <-
temp : T > =>
    < S : Sensor | mode : sleep, average : (A * N + T)/(N + 1), count : N + 1 >
    [D, < S <- check >] with probability D := Exponential(1) .

rl  < S : Sensor | mode : sleep, room : R > < S <- check > =>
    < S : Sensor | mode : wait, room : R > < R <- report(S) > .
endshy
```

A SHYMaude specification can be desugared into a corresponding PMaude specification. Since probabilistic rewrite rules have extra variables in their right-hand sides, they are not directly executable. However, as explained in [1], provided sampling functions for the corresponding probability measures have been implemented in the underlying Maude, a PMaude specification can be *simulated* by an ordinary rewrite theory in Maude, in which the probabilistic choice is realized by the corresponding sampling function. In this way, SHYMaude specifications can be simulated in the underlying Maude system. The Maude translation of a SHYMaude module approximates the SDE dynamics using the Euler-Maruyama method. In this way, Monte Carlo simulations of the OBSHS specification can be performed. Furthermore, such simulations can be input to a statistical model checker like VeStA [29] to formally verify system properties.

5   Statistical Model Checking of OBSHS's

Developing formal verification methods for stochastic hybrid system properties that go beyond current simulation methods is an important research issue. Probabilistic temporal logics are possible candidates to state properties; but they are somewhat restrictive: they give a true or false answer when one would often be interested in a *quantitative* answer. For this reason, we use the QuaTEx language of *Quantitative Temporal Expressions* proposed in [1]. This language is supported by the VeStA tool [29], which has an interface to Maude allowing PMaude and SHYMaude specifications to be model checked with respect to QuaTEx properties using their Maude translations.

The key idea of QuaTEx is to generalize probabilistic temporal logic formulas from Boolean-valued expressions to real-valued expressions. The Boolean interpretation is preserved as a special case using the real numbers 0 and 1. As usual, QuaTEx has *state expressions*, evaluated on states, and (real-valued) *path expressions* evaluated on computation paths. The notion of state predicates is now generalized to that of *state functions*, which can evaluate quantitative properties of a state. QuaTEx is particularly expressive because of the possibility of defining recursive expressions. In this way, only the next operator $\bigcirc$ (represented as # in the VeStA syntax) and conditional branching *if Bexp then Pexp then Pexp'* *fi*, with *Bexp* Boolean and *Pexp, Pexp'* path expressions, are needed to define more complex operators like the until $\mathcal{U}$ of probabilistic computational tree logic (PCTL) and of continuous stochastic logic (CSL) [5], and the CSL bounded until $\mathcal{U}^{\leq t}$. We refer to [1] for a detailed account of QuaTEx and its semantics. We give a flavor for it here by means of one of the QuaTEx expressions that we have evaluated in one of the case studies described below (an auction). The expression in question, numToGet(n,id), computes the number of times that a bidder named id has to compete in a repeated auction to get the auctioned item n times. This is an expression evaluated on computation paths. The two auxiliary state functions in this case are won(id), counting the number of times that id has already won a bid, and numberOfAuctions(id), counting the number of auctions id has participated in. The corresponding QuaTEx expression is

```
numToGet(n,id) = if won(id) = n then numberOfAuctions(id) else #numToGet(n,id) fi;
```

VeStA performs *statistical model checking* on a probabilistic system by evaluating QuaTEx expressions on computation paths obtained by Monte Carlo simulations. For the above formula the VeStA command is E[numToGet(n,id)]. Two other parameters α and δ are also provided to the tool. VeStA then responds with a real number v, which is the estimated value of the expression with a $(1 - \alpha)100\%$ confidence interval bounded by δ. Depending on the tightness of the parameters, VeStA may need a greater or smaller number of sample runs to compute such a value.

5.1 Repeated Second-Price Auction

We have specified and analyzed a model of consecutive second-price online auctions repeated on similar items inspired by [27]. During each auction a similar item is on sale and throughout the auction the second highest bid is posted. To overbid the current bid a bidder must submit a bid higher then the current winning bid (which is not public). The winner pays the second highest bid. We enrich the model with the assumption that the bidders reside in different countries and hence the exchange rates (which fluctuate over time and whose dynamics we can model using SDE's [32]) must be used. The specification of the system consists of several object classes: a class of auctioneer who receives bids and updates the current state of the auction, the agency who provides the exchange rate modeling them using the appropriate SDE's, and two classes of bidders one being a class of "normal" bidders who bid throughout the auction with a certain probability and the other being a class of "experts" who bid at the very end of the auction with the price which they consider to be appropriate.

VeStA Analysis. We have used VeStA to estimate a quantitative property of the system. In the analysis we considered a system consisting of 1 auctioneer, 3 early bidders with 1 domestic and 2 in different foreign countries, and one foreign sniper.

The quantitative property was the expected number of auctions for a bidder to get N items. The QuaTEx query for this quantitative property was explained above. The results of estimating this quantitative property for **n** = 2 with 95% confidence were: (i) for the domestic bidder the interval $[6.8, 7.5]$, (ii) for a foreign bidder $[8.2, 9.1]$, and (iii) for the sniper $[7.8, 8.6]$.

5.2 Thermostat

We have specified and analyzed a system consisting of N rooms, each equipped with a thermostat and a central server unit controlling them. Each thermostat can be in one of three modes: heating, cooling, and idle. The temperature in each room changes randomly according to the SDE $dT = I dt + I_n dW_t$, where I depends on the thermostat mode and is either the rate of heating I_h, the rate of cooling I_c, or equal to zero in the idle mode. The server checks the temperature in each room at random times and sends commands to the thermostat according to three rules: (i) if the temperature T in a room is $T > T_{max}$, then it sends a messages to to start cooling, (ii) if $T < T_{min}$, then it sends a message to start heating, (iii) if the temperature is in the region close to T_0 with $T_0 = (T_{max} + T_{min})/2$, then it sends a message to go to the idle mode.

VeStA Analysis. We used VeStA to estimate a quantitative property of the thermostat system. The property was the probability that if during a run the temperature goes out of some desired interval $I_D = [T_0-\Delta, T_0+\Delta] \subseteq [T_{min}, T_{max}]$ in a specific room it will return to the desired interval in a specified amount of time. The QuaTEx query for this probability is

```
Eventually(t,id) = if time() >= T then 0
                   else if time() > t + I then 0
                       else if InInterval(id) = 1 then #Always(id)
                                  else #Eventually(t,id) fi fi ;
Always(id) = if time() > T then 1
             else if InInterval(id) = 1 then #Always(id)
                        else #Eventually(time(),id) fi fi ;
eval E[Always(id)];
```

where T bounds the lengths of paths, and I defines the interval during which the temperature has to return to the desired interval after leaving it. The function InInterval returns 1 if the temperature of the room with the identifier id is in the desired interval I_D and 0 otherwise. The function Always returns 1 if the path satisfies the property stated above and 0 otherwise. Thus the expectation of this function is the desired quantitative property [1]. We used T = 20 minutes and I = 60 seconds. As in the previous property we used $T_{max} = 74$, $T_{min} = 70$, $\Delta = 1$. Using this values we obtained that with 95% confidence the desired probability lies in the confidence interval [0.31,0.34].

6   Related Work and Conclusions

Since under Assumption 3 the OBSHS model can be mapped into the GSHS model, the relation to less general models — including PDP [8], SHS [17], and SDP [14] — which are encompassed by GSHS as special cases is then very direct. We refer to [28] for a recent survey of stochastic hybrid system models, and focus instead on the relation of OBSHS to the three other stochastic hybrid system models addressing concurrency and composition that we are aware of, namely: (i) the model presented in [2], with associated Charon specifications; (ii) communicating piecewise deterministic Markov processes (CPDP) [31]; and (iii) stochastically and dynamically colored Petri nets (SDCPN) [12].

Like OBSHS specifications, the Charon specifications in [2] also support stochastic hybrid objects (called agents in Charon) and object composition; however, the forms of composition supported in each model are orthogonal and complementary. Charon objects can be composed out of subobjects that communicate instantaneously with each other by sharing variables. Once a closed object is thus composed, no dynamic object creation is possible; also, no support for non-instantaneous asynchronous message passing is provided. By contrast, in OBSHS objects are composed into distributed configurations by means the _||_ operator. We view these composition operations as serving different purposes: Charon object composition is best suited for building a single object out of tightly coupled subobjects that are contiguouous to each other and can communicate instantaneously. OBSHS composition is best suited for asynchronous distributed object composition. We believe that the methods presented in this paper could be generalized to encompass both Charon and OBSHS compositions, essentially by viewing composed Charon objects as "Russian doll" objects [26] that could then communicate asynchronously with other such objects by messages in the OBSHS style.

The CPDP model [31] is a hybrid automaton formalism with two types of synchronization: on shared events, and on active-passive events with complementary labels. Composition is then synchronous parallel automaton composition. As in the PDP model [8], to which CPDP models can be reduced if their nondeterminism is eliminated by means of a scheduler, no diffusion is allowed, and no dynamic process creation is possible. Also, all communication (which can be value-passing) is assumed to be instantaneous. Therefore, CPDP models seem best suited for composing tightly coupled stochastic processes, not involving diffusion, out of simpler subprocesses.

The SDCPN model [12] has some similarities and some differences with respect to OBSHS. Both models map to GSHS. Both have distributed states formed by multiset union. In fact, by using the formalization of Petri nets as rewrite theories presented in [30], SDCPN transitions can be understood as probabilistic rewrite rules that perform multiset rewriting in the current marking multiset. In both models, both instantaneous and delayed interactions are possible (the analogous role of scheduled messages in OBSHS is played by delay transitions in SDCPN). But SDCPN models do not directly support objects and asynchronous message passing. In our view, SDCPN and OBSHS models, while having a comparable expressive power at the level of their GSHS translations, support quite different specification styles. We think that the most fruitful way of relating these models would be by unifying them within a more general model that specifies transitions as probabilistic rewrite rules.

We can summarize the work just presented as the first proposal we are aware of for a formal model and specification language for distributed object-based stochastic hybrid systems that communicate by asynchronous message passing; and for analyzing such systems by statistical model checking. We view explicit modeling of asynchronous communication as essential for many classes of applications in which objects are physically distributed over non-negligible distances. Furthermore, network communication makes message delays unavoidable. Compositionality is supported in OBSHS at two different levels: at the object level by the parallel object composition operator $\_\|\_$, and at the class level by multiple inheritance.

The work presented here is a first step. Further work is needed in several directions, including: (i) further advancing the design and implementation of our OBSHS specification language; (ii) experimenting with a wider class of applications, including Bioinformatics applications; and (iii) developing, as suggested above, a more general formalism for stochastic hybrid system specification based on probabilistic rewrite rules that can combine the benefits of the OBSHS model with those of other models such as those proposed in [2, 12].

Acknowledgement. Research partially supported by grants NSF CNS 05-24516 and ONR N00014-02-1-0715. We cordially thank Koushik Sen for helping us in the use of the VeStA tool, and Rajeev Alur, Mikhail Bernadsky, Manuela

Bujorianu, John Lygeros, Prakash Panangaden, and Richard Sowers for many helpful comments that allowed us to improve the paper.

References

1. G. Agha, J. Meseguer, and K. Sen. PMaude: Rewrite-based specification language for probabilistic object systems. In *3rd Workshop on Quantitative Aspects of Programming Languages (QALP'05) ENTCS, http://osl.cs.uiuc.edu/~ksen/publications.html*, 2005.
2. R. Alur, M. Bernadsky, and R. Sharykin. Structured modeling of concurrent stochastic hybrid systems. In *FORMATS/FTRTFT, Springer LNCS 3253*, pages 309–324, 2004.
3. R. Alur, C. Courcoubetis, N. Halbwachs, T. A. Henzinger, P.-H. Ho, X. Nicollin, A. Olivero, J. Sifakis, and S. Yovine. The algorithmic analysis of hybrid systems. *Theoretical Computer Science*, 138:3–34, 1995.
4. R. Alur, T. Dang, J. M. Esposito, Y. Hur, F. Ivancic, V. Kumar, I. Lee, P. Mishra, G. J. Pappas, and O. Sokolsky. Hierarchical modeling and analysis of embedded systems. *Proceedings of the IEEE*, 91(1):11–28, 2003.
5. A. Aziz, K. Sanwal, V. Singhal, and R. Brayton. Model-checking continuous-time markov chains. *ACM Trans. Comput. Logic*, 1(1):162–170, 2000.
6. M. L. Bujorianu and J. Lygeros. Toward a general theory of stochastic hybrid systems. *Final Project Report, HYBRIDGE*, 2005.
7. M. Clavel, F. Durán, S. Eker, P. Lincoln, N. Martí-Oliet, J. Meseguer, and J. Quesada. Maude: specification and programming in rewriting logic. *Theoretical Computer Science*, 285:187–243, 2002.
8. M. H. A. Davis. *Markov Processes and Optimization*. Chapman & Hall, 1993.
9. M. H. A. Davis and M. H. Vellekoop. Permanent health insurance: a case study in piecewise-deterministic markov modelling. *Mitteilungen der Schweiz. Vereiningung der Versicherungsmathematiker*, 2:177–212, 1995.
10. N. Dershowitz and J.-P. Jouannaud. Rewrite systems. In J. van Leeuwen, editor, *Handbook of Theoretical Computer Science, Vol. B*, pages 243–320. North-Holland, 1990.
11. S. Eker, M. Knapp, K. Laderoute, P. Lincoln, J. Meseguer, and K. Sonmez. Pathway logic: Symbolic analysis of biological signaling. In *Proceedings of the Pacific Symposium on Biocomputing*, pages 400–412, January 2002.
12. M. H. C. Everdij and H. A. P. Blom. Hybrid Petri nets with diffusion that have into-mappings with generalised stochastic hybrid processes. *Final Project Report, HYBRIDGE*, 2005.
13. M. K. Ghosh, A. Arapostathis, and S. I. Marcus. Optimal control of switching diffusions with application to flexible manufacturing systems. *SIAM Journal on Control Optimization*, 35:1183–1204, 1993.
14. M. K. Ghosh, A. Arapostathis, and S. I. Marcus. Ergodic control of switching diffusions. *SIAM J. Control Optim.*, 35(6):1952–1988, 1997.
15. P. J. Goss and J. Peccoud. Quantitative modeling of stochastic systems in molecular biology using stochastic Petri nets.. *Proc. Natl. Acad. Sci. U.S.A.*, 1998.
16. J. P. Hespanha. Stochastic hybrid systems: Application to communication network. *Hybrid Systems: Computation and Control, number 1790 in LNCS*, pages 160–173, 2000.

17. J. Hu, J. Lygeros, and S. Sastry. Towars a theory of stochastic hybrid systems. In *HSCC, Springer LNCS 1790*, pages 160–173, 2000.

18. I. Hwang, J. Hwang, and C. J. Tomlin. Flight-model-based aircraft conflict detection using a residual-mean interacting multiple model algorithm. *In AIAA Guidance, Navigation, and Control Conference, AIAA-2003-5340*, 2003.

19. HYBRIDGE.   Final   project   report,   http://hosted.nlr.nl/public/hosted-sites/hybridge/. 2005.

20. N. Kumar, K. Sen, J. Meseguer, and G. Agha. A rewriting based model of probabilistic distributed object systems. Proc. of Formal Methods for Open Object-Based Distributed Systems, FMOODS 2003, Springer LNCS Vol. 2884, 2003.

21. P. Lincoln and A. Tiwari. Symbolic systems biology: Hybrid modeling and analysis of biological networks. In *HSCC*, pages 660–672, 2004.

22. N. Lynch, R. Segala, and F. Vaandrager. Hybrid i/o automata. *Inf. Comput.*, 185(1):105–157, 2003.

23. O. Maler, Z. Manna, and A. Pnueli. From timed to hybrid systems. In *Proceedings of the Real-Time: Theory in Practice, REX Workshop*, pages 447–484, London, UK, 1992. Springer-Verlag.

24. J. Meseguer. Conditional rewriting logic as a unified model of concurrency. *Theoretical Computer Science*, 96(1):73–155, 1992.

25. J. Meseguer and R. Sharykin. Specification and analysis of distributed object-based stochastic hybrid systems. *UIUCDCS-R-2005-2649, Technical Report, Computer Science, University of Illinois at Urbana-Champaign*, 2005.

26. J. Meseguer and C. Talcott. Semantic models for distributed object reflection. In *Proceedings of ECOOP'02, Málaga, Spain, June 2002*, pages 1–36. Springer LNCS 2374, 2002.

27. H. Mizuta and K. Steiglitz. Agent-based simulation of dynamic online auctions. In *Winter Simulation Conference*, pages 1772–1777, 2000.

28. G. Pola, M. L. Bujorianu, J. Lygeros, and M. D. D. Benedetto. Stochastic hybrid models: an overview. *Proc. of the IFAC Conference on Analysis and Design of Hybrid Systems*, pages 45–50, 2003.

29. K. Sen, M. Viswanathan, and G. Agha. On statistical model checking of stochastic systems. In *CAV*, pages 266–280, 2005.

30. M.-O. Stehr, J. Meseguer, and P. Ölveczky. Rewriting logic as a unifying framework for Petri nets. In *Unifying Petri Nets*, pages 250–303. Springer LNCS 2128, 2001.

31. S. Straube and A. van der Schaft. Communicating piecewise deterministic Markov processes. *Final Project Report, HYBRIDGE*, pages http://hosted.nlr.nl/public/hosted–sites/hybridge/, 2005.

32. H. D. Vinod. Forecasting exchange rate dynamics using gmm, estimating functions and numerical conditional variance methods. Fordham University.

Verifying Average Dwell Time by Solving Optimization Problems*

Sayan Mitra[1], Nancy Lynch[1], and Daniel Liberzon[2]

[1] Computer Science and AI Laboratory, Massachusetts Inst. of Technology,
32 Vassar Street, Cambridge, MA 02139
{lynch, mitras}@csail.mit.edu
[2] Coordinated Science Laboratory, Univ. of Illinois at Urbana-Champaign,
Urbana, IL 61821
liberzon@uiuc.edu

Abstract. A switched system is a hybrid system whose discrete mechanisms are abstracted away in terms of an exogenous switching signal which brings about the mode switches. For switched systems, the *Average Dwell time (ADT)* property defines restricted classes of switching signals which can be used for proving stability. In this paper, we develop optimization-based methods for automatically verifying ADT properties of hybrid systems. This enables us to prove stability of hybrid systems, provided the individual modes of the system are stable. For two special classes of hybrid systems, we show that the resulting optimization problems can indeed be solved efficiently using standard mathematical programming techniques. We also present simulation relation-based proof methods for establishing equivalence of hybrid systems with respect to ADT. The proposed methods are applied to verify ADT properties of a linear hysteresis switch and a nondeterministic thermostat.

1 Introduction

In order to accurately represent hybrid phenomena that arise in typical applications, hybrid system models must provide discrete and continuous valued state variables and must have mechanisms to capture both instantaneous state transitions and state trajectories spanning time intervals. The standard approach for describing hybrid behavior is to assume that every state of the system belongs to one of $\mathcal{P}$ *modes*, where $\mathcal{P}$ is a finite index set. When the state is in mode p, for some $p \in \mathcal{P}$, the continuous variables $\mathbf{x}$ evolve according to $\dot{\mathbf{x}} = f_p(\mathbf{x})$ and the discrete variables remain constant. Discrete transitions alter both continuous and discrete variables, which may lead to mode change. Analyzing the stability of hybrid systems is challenging because the stability of the continuous dynamics of each individual mode does not necessarily imply the stability of the whole system (see [1] for an example). The basic tool for studying stability of hybrid systems relies on the existence of a *Common Lyapunov function*, whose derivative along the trajectories of all the modes must satisfy suitable

---

* Supported by the MURI project:DARPA/AFOSR MURI F49620-02-1-0325 grant.

João Hespanha and A. Tiwari (Eds.): HSCC 2006, LNCS 3927, pp. 476–490, 2006.

inequalities. When such a function is not known or does not exist, *Multiple Lyapunov* functions [1] are useful for proving stability of a chosen execution. These and many other stability results are based on the *switched system* [2, 3] view of hybrid systems. Switched systems may be seen as higher-level abstractions of hybrid systems. A switched system model neglects the details of the discrete behavior of a hybrid system and instead relies on an exogenous switching signal to bring about the mode switches. If the individual modes of the system are stable, then the *Dwell Time* [4] and the more general *Average Dwell Time (ADT)* criteria, introduced by Morse and Hespanha [5], define restricted classes of switching signals that guarantee stability of the whole system. In this paper, we present techniques for automatically verifying ADT properties using a model for hybrid systems that captures both their discrete and continuous mechanisms. Thus we provide a missing piece in the toolbox for analysis of stability of hybrid systems.

We use the *Hybrid Input/Output Automaton (HIOA)* framework of Lynch, Segala, and Vaandrager [6] to develop methods for checking ADT properties. A hybrid system $\mathcal{A}$ has ADT τ_a if, in every execution fragment of $\mathcal{A}$, any τ_a interval of time, on an average, has at most one mode switch. A large ADT means that the system spends enough time in each mode to dissipate the transient energy gained through mode switches. Having a large ADT itself is not sufficient for stability; in addition, the individual modes of the automaton must also be stable. In fact, the problem of testing the stability of a hybrid system can be broken down into (a) finding Lyapunov functions for the individual modes and (b) checking the ADT property. We assume that a solution to part (a)—a set of Lyapunov functions for the individual modes—is known from existing techniques, and we present automatic methods for part (b).

Our approach for checking if a given automaton $\mathcal{A}$ has ADT τ_a, is to formulate an optimization problem $\mathsf{OPT}(\tau_a)$. From the solution of $\mathsf{OPT}(\tau_a)$ we can either get a counterexample execution fragment of $\mathcal{A}$ that violates the ADT property τ_a, or else we can conclude that no such counterexample exists and that $\mathcal{A}$ has ADT τ_a. We show that for certain useful classes of HIOA, $\mathsf{OPT}(\tau_a)$ can indeed be formulated and solved using standard mathematical programming techniques. We also present a simulation relation-based proof technique for showing that ADT of a given HIOA is no less than (or equal to) that of another HIOA. This proof technique enables us to verify ADT of automata for which $\mathsf{OPT}(\tau_a)$ may not be solvable directly. For example, we can abstract such an automaton $\mathcal{A}$ in terms of another automaton $\mathcal{B}$ for which $\mathsf{OPT}(\tau_a)$ *can* be solved efficiently, such that ADT of $\mathcal{A}$ is no less than that of $\mathcal{B}$. Then, by verifying that $\mathcal{B}$ has ADT τ_a we can conclude that the ADT of $\mathcal{A}$ is at least τ_a. We do not address the problem of constructing such an abstract automaton $\mathcal{B}$ in this paper; this direction will be pursued in the future.

In [7], an invariant-based method for proving ADT is proposed. This method transforms the given automaton $\mathcal{A}$ to a new automaton $\mathcal{A}_{\tau_a}$, so that $\mathcal{A}$ has ADT τ_a if and only if $\mathcal{A}_{\tau_a}$ has a particular invariant property $\mathcal{I}_{\tau_a}$. This method is applicable to any HIOA; however, for general HIOA, the invariant $\mathcal{I}_{\tau_a}$ cannot be checked automatically. The optimization-based approach presented here is automatic and complements the invariant method of [7] because the two can be used in combination to find the ADT of hybrid systems. We can start with some candidate value of $\tau_a > 0$ and search for a counterexample execution fragment for it, using the optimization-based approach. If such an execution fragment is found, then we decrease τ_a (say, by a factor of 2) and try again. If eventually the optimization approach fails to find a counterexample execution fragment for a particular value of τ_a, then we use the invariant approach to prove that this value of τ_a is an ADT for the given system.

Contributions and overview. In Section 2 we introduce a specialization of HIOA called *Structured Hybrid Automaton (SHA)* and define the Average Dwell Time (ADT) property in terms of this model. In Section 3 we introduce the optimization problem $\mathsf{OPT}(\tau_a)$. We formally define what it means for two SHA to be ADT-equivalent and present a new type of simulation relation, called *switching simulation*, that provides sufficient conditions for establishing the ADT equivalence. In Section 4 we explore the class of One-clock initialized SHA, and we show that solving $\mathsf{OPT}(\tau_a)$ for this class reduces to detecting a negative cost cycle in a weighted graph. We verify the ADT property of a linear, scale-independent hysteresis switch taken from [8] by first finding a SHA $\mathcal{B}$ that is ADT-equivalent to it and then showing how $\mathsf{OPT}(\tau_a)$ for $\mathcal{B}$ can be solved efficiently using standard graph algorithms, like Karp's algorithm for minimum mean-weight cycle [9]. In Section 5, we study the more general class of Initialized SHA and show that $\mathsf{OPT}(\tau_a)$ can be solved by detecting a cyclic execution fragment with "extra" mode switches. We show that for rectangular initialized SHA, $\mathsf{OPT}(\tau_a)$ can be formulated as a Mixed Integer Linear Program. We use this formulation along with switching simulations to verify the ADT property of a nondeterministic thermostat.

2   Hybrid System Model and Stability Definitions

The Hybrid Input/Output Automaton (HIOA) model [6] with its invariant and simulation based proof methods has been used to verify the safety properties of several hybrid systems (see, e.g., [10, 11, 12]). In this paper, we are concerned with internal stability of hybrid systems, so we use a specialization of the HIOA model called *Structured Hybrid Automata (SHA)*, that does not have input/output variables and does not distinguish among input, output, and internal actions. On the other hand, SHA have extra structure called "state models" for describing the trajectories using differential and algebraic equations.

2.1   Structured Hybrid Automaton Model

We denote the domain of a function f by $f.dom$. For a set $S \subseteq f.dom$, we write $f \lceil S$ for the restriction of f to S. If f is a function whose range is a set of functions containing Y, then we write $f \downarrow Y$ for the function g with $g.dom = f.dom$ such that for each $c \in g.dom$, $g(c) = f(c) \lceil Y$. For a tuple or an array b with n elements, we refer to its ith element by $b[i]$.

We fix the *time axis* T to be $\mathbb{R}_{\geq 0}$. Let X be a set of state variables; X is partitioned into X_d, the set of discrete variables, and X_c, the set of continuous variables. Each variable $x \in X$ is associated with a *type*, which is the set of values that x can assume. Each $x \in X_d$ (respectively, X_c) has *dynamic type*, which is the pasting closure of the set of constant (resp. continuous) functions[1] from left-closed intervals in T to the type of x. A *valuation* $\mathbf{x}$ for the set of variables X is a function that associates each $x \in X$ to a value in its type. The set of all valuations of X is denoted by $val(X)$. A *trajectory* $\tau : J \to val(X)$ specifies the values of all variables X on a time interval J with left endpoint of J equal to 0, with the constraint that evolution of each $x \in X$ over the trajectory should be consistent with its dynamic type. A trajectory with domain $[0,0]$ is called a *point trajectory*. If $\tau.dom$ is right closed then τ is *closed* and its *limit time* is the supremum of $\tau.dom$ and is written as $\tau.ltime$. The *first valuation* of τ, $\tau.fval$ is $\tau(0)$, and if τ is closed, then the *last valuation* of τ, $\tau.lval$, is $\tau(\tau.ltime)$.

Definition 1. *A state model F for a set of variables X is a set of differential equations for X_c of the form $\dot{\mathbf{x}}_c = f(\mathbf{x}_c)$, such that: (1) For every $\mathbf{x} \in val(X)$, there exists a trajectory τ with $\tau.fval = \mathbf{x}$, with the property that $\tau \downarrow X_c$ satisfies F, and (2) for all $t \in \tau.dom$, $(\tau \downarrow X_d)(t) = (\tau \downarrow X_d)(0)$. The prefix and suffix closure of the set of trajectories of X that satisfy the above conditions is denoted by $traj(X,F)$.*

Definition 2. *A* Structured Hybrid Automaton *(SHA) is a tuple $\mathcal{A}=(X,Q,\Theta,$- $A,\mathcal{D},P)$, where (1) X is a set of variables, including a special discrete variable called* mode*. (2) $Q \subseteq val(X)$ is the set of states, (3) $\Theta \subseteq Q$ is a nonempty set of start states, (4) A is a set of actions, (5) $\mathcal{D} \subseteq Q \times A \times Q$ is a set of discrete transitions, and (6) P is an indexed family F_i, $i \in \mathcal{P}$, of state models, where $\mathcal{P}$ is an index set.*

A transition $(\mathbf{x}, a, \mathbf{x}') \in \mathcal{D}$ is written in short as $\mathbf{x} \xrightarrow{a}_{\mathcal{A}} \mathbf{x}'$ or as $\mathbf{x} \xrightarrow{a} \mathbf{x}'$ when $\mathcal{A}$ is clear from the context. A transition $\mathbf{x} \xrightarrow{a} \mathbf{x}'$ is a *mode switch* if $\mathbf{x} \lceil mode \neq \mathbf{x}' \lceil mode$. The set of *mode switching transitions* is denoted by M. The *guard predicate* of action a is $G_a \triangleq \{\mathbf{x} \in Q \mid \exists \mathbf{x}', \mathbf{x} \xrightarrow{a} \mathbf{x}' \in \mathcal{D}\}$. In this paper, we assume that the right hand sides of the differential equations in the state models are well behaved (locally Lipschitz), and the differential equations have solutions defined globally in time. Therefore, for each F_i, $i \in \mathcal{P}$ and $\mathbf{x} \in Q$ with $\mathbf{x} \lceil mode = i$, there exists a trajectory τ starting from $\mathbf{x}$ that satisfies F_i and if, $\tau.dom$ is finite then $\tau.lval \in G_a$ for some $a \in A$. The set $\mathcal{T}$ of trajectories of SHA $\mathcal{A}$ is defined as $\mathcal{T} \triangleq \bigcup_{i \in \mathcal{P}} traj(X, F_i)$. An *execution fragment* of an SHA $\mathcal{A}$ is an alternating sequence of actions and trajectories $\alpha = \tau_0 a_1 \tau_1 a_2 \ldots$, where (1) each $\tau_i \in \mathcal{T}$, and (2) if τ_i is not the last trajectory then $\tau_i.lstate \xrightarrow{a_{i+1}} \tau_{i+1}.fstate$. The *first state* of an execution fragment α, $\alpha.fstate$, is $\tau_0.fstate$. An execution fragment α is an *execution* of $\mathcal{A}$ if $\alpha.fstate \in \Theta$. The *length* of a finite execution

---

[1] This set of functions must be closed under time-shift, restriction to subintervals, and pasting. See [13] for formal definition of these closure properties.

fragment α is the number of actions in α. An execution fragment is *closed* if it is a finite sequence, and the domain of the last trajectory is closed. Given a closed execution fragment $\alpha = \tau_0, a_1, \ldots, \tau_n$, its *last state*, $\alpha.lstate$, is $\tau_n.lstate$ and its *limit time*, $\alpha.ltime$, is defined as $\sum_i^n \tau_i.ltime$. We define the following shorthand notation for the valuation of the variables of $\mathcal{A}$ at $t \in [0, \alpha.ltime]$: $\alpha(t) = \alpha'.lstate$, where α' is the longest prefix of α with $\alpha'.ltime = t$. A state $\mathbf{x} \in Q$ is *reachable* if it is the last state of some execution of $\mathcal{A}$. An execution fragment α is *reachable* if $\alpha.fstate$ is reachable. A closed execution fragment α of SHA $\mathcal{A}$ is a *cycle* if $\alpha.fstate = \alpha.lstate$.

2.2   Stability and Average Dwell Time

Stability is a property of the continuous variables of SHA $\mathcal{A}$ with respect to the standard Euclidean norm in $\mathbb{R}^n$. At a given state $\mathbf{x} \in Q$, we write the norm of the continuous variables $|\mathbf{x} \lceil X_c|$ in short as $|\mathbf{x}|$. We assume that for each $i \in \mathcal{P}$, the origin is an equilibrium point for the state model $\dot{\mathbf{x}}_c = f_i(\mathbf{x}_c)$ of $\mathcal{A}$.

SHA $\mathcal{A}$ is *stable* (also called stable in the sense of Lyapunov), if for every $\epsilon > 0$, there exists a $\delta > 0$, such that for every closed execution α of $\mathcal{A}$, for all $t \in [0, \alpha.ltime]$, $|\alpha(0)| \leq \delta$ implies $|\alpha(t)| \leq \epsilon$. $\mathcal{A}$ is *asymptotically stable* if it is stable and δ can be chosen so that, $|\alpha(0)| \leq \delta$ implies $\alpha(t) \to 0$ as $t \to \infty$. If the above condition holds for all δ then $\mathcal{A}$ is *globally asymptotically stable*.

Uniform stability guarantees that the stability property in question holds for execution fragments and not only for executions. $\mathcal{A}$ is *uniformly stable* if for every $\epsilon > 0$ there exists a constant $\delta > 0$, such that for any execution fragment α, $|\alpha.fstate| \leq \delta$ implies $|\alpha.lstate| \leq \epsilon$. An SHA $\mathcal{A}$ is said to be *uniformly asymptotically stable* if it is uniformly stable and there exists a $\delta > 0$, such that for every $\epsilon > 0$ there exists a T, such that for any execution fragment α with $\alpha.ltime \geq T$, $\forall t \geq T$, $|\alpha.fstate| \leq \delta$ implies $|\alpha(t)| \leq \epsilon$. It is said to be *globally uniformly asymptotically stable* if the above holds for all δ, with $T = T(\delta, \epsilon)$.

It is well known that a hybrid system is stable if all the individual modes of the system are stable and the switching is sufficiently slow, so as to allow the dissipation of the transient effects after each switch. The *dwell time* [4] and the *average dwell time* [5] criteria define restricted classes of switching patterns, based on switching speeds, and one can conclude the stability of a system with respect to these restricted classes.

Definition 3. *Given a duration of time $\tau_a > 0$, SHA $\mathcal{A}$ has* Average Dwell Time (ADT) τ_a *if there exists a positive constant N_0, such that for every reachable execution fragment α, $N(\alpha) \leq N_0 + \alpha.ltime/\tau_a$, where $N(\alpha)$ is the number of mode switches in α. The number of extra switches of α with respect to τ_a is $S_{\tau_a}(\alpha) \triangleq N(\alpha) - \alpha.ltime/\tau_a$.*

Theorem 1 from [5], adapted to SHA, gives a sufficient condition for stability based on ADT. Roughly, it states that a hybrid system is stable if the modes are individually stable and the switches do not occur too frequently on the average. See Section 3.2 of [2] for a proof.

Theorem 1. *If there exist positive definite, radially unbounded, and continuously differentiable functions $\mathcal{V}_i : \mathbb{R}^n \to \mathbb{R}^n$, for each $i \in \mathcal{P}$, and positive numbers λ_0 and μ such that:*

$$\frac{\partial \mathcal{V}_i}{\partial \mathbf{x}_c} f_i(\mathbf{x}_c) \leq -\lambda_0 \mathcal{V}_i(\mathbf{x}_c), \quad \forall \mathbf{x}_c, \ \forall i \in \mathcal{P}, and$$

$$\mathcal{V}_i(\mathbf{x}_c') \leq \mu \mathcal{V}_j(\mathbf{x}_c), \quad \forall \mathbf{x} \xrightarrow{a}_\mathcal{A} \mathbf{x}', \ where \ i = \mathbf{x}' \lceil mode \ and \ j = \mathbf{x} \lceil mode.$$

Then, $\mathcal{A}$ is globally uniformly asymptotically stable if it has an ADT $\tau_a > \frac{\log \mu}{\lambda_0}$.

This stability condition effectively allows us to decouple the construction of Lyapunov functions—the $\mathcal{V}_i$'s for each $i \in \mathcal{P}$, which we assume are known from available methods of system theory—from the problem of checking that the automaton has a certain ADT, which we discuss in the rest of the paper.

3   ADT: Optimization and Equivalence

From Definition 3 it follows that a given $\tau_a > 0$ is *not* an ADT of a given SHA $\mathcal{A}$ if and only if, for every $N_0 > 0$ there exists a reachable execution fragment α of $\mathcal{A}$ such that $S_{\tau_a}(\alpha) > N_0$. Thus, if we solve the following optimization problem:

$$\mathsf{OPT}(\tau_a): \quad \alpha^* \in \arg\max S_{\tau_a}(\alpha)$$

over all the execution fragments of $\mathcal{A}$, and the optimal value $S_{\tau_a}(\alpha^*)$ turns out to be bounded, then we can conclude that $\mathcal{A}$ has ADT τ_a. Otherwise, if $S_{\tau_a}(\alpha^*)$ is unbounded and α^* is reachable then we can conclude that τ_a is not an ADT for $\mathcal{A}$. However, the optimization problem $\mathsf{OPT}(\tau_a)$ may not be solvable because, among other things, the executions of $\mathcal{A}$ may not have finite descriptions. In Sections 4 and 5 we study particular classes of SHA for which $\mathsf{OPT}(\tau_a)$ can be solved efficiently. In the remainder of this section we develop a simulation relation-based method for proving that any given SHA $\mathcal{A}$ is equivalent to another SHA $\mathcal{B}$, with respect to ADT properties. As we shall see in Sections 4 and 5, this simulation method enables us to use the optimization based technique to verify ADT of even those SHA for which $\mathsf{OPT}(\tau_a)$ cannot be solved directly.

Definition 4. *A switching simulation relation from $\mathcal{A}$ to $\mathcal{B}$ is a relation $\mathcal{R} \subset Q_\mathcal{A} \times Q_\mathcal{B}$ satisfying the following conditions:*

1. *If $\mathbf{x} \in \Theta_\mathcal{A}$ then there exists $\mathbf{y} \in \Theta_\mathcal{B}$ such that $\mathbf{x} \mathcal{R} \mathbf{y}$.*
2. *If $\mathbf{x} \mathcal{R} \mathbf{y}$ and α is an execution fragment of $\mathcal{A}$ consisting of a single action surrounded by two point trajectories with $\alpha.fstate = \mathbf{x}$, then $\mathcal{B}$ has a closed execution fragment β, such that $\beta.fstate = \mathbf{y}$, $N(\beta) \geq N(\alpha)$, $\beta.ltime = 0$, and $\alpha.lstate \mathcal{R} \beta.lstate$. Here $N(\beta)$ is the number of mode switches in β.*
3. *If $\mathbf{x} \mathcal{R} \mathbf{y}$ and α is an execution fragment of $\mathcal{A}$ consisting of a single closed trajectory with $\alpha.fstate = \mathbf{x}$, then $\mathcal{B}$ has a closed execution fragment β, such that $\beta.fstate = \mathbf{y}$, $\beta.ltime \leq \alpha.ltime$, and $\alpha.lstate \mathcal{R} \beta.lstate$.*

Lemma 1. *Let $\mathcal{R}$ be a switching simulation relation from SHA $\mathcal{A}$ to $\mathcal{B}$. Then, for all $\tau_a > 0$ and for every reachable execution fragment α of $\mathcal{A}$, there exists a reachable execution fragment β of $\mathcal{B}$, such that $S_{\tau_a}(\beta) \geq S_{\tau_a}(\alpha)$.*

Owing to space limitations most of the proofs are omitted from this paper; complete proofs for all the results are available in the full version [14]. The above lemma is proved by inductively defining a sequence $\beta_0\beta_1\beta_2\ldots$ of closed execution fragments of $\mathcal{B}$ for a given an execution fragment $\alpha = \tau_0 a_1 \tau_1 a_2 \tau_2 \ldots$ of $\mathcal{A}$, such that for all i, $\beta_i.lstate = \beta_{i+1}.fstate$, $\alpha_i.lstate \; \mathcal{R} \; \beta_i.lstate$, and $S_{\tau_a}(\beta) \geq S_{\tau_a}(\alpha)$. We use Property 3 of the definition of switching simulation for the construction of the β_i's with i even. This gives us $\beta_i.ltime \leq \alpha_i.ltime$ for every even i. We use Property 2 of the definition of switching simulation for the construction of the β_i's with i odd. This gives us $\beta_i.ltime = \alpha_i.ltime$ and $N(\beta_i) \geq N(\alpha_i)$ for every odd i.

Suppose for every $\tau_a > 0$, if $\mathcal{B}$ has ADT τ_a then $\mathcal{A}$ also has ADT τ_a; we write this as $\mathcal{A} \geq_{ADT} \mathcal{B}$. If $\mathcal{A} \geq_{ADT} \mathcal{B}$ and $\mathcal{B} \geq_{ADT} \mathcal{A}$, then we write $\mathcal{A} =_{ADT} \mathcal{B}$. Intuitively, $\mathcal{A} \geq_{ADT} \mathcal{B}$ means that $\mathcal{B}$ switches faster than $\mathcal{A}$ on an average, and $\mathcal{A} =_{ADT} \mathcal{B}$ means that $\mathcal{A}$ and $\mathcal{B}$ have the same average switching speeds. We use Theorem 2 for proving $\mathcal{B} \geq_{ADT} \mathcal{A}$.

Theorem 2. *If $\mathcal{R}$ is a switching simulation relation from $\mathcal{A}$ to $\mathcal{B}$, then $\mathcal{B} \geq_{ADT} \mathcal{A}$.*

Corollary 1. *If $\mathcal{R}_1$ be a switching simulation from $\mathcal{A}$ to $\mathcal{B}$ and $\mathcal{R}_2$ is a switching simulation from $\mathcal{B}$ to $\mathcal{A}$, then, $\mathcal{A} =_{ADT} \mathcal{B}$.*

4 One-Clock Initialized SHA

In this section we study a special class of SHA, called *one-clock initialized SHA*, for which $\mathsf{OPT}(\tau_a)$ (see Section 3) can be solved using classical graph algorithms. Consider a graph G defined by: a set of vertices $\mathcal{V}$, a set of directed edges $\mathcal{E} \subseteq \mathcal{V} \times \mathcal{V}$, a cost function $w : \mathcal{E} \to \mathbb{R}_{\geq 0}$ for the edges, and a special start edge $e_0 \in \mathcal{E}$. The cost of a path in G is the sum of the costs of the edges in the path. Given $G = (\mathcal{V}, \mathcal{E}, w, e_0)$, the corresponding one-clock initialized SHA $Aut(G)$ is specified by the code in Figure 1. The source and the target vertices of an edge e are denoted by $e[1]$ and $e[2]$, respectively.

The discrete transitions are written using the standard precondition-effect style. Each *trajdef* d defines a set of trajectories $\mathcal{T}_d$ in terms of the invariant $inv(d)$, the stopping condition $stop(d)$, and the state model written as an evolve clause $evolve(d)$. A trajectory τ is in $\mathcal{T}_d$, if an only if (1) τ satisfies $evolve(d)$, (2) $\forall \, t \in \tau.dom$, $\tau(t) \in inv(d)$, and (3) $\exists \, t \in \tau.dom$, $\tau(t) \in stop(d) \to t = \tau.ltime$. The set of trajectories of $Aut(G)$ is the union of the sets of trajectories defined by each trajdef.

Intuitively, the state of $Aut(G)$ captures the motion of a particle moving with unit speed along the edges of the graph G. The position of the particle is given by the *mode*, which is the edge it resides on, and the value of x, which is its distance from the source vertex of the edge G. Thus, a switch from mode e to mode e' of $Aut(G)$ corresponds to the particle arriving at vertex $e[2]$ via edge e, and

Variables:
  $mode \in \mathcal{E} \subset \mathcal{V} \times \mathcal{V}$, *initialy* e_0
  $x \in R$, *initially* 0

Actions:
  switch(e,e'), $e,e' \in \mathcal{E}$

Transitions:
  switch(e,e')

Precondition
  $mode = e \wedge e[2] = e'[1] \wedge x = w(e)$
Effect
  $mode \leftarrow e'$, $x \leftarrow 0$

Trajectories:
  Trajdef edge$(mode)$
  Evolve $d(x) = 1$
  Invariant $x \leq w(mode)$
  Stop when $x = w(mode)$

Fig. 1. Automaton $Aut(G)$, where $G = (\mathcal{V}, \mathcal{E} \subseteq \mathcal{V} \times \mathcal{V}, w : \mathcal{E} \to \mathbb{R}_{\geq 0}$, and e_0)

departing on edge e'. Within edge e the particle moves at unit speed from $e[1]$, where $x = 0$ to $e[2]$, where $x = w(e)$. The next theorem implies that to search for an execution of $Aut(G)$ that violates a ADT property τ_a, it is necessary and sufficient to search over the space of the cycles of G. See [14] for a proof.

Theorem 3. *Consider* $\tau_a > 0$ *and a one-clock initialized SHA* $Aut(G)$. $\mathcal{A}$ *has average dwell time* τ_a *if and only if for all* $m > 1$, *the cost of any reachable cycle of* G *with* m *segments is at least* $m\tau_a$.

Thus, the problem of solving $\mathsf{OPT}(\tau_a)$ for $Aut(G)$ reduces to checking whether G contains a cycle of length m, for some $m > 1$, with cost less than $m\tau_a$. This is a standard problem for directed graphs and can be solved efficiently using Bellman-Ford algorithm or Karp's minimum mean-weight cycle algorithm [9].

Example 1: Linear hysteresis switch. We verify the ADT properties of a linear, scale-independent hysteresis switch which is a subsystem of an adaptive supervisory control system taken from [8] (also Chapter 6 of [2]). An adaptive supervisory controller consists of a family of candidate controllers $u_i, i \in \mathcal{P}$, which correspond to the parametric uncertainty range of the plant in a suitable way. The controller operates in conjunction with a set of on-line estimators that provide *monitoring signals* $\mu_i, i \in \mathcal{P}$; intuitively, smallness of μ_i indicates high likelihood that i is the actual parameter value. Based on these signals, the switching logic unit changes the variable *mode*, which in turn determines the controller to be applied to the plant. Average dwell time property of this switching logic guarantees stability of the overall supervisory control system.

In building the linear SHA model $\mathcal{A}$ (shown in Figure 2), we consider monitoring signals generated by linear differential equations, such that for each $i \in \mathcal{P}$, if $mode = i$, then $d(\mu_i) = c_i\mu_i$, otherwise $d(\mu_i) = 0$. The switching logic unit implements scale independent hysteresis switching as follows: at an instant of time when controller k is operating, that is, $mode = k$ for some $k \in \mathcal{P}$, if there exists an $i \in \mathcal{P}$ such that $\mu_i(1 + h) \leq \mu_k$ for some fixed hysteresis constant h, then the switching logic sets $mode = i$ and applies output of controller i to the plant.

As $\mathcal{A}$ is not a one-clock initialized SHA, we cannot apply Theorem 3 to verify its ADT directly. However, we notice that the switching behavior of $\mathcal{A}$, does not depend on the value of the μ_i's, but on the ratio of $\frac{\mu_i}{\mu_{min}}$, which is always within

---

Variables:
  $mode \in \mathcal{P}$, initially p_0
  $\mu_p \in \mathbb{R}, p \in \mathcal{P}$,
    initialy $\mu_{p_0} = (1+h)C_0$
    for all $i \neq p_0$, $\mu_i = C_0$
  derived
    $\mu_{min} = Min_{i \in \mathcal{P}} \mu_i$

Actions:
  switch(p,q), $p,q \in \mathcal{P}$

Transitions:
  switch(p,q)
  Precondition
    $mode = p \wedge (1+h)\mu_q \leq \mu_p$
  Effect $mode \leftarrow q$

Trajectories:
  Trajdef mode(p)
  Evolve for all $i \in \mathcal{P}$,
    if $i = p$ then $d(\mu_p) = c_p \mu_p$ else $d(\mu_i) = 0$
  Stop when
    $\exists\, q \in \mathcal{P}$ such that $(1+h)\mu_q \leq \mu_p$

Fig. 2. Linear hysteresis switch with parameters $\mathcal{P}, C_0, h$ and c_i for each $i \in \mathcal{P}$

$[1, (1+h)]$. When $\mathcal{A}$ is in mode $p \in \mathcal{P}$, all the ratios remain constant, except $\frac{\mu_p}{\mu_{min}}$ which increases monotonically from 1 to either $(1+h)$ or to $(1+h)^2$, in time $\frac{1}{c_p}\ln(1+h)$ or $\frac{2}{c_p}\ln(1+h)$, respectively. Thus, we will first show that there exists a one-clock initialized automaton $\mathcal{B}$, that is equivalent to $\mathcal{A}$ with respect to ADT, and then we will solve $\mathsf{OPT}(\tau_a)$ for $\mathcal{B}$.

Consider a graph $G = (\mathcal{V}, \mathcal{E}, w, e_0)$, where:

1. $\mathcal{V} \subset \{1, (1+h)\}^n$, such that for any $v \in V$, all the n-components are not equal. We denote the ith component of $v \in V$, by $v[i]$.
2. An edge $(u,v) \in \mathcal{E}$ if and only if, one of the following conditions hold:
   (a) There exists $j \in \{1,\ldots,n\}$, such that, $u[j] \neq v[j]$ and for all $i \in \{1,\ldots,n\}$, $i \neq j$, $u[i] = v[i]$. The cost of the edge $w(u,v) \triangleq \frac{1}{c_j}\ln(1+h)$ and we define $\zeta(u,v) \triangleq j$.
   (b) There exists $j \in \{1,\ldots,n\}$ such that $u[j] = 1, v[j] = (1+h)$ and for all $i \in \{1,\ldots,n\}$, $i \neq j$ implies $u[i] = (1+h)$ and $v[i] = 1$. The cost of the edge $w(u,v) \triangleq \frac{2}{c_j}\ln(1+h)$ and we define $\zeta(u,v) \triangleq j$.
3. $e_0 \in \mathcal{E}$, such that $e_0[1][p_0] = (1+h)$ and for all $i \neq p_0$, $e_0[1][i] = 1$.

As an example, the graph for $n = 3$ is shown in Figure 3. Let $\mathcal{B}$ be the automaton $Aut(G)$. Each edge of G corresponds to a mode of $\mathcal{A}$. In fact, $mode$ of $\mathcal{A}$ equals $\zeta(e)$, where e is the edge corresponding to the $mode$ of $\mathcal{B}$.

We define a relation $\mathcal{R}$ on the state spaces on $\mathcal{A}$ and $\mathcal{B}$. Each vertex of G is an n-tuple; the ith component of the source vertex of e is denoted by $e[1][i]$.

Definition 5. *For any* $\mathbf{x} \in Q_\mathcal{A}$ *and* $\mathbf{y} \in Q_\mathcal{B}$, $\mathbf{x}\,\mathcal{R}\,\mathbf{y}$ *if and only if:*

1. $\zeta(\mathbf{y} \lceil mode) = \mathbf{x} \lceil mode$
2. *For all* $j \in \{1,\ldots,n\}$, *if* $j = \zeta(\mathbf{y} \lceil mode)$ *then* (a) $\frac{\mathbf{x}\lceil\mu_j}{\mathbf{x}\lceil\mu_{min}} = e^{c_j(\mathbf{y}\lceil x)}$ *else* (b) $\frac{\mathbf{x}\lceil\mu_j}{\mathbf{x}\lceil\mu_{min}} = (\mathbf{y} \lceil mode)[1][j]$ *and* $\frac{\mathbf{x}\lceil\mu_j}{\mathbf{x}\lceil\mu_{min}} = (\mathbf{y} \lceil mode)[2][j]$.

Part 1 of Definition 5 states that if $\mathcal{A}$ is in mode j and $\mathcal{B}$ is in mode e, then $\zeta(e) = j$. Part 2 states that for all $j \neq \zeta(e)$, the jth component of $e[1]$ and $e[2]$ are the same, and are equal to μ_j/μ_{min}, and for $j = \zeta(e)$, $\mu_j = \mu_{min}e^{c_j x}$. The next lemma states that $\mathcal{R}$ is a switching simulation relation from $\mathcal{A}$ and $\mathcal{B}$ and

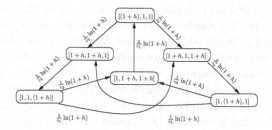

Fig. 3. Graph G with 3 modes. Here h and c_i's are the parameters from the hysteresis switch automaton $\mathcal{A}$.

from $\mathcal{B}$ to $\mathcal{A}$. The first part is proved by showing that every start state of $\mathcal{A}$ is related to some state of $\mathcal{B}$ and that every action and trajectory of $\mathcal{A}$ can be emulated by an execution fragment of $\mathcal{B}$ with more extra switches. The second part is proved using identical steps by interchanging $\mathcal{A}$ and $\mathcal{B}$.

Lemma 2. $\mathcal{R}$ *is a switching simulation relation from* $\mathcal{A}$ *to* $\mathcal{B}$ *and from* $\mathcal{B}$ *to* $\mathcal{A}$.

Remark 1. From Corollary 1 it follows that SHA $\mathcal{A}$ and $\mathcal{B}$ are ADT-equivalent. As $\mathcal{B}$ is one-clock initialize, its ADT properties can be verified using Karp's algorithm.

5 Initialized SHA and Mixed Integer Linear Programming

In this section we study ADT properties of *Initialized SHA*. A SHA $\mathcal{A}$ is *initialized* if every $a \in A$ is associated with a set $R_a \subseteq Q$, such that $\mathbf{x} \xrightarrow{a} \mathbf{x}'$ is a mode switching transition if and only if $\mathbf{x} \in G_a$ and $\mathbf{x}' \in R_a$. The set R_a is called the *initialization predicate* of a. A SHA is *rectangular* if the differential equations in the state models have constant right hand sides, and the guard and the initialization predicates (restricted to the set of continuous variables) are polyhedra.

Our next theorem implies that for an initialized SHA $\mathcal{A}$, it is necessary and sufficient to solve $\mathsf{OPT}(\tau_a)$ over the space of the cyclic fragments of $\mathcal{A}$ instead of the larger space of all execution fragments.

Theorem 4. *Given* $\tau_a > 0$ *and initialized SHA* $\mathcal{A}$, τ_a *is an ADT for* $\mathcal{A}$ *if and only if* $\mathcal{A}$ *does not have any cycles with extra switches with respect to* τ_a.

Here we sketch a proof of this theorem and refer the reader to [14] for the complete proof. Existence of a cycle α of $\mathcal{A}$ with $S_{\tau_a}(\alpha) > 0$ implies that τ_a is not an ADT, because by concatenating many α's we can construct an execution fragment $\alpha \frown \alpha \frown \alpha \dots$ with an arbitrarily large S_{τ_a}. To prove that the existence of a cycle with extra switches is also necessary for violating the ADT property, we assume that τ_a is not an ADT for $\mathcal{A}$ and that $\mathcal{A}$ does not have any cycles with extra switches. We choose $N_0 > |\mathcal{P}|^3$; from the definition of ADT we know that there exists an execution fragment γ, such that $S_{\tau_a}(\gamma) > N_0$. Let $\alpha = \tau_0 a_1 \tau_1 \ldots \tau_n$ be the shortest such execution fragment. Since $N(\alpha \geq |\mathcal{P}|^3$ mode switches and $\mathcal{A}$ is initialized, α must contain a cycle. As $\mathcal{A}$ does not have any cycles with extra switches, we get a contradiction to the assumption that α is the shortest execution fragment with more than N_0 extra switches.

Lemma 3 allows us to limit the search for cycles with extra switches to cycles with at most $|\mathcal{P}|^3$ mode switches. It is proved by showing that any cycle with extra switches that has more than $|\mathcal{P}|^3$ mode switches, can be decomposed into two smaller cycles, one of which must also have extra switches.

Lemma 3. *If initialized SHA $\mathcal{A}$ has a cycle with extra switches, then it has a cycle with extra switches that has fewer than $|\mathcal{P}|^3$ mode switches.*

MILP formulation of OPT(τ_a). We use the above results to solve the ADT verification problem for rectangular initialized SHA with Mixed Integer Linear Programming (MILP). Figure 4 shows the specification of a generic Initialized rectangular SHA $\mathcal{A}$. The automaton $\mathcal{A}$ has a single discrete variable called *mode* which takes values in the index set $\mathcal{P} = \{1, \ldots, N\}$, and a continuous variable vector $\mathbf{x} \in \mathbb{R}^n$. For any $p, q \in \mathcal{P}$, the action that changes the mode from p to q is called *switch*(p, q). The guard and the initialization predicates of this action are given by sets of linear inequalities on the continuous variables, represented in the matrix notation by: $G[p,q]\mathbf{x} \leq g[p,q]$ and $R[p,q]\mathbf{x} \leq r[p,q]$, respectively, where $G[p,q]$ and $R[p,q]$ are constant matrices with n columns and $g[p,q], r[p,q]$ are constant vectors.

For each mode $p \in P$ of automaton $\mathcal{A}$, the invariant is stated in terms of linear inequalities of the continuous variables $A[p]\mathbf{x} \leq a[p]$, where $A[p]$ is a constant matrix with n columns and $a[p]$ is a constant vector. The evolve clause is given by a single differential equation $d(\mathbf{x}) = c[p]$, where the right hand side $c[p]$ is a constant vector.

We describe a MILP formulation $\mathsf{MOPT}(K, \tau_a)$ for finding a cyclic execution with K mode switches that maximizes the number of extra switches with respect to τ_a. If the optimal value is positive, then the optimal solution represents a cycle with extra switches with respect to τ_a, and we conclude that τ_a is not an ADT for $\mathcal{A}$. On the other hand, if the optimal value is not positive, then we conclude that there are no cycles with extra switches of length K. To verify ADT of

---

Variables:
  mode $\in \mathcal{P}$, *initially* p
  $\mathbf{x} \in R^n$, *initially* $\mathbf{x}_0$

Actions
  switch(p,q), $p, q \in \mathcal{P}$

Transitions:
  switch(p,q)

Precondition
  mode $= p \wedge G[p,q]\mathbf{x} \leq g[p,q]$
Effect
  mode $\leftarrow q$
  $\mathbf{x} \leftarrow \mathbf{x}'$ such that $R[p,q]\mathbf{x}' \leq r[p,q]$

Trajectories:
  Trajdef *mode*(p)
  Invariant $A[p]\mathbf{x} \leq a[p]$
  Evolve $d(\mathbf{x}) = c[p]$

Fig. 4. Generic rectangular initialized SHA with parameters $\mathcal{P}, G, A, R, q, a, r, c$

Objective function: $S_{\tau_a} : \dfrac{K}{2} - \dfrac{1}{\tau_a} \displaystyle\sum_{i=0,2,\ldots}^{K} t_i$

Mode: $\forall\, i \in \{0,2,\ldots,K\},\ \displaystyle\sum_{j=1}^{N} m_{ij} = 1\ and\ \forall\, i \in \{1,3,\ldots,K-1\},\ \displaystyle\sum_{j=1}^{N}\sum_{k=1}^{N} p_{ijk} = 1$

$$(1)$$

Cycle: $\mathbf{x}_0 = \mathbf{x}_K$ and $\forall\, j \in \{1,\ldots,N\}, m_{0j} = m_{Kj}$ \hfill (2)

Preconds: $\forall\, i \in \{1,3,\ldots,K-1\},\ \displaystyle\sum_{j=1}^{N}\sum_{k=1}^{N} G[j,k].p_{ijk}.\mathbf{x}_i \le \displaystyle\sum_{j=1}^{N}\sum_{k=1}^{N} p_{ijk}.g[j,k]$ \hfill (3)

Initialize: $\forall\, i \in \{1,3,\ldots,K-1\},\ \displaystyle\sum_{j=1}^{N}\sum_{k=1}^{N} R[j,k].p_{ijk}.\mathbf{x}_{i+1} \le \displaystyle\sum_{j=1}^{N}\sum_{k=1}^{N} p_{ijk}.r[j,k]$ \hfill (4)

Invariants: $\forall\, i \in \{0,2,\ldots,K\},\ \displaystyle\sum_{j=1}^{N} A[j].m_{ij}.\mathbf{x}_i \le \displaystyle\sum_{j=1}^{N} m_{ij}.a[j]$ \hfill (5)

Evolve: $\forall\, i \in \{0,2\ldots,K\},\ \mathbf{x}_{i+1} = \mathbf{x}_i + \displaystyle\sum_{j=1}^{N} c[j].m_{ij}.t_i$ \hfill (6)

Fig. 5. The objective function and the linear and integral constraints for $\mathsf{MOPT}(K,\tau_a)$

$\mathcal{A}$, we solve a sequence of $\mathsf{MOPT}(K,\tau_a)$'s with $K = 2,\ldots,|\mathcal{P}|^3$. If the optimal values are not positive for any of these, then we conclude that τ_a is an ADT for $\mathcal{A}$. By adding extra variables and constraints we are able to formulate a single MILP that maximizes the extra switches over all cycles with K or less mode switches, but for simplicity of presentation, we discuss sf $\mathsf{MOPT}(\tau_a)$ instead of this latter formulation. The following are the decision variables for $\mathsf{MOPT}(K,\tau_a)$; the objective function and the constraints are shown in Figure 5.

- $\mathbf{x}_i \in \mathbb{R}^n$, $i \in \{0\ldots,K\}$, value of continuous variables
- $t_i \in R$, $i \in \{0,2,4,\ldots,K\}$, length of ith trajectory
- $m_{ij} = \begin{cases} 1, & \text{if mode over } i^{th} \text{ trajectory is } j \\ 0, & \text{otherwise.} \end{cases}$ for each $i \in \{0,2,\ldots,K\}, j \in \{1,\ldots,N\}$
- $p_{ijk} = \begin{cases} 1, & \text{if mode over } (i-1)^{st} \text{ trajectory is } j \text{ and over } (i+1)^{st} \text{ trajectory is } k \\ 0, & \text{otherwise.} \end{cases}$ for each $i \in \{0,2,4,\ldots,K\}, j,k \in \{1,\ldots,N\}$

In $\mathsf{MOPT}(K,\tau_a)$, an execution fragment with K mode switches is represented as a sequence $\mathbf{x}_0, \mathbf{x}_1, \ldots, \mathbf{x}_K$ of K valuations for the continuous variables. For each even i, $\mathbf{x}_i$ goes to $\mathbf{x}_{i+1}$ by a trajectory of length t_i. If this trajectory is in mode j, for some $j \in \{1,\ldots,N\}$, then $m_{ij} = 1$, else $m_{ij} = 0$. For each odd i, $\mathbf{x}_i$ goes to $\mathbf{x}_{i+1}$ by a discrete transition. If this transition is from mode j to mode k, for some $j,k \in \{1,\ldots,N\}$, then $p_{ijk} = 1$, else $p_{ijk} = 0$. These constraints are specified by Equation (1) in Figure 5. For each odd i, Constraints (3) and (4) ensure that $(\mathbf{x}_i, switch(j,k), \mathbf{x}_{i+1})$ is a valid mode switching transition. These constraints reduce to the inequalities $G[j,k]\mathbf{x}_i \le g[j,k]$ and $R[j,k]\mathbf{x}_{i+1} \le r[j,k]$ which correspond to the guard and the initialization conditions on the pre- and the post-state of the transition. For each even i, $\mathbf{x}_i$ evolves to $\mathbf{x}_{i+1}$ through a trajectory in some mode, say j. Constraint (5) ensures that $\mathbf{x}_i$ satisfies the invariant of mode j described by the inequality $A[j]\mathbf{x}_i \leq a[j]$. An identical constraint for $\mathbf{x}_{i+1}$ is written by replacing $\mathbf{x}_i$ with $\mathbf{x}_{i+1}$ in (5). Since the differential equations have constant right hand sides and the invariants describe pohyhedra in $\mathbb{R}^n$, the above conditions ensure that all the intermediate states in the trajectory satisfy the mode invariant. Equation (6) ensures that, for each even i, $\mathbf{x}_i$ evolves to $\mathbf{x}_{i+1}$ in t_i time according to the differential equation $d(\mathbf{x}) = c[j]$.

Some of these constrains involve nonlinear terms. For example, $m_{ij}\mathbf{x}_i$ in (5) is the product of real variable $\mathbf{x}_i$ and boolean variable m_{ij}. Using the "big M" method [15] we can linearize this equation by replacing $m_{ij}\mathbf{x}_i$ with $\mathbf{y}_i$, and adding the following linear inequalities: $\mathbf{y}_i \geq m_{ij}\delta$, $\mathbf{y}_i \leq m_{ij}\Delta$, $\mathbf{y}_i \leq \mathbf{x}_i - (1 - m_{ij})\delta$, and $\mathbf{y}_i \geq \mathbf{x}_i - (1 - m_{ij})\Delta$, where δ and Δ are the lower and upper bounds on the values of $\mathbf{x}_i$.

Example 2: Thermostat. We use the MILP technique together with switching simulation relations to verify the ADT of a thermostat with nondeterministic switches. The thermostat SHA $\mathcal{A}$ (see Figure 6 *Left*) has two modes l_0, l_1, two continuous variables x and z, and real parameters $h, K, \theta_1, \theta_2, \theta_3, \theta_4$, where $0 < \theta_1 < \theta_2 < \theta_3 < \theta_4 < h$. In l_0 mode the heater is off and the temperature x decreases according to the differential equation $d(x) = -Kx$. While the temperature x is between θ_2 and θ_1, the on action *must* occur. As a result of which the mode changes to l_1. In mode l_1, the heater is on and the x rises according to the $d(x) = K(h - x)$, and while x is between θ_3 and θ_4, the offaction must occur. The continuous variable z measures the total time spent in mode l_1.

The thermostat SHA $\mathcal{A}$ is neither initialized nor rectangular; however, there is a rectangular initialized SHA $\mathcal{B}$, such that $\mathcal{B} \geq_{ADT} \mathcal{A}$. Consider the SHA $\mathcal{B}$ of Figure 6 (*Right*) with parameters L_0 and L_1. Automaton $\mathcal{B}$ has a clock t and two modes l_0 and l_1, in each of which t increases at a unit rate. When t reaches L_i in mode l_i, a switch to the other mode *may* occur and if it does then t is set to zero. We define a relation $\mathcal{R}$ on the state spaces of $\mathcal{A}$ an $\mathcal{B}$ such that with appropriately chosen values of L_0 and L_1, $\mathcal{B}$ captures the fastest switching behavior of $\mathcal{A}$.

Definition 6. *For any $\mathbf{x} \in Q_\mathcal{A}$ and $\mathbf{y} \in Q_\mathcal{B}$, $\mathbf{x}\,\mathcal{R}\,\mathbf{y}$ if and only if: (1) $\mathbf{x} \lceil mode = \mathbf{y} \lceil mode$, and (2) if $\mathbf{x} \lceil mode = l_0$ then $\mathbf{y} \lceil t \geq \frac{1}{k}\ln \frac{\theta_3}{\mathbf{x}\lceil x}$ else $\mathbf{y} \lceil t \geq \frac{1}{k}\ln \left(\frac{h - \theta_2}{h - \mathbf{x}\lceil x} \right)$.*

Lemma 4. *If we set $L_0 = \frac{1}{k}\ln \frac{\theta_3}{\theta_2}$ and $L_1 = \frac{1}{k}\ln \frac{h - \theta_2}{h - \theta_3}$, then the relation $\mathcal{R}$ is a switching simulation from $\mathcal{A}$ to $\mathcal{B}$.*

The proof of this lemma is like that of Lemma 2 ; we show that every state of $\mathcal{A}$ is related to some state of $\mathcal{B}$ and that every action and trajectory of $\mathcal{A}$ can be emulated by an execution fragment of $\mathcal{B}$ with more extra switches. Lemma 4 implies that $\mathcal{A} \geq_{ADT} \mathcal{B}$, that is, for any $\tau_a > 0$ if τ_a is an ADT for $\mathcal{B}$ then τ_a is also an ADT for $\mathcal{A}$. Since $\mathcal{B}$ is rectangular and initialized, we can use Theorem 4 and the MILP technique to check any ADT property of $\mathcal{B}$.

Variables: $mode \in \{l_0, l_1\}$, *initially* l_0 $x, z \in R$, *initially* $x = \theta_4, z = 0$	Variables: $mode \in \{l_0, l_1\}$, *initially* l_0 $r \in R$, *initially* $r = L_1$
Actions on, off	**Actions** switchto$_i$, $i \in \{0,1\}$
Transitions: on **Precondition** $mode = l_0 \wedge x \leq \theta_2$ **Effect** $mode \leftarrow l_1$	**Transitions:** switchto$_1$ **Precondition** $mode = l_0 \wedge r \geq L_0$ **Effect** $mode \leftarrow l_1, r \leftarrow 0$
off **Precondition** $mode = l_1 \wedge x \geq \theta_3$ **Effect** $mode \leftarrow l_0$	switchto$_0$ **Precondition** $mode = l_1 \wedge r \geq L_1$ **Effect** $mode \leftarrow l_0, r \leftarrow 0$
Trajectories: **Trajdef** l_0 **Evolve** $d(x) = -Cx;\; d(z) = 0$ **Invariant** $x \geq \theta_1$ **Stop when** $x = \theta_1$	**Trajectories:** **Trajdef** l_0 **Evolve** $d(r) = 1$
Trajdef l_1 **Evolve** $d(x) = C(h\text{-}x);\; d(z) = 1$ **Invariant** $x \leq \theta_4$ **Stop when** $x = \theta_4$	**Trajdef** l_1 **Evolve** $d(r) = 1$

Fig. 6. *Left:*Thermostat SHA $\mathcal{A}$ with parameters $\theta_1, \theta_2, \theta_3, \theta_4, K$, and h. *Right:* Rectangular SHA $\mathcal{B}$ with parameters L_0, L_1.

We formulated the MOPT(K, τ_a) for automaton $\mathcal{B}$ and used the GNU Linear Programming Kit [16] to solve it. Solving for $K = 4, L_0 = 40, L_1 = 15$, and $\tau_a = 25, 27, 28$, we get optimal costs $-0.4, -4.358E^{-13}(\approx 0)$ and 0.071, respectively. We conclude that the ADT of $\mathcal{B}$ is $\geq 25, \geq 27$, and < 28. Since $\mathcal{B} \geq_{ADT} \mathcal{A}$, we conclude that the ADT of the thermostat is no less than 27.

Remark 2. For finding counterexample execution fragments of proposed ADT properties, the MILP approach can be applied to non-initialized rectangular SHA as well. In such applications, however, the necessity part of Theorem 4 will not hold and from the failure to find a counterexample alone we cannot conclude that the automaton satisfies the ADT property in question.

6   Conclusions

We have presented optimization-based methods for automatically verifying Average Dwell Time (ADT) properties of certain classes of hybrid systems, which provides a tool for proving (uniform) stability. We have also defined equivalence of hybrid systems with respect to ADT and have presented a simulation relation-based method for proving these equivalence relationships. The proposed methods have been applied to verify ADT of a linear, scale-independent hysteresis switch and a nondeterministic thermostat.

In this paper we examined internal stability only; however, the input and output variables of HIOA make the framework suitable for studying input-output properties of hybrid systems. Another direction of future research is to extend the ADT verification technique to probabilistic hybrid systems.

Acknowledgments. We thank Debasish Chatterjee and the anonymous reviewers for making several constructive suggestions which helped us improved the paper. In particular we thank the reviewer for suggesting Karp's algorithm as an alternative to the Bellman-Ford for solving the optimization problem of Section 4.

References

1. Branicky, M.: Multiple lyapunov functions and other analysis tools for switched and hybrid systems. IEEE Transactions on Automatic Control **43** (1998) 475–482
2. Liberzon, D.: Switching in Systems and Control. Systems and Control: Foundations and Applications. Birkhauser, Boston (2003)
3. van der Schaft, A., Schumacher, H.: An Introduction to Hybrid Dynamical Systems. Springer, London (2000)
4. Morse, A.S.: Supervisory control of families of linear set-point controllers, part 1: exact matching. IEEE Transactions on Automatic Control **41** (1996) 1413–1431
5. Hespanha, J., Morse, A.: Stability of switched systems with average dwell-time. In: Proceedings of 38th IEEE Conference on Decision and Control. (1999) 2655–2660
6. Lynch, N., Segala, R., Vaandrager, F.: Hybrid I/O automata. Information and Computation **185**(1) (2003) 105–157
7. Mitra, S., Liberzon, D.: Stability of hybrid automata with average dwell time: an invariant approach. In: Proceedings of the 43rd IEEE Conference on Decision and Control, Paradise Island, Bahamas (2005)
8. Hespanha, J., Liberzon, D., Morse, A.: Hysteresis-based switching algorithms for supervisory control of uncertain systems. Automatica **39** (2003) 263–272
9. Cormen, T.H., Leiserson, C.E., Rivest, R.L.: Introduction to Algorithms. MIT Press/McGraw-Hill (1990)
10. Livadas, C., Lygeros, J., Lynch, N.A.: High-level modeling and analysis of TCAS. In: Proceedings of the 20th IEEE Real-Time Systems Symposium (RTSS'99),Phoenix, Arizona. (1999) 115–125
11. Mitra, S., Wang, Y., Lynch, N., Feron, E.: Safety verification of model helicopter controller using hybrid Input/Output automata. In: HSCC'03, Hybrid System: Computation and Control, Prague, the Czech Republic (2003)
12. Heitmeyer, C., Lynch, N.: The generalized railroad crossing: A case study in formal verification of real-time system. In: Proceedings of the 15th IEEE Real-Time Systems Symposium, San Juan, Puerto Rico, IEEE Computer Society Press (1994)
13. Kaynar, D., Lynch, N., Segala, R., Vaandrager, F.: The theory of timed I/O automata. Technical Report MIT/LCS/TR-917a, MIT Laboratory for Computer Science (2004) Available at `http://theory.lcs.mit.edu/tds/reflist.html`.
14. Mitra, S., Lynch, N., Liberzon, D.: Verifying average dwell time by solving optimization problems (2005) Available from: `http://theory.lcs.mit.edu/ mitras/ research/hscc06-full.pdf`.
15. Williams, H.: Model building in mathematical programming. J. Wiley, New York (1990) third edition.
16. Makhorin, A.: GLPK - GNU linear programming kit (2003) Available from `http://www.gnu.org/directory/libs/glpk.html`.

Interchange Format for Hybrid Systems: Abstract Semantics

Alessandro Pinto[1], Luca P. Carloni[3], Roberto Passerone[2],
and Alberto Sangiovanni-Vincentelli[1]

[1] University of California at Berkeley, Berkeley, CA 94720
{apinto, alberto}@eecs.berkeley.edu
[2] University of Trento, Trento, Italy
roby@dit.unitn.it
[3] Columbia University in the City of New York, NY 10027-7003
luca@cs.columbia.edu

Abstract. In [1] we advocated the need for an interchange format for
hybrid systems that enables the integration of design tools coming from
many different research communities. In deriving such interchange format the main challenge is to define a language that, while presenting
a particular formal semantics, remains general enough to accommodate
the translation across the various modeling approaches used in the existing tools. In this paper we give a formal definition of the syntax and
semantics for the proposed interchange format. In doing so, we clearly
separate the structure of a hybrid system from the semantics attached to
it. The semantics can be considered an "abstract semantics" in the sense
that it can be refined to yield the model of computation, or "concrete
semantics", which, in turn, is associated to the existing languages that
are used to specify hybrid systems. We show how the interchange format
can be used to capture the essential information across different modeling approaches and how such information can be used in the translation
process.

1 Introduction

While the main concept behind the term *hybrid system* is commonly accepted by
the control theory community and the computer science community, there is a
mismatch in the interpretation of hybrid system models. The original definition
of hybrid systems captures the discrete dynamics as a graph representing a state
machine [2]. A function associates a continuous dynamics to each discrete state.
These dynamics, which are expressed in terms of differential equations, may
vary across different states. Transitions from a source state to a target state are
enabled, or triggered, by the continuous evolution of the system's variables and
each transition can also set the initial conditions for the system of differential
equations associated with the target state. Following a *denotational* approach,
control theorists use such model to complete a formal analysis of a hybrid system
and derive necessary and/or sufficient conditions for its stability, safety, and
reachability. Computer scientists, instead, use such model as a reference while

João Hespanha and A. Tiwari (Eds.): HSCC 2006, LNCS 3927, pp. 491–506, 2006.
© Springer-Verlag Berlin Heidelberg 2006

following an *operational* approach. Their main concern is to develop software programs that designers can use to simulate and verify hybrid systems. Generally, this entails the definition of a language, whose syntax defines the words and sentences that can be written in a program while its semantics defines their meaning. In fact, the language semantics should formally define the steps that an idealized computer must follow in order to produce a meaningful result while processing the program. In particular, for tools that target simulation, to define the semantics of their language corresponds to formally specify the algorithm that will produce the simulation trace. An excellent example of the definition of operational semantics of hybrid systems is given in [3].

Each language defines a *programming style* to describe hybrid systems based on its specific purpose, e.g. simulation, verification, or synthesis. Moreover, different algorithms require different data structures and the language is usually tailored to simplify the translation from the input language description to the internal data structure used by the algorithms. MODELICA, for instance, provides a language for describing systems in terms of implicit equations [4, 5]. The language is object-oriented and objects can be instantiated inside other object to model hierarchy. HYVISUAL gives a graphical syntax and a rich library of predefined actors that can be composed to model dynamical systems [6]. A hybrid system is described as a state machine in which states are refined into interconnection of continuous time actors. CHECKMATE [7], like HYSDEL [8], uses the interconnection of a state machine and a set of dynamical systems where the state machine selects one of the dynamics depending on the value of the system variables. Finally, a language also defines the class of hybrid systems that can be described. For instance, tools that target verification only allow linear dynamics and convex guards and invariants.

A system is usually described as a composition of objects. Compositionality and hierarchy are desirable features for the design of complex systems. While composing objects at the denotational level corresponds to composing functions, giving a semantically sound definition of composition in terms of a programming language is not a trivial task. The semantics of CHARON, a high-level language for modular specification of multiple, interacting hybrid systems, is indeed *compositional* in the sense that the semantics of one of its components (possibly the entire hybrid system) is entirely specified in terms of the semantics of its subcomponents [9, 10]. An interesting aspect of composition for simulation purposes is how to schedule the execution of a system across multiple interacting components. Consider, for instance, a system where component A feeds two components B and C and, furthermore, C also receives the output of B as input. After executing A, the simulator must choose whether to execute B or C first. The two possible choices would likely give different simulation results.

Another interesting issue involves solving a system of differential algebraic equations. The solution is typically represented inside a computer as a finite subset of value-time pairs (x, t). Since the computer resources are discrete and finite, two problems must be addressed: (1) how to select a subset that makes the result meaningful and (2) how to compute the value of x at time t for a generic system of differential equations without relying on the analytical solution [3]. Further, if instead of a single equation we have a system of differential and algebraic equations, then there are many variables that must be computed and the order in which equations are evaluated becomes relevant. Finally, support for expressing algebraic equations makes things more complex due to the possibility of generating algebraic loops. In fact, some languages like MODEL-ICA do not define the meaning of an algebraic loop and leave the decision of how to compute the solution of such equations to the simulation engine. Other tools like SIMULINK/STATEFLOW and HyVISUAL return an error message whenever they detect the presence of algebraic loops.

Contributions. Researchers in industry and academia have developed several tools for the simulation, verification and synthesis of hybrid systems. In their development efforts, they had to address all the important issues mentioned above and, generally, they have made different implementation decisions. In [1] we advocated the need for an interchange format for hybrid systems that makes it possible to integrate design tools coming from many different research communities. While to define the syntax of the interchange format is an important step, and there are already interesting approaches in this direction [11], the definition of its semantics is the key to enable unambiguous translation of models across tools. In order to capture all the different models, we define an *abstract* semantics that can be refined in the *concrete* semantics of each language, we specify a set of functions that can be applied to perform such refinement, and we show the effectiveness in translating to and from the interchange format. Our approach allows us to better understand the structure of the exisisting languages for hybrid systems, to capture the semantic differences among them, and to develop algorithms for interchanging models.

2 Preliminaries

Metropolis Meta-Model Interchange Format. In [1] we reviewed a number of languages and tools for hybrid systems. Based on the outcome of our comparative summary, we highlighted the differences among tools and also a set of desirable features that a language for hybrid systems should provide. We then offered a proposal for an interchange format for hybrid systems whose formal semantics is based on the Metropolis Meta-Model [12]. The main challenge in defining an interchange format is to define a language with a formal semantics that remains general enough as it provides and easy translation path to/from all other languages of interest. Accordingly, the proposed interchange format defines *processes* for the solution of equations and *media* for communicating results among processes. The way in which the computation is performed is described in a separate view of the specification that consists of a collection of schedulers. Processes, media and schedulers can be hierarchically organized as shown in Figure 1. The hierarchy of a hybrid system has three levels: the *transition level*, *the dynamical system level* and the *equation level*. At the transition level, a scheduler (TM) selects a set of continuous-time processes whose composition forms

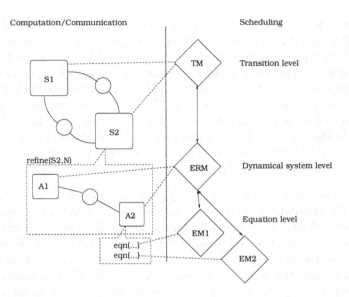

Fig. 1. Organization of the interchange format presented in [1]

a dynamical system. At the dynamical system level, a scheduler (ERM) selects a set of equations and orders their execution. At the equation level, the execution of each equation is governed by equation managers EM. Across the three hierarchical levels, the network of schedulers restricts the possible executions of the process network by (1) selecting a set of active processes at the transition level, (2) scheduling the execution of continuous time processes at the dynamical system level and (3) scheduling the solution of the equations at the equation level.

Notation Basics. For a tuple $W = (w_1, ..., w_n)$, we denote the component w_i of W with $W.w_i$. Given a variable with name v, its value is denoted by $val(v)$ where val is a valuation function. If V is the tuple $(v_1, ..., v_n)$ then $val(V) = (val(v_1), ..., val(v_n))$. If, instead, V is the set $\{v_1, ..., v_n\}$ then its valuation is the multi-set $val(V) = \{val(v_1), ..., val(v_n)\}$. For a set of variables V, the set of all possible valuations of V is denoted by $\mathcal{R}(V)$. Given a subset $D \subseteq \mathcal{R}(V)$ of the possible values of the set of variables V, and given another set $V' \supseteq V$, the lifting of D to V' is given by the operator $\mathcal{L}(V')(D) = \{p' \in \mathcal{R}(V') : p'|_V \in \mathcal{R}V\}$, where $p'|_V$ denotes the restriction of the valuation p' to only the variables in V.

Running Example. The diagram in Figure 2 represents a *half-wave rectifier circuit,* a simple electronic circuit that can be modeled as a hybrid system and will be used throughout the paper to illustrate the proposed interchange format. In particular, we model the diode by dividing the voltage across its endpoints in two regions of operation: if $v_a - v_k < 0$ the diode behaves as a constant current source of value $-I_0$; if $v_a - v_k \geq 0$ the diode behaves like a resistor of value R_d. The half-wave rectifier can be "structurally" represented by the block diagram in Figure 3. The three currents i_d, i_R and i_C must satisfy the Kirchoff's

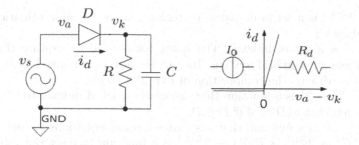

Fig. 2. Half-wave rectifier used as running example in this paper

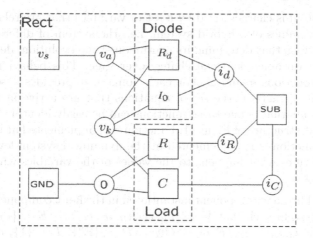

Fig. 3. Block diagram representing the half-wave rectifier

current law that states that the sum of all currents of components attached to the same node is equal to zero. This constraint is implemented by the block SUB in Figure 2.

3 Interchange Format Syntax

With the term syntax we refer to the language constructs that are provided by the interchange format to express hybrid systems. Our definitions are based on sets and functions that have a direct connection to the syntax defined in [1]. To simplify our notation, and without loss of generality, all components in our model are already instantiated and unique. The introduction of renaming functions and instantiation is straightforward in this context. We describe the syntax of a hybrid system as a tuple $H = (V, E, \mathcal{D}, I, \sigma, \omega, \rho)$ where:

- $V = \{v_1, ..., v_n\}$ is a set of variables;
- $E = \{e_1, ..., e_m\}$ is a set of equations in the variables V. An equation e_i is of the form $l(V) = r(V)$ (or equivalently $l(V) = 0$) where $l(V)$ and $r(V)$ are expressions;

- $\mathcal{D} \subseteq 2^{\mathcal{R}(V)}$ is a set of domains, or regions, of the possible valuations of the variables V;
- $I \subseteq \mathbb{N}$ is a set of indexes. The index set is used to capture the distinct dynamics of a hybrid system. Its precise role is explained in detail later when we discuss the composition of hybrid systems;
- $\sigma : 2^{\mathcal{R}(V)} \rightarrow 2^I$ is a function that associates a set of indexes to each domain and such that $\sigma(D) = \emptyset$ if $D \notin \mathcal{D}$;
- $\omega : I \rightarrow 2^E$ is a function that associates a set of equations to each index;
- $\rho : 2^{\mathcal{R}(V)} \times 2^{\mathcal{R}(V)} \times \mathcal{R}(V) \rightarrow 2^{\mathcal{R}(V)}$ is a function to reset the values of the variables (after a transition between two domains has happened) and such that $\rho(D_1, D_2, val(v)) = \emptyset$ if $D_1 \notin \mathcal{D} \vee D_2 \notin \mathcal{D}$.

A hybrid system is characterized by a set of variables that are related by equations. The dynamics of a hybrid system, i.e., the system of differential and algebraic equations that determine its continuous-time evolution, depends on the values of the variables, and can change over time. This behavior is captured by the two functions σ and ω. For each domain, σ provides a set of indexes J. The union $\cup_{i \in J} \omega(i)$ is the set of equations that are active in that domain. The components that define these functions can be easily identified in the interchange format structure of Figure 1. Function σ is implemented at the transition level while function ω is implemented at the dynamical system level. The reset function describes what happens to the values of the variables when the active domain changes.

Example 1. The Load component instantiated in the Rect component of Figure 2 is a hybrid system such that $V = \{v_R, v_C, i_R, i_C, v_k, i_d\}$, $E = \{v_R = v_C, v_R = v_k, i_C + i_R = i_d, i_R = v_R/R, i_C = C\dot{v}_C\}$, $\mathcal{D} = \{\mathbb{R}^6\}$, $I = \{1\}$, $\sigma(\mathbb{R}^6) = \{1\}$, $\omega(1) = E$. The reset function ρ acts as the identity on the values of the variables V: $\rho(\mathbb{R}^6, \mathbb{R}^6, val(V)) = val(V)$.   □

In the previous example, a continuous time system is described as a hybrid system with one domain, where all equations are active, and a trivial reset map. The following example shows a system with two domains and a more elaborated reset map.

Example 2. A bouncing ball is a hybrid system whose dynamics is described by two variables: the vertical position y and the vertical velocity v. Every time the ball touches the ground, the sign of the velocity is reversed and the value is scaled by a factor called the restitution factor, and denoted by ϵ, that accounts for the energy loss due to the impact. A bouncing ball can be modeled as a hybrid system with $V = \{y, v\}$, $E = \{\dot{v} = -g, \dot{y} = v\}$. The set of possible valuations of the variables V is partitioned in two subsets: $D_1 = \{\{val(y), val(v)\} : val(y) \leq 0 \wedge val(v) < 0\}$ and $D_2 = \overline{D_1} = \{\{val(y), val(v)\} : val(y) > 0 \vee val(v) \geq 0\}$, hence $\mathcal{D} = \{D_1, D_2\}$; $I = \{1\}$, $\sigma(D_1) = \sigma(D_2) = \{1\}$, $\omega(1) = E$. The reset function is defined as follows: $\rho(D_2, D_1, val(V)) = \{val(y), -\epsilon val(v)\}$ and $\rho(D_1, D_2, val(V)) = \{val(y), val(v)\}$.   □

Both these examples show hybrid systems where the index set is a singleton. The reason is that the dynamics of the hybrid system is the same in each domain.

Hybrid systems for which the dynamics changes depending on the domain, or hybrid systems resulting from the composition of other hybrid systems, will have non-singleton index sets.

Equation ordering and temporary variables. Before defining the composition of hybrid systems, we extend the hybrid system tuple by adding two more elements: a set of temporary variables V_t, which store the intermediate results of a computation, and a function $\pi : E \rightarrow \{1, 2, \ldots, |E|\}$ that fixes an order on the set of equations[1]. Hence, the tuple denoting a hybrid system that was defined in the previous section is extended as follows: $H = (V, V_t, E, \mathcal{D}, I, \sigma, \omega, \rho, \pi)$.

Temporary variables are used in algorithms like fixed-point computation or event detection, i.e., whenever the system of equations must be solved multiple times before reaching the desired result. Also, as discussed in the introduction, an important task in solving the systems of equations is to properly order them.

Composition of hybrid systems. Given two hybrid systems $H_1 = (V_1, V_{t1}, E_1, \mathcal{D}_1, I_1, \sigma_1, \omega_1, \rho_1, \pi_1)$ and $H_2 = (V_2, V_{t2}, E_2, \mathcal{D}_2, I_2, \sigma_2, \omega_2, \rho_2, \pi_2)$, we define their composition as a new hybrid system $H = H_1 \parallel H_2$ such that:

- the variable, equation and domain sets are the union of the corresponding sets of the two hybrid systems H_1 and H_2:

$$V = V_1 \cup V_2, \ V_t = V_{t1} \cup V_{t2}, \ E = E_1 \cup E_2, \ \mathcal{D} = \mathcal{L}(V)(\mathcal{D}_1) \cup \mathcal{L}(V)(\mathcal{D}_2)$$

  where domains are lifted as the new set of variables contains V_1 and V_2;
- the index set is the juxtaposition of the two index sets

$$I = \{1, \ldots, |I_1| + |I_2|\}$$

  which takes into account the fact that the number of dynamics and components is equal to the sum of the number of the dynamics and components coming from the two hybrid systems H_1 and H_2;
- for a given domain, the set of enabled dynamics (which is a subset of the index set) is the union of the sets of enabled dynamics of H_1 and H_2:

$$\forall D \in 2^{\mathcal{R}(V)}, \ \sigma(D) = \sigma_1(D|_{V_1}) \cup (\sigma_2 + |I_1| + 1)(D|_{V_2})$$

  where $(\sigma + k)(D) = \{n + k : n \in \sigma(D)\}$ is a shifting of the indexes;
- the set of equations associated with each given index (and, therefore, the set of equations associated with the dynamics denoted by that index) is the same as in H_1 and H_2 (after a suitable shifting of the indexes):

$$\omega(i) = \omega_1(i), \qquad \text{if } 1 \leq i \leq |I_1|,$$
$$\omega(i) = \omega_2(i - |I_1|), \quad \text{if } |I_1| + 1 \leq i \leq |I_1| + |I_2|$$

---

[1] Note that π is not necessarily an injective function. For instance, for languages like MODELICA that do not define any specific equation ordering all the equations are mapped to the same integer.

– the equations order is directly derived form the orders in H_1 and H_2. The new order must preserve the original order within the two sets E_1 and E_2 such that equations in E_1 precede equations in E_2:

$$\pi(e) = \begin{cases} \pi_1(e) & if\ e \in E_1 \\ \pi_2(e) + |I_2| + 1 & if\ e \in E_2 \end{cases}$$

– the two reset functions ρ_1 and ρ_2 give a set of new possible values for the variables as a function of the domains and the variables themselves. If the two hybrid systems share the same variables and if the two reset functions assign different values for the same domain transition, then both resets should be considered. If the two reset functions agree on the resets then only one value should be considered. This operation is implemented by the set union. Given $D_i,\ D_j \in 2^{\mathcal{R}(V)}$

$$\rho(D_i, D_j, val(V)) = \mathcal{L}(V)(\rho_1(D_i|_{V_1}, D_j|_{V_1}, val(V_1)) \cup \\ \mathcal{L}(V)(\rho_2(D_i|_{V_2}, D_j|_{V_2}, val(V_2))$$

The composition of hybrid systems is associative but it is not commutative because the equation ordering depends on the position of the hybrid systems in the composition. The n-ary composition of n hybrid systems $H_1, \ldots, H_n$ is another hybrid system $H = H_1\ ||\ \ldots\ ||\ H_n = (((H_1\ ||\ H_2)\ ||\ H_3)\ ||\ \ldots H_n)$.

Example 3. We model here the diode of Figure 2. Resistor R_d is a hybrid system such that $R_d.V = \{v_a, v_k, i_d\}$, $R_d.E = \{e_1\} = \{i_d = (v_a - v_k)/R_d\}$, $D_1 = \{p \in \mathcal{R}(R_d.V) : val(v_a) - val(v_k) \geq 0\}$ and $R_d.\mathcal{D} = \{D_1\}$, $R_d.I = \{1\}$, $R_d.\sigma(D_1) = \{1\}$, $\omega(1) = R_d.E$, $\pi(e_1) = 1$ and $R_d.\rho$ acts as the identity on the values of the variables.

The current source I_d is a hybrid system such that $I_d.V = \{v_a, v_k, i_d\}$, $I_d.E = \{e_2\} = \{i_d = -I_0\}$, $D_2 = \{p \in \mathcal{R}(I_d.V) : val(v_a) - val(v_k) < 0\}$ and $I_d.\mathcal{D} = \{D_2\}$, $I_d.I = \{1\}$, $I_d.\sigma(D_1) = \{1\}$, $\omega(1) = I_d.E$, $\pi(e_2) = 1$ and $I_d.\rho$ acts as the identity on the values of the variables.

A `diode` is the parallel composition $R_d\ ||\ I_d = diode$ that results in the hybrid system with the following properties: $diode.V = \{v_a, v_k, i_d\}$, $diode.E = \{e_1, e_2\}$, $diode.\mathcal{D} = \{D_1, D_2\}$, $I = \{1, 2\}$ $diode.\sigma(D_1) = \{1\}$, $diode.\sigma(D_2) = \{2\}$, $\omega(1) = e_1, \omega(2) = e_2, \pi(e_1) = 1, \pi(e_2) = 2$ and $diode.\rho$ acts as the identity on the values of the variables. □

In the previous example D_1 and D_2 are disjoint, therefore the ordering among the various equations is irrelevant because they will never belong to the same system of equations. The following example, instead, is a case where the order is relevant.

Example 4. The entire rectifier is the parallel composition $rect = V_s||diode||load$. The reader can verify that such composition has three domains: the entire set of possible valuation coming from the voltage source and the load, and the two domains D_1 and D_2 defined by the diode. Moreover, equations are ordered with $V_s.E$ coming before $diode.E$ which, in turn, come before $load.E$. □

4   Interchange Format Semantics

We define the semantics of a hybrid system H with a tuple $(H, B, T, \mathtt{resolve},$ $\mathtt{init}, \mathtt{update})$. The set B is a set of pairs (γ, t) where $\gamma \in \mathcal{R}(H.V)$ is a multi-set of possible values of the hybrid system variables and $t \in \mathbb{R}_+$ is a time stamp. The computation of the time stamps is controlled by the abstract finite state machine T (the *time stamper*), whose transition diagram is reported in Figure 4. Furthermore, T governs the valuation of the system variables for a given time stamp. In other words, T is in charge of both selecting the next time stamp and deciding whether the pair (val, t) can be added to the set B. Both tasks are performed by T through the invocation of three algorithms ($\mathtt{init}$, $\mathtt{resolve}$ and $\mathtt{update}$). This invocation follows a specific sequence that is encoded in the transition diagram. For different time-stamp-control methods, predicates and actions on the arcs of the abstract state machine change, while the three algorithms remain the same.

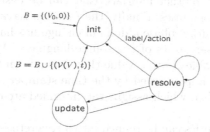

Fig. 4. Time stamper finite state machine

The set of actions that can be used to "customize" the time stamper are: $\mathtt{next}$, which selects the next time stamp, and $\mathtt{resolve}$, $\mathtt{init}$ and $\mathtt{update}$ that are each used to invoke the execution of the corresponding homonymous algorithms. The set of predicates that can be used are $\mathtt{true}$, $\mathtt{false}$, thresholds on the integration error, and $\mathtt{domainchange}$, which checks if the values of the variables $H.V$ have caused a domain change. Depending on how such predicates and actions are positioned on the arcs of the state machine, and depending on the implementation of $\mathtt{next}$, several execution semantics can be implemented that lead to different sets B.

The set B is initialized with a pair $(V_0, 0)$ representing the initial condition of the hybrid system H. In the initial state $\mathtt{init}$ the time stamper T invokes the initialization of H. This is carried out by executing the $\mathtt{init}$ algorithm. In the $\mathtt{resolve}$ state, T invokes the execution of the $\mathtt{resolve}$ algorithm that produces a valuation of all the variables of H. Finally, in the $\mathtt{update}$ state, T invokes the execution of the $\mathtt{update}$ algorithm and adds a new pair (γ, t) to the set B.

In the $\mathtt{resolve}$ algorithm (Algorithm 4), the $\mathtt{solve}$ method takes an equation and computes the value of the unknown variables at time t. Computation is done on the auxiliary set V_t. Depending on the equation ordering, it might happen that the equation admits more than one solution. In this case, $\mathtt{solve}$

Algorithm 1. `resolve` algorithm

```
resolve(t)
D' ⇐ {D ∈ 𝒟 | val(Vₜ) ∈ D}                    // Compute the set of active domains.
I ⇐ ∅, Eₜ ⇐ ∅
I ⇐ ∪_{D∈𝒟'} σ(D)                              // Collect all active dynamics and components.
for all i ∈ I do
    Eₜ = Eₜ ∪ ω(i)                              // Collect all active equations.
end for
sort(Eₜ, π)                                     // Order the equations.
for all eᵢ ∈ Eₜ  do
    solve(eᵢ,t)
end for
D'' ⇐ {D ∈ 𝒟 | val(Vₜ) ∈ D}                   // Set of active domains after the computation.
markchange(D', D'')                            // Check if the set of active domains has changed.
```

---

has several options: it could assign a special value *any* to all variables to indicate that a unique solution could not be computed; it could return a set of solutions; it could pick one solution depending on specific criteria. In fact, `solve` can be seen as another interface that can be customized depending on the source-language semantics. Finally, the function `markchange` checks if during the equation resolution phase a domain change has happened. This decision also depends on the semantics of the source language. Algorithm `init` initializes the auxiliary variables V_t to a value that depends on the reset function $H.\rho$ and on the algorithm implemented by the time stamper. Algorithm `update` executes $val(V) = val(V_t)$, which assigns the intermediate-computation values to the system variables.

The abstract semantics can be refined into a concrete semantics by fully specifying the algorithms and functions that we have described in this section. Some of them, e.g. equation ordering, are easy to specify while others like `solve` and `next` have usually very complicated implementations. Consequently, for these functions we foresee the development of standard libraries that can be selected in the translation from one language to the interchange format. Tools for simulation map directly onto the scheduling specification. Tools for verification and synthesis can also be applied by taking advantage of the trace semantics B discussed in Section 4 and of the underlying Metropolis Meta-Model [12], which defines a formal semantics for the schedulers that is suitable for analysis. The use of libraries can further simplify the analysis with the use of pre-characterized components. The Meta-Model also supports declarative properties and constraints, which can be used as links to tools and components described in other models of computation.

Back-tracking and Algebraic Loops. As shown in Figure 4, a time stamper can invoke the `resolve` algorithm of a hybrid system multiple times. It is also possible to re-initialize the system before updating the values of the variables. Such iterations can be used for back-traking or to reach a fixed-point in case of algebraic loops. Many iterations are also required for event detection. This is the main reason for having auxiliary variables and separating the resolution step from the update step as it is also defined by the *stateful* firing abstract semantics of PTOLEMY [13].

5   Partitioning Structure and Semantics

In Section 3 and 4 we defined the syntax and abstract semantics of the interchange format and we showed how the abstract semantics can be refined into many concrete semantics. In this section we show 1) how the semantics can still be formally defined by partitioning the `resolve` algorithm among components and 2) how structure and semantics can be clearly separated such that it is possible to assign different semantics to hybrid systems having the same structure. In order to keep structure and semantics well separated and also to clearly represent the hierarchical structure of a design, we partition a hybrid system into components and schedulers and we organize them into a tree that has both a structural as well as an algebraic interpretation. This section formalizes and justifies the structure of the interchange format presented in [1] and shown in Figure 1.

A hybrid system is a pair $H = (c, s)$ where c is a component and s is a scheduler. The component is a tuple $c = (V, E, \mathcal{D})$ of variables and equations while the scheduler is a tuple $s = (I, \sigma, \omega, \rho, \pi)$. Let $\mathcal{C}$ be the set of all component instances and $\mathcal{S}$ be the set of all scheduler instances for a hybrid system H. Then, $\mathcal{I} : \mathcal{C} \to \mathcal{S}$ is a bijection that for each component c returns its associated scheduler. Note that we use instances of components and schedulers instead of objects. Also note that the same symbol H has been used here and in Section 3, but this should not confuse the reader since the object and the elements in the tuple are the same, while the tuple is just partitioned in a component and a scheduler.

The n-way composition for components and schedulers can be easily derived from the composition of hybrid systems defined in Section 3. Let $||^c$ and $||^s$ be such operations, respectively. Given two hybrid systems $H_1 = (c_1, s_1)$ and $H_2 = (c_2, s_2)$, their composition is $H = H_1 \parallel H_2 = (c_1 \parallel^c c_2, s_1 \parallel^s s_2)$.

We now consider the hierarchical structure of hybrid systems. A hybrid system structure $\mathcal{H} = (C, S)$ is a pair where C is a rooted tree of components and S is a rooted tree of schedulers. $C = (C_N, C_E)$ where C_N is a set of components and $C_E \subset C_N \times C_N$ is a binary relation (the edges of the tree). If $r = (c_i, c_j) \in C_E$ we say that c_j is instantiated in c_i.

The tree of schedulers has the following structure: $S = (S_N, S_E)$ where S_N is a set of schedulers and $S_E \subset S_N \times S_N$ is a set of connections among schedulers. $S_N = T \cup S_N'$ where T is a time-stamper. The subtree induced[2] by S_N' is isomorphic to C, and the isomorphism is $\mathcal{I}$. Also, if $s \in S_N'$ is the root of such induced subtree, then $(T, s) \in S_E$ and it is the only outgoing edge of T. The input degree of T is always equal to zero.

We illustrate this concept using the example in Figure 2.

Example 5. Figure 5, which shows the structure of the rectifier, has two interpretations:

---

[2] A subgraph induced by a set of vertices of a graph G is the set of vertices together with any edge whose endpoints are both in the subset.

- it captures the organization of a design. For instance, component Diode contains two instances: component R_d and component I_0;
- it represents the parse tree of the algebraic composition

$$Rect = v_s \,\|\, Diode \,\|\, \text{GND} \,\|\, \text{SUB} \,\|\, Load = v_s \,\|\, (R_d \,\|\, I_0) \,\|\, \text{GND} \,\|\, \text{SUB} \,\|\, (R \,\|\, C)$$

□

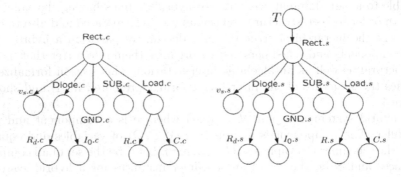

Fig. 5. Structural representation of the half-wave rectifier

Being able to capture hierarchies in a formal way is extremely important for an interchange format in order to retain the structure of the original specification and to allow "back translation" without loss of information.

Let $\mathcal{G} : S_N \to 2^{S_N}$ be a function that associates to each scheduler the set of its children, and let $\Pi : S_N \to \{1, ..., |S_N|\}$ be a global ordering of the nodes. Such ordering depends on the order in which hybrid systems are composed. Each scheduler implements three algorithms: init, resolve, and update.

The time stamper, which has been presented in Section 4, invokes the init, resolve and update functions on the "root scheduler" of S_N for a given time

---

Algorithm 2. resolve algorithm of $s \in S_N$

```
resolve(t)
children ⇐ 𝒢(s)
if children = ∅ then
    // s is a leaf, proceed to solve the equations and end recursion
    𝒟' ⇐ {D ∈ ℐ⁻¹(s).𝒟 | val(ℐ⁻¹(s).Vₜ) ∈ D}
    J ⇐ ∪_{D∈𝒟'} s.σ(D)
    Eₜ ⇐ ∪_{i∈J} s.ω(i)
    Eₜ ⇐ sort(Eₜ, s.π)
    for all eᵢ ∈ Eₜ do
        solve(eᵢ, t)
    end for
    markchange ( 𝒟', val(ℐ⁻¹(s).Vₜ) )
else
    // s is not a leaf, continue the recursion
    children ⇐ sort(children, Π)
    for all sᵢ ∈ children do
        sᵢ.resolve(t)
    end for
end if
```

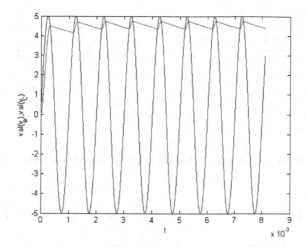

Fig. 6. Simulation result of the rectifier circuit

stamp t. In particular, the `resolve` algorithm (Algorithm 2) proceeds as follows: first, the set of all children of the scheduler s is computed. If s is a leaf then the active equations are selected and solved, while if s is not a leaf the recursion along the trees calls the `resolve` method on all children of s in the order specified by Π. Notice that Π together with ordering π defined in the leaves implement the ordering $H.\pi$.

The `init` and `update` algorithms recursively call the `init` and `update` along the tree using the ordering in Π. They simply initialize variables to a given value and copy the auxiliary variable V_t into V, respectively.

We have implemented the rectifier circuit in the METROPOLIS framework and the simulation results can be observed in Figure 6. We used a fixed step size solver as a time stamper and simulated the rectifier for $C = 10^{-4}\mu F, R = 100\Omega$, and for an input voltage $v_s(t) = 5\sin(2\pi 10^3 t)$.

6 Applications

The structure of the interchange format introduced in Section 5 and its abstract semantics are very effective in 1) representing models coming from different languages, 2) developing algorithms for the translation of models to and from different tools and 3) understanding the concrete semantics of different languages for hybrid systems.

Figure 7 a) shows the structure of a language that supports neither hierarchy nor composition. Examples of languages belonging to this class are CHECK-MATE [7], d/dt [14], and HYSDEL [8]. The tree of components has only one node which is the entire hybrid system described as a single monolithic component. In CHECKMATE, c is a switched dynamical system and a set of linear inequalities that defines the domains implemented in SIMULINK. The scheduler is implemented by a STATEFLOW chart and the time stamper is provided by the SIMULINK solvers.

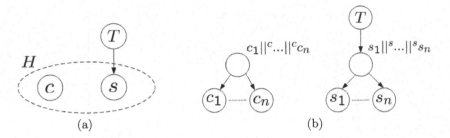

Fig. 7. Structure of the programs that do not support a) hierarchy and composition, b) hierarchy

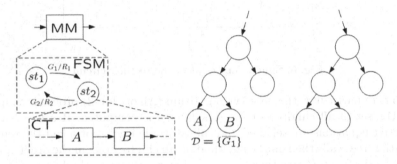

Fig. 8. Structure of a HYVISUAL modal model

Figure 7 b) shows the structure of programs that support composition but not hierarchy. Examples of languages belonging to this class are HYTECH [15] and HSIF [16]. Each child of the root node is a hybrid system. For HSIF programs, hybrid automata are ordered with respect to a dependency graph. The graph nodes are are hybrid automata and there is an edge $H_i \rightarrow H_j$ if an output of H_j is used in some equation, invariant, guard or assignment of H_j. The dependency graph, which is required to be acyclic, can be used to order the automata. Moreover, differential equations precede algebraic equations in the order.

Figure 8 shows the structure of a HYVISUAL *modal model* [17]. A modal model is described by a state machine with guards and reset maps on the edges. Each state of the state machine is refined into a continuous time system that is an interconnection of continuous time actors. The topological sort of the actor graph gives their order of execution. Also, since guards have a triggering semantics, a transition must be taken as soon as a guard is satisfied (i.e., there is a domain change as soon as the values of the variables fall outside a domain). Modal models can be connected together as indicated by the dotted lines in Figure 8. CHARON [9] programs lead to a similar structure but guard conditions have different enabling semantics: these impact the way in which the time stamper processes the `domainchange` condition in order to decide whether a pair (val, t) is valid or not.

The interchange of models between simulation tools like HYVISUAL or MODELICA and verification tools like CHECKMATE, requires to check several conditions. First, the pair (C, S) of component and scheduler trees must be compacted into only three nodes: one component, one scheduler and a time stamper. This implies the explicit computation of the parallel composition defined in Section 3. Second, the domains must be defined as intersection of polyhedra. The inverse translation leaves many choices, the most natural among which would be to have a root node connected to as many dynamical systems as there are domains in the original CHECKMATE model.

For each language, the interchange format representation also highlights semantic and structural properties such as scheduling decisions, transition semantics, composition, representation of discrete and continuous dynamics interaction, hierarchy and solution methods. Some of these properties could be unspecified or not supported in a particular language and such information is directly reflected in the interchange format. Hierarchy is one example that we have already discussed. Ordering of equations and scheduling of hybrid systems is another good example. For instance, MODELICA does not define how a system of differential and algebraic equations is sorted and solved. A MODELICA model represented in the interchange format would have $\pi(e) = 1$, $\forall e \in H.E$. The translation of such model to HSIF would first require the reduction of the tree representation to a one-level tree and then the decision on how automata and equations are ordered. On the other hand, the inverse translation would disregard such order.

7 Conclusions

We discussed the importance of an abstract semantics as the foundation of an interchange format for hybrid system design. In particular, we defined an abstract semantics for the interchange format that we first proposed in [1]. The abstract semantics can be refined into various concrete semantics, each capturing the model used by a different language for the specification of hybrid systems. We also showed how a structural representation that keeps semantics and structure clearly separated is effective in highlighting the differences among such languages. We illustrated the use of the abstract semantics and its structural representation by applying them to various existing languages. We implemented the proposed interchange format within the METROPOLIS framework and we verified with a simple example the viability of our approach. In particular, thanks to its modularity, this approach makes it possible not only to translate the model of an hybrid system from one language to another, but also to combine models written in different languages.

References

1. Pinto, A., Sangiovanni-Vincentelli, A.L., Carloni, L.P., Passerone, R.: Interchange formats for hybrid systems: review and proposal. In Morari, M., Thiele, L., eds.: HSCC 05: Hybrid Systems—Computation and Control. Volume 3414 of Lecture Notes in Computer Science., Springer-Verlag (2005) 526–541

2. Lygeros, J., Tomlin, C., Sastry, S.: Controllers for reachability specifications for hybrid systems. In: Automatica. Volume 35. (1999)

3. Lee, E.A., Zheng, H.: Operational semantics of hybrid systems. In: HSCC. (2005) 25–53

4. Fritzson, P.: Principles of object-oriented modeling and simulation with Modelica 2.1. J. Wiley & Sons (2004)

5. Tiller, M.M.: Introduction to physical modeling with Modelica. Kluwer Academic Publishers (2001)

6. Hylands, C., Lee, E.A., Liu, J., Liu, X., Neuendorffer, S., Zheng, H.: Hyvisual: A hybrid system visual modeler. Technical Report UCB/ERL M03/1, UC Berkeley (2003) available at http://ptolemy.eecs.berkeley.edu/hyvisual/.

7. Silva, B.I., Richeson, K., Krogh, B., Chutinan, A.: Modeling and verifying hybrid dynamic systems using CheckMate. In: Proceedings of 4th International Conference on Automation of Mixed Processes. (2000) 323–328

8. Torrisi, F.D., Bemporad, A.: HYSDEL - a tool for generating computational hybrid models for analysis and synthesis problems. IEEE Transactions on Control Systems Technology **12**(2) (2004) 235–249

9. Alur, R., Grosu, R., Hur, Y., Kumar, V., Lee, I.: Modular specification of hybrid systems in Charon. In Lynch, N., B.H, K., eds.: Proc. of the Third Intl. Work. on Hybrid Systems: Computation and Control. Volume 1790 of Lecture Notes in Computer Science., Springer-Verlag (2000) 6–19

10. Alur, R., Grosu, R., Lee, I., Sokolsky, O.: Compositional refinement for hierarchical hybrid systems. In Benedetto, M.D., Sangiovanni-Vincentelli, A., eds.: Hybrid Systems: Computation and Control. Volume 2034 of Lecture Notes in Computer Science., Springer-Verlag (2001)

11. Sprinkle, J., Ames, A.D., Pinto, A., Zheng, H., Sastry, S.S.: On the partitioning of syntax and semantics for hybrid systems tools. In: 44th IEEE Conference on Decision and Control and European Control Conference ECC 2005 (CDC-ECC'05), (accepted for publication) (2005)

12. Team, T.M.P.: The Metropolis meta model version 0.4. Technical Report UCB/ERL M04/38, University of California, Berkeley (2004)

13. Davis, J., Goel, M., Hylands, C., Kienhuis, B., Lee, E., Liu, J., Liu, X., Muliadi, L., Neuendorffer, S., Reekie, J., Smyth, N., Tsay, J., Xiong, Y.: Overview of the Ptolemy project. Technical Report UCB/ERL M99/37, Univ. of California at Berkeley (1999)

14. Asarin, E., Dang, T., Maler, O.: The d/dt tool for verification of hybrid systems. In: Proc. of the 14th Intl. Conf. on Computer-Aided Verification. (2002) 365–370

15. Henzinger, T.A., Ho, P.H., Wong-Toi, H.: HYTECH: A model checker for hybrid systems. International Journal on Software Tools for Technology Transfer **1**(1–2) (1997) 110–122

16. Group, M.: Hsif semantics (version 3, synchronous edition). Internal document, The University of Pennsylvania (August 22, 2002)

17. Brooks, C., Cataldo, A., Lee, E.A., Liu, J., Liu, X., Neuendorffer, S., Zheng, H.: Hyvisual: A hybrid system visual modeler. Technical Report UCB/ERL M04/18, UC Berkeley (2004) available at http://ptolemy.eecs.berkeley.edu/hyvisual/.

Model Checking of Hybrid Systems: From Reachability Towards Stability[*]

Andreas Podelski and Silke Wagner

Max-Planck-Institut für Informatik, Saarbrücken, Germany

Abstract. We call a hybrid system *stable* if every trajectory inevitably ends up in a given region. Our notion of stability deviates from classical definitions in control theory. In this paper, we present a model checking algorithm for stability in the new sense. The idea of the algorithm is to reduce the stability proof for the whole system to a set of (smaller) proofs for several one-mode systems.

1 Introduction

Consider a heating system for a plant that consists of a heater and an internal engine. The internal engine may overheat and switch off the heater temporarily, even though the desired temperature is not yet reached. This means that, starting from low, the temperature will not increase strictly monotonically but it will also decrease during some (relatively short) periods of time. We do not know when exactly such periods start and how long they will be. A sample trajectory of the system is shown in Fig. 1.

When does such a system behaves correctly? Informally, we expect that the heating system will bring the temperature of the plant to a range between 20 and 25 degrees and then keep it there, whatever the initial temperatures of the plant and the heater are and whatever the exact time points are when the controller switches the heater from "on" to "off" and back. In this paper we introduce a new notion of stability that allows one to formalize the corresponding notion of correctness. We will then give an algorithm to verify that a hybrid system is stable in our sense. The algorithm is parameterized by the constraint solver that it calls as a subroutine in each of its different steps. Using a constraint solver for linear constraints, we obtain a specific algorithm for linear hybrid systems.

The contribution of this paper is threefold. First, our notion of stability fills the need to specify correctness properties of hybrid systems that cannot be formalized by "classical" notions like asymptotic or exponential stability [2, 17, 23]. An example of such a system is the above mentioned heating system. Another example may be an aircraft that oscillates around an optimal course within a certain allowance. Any realistic model of such a system does not satisfy a stability property in the classical sense yet the performance of the aircraft is acceptable.

Second, we use existing reachability tools to reduce the stability proof for the whole system to a set of proofs for one-mode systems [12, 11, 29]. We also show (and this is

---

[*] This work was partly supported by the German Research Council (DFG) as part of the Transregional Collaborative Research Center "Automatic Verification and Analysis of Complex Systems" (SFB/TR 14 AVACS). See www.avacs.org for more information.

João Hespanha and A. Tiwari (Eds.): HSCC 2006, LNCS 3927, pp. 507–521, 2006.

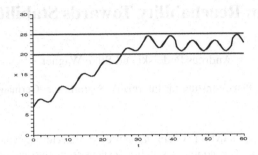

Fig. 1. Sample trajectory of the heating system

the third part of our contribution) how one can carry over techniques that are used in program analysis for termination proofs to stability proofs for one-mode hybrid systems [25, 26, 9, 4].

2   Related Work

In this section, we discuss the relation between our and classical notions of stability in control theory, and the relation between our algorithm and verification methods in control theory and model checking.

Stability is a central themes in control theory. There are many different variations of this property, such as asymptotical stability or exponential stability [2, 3, 17, 19, 21]. These classical notions of stability refer to a single equilibrium point. As we have pointed out in the introduction, stability with respect to one point does not seem to be always adequate. In the example of the heating system, where the temperature is specified by upper and lower bounds, such an equilibrium point does not even exist.

The example of the heating system shows that it is not always possible to express stability with respect to a region in terms of e.g. asymptotical stability. The other way round, asymptotical stability with respect to a point x_0 is expressible as stability with respect to *every* region $(x_0 - \varepsilon, x_0 + \varepsilon)$, for $\varepsilon > 0$. However, it does not seem clear how to compare these notions of stability. In particular we don't see how one could use existing techniques for proving classical stability (e.g. [2, 3, 18, 19, 20]) to prove that a hybrid system is stable with respect to a given region.

Verification methods for non-reachability properties (or properties that can be reduced to non-reachability) for hybrid systems have been intensively studied by both computer scientists and control theorists [32, 10, 34, 8, 27] and have lead to popular verification systems such as PHAVer [12], HSolver [29], d/dt [11] and CheckMate [7]. Stability properties (in the classical as well as in our sense) are fundamentally different from (non-)reachability. The methods used in reachability analysis are inherently not applicable to stability. This means it is not possible to check stability with existing tools for reachability.

The open problem that this paper attacks is the question whether model checking for our new definition of stability is possible. Our results together with preliminary experiments in a prototypical implementation implicate that this is possible in principle.

3 Preliminaries: Hybrid Systems and Trajectories

In this section, we rephrase the classical definitions of the syntax and semantics of hybrid systems [1, 13, 14].

A **hybrid system** is a tuple (fixed from now on)

$$A = (L, V, (jump_{\ell,\ell'})_{\ell,\ell' \in L}, (flow_\ell)_{\ell \in L}, (inv_\ell)_{\ell \in L}, (init_\ell)_{\ell \in L})$$

consisting of the following components:

1. a finite set L of locations.
2. a finite set V of real-valued variables, including a variable t that denotes the time.
3. a family $(jump_{\ell,\ell'})_{\ell,\ell' \in L}$ of formulas over V representing the possible jumps from location ℓ to location ℓ'.
4. a family $(flow_\ell)_{\ell \in L}$ of formulas over V and $\dot{V}$ specifying the continuous variable update in location ℓ. We use $\dot{V} = \{\dot{x}_1, \dot{x}_2, \ldots\}$ for the set of dotted variables. A variable $\dot{x}$ represents the first derivative of x with respect to time, i.e. $\dot{x} = dx/dt$. Especially the derivative of time t with respect to itself is always equal to 1, $\dot{t} = 1$.
5. a family $(inv_\ell)_{\ell \in L}$ of formulas over V representing the invariant condition in location ℓ.
6. a family $(init_\ell)_{\ell \in L}$ of formulas over V representing the initial states of the system.

A **state** s is a pair (ℓ, v) consisting of a location ℓ of L and a valuation v of all variables over the set V. We write Σ_V for the set of all variables valuations v and $\Sigma = L \times \Sigma_V$ for the set of all states. A set of states is also called a **region**. A valuation over the set $\dot{V}$ of dotted variables is denoted by $\dot{v}$.

Note that a linear flow formula $flow_\ell$ can also be specified over V and V' (instead of V and $\dot{V}$). A formula $flow_\ell(x_1, \ldots, t, x'_1, \ldots, t')$ represents the flow of duration $t' - t$ in location ℓ, where the values of the continuous variables change from $x_1, \ldots, t$ to $x'_1, \ldots, t'$.

A **trajectory** τ of a hybrid system A is a function mapping time points t in $\mathbb{R}^+$ to states in Σ such that the following conditions hold:

Let v be the real-valued component of τ at time point t.

1. If $\tau(0)$ has location ℓ, then $\tau(0)$ must satisfy the initial condition of that location, formally

$$\tau(0) \models init_\ell .$$

2. If v is differentiable at t, and both $\tau(t)$ and the left-limit of τ at t,

$$\lim_{t' \to t_-} \tau(t') ,$$

have an equal location ℓ, then the pair $(v, \dot{v})$ of variable valuation and valuation of the first derivatives satisfies the invariant and the flow condition of location ℓ, formally

$$(v, \dot{v}) \models inv_\ell \wedge flow_\ell .$$

3. If the left-limit of τ at t has location ℓ and $\tau(t)$ has a different location ℓ', then the real-valued component of the left-limit of τ at t must satisfy the jump condition from location ℓ to location ℓ', formally The values of the continuous variables remain unchanged during a jump.

$$\lim_{t' \to t_-} \tau(t') \models jump_{\ell,\ell'} .$$

The values of the continuous variables remain unchanged during a jump.

Example:

We take a simplified model of a temperature controller with an internal engine which we depict in Fig.2.

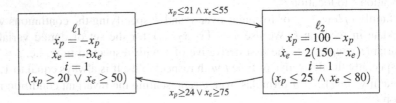

Fig. 2. Temperature controller

The temperature of a plant is controlled through a thermostat, which continuously senses the temperature and turns a heater on and off. The system has three *variables* x_p, x_e and t,

$$\mathcal{V} = \{x_p, x_e, t\} ,$$

where x_p models the temperature of the plant, x_e models the temperature of the internal engine and t models the total elapse of time. The two states "on" and "off" of the heater correspond to the two *locations* ℓ_1 and ℓ_2 of the overall system,

$$\mathcal{L} = \{\ell_1, \ell_2\} .$$

The temperature fall resp. rise is governed by differential equations. Namely, in location ℓ_1, where the heater is off, the temperature falls according to the *flow condition* $flow_{\ell_1}$.

$$flow_{\ell_1}(x_p, x_e, t, \dot{x}_p, \dot{x}_e, \dot{t}) \equiv (\dot{x}_p = -x_p \wedge \dot{x}_e = -3x_e \wedge \dot{t} = 1)$$

In location ℓ_2, where the heater is on, the temperature rises as specified by $flow_{\ell_2}$.

$$flow_{\ell_2}(x_p, x_e, t, \dot{x}_p, \dot{x}_e, \dot{t}) \equiv (\dot{x}_p = 100 - x_p \wedge \dot{x}_e = 2(150 - x_e) \wedge \dot{t} = 1)$$

The heater itself has an engine that may overheat. The heater is turned off not only when the plant gets too hot but also when the engine is overheated. We assume that a ventilator aids cooling down the engine; that is it cools down faster than it heats up. The engine is overheated if its temperature exceeds 80 degrees; if it is cooled down to 55 degrees, the heater can again be turned on.

The controller can switch the heater from "off" to "on" and back (which corresponds to switches between the modes for the overall system) according to the *jump conditions* on the edges between the two modes.

$$jump_{\ell_1,\ell_2}(x_p,x_e,t) \equiv (x_p \leq 21 \wedge x_e \leq 55)$$
$$jump_{\ell_2,\ell_1}(x_p,x_e,t) \equiv (x_p \geq 24 \vee x_e \geq 75)$$

The controller *must* switch the heater from "off" to "on" and thus trigger a switch of the locations ℓ_1 and ℓ_2 before the *invariant condition* of the location ℓ_1 is violated (i.e. before the temperature of the plant is below 20 and the temperature of the heater is below 50).

$$inv_{\ell_1} \equiv (x_p \geq 20 \vee x_e \geq 50)$$

Similarly, the controller must switch from "on" to "off" before the temperature of the plant is above 25 or the temperature of the heater is above 80.

$$inv_{\ell_2} \equiv (x_p \leq 25 \wedge x_e \leq 80)$$

4   Stability

In this section, we introduce our notion of stability and investigate its expressiveness.

Definition 1 (Stability). *We call a hybrid system stable with respect to a given region φ if for every trajectory τ there exists a point of time t_0 such that from then on, the trajectory is always in the region φ.*

$$\forall \tau \, \exists t_0 \, \forall t \geq t_0 \, : \, \tau(t) \in \varphi$$

In the example of the heating system, the correctness property we are interested in is this: whatever the initial temperature of the plant is and whatever the initial temperature of the heater is and whatever the exact time points are when the controller switches the heater from "off" to "on" and back, the temperature of the plant will finally be between 20 and 25 degrees (and it may oscillate between these bounds). We can now formalize this correctness property as the stability wrt. the region $\varphi \equiv x_p \in [20, 25]$.

We can express stability in temporal logic, in LTL or in CTL*. In CTL*, for example, one would say that *all* trajectories *finally globally* are in the region φ.

$$A(FG)\,\varphi$$

One might think of verifying stability by applying a CTL* model checker to a finite state abstraction of the given hybrid system. However, there exist no abstraction techniques that would preserve the stability property (except for trivial cases).

The following CTL formula is stronger than, but not implied by stability.

$$AF\,AG\,\varphi$$

The hybrid system below is stable with respect to the region $x = 0$. However, it does not satisfy $AF\,AG\,(x = 0)$; if the system stays in location ℓ_0 forever, it always has the option to switch to location ℓ_1 where it would go outside the region $x = 0$.

$$\xrightarrow[y=0]{x=0} \boxed{\begin{array}{c} \ell_0 \\ \dot{x}=0 \\ \dot{y}=0 \end{array}} \xrightarrow{x=0} \boxed{\begin{array}{c} \ell_1 \\ \dot{x}=\cos(y) \\ \dot{y}=1 \\ x \geq 0 \end{array}} \xrightarrow{x\leq 0} \boxed{\begin{array}{c} \ell_2 \\ \dot{x}=0 \\ \dot{y}=0 \end{array}}$$

One might think of verifying stability wrt. φ by using fixpoint iteration in order to compute the set of states satisfying the formula $\neg EG \neg EF \neg\varphi$, which is equivalent to $AF\,AG\,\varphi$. The problem here would be to find practical approximation techniques for greatest fixpoint iteration which is needed for the computation of $\neg EG$.

We will now introduce yet another property that is stronger than stability (and stronger than $AF\,AG\,\varphi$). Our algorithm to prove stability is based on this property.

Definition 2 (Strong Attractor). *We call a region φ a strong attractor of a hybrid system A if every trajectory τ of A will (1) finally reach the attractor φ and (2) once in φ it will never leave the region again.*

$$\exists t_0 \in \mathbb{R}^+ \begin{cases} \forall t < t_0 : \tau(t) \notin \varphi \\ \forall t \geq t_0 : \tau(t) \in \varphi \end{cases}$$

Our terminology refers to the notion of attractor in the theory of dynamical systems, where the *basin of attraction* is a specified region (and not necessarily the whole state space, as with strong attractors) and where trajectories are required to converge towards the given region φ (and need not finally reach φ).

The region $\varphi \equiv x \leq 0$ is not a strong attractor for the hybrid system below, which, however, satisfies the temporal property $AF\,AG\,\varphi$.

$$\xrightarrow{x\leq 0} \boxed{\begin{array}{c} \ell_0 \\ \dot{x}=1 \\ x \leq 1 \end{array}} \xrightarrow{x\geq 1} \boxed{\begin{array}{c} \ell_1 \\ \dot{x}=-1 \end{array}}$$

A hybrid system can be stable wrt. a region without having that region as a strong attractor. For example a slightly damped pendulum that oscillates around the origin with initial amplitude $x = 100$ is certainly stable wrt. $x < 1$, but the region $x < 1$ is not a strong attractor of the system. In fact, this system does not have any strong attractor at all.

5   Algorithm

In this section we describe in detail our algorithm.

The input of the algorithm is a hybrid system A and a region φ. The output is a "yes/don't know" answer. If the the answer is "yes", the system A is stable wrt. φ. If the algorithm answers "don't know", the system may be stable or unstable.

Again, our algorithm doesn't check directly whether the system A is stable with respect to the region φ, but it checks whether φ is a strong attractor of A with the whole state space as its basin of attraction, which implies stability.

The algorithm proceeds in four steps.

Step 1: Transformation $\mathbf{A} \mapsto \mathbf{A}^\tau$

The first step of the algorithm is to transform the given hybrid system into a new one. Program transformation has been used recently in program analysis for termination proofs for finite state systems and infinite programs [4, 9]. For the example of the heating system, Fig.3 shows the relevant part of the transformed system.

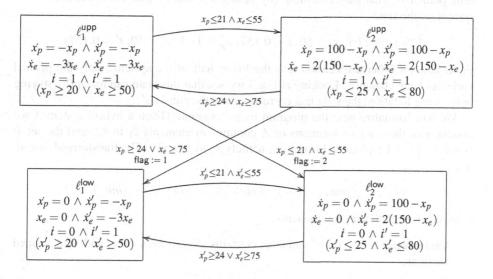

Fig. 3. Transformed system

We will explain next the characteristics of the transformation. Each state of the new system corresponds to a pair (s, s') of states s and s' of the original system. Whenever the state s' is reachable from the state s in the original system, where s is a state just after a discrete jump, then the state corresponding to the pair (s, s') is reachable in the new system. We refer to this property as *binary reachability*, i.e. a pair of states (s, s') is called binary reachable in a hybrid system A, if there exists a trajectory τ of A such that

1. s is a state on τ at time point t: $s = \tau(t)$;
2. s' is a state on τ at time point t': $s' = \tau(t')$;
3. $t < t'$.

Take the states $s = (\ell_2; x_p = 17.1, x_e = 50, t = 0.157)$ and $s' = (\ell_2; x_p = 21.4, x_e = 60, t = 0.209)$. The state s can reach the state s' (both the temperature of the plant and the engine increase in a time period of 5) in a trajectory of the original system; the trajectory starts in the initial state $s_0 = (\ell_1; x_p = 20, x_e = 80, t = 0)$. The state

$$(\ell_2^{low}; x_p = 17.1, x_e = 50, t = 0.157, x'_p = 21.4, x'_e = 60, t' = 0.209)$$

of the new system corresponds to the pair (s, s'). We will now see that this state is reachable (in the transformed system). The state

$$(\ell_1^{upp}; x_p = 20, x_e = 80, t = 0, x'_p = 20, x'_e = 80, t' = 0)$$

is an initial state of the transformed system; it corresponds to the pair (s_0, s_0). Looking at Fig.3 we see that it can reach the state

$$(\ell_1^{upp}; x_p = 17.1, x_e = 50, t = 0.157, x'_p = 17.1, x'_e = 50, t' = 0.157)$$

(namely, when the transformed system stays in the location ℓ_1^{upp} from time point 0 to time point 10). That state can jump (by taking a transition into the lower half of the system) to the state

$$(\ell_2^{low}; x_p = 17.1, x_e = 50, t = 0.157, x'_p = 17.1, x'_e = 50, t' = 0.157).$$

From now on (after a transition into the lower half of the system), only the primed variables keep changing. Looking at Fig.3 we see that this state can reach (by staying in the same location) the state that corresponds to the pair (s, s').

We will formalize next the program transformation. Given a hybrid system A we assume that the set L of locations of A contains m elements ℓ_1 to ℓ_m, and the set $\mathcal{V}$ consists of $n+1$ real-valued variables, namely x_1 to x_n and t. The transformed system A^T,

$$A^T = (L^T, \mathcal{V}^T, (jump_{\ell,\ell'}^T)_{\ell,\ell' \in L_T}, (flow_\ell^T)_{\ell \in L_T}, (inv_\ell^T)_{\ell \in L_T}, (init_\ell^T)_{\ell \in L_T}),$$

consists of the following components.

1. **Variables:** The set $\mathcal{V}^T$ of variables contains all variables of $\mathcal{V}$, and their primed versions.

$$\mathcal{V}^T = \{x_1, \ldots, x_n, t, x'_1, \ldots, x'_n, t'\}$$
$$= \mathcal{V} \cup \mathcal{V}'$$

2. **Locations:** Each location of the original system is duplicated, i.e. a location ℓ of the original system corresponds to two locations ℓ^{upp} and ℓ^{low} in the transformed system. We refer to the set of all locations from ℓ_1^{upp} to ℓ_m^{upp} as L^{upp},

$$L^{upp} = \{\ell_1^{upp}, \ldots, \ell_m^{upp}\}$$

and to the set of locations from ℓ_1^{low} to ℓ_m^{low} as L^{low}.

$$L^{low} = \{\ell_1^{low}, \ldots, \ell_m^{low}\}$$

In addition, the transformed system has a location ℓ^{init}. Altogether, the set L^T of locations of the transformed system consists of the following components:

$$L^T = \{\ell^{init}\} \cup L^{upp} \cup L^{low}.$$

3. **Initial conditions:** Initially, each variable x_i has the same value as x'_i and the value of t is equal to the value of t'; the system starts in ℓ^{init}.

$$init_\ell^T(x_1, \ldots, t') \equiv \begin{cases} \{(x_1, \ldots, t') \in \Sigma_{\mathcal{V}^T} : x_1 = x'_1 \wedge \ldots \wedge t = t'\} & \text{, if } \ell = \ell^{init} \\ false & \text{, otherwise} \end{cases}$$

4. **Jump conditions:** There are two types of switches in the transformed system. The first type occurs between two locations of $\mathcal{L}^{upp}$ or between two locations of $\mathcal{L}^{low}$, respectively. A jump condition between location ℓ_i^{upp} and location ℓ_j^{upp} for the variables $(x_1,\ldots,t,x_1',\ldots,t')$ conforms to the jump condition between the locations ℓ_i and ℓ_j of the original system A for the variables $(x_1,\ldots,t)$. Analogously, a jump condition between the locations ℓ_i^{low} and ℓ_j^{low} of the transformed system corresponds to the jump condition from location ℓ_i to ℓ_j of the original system after replacing the variables $x_1,\ldots,t$ by their primed versions.

$$(jump_{\ell,\ell'}^{\mathcal{T}})(x_1,\ldots,t,x_1'\ldots,t') \equiv \begin{cases} (jump_{\ell,\ell'})(x_1,\ldots,t) & , \text{ if } \ell,\ell' \in \mathcal{L}^{upp} \\ (jump_{\ell,\ell'})(x_1',\ldots,t') & , \text{ if } \ell,\ell' \in \mathcal{L}^{low} \end{cases}$$

The second type of switches are nondeterministic jumps either between the location ℓ^{init} and a location of $\mathcal{L}^{upp}$, or between a location of $\mathcal{L}^{upp}$ and a location of $\mathcal{L}^{low}$. A jump is always possible from the location ℓ^{init} to any location of $\mathcal{L}^{upp}$, if the invariant condition of the target location is fulfilled.

$$(jump_{\ell^{init},\ell'}^{\mathcal{T}})(x_1,\ldots,t,x_1'\ldots,t') \equiv (inv_{\ell'}^{\mathcal{T}})(x_1,\ldots,t,x_1'\ldots,t') \text{ , if } \ell' \in \mathcal{L}^{upp}$$

A jump from a location ℓ_i^{upp} to a location ℓ_j^{low} is possible whenever the jump condition from ℓ_i to ℓ_j is fulfilled in the original system. We use the variable flag $\notin \mathcal{V}^{\mathcal{T}}$ as a discrete variable that ranges over the set $\{1,\ldots,m\}$ of indices of the locations of the system. During the jump, the index j of the target location is memorized in the variable flag.

$$(jump_{\ell_i^{upp},\ell_j^{low}}^{\mathcal{T}})(x_1,\ldots,t,x_1'\ldots,t') \equiv (jump_{\ell_i,\ell_j})(x_1,\ldots,t) \wedge \text{flag} := j$$

If there is no jump outgoing from ℓ_i possible in the original system, the jump condition from ℓ_i^{upp} to ℓ_i^{low} in the transformed system is true.

$$\forall j \neq i : (jump_{\ell_i,\ell_j})(x_1,\ldots,t) \equiv \text{false} \Rightarrow (jump_{\ell_i^{upp},\ell_i^{low}}^{\mathcal{T}})(x_1,\ldots,t,x_1'\ldots,t') \equiv \text{true}$$

All other jump conditions are false.

5. **Flow conditions:** First, in the locations ℓ^{init} no flow of the continuous variables proceeds.

$$(flow_\ell^{\mathcal{T}})(x_1,\ldots,t',\dot{x}_1,\ldots,\dot{t}') \equiv \bigwedge_{x\in\mathcal{V}^{\mathcal{T}}} \dot{x} = 0 \text{ , } \quad \text{if } \ell = \ell^{init}$$

In each location ℓ_i^{upp} of $\mathcal{L}^{upp}$, the flow of the variables $x_1,\ldots,t$ in the transformed system is the same as the flow of $x_1,\ldots,t$ in the original system; each variable $x_1',\ldots,t'$ behaves exactly like its unprimed version, that is the flow of $x_1',\ldots,t'$ is equal to the flow of the original system after replacing the variables $x_1,\ldots,t$ by their primed versions $x_1',\ldots,t'$.

$$(flow_\ell^{\mathcal{T}})(x_1,\ldots,t',\dot{x}_1,\ldots,\dot{t}') \equiv flow_\ell(x_1,\ldots,\dot{t}) \wedge flow_\ell(x_1',\ldots,\dot{t}'), \text{if } \ell \in \mathcal{L}^{upp}$$

In each location of L^{low} the values of the variables $x_1,\ldots,t$ are fixed, i.e. the flow of them is constant. The variables $x'_1,\ldots,t'$ keep on evolving as before.

$$(flow^{\mathcal{T}}_\ell)(x_1,\ldots,t',\dot{x}_1,\ldots,\dot{t}') \equiv \bigwedge_{x\in\mathcal{V}} \dot{x}=0 \wedge flow_\ell(x'_1,\ldots,\dot{t}'), \quad \text{if } \ell \in L^{low}$$

6. **Invariant conditions:** For the location ℓ^{init}, the invariant condition is true.

$$(inv^{\mathcal{T}}_\ell)(x_1,\ldots,t,x'_1,\ldots,t') \equiv \text{true}, \quad \text{if } \ell = \ell^{init}$$

For a location ℓ^{upp}_i in L^{upp} (or ℓ^{low}_i in L^{low}, respectively), the invariant condition over $x_1,\ldots,t,x'_1,\ldots,t'$ is the same as the invariant condition of the original system A for ℓ_i over $x_1,\ldots,t$ (or $x'_1,\ldots,t'$, respectively).

$$(inv^{\mathcal{T}}_\ell)(x_1,\ldots,t,x'_1,\ldots,t') \equiv \begin{cases} inv_\ell(x_1,\ldots,t) & , \quad \text{if } \ell \in L^{upp} \\ inv_\ell(x'_1,\ldots,t') & , \quad \text{if } \ell \in L^{low} \end{cases}$$

Step 2: Reachability analysis

In the second step, our algorithm applies a procedure on the transformed system that computes an overapproximation of the set of all reachable states of the transformed system. The procedure is implemented by existing reachability tools as PHAVer [12], d/dt [11] or HSolver [29]. As result we obtain a set of constraints, given by a disjunction of conjunctions of linear inequalities in case of PHAVer. Each constraint is marked by the location of the transformed system it is related to. In the example of the heating system, one constraint in the output of PHAVer is e.g.

$$\ell^{low}_2: \quad flag = 2, \, x_p \geq 20, \, -x_p \geq -21, \, x_e \geq 0, \, -x_e \geq -55,$$
$$-x'_p > -20, \, -x'_e \geq -80, \, -x'_e + 300(t'-t) \geq 245, \, t'-t \geq 1,$$
$$x'_e - 140(t'-t) \geq -90, \, x'_p - 75(t'-t) \geq -75$$

In our notation, we identify a constraint with the relation that it denotes. We view a unary relation over the variables $\mathcal{V}^{\mathcal{T}}$ of the transformed system as a binary relation over the values of the variables $\mathcal{V}$ and their primed versions $\mathcal{V}'$ of the original system. Each relation refers to pairs of valuations (v,v'), where the pair of states $((\ell,v),(\ell',v'))$ is binary reachable in the original system for some ℓ and ℓ'.

In the remainder of this paper we only talk about binary relations over pairs of valuations of the original system (and not about unary relations over valuations of the transformed system) when we refer to relations in the output of the reachability tool.

Step 3: Computation of a Lyapunov-like function

For the third step of the algorithm we consider the finite subset C of disjuncts in the output of the reachability tool where the value of the variable flag is equal to the index of the location the relation is related to. These relations refer to pairs of valuations (v,v') such that the pair of states $((\ell_i,v),(\ell_i,v'))$ is binary reachable in the original system for the location ℓ_i whose index i is equal to the value of the variable flag.

We prove for each single relation c of C that its conjunction with the negation of the region φ and with $t' - t \geq \delta$

$$c \wedge \neg\varphi \wedge (t' - t \geq \delta)$$

is well-founded, where $\delta > 0$ is arbitrarily small. *Well-founded* means that there is no infinite sequence of states $s_1, s_2, s_3, \ldots$ such that each pair of consecutive states (s_i, s_{i+1}) satisfies the relation.

To show that a relation is well-founded, the algorithm applies a procedure that automatically constructs a *Lyapunov-like* function for the relation. By a Lyapunov-like function we mean a function r over the real-valued variables v, such that (1) $r(x_1, \ldots, x_n, t) \geq 0$ for all $(x_1, \ldots, x_n, t)$, and (2) $r(x_1, \ldots, x_n, t)$ $< r(x'_1, \ldots, x'_n, t')$ for all $(x_1, \ldots, x_n, t, x'_1, \ldots, x'_n, t')$ that fulfill the considered constraint. For relations that are given by conjunctions of linear inequalities, the algorithm computes a Lyapunov-like function using RankFinder [31], a tool for synthesizing linear ranking functions [24, 5, 6].

In section 6, we will prove that this condition suffices to show, that every trajectory of the original system A inevitably reaches the region φ.

For the sample formula above, we obtain the result "Ranking: $r = [1, 0, 0]$" which means that the Lyapunov-like function

$$r(x_p, x_e, t) = x_p$$

is a witness for *inevitability* of the evolution towards φ.

Step 4: Invariance
In a final step our algorithm checks the entailment between constraints in the form below, where c is a constraint given by the output of the reachability tool in Step 2 of the algorithm (the renaming of all variables in φ to their primed versions yields φ').

$$\varphi \wedge c \models \varphi'$$

This check proves that the region φ is an invariant of the system, i.e. each evolution of a state in the region leads to another state that is in the region again. For linear constraints c the algorithm uses the linear constraint solver clp(Q,R) [16] for this entailment check.

6 Correctness

In this section we investigate the correctness of the algorithm. The algorithm is sound (its definite answers are correct) and not complete (it may return don't know answers).

Soundness. The hybrid system A is stable wrt. φ if (1) every trajectory of A must reach the region φ after a amount of finite time, and (2) from then on it will never leave the region again.

Assume that the set C contains all relations c in the output of the reachability analysis for the transformed system (computed in Step 2 of the algorithm) where the value of the variable flag is equal to the index of the location the relation is related to. Again, these relations refer to pairs of valuations (v, v') such that the pair of states $((\ell, v), (\ell, v'))$ is binary reachable in the original system for the same location ℓ. We must show that property (1) holds for A if the conjunction of each relation c in the set C with the negation of the region φ and with $t' - t \geq \delta$ (for any arbitrary small $\delta > 0$)

$$c \wedge \neg\varphi \wedge (t' - t \geq \delta)$$

is well founded.

The well-known combinatorial argument used to show that this is indeed sufficient (and that the algorithm is correct) is standard in the theory of Büchi automata and has been used so far only for linear temporal properties of discrete systems [28, 25, 26].

Theorem 1. *Assume a hybrid system A and a solution of the reachability analysis for the transformed system A^τ such that the set C consists of all relations c of the solution where the value of the variable* flag *is equal to the index of the location the relation is related to.*

The hybrid system A reaches a region φ in every trajectory after a finite amount of time if C is a finite set of relations where the conjunction of each relation c of C with the negation of the region φ and with $t' - t \geq \delta$

$$c \wedge \neg\varphi \wedge (t' - t \geq \delta)$$

is well-founded for any arbitrary small $\delta > 0$.

Proof. For a proof by contradiction we assume that each relation $c \wedge \neg\varphi \wedge (t' - t \geq \delta)$, for c in c, is well-founded but A does not reach the region φ in every trajectory. Let τ be a trajectory of the system A that does not reach φ.

We consider a *discretization* of the trajectory τ by a time interval $\delta > 0$, that is the infinite sequence

$$\tau(0), \tau(\delta), \tau(2\delta), \ldots$$

The sequence is infinite, but we have only finitely many locations. Hence, at least one location, say ℓ, appears infinitely often in the sequence. This means that we can build an infinite subsequence $\tau_0, \tau_1, \tau_2, \ldots$ of the sequence $\tau(0), \tau(\delta), \tau(2\delta), \ldots$, such that all states on the subsequence have the same location ℓ.

We now use the assumption that c is a finite union of relations, say

$$C = c_1 \cup \ldots \cup c_k$$

such that for each relation c_j of c its conjunction with the negation of the region φ and with $t' - t \geq \delta$

$$c_j \wedge \neg\varphi \wedge (t' - t \geq \delta)$$

is well-founded.

We define a function g with finite range that maps an ordered pair of indices of the sequence $\tau_0, \tau_1, \tau_2, \ldots$ to the index j of the relation c_j that contains the corresponding pair of states.

$$g(k, l) \overset{\text{def}}{=} j \quad \text{if} \quad (\tau_k, \tau_l) \in c_j$$

Furthermore the function g induces an equivalence relation $\sim$ on pairs of indices of the sequence $\tau_0, \tau_1, \tau_2, \ldots$.

$$(k_1, l_1) \sim (k_2, l_2) \quad \overset{\text{def}}{\Longleftrightarrow} \quad g(k_1, l_1) = g(k_2, l_2)$$

The index of $\sim$ is finite since the range of g is finite. By Ramsey's Theorem [28], there exists an infinite set of indices K such that all pairs from K belong to the same equivalence class. Thus, there exists m and n in K, with $m < n$, such that for every k and l in K, with $k < l$, we have $(k, l) \sim (m, n)$. Let $k_1, k_2, \ldots$ be the ascending sequence of elements of K. Hence, for the infinite sequence $\tau_{k_1}, \tau_{k_2}, \ldots$ we have

$$\left(\tau_{k_i}, \tau_{k_{i+1}} \right) \in c_j \quad \text{for all } i \geq 1$$

By our assumption that τ does not reach φ, each state τ_{k_i} is not in the region φ, which yields that

$$\left(\tau_{k_i}, \tau_{k_{i+1}} \right) \in c_j \wedge \neg \varphi \quad \text{for all } i \geq 1$$

Because we have chosen a discretization of τ by δ, this is a contradiction to the well-foundedness of $c_j \wedge \neg \varphi \wedge (t' - t \geq \delta)$. □

Incompleteness. The algorithm may fail to prove the stability of a correct system (and return a don't know answer) for one of the following three reasons.

First, the output of the existing reachability tools (that we use in Step 2 of our algorithm) is only an overapproximation of the set of all reachable states (and not the set itself) due to the fact that reachability in general is undecidable.

The second point is the incompleteness of general well-foundedness tests (used in Step 3 of the algorithm). Complete tests exist only in some restricted cases (e.g. in the form of termination checkers for small classes of programs [24, 33]).

The third source of incompleteness is that the algorithm checks whether a region φ is a strong attractor of the system, which is only a sufficient but not necessary condition for stability wrt. φ; see Section 4.

7 Conclusion and Future Work

Previous notions of stability refer to a single equilibrium point. We have introduced a new notion of stability that refers to a region instead. For some cases of hybrid systems, this gives the appropriate formalization of their correctness. We have situated our notion in the landscape of related properties in control theory and model checking.

Verification methods for non-reachability properties (or properties that can be reduced to non-reachability) for hybrid systems have been intensively studied by both computer scientists and control theorists [32, 10, 34, 8, 27] and have lead to popular verification systems such as PHAVer [12], HSolver [29], d/dt [11] and CheckMate [7].

There are many methods for the verification of hybrid systems for non-reachability properties or properties that can be reduced to non-reachability; stability does not belong to them. We have given an algorithm to verify stability properties (in the new sense) for general hybrid systems. The algorithm is parameterized by the constraint solver that it calls as a subroutine in each of its different steps. Using a constraint solver for linear constraints, we obtain a specific algorithm for linear hybrid systems.

The crucial step of the algorithm is the computation of binary reachability (a precise enough approximation of the binary reachability relation). Thanks to a source-to-source transformation, this step can be implemented using an off-the-shelf tool for (unary) reachability. Future work consists of evaluating existing (or new) reachability tools in our context, where we use them not for safety but for stability.

In preliminary experiments, we have run the different steps on a number of examples (using PHAVer [12] and RankFinder [31]), including the example of the heating system. The experiments indicate a promising potential of our method.

Out of the three sources of incompleteness of our algorithm, two are inherent due to recursion-theoretic properties. The question is whether the third source of incompleteness can be circumvented by an alternative to our present definition of strong attractors and ways to compute them.

Acknowledgment

We thank Oded Maler and Thao Dang for numerous insightful discussions on reachability and stability analysis for hybrid system, Stefan Ratschan for comments and suggestions on this paper, and Li Hong and Goran Frehse for their help with the first practical experiments. We thank Oliver Theel, Martin Fränzle and their students for discussions during the AVACS meetings.

References

1. R. Alur, C. Courcoubetis, T.A. Henzinger, and P.-H. Ho. Hybrid Automata. An Algorithmic Approach to the Specification and Verification of Hybrid Systems. In Hybrid Systems: Computation and Control, 1993.
2. M.S. Branicky. Stability of hybrid systems: State of the art. In Conference on Decision and Control, 1997.
3. M.S. Branicky. Multiple Lyapunov functions and other analysis tools for switched and hybrid systems. In Trans. on Automatic Control, 1998.
4. A. Biere, C. Artho, and V. Schuppan. Liveness checking as safety checking. In Formal Methods for Industrial Critical Systems (FMICS), 2002.
5. A. Bradley, Z. Manna, and H.B. Sipma. Linear Ranking with Reachability. In Computer Aided Verification (CAV), 2005.
6. A. Bradley, Z. Manna, and H.B. Sipma. The Polyranking Principle. In International Colloquium on Automata, Languages and Programming (ICALP), 2005.
7. A. Chutinan, A. Fehnker, Z. Han, J. Kapinski, R. Kumar, B.H. Krogh, and O. Stursberg. CheckMate, http://www.ece.cmu.edu/ webk/checkmate.
8. E.M. Clarke, A Fehnker, Z. Han, B. Krogh, O. Stursberg, and M. Theobald. Verification of Hybrid Systems Based on Counterexample-Guided Abstraction Refinement. In Tools and Algorithms for the Construction and Analysis of Systems (TACAS), 2003.
9. B. Cook, A. Podelski, A. Rybalchenko. Termination Proofs for Systems Code. Submitted to Conference on Programming Language Design and Implementation (PLDI), 2006.
10. M. Colon, S. Sankaranarayanan, and H. Sipma. Linear invariant generation using non-linear constraint solving. In Computer Aided Verification (CAV), 2003.

11. T. Dang and O. Maler. d/dt, http://www-verimag.imag.fr/ tdang/Tool-ddt/ddt.html.
12. G. Frehse. PHAVer , http://www.cs.ru.nl/ goranf.
13. T.A. Henzinger. The Theory of Hybrid Automata. In Logic in Computer Science (LICS), 1996.
14. T.A. Henzinger, P.-H. Ho, and H. Wong-Toi. Algorithmic analysis of nonlinear hybrid systems. In Automatic Control, 1998.
15. T. Henzinger, P.-H. Ho, and H. Wong-Toi. HyTech, http://www-cad.eecs.berkeley.edu/ tah/HyTech.
16. C. Holzbaur. clp(Q,R), http://www.ai.univie.ac.at/clpqr.
17. D. Liberzon. Switching in Systems and Control. Birkhäuser, 2003.
18. D. Liberzon, and A.A. Agrachev. Lie-algebraic stability criteria for switched systems. In Control and Optimization, 2001.
19. D. Liberzon, J.P. Hespanha, and A.S. Morse. Stability of switched systems: a Lie-algebraic condition. In Systems and Control Letters, 1999.
20. D. Liberzon, and M. Margaliot. Lie-algebraic stability conditions for nonlinear switched systems and differential inclusions, Systems and Control Letters, to appear.
21. V. Lakshmikantham, S. Leela, and A.A. Martynyuk. Practical Stability of Nonliear Systems. World Scientific Pub Co Inc, 1990.
22. A. Papachristodoulou, and S. Prajna. On the Construction of Lyapunov Functions using the Sum of Squares Decomposition. In Conference on Decision and Control (CDC), 2002.
23. S. Pettersson. Analysis and Design of Hybrid Systems. Ph.D. Thesis, Chalmers University of Technology, Göteborg, Sweden, 1999.
24. A. Podelski, and A. Rybalchenko. A complete Method for the Synthesis of Linear Ranking Functions. In Verification, Model Checking and Abstract Interpretation (VMCAI), 2004.
25. A. Podelski, and A. Rybalchenko. Transition invariants. In Logic in Computer Science (LICS), 2004.
26. A. Podelski, and A. Rybalchenko. Transition Predicate Abstraction and Fair Termination. In Principles of Programming Language (POPL), 2005.
27. S. Prajna, and A. Jadbabaie. Safety Verification of Hybrid Systems Using Barrier Certificates. In Hybrid Systems: Computation and Control, 2004.
28. F.P. Ramsey. On a problem of formal logic. In Proc. of the London Mathematical Society 30, 1930.
29. S. Ratschan, and Z. She. HSolver, http://www.mpi-sb.mpg.de/ ratschan/hsolver.
30. S. Ratschan, and Z. She. Safety Verification of Hybrid Systems by Constraint Propagation Based Abstraction Refinement. In Hybrid Systems: Computation and Control, 2005.
31. A. Rybalchenko. RankFinder, http://www.mpi-inf.mpg.de/ rybal/rankfinder.
32. S. Sankaranarayanan, H. Sipma, and Z. Manna. Constructing Invariants for Hybrid Systems. In Hybrid Systems: Computation and Control, 2004.
33. A. Tiwari. Termination of linear programs. In Computer Aided Verification (CAV), 2004.
34. A. Tiwari, H. Ruess, H. Saidi and N. Shankar. Automatic Generation of Invariants. In Tools and Algorithms for the Construction and Analysis of Systems (TACAS), 2001.

A Feedback Control Motivation for Generalized Solutions to Hybrid Systems*

Ricardo G. Sanfelice, Rafal Goebel, and Andrew R. Teel

Center for Control, Dynamical Systems, and Computation,
Department of Electrical and Computer Engineering,
University of California, Santa Barbara, CA 93106-9560
{rsanfelice, rafal, teel}@ece.ucsb.edu

Abstract. Several recent results in the area of robust asymptotic stability of hybrid systems show that the concept of a generalized solution to a hybrid system is suitable for the analysis and design of hybrid control systems. In this paper, we show that such generalized solutions are exactly the solutions that arise when measurement noise is present in the system.

1 Introduction

1.1 Motivation

Hybrid dynamical systems comprise a rich class of systems in which the state can both evolve continuously (flow) and discontinuously (jump). Over the last ten years or more, in research areas such as computer science, feedback control, and dynamical systems, researchers have given considerable attention to modeling and solution definitions for hybrid systems. Some notable references include [41, 38, 4, 9, 8, 28, 40].

In the paper [19], motivated by robust stability issues in hybrid control systems, the authors introduced the notion of a generalized solution to a hybrid system and outlined some stability theory consequences that followed from this solution concept. These included results on "for free" robustness of stability, a generalization of LaSalle's invariance principle, and the existence of smooth Lyapunov functions for asymptotically stable hybrid systems. More details about these results and generalizations were given in the subsequent conference papers [20] (see also [21]), [35] and [10], respectively.

The purpose of the current paper is to motivate further the use of generalized hybrid solutions by considering the effect of arbitrary small measurement noise in hybrid control systems. In this paper we show that, for hybrid systems arising from using hybrid feedback control, generalized hybrid solutions agree with the

* Research partially supported by the Army Research Office under Grant no. DAAD19-03-1-0144, the National Science Foundation under Grant no. CCR-0311084 and Grant no. ECS-0324679, and by the Air Force Office of Scientific Research under Grant no. F49620-03-1-0203.

João Hespanha and A. Tiwari (Eds.): HSCC 2006, LNCS 3927, pp. 522–536, 2006.

limits (in an appropriate sense) of solutions generated by arbitrarily small measurement noise in the hybrid control system. This result generalizes to hybrid
systems a similar result for differential equations initially reported by Hermes
in [23] and expanded upon by Hàjek in [22]. It contains, as a special case, an
analogous result for difference equations that, to the best of our knowledge, has
not appeared in the literature.

1.2   Controversy?

In continuous-time systems, generalized solutions to discontinuous differential
equations are shunned at times because using such a solution precludes solving
certain nonlinear control problems. For example, for asymptotically controllable
nonlinear systems, it is possible to solve the stabilization problem by state feedback when using weak notions of solution for discontinuous differential equations
(e.g., Caratheodory solutions, Euler solutions, etc.) (see [13]) but it is impossible to solve this problem in general when using generalized solutions such as
those due to Krasovskii [25], Filippov [18], or Hermes [23]; for further details
see [11].

The feedback stabilization problem does not provide the same motivation for
avoiding generalized solutions to hybrid systems. Indeed, it is possible to robustly
stabilize asymptotically controllable nonlinear systems using hybrid feedback
and using generalized solutions to hybrid systems. See, for example, [31].

Despite our opinion that the use of generalized solutions to hybrid systems
will never diminish the capabilities of hybrid control, we would not be surprised
to see some resistance to the use of generalized hybrid solutions to hybrid control
systems. We expect the main sticking point to be how the notion of generalized
solutions affects the "semantics" of a hybrid control system. We now elaborate
on what we mean.

For the purposes of this paper, a hybrid system is specified by the data $\mathcal{H} =
(f, g, C, D, O)$ where the open set $O \subset \mathbb{R}^n$ is the state space of the hybrid system
$\mathcal{H}$, f is a function from C to $\mathbb{R}^n$ called the "flow map", g is a function from D
to $C \cup D$ called the "jump map", C is a subset of O called the "flow set" and
indicates where in the state space flow may occur, D is a subset of O called the
"jump set" and indicates from where in the state space jumps may occur. At
times, we write the data in the suggestive form

$$\mathcal{H} \begin{cases} \dot{x} = f(x) & x \in C \\ x^+ = g(x) & x \in D \end{cases} \tag{1}$$

where x is the state of the hybrid system (with discrete modes already embedded
in it). Several models for hybrid systems available in the literature (see e.g.
[8], [28], [40]), under certain assumptions, can be fit in such framework. The
particular concept of a solution to a hybrid system we use will be made precise
in Section 2; it is not relevant for the discussion below.

Generalized solutions to $\mathcal{H}$ are solutions to a hybrid system with regularized
data $\overline{\mathcal{H}} = (\overline{f}, \overline{g}, \overline{C}, \overline{D}, O)$, where $\overline{f}$ and $\overline{g}$ are constructed from f and g in a
manner that will be made precise later (see Definition 3) and $\overline{C}$ and $\overline{D}$ denote

the closures of C and D, respectively, relative to O. In particular this means that if $C \cup D = O$ then $\overline{C} \cap \overline{D}$ is not empty[1] even if $C \cap D$ is empty. It turns out that many models of hybrid systems insist on having $C \cap D$ empty. For example, one has $C = O \backslash D$ in the definition of state-dependent impulsive systems in [5] (see also [6] and [12]). The condition $C = O \backslash D$ is also used in many of the hybrid models considered in [8]. Making $C \cap D$ empty is one way to guarantee that jumps are enforced in the jump set rather than simply enabled. (Some researchers use the phrases " 'as is' semantics" and "enabling semantics" for these two respective situations, see [36].) Moreover, it is a way to guarantee that solutions, if they exist, are unique when the flow map f is locally Lipschitz. See, for example, [29].

As we pointed out in [19], changing C and D to their relative closures can have a dramatic effect on the solutions to the hybrid control system. For example, if D has measure zero, perhaps being a surface on which jumps are enforced, and $C = O \backslash D$ (see, for example, the model of reset control systems used in [6] and the references therein) then the relative closure of C will be equal to the entire state space. This may enable solutions that never jump, circumventing the reason for hybrid control in the first place. However, the point we are making in this paper is that the new behavior that appears when taking the relative closures can manifest itself due to measurement noise in a feedback control system. In this sense, this new behavior should be taken into account.

There are many motivations for not taking the flow set C and the jump set D to be sets that are closed relative to O in the definition of a hybrid system. However, in the context of hybrid control systems, we hope that the robust stability motivation given in [19], the solution properties reported in [20], the stability theory corollaries reported in [20] and [35], and the new results reported here on the equivalence between generalized solutions and the limit of solutions due to measurement noise continue to motivate the development of hybrid control system models that use jump and flow sets that are closed relative to the state space. An example in this direction is the work of [42, 30] which revisits the reset control systems considered in [6] and finds a natural definition of the flow set and jump set so that they are closed and yet still force jumps at the appropriate locations in the state space.

2   Definition of Generalized Solutions

In what follows we write $\mathbb{R}_{\geq 0}$ for $[0, +\infty)$, $\mathbb{N}$ for $\{0, 1, 2, ...\}$, and $|\cdot|$ for the Euclidean vector norm.

2.1   Generalized Time Domain

In what could be described as the "classical" approach to hybrid systems, a solution to $\mathcal{H} = (f, g, C, D, O)$ is, vaguely, a piecewise continuous function ξ that

---

[1] This is true unless either C is empty or D is empty, in which case the original system was not truly hybrid in the first place.

is left-continuous and such that, on each interval of continuity satisfies $\xi(t) \in C$ and $\dot{\xi} = f(\xi(t))$, while at each point τ of discontinuity satisfies $\lim_{t \to \tau^-} \xi(t) \in D$ and $\xi(\tau) = g(\lim_{t \to \tau^-} \xi(t))$ (so, more compactly, $\xi^- \in D$, $\xi^+ = g(\xi^-)$). By design, such concept of a solution excludes multiple jumps at a single time instant. Furthermore, it makes it troublesome (or impossible) to discuss limits of solutions; see Example 1. These issues can be overcome by using a "generalized" time domain, as defined below.

Definition 1 (hybrid time domain). *A subset* $\mathcal{D} \subset \mathbb{R}_{\geq 0} \times \mathbb{N}$ *is a* compact hybrid time domain *if*

$$\mathcal{D} = \bigcup_{j=0}^{J-1} ([t_j, t_{j+1}], j)$$

for some finite sequence of times $0 = t_0 \leq t_1 \leq t_2 \ ... \leq t_J$. *It is a* hybrid time domain *if for all* $(T, J) \in \mathcal{D}$, $\mathcal{D} \cap ([0,T] \times \{0, 1, ...J\})$ *is a compact hybrid domain.*

Hybrid time domains are similar to hybrid time trajectories in [28],[29], and [3], and to the concept of time evolution in [40], but give a more prominent role to the number of jumps j (c.f. the definition of hybrid time set by Collins in [15]). On each hybrid time domain there is a natural ordering of points: we write $(t, j) \preceq (t', j')$ for $(t, j), (t', j') \in \mathcal{D}$ if $t \leq t'$ and $j \leq j'$.

Definition 2 (hybrid arc). *A* hybrid arc *is a pair* $(x, \operatorname{dom} x)$ *consisting of a hybrid time domain* $\operatorname{dom} x$ *and a function* x *defined on* $\operatorname{dom} x$ *that is locally absolutely continuous in* t *on* $\operatorname{dom} x \cap (\mathbb{R}_{\geq 0} \times \{j\})$ *for each* $j \in \mathbb{N}$.

We will not mention $\operatorname{dom} x$ explicitly, and understand that with each hybrid arc x comes a hybrid time domain $\operatorname{dom} x$. In this way, hybrid arcs x are parameterized by $(t, j) \in \operatorname{dom} x$, with $x(t, j)$ being the value of x at the "hybrid instant" given by (t, j). A hybrid arc ξ is said to be *nontrivial* if $\operatorname{dom} \xi$ contains at least one point different from $(0, 0)$, *complete* if $\operatorname{dom} \xi$ is unbounded, and *Zeno* if it is complete but the projection of $\operatorname{dom} \xi$ onto $\mathbb{R}_{\geq 0}$ is bounded.

Example 1. Consider a hybrid system on $\mathbb{R}^2$ given by $D = (0, 1) \times \{0\}$, $C = \mathbb{R}^2 \setminus D$, $f(x_1, x_2) = (x_2, -x_1)$, $g(x) = x/2$. For any point ξ^0 with $0 < |\xi^0| < 1$, $\xi^0 \notin D$, a "classical" solution from ξ^0 (the solution is unique!) rotates clockwise until it hits D, then via a jump has its magnitude divided by 2, then rotates again for time 2π until it jumps again, etc; see Figure 1(a). In the presence of arbitrarily small noise, a "classical" solution may jump almost immediately after the first jump. That is, if τ is the time of the first jump, a solution to $\dot{x} = f(x+e)$, $x \in C$ while $x^+ = g(x^- + e^-)$, $x^- \in D$ will jump at τ and then again when $x_2 = -\varepsilon$, if one considers the noise $e(t) = (0, 0)$ if $t \leq \tau$, $e(t) = (0, \varepsilon)$ for $t > \tau$. In this fashion, one can in fact construct a "classical" solution and arbitrarily small noise so that the solution jumps arbitrarily many times (even infinitely many) in arbitrary short time (so it may be a Zeno solution). One can then ask what the limit of such solutions is (with the noise size decreasing to 0), and it would be reasonable to expect that the limit is a solution that jumps infinitely

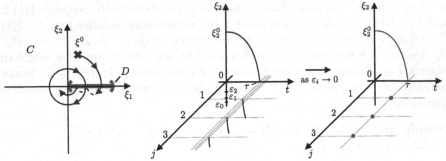

(a) One possible "classical" solution

(b) Convergence of solutions when the noise approaches zero. The value of the noise e at the i-th jump is given by $(0, \varepsilon_i)$ where $\varepsilon_i \to 0$ as $i \to \infty$.

Fig. 1. Solutions and their convergence under the presence of measurement noise for the system in Example 1

many times at time τ. Figure 1(b) shows this on hybrid time domains. Of course, such solution is not a "classical" solution, in fact, it can not be represented using regular time. However, it is a hybrid arc (in the sense of Definition 2) defined on a hybrid time domain.

2.2   Generalized Solutions a La Krasovskii

The regularization of the hybrid system $\mathcal{H}$ is defined below. We remind the reader that for a set $C \subset O$, its closure relative to O is equal to the closure of C intersected with O, and is the smallest relatively closed subset of O that contains C.

Definition 3 (regularized hybrid system $\overline{\mathcal{H}}$). *Given a hybrid system $\mathcal{H} = (f, g, C, D, O)$, its regularization (a la Krasovskii) is denoted by $\overline{\mathcal{H}} = (\overline{f}, \overline{g}, \overline{C}, \overline{D}, O)$ where, for every $x \in O$,*

$$\overline{f}(x) := \bigcap_{\delta > 0} \overline{co} f((x + \delta \mathbb{B}) \cap C), \quad \overline{g}(x) := \bigcap_{\delta > 0} \overline{g((x + \delta \mathbb{B}) \cap D)} \quad (2)$$

and $\overline{C}, \overline{D}$ are the relative closures of the sets C, D with respect to the state space O, respectively.

Regarding the function f, the regularization corresponds to the one proposed by Krasovskii in [26] for discontinuous differential equations. (An equivalent description of $\overline{f}(x)$ would say that it is the smallest closed convex set containing all limits of $f(x_i)$ as $x_i \to x$, $x_i \in C$.) We note that the regularization of f as proposed by Filippov in [18] ignores the behavior of f on sets of measure zero, and thus proves to be unsuitable for hybrid systems (and even for constrained differential equations). Indeed, for example, a set C with zero measure leads to an "empty" regularization. Regarding g, the regularization is the one used in [24]; due to the nature of discrete time, the convexification is not needed.

Following the compact form for hybrid systems $\mathcal{H} = (f, g, C, D, O)$ given in (1), we can write its regularized version $\overline{\mathcal{H}} = (\overline{f}, \overline{g}, \overline{C}, \overline{D}, O)$ as

$$\overline{\mathcal{H}} \begin{cases} \dot{x} \in \overline{f}(x) & x \in \overline{C} \\ x^+ \in \overline{g}(x) & x \in \overline{D}. \end{cases} \tag{3}$$

Note that the differential and difference equations in $\mathcal{H}$ are replaced by differential and difference inclusions, since $\overline{f} : O \rightrightarrows \mathbb{R}^n$, $\overline{g} : O \rightrightarrows O$, by their very definitions, are in general set-valued mappings and not functions. A formal definition of Krasovskii solutions follows.

Definition 4 (hybrid Krasovskii solution to $\mathcal{H}$). *A hybrid arc $\psi : \mathrm{dom}\,\psi \to O$ is a hybrid Krasovskii solution to the hybrid system $\mathcal{H} = (f, g, C, D, O)$ with regularization given by $\overline{\mathcal{H}} = (\overline{f}, \overline{g}, \overline{C}, \overline{D}, O)$ if $\psi(0, 0) \in \overline{C} \cup \overline{D}$ and:*

(K1) for all $j \in \mathbb{N}$ and almost all t such that $(t, j) \in \mathrm{dom}\,\psi$,

$$\psi(t, j) \in \overline{C}, \quad \dot{\psi}(t, j) \in \overline{f}(\psi(t, j)); \tag{4}$$

(K2) for all $(t, j) \in \mathrm{dom}\,\psi$ such that $(t, j + 1) \in \mathrm{dom}\,\psi$,

$$\psi(t, j) \in \overline{D}, \quad \psi(t, j + 1) \in \overline{g}(\psi(t, j)). \tag{5}$$

Under minor assumptions on f and g, the system $\overline{\mathcal{H}} = (\overline{f}, \overline{g}, \overline{C}, \overline{D}, O)$ has the regularity properties (stated below, in Theorem 1) that were imposed on the hybrid systems by the authors et al. in [19] and in [20] and led to results on sequential compactness of the sets of solutions to hybrid systems. In particular, such properties guarantee that an appropriately understood limit of a sequence of solutions to a hybrid system is itself a solution.

A function $\phi : O \to \mathbb{R}^n$ (or a set-valued mapping $\phi : O \rightrightarrows \mathbb{R}^n$) is locally bounded on O if for each compact set $K \subset O$ there exists a compact set $K' \subset \mathbb{R}^n$ such that $\phi(K) \subset K'$. It is locally bounded with respect to O on O if we request that $K' \subset O$.

Assumption 1. *The function f is locally bounded on O. The function g is locally bounded with respect to O on O.*

A set valued mapping $\phi : O \rightrightarrows \mathbb{R}^n$ (or $\phi : O \rightrightarrows O$) is outer semicontinuous if for any sequence $\{x_i\}_{i=1}^{\infty}$ with $\lim_{i \to \infty} x_i = x \in O$ and any sequence $\{y_i\}_{i=1}^{\infty}$ with $y_i \in \phi(x_i)$ and $\lim_{i \to \infty} y_i = y$ we have $y \in \phi(x)$.

Theorem 1 (basic properties of $\overline{\mathcal{H}}$). *Under Assumption 1, the regularized hybrid system $\overline{\mathcal{H}} = (\overline{f}, \overline{g}, \overline{C}, \overline{D}, O)$ satisfies*

(A0) $O \subset \mathbb{R}^n$ is an open set.
(A1) $\overline{C}$ and $\overline{D}$ are relatively closed sets in O.

(A2) $\overline{f} : O \rightrightarrows \mathbb{R}^n$ *is outer semicontinuous and locally bounded, and* $\overline{f}(x)$ *is nonempty and convex for all* $x \in \overline{C}$.

(A3) $\overline{g} : O \rightrightarrows O$ *is outer semicontinuous and* $\overline{g}(x)$ *is nonempty for all* $x \in \overline{D}$.

One of the benefits of these properties is that, for systems that possess them, very general conditions for existence of solutions can be given, and maximal solutions behave as expected: that is, they are either complete or "blow up" in finite hybrid time (a solution is complete if its domain is unbounded). More specifically, under Assumption 1, and hence in presence of the properties listed in Theorem 1, the following is true: if $\psi^0 \in D$ or the following condition holds:

(VC) $\psi^0 \in C$ and for some neighborhood U of ψ^0, for all $\psi' \in U \cap C$, $T_C(\psi') \cap F(\psi') \neq \emptyset$,

then there exists a nontrivial Krasovskii solution ψ to $\mathcal{H}$ with $\psi(0,0) = \psi^0$. If (VC) holds for all $\psi^0 \in C \backslash D$, then for any maximal solution ψ with $\psi(0,0) = \psi^0$ (a Krasovskii solution ψ is said to be *maximal* if there does not exist another Krasovskii solution ψ' such that ψ is a truncation of ψ' to some proper subset of dom ψ') at least one of the following statements is true:

  (i) ψ is complete;
 (ii) ψ eventually leaves every compact subset of O: for any compact $K \subset O$, there exists $(T, J) \in$ dom ψ such that for all $(t, j) \in$ dom ψ with $(T, J) \prec (t, j)$, $\psi(t, j) \notin K$;
(iii) for some $(T, J) \in$ dom ψ, $(T, J) \neq (0, 0)$, we have $\psi(T, J) \notin C \cup D$.

If additionally

(VD) for all $\psi^0 \in D$, $G(\psi^0) \subset C \cup D$,

then case (iii) above does not occur. For details, see [21, Proposition 2.5].

Note that the viability condition (VC) for the continuous evolution is automatically satisfied at each point ψ^0 in the interior of C. Therefore, when $C \cup D = O$ (a condition that is common in many models for hybrid systems, see the Introduction), (VC) holds for all $\psi^0 \in C \setminus D$ since $C \setminus D = O \setminus D$ and the latter set is open. Consequently, if $C \cup D = O$, for all $\psi^0 \in O$ there exists a nontrivial solution ψ with $\psi(0,0) = \psi^0$.

Example 2. Consider the system from Example 1. Since the set D is thin, arbitrarily small noise can cause "classical" solutions, or solutions understood as hybrid arcs satisfying (1), starting from initial points ξ^0 with $0 < |\xi^0| < 1$, $\xi \notin D$, to miss D and never jump. On the other hand, arbitrarily small noise can cause solutions from ξ^0 with $|\xi^0| = 1$ to jump (to a point near $(0.5, 0)$) when the solution is near $(1, 0)$. Finally, once a solution ξ is such that $0 < |\xi(t)| < 1$, arbitrarily small noise can cause it to miss D and rotate, jump several times in arbitrarily short time, or display any combination of these behaviors. (So in particular, when limits of such solutions under vanishing noise are considered, uniqueness – present for "classical" solutions – is lost.)

Such potential effects of noise on the system are captured by its Krasovskii regularization. Here, we get $\overline{C} = \mathbb{R}^2$, $\overline{D} = [0, 1] \times \{0\}$, while $\overline{f} = f$, $\overline{g} = g$. The fact that $\overline{C} = \mathbb{R}^2$ results in Krasovskii solutions that only flow, or rotate around the origin an arbitrary number of times in between jumps. The point $(1, 0)$ being in $\overline{D}$ leads to solutions starting with $|\xi(0)| = 1$ that jumps at some time. These features, and the generality of hybrid time domains, capture the behavior of the original system under (arbitrarily small) noise.

2.3   Generalized Solutions a La Hermes

To define hybrid Hermes solutions to a hybrid system, we need a concept of convergence of hybrid arcs that admits sequences of arcs with potentially different domains. Consequently, we will rely on graphical convergence. Given a hybrid arc x with domain $\operatorname{dom} x$, its graph is the set

$$\operatorname{gph} x := \{(t, j, x(t, j)) \in \mathbb{R}_{\geq 0} \times \mathbb{N} \times O \mid (t, j) \in \operatorname{dom} x\} \ .$$

A sequence of hybrid arcs $\{x_i\}_{i=1}^{\infty}$ *converges graphically* to a hybrid arc x if the sequence of graphs $\{\operatorname{gph} x_i\}_{i=1}^{\infty}$ converges to $\operatorname{gph} x$ in the sense of set convergence. The latter concept is well-established and often used in set-valued and nonsmooth analysis; see [32, 2]. For precise definitions of general set and graphical convergence we refer the reader to [32, Chapters 4,5]; below we state a version of [32, Exercise 5.34] relevant for our purposes. For further details on graphical convergence of hybrid arcs we recommend [20]. Finally, we add that graphical convergence is closely related to convergence in the Skorokhod topology used in [15].

Lemma 1 (graphical convergence of hybrid arcs). *Let x be a hybrid arc with compact $\operatorname{dom} x$, and let (T, J) be the supremum of $\operatorname{dom} x$. A sequence $\{x_i\}_{i=1}^{\infty}$ of hybrid arcs with $\operatorname{dom} x_i \subset \mathbb{R}_{\geq 0} \times \{0, 1, \dots, J\}$, $i = 1, 2, \dots$, converges graphically to x if and only if for all $\varepsilon > 0$, there exists $i_0 \in \mathbb{N}$ such that, for all $i > i_0$*

(a) for all $(t, j) \in \operatorname{dom} x$ there exists s such that $(s, j) \in \operatorname{dom} x_i$, $|t - s| < \varepsilon$, and $|x(t, j) - x_i(s, j)| < \varepsilon$,

(b) for all $(t, j) \in \operatorname{dom} x_i$ there exists s such that $(s, j) \in \operatorname{dom} x$, $|t - s| < \varepsilon$, and $|x_i(t, j) - x(s, j)| < \varepsilon$.

In particular, a sequence $\{x_i\}_{i=1}^{\infty}$ of hybrid arcs with $\operatorname{dom} x_i \subset \operatorname{dom} x$, $i = 1, 2, \dots$, converges graphically to x if for all $\varepsilon > 0$ there exists $i_0 \in \mathbb{N}$ such that, for all $i > i_0$, all $(t, j) \in \operatorname{dom} x$, we have $(t, j) \in \operatorname{dom} x_i$ and $|x(t, j) - x_i(t, j)| < \varepsilon$.

Equipped with graphical convergence, we generalize the definition of Hermes solutions discussed by Hermes in [23] and later defined by Hàjek in [22].

Definition 5 (hybrid Hermes solution to $\mathcal{H}$). *A hybrid arc $\varphi : \operatorname{dom} \varphi \to O$ is a hybrid Hermes solution to $\mathcal{H} = (f, g, C, D, O)$ if for each compact hybrid time domain $\mathcal{D} \subset \operatorname{dom} \varphi$ and the truncation $\varphi^{\mathcal{D}}$ of φ to $\mathcal{D}$, there exists a sequence of hybrid arcs $\varphi_i : \operatorname{dom} \varphi_i \to O$ and measurable functions $e_i : \operatorname{dom} e_i \to \mathbb{R}^n$, $\operatorname{dom} e_i = \operatorname{dom} \varphi_i$, that satisfy, for each i,*

(H1) for all $j \in \mathbb{N}$ and almost all t such that $(t, j) \in \operatorname{dom} \varphi_i$,

$$\varphi_i(t,j) + e_i(t,j) \in C, \quad \dot{\varphi}_i(t,j) = f(\varphi_i(t,j) + e_i(t,j)); \qquad (6)$$

(H2) for all $(t,j) \in \operatorname{dom} \varphi_i$ such that $(t, j+1) \in \operatorname{dom} \varphi_i$,

$$\varphi_i(t,j) + e_i(t,j) \in D, \quad \varphi_i(t,j+1) = g(\varphi_i(t,j) + e_i(t,j)) \qquad (7)$$

with the property that $\lim_{i \to \infty} \varphi_i(0,0) = \varphi(0,0)$, $\{\varphi_i\}_{i=0}^{\infty}$ converges graphically to $\varphi^{\mathcal{D}}$, for each i we have $\sup_{(t,j) \in \operatorname{dom} e_i} |e_i(t,j)| =: \varepsilon_i < +\infty$, and the sequence $\{\varepsilon_i\}_{i=0}^{\infty}$ converges to 0.

To illustrate what graphical convergence (vs. classical convergence notions) grants us, we give two somewhat extreme, but important, examples.

Example 3. Consider the system from Example 1, and a sequence of points on the line $x_1 = x_2$ converging to $(0,0)$. From each such point, one can find noise e_i and a "classical" solution ξ_i so that ξ_i rotates to D, and then jumps infinitely many times, with jumps separated by less than $1/i$ amount of time. (We argued that this is possible in Example 1.) The resulting sequence of hybrid arcs ξ_i converges graphically to a hybrid arc ξ with $\operatorname{dom} \xi = \{0\} \times \mathbb{N}$ (that is, ξ never flows) and for all $j \in \mathbb{N}$, $\xi(0,j) = (0,0)$. Such ξ is a Hermes solution. It is also a Krasovskii solution, since $(0,0) \in \overline{D}$ and $\bar{g}(0,0) = (0,0)$. (Recall though that $(0,0) \notin D$!)

Example 4. Consider a hybrid system on $\mathbb{R}^2$ given by $D = \mathbb{R}^2$; $C = [0, +\infty) \times \{0\}$; $f(x_1, x_2) = (1,1)$ for every point (x_1, x_2) where x_1 is rational, otherwise $f(x_1, x_2) = (1, -1)$; and $g(x) = 0$. For any point $\xi^0 \in C$ every classical solution cannot flow since it would be pushed away from the set C. On the other hand, in the presence of arbitrarily small noise, a "classical" solution can flow along the C set towards $+\infty$. Note that such a solution is also a Krasovskii solution since the regularization of f is given by $\overline{f}(x_1, x_2) = (1, [-1, 1])$.

In many control applications, the state of the system cannot be measured exactly since it is corrupted by noise. The measurement noise can appear in some but not every component of the state (e.g. when state feedback is implemented, noise appears only on states measured with specific sensors). To account for such cases, we consider functions f and g given as

$$\forall x \in C \quad f(x) := f'(x, \kappa_c(x)), \quad \forall x \in D \quad g(x) := g'(x, \kappa_d(x)) \qquad (8)$$

where $f' : O \times U \to \mathbb{R}^n$ and $g' : O \times U \to O$, $\kappa_c : C \to U$, and $\kappa_d : D \to U$, $U \subset O$. We allow for κ_c, κ_d to be discontinuous.

The notion of Hermes solution in Definition 5 changes for a hybrid system $\mathcal{H} = (f, g, C, D, O)$ with f and g given by (8) since the noise is affecting the differential and difference equations only through the function κ_c and κ_d.

Definition 6 (hybrid control-Hermes solution to $\mathcal{H}$). *A hybrid arc φ : $\operatorname{dom} \varphi \to O$ is a hybrid control-Hermes solution to $\mathcal{H} = (f, g, C, D, O)$ with f*

and g given in (8) if for each compact hybrid time domain $\mathcal{D} \subset \operatorname{dom} \varphi$ and the truncation $\varphi^{\mathcal{D}}$ of φ to $\mathcal{D}$, there exists a sequence of hybrid arcs $\varphi_i : \operatorname{dom} \varphi_i \to O$ and measurable functions $e_i : \operatorname{dom} e_i \to \mathbb{R}^n$, $\operatorname{dom} e_i = \operatorname{dom} \varphi_i$, that satisfy, for each i,

(cH1) for all $j \in \mathbb{N}$ and almost all t such that $(t, j) \in \operatorname{dom} \varphi_i$,

$$\varphi_i(t,j) + e_i(t,j) \in C, \quad \dot{\varphi}_i(t,j) = f'(\varphi_i(t,j), \kappa_c(\varphi_i(t,j) + e_i(t,j))); \quad (9)$$

(cH2) for all $(t, j) \in \operatorname{dom} \varphi_i$ such that $(t, j + 1) \in \operatorname{dom} \varphi_i$,

$$\varphi_i(t,j) + e_i(t,j) \in D, \quad \varphi_i(t, j+1) = g'(\varphi_i(t,j), \kappa_d(\varphi_i(t,j) + e_i(t,j))) \quad (10)$$

with the property that $\lim_{i \to \infty} \varphi_i(0,0) = \varphi(0,0)$, $\{\varphi_i\}_{i=0}^{\infty}$ converges graphically to $\varphi^{\mathcal{D}}$, for each i we have $\sup_{(t,j) \in \operatorname{dom} e_i} |e_i(t,j)| =: \varepsilon_i < +\infty$, and the sequence $\{\varepsilon_i\}_{i=0}^{\infty}$ converges to 0.

3   Statement of Main Results

Following the work by Hermes [23] and Hàjek [22], we show that hybrid Krasovskii solutions to $\mathcal{H}$ are equivalent to hybrid Hermes solutions to $\mathcal{H}$.

Theorem 2 (Krasovskii solutions $\equiv$ Hermes solutions). *Under Assumption 1, a hybrid arc is a hybrid Krasovskii solution to $\mathcal{H}$ if and only if it is a hybrid Hermes solution to $\mathcal{H}$.*

The two implications are stated and proved as Corollary 4.4 and Corollary 5.2 in [34].

We note that Theorem 2 generalizes, to the hybrid framework, the result by Hàjek [22] given for differential equations. In proving the theorem, we first extend some results by Hàjek to differential equations with a constraint (and we give a proof quite different from that by Hàjek). We will also rely on results on perturbations of hybrid systems given in [20].

Assumption 2. *The functions f' is locally Lipschitz in the first argument uniformly in the second argument. The function g' is continuous in the first argument uniformly in the second argument.*

The result below is a generalization to the hybrid framework of the result given by Coron and Rosier [16] in the context of robust stabilizability of nonlinear systems with time-varying feedback laws.

Theorem 3 (Krasovskii solutions $\equiv$ control-Hermes solutions). *Under Assumptions 1 and 2, for a hybrid system $\mathcal{H}$ with f and g given in (8), a hybrid arc is a hybrid Krasovskii solution to $\mathcal{H}$ if and only if it is a hybrid control-Hermes solution to $\mathcal{H}$.*

The two implications are stated and proved as Corollary 4.7 and Proposition 5.1 in [34] (One of them naturally follows from Theorem 2.)

4   Examples

Here we discuss examples that illustrate that generalized solutions to hybrid systems play a very important role in the robust stabilization problem.

Example 5 (reset and impulsive control systems). For the problem of stabilizing dynamical systems with state feedback, controllers that have states that jump when certain conditions are satisfied have been proposed in the literature as it is the case of reset and impulsive control systems, see e.g. [14], [27], [6], [42]. A reset controller is a linear system with the property that its output is reset to zero whenever its input and output satisfy certain algebraic condition. The first reset integrator was introduced in [14] in order to improve the performance of linear systems. Several models for reset control systems and various design tools are currently available in the literature. One of the models for (closed-loop) reset control systems that has been widely used in the literature, see e.g. [6] and the references therein, assumes the form

$$\dot{x} = A_{cl}x + B_{cl}d \quad x \notin \mathcal{M} \tag{11}$$
$$x^+ = A_R x \qquad x \in \mathcal{M} \tag{12}$$

where $\mathcal{M} := \{x \in \mathbb{R}^n \mid C_{cl}x = 0, (I - A_R)x \neq 0\}$; A_{cl}, B_{cl}, C_{cl} are the closed-loop system matrices; A_R is the reset control matrix; x is the state of the system; and d is an exogenous signal. The set where resets are possible is a subset of $\{x \in \mathbb{R}^n \mid C_{cl}x = 0\}$ and is given by $D := \mathcal{M}$, while the set where the flows are active is given by $C := \mathbb{R}^n \setminus \mathcal{M}$. Note that the latter set corresponds to almost every point in the state space. It follows that for every trajectory of the system it is possible to construct an arbitrarily small measurement noise signal so that the measurement of the state never belongs to the jump set $\mathcal{M}$, so that the solution never jumps.

Therefore, in the presence of arbitrary small measurement noise, there exist solutions to the reset control system that never jump. Note that since the measurement noise can be picked arbitrarily small, a sequence of solutions converging to a solution that never jumps under the presence of measurement noise with magnitude converging to zero can be constructed, a Hermes solution to the reset control system. The limiting solution corresponds to a Krasovskii solution to the reset control system and it satisfies (K1) and (K2) in Definition 4 on the regularized sets $\overline{C} = \mathbb{R}^n$ and $\overline{D} = \mathcal{M}$, respectively.

This lack of robustness not only arises in situations where exogenous signals are present in the system but also in numerical simulation. When the reset control system (11)-(12) is implemented in Simulink with an integrator with reset and simple function blocks, the discretization in time produced by the ODE solver may prevent the resets from being triggered and one has to appeal to special Simulink blocks with zero-crossing detection. These special blocks confer certain robustness properties to the closed loop and, in some situations, make the simulation possible while affecting the model considered in the first place.

Now consider the state-dependent impulsive dynamical system first introduced in [5] that is modeled as (see also [12] and the references therein)

$$\dot{x} = f_c(x) \qquad\qquad x \notin \mathcal{M} \qquad\qquad (13)$$
$$x^+ = x + f_d(x) \qquad\qquad x \in \mathcal{M} \qquad\qquad (14)$$

where the function f_c defines the continuous dynamics, the function f_d defines the discrete dynamics, and $\mathcal{M}$ is the reset set. In most applications of state-dependent impulsive dynamical systems, the reset set $\mathcal{M}$ defines a surface in $\mathbb{R}^n$ (for example, see the modeling examples in [12] or the feedback control strategies proposed in [37, 33]). In such situations, it is also the case that arbitrarily small measurement noise in the state x can prevent every solution to the closed-loop system from jumping.

Example 6 (optimal control). In many robotics applications, optimal navigation algorithms for mobile robots are designed by switching between several feedback laws when the state of the system reaches the switching surface corresponding to the current operation mode, see e.g. [1],[17], [7]. Since the switches between modes occur when the state reaches the switching surface, arbitrarily small measurement noise can prevent the switches from occurring, and consequently, can cause the navigation task to fail.

Consider the example given in [7, Section 3] where a mobile robot of the unicycle type is optimally steered from its initial location to a target (by optimality the authors mean that the vehicle reaches the target while avoiding obstacles so that it minimizes a cost function that penalizes the distance from the obstacle and the proximity to the target). In this case, a hysteresis-type switching scheme is designed around a circular obstacle by defining two circular surfaces given by $g_i(x, y, a_i) = (x_0 - x)^2 + (y_0 - y)^2 - a_i^2$, $i = 1, 2$, $a_2 > a_1$. When the surface g_1 is reached with the vector field pointing inwards, the control law switches to the one that drives the vehicle away from the obstacle while when the surface g_2 is reached with the vector field pointing outwards, the control law is switched to the one that steers the vehicle to the target. Figure 2 depicts this scenario. Even

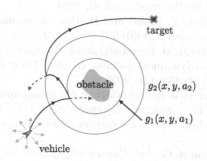

Fig. 2. Steering a vehicle to its target: the circles represent the switching surfaces for the control strategy. "Classical" (solid) and generalized (dashed) solutions to the optimal control problem in Example 6.

though this strategy solves the chattering problem when only one switching surface is considered, arbitrary small measurement noise can prevent the switch on the surface g_1 from happening (causing the vehicle to crash against the obstacle) or it can also preclude the switch on the other surface to occur (causing the vehicle to miss its target). Note that the nonrobustness phenomenon in this example is not due to the existence of obstacles itself (see [39]), it is mainly related to the fact that the concept of solution and the modeling framework were not designed for asymptotic stability to be robust.

5   Conclusions

In this paper, motivated by the problem of robust stabilization of hybrid systems, we have discussed the concepts of hybrid Krasovskii, Hermes, and control-Hermes solutions. We have established that these three concepts of generalized solutions are equivalent. This equivalence implies that hybrid Krasovskii solutions can be approximated with arbitrary precision by solutions to the unregularized system with (arbitrarily small) measurement noise. By examples of theoretical and practical relevance, we have motivated the use of generalized solutions in the design of robust hybrid control systems.

References

1. R.C. Arkin. *Behavior Based Robotics.* The MIT Press, 1998.
2. J.-P. Aubin and A. Cellina. *Differential Inclusions.* Springer-Verlag, 1984.
3. J.-P. Aubin, J. Lygeros, M. Quincampoix, S. S. Sastry, and N. Seube. Impulse differential inclusions: a viability approach to hybrid systems. *IEEE Trans. Aut. Cont.,* 47(1):2–20, 2002.
4. A. Back, J. Guckenheimer, and M. Myers. A dynamical simulation facility for hybrid systems. In *Hybrid Systems volume 36 of Lecture Notes in Computer Science,* pages 255–267, 1993.
5. D. D. Bainov and P.S. Simeonov. *Systems with Impulse Effect: Stability, Theory, and Applications.* Ellis Horwood Limited, 1989.
6. O. Beker, C.V. Hollot, Y. Chait, and H. Han. Fundamental properties of reset control systems. *Automatica,* 40(6):905–915, 2004.
7. M. Boccadoro, Y. Wardi, M. Egerstedt, and E. Verriest. Optimal control of switching surfaces in hybrid dynamical systems. *Discrete Event Dynamic Systems-Theory and Applications,* 15(4):433–448, 2005.
8. M. S. Branicky. Studies in hybrid systems: Modeling, analysis, and control. *Ph.D. dissertation, Dept. Elec. Eng. and Computer Sci., MIT,* 1995.
9. R. W. Brocket. Hybrid models for motion control systems. In *Essays in control,* pages 29–53, 1993.
10. C. Cai, A.R. Teel, and R. Goebel. Converse Lyapunov theorems and robust asymptotic stability for hybrid systems. In *Proc. 24th American Control Conference,* pages 12–17, 2005.
11. F. Ceragioli. Some remarks on stabilization by means of discontinuous feedbacks. *Systems Control Lett.,* 45(4):271–281, 2002.

12. V. Chellaboina, S.P. Bhat, and W.H. Haddad. An invariance principle for nonlinear hybrid and impulsive dynamical systems. *Nonlin. Anal.*, 53:527–550, 2003.
13. F.H. Clarke, Y.S. Ledyaev, E.D. Sontag, and A.I. Subbotin. Asymptotic controllability implies feedback stabilization. *IEEE Trans. Aut. Cont.*, 42(10):1394–1407, 1997.
14. J. C. Clegg. A nonlinear integrator for servomechanisms. *Transactions A.I.E.E.*, 77 (Part II):41–42, 1958.
15. P. Collins. A trajectory-space approach to hybrid systems. In *Proc. 16th MTNS*, 2004.
16. J-M. Coron and L. Rosier. A relation between continuous time-varying and discontinuous feedback stabilization. *Journal of Math. Sys., Est., and Control*, 4(1): 67–84, 1994.
17. M. Egerstedt. Behavior based robotics using hybrid automata. *Hybrid Systems: Computation and Control Lecture Notes in Computer Science*, 1790:103–116, 2000.
18. A.F. Filippov. Differential equations with discontinuous right-hand sides (english). *Matemat. Sbornik.*, 51(93):99–128, 1960.
19. R. Goebel, J.P. Hespanha, A.R. Teel, C. Cai, and R.G. Sanfelice. Hybrid systems: Generalized solutions and robust stability. In *Proc. 6th IFAC NOLCOS*, pages 1–12, 2004.
20. R. Goebel and A.R. Teel. Results on solution sets to hybrid systems with applications to stability theory. In *Proc. 24th American Control Conference*, pages 557–562, 2005.
21. R. Goebel and A.R. Teel. Solutions to hybrid inclusions via set and graphical convergence with stability theory applications. To appear in Automatica, 2006.
22. O. Hàjek. Discontinuous differential equations I. *Journal of Diff. Eqn.*, 32:149–170, 1979.
23. H. Hermes. Discontinuous vector fields and feedback control. *Diff. Eqn. & Dyn. Systems*, pages 155–165, 1967.
24. C. M. Kellet and A. R. Teel. Smooth Lyapunov functions and robustness of stability for differential inclusions. *Sys. & Cont. Lett.*, 52:395–405, 2004.
25. N.N. Krasovskii. *Game-Theoretic Problems of Capture*. Nauka, Moscow, 1970.
26. N.N. Krasovskii and A.I. Subbotin. *Game-Theoretical Control Problems*. Springer-Verlag, 1988.
27. K.R. Krishnan and I.M. Horowitz. Synthesis of a non-linear feedback system with significant plant-ignorance for prescribed system tolerances. *International Journal of Control*, 19:689–706, 1974.
28. J. Lygeros, K.H. Johansson, S. S. Sastry, and M. Egerstedt. On the existence of executions of hybrid automata. In *Proc. 38th IEEE Conference on Decision and Control*, pages 2249–2254, 1999.
29. J. Lygeros, K.H. Johansson, S.N. Simić, J. Zhang, and S. S. Sastry. Dynamical properties of hybrid automata. *IEEE Trans. Aut. Cont.*, 48(1):2–17, 2003.
30. D. Nesic, L. Zaccarian, and A.R. Teel. Stability properties of reset systems. In *Proc. 16th IFAC World Congress in Prague*, 2005.
31. C. Prieur, R. Goebel, and A. R. Teel. Results on robust stabilization of asymptotically controllable systems by hybrid feedback. In *Proc. 44th IEEE Conference on Decision and Control and European Control Conference*, pages 2598–2603, 2005.
32. R.T. Rockafellar and R. J-B Wets. *Variational Analysis*. Springer, 1998.
33. A.V. Roup, D.S. Bernstein, S.G. Nersesov, W.M. Haddad, and V. Chellaboina. Limit cycle analysis of the verge and foliot clock escapement using impulsive differential equations and poincare maps. *International Journal of Control*, 76(17): 1685–1698, 2003.

34. R.G. Sanfelice, R. Goebel, and A.R. Teel. Generalized solutions to hybrid dynamical systems. *Submitted*, 2005.
35. R.G. Sanfelice, R. Goebel, and A.R. Teel. Results on convergence in hybrid systems via detectability and an invariance principle. In *Proc. 24th American Control Conference*, pages 551–556, 2005.
36. J. Sprinkle, A. D. Ames, A. Pinto, H. Zheng, and S. S. Sastry. On the partitioning of syntax and semantics for hybrid systems tools. In *Proc. 44th IEEE Conference on Decision and Control and European Control Conference*, 2005.
37. S.Y. Tang and R.A. Cheke. State-dependent impulsive models of integrated pest management (IPM) strategies and their dynamic consequences. *Journal of Mathematical Biology*, 50(3):257–292, 2005.
38. L. Tavernini. Differential automata and their discrete simulators. *Nonlin. Anal.*, 11(6):665–683, 1987.
39. S. E. Tuna, R. G. Sanfelice, M. J. Messina, and A. R. Teel. Hybrid MPC: Open-minded but not easily swayed. In *International Workshop on Assessment and Future Directions of Nonlinear Model Predictive Control*, 2005.
40. A. van der Schaft and H. Schumacher. *An Introduction to Hybrid Dynamical Systems*. Lecture Notes in Control and Information Sciences, Springer, 2000.
41. H. S. Witsenhausen. A class of hybrid-state continuous-time dynamic systems. *IEEE Trans. Aut. Cont.*, 11(2):161–167, 1966.
42. L. Zaccarian, D. Nesic, and A.R. Teel. First order reset elements and the Clegg integrator revisited. In *Proc. 24th American Control Conference*, pages 563–568, 2005.

Fixed Point Iteration for Computing the Time Elapse Operator

Sriram Sankaranarayanan[1,2], Henny B. Sipma[2], and Zohar Manna[2,*]

[1] NEC Laboratories America, Princeton, NJ
srirams@nec-labs.com
[2] Computer Science Department, Stanford University
{sipma, zm}@theory.stanford.edu

Abstract. We investigate techniques for automatically generating symbolic approximations to the time solution of a system of differential equations. This is an important primitive operation for the safety analysis of continuous and hybrid systems. In this paper we design a *time elapse operator* that computes a symbolic over-approximation of time solutions to a continuous system starting from a given initial region. Our approach is iterative over the cone of functions (drawn from a suitable universe) that are non negative over the initial region. At each stage, we iteratively remove functions from the cone whose Lie derivatives do not lie inside the current iterate. If the iteration converges, the set of states defined by the final iterate is shown to contain all the time successors of the initial region. The convergence of the iteration can be forced using abstract interpretation operations such as widening and narrowing.

We instantiate our technique to linear hybrid systems with piecewise-affine dynamics to compute polyhedral approximations to the time successors. Using our prototype implementation TimePass, we demonstrate the performance of our technique on benchmark examples.

1 Introduction

An invariant is a predicate that holds on every reachable state of the system. By generating invariants, it is possible to prove a system safe or find potential bugs in systems. For discrete systems, the generation of invariants can be performed by a static analysis of the system; forward propagation is used to explore the reachable states of the system starting from the initial states of the system until an over-approximation of the reach set is generated, excluding the unsafe region. This idea has been explored for restricted classes of hybrid systems by popular tools such as Hytech, DDT, CheckMate and Charon.

To apply the forward propagation scheme to hybrid systems, we need a *time elapse operator*; an operator that, given an initial region Θ and a vector field D describing the continuous dynamics, computes an over-approximation of the

---

* This research was supported in part by NSF grants CCR-01-21403, CCR-02-20134, CCR-02-09237, CNS-0411363, and CCF-0430102, by ARO grant DAAD19-01-1-0723, and by NAVY/ONR contract N00014-03-1-0939.

João Hespanha and A. Tiwari (Eds.): HSCC 2006, LNCS 3927, pp. 537–551, 2006.

time successors of Θ under D for a potentially infinite time horizon. The construction of the reachable set consists of alternate applications of such a time elapse operator for each mode, along with the standard *post condition (image)* operator for discrete mode changes. To be useful, this time elapse operator must be as accurate as possible. This paper presents a novel method to construct such a time elapse operator.

Our method iteratively constructs a set of functions $\{f_1, \ldots, f_m\}$ over the system variables drawn from a given universe of functions U, such that the corresponding assertion $f_1 \geq 0 \wedge \ldots \wedge f_m \geq 0$ holds for all time successors of Θ. We start with the set of all functions in U that are nonnegative over Θ, and then iteratively remove those functions whose Lie derivative with respect to the system's vector field D does not support the corresponding invariant assertion until a fixed point is reached. We show that the fixed point is guaranteed to correspond to an invariant assertion. Standard techniques from abstract interpretation such as widening and narrowing [5,6] are used to force convergence in a finite number of steps to a set of functions that are guaranteed to be nonnegative on all the time successors of Θ.

The method is presented as a general framework, parameterized by an abstract *refinement operator* that performs the removal of functions from the set at each iteration. Specialization of the refinement operator allows the method to be applied to different function domains, thus generating different types of inequalities. To illustrate the method we describe a concrete instance of the framework for the domain of affine functions, providing an alternative way of polyhedral analysis. We have implemented this approach in our prototype tool TIMEPASS with encouraging results over benchmark examples.

Related Work

The time elapse operator can be analytically computed for polyhedral initial regions and piecewise constant dynamics. The computation is *hard* for linear systems and *harder* for nonlinear systems. The polyhedral flowpipe approximation approach of Krogh et al. can solve the bounded time elapse problem for arbitrary differential equations. The approach has been implemented in their tool CheckMate [18] and used for complex systems with both linear and nonlinear dynamics. The DDT system due to Dang et al. uses orthogonal polyhedra and face lifting to compute the time elapse [1]. The PHAVer tool due to Frehse [9] presents a technique for the safety analysis of linear system using a sophisticated flowpipe construction for linear differential equations. Nevertheless, these technique can approximate flowpipes only upto a time bound. They also rely on numerical integration using ODE solvers to solve a hard non convex optimization problem numerically. Piazza et al. [13] and Ratschan et al. [15] propose approximations to the time-elapse based on quantifier elimination over the reals along with Taylor series expansions.

The time solutions can be symbolically computed for certain affine systems. However, the solution typically contains terms involving exponentiations, sines and cosines. It is computationally expensive to draw inferences from these results.

Extracting polyhedral over-approximations from the solution of linear systems is a formidable challenge. The work of Lafferriere et al. [12] and Tiwari [19] present interesting techniques for proving safety by integrating the dynamics of the system. Recently, symbolic techniques for generating invariants without the use of an explicit time elapse operator have been proposed, including the generation of nonlinear equality invariants for systems with polynomial dynamics [17,20,16]. These techniques can handle interesting nonlinear systems beyond the reach of traditional automatic techniques, but the theory has so far been restricted to equality invariants. Prajna and Jadbabaie [14] propose a method for the synthesis of barrier functions (inequalities) to justify invariants of nonlinear systems using convex optimization. These barrier functions are generated by solving equations on the unknown coefficients of a parametric polynomial; in contrast, in this paper we iteratively compute a set of functions starting from the initial region.

2   Preliminaries

Let $\mathcal{R}$ denote the set of reals. A function $f : \mathcal{R}^n \mapsto \mathcal{R}$ is said to be *smooth* if it is continuous and differentiable to any degree. Examples of such functions include polynomials and other analytical functions. Throughout this paper, we consider assertions $\varphi : \bigwedge_{i=1}^m f_i \geq 0$, such that each $f_i : \mathcal{R}^n \mapsto \mathcal{R}$ is smooth.

Let $\varphi : \bigwedge_{i=1}^m f_i \geq 0$ be such an assertion. We denote the set of values satisfying φ by $[[\varphi]]$, i.e, $[[\varphi]] = \{x \in \mathcal{R}^n \mid \varphi(x)\}$. An assertion φ_1 *semantically entails* φ_2, written $\varphi_1 \models \varphi_2$ iff $[[\varphi_1]] \subseteq [[\varphi_2]]$.

Definition 1 (Cone). *Let $G = \{f_1, \ldots, f_i, \ldots\}$ be a set of smooth functions. The cone generated by G is given by*

$$Cone(G) = \left\{ \lambda_0 + \sum_{i=1}^N \lambda_i f_i \mid \lambda_i \geq 0, \ 0 \leq i \leq N, \ N > 0 \right\}.$$

Each $f_i \in G$ is said to be a generator of the cone. The cone I is said to be finitely generated iff $I = Cone(G)$ for some finite set G. Given an assertion $\varphi : \bigwedge_{i=1}^m f_i \geq 0$, the expression $Cone(\varphi)$ denotes $Cone(\{f_1, \ldots, f_m\})$.

A cone I defines a region $[[I]] = \{x \in \mathcal{R}^n \mid f_i(x) \geq 0, \ \forall f_i \in I\}$. Given cones I, J, note that $I \subseteq J$ iff $[[J]] \subseteq [[I]]$.

Lemma 1. *Given $\varphi : \bigwedge_{i=1}^m f_i \geq 0$, if $g \in Cone(\varphi)$ then $\varphi \models (g \geq 0)$.*

Example 1. Consider $J = Cone(\varphi : x \geq 0 \wedge y \geq 0)$. We note that $3x + 4y \in J$. Thus $\varphi \models 3x + 4y \geq 0$. On the other hand, $\varphi \models x^2 + y \geq 0$. However, $x^2 + y \notin J$; $Cone(\varphi)$ is not necessarily a complete set of consequences.

The intersection of two cones is also a cone. However, the union of two cones fails to be a cone. We define the *conic hull* $I_1 \uplus I_2$, to be the smallest cone containing $I_1 \cup I_2$. Let $I_1 = Cone(f_1, \ldots, f_k)$ and $I_2 = Cone(g_1, \ldots, g_m)$, then $I_1 \uplus I_2 = Cone(f_1, \ldots, f_k, g_1, \ldots, g_m)$. Therefore, $Cone(\varphi_1 \wedge \varphi_2) = Cone(\varphi_1) \uplus Cone(\varphi_2)$

Continuous and Hybrid Systems

A vector field D over $\mathcal{R}^n$ associates each point $\boldsymbol{x}$ with a direction $D(\boldsymbol{x}) \in \mathcal{R}^n$. Given a system of differential equations of the form $\dot{x}_i = f_i(x_1, \ldots, x_n)$, we associate a vector field $D(\boldsymbol{x}) = \langle f_1(\boldsymbol{x}), \ldots, f_n(\boldsymbol{x}) \rangle$.

Definition 2 (Continuous System). *A continuous system $\langle V, D(\cdot), X, \Theta \rangle$ consists of a set of real-valued continuous variables V, such that $|V| = n$; a vector field $D(\cdot)$ over $\mathcal{R}^n$ defining the dynamics of the system; an invariant predicate (domain) X restricting the state space of the system and an initial region Θ such that $[[\Theta]] \subseteq [[X]]$.*

A *time trajectory* of a continuous system is a function $\tau : [0, \delta) \mapsto \mathcal{R}^n$ for some time $\delta > 0$ such that

(a) $\tau(0) \in [[\Theta]]$,
(b) $\tau(t) \in [[X]]$, for all $t \in [0, \delta)$, and
(c) $\dot{\tau}(t) = D(\tau(t))$.

Definition 3 (Lie Derivative). *Let $V(\boldsymbol{x}) = \langle p_1(\boldsymbol{x}), \ldots, p_n(\boldsymbol{x}) \rangle$ be a vector field in $\mathcal{R}^n$. Let $f : \mathcal{R}^n \mapsto \mathcal{R}$ be continuous and differentiable. The* Lie derivative *of f over V is given by $\mathcal{L}_V(f) = (\nabla f) \cdot V(\boldsymbol{x}) = \sum_{i=1}^{n} \frac{\partial f}{\partial x_i} \cdot p_i(\boldsymbol{x})$.*

Let τ be some time trajectory of a continuous system with dynamics given by $D(\cdot)$. Consider the function $u(t) = f(\tau(t))$. The time derivative $\dot{u}(t)$ is given by the Lie derivative $\mathcal{L}_D(f)$ evaluated at $\boldsymbol{x} = \tau(t)$.

Hybrid systems generalize continuous systems by providing finitely many modes, each with possibly different dynamics and discrete mode changes. A state is *reachable* if it occurs in some computation. The set of all reachable states of a hybrid system is denoted $\mathsf{Reach}(H)$. The safety analysis problem given a safe set S, asks if $\mathsf{Reach}(H) \subseteq S$. Alternatively, the reachability problem given an unsafe set U, decides $\mathsf{Reach}(H) \cap U = \emptyset$.

The safety analysis problem is undecidable for a general hybrid system. In practice, it is solved by generating an over-approximation of the set $\mathsf{Reach}(H)$, also known as an *invariant*. The standard technique for generating invariants is based on a symbolic simulation of the system using assertions to represent sets of states. These techniques require the fundamental primitive of computing *time elapse* on a given region.

Definition 4 (Time Elapse Problem). *Given a system $\langle V, D(\cdot), X, \Theta \rangle$, compute an assertion ψ that contains all the time trajectories of the system starting from any state $\boldsymbol{x}_0 \in [[\Theta]]$.*

This problem is hard to solve in general. However, for restricted cases such as piecewise constant differential equations and polyhedral assertions, there have been many successful approaches to approximating the time elapse operation. In this paper, we provide a general iterative approach to computing the time elapse operator.

3   Algorithm

We first present the general framework to construct the time elapse operator without the use of invariant regions. After specializing this framework for the domain of affine functions, we refine the general framework to the case of systems with invariant regions. Proofs of theorems have been omitted in this version. They may be obtained in an extended version of this paper.

3.1   General Framework

Let x be a vector of system variables, $\Theta: f_1 \geq 0 \wedge \cdots \wedge f_m \geq 0$ be the initial region. Differential equations $\dot{x}_i = p_i(x)$, $1 \leq i \leq n$ specify the dynamics. Recall that the dynamics induce a vector field D such that $D(x) = \langle p_1(x), \ldots, p_n(x) \rangle$. Assume $p_1, \ldots, p_n$ Lipschitz continuous.

Let U be a class of continuous and differentiable functions. Typically, U is suggested by the class of inequalities $f_i \geq 0$ that appear in the system description and those inequalities sought as potential invariants. We assume that U is a vector space of functions, i.e, closed under addition of functions and scaling by a real. Examples of U include the set of all affine functions over x, the set of all polynomials of degree at most k, and the set of all polynomials.

We shall begin by formulating the notion of invariants that over-approximate the reachable states of the continuous system. The time elapse operator that we seek is nothing but a process of computing such invariants automatically.

Definition 5 (Bounding Invariant). *An assertion* $\varphi: g_1 \geq 0 \wedge \cdots \wedge g_m \geq 0$ *is a* bounding invariant *iff (a)* $\Theta \models \varphi$ *and (b)* $g_1 \geq 0 \wedge \cdots \wedge \mathbf{g_i} = \mathbf{0} \wedge \cdots \wedge g_m \geq 0 \models \mathcal{L}_D(g_i) > 0$, *for all* $1 \leq i \leq m$.

Bounding invariants contain the time trajectories of the system starting from Θ.

Lemma 2 (Soundness). *If* φ *is a bounding invariant then all time trajectories starting from* $x_0 \in [[\varphi]]$ *satisfy* φ.

The set of all functions that are bounding invariants need not be convex. For instance, if $g_1 \geq 0$ and $g_2 \geq 0$ are bounding invariants, then $g_1 + g_2 \geq 0$ is invariant but not necessarily a bounding invariant. The notion of a *relaxed invariant* provides a stronger condition that is convex.

Definition 6 (Relaxed Invariant). *An assertion* $\varphi: \bigwedge_{i=1}^m g_i \geq 0$ *is a relaxed invariant for a scale factor* $\lambda \in \mathcal{R}$ *iff (a)* $\Theta \models \varphi$ *and (b)* $\varphi \models \mathcal{L}_D(g_i) + \lambda g_i > 0$, *for each* $1 \leq i \leq m$.

Lemma 3. *If* φ *is a relaxed invariant then it is also a bounding invariant.*

We now extend the notion of a relaxed invariant to a cone of functions.

Definition 7 (Invariant Cone). *Let* $I = Cone(\{g_1, \ldots, g_m\})$ *be a finitely generated cone of functions such that* $I \subseteq U$. *Let* $\lambda \in \mathcal{R}$ *be a scale factor. We say that* I *is an* invariant cone *iff it satisfies the initiation and closure condition*

(1) Initiation: $I \subseteq Cone(\Theta)$, *(thus* $[[\Theta]] \subseteq [[I]]$*)*,

(2) Lie derivative closure: $(\forall \, f \in I) \, (\exists \epsilon > 0) \, (\mathcal{L}_D(f) + \lambda f - \epsilon \in I)$.

Lemma 4 (Soundness). *Let* $I = Cone(\{g_1, \ldots, g_m\})$ *be an invariant cone for scale factor* λ. *The assertion* $\varphi: \; g_1 \geq 0 \wedge \ldots \wedge g_m \geq 0$ *is a relaxed invariant.*

Lemma 5. *If* I_λ *is an invariant cone for scale factor* λ, *then it is also invariant for any scale factor* $\mu \geq \lambda$.

The key computational step in our scheme is that of a refinement operator:

Definition 8 (Refinement Operator). *Given a cone* I, *a vector field* D *and a scale factor* λ, *we define the set*

$$\partial_\lambda I = \{f \in U \mid \lambda f + \mathcal{L}_D(f) - \epsilon \in I, \; \epsilon > 0\} \,.$$

Thus, $\partial_\lambda I$ *consists of all the functions* $f \in U$ *such that* $\mathcal{L}_D(f) + \lambda f - \epsilon \in I$.

The notion of an invariant may be recast as follows: A cone I is invariant for scale factor λ iff $I \subseteq Cone(\Theta) \cap \partial_\lambda I$. Consider the monotonic function $\mathfrak{F}_\lambda$ over cones, defined by $\mathfrak{F}_\lambda(I) = I \cap \partial_\lambda I \cap Cone(\Theta)$. A cone I is said to be a *fixed point* for $\mathfrak{F}_\lambda$ iff $\mathfrak{F}_\lambda(I) = I$.

Theorem 1. *Given a cone* I, *and the refinement operator* ∂_λ,

1. $\partial_\lambda I$ *is a cone.*
2. *The function* $\mathfrak{F}_\lambda(I) = I \cap (\partial_\lambda I) \cap (Cone(\Theta))$ *is monotonic and decreasing in the lattice of cones ordered by set inclusion, i.e.,* $\mathfrak{F}_\lambda(I) \subseteq I$.
3. *If* $\mathfrak{F}_\lambda(I) = I$, *i.e.,* I *is a fixed point of* $\mathfrak{F}_\lambda$, *then* I *is an invariant cone.*
4. *If* $\lambda \leq \mu$ *then* $\partial_\lambda I \subseteq \partial_\mu I$. *Thus,* $\mathfrak{F}_\lambda(I) \subseteq \mathfrak{F}_\mu(I)$.

The space of all cones $I \subseteq U$ forms a complete lattice and furthermore, $\mathfrak{F}_\lambda$ is a monotonic function. Tarski's theorem (see [7]) guarantees the existence of a greatest fixed point of $\mathfrak{F}_\lambda$: $I_\lambda^* = \bigcap_{i \geq 0} \partial_\lambda^i Cone(\Theta)$.

If I_λ^* is finitely generated then its generators correspond to an invariant assertion. Note that $I_\lambda^* \subseteq I_\mu^*$ for $\mu \geq \lambda$. Thus, it follows that $[[I_\mu^*]] \subseteq [[I_\lambda^*]]$. A larger value of λ, yields a stronger invariant.

In practice, the greatest fixed point is frequently not computable and even when it can be analytically computed, it may not be finitely generated. Therefore, we seek fixed points that are not necessarily the greatest fixed points. Note that such fixed points are also guaranteed to be invariant cones. This is performed by under-approximating I_λ^* as the limit of the following iteration:

$$I^{(0)} = U$$
$$I^{(i+1)} = \mathfrak{F}_\lambda(I^{(i)}) = I^{(i)} \cap (\partial_\lambda I^{(i)}) \cap Cone(\Theta)$$

It follows from the monotonicity of $\mathfrak{F}_\lambda$ that each $I^{(i+1)} \subseteq I^{(i)}$. The iteration converges if $I^{(i+1)} = I^{(i)}$. If convergence occurs in finitely many steps then the result is a fixed point. Additionally, if the result is finitely generated then it is also an invariant. On the other hand, convergence is not guaranteed in all domains. Therefore, we use the narrowing operator $\triangle$ to force convergence [5, 6].

Definition 9 (Narrowing Operator [5, 6]). *Let I_1, I_2 be two cones such that $I_1 \supseteq I_2$. The narrowing $I_1 \triangle I_2$ is a cone defined as follows*

1. $I_1 \triangle I_2 \subseteq I_1 \cap I_2 \subseteq I_2$.
2. *Given any monotonically decreasing sequence $I_0 \supseteq I_1 \supseteq \cdots$, the sequence $J_0 = I_0$, $J_i = J_{i-1} \triangle I_i$ converges in finitely many steps.*

The convergence of the iterative strategy to some fixed point can now be ensured by repeated application of narrowing. For instance, consider the strategy

$$
\begin{aligned}
I_0 &= U \\
I_{j+1} &= \mathfrak{F}_\lambda(I_j), && \text{if } 0 \le j \le K \\
I_{k+1} &= I_k \triangle \mathfrak{F}(I_k), \text{if } k > K
\end{aligned}
$$

This strategy known as the *naive iteration* computes the regular iteration sequence until a fixed limit K. If convergence is not achieved within this bound, the repeated application of the narrowing operator guarantees convergence. Starting from a finitely generated cone $Cone(\Theta)$, and forcing convergence in finitely many steps (either naturally or through narrowing), we are guaranteed a finitely generated invariant cone I.

3.2   Polyhedral Analysis of Affine Systems

As a concrete instance of the framework defined in Section 3.1, we now present algorithms for the special case when the universe is the set of all affine expressions $c^T x + c_0$, the initial set Θ is a polyhedron of the form $Ax + b \ge 0$, and the dynamics are affine, of the form $\dot{x} = Px + q$. The Lie derivative is given by $\mathcal{L}_D(c^T x + c_0) = c^T P x + c^T q$.

Definition 10 (Finitely generated (polyhedral) cones). *A cone $I \subseteq U$ is said to be* finitely generated *iff $I = Cone(g_1, \ldots, g_m)$. The functions $g_1, \ldots, g_m$ are said to be its* generators. *Let I be a finitely generated cone of affine expressions. We may represent I in the form of a polyhedron $I = \{c^T x + c_0 \mid Ac \ge 0\}$, for a $m \times (n+1)$ matrix A.*

More generally, the coefficients of each expression in I satisfy a linear constraint of the form $Ac \ge 0$. Note that the vector c contains coefficient c_i for variables x_i along with the coefficient c_0 for the constant term.

Example 2. Consider the set of all affine expressions with nonnegative coefficients. We may represent such a set as

$$
N = \{c^T x + c_0 \mid c_0 \ge 0 \ \wedge \ c_1 \ge 0 \ \wedge \ \cdots \ c_n \ge 0\}.
$$

This set is finitely generated by the expressions $\{x_1, x_2, \ldots, x_n\}$. Consider the assertion $\Theta : x = 0 \ \wedge \ y \ge 0 \ \wedge \ y \le 1$. We may represent $Cone(\Theta)$ in two ways:

$$
\begin{aligned}
Cone(\Theta) &= Cone(\{x, -x, y, 1-y\}) \\
&= \{c_0 + c_1 x + c_2 y \mid c_0 \ge 0 \ \wedge \ c_0 + c_2 \ge 0\}
\end{aligned}
$$

Conversion between representations is achieved through a vertex enumeration.

The refinement operator can be computed in a straightforward manner for finitely generated cones of affine expressions, as suggested by the following lemma

Lemma 6. *Let $I = \{c^T x + c_0 \mid \varphi(c, c_0)\}$ and $\epsilon > 0$. The refinement $\partial_\lambda I$ for a field $D(x) = Px + q$ is a finitely generated cone given by*

$$\partial_\lambda I = \{c^T x + c_0 \mid \varphi(P^T c + \lambda c, \lambda c_0 + q^T c - \epsilon)\}.$$

Proof. The Lie derivative $\mathcal{L}_D(c^T x + c_0) = c^T P x + q^T c$. Therefore, given an expression $f : c^T x + c_0 \in U$, $(\mathcal{L}_D(f) + \lambda f - \epsilon) \in I : \{c^T x + c_0 \mid \varphi(c, c_0)\}$ iff $\psi : \varphi(\lambda c + P^T c, \lambda c_0 + q^T c - \epsilon)$ holds.

Note: The set $I = \{c^T x + c_0 \mid A(c, c_0)^T + b \geq 0\}$ is convex but not a cone unless $b = 0$. If ϵ were given a fixed value such as 0.001 in our theory, the resulting constraints after refinement are not homogeneous. In theory, we introduce ϵ as a new variable and eliminate it from the final result. This is common in polyhedral libraries implementing strict inequalities.

The intersection of two sets $\{c^T x + c_0 \mid \varphi_1\}$ and $\{c^T x + c_0 \mid \varphi_2\}$ is given by $\{c^T x + c_0 \mid \varphi_1 \wedge \varphi_2\}$. We have now defined all the basic primitives needed to carry out the fixed point iteration for this domain.

Example 3. Consider the system $\dot{x} = 2x - y$, $\dot{y} = -x + 2y$. We perform the iterator for scale factor $\lambda = 0$. The Lie derivative of an expression $c_0 + c_1 x + c_2 y$ is given by $(2c_1 - c_2)x + (2c_2 - c_1)y$. Consider the initial region $\Theta : x = 0$, $0 \leq y \leq 1$.

$$Cone(\Theta) = \{c_0 + c_1 x + c_2 y \mid c_0 \geq 0 \wedge c_0 + c_2 \geq 0\}.$$

Let $I^{(0)} = U$, the set of all affine expressions. It follows that $\partial_0 I^{(0)} = U$. Therefore, $I^{(1)} = \mathfrak{F}(I) = Cone(\Theta) \cap (\partial_0 I^{(0)}) \cap I^{(0)} = Cone(\Theta)$.

$$\begin{aligned} \partial_0 I^{(1)} &= \partial_0 \{c_0 + c_1 x + c_2 y \mid c_0 \geq 0 \wedge c_0 + c_2 \geq 0\} \\ &= \{c_0 + c_1 x + c_2 y \mid 2c_2 - c_1 \geq \epsilon\} \\ I^{(2)} &= \{c_0 + c_1 x + c_2 y \mid c_0 \geq 0 \wedge c_0 + c_2 \geq 0 \wedge 2c_2 - c_1 \geq \epsilon, \epsilon > 0\} \end{aligned}$$

Table shows the cones encountered along the iteration, visualized in Figure 1(a). The fixed point I_∞ is not reached in finitely many iterations. The following table shows the fixed points for different values of the scale factor λ. Convergence was forced by the narrowing heuristics described below. Figure 1(b) depicts the fixed point for the case $\lambda = 1$.

λ	I_λ fixed point generators
-1	$x + y \geq 0,\ x \leq 0$
1	$x + y \geq 0,\ x \leq 0,\ 2x + y \leq 1,\ 7x + 5y \leq 8,$ $13x + 11y \leq 32, 25x + 23y \leq 128, 49x + 47y \leq 512$
2	$x + y \geq 0, x \leq 0, 2x + y \leq 1, 6x + 4y \leq 5,$ $56x + 44y \leq 75, 536x + 464y \leq 1125$

Table 1. Iterates for Examples 3 for $\lambda = 0$

#	constraints	generators
1	$c_0 \geq 0,\ c_0 + c_2 \geq 0$	$x = 0,\ 0 \leq y \leq 1$
2	$c_0 \geq 0,\ c_0 + c_2 \geq 0,\ 2c_2 - c_1 \geq \epsilon$	$x \leq 0, y \geq 0, 0 \leq 2x + y \leq 1$
3	$c_0 \geq 0,\ c_0 + c_2 \geq 0,$ $2c_2 - c_1 \geq \epsilon,\ 5c_2 - 4c_1 \geq 0$	$x \leq 0, y \geq 0,$ $2x + y \leq 1, 4y + 5x \geq 0$
4	$c_0 \geq 0,\ c_0 + c_2 \geq 0,$ $2c_2 - c_1 \geq \epsilon,\ 14c_2 - 13c_1 \geq 0$	$x \leq 0, y \geq 0,$ $2x + y \leq 1, 13y + 14x \geq 0$
$\vdots$	$\vdots$	$\vdots$
∞	$c_0 \geq 0,\ c_0 + c_2 \geq 0,$ $2c_2 - c_1 \geq \epsilon, c_2 - c_1 \geq 0$	$x \leq 0, y \geq 0,$ $2x + y \leq 1,$ $y + x \geq 0$

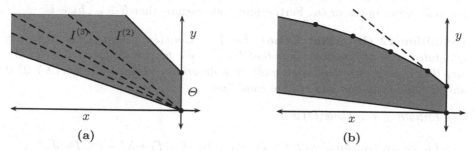

Fig. 1. Fixed points for Example 3: (a) $\lambda = 0$, (b) $\lambda = 1$. The shaded figure represents the final fixed point (not to scale). Dashed line in (b) represents upper solid line in (a).

Note that the invariant for a larger value of λ subsumes that for a smaller value. In general, the iteration does not necessarily terminate in a finite number of steps. Furthermore, the resulting cone I may not be finitely generated. Therefore, approximations in the form of narrowing are required to force termination in a finite number of steps. For any two finitely generated cones, it is possible to define a *standard narrowing* by dropping generators [5].

Definition 11 (Standard Narrowing). *Consider two cones $I_1 = Cone(g_1, \ldots, g_m)$ and $I_2 = Cone(h_1, \ldots, h_k)$ such that $I_1 \supseteq I_2$. The standard narrowing $I = I_1 \triangle I_2$ is defined as $I = Cone(g_i \mid g_i \in I_2)$. In other words, the standard narrowing drops from I_1 all those generators that do not belong to the cone I_2.*

Each application of the standard narrowing results either in convergence or the removal of at least one generator from the first argument. This guarantees convergence of the naive iteration strategy in finitely many steps.

Example 4. Consider two successive iterates from Example 3.

$$I_1 = \begin{pmatrix} c_0 \geq 0,\ c_0 + c_2 \geq 0, \\ 2c_2 - c_1 \geq 0,\ 11c_2 - 10c_1 \geq 0 \end{pmatrix} = Cone(x, -y, 2x + y - 1, 10y + 11x)$$

$$I_2 = \begin{pmatrix} c_0 \geq 0, \ c_0 + c_2 \geq 0, \\ 2c_2 - c_1 \geq 0, \ 33c_2 - 32c_1 \geq 0 \end{pmatrix} = Cone(x, -y, 2x + y - 1, 32x + 33y)$$

Note that all but one generator $(10x + 11y)$ in I_1 also belong to I_2. Therefore, narrowing drops this generator resulting in

$$I_1 \bigtriangleup I_2 = \begin{pmatrix} c_0 \geq 0, \ c_1 \leq 0, \\ c_0 + c_2 \geq 0, \ 2c_2 - c_1 \geq 0 \end{pmatrix} = Cone(x, -y, 2x + y - 1)$$

3.3 Adding Invariant Regions

We now extend the general framework by considering the evolution restricted to an invariant region of the form $X : h_1 \geq 0 \ \wedge \ h_2 \geq 0 \ \cdots h_k \geq 0$ such that $\Theta \models X$. Let $J = Cone(X) = Cone(h_1, \ldots, h_k)$. As in Section 3.1, we assume that U is a universe, Θ is the initial condition and D is a differential field, with the refinement operator ∂_λ. Furthermore, we assume that $h_1, \ldots, h_k \in U$.

Definition 12 (Invariant Cone). *Let $I = Cone(\{g_1, \ldots, g_m\})$ be a finitely generated cone of functions such that $I \subseteq U$. We fix a scale factor $\lambda \in \mathcal{R}$. We say that I is an invariant cone under the invariant region $J = Cone(X)$ iff it satisfies the initiation and closure condition*

(1) Initiation: $I \subseteq Cone(\Theta) \uplus J$,

(2) Lie derivative closure: $(\forall \ f \in I) \ (\exists \ \epsilon > 0) \ (\mathcal{L}_D(f) + \lambda f - \epsilon \in I \uplus J)$.

Lemma 7 (Soundness). *Let $\tau : [0, \delta)$ be any time trajectory starting from $x_0 \in [[\Theta]]$, under the vector field D and the invariant region X. Let I be an invariant cone (under X). It follows that for all $t \in [0, \delta)$, $g_i(\tau(t)) \geq 0$.*

Algorithm 1. Algorithmic scheme for computing Time Elapse

K: Number of steps of initial iteration. λ: Appropriate value of λ for refinement.
Narrow: function implementing narrowing scheme for forcing convergence
function **ComputeTimeElapse**(Θ : predicate, D: dynamics, ψ: invariant)
$I(0) := \mathsf{ConeOfConsequences}(\Theta)$ { Form the initial cone by dualization }
$J := \mathsf{ConeOfConsequences}(\psi)$ { Form the cone for the invariant region}
for $i = 1$ to K do
    {Initial iteration for K steps}
    $I(i) := (I(i-1) \cap \mathsf{Refinement}(I(i-1), D, \lambda)) \uplus J$
end for
$I := I(K)$
{Start Narrowing to enforce convergence}
repeat
    $I' := (I \cap \mathsf{Refinement}(I, D, \lambda)) \uplus J$ {Refine I w.r.t. dynamics. assert($I' \subseteq I$)}
    $I := \mathsf{Narrow}(I, I')$ { Narrow successive iterations. assert($I \subseteq I'$)}
until $I' \equiv I$
return$[[I]]$

Algorithm 2. Compute reach-set for hybrid system using time elapse operator

list *wlist* : worklist consisting of unprocessed modes and predicates.
map *reachmap* : maps each location to its current *reachability predicate*.

function **analyze-hybrid-system** { compute reachable state (predicates) }
{initialize the worklist and reachmap}
wlist := {$\langle m_{initial}, \Theta \rangle$} {add initial mode and start predicate to the worklist}
($\forall$ mode m) *reahmap*(m) := *false*
{initial reachable region is empty for each mode}
while *wlist* $\neq \emptyset$ **do**
    $\langle m, \varphi \rangle$:= pop(*wlist*) {pop an unprocessed mode/predicate from worklist.}
    if $[[\varphi]] \not\subseteq [[reachmap(m)]]$ **then**
        {if the states in the popped predicate have not already been visited}
        visit(m, φ) {process unvisited states}
    end if
end while
{No more unprocessed predicates. Hence, all states have been visited.}
end function {analyze-hybrid-system}

function **visit**(m :mode, φ : predicate) {mode m is entered with state set φ}
φ' := computeTimeElapse$(\varphi, \text{inv}(m), \text{dynamics}(m))$
{apply time elapse operator to φ}
reachmap(m) := *reachmap*$(m) \vee \varphi'$
{add φ' to reachmap. If φ' is polyhedral, $\vee$ may be approximated by convex hull. }
for all $\tau : m \to m'$ outgoing discrete transitions of mode m **do**
    ψ' := post(φ', τ) {compute post condition}
    wlist := *wlist* $\cup \langle m', \psi' \rangle$ { enqueue new $\langle$location, predicate$\rangle$ pair}
end for
end function {visit}

We now extend the iterative solution in the presence of an invariant region cone J. Let us assume a fixed scale factor λ. Let $\mathfrak{F}_X(I) = J \uplus (\mathfrak{F}_\lambda(I))$. Also, let $I^{(0)} = U$ be the initial iterate. We refine each iterate using

$$I^{(i+1)} = \mathfrak{F}_X(I^{(i)}) = J \uplus (I^{(i)} \cap (\partial_\lambda I^{(i)}) \cap Cone(\Theta)).$$

$\mathfrak{F}_X$ is monotonic, and furthermore, its fixed point is an invariant under the region X. Therefore, as before, we may use the iterative technique with heuristic narrowing to force convergence. Algorithm 1 depicts the computation.

Given two cones $I_1 = \{c^T x + c_0 | A_1 c \geq 0\}$ and $I_2 = \{c^T x + c_0 | A_2 c \geq 0\}$, their union is given by $I_1 \uplus I_2 = \{c^T x + c_0 \mid (A_1 c \geq 0) \sqcup (A_2 c \geq 0)\}$, where $\sqcup$ denotes the polyhedral convex hull of two polyhedra.

Hybrid Systems Analysis. The time elapse operator presented so far can be used as a primitive to perform approximate reachability analysis of hybrid systems. While the time elapse operator is used inside each mode to compute the time successors, the standard *post condition* operator is used to compute the image of a set of reachable states under a discrete transition. Algorithm 2 presents the use of our time elapse operator for the analysis of hybrid system. This algorithm is widely used in the analysis of hybrid systems [11]. Note that the convergence of this algorithm is not guaranteed for all hybrid systems. It is possible to modify Algorithm 2 to use widening/narrowing along the lines of Algorithm 1 (see [10]). However the loss in precision due to widening could make it less useful in practice. We have implemented the algorithm for systems with affine dynamics and polyhedral guards/invariants maps in our prototype tool TIMEPASS.

3.4   Discussion

The technique, so far, has many parameters that need to be adjusted for its proper working. We list a few important issues that arise in practice.

Narrowing. Repeated applications of standard narrowing guarantees the termination of the iteration. However, the standard narrowing is a poor strategy for forcing convergence. More heuristic strategies such as extrapolation are based on "guessing" the ultimate limits of an iteration. For instance, the evolution of a generator across successive iterations $4y + 5x$, $13y + 14x$, $40y + 41x$, $\cdots$ observed in Example 3 suggests the limit $x + y$, leading us to the actual fixed point. The problem of designing precise narrowing/widening operators for polyhedral iterates has received a lot of attention in the (discrete) program analysis community [4, 10, 2]. Our own narrowing strategy maps generators across successive iterates using a distance metric such as the euclidean distance. It then guesses the ultimate limit as a weighted sum of the mapped pairs of generators rounded to a fixed precision limit.

Iteration Scheme. There has been a significant amount of work in the program analysis community on choosing iteration schemes for fixed point iterations. In this paper, however, we choose the "naive iteration" scheme (Algorithm 1). The scheme uses a pre-determined number (K) of initial iteration steps followed by narrowing/extrapolation until convergence. The value of K needs to be sufficiently large to allow our extrapolation scheme to guess the right limit to the iteration. However, higher values of K lead to large and complex polyhedra.

Choosing λ. In theory, a larger value of λ produces a stronger invariant. This may fail to hold due to the approximate nature of the narrowing operator. Nevertheless, the result holds in most examples encountered in practice. Unfortunately, a larger value of λ yields extremely complex cones with large coefficients in its representation. In practice, we perform many time elapses in stages, starting from a coarser grained approximation with smaller values of λ and improving using larger values. Such an approach provides means of focusing our narrowing heuristic at each stage to perform no worse than the previous one. For linear systems, using $\lambda = 0$ discovers the rays (infinite directions) of the time elapse operator, useful for computing time elapses over infinite time horizons.

4 Applications

Our tool TIMEPASS implements the algorithms described in this paper for the case of hybrid automata with affine dynamics and updates. Mode invariants, transition guards and initial regions are all assumed polyhedral. Our implementation is based on the Parma Polyhedral Library [2]. The library uses exact arithmetic to represent the coefficients of polyhedra. By default, the reachable set is represented as a list of polyhedra. However, it is possible to speed convergence of Algorithm 2 by using a single polyhedron per location.

Example 5. We consider the NAV benchmark examples standardized by Fehnker and Ivančić [8]. These benchmarks consist of an object moving through rectangular cells on a plane, each with different target velocities. Instances of these benchmarks have been standardized and are available online[1]. We refer the reader to this online repository for a detailed description. For each benchmark, we allowed our tool 45 minutes to converge. Figure 2 depicts the final reach sets computed for NAV-04 and NAV-06. In each case, the square at the top left corner is the forbidden region whose unreachability needs to be proved. Table 2 shows the running times and memory consumption recorded on an Intel Pentium III laptop with 512 Mb RAM. We were able to prove unreachability of the forbidden

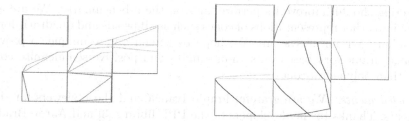

Fig. 2. Reachable regions for benchmarks NAV-04 (left) and NAV-06(right). Top left rectangle shows the unsafe region.

Table 2. Resource utilization for the NAV benchmark examples

#	$\lambda = 0,10$			$\lambda = 0,100$		
	Time	Mem (Mb)	Proved	Time	Mem (Mb)	Proved
NAV-01	4.4s	2.1	Yes	1m28s	5.2	Yes
NAV-02	1m13s	5.2	Yes	20m12s	18	Yes
NAV-03	1m18s	5	Yes	17m51s	16	Yes
NAV-04	19m51s	16	Yes	$\geq 45m$	≥ 60	No
NAV-05	2m39s	8.5	No	11m49s	30	No
NAV-06	$\geq 45m$	≥ 35	No	12m14s	21	No

---

[1] see http://www.cse.unsw.edu.au/~ansgar/benchmark/nav_inst.txt

region for benchmarks NAV-01 to NAV-04. For NAV-06, the entire forbidden region but for the right most corner of the forbidden region is unreachable. As expected, there is a performance penalty for a higher value of λ. However for the case of NAV-06, we observe a reversal of this trend. A more accurate time elapse operator forces convergence of Algorithm 2 faster for this case.

5 Conclusion

We have presented a general framework for over approximating the flowpipe of a continuous system given a starting region. We have provided an instance of this framework for affine systems and polyhedral approximations. Our technique is entirely symbolic and works by computing a greatest fixed point in the space of finitely generated cones. As an advantage, our technique can handle unbounded domains and construct approximations that hold without any time bounds. Our approach is independent of the eigenstructure of the equation. On the other hand, the technique presents many parameters, chiefly the "scale factor" involved in the iteration. A larger value provably yields a more precise answer at the cost of performance.

We have engineered a prototype TIMEPASS for the analysis of affine hybrid systems using polyhedra to represent sets of states. Our initial results with benchmarks results are encouraging. Better narrowing strategies and careful engineering should improve its performance on these benchmarks. We are also looking into other representations of cones such as ellipsoids and quadratic forms for handling non-linear systems. We hope to extend our technique to provide a stronger framework based on sum-of-squares and positive semidefinite cones rather than polyhedral cones.

Acknowledgments. We are grateful Franjo Ivančić and the reviewers for their comments. Thanks to the developers of the PPL library [3] and Aaron Bradley for the Mathematica interface to PPL.

References

1. ASARIN, E., DANG, T., AND MALER, O. The d/dt tool for verification of hybrid systems. In *Proc. 14th Intl. Conference on Computer Aided Verification* (2002), vol. 2404 of *Lecture Notes in Computer Science*, Springer–Verlag, pp. 365–370.
2. BAGNARA, R., HILL, P. M., RICCI, E., AND ZAFFANELLA, E. Precise widening operators for convex polyhedra. In *Static Analysis Symposium* (2003), vol. 2694 of *Lecture Notes in Computer Science*, Springer–Verlag, pp. 337–354.
3. BAGNARA, R., RICCI, E., ZAFFANELLA, E., AND HILL, P. M. Possibly not closed convex polyhedra and the Parma Polyhedra Library. In *Static Analysis Symposium* (2002), vol. 2477 of *Lecture Notes in Computer Science*, Springer–Verlag, pp. 213–229.
4. BESSON, F., JENSEN, T., AND TALPIN, J.-P. Polyhedral analysis of synchronous languages. In *Static Analysis Symposium* (1999), vol. 1694 of *Lecture Notes in Computer Science*, Springer–Verlag, pp. 51–69.

5. COUSOT, P., AND COUSOT, R. Abstract Interpretation: A unified lattice model for static analysis of programs by construction or approximation of fixpoints. In *ACM Principles of Programming Languages* (1977), pp. 238–252.

6. COUSOT, P., AND COUSOT, R. Comparing the Galois connection and widening/narrowing approaches to Abstract interpretation, invited paper. In *PLILP '92* (1992), vol. 631 of *Lecture Notes in Computer Science*, Springer–Verlag, pp. 269–295.

7. DAVEY, B. A., AND PRIESTLY, H. A. *Introduction to Lattices and Order*. Cambridge University Press, 1990.

8. FEHNKER, A., AND IVANČIĆ, F. Benchmarks for hybrid systems verification. In *Hybrid Systems: Computation and Control (HSCC 2004)* (2004), vol. 2993 of *Lecture Notes in Computer Science*, Springer–Verlag, pp. 326–341.

9. FREHSE, G. PHAVer: Algorithmic verification of hybrid systems past HyTech. In *Hybrid Systems: Computation and Control (HSCC 2005)* (2005), vol. 2289 of *Lecture Notes in Computer Science*, Springer–Verlag, pp. 258–273.

10. HALBWACHS, N., PROY, Y., AND ROUMANOFF, P. Verification of real-time systems using linear relation analysis. *Formal Methods in System Design 11*, 2 (1997), 157–185.

11. HENZINGER, T., AND HO, P.-H. Algorithmic analysis of nonlinear hybrid systems. In *Computer-Aided Verification*, P. Wolper, Ed., vol. 939 of *Lecture Notes in Computer Science*. Springer–Verlag, 1995, pp. 225–238.

12. LAFFERRIERE, G., PAPPAS, G., AND YOVINE, S. Symbolic reachability computation for families of linear vector fields. *J. Symbolic Computation 32* (2001), 231–253.

13. PIAZZA, C., ANTONIOTTI, M., MYSORE, V., POLICRITI, A., WINKLER, F., AND MISHRA, B. Algorithmic algebraic model checking I: Challenges from systems biology. In *Computer-aided Verification* (2005), vol. 3576 of *Lecture Notes in Computer Science*, Springer–Verlag, pp. 5–19.

14. PRAJNA, S., AND JADBABAIE, A. Safety verification using barrier certificates. In *Hybrid Systems: Computation and Control* (2004), vol. 2993 of *Lecture Notes in Computer Science*, Springer–Verlag, pp. 477–492.

15. RATSCHAN, S., AND SHE, Z. Safety verification of hybrid systems by constraint propagation based abstraction refinement. In *HSCC* (2005), vol. 3414 of *Lecture Notes in Computer Science*, Springer–Verlag, pp. 573–589.

16. RODRIGUEZ-CARBONELL, E., AND TIWARI, A. Generating polynomial invariants for hybrid systems. In *Hybrid Systems: Computation and Control, HSCC 2005* (2005), vol. 3414 of *LNCS*, Springer, pp. 590–605.

17. SANKARANARAYANAN, S., SIPMA, H. B., AND MANNA, Z. Constructing invariants for hybrid systems. In *Hybrid Systems: Computation and Control (HSCC 2004)* (march 2004), vol. 2993 of *Lecture Notes in Computer Science*, Springer–Verlag, pp. 539–555.

18. SILVA, B., RICHESON, K., KROGH, B. H., AND CHUTINAN, A. Modeling and verification of hybrid dynamical system using checkmate. In *ADPM 2000* (2000). available online from http://www.ece.cmu.edu/~webk/checkmate.

19. TIWARI, A. Approximate reachability for linear systems. In *Hybrid Systems: Computation and Control HSCC* (2003), vol. 2623 of *Lecture Notes in Computer Science*, Springer–Verlag, pp. 514–525.

20. TIWARI, A., AND KHANNA, G. Non-linear systems: Approximating reach sets. In *Hybrid Systems: Computation and Control* (2004), vol. 2993 of *Lecture Notes in Computer Science*, Springer–Verlag, pp. 477–492.

Mixed Initial-Boundary Value Problems for Scalar Conservation Laws: Application to the Modeling of Transportation Networks

Issam S. Strub and Alexandre M. Bayen

Civil Systems, Department of Civil and Environmental Engineering,
University of California, Berkeley, CA, 94720-1710
strub@ce.berkeley.edu
Civil Systems, Department of Civil and Environmental Engineering,
University of California, Berkeley, CA, 94720-1710
bayen@ce.berkeley.edu
Tel.: (510)-642-2468; Fax:(510)-643-5264

Abstract. This article proves the existence and uniqueness of a weak solution to a scalar conservation law on a bounded domain. A weak formulation of hybrid boundary conditions is needed for the problem to be well posed. The boundary conditions are represented by a hybrid automaton with switches between the modes determined by the direction of characteristics of the system at the boundary. The existence of the solution results from the convergence of a Godunov scheme derived in this article. This weak formulation is written explicitly in the context of a strictly concave flux function (relevant for highway traffic). The numerical scheme is then applied to a highway scenario with data from the I210 highway obtained from the California PeMS system. Finally, the existence of a minimizer of travel time is obtained, with the corresponding optimal boundary control.

Keywords: Weak solution of scalar conservation laws, Weak hybrid boundary conditions, LWR PDE, Highway traffic modeling, Boundary control.

1   Introduction

This article is motivated by recent research efforts which investigate the problem of controlling highway networks with metering strategies that can be applied at the on-ramps of the highway (see in particular [46] and references therein). The seminal models of highway traffic go back to the 1950's with the work of Lighthill-Whitham [36] and Richards [43] who tried to use fluid dynamics equations to model traffic flow. The resulting theory, called *Lighthill-Whitham-Richards* (LWR) theory relies on a scalar hyperbolic conservation law, with a concave flux function. Very few approaches have tackled the problem of boundary control of scalar conservation laws in bounded domains in an explicit manner directly applicable for engineering. Unlike the viscous Burgers equation, which has been is focus of numerous ongoing studies, very few results exist for the

João Hespanha and A. Tiwari (Eds.): HSCC 2006, LNCS 3927, pp. 552–567, 2006.

inviscid Burgers equation, which is traditionally used as a model problem for hyperbolic conservation laws. Differential flatness [42] and Lyapunov theory [30] have been explored and appear as promising directions to investigate.

The proper notion of weak solution for the LWR partial differential equation (PDE), called *entropy solution* was first defined by Oleinik [39] in 1957. Even though this work was known to the traffic community, it does not (as far as we know) appear explicitly in the transportation literature before the 1990's with the work of Ansorge [4]. The entropy solution has been since acknowledged as the proper weak solution to the LWR PDE [18] for traffic models. Unfortunately the work of Oleinik in its initial form [39] does not hold for bounded domains, i.e. it would only work for infinitely long highways with no on-ramps or off-ramps. Bounded domains, i.e. highways of finite length (required to model on and off-ramps) imply the use of boundary conditions, for which the existence and uniqueness of a weak solution is not straightforward.

The first result of existence and uniqueness of a weak solution of the LWR PDE in the presence of boundary conditions follows from the work of Bardos, Leroux and Nedelec [8], in the more general context of a first order quasilinear PDE on a bounded open set of $\mathbb{R}^n$. In particular, they introduce a weak formulation of the boundary conditions for which the initial-boundary value problem is well-posed.

We begin this article by explaining that in general, one cannot expect the boundary conditions to be fulfilled pointwise a.e. and we provide several examples to illustrate this fact. We then turn to the specific case of highway traffic flow, for which we are able to state a simplified weak hybrid formulation of the boundary conditions, and prove the existence and uniqueness of a weak solution to the LWR PDE, the former resulting from the convergence of the associated Godunov scheme to the entropy solution of the PDE. This represents a major improvement from the existing traffic engineering literature, where boundary conditions are expected to be fulfilled pointwise and therefore existence of a solution and convergence of the numerical schemes to this solution are not guaranteed. We illustrate the applicability of the method and the numerical scheme developed in this work with a highway scenario, using data for the I210 highway, obtained from the California PeMS system. In particular, we show that the model is able to reproduce flow variations on the highway with a good accuracy over a period of five hours. The last part of the article is devoted to the boundary control of the LWR PDE and its application to a highway optimization problem, in which boundary control is used to minimize travel time on a given stretch of the highway.

2 The Need for a Weak Formulation of Hybrid Boundary Conditions

This section shows three examples of the sort of trouble one runs into when prescribing the boundary conditions in the strong sense. Numerous articles solve a discrete version of this type of problems. Regardless of the numerical schemes used (Godunov [22], Jameson-Schmidt-Turkel [25, 26], Daganzo [17, 18]), these methods suffer from the same difficulties: the authors solve a discrete problem with strong boundary conditions which entails that the corresponding continuous problem is usually ill-posed, i.e. does not have a solution. While the numerical schemes listed above might still yield a numerical output, this numerical data would be meaningless since the initial boundary-value problem does not have a solution in the first place. The object of this work is not to make an endless list of engineering articles which exhibit such shortcomings: we will just mention a previous paper from one of the authors [9] and let the reader discover that this is far from being an exception... To sum up, boundary conditions may only be prescribed on the part of the boundary where the characteristics are incoming, that is entering the domain.

Example 1: Advection equation. We start by considering the simple example where the propagation speed is a constant c,

$$\frac{\partial \rho}{\partial t} + c\frac{\partial \rho}{\partial x} = 0 \text{ for } (x,t) \in (a,b) \times (0,T).$$

In that case, one can clearly see that the boundary condition is either prescribed on the left $(x = a)$ if the speed c is positive or the right $(x = b)$ if the speed is negative. While finding the sign of the speed is quite simple in the linear case, it becomes more subtle when dealing with a nonlinear conservation law such as the LWR PDE as this sign is no longer constant.

Example 2: LWR PDE, shock wave back-propagation due to a bottleneck. For this example, we consider the LWR PDE with a Greenshields flux function [24]:

$$\frac{\partial \rho}{\partial t} + v\left(1 - \frac{2\rho}{\rho^*}\right)\frac{\partial \rho}{\partial x} = 0 \tag{1}$$

where $\rho = \rho(x,t)$ is the vehicle density on the highway, ρ^* is the *jam density* and v is the *free flow density* (see [17, 18] for more explanations on the interpretation of these parameters). We consider a road of length $L = 30$, $\rho^* = 4$ and $v = 1$ (dummy values), and an initial density profile given by $\rho_0(x) \triangleq \rho(x,0) = 2$ if $x \in [0,10]$, $\rho_0(x) \triangleq \rho(x,0) = 4$ if $x \in (10,20]$, $\rho_0(x) \triangleq \rho(x,0) = 1$ if $x > 20$. The highway might be bounded or unbounded on the right at $x = L = 30$ (it does not matter for our problem). We assume free flow conditions at $x = L$, that we can control the inflow at $x = 0$, and we try to prescribe it pointwise, i.e. $\rho(0,t) = 2$ for all t (this corresponds to sending the maximum flow onto the highway). The solution to this problem can easily be computed by hand (for example by the method of characteristics, see Figure 1, left). The solution to this problem reads

$$\begin{cases} \rho(x,t) = 2 & \text{if } t \le 2(10-x) & \text{AC: shock} \\ \rho(x,t) = 4 & \text{if } 2(10-x) \le t \le 20 - x & \text{BC: left edge of exp. wave} \\ \rho(x,t) = 2(1-(x-20)/t) & \text{if } t \ge \max\{20-x, 2(x-20)\} & \text{CBD is an expansion wave} \\ \rho(x,t) = 1 & \text{if } t \le 2(x-20) & \text{BD: right edge of exp. wave} \end{cases}$$

As can be seen, $\lim_{x \to 0^+} \rho(x,t) = 2$ for $t \le 20$ and $\lim_{x \to 0^+} \rho(x,t) = 2(1+20/t)$ for $t > 20$. Thus, the boundary condition $\rho(0,t) = 2$ is no longer verified as soon

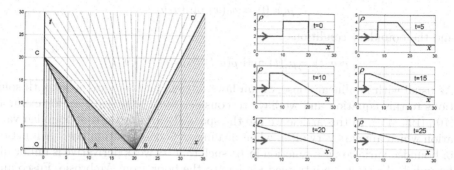

Fig. 1. Left: Characteristics for the solution of the LWR PDE for Example 2. **Right:** corresponding value of the solution at successive times. The arrow represents the value of the input at $x = 0$, which becomes irrelevant for $t \geq 20$.

as $t \geq 20$. This phenomenon is crucial in traffic flow models: it represents the back-propagation of congestion (i.e. upstream). If the location $x = 0$ was the end of a link merging into the highway (that we could potentially control), the case when $\rho(0^+, t) > \rho^*$ is congested would correspond to a situation in which the upstream flow ($x = 0^-$) is imposed by the downstream flow ($x = 0^+$), i.e. the boundary condition on the left becomes irrelevant. When $\rho(0^+, t) < \rho^*$ is not congested, the boundary condition is relevant and can be imposed pointwise.

Example 3: Burgers equation. We now consider the inviscid Burgers equation on $(0, 1) \times (0, T)$. If we try to prescribe strong boundary conditions at both ends, the problem becomes ill-posed. Burgers equation reads:

$$\frac{\partial u}{\partial t} + u \frac{\partial u}{\partial x} = 0 \qquad (2)$$

The initial value is $u(x, 0) = 1$, and the boundary conditions $u(0, t) = u(1, t) = 0$ on $[0, 1]$. The solution of (2) with these boundary conditions is for $t < 1$:

$$\begin{cases} u(x, t) = \frac{x}{t} \text{ if } x < t \text{ self similar expansion wave} \\ u(x, t) = 1 \text{ if } x > t \text{ convection to the right with speed 1} \end{cases}$$

We notice that the boundary condition is not satisfied at $x = 1$. Since the data propagates at speed u, they are leaving $[0, 1]$ at $x = 1$ while they stay in $[0, 1]$ as a rarefaction wave at $x = 0$.

3   Traffic Flow Equation with Hybrid Boundary Conditions

We consider a mixed initial-boundary value problem for a scalar conservation law on $(a, b) \times (0, T)$.

$$\frac{\partial \rho}{\partial t} + \frac{\partial q(\rho)}{\partial x} = 0 \qquad (3)$$

with the initial condition

$$\rho(x,0) = \rho_0(x) \text{ on } (a,b)$$

and the boundary conditions

$$\rho(a,t) = \rho_a(t) \text{ and } \rho(b,t) = \rho_b(t) \text{ on } (0,T).$$

As usual with nonlinear conservation laws, in general there are no smooth solutions to this equation and we have to consider weak solutions (see for example [10], [19], [45]). In this article we use the space BV of functions of bounded variation which appears very often when dealing with conservation laws. A function of bounded variation is a function in L^1 such that its weak derivative is uniformly bounded. We refer the intrigued readers to the book from Ambrosio, Fusco and Pallara [1] for many more properties and applications of BV functions. Other valuable references on BV functions include the article by Vol'pert [48] and the book from Evans and Gariepy [20].

In our problem, we make the assumption that the flux q is continuous and that the initial and boundary conditions ρ_0, ρ_a, ρ_b are functions of bounded variation. When the flux q models the flux of cars in terms of the car density ρ we obtain the LWR PDE. As explained earlier on, boundary conditions may not be fulfilled pointwise a.e., thus following [8], we shall require that an entropy solution of (3) satisfy a weak formulation of the boundary conditions:

$$L(\rho(a,t), \rho_a(t)) = 0 \text{ and } R(\rho(b,t), \rho_b(t)) = 0$$

where

$$L(x,y) = \sup_{k \in I(x,y)} (sg(x-y)(q(x) - q(k))) \text{ and}$$

$$R(x,y) = \inf_{k \in I(x,y)} (sg(x-y)(q(x) - q(k))) \text{ for } x, y \in \mathbb{R}$$

and $I(x,y) = [\inf(x,y), \sup(x,y)]$ with sg denoting the sign function. In the case of a strictly concave flux (such as the Greenshields [24] and Greenberg [23] models used in traffic flow modeling), the boundary conditions can be written as (Le Floch gives analogous conditions in the case of a strictly convex flux in [33]):

$$\begin{cases} \rho(a,t) = \rho_a(t) \text{ or} \\ q'(\rho(a,t)) \leqslant 0 \text{ and } q'(\rho_a(t)) \leqslant 0 \text{ or} \\ q'(\rho(a,t)) \leqslant 0 \text{ and } q'(\rho_a(t)) \geqslant 0 \text{ and } q(\rho(a,t)) \leqslant q(\rho_a(t)) \end{cases} \quad (4)$$

Similarly, the boundary condition at b is:

$$\begin{cases} \rho(b,t) = \rho_b(t) \text{ or} \\ q'(\rho(b,t)) \geqslant 0 \text{ and } q'(\rho_b(t)) \geqslant 0 \text{ or} \\ q'(\rho(b,t)) \geqslant 0 \text{ and } q'(\rho_b(t)) \leqslant 0 \text{ and } q(\rho(b,t)) \geqslant q(\rho_b(t)) \end{cases} \quad (5)$$

As noticed in [33], we can always assume the boundary data are entering the domain at both ends. Indeed, if for example $q'(\rho_a(t)) < 0$ on a subset I of $\mathbb{R}_+$ of positive measure, the boundary data:

$$\tilde{\rho}_a(t) = \begin{cases} q'^{-1}(0) \text{ if } t \in I \\ \rho_a(t) \text{ otherwise} \end{cases} \tag{6}$$

will yield the same solution. With this assumption the boundary conditions can be written as:

$$\begin{cases} \rho(a,t) = \rho_a(t) \text{ or} \\ q'(\rho(a,t)) \leqslant 0 \text{ and } q(\rho(a,t)) \leqslant q(\rho_a(t)) \end{cases} \tag{7}$$

and

$$\begin{cases} \rho(b,t) = \rho_b(t) \text{ or} \\ q'(\rho(b,t)) \geqslant 0 \text{ and } q(\rho(b,t)) \geqslant q(\rho_b(t)) \end{cases} \tag{8}$$

We can now define an notion of entropy solution for a scalar conservation law (3) with initial and boundary conditions.

Interpretation of the hybrid automaton for concave flux functions. Figure 2 (left) shows the three-mode automaton corresponding to (4). The first mode, $\rho(a,t) = \rho_a(t)$ corresponds to the situation in which the boundary condition $\rho_a(t)$ is effectively applied (as in the strong sense). The second mode $q'(\rho(a,t)) \leqslant 0$ and $q'(\rho_a(t)) \leqslant 0$ corresponds to a situation in which the characteristics exit the domain at $x = a$ for both the solution $\rho(a,t)$ and the prescribed boundary condition $\rho_a(t)$ (therefore the boundary condition does not 'affect' the solution). The third mode corresponds to a supercritical $\rho(a,t)$, i.e. $\rho(a,t) \geq \rho_c$ (see Figure 3 and [17, 18]), a subcritical $\rho_a(t)$, i.e. i.e. $\rho_a(t) \leq \rho_c$, and a prescribed inflow $q(\rho_a(t))$ greater than the actual flow $q(\rho(a,t))$ at $x = a$. This corresponds to a shock moving to the left (to see this, plug the previous quantities in the Rankine-Hugoniot conditions), which means that the prescribed boundary condition does

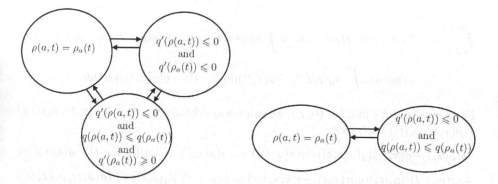

Fig. 2. Left: Hybrid automaton encoding the boundary conditions at $x = a$, corresponding to (4). A similar automaton can be constructed for (5). **Right:** Simplification of the automaton corresponding to the transformation of (4) into (7). A similar automaton can be constructed for (8) from (5).

not 'affect' the solution. The guards for this hybrid systems are thus determined by the sign of the flux derivative $q'(\cdot)$ and the values of the flux $q(\cdot)$ at $x = a$.

Definition: A solution of the mixed initial-boundary value problem for the PDE (3) is a function $\rho \in L^\infty((a,b) \times (0,T))$ such that for every $k \in \mathbb{R}$, $\varphi \in C_c^1((0,T))$, the space of C^1 functions with compact support, and $\psi \in C_c^1((a,b) \times (0,T))$ with φ and ψ nonnegative:

$$\int_a^b \int_0^T (|\rho - k|\frac{\partial \psi}{\partial t} + sg(\rho - k)(q(\rho) - q(k))\frac{\partial \psi}{\partial x})dxdt \geqslant 0$$

and there exist E_0, E_L, E_R three sets of measure zero such that :

$$\lim_{t \to 0, t \notin E_0} \int_a^b |\rho(x,t) - \rho_0(x)|dx = 0$$

$$\lim_{x \to a, x \notin E_L} \int_0^T L(\rho(x,t), \rho_a(t))\varphi(t)dt = 0$$

$$\lim_{x \to b, x \notin E_R} \int_0^T R(\rho(x,t), \rho_b(t))\varphi(t)dt = 0$$

With this definition, we now establish the uniqueness by proving an L^1- semigroup property following the method introduced by Kružkov [31] (see also the articles from Keyfitz [28] and Schonbek [44]).

Let ρ, σ be two solutions of (3), φ and ψ two test functions in $C_c^1((0,T))$ and $C_c^1((a,b))$ respectively and nonnegative; the aforementioned definition yields:

$$\int_a^b \int_0^T (|\rho(x,t) - \sigma(x,t)|\psi(x)\varphi'(t) + sg(\rho(x,t) - \sigma(x,t))(q(\rho(x,t)) - q(\sigma(x,t)))\varphi(t)\psi'(x)))dxdt \geqslant 0$$

For ψ approximating $\chi|_{[a,b]}$, the characteristic function of the interval $[a,b]$, we have:

$$\int_a^b \int_0^T |\rho(x,t) - \sigma(x,t)|\varphi'(t)dt \geqslant \liminf_{x \to b} \int_0^T sg(\rho(x,t) - \sigma(x,t))(q(\rho(x,t) - q(\sigma(x,t)))\varphi(t)dt$$

$$- \limsup_{x \to a} \int_0^T sg(\rho(x,t) - \sigma(x,t))(q(\rho(x,t)) - q(\sigma(x,t)))\varphi(t)dt.$$

For a fixed $x \notin E_L$ and $t \in (0,T)$, we can always define $k(x,t) \in I(\sigma(x,t), \rho_a(t)) \cap I(\rho(x,t), \rho_a(t))$ such that:

$$sg(\rho(x,t) - \sigma(x,t))(q(\rho(x,t)) - q(\sigma(x,t))) = sg(\rho(x,t) - \rho_a(t))(q(\rho(x,t)) - q(k(x,t)))$$

$$+ sg(\sigma(x,t) - \rho_a(t))(q(\sigma(x,t)) - q(k(x,t))) \leqslant L(\rho(x,t), \rho_a(x,t)) + L(\sigma(x,t), \rho_a(x,t)).$$

The situation is similar in a neighborhood of b which eventually yields:

$$\int_a^b \int_0^T |\rho(x,t) - \sigma(x,t)|\varphi'(t)dtdx \geqslant 0.$$

Therefore, for $0 < t_0 < t_1 < T$,

$$\int_a^b |\rho(x,t_1) - \sigma(x,t_1)|dx \leqslant \int_a^b |\rho(x,t_0) - \sigma(x,t_0)|dx$$

which proves the L^1-semigroup property from which the uniqueness follows.

4 Numerical Methods for the Initial-Boundary Value Problem

In this section, we prove the existence of a solution to equation (3) through the convergence of the Godunov scheme. Let $h = \frac{b-a}{M}$ and $I_i = [a + h(i - \frac{1}{2}), a + h(i + \frac{1}{2}))$ for $i \in \{0, ..., M\}$. For $r > 0$, let $J_n = [(n - \frac{1}{2})rh, (n + \frac{1}{2})rh)$ with $n \in \{0, 1, ..., N = E(1 + \frac{T}{rh})\}$. We approximate the solution ρ by ρ_i^n on each cell $I_i \times J_n$, with ρ_h the resulting function on $[a, b] \times [0, T]$. The initial and boundary conditions can be written as:

$$\begin{cases} \rho_i^0 = \frac{1}{h} \int_{I_i} \rho_0(x)dx \ , \ 0 \leqslant i \leqslant M \\ \rho_0^n = \frac{1}{rh} \int_{J_n} \rho_a(t)dt \text{ and } \rho_M^n = \frac{1}{rh} \int_{J_n} \rho_b(t)dt \ , \ 0 \leqslant n \leqslant N \end{cases}$$

According to the Godunov scheme [22], ρ_i^{n+1} is computed from ρ_i^n by the following algorithm:

$$\begin{cases} \rho_{i+\frac{1}{2}}^n \text{ is an element } k \text{ of } I(\rho_i^n, \rho_{i+1}^n) \text{ such that } sg(\rho_{i+1}^n - \rho_i^n)q(k) \text{ is minimal} \\ \rho_i^{n+1} = \rho_i^n - r(q(\rho_{i+\frac{1}{2}}^n) - q(\rho_{i-\frac{1}{2}}^n)) \end{cases}$$

Let $M_0 = \max(\|\rho_0\|_\infty, \|\rho_a\|_\infty, \|\rho_b\|_\infty)$; if the CFL (Courant-Friedrichs-Lewy) condition ([35])

$$r \sup_{|k| < M_0} |q'(k)| \leqslant 1$$

is verified, ρ_h converges in $L^1((a, b) \times (0, T))$ to a solution $\rho \in BV((a, b) \times (0, T))$. The CFL condition yields the following estimates:

$$|\rho_i^{n+1}| \leqslant (1 + C_0 h) \sup(|\rho_{i-\frac{1}{2}}^n|, |\rho_i^n|, |\rho_{i+\frac{1}{2}}^n|) + C_1 h \text{ for every } i \in \mathbb{Z}$$

$$\sum_{1 \leqslant i \leqslant M} |\rho_{i+1}^{n+1} - \rho_i^{n+1}| \leqslant (1 + C_2 h) \sum_{|i| \leqslant M+1} |\rho_{i+1}^n - \rho_i^n| + C_3 M h^2 \text{ for every } M \in \mathbb{N}$$

$$\sum_{|i| \leqslant M} |\rho_i^{n+1} - \rho_i^n| \leqslant \sum_{|i| \leqslant M+1} |\rho_{i+1}^n - \rho_i^n| + C_4 M h (1 + \sup_{i \in \mathbb{Z}} |\rho_i^n|) \text{ for every } M \in \mathbb{N}$$

from which we can deduce that a subsequence ρ_{h_n} converges strongly to a function $\rho \in L^\infty((a, b) \times (0, T))$ of bounded variation and verifying the initial condition. We also have for k of $I(\rho_i^n, \rho_{i+1}^n)$

$$|\rho_i^{n+1} - k| \leqslant |\rho_i^n - k| - r(sg(\rho_{i+\frac{1}{2}}^n - k)(q(\rho_{i+\frac{1}{2}}^n) - q(k)) - sg(\rho_{i-\frac{1}{2}}^n - k)(q(\rho_{i-\frac{1}{2}}^n) - q(k)))$$

which shows that ρ is a weak solution of (3). If $\varphi^n = \frac{1}{rh} \int_{I_n} \varphi(t)dt$ for $\varphi \in C_c^1((0,T))$, non negative, we have:

$$\sum_{0 \leqslant n \leqslant N} sg(\rho_{i+\frac{1}{2}}^n - k)(q(\rho_{i+\frac{1}{2}}^n) - q(k))\varphi^n rh \leqslant \sum_{0 \leqslant n \leqslant N} sg(\rho_{\frac{1}{2}}^n - k)(q(\rho_{\frac{1}{2}}^n) - q(k))\varphi^n rh +$$

$$+ih\|\varphi'\|_\infty T(M_0 + |k|).$$

Let $\lambda(t)$ be the weak $*$ limit in $L^\infty((0,T))$ of a subsequence of $q(\rho_{\frac{1}{2}}^i)$; the following inequality holds:

$$\int_0^T sg(\rho(x,t) - k)(q(\rho(x,t)) - q(k))\varphi(t)dt \leqslant \int_0^T sg(\rho_a(t) - k)(\lambda(t) - q(k))\varphi(t)dt +$$

$$+|x - a|\|\varphi'\|_\infty T(M_0 + |k|),$$

using that $sg(\rho_{\frac{1}{2}}^n - k)(q(\rho_{\frac{1}{2}}) - q(k)) \leqslant sg(\rho_0^n - k)(q(\rho_{\frac{1}{2}}) - q(k))$.

$\rho(x,.)$ is of bounded variation, therefore it converges strongly in L^1 sense to a limit $\alpha \in L^\infty((0,T))$ and it verifies:

$$sg(\alpha(t) - k)(q(\alpha(t)) - q(k)) \leqslant sg(\rho_a(t) - k)(\lambda(t) - q(k))$$

for every $k \in \mathbb{R}$ and a.e. $t \in (0,T)$. This inequality shows that $\lambda = q(\alpha)$ a.e. and $L(\alpha(t), \rho_a(t)) \leqslant 0$ and ρ verifies the weak boundary condition at $x = a$. Similarly, ρ verifies the corresponding condition at $x = b$ and the existence is proved.

5   Implementation and Simulations for I201W

We now turn to the practical implementation of the Godunov scheme for the LWR PDE. The scheme is written as follows:

$$\rho_i^{n+1} = \rho_i^n - r(q_G(\rho_i^n, \rho_{i+1}^n) - q_G(\rho_{i-1}^n, \rho_i^n))$$

If the flux q is strictly concave, which is often the case in traffic flow modeling, it reaches its only maximum at a point ρ_c (see Figure 3) and the numerical flux is defined by:

$$q_G(\rho_1, \rho_2) = \begin{cases} \min(\rho_1, \rho_2) & \text{if } \rho_1 \leqslant \rho_2, \\ q(\rho_1) & \text{if } \rho_2 < \rho_1 < \rho_c, \\ q(\rho_c) & \text{if } \rho_2 < \rho_c < \rho_1, \\ q(\rho_2) & \text{if } \rho_c < \rho_2 < \rho_1. \end{cases}$$

The boundary conditions are treated via the insertion of a ghost cell on the left and on the right of the domain, that is:

$$\rho_0^{n+1} = \rho_0^n - r(q_G(\rho_0^n, \rho_1^n) - q_G(\rho_{-1}^n, \rho_0^n))$$

with $\rho_{-1}^n = \frac{1}{rh} \int_{J_n} \rho_a(t)dt$, $0 \leqslant n \leqslant N$ for the left boundary condition and

$$\rho_M^{n+1} = \rho_M^n - r(q_G(\rho_M^n, \rho_{M+1}^n) - q_G(\rho_{M-1}^n, \rho_M^n))$$

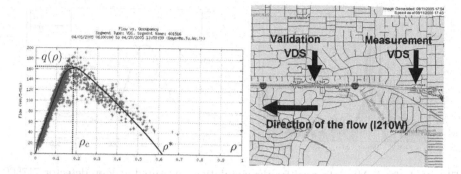

Fig. 3. Left: Illustration of the empirical data obtained from the PeMS system. The horizontal axis represents the normalized density ρ (i.e. occupancy, see [41, 38] for more details). The vertical axis represents the flux $q(\cdot)$. Each track corresponds to a loop detector measurement. This data can easily be modelled with a strictly concave flux function (solid fit), for which we display the critical density ρ_c and the jam density, ρ^*. **Right:** Location of the loop detectors used for measurement and validation purposes.

with $\rho_{M+1}^n = \frac{1}{rh} \int_{J_n} \rho_b(t) dt$, $0 \leqslant n \leqslant N$ on the right of the domain. We illustrate an application of this Godunov scheme to the simulation of highway traffic. A comparison of the density obtained numerically with the corresponding experimental density measured by the loop detectors is performed. We consider I210 West in Los Angeles and focus on a stretch going from the Santa Anita on-ramp 1 to the Baldwin on-ramp 2 in free-flow conditions between midnight and 05:00 a.m. The data measured by the loop detectors is accessible through the PeMS system (Performance Measurement System [41]); in our case the two detectors ID are 764669 and 717664.

We measure the flow at the loop detector 764669 (left subfigure in Figure 4). The need for signal processing is quite visible; for this example, it was done using Fast Fourier Transform methods. Noise levels are a very important issue with PeMS measurements, that has been covered extensively in the literature and is out of the scope of this work. The comparison with the actual measurements is performed at the next downstream loop detector (detector 717664), see right subfigure in Figure 4. The results shown in this figure illustrate the fact that the method is able to reproduce traffic flow patterns over an extended period of time (5 hours in the present case). The numerical simulation was done with FORTRAN codes from the CLAWPACK software developed by LeVeque and available at [12], implemented on a Sun Blade workstation. Further model refinements would be needed to obtain an enhanced matching of the two curves. This is also out of the scope of this article (the reader is referred to [38] for more on this topic).

6 Optimization of Travel Time Via Boundary Control

Our next endeavor is directed towards the minimization of the mean time spent by cars traveling through a stretch of highway between $x = x_0$ and $x = x_1$ via

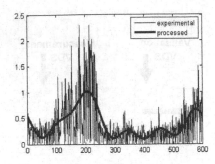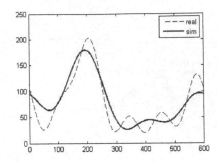

Fig. 4. Left: PeMS data used for the simulation, measured at loop detector 717669. The horizontal axis represents time, the vertical axis represents the inflow at the left boundary. **Right:** Comparison between loop detector measurements 717664 and flux simulations predicted by the model at the same location. The horizontal axis is time; the vertical axis is the vehicle flux. Source [41] .

the adjustment of the density of cars entering the highway. The results from Ancona and Marson ([2], [3]) enable us to solve this problem. The first step consists in studying the attainable set at a fixed point in space x_1:

$A(x_1, \mathcal{C}) = \{\rho(x_1, .)\}$, ρ being a solution of the LWR PDE with $\rho_0 = 0$ and $\rho_a \in \mathcal{C}$ for a given set of admissible controls $\mathcal{C} \subset L^1_{loc}$.

Using the method of generalized characteristics introduced by Dafermos ([15], [16]), the attainable set is shown to be compact, the key argument being that the set of fluxes $\{q(\rho_a), \rho_a \in \mathcal{C}\}$ is weakly compact in L^1 (see [32] for functional analysis in L^p spaces). The compactness of the attainable set in turn yields the existence of a solution to the optimal control problem

$$\min_{\rho_a \in \mathcal{C}} F(S_{(.)}\rho_a(x_1))$$

for $F : L^1([0, T]) \to \mathbb{R}$ a lower semicontinuous functional and $\mathcal{C}$ a set of admissible controls. We use the semigroup notation $S_t\rho_a$ to designate the unique solution of the LWR PDE at time t (we refer to the textbook [19] for more on semigroup theory). In the case of traffic modeling on a highway, we wish to minimize the difference between the average incoming time of cars at $x = x_1$ and at $x = x_0$ which can be written as:

$$\min_{\rho_a \in \mathcal{C}} \left(\int_0^{+\infty} tq(S_t\rho_a(x_1))dt - \int_0^{+\infty} tg(t)dt \right) \left(\int_0^{+\infty} g(t)dt \right)^{-1}$$

where $g(t)$ represents the number of cars entering the stretch of highway per unit of time. This amounts to solving the equivalent problem:

$$\min_{\rho_a \in \mathcal{C}} \int_0^{+\infty} tq(S_t\rho_a(x_1))dt$$

For this particular problem, we make the following additional assumptions:

- the net flux of cars entering the highway is equal to the total number of cars arriving at the entry:

$$\int_0^{+\infty} q(\rho_a(s))ds = \int_0^{+\infty} g(s)ds$$

- for every time $t > 0$ the total number of cars which have entered the highway is smaller than or equal to the total number of cars that have arrived at the entry from time 0 to t:

$$\int_0^t q(\rho_a(s))ds \leqslant \int_0^t g(s)ds$$

- the number of cars entering the highway is at most equal to the maximum density of cars on the highway:

$$\rho_a(t) \in [0, \rho_m]$$

- after a given time T no cars enter the highway:

$$\rho_a(t) = 0 \text{ for } t > T.$$

The map $F : \rho \rightarrow \int_0^T q(\rho(t))dt$ is obviously a continuous functional on L^1_{loc} ($[0,T]$), hence the existence of a solution of an optimal control ρ_a.

Furthermore, a comparison principle for solutions of scalar nonlinear conservation laws with boundary conditions established by Terracina in [47] will allow us to find an explicit expression of the optimal control. Indeed if $\rho(x,t)$ is a weak solution of the LWR PDE, $u(x,t) = -\int_x^{+\infty} \rho(y,t)dy$ is the viscosity solution ([14]) of the Hamilton-Jacobi equation

$$\frac{\partial u}{\partial t} + q(\frac{\partial u}{\partial x}) = q(0).$$

Since viscosity solutions verify a comparison property [13], so will the solution of the LWR PDE.

Since $\int_0^T tq(S_t\rho_a(x_1))dt = T\int_0^T q(S_t\rho_a(x_1))dt - \int_0^T \int_0^t q(S_s\rho_a(x_1))dsdt$, the boundary control problem can be rewritten as:

$$\max_{\rho_a \in C} \int_0^T \int_0^t q(S_s\rho_a(x_1))dsdt.$$

As we can assume that the boundary data is always incoming, the comparison principle shows that the optimal control $\tilde{\rho}$ should verify:

$$\int_0^t q(\tilde{\rho}(s))ds \geqslant \int_0^t q(\rho_a(s))ds, \text{ for every } t > 0 \text{ and } \rho_a \in C.$$

Eventually we obtain the following expression of the optimal control $\tilde{\rho}$:

$$\tilde{\rho}(t) = \begin{cases} q^{-1}(\rho_m) & \text{if } g(t) \leqslant q(\rho_m) \text{ and } \int_0^t q(\tilde{\rho}(s))ds < \int_0^t g(s)ds \text{ or } g(t) > q(\rho_m) \\ q^{-1}(g(t)) & \text{if } g(t) \leqslant q(\rho_m) \text{ and } \int_0^t q(\tilde{\rho}(s))ds = \int_0^t g(s)ds \end{cases}$$

7   Conclusion

We have proved the existence and uniqueness of a weak solution to a scalar conservation law on a bounded domain. The proof relies on the weak formulation of the hybrid boundary conditions which is necessary for the problem to be well posed. For strictly concave flux functions, the simplified expression of the weak formulation of the hybrid boundary conditions was written explicitly. The corresponding Godunov scheme was developed and applied on a highway traffic flow application, using PeMS data for the I210W highway in Pasadena. The numerical scheme and the parameters identified for this highway were validated experimentally against measured data. Finally, the existence of a minimizer of travel time was obtained, with corresponding optimal boundary control.

The hybridness of the boundary conditions is closely linked to the one-dimensional nature of the problem (i.e. to the direction of the characteristics and the corresponding values of the fluxes). The switches between the modes occur based on the value of the solution, which itself acts as a guard. The boundary conditions derived in this article should thus be viewed as an instantiation of the more general weak boundary conditions given in [8], for which a clear hybrid structure appears in the one dimensional case, through a modal behavior.

This article should be viewed as a first step towards building sound metering control strategies for highway networks: it defines the mathematical solution, and appropriate hybrid boundary conditions to apply in order to pose and solve the optimal control problem properly. Not using the framework developed here while computing numerical solutions of the LWR PDE would lead to ill-posed problems and therefore the data obtained through a numerical scheme would be meaningless.

Our result is crucial for highway performance optimization, since by nature, in most highways, traffic flow control is achieved by on-ramp metering, i.e. boundary control. However, results are still lacking in order to generalize our approach to a real highway network. For such a network, PDEs are coupled through boundary conditions, which makes the problem harder to pose. Furthermore, optimization problems arising in transportation networks often cannot be solved as the problem derived in the last section of this article. In fact, several approaches have to rely on the computation of the gradient of the optimization functional, which for example could be achieved using adjoint-based techniques. Obtaining the proper formulation of the adjoint problem, and the corresponding proofs of existence and uniqueness of the resulting solutions represents a challenge for which the present result is a building block.

Acknowledgements. We are grateful to Antoine Bonnet and Remy Nollet for their help with the PeMS data. We acknowledge fruitful discussions with Professor Roberto Horowitz on highway traffic control problems. I. Strub wishes to thank Professor F. Rezakhanlou for his helpful remarks and bibliographical references.

References

1. L. AMBROSIO, N. FUSCO, D. PALLARA. *Functions of bounded variation and free discontinuity problems.* Oxford Mathematical Monographs. The Clarendon Press, Oxford University Press, New York, 2000.
2. F. ANCONA, A. MARSON. On the attainable set for scalar nonlinear conservation laws with boundary control. *SIAM J. Control Optim.*, 36(1):290–312, 1998.
3. F. ANCONA, A. MARSON. Scalar non-linear conservation laws with integrable boundary data. *Nonlinear Analysis*, 35:687–710, 1999.
4. R. ANSORGE. What does the entropy condition mean in traffic flow theory? *Transportation Research*, 24B(2):133–143, 1990.
5. J. A. ATWELL, J. T. BORGGAARD, B. B. KING. Reduced order controllers for Burgers' equation with a nonlinear observer. *Applied Mathematics and Computational Science*, 11(6):1311–1330, 2001.
6. J. BAKER, A. ARMAOU, P. D. CHRISTOFIDES. Nonlinear control of incompressible fluid flow: Application to burgers' equation and 2d channel flow. *Journal of Mathematical Analysis and Applications*, 252:230–255, 2000.
7. A. BALOGH, M. KRSTIC. Burgers' equation with nonlinear boundary feedback: H_1 stability, well posedness, and simulation. *Mathematical Problems in Engineering*, 6:189–200, 2000.
8. C. BARDOS, A. Y. LEROUX, J. C. NEDELEC. First order quasilinear equations with boundary conditions. *Comm. Part. Diff. Eqns*, 4(9):1017–1034, 1979.
9. A. M. BAYEN, R. L. RAFFARD, C. J. TOMLIN. Network congestion alleviation using adjoint hybrid control: application to highways. In R. Alur and G. J. Pappas, editors, *Hybrid Systems: Computation and Control*, Lecture Notes in Computer Science 2993, pages 95–110. Springer-Verlag, 2004.
10. A. BRESSAN. *Hyperbolic systems of conservation laws: the one dimensional Cauchy problem.* Oxford Lecture Series in Mathematics and its Applications, 20. Oxford University Press, 2000.
11. C. I. BYRNES, D. S. GILLIAM, V. I. SHUBOV. Semiglobal stabilization of a boundary controlled viscous burgers' equation. In *Proceedings of the 38th IEEE Conference on Decision and Control*, pages 680–681, Phoenix, AZ, Dec. 1999.
12. CLAWPACK 4.2, http://www.amath.washington.edu/~claw/
13. M. G. CRANDALL. Viscosity solutions: a primer. In *Viscosity solutions and applications*, Lecture Notes in Mathematics 1660, pages 1–43. Springer, Berlin, 1997.
14. M. G. CRANDALL, L. C. EVANS, P.-L. LIONS. Some properties of viscosity solutions of Hamilton-Jacobi equations. *Trans. Amer. Math. Soc.*, 282:487–502, 1984.
15. C. DAFERMOS Generalized characteristics and the structure of solutions of hyperbolic conservation laws. *Indiana Math. J.*, 26:1097–1119, 1977.
16. C. DAFERMOS *Hyberbolic conservation laws in continuum physics.* Grundlehren der Mathematischen Wissenschaften, 325. Springer-Verlag, 2000.
17. C. DAGANZO. The cell transmission model: a dynamic representation of highway traffic consistent with the hydrodynamic theory. *Transportation Research*, 28B(4):269–287, 1994.
18. C. DAGANZO. The cell transmission model, part II: network traffic. *Transportation Research*, 29B(2):79–93, 1995.
19. L. C. EVANS. *Partial differential equations.* Graduate studies in Mathematics, 19. A.M.S. 2002.
20. L. C. EVANS, R. F. GARIEPY. *Measure theory and fine properties of functions.* CRC Press, 1991.

21. D. C. GAZIS. *Traffic theory.* International series in Operations Research and Management Science, Boston, Kluwer Academic, 2002.
22. S. K. GODUNOV. A difference method for numerical calculation of discontinuous solutions of the equations of hydrodynamics. *Math. Sbornik*, 47:271–306, 1959.
23. H. GREENBERG. An analysis of traffic flow. *Operation Res.*, 7(1):79–85, 1959.
24. B. D. GREENSHIELDS A study of traffic capacity. *Proc. Highway Res. Board*, 14:448–477, 1935.
25. A. JAMESON. Analysis and design of numerical schemes for gas dynamics 1: Artificial diffusion, upwind biasing, limiters and their effect on accuracy and multigrid convergence. *International Journal of Computational Fluid Dynamics*, 4:171–218, 1995.
26. A. JAMESON. Analysis and design of numerical schemes for gas dynamics 2: Artificial diffusion and discrete shock structure. *International Journal of Computational Fluid Dynamics*, 4:1–38, 1995.
27. K. T. JOSEPH, G. D. VEERAPPA GOWDA. Explicit formula for the solution of convex conservation laws with boundary condition. *Duke Math. J.*, 62(2):401–416, 1991.
28. B. L. KEYFITZ. Solutions with shocks. *Comm. Pure and Appl. Math.*, 24:125–132, 1971.
29. T. KOBAYASHI. Adaptive regulator design of a viscous Burgers' system by boundary control. *IMA Journal of Mathematical Control and Information*, 18(3):427–437, 2001.
30. M. KRSTIĆ. On global stabilization of Burgers' equation by boundary control. *Systems and Control Letters*, 37:123–142, March 1999.
31. S. N. KRUŽKOV. First order quasilinear equations in several independent variables. *Math. USSR Sbornik*, 10:217–243, 1970.
32. P. D. LAX. *Functional analysis.* Wiley-Interscience, 2002.
33. P. LE FLOCH. Explicit formula for scalar non-linear conservation laws with boudary condition. *Math. Meth. Appl. Sci.*, 10:265–287, 1988.
34. A. Y. LEROUX. Vanishing viscosity method for a quasilinear first order equation with boundary conditions. *Conference on the Numerical Analysis of Singular Perturbation Problems*, Nijnegen, Academic Press, 1978.
35. R. J. LEVEQUE. *Finite volume methods for hyperbolic problems.* Cambridge University Press, Cambridge, 2002.
36. M. J. LIGHTHILL, G. B. WHITHAM. On kinematic waves. II. A theory of traffic flow on long crowded roads. *Proceedings of the Royal Society of London*, 229(1178): 317–345, 1956.
37. H. LY, K. D. MEASE, E. S. TITI. Distributed and boundary control of the viscous burgers' equation. *Numerical Functional Analysis and Optimization*, 18(1-2): 143–188, 1997.
38. R. NOLLET. Technical report, July 2005.
39. O. A. OLEINIK. On discontinuous solutions of nonlinear differential equations. *Uspekhi Mat. Nauk.*, 12:3–73, 1957. English translation: *American Mathematical Society*, Ser. 2 No. 26 pp. 95–172, 1963.
40. M. ÖNDER, E. ÖZBAY. Low dimensional modelling and dirichlet boundary controller design for burgers equation. *International Journal of Control*, 77(10): 895–906, 2004.
41. Freeway performance measurement system, http://pems.eecs.berkeley.edu
42. N. PETIT. *Systèmes à retard. Platitude en génie des procédés et contrôle de certaines équations des ondes.* PhD thesis, Ecole Nationale Supérieure des Mines de Paris, 2000.

43. P. I. RICHARDS. Shock waves on the highway. *Operations Research*, 4(1):42–51, 1956.
44. M. E. SCHONBEK. Existence of solutions to singular conservation laws. *J. Math. Anal.*, 15(6):1125–1139, 1984.
45. D. SERRE. *Systems of conservation laws. Volume 1: Hyperbolicity, entropies, shock waves.* Cambridge University Press, Cambridge, 1999.
46. X. SUN and R. HOROWITZ. Localized switching ramp-metering controller with queue length regulator for congested freeways. In *2005 American Control Conference*, pages 2141–2146, Portland, OR, June 2005.
47. A. TERRACINA. Comparison properties for scalar conservation laws with boundary conditions. *Nonlinear Anal. Theory Meth. Appl.*, 28:633–653, 1997.
48. A. I. VOL'PERT. The spaces *BV* and quasilinear equations. *Math. USSR Sbornik*, 2:225–267, 1967.

Beyond Zeno: Get on with It!*

Haiyang Zheng, Edward A. Lee, and Aaron D. Ames

Center for Hybrid and Embedded Software Systems (CHESS),
Department of Electrical Engineering and Computer Sciences,
University of California, Berkeley, 94720, USA
hyzheng@eecs.berkeley.edu, eal@eecs.berkeley.edu,
adames@eecs.berkeley.edu

Abstract. In this paper we propose a technique to extend the simulation of a Zeno hybrid system beyond its Zeno time point. A Zeno hybrid system model is a hybrid system with an execution that takes an infinite number of discrete transitions during a finite time interval. We argue that the presence of Zeno behavior indicates that the hybrid system model is incomplete by considering some classical Zeno models that incompletely describe the dynamics of the system being modeled. This motivates the systematic development of a method for completing hybrid system models through the introduction of new *post-Zeno* states, where the completed hybrid system transitions to these post-Zeno states at the Zeno time point. In practice, simulating a Zeno hybrid system is challenging in that simulation effectively halts near the Zeno time point. Moreover, due to unavoidable numerical errors, it is not practical to exactly simulate a Zeno hybrid system. Therefore, we propose a method for constructing approximations of Zeno models by leveraging the completed hybrid system model. Using these approximation, we can simulate a Zeno hybrid system model beyond its Zeno point and reveal the complete dynamics of the system being modeled.

1 Introduction

The dynamics of physical systems at the macro scale level (not considering effects at the quantum level) are continuous in general. Even in a digital computer that performs computation in a discrete fashion, its fundamental computing elements (transistors) have continuous dynamics. Therefore, it is a natural choice to model the dynamics of physical systems with ordinary differential equations (ODEs) or partial differential equations (PDEs). However, modeling a physical system with only continuous dynamics may generate a stiff model, because the system dynamics might have several time scales of different magnitudes. Simulating such

---

* This work was supported in part by the Center for Hybrid and Embedded Software Systems (CHESS) at UC Berkeley, which receives support from the National Science Foundation (NSF award #CCR-0225610), the State of California Micro Program, and the following companies: Agilent, DGIST, General Motors, Hewlett Packard, Infineon, Microsoft, and Toyota.

João Hespanha and A. Tiwari (Eds.): HSCC 2006, LNCS 3927, pp. 568–582, 2006.
© Springer-Verlag Berlin Heidelberg 2006

stiff models in general is difficult in that it takes a lot of computation time to get a reasonably accurate simulation result.

Hybrid system modeling offers one way to resolve the above problem by introducing abstractions on dynamics. In particular, slow dynamics are modeled as piecewise constant while fast dynamics are modeled as instantaneous changes, i.e., discretely. In this way, the remaining dynamics will have time scales of about the same magnitude and the efficiency of simulation, especially the simulation speed, is greatly improved. However, special attention must be devoted to hybrid system models because Zeno hybrid system models may arise from the abstractions.

An execution of a Zeno hybrid system has an infinite number of discrete transitions during a finite time interval. The limit of the set of switching time points of a Zeno execution is called the *Zeno time*. The states of the model at the Zeno time point are called the *Zeno states*. Because each discrete transition takes a non-zero and finite computation time, the simulation of a Zeno hybrid system inevitably halts near the Zeno time point.

Some researchers have treated Zeno hybrid system models as over abstractions of the physical systems and tried to rule them out by developing theories to detect Zeno models [1, 2, 3]. However, because of the intrinsic complexity of interactions between continuous and discrete dynamics of hybrid systems, a general theory, which can give the sufficient and necessary conditions for the existence of Zeno behaviors of hybrid system models with nontrivial dynamics, is still not available (and does not appear to be anywhere on the horizon).

Some researchers have tried to extend the simulation of Zeno systems beyond the Zeno point by regularizing the original system [4, 5] or by using a sliding mode simulation algorithm [6]. The regularization method requires modification of the model structure by introducing some lower bound of the interval between consecutive discrete transitions. However, the newly introduced lower bound invalidates the abstractions and assumptions of the instantaneity of discrete transitions. Consequently, the simulation performance might suffer from the resulting stiff models. Furthermore, different behaviors after the Zeno time may be generated depending on the choices of regularizations. This may not be desirable because the physical system being modeled typically has a unique behavior. The sliding mode algorithm tends to be more promising in simulation efficiency and uniqueness of behaviors, but it only applies to special classes of hybrid system models.

A new technique to extend simulations beyond the Zeno time point is presented in [7], where a special class of hybrid systems called *Lagrangian* hybrid systems are considered. Rather than using regularizations or a sliding mode algorithm, the dynamics of a Lagrangian hybrid system before and after the Zeno time point are derived under different constraints. In this paper, we extend the results in [7] to more general hybrid system models.

Before we get into the details of the algorithm on extending simulation beyond Zeno time points, we would like to investigate some classical Zeno hybrid system models including the bouncing ball model [8] and the water tank model [4], and show that they do not completely describe the behavior of the original physical systems.

1.1 Bouncing Ball

Considering a ball bouncing on the ground, where bounces happen instantaneously with a restitution coefficient $e \in [0, 1]$. A hybrid system model for this system is shown in Fig. 1. This model has only one state q_1 associated with a second-order differential equation modeling the continuous dynamics, where the variables x_1 and x_2 represent the ball's position and velocity respectively, and $\dot{x}_1 = x_2$, $\dot{x}_2 = -g$. From this one state, there is a transition e_1 that goes back to itself. The transition has a guard expression, $x_1 = 0 \wedge x_2 \leq 0$, and a reset map, $x_2 := -e \cdot x_2$.[1]

Note that the above guard expression declares that a bounce happens when the ball touches the ground and its velocity x_2 is non-positive, meaning either it is still or it is moving towards the ground. However, further analysis of the model reveals that when the following condition holds, $x_1 = 0 \wedge x_2 = 0$, meaning that the ball is at reset on the ground, the supporting force from the ground cancels out the gravity force. Therefore, the acceleration of the ball should be 0 rather than the acceleration of gravity. Under this circumstance, the ball in fact has a rather different dynamics given by $\dot{x}_1 = x_2$, $\dot{x}_2 = 0$.

This suggests that new dynamics might be necessary to describe the model's behavior. Consequently, the complete description of the dynamics of the bouncing ball system should include both an extra state associated with the new dynamics and a transition that drives the model into that state. One design of such hybrid system models is shown in Fig. 2, where q_2 and e_2 are the new state and transition.

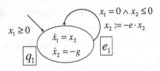

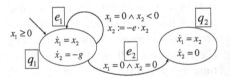

Fig. 1. A hybrid system model of a simple bouncing ball

Fig. 2. A more complete hybrid system model of the bouncing ball

1.2 Water Tank

The second model that we will consider is the water tank system consisting of two tanks. We use x_1 and x_2 for the water levels, r_1 and r_2 for the critical water level thresholds, and v_1 and v_2 for the constant flow of water out of the tanks. There is a constant input flow of water w, which goes through a pipe and into either tank at any particular time point. We assume that $(v_1 + v_2) > w$, meaning that the sum of the output flow in both tanks is greater than the input flow. Therefore, the water levels of both tanks keep dropping. If the water level of any tank drops below its

---

[1] Identity reset maps, such as $x_1 := x_1$, are not explicitly shown.

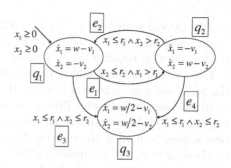

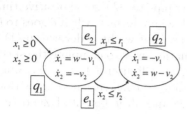

Fig. 3. A hybrid system model of a water tank system

Fig. 4. A more complete hybrid system model of the water tank system

critical threshold, the input water gets delivered into that tank. The process of switching the pipe from one tank to the other takes zero time.

One hybrid system model that describes such system is shown in Fig. 3. This model has two states q_1 and q_2 corresponding to the different dynamics of the system when the input water flows into either of the two tanks. Transitions e_1 and e_2 specify switching conditions between states.

Note that the guard expressions between those two states are not mutually exclusive, meaning that the guards $x_1 \leq r_1$ and $x_2 \leq r_2$ may be enabled at the same time. A trivial example will be that the two tanks have initial water levels $x_1 = r_1$ and $x_2 = r_2$. If the two tanks have initial water levels $x_1 > r_1$ and $x_2 > r_2$, then the water levels of both tanks will drop and the water pipe will switch between the two tanks. As more and more water flows out of tanks, we will see that the frequency of the pipe switching becomes higher and higher. In the limit, when this frequency reaches infinity, both guards become enabled at the same time.

When both guards are enabled, the water tank system will have a different dynamics. Recall the assumption that the switching speed of the water pipe is infinitely fast, the pipe should inject water into both tanks at the same time. In other words, there are virtually two *identical* pipes injecting water into both tanks. Also note that the input water flow is a constant and the pipe cannot hold water, therefore one possible scenario will be that each tank gets *half* of the input water. Therefore, at this time point, the whole system will have a rather different dynamics given by

$$\dot{x}_1 = w/2 - v_1, \quad \dot{x}_2 = w/2 - v_2. \tag{1}$$

We introduce a new state associated with the above dynamics and complete the transitions going from the existing states to the newly added state. The new design of the complete hybrid system model for the water tank system is shown in Fig. 4, where q_3 is the new state, e_3 and e_4 are the newly added transitions. Note that for simplicity we allow the water levels to have negative values. Otherwise, we will need some other discrete states to show that once a tank is empty, it is always empty.

The hybrid system model in Fig. 4 is similar to the *temporal* regularization results proposed in [4]. One of the key differences is that the temporal regularization solution requires the process of switching pipe to take some positive time ϵ. The amount of this ϵ affects the resulting behaviors. In fact, when ϵ goes to 0, the temporal regularization result is the same as what we have derived in (1).

In the next section, we will propose a systematical way to complete the specification of hybrid system models. In particular, we will discuss how to introduce new states, to modify the existing transitions, and to construct new transitions to these new states for model behaviors before and after potential Zeno time points. In Sect. 3, we will develop a feasible simulation algorithm to approximate the exact behaviors of Zeno hybrid system models. Conclusions will be given in Sect. 4.

2   Completing Hybrid System Models

The purpose of this section is to introduce an algorithm for completing hybrid system models with the goal of carrying executions past the Zeno point. This algorithm can be thought of as a combination of the currently known conditions for the existence (or nonexistence) of Zeno behavior in hybrid systems. Of course, the characterization of Zeno behavior in the literature is by no means complete, so we cannot claim that the procedure outlined here is the only way to complete a hybrid system, nor that the resulting hybrid system is the canonical completed hybrid system. We only claim that, given the current understanding of Zeno behavior, this method provides a reasonably satisfying method for completing hybrid systems. We dedicate the latter half of this section to examples, where we carry out the completion process.

2.1   Hybrid System Completion

Define a *hybrid system* as a tuple,

$$\mathscr{H} = (\Gamma, D, G, R, F),$$

where

- $\Gamma = (Q, E)$ is a finite oriented graph, where Q represents the set of discrete states and E represents the set of edges connecting these states. There are two maps $s : E \to Q$ and $t : E \to Q$, which are the source and target maps respectively. That is $s(e)$ is the source of the edge e and $t(e)$ is its target.
- $D = \{D_q \subseteq \mathbb{R}^n \mid q \in Q\}$ is a set of *domains*, one for each state $q \in Q$. While the hybrid system is in state q, the dynamics of the hybrid system is a trajectory in D_q.
- $G = \{G_e \subseteq D_{s(e)} \mid e \in E\}$ is a set of *guards*, where G_e is a set associated with the edge e and determines the switching behavior of the hybrid system at state $s(e)$. When the trajectory intersects with the guard set G_e, a transition is triggered and the discrete state of the hybrid system changes to $t(e)$.

$G_q = \bigcup_{s(e)=q} G_e$ is the union of the guards associated with the outgoing edges from the same state q. We assume that G_q is closed, i.e., that every Cauchy sequence converges to an element in G_q.

- $R = \{R_e : G_e \to D_{t(e)} \mid e \in E\}$ is a set of *reset maps*. We write the image of R_e as $R_e(G_e) \subseteq D_{t(e)}$. These reset maps specify the initial continuous states of trajectories in the target discrete states.
- $F = \{f_q : D_q \to \mathbb{R}^n \mid q \in Q\}$ is a set of *vector fields*, which specify the dynamics of the hybrid system when it is in a discrete state q. We assume f_q is Lipschitz when restricted to D_q.

In this paper, we will not explicitly define hybrid system behavior and Zeno behavior, as these definitions are well-known and can be found in a number of references (cf. [1, 2, 4, 9]).

The goal of this section is to complete a hybrid system $\mathscr{H}$, i.e., we want to form a new hybrid system $\overline{\mathscr{H}}$ in which executions are carried beyond the Zeno point. We begin by constructing this system theoretically and then discuss how to implement it practically. The theoretical completion of a hybrid system is carried out utilizing the following process:

- Augment the graph Γ of $\mathscr{H}$, based on the existence of *higher order cycles*, to include *post-Zeno* states, and edges to these post-Zeno states.
- Specify the domains of the post-Zeno states.
- Specify the guards on the edges to the post-Zeno states.
- Specify the vector fields on the post-Zeno states, based on the vector fields on the pre-Zeno states.

Before carrying out this process, it is necessary to introduce the notion of *higher order cycles* in Γ. We call a finite string consisting of states and edges in Γ a *finite path*,

$$q_1 \xrightarrow{e_1} q_2 \xrightarrow{e_2} q_3 \xrightarrow{e_3} \cdots \xrightarrow{e_{k-1}} q_k,$$

with $e_i \in E$ and $q_i \in Q$, s.t., $s(e_i) = q_i$ and $t(e_i) = q_{i+1}$. We denote such a path by $\langle q_1; e_1, e_2, \ldots, e_{k-1}; q_k \rangle$.

For simplicity, we only consider paths with distinct edges. We could have considered paths with repeated edges, but that will result in an unbounded number of paths, each of which is arbitrarily long. This makes the problem intractable. The number and length of paths with distinct edges are finite. In the worst case scenario, the number of paths is $|Q| \, 2^{|E|}$, where $|Q|$ and $|E|$ are the number of states and edges.

Although we only consider paths with distinct edges, we do not require a path to contain distinct states. In particular, if the starting state is the same as the ending state, such as $\langle q_1; e_1, e_2, \ldots, e_{k-1}; q_1 \rangle$, we call such a path a *finite cyclic path*. The set of all finite cyclic paths is called the *higher order cycles* in Γ and denoted by C. Formally,

$$C = \{\langle q; e_1, e_2, \ldots, e_{k-1}; q \rangle \mid \forall i, j, \ i \neq j \Rightarrow e_i \neq e_j, \ e_i, e_j \in E, \ q \in Q\}. \quad (2)$$

To ease future discussion, we define two operators, π_Q and π_E, on a cyclic path $c \in C$, where $\pi_Q(c)$ gives the starting and ending state of the path and $\pi_E(c)$

gives the first edge appearing in the path. When applied to a path in (2), $\pi_Q(c) = q$ and $\pi_E(c) = e_1$.

For a cyclic path $c \in C$, where $\pi_Q(c) = q$ and $\pi_E(c) = e_1$, we define the following map $R_c^* : G_{e_1} \to D_q$, where $G_{e_1} \subseteq D_q$, by

$$R_c^* = R_{(q;e_1,e_2,\ldots,e_{k-1};q)}^* = R_{e_{k-1}} \circ R_{e_{k-2}} \circ \cdots \circ R_{e_2} \circ R_{e_1}.$$

R_c^* is the composition of the reset maps along the path c. We write the image of R_c^* as $R_c^*(G_{e_1}) \subseteq D_q$.

For a cyclic path $c \in C$, where $\pi_E(c) = e_1$, let

$$Z_c = G_{e_1} \cap R_c^*(G_{e_1}), \tag{3}$$

then,

$$R_c^*(z) = z, \ \forall z \in Z_c. \tag{4}$$

Equation (4) states that if a trajectory intersects with the guard set G_{e_1} at an element $z \in Z_c$, then after a series of reset maps, R_c^*, the initial continuous state of the new trajectory is again z. Since transitions happen instantaneously, there will be an infinite number of transitions happening at the same time point. Therefore, the existence of a nonempty set Z_c indicates the possible existence of Zeno equilibria (cf. [1]). This motivates the construction of the completed hybrid system based on a subset of cyclic paths, $C' = \{c \in C \mid Z_c \neq \emptyset\}$.

For a hybrid system $\mathscr{H}$, define the corresponding *completed hybrid system* $\overline{\mathscr{H}}$ by

$$\overline{\mathscr{H}} = (\overline{\Gamma}, \overline{D}, \overline{G}, \overline{R}, \overline{F}),$$

where

- $\overline{\Gamma} = (\overline{Q}, \overline{E})$, where $\overline{\Gamma}$ has more discrete states and edges than Γ. The set of extra states is $Q' = \overline{Q} \setminus Q$, where Q' is called the set of *post-Zeno states*. The set of extra edges is $E' = \overline{E} \setminus E$. We pick the extra states and edges to be in bijective correspondence with Q', i.e., there exist bijections $g : Q' \to C'$ and $h : E' \to C'$. Consequently, $\forall c \in C'$, there always exist a unique $q \in Q'$ and a unique $e \in E'$.

  We define the source and target maps, $\overline{s} : \overline{E} \to \overline{Q}$ and $\overline{t} : \overline{E} \to \overline{Q}$ for $e \in \overline{E}$ by

$$\overline{s}(e) = \begin{cases} s(e) & \text{if } e \in E \\ \pi_Q(h(e)) & \text{if } e \in E' \end{cases}, \quad \text{and} \quad \overline{t}(e) = \begin{cases} t(e) & \text{if } e \in E \\ g^{-1}(h(e)) & \text{if } e \in E' \end{cases}.$$

  Intuitively, for each cyclic path $c \in C'$ found in Γ, we can find a new discrete state $q = g^{-1}(c) \in Q'$ and a new edge $e = h^{-1}(c) \in E'$ that goes from $\pi_Q(c)$ to q in $\overline{\Gamma}$.

- Define $\overline{D} = D \cup D'$, where D' is the set of domains of post-Zeno states, defined as $D' = \{D_q' \subseteq \mathbb{R}^n \mid q \in Q'\}$. For each $c \in C'$, D_q' is defined by

$$D_q' = Z_c, \quad \text{where } q = g^{-1}(c) \in Q'. \tag{5}$$

Note that D_q' is not only the domain for post-Zeno state q but also the guard set that triggers the transition from the pre-Zeno state $\pi_Q(c)$ to the post-Zeno state q.

– In order to define $\overline{G}$, we first modify the guard G_e in G by subtracting Z_c from G_e, where $c \in C'$ with $\pi_Q(c) = \overline{s}(e)$. Define, for all $e \in E$,

$$\widetilde{G}_e = G_e \backslash \bigcup_{c \in C' \text{ s.t. } \pi_Q(c) = \overline{s}(e)} Z_c, \tag{6}$$

and define, for all $e \in E'$,

$$G'_e = D'_q, \quad \text{where } q = \overline{t}(e). \tag{7}$$

Then the complete definition of $\overline{G}$ is $\overline{G} = \{\widetilde{G}_e \mid e \in E\} \cup \{G'_e \mid e \in E'\}$.

– $\overline{R} = \{R_e : \widetilde{G}_e \rightarrow D_{\overline{t}(e)} \mid e \in E\} \cup \{R'_e : G'_e \rightarrow D_{\overline{t}(e)} \mid e \in E'\}$, where the reset map R'_e is the identity map.

– $\overline{F} = F \cup \{f'_q : D'_q \rightarrow \mathbb{R}^n \mid q \in Q'\}$, where f'_q is the vector field on D'_q. This vector field may be application-dependent, but in some circumstances, it can be obtained from the vector field $f_{q'}$ on $D_{q'}$, where $q' = \pi_Q(g(q)) \in Q$.

Upon inspection of the definition of the completed hybrid system, it is evident that we have explicitly given a method for computing every part of this system except for the vector fields on the post-Zeno states. We do not claim to have an explicit method for generally computing f'_q, because this would depend on the constraints imposed by D'_q which we do not assume are of any specific form. However, in some special cases, it is possible to find such a vector field. In the next subsection, we will demonstrate how to carry out the process of completing hybrid systems by revisting the examples discussed in Sect. 1.

2.2   Examples

Example 1: Bouncing Ball. We first revisit the bouncing ball example shown in Fig. 1. Write this example hybrid system as a tuple, $\mathcal{H} = ((Q, E), D, G, R, F)$. We have the discrete state set $Q = \{q_1\}$, the edge set $E = \{e_1\}$, the set of guards $G = \{G_{e_1}\}$, where $G_{e_1} = \{(x_1, x_2) \in \mathbb{R}^2 \mid x_1 = 0 \wedge x_2 \leq 0\}$, and the set of the reset maps $R = \{R_{e_1}\}$, where R_{e_1} is defined by $R_{e_1}(x_1, x_2) = (x_1, -e \cdot x_2)$, $\forall (x_1, x_2) \in G_{e_1}$.

There is only one element, $c = \langle q_1; e_1; q_1 \rangle$, in the set C of cyclic paths. For path c, the composition of reset maps along c is $R^*_c = R_{e_1}$ and $\pi_E(c) = e_1$. Evaluating (3) with the guard G_{e_1}, we get

$$\begin{aligned} Z_c &= G_{e_1} \cap R_{e_1}(G_{e_1}) \\ &= \{(x_1, x_2) \mid x_1 = 0 \wedge x_2 \leq 0\} \cap \{(x_1, x_2) \mid x_1 = 0 \wedge x_2 \geq 0\} \\ &= \{(x_1, x_2) \mid x_1 = 0 \wedge x_2 = 0\} \\ &= \{(0, 0)\}. \end{aligned}$$

Since Z_c is nonempty, we introduce a new state q_2 and a new edge e_2 such that $\overline{Q} = \{q_1, q_2\}$ and $\overline{E} = \{e_1, e_2\}$. The source and target maps are

$$\overline{s}(e) = q_1, \forall e \in \overline{E}, \quad \text{and} \quad \overline{t}(e) = \begin{cases} q_1 \text{ if } e = e_1 \\ q_2 \text{ if } e = e_2 \end{cases}.$$

The domain for discrete state q_2 is $D'_{q_2} = Z_c$. Then $\overline{D} = D \cup \{D'_{q_2}\}$. Since the set D'_{q_2} only contains one element, the dynamics (vector fields) of the hybrid system is trivial, where $\dot{x}_1(t) = 0$, $\dot{x}_2(t) = 0$. This simply means that the ball cannot move at all, which is exactly the same as what we got in the introduction.

We must point out that the domain for a post-Zeno state may contain more than one element. In this case, the dynamics in general cannot be computed without a model designer's expertise. However, in some special cases such as mechanical systems, the vector fields describe the equations of motion for these systems. If in addition, the guards are derived from unilateral constraints on the configuration space, then the vector fields on the post-Zeno states can be obtained from the vector fields on the pre-Zeno states via holonomic constraints. In fact, the vector fields on the post-Zeno state of the above example can be obtained from a *hybrid Lagrangian* [7]. A detailed explanation of the process for computing vector fields and more examples can be found in [7].

Note that D'_{q_2} is also the guard set of e_2 that specifies the switching condition from q_1 to q_2, meaning $G'_{e_2} = \{(x_1, x_2) \in \mathbb{R}^2 \mid x_1 = 0 \wedge x_2 = 0\}$. Following (6), we get a modified $\widetilde{G_{e_1}} = \{(x_1, x_2) \in \mathbb{R}^2 \mid x_1 = 0 \wedge x_2 < 0\}$. The set of these two guard sets gives $\overline{G} = \{\widetilde{G_{e_1}}, G'_{e_2}\}$.

Finally, $\overline{R} = \{R_{e_1}, R'_{e_2}\}$, where R'_{e_2} is just the identity map.

In summary we get the completed hybrid system $\overline{\mathscr{H}} = ((\overline{Q}, \overline{E}), \overline{D}, \overline{G}, \overline{R}, \overline{F})$, which is the same as the model shown in Fig. 2.

Example 2: Water Tank. Now let us revisit the water tank example shown in Fig. 3. Write this example hybrid system as a tuple, $\mathscr{H} = ((Q, E), D, G, R, F)$. We have the discrete state set $Q = \{q_1, q_2\}$, the edge set $E = \{e_1, e_2\}$, the set of guards $G = \{G_{e_1}, G_{e_2}\}$, where $G_{e_1} = \{(x_1, x_2) \in \mathbb{R}^2 \mid x_2 \leq r_2\}$ and $G_{e_2} = \{(x_1, x_2) \in \mathbb{R}^2 \mid x_1 \leq r_1\}$, and the set of the reset maps $R = \{R_{e_1}, R_{e_2}\}$, where both reset maps are identity maps.

There are two elements, $c_1 = \langle q_1; e_1, e_2; q_1 \rangle$ and $c_2 = \langle q_2; e_2, e_1; q_2 \rangle$, in the set C that contains cyclic paths. For path c_1, the composition of reset maps along c_1 is $R^*_{c_1} = R_{e_2} \circ R_{e_1}$ and $\pi_E(c_1) = e_1$. Evaluating (3) with the guard G_{e_1}, we get

$$
\begin{aligned}
Z_{c_1} &= G_{e_1} \cap R_{e_2}(R_{e_1}(G_{e_1})) \\
&= G_{e_1} \cap G_{e_2} \\
&= \{(x_1, x_2) \mid x_2 \leq r_2\} \cap \{(x_1, x_2) \mid x_1 \leq r_1\} \\
&= \{(x_1, x_2) \mid x_1 \leq r_1 \wedge x_2 \leq r_2\}.
\end{aligned}
$$

Similarly, for path c_2, we get $Z_{c_2} = \{(x_1, x_2) \mid x_1 \leq r_1 \wedge x_2 \leq r_2\}$, which is the same as Z_{c_1}.

Since both Z_{c_1} and Z_{c_2} are nonempty, we introduce two new states q_3 and q_4 and two new edges e_3 and e_4 such that $\overline{Q} = \{q_1, q_2, q_3, q_4\}$ and $\overline{E} = \{e_1, e_2, e_3, e_4\}$. The source and target maps are

$$
\overline{s}(e) = \begin{cases} q_1 \text{ if } e = e_1 \vee e = e_3 \\ q_2 \text{ if } e = e_2 \vee e = e_4 \end{cases}, \quad \text{and} \quad \overline{t}(e) = \begin{cases} q_2 \text{ if } e = e_1 \\ q_1 \text{ if } e = e_2 \\ q_3 \text{ if } e = e_3 \\ q_4 \text{ if } e = e_4 \end{cases}.
$$

The domain for discrete state q_3 is $D'_{q_3} = Z_{c_1}$, and the domain for discrete state q_4 is $D'_{q_4} = Z_{c_2}$. Then $\overline{D} = D \cup \{D'_{q_3}, D'_{q_4}\}$.

As we pointed out earlier in the previous example, in order to derive the dynamics for post-Zeno states, a careful analysis has to be performed by model designers, and the resulting dynamics may not be unique. For example, one might think that $3/4$ of the input flow goes into the first tank and the rest goes into the second tank. This dynamics is different from what we had in the introduction section. We do not (in fact, we cannot) determine which result is better.

Note that D'_{q_3} is also the guard set of e_3 that specifies the switching condition from q_1 to q_3, meaning $G'_{e_3} = \{(x_1, x_2) \in \mathbb{R}^2 \mid x_1 \le r_1 \wedge x_2 \le r_2\}$. Following (6), we get a modified $\widetilde{G_{e_1}} = \{(x_1, x_2) \in \mathbb{R}^2 \mid x_1 \le r_1 \wedge x_2 > r_2\}$. Similarly, we get $G'_{e_4} = \{(x_1, x_2) \in \mathbb{R}^2 \mid x_1 \le r_1 \wedge x_2 \le r_2\}$, and a modified $\widetilde{G_{e_2}} = \{(x_1, x_2) \in \mathbb{R}^2 \mid x_2 \le r_2 \wedge x_1 > r_1\}$. The set of these two guard sets gives $\overline{G} = \{\widetilde{G_{e_1}}, \widetilde{G_{e_2}}, G'_{e_3}, G'_{e_4}\}$.

Finally, $\overline{R} = \{R_{e_1}, R_{e_2}, R'_{e_3}, R'_{e_4}\}$, where all reset maps are identity maps.

In summary we get the completed hybrid system $\overline{\mathscr{H}} = ((\overline{Q}, \overline{E}), \overline{D}, \overline{G}, \overline{R}, F)$, which is slightly different from the model shown in Fig. 4 in that $\overline{\mathscr{H}}$ contains 4 discrete states. However, if we choose the same dynamics such as (1) for discrete states q_3 and q_4, then q_3 and q_4 are the same. Thus we get a model with the same dynamics as that of the model in Fig. 4.

3 Approximate Simulation

In [10], we proposed an operational semantics for simulating hybrid system models. The key idea of the operational semantics is to treat a complete simulation as a sequence of unit executions, where a unit execution consists of two phases. The discrete phase of execution handles all discrete events at the same time point, and the continuous phase resolves the continuum between two consecutive discrete events.

When simulating a Zeno hybrid system model, we meet more challenging practical issues. The first difficulty is that before the Zeno time point, there will be an infinite number of discrete transitions (events). A discrete phase of execution needs to be performed for each time point when a discrete event occurs, which takes a non-zero time. So it is impossible to handle all discrete transitions in a finite time interval. In other words, the simulation gets stuck near the Zeno time point. The second difficulty is caused by numerical errors, which make it impractical to get an exact simulation. We will first elaborate on the second issue, and then we will come back to the first issue in subsection 3.3.

3.1 Numerical Errors

There are two sources of numerical errors: round-off error and truncation error[2]. Round-off error arises from using a finite number of bits in a computer to

---

[2] We will not give a thorough discussion of numerical errors, which have been extensively studied, e.g. in [11]. We would rather briefly review and explain the important trade-offs when choosing integration step sizes.

represent a real value. We denote this kind of difference as η. Then we can say that each integration operation will incur a round-off error of order η, denoted as $O(\eta)$. Round-off error accumulates. Suppose we integrate with a fixed step-size solver with a integration step size as h. In order to simulate over a unit time interval, we need h^{-1} integration steps, then the total round-off error is $O(\eta/h)$. Clearly, the bigger the step size, the fewer integration steps, the smaller the total round-off error. Similar results can be drawn for variable step-size solvers.

Truncation error comes from the integration algorithms used by practical ODE solvers. For example, an nth-order explicit Runge-Kutta method, which is derived to match the first $n+1$ terms of Taylor's expansion, has a *local* truncation error of $O(h^{n+1})$ and an *accumulated* truncation error of $O(h^n)$. Note that both truncation errors decrease as h decreases. Ideally we will get no truncation errors as $h \to 0$.

The total numerical error ε for an ODE solver using an nth-order explicit Runge-Kutta method is the sum of the round-off error and truncation error,

$$\varepsilon \sim \eta/h + h^n. \tag{8}$$

We can see that with a big integration step size h, the total error is dominated by truncation error, whereas round-off error dominates with a small step size. Therefore, although it is desirable to choose a small step size to reduce truncation error, the accuracy of a calculation result may not be increased due to the accumulation of round-off error. If we take the derivative of (8) with respect to h, then we get that when $h \sim \eta^{1/(n+1)}$ the total error ε reaches its minimum $O(\eta^{n/(n+1)})$. Therefore, in practice, we need to set a lower bound for both the integration step size and error tolerance (or value resolution) of integration results. We denote them as h_0 and ε_0 respectively, where

$$h_0 \sim \eta^{1/(n+1)}, \quad \varepsilon_0 \sim \eta^{n/(n+1)}.$$

For a good simulation, accuracy is one concern and efficiency is another objective. Efficiency for numerical integration is usually measured in terms of computation time or the number of computing operations. Using a big integration step size is an effective way to improve efficiency but with the penalty of loss of accuracy. So there is a trade-off. Furthermore, step sizes have upper bounds that are enforced by the consistency, convergence, and stability requirements when deploying practical integration methods on concrete ODEs [11]. Therefore, most practical *adaptive* ODE solvers embed a mechanism inside the integration process to adjust the step size according to the changing speed (derivative) of integration results, so that efficiency gets improved while maintaining the required accuracy at the same time.

In summary, a practical ODE solver usually specifies a minimum integration step size h_0, some small error tolerance ε_0, and an algorithm to adapt step size to meet requirements on both efficiency and accuracy.

3.2   Computation Difficulties

It is well-known that numerical integration in general can only deliver an approximation to the exact solution of an initial value ODE. However, the distance of the approximation from the exact solution is controllable for certain kinds of vector fields. For example, if a vector field satisfies a Lipschitz condition along the time interval where it is defined, we can constrain the integration results to reside within a neighborhood of the exact solution by introducing more bits for representing values to get better precision and integrating with a small step size.

The same difficulties that arise in numerical integration also appear in event detection. A few algorithms have been developed to solve this problem [12, 13, 14]. However, there is still a fundamental unsolvable difficulty: we can only get the simulation time close to the time point where an event occurs, but we are not assured of being able to determine that point precisely.

Simulating a Zeno hybrid system poses another fundamental difficulty. We will first explain it through a simple continuous-time example with dynamics

$$\dot{x}(t) = 1/(t-1), \ x(0) = 0, \ t \in [0,2]. \tag{9}$$

We can analytically find the solution for this example, $x(t) = \ln|t-1|$. However, getting the same result through simulation is difficult. Suppose the simulation starts with $t = 0$. As t approaches 1, the derivative $\dot{x}(t)$ keeps decreasing without bound. To satisfy the convergence and stability requirements, the step size h has to be decreased. When the step size becomes smaller than h_0, round-off error is not neglectable any more and the simulation results become unreliable. Trying to reduce the step size further doesn't help, because the disturbance from round-off error will dominate.

A similar problem arises when simulating Zeno hybrid system models. Recall that Zeno executions have an infinite number of discrete events (transitions) before reaching the Zeno time point, and the time intervals between two consecutive transitions shrink to 0. When the time interval becomes less than h_0, round-off errors again dominate.

In summary, it is impractical to precisely simulate the behavior of a Zeno model. Therefore, similar to numerical integration, we need to develop a computationally feasible way to approximate the exact model behavior. The objective is to give a close approximation under the limits enforced by numerical errors. We will do this in the next subsection.

3.3   Approximating Zeno Behaviors

In Sect. 2, we have described how to specify the behaviors of a Zeno hybrid system before and after the Zeno time point and how to develop transitions from pre-Zeno states to post-Zeno states. The construction procedure works for guards which are arbitrary sets. However, assuming that each guard is the sub-levelset of a function (or collection of functions) simplifies the framework for studying transitions to post-Zeno states. Therefore, we assume that a transition going from a pre-Zeno state to a post-Zeno state has a guard expression of form,

$$G_{e_c} = \{x \in \mathbb{R}^n \mid g_{e_c}(x) \leq 0\}, \tag{10}$$

for every $c \in C$, where $e_c = h^{-1}(c)$ and $g_{e_c} : \mathbb{R}^n \to \mathbb{R}^k$. Furthermore, we assume that $g_{e_c}(x)$ is continuously differentiable.

In this section, we will develop an algorithm such that the complete model behavior can be simulated. As the previous subsection pointed out, we can only approximate the model behaviors before the Zeno time point. Therefore, the first issue is to be able to tell how close the simulation results are to the exact solutions before the Zeno time point. This will decide when the transitions from pre-Zeno states to post-Zeno states are taken. The second issue is how to establish the initial conditions of the dynamics after the Zeno time point from the approximated simulation results.

Issue 1: Relaxing Guard Expressions. To solve the first issue, we first relax the guard conditions defining the transitions from the pre-Zeno states to the post-Zeno states; if the current states fall into a neighborhood of the Zeno states (the states at the Zeno time point), the guard is enabled and transition is taken. Note that when the transition is taken, the system has a new dynamics and the rest of the events before the Zeno time point, which are infinite in number, are discarded. Therefore the computation before the approximated Zeno time point can be finished in finite time.

A practical problem now is to define a good neighborhood such that the approximation is "close enough" to the exact Zeno behavior. We propose two criteria. The first criterion is based on the error tolerance ε_0[3]. We rewrite (10) as

$$G_{e_c}^{\varepsilon_0} = \{x \in \mathbb{R}^n \mid g_{e_c}(x) \leq \varepsilon_0\}, \tag{11}$$

meaning if $x(t)$ is the solution of $\dot{x} = f_q(x)$ with $q = \overline{s}(e_c)$, and if the evaluation result of $g_{e_c}(x(t))$ falls inside $[0, \varepsilon_0]$, the simulation results of $x(t)$ will be thought as close enough to the exact solution at the Zeno time point, and the transition will be taken. In fact, because ε_0 is the smallest amount that can be reliably distinguished, any value in $[0, \varepsilon_0]$ will be treated the same.

The second criterion is based on the minimum step size h_0. Suppose the evaluation result of $g_{e_c}(x(t))$ is outside of the range $[0, \varepsilon_0]$. If it takes less than h_0 time for the dynamics to drive the value of $g_{e_c}(x(t))$ down to 0, then we will treat the current states as close enough to the Zeno states. This criterion prevents the numerical integration from failing with a step size smaller than h_0, which may be caused by some rapidly changing dynamics, such as those in (9).

We first get a linear approximation to function $g_{e_c}(x(t))$ around t_0 (cf. [12],[14]),

$$g_{e_c}(x(t_0 + h)) = g_{e_c}(x(t_0)) + \frac{\partial g_{e_c}(x)}{\partial x} \cdot f_q(x) \mid_{x = x(t_0)} \cdot h + O(h^2), \tag{12}$$

where h is the integration step size. Because we are interested in the model's behavior when h is close to h_0, where h is very small, we can discard the $O(h^2)$

---

[3] If $g_{e_c}(x)$ is a vector valued function, then ε_0 is a vector with ε_0 as the elements.

term in (12). We are interested in how long it takes for the value of function $g_{e_c}(x(t_0))$ to go to 0, so we calculate the required step size by solving (12),

$$h = -\frac{g_{e_c}(x(t_0))}{\frac{\partial g_{e_c}(x)}{\partial x} \cdot f_q(x) \mid_{x=x(t_0)}}. \tag{13}$$

Now we say that if $h < h_0$, the states are close enough to the Zeno point. So we rewrite the boolean expression (10) as

$$G_{e_c}^{h_0} = \left\{ x \in \mathbb{R}^n \mid -\frac{g_{e_c}(x)}{\frac{\partial g_{e_c}(x)}{\partial x} \cdot f_q(x)} \leq h_0 \right\}. \tag{14}$$

In the end, we give a complete approximated guard expression of the transition e_c from a pre-Zeno state to a post-Zeno state:

$$G_{e_c}^{\text{approx}} = G_{e_c}^{\varepsilon_0} \cup G_{e_c}^{h_0}.$$

This means that if either guard expression in (11) and (14) evaluates to be true, the transition will be taken. Performing this process on each guard in the set $\{G_{e_c} \mid c \in C\}$ we obtain the set $\{G_{e_c}^{\text{approx}} \mid c \in C\}$. Note that to ensure deterministic transitions, we also subtract the same set from the original guard sets defined in (6). Replacing the guard expressions given in Sect. 2 with these approximated ones, we obtain an approximation to the completed hybrid system $\mathcal{H}$, $\overline{\mathcal{H}}^{\text{approx}}$. This is the completed hybrid system that is implemented for simulation.

Issue 2: Reinitialization. The other issue is how to reinitialize the initial continuous states of the new dynamics defined in a post-Zeno state. Theoretically, these initial continuous states are just the states at the Zeno time point, meaning that they satisfy the guard expression in (10). This is guaranteed by the identity reset maps associated with the transitions.

In some circumstances, like the examples discussed in this paper, the initial continuous states can be explicitly and precisely calculated. However, in general, if there are more variables involved in guard expressions than the constraints enforced by guard expressions, we cannot resolve all initial states. In this case, we have to use the simulation results as part of the initial states. Clearly, since in simulation we do not actually reach the Zeno time point, the initial states are just approximations. Consequently, the simulation of the dynamics of post-Zeno states will be approximation too.

4   Conclusions

We have introduced a systematic method for completing hybrid systems through the introduction of new post-Zeno states and transitions to these states at the Zeno point. We have developed a way to approximate model behaviors at Zeno points such that the simulation does not halt nor break down. With these solutions, we can simulate a Zeno hybrid system model beyond its Zeno point and reveal its dynamics completely. In the end, we want to thank the anonymous reviewers for their valuable and constructive comments.

References

1. Zhang, J., Johansson, K.H., Lygeros, J., Sastry, S.: Zeno hybrid systems. Int. J. Robust and Nonlinear Control **11**(2) (2001) 435–451
2. Ames, A.D., Sastry, S.: Sufficient conditions for the existence of zeno behavior. 44th IEEE Conference on Decision and Control and European Control Conference ECC (2005)
3. Ames, A.D., Tabuada, P., Sastry, S.: (On the stability of Zeno equilibria) To appear in Hybrid Systems: Computation and Control, 2006.
4. Johansson, K.H., Lygeros, J., Sastry, S., Egerstedt, M.: Simulation of zeno hybrid automata. In: Proceedings of the 38th IEEE Conference on Decision and Control, Phoenix, AZ (1999)
5. Ames, A.D., Sastry, S.: Blowing up affine hybrid systems. 43rd IEEE Conference on Decision and Control (2004)
6. Mosterman, P.: An overview of hybrid simulation phenomena and their support by simulation packages. In Varager, F., Schuppen, J.H.v., eds.: Hybrid Systems: Computation and Control (HSCC). Volume LNCS 1569., Springer-Verlag (1999) 165–177
7. Ames, A.D., Zheng, H., Gregg, R.D., Sastry, S.: Is there life after zeno? taking executions past the breaking (zeno) point. In: Sumbitted to the 2006 American Control Conference. (2006)
8. van der Schaft, A., Schumacher, H.: An Introduction to Hybrid Dynamical Systems. Lecture Notes in Control and Information Sciences 251. Springer-Verlag (2000)
9. Lygeros, J.: Lecture Notes on Hybrid Systems. ENSIETA 2-6/2/2004 (2004)
10. Lee, E.A., Zheng, H.: Operational semantics of hybrid systems. In Morari, M., Thiele, L., eds.: Hybrid Systems: Computation and Control (HSCC). Volume LNCS 3414., Zurich, Switzerland, Springer-Verlag (2005) 25–53
11. Burden, R.L., Faires, J.D.: Numerical analysis, 7th ed. Brroks/Cole (2001)
12. Shampine, L.F., Gladwell, I., Brankin, R.W.: Reliable solution of special event location problems for odes. ACM Trans. Math. Softw. **17**(1) (1991) 11–25
13. Park, T., Barton, P.I.: State event location in differential-algebraic models. ACM Transactions on Modeling and Computer Simulation (TOMACS) **6**(2) (1996) 137–165
14. Esposito, J.M., Kumar, V., Pappas, G.J.: Accurate event detection for simulating hybrid systems. In: Hybrid Systems: Computation and Control (HSCC). Volume LNCS 2034., London, UK, Springer-Verlag (2001) 204–217

Author Index

Lecture Notes in Computer Science

For information about Vols. 1–3819

please contact your bookseller or Springer

Vol. 3868: K. Römer, H. Karl, F. Mattern (Eds.), Wireless Sensor Networks. XI, 342 pages. 2006.

Vol. 3866: T. Dimitrakos, F. Martinelli, P.Y.A. Ryan, S. Schneider (Eds.), Formal Aspects in Security and Trust. X, 259 pages. 2006.

Vol. 3865: W. Shen, K.-M. Chao, Z. Lin, J.-P.A. Barthès (Eds.), Computer Supported Cooperative Work in Design II. XII, 359 pages. 2006.

Vol. 3863: M. Kohlhase (Ed.), Mathematical Knowledge Management. XI, 405 pages. 2006. (Sublibrary LNAI).

Vol. 3862: R.H. Bordini, M. Dastani, J. Dix, A.E.F. Seghrouchni (Eds.), Programming Multi-Agent Systems. XIV, 267 pages. 2006. (Sublibrary LNAI).

Vol. 3861: J. Dix, S.J. Hegner (Eds.), Foundations of Information and Knowledge Systems. X, 331 pages. 2006.

Vol. 3860: D. Pointcheval (Ed.), Topics in Cryptology – CT-RSA 2006. XI, 365 pages. 2006.

Vol. 3858: A. Valdes, D. Zamboni (Eds.), Recent Advances in Intrusion Detection. X, 351 pages. 2006.

Vol. 3857: M.P.C. Fossorier, H. Imai, S. Lin, A. Poli (Eds.), Applied Algebra, Algebraic Algorithms and Error-Correcting Codes. XI, 350 pages. 2006.

Vol. 3855: E. A. Emerson, K.S. Namjoshi (Eds.), Verification, Model Checking, and Abstract Interpretation. XI, 443 pages. 2005.

Vol. 3854: I. Stavrakakis, M. Smirnov (Eds.), Autonomic Communication. XIII, 303 pages. 2006.

Vol. 3853: A.J. Ijspeert, T. Masuzawa, S. Kusumoto (Eds.), Biologically Inspired Approaches to Advanced Information Technology. XIV, 388 pages. 2006.

Vol. 3852: P.J. Narayanan, S.K. Nayar, H.-Y. Shum (Eds.), Computer Vision – ACCV 2006, Part II. XXXI, 977 pages. 2006.

Vol. 3851: P.J. Narayanan, S.K. Nayar, H.-Y. Shum (Eds.), Computer Vision – ACCV 2006, Part I. XXXI, 973 pages. 2006.

Vol. 3850: R. Freund, G. Păun, G. Rozenberg, A. Salomaa (Eds.), Membrane Computing. IX, 371 pages. 2006.

Vol. 3849: I. Bloch, A. Petrosino, A.G.B. Tettamanzi (Eds.), Fuzzy Logic and Applications. XIV, 438 pages. 2006. (Sublibrary LNAI).

Vol. 3848: J.-F. Boulicaut, L. De Raedt, H. Mannila (Eds.), Constraint-Based Mining and Inductive Databases. X, 401 pages. 2006. (Sublibrary LNAI).

Vol. 3847: K.P. Jantke, A. Lunzer, N. Spyratos, Y. Tanaka (Eds.), Federation over the Web. X, 215 pages. 2006. (Sublibrary LNAI).

Vol. 3846: H. J. van den Herik, Y. Björnsson, N.S. Netanyahu (Eds.), Computers and Games. XIV, 333 pages. 2006.

Vol. 3845: J. Farré, I. Litovsky, S. Schmitz (Eds.), Implementation and Application of Automata. XIII, 360 pages. 2006.

Vol. 3844: J.-M. Bruel (Ed.), Satellite Events at the MoDELS 2005 Conference. XIII, 360 pages. 2006.

Vol. 3843: P. Healy, N.S. Nikolov (Eds.), Graph Drawing. XVII, 536 pages. 2006.

Vol. 3842: H.T. Shen, J. Li, M. Li, J. Ni, W. Wang (Eds.), Advanced Web and Network Technologies, and Applications. XXVII, 1057 pages. 2006.

Vol. 3841: X. Zhou, J. Li, H.T. Shen, M. Kitsuregawa, Y. Zhang (Eds.), Frontiers of WWW Research and Development - APWeb 2006. XXIV, 1223 pages. 2006.

Vol. 3840: M. Li, B. Boehm, L.J. Osterweil (Eds.), Unifying the Software Process Spectrum. XVI, 522 pages. 2006.

Vol. 3839: J.-C. Filliâtre, C. Paulin-Mohring, B. Werner (Eds.), Types for Proofs and Programs. VIII, 275 pages. 2006.

Vol. 3838: A. Middeldorp, V. van Oostrom, F. van Raamsdonk, R. de Vrijer (Eds.), Processes, Terms and Cycles: Steps on the Road to Infinity. XVIII, 639 pages. 2005.

Vol. 3837: K. Cho, P. Jacquet (Eds.), Technologies for Advanced Heterogeneous Networks. IX, 307 pages. 2005.

Vol. 3836: J.-M. Pierson (Ed.), Data Management in Grids. X, 143 pages. 2006.

Vol. 3835: G. Sutcliffe, A. Voronkov (Eds.), Logic for Programming, Artificial Intelligence, and Reasoning. XIV, 744 pages. 2005. (Sublibrary LNAI).

Vol. 3834: D.G. Feitelson, E. Frachtenberg, L. Rudolph, U. Schwiegelshohn (Eds.), Job Scheduling Strategies for Parallel Processing. VIII, 283 pages. 2005.

Vol. 3833: K.-J. Li, C. Vangenot (Eds.), Web and Wireless Geographical Information Systems. XI, 309 pages. 2005.

Vol. 3832: D. Zhang, A.K. Jain (Eds.), Advances in Biometrics. XX, 796 pages. 2005.

Vol. 3831: J. Wiedermann, G. Tel, J. Pokorný, M. Bieliková, J. Štuller (Eds.), SOFSEM 2006: Theory and Practice of Computer Science. XV, 576 pages. 2006.

Vol. 3830: D. Weyns, H. V.D. Parunak, F. Michel (Eds.), Environments for Multi-Agent Systems II. VIII, 291 pages. 2006. (Sublibrary LNAI).

Vol. 3829: P. Pettersson, W. Yi (Eds.), Formal Modeling and Analysis of Timed Systems. IX, 305 pages. 2005.

Vol. 3828: X. Deng, Y. Ye (Eds.), Internet and Network Economics. XVII, 1106 pages. 2005.

Vol. 3827: X. Deng, D.-Z. Du (Eds.), Algorithms and Computation. XX, 1190 pages. 2005.

Vol. 3826: B. Benatallah, F. Casati, P. Traverso (Eds.), Service-Oriented Computing - ICSOC 2005. XVIII, 597 pages. 2005.

Vol. 3824: L.T. Yang, M. Amamiya, Z. Liu, M. Guo, F.J. Rammig (Eds.), Embedded and Ubiquitous Computing – EUC 2005. XXIII, 1204 pages. 2005.

Vol. 3823: T. Enokido, L. Yan, B. Xiao, D. Kim, Y. Dai, L.T. Yang (Eds.), Embedded and Ubiquitous Computing – EUC 2005 Workshops. XXXII, 1317 pages. 2005.

Vol. 3822: D. Feng, D. Lin, M. Yung (Eds.), Information Security and Cryptology. XII, 420 pages. 2005.

Vol. 3821: R. Ramanujam, S. Sen (Eds.), FSTTCS 2005: Foundations of Software Technology and Theoretical Computer Science. XIV, 566 pages. 2005.

Vol. 3820: L.T. Yang, X.-s. Zhou, W. Zhao, Z. Wu, Y. Zhu, M. Lin (Eds.), Embedded Software and Systems. XXVIII, 779 pages. 2005.